Privacy Law and Society

Second Edition

■ ■ ■

By
Anita L. Allen

Henry R. Silverman Professor of Law
and Professor of Philosophy
University of Pennsylvania Law School

With contributions by
Dr. Rok Lampe, LL.M. Professor of Law
European Faculty of Law and Gea College, Slovenia
Director of the Human Rights Institute Maribor, Slovenia

AMERICAN CASEBOOK SERIES®

WEST®
A Thomson Reuters business

Mat #41056563

American Casebook Series is a trademark registered in the U.S. Patent and Trademark Office.

© West, a Thomson business, 2007
© 2011 Thomson Reuters
 610 Opperman Drive
 St. Paul, MN 55123
 1–800–313–9378
Printed in the United States of America

ISBN: 978–0–314–26703–0

To Paul, Adam and Ophelia

PREFACE

This textbook is a comprehensive introduction to the privacy law of the United States. Its purpose is to convey and assess the role that the concept of privacy plays in American law. Like typical textbooks geared for American law schools, it is a compilation of judicial opinions, legislated rules and commentary. Unlike typical law school textbooks, it deals with a subject matter that is inherently interdisciplinary.

The book is organized into four major chapters, representing the main legal sources of the nation's privacy law: the common law; the Constitution; and, in two chapters, federal legislation.

The book is designed primarily to support an intellectually rewarding three-credit hour law school course surveying the entire field of privacy law. It is important to note that the content of this textbook is not limited to, but includes, "information law". Information law is an important subset of privacy law. It is the component that grapples with data-protection problems facing consumers, government and business. Because the content of this book is broader than information law, students get a picture of the common values and historical connections among the various bodies of law that prominently feature the concept of privacy.

Instructors can design "perspectives" courses around this textbook. The textbook can also complement traditional law school offerings, especially torts, constitutional law and legislation. However, Privacy Law and Society offers a more detailed overview of the privacy torts than any tort law text; a fuller encounter with the Constitution's privacy jurisprudence than a typical constitutional law text; and more extensive analysis of communications, electronic and internet privacy policies than existing legislation or administrative law texts.

Each of the book's four main chapters is sufficiently self-contained, potentially to serve as a text for a seminar or two-credit hour course in a law school. For example, Chapter 1 could form the basis of an advanced torts course or seminar with invasion of privacy and confidentiality as its theme. Chapter 2 could support a thorough constitutional privacy course or seminar. Chapter 3 could support a U.S. information law course or seminar. Combined with the section of Chapter 2 that treats the Fourth Amendment, Chapter 4 could form the basis of a complete course on government surveillance.

For students of law, government, business, technology, journalism, or communications, the book provides an accessible window into the history, content, and methods of one of the most fascinating and important areas of contemporary law.

Here are a few suggestions for courses using this textbook that would work outside of a law school setting.

1. Undergraduate Constitutional Law. Chapter 2 would work well as the text for an undergraduate constitutional law course focusing on substantive protections for individual rights, including rights respecting religion, marriage, families, sex, reproduction, and death. I have enjoyed success teaching such a course to undergraduates at the University of Pennsylvania and as a freshman seminar at Princeton.

2. Personal Decision-making. A course or seminar examining constitutional protection for personal decision-making about private life, including sex, marriage, family, reproduction, lifestyles and the right to die would rely primarily on Chapter 2. The sections in Chapter 2 that cover the Fourth and Fifth Amendments should be omitted in such a course.

3. Information Society. An instructor who wished to teach a course or seminar concentrating on informational privacy and data-protection would rely primarily on Chapter 3.

4. Surveillance Society. A timely course on contemporary problems of law enforcement, national security, and surveillance, would rely on the Fourth and Fifth Amendment sections of Chapter 2, and Chapter 4.

5. Journalism and First Amendment. Materials relating to the press are scattered throughout the book. A course or seminar on the topic of privacy issues in journalism and the media, would primarily utilize Chapter 1; the section of Chapter 2 that covers the First Amendment; and sections of Chapter 3 that relate to First Amendment challenges to the application of data privacy laws, open records laws, and internet-access regulations.

I would be happy to provide prospective college, university or law school instructors with appropriate model syllabi for their courses. In addition, a Teacher's Manual that includes suggested syllabi and other pedagogical aids will be available from the Publisher.

A few additional prefatory points are in order. First, this textbook on U.S. privacy law includes international human rights and European law perspectives. Second, in the instance of the judicial opinions excerpted in the book, I have freely removed inessential case citations and footnotes. I have indicated all other elisions from excerpted materials by insertion of the notation, * * *, in their places. Finally, with the exception of government documents, substantially quoted copyrighted materials appear with permission.

ACKNOWLEDGEMENTS

The late Professor Richard C. Turkington served on the faculty of Villanova University School of Law for many years. He was the principal author of the privacy law textbook we published jointly under our names, Richard C. Turkington and Anita L. Allen, <u>Privacy Law: Cases and Materials</u> (2nd ed., 2002).

"There is a lot of intellectual property in that book," he once said to me, calling attention to the fact that <u>Privacy Law: Cases and Materials</u> was no mere utilitarian compilation of government documents. Professor Turkington's textbook commentaries on privacy law were original contributions.

Left undisturbed by me, the scholarly labor Professor Turkington poured into <u>Privacy Law: Cases and Materials</u> will have enduring value.

<u>Privacy Law and Society</u> is thus a brand new privacy law textbook with a structure and content of its own. I am grateful to Greg Hall, Brielle Madje, Colleen Rutledge and Daniel Alan Spitzer, my research assistants at the University of Pennsylvania School of Law, for their help in the preparation of the manuscript. I thank Lauren Murphy Pringle for assistance with the Teacher's Manual.

ACKNOWLEDGEMENTS TO THE
SECOND EDITION

I am greatly indebted to Dr. Rok Lampe, LLM., Professor of Law, European Faculty of Law and Gea College, Slovenia, Director of the Human Rights Institute Maribor, Slovenia. Dr. Lampe is responsible for the selection and editing of the international human rights and European materials incorporated into the second edition.

Without the help of Erez Aloni, LLM, SJD (candidate), a timely second edition of <u>Privacy Law and Society</u> would not have been possible. For his research and editing assistance, I am also greatly indebted.

Summary of Contents

TABLE OF C

TABLE OF CASES

The principal cases are in bold type. Cases cited or discussed in the text are in roman type. References are to pages. Cases cited in principal cases and within other quoted materials are not included.

PRIVACY LAW
AND SOCIETY

Second Edition

An Introduction to Privacy Law

The subject matter of this textbook is the privacy and privacy-related confidentiality, publicity and data protection law of the United States. I will refer to this body of law as "privacy law," for short. Privacy law is not found in a single document or code. It is located instead in state common law, within state and federal constitutional law, and in a multitude of local, state and federal statutes and rules.

This textbook comprehensively surveys major sources of federal and state privacy law. Its broad aim is to impart a critical understanding of the varied roles the concept of privacy has come to play in American law and society. Such an understanding is particularly important today, as new technologies of communication and surveillance are coming to dominate everyday life. To invite contrast and comparison, examples of international and European approaches to privacy law are interspersed throughout the textbook.

A. The Study of Privacy Law

Our study begins with state common law. State common law is an historic source of privacy protections. Chapter 1 examines the origins of state privacy law in the late 19th century and its subsequent growth until today. The chapter considers the four common law invasion of privacy torts recognized in most states and by the American Law Institute's *Restatement (Second) of Torts*. The chapter also examines the closely affiliated state common law of publicity and confidentiality. Chapter 1 samples major statutes enacted by state legislatures. State statutes create and supplement privacy rights akin to those recognized in the common law.

We move next to the federal constitution, a key source of socially important privacy law. Chapter 2 takes on the voluminous privacy jurisprudence spawned by the Bill of Rights. The First and Fourth Amendment jurisprudence of associational, physical, and informational privacy is especially rich. Chapter 2 also features the often-controversial Fourteenth Amendment equal protection and substantive due process decisional privacy jurisprudence. Conceptions of privacy at play in Second, Fifth, Eighth and Twenty-first Amendment jurisprudence are briefly considered. Chapter 2 concludes with a consideration of state constitutions which, as state courts have held, significantly expand privacy protection beyond federal limits.

The journey ends after an encounter with the federal privacy statutes, a dynamic source of privacy and data protection law. Chapters 3 and 4 examine more than a dozen federal privacy statutes, and the agency rules and case law that implement them. Chapter 3 covers rules regarding government record management; health, education, and financial data; video rentals; telecommunications; and the internet. Chapter 3 introduces the European Union's comprehensive "omnibus" approach to data protection, a contrast to our own "sectoral" approach. Chapter 4 focuses on public and private surveillance, with particular emphasis on electronic communications and foreign intelligence gathering. Chapters 3 and 4 also touch on state law counterparts to federal laws.

B. Objectives

The study of privacy law serves several purposes. Most basically, it introduces students to an important area of legal practice. Not only is privacy law now a recognized area of legal practice in its own right, knowledge of privacy law is frequently called for in the practice of health, business, civil rights, civil liberties and intellectual property law.

But there is more. These materials display a spectrum of typical methods of legal reasoning and analysis. In Chapter 1, precedent-based and policy-driven common law reasoning features heavily. In Chapter 2, the structure of constitutional analysis is on view, replete with its famous balancing tests, degrees of scrutiny, and fundamental rights analysis. Chapters 3 and 4 highlight approaches to statutory interpretation, including both plain-meaning analysis, and resort to legislative history, intent and purposes.

The study of privacy law serves a final purpose: developing an understanding of the concept of privacy and the controversies—some ethnical, some philosophical, some political—surrounding its application in the law.

C. Political and Philosophical Controversy

1. Politics

Politically, "the right to privacy" has been on the frontlines of the U.S. culture wars. By "cultural wars," I mean the acrid, divisive debates over values repeatedly played out in town halls, the media and the courts. When the foes in a skirmish are social conservatives and traditionalists, on the one hand, and social liberals and progressives on the other, it is not always clear which side gets the most mileage out of appeals to privacy rights. In fact, a careful study of privacy law reveals that "the right to privacy" has proven to be a double-edged sword in battles between many sets of political enemies.

As you will see in the pages of this book, in the old South, segregationists used the "right to privacy" to maintain white-only social clubs; but integrationists, like the NAACP, used the same "right to privacy" to fight off state efforts to foil the civil rights movement through intimidation. More recently, social conservatives who wished to exclude homosexuals from their parades and civic groups employed "the right to privacy" to win cherished rights of exclusion. But "the right to privacy" is also the banner under which permissive abortion rights and homosexual freedoms have been won.

Feminist lawyers strategically embraced "the right to privacy," hoping to prevail in reproductive rights cases, but were disappointed that variants of the public-privacy distinction stood in the way of mandatory government abortion funding for the poor and protections against violence and denigrating pornography. Civil libertarians have been staunch defenders both of free speech and "the right to privacy." But their efforts to learn the identities of suspects detained in the post–9/11 campaign against terrorism were rebuffed by government officials asserting the "right to privacy" of prisoners.

Civil libertarians have advocated for strong rights of privacy against government. But public interest advocates have discovered that governments will use the privacy of its citizens, employees and work product as reasons not to respond eagerly to freedom of information law requests.

2. Ethics and Philosophy

Moral, legal and political philosophers have often greeted the term "privacy" as if it were an unruly beast at the door of modern thought. Can "privacy" be tamed? Does it really need to be? Describing "privacy" as elusive, vague and confusing, academic theorists have attempted to prescribe conceptual rigor. Efforts at imposing rigor through precise definitions go back to the 1960's. See, e.g., Alan P. Bates, Privacy—A Useful Concept? 42 *Social Forces* 429 (1964); Alan F. Westin, *Privacy and Freedom* (1967).

"The right to privacy" frustrates theorists who believe the law's use of the term "privacy" is especially confusing. Of particular concern has been the use of "privacy" in connection with (1) the "false light" and "appropriation" torts, examined here in Chapter 1; (2) the interpretation of 14th Amendment liberty, examined in Chapter 2; and (3) high-tech data protection and security, examined in Chapters 3 and 4. Regarding (3), to avoid further expansion of privacy discourse as society moves to address the ethical and legal implications of surveillance and computers, some theorists prefer to speak of a "right to control data" or a "right to manage information flow" rather than a "right to privacy."

Yet individuals, families and groups boldly claim "privacy" rights. Litigants appeal to the "privacy" rights embodied in judge-made law. Legislators enact what they call "privacy" statutes. Lawyers and law firms boast specialties in "privacy" law. Professional organizations and legal advocacy groups make "privacy" their particular focus. A forest of privacy-promoting rules, principles and policies has grown up around a thicket of theoretical debates about how, if at all, the word "privacy" should be used in the law.

Forty years ago, when the body of what this textbook terms "privacy law" was substantially smaller, scholarly attempts to prescribe a more limited usage of "privacy" may have made some headway. But monumental growth in the volume of "privacy" statutes, combined with the popularity of the word "privacy" in everyday life has undercut the usefulness of calls for linguistic purity. A better agenda for theorists today is (1) to distinguish the varied uses of "privacy" in the law, hoping to reduce the potential for confusion in the minds of newcomers to the field; and (2) to clearly explicate the costs, benefits and values associated with whatever "privacy" is intended to denote.

D. What "Privacy" Means in the Law

Consider the diverse range of things ordinary people and legal professionals refer to when they speak of privacy. In everyday parlance, invasions of "privacy" include: (1) physical intrusions, such as a voyeuristic landlord hiding in a tenant's bedroom; (2) informational intrusions, such as a curious employer reading an employee's personal email just for fun; (3) decisional intrusions, such as states banning assisted suicide or gay marriages; (4) proprietary intrusions, such as an advertiser using someone's photograph without permission; and (5) associational intrusions, such as an unwelcome person demanding membership in an exclusive club. Cf. Anita L. Allen, Privacy, *Encyclopedia of Privacy* (ed. William Staples, 2007), distinguishing several senses of privacy. Profession Neil Richards and others discern another notion of privacy invasion immanent in the law, namely, invasion of (6) intellectual privacy, such as criminal prosecution for viewing materials depicting cruelty to animals. Cf. Neil Richards, Intellectual Privacy, 87 *Texas Law Review* 387 (2008).

1. Examples of Everyday Usage

Physical Privacy. Peeping into someone else's bedroom and planting secret recording devices are described as invasions of privacy. Solitude and intimate seclusion can be vital to the enjoyment of privacy in a physical, bodily, territorial or spatial sense. Though no guarantor of repose, the home is often the heart of private life, and a domain culturally marked for the enjoyment of the highest expectations of physical privacy from strangers. The desire for physical privacy often drives legal complaints about unlawful search and seizure, peeping Toms, trespass, and "ambush" journalism. Bodily integrity, an important, additional physical privacy concern, comes up in legal discussions of everything from the right to refuse medical care to roadside sobriety testing.

Informational Privacy. The law allows employers access to employee emails in the workplace. Yet employers who read employees' personal email messages without a legitimate business purpose offend morals and manners, violating expectations of privacy in an informational sense. Confidentiality, data protection, data encryption, data security, secrecy, anonymity and adherence to fair information practice standards comprise an informational dimension of privacy. Regulating informational privacy is the overwhelming focus of the federal privacy statutes, especially the statutes governing law enforcement access to electronic databases and telephonic communications.

Decisional Privacy. Same-sex marriage and polygamy bans illustrate a denial by government of privacy in a decisional sense of the term. Not without heated controversy in jurisprudential circles, the term "privacy" has come to denote freedom from government interference with personal life. Like it or not, the rights of individuals, married couples, and families to direct their own lives are commonly styled as privacy rights. Disagreements about the proper limits of decisional privacy fuel moral debates over gay rights, abortion and physician-assisted suicide.

Proprietary Privacy. Advertisers making use of photographs without permission illustrate a loss of privacy in a proprietary sense. In general, the rights of celebrities and others to control the attributes of their personal identities—their likenesses, names, monikers, voices, trademarks, DNA and social security numbers—are commonly styled as privacy concerns. Government regulators and the general public characterize "identity theft" as a privacy problem. Because it entails seizing otherwise confidential information and personal identifiers, identify theft evokes notions of both informational and proprietary privacy.

Associational Privacy. Seeking membership, inclusion or access to an otherwise closed group invades privacy in an associational sense. The ability to meet alone with selected individuals of one's own choosing is described as privacy, whether the purpose of meeting is sexual, political, civic, cultural or religious. Discriminatory exclusion makes people uncomfortable, but the rhetoric of "privacy" has been used in asserting entitlement to shut out people with unwanted races, religions, sexes, or sexual orientations. Associational privacy is buttressed by strong rights of physical, informational and decisional privacy.

Intellectual privacy. Mental repose is a kind of privacy. And when the aim of letting others alone with their thoughts is to grant them freedom to think forbidden thoughts, mull over controversial ideas, produce creative works, or engage in intimate discussion, we can speak of intellectual privacy. The point of intellectual privacy is not to enable everyone to write the great novel, blog or political manifesto. The kind of intellectual freedom courts and lawyers often defend is a freedom that could as easily be put to enjoying homemade pornography as to pondering Nobel prize-winning physics.

All six of the foregoing everyday senses of "privacy" have wide currency in contemporary legal discourse. Indeed, privacy law could be summed up as the set of legal rules, principles and policies that regulate physical, informational, decisional, proprietary, associational and intellectual privacies. Cf. Neil Richards, The Information Privacy Law Project, 94 *Geo. L.J.* 1087 (2006), distinguishing informational and decisional privacy as the major subject-matters of privacy law and arguing that common values warrant protecting both; Daniel Solove, A Taxonomy of Privacy, 154 *U. Pa. L. Rev.* 477 (2006), attempting a prescriptive new formulation of legal privacy.

No single Definition

Its varied meanings in the law have confounded repeated attempts to come up with a single useful definition of "privacy" or the right to it. See, e.g., W. A. Parent, Privacy, Morality and the Law, 12 *Philosophy and Public Affairs*, 269 (1983). Legal privacy has been defined as the right to be let alone, the right to control information, the condition of limited accessibility and the contexual integrity of data flows. It has been identified with autonomy, intimacy, liberty and property. Privacy has been described for decades now as a general or "umbrella" concept encompassing solitude, seclusion, confidentiality, secrecy, anonymity, data protection, data security, fair information practices, modesty and reserve. One commentator has concluded that because "[p]rivacy is a generic label for a grab bag of values and rights, [t]o arrive at a general definition of privacy would be no easier today than finding a consensus on a definition of freedom." See Simon G. Davies, Re–Engineering the Right to Privacy: How Privacy has been Transformed from a Right to a Commodity, in *Technology and Privacy: the New Landscape* 143, 153 (eds., Philip E. Agre & Marc Rotenberg 1997).

2.   No Purely Private Sphere

"Privacy" is used in a number of distinct ways in the law, and so is the distinction between "public" and "private." The distinction variously dichotomizes the governmental and the non-governmental; the official and the unofficial; the open and the secret; the societal and the individual; and the communal and the personal. See generally, Howard B. Radest, The Public and the Private: An American Fairy Tale, 89 *Ethics* 280, 280–88 (1979).

A sacrosanct private sphere is a tempting moral construct. But a walled-off private domain does not exist in the law. Virtually every aspect of nominally private life is a focus of direct or indirect government regulation. Marriage is considered a private relationship, yet governments require licenses and medical tests, impose age limits, and prohibit polygamous and incestuous marriages. Procreation and childrearing are considered private, but government child-abuse and neglect laws regulate, if at times inadequately, how parents and guardians must exercise their responsibilities. The private sphere, for legal purposes, can only be understood as the ability of ordinary citizens to make many choices and live lives that are relatively free of the most direct forms of outside intrusion, interference and constraint.

As explained by philosopher Hannah Arendt, the Greeks distinguished the "public" sphere of the polis, or city-state, from the "private" sphere of the *oikos*, or household. The Romans similarly distinguished *res publicae*, concerns of the community, from *res privatae*, concerns of individuals and families. The ancients celebrated the public sphere as the sphere of political freedom for citizens. By contrast, the private realm was the sector of economic and biologic necessity. Wives, children, and slaves were denizens of the private sphere, living as subordinates to more autonomous male caretakers. See Hannah Arendt, *The Human Condition* 38–78 (1958). See also Jurgen Habermas, *The Structural Transformation of the Public Sphere* 3–4 (1962) (echoing Arendt). These ancient distinctions may have a relevant legacy: many of the characteristic activities of the household carry the aura of appropriately private activities, even though the modern state respects no impervious boundary at the threshold. Collective welfare, sometimes construed broadly to include economic, social and moral welfare, prompts incursions into home life and the presumptively "hands-off" territories of personal identity, free expression and autonomous moral responsibility.

E. Competing Values

Explicit privacy rights emerged in the 19th century in response to problems of unwanted publicity and physical intrusion; expanded in the 20th century in response to problems of unwanted surveillance and social control; and continue in the 21st century as reactions to consumer, corporate and governmental applications of information technology. It is likely that "the right to privacy" will be an enduring feature of American law.

1. The Case for Privacy Protection

Scholars argue that various forms of privacy are conditions, values and social practices, well worth legal protection. See, e.g., Helen Nissenbaum, *Privacy in Context: Technology, Policy and the Integrity of Social Life* (2009); Daniel Solove, *The Digital Person: Technology and Privacy in the Information Age* (2004); Judith W. DeCew, *In Pursuit of Privacy: Law, Ethics and the Rise of Technology* (1997); Patricia Boling, *Privacy and the Politics of Intimate Life* (1996); Anita L. Allen, *Uneasy Access: Privacy for Women in a Free Society* (1988); Ferdinand Schoeman, *Philosophical Dimensions of Privacy: An Anthology* (1984); Alan F. Westin, *Privacy and Freedom* (1967); and Glenn Negley, Philosophical Views on the Value of Privacy, 31 *Law and Contemporary Problems* 319 (1966).

To briefly summarize the essence of a subtle literature, opportunities for privacy are said to allow individuals better to express their true personalities, preserve their reputations, relax, create, and reflect. Opportunities for privacy are thought to enable individuals to keep some people at a distance, so that they can enjoy intense intimate relationships with others on their own terms. See Jeffrey Rosen, *The Unwanted Gaze: The Destruction of Privacy in America* (2000). Cf. Erving Goffman, *The Presentation of Self in Everyday Life* (1959).

Privacy affords the individual and groups of like-minded individuals the opportunity to plan undertakings and live in harmony with their own preferences and traditions. See Ferdinand Schoeman, *Privacy and Social Freedom* (1992). Privacy norms sustain civility by condemning behaviors that offend courtesy, honor and appropriateness. See Robert Post, The Social Foundations of Privacy: Community and Self in the Common Law, 77 *Calif. L. Rev.* 957 (1989). Cf. James Q. Whitman, Two Western Cultures of Privacy: Dignity v. Liberty, 113 *Yale L.J.* 1151 (2004).

Philosophers have argued that respect for privacy is, in many ways, respect for human dignity itself. See Edward Bloustein, Privacy as an

Aspect of Human Dignity: An Answer to Dean Prosser, 39 *N.Y.U.L. Rev.* 34 (1967); see also Stanley I. Benn, Privacy, Freedom and Respect for Persons, *Nomos VIII: Privacy* (eds. J. Roland Pennock & John W. Chapman, 1971). Respect for privacy has also been described as regard for social practices that constitute a society of distinct individuals. See Jeffrey Reiman, "Privacy, Intimacy and Personhood," 6 *Philosophy and Public Affairs* 26 (1976).

Privacy rights against government demand that state power is limited and unobtrusive, as liberal democracy requires. See Jed Rubenfeld, The Right to Privacy, 102 *Harv. L. Rev.* 737 (1989), (arguing that privacy rights protect against totalitarian government). Privacy rights demand that government tolerate differences. See David A.J. Richards, *Toleration and the Constitution* (1986). Privacy rights aim to insure that those who disagree with fellow citizens will not be permitted by the state to impose their values on them, or force them to live as they live. See Joel Feinberg, The Nature and Value of Rights, 4 *J. Value Inquiry* 243, 252 (1970). An aspect of liberty, privacy thus fosters the development and exercise of moral autonomy. See James Rachels, Why Privacy is Important, 4 *Philosophy and Public Affairs* 323–33 (1975). But see Catharine A. Mackinnon, *Feminism Unmodified: Discourses on Life and Law* 96–102 (1987), arguing that abortion privacy furthers male autonomy more than female autonomy or equality.

Is privacy a purely individualistic value, at odds with ideals of cooperative, efficient, democratic community? It has been argued that privacy makes us more fit for our social responsibilities and participation in group life. To the extent that self-governing communities benefit from the psychological well-being and independent judgments of their members, privacy is a distinctly social good. See C. Keith Boone, Privacy and Community, 9 *Social Theory and Practice* 1, 6–24 (1983).

Opinion polls suggest that ordinary Americans value their privacy. See   http://epic.org/privacy/survey/;   cf.   http://www.privacilla.org/ fundamentals/privacypolls.html. Yet, not every group values the same forms of privacy equally. See Oscar H. Gandy, African Americans and Privacy: Understanding the Black Perspective in the Emerging Policy Debates, 24 *J. of Black Studies* 178 (1993). Moreover, the same individual may value his or her own privacy inconsistently. Privacy norms are complex and highly contextual: "Privacy is structured by situational contexts". See Alan P. Bates, Privacy—A Useful Concept? 42 *Social Forces* 429 (1964). See also Helen Nissenbaum, Privacy as Contextual Integrity, 79 *Wash. L. Rev.* 119, 136–143 (2004). Cf. Anita L. Allen, *Why Privacy Isn't Everything: Feminist Reflections on Personal Accountability* (2003), arguing that context-specific norms of accountability and privacy mark interpersonal relationships. The person who speaks about her medical problems on a cell phone in public places might balk at the thought that her physician would reveal confidential medical information to a third-party without her consent. The same person who would not wish his bank to reveal his checking account balance to a stranger might choose to appear on television and detail his financial woes to an empathetic talk show host. The proliferation of tell-all books, reality television shows, blogs and social networking websites suggests that people value opportunities both for intimate confidential disclosure and reckless exhibitionism.

2. The Case Against Privacy Protection

Not every wounded privacy interest is tended by the law. As you are about to learn, the law provides a remedy only against intrusions and publications that are "highly offensive". It protects only "reasonable expectations of privacy" and bars state interference only if it is wholly irrational or "unduly burdensome".

Students of American privacy law come quickly to appreciate that privacy rights are not absolute. But see Amitai Etzioni, *The Limits of Privacy* (1999), arguing that U.S. law treats privacy rights as absolute at the expense of the common good. Not only do legal privacy rights provide less than absolute protection of privacy interests, some privacy laws were enacted to *regulate* access to people and information, not to *prohibit* such access. At their strongest, government privacy regulations—and corporate privacy policies—adhere to widely promulgated Fair Information Practice Standards whose scope and origin are detailed in Chapter 3.

From a legal perspective, interests opposing privacy interests matter too, as they must in a well-ordered society. In crafting privacy rules, U.S. courts, legislatures and regulatory authorities balance privacy interests against others with which they compete. In constitutional law, even "fundamental" privacy rights give way to interests that are "compelling". Generally, freedom from unwanted publicity competes with accountability, newsworthiness, and freedom of speech. The interest in private conversation and anonymous travel competes with the interest in law enforcement and national security. The interest in the confidentiality of health records competes with the need for public health research and insurance integrity. The employee's interest in workplace privacy completes with the employer's need for efficiency and supervision.

Although some experts believe the U.S. needs more privacy laws, other experts believes it already has too many. As a practical matter, privacy rights potentially keep socially valuable information out of the hands of people who could use and learn from it. Privacy rights also may introduce economic inefficiencies into society. See Richard A. Posner, The Right to Privacy, 12 *Ga. L. Rev.* 393 (1987); The Economics of Privacy, 71 *Amer. Econ. Rev.* 405 (1981). But see Kim L. Scheppele, *Legal Secrets* (1988), defending strong privacy rights for individuals from a contractarian perspective. Cf. Jim Harper, Understanding Privacy—and the Real Threats to It, *Policy Analysis*, No. 520 (August 4, 2004), arguing that weak rather than strong privacy regulation could in some cases be better for consumers. Harper maintains that legal privacy rights conferred by government may actually undermine important privacy interests. But see Marc Rotenberg, Privacy and Secrecy After September 11, 86 *Minn. L. Rev.* 1115 (2002), defending privacy laws, but calling for more government accountability.

F. International and European Privacy Law

Privacy law is a prominent feature of the US and Canadian legal systems. But "the right to privacy" is by no means a North American or exclusively western phenomenon. See Marc Rotenberg, *Privacy Law Sourcebook* (2006), compiling representative international laws and standards. See also Andrew T. Kenyon and Megan Richardson, *New Dimensions in Privacy Law: International and Comparative Perspectives* (2006).

Privacy protection is recognized as a human right in the 1948 U.N. Declaration on Human Rights. Article 12 of the Declaration provides that "No one shall be subjected to arbitrary interference with his privacy, family, home or correspondence, nor to attacks upon his honour and reputation. Everyone has the right to the protection of the law against such interference or attacks." Similarly, Article 17 of the binding Covenant on Civil and Political Rights provides that: "No one shall be subjected to arbitrary or unlawful interference with his privacy, family, home or correspondence, nor to unlawful attacks on his honour and reputation."

The Council of Europe's Convention on Human Rights and Fundamental Freedoms (ECHR) at Article 8 echoes the theme: "Everyone has a right to respect for his private and family life, his home and his correspondence." The European Union Parliament and Council enacted a data privacy directive, Directive 95/46/EC "on the protection of individuals with regard to the processing of personal data and on the free movement of such data." Along with subsequent Directives governing telecommunication, electronic communications and data retention, Directive 95/46/EC provides a strong, comprehensive foundation, shaping and harmonizing privacy law within and among the 27 member states comprising the union.

Lawyers whose corporate clients operate abroad require detailed knowledge of foreign privacy laws. Unfortunately, a single textbook of reasonable length cannot thoroughly survey both US privacy law and the vast sweep of international privacy law. Yet each chapter of this book invites comparisons between US law and international or European privacy and data protection standards. For example, Chapter 1 includes a Council of Europe response to the problem of media attention given to private life. Chapter 2 considers privacy as a human right in connection with the rights of homosexuals, transgender persons and medical consumers; it also examines European approaches both to the right to die and to government search and seizure. Chapter 3 identifies basic differences between American and European data protection standards. In particular, it describes the negotiated "Safe Harbor" agreement which permits U.S. multi-national firms committed to fair information practices to engage in trans-border data transactions from Europe, despite US non-conformity to European data-protection requirements.

CHAPTER 1

PRIVACY IN TORT LAW

■ ■ ■

Introduction

We begin with the four "invasion of privacy" torts—intrusion upon seclusion, publication of private fact, false light publication and misappropriation of name or likeness. The four invasion of privacy torts aim to deter and redress certain kinds of highly offensive conduct that wounds feelings and damages reputations. In addition to exploring the four invasion of privacy torts, this chapter also examines privacy-related civil remedies for wrongful publicity and breaches of confidentiality. Most states now recognize one or more causes of action for invasion of privacy, wrongful publicity and breach of confidence.

Vigorous protection of privacy sometimes impairs constitutionally protected freedoms. Indeed, how can the United States, a country that values free enterprise, along with freedom of the press, speech and expression place individuals in effective control of personal information sought by others? Even assuming that liability for uninvited voyeurism and snooping makes sense, does liability for publishing embarrassing truths make equal sense? Are the privacy torts noble expressions of a deep commitment to civility, dignity and autonomy; or are they prickly eruptions of intolerance for the rough and tumble of an open society? Do torts born in the 19th and early 20th centuries have a role to play in the networked and linked-in Information Age? As noted in a still relevant 2002 Report, *The Privacy Torts: How U.S. State Law Quietly Leads the Way in Privacy Protection:* "The existence and meaning of the state privacy torts is one of many factors that remain to be considered in our collective effort to respond to the privacy challenges we face in the Information Age." http://www.privacilla.org/releases/Torts_Report.pdf.

A. BEFORE THE FOUR "RIGHT TO PRIVACY" TORTS

Before tort law expressly recognized a "right to privacy," many Americans already regarded themselves as entitled to privacy and private lives free of government intrusion. Represented here by James Otis and

John Adams, prominent members of the founding generation of Americans recognized domestic seclusion and mental reserve as privacies worthy of moral and perhaps legal protection.

How accessible must citizens' homes and papers be to their government? In a famous oration on behalf of colonists against British "writs of assistance," Otis defended the privacy of the home, not only from ordinary common law trespass, but also from unwanted government intrusion. The Fourth Amendment to the U.S. Constitution would enshrine the principle of freedom from warrantless searches and seizures.

How open must I be with others about my thoughts, feelings and opinions? In one of his remarkable personal diaries, Adams defended a pragmatic understanding of the ethics of self-disclosure. While in most instances mental reserve and secrecy are wise acts of virtue, public duties sometimes call for bold disclosures, Adams declared.

JAMES OTIS, ORATION IN *PAXTON'S CASE* AGAINST WRITS OF ASSISTANCE

(Boston, February 1761).

Now, one of the most essential branches of English liberty is the freedom of one's house. A man's house is his castle; and whilst he is quiet, he is as well guarded as a prince in his castle. This writ, if it should be declared legal, would totally annihilate this privilege. Custom-house officers may enter our houses when they please; we are commanded to permit their entry. Their menial servants may enter, may break locks, bars, and everything in their way; and whether they break through malice or revenge, no man, no court may inquire. Bare suspicion without oath is sufficient.

JOHN ADAMS, DIARY OF JOHN ADAMS

1770 Aug. 20. Monday
http://www.masshist.org/digitaladams.

The first maxim of worldly wisdom, constant dissimulation, may be good or evil as it is interpreted. If it means only a constant concealment from others of such of our sentiments, actions, desires, and resolutions, as others have not a right to know, it is not only lawful but commendable—because when these are once divulged, our enemies may avail themselves of the knowledge of them, to our damage, danger and confusion. So that some things which ought to be communicated to some of our friends, that they may improve them to our profit or honour or pleasure, should be concealed from our enemies, and from indiscreet friends, least they should be turned to our loss, disgrace or mortification. I am under no moral or other obligation to publish to the world, how much my expenses or my incomes amount to yearly. There are times when and persons to whom, I am not obliged to tell what are my principles and opinions in politics or religion. There are persons whom in my heart I despise; others I abhor.

Yet I am not obliged to inform the one of my contempt, nor the other of my detestation.

This kind of dissimulation, which is no more than concealment, secrecy, and reserve, or in other words, prudence and discretion, is a necessary branch of wisdom, and so far from being immoral and unlawful, that [it] is a duty and a virtue.

Yet even this must be understood with certain limitations, for there are times, when the cause of religion, of government, of liberty, the interest of the present age and of posterity, render it a necessary duty for a man to make known his sentiments and intentions boldly and publicly. So that it is difficult to establish any certain rule, to determine what things a man may and what he may not lawfully conceal, and when. But it is no doubt clear, that there are many things which may lawfully be concealed from many persons at certain times; and on the other hand there are things, which at certain times it becomes mean and selfish, base, and wicked to conceal from some persons.

NOTE: JURISTS WEIGH IN

Nineteenth century American judges recognized strong legal interests in private relationships free from government interference. Two examples from North Carolina are troubling defenses of the right to use private violence to control slaves, *State v. Mann* (1829), and spouses, *State v. Rhodes* (1868). In a more benign vein, the decision of the Supreme Court of Michigan, *De May v. Roberts* (1881), validated expectations of privacy during labor and childbirth: "The plaintiff had a legal right to the privacy of her apartment at such a time, and the law secures to her this right by requiring others to observe it, and to abstain from its violation."

STATE v. MANN

13 N.C. 263 (N.C. 1829).

RUFFIN, J.

[On the trial it appeared that the Defendant had hired the slave for a year—that during the term, the slave had committed some small offence, for which the Defendant undertook to chastise her—that while in the act of so doing, the slave ran off, whereupon the Defendant called upon her to stop, which being refused, he shot at and wounded her. * * *]

The power of the master must be absolute, to render the submission of the slave perfect. I most freely confess my sense of the harshness of this proposition, I feel it as deeply as any man can. And as a principle of moral right, every person in his retirement must repudiate it. But in the actual condition of things, it must be so. There is no remedy. This discipline belongs to the state of slavery. They cannot be disunited, without abrogating at once the rights of the master, and absolving the slave from his subjection. It constitutes the curse of slavery to both the bond and free portions of our population. But it is inherent in the relation of master and slave. * * *

That there may be particular instances of cruelty and deliberate barbarity, where, in conscience the law might properly interfere, is most probable. The difficulty is to determine, where *a Court* may properly begin. * * * We cannot allow the right of the master to be brought into discussion in the Courts of Justice. The slave, to remain a slave, must be made sensible, that there is no appeal from his master; that his power is in no instance, usurped; but is conferred by the laws of man at least, if not by the law of God. The danger would be great indeed, if the tribunals of justice should be called on to graduate the punishment appropriate to every temper, and every dereliction of menial duty. No man can anticipate the many and aggravated provocations of the master, which the slave would be constantly stimulated by his own passions, or the instigation of others to give; or the consequent wrath of the master, prompting him to bloody vengeance, upon the turbulent traitor—a vengeance generally practised with impunity, by reason of its privacy. The Court therefore disclaims the power of changing the relation, in which these parts of our people stand to each other.

Judgment reversed, and judgment entered for the Defendant.

STATE v. RHODES

61 N.C. 453 (NC 1868).

READE, J.

[The defendant was indicted for an assault and battery for striking his wife, Elizabeth Rhodes, three times. The trial court opined that "the defendant had a right to whip his wife with a switch no larger than his thumb." Judgment in favor of the defendant husband was accordingly entered and the State appealed.]

The violence complained of would without question have constituted a battery if the subject of it had not been the defendant's wife. The question is how far that fact affects the case.

The courts have been loath to take cognizance of trivial complaints arising out of the domestic relations—such as master and apprentice, teacher and pupil, parent and child, husband and wife. Not because those relations are not subject to the law, but because the evil of publicity would be greater than the evil involved in the trifles complained of; and because they ought to be left to family government. * * *

In this case no provocation worth the name was proved. The fact found was that it was "without any provocation except some words which were not recollected by the witness." The words must have been of the slightest import to have made no impression on the memory. We must therefore consider the violence as unprovoked. The question is therefore plainly presented, whether the court will allow a conviction of the husband for moderate correction of the wife without provocation. * * *

Blackstone says "that the husband, by the old law, might give the wife moderate correction, for as he was to answer for her misbehavior, he ought to have the power to control her; but that in the polite reign of Charles the Second, this power of correction began to be doubted." 1 Black 444. * * * The old law of moderate correction has been questioned even in England, and has been repudiated in Ireland and Scotland. The old rule is approved in Mississippi, but it has met with but little favor elsewhere in the United States. * * * In looking into the discussions of the other States we find but little uniformity. * * *

Our conclusion is that family government is recognized by law as being as complete in itself as the State government is in itself, and yet subordinate to it; and that we will not interfere with or attempt to control it, in favor of either husband or wife, unless in cases where permanent or malicious injury is inflicted or threatened, or the condition of the party is intolerable. For, however great are the evils of ill temper, quarrels, and even personal conflicts inflicting only temporary pain, they are not comparable with the evils which would result from raising the curtain, and exposing to public curiosity and criticism, the nursery and the bed chamber. Every household has and must have, a government of its own, modeled to suit the temper, disposition and condition of its inmates. Mere ebullitions of passion, impulsive violence, and temporary pain, affection will soon forget and forgive, and each member will find excuse for the other in his own frailties. But when trifles are taken hold of by the public, and the parties are exposed and disgraced, and each endeavors to justify himself or herself by criminating the other, that which ought to be forgotten in a day, will be remembered for life.

It is urged in this case that as there was no provocation the violence was of course excessive and malicious; that every one in whatever relation of life should be able to purchase immunity from pain, by obedience to authority and faithfulness in duty. * * *

If in every such case we are to hunt for the provocation, how will the proof be supplied? Take the case before us. The witness said there was no provocation except some slight words. But then who can tell what significance the trifling words may have had to the husband? Who can tell what had happened an hour before, and every hour for a week? To him they may have been sharper than a sword * * * Suppose a case coming up to us from a hovel, where neither delicacy of sentiment nor refinement of manners is appreciated or known. The parties themselves would be amazed, if they were to be held responsible for rudeness or trifling violence. What do they care for insults and indignities? In such cases what end would be gained by investigation or punishment? Take a case from the middle class, where modesty and purity have their abode, but nevertheless have not immunity from the frailties of nature, and are sometimes moved by the mysteries of passion. What could be more harassing to them, or injurious to society, than to draw a crowd around their seclusion? Or take a case from the higher ranks, where education and culture have so refined nature, that a look cuts like a knife, and a word strikes like a hammer; where the most delicate attention gives pleasure, and the slightest neglect pain; where an indignity is disgrace and exposure is ruin. Bring all these cases into court side by side, with the same offense charged and the same proof made; and what conceivable charge of the court to the jury would be alike appropriate to all the cases, except that they all have domestic government, which they have formed for themselves, suited to their own peculiar conditions, and that those governments are supreme, and from them there is no appeal except in cases of great importance requiring the strong arm of the law, and that to those governments they must submit themselves.

It will be observed that the ground upon which we have put this decision is not that the husband has the *right* to whip his wife much or little; but that we will not interfere with family government in trifling cases. We will no more interfere where the husband whips the wife than where the wife whips the husband; and yet we would hardly be supposed to hold that a wife has a *right* to whip her husband. We will not inflict upon society the greater evil of raising the curtain upon domestic privacy, to punish the lesser evil of trifling violence. * * *

DE MAY v. ROBERTS

46 Mich. 160, 9 N.W. 146 (Mich. 1881).

MARSTON, C.J.

[The facts are as follows. On a dark, stormy evening, Dr. John H. De May was summoned to the house of Mrs. Alvira Roberts to assist in childbirth. The roads were so bad that a horse could not be ridden or driven over them. The doctor was sick and fatigued from overwork. He therefore asked Alfred B. Scattergood to assist him in carrying a lantern, umbrella and other necessary articles. Upon arrival at the small, one-room house, the doctor knocked on the door and Mrs. Roberts' husband answered. De May told him he had brought a friend along to help carry his things, and Mr. Roberts seemed perfectly satisfied. They were asked to enter and treated kindly. De May and Scattergood were fed supper and allowed to warm themselves and nap. As the time of delivery neared, Dr. De May tended Mrs. Roberts, assisted by a woman named Mrs. Parks. Scattergood sat uninvolved by the stove. At some point, Mrs. Parks briefly stepped outside. While Mrs. Parks was away, Dr. De May requested that Scattergood take hold of Mrs. Roberts' hand during a paroxysm of pain that might have caused her to fall. When the child was eventually born, both mother and child were cared for and the men left. Mr. and Mrs. Roberts later learned that Scattergood was not a medical professional. They sued the pair for deceit and other wrongs. Mrs. Roberts prevailed in a trial by jury and the defendants appealed.]

Dr. De May therefore took an unprofessional young unmarried man with him, introduced and permitted him to remain in the house of the plaintiff, when it was apparent that he could hear at least, if not see all that was said and done, and as the jury must have found, under the

instructions given, without either the plaintiff or her husband havi
knowledge or reason to believe the true character of such third pa
would be shocking to our sense of right, justice and propriety to
even but that for such an act the law would afford an ample remeuy. ɪo
the plaintiff the occasion was a most sacred one and no one had a right to
intrude unless invited or because of some real and pressing necessity
which it is not pretended existed in this case. The plaintiff had a legal
right to the privacy of her apartment at such a time, and the law secures
to her this right by requiring others to observe it, and to abstain from its
violation. The fact that at the time, she consented to the presence of
Scattergood supposing him to be a physician, does not preclude her from
maintaining an action and recovering substantial damages upon afterwards ascertaining his true character. In obtaining admission at such a
time and under such circumstances without fully disclosing his true
character, both parties were guilty of deceit, and the wrong thus done
entitles the injured party to recover the damages afterwards sustained,   *Affirmed*
from shame and mortification upon discovering the true character of the
defendants.

NOTE: "THE PRIVACY OF HER APARTMENT"

The *De May* case contains elements that appear again and again in the
privacy tort cases, though rarely all at once: a private home violated, a
married couple mortified, a woman's modesty compromised, the intimate body
observed, health information disclosed, and, most fundamentally, someone's
expectations of privacy shattered.

Consider Mr. and Mrs. Roberts' expectations. Were they reasonable under
the circumstances? De May and Scattergood believed exigent circumstances—
the doctor's illness and fatigue, inclement weather, and Mrs. Roberts' prolonged, difficult labor—excused the young man's presence. Mr. Roberts had
not raised questions about Scattergood before admitting him into his home.
Yet the court concluded that Mrs. Roberts had been wronged, and that
denying her a legal remedy would be "shocking to our sense of right, justice
and propriety".

Childbirth was not a solitary affair in the 19th century. However, there
were customs governing who could observe a delivery. Women typically gave
birth at home, assisted by other women, a professional midwife or physician.
It was not common practice for a male who was not a physician to attend the
birth of another man's wife. Scattergood—a young, unmarried, unprofessional
man—was a quadruple threat to Mr. Roberts' honor as a husband and Mrs.
Roberts' modesty as a wife. For a discussion of gender norms in the emergence of privacy law see Anita L. Allen and Erin Mack, How Privacy Got its
Gender, 10 *N. Ill. U. L. Rev.* 441–78 (1990). See also Susan E. Gallagher's
online illustrated history of women in the growth of privacy law, **http://
historyofprivacy.net**/, *"A Man's Home: Rethinking the Origins of the Pub-
lic/Private Dichotomy in American Law."*

Judge Marston referred to the "privacy" of Mrs. Roberts' apartment.
What was he referring to? Physical seclusion in her fourteen by sixteen feet

home? Intimate association with her husband? The right to decide who would be included and excluded?

Did Scattergood catch a glimpse of Mrs. Roberts' genitals? Did he witness her infant's passage through the birth canal? According to one anthropologist, although privacy customs vary dramatically from culture to culture, the female genitals are shrouded in privacy virtually everywhere. See Barrington Moore, *Privacy: Studies in Social and Cultural History* (1984). However, it is not unusual today for U.S. families to film childbirth. Nor is it unusual to see graphic images of live childbirth on cable television or the web. See, e.g., unassistedbirth.com/

B. ORIGINS OF THE RIGHT TO PRIVACY TORTS

NOTE: A VERY PERSUASIVE ESSAY

An essay in the *Harvard Law Review* launched the idea of an express "right to privacy" tort. Jointly published by Boston lawyers Samuel D. Warren and Louis D. Brandeis in 1890, "The Right to Privacy," mapped out a new invasion of privacy tort. A generous excerpt from the article appears below, after some background.

It is believed that the article was largely executed by Brandeis but prompted by Warren's strong distaste for the attention paid by the press to his upper-crust lifestyle. See generally, MELVIN I. UROFSKY, LOUIS D. BRANDEIS: A LIFE 46–104 (2009). "Naturally," according to Urofsky, "the penny press of the era wanted to report on the doings of [Warren's circle of family and friends] . . . men and women who seemed to party constantly, had homes in the city and country, rode to the hounds, sailed, and had money to support such a lifestyle." *Id.* at 98. Warren's lifestyle was so exclusive, that he did not even invite his friend (and future Supreme Court Justice) Louis Brandeis to his wedding—Warren's snobbish bride did not want to celebrate with a Jew. *Id.* at 97.

Warren and Brandeis argued for explicit recognition of a right to privacy, "a right to be let alone," they called it, borrowing the term from prominent nineteenth century tort scholar Thomas Cooley. The right to privacy would protect the individual's interest in "inviolate personality". Warren and Brandeis sounded an alarm against the threat to privacy posed by prurient curiosity, gossip-laden journalism, and the technology of the instantaneous photograph. As a result of their article's persuasive genius, the American courts installed the right to privacy in the common law within a single generation.

Warren and Brandeis refer in their article to the "sacred precincts of private and domestic life". Yet, physical intrusion into the home of the sort alleged in *De May v. Roberts* was not the precise threat to personality they emphasized. They made their case for a privacy tort by stressing the problem of unwanted publicity about private life rather than unwanted physical intrusion into the home. Accordingly, the initial cases in which the courts recognized the Warren and Brandeis invasion of privacy tort dealt with unwanted publicity rather than physical intrusion.

NOTE: *MANOLA V. STEVENS—MODESTY AND AUTONOMY*

A New York judge decided an unusual unwanted publicity case, *Manola v. Stevens*, just in time for Warren and Brandeis to cite it in their article. Marion Manola was a popular New York City stage performer. She sued a theatrical manager and photographer who colluded to photograph her wearing a theatrical costume that included tights. Well into the twentieth century, photographs of women wearing tights was considered somewhat risqué. Manola successfully filed for an injunction against the use of her photograph. On the ground that the picture offended the "modesty" of the lady, the judge granted Manola's request for a permanent injunction forever barring display of the photo. Viewed as a bid for modesty, Manola's suit seems quaint by today's standards. Nude and nearly nude entertainment is commonplace. If anything, today's female entertainers want the right to be more revealing than authorities see fit. See *City of Erie v. Pap's A.M.*, 529 U.S. 277 (2000) and *Barnes v. Glen Theater*, 501 U.S. 560 (1991) (upholding restrictions on totally nude dancing).

The *Manola* case was not reported in the official law reports. However, it did make the local Manhattan and Brooklyn newspapers. Warren and Brandeis noted the *"New York Times"* coverage of June 15–21, 1890, this way: "There the complainant alleged that while she was playing in the Broadway Theatre, in a rôle which required her appearance in tights, she was, by means of a flash light, photographed surreptitiously and without her consent, from one of the boxes by defendant Stevens, the manager of the 'Castle in the Air' company, and defendant Myers, a photographer, and prayed that the defendants might be restrained from making use of the photograph taken. A preliminary injunction issued ex parte, and a time was set for argument of the motion that the injunction should be made permanent, but no one then appeared in opposition."

Manola's case provided the evidence Warren and Brandeis needed that modern courts were already open to recognizing privacy rights against unwanted publicity. It is of no consequence that the *Brooklyn Daily Eagle* (July 9, 1890) expressed skepticism about the merits of Manola's suit. The *Eagle* claimed that the diva had been photographed many times and that numerous photographs of her wearing tights were already in circulation. But Warren and Brandeis saw in Manola's suit a court's extraordinary willingness to protect privacy—here, a female public figure's modesty and, as important, her desire for sufficient autonomy to control the use of her likeness.

NOTE: *"THE FINE FLOWER OF CIVILIZATION"*

The outcome of the *Manola* case worked to the advantage of Warren and Brandeis. It prepared the way for an out-right defense of a legal right to privacy. The stage for Warren and Brandeis was further set by an essay by Edwin L. Godkin, a leading lawyer and intellectual. In July 1890, Godkin published a high-toned ethical defense of privacy in the popular *Scribner's* magazine.

Godkin doubted that the law could adequately incorporate a right protecting so ethereal a quality as the sense of privacy. But he made a memorable argument for the importance of privacy, nonetheless. See James H. Barron, Warren and Brandeis, The Right to Privacy: Demystifying a Landmark Citation, 13 *Suffolk U. L. Rev.* 875, 887 (1979); Elbridge L. Adams, The Right to Privacy, and its Relation to the Law of Libel, 39 *Am U. L. Rev.* 37 (1905).

Godkin's encomium to privacy embraced both the "privacy of [the] apartment" (at issue in *De May v. Roberts*) and freedom from unwanted publicity (at issue in *Manola v. Stevens*). Godkin contended that the popularity of home-ownership and solitary rooms evidenced a growing devotion to privacy. He argued that people seek houses with rooms of their own to achieve freedom from public exposure. Freedom from public exposure in turn protects reputations and affords solace. Cf. Nelson Lasson, *The History and Development of the Fourth Amendment to the United States Constitution* 13–15 (1937), tracing the Judeo–Christian roots of "the peculiar immunity that the law has thrown around the dwelling house of man."

A brief excerpt from Godkin's article follows, and just after it, "The Right to Privacy," by Warren and Brandeis. Assess Godkin's claim that lovers of privacy are "the element in society which most contributes to its moral and intellectual growth". To whom was he alluding? Did Warren and Brandeis agree? Was the "right to privacy" a product of elitism and snobbery? Does it matter?

EDWIN L. GODKIN, THE RIGHTS OF THE CITIZEN TO HIS REPUTATION

8 Scribner's Mag. 58, 65 (1890).

Privacy is a distinctly modern product, one of the luxuries of civilization, which is not only unsought for but unknown in primitive or barbarous societies. The savage cannot have privacy, and does not desire or dream it. To dwellers in tents and wigwams, it must have been unknown. The earliest houses of our Anglo-saxon ancestors in England, even among the Thanes, consisted of only one large room in which master and mistress, and retainers, cooked, ate and slept. The first sign of material progress was the addition of sleeping rooms, and afterward of "withdrawing-rooms" into which it was possible for the heads of the household to escape from the noise and publicity of the outer hall. One of the greatest attractions of the dwellings of the rich is the provision they make for the segregation of the occupants. All of the improvements, too, of recent years to the dwellings of the poor, have been in the direction, not simply of more space, but of separate rooms. * * * To have a house of one's own is the ambition of nearly all civilized men and women, and the reason which most makes them enjoy it is the opportunity it affords to deciding for themselves how much or how little publicity should surround their daily lives.

The right to decide how much knowledge of * * * personal thought and feeling, and how much knowledge, therefore, of his tastes, and habits, of his own private doings and affairs, and those of his family living under his roof, the public at large shall have is as much one of his natural rights as his right to decide how he shall eat and drink, what he shall wear, and in what manner he shall pass his leisure hours.

Of course, the importance attached to this privacy varies in individuals. Intrusion on it afflicts or annoys different persons in different degrees. It annoys women more than men, and some men very much more than others. To some persons it causes exquisite pain to have their private life laid bare to the world, others rather like it; but it may be laid down as a general rule that the former are the element in society which most contributes to its moral and intellectual growth, and that which the state is most interested in cherishing and protecting. Personal dignity is the fine flower of civilization, and the more of it there is in a community, the better off the community is.

1. WARREN AND BRANDEIS MAP IT OUT

SAMUEL D. WARREN AND LOUIS D. BRANDEIS, THE RIGHT TO PRIVACY

4 Harvard Law Review 193 (1890).

That the individual shall have full protection in person and in property is a principle as old as the common law; but it has been found necessary from time to time to define anew the exact nature and extent of such protection. Political, social, and economic changes entail the recognition of new rights, and the common law, in its eternal youth, grows to meet the demands of society. * * *

Recent inventions and business methods call attention to the next step which must be taken for the protection of the person, and for securing to the individual what Judge Cooley calls the right "to be let alone." Instantaneous photographs and newspaper enterprise have invaded the sacred precincts of private and domestic life; and numerous mechanical devices threaten to make good the prediction that "what is whispered in the closet shall be proclaimed from the house-tops." For years there has been a feeling that the law must afford some remedy for the unauthorized circulation of portraits of private persons; and the evil of the invasion of privacy by the newspapers, long keenly felt, has been but recently discussed by an able writer [E.L. Godkin]. The alleged facts of a somewhat notorious case [Manola v. Stevens] brought before an inferior tribunal in New York a few months ago, directly involved the consideration of the right of circulating portraits; and the question whether our law will recognize and protect the right to privacy in this and in other respects must soon come before our courts for consideration.

Of the desirability—indeed of the necessity—of some such protection, there can, it is believed, be no doubt. The press is overstepping in every direction the obvious bounds of propriety and of decency. Gossip is no longer the resource of the idle and of the vicious, but has become a trade, which is pursued with industry as well as effrontery. To satisfy a prurient taste the details of sexual relations are spread broadcast in the columns of the daily papers. To occupy the indolent, column upon column is filled with idle gossip, which can only be procured by intrusion upon the domestic circle. The intensity and complexity of life, attendant upon advancing civilization, have rendered necessary some retreat from the world, and man, under the refining influence of culture, has become more sensitive to publicity, so that solitude and privacy have become more essential to the individual; but modern enterprise and invention have, through invasions upon his privacy, subjected him to mental pain and distress, far greater than could be inflicted by mere bodily injury. Nor is the harm wrought by such invasions confined to the suffering of those who may be made the subjects of journalistic or other enterprise. In this, as in other branches of commerce, the supply creates the demand. Each crop of unseemly gossip, thus harvested, becomes the seed of more, and, in direct proportion to its circulation, results in a lowering of social standards and of morality. Even gossip apparently harmless, when widely and persistently circulated, is potent for evil. It both belittles and perverts. It belittles by inverting the relative importance of things, thus dwarfing the thoughts and aspirations of a people. When personal gossip attains the dignity of print, and crowds the space available for matters of real interest to the community, what wonder that the ignorant and thoughtless mistake its relative importance. Easy of comprehension, appealing to that weak side of human nature which is never wholly cast down by the misfortunes and frailties of our neighbors, no one can be surprised that it usurps the place of interest in brains capable of other things. Triviality destroys at once robustness of thought and delicacy of feeling. No enthusiasm can flourish, no generous impulse can survive under its blighting influence.

It is our purpose to consider whether the existing law affords a principle which can properly be invoked to protect the privacy of the individual; and, if it does, what the nature and extent of such protection is. * * *

It is not, however, necessary, in order to sustain the view that the common law recognizes and upholds a principle applicable to cases of invasion of privacy, to invoke the analogy, which is but superficial, to injuries sustained, either by an attack upon reputation or by what the civilians called a violation of honor; for the legal doctrines relating to infractions of what is ordinarily termed the common-law right to intellectual and artistic property are, it is believed, but instances and applications of a general right to privacy, which properly understood afford a remedy for the evils under consideration.

The common law secures to each individual the right of determining, ordinarily, to what extent his thoughts, sentiments, and emotions shall be communicated to others. Under our system of government, he can never be compelled to express them (except when upon the witness stand); and even if he has chosen to give them expression, he generally retains the power to fix the limits of the publicity which shall be given them. The existence of this right does not depend upon the particular method of expression adopted. It is immaterial whether it be by word or by signs, in painting, by sculpture, or in music. * * *

What is the nature, the basis, of this right to prevent the publication of manuscripts or works of art? * * * They certainly possess many of the attributes of ordinary property: they are transferable; they have a value; and publication or reproduction is a use by which that value is realized. But where the value of the production is found not in the right to take the profits arising from publication, but in the peace of mind or the relief afforded by the ability to prevent any publication at all, it is difficult to regard the right as one of property, in the common acceptation of that term. * * *

[T]he protection afforded to thoughts, sentiments, and emotions, expressed through the medium of writing or of the arts, so far as it consists in preventing publication, is merely an instance of the enforce-ment of the more general right of the individual to be let alone * * *.

If we are correct in this conclusion, the existing law affords a principle which may be invoked to protect the privacy of the individual from invasion either by the too enterprising press, the photographer, or the possessor of any other modern device for recording or reproducing scenes or sounds. * * * If, then, the decisions indicate a general right to privacy for thoughts, emotions, and sensations, these should receive the same protection, whether expressed in writing, or in conduct, in conversation, in attitudes, or in facial expression.

It may be urged that a distinction should be taken between the deliberate expression of thoughts and emotions in literary or artistic compositions and the casual and often involuntary expression given to them in the ordinary conduct of life. In other words, it may be contended that the protection afforded is granted to the conscious products of labor, perhaps as an encouragement effort. This contention, however plausible, has, in fact, little to recommend it. If the amount of labor involved be adopted as the test, we might well find that the effort to conduct one's self properly in business and in domestic relations had been far greater than that involved in painting a picture or writing a book; one would find that it was far easier to express lofty sentiments in a diary than in the conduct of a noble life. If the test of deliberateness of the act be adopted, much casual correspondence which is now accorded full protection would be excluded from the beneficent operation of existing rules * * *.

It should be stated that, in some instances where protection has been afforded against wrongful publication, the jurisdiction has been asserted, not on the ground of property, or at least not wholly on that ground, but upon the ground of an alleged breach of an implied contract or of a trust or confidence. * * *

A similar groping for the principle upon which a wrongful publication can be enjoined is found in the law of trade secrets. There, injunctions have generally been granted on the theory of a breach of contract, or of an abuse of confidence. * * *

We * * * conclude that the rights, so protected, whatever their exact nature, are not rights arising from contract or from special trust, but are rights as against the world; and, as above stated, the principle which has been applied to protect these rights is in reality not the principle of private property, unless that word be used in an extended and unusual sense. The principle which protects personal writings and any other productions of the intellect or of the emotions, is the right to privacy, and the law has no new principle to formulate when it extends this protection to the personal appearance, sayings, acts, and to personal relations, domestic or otherwise. * * *

The right of one who has remained a private individual, to prevent his public portraiture, presents the simplest case for such extension; the right to protect one's self from pen portraiture, from a discussion by the press of one's private affairs, would be a more important and far-reaching one. If casual and unimportant statements in a letter, if handiwork, however inartistic and valueless, if possessions of all sorts are protected not only against reproduction, but against description and enumeration, how much more should the acts and sayings of a man in his social and domestic relations be guarded from ruthless publicity. If you may not reproduce a woman's face photographically without her consent, how much less should be tolerated the reproduction of her face, her form, and her actions, by graphic descriptions colored to suit a gross and depraved imagination.

The right to privacy, limited as such right must necessarily be, has already found expression in the law of France.

It remains to consider what are the limitations of this right to privacy, and what remedies may be granted for the enforcement of the right. * * *

First. The right to privacy does not prohibit any publication of matter which is of public or general interest. * * *

The design of the law must be to protect those persons with whose affairs the community has no legitimate concern, from being dragged into an undesirable and undesired publicity and to protect all persons, whatsoever their position or station, from having matters which they may properly prefer to keep private, made public against their will. * * *

In general, then, the matters of which the publication should be repressed may be described as those which concern the private life, habits, acts, and relations of an individual, and have no legitimate connection with his fitness for a public office which he seeks or for which he is suggested, or for any public or quasi-public position which he seeks or for which he is suggested, and have no legitimate relation to or bearing upon any act done by him in a public or quasi-public capacity. * * *

Second. The right to privacy does not prohibit the communication of any matter, though in its nature private, when the publication is made under circumstances which would render it a privileged communication according to the law of slander and libel.

Under this rule, the right to privacy is not invaded by any publication made in a court of justice, in legislative bodies, or the committees of those bodies; in municipal assemblies, or the committee of such assemblies, or practically by any communication made in airy other public body, municipal or parochial, or in any body quasi-public, like the large voluntary associations formed for almost every purpose of benevolence, business, or other general interest; and (at least in many jurisdictions) reports of any such proceedings would in some measure be accorded a like privilege. Nor would the rule prohibit any publication made by one in the discharge of some public or private duty, whether legal or moral, or in conduct of one's own affairs, in matters where his own interest is concerned.

Third. The law would probably not grant any redress for the invasion of privacy by oral publication in the absence of special damage. * * *

Fourth. The right to privacy ceases upon the publication of the facts by the individual, or with his consent. * * *

Fifth. The truth of the matter published does not afford a defense.

Obviously this branch of the law should have no concern with the truth or falsehood of the matters published. It is not for injury to the individual's character that redress or prevention is sought, but for injury to the right of privacy. For the former, the law of slander and libel provides perhaps a sufficient safeguard. The latter implies the right not merely to prevent inaccurate portrayal of private life, but to prevent its being depicted at all.

Sixth. The absence of "malice" in the publisher does not afford a defense. * * *

The remedies for an invasion of the right of privacy are also suggested by those administered in the law of defamation, and in the law of literary and artistic property, namely:

1. An action of tort for damages in all cases. Even in the absence of special damages, substantial compensation could be allowed for injury to feelings as in the action of slander and libel.

2. An injunction, in perhaps a very limited class of cases. * * *

The common law has always recognized a man's house as his castle, impregnable, often even to its own officers engaged in the execution of its commands. Shall the courts thus close the front entrance to constituted authority, and open wide the back door to idle or prurient curiosity?

NOTE: REALISM ABOUT "OUR FOND IDEAL"

The Warren and Brandeis article begins decrying "[r]ecent inventions and business methods," and in the end resorts to the old adage recited by James Otis that "[a] man's house [is] his castle". Is freedom from invasive publicity won through home ownership? What happens to privacy when a "man's" house is too accessible to be likened to a citadel?

If individuals are unmolested by the press, nosey neighbors or other outsiders, do they necessarily enjoy privacy inside their homes? As Godkin understood, the amount of privacy found at home depends upon the size and configuration of the house. But that is not all. It also depends upon the economic and social organization of the household.

Many family homes bustle with life. They are not hermetically sealed havens for the people who live there. Home dwellers conduct social lives and receive professional services at home. Friends, relatives, clergy, painters, electricians, plumbers, housekeepers, social workers and hospice care workers come and go. Being at home did not spare Mrs. Roberts and her husband. They needed to call in Dr. De May and Mrs. Parks. And Dr. De May needed the help of Scattergood. Is the lesson here that the privacy of the home is a sentimental myth?

In an 1898 book, *Women and Economics,* the utopian feminist Charlotte Perkins Gilman, took on the myth of homes as intimate havens. She explained that how much privacy and intimacy a person is able to enjoy at home depends not only on the architecture of the home and the ability to avoid the attention of newspapers and gossips, but also on the responsibilities, personalities, needs, ages and genders of a home's co-inhabitants.

Gilman proposed radical changes in domestic organization and the status of women to increase genuine privacy at home and to better realize the "fond ideal" of the family home. Her beef was not with "loving home" but with the perpetuation of a certain "kind of a home and in the kind of womanhood that it fosters." Explain what Gilman meant when she wrote that: "Only as we live, think, feel, and work outside the home, do we become humanly developed, civilized, socialized." Does "family privacy" compromise "individual privacy"? How?

CHARLOTTE PERKINS GILMAN WOMEN AND ECONOMICS (1898)

Chapter 10–11.

A home is a permanent dwelling-place, whether for one, two, forty, or a thousand, for a pair, a flock, or a swarm. The hive is the home of the bees as literally and absolutely as the nest is the home of mating birds in their season. Home and the love of it may dwindle to the one chamber of the bachelor or spread to the span of a continent, when the returning traveller sees land and calls it "home." There is no sweeter word, there is no dearer fact, no feeling closer to the human heart than this. * * *

A place to be safe in; a place to be warm and dry in; a place to eat in peace and sleep in quiet; a place whose close, familiar limits rest the nerves from the continuous hail of impressions in the changing world outside; the same place over and over,—the restful repetition, rousing no keen response, but healing and soothing each weary sense,—that "feels like home." All this from our first consciousness. All this for millions and millions of years. No wonder we love it.

Then comes the gradual addition of tenderer associations, family ties of the earliest. Then, still primitive, but not yet outgrown, the groping religious sentiment of early ancestor-worship, adding sanctity to safety, and driving deep our sentiment for home. It was the place in which to pray, to keep alight the sacred fire, and pour libations to departed grandfathers * * *. Upon this deep foundation we have built a towering superstructure of habit, custom, law; and in it dwell together every deepest, oldest, closest, and tenderest emotion of the human individual. No wonder we are blind and deaf to any suggested improvement in our lordly pleasure-house.

But look farther. Without contradicting any word of the above, it is equally true that the highest emotions of humanity arise and live outside the home and apart from it. While religion stayed at home, in dogma and ceremony, in spirit and expression, it was a low and narrow religion. It could never rise till it found a new spirit and a new expression in human life outside the home, until it found a common place of worship, a ceremonial and a morality on a human basis. Science, art, government, education, industry,—the home is the cradle of them all, and their grave, if they stay in it. Only as we live, think, feel, and work outside the home, do we become humanly developed, civilized, socialized. * * *

Consider, for instance, that long-standing popular myth known as "the privacy of the home." * * *

May we not smile a little bitterly at our fond ideal of "the privacy of the home"? The swift progress of professional sweepers, dusters, and scrubbers, through rooms where they were wanted, and when they were wanted, would be at least no more injurious to privacy than the present method. Indeed, the exclusion of the domestic servant, and the entrance of woman on a plane of interest at once more social and more personal, would bring into the world a new conception of the sacredness of privacy, a feeling for the rights of the individual as yet unknown. * * *

The free woman, having room for full individual expression in her economic activities and in her social relation, will not be forced so to pour out her soul in tidies and photograph holders. The home will be her place of rest, not of uneasy activity; and she will learn to love simplicity at last. This will mean better sanitary conditions in the home, more beauty and less work. * * *

Such privacy as we do have in our homes is family privacy, an aggregate privacy; and this does not insure—indeed it prevents—individual privacy * * *.

The progressive individuation of human beings requires a personal home, one room at least for each person. * * * The home is the one place on earth where no one of the component individuals can have any privacy. A family is a crude aggregate of persons of different ages, sizes, sexes, and temperaments, held together by sex-ties and economic necessity; and the affection which should exist between the members of a family is not increased in the least by the economic pressure, rather it is lessened. Such affection as is maintained by economic forces is not the kind which humanity most needs.

At present any tendency to withdraw and live one's own life on any plane of separate interest or industry is naturally resented, or at least regretted, by the other members of the family. This affects women more than men, because men live very little in the family and very much in the world. The man has his individual life, his personal expression and its rights, his office, studio, shop: the women and children live in the home— because they must. For a woman to wish to spend much time elsewhere is considered wrong, and the children have no choice. The historic tendency of women to "gad abroad," of children to run away, to be forever teasing for permission to go and play somewhere else; the ceaseless, futile, well-meant efforts to "keep the boys at home,"—these facts, together with the definite absence of the man of the home for so much of the time, constitute a curious commentary upon our patient belief that we live at home, and like it. Yet the home ties bind us with a gentle dragging hold that few can resist. Those who do resist, and who insist upon living their individual lives, find that this costs them loneliness and privation; and they lose so much in daily comfort and affection that others are deterred from following them.

There is no reason why this painful choice should be forced upon us, no reason why the home life of the human race should not be such as to allow—yes, to promote—the highest development of personality. * * *

A home life with a dependent mother, a servant-wife, is not an ennobling influence. We all feel this at times. The man, spreading and growing with the world's great growth, comes home, and settles into the tiny talk and fret, or the alluring animal comfort of the place, with a distinct sense of coming down. It is pleasant, it is gratifying to every sense, it is kept warm and soft and pretty to suit the needs of the feebler and smaller creature who is forced to stay in it. It is even considered a virtue for the man to stay in it and to prize it, to value his slippers and his newspaper, his hearth fire and his supper table, his spring bed, and his clean clothes above any other interests.

The harm does not lie in loving home and in staying there as one can, but in the kind of a home and in the kind of womanhood that it fosters, in the grade of industrial development on which it rests.

2. WHY THEN? PRIVACY AND HISTORY

By the close of the nineteenth century the concept of a right to privacy had begun to garner adherents. It garnered even more adherents in the early years of the twentieth century, moving from the musings of a few visionary journalists, lawyers, and feminists into the hearts and minds of the general public. But why? Why then? Historians of privacy have proposed a number of theories to explain the emergence of concerns about privacy and the right to it.

Population Density. The number and percentage of people living in towns and cities increased several fold after the civil war. Northern industrial cities could feel crowded. Perhaps the growing population density in urban areas made Americans in the northeast more conscious of physical privacy and forced intimacy. City life afforded a degree of anonymity when compared to rural life, but it also placed people in closer proximity to neighbors and family members. See Edward Shils, Privacy: Its Constitution and Vicissitudes, 31 *Law and Contemp. Probs.* 281 (1966).

Closing of the West. In 1893, historian Frederick Jackson Turner declared that the period of the American Frontier had come to an end. The U.S. was a nation "from sea to shining sea." The gradual closing of the western frontier symbolized a loss of opportunity for independence and secluded lifestyles. See Robert Copple, Privacy and the Frontier Thesis: An American Intersection of Self and Society, 34 *Am. J. of Juris.* 87–104 (1989). There was no actual geographic land scarcity in the U.S. Still, Copple argued, Americans believed that one could no longer "go west" to make it on their own, to live autonomous, solitary lives. The result of their belief was a preoccupation with privacy and laws to protect it.

Popular Literacy. Increased literacy and the rise in the number of mass-circulated newspapers between 1880 and 1890 may have made Americans of all social classes more concerned about informational privacy and publicity. Lurid, graphic stories sold well, creating a market in personal information as never before. Patrician Bostonians like Samuel Warren may have felt a special threat to the privacy of their interesting families, although the scandals and misfortunes that befell the poor made for good reading, too. See Donald R. Pember, *Privacy and the Press* (1972). Literacy, combined with crowded urban living in the northeast, created the possibility of a truly "popular culture". Cultivated intellectual and social elites, Warren, Brandeis, and Godkin lashed out against the supposed coarsening effects of low-brow popular journalism. They resented the decline in traditional modes of civility. Their attacks on the press were in one sense personal; but they seemed to have struck a cord with others.

Threat of Technology. A final explanation for attention to privacy focuses on the rise of new technology, starting with the camera. Photography is a technology of nostalgia, art, news and surveillance. Dry-plate film technology perfected by the Kodak company made possible the "instantaneous photography" that worried Warren and Brandeis. Publicity-conscious people in Warren and Brandeis' social milieu complained about "kodakers lying in wait," much as we complain today about paparazzi and people snapping video with their cell phones. See Robert E. Mensel, *"Kodakers Lying in Wait": Amateur Photography and the Right of Privacy in New York, 1885–1915*, 43 American Quarterly 24–45 (1991):

> The inventor of the Kodak, George Eastman, was the consummate entrepreneur. His goal was nothing less than to build the largest photographic supply business in the country. He understood that "in order to make a large business we would have to reach the general public and create a new class of patrons." His deliberate effort to

create consumer demand for a new product was enormously success-ful. While other manufacturers built and marketed small cameras that were sufficiently simple and inexpensive to be suitable for a broad middle-class clientele, Eastman's product became the standard of the industry, and its name provided a slang term for all amateur photographers: kodakers. The most important cultural consequence of the technological and marketing strategy which produced the Kodak was that it completely changed the conception of who was to practice photography. Photography was no longer the province of the professional and affluent amateur, but was practiced by thousands upon thousands of people. The newspapers of the period indicate that there was a startling increase in the number of amateur photographers in New York. By 1889, the New York Tribune was able to report that "[a]mateur photography is rapidly approaching, if it has not already reached, the dignity of a 'craze.' " The *New York Times* also reported a remarkable increase in the popularity of photography as a hobby. By the end of 1889, the Times carried regular notes on amateur photography in its Monday editions. The boom in amateur photography was much more than a triumph of American consumer culture. In the late 1880s and early 1890s, New Yorkers responded to amateur photographers with exceptionally intense and remarkable feelings. The amateurs were positively Mephistophelean: they belonged to a class of minor demons known as "camera fiends," or "Kodak fiends," and were said "to be in league with some evil spirit." Their activities were mysterious, seductive, and intoxicating.

Id. at 28–9.

Early in the 20th century, the telephone came into widespread use. Party lines (multiple households sharing a single phone line) and wire-tapping made eavesdropping simple. Microphones and voice recorders came along to make telephone surveillance an attractive tool for law enforcement. Motion picture photography was a leap forward, and not just in the field of entertainment. Anxieties about social control through television surveillance popularized by novelist George Orwell were not long in coming.

NOTE: CAMERAS, TELEGRAMS AND POST CARDS

Ex parte Jackson, 96 U.S. 727 (1878), established the privacy of the mails, holding that a search warrant was necessary if government authorities wished to open sealed letters and packages.

As Warren and Brandeis stressed, the invention of modern photography and printing had a major impact on the ability of ordinary people to keep their lives private. Frederick S. Lane tells an engaging story of how a number of 19th century and early 20th century inventions changed expectations of privacy. Using the example of the telegraph and the post card, Lane argued in his book, *American Privacy: The 400 Year History of Our Most Contested Right* (2009), that Americans have often been willing to give up privacy for the sake of quicker, more convenient, or less expensive modes of communication. Is his argument convincing?

The telegram quickly became an indispensable instrument of business and social life, but the cost to privacy was high:

> [T]he use of the telegraph to transmit messages necessarily required the disclosure of the contents of the message to a third party: the telegraph company and its employees. Moreover, telegraph companies themselves quickly developed the practice, largely for accounting purposes, of keeping copies (at least temporarily) of messages sent from one office to another. Much like e-mail today, at any given time, a copy of the particular telegram might exist in at least three or four separate locations. * * *

> In the absence of any federal statutory protections, the privacy and confidentiality of telegrams were dependent on the contractual relationship between the telegraph company and the sender. (A few states did pass laws imposing a duty of confidentiality on telegraph companies and their employees * * *. Over time, however, a substantial body of case law developed making it clear that * * * telegraph companies had a duty of confidentiality for their customers.)

Id. 21ff. Postcards were an overnight sensation despite the inability of the messages they contained to be kept secret:

> When the cards were first offered for sale in New York City on May 15, 1873, more than 200,000 cards were purchased in the first two hours. * * * [In 1908, when the U.S. population numbered 90 million, U.S postal carriers delivered 677,777,798 postcards.] The postcard phenomenon convincingly demonstrated that from the start, Americans were willing to give up a certain amount of privacy in exchange for the fun and convenience of using the cards. The postcards also demonstrated one other critical element of the ongoing privacy debate in this country: the fact that the definition of "privacy" is a highly individual concept. As any postcard collector will tell you, every stack of cards is a fascinating cultural and social record, containing revelations ranging from the briefest travel diaries to heartrending health updates, from banal restaurant reviews and weather reports to the most endearing expressions of love. * * *

From the American experience with telegrams, postcards and other privacy diminishing innovations, Lane boldly concludes that:

> The sheer variety of personal disclosures makes it clear that it is next to impossible to create a "right to privacy" that encompasses every type of personal disclosures; what one might consider a trivial disclosure, another might find mortifying. Taken together, the common types of 19th-century communication—the letter, the telegram, the photograph, the postcard—illustrate that a "right to privacy" encompasses the *choice* to disclose private information, rather than what is actually revealed. It is the individual decision to seal one's thoughts in a letter or scrawl those same thoughts on the back of a card for the world to see that is the essence of the right to privacy.

Id. at 32. Do you agree that privacy rights should protect idiosyncratic choices rather than specific categories of sensitive information?

3. FORMAL RECOGNITION OF PRIVACY RIGHTS BY COURTS AND LEGISLATURES

NOTE: AN EXPLICIT RIGHT OF PRIVACY

The cases excerpted in this Section trace the development of the privacy tort in the years just after Warren and Brandeis published "The Right to Privacy" (1890).

In 1891, the U.S. Supreme Court endorsed the notion that a "right to be let alone" is embodied in the common law. The case was *Union Pacific Railway Company v. Botsford*, in which the Court held that a plaintiff cannot be required to submit to a medical examination by defense counsel in a tort action. Although the case has little value as precedent either in the field of civil procedure or privacy law, it is striking evidence of Warren's and Brandeis' immediate influence among jurists.

The invasion of privacy tort advocated by Warren and Brandeis took off in the state courts within a few years' time. It was cited with approval by a New York court in 1895 in *Schuyler v. Curtis*, only to be rejected by the New York high court in 1902 in *Roberson v. Rochester Folding Box Co.* However, the privacy tort was fully embraced by the supreme court of Georgia in 1905 in an unwanted publicity case, *Pavesich v. New England Life Insurance Company*. The *Pavesich* court argued that a right to control the extent of exposure to the public is a natural liberty to which the courts of a civilized society ought to extend legal protection. The court allowed to stand Mr. Pavesich's privacy suit against an insurance company which used his photograph in an advertisement without his permission.

UNION PACIFIC RAILWAY COMPANY v. BOTSFORD

141 U.S. 250 (1891).

MR. JUSTICE GRAY

[Clara L. Botsford sued the Union Pacific Railway Company for negligence. She alleged that the upper berth of a sleeping car fell on her head, causing pain and permanent injuries. Three days before trial, the railroad asked the court to compel plaintiff Botsford to submit to a medical examination. The court denied the railroad's motion, the trial went forward, and the jury awarded Mrs. Botsford $10,000. The railroad appealed, arguing that the motion to compel a medical examination to determine the extent of Botsford's injuries ought to have been granted.]

No right is held more sacred, or is more carefully guarded, by the common law, than the right of every individual to the possession and control of his own person, free from all restraint or interference of others, unless by clear and unquestionable authority of law. As well said by Judge Cooley, "The right to one's person may be said to be a right of complete immunity: to be let alone." Cooley on Torts, 29. * * *

The inviolability of the person is as much invaded by a compulsory stripping and exposure as by a blow. To compel any one, and especially a woman, to lay bare the body, or to submit it to the touch of a stranger, without lawful authority, is an indignity, an assault and a trespass; and no order or process, commanding such an exposure or submission, was ever known to the common law in the administration of justice between individuals, except in a very small number of cases, based upon special reasons, and upon ancient practice, coming down from ruder ages, now mostly obsolete in England, and never, so far as we are aware, introduced into this country. * * *

The order moved for, subjecting the plaintiff's person to examination by a surgeon, without her consent and in advance of the trial, was not according to the common law, to common usage, or to the statutes of the United States. * * * Judgment affirmed.

SCHUYLER v. CURTIS

15 N.Y.S. 787 (1891).

O'BRIEN, J. * * *

The defendants, except Hartley, who is the sculptor engaged to execute the statue, are members of the "Woman's Memorial Fund Association," which has undertaken to raise money by public subscription for a life-size statue of Mrs. Schuyler, to be designated as the "Typical Philanthropist," and has publicly announced its intention of placing this statue on public exhibition at the Columbian Exposition to be held in Chicago in 1893, as a companion piece to a bust of the well-known agitator, Susan B. Anthony, which bust is to be designated as the "Typical Reformer." Neither Mrs. Schuyler in her life-time, nor her husband after her death, knew or consented to the project; and, in view of the attitude assumed by plaintiff on behalf of her nearest living relatives, it must be concluded that, so far as the family is concerned, the project is unauthorized. * * *

It has not been shown that Mrs. Schuyler ever came within the category of what might be denominated "public characters." She was *Not a public figure* undoubtedly a woman of rare gifts and of a broad and philanthropic nature; but these she exercised as a private citizen, in an unobtrusive way. There is no refutation of the status given her by the complaint, which alleges that "she was in no sense either a public character or even a person generally known either in the community in which she lived or throughout the United States, but that her life was preeminently the life of a private citizen; that she was a woman of great refinement and cultivation; that notoriety in any form was both extremely distasteful to her and wholly repugnant to her character and disposition; and that throughout her life she neither sought nor desired it in any way." Such a person, thus described, does not lose her character as a private citizen merely because she engaged in private works of philanthropy. [The cases cited by Warren and Brandeis, including Manola v. Stevens,] are a clear recognition of the principle that the right to which protection is given is the right to privacy.

Upon the facts presented on the motion, and the law applicable thereto, the motion to continue injunction until the trial should be granted.

ROBERSON v. ROCHESTER FOLDING BOX CO.

171 N.Y. 538 (N.Y. 1902).

PARKER, J. * * *

[The Franklin Mills Co.was engaged in the manufacture and sale of flour, packaged in boxes made by the Rochester Folding Box Company. Without consent, the defendants placed a photographic likeness of the plaintiff on product labels and advertisements for Franklin Mills' flour. Above the plaintiff's portrait, the words, "Flour of the Family" were printed. Altogether, 25,000 likenesses were made. The plaintiff alleged that she was subjected to humiliation, jeers, loss of reputation and emotional and physical pain requiring medical attention. She sought an injunction against further use of her picture and damages of $15,000. Relying on Schuyler v. Curtis, the Appellate Division reached the conclusion that plaintiff had a valid cause of action against defendants for invasion of her "right of privacy," but the defendants successfully appealed to the state high court, the Court of Appeals.]

The so-called right of privacy is, as the phrase suggests, founded upon the claim that a man has the right to pass through this world, if he wills, without having his picture published, his business enterprises discussed, his successful experiments written up for the benefit of others, or his eccentricities commented upon either in handbills, circulars, catalogues, periodicals or newspapers, and, necessarily, that the things which may not be written and published of him must not be spoken of him by his neighbors, whether the comment be favorable or otherwise. * * *

The legislative body could very well interfere and arbitrarily provide that no one should be permitted for his own selfish purpose to use the picture or the name of another for advertising purposes without his consent. * * * The courts, however, being without authority to legislate, are required to decide cases upon principle * * *.

The history of the phrase "right of privacy" in this country seems to have begun in 1890 in a clever article in the Harvard Law Review * * * in which a number of English cases were analyzed, and, reasoning by analogy, the conclusion was reached that—notwithstanding the unanimity of the courts in resting their decisions upon property rights in cases where publication is prevented by injunction—in reality such prevention was due to the necessity of affording protection to thoughts and sentiments expressed through the medium of writing, printing and the arts, which is like the right not to be assaulted or beaten; in other words, that the principle, actually involved though not always appreciated, was that of an inviolate personality, not that of private property. * * *

An examination of the authorities leads us to the conclusion that the so-called "right of privacy" has not as yet found an abiding place in our jurisprudence, and, as we view it, the doctrine cannot now be incorporated without doing violence to settled principles of law by which the profession and the public have long been guided. * * *

GRAY, J. (dissenting). * * *

The right of privacy, or the right of the individual to be let alone, is a personal right, which is not without judicial recognition. It is the complement of the right to the immunity of one's person. The individual has always been entitled to be protected in the exclusive use and enjoyment of that which is his own. The common law regarded his person and property as inviolate, and he has the absolute right to be let alone. (Cooley on Torts.) The principle is fundamental and essential in organized society that every one, in exercising a personal right and in the use of his property, shall respect the rights and properties of others.

NOTE: A LEGISLATIVE REPLY TO ROBERSON: N.Y. CIVIL RIGHTS LAW §§ 50 AND 51

On the slim basis of scholarship and precedent at its disposal, the *Roberson* court refused to recognize a right of privacy. Not even a year passed, however, before the New York legislature enacted a statute creating such a right. The statute remains in effect today: "A person, firm or corporation that uses for advertising purposes, or for the purposes of trade, the name, portrait or picture of any living person without having first obtained the written consent of such person, or if a minor of his or her parent or guardian, is guilty of a misdemeanor."

Under this statute, could a valid lawsuit for invasion of privacy be brought against a "peeping Tom"? What about a suit against a newspaper that published an embarrassing story about a reclusive woman's divorce? Would the statute help plaintiffs in a case identical to *Schuyler v. Curtis*?

PAVESICH v. NEW ENGLAND LIFE INSURANCE CO.

122 Ga. 190, 50 S.E. 68 (Ga. 1905).

COBB, J. * * *

[This case was brought by an Atlanta artist whose photograph was used without his permission in an advertisement which appeared in one of the city's leading newspaper. The text of the advertisement falsely implied that the plaintiff had purchased defendant's insurance.] * * *

The liberty which he derives from natural law * * * embraces far more than freedom from physical restraint. * * * Liberty includes the right to live as one will, so long as that will does not interfere with the rights of another or of the public. One may desire to live a life of seclusion;

another may desire to live a life of publicity; still another may wish to live a life of privacy as to certain matters and of publicity as to others. * * * All will admit that the individual who desires to live a life of seclusion can not be compelled, against his consent, to exhibit his person in any public place, unless such exhibition is demanded by the law of the land. He may be required to come from his place of seclusion to perform public duties,— to serve as a juror and to testify as a witness, and the like; but when the public duty is once performed, if he exercises his liberty to go again into seclusion, no one can deny him the right. * * *

Under the Roman law, "to enter a man's house against his will, even to serve a summons, was regarded as an invasion of his privacy." * * * This conception is the foundation of the common-law maxim that "every man's house is his castle;" and in Semayne's case (5 Coke, 91), 1 Smith's Lead. Cas. 228, where this maxim was applied, one of the points resolved was "That the house of every one is to him as his castle and fortress, as well for his defence against injury and violence as for his repose." "Eavesdroppers, or such as listen under walls or windows or the eaves of a house to hearken after discourse, and thereupon to frame slanderous and mischievous tales," were a nuisance at common law and indictable, and were required, in the discretion of the court, to find sureties for their good behavior. * * * The offense consists in lingering about dwelling-houses and other places where persons meet for private intercourse and listening to what is said, and then tattling it abroad. * * * A common scold was at common law indictable as a public nuisance to her neighborhood. * * * And the reason for the punishment of such a character was not the protection of any property right of her neighbors, but the fact that her conduct was a disturbance of their right to quiet and repose, the offense being complete even when the party indicted committed it upon her own premises. Instances might be multiplied where the common law has both tacitly and expressly recognized the right of an individual to repose and privacy. The right of the people to be secure in their persons, houses, papers, and effects against unreasonable searches and seizures, which is so fully protected in the constitutions of the United States and of this State (Civil Code, §§ 6017, 5713), is not a right created by these instruments, but is an ancient right which, on account of its gross violation at different times, was preserved from such attacks in the future by being made the subject of constitutional provisions.

The right of privacy, however, like every other right that rests in the individual, may be waived by him, or by any one authorized by him, or by any one whom the law empowers to act in his behalf, provided the effect of his waiver will not be such as to bring before the public those matters of a purely private nature which express law or public policy demands shall be kept private. * * * The most striking illustration of a waiver is where one either seeks or allows himself to be presented as a candidate for public office. He thereby waives any right to restrain or impede the public in any proper investigation into the conduct of his private life which may throw light upon his qualifications for the office or the advisability of imposing upon him the public trust which the office carries. * * *

It may be said that to establish a liberty of privacy would involve in numerous cases the perplexing question to determine where this liberty ended and the rights of others and of the public began. This affords no reason for not recognizing the liberty of privacy and giving to the person aggrieved legal redress against the wrong-doer in a case where it is clearly shown that a legal wrong has been done. * * *

Privacy * * * is not only essential to the welfare of the individual, but also to the well-being of society. The law stamping the unbreakable seal of privacy upon communications between husband and wife, attorney and client, and similar provisions of the law, is a recognition, not only of the right of privacy, but that for the public good some matters of private concern are not to be made public even with the consent of those interested. * * *

The stumbling block which many have encountered in the way of a recognition of the existence of a right of privacy has been that the recognition of such right would inevitably tend to curtail the liberty of speech and of the press. The right to speak and the right of privacy have been coexistent. Each is a natural right, each exists, and each must be recognized and enforced with due respect for the other. * * *

It seems that the first case in this country where the right of privacy was invoked as a foundation for an application to the courts for relief was the unreported case of Manola v. Stevens, which was an application for injunction to the Supreme Court of New York, filed on June 15, 1890. [A famous article referring to Manola v. Stevens appeared in 1890, written by Samuel D. Warren and Louis D. Brandeis.] In it the authors ably and forcefully maintained the existence of a right of privacy, and the article attracted much attention at the time. * * * The first reported case in which the right of privacy was expressly recognized was the case of Schuyler v. Curtis (1892), 15 N.Y.S. 787, where Justice O'Brien of the Supreme Court of New York granted an injunction to restrain the making and public exhibition of a statue of a deceased person, upon the ground that it was not shown that she was a public character. * * *

In Roberson v. Rochester Folding Box Company * * * it appeared that lithographic likenesses of a young woman, bearing the words "Flour of the Family," were without her consent printed and used by a flour milling company to advertise its goods. * * * This is the first and only decision by a court of last resort involving directly the existence of a right of privacy. * * *

We think that what should have been a proper judgment in the Roberson case was that contended for by Judge Gray in his dissenting opinion * * *.

Nothing appears from which it is to be inferred that [Mr. Pavesich] has waived his right to determine for himself where his picture should be displayed in favor of the advertising right of the defendants. The mere fact that he is an artist does not of itself establish a waiver of this right, so that his picture might be used for advertising purposes. If he displayed in public his works as an artist, he would of course subject his works and his character as an artist, and possibly his character and conduct as a man, to such scrutiny and criticism as would be legitimate and proper to determine whether he was entitled to rank as an artist and should be accorded recognition as such by the public. But it is by no means clear that even this would have authorized the publication of his picture. * * *

What we have ruled can not be in any sense construed as an abridgment of the liberty of speech and of the press as guaranteed in the constitution. * * * There is in the publication of one's picture for advertising purposes not the slightest semblance of an expression of an idea, a thought, or an opinion, within the meaning of the constitutional provision which guarantees to a person the right to publish his sentiments on any subject. Such conduct is not embraced within the liberty to print, but is a serious invasion of one's right of privacy, and may in many cases, according to the circumstances of the publication and the uses to which it is put, cause damages to flow which are irreparable in their nature. The knowledge that one's features and form are being used for such a purpose and displayed in such places as such advertisements are often liable to be found brings not only the person of an extremely sensitive nature, but even the individual of ordinary sensibility, to a realization that his liberty has been taken away from him, and, as long as the advertiser uses him for these purposes, he can not be otherwise than conscious of the fact that he is, for the time being, under the control of another, that he is no longer free, and that he is in reality a slave without hope of freedom, held to service by a merciless master * * *.

NOTE: THE RHETORIC OF FREEDOM AND SLAVERY

The *Pavesich* opinion grounds the case for a right of privacy, there, the right to control whether one's photograph is published, on human freedom. Is the protection of privacy as important as that? Is it a matter of liberty? Judge Cobb drew broadly on principles of Roman law, English and American common law, and the U.S. constitution as persuasive authority for his historic recognition of a right to privacy.

At the end of his opinion, Judge Cobb, suggested that privacy invasions are tantamount to slavery. The victim of a privacy invasion: "is in reality a slave without hope of freedom, held to service by a merciless master." This is remarkable rhetoric. Cf. *State v. Mann*, 13 N.C. 263 (N.C.1829), holding that intervening on behalf of an abused slave would violate private property rights of their owners. Actual chattel slavery of African–Americans had ended in Georgia forty years earlier. Indeed, in 1905, virtually all schools, neighborhoods, and places of accommodation were still legally segregated by race in Georgia.

Was the wrong Mr. Pavesich suffered comparable to slavery? Was it more like bad manners than slavery?

NOTE: POSITIVISM AND NATURAL LAW

In *Pavesich*, Judge Cobb asserted that privacy is an aspect of liberty and that liberty is a requirement of natural law. What is natural law? See John Finnis, *Natural Law and Natural Rights* (1980). See also Ronald Dworkin, Natural Law Revisited, 34 *Fla. L. Rev.* 165 (1982). Natural laws are principles of right conduct discernable by faculties of reason, intuition or faith. When a judge appeals to natural law he or she is appealing to "higher" values that may not have found their way into case precedent or legislation. Can two good judges disagree about how natural law requires them to decide a case? Assuming, for the sake of argument, that there really are natural laws, might there be a good reason not to appeal to them directly when deciding cases?

Why didn't Judge Parker turn to natural law in the *Roberson* case? Judge Parker seemed implicitly to adhere to an approach to adjudication often described as "positivism". Positivism most commends judges who decide cases by strictly applying rules put into place by real-world legal authorities. Positivist judges look to preexisting rules or enactments, rather than natural laws, moral values or attractive public policies. Is positivistic adjudication potentially more democratic than natural law adjudication? Is natural law adjudication potentially more humane?

Philosophers have argued that the law ought to include rights of privacy, whether "created" by legislation or "recognized" through the common law. One compelling argument for privacy rights relies on the ideal of respect for persons rooted in the moral thought of Immanuel Kant (1724–1804). S.I. Benn was one of the first influential proponents of the perspective that the principle of respect for persons is an ethical rationale for privacy protection.

S.I. BENN, PRIVACY, FREEDOM, AND RESPECT FOR PERSONS

Nomos XIII (ed. Pennock and Chapman (1971)) 8–9.

I am suggesting that a general principle of privacy might be grounded on the more general principle of respect for persons. By a person I understand a subject with a consciousness of himself as agent, one who is capable of having projects, and assessing his achievements in relation to them. To conceive someone as a person is to see him as actually or potentially a chooser, as one attempting to steer his own course through the world, adjusting his behavior as his apperception of the world changes, and correcting course as he perceives his errors. It is to understand that his life is for him a kind of enterprise like one's own, not merely a succession of more or less fortunate happenings, but a record of achievements and failures; and just as one cannot describe one's own life in these terms without claiming that what happens is important, so to see another's in the same light is to see that for him at least this must be important. * * * To respect someone as a person is to concede that one ought to take account of the way in which his enterprise might be affected by one's decision.

NOTE: FOUR PRIVACY TORTS

In 1960, William Prosser looked back at all the cases the courts had decided under the right to privacy rubric since *Pavesich*. He grouped the cases into four categories. One category—the intrusion cases—were efforts by plaintiffs to recover against people who had entered concealed and secluded spaces. The other three categories of cases were efforts by plaintiffs to cover against people for wrongful publications and publicity. Prosser concluded that, all combined, the privacy cases reflected the emergence of a right to privacy protected by four distinct privacy torts.

The American Law Institute incorporated Prosser's analysis of the invasion of privacy torts into the *Restatement (Second) of Torts*. Most states have now adopted the some or all of the invasion of privacy torts recognized in the *Restatement*. One of the four torts, the "false light" tort, has proven less popular with the courts than the others, for reasons we shall soon see.

WILLIAM L. PROSSER, PRIVACY

48 California Law Review 383, 388–89 (1960).

In nearly every jurisdiction the first decisions were understandably preoccupied with the question whether the right to privacy existed at all, and give little or no consideration to what it would amount to if it did. It is only in recent years, and largely through legal writers that there has been any attempt to inquire what interests are we protecting, and against what conduct. Today, with something over three hundred cases in the books, the holes in the jigsaw have been largely filled in, and some rather definite conclusions are possible.

What has emerged from the decisions is no simple matter. It is not one tort, but a complex of four. The law of privacy comprises four distinct kinds of invasion of four different interests of the plaintiff, which are tied together by the common name, but otherwise have almost nothing in common except that each represents an interference with the right of the plaintiff, in the phrase coined by Judge [Thomas] Cooley, "to be let alone." Without any attempt to exact definition, these four torts may be described as follows: 1. Intrusion upon the plaintiff's seclusion or into his private affairs. 2. Public disclosure of embarrassing private facts about the plaintiff. 3. Publicity which places the plaintiff in a false light in the public eye. 4. Appropriation, for the defendant's advantage, of the plaintiff's name or likeness.

AMERICAN LAW INSTITUTE RESTATEMENT (SECOND) OF TORTS

Invasion of Privacy—Sections 652 A, B, C, D and E.

652A. General Principle

(1) One who invades the right of privacy of another is subject to liability for the resulting harm to the interests of the other.

(2) The right of privacy is invaded by:

(a) unreasonable intrusion upon the seclusion of another, as stated in 652B; or

(b) appropriation of the other's name or likeness, as stated in 652C; or

(c) unreasonable publicity given to the other's private life, as stated in 652D; or

(d) publicity that unreasonably places the other in a false light before the public, as stated in 652E.

NOTE: WHY PRIVACY MATTERS—LIBERAL TRADITIONS

S.I. Benn argued, *supra*, that respect for persons mandates respect for privacy. If he is right, a society potentially satisfies a moral mandate of respect for persons when it creates or recognizes legal privacy rights. Does a society which fails to recognize even one of the four privacy torts fail fully to respect persons? Does "respect for persons" capture all the benefits that a society gets out of privacy?

Philosopher Gary Marx's "top ten" list of reasons that privacy is important cites moral, psychological, social and political benefits. See Gary T. Marx, *Privacy and Technology*, http://www.garymarx.net. Marx argued, consistent with Benn, that "The ability to control information is linked to the dignity of the individual, self-respect and the sense of personhood. Self-presentations and back-stage behavior are dependent on such control." But he also argued that "Group boundaries are maintained partly by control over information;" that "Privacy makes possible the American ideal of * * * the fresh start;" and that "Privacy can help provide the solitude and peace necessary to mental health and creativity in a dynamic society."

Moreover, privacy has symbolic value in liberal society, Marx maintained: "There is a broader, all encompassing symbolic meaning of practices that protect privacy. Such practices say something about what a nation stands for and are vital to individualism. By contrast, a thread running through all totalitarian systems from the prison to the authoritarian state is lack of respect for the individual's right to control information about the self. It has been said that the mark of a civilization can be seen in how it treats its prisoners; it might also be seen in how it treats personal privacy."

The *Pavesich* court, again, the first state supreme court to expressly recognize a right to privacy tort, analogized privacy invasions to slavery—a radical lack of liberty. Is respecting privacy only possible in a society that is broadly speaking "liberal"?

By definition * * * 'a liberal is a man who believes in liberty'. In two different ways, liberals accord liberty primacy as a political value. (i) Liberals have typically maintained that humans are naturally in 'a *State of perfect Freedom* to order their Actions ... as they think fit ... without asking leave, or depending on the Will of any other Man' (Locke * * *). Mill too argued that 'the burden of proof is supposed to be with those who are against liberty; who contend for any restriction or prohibition....

The *a priori* assumption is in favour of freedom...' * * *. Recent liberal thinkers such as Joel Feinberg * * *, Stanley Benn * * * and John Rawls * * * agree. This might be called the *Fundamental Liberal Principle* * * *: freedom is normatively basic, and so the onus of justification is on those who would limit freedom, especially through coercive means. It follows from this that political authority and law must be justified, as they limit the liberty of citizens. * * * (ii) The Fundamental Liberal Principle holds that restrictions on liberty must be justified.

Gerald F. Gaus, Liberalism, *Stanford Encyclopedia of Philosophy*, http://plato. stanford.edu/entries/liberalism/. If liberals understand privacy as a form or requirement of liberty, what kinds of privacy protections are required of a just liberal state? Are privacy torts essential protections?

NOTE: *MASTERING THE DOCTRINE*

The remainder of this chapter will introduce each of the four privacy torts, one at a time. It will also provide an opportunity to learn common law confidentiality rules, and how celebrities use the right to publicity to protect their fame and work products. As you read through the cases, take careful note of the doctrinal aspects of the privacy torts.

First, who has standing to sue for invasion of someone's privacy? Can a family member sue? What about an employer? Can a corporation sue for invasion of its own privacy? What monetary damages and/or equitable remedies are available to privacy plaintiffs?

Second, what elements must plaintiffs prove in order to prevail? Must they prove intent? What is the burden of proof? Must the plaintiff always show a "highly offensive" act and prove it by a preponderance of the evidence?

Third, what are the affirmative defenses and privileges on which a defendant may rely? What kinds of unwanted informational disclosures and publications may be privileged by newsworthiness and the First Amendment?

Fourth, does a lawsuit for invasion of privacy continue if the plaintiff dies before the suit has been resolved? Can a suit for invasion of privacy be instituted after the person whose privacy was invaded has died?

Fifth, what values do the courts cite in the privacy torts cases? What moral or policy purposes do the rules and rulings serve?

Finally, jurists and legal scholars who assert that privacy is a legal right uniformly agree that privacy rights are not and cannot be absolute. It is common for courts to "balance" privacy interests against interests in, inter alia, open government, law enforcement, public health, national security, business, efficiency, and the public's right to know. In constitutional cases courts have held that even where privacy interests are "fundamental," they can be overcome by "compelling state interests" and burdens that are not "unduly burdensome." Pay careful attention to what interests are most typically pitted against privacy interests in the tort cases, and just how weak or strong the courts take privacy interests to be.

C. THE INTRUSION TORT

1. AMERICAN LAW INSTITUTE, RESTATEMENT (SECOND) OF TORTS, § 652B

§ 652B. Intrusion Upon Seclusion

One who intentionally intrudes, physically or otherwise, upon the solitude or seclusion of another or his private affairs or concerns, is subject to liability to the other for invasion of his privacy, if the intrusion would be highly offensive to a reasonable person.

2. LISTENING AND LOOKING

HAMBERGER v. EASTMAN

106 N.H. 107 (N.H. 1964).

KENISON, J.

[The defendant planted a listening device in the bedroom of a married couple, who sued for invasion of privacy. The defendant moved to dismiss the lawsuit.] The question presented is whether the right of privacy is recognized in this state. * * *

In capsule summary the invasion of the right of privacy developed as an independent and distinct tort from the classic and famous article by Warren and Brandeis, The Right to Privacy, 4 Harv. L. Rev. 193 (1890), although Judge Cooley had discussed "the right to be let alone" some years previously. Cooley, Torts 29 (1st ed. 1879). In 1902 the New York Court of Appeals decided that the right of privacy did not have "an abiding place in our jurisprudence." Roberson v. Rochester Folding Box Co., 171 N. Y. 538, 556. The following year the New York Legislature acted promptly to remedy this deficiency. Laws of N. Y. 1903, ch. 132; N. Y. Civil Rights Law, ss. 50 and 51. Shortly thereafter in 1905 Pavesich v. New England Life Ins. Co., 122 Ga. 190, upheld the right of privacy and became the leading case on the subject. Since that time the right of privacy has been given protection in a majority of the jurisdictions in this country, generally without benefit of statute, and only a small minority have rejected the concept and some of these minority decisions are not recent. * * * "What has emerged is * * * not one tort, but a complex of four. The law of privacy comprises four distinct kinds of invasion of four different interests of the plaintiff which are tied together by the common name, but otherwise have almost nothing in common except that each represents an interference with the right of the plaintiff 'to be let alone.' " Prosser, Torts, s. 112, p. 832 (3d ed. 1964).

The four kinds of invasion comprising the law of privacy include: (1) intrusion upon the plaintiff's physical and mental solitude or seclusion; (2) public disclosure of private facts; (3) publicity which places the plaintiff in a false light in the public eye; (4) appropriation, for the defendant's benefit or advantage, of the plaintiff's name or likeness. In the present case, we are concerned only with the tort of intrusion upon the plaintiffs' solitude or seclusion. * * *

The tort of intrusion upon the plaintiff's solitude or seclusion is not limited to a physical invasion of his home or his room or his quarters. As Prosser points out, the principle has been carried beyond such physical intrusion "and extended to eavesdropping upon private conversations by means of wire tapping and microphones." * * *

We have not searched for cases where the bedroom of husband and wife has been "bugged" but it should not be necessary—by way of understatement—to observe that this is the type of intrusion that would be offensive to any person of ordinary sensibilities. What married "people do in the privacy of their bedrooms is their own business so long as they are not hurting anyone else." * * *

The defendant contends that the right of privacy should not be recognized on the facts of the present case as they appear in the pleadings because there are no allegations that anyone listened or overheard any sounds or voices originating from the plaintiffs' bedroom. The tort of intrusion on the plaintiffs' solitude or seclusion does not require publicity and communication to third persons although this would affect the amount of damages * * *. The defendant also contends that the right of privacy is not violated unless something has been published, written or printed and that oral publicity is not sufficient. Recent cases make it clear that this is not a requirement. * * *

If the peeping Tom, the big ear and the electronic eavesdropper (whether ingenious or ingenuous) have a place in the hierarchy of social values, it ought not to be at the expense of a married couple minding their own business in the seclusion of their bedroom who have never asked for or by their conduct deserved a potential projection of their private conversations and actions to their landlord or to others. Whether actual or potential such "publicity with respect to private matters of purely personal concern is an injury to personality. It impairs the mental peace and comfort of the individual and may produce suffering more acute than that produced by a mere bodily injury." III Pound, Jurisprudence 58 (1959). The use of parabolic microphones and sonic wave devices designed to pick up conversations in a room without entering it and at a considerable distance away makes the problem far from fanciful. Dash, Schwartz & Knowlton, The Eavesdroppers pp. 346–358 (1959). * * *

For the purposes of the present case it is sufficient to hold that the invasion of the plaintiffs' solitude or seclusion, as alleged in the pleadings, was a violation of their right of privacy and constituted a tort for which the plaintiffs may recover damages to the extent that they can prove them.

BORING v. GOOGLE, INC.

598 F.Supp.2d 695 (W.D. Pennsylvania 2009).

HAY, UNITED STATES MAGISTRATE JUDGE.

In April 2008, Pennsylvania residents, Aaron and Christine Boring ("the Plaintiffs" or "the Borings"), filed a five count Complaint against Google, Inc. ("the Defendant" or "Google"), a Delaware corporation, in the Court of Common Pleas of Allegheny County, Pennsylvania. The Borings alleged entitlement to compensatory and punitive damages based on four tort-based causes of action [including] Count I—invasion of privacy * * *. * * * Because the Plaintiffs have failed to state a claim under any count, the Amended Complaint will be dismissed.

Background

Google describes itself as the operator of a "well-known internet search engine" that maintains the world's largest and most comprehensive index of web sites and other online content. * * * One of the services offered by Google is comprehensive online map access. "Google Maps gives users the ability to look up addresses, search for businesses, and get point-to point driving directions—all plotted on interactive street maps" made up of satellite or aerial images. * * * In May 2007, Google introduced "Street View" to its map options. Street View permits users to see and navigate within 360 degree street level images of a number of cities, including Pittsburgh. These images were generated by Google drivers who traversed the covered cities in passenger vehicles equipped with continuously filming digital panoramic cameras. * * * According to Google, "the scope of Street View was public roads." *Id.* Google included in the Street View program an option for those objecting to the content of an image to have it removed from view. * * *

The Borings, who live on a private road north of Pittsburgh, discovered that "colored imagery" of their residence, outbuildings, and swimming pool, taken "from a vehicle in their residence driveway ... without ... waiver or authorization," had been included on Street View. * * * The Plaintiffs allege that the road on which their home is located is unpaved and clearly marked with "Private Road" and "No Trespassing" signs. * * * They contend that Google, in taking the Street Search pictures from their driveway at a point past the signs, and in making those photographs available to the public, "significantly disregarded [their] privacy interests." * * * The Court addresses the sufficiency of the Borings' claims seriatim. * * *

A. The Claims for Invasion of Privacy

The action for invasion of privacy embraces four analytically distinct torts: (1) intrusion upon seclusion; (2) publicity given to private life; (3) appropriation of name or likeness; and (4) publicity placing a person in a false light. *Borse v. Piece Goods Shop, Inc.,* 963 F.2d 611, 621 n. 9 (3d Cir.1992). The Borings do not identity the tort or torts underlying their invasion of privacy claim. Appropriation of name or likeness and false light publicity clearly do not apply. Since the remaining torts have an arguable relationship to the facts alleged, the Court will discuss each.

1. Intrusion Upon Seclusion

This tort is established where a plaintiff is able to show: (1) physical intrusion into a place where he has secluded himself; (2) use of the defendant's senses to oversee or overhear the plaintiff's private affairs; or (3) some other form of investigation into or examination of the plaintiff's private concerns. *Id.* at 621. "Liability attaches only when the intrusion is substantial and would be highly offensive to 'the ordinary reasonable person.'" *Id.* (quoting *Harris by Harris v. Easton Publ'g Co.,* 335 Pa.Super. 141, 483 A.2d 1377, 1383–84 (1984)). *See also* Restatement (Second) of Torts § 652B (same). In order to show that an intrusion was highly offensive, the plaintiff must allege facts sufficient to establish that the intrusion could be expected to cause "mental suffering, shame, or humiliation to a person of ordinary sensibilities." *Pro Golf Mfg., Inc. v. Tribune Review Newspaper Co.,* 570 Pa. 242, 809 A.2d 243, 247 (2002) (*quoting McGuire v. Shubert,* 722 A.2d 1087 (Pa.Super.1998)). This is a stringent standard. *Wolfson v. Lewis,* 924 F.Supp. 1413, 1420 (E.D.Pa.1996). While it is easy to imagine that many whose property appears on Google's virtual maps resent the privacy implications, it is hard to believe that any—other than the most exquisitely sensitive—would suffer shame or humiliation. The Plaintiffs have not alleged facts to convince the Court otherwise.

Although the Plaintiffs have alleged intrusion that was substantial and highly offensive to them and have asserted that others would have a similar reaction, they have failed to set out facts to substantiate this claim. This is especially true given the attention that the Borings have drawn to themselves and the Street View images of their property. The Borings do not dispute that they have allowed the relevant images to remain on Google Street View, despite the availability of a procedure for having them removed from view. Furthermore, they have failed to bar others' access to the images by eliminating their address from the pleadings, or by filing this action under seal. "Googling" the name of the Borings' attorney demonstrates that publicity regarding this suit has perpetuated dissemination of the Borings' names and location, and resulted in frequent re-publication of the Street View images. The Plaintiffs' failure to take readily available steps to protect their own privacy and mitigate their alleged pain suggests to the Court that the intrusion and the their suffering were less severe than they contend.

NOTE: *BORING V. GOOGLE ON APPEAL*

The Borings appealed the decision of the District Court. See *Boring v. Google, Inc.,* 362 Fed.Appx. 273, 2010 WL 318281 (C.A.3 (Pa.)). In its unpublished opinion filed Jan. 28, 2010, the Third Circuit Court of Appeals affirmed the dismissal of the privacy claims. On the intrusion theory, the court found that: "No person of ordinary sensibilities would be shamed, humiliated, or have suffered mentally as a result of a vehicle entering into his or her ungated driveway and photographing the view from there. The Restatement cites knocking on the door of a private residence as an example of conduct that would not be highly offensive to a person of ordinary sensibilities. *See* RESTATEMENT (SECOND) OF TORTS, § 652B cmt. d. The Borings' claim is pinned to an arguably less intrusive event than a door knock. Indeed, the privacy allegedly intruded upon was the external view of the Borings' house, garage, and pool—a view that would be seen by any person who entered onto their driveway, including a visitor or a delivery man. Thus, what really seems to be at the heart of the complaint is not Google's fleeting presence in the driveway, but the photographic image captured at that time. The existence of that image, though, does not in itself rise to the level of an intrusion that could reasonably be called highly offensive. * * * In sum, accepting the Borings' allegations as true, their claim for intrusion upon seclusion fails as a matter of law, because the alleged conduct would not be highly offensive to a person of ordinary sensibilities."

DALLEY v. DYKEMA GOSSETT ET AL.

788 N.W.2d 679 (Mich.App.2010).

* * * This case finds its genesis in a dispute between an insurance company and its agent. On April 13, 2004, defendants Lincoln National Life Insurance Company and Lincoln Financial Advisors Corporation (collectively Lincoln) sued Rodney Ellis, a Lincoln agent, and Lucasse, Ellis, Inc. (Lucasse), a company partially owned by Ellis, in the United States District Court for the Western District of Michigan. Lincoln's federal court complaint alleged fraud, breach of fiduciary duty, conversion, breach of contract, and tortious interference with business expectancies or relations. * * * [Plaintiff Scott Dalley was a consultant for Lucasse.]

On April 15, 2004, a federal judge entered a temporary restraining order (TRO) prohibiting Ellis, Lucasse, and instant plaintiff Dalley from "deleting, erasing, destroying, shredding, secreting, removing, modifying, overwriting, replacing, or 'wiping' " any computer data or files containing information related to Lincoln's customers and financial records. * * *

On April 19, 2004, Lincoln's agents served plaintiff with the TRO in his Kentwood apartment, and with the assistance of personnel employed by defendant Guidance Software, Inc. (Guidance Software), copied all the data from all of plaintiff's computers. The events surrounding defendants' entry into plaintiffs' home and the copying of his computer data form the basis of the instant lawsuit. * * *

The amended complaint avers that in April 2004, plaintiff worked out of his apartment as an independent computer consultant for several small businesses, including Lucasse. The computers in his apartment provided his livelihood and held confidential information concerning all his clients, such as their user identifications and passwords. Plaintiff, who suffers from AIDS, also stored on his computers highly personal information, medical records, photographs, and tax returns.

On April 19, 2004, plaintiff's doorbell rang and someone requested that plaintiff permit entry into his apartment building. Because plaintiff was not expecting visitors, he did not respond. At approximately 11:00 a.m., loud pounding on his door "jolted" plaintiff awake and he "realized that the men outside had managed to slip through the security system downstairs." Plaintiff saw papers slide under his door, and he read them after the men had departed. The papers included the TRO, which "completely blindsided" plaintiff. Soon thereafter, plaintiff's telephone rang, but he did not answer it. The caller, Ferroli, left a message declaring that a federal court subpoena allowed him and others to enter plaintiff's apartment "to either take his computers and hard drives or copy what was on them." Plaintiff "reasonably believed that he could not let Ferroli simply walk out the door with the computers," and that "he had no choice and would go to jail" if he refused Ferroli access to his computers. Plaintiff thus "returned Ferroli's call and agreed to" allow Ferroli "to copy the information on his computers."

Ferroli and several Guidance Software employees arrived, and plaintiff "led the group to the master bedroom where he kept two computers and four hard drives and, having seen from the subpoena that the case had something to do with Lincoln and Ellis, pointed them to the one and only hard drive that would contain Lincoln data." But "[t]he intruders . . . demanded everything." The Guidance Software personnel connected laptop computers to plaintiff's machines and transferred "every bit of information on all [plaintiff's] computers and hard drives." Only a "small percentage" of the information copied by Guidance Software personnel related to Ellis, Lucasse, or Lincoln. The data transfer and copying process consumed 11 hours, during which period Ferroli "wandered in and out." In frail health and underweight, plaintiff "did not sleep for several days thereafter." * * *

The amended complaint sets forth five intentional tort claims: invasion of privacy in the form of intrusion on seclusion or into private affairs; trespass; intentional or reckless infliction of emotional distress; abuse of process; and tortious interference with business relationships or expectancies. All defendants sought summary disposition of plaintiff's claims * * *.

Plaintiff challenges the circuit court's grant of summary disposition regarding all five counts of his complaint. This Court reviews de novo a circuit court's summary disposition ruling. * * *

B. Invasion of Privacy

"Michigan has long recognized the common-law tort of invasion of privacy." *Lewis v. LeGrow,* 258 Mich.App 175, 193; 670 NW2d 675 (2003). Dean Prosser has identified a Michigan case, *DeMay v. Roberts,* 46 Mich. 160; 9 NW 146 (1881), as among the first reported decisions allowing relief premised on an invasion of privacy theory. Prosser, *Privacy,* 48 Cal L Rev 383, 389 (1960). * * *

There are three necessary elements to establish a prima facie case of intrusion upon seclusion: (1) the existence of a secret and private subject matter; (2) a right possessed by the plaintiff to keep that subject matter private; and (3) the obtaining of information about that subject matter through some method objectionable to a reasonable man. [*Doe v. Mills,* 212 Mich.App 73, 88; 536 NW2d 824 (1995).]

elements

The circuit court granted summary disposition of plaintiff's intrusion of seclusion claim on the basis that the complaint failed to set forth facts "that show that he had a right to privacy in those areas of the apartment necessary to carry out the mandate of the TRO." Relying on this Court's opinion in *Saldana v. Kelsey–Hayes Co,* 178 Mich.App 230; 443 NW2d 382 (1989), the circuit court added that the TRO deprived plaintiff of a right to privacy in his computers and hard drives * * *.

We find *Saldana* readily distinguishable from this case. In *Saldana,* the nature of the parties' relationship limited the plaintiff's right to privacy concerning the matter the defendant investigated: whether the plaintiff suffered from work-related disabilities. Here, defendants and plaintiff shared no special relationship, business or otherwise, and defendants possessed no legitimate interest in viewing plaintiff's apartment or copying computer data unrelated to Lincoln. * * * The TRO afforded defendants no right whatsoever to enter or search plaintiff's apartment. Regarding plaintiff's computers, the TRO entitled Lincoln's agent to copy hard drives and other electronic media "which contain any Lincoln Customer Records." But no provision in the TRO authorized defendants to copy personal computer data unrelated to Lincoln. * * *

The plain language of the TRO in no way renders unenforceable plaintiff's intrusion on seclusion claim.

Defendants alternatively maintain that plaintiff expressly or impliedly consented to the intrusion on his seclusion by allowing Ferroli and the Guidance Software personnel into his apartment and permitting them to copy his computer data. We resolve this contention by referring to our Supreme Court's landmark decision in *DeMay,* 46 Mich. 160, and this Court's analysis in *Lewis,* 258 Mich.App 175. The defendant in *DeMay,* a physician, set out on "a dark and stormy" night to attend the plaintiff, a patient in labor. *Id.* at 162. Because Dr. DeMay "was sick and very much fatigued from overwork," he asked a codefendant named Scattergood, "a young unmarried man, a stranger to the plaintiff and utterly ignorant of the practice of medicine," to accompany and assist him. *Id.* at 161–162. When they arrived at the plaintiff's home, Dr. DeMay told the plaintiff's husband, " 'I had fetched a friend along to help carry my things'. . . ." *Id.* at 162. Neither the plaintiff nor her husband objected to Scattergood's presence, and during most of the plaintiff's labor Scattergood sat facing a wall. *Id.* at 162, 165. At one point, Dr. DeMay asked Scattergood to assist by holding the plaintiff's hand "during a paroxysm of pain." *Id.* at 162.

The plaintiff brought suit when she ascertained Scattergood's true identity and lack of medical training, contending that Dr. DeMay deceived her into believing that Scattergood "was an assistant physician." *Id.* at 161.

The Supreme Court held that "the plaintiff had a legal right to the privacy of her apartment at such a time, and the law secures to her this right by requiring others to observe it, and to abstain from its violation." *DeMay,* 46 Mich. at 165–166. Notwithstanding that Scattergood and Dr. DeMay "were bidden to enter, treated kindly and no objection whatever [was] made to the presence of defendant Scattergood," *id.* at 162, the Supreme Court declined to hold that the plaintiff had consented to Scattergood's intrusion on her privacy:

> The fact that at the time, she consented to the presence of Scattergood supposing him to be a physician, does not preclude her from maintaining an action and recovering substantial damages upon afterwards ascertaining his true character. In obtaining admission at such a time and under such circumstances without fully disclosing his true character, both parties were guilty of deceit, and the wrong thus done entitles the injured party to recover the damages afterwards sustained, from shame and mortification upon discovering the true character of the defendants. [*Id.* at 166.]

This Court revisited *DeMay* in *Lewis,* 258 Mich.App 175, a case that "involve[d] the surreptitious, nonconsensual videotaping of intimate acts of sexual relations in defendant['s] . . . bedroom." *Id.* at 178. A jury found that the defendant had violated the plaintiffs' common-law rights to privacy. The defendant argued on appeal that because the plaintiffs had consented to having sex with him, as a matter of law he had not invaded their privacy. *Id.* at 191. This Court acknowledged that "there can be no invasion of privacy under the theory of intrusion upon the seclusion of plaintiffs if plaintiffs consented to defendant's intrusion (videotaping)." *Id.* at 194. However, "[t]he question of waiver or consent . . . does not have a zero-sum answer but, rather, presents an issue of the degree or extent of waiver or consent granted, which depends on the facts and circumstances of the case." *Id.* at 194. Because the evidence in *Lewis* supported that the defendant had videotaped the plaintiffs without their knowledge or consent, this Court concluded that a factual question existed on which reasonable minds could differ with respect to the scope of the plaintiffs' consent to the taping. * * *

Here, plaintiff's amended complaint alleges that defendants obtained consent to enter the apartment through a combination of subterfuge and threat: "Ferroli said he had a federal court subpoena that allowed him and the other men to come inside [plaintiff's] apartment to either take his computers and hard drives or copy what was on them." The amended complaint also avers that plaintiff withheld consent to defendants' copying of anything other than "the one and only hard drive that would contain Lincoln data." These averments fall squarely within the legal analyses and holdings presented in *DeMay* and *Lewis.* As described in the amended complaint, the circumstances surrounding defendants' entry into plaintiff's apartment and the copying of his computer hard drives reasonably suggest that defendants' artifice and dishonesty enticed plaintiff's consent. "Generally, the scope of a waiver or consent will present a question of fact for the jury[.]" *Lewis,* 258 Mich.App at 195. As in *Lewis, id.,* when viewed in the light most favorable to plaintiff, the amended complaint presents factual questions on which reasonable minds could differ with respect to whether defendants gained admission to plaintiff's premises by deceit, as in *DeMay,* or exceeded the scope of the consent plaintiff extended, as in *Lewis* and *Earp.*

Defendants lastly argue regarding the invasion of privacy count that plaintiff's complaint contains no facts supporting that defendants obtained private information through a method that might be objectionable to a reasonable person, or that defendants ever viewed the information they copied. Whether a reasonable person would find an intrusion objectionable constitutes a factual question best determined by a jury. * * *

In summary, because plaintiff's amended complaint adequately sets forth a claim for invasion of privacy by intrusion on seclusion, we conclude that the circuit court improperly granted defendants summary disposition of this claim under MCR 2.116(C)(8).

ELMORE v. ATLANTIC ZAYRE

178 Ga.App. 25, 341 S.E.2d 905 (1986).

CARLEY, JUDGE.

A customer made a complaint that homosexual activity was occurring in a rest room that appellee-defendant Zayre's maintained for the convenience of its patrons. In response, appellee-defendant Cox, who is Zayre's loss prevention manager, inspected the rest room and observed an exhibition of highly suspicious behavior therein. He and another member of the security staff then determined to verify that criminal activity was occurring behind the door of a closed stall. For that purpose, they went to a location in a storage area above the rest room, where a crack in the ceiling provided a vantage point. Based on their observations, appellant-plaintiff was arrested and charged with sodomy. * * * [A]ppellant pled guilty without admitting the commission of sodomy and received a probated first offender sentence. Appellant then brought the instant civil action, alleging that appellees had invaded his privacy by "spying on him in a private place." This appeal is from the grant of summary judgment in favor of appellees. Appellant contends that the trial court erred in granting summary judgment because the following genuine issues of material fact remain: whether appellees invaded his privacy by peeking through a crack in the bathroom ceiling; whether any homosexual activity actually took place in the bathroom prior to appellees' surveillance of appellant; and, whether appellant actually committed any homosexual or other criminal act. * * *

Appellant asserts that appellees' act of "spying" on him while he was in the private seclusion of the toilet stall constituted such an actionable invasion of privacy. An individual clearly has an interest in privacy within a toilet stall. See *Wylie v. State,* 164 Ga.App. 174, 296 S.E.2d 743 (1982). "However, the law recognizes that the right of privacy is not absolute.... 'But it [right of privacy] must be kept within its proper limits, and in its exercise must be made to accord with the rights of those who have other liberties, *as well as the rights of any person who may be properly interested in the matters which are claimed to be of purely private concern.*' [*Pavesich v. New England Life Ins. Co.,* 122 Ga. 190, 201 (50 SE 68) (1905).]" * * *

In the instant case, the toilet stall which appellant was occupying was in a restroom provided by appellee Zayre's for use by its customers. Thus, appellee Zayre's had an overriding responsibility to its patrons to keep that restroom free of crime, safe, and available for its intended purpose. The evidence is uncontradicted that appellees' investigation was prompted by a customer complaint of homosexual activity in the restroom. Acting solely upon this complaint, appellee Cox inspected the restroom. There, his own suspicion was alerted by seeing three or four men along the wall seemingly waiting for the second and third stalls, both of which were occupied, even though the first stall was empty and in working order. Only then was the decision made to go above the restroom and determine if any criminal activity was in fact occurring. * * * Under similar circumstances to those which exist in the case sub judice, police surveillance has been held not to constitute an invasion of the right of privacy. "Where, 'as here, the police have reasonable cause to believe that public toilet stalls are being used in the commission of crime, and when, as here, they confine their activities to the times when such crimes are most likely to occur, they are entitled to institute clandestine surveillance, even though they do not have probable cause to believe that the particular persons whom they may thus catch in flagrante delicto have committed or will commit the crime. The public interest in its privacy, we think, must, to that extent, be subordinated to the public interest in law enforcement.' [Cit.]" *Mitchell v. State,* 120 Ga.App. 447, 170 S.E.2d 765 (1969). * * *

Appellant contends, however, that even if law enforcement officers would have been authorized to surveil the toilet stalls, private citizens were not. OCGA § 16–11–62 does provide that "[i]t shall be unlawful for ... (3) Any person to go on or about the premises of another or any private place for the purpose of invading the privacy of another by ... secretly observing their activities." See also OCGA § 16–11–61. However, appellant was not in a private bathroom. He was in a stall of a public restroom on premises belonging to appellee Zayre's. The employees of appellee Zayre's were thus upon their employer's own premises. It is likewise uncontroverted that the observations were made, not for the purpose of personally invading the privacy of others, but while investigating suspected criminal activity on those premises. Accordingly, the general proscription of OCGA § 16–11–61 and 16–11–62(3) is in no way applicable to appellees' acts.

HOUGUM v. VALLEY MEMORIAL HOMES

574 N.W.2d 812 (N.D.,1998).

NEUMANN, JUSTICE.

Daniel Hougum appealed from a summary judgment dismissing his *PH* action against Valley Memorial Homes (VMH), Sears Inc., and Shane Moran. We hold Hougum failed to raise disputed factual issues to support *Decision* his claim against Moran and Sears for intrusion upon seclusion. * * *

[An ordained minister, Hougum lost his job as a chaplain for a Christian retirement community after pleading guilty to disorderly conduct. Mr. Hougun was arrested for masturbating in a Sear's department store restroom stall. He had been observed masturbating by a store employee who watched him briefly through an opening in an adjacent stall.]

Under the Restatement, a claim for intrusion upon seclusion [must *elements* allege] * * *(1) an intentional intrusion by the defendant, (2) into a matter the plaintiff has a right to keep private, (3) which is objectionable to a reasonable person. * * * Generally, there are two primary factors for analyzing a claim for intrusion upon seclusion: (1) the means used for the intrusion, and (2) the defendant's purpose for obtaining the information. *Prosser and Keeton* at § 117, p. 856.

In tort claims for intrusion upon seclusion in a public restroom, the intrusion generally involves a preconceived or planned intrusion by surveillance equipment, or by surreptitious observations. *See Elmore v. Atlantic Zayre, Inc.,* 178 Ga.App. 25, 341 S.E.2d 905, 906–07 (1986); *Harkey,* 346 N.W.2d at 75. * * *

In *Harkey,* patrons at a roller rink alleged the rink had installed see-through panels in a restroom ceiling which permitted surreptitious surveillance of patrons using the restroom. The Michigan Court of Appeals held the patrons had a right to privacy in the public restroom, and the installation of hidden viewing devices constituted an interference with privacy that a reasonable person would find highly offensive. *Harkey,* 346 N.W.2d at 76. In *Harkey,* the means of the intrusion demonstrated a preconceived and intentional effort to intrude upon the privacy of another by a method that served no legitimate purpose and was objectionable to a reasonable person. * * *

In *Kjerstad,* there was evidence a male employer used a vacant room next to a workplace restroom on several occasions to observe three female employees through a hole in the wall. The court held the evidence was sufficient to submit the invasion of privacy claim to the jury. *Kjerstad,* 517 N.W.2d at 424.

Here, there was no evidence Moran or Sears drilled the hole in the partition between the two stalls, and there was evidence Sears had, on several occasions, placed a metal plate over the hole, but unidentified persons had removed the plate. According to Moran, he thought the restroom was empty, and while reaching for toilet paper, he saw movement through the hole, which was located about four to five inches directly above the toilet paper dispenser, and inadvertently observed an unidentified individual masturbating for "maybe ten seconds . . . [p]ossibly more or less." According to Moran, his line-of-sight angle permitted him to inadvertently observe the individual through the hole without "stick[ing his] eye down [to] look through the hole."

Moran's visual intrusion was limited in time and scope, and it was not recorded, nor seen by others. As a Sears employee, he was not required to ignore the possibility of shoplifting or vandalism in his employer's public restroom, which he believed was unoccupied, and his relatively brief visual intrusion was consistent with his work responsibilities.

Under the circumstances presented in this record, we decline to elevate the actions by Moran and Sears in this public restroom to an intentional intrusion upon Hougum's interest in seclusion by a method which is objectionable to a reasonable person. Issues about intent and the reasonable person standard are ordinarily questions of fact * * * We hold as a matter of law, reasonable persons could only conclude the manner and purpose of the intrusion by Moran and Sears was not an intentional intrusion upon seclusion by a method which was objectionable to a reasonable person. We therefore conclude summary judgment was proper on Hougum's invasion of privacy claim.

ROBERT POST, THE SOCIAL FOUNDATIONS OF PRIVACY: COMMUNITY AND SELF IN THE COMMON LAW TORT

77 California Law Review 957, 959, 961–3, 973 (1989).

The conceptual structure that underlies the branch of the tort which regulates unreasonable intrusion can be illuminated by consideration of an elementary case, *Hamberger v. Eastman*. Eastman was decided by the New Hampshire Supreme Court in 1964, and constituted the state's first official recognition of the tort of invasion of privacy. I choose the case because it is so entirely unexceptional and representative in its reasoning and conclusions. The plaintiffs were a husband and wife who alleged that the defendant, their landlord and neighbor, had installed an eavesdropping device in their bedroom. * * *

[My proposed] * * * characterization of the conceptual structure underlying Eastman is that a plaintiff is entitled to relief if it can be demonstrated that a defendant has transgressed the kind of social norms whose violation would properly be viewed with outrage or affront, and that the function of this relief is to redress "injury to personality." This legal structure typifies the tort of intrusion. It rests on the premise that the integrity of individual personality is dependent upon the observance of certain kinds of social norms.

This premise, of course, also underlies much of sociological thought. For purposes of analyzing the privacy tort, the most systematic and helpful explication of the premise may be found in the work of Erving Goffman. He most explicitly states the premise in his early article on *The Nature of Deference and Demeanor*, where he offers an image of social interactions as founded on rules of "deference and demeanor." Rules of deference define conduct by which a person conveys appreciation "to a recipient or of this recipient, or of something of which this recipient is taken as a symbol, extension, or agent." Rules of demeanor define conduct by which a person expresses "to those in his immediate presence that he is a person of certain desirable or undesirable qualities."

Taken together, rules of deference and demeanor constitute "rules of conduct which bind the actor and the recipient together" and "are the bindings of society." By following these rules, individuals not only confirm the social order in which they live, but they also establish and affirm "ritual" and "sacred" aspects of their own and others' identities. Thus Goffman states that each "individual must rely on others to complete the picture of him of which he himself is allowed to paint only certain parts":

> Each individual is responsible for the demeanor image of himself and the deference image of others, so that for a complete man to be expressed, individuals must hold hands in a chain of ceremony, each giving deferentially with proper demeanor to the one on the right what will be received deferentially from the one on the left. While it may be true that the individual has a unique self all his own, evidence of this possession is thoroughly a product of joint ceremonial labor, the part expressed through the individual's demeanor being no more significant than the part conveyed by others through their deferential behavior toward him.

According to Goffman, then, we must understand individual personality as constituted in significant aspects by the observance of rules of deference and demeanor; or, to return to the more prosaic language of Eastman, by the rules of decency recognized by the reasonable man, Violation of these rules can thus damage a person by discrediting his identity and injuring his personality. Breaking "the chain of ceremony" can deny an individual the capacity to become "a complete man" and hence "disconfirm" his very "self."

It is for this reason that the law regards the privacy tort as simultaneously upholding social norms and redressing "injury to personality." We must be clear, however, that in any particular case individuals may or may not have internalized pertinent rules of deference and demeanor, and hence may or may not suffer actual injury to personality. But the device of the reasonable person focuses the law not on actual injury to the personality of specific individuals, but rather on the protection of that personality which would be constituted by full observance of the relevant rules of deference and demeanor, those whose violation would appropriately cause outrage or affront. I shall call such rules "civility rules," and I shall call the personality that would be upheld by these civility rules "social personality."

The concept of social personality points simultaneously in two distinct directions. On the one hand, the actual personalities of well-socialized individuals should substantially conform to social personality, for such individuals have internalized the civility rules by which social personality is defined. It is for this reason that the tort of intrusion, even though formally defined in terms of the expectations of the "reasonable person," can in practice be expected to offer protection to the emotional well-being of real plaintiffs. But, on the other hand, social personality also subsists in a set of civility rules that, when taken together, give normative shape and substance to the very society that shares them. In fact these rules can be said to define the very "community" which the "reasonable person" inhabits. * * *

Goffman's analysis suggests that by lending authoritative sanction to the territories of the self, the tort of intrusion performs at least three distinct functions. First, it safeguards the respect due individuals by virtue of their territorial claims. Second, it maintains the language or "ritual idiom" constituted by territories, thus conserving the particular meanings carried by that language. Third, the tort preserves the ability of individuals to speak through the idiom of territories, and this ability, as Goffman notes: "is somehow central to the subjective sense that the individual has concerning his selfhood, his ego, the part of himself with which he identifies his positive feelings." And here the issue is not whether a preserve is exclusively maintained, or shared, or given up entirely, but rather the role the individual is allowed in determining what happens to his claim. An individual's ability to press or to waive territorial claims, his ability to choose respect or intimacy, is deeply empowering for his sense of himself as an independent or autonomous person. As Jeffrey Reiman has noted, "[p]rivacy is an essential part of the complex social practice by means of which the social group recognizes—and communicates to the individual—that his existence is his own. And this is a precondition of personhood".

NOTE: PRIVACY AS A SOCIAL RITUAL

Professor Robert Post's selection ends with a quotation from an article by philosopher Jeffrey Reiman, whose unique account of the nature and value of privacy merits attention. For Reiman, privacy recognition does not simply "enhance" personhood—the claim of many who defend privacy. Rather, privacy is a precondition for personhood. Reiman argued that it is through privacy practices that human young learn that their bodies are their own and that they have "moral title" to their existence. See generally Jeffrey Reiman, "Privacy, Intimacy and Personhood," 6 *Philosophy and Public Affairs* 26 (1976). If privacy is all about "moral title" to our existence, does this suggest that Judge Cobb's slavery rhetoric near the end of the *Pavesich* case was on point?

The plaintiffs in the *Eastman* case were innocent victims of an egregious act of uncivil intrusion. The defendant was a simple auditory voyeur. See Clay

Calvert, *Voyeur Nation: Media, Privacy, and Peering in Modern Culture* (2000). Does Post's civility theory explain the plaintiffs' sense of wrong in *Elmore* and *Hougum*? In the next case, *Plaxico v. Michael*, the defendant is not a mere voyeur and the plaintiff is an "illicit" lover. Is intrusion uncivil if, as in *PETA v. Berosini, Ltd.*, below, the plaintiff is allegedly cruel to animals when he thinks no one is looking and ethically should be stopped?

PLAXICO v. MICHAEL

735 So. 2d 1036 (Miss. 1999).

SMITH, J.

This is an appeal from a judgment of the Circuit Court of Tippah County, Mississippi, dismissing with prejudice, Rita Plaxico's invasion of privacy claim which is based upon the sub-tort of intentional intrusion upon seclusion or solitude. * * *

Glenn Michael and his wife were divorced. They had one female child who was about six (6) years old at the time of trial. The Chancellor gave custody of the child to Michael's wife in the Divorce Decree. Michael's former wife and child lived in a cabin that had been rented by Michael as the family home prior to their divorce. Plaxico moved into the cabin with Michael's former wife and his child sometime after the divorce.

Michael was later informed that his ex-wife was having a [lesbian] relationship with the Plaintiff, Rita Plaxico. Michael wanted to modify the child custody based on the fact that his former wife and Plaxico were romantically involved with each other.

One night in June, 1993, Michael slipped up to a window in the cabin through which he witnessed Plaxico and his former wife having sexual relations. He left to retrieve a camera from his vehicle. After doing so, he returned and took three (3) photographs of Plaxico, who was sitting in bed naked. However, the bed covers covered her from the waist down.

Michael had the photographs developed and delivered the pictures to his attorney. He then, on November 16, 1993, filed for modification of child custody. Michael testified that he did not show the photographs to anyone other than his lawyer. His lawyer produced the photographs to Michael's former wife's attorney in response to discovery requests in the child custody matter pending between Michael and his former wife in which the Chancellor granted Michael the custody of his child. Plaxico became aware of the photographs through Michael's former wife's attorney, who represented both Plaxico and Mrs. Michael.

Plaxico subsequently filed suit for invasion of privacy. She claimed that Michael intentionally intruded upon her seclusion and solitude, and she suffered damages as a result of this tort. She further testified and acknowledged that she and Michael's former wife were lovers and had engaged in sexual relations. Plaxico's complaint and action were dismissed by the Circuit Court of Tippah County, Mississippi, and appealed to this Court. * * *

In order for Plaxico to prevail in this action, she must prove all elements of the sub-tort to invasion of privacy, intentional intrusion upon seclusion or solitude. In Candebat v. Flanagan, we stated that actions for the invasion of privacy as a tort have received universal recognition in the United States. Candebat v. Flanagan, 487 So. 2d 207, 209 (Miss. 1986). In fact, every state except Rhode Island provides either statutory or common law relief for it. * * * Mississippi gave explicit recognition to the tort of invasion of privacy in Deaton v. Delta Democrat Publishing Co., 326 So. 2d 471, 473 (Miss. 1976). * * *

Candebat is our only case that deals specifically with the sub-tort of intentional intrusion upon the solitude or seclusion of another. There we stated that to recover for an invasion of privacy, a plaintiff must meet a heavy burden of showing a substantial interference with his seclusion of a kind that " 'would be highly offensive to the ordinary, reasonable man, as the result of conduct to which the reasonable man would strongly object.' " Id. (quoting Restatement Second of Torts, § 652B, comt. d (1977)). Further, the plaintiff must show some bad faith or utterly reckless prying to recover on an invasion of privacy cause of action. 487 So. 2d at 209. However, the general rule is that there is no requirement of publication or communication to a third party in cases of intrusion upon a plaintiff's seclusion or solitude. Fowler v. Southern Bell Tel. & Tel. Co., 343 F.2d 150, 156 (5th Cir. 1965).

In the present case, Plaxico did not prove each element of intentional intrusion upon solitude or seclusion of another. Plaxico was in a state of solitude or seclusion in the privacy of her bedroom where she had an expectation of privacy. However, we conclude that a reasonable person would not feel Michael's interference with Plaxico's seclusion was a substantial one that would rise to the level of gross offensiveness as required to prove the sub-tort of intentional intrusion upon seclusion or solitude. * * *

Here, Michael became concerned about the welfare of his daughter, who was in the custody of his former wife. Michael's former wife subleased a cabin from him, and invited Plaxico to be her roommate. His concern was based on numerous rumors of an illicit lesbian sexual relationship between Plaxico and his former wife. Michael decided that it was not in the best interests of his daughter to allow her to remain in the custody of her mother, and he wanted to obtain custody of the child. It is of no consequence that the mother was having an affair with another woman. She could have been carrying on an illicit affair with a man in the home where the child was, and any father would feel that this too was inappropriate behavior to be carried on in the presence of the child. A modification would still be desired by the parent.

In the present case, Michael did want to file for modification of child custody. However, he had no proof that there actually was lesbian sexual relationship which could be adversely affecting his minor child. In order to obtain such proof, he went to the cabin, peered through the window and took pictures of the two women engaged in sexual conduct. Three pictures were actually developed which were of Plaxico in a naked state from her waist up in her bed. Michael believed that he took these pictures for the sole purpose to protect his minor child. Although these actions were done without Plaxico's consent, this conduct is not highly offensive to the ordinary person which would cause the reasonable person to object. In fact, most reasonable people would feel Michael's actions were justified in order to protect the welfare of his minor child. Therefore, the elements necessary to establish the tort of intentional intrusion upon solitude or seclusion are not present. * * *

BANKS, J., dissenting

In my view, peeping into the bedroom window of another is a gross invasion of privacy which may subject one to liability for intentional intrusion upon the solitude or seclusion of that other. See *Candebat v. Flanagan, 487 So. 2d 207, 209–10 (Miss. 1986);* RESTATEMENT (SECOND) OF TORTS § 652B cmt. b, illus. 2 (1977) (invasion of privacy would occur if private investigator, seeking evidence for use in a lawsuit, looks into plaintiff's bedroom window with telescope for two weeks and takes intimate photographs).

The trial court found refuge in what it found to be a qualified privilege to see to the best interest of a child. Neither rumors concerning an ex-wife's lifestyle nor a parent's justifiable concern over the best interests of his child, however, gave Michael license to spy on a person's bedroom, take photographs of her in a semi-nude state and have those photographs developed by third parties and delivered to his attorney thereby exposing them to others. * * *

In another context, we have observed that "the end does not justify the means. * * * Our society is one of law, not expediency. This message must be repeated at every opportunity ..." Mississippi Bar v. Robb, 684 So. 2d 615, 623 (Miss. 1996). I regret that today's majority here does not follow these worthy ideals.

McRAE, J., dissenting

While the majority did not reach the issue, it impliedly affirms the lower court's finding that Michael had a qualified privilege to take the semi-nude photographs of Plaxico to obtain information helpful to him in his custody battle with his former wife. Ms. Plaxico, the paramour of Michael's ex-wife, however, was not a party to the custody proceedings. As the majority points out, it matters not whether Michael's former wife was involved in a lesbian or a heterosexual relationship. Michael was not at liberty to peek in the women's bedroom window, an act that can only be characterized as voyeuristic. Nor was he at liberty to take photographs of Plaxico and share them with his attorney. At best, only pictures of his former wife could possibly be characterized as helpful to Michael's case. As to Plaxico, any privilege allowed Michael is misplaced. Accordingly, I dissent.

NOTE: GEOGRAPHIZATION OF SEXUAL LIBERTY

The Supreme Court's decision in *Lawrence v. Texas,* 539 U.S. 558 (2003), struck down laws criminalizing consensual sexual acts between same-sex adults. Lawrence had been charged with criminal sodomy after police found him with a partner in his own bedroom. Professor Carlos Ball has argued that "The Court's geographization of sexual liberty has resulted in the protection of sexual conduct that takes place in the home (and, presumably, in analogous sites such as hotel rooms) while leaving unprotected sexual conduct that occurs in public sites" such as restrooms. Carlos Ball, *Privacy, Property, and Public Sex*, 18 COLUMBIA JOURNAL OF GENDER AND LAW 1 (2008). Does *Plaxico v. Michael,* above, suggest that the private home is not a sanctuary for intimate sex for LGBT individuals, where courts view homosexual relationships as illicit? Are gay and lesbian relationships still considered "illicit?" Would *Lawrence*, the expansion of civil unions, and/or the legalization of same-sex marriages preclude a loss by a plaintiff in Rita Plaxico's shoes, today?

PEOPLE FOR THE ETHICAL TREATMENT OF ANIMALS v. BOBBY BEROSINI, LTD.

111 Nev. 615 (Nev. 1995).

SPRINGER, J.

In this litigation respondent [Bobby Berosini, Ltd.] claims that two animal rights organizations, People for the Ethical Treatment of Animals (PETA) and Performing Animal Welfare Society (PAWS), and three individuals * * * invaded his privacy. [A jury awarded the respondent $4.2 million.] This appeal followed. We conclude that the evidence was insufficient to support the jury's verdict and, accordingly, reverse the judgment. * * *

The focus, then, of Berosini's intrusion upon seclusion claim is Gesmundo's having "trespassed onto the Stardust Hotel with a video camera" and having "unlawfully filmed Plaintiff Berosini disciplining the orangutans without the Plaintiff's knowledge or consent." It is of no relevance to the intrusion tort that Gesmundo trespassed onto the Stardust Hotel, and it is of no moment that Gesmundo might have "unlawfully" filmed Berosini, unless at the same time he was violating a justifiable expectation of privacy on Berosini's part. The issue, then, is whether, when Gesmundo filmed Berosini "disciplining the orangutans without the Plaintiff's knowledge or consent," Gesmundo was intruding on "the solitude or seclusion" of Berosini.

The primary thrust of Berosini's expectation of privacy backstage at the Stardust was that he be left alone with his animals and trainers for a period of time immediately before going on stage. Berosini testified that "as part of his engagement with the Stardust," he demanded that "the animals be left alone prior to going on stage." Throughout his testimony, over and over again, he stresses his need to be alone with his animals before going on stage. * * * Significantly, Berosini testified that his "concern for privacy was based upon the animals" and that his "main concern is that [he] have no problems going on stage and off stage," that is to say that no one interfere with his animals in any way immediately before going on stage.

Berosini was concerned that backstage personnel not "stare at the orangutans in their faces. The orangutans will interpret [this] as a challenge." It is clear that Berosini's "main concern" was that he be provided with an area backstage in which he could get the animals' undistracted attention before going on stage. He never expressed any concern about backstage personnel merely seeing him or hearing him during these necessary final preparations before going on stage; his only expressed concern was about possible interference with his pre-act training procedures and the danger that such interference might create with respect to his control over the animals. Persons who were backstage at the Stardust could hear what was going on when "Berosini [was] disciplining his animals," and, without interfering with Berosini's activities, could, if they wanted to, get a glimpse of what Berosini was doing with his animals as he was going on stage.

What is perhaps most important in defining the breadth of Berosini's expectation of privacy is that in his own mind there was nothing wrong or untoward in the manner in which he disciplined the animals, as portrayed on the videotape, and he expressed no concern about merely being seen or heard carrying out these disciplinary practices. To Berosini all of his disciplinary activities were completely "justified." He had nothing to hide—nothing to be private about. Except to avoid possible distraction of the animals, he had no reason to exclude others from observing or listening to his activities with the animals. Berosini testified that he was not "ashamed of the way that [he] controlled [his] animals"; and he testified that he "would have done the same thing if people were standing there because if anybody would have been standing there, it was visible. It was correct. It was proper. It was necessary."

As his testimony indicates, Berosini's "concern for privacy was based upon the animals," and not upon any desire for sight/sound secrecy or privacy or seclusion as such; and he "would have done the same thing if people were standing there." The supposed intruder, Gesmundo, was in a real sense just "standing there." By observing Berosini through the eye of his video camera, he was merely doing what other backstage personnel were also permissibly doing. The camera did not interfere in any way with Berosini's pre-act animal discipline or his claimed interest in being "secured from the other cast members and people before [he] went on stage." Having testified that he would have done the same thing if people were standing there, he can hardly complain about a camera "standing there."

If Berosini's expectation was, as he says it is, freedom from distracting intrusion and interference with his animals and his pre-act disciplinary procedures, then Gesmundo's video "filming" did not invade the scope of this expectation. Gesmundo did not intrude upon Berosini's expected seclusion. * * *

On the question of whether Gesmundo's camera was highly offensive to a reasonable person, we first note that this is a question of first impression in this state. As might be expected, "the question of what kinds of conduct will be regarded as a 'highly offensive' intrusion is largely a matter of social conventions and expectations." J. Thomas McCarthy, The Rights of Publicity and Privacy, § 5.10(A)(2) (1993). For example, while questions about one's sexual activities would be highly offensive when asked by an employer, they might not be offensive when asked by one's closest friend. See Phillips v. Smalley Maint. Services, 435 So. 2d 705 (Ala. 1983). * * * A court considering whether a particular action is "highly offensive" should consider the following factors: "the degree of intrusion, the context, conduct and circumstances surrounding the intrusion as well as the intruder's motives and objectives, the setting into which he intrudes, and the expectations of those whose privacy is invaded." Miller, 232 Cal. Rptr. at 679; 5 B. E. Witkin, Summary of California Law, Torts § 579 at 674 (9th ed. 1988). * * *

[I]n Estate of Berthiaume, 365 A.2d at 796, the court held that a doctor who photographed a dying patient against his will could be held liable for intrusion, in part because the doctor was not seeking to further the patient's treatment when he photographed him. * * *

While we could reverse Berosini's intrusion upon seclusion judgment solely on the absence of any intrusion upon his actual privacy expectation, we go on to conclude that even if Berosini had expected complete seclusion from prying eyes and ears, Gesmundo's camera was not "highly offensive to a reasonable person" because of the nonintrusive nature of the taping process, the context in which the taping took place, and Gesmundo's well-intentioned (and in the eyes of some, at least, laudable) motive. If Berosini suffered as a result of the videotaping, it was not because of any tortious intrusion, it was because of subsequent events that, if remediable, relate to other kinds of tort actions than the intrusion upon seclusion tort.

NOTE: PRIVACY IN PUBLIC PLACES

Berosini was backstage but not at home in his bedroom. Is being monitored outside the home a burdensome intrusion? People may feel that others in the world around them are invading their privacy by staring, stalking, using cell phone cameras, or operating security cameras on the streets and in businesses. Are such feelings reasonable and open to legal validation? A while back Seattle, Washington outlawed using cell phones for "upskirting"—bending or reaching to photograph a woman's undergarments. The Seattle ordinance was a response to a joint court decision, *Washington v. Glas* and *Washington v. Sorrells*, 54 P.3d 147 (Wash. 2002), which overturned the voyeurism conviction of two men who upskirted. The very specific ordinance seems a little silly. But there are larger issues of harassment and stalking in public places to consider.

Is there a legal right to privacy in public? Courts in tort cases have generally said that there is not. Leaving our homes constitutes consent to public exposure and the end of expectations of privacy. Critics of this view argue that the "bifurcation between public and private places in privacy law is based on a fallacious view of privacy as an all or nothing concept." See Elizabeth Paton–Simpson, Privacy and the Reasonable Paranoid: The Protection of Privacy in Public Places, 50 *Univ. of Toronto L.J.* 305 (2000). Paton–Simpson points out there are differences the law could countenance between causal observance and systematic surveillance, between looking and recording, and between photographing and stalking. Privacy in public, she argues, is important to the ideals of free association and equality, too, since some people cannot choose to seclude themselves as easily as others. Cf. Joseph Siprut, Privacy through Anonymity: an Economic Argument for Expanding the Right of Privacy in Public Places, 33 *Pepp. L. Rev.* 311 (2006).

Private investigators are permitted to shadow people in public places. But there is a limit to just how much snooping around in public is tolerable. In a famous case, General Motors was sued by consumer rights activist Ralph Nader, who had published a report questioning the safety of some automobiles GM manufactured. Attempting to discredit Mr. Nader, General Motors had him followed by prostitutes, by whom the company hoped he would be seduced to discredit his moral reputation. The company's investigators tapped Nader's phone and also closely questioned Nader's friends and neighbors in a vain search for "dirt". See *Nader v. General Motors Corp.,* 307 N.Y.S.2d 647 (N.Y. 1970). Nader won more than $200,000 in a successful suit alleging overzealous surveillance. Does Helen Nissenbaum's contextual understanding of privacy norms help to illuminate Nader's victory? See below and Helen Nissenbaum, Protecting Privacy in an Information Age: The Problems of Privacy in Public, 17 *Law and Philosophy* 559 (1998).

HELEN NISSENBAUM, PRIVACY AS CONTEXTUAL INTEGRITY

79 Wash. L. Rev. 119, 136–143 (2004).

Contexts, or spheres, offer a platform for a normative account of privacy in terms of contextual integrity. * * * [C]ontexts are partly constituted by norms, which determine and govern key aspects such as roles, expectations, behaviors, and limits. There are numerous possible sources of contextual norms, including history, culture, law, convention, etc. Among the norms present in most contexts are ones that govern information, and, most relevant to our discussion, information about the people involved in the contexts. I posit two types of informational norms: norms of appropriateness, and norms of flow or distribution. Contextual integrity is maintained when both types of norms are upheld, and it is violated when either of the norms is violated. [T]he benchmark of privacy is contextual integrity; that in any given situation, a complaint that privacy has been violated is sound in the event that one or the other types of the informational norms has been transgressed.

A. Appropriateness

As the label suggests, norms of appropriateness dictate what information about persons is appropriate, or fitting, to reveal in a particular context. Generally, these norms circumscribe the type or nature of information about various individuals that, within a given context, is allowable, expected, or even demanded to be revealed. In medical contexts, it is appropriate to share details of our physical condition or, more specifically, the patient shares information about his or her physical condition with the physician but not vice versa; among friends we may pour over romantic entanglements (our own and those of others); to the bank or our creditors, we reveal financial information; with our professors, we discuss our own grades; at work, it is appropriate to discuss work-related goals and the details and quality of performance. * * *

While norms of appropriateness are robust in everyday experience, the idea that such norms operate has not been explicitly addressed in most of the dominant research and scholarship that feed into public deliberations of privacy policy in the United States. Within the philosophical literature of the past few decades, however, we find recognition of similar notions. * * *

B. Distribution

In addition to appropriateness, another set of norms govern what I will call flow or distribution of information—movement, or transfer of information from one party to another or others. * * * What matters is not only whether information is appropriate or inappropriate for a given context, but whether its distribution, or flow, respects contextual norms of information flow.

Let us [consider]the context of friendship, * * * to consider some examples of norms of flow. [R]elatively few general norms of appropriateness apply, though practices may vary depending on whether the friends are close, have known each other for a long time, and so on. Information that is appropriate to friendship can include mundane information about day-to-day activities, likes and dislikes, opinions, relationships, character, emotions, capacity for loyalty, and much more. The same open-endedness, however, does not hold for norms of flow, which are quite substantial. In friendship, generally, information is either shared at the discretion of the subject in a bidirectional flow—friends choose to tell each other about themselves—or is inferred by one friend of another on the basis of what the other has done, said, experienced, etc. But that is not all. Confidentiality is generally the default—that is, friends expect what they say to each other to be held in confidence and not arbitrarily spread to others. * * *

Free choice, discretion, and confidentiality, prominent among norms of flow in friendship, are not the only principles of information distribution. Others include need, entitlement, and obligation—a list that is probably open-ended. * * * Other cases of information practices following rational norms of flow include, for example, transactions between customers and mail-order merchants. In such transactions, customers are required to provide sufficient and appropriate information to satisfy companies that they can pay, and provide an address indicating where packages should be sent. Police are bound by law to abide by various regulations governing modes of acquiring information and how to deal with its flow thereafter. However, suspects arrested by police on criminal charges may volunteer certain categories of information beyond those that they are compelled to provide. A sexual partner may be entitled to information about the other's HIV status, although the same demand by a friend is probably not warranted. A job applicant may volunteer information she considers evidence of her ability to do the job. Candidates for political office volunteer proof of professional competence, political loyalty, personal integrity, political connections, and past political activities. But it is accepted that employers and voters, respectively, might choose to conduct independent investigations as to fitness and competence. These cases are intended merely to illustrate the many possible configurations of informational norms we are likely to encounter, and they just begin to scratch the surface.

3. INVESTIGATIVE JOURNALISM AND THE MEDIA

DIETEMANN v. TIME, INC.

449 F.2d 245 (9th Cir. 1971).

HUFSTEDLER, CIRCUIT JUDGE:

The facts, as narrated by the district court, are these:

"Plaintiff, a disabled veteran with little education, was engaged in the practice of healing with clay, minerals, and herbs—as practiced, simple quackery.

"Life Magazine entered into an arrangement with the District Attorney's Office of Los Angeles County whereby Life's employees would visit plaintiff and obtain facts and pictures concerning his activities. Two employees of Life, Mrs. Jackie Metcalf and Mr. William Ray, went to plaintiff's home on September 20, 1963. When they arrived at a locked gate, they rang a bell and plaintiff came out of his house and was told by Mrs. Metcalf and Ray that they had been sent there by a friend, a Mr. Johnson. The use of Johnson's name was a ruse to gain entrance. Plaintiff admitted them and all three went into the house and into plaintiff's den.

"The plaintiff had some equipment which could at best be described as gadgets, not equipment which had anything to do with the practice of medicine. Plaintiff, while examining Mrs. Metcalf, was photographed by Ray with a hidden camera without the consent of plaintiff. One of the pictures taken by him appeared in Life Magazine showing plaintiff with his hand on the upper portion of Mrs. Metcalf's breast while he was looking at some gadgets and holding what appeared to be a wand in his right hand. Mrs. Metcalf had told plaintiff that she had a lump in her breast. Plaintiff concluded that she had eaten some rancid butter 11 years, 9 months, and 7 days prior to that time. Other persons were seated in the room during this time.

"The conversation between Mrs. Metcalf and plaintiff was transmitted by radio transmitter hidden in Mrs. Metcalf's purse to a tape recorder in a parked automobile occupied by Joseph Bride, Life employee, John Miner of the District Attorney's Office, and Grant Leake, an investigator of the State Department of Public Health. While the recorded conversation was not quoted in the article in Life, it was mentioned that Life correspondent Bride was making notes of what was being received via the radio transmitter, and such information was at least referred to in the article.

"The foregoing events were photographed and recorded by an arrangement among Miner of the District Attorney's Office, Leake of the State Department of Public Health, and Bride, a representative of Life. It had been agreed that Life would obtain pictures and information for use as evidence, and later could be used by Life for publication.

"Prior to the occurrences of September 20, 1963, on two occasions the officials had obtained recordings of conversations in plaintiff's home; however, no pictures had been secured. Life employees had not participated in obtaining the recordings on these occasions.

"On October 15, 1963, plaintiff was arrested at his home on a charge of practicing medicine without a license in violation of Section 26280, California Health and Safety Code. At the time of his arrest, many pictures were made by Life of plaintiff at his home. Plaintiff testified that he did not agree to pose for the pictures but allowed pictures because he thought the officers could require it. Also present were newspaper men who had also been invited by the officials to be present at the time of arrest.

"Defendant contends that plaintiff posed for pictures at the time of his arrest and thus permission was given to take those pictures. As hereinafter pointed out, it is unnecessary to decide whether or not permission was given to take pictures at the time of his arrest.

"Plaintiff, although a journeyman plumber, claims to be a scientist. Plaintiff had no listings and his home had no sign of any kind. He did not advertise, nor did he have a telephone. He made no charges when he attempted to diagnose or to prescribe herbs and minerals. He did accept contributions.

"Life's article concerning plaintiff was not published until after plaintiff was arrested but before his plea on June 1, 1964 of nolo contendere for violations of Section 2141 of the California Business and Professions Code and Section 26280 of the California Health and Safety Code (misdemeanors).

"Defendant's claim that the plaintiff's house was open to the public is not sustained by the evidence. The plaintiff was administering his so-called treatments to people who visited him. He was not a medical man of any type. He did not advertise. He did not have a phone. He did have a lock on his gate. To obtain entrance it was necessary to ring a bell. He conducted his activities in a building which was his home. The employees of defendant gained entrance by a subterfuge." * * *

Although the issue has not been squarely decided in California, we have little difficulty in concluding that clandestine photography of the plaintiff in his den and the recordation and transmission of his conversation without his consent resulting in his emotional distress warrants recovery for invasion of privacy in California. * * *

Decision

Plaintiff's den was a sphere from which he could reasonably expect to exclude eavesdropping newsmen. He invited two of defendant's employees to the den. One who invites another to his home or office takes a risk that the visitor may not be what he seems, and that the visitor may repeat all he hears and observes when he leaves. But he does not and should not be required to take the risk that what is heard and seen will be transmitted by photograph or recording, or in our modern world, in full living color and hi-fi to the public at large or to any segment of it that the visitor may select. A different rule could have a most pernicious effect upon the dignity of man and it would surely lead to guarded conversations and conduct where candor is most valued, e.g., in the case of doctors and lawyers.

The defendant claims that the First Amendment immunizes it from liability for invading plaintiff's den with a hidden camera and its concealed electronic instruments because its employees were gathering news and its instrumentalities "are indispensable tools of investigative reporting." We agree that newsgathering is an integral part of news dissemination. * * * The First Amendment has never been construed to accord newsmen immunity from torts or crimes committed during the course of newsgathering. The First Amendment is not a license to trespass, to steal, or to intrude by electronic means into the precincts of another's home or office. It does not become such a license simply because the person subjected to the intrusion is reasonably suspected of committing a crime. * * *

No interest protected by the First Amendment is adversely affected by permitting damages for intrusion * * *.

NOTE: AMBUSH

Another example of the conflict between the desire for privacy and the desire for publication is *Food Lion, Inc. v. Capital Cities/ABC, Inc.*, 964 F. Supp. 956 (M.D.N.C. 1997). Employees of ABC News's Prime Time Live lied on resumés submitted to obtain jobs at a Food Lion supermarket for the purpose of an undercover investigation of charges of adulteration of food products. Hidden cameras revealed Food Lion employees engaging in questionable practices mandated by store management, including repackaging unsold, out-of-date meat. Food Lion initially won a multimillion dollar jury award in a lawsuit for fraud, breach of loyalty and trespass. Ultimately, the interest in public health and information seemed to outweigh the privacy and employee loyalty preferences of Food Lion management and employees. The Court of Appeals reduced Food Lion's damage award to $2.00.

In a similar case, *Desnick v. ABC*, 44 F.3d 1345 (7th Cir. 1995) a federal court held valid the fraudulently obtained consent Prime Time Live used to gain access to the offices of two eye surgeons who had performed more than 10,000 cataract operations in a single year. Although ABC promised the doctors that they would not be subjected to ambush journalism or undercover surveillance, it sent agents disguised as patients and carrying concealed cameras to see the doctors. ABC broadcast a program suggesting that the doctors were performing unnecessary surgery. The surgeons unsuccessfully sued for privacy intrusion and trespass.

The First Amendment protects speech about "daily life matters" as well as political matters. Eugene Volokh has argued that "in a free speech regime, others' definitions of me should primarily be molded by their own judgments, rather than by my using legal coercion to keep them in the dark." See Eugene Volokh, Freedom of Speech and Information Privacy: The Troubling Implications of a Right to Stop People From Speaking About You, 52 *Stanford L. Rev.* 1049 (2000).

NOTE: *JOURNALISTIC ETHICS*

Historically, the professional standards of print and broadcast journalism called for respect for privacy. For example, the Code of Ethics promulgated by the Society of Professional Journalists in 1996 exhorted members to avoid "intrusion into anyone's privacy." See http://www.spj.org/ethicscode.asp. Shouldering the burden of respecting privacy grows increasingly impractical as the information demands of our complex society multiply and as diverse, pluralistic conceptions of "the private" flourish. Notions of privacy vary from cultural group to cultural group and from individual to individual. A cultural group's consensus may be obtainable from "community leaders" or ethnographers, but these may err, innocently or otherwise, and it may be difficult to determine their relevance to a particular news subject. The burdens of impracticality and principle might be thought to justify journalism's abandonment of privacy values, both in theory and in practice.

The Associated Press Managing Editors Code of Ethics, updated in 1995, urges newspapers to "respect the individual's right to privacy." In the 1920s, the American Society of Newspaper Editors, in its Canons of Journalism, affirmed that "[a] newspaper should not involve private rights or feeling without sure warrant of public right as distinguished from public curiosity." Some professional journalists have already jettisoned privacy even as a hortatory ethical ideal. The guidelines for ethical newsgathering adopted in 1999 by the Gannett Company, publishers of U.S.A. Today and numerous local newspapers, expressed a commitment to "[s]eeking and reporting the truth" in the public interest and "uphold[ing] First Amendment principles," but does not even mention the word privacy. See generally Craig LeMay (ed.), *Journalism and the Debate Over Privacy* (2003).

SHULMAN v. GROUP W PRODUCTIONS, INC.

18 Cal. 4th 200 (Cal. 1998).

WERDEGAR, J.

In the present case, we address the balance between privacy and press freedom in the commonplace context of an automobile accident. * * *

On June 24, 1990, plaintiffs Ruth and Wayne Shulman, mother and son, were injured when the car in which they and two other family members were riding on interstate 10 in Riverside County flew off the highway and tumbled down an embankment into a drainage ditch on state-owned property, coming to rest upside down. Ruth, the most seriously injured of the two, was pinned under the car. Ruth and Wayne both had to be cut free from the vehicle by the device known as "the jaws of life."

A rescue helicopter operated by Mercy Air was dispatched to the scene. The flight nurse, who would perform the medical care at the scene and on the way to the hospital, was Laura Carnahan. Also on board were the pilot, a medic and Joel Cooke, a video camera operator employed by defendants Group W Productions, Inc., and 4MN Productions. Cooke was recording the rescue operation for later broadcast.

Cooke roamed the accident scene, videotaping the rescue. Nurse Carnahan wore a wireless microphone that picked up her conversations with both Ruth and the other rescue personnel. Cooke's tape was edited into a piece approximately nine minutes long, which, with the addition of narrative voice-over, was broadcast on September 29, 1990, as a segment of On Scene: Emergency Response. * * *

The accident left Ruth a paraplegic. When the segment was broadcast, Wayne phoned Ruth in her hospital room and told her to turn on the television because "Channel 4 is showing our accident now." Shortly afterward, several hospital workers came into the room to mention that a videotaped segment of her accident was being shown. Ruth was "shocked, so to speak, that this would be run and I would be exploited, have my privacy invaded, which is what I felt had happened." She did not know her rescue had been recorded in this manner and had never consented to the recording or broadcast. Ruth had the impression from the broadcast "that I was kind of talking nonstop, and I remember hearing some of the things I said, which were not very pleasant." Asked at deposition what part of the broadcast material she considered private, Ruth explained: "I think the whole scene was pretty private. It was pretty gruesome, the parts that I saw, my knee sticking out of the car. I certainly did not look my best, and I don't feel it's for the public to see. I was not at my best in what I was thinking and what I was saying and what was being shown, and it's not for the public to see this trauma that I was going through."

Ruth and Wayne sued the producers of On Scene: Emergency Response, as well as others. The first amended complaint included two causes of action for invasion of privacy, one based on defendants' unlawful intrusion by videotaping the rescue in the first instance and the other based on the public disclosure of private facts, i.e., the broadcast. * * *

Of the four privacy torts identified by Prosser, the tort of intrusion into private places, conversations or matter is perhaps the one that best captures the common understanding of an "invasion of privacy." It encompasses unconsented-to physical intrusion into the home, hospital room or other place the privacy of which is legally recognized, as well as unwarranted sensory intrusions such as eavesdropping, wiretapping, and visual or photographic spying * * *.

Despite its conceptual centrality, the intrusion tort has received less judicial attention than the private facts tort, and its parameters are less clearly defined. The leading California decision is Miller v. National Broadcasting Co., supra, 187 Cal.App.3d 1463 (Miller). Miller, which like the present case involved a news organization's videotaping the work of emergency medical personnel, adopted the Restatement's formulation of the cause of action * * *.

elements

As stated in Miller and the Restatement, therefore, the action for intrusion has two elements: (1) intrusion into a private place, conversation or matter, (2) in a manner highly offensive to a reasonable person. * * *

Two aspects of defendants' conduct * * * raise triable issues of intrusion on seclusion. First, a triable issue exists as to whether both plaintiffs had an objectively reasonable expectation of privacy in the interior of the rescue helicopter, which served as an ambulance. Although the attendance of reporters and photographers at the scene of an accident is to be expected, we are aware of no law or custom permitting the press to ride in ambulances or enter hospital rooms during treatment without the patient's consent. * * *

Second, Ruth was entitled to a degree of privacy in her conversations with Carnahan and other medical rescuers at the accident scene, and in Carnahan's conversations conveying medical information regarding Ruth to the hospital base. Cooke, perhaps, did not intrude into that zone of privacy merely by being present at a place where he could hear such conversations with unaided ears. But by placing a microphone on Carnahan's person, amplifying and recording what she said and heard, defendants may have listened in on conversations the parties could reasonably have expected to be private. * * *

We turn to the second element of the intrusion tort, offensiveness of the intrusion. In a widely followed passage, the Miller court explained that determining offensiveness requires consideration of all the circumstances of the intrusion, including its degree and setting and the intruder's "motives and objectives." * * * The Miller court concluded that reasonable people could regard the camera crew's conduct in filming a man's emergency medical treatment in his home, without seeking or obtaining his or his wife's consent, as showing "a cavalier disregard for ordinary citizens' rights of privacy" and, hence, as highly offensive. (Miller, supra, 187 Cal.App.3d at p. 1484.)

We agree with the Miller court that all the circumstances of an intrusion, including the motives or justification of the intruder, are pertinent to the offensiveness element. Motivation or justification becomes particularly important when the intrusion is by a member of the print or broadcast press in the pursuit of news material. * * *

In deciding, therefore, whether a reporter's alleged intrusion into private matters (i.e., physical space, conversation or data) is "offensive" and hence actionable as an invasion of privacy, courts must consider the extent to which the intrusion was, under the circumstances, justified by the legitimate motive of gathering the news. * * *

The mere fact the intruder was in pursuit of a "story" does not, however, generally justify an otherwise offensive intrusion; offensiveness depends as well on the particular method of investigation used. At one extreme, " 'routine * * * reporting techniques,' " such as asking questions of people with information ("including those with confidential or restricted information") could rarely, if ever, be deemed an actionable intrusion. * * *

On this summary judgment record, we believe a jury could find defendants' recording of Ruth's communications to Carnahan and other rescuers, and filming in the air ambulance, to be " 'highly offensive to a reasonable person.' " * * * With regard to the depth of the intrusion * * *, a reasonable jury could find highly offensive the placement of a microphone on a medical rescuer in order to intercept what would otherwise be private conversations with an injured patient. In that setting, as defendants could and should have foreseen, the patient would not know her words were being recorded and would not have occasion to ask about, and object or consent to, recording. Defendants, it could reasonably be said, took calculated advantage of the patient's "vulnerability and confusion." * * * Arguably, the last thing an injured accident victim should have to worry about while being pried from her wrecked car is that a television producer may be recording everything she says to medical personnel for the possible edification and entertainment of casual television viewers.

For much the same reason, a jury could reasonably regard entering and riding in an ambulance—whether on the ground or in the air—with two seriously injured patients to be an egregious intrusion on a place of expected seclusion. Again, the patients, at least in this case, were hardly in a position to keep careful watch on who was riding with them, or to inquire as to everyone's business and consent or object to their presence. A jury could reasonably believe that fundamental respect for human dignity requires the patients' anxious journey be taken only with those whose care is solely for them and out of sight of the prying eyes (or cameras) of others.

Nor can we say as a matter of law that defendants' motive—to gather usable material for a potentially newsworthy story—necessarily privileged their intrusive conduct as a matter of common law tort liability. A reasonable jury could conclude the producers' desire to get footage that would convey the "feel" of the event—the real sights and sounds of a difficult rescue—did not justify either placing a microphone on Nurse Carnahan or filming inside the rescue helicopter. Although defendants' purposes could scarcely be regarded as evil or malicious (in the colloquial sense), their behavior could, even in light of their motives, be thought to show a highly offensive lack of sensitivity and respect for plaintiffs' privacy. * * *

Turning to the question of constitutional protection for newsgathering, one finds the decisional law reflects a general rule of nonprotection: the press in its newsgathering activities enjoys no immunity or exemption from generally applicable laws. * * *

In contrast to the broad privilege the press enjoys for publishing truthful, newsworthy information in its possession, the press has no recognized constitutional privilege to violate generally applicable laws in pursuit of material. Nor, even absent an independent crime or tort, can a highly offensive intrusion into a private place, conversation, or source of information generally be justified by the plea that the intruder hoped thereby to get good material for a news story. Such a justification may be available when enforcement of the tort or other law would place an impermissibly severe burden on the press, but that condition is not met in this case.

In short, the state may not intrude into the proper sphere of the news media to dictate what they should publish and broadcast, but neither may the media play tyrant to the people by unlawfully spying on them in the name of newsgathering. Summary judgment for the defense was * * * improper as to the cause of action for invasion of privacy by intrusion * * *.

SANDERS v. AMERICAN BROADCASTING COMPANIES

20 Cal. 4th 907 (Cal. 1999).

WERDEGAR, J. * * *

Defendant Stacy Lescht, employed by defendant ABC in an investigation of the telepsychic industry, obtained employment as a psychic in PMG's Los Angeles office. When she first entered the PMG office to apply for a position, she was not stopped at the front door or greeted by anyone until she found and approached the administration desk. Once hired, she sat at a cubicle desk, where she gave telephonic readings to customers. Lescht testified that while sitting at her desk she could easily overhear conversations conducted in surrounding cubicles or in the aisles near her cubicle. When not on the phone, she talked with some of the other psychics in the phone room. Lescht secretly videotaped these conversations with a "hat cam," i.e., a small camera hidden in her hat; a microphone attached to her brassiere captured sound as well. Among the conversations Lescht videotaped were two with Sanders, the first at Lescht's cubicle, the second at Sanders's. * * *

Sanders pled two causes of action against Lescht and ABC ᵇ the videotaping itself * * *.

[T]he jury found defendants liable on the cause of action for i of privacy by intrusion. In subsequent trial phases, the jury fixed ᴄᴏᴍᴘᴇɴ satory damages at $335,000; found defendants had acted with malice, fraud or oppression; and awarded exemplary damages of about $300,000. * * *

May a person who lacks a reasonable expectation of complete privacy in a conversation because it could be seen and overheard by coworkers (but not the general public) nevertheless have a claim for invasion of privacy by intrusion based on a television reporter's covert videotaping of that conversation? * * *

This case squarely raises the question of an expectation of limited privacy. On further consideration, we adhere to the view suggested in Shulman: privacy, for purposes of the intrusion tort, is not a binary, all-or-nothing characteristic. There are degrees and nuances to societal recognition of our expectations of privacy: the fact that the privacy one expects in a given setting is not complete or absolute does not render the expectation unreasonable as a matter of law. Although the intrusion tort is often defined in terms of "seclusion" * * *, the seclusion referred to need not be absolute. "Like 'privacy,' the concept of 'seclusion' is relative. The mere fact that a person can be seen by someone does not automatically mean that he or she can legally be forced to be subject to being seen by everyone." (1 McCarthy, The Rights of Publicity and Privacy (1998) § 5.10[A][2], p. 5–120.1.) * * *

Finally, defendants rely on * * * Desnick v. American Broadcasting Companies, Inc. (7th Cir. 1995) 44 F.3d 1345. * * *

In Desnick, the question was whether the covert videotaping by "testers" posing as patients was a tortious invasion of privacy. The appellate court held it was not, partly because "the only conversations that were recorded were conversations with the testers themselves." "The test patients entered offices that were open to anyone expressing a desire for ophthalmic services and videotaped physicians engaged in professional, not personal, communications with strangers (the testers themselves)." * * *

The Desnick court characterized the doctor-patient relationship as one between a service provider and a customer and therefore viewed these parties' conversations in the medical office as essentially public conversations between strangers. We need not agree or disagree with this characterization in order to see that it renders the decision's reasoning inapplicable to the question before us. We are concerned here with interactions between coworkers rather than between a proprietor and customer. As the briefed question is framed, the interactions at issue here could not have been witnessed by the general public, although they could have been overheard or observed by other employees in the shared workplace. * * *

To summarize, we conclude that in the workplace, as elsewhere, the reasonableness of a person's expectation of visual and aural privacy depends not only on who might have been able to observe the subject interaction, but on the identity of the claimed intruder and the means of intrusion. * * * For this reason * * * a person who lacks a reasonable expectation of complete privacy in a conversation, because it could be seen and overheard by coworkers (but not the general public), may nevertheless have a claim for invasion of privacy by intrusion based on a television reporter's covert videotaping of that conversation.

Defendants warn that "the adoption of a doctrine of per se workplace privacy would place a dangerous chill on the press' investigation of abusive activities in open work areas, implicating substantial First Amendment concerns." * * * We hold only that the possibility of being overheard by coworkers does not, as a matter of law, render unreasonable an employee's expectation that his or her interactions within a nonpublic workplace will not be videotaped in secret by a journalist. In other circumstances, where, for example, the workplace is regularly open to entry or observation by the public or press, or the interaction that was the subject of the alleged intrusion was between proprietor (or employee) and customer, any expectation of privacy against press recording is less likely to be deemed reasonable. * * *

4. INTRUSION AND HEALTH SERVICES

NOTE: MEDICAL PRIVACY

Health-related intrusions have resulted in suits against laypersons and professionals, including physicians. In the first case in this section, the court considers whether a medical doctor invades his dying patient's privacy when he enters his hospital room and, over his objections, photographs the man's surgical wound. Perhaps we could all agree that there are times in life when individuals are entitled to privacy. One such time is arguably the final stages of dying. What, though, of a soldier suffering injury or agony on a battlefield in the midst of a politically controversial war; would it be intrusive for a news photographer to snap a photograph at close range? From a privacy perspective, what is appropriate treatment of a hospital patient who is dying?

The second case in this section, *Knight v. Penobscot Bay Medical Center*, is reminiscent of *De May v. Roberts*. A stranger to the plaintiff observes her giving birth. In *De May* the court concluded that a woman was entitled to the privacy of her apartment "at such a time," meaning at the time of labor and delivery of a child. In *Doe v. High–Tech Inst.*, a third case, a professor has one of her students secretly tested for the virus that causes AIDS. In a final case, an accident victim is placed under surveillance to ascertain the extent of insurable injuries.

What do all the medical intrusion cases suggest about the extent of meaningful health privacy? In Chapter 3 of this textbook, we will consider the information privacy and security provisions of the Health Insurance Portability and Accountability Act ("HIPAA"). HIPAA does not address many of the health-related intrusions arising in daily life, and does not grant a patients a right to sue. How useful is the invasion of privacy addressing felt invasions of health privacy?

ESTATE OF BERTHIAUME v. PRATT

365 A.2d 792 (Me. 1976).

POMEROY, J.

The appellant, as administratrix, based her claim of right to damages P on an alleged invasion of her late husband's "right to privacy" and on an alleged assault and battery of him. * * *

The appellee is a physician and surgeon practicing in Waterville, D Maine. It was established at trial without contradiction that the deceased, Henry Berthiaume, was suffering from a cancer of his larynx. Appellee, an otolaryngologist, had treated him twice surgically. A laryngectomy was performed; and later, because of a tumor which had appeared in his neck, a radical neck dissection on one side was done. No complaint is made with respect to the surgical interventions.

During the period appellee was serving Mr. Berthiaume as a surgeon, many photographs of Berthiaume had been taken by appellee or under his direction. * * *

At all times material hereto Mr. Berthiaume was the patient of a physician other than appellee. Such other physician had referred the patient to appellee for surgery. On September 2, 1970, appellee saw the patient for the last time for the purpose of treatment or diagnosis. * * * The incident which gave rise to this lawsuit occurred on September 23, 1970.

It was also on that day Mr. Berthiaume died.

Although appellee disputed the evidence appellant produced at trial in many material respects, the jury could have concluded from the evidence that shortly before Mr. Berthiaume died on the 23rd, the appellee and a nurse appeared in his hospital room. In the presence of Mrs. Berthiaume and a visitor of the patient in the next bed, either Dr. Pratt or the nurse, at his direction, raised the dying Mr. Berthiaume's head and placed some blue operating room toweling under his head and beside him on the bed. The appellee testified that this blue toweling was placed there for the purpose of obtaining a color contrast for the photographs which he proposed to take. He then proceeded to take several photographs of Mr. Berthiaume.

The jury could have concluded from the testimony that Mr. Berthiaume protested the taking of pictures by raising a clenched fist and moving his head in an attempt to remove his head from the camera's range. The appellee himself testified that before taking the pictures he had been told by Mrs. Berthiaume when he talked with her in the corridor before entering the room that she "didn't think that Henry wanted his picture taken."

It is the raising of the deceased's head in order to put the operating room towels under and around him that appellant claims was an assault and battery. It is the taking of the pictures of the dying Mr. Berthiaume that appellant claims constituted the actionable invasion of Mr. Berthiaume's right to privacy. * * *

By our decision in this case we join a majority of the jurisdictions in the country in recognizing a "right to privacy." We also declare it to be the rule in Maine that a violation of this legally protected right is an actionable tort.

Decision

Specifically in this case we rule an unauthorized intrusion upon a person's physical and mental solitude or seclusion is a tort for the commission of which money damages may be had. * * *

All cases so far decided on the point agree that the plaintiff need not plead or prove special damages. Punitive damages can be awarded on the same basis as in other torts where a wrongful motive or state of mind appears * * * but not in cases where the defendant has acted innocently as, for example, in the mistaken but good faith belief that the plaintiff has given his consent. * * *

In this case we are concerned only with a claimed intrusion upon the plaintiff's intestate's physical and mental solitude or seclusion. The jury had a right to conclude from the evidence that plaintiff's intestate was dying. It could have concluded he desired not to be photographed in his hospital bed in such condition and that he manifested such desire by his physical motions. The jury should have been instructed, if it found these facts, that the taking of pictures without decedent's consent or over his objection was an invasion of his legally protected right to privacy, which invasion was an actionable tort for which money damages could be recovered. * * *

We recognize the benefit to the science of medicine which comes from the making of photographs of the treatment and of medical abnormalities found in patients. However, we agree with the reasoning expressed by Alessandroni, J., sitting in the Court of Common Pleas in Pennsylvania, when in writing of a fact situation almost identical to that now before us, he said in Clayman v. Bernstein, 38 Pa.D. & C. 543 (1940): * * *

"A man may object to any invasion, as well as to an unlimited invasion. Widespread distribution of a photograph is not essential nor can it be said that publication in its common usage or in its legal meaning is necessary. * * * Plaintiff's picture was taken without her authority or consent. Her right to decide whether her facial characteristics should be recorded for another's benefit or by reason of another's capriciousness has been violated. The scope of the authorization defines the extent of the acts necessary to constitute a violation. If plaintiff had consented to have her photograph taken only for defendant's private files certainly he would have no right to exhibit it to others without her permission. Can it be said that his rights are equally extensive when even that limited consent has not been given?" * * *

Because there were unresolved, disputed questions of f decided by the fact finder in favor of the plaintiff, would ha verdict for the plaintiff, it was reversible error to have dire for the defendant. * * *

KNIGHT v. PENOBSCOT BAY MEDICAL CEI . . . . . .

420 A.2d 915 (Me. 1980).

WERNICK, J. * * *

[Plaintiff and her husband appeal an unfavorable jury verdict denying *P, PH* them damages sought for invasion of privacy.] Nurse Robie's husband, the *D* defendant Theodore Robie, anticipating that his wife would leave the hospital at the end of her regular shift, had come to the hospital to meet her and take her home. When he learned that she would be detained, he decided to stay at the hospital until she finished her work. To give her husband something interesting to do while he was waiting for her, Nurse Robie asked Dr. Lantinen for permission to have her husband witness a birth. * * *

Mrs. Allen's pregnancy had been difficult. As the time approached for her to deliver, Dr. Lantinen realized that he would face complications. He decided that it would be better to have Mr. Robie witness a normal birth, and so he stationed Mr. Robie, who had put on hospital attire, where he could watch Kathleen Knight instead of Mrs. Allen.

Mr. Robie stood behind a viewing window in the surgical corridor, approximately twelve feet from the delivery table. From where he stood, Mr. Robie had a side view of Mrs. Knight's body, and her body was entirely covered by draping, except for her face and hands. Hence, Mr. Robie did not witness the actual process of delivering; what he saw was the baby being lifted up and then being placed on the mother's abdomen. * * *

Both Mr. and Mrs. Robie testified that they believed that Mr. Robie's presence had been authorized, that they were entirely unaware that his presence in the surgical corridor was offensive or intrusive to either patient, and that they had no intent to intrude. Similarly, Dr. Lantinen testified that he had no intention to "intrude upon anyone's privacy." During her stay in the hospital, Kathleen Knight never expressed any concern about Fred Robie's having been present at the window in the delivery area. * * *

The extent to which the law of Maine holds conduct tortious as an invasion of "privacy" is set forth in * * * Estate of Berthiaume v. Pratt * * *. Within the formulation enunciated * * *, the "privacy" interest asserted in the case at bar is * * * the interest that one's solitude or seclusion be protected against particular kinds of intrusion. * * *

Here, the presiding Justice used this language in instructing the jury. He thus formulated for the jury the elements, under the law of Maine, of the tort of invasion of privacy that is involved in this case. In concluding, as he did, that further amplification focusing upon particular factual aspects of the case was unnecessary, or might risk improperly influencing the jury in its function as factfinder, the presiding Justice acted within the proper bounds of discretion. * * *

More specifically, the Justice acted correctly in refusing to instruct in accordance with plaintiffs' requested instruction #8 because it was erroneous in three respects.

First, it failed to refer to the essential element that the defendant must intend as the result of his conduct that there be an intrusion upon another's solitude or seclusion.

Second, in reference to whether Mr. Robie's presence in the delivery area was "unnecessary" to serve the functional purpose involved, requested instruction #8 * * * erroneously stated that Mr. Robie's "unnecessary" presence in the delivery area was sufficient, without more, to establish as a matter of law that Mr. Robie had unlawfully intruded upon the plaintiffs' interest in seclusion.

Third, requested instruction #8 failed to differentiate between Kathleen Knight's interest in solitude or seclusion while giving birth and her husband's separate interest as arising from his being present at the time of birth. Since the interest in solitude or seclusion is protected as a personal interest, Mr. Knight could not properly claim an invasion of his separate personal interest merely because he was Kathleen Knight's husband. * * *

Here, the jury had before it testimony concerning such relevant factors as the agency relationships and scopes of authority of the various defendants, the location of the observer, Mr. Robie, relative to the plaintiffs, what was visible in the delivery room during the time Mr. Robie was observing it, the intentions of the participants and so forth. Hence, the presiding Justice acted correctly in leaving for jury determination whether in light of all the circumstances any of the defendants had intentionally intruded on the solitude, or seclusion, of either of the plaintiffs in a manner highly offensive to a reasonable person. * * * Appeal denied; the judgment of the Superior Court is affirmed.

NOTE: DE MAY, AGAIN

Compare the *Knight* case to *De May v. Roberts*. How did the passage of time affect the facts and circumstances of these two cases about a man who witnesses childbirth without the family's consent?

DOE v. HIGH–TECH INST., INC.
972 P.2d 1060 (Colo. Ct. App. 1998).

JUDGE DAVIDSON * * *

According to his complaint, plaintiff was a student in Cambridge's medical assistant training program. Shortly after the beginning of a class,

he informed the instructor that he had tested positive for hum
deficiency virus (HIV) as the result of an anonymous bloc
requested the instructor to treat that information as confidenti

That same month, the instructor informed the class that
at Cambridge were required to be tested for rubella. Each s
given a consent form indicating that such test would be performed on a
blood sample. Plaintiff signed and returned the consent form with the
understanding that his blood sample would be tested only for rubella.
Without plaintiff's knowledge, the instructor requested the laboratory
doing the testing also to test plaintiff's blood sample for HIV. She did not
request this test for any other student. The test yielded a positive result
for HIV. The laboratory, as required under 25–4–1402, C.R.S. 1997,
reported plaintiff's name, address, and positive HIV status to the Colorado
Department of Health and informed Cambridge of the test results. * * *

According to Restatement (Second) of Torts 625B (1981), to prevail on
a claim for intrusion upon seclusion as a violation of one's privacy, a
plaintiff must show that another has intentionally intruded, physically or
otherwise, upon the plaintiff's seclusion or solitude, and that such intrusion would be considered offensive by a reasonable person. * * *

elements

On the other hand, to prevail on a claim for unreasonable disclosure
of private facts, a plaintiff must establish that: (1) the fact disclosed was
private in nature; (2) the disclosure was made to the public; (3) the
disclosure was one which would be highly offensive to a reasonable person;
(4) the disclosed fact was not of legitimate concern to the public; and (5)
the one who disclosed the fact did so with reckless disregard of the private
nature of the fact disclosed.

2nd Tort elements

Thus, not only do the two claims contain different elements that must
be established, but here, each claim arises under differing circumstances
and is established by different facts. The basis for plaintiff's claim for
intrusion upon seclusion is the improper appropriation of private information resulting from the HIV test that was performed without his knowledge or consent. In contrast, plaintiff's claim for unreasonable disclosure
of private facts arose from the laboratory's reporting of the results of the
unauthorized blood test to the department of health and Cambridge's
disclosure of the results to third parties. * * *

Generally, a plaintiff may not receive a double recovery for the same
wrong. Lexton–Ancira Real Estate Fund v. Heller, 826 P.2d 819 (Colo.
1992). However, as discussed, the claims made by plaintiff, while based on
events occurring close in time, are not supported by identical evidence and
do not comprise the same wrong. Accordingly, plaintiff is not seeking
duplicative damages for the same loss under an alternative theory. Rather,
he seeks damages for Cambridge's conduct prior to and apart from any
disclosure of his HIV status. Thus, the fact that plaintiff received a
judgment on one claim does not render moot his appeal of the dismissal of
the other claim. * * *

Here, reversal of the dismissal of the intrusion upon seclusion claim does not require reversal of the judgment for plaintiff for his claim of unreasonable public disclosure of private facts. The two claims are not mutually dependent. As discussed, they are distinct and discrete claims and are established by different facts.

Additionally, that plaintiff has received damages for his claim of unreasonable public disclosure of private facts does not preclude an award of damages for his claim of intrusion upon seclusion.

One who suffers an intrusion upon his or her seclusion is entitled to recover damages for the harm to the particular privacy interest that has been invaded. * * *

And, such damages for that invasion may include: (1) general damages for harm to a plaintiff's interest in privacy resulting from the invasion; (2) damages for mental suffering; (3) special damages; and (4) nominal damages if no other damages are proven. * * *

[W]e conclude that a person has a privacy interest in his or her blood sample and in the medical information that may be obtained from it. We further conclude that an additional, unauthorized test, such as alleged here, can be sufficient to state a claim for relief for intrusion upon seclusion. * * *

[T]here is a generally recognized privacy interest in a person's body. Because personal information concerning a person's health may be obtained through one's blood, urine, and other bodily products, such products cannot be extracted from a person or initially tested without either consent or proper authorization. See Skinner v. Railway Labor Executives' Ass'n, 489 U.S. 602 (1989).

Similarly, there is a generally recognized privacy interest in information concerning one's health. * * *

For these reasons, we conclude that an unauthorized HIV test, under the circumstances as set forth in plaintiff's complaint, would be considered by a reasonable person as highly invasive, and therefore, such is sufficient to constitute an unreasonable or offensive intrusion. * * *

 The judgment is reversed and the cause is remanded for further proceedings consistent with the views expressed herein.

I.C.U. INVESTIGATIONS, INC. v. JONES

780 So. 2d 685 (Ala. 2000).

BROWN, J.

Jones was employed by Alabama Power Company ("APCo") as a groundman and winch-truck driver. While working on February 26, 1990, he suffered an electric shock and fell from the bed of the truck, dislocating and fracturing his left shoulder. Following his injury, he underwent five operations for problems with his shoulder, neck, back, and ribs. Jones sued APCo for workers' compensation benefits; APCo disputed the extent of his disability. * * *

[T]his case requires that we first determine the purpose for the investigation and whether " 'the thing into which there is intrusion or prying [is], and [is] entitled to be, private.' " * * * In Alabama Electric Co-operative, Inc. v. Partridge, 284 Ala. 442, 445, 225 So. 2d 848, 851 (1969), this Court noted, with approval, that plaintiffs making personal-injury claims " 'must expect reasonable inquiry and investigation to be made of [their] claims and [that] to this extent [their] interest in privacy is circumscribed.' "

The key issue in Jones's workers' compensation case was the extent of his injury. Jones, therefore, should have expected a reasonable investigation regarding his physical capacity. * * *

Hand [who was employed as a private investigator to verify the plaintiff's health condition] watched Jones and taped his activities while Jones was outside his home, in his front yard, where he was exposed to public view. Indeed, Jones's front yard was located at the intersection of two public roads. At no time did Hand enter or tape activities conducted inside Jones's own home. Because the activities Jones carried on in his front yard could have been observed by any passerby, we conclude that any intrusion by [the private investigator] into Jones's privacy was not "wrongful" and, therefore, was not actionable.

5. SNOOPING THROUGH TRASH

DANAI v. CANAL SQUARE ASSOCS.

862 A.2d 395 (D.C. 2004).

REID, ASSOCIATE JUDGE * * *

Ms. Danai is the President and Chief Executive Officer of PERS Travel, Inc. ("PERS"). On August 14, 1994, she entered into a five-year renewable lease with Canal for office space in a building located in the Northwest quadrant of the District of Columbia. On October 1, 1999, Canal filed a complaint for possession against PERS, claiming that PERS failed to renew its lease in a timely manner. During a bench trial on its complaint, Canal used a letter, which it had obtained from trash discarded by PERS, to impeach Ms. Danai's testimony as to her understanding of the renewal provision in her lease agreement. The trial court rendered judgment in favor of Canal. Subsequently, Ms. Danai filed a complaint against Canal on July 3, 2000, alleging invasion of privacy and intentional infliction of emotional distress. * * *

At least since *Pearson v. Dodd*, 133 U.S. App. D.C. 279, 410 F.2d 701 (1969), the District of Columbia has recognized intrusion upon seclusion as one type of invasion of privacy. * * *

We have not considered previously whether the tort of intrusion upon seclusion occurs when an item is taken that has been collected from the wastepaper basket in a person's office and placed with trash from other offices in a locked community trash room under the control of the property managers for disposal of off-site. * * *

Ms. Danai tore a March 30, 1999, letter she had written to Canal into large pieces and placed the pieces in a wastepaper basket in her office. According to an affidavit provided by her in opposition to Canal's motion for summary judgment, "trash [from her office and others in the building] was picked up daily by crews under the supervision of RB Associates, the property managers for Canal." The trash was taken to "a locked room under the control of the property managers." Ms. Danai did not indicate that she had requested segregation of her trash, or that she had a key to this trash room and could readily retrieve the trash collected from her wastepaper basket after it was placed in the community trash room. On April 1, 1999, the Vice President of RB Associates, Ted Vogel, went through the trash taken from Ms. Danai's office and retrieved the torn letter addressed to Canal. The letter was used in Canal's suit against Ms. Danai to show she was aware of her failure to give timely notice of intent to renew her lease, and therefore, her eviction was justified.

To prevail upon her claim of intrusion upon seclusion, Ms. Danai must establish not merely the first element of the tort, that is, "an invasion or interference by physical intrusion," Wolf, supra, 553 A.2d at 1217, here the rummaging through her trash by Canal's agent, Mr. Vogel of RB Associates and the taking of the discarded letter, but also must show, under the second element, that the invasion or physical intrusion was "into a place where [she] secluded [herself], or into [her] private or secret concerns." Although there was an invasion into Ms. Danai's trash, it did not occur in her office. Rather it took place in the community trash room, which was a place of seclusion for neither Ms. Danai nor her trash. Indeed, other trash from the building was placed in the same room, and according to Ms. Danai's affidavit, the locked trash room was "under the control of the property managers." There is no evidence that she possessed a key to the locked room, nor gave instructions to the property managers to keep her trash intact and under seal. Thus, Ms. Danai had no "legitimate expectation of privacy in the invaded place," the locked community trash room. *Godfrey v. United States*, 408 A.2d 1244, 1245.

Since Ms. Danai cannot establish that the community trash room was a place of seclusion for her or her trash, she must demonstrate that the torn letter retrieved by Canal's agent constituted an intrusion into her private or secret concerns. Her affidavit states: "much of my private, personal correspondence was done by me in hand-written letters or memos, which I would fax to the recipient and then throw away the original (into the wastepaper basket)." In essence, she contends she had a subjective expectation of privacy with respect to her discarded papers. * * *

[Ms. Danai had a subjective expectation of privacy. But, as Fourth Amendment cases suggest, subjective expectations of privacy that are not also "reasonable" expectations of privacy do not mandate protection.]

"The vast majority of courts have ruled that * * * the individual who placed [the] garbage [or trash] for collection either abandoned it or has no reasonable expectation of privacy therein, thus rendering any search and seizure of that trash lawful." Kimberly J. Winbush, Annotation, Searches and Seizures: Reasonable Expectation of Privacy in Contents of Garbage or Trash Receptacle, 62 A.L.R. 5th 1 (1998); Gordon J. MacDonald, Stray Katz: Is Shredded Trash Private? 79 *Cornell L. Rev.* 452, 464 (1994). Here, Ms. Danai knowingly and voluntarily abandoned objects she placed in her trash. She relinquished control over them, knowing that they were readily accessible to a third party, the property managers and the landlord, upon collection from her office for mixing with other trash in a community trash room, and ultimately accessible to others when the trash was removed and discarded off-site. The fact that the community trash room was locked by itself does not support an objective, reasonable expectation of privacy on Ms. Danai's part. Public trash cans and dumps often are locked or bolted to some extent to prevent their contents from being disturbed, for example, by animals or scavengers. * * *

It is common knowledge that plastic garbage bags left on or at the side of a public street are readily accessible to animals, children, scavengers, snoops, and other members of the public. Moreover, respondents placed their refuse at the curb for the express purpose of conveying it to a third party, the trash collector, who might himself have sorted through respondent's trash or permitted others, such as the police, to do so. Accordingly, having deposited their garbage "in an area particularly suited for public inspection and, in a manner of speaking, public consumption, for the express purpose of having strangers take it," *United States v. Reicherter*, 647 F.2d 397, 399 (3d Cir. 1981), respondents could have had no reasonable expectation of privacy in the * * * items that they discarded.

Here, admittedly Ms. Danai did not place her garbage "at the curb" but she did convey it to a third party, the property managers, who in turn made arrangements for discarding it to yet another party, the outside trash collector. * * * A locked community trash room under the control of property managers is not akin to "the curtilage" of Ms. Danai's office space. That is, it is not "the area to which extends the intimate activity associated with the sanctity of a [person's] * * * privacies of life." *California v. Ciraolo*, 476 U.S. 207, 212 (1986) (citations omitted). * * *

Accordingly, for the foregoing reasons, we affirm the judgment of the trial court.

NOTE: SEARCHING IN TRASH TO DETERMINE PATERNITY

In 2002, billionaire Kirk Kerkorian, the 84-year-old owner of MGM, sent a private investigator to search film producer Steve Bing's trash. According to a lawsuit filed by Bing, the private detective sought evidence that Bing was the biological father of Kerkorian's daughter Kira. At the time, Kira's mother had filed a lawsuit against Kerkorian seeking increased child support payments for Kira. In response, Kerkorian hired the aforementioned private detective. The investigator found Bing's discarded dental floss in Bing's trash bins and Kerkorian hired a firm to perform a DNA test. Based on the test results, Kerkorian argued that Bing was Kira's father. Bing filed a one billion dollar lawsuit against Kerkorian, alleging invasion of privacy and trespassing. Later Bing dropped the case. According to Bing's publicist, "Kirk Kerkorian and Steve Bing jointly announced that they have amicably resolved all outstanding differences between them. * * *"

Does the fact that trash bins contain vast quantities of human DNA, which if collected could convey a wealth of personal health information, suggest a need to rethink the privacy of rubbish? Genetic materials can reveal, not only our biological ancestry, but our biological sex, diseases, abnormalities and susceptibilities.

6. A REMEDY FOR SEXUAL HARASSMENT?

NOTE: HARASSMENT AND STALKING

In the next few cases, women who have been sexually harassed bring suits alleging wrongful intrusion. Consider the social context of each case, and how evolving attitudes about female modesty, sexual harassment, stalking and data security may have affected the courts' decisions. Note the procedural barrier in *Vescovo* faced by a parent's suit on behalf of her young daughter. Does it make sense to hold newspapers liable for acts of harassment committed by third-parties whose behavior they cannot control?

In *Phillips v. Smalley Maintenance Services* an employer is sued, in part, because he peppered a female employee with sexually explicit questions. Should the invasion of privacy tort apply in a case where a person just asks offensive questions that never get answered? In *Remsburg v. Docusearch* the intrusion tort is aimed at defendants who relied upon pretexting and identity theft to obtain a social security number and other information a customer used to locate and murder an innocent woman. Do legal privacy rights help women? See Sally F. Goldfarb, Violence Against Women and the Persistence of Privacy, 61 *Ohio St. L.J.* 1 (2000).

VESCOVO v. NEW WAY ENTERPRISES, LTD.

60 Cal. App. 3d 582 (Cal. Ct. App. 1976).

ASHBY J. * * *

The factual allegations of the first amended complaint are as follows: Plaintiff Norma Jean Vescovo is the wife of plaintiff Albert Vescovo, and they are the parents of plaintiff Frankie Renee Vescovo, a minor, who was 14 years old at the time of defendants' alleged acts. Plaintiffs all resided together. Defendants are publishers and officers of the Los Angeles Free Press.

In the June 15, 1973, issue of the Los Angeles Free Press the following classified advertisement appeared, giving plaintiff's address:

"Hot Lips—Deep Throat Sexy young bored housewife Norma—[plaintiffs' address]".

After the appearance of this advertisement, Norma received letters from inmates in penal institutions and numerous other persons soliciting her to perform lewd, immoral and criminal sexual acts; in excess of 100 persons wrongfully entered on plaintiffs' residential property without consent, both during the day and night, demanding to see Norma, creating disturbances, and using lewd, abusive and threatening language upon being asked to leave; in excess of 150 motor vehicles stopped in front of or cruised slowly by plaintiffs' residence, harassing, annoying and frightening plaintiffs.

Alleging that neither Norma nor anyone acting in her behalf requested, consented, or gave permission to defendants to publish the advertisement, plaintiffs set forth 10 alleged causes of action. * * *

The question on this appeal is whether the first amended complaint stated a valid cause of action on behalf of Frankie for invasion of privacy, intentional infliction of emotional harm, and negligent infliction of emotional harm. * * *

[I]t is alleged that "[as] a direct and proximate result of the publication of said classified advertisement, plaintiff Frankie Renee Vescovo's right to privacy has been violated in that said plaintiff's physical solitude and home have been wrongfully invaded by innumerable undesirable and unsavory persons, who in responding to said malicious advertisement, have harassed, annoyed and frightened plaintiff Frankie Renee Vescovo, all of which have resulted in the disruption of said plaintiff's life and the peace and tranquility of her mind, and have made her subject to contempt and ridicule of her neighbors and friends, and who have invaded and impaired the seclusion of said plaintiff's private life and her said residence, and have caused and will continue to cause plaintiff Frankie Renee Vescovo injury to her mental health, strength, activity and body and have caused and will continue to cause said plaintiff great mental, physical and nervous pain and suffering, all to her general damage in the sum of $50,000.00."

Plaintiffs contend that the * * * cause of action adequately states a cause of action for that aspect of invasion of privacy involving intrusion on the plaintiff's physical solitude or seclusion. * * *

Defendants contend that there is no relational right to privacy, i.e., even a close relative may not recover for the invasion of privacy of another. * * * In this respect defendants' argument misses the mark. Frankie does not seek to recover based upon the derogatory information implied about Norma in the advertisement. Frankie seeks to recover for the physical intrusion by various unsavory characters on her own solitude in her own home. As stated by Prosser, "[Plaintiff's] right is a personal one, which does not extend to members of his family, unless, as is obviously possible, their own privacy is invaded along with his." * * *

It is alleged in the first amended complaint that defendants published the advertisement "with intent and design to injure, disgrace and aggrieve plaintiff Frankie Renee Vescovo and disregarding the comfort of said plaintiff's life and the peace and tranquility of her mind, and to invade and impair the seclusion of said plaintiff's private life * * *. Under the circumstances a cause of action for invasion of privacy was stated.

Decision

NOTE: STANDING TO SUE

Generally, a person will only have standing to sue to vindicate his or her own legal rights. In common law privacy suits, the general rule is that the person who suffers the alleged invasion must herself sue. Frankie Lee Vescovo had standing to sue for invasion of privacy, even though the fraudulent "Hot Lips" ad named her mother Norma Vescovo. Why? Because Frankie, along with her mother, experienced intrusions as a result of the ad.

Family members generally lack standing to sue to recover for the invasion of a relative's privacy. As in *Vescovo*, Courts have sometimes found that intrusions or disclosures concerning one person in the family amount to intrusions or disclosures concerning another. If someone reveals a man's positive HIV status to the public, should his HIV-negative status wife and children have standing to sue for invasions of their privacy? See *Doe v. Barrington*, 729 F. Supp. 376 (D.N.J. 1990).

In most states the privacy claims of deceased persons based on wrongs committed in their lifetimes survive their deaths and can continue as suits of the estate. Thus a dying man, whose photograph is taken against his will just prior to passing, has a privacy claim that survives as a claim of his estate, as in *Estate of Berthiaume*.

Posthumous celebrity publicity rights are recognized in many states. However, ordinary privacy actions for intrusion, publication of embarrassing facts, false light and appropriation cannot be brought for posthumous "invasions". The dead have no feelings, and no privacy.

Occasionally an employer will be granted standing to sue on behalf of its employees. This might be permitted, for example, where a third-party intrudes into the affairs of a company in a way that injures employees as a group. In the constitutional arena, the standing rules are flexible. In abortion cases, for example, the Supreme Court has held that health care providers have third-party standing to sue to vindicate the privacy rights of their actual and potential patients. Accord *Northwestern Memorial Hospital v. Ashcroft*, 362 F.3d 923 (7th Cir. 2004).

PHILLIPS v. SMALLEY MAINTENANCE SERVICES, INC.

435 So. 2d 705 (Ala. 1983).

JONES, J. * * *

Plaintiff Brenda Phillips (Phillips) was formerly employed by Defendant Smalley Maintenance Services, Inc. (SMS). SMS and the president and principal owner of SMS, Appellant Ray Smalley (Smalley), were found

by the trial judge, after a special advisory verdict by the jury, to have PH
wrongfully discharged Phillips in violation of Title VII for her refusal to
engage in sexual activities with Smalley. On this claim, Phillips was
awarded lost wages of $2,666.40. The trial judge also found that she had
been subjected to actionable sexual harassment prior to the wrongful
discharge, but that no actual damages arose from this Title VII violation.
Pursuant to the exercise of pendent jurisdiction, the jury found that on
one occasion Smalley had touched Phillips without her consent in an
angry, hostile or offensive manner and awarded her $10 as nominal
damages for common law battery. The jury also found that Smalley had
wrongfully intruded into Phillips's private activities so as to cause outrage
or mental suffering, shame, or humiliation to a person of ordinary sensibilities. Compensatory damages of $25,000 were awarded on this Alabama
state law "invasion of privacy" claim.

Phillips began working as an "overhead cleaner" for SMS on July 30,
1979. SMS provided cleaning, janitorial, and other miscellaneous services
at a Monsanto plant in Marshall County, Alabama. Phillips was transferred between jobs of various descriptions, primarily on her request, to
avoid sexually oriented discussions with male co-workers.

At trial Phillips testified that within a few weeks of beginning her job,
Smalley called her into his office and locked the door. He questioned her
about how she was getting along with her husband and told her his wife
was ill. The conversation ended when Phillips said she must return to
work. A few days later he again called her into his office, locked the door,
and this time inquired how often Phillips and her husband had sex and
what "positions" they used. Phillips told Smalley it was none of his
business and left the office. This form of intrusive interrogation continued
two to three times a week. On repeated occasions, calling Phillips away
from her work, into his office and locking the door, Smalley asked her
whether she had ever engaged in oral sex.

At one time, he invited her to have a drink with him on a Saturday.
She refused. In later conversations he insisted that she engage in oral sex
with him on penalty of losing her job, upon which he knew she and her
family were significantly financially dependent. She consistently resisted
his advances. Shortly before the termination of her employment, he again
called her into his office, showing anger toward her, beating on his desk,
and insisted that she engage in oral sex with him at least three times a
week. He then began to cover the window in the office door with paper to
prohibit anyone from seeing inside. Phillips forced her way out of the
office. As she was leaving, Smalley hit her "across the bottom" with the
back of his hand. Phillips testified that this treatment made her nervous
and unable to adequately perform her work.

On October 23, 1979, Smalley once more called Phillips into his office
and asked her if she was going to show her gratitude to him for hiring her
by engaging in certain sexual acts. She again refused. She testified that
she was already upset by virtue of having learned the day before that she

was possibly going to have surgery. After the incident with Smalley, Phillips said she "tried to work, and * * * got so upset that [she] couldn't." She told her supervisor and Smalley that she was going home early. Smalley asked for her gate pass; she would not give it to him and said she was not quitting the job. The next day her gate pass would no longer work to admit her to the plant.

She then went to see a lawyer, returned to the plant, and talked by phone to Smalley, who brought her pay check. When she asked Smalley why she had been fired, he said she had not been fired but was "laid off," because the work for which she was hired was completed. Testifying at trial, Smalley made it clear that even if she were only "laid off" he had no intention of calling her back when more work was available. The distinction between "laying off" and "firing" in his mind was relevant only to the terminated employee's ability to collect unemployment benefits. * * *

The testimony of a family practice physician and of a psychiatrist was introduced at trial to the effect that Phillips experienced chronic anxiety in the months following her termination from SMS. She underwent treatment and was placed on medication. According to her husband, she had contemplated suicide and her relationships with family and friends were disrupted. In addition, she experienced physical problems, basically unrelated to her termination but resulting in surgery. The medical experts, expressing their expert opinion, testified that her anxiety was related to the events surrounding her termination and was not caused by her physical problems. * * *

Since 1948, beginning with the case of Smith v. Doss, 251 Ala. 250, 37 So. 2d 118 (1948), Alabama has recognized the tort of "invasion of the right to privacy." * * *

The parties concede that Plaintiff's action is premised upon that species of the privacy realm known as a "wrongful intrusion into one's private activities." * * * Despite previous recognition and description of the "wrongful intrusion" tort, we have never, up to now, specifically adopted the language of Restatement (Second) of Torts, § 652B (1977), as the law of this State. * * *

We hold that acquisition of information from a plaintiff is not a requisite element of a § 652B cause of action. * * *

Although Defendants vigorously insist to the contrary, we cannot agree that 652B's application must be triggered by some "communication" or "publication" by a defendant to a third party of any private information elicited from a plaintiff. * * *

In Estate of Berthiaume v. Pratt, 365 A. 2d 792 (Me. 1976), a cause of action for invasion of privacy was held stated where the defendant, a physician, had photographed a dying man in his hospital bed, over his objections. * * *

Defendants argue that, if the claimed invasion of one's right to privacy is the attempted acquisition of information about a plaintiff's private matters or affairs, then it necessarily follows that such attempted acquisition must be made "surreptitiously." We disagree.

While conduct undertaken surreptitiously may form the basis of a different actionable claim, we find no authority for the proposition that this is an element of the "wrongful intrusion" tort.

In Bennett [v. Norban, a Pennsylvania case] * * * the plaintiff was stopped outside defendant's store by the assistant manager of the store: "He put his hand on her shoulder, put himself in position to block her path, and ordered her to take off her coat, which, being frightened, she did. He then said: 'What about your pockets?' and reached into two pockets on the sides of her dress. Not finding anything, he took her purse from her hand, pulled her things out of it, peered into it, replaced the things, gave it back to her, mumbled something, and ran back into the store." 151 A. 2d at 477. Although no surreptitious conduct was involved, and no information of the plaintiff's private activities was obtained, the Court held that the plaintiff did have an invasion of privacy action. "The angry performance of defendant's agent was an unreasonable and serious interference with appellant's desire for anonymity and an intrusion beyond the limits of decency." 151 A. 2d at 479. * * *

[W]e find that Smalley's intrusive and coercive sexual demands upon Brenda Phillips were such an "examination" into her "private concerns," that is, improper inquiries into her personal sexual proclivities and personality. * * *

Do the facts of this case support a claim under Alabama law for "the wrongful intrusion into one's private activities in such manner as to outrage or cause mental suffering, shame or humiliation to a person of ordinary sensibilities?" We hold they do.   *Decision*

REMSBURG v. DOCUSEARCH, INC.

149 N.H. 148 (N.H. 2003).

DALLIANIS, J. * * *

Docusearch, Inc. and Wing and a Prayer, Inc. (WAAP) jointly own and operate an Internet-based investigation and information service known as Docusearch.com. Daniel Cohn and Kenneth Zeiss each own 50% of each company's stock. Cohn serves as president of both companies and Zeiss serves as a director of WAAP. Cohn is licensed as a private investigator by both the State of Florida and Palm Beach County, Florida.

On July 29, 1999, New Hampshire resident Liam Youens contacted Docusearch through its Internet website and requested the date of birth for Amy Lynn Boyer, another New Hampshire resident. Youens provided Docusearch his name, New Hampshire address, and a contact telephone number. He paid the $20 fee by credit card. Zeiss placed a telephone call to Youens in New Hampshire on the same day. Zeiss cannot recall the reason for the phone call, but speculates that it was to verify the order. The next day, July 30, 1999, Docusearch provided Youens with the birth dates for several Amy Boyers, but none was for the Amy Boyer sought by Youens. In response, Youens e-mailed Docusearch inquiring whether it would be possible to get better results using Boyer's home address, which he provided. Youens gave Docusearch a different contact phone number.

Later that same day, Youens again contacted Docusearch and placed an order for Boyer's social security number (SSN), paying the $45 fee by credit card. On August 2, 1999, Docusearch obtained Boyer's social security number from a credit reporting agency as a part of a "credit header" and provided it to Youens. A "credit header" is typically provided at the top of a credit report and includes a person's name, address and social security number. The next day, Youens placed an order with Docusearch for Boyer's employment information, paying the $109 fee by credit card, and giving Docusearch the same phone number he had provided originally. Docusearch phone records indicate that Zeiss placed a phone call to Youens on August 6, 1999. The phone number used was the one Youens had provided with his follow-up inquiry regarding Boyer's birth date. The phone call lasted for less than one minute, and no record exists concerning its topic or whether Zeiss was able to speak with Youens. On August 20, 1999, having received no response to his latest request, Youens placed a second request for Boyer's employment information, again paying the $109 fee by credit card. On September 1, 1999, Docusearch refunded Youens' first payment of $109 because its efforts to fulfill his first request for Boyer's employment information had failed.

With his second request for Boyer's employment information pending, Youens placed yet another order for information with Docusearch on September 6, 1999. This time, he requested a "locate by social security number" search for Boyer. Youens paid the $30 fee by credit card, and received the results of the search—Boyer's home address—on September 7, 1999.

On September 8, 1999, Docusearch informed Youens of Boyer's employment address. Docusearch acquired this address through a subcontractor, Michele Gambino, who had obtained the information by placing a "pretext" telephone call to Boyer in New Hampshire. Gambino lied about who she was and the purpose of her call in order to convince Boyer to reveal her employment information. Gambino had no contact with Youens, nor did she know why Youens was requesting the information.

On October 15, 1999, Youens drove to Boyer's workplace and fatally shot her as she left work. Youens then shot and killed himself. A subsequent police investigation revealed that Youens kept firearms and ammunition in his bedroom, and maintained a website containing references to stalking and killing Boyer as well as other information and statements related to violence and killing.

All persons have a duty to exercise reasonable care not to subject others to an unreasonable risk of harm. * * *

In situations in which the harm is caused by criminal misconduct, however, determining whether a duty exists is complicated by the competing rule "that a private citizen has no general duty to protect others from the criminal attacks of third parties." * * *

In certain limited circumstances, however, we have recognized that there are exceptions to the general rule where a duty to exercise reasonable care will arise. * * * We have held that such a duty may arise because: (1) a special relationship exists; (2) special circumstances exist; or (3) the duty has been voluntarily assumed. Id. The special circumstances exception includes situations where there is "an especial temptation and opportunity for criminal misconduct brought about by the defendant." * * *

Thus, if a private investigator or information broker's (hereinafter "investigator" collectively) disclosure of information to a client creates a foreseeable risk of criminal misconduct against the third person whose information was disclosed, the investigator owes a duty to exercise reasonable care not to subject the third person to an unreasonable risk of harm. In determining whether the risk of criminal misconduct is foreseeable to an investigator, we examine two risks of information disclosure implicated by this case: stalking and identity theft.

It is undisputed that stalkers, in seeking to locate and track a victim, sometimes use an investigator to obtain personal information about the victims. * * *

Public concern about stalking has compelled all fifty States to pass some form of legislation criminalizing stalking. Approximately one million women and 371,000 men are stalked annually in the United States. * * *

Identity theft, i.e., the use of one person's identity by another, is an increasingly common risk associated with the disclosure of personal information, such as a SSN. * * *

Like the consequences of stalking, the consequences of identity theft can be severe. The best estimates place the number of victims in excess of 100,000 per year and the dollar loss in excess of $2 billion per year. * * * Victims of identity theft risk the destruction of their good credit histories. This often destroys a victim's ability to obtain credit from any source and may, in some cases, render the victim unemployable or even cause the victim to be incarcerated. * * *

The threats posed by stalking and identity theft lead us to conclude that the risk of criminal misconduct is sufficiently foreseeable so that an investigator has a duty to exercise reasonable care in disclosing a third person's personal information to a client. And we so hold. This is especially true when, as in this case, the investigator does not know the client or the client's purpose in seeking the information. * * *

A tort action based upon an intrusion upon seclusion must relate to something secret, secluded or private pertaining to the plaintiff. * * * Moreover, liability exists only if the defendant's conduct was such that the defendant should have realized that it would be offensive to persons of ordinary sensibilities. "It is only where the intrusion has gone beyond the limits of decency that liability accrues." * * *

In addressing whether a person's SSN is something secret, secluded or private, we must determine whether a person has a reasonable expectation of privacy in the number. * * * SSNs are available in a wide variety of contexts. * * * SSNs are used to identify people to track social security benefits, as well as when taxes and credit applications are filed. * * * "[T]he widespread use of SSNs as universal identifiers in the public and private sectors is one of the most serious manifestations of privacy concerns in the Nation." * * * [A] person's interest in maintaining the privacy of his or her SSN has been recognized by numerous federal and state statutes. As a result, the entities to which this information is disclosed and their employees are bound by legal, and, perhaps, contractual constraints to hold SSNs in confidence to ensure that they remain private. * * *

Thus, while a SSN must be disclosed in certain circumstances, a person may reasonably expect that the number will remain private.

Whether the intrusion would be offensive to persons of ordinary sensibilities is ordinarily a question for the fact-finder and only becomes a question of law if reasonable persons can draw only one conclusion from the evidence. * * * The evidence underlying the certified question is insufficient to draw any such conclusion here, and we therefore must leave this question to the fact-finder. In making this determination, the fact-finder should consider "the degree of intrusion, the context, conduct and circumstances surrounding the intrusion as well as the intruder's motives and objectives, the setting into which he intrudes, and the expectations of those whose privacy is invaded." * * * Accordingly, a person whose SSN is obtained by an investigator from a credit reporting agency without the person's knowledge or permission may have a cause of action for intrusion upon seclusion for damages caused by the sale of the SSN, but must prove that the intrusion was such that it would have been offensive to a person of ordinary sensibilities.

We next address whether a person has a cause of action for intrusion upon seclusion where an investigator obtains the person's work address by using a pretextual phone call. We must first establish whether a work address is something secret, secluded or private about the plaintiff. * * *

In most cases, a person works in a public place. "On the public street, or in any other public place, [a person] has no legal right to be alone." W. Page Keeton et al., Prosser and Keeton on the Law of Torts § 117, at 855 (5th ed. 1984). A person's employment, where he lives, and where he works are exposures which we all must suffer. We have no reasonable expectation of privacy as to our identity or as to where we live or work. Our commuting to and from where we live and work is not done clandestinely and each place provides a facet of our total identity. * * *

Thus, where a person's work address is readily observable by members of the public, the address cannot be private and no intrusion upon seclusion action can be maintained.

7. PERSONAL COMPUTERS AND INTRUSION

NOTE: COOKIES AS CYBER-INTRUSION

"A 'cookie' is an electronic file that online companies, including Intuit, implant upon computer users' hard drives when those users visit Internet Web sites. * * * Cookies, which Internet companies can differentiate between by assigning unique identification numbers to each computer user, can contain virtually any kind of information. Cookies generally perform many convenient and innocuous functions, such as keeping track of items Web site visitors may purchase. Cookies are also commonly used to keep track of usernames and passwords to make it easier for people to access Web sites that require authentication to view certain Web pages." See *In re Intuit Privacy Litigation*, 138 F.Supp.2d 1272 (C.D. Cal. 2001). Suppose the operator of a website you visited to purchase tax preparation software placed a cookie on your computer. Do you have a cause of action for intrusion upon seclusion? If the question seems fanciful, see Id., in which computer users asserted a number of statutory and common law privacy-based claims against a defendant they say placed cookies on their computers.

Commentators have considered whether the intrusion tort might be useful against bothersome "adware" and "spyware." In Chapter 3 we will look more closely at annoyances like spyware and spam, which pending and enacted legislation seek to address. See generally Paul M. Schwartz, Privacy, Inalienability and the Regulation of Spyware, 20 *Berkeley Tech. L.J.* 1269 (2005). See also Alan F. Blakely et. al., Why the Law Doesn't Adequately Address Computer Spyware, 2005 *Duke J. L. & Tech* 0025 (2005).

DANIEL B. GARRIE, THE LEGAL STATUS OF SPYWARE
59 Fed. Comm. L.J. 157 (2006).

Legal Treatment of Spyware

Spyware victims pursuing civil remedies can currently pursue five theories of recovery: (1) trespass to chattels; (2) the Stored Wire and Electronic Communications and Transactional Records Act ("Stored Communications Act"); (3) the Computer Fraud and Abuse Act ("CFAA"); (4) invasion of privacy; and (5) the Wiretap Act. Each of these theories of recovery has varying levels of success depending on the facts of the litigation, amount of damages, data mining methods, and the nature of consent inferred from the plaintiff's conduct. A complaint should allege any and all of these causes of action applicable, since the inner workings of the specific spyware program may not be known until after discovery.

First, spyware victims can assert a cause of action under the common law tort theory of trespass to chattels. By inserting a code into another person's computer system, the spyware perpetrator enters an end-user's computer by intermeddling with it: One who commits a trespass to chattel is subject to liability to the possessor of the chattel if, but only if, * * * (b) the chattel is impaired as to its condition, quality, or value, or (c) the possessor is deprived of the use of the chattel for a substantial time * * *.

Trespass to chattels claims arise under state common law, and therefore, their usefulness depends on whether a particular jurisdiction is willing to classify spyware violations as trespasses, as well as the requirements that individual jurisdictions may have for proving trespass to chattels. Trespass to chattels claims can also be hindered if a court finds that an end-user granted consent. As such, trespass to chattels claims present a strong cause of action against certain types of spyware in certain jurisdictions, and they should be asserted if applicable.

Second, spyware victims can assert claims under the CFAA if the aggregate damages over the course of a year exceed $5,000 or the spyware causes physical injury to any person. The CFAA contains eight powerful civil and criminal causes of action designed to prevent unauthorized access to "protected computers" of U.S. government agencies, financial institutions, and private end-users. As long as an end-user's computer is used in interstate commerce, it constitutes a "protected computer" and the end-user can bring an action for spyware violations under this Act. Litigants alleging claims under the CFAA face two potential drawbacks: (1) end-users frequently authorize spyware data mining when they install the associated programs on their computers; and (2) spyware is unlikely to cause over $5,000 worth of damages unless a company has been victimized or multiple victims aggregate their damages. Companies victimized by spyware will usually be able to meet the $5,000 damage requirement assuming they either have in-house staff or they hire a technology consultant to perform general system maintenance to eliminate the spyware and plug any holes it has created. The CFAA provides the strongest cause of action available for businesses but does not afford the vast majority of end-users sufficient protection due to its high $5,000 jurisdictional requirement.

Third, spyware victims may be able to assert causes of action under the Stored Communications Act which protects end-user digital privacy, be it email, IM, file transfer protocol, or other Internet-based communications when the information is stored on the end-user's machine. A spyware victim alleging a violation of the Stored Communications Act must prove that the spyware program (1) intentionally, (2) in an unauthorized fashion, (3) gained access to a facility providing electronic communications, (4) obtained electronic or wire communications, and (5) the data acquired by the spyware program was in electronic storage. Spyware programs mine data that resides electronically on end-users' machines. Spyware violates the Stored Communications Act if it mines information in temporary storage intended to be an electronic communication without consent. Two drawbacks to the Stored Communications Act are that (1) personal data is not protected unless it is an electronic communication, and (2) spyware can mine any data on an end-user's machine as long as the end-user gives consent to mine data when the spyware is installed along with another freeware or shareware program. As a result, the Stored Communications Act gives spyware victims a rather limited cause of action when a stored electronic communication is mined without consent.

Fourth, spyware victims may have a cause of action under the tort of invasion of privacy, or as Restatement (Second) of Torts calls it, "intrusion upon seclusion." The victim will claim that the spyware perpetrator, by inserting the spyware without the victim's permission, "intrudes * * * upon the solitude or seclusion of another or his private affairs or concerns," and there will be liability "if the intrusion would be highly offensive to a reasonable person." The authors of the restatement specifically envision intrusions that are not physical. The restatement specifies that the intrusion "may be by some other form of investigation or examination into his private concerns, as by opening his private and personal mail, searching his safe or his wallet, examining his private bank account * * *." The only concern may be to show that "the intrusion has gone beyond the limits of decency" leading to liability on the part of the perpetrator. Spyware victims, therefore, will be more likely to recover under an invasion of privacy theory if the spyware steals personally identifiable information, such as private bank accounts, credit card numbers, and social security numbers.

Fifth, spyware victims may be able to assert a cause of action under the Federal Wiretap Act if the spyware intercepts an oral, wire, or electronic communication without consent. Even though spyware's primary functional purpose is to make unauthorized interceptions of electronic communications, spyware developers have designed spyware programs capable of evading the Wiretap Act's reach. Spyware makers have accomplished this evasion by engineering their software to record stored end-user files and end-user inputs before they are transmitted to another communicant. In certain situations, however, spyware victims could successfully argue that while the spyware is merely tracking communications input by the end-user onto his or her own computer, the time between the end-user's input and the actual transmission of the bits of data to the other communicant is so short, on the order of milliseconds, that the communication begins contemporaneously with the end-user's input. The courts have not yet credited this argument. However, if they did, then a majority of spyware programs installed without actual consent could be found to violate the Wiretap Act, and consumers could have another cause of action against spyware proliferators.

In all five causes of action, damages can run the gamut from the minor annoyance of uninstalling or otherwise removing the spyware, to disposal of a computer that seems to have acquired a disease similar to syphilis—eating its brain away—to thousands of dollars of damage caused by the harvesting and exploitation of an end-user's personal information or identity. Since most consumers are unlikely to have damages in amounts sufficient to justify litigation, the class action device may be most useful, especially under the CFAA, which offers powerful civil causes of action as long as the victims can allege $5,000 in damages. Since the spyware perpetrator's actions are the only actions relevant, and the cause of injuries arise from the single course of conduct under the control of the spyware perpetrator, courts may be more willing to certify these class actions. Companies, however, will easily be able to meet the damages requirement given the loss in time, computing, people, and business resulting from malicious spyware operating on their systems.

8. CHASING CELEBRITIES

NOTE: PAPARAZZI

Former First Lady and wife of a Greek billionaire, the glamorous Jacqueline Kennedy Onassis was hounded by photographers. She sued one of them, Ronald Galella, a free-lance photographer who virtually stalked her hoping to take commercially valuable pictures. A federal court issued an injunction ordering Mr. Galella to keep a certain distance from Mrs. Onassis and her children, John and Caroline Kennedy. The court found that Galella had "insinuated himself into the very fabric of Mrs. Onassis' life". Although the intrusion and private fact torts do not exist in New York, the court framed its relief around "the need to prevent further invasion of the defendant's privacy," reachable through the New York's laws against harassment. Galella unsuccessfully fought the injunction, and sued Onassis' Secret Service body guards. See *Galella v. Onassis*, 487 F.2d 986 (2d Cir. 1973).

After the death of Princess Diana of Great Britain in 1998 drew attention to the dangers of chasing celebrities, California enacted a statute designed to keep photographers away from famous people. Primarily the law protects public officials and public figures engaged in family activities at their homes. Still, the law has been controversial. See Note, Privacy, Technology, and the California "Anti–Paparazzi" Statute, 112 *Harv. L. Rev* 1367 (1999); Lisa Vance, Amending its Anti–Paparazzi Statute: California's Latest Baby Step in its Attempt to Curb the Aggressive Paparazzi, 29/1 *Comm/Ent: Hastings Comm. and Entert. L. J.* (2006)

ANN LOEB AND JONATHAN E. STERN, PAPARAZZI EXPOSED TO EXPANDED LIABILITY

Los Angeles Lawyer, May, 2006.

In the wake of several widely reported perilous encounters between celebrities and paparazzi, the California Legislature has amended a statute so that, effective January 1, 2006, paparazzi face an increased risk of enhanced penalties for their unlawful actions.

With the value of candid celebrity photos climbing to more than $100,000, and with a greater number of paparazzi in search of the next big "money shot," the competition for those six-figure photos has become increasingly fierce. Indeed, an alarming number of photographers appear ready, willing, and able to resort to highly aggressive means to be the first to locate, pursue, and corner their celebrity prey, including tailgating celebrities at speeds in excess of 100 miles per hour, intentionally ramming vehicles in which celebrities are traveling, and physically assaulting celebrities and their companions traveling on foot.

In September 2005, [photographer Todd] Wallace was arrested and charged with battery and child endangerment after he allegedly accosted recent Academy Award winner Reese Witherspoon, her children, and some close friends during a visit to Disney's California Adventure theme park. When Witherspoon refused to pose for him, Wallace allegedly hit one of the children with his camera and battered the child's mother (a friend of Witherspoon's), along with two theme park employees. The incident left some of the children in tears. The following month, Wallace was ordered to stay at least 300 yards from Witherspoon as a result of his conduct at the theme park. Arrest warrants were issued after Wallace missed a December 2005 bail hearing in the Witherspoon case, as well as an arraignment on a separate felony petty theft charge.

Unfortunately for Hollywood celebrities, this is by no means an isolated incident. Actress Scarlett Johansson, for example, sideswiped a car in 2005 while fleeing paparazzi who had pursued her for over an hour. Months earlier, actress Lindsay Lohan was chased in her car by a swarm of paparazzi and wound up on a dead-end street. When she attempted to make a U-turn, paparazzo Galo Ramirez smashed his minivan into her vehicle, causing Lohan to suffer multiple cuts and bruises. The incident was photographed by other members of the pursuing paparazzi and immediately found its way into the tabloids. Ramirez was subsequently arrested for assault on suspicion that the collision was deliberate. The Los Angeles County District Attorney's Office ultimately decided not to charge Ramirez, finding that there was insufficient evidence to prove that he intentionally rammed Lohan's car.

Notwithstanding such incidents, historically it has been difficult to generate much public sympathy for a celebrity complaining of a loss of privacy. In light of the many benefits—fortune and otherwise—that accompany fame, to many celebrity watchers a loss of privacy seems a very small price to pay. It is perhaps this general lack of public outrage that has until recently left besieged celebrities without the protection of a statutory or even common law remedy to effectively thwart any but the most egregious offenders. And the remedies that were available carried only modest penalties that many paparazzi likely viewed as simply the cost of doing business. The minimal risk of a fine or restraining order was far outweighed by the potential for a massive payday. Consequently, these remedies did little to dissuade aggressive conduct by the paparazzi.

A 1998 statute, Civil Code Section 1708.8, attempted to expand the liability of the paparazzi by creating a specific cause of action targeting individuals who commit a physical trespass or "constructive invasion of privacy" with the intent to capture a photograph or other image of a person engaged in a "personal or familial activity" and if the invasion occurs in a manner that is "offensive to a reasonable person." Although that statute established enhanced penalties for this type of trespass or invasion of privacy—specifically, punitive damages, the disgorgement of proceeds, and employer or agency liability—it was entirely inapplicable to the most dangerous conduct of the paparazzi occurring on streets and freeways and in other public locales. Thus, while the 1998 version of Section 1708.8 may have discouraged some paparazzi from scaling the walls of celebrity homes or utilizing telephoto lenses to snap topless sunbathing photos from afar, it almost certainly had no deterrent effect on aggressive tactics in places where celebrities have no reasonable expectation of privacy (for example, at theme parks or in their cars).

The amendment to Section 1708.8—effective January 1, 2006—extends the enhanced penalties of the section to any assault committed by an individual with the intent to capture a photograph or other image of another person, without regard to whether the subject of the photograph has an expectation of privacy at the time of the assault or whether he or she is participating in a personal or familial activity at that time. In theory, by drastically increasing the penalties on a paparazzo who engages in aggressive conduct, the risk of being identified as the individual who committed an assault—or the employer of that individual—no longer can be dismissed as the cost of doing business. In reality, the deterrent impact of the amended Section 1708.8 will depend entirely upon the frequency with which it is successfully invoked by celebrities, which in turn depends upon counsel to celebrities understanding how the statute operates, including the evidence needed to establish a claim.

NOTE: ROK LAMPE, THE MEDIA AND PRIVACY: A RESOLUTION OF THE PARLIAMENTARY ASSEMBLY OF THE COUNCIL OF EUROPE

In 1998, the Parliamentary Assembly of the Council of Europe produced a major statement on privacy and the media—Resolution 1165. It was prompted by the death of the Princess of Wales in an automobile accident caused, it was believed, by reckless efforts to escape the glare of the media. The Resolution must be understood in the full context of its remarkable source.

The Council of Europe is an European regional organization of 47 member countries formed in 1949 through the Statute of the Council of Europe (which defines the organizational structure of the Council, see http://www.coe.int/) and spirited by the European Convention for the Protection of Human Rights and Fundamental Freedoms. This Convention was adopted in Rome in 1950 and is today the central European document for human rights protection.

Pursuant to the Convention for the Protection of Human Rights and Fundamental Freedoms, the European Court of Human Rights in Strasbourg, France was established. The European Court of Human Rights is arguably today the most effective international (although regional) institution monitoring States' progress toward fulfilling their obligations regarding human rights protection. The European Convention on Human Rights and Fundamental

Freedoms ("ECHR" or "Convention") demands from each State party compliance with its provisions—those which create negative obligations, to refrain from violating rights granted by the Convention to each individual in its jurisdiction and those which create positive obligations, to establish a legal environment wherein each individual can exercise his or her rights.

The ECHR and its Protocols (see http://www.conventions.coe.int/) include procedural provisions setting out rules for bringing a complaint before the European Court of Human Rights. The substantive provisions of the ECHR are a catalogue of human rights, whose language is derived more or less directly from the United Nations Universal Declaration of Human Rights. It grants basic human rights (including a right to life; prohibition of torture and cruel and unusual punishment; prohibition of slavery and forced labor; the right to fair trial and other procedural guarantees; prohibition of discrimination; religious freedoms; freedom of speech; right to assembly; etc.).

Most important, for present purposes, Article 8 of the Convention calls for respect for private and family life, home and correspondence:

Article 8—Right to respect for private and family life

1. Everyone has the right to respect for his private and family life, his home and his correspondence.

2. There shall be no interference by a public authority with the exercise of this right except such as is in accordance with the law and is necessary in a democratic society in the interests of national security, public safety or the economic well-being of the country, for the prevention of disorder or crime, for the protection of health or morals, or for the protection of the rights and freedoms of others.

Article 8 derives from Article 12 of the Universal Declaration of Human Rights and Article 17 of the United Nations Covenant on Civil and Political Rights. The right to privacy based on Article 8 of the Convention is closely connected to other rights and freedoms set forth in the Convention. Primarily it intersects with Article 12 of the Convention (right to marry and to found a family); Article 2 of the First Protocol to the Convention (parental control over children); Article 5 of the 7th Protocol to the Convention (equality of spouses); Article 5 (personal security); Article 9 (freedom of conscience); Article 10 (freedom of speech); and Article 11 (freedom of assembly).

A conference of the International Commission of Jurists, an international human rights non-governmental organization, was convened in 1976 in Stockholm to elaborate the meaning and implications of Article 8.

CONCLUSIONS OF THE CONFERENCE (1976)

International Commission of Jurists' Conference on the Right to Privacy.

The Right to Privacy, being of paramount importance to human happiness, should be recognized as a fundamental right of mankind. It protects the individual against public authorities, the public in general and other individuals.

The Right to Privacy is the right to be let alone to live one's own life with a minimum degree of interference. In expanded form, it means:

The right of the individual to lead his own life protected against:

- interference with his private life, family and home life;
- interference with his physical or mental integrity or his moral or intellectual freedom;
- attacks on his honour and reputation;
- being placed in a false light;
- the disclosure of irrelevant embarrassing facts relating to his private life;
- to use his name, identity or likeness;
- spying, praying, watching and besetting;
- interference with his correspondence;
- misuse of his private communications, written or oral; disclosure of information given or received by him in circumstances of professional confidence.

For practical purposes, the above definition is intended to cover (among other matters) the following:

- search of the person;
- entry on and search premises or other property;
- medical examinations, psychological and physical tests;
- untrue or irrelevant embarrassing statements about a person;
- interception of correspondence;
- wire or telephone tapping;
- use of electronic surveillance or other "bugging" devices;
- recording, photographing or filming;
- importuning; by the press or by agents of other mass media;
- public disclosure of private facts;
- disclosure of information given to, or received from, professional advisers or to public authorities bound to observe secrecy;
- harassing a person (e.g. watching and besetting him or subjecting him to nuisance calls on the phone).

COUNCIL OF EUROPE

Resolution 1165 (1998) on the Right to Privacy.

Right to privacy

1. The Assembly recalls the current affairs debate it held on the right to privacy during its September 1997 session, a few weeks after the accident which cost the Princess of Wales her life.

2. On that occasion, some people called for the protection of privacy, and in particular that of public figures, to be reinforced at the European level

by means of a convention, while others believed that privacy was suffi-ciently protected by national legislation and the European Convention on Human Rights, and that freedom of expression should not be jeopardised.

3.   In order to explore the matter further, the Committee on Legal Affairs and Human Rights organised a hearing in Paris on 16 December 1997 with the participation of public figures or their representatives and the media.

4.   The right to privacy, guaranteed by Article 8 of the European Conven-tion on Human Rights, has already been defined by the Assembly in the declaration on mass communication media and human rights, contained within Resolution 428 (1970), as "the right to live one's own life with a minimum of interference".

5.   In view of the new communication technologies which make it possible to store and use personal data, the right to control one's own data should be added to this definition.

6.   The Assembly is aware that personal privacy is often invaded, even in countries with specific legislation to protect it, as people's private lives have become a highly lucrative commodity for certain sectors of the media. The victims are essentially public figures, since details of their private lives serve as a stimulus to sales. At the same time, public figures must recognise that the position they occupy in society—in many cases by choice—automatically entails increased pressure on their privacy.

7.   Public figures are persons holding public office and/or using public resources and, more broadly speaking, all those who play a role in public life, whether in politics, the economy, the arts, the social sphere, sport or in any other domain.

8.   It is often in the name of a one-sided interpretation of the right to freedom of expression, which is guaranteed in Article 10 of the European Convention on Human Rights, that the media invade people's privacy, claiming that their readers are entitled to know everything about public figures.

9.   Certain facts relating to the private lives of public figures, particularly politicians, may indeed be of interest to citizens, and it may therefore be legitimate for readers, who are also voters, to be informed of those facts.

10.   It is therefore necessary to find a way of balancing the exercise of two fundamental rights, both of which are guaranteed in the European Convention on Human Rights: the right to respect for one's private life and the right to freedom of expression.

11.   The Assembly reaffirms the importance of every person's right to privacy, and of the right to freedom of expression, as fundamental to a democratic society. These rights are neither absolute nor in any hierarchi-cal order, since they are of equal value.

12.   However, the Assembly points out that the right to privacy afforded by Article 8 of the European Convention on Human Rights should not

only protect an individual against interference by public authorities, but also against interference by private persons or institutions, including the mass media.

13. The Assembly believes that, since all member states have now ratified the European Convention on Human Rights, and since many systems of national legislation comprise provisions guaranteeing this protection, there is no need to propose that a new convention guaranteeing the right to privacy should be adopted.

14. The Assembly calls upon the governments of the member states to pass legislation, if no such legislation yet exists, guaranteeing the right to privacy containing the following guidelines, or if such legislation already exists, to supplement it with these guidelines:

i. the possibility of taking an action under civil law should be guaranteed, to enable a victim to claim possible damages for invasion of privacy;

ii. editors and journalists should be rendered liable for invasions of privacy by their publications, as they are for libel;

iii. when editors have published information that proves to be false, they should be required to publish equally prominent corrections at the request of those concerned;

iv. economic penalties should be envisaged for publishing groups which systematically invade people's privacy;

v. following or chasing persons to photograph, film or record them, in such a manner that they are prevented from enjoying the normal peace and quiet they expect in their private lives or even such that they are caused actual physical harm, should be prohibited;

vi. a civil action (private lawsuit) by the victim should be allowed against a photographer or a person directly involved, where paparazzi have trespassed or used "visual or auditory enhancement devices" to capture recordings that they otherwise could not have captured without trespassing;

vii. provision should be made for anyone who knows that information or images relating to his or her private life are about to be disseminated to initiate emergency judicial proceedings, such as summary applications for an interim order or an injunction postponing the dissemination of the information, subject to an assessment by the court as to the merits of the claim of an invasion of privacy;

viii. the media should be encouraged to create their own guidelines for publication and to set up an institute with which an individual can lodge complaints of invasion of privacy and demand that a rectification be published.

15. It invites those governments which have not yet done so to ratify without delay the Council of Europe Convention for the Protection of Individuals with regard to Automatic Processing of Personal Data.

16.   The Assembly also calls upon the governments of the member states to:

i.   encourage the professional bodies that represent journalists to draw up certain criteria for entry to the profession, as well as standards for self-regulation and a code of journalistic conduct;

ii.   promote the inclusion in journalism training programmes of a course in law, highlighting the importance of the right to privacy vis-à-vis society as a whole;

iii.   foster the development of media education on a wider scale, as part of education about human rights and responsibilities, in order to raise media users' awareness of what the right to privacy necessarily entails;

iv.   facilitate access to the courts and simplify the legal procedures relating to press offences, in order to ensure that victims' rights are better protected.

D.   THE PUBLICATION OF PRIVATE FACTS TORT

1.   AMERICAN LAW INSTITUTE, RESTATEMENT (SECOND) OF TORTS § 652D

§ 652D. Publicity Given To Private Life

One who gives publicity to a matter concerning the private life of another is subject to liability to the other for invasion of his privacy, if the matter publicized is of a kind that

(a) would be highly offensive to a reasonable person, and

(b) is not of legitimate concern to the public.

2.   DREDGING UP THE PAST

MELVIN v. REID

112 Cal. App. 285 (Cal. Ct. App. 1931) (superceded by statute).

MARKS, J. * * *

It is alleged that appellant's maiden name was Gabrielle Darley; that a number of years ago she was a prostitute and was tried for murder, the trial resulting in her acquittal; that during the year 1918, and after her acquittal, she abandoned her life of shame and became entirely rehabilitated; that during the year 1919, she married Bernard Melvin and commenced the duties of caring for their home, and thereafter at all times lived an exemplary, virtuous, honorable and righteous life; that she assumed a place in respectable society and made many friends who were not aware of the incidents of her earlier life; that during the month of July, 1925, the defendants, without her permission, knowledge or consent, made, photographed, produced and released a moving picture film entitled

"The Red Kimono" and thereafter exhibited it in moving picture houses in California, Arizona, and throughout many other states; that this moving picture was based upon the true story of the past life of appellant and that her maiden name, Gabrielle Darley, was used therein; that defendants featured and advertised that the plot of the film was the true story of the unsavory incidents in the life of appellant; that Gabrielle Darley was the true name of the principal character, and that Gabrielle Darley was appellant; that by the production and showing of the picture, friends of appellant learned for the first time of the unsavory incidents of her early life. This caused them to scorn and abandon her and exposed her to obloquy, contempt, and ridicule, causing her grievous mental and physical suffering to her damage in the sum of fifty thousand dollars. These allegations were set forth in the first cause of action. * * *

The law of privacy is of recent origin. * * * It did not gain prominence or notice of the bench or bar until an article appeared in 4 Harvard Law Review, page 193, written by the Honorable Louis D. Brandeis in collaboration with Samuel D. Warren. * * *

[T]he use of the incidents from the life of appellant in the moving picture is in itself not actionable. These incidents appeared in the records of her trial for murder which is a public record open to the perusal of all. The very fact that they were contained in a public record is sufficient to negative the idea that their publication was a violation of a right of privacy. When the incidents of a life are so public as to be spread upon a public record they come within the knowledge and into the possession of the public and cease to be private. Had respondents, in the story of "The Red Kimono", stopped with the use of those incidents from the life of appellant which were spread upon the record of her trial, no right of action would have accrued. They went further and in the formation of the plot used the true maiden name of appellant. If any right of action exists it arises from the use of this true name in connection with the true incidents from her life together with their advertisements in which they stated that the story of the picture was taken from true incidents in the life of Gabrielle Darley who was Gabrielle Darley Melvin. * * *

Section 1 of article I of the Constitution of California provides as follows: "All men are by nature free and independent, and have certain inalienable rights, among which are those of enjoying and defending life and liberty; acquiring, possessing and protecting property; and pursuing and obtaining safety and happiness."

The right to pursue and obtain happiness is guaranteed to all by the fundamental law of our state. This right by its very nature includes the right to live free from the unwarranted attack of others upon one's liberty, property, and reputation. Any person living a life of rectitude has that right to happiness which includes a freedom from unnecessary attacks on his character, social standing or reputation.

The use of appellant's true name in connection with the incidents of her former life in the plot and advertisements was unnecessary and indelicate and a wilful and wanton disregard of that charity which should actuate us in our social intercourse and which should keep us from unnecessarily holding another up to the scorn and contempt of upright members of society. * * *

One of the major objectives of society as it is now constituted, and of the administration of our penal system, is the rehabilitation of the fallen and the reformation of the criminal. Under these theories of sociology it is our object to lift up and sustain the unfortunate rather than tear him down. Where a person has by his own efforts rehabilitated himself, we, as right-thinking members of society, should permit him to continue in the path of rectitude rather than throw him back into a life of shame or crime. Even the thief on the cross was permitted to repent during the hours of his final agony.

We believe that the publication by respondents of the unsavory incidents in the past life of appellant after she had reformed, coupled with her true name, was not justified by any standard of morals or ethics known to us and was a direct invasion of her inalienable right guaranteed to her by our Constitution, to pursue and obtain happiness. Whether we call this a right of privacy or give it any other name is immaterial because it is a right guaranteed by our Constitution that must not be ruthlessly and needlessly invaded by others. * * *

SIDIS v. F–R PUB. CORP.

113 F.2d 806 (2d Cir. 1940).

CLARK, CIRCUIT JUDGE * * *

William James Sidis was a famous child prodigy in 1910. His name and prowess were well known to newspaper readers of the period. At the age of eleven, he lectured to distinguished mathematicians on the subject of Four–Dimensional Bodies. When he was sixteen, he was graduated from Harvard College, amid considerable public attention. Since then, his name has appeared in the press only sporadically, and he has sought to live as unobtrusively as possible. Until the articles objected to appeared in The New Yorker, he had apparently succeeded in his endeavor to avoid the public gaze.

Among The New Yorker's features are brief biographical sketches of current and past personalities. In the latter department, which appears haphazardly under the title of "Where Are They Now?" the article on Sidis was printed with a subtitle "April Fool." The author describes his subject's early accomplishments in mathematics and the wide-spread attention he received, then recounts his general breakdown and the revulsion which Sidis thereafter felt for his former life of fame and study. The unfortunate prodigy is traced over the years that followed, through his attempts to conceal his identity, through his chosen career as an insignificant clerk who would not need to employ unusual mathematical talents, and through the bizarre ways in which his genius flowered, as in his enthusiasm for collecting streetcar transfers and in his proficiency with an adding machine. The article closes with an account of an interview with Sidis at his present lodgings, "a hall bedroom of Boston's shabby south end." The untidiness of his room, his curious laugh, his manner of speech, and other personal habits are commented upon at length, as is his present interest in the lore of the Okamakammessett Indians. The subtitle is explained by the closing sentence, quoting Sidis as saying "with a grin" that it was strange, "but, you know, I was born on April Fool's Day." Accompanying the biography is a small cartoon showing the genius of eleven years lecturing to a group of astounded professors.

It is not contended that any of the matter printed is untrue. Nor is the manner of the author unfriendly; Sidis today is described as having "a certain childlike charm." But the article is merciless in its dissection of intimate details of its subject's personal life, and this in company with elaborate accounts of Sidis' passion for privacy and the pitiable lengths to which he has gone in order to avoid public scrutiny. The work possesses great reader interest, for it is both amusing and instructive; but it may be fairly described as a ruthless exposure of a once public character, who has since sought and has now been deprived of the seclusion of private life.

The article of December 25, 1937, was a biographical sketch of another former child prodigy, in the course of which William James Sidis and the recent account of him were mentioned. The advertisement published in the New York World–Telegram of August 13, 1937, read: "Out Today. Harvard Prodigy. Biography of the man who astonished Harvard at age 11. Where are they now? by J. L. Manley. Page 22. The New Yorker." * * *

Under the first "cause of action" we are asked to declare that this exposure transgresses upon plaintiff's right of privacy * * *.

William James Sidis was once a public figure. As a child prodigy, he excited both admiration and curiosity. Of him great deeds were expected. In 1910, he was a person about whom the newspapers might display a legitimate intellectual interest, in the sense meant by Warren and Brandeis, as distinguished from a trivial and unseemly curiosity. But the precise motives of the press we regard as unimportant. And even if Sidis had loathed public attention at that time, we think his uncommon achievements and personality would have made the attention permissible. Since then Sidis has cloaked himself in obscurity, but his subsequent history, containing as it did an answer to the question of whether or not he had fulfilled his early promise, was still a matter of public concern. The article in The New Yorker sketched the life of an unusual personality, and it possessed considerable popular news interest.

We express no comment on whether or not the news worthiness of the matter printed will always constitute a complete defense. Revelations may be so intimate and so unwarranted in view of the victim's position as to outrage the community's notions of decency. But when focused upon public characters, truthful comments upon dress, speech, habits, and the ordinary aspects of personality will usually not transgress this line. Regrettably or not, the misfortunes and frailties of neighbors and "public figures" are subjects of considerable interest and discussion of the rest of the population. And when such are the mores of the community, it would be unwise for a court to bar their expression in the newspapers, books, and magazines of the day.

BRISCOE v. READER'S DIGEST ASS'N

4 Cal. 3d 529 (Cal. 1971).

PETERS, J.

Plaintiff Marvin Briscoe filed suit against defendant Reader's Digest Association, alleging that defendant had willfully and maliciously invaded his privacy by publishing an article which disclosed truthful but embarrassing private facts about plaintiff's past life. * * *

One sentence in the article refers to plaintiff: "Typical of many beginners, Marvin Briscoe and [another man] stole a 'valuable-looking' truck in Danville, Ky., and then fought a gun battle with the local police, only to learn that they had hijacked four bowling-pin spotters." There is nothing in the article to indicate that the hijacking occurred in 1956.

As the result of defendant's publication, plaintiff's 11–year–old daughter, as well as his friends, for the first time learned of this incident. They thereafter scorned and abandoned him.

Conceding the truth of the facts published in defendant's article, plaintiff claims that the public disclosure of these private facts has humiliated him and exposed him to contempt and ridicule. Conceding that the subject of the article may have been "newsworthy," he contends that the use of his name was not, and that the defendant has thus invaded his right to privacy. * * *

Acceptance of the right to privacy has grown with the increasing capability of the mass media and electronic devices with their capacity to destroy an individual's anonymity, intrude upon his most intimate activities, and expose his most personal characteristics to public gaze.

In a society in which multiple, often conflicting role performances are demanded of each individual, the original etymological meaning of the word "person"—mask—has taken on new meaning. Men fear exposure not only to those closest to them; much of the outrage underlying the asserted right to privacy is a reaction to exposure to persons known only through business or other secondary relationships. The claim is not so much one of total secrecy as it is of the right to define one's circle of intimacy—to choose who shall see beneath the quotidian mask. Loss of control over which "face" one puts on may result in literal loss of self-identity (Westin, supra, at p. 1023; cf. Fried, Privacy (1968) 77 Yale L.J. 475), and is humiliating beneath the gaze of those whose curiosity treats a human being as an object. * * *

The central purpose of the First Amendment "is to give to every voting member of the body politic the fullest possible participation in the understanding of those problems with which the citizens of a self-governing society must deal * * *." (A. Meiklejohn, Political Freedom: The Constitutional Powers of the People (1960) p. 75.) * * *

We have no doubt that reports of the facts of past crimes are newsworthy. Media publication of the circumstances under which crimes were committed in the past may prove educational in the same way that reports of current crimes do. The public has a strong interest in enforcing the law, and this interest is served by accumulating and disseminating data cataloguing the reasons men commit crimes, the methods they use, and the ways in which they are apprehended. Thus in an article on truck hijackings, Reader's Digest certainly had the right to report the facts of plaintiff's criminal act. * * *

The Restatement of Torts some time ago balanced the considerations relevant here, concluding that criminals "are the objects of legitimate public interest during a period of time after their conduct * * * has brought them to the public attention; until they have reverted to the lawful and unexciting life led by the great bulk of the community, they are subject to the privileges which publishers have to satisfy the curiosity of the public as to their leaders, heroes, villains and victims." (§ 867, com. c.) Where a man has reverted to that "lawful and unexciting life" led by others, the Restatement implies that he no longer need "satisfy the curiosity of the public."

Another factor militating in favor of protecting the individual's privacy here is the state's interest in the integrity of the rehabilitative process. Our courts recognized this issue four decades ago in Melvin v. Reid, supra, 112 Cal.App. 285. There, plaintiff had been a prostitute. She was charged with murder and acquitted after a long and very public trial. She thereafter abandoned her life of shame, married, and assumed a place in respectable society, making many friends who were not aware of the incidents of her earlier life. * * *

One of the premises of the rehabilitative process is that the rehabilitated offender can rejoin that great bulk of the community from which he has been ostracized for his anti-social acts. In return for becoming a "new man," he is allowed to melt into the shadows of obscurity.

We are realistic enough to recognize that men are curious about the inner sanctums of their neighbors—that the public will create its heroes and villains. We must also be realistic enough to realize that full disclosure of one's inner thoughts, intimate personal characteristics, and past life is neither the rule nor the norm in these United States. We have developed a variegated panoply of professional listeners to whom we confidentially "reveal all"; otherwise we keep our own counsel. * * *

In a nation built upon the free dissemination of ideas, it is always difficult to declare that something may not be published. But the great general interest in an unfettered press may at times be outweighed by other great societal interests. As a people we have come to recognize that one of these societal interests is that of protecting an individual's right to privacy. The right to know and the right to have others not know are, simplistically considered, irreconcilable. But the rights guaranteed by the First Amendment do not require total abrogation of the right to privacy. The goals sought by each may be achieved with a minimum of intrusion upon the other. * * *

We have previously set forth criteria for determining whether an incident is newsworthy. We consider "[1] the social value of the facts *elements* published, [2] the depth of the article's intrusion into ostensibly private affairs, and [3] the extent to which the party voluntarily acceded to a position of public notoriety. * * *" " * * *

On the assumed set of facts before us we are convinced that a jury could reasonably find that plaintiff's identity as a former hijacker was not newsworthy. First, as discussed above, a jury could find that publication of plaintiff's identity in connection with incidents of his past life was in this case of minimal social value. There was no independent reason whatsoever for focusing public attention on Mr. Briscoe as an individual at this time. A jury could certainly find that Mr. Briscoe had once again become an anonymous member of the community. Once legal proceedings have concluded, and particularly once the individual has reverted to the lawful and unexciting life led by the rest of the community, the public's interest in knowing is less compelling.

Second, a jury might find that revealing one's criminal past for all to see is grossly offensive to most people in America. Certainly a criminal background is kept even more hidden from others than a humiliating disease * * * or the existence of business debts * * *. The consequences of revelation in this case—ostracism, isolation, and the alienation of one's family—make all too clear just how deeply offensive to most persons a prior crime is and thus how hidden the former offender must keep the knowledge of his prior indiscretion.

Third, in no way can plaintiff be said to have voluntarily consented to the publicity accorded him here. He committed a crime. He was punished. He was rehabilitated. And he became, for 11 years, an obscure and law-abiding citizen. His every effort was to forget and have others forget that he had once hijacked a truck.

Finally, the interests at stake here are not merely those of publication and privacy alone, for the state has a compelling interest in the efficacy of penal systems in rehabilitating criminals and returning them as productive and law-abiding citizens to the society whence they came. A jury might well find that a continuing threat that the rehabilitated offender's old identity will be resurrected by the media is counter-productive to the goals of this correctional process. * * *

We do not hold today that plaintiff must prevail in his action. It is for the trier of fact to determine (1) whether plaintiff had become a rehabilitated member of society, (2) whether identifying him as a former criminal would be highly offensive and injurious to the reasonable man, (3) whether defendant published this information with a reckless disregard for its offensiveness, and (4) whether any independent justification for printing plaintiff's identity existed. We hold today only that, as pleaded, plaintiff has stated a valid cause of action, sustaining the demurrer to plaintiff's complaint was improper, and that the ensuing judgment must therefore be reversed.

CONRADT v. NBC UNIVERSAL

536 F.Supp.2d 380 (2008).

CHIN, DISTRICT JUDGE.

On November 5, 2006, Louis William Conradt, Jr. ("Conradt")—an assistant district attorney in Texas—shot himself in his home as he was about to be arrested by the police for attempting to solicit a minor online. Waiting outside the house were members of the cast and crew of the national television news show Dateline NBC ("Dateline"). They were there to film Conradt's arrest for a segment of "To Catch A Predator"—a show that works with local police departments and an on-line "watchdog" group called Perverted Justice to identify and arrest "sexual predators." Apparently unable to face the humiliation of the public spectacle that faced him, Conradt took his own life.

 In this case, Conradt's sister, Patricia Conradt, sues defendant NBC Universal Inc. ("NBC"), alleging that Dateline is responsible for her brother's death and the harm to his reputation and "good name." On behalf of herself and his estate (the "Estate"), she seeks in excess of $100 million in compensatory and punitive damages. * * *

Plaintiff asserts four claims on her own behalf: intentional intrusion on the right to be left alone (fifth cause of action), intentional disclosure of private facts (sixth cause of action), intentional infliction of emotional distress (seventh cause of action), and negligence (eighth cause of action).

The fifth and sixth causes of action are dismissed because plaintiff lacks standing to assert these claims in her own name. Under Texas law, claims for injury to reputation and invasion of the right to privacy may only be brought by or on behalf of the individuals who are actually the subject of the wrongful acts. *See, e.g., Ritzmann v. Weekly World News, Inc.,* 614 F.Supp. 1336, 1339 (N.D.Tex.1985) ("unless the plaintiff herself is the particular person with references to whom defamatory statements were made, she has no cause of action"); *Moore v. Charles B. Pierce Film Enters., Inc.,* 589 S.W.2d 489, 491 (Tex.Civ.App.1979) (privacy is personal right and action for invasion of privacy "terminates upon the death of the person whose privacy is invaded"); *Gonzales v. Times Herald Printing Co.,* 513 S.W.2d 124, 126 (Tex.Civ.App.1974) ("a libel upon the memory of a deceased person * * * does not give [his relatives] any right of action, although they may have thereby suffered mental anguish or sustained an impairment of their social standing"); *Renfro Drug v. Lawson,* 138 Tex.

434, 160 S.W.2d 246, 249 (Tex.Com.App.1942) ("[T]he law does not contemplate ... defamation of the dead [ ] as causing any special damage to another individual, though related to the deceased, and therefore it cannot be made the basis of recovery in a civil action."). Under Texas law, where the invasion was directed primarily at the deceased, a relative of the deceased has no claim for invasion of privacy. *Justice v. Belo Broad. Corp.*, 472 F.Supp. 145, 147 (N.D.Tex.1979).

The seventh cause of action is dismissed, for Texas law does not permit a plaintiff to sue for intentional infliction of emotional distress unless the defendant's conduct is "about or directed at" the plaintiff. *Doe v. Mobile Video Tapes, Inc.*, 43 S.W.3d 40, 49 (Tex.App.2001); *see also Mineer v. Williams*, 82 F.Supp.2d 702, 707 (E.D.Ky.2000) (statements made in broadcast about plaintiff's son did not give rise to claim for intentional infliction of emotional distress for her).

CATSOURAS v. DEPARTMENT OF CALIFORNIA HIGHWAY PATROL ET AL.

181 Cal.App.4th 856, 104 Cal.Rptr.3d 352 (2010).

MOORE, J.

Nicole Catsouras (decedent) suffered a tragic end to her young life. At age 18, she was decapitated in an automobile accident. With her demise, the torment of her family members began. They endured not only her death, and the hideous manner of it, but also the unthinkable exploitation of the photographs of her decapitated remains. Those photographs were strewn about the Internet and spit back at the family members, accompanied by hateful messages.

In a second amended complaint against the State of California Highway Patrol (CHP) and two of its peace officers, Thomas O'Donnell (O'Donnell) and Aaron Reich (Reich), decedent's father, mother and sisters (plaintiffs) alleged that O'Donnell and Reich had e-mailed the horrific photographs of decedent's mutilated corpse to members of the public unrelated to the accident investigation. Plaintiffs alleged more specifically, in their opposition to a demurrer, that O'Donnell and Reich had e-mailed nine gruesome death images to their friends and family members on Halloween—for pure shock value. Once received, the photographs were forwarded to others, and thus spread across the Internet like a malignant firestorm, popping up in thousands of Web sites. Plaintiffs further alleged that Internet users at large then taunted them with the photographs, in deplorable ways.

The trial court, finding no duty on behalf of O'Donnell and Reich running in favor of plaintiffs, and no basis for a title 42 United States Code section 1983 (section 1983) cause of action * * * entered judgments of dismissal as to [O'Donnell and Reich] * * * and a judgment on the pleadings in favor of the CHP. We reverse.

California law clearly provides that surviving family members have no right of privacy in the context of written media discussing, or pictorial media portraying, the life of a decedent. Any cause of action for invasion of privacy in that context belongs to the decedent and expires along with him or her. (*Flynn v. Higham* (1983) 149 Cal.App.3d 677, 197 Cal.Rptr. 145 (*Flynn*).) The publication of death images is another matter, however. How can a decedent be injured in his or her privacy by the publication of death images, which only come into being once the decedent has passed on? The dissemination of death images can only affect the living. As cases from other jurisdictions make plain, family members have a common law privacy right in the death images of a decedent, subject to certain limitations.

NOTE: SOCIAL NETWORKS

In an original article, Lior Jacob Strahilevitz introduced what he calls a "social networks" theory of privacy. See A Social Networks Theory of Privacy, 72 *U. Chi. L. Rev.* 919 (2005). His ambition was a theory that can replace "the common law's vagueness with a relatively objective, testable, rigorous, and principled approach." Id. at 988. The approach works like this: "Where a defendant's disclosure materially alters the flow of otherwise obscure information through a social network, such that what would have otherwise remained obscure becomes widely known, the defendant should be liable for public disclosure of private facts." Id. A social network is a set of people and the links between and among them. Does this approach sound promising? Does it suggest a way of resolving the "dredging up the past" suits? What about suits in which plaintiffs complain of revelations of recent and current embarrassing events, like *Hall v. Post* and *Yath v. Fairview Clinics*, below?

YATH v. FAIRVIEW CLINICS
767 N.W.2d 34 (Ct. App. Minn. 2009).

ROSS, JUDGE.

This invasion-of-privacy case involves the Internet posting of embarrassing personal information taken surreptitiously from a patient's medical file. A Fairview Cedar Ridge Clinic employee saw a personal acquaintance at the clinic and read her medical file, learning that she had a sexually transmitted disease and a new sex partner other than her husband. The employee disclosed this information to another employee, who then disclosed it to others, including the patient's estranged husband. Then someone created a MySpace.com webpage posting the information on the Internet. The patient sued the clinic and the individuals allegedly involved in the disclosure under various legal theories. The district court granted summary judgment to the defendants on most of the claims. * * *

We * * * conclude that the invasion-of-privacy claim was correctly resolved by summary judgment for lack of evidence. * * *

Yath contests the district court's summary-judgment decision dismissing her invasion-of-privacy claim. She argues that the district court erroneously concluded that the temporary posting of data gleaned from her medical file on MySpace.com "failed to meet the 'publicity' requirements for a successful claim." The argument is persuasive.

Minnesota recognizes the tort of invasion of privacy on three alternative theories: intrusion of seclusion, appropriation of a name or likeness of another, and publication of private facts. *Bodah v. Lakeville Motor Express, Inc.*, 663 N.W.2d 550, 553 (Minn.2003). Yath's invasion-of-privacy claim is based on the publication of private facts, so the claim can survive summary judgment only if the record contains evidence that (1) a defendant gave "publicity" to a matter concerning Yath's private life, (2) the *elements* publicity of the private information would be highly offensive to a reasonable person, and (3) the matter is not of legitimate concern to the public. *Id.* (quotation omitted). The district court held that Yath's private information was not given "publicity" within the meaning of the tort of invasion of privacy because Yath had not proven a sufficient number of people had seen the webpage. We reach a different legal conclusion.

"Publicity," for the purposes of an invasion-of-privacy claim, means that "the matter is made public, by communicating it to the public at large, or to so many persons that the matter must be regarded as substantially certain to become one of public knowledge." *Id.* at 557 (quoting from Restatement (Second) of Torts § 652D cmt. a (1977)). In other words, there are two methods to satisfy the publicity element of an invasion-of-privacy claim: the first method is by proving a single communication to the public, and the second method is by proving communication to individuals in such a large number that the information is deemed to have been communicated to the public.

The supreme court's analysis and application in *Bodah* is illuminating. The *Bodah* court held that the publicity element was not satisfied when an employer disseminated employee names and social security numbers to sixteen managers in six states. *Id.* at 557–58. The employer disseminated the information by private means, specifically, by facsimile. The private rather than public nature of this communication caused the *Bodah* court to consider whether the communication was to a large enough number of recipients to support a determination of "publicity" under the second method. It held that dissemination of information to the relatively small group of individuals did not satisfy the publicity element because the disseminated information could not "be regarded as substantially certain to become public." *Id.*

But in reaching the conclusion, the supreme court explained the type of communication that would constitute publicity under the first method. It approvingly acknowledged the Restatement of Torts explanation that "any publication in a newspaper or a magazine, even of small circulation . . . or any broadcast over the radio, or statement made in an address to a large audience," would meet the publicity element of an invasion-of-privacy claim. *Id.* at 554. It also relied on the Restatement for the proposition that posting private information in a shop window viewable by passers-by constitutes "publicity." *Id.* The Restatement explains that "[t]he distinction ... is one between private and public communication." *Id.* This explanation informs our judgment that the challenged communication here constitutes publicity under the first method, or publicity per se. Unlike *Bodah,* where the private information went through a private medium to reach a finite, identifiable group of privately situated recipients, Yath's private information was posted on a public MySpace.com webpage for anyone to view. This Internet communication is materially similar in nature to a newspaper publication or a radio broadcast because upon release it is available to the public at large.

The district court appears to have accepted Fairview and Phat's argument that the publicity element was not satisfied because Yath proved only that a small number of people actually viewed the MySpace.com webpage and that the webpage was available only 24 to 48 hours. A similar argument could be made about a newspaper having only a small circulation, or a radio broadcast at odd hours when few were listening. The district court therefore mistakenly analyzed "publicity" using the second method, which applies only to privately directed communication and requires an assessment based on the number of actual viewers. But when the communication is made by offering the information in a public forum, the first method applies and the tort is triggered when the discloser makes the private information publicly available, not when some substantial number of individuals actually get the information. Like the temporary posting of information in a shop window, the MySpace.com webpage put the information in view of any member of the public—in large or small numbers—who happened by. The number of actual viewers is irrelevant. *See id.* at 554–57 (adopting the Restatement definition of publicity which explains that the distinction is "between private and public communication," and that the publicity element is satisfied when information is "disseminat[ed] to the public at large").

Fairview argues that posting information on a "social networking" website such as MySpace.com should be treated only as a private communication because Myspace.com webpages are not of "general interest" like online newspaper websites. But *Bodah's* analysis of the publicity element renders this claimed distinction meaningless. The determination does not depend on whether the content offered through the medium is of general interest to the public, but on whether the content is conveyed through a medium that delivers the information directly to the public. The supreme court's other example of publicity, albeit offered in dicta, is consistent with this approach. The court expressly opined that the posting of private employee information on the Internet would constitute "publicity." *Id.* at 554 (approvingly citing dictum of *Purdy v. Burlington N. & Santa Fe Ry. Co.,* No. 98–833, slip op. at 6, 2000 WL 34251818 (D.Minn. Mar. 28, 2000)). By focusing on the number of people who were exposed to the information, the district court revealed that it erroneously treated the nature of the medium as private, which would constitute publicity only if the information would likely be retold publicly. We hold that the publicity element of an invasion-of-privacy claim is satisfied when private information is posted on a publicly accessible Internet website.

The MySpace.com webpage that triggers Yath's claim was such a site. Access to it was not protected, as some webpages are, by a password or some other restrictive safeguard. It was a window that Yath's enemies propped open for at least 24 hours allowing any internet-connected voyeur access to private details of her life. The claim therefore survives the "publicity" challenge.

The concurring opinion maintains that we should analyze this case under the second theory of publicity, but not the first. The concurrence's reason is that a finding of publicity depends on the matter being communicated to such a large number of people that it becomes public knowledge. This is a correct statement of the law describing only the second theory of publicity, but it ignores the first theory. The Restatement and caselaw teach that proof of publicity under the first theory does not require evidence that the information has been communicated to a large number of people. Rather, the question is whether the information has been communicated *"to the public at large." Bodah,* 663 N.W.2d at 553–54 (citing Restatement (Second) of Torts § 652D cmt. a). That the Internet vastly enlarges both the amount of information publicly available and the number of sources offering information does not erode the reasoning leading us to hold that posting information on a publicly accessible webpage constitutes publicity. If a late-night radio broadcast aired for a few seconds and potentially heard by a few hundred (or by no one) constitutes publicity as a matter of law, a maliciously fashioned webpage posted for one or two days and potentially read by hundreds, thousands, millions (or by no one) also constitutes publicity as a matter of law.

It is true that mass communication is no longer limited to a tiny handful of commercial purveyors and that we live with much greater access to information than the era in which the tort of invasion of privacy developed. A town crier could reach dozens, a handbill hundreds, a newspaper or radio station tens of thousands, a television station millions, and now a publicly accessible webpage can present the story of someone's private life, in this case complete with a photograph and other identifying features, to more than one billion Internet surfers worldwide. This extraordinary advancement in communication argues for, not against, a holding that the MySpace posting constitutes publicity.

Contrary to the concurring opinion, as the Restatement examples illustrate, publicity under the first theory occurs at the point when the communication is made to the public at large, not to a large number of the public: "any *publication* in a newspaper or a magazine, even of small circulation" (not *any information that a large number of persons actually read in the newspaper*); "in a handbill *distributed to* a large number of persons" (not *a handbill actually read by a large number of persons*); "any broadcast over the radio" (not *any broadcast actually heard by a significant audience*). Restatement (Second) of Torts § 652D cmt. a. "Publicity" therefore occurs on the act that disseminates the information "to the public at large," which is the printing, distribution, or utterance in the public forum. Although the damages calculation for invasion of privacy might be influenced by the extent to which the publicity was effective, *see* Restatement (Second) of Torts § 652H cmt. b (explaining that damages recoverable under an invasion-of-privacy claim closely resemble damages recoverable for defamation); *cf. Longbehn v. Schoenrock,* 727 N.W.2d 153, 160 (Minn.App.2007) (permitting recovery in defamation for the injury to reputation), a determination that publicity occurred does not require a large actual audience.

We acknowledge that some public webpages might get little actual attention. But the same may be said of a card posted on the door of a residence or a poster displayed in a shop window, each of which constitutes publicity. *See Thompson v. Adelberg & Berman, Inc.,* 181 Ky. 487, 205 S.W. 558 (1918) (reversing judgment against plaintiff who alleged that the defendant clothing store had posted cards for several hours on the front door and side windows of her house and on a stick near the public sidewalk indicating that the plaintiff had failed to pay a store debt); *see also Brents v. Morgan,* 221 Ky. 765, 299 S.W. 967 (1927) (citing *Thompson* and holding that poster in a shop window identifying debtor to passers-by was actionable as an invasion of privacy). The unrestricted MySpace.com webpage posting likewise constitutes publicity.

Fairview and Phat argue alternatively that we could affirm the district court's dismissal of Yath's invasion-of-privacy claim on other grounds. "This court can, if it needs to, affirm summary judgment on alternative theories presented but not ruled on at the district court level." *Nelson v. Short–Elliot–Hendrickson, Inc.,* 716 N.W.2d 394, 402 (Minn.App. 2006). Fairview and Phat argued in the district court, and again on appeal, that Yath's invasion-of-privacy claim is also subject to summary judgment because Yath did not produce any evidence that Phat or Fairview were involved in creating the MySpace.com webpage. This argument is convincing.

Summary judgment is proper "when the record is devoid of proof on an essential element of the plaintiff's claim." *Cargill,* 719 N.W.2d at 232. Yath conceded at oral argument that there is nothing in the record, except her allegation that "Phat is a liar," to establish that Phat or Fairview were involved in creating or sustaining the MySpace.com webpage. Our independent examination of the record confirms Yath's concession. Because MySpace.com is a "blocked" site at Fairview's Cedar Ridge Clinic and at Fairview Ridges Hospital, the webpage could not have been created at Fairview. And Yath actually traced the creation of the webpage to the IP address of an Eagan business's computer. Tek's sister, Molyka Mao, worked at the business. At most, the record suggests that Mao created the website possibly with Tek's assistance. It appears that the district court may have improperly addressed the claim as it regards these two. But Yath dismissed Mao and Tek from this suit and the record reveals no communication between Mao and Phat and no affiliation between Mao and Fairview. It is true that these defendants remained part of the case through summary judgment. But their dismissal occurred before the appeal. That Mao and Tek may be liable if the invasion-of-privacy claims against them are revived does not prevent us from affirming summary judgment.

Because Yath failed to produce any evidence on an essential element of her claim—specifically, that any of the defendants surviving on appeal were involved in creating or sustaining the disparaging MySpace.com webpage—her invasion-of-privacy claim fails.

3.   EMBARRASSING TRUTHS—NORTH CAROLINA REJECTS PRIVATE FACT TORT

HALL v. POST

323 N.C. 259 (N.C. 1988).

MITCHELL, J. * * *

The plaintiffs, Susie Hall and her adoptive mother, Mary Hall, brought separate civil actions against the defendants for invasion of privacy. The actions were based upon two articles printed in The Salisbury Post and written by its special assignment reporter, Rose Post. * * *

The article concerned the search by Lee and Aledith Gottschalk for Aledith's daughter by a previous marriage, whom she and her former husband had abandoned in Rowan County in September of 1967. The article told of Aledith's former marriage to a carnival barker named Clarence Maxson, the birth of their daughter in 1967, their abandonment of the child at the age of four months, events in Aledith's life thereafter, and her return to Rowan County after seventeen years to look for the child. The article indicated that Clarence Maxson had made arrangements in 1967 for a babysitter named Mary Hall to keep the child for a few weeks. Clarence and Aledith then moved on with the carnival, and Clarence later told Aledith that he had signed papers authorizing the baby's adoption.

Aledith was married to Lee Gottschalk in 1984, and they decided to travel to Rowan County to look for Aledith's child. The newspaper article of 18 July 1984 related the details of their unsuccessful search and then stated: "If anyone, they say, knows anything about a little blonde baby left here when the county fair closed and the carnies moved on in September 1967, Lee and Aledith Gottschalk can be reached in Room 173 at the Econo Motel."

Shortly after the article was published, the Gottschalks were called at the motel and informed of the child's identity and whereabouts.

The defendants published a second article on 20 July 1984 reporting that the Gottschalks had located the child with the aid of responses to the earlier article. The second article identified the child as Susie Hall and identified her adoptive mother as Mary Hall. The article related the details of a telephone encounter between the Gottschalks and Mrs. Hall and described the emotions of both families.

The plaintiffs alleged that they fled their home in order to avoid public attention resulting from the articles. Each plaintiff alleged that she sought and received psychiatric care for the emotional and mental distress caused by the incident.

The defendants have contended at all times that the imposition of civil liability for their truthful public disclosure of facts about the plaintiffs would violate the First Amendment to the Constitution of the United States. The defendants have contended in the alternative that this Court should refuse to adopt any tort which imposes liability for such conduct as a part of the common law of this State.

In the present case, we consider for the first time that branch of the invasion of privacy tort which is most commonly referred to as the "public disclosure of private facts." The plaintiffs have at all times acknowledged that the facts published about them by the defendants were true and accurate in every respect, but they contend, nevertheless, that they are entitled to recover.

elements

Under the definition of the private facts tort set out in the Restatement (Second) of Torts, liability will be imposed for publication of "private facts" when "the matter publicized is of a kind that (a) would be highly offensive to a reasonable person, and (b) is not of legitimate concern to the public." Restatement (Second) of Torts § 652D (1977). That definition includes four elements: (1) publicity; (2) private facts; (3) offensiveness; and (4) absence of legitimate public concern. * * *

Although expressing constitutional and other reservations, this Court has recognized a general right of privacy as a part of the tort law of this State. See Flake v. News Co., 212 N.C. 780, 195 S.E. 55 (1938) (recognizing the "appropriation" branch of the tort). However, we have not recognized or applied either of the two branches of the tort which, because they arise from publicity, most directly affect First Amendment speech and press rights. Quite to the contrary, we have refused to recognize the branch of the invasion of privacy tort arising from publicity by which the defendant places the plaintiff in a false light in the public eye. Renwick v. News and Observer, 310 N.C. 312, 312 S.E. 2d 405. We did so because "false light" claims often would duplicate or overlap existing claims for relief. Id. at 323, 312 S.E. 2d at 412. Additionally, "recognition of a separate [false light] tort * * * would tend to add to the tension already existing between the First Amendment and the law of torts * * *." Id. For the same reasons, we now hold that claims for invasions of privacy by publication of true but "private" facts are not cognizable at law in this State.

In North Carolina, the tort of intentional infliction of emotional distress, consists of (1) extreme and outrageous conduct, (2) which is intended to cause and does cause (3) severe emotional distress to another. The tort may also exist where defendant's actions indicate a reckless indifference to the likelihood that they will cause severe emotional distress. Recovery may be had for the emotional distress so caused and for any other bodily harm which proximately results from the distress itself. * * *

We conclude that any possible benefits which might accrue to plaintiffs are entirely insufficient to justify adoption of the constitutionally suspect private facts invasion of privacy tort which punishes defendants for the typically American act of broadly proclaiming the truth by speech or writing. Accordingly, we reject the notion of a claim for relief for invasion of privacy by public disclosure of true but "private" facts.

4.   RAPE PUBLICITY

COX BROADCASTING CORP. v. COHN
420 U.S. 469 (1975).

MR. JUSTICE WHITE delivered the opinion of the Court. * * *

In August 1971, appellee's 17–year–old daughter was the victim of a rape and did not survive the incident. Six youths were soon indicted for murder and rape. Although there was substantial press coverage of the crime and of subsequent developments, the identity of the victim was not disclosed pending trial, perhaps because of Ga. Code Ann. § 26–9901 (1972), which makes it a misdemeanor to publish or broadcast the name or identity of a rape victim. In April 1972, some eight months later, the six defendants appeared in court. Five pleaded guilty to rape or attempted rape, the charge of murder having been dropped. The guilty pleas were accepted by the court, and the trial of the defendant pleading not guilty was set for a later date.

In the course of the proceedings that day, appellant Wassell, a reporter covering the incident for his employer, learned the name of the victim from an examination of the indictments which were made available for his inspection in the courtroom. That the name of the victim appears in the indictments and that the indictments were public records available for inspection are not disputed. Later that day, Wassell broadcast over the facilities of station WSB–TV, a television station owned by appellant Cox Broadcasting Corp., a news report concerning the court proceedings. The report named the victim of the crime and was repeated the following day.

In May 1972, appellee brought an action for money damages against appellants, relying on § 26–9901 and claiming that his right to privacy had been invaded by the television broadcasts giving the name of his deceased daughter. Appellants admitted the broadcasts but claimed that they were privileged under both state law and the First and Fourteenth Amendments. * * *

The version of the privacy tort now before us—termed in Georgia "the tort of public disclosure," 231 Ga., at 60, 200 S. E. 2d, at 130—is that in which the plaintiff claims the right to be free from unwanted publicity about his private affairs, which, although wholly true, would be offensive to a person of ordinary sensibilities. Because the gravamen of the claimed injury is the publication of information, whether true or not, the dissemination of which is embarrassing or otherwise painful to an individual, it is here that claims of privacy most directly confront the constitutional freedoms of speech and press. * * *

Appellee has claimed in this litigation that the efforts of the press have infringed his right to privacy by broadcasting to the world the fact that his daughter was a rape victim. The commission of crime, prosecutions resulting from it, and judicial proceedings arising from the prosecutions, however, are without question events of legitimate concern to the public and consequently fall within the responsibility of the press to report the operations of government. * * *

[T]he prevailing law of invasion of privacy generally recognizes that the interests in privacy fade when the information involved already appears on the public record. The conclusion is compelling when viewed in terms of the First and Fourteenth Amendments and in light of the public interest in a vigorous press. The Georgia cause of action for invasion of privacy through public disclosure of the name of a rape victim imposes sanctions on pure expression—the content of a publication—and not conduct or a combination of speech and nonspeech elements that might otherwise be open to regulation or prohibition. See United States v. O'Brien, 391 U.S. 367, 376–377 (1968). The publication of truthful information available on the public record contains none of the indicia of those limited categories of expression, such as ''fighting'' words, which ''are no essential part of any exposition of ideas, and are of such slight social value as a step to truth that any benefit that may be derived from them is clearly outweighed by the social interest in order and morality.'' Chaplinsky v. New Hampshire, 315 U.S. 568, 572 (1942).

By placing the information in the public domain on official court records, the State must be presumed to have concluded that the public interest was thereby being served. Public records by their very nature are of interest to those concerned with the administration of government, and a public benefit is performed by the reporting of the true contents of the records by the media. The freedom of the press to publish that information appears to us to be of critical importance to our type of government in which the citizenry is the final judge of the proper conduct of public business. In preserving that form of government the First and Fourteenth Amendments command nothing less than that the States may not impose sanctions on the publication of truthful information contained in official court records open to public inspection.

We are reluctant to embark on a course that would make public records generally available to the media but forbid their publication if offensive to the sensibilities of the supposed reasonable man. Such a rule would make it very difficult for the media to inform citizens about the public business and yet stay within the law. The rule would invite timidity and self-censorship and very likely lead to the suppression of many items that would otherwise be published and that should be made available to the public.

Under these circumstances, the protection of freedom of the press provided by the First and Fourteenth Amendments bars the State of Georgia from making appellants' broadcast the basis of civil liability.

FLORIDA STAR v. B. J. F.

491 U.S. 524 (1989).

JUSTICE MARSHALL delivered the opinion of the Court.

Florida Stat. § 794.03 (1987) makes it unlawful to "print, publish, or broadcast * * * in any instrument of mass communication" the name of the victim of a sexual offense. Pursuant to this statute, appellant The Florida Star was found civilly liable for publishing the name of a rape victim which it had obtained from a publicly released police report. The issue presented here is whether this result comports with the First Amendment. We hold that it does not. * * *

The Florida Star is a weekly newspaper which serves the community of Jacksonville, Florida, and which has an average circulation of approximately 18,000 copies. A regular feature of the newspaper is its "Police Reports" section. That section, typically two to three pages in length, contains brief articles describing local criminal incidents under police investigation.

On October 20, 1983, appellee B. J. F. reported to the Duval County, Florida, Sheriff's Department (Department) that she had been robbed and sexually assaulted by an unknown assailant. The Department prepared a report on the incident which identified B. J. F. by her full name. The Department then placed the report in its pressroom. The Department does not restrict access either to the pressroom or to the reports made available therein.

A Florida Star reporter-trainee sent to the pressroom copied the police report verbatim, including B. J. F.'s full name, on a blank duplicate of the Department's forms. A Florida Star reporter then prepared a one-paragraph article about the crime, derived entirely from the trainee's copy of the police report. The article included B. J. F.'s full name. It appeared in the "Robberies" subsection of the "Police Reports" section on October 29, 1983, one of 54 police blotter stories in that day's edition. The article read:

"[B. J. F.] reported on Thursday, October 20, she was crossing Brentwood Park, which is in the 500 block of Golfair Boulevard, enroute to her bus stop, when an unknown black man ran up behind the lady and placed a knife to her neck and told her not to yell. The suspect then undressed the lady and had sexual intercourse with her before fleeing the scene with her 60 cents, Timex watch and gold necklace. Patrol efforts have been suspended concerning this incident because of a lack of evidence."

In printing B. J. F.'s full name, The Florida Star violated its internal policy of not publishing the names of sexual offense victims. * * *

The tension between the right which the First Amendment accords to a free press, on the one hand, and the protections which various statutes and common-law doctrines accord to personal privacy against the publication of truthful information, on the other, is a subject we have addressed several times in recent years. Our decisions in cases involving government attempts to sanction the accurate dissemination of information as invasive of privacy, have not, however, exhaustively considered this conflict. On the contrary, although our decisions have without exception upheld the press' right to publish, we have emphasized each time that we were resolving this conflict only as it arose in a discrete factual context. * * *

It is undisputed that the news article describing the assault on B. J. F. was accurate. In addition, appellant lawfully obtained B. J. F.'s name. Appellee's argument to the contrary is based on the fact that under Florida law, police reports which reveal the identity of the victim of a sexual offense are not among the matters of "public record" which the public, by law, is entitled to inspect. * * * But the fact that state officials are not required to disclose such reports does not make it unlawful for a newspaper to receive them when furnished by the government. Nor does the fact that the Department apparently failed to fulfill its obligation under [state law] not to "cause or allow to be * * * published" the name of a sexual offense victim make the newspaper's ensuing receipt of this information unlawful. Even assuming the Constitution permitted a State to proscribe receipt of information, Florida has not taken this step. It is, clear, furthermore, that the news article concerned "a matter of public significance," * * *. That is, the article generally, as opposed to the specific identity contained within it, involved a matter of paramount public import: the commission, and investigation, of a violent crime which had been reported to authorities * * *.

Appellee argues that a rule punishing publication furthers three closely related interests: the privacy of victims of sexual offenses; the physical safety of such victims, who may be targeted for retaliation if their names become known to their assailants; and the goal of encouraging victims of such crimes to report these offenses without fear of exposure. * * *

At a time in which we are daily reminded of the tragic reality of rape, it is undeniable that these are highly significant interests, a fact underscored by the Florida Legislature's explicit attempt to protect these interests by enacting a criminal statute prohibiting much dissemination of victim identities. We accordingly do not rule out the possibility that, in a proper case, imposing civil sanctions for publication of the name of a rape victim might be so overwhelmingly necessary to advance these interests * * *.

Our holding today is limited. We do not hold that truthful publication is automatically constitutionally protected, or that there is no zone of personal privacy within which the State may protect the individual from intrusion by the press, or even that a State may never punish publication of the name of a victim of a sexual offense. We hold only that where a newspaper publishes truthful information which it has lawfully obtained, punishment may lawfully be imposed, if at all, only when narrowly tailored to a state interest of the highest order, and that no such interest is satisfactorily served by imposing liability under § 794.03 to appellant under the facts of this case. The decision below is therefore [r]eversed.

JUSTICE WHITE, with whom the CHIEF JUSTICE and JUSTICE O'CONNOR join, dissenting.

"Short of homicide, [rape] is the 'ultimate violation of self.' " Coker v. Georgia, 433 U.S. 584, 597 (1977) (opinion of White, J.). For B. J. F., however, the violation she suffered at a rapist's knifepoint marked only the beginning of her ordeal. A week later, while her assailant was still at large, an account of this assault—identifying by name B. J. F. as the victim—was published by The Florida Star. As a result, B. J. F. received harassing phone calls, required mental health counseling, was forced to move from her home, and was even threatened with being raped again. Yet today, the Court holds that a jury award of $75,000 to compensate B. J. F. for the harm she suffered due to the Star's negligence is at odds with the First Amendment. I do not accept this result. * * *

At issue in this case is whether there is any information about people, which—though true—may not be published in the press. By holding that only "a state interest of the highest order" permits the State to penalize the publication of truthful information, and by holding that protecting a rape victim's right to privacy is not among those state interests of the highest order, the Court accepts appellant's invitation, to obliterate one of the most noteworthy legal inventions of the 20th century: the tort of the publication of private facts.

NOTE: RAPE DETAILS OTHER THAN IDENTITY

Public disclosure of the name of a rape victim was at issue in *Florida Star*. What if a surviving rape victim does not mind that her identity is disclosed, but objects to public disclosure of the humiliating details of her ordeal? Does she have a claim? Cf. *Bloch v. Ribar*, 156 F.3d 673 (6th Cir. 1998), holding that although the qualified sovereign immunity doctrine limiting the liability of public officials foreclosed liability in the instant case, a rape victim has a constitutional interest in law enforcement's keeping the specific sexual details of a sexual assault quiet.

Cynthia Bloch reported to the Medina County Sheriff's Department that she had been raped by an unknown assailant. Eighteen months later, the *Cleveland Plain Dealer* published a series of articles criticizing the Sheriff's Department and Sheriff L. John Ribar for sluggish investigation of the rape. Bloch was interviewed for the articles and she condemned the pace of the investigation. In response, Sheriff Ribar called a press conference to announce that he was asking a grand jury to investigate Bloch's rape charges. During the press conference he revealed very personal and embarrassing details of the alleged rape. Bloch believed Sheriff Ribar made the disclosures solely to get back at her for criticizing his Department. She brought a civil lawsuit for invasion of her constitutional privacy rights and for unlawful retaliation.

Citing *Whalen v. Roe*, 429 U.S. 589 (1977), which concerned state mandated disclosure of prescription drug purchases, the court argued that officials' disclosures of personal information may violate the Fourteenth Amendment. Sexual information, including the details of a sexual assault, is protected personal information.

Are the details of a rape private? The court approvingly cited an article "quoting Professor Anita Allen [*Uneasy Access: Privacy for Women in a Free Society*, 1988] as stating: 'Rape is an act of physical violence which by its very nature is an affront to privacy. It represents forcible exposure of aspects of oneself that are protected by conventions of limited access. These conventions are normally adhered to out of regard for well-being and respect for personal privacy.'" But do the conventions in question apply, whether in a common law or in a constitutional law context, if the victim has voluntarily publicized her victim status in a series of provocative articles appearing in a major city newspaper? Can a rape victim who has voluntarily revealed her identity in the newspaper nonetheless assert that publishing the details of her rape is "highly offensive to a reasonable person" in the sense required by the public disclosure tort? Professor Susan Brison revealed and philosophically assessed the details of a brutal sexual assault she suffered while visiting France in 1990. Her attacker left her for dead. See Susan Brison, *Aftermath: Violence and the Remaking of a Self* (2003). Does the writing and publication of Brison's book imply that graphic disclosures of sexual assault should not, in our day and age, be classed as highly offensive to a reasonable person?

NOTE: SURVIVING RAPE

How do the privacy interests of rape victims who survive differ from the privacy interests of the families of rape victims who are murdered? Do you agree with Justice White's dissent in *Florida Star*?

Should the rules of tort law aim at removing the stigma of rape? Is there a public policy argument to be made that victims of rape, like homosexuals, should not be shielded in privacy?

5. SEXUAL ORIENTATION AS A PRIVATE FACT

URANGA v. FEDERATED PUBLS.

138 Idaho 550 (Id. 2003).

EISMANN, J.

On Sunday, October 15, 1995, the Statesman published a front-page story entitled "The Boy Most Likely" concerning events that occurred in Boise in 1955 and 1956 surrounding an investigation that began with allegations that adult homosexual men were propositioning teenage boys at the YMCA. * * * The events became known as the "Boys of Boise" scandal.

The Statesman story centered upon Frank Jones, the son of a Boise City Councilman, who had been accepted to the United States Military Academy at West Point. According to the story, six months after Frank entered West Point a man named Melvin Dir was charged with a felony for allegedly performing oral sex upon Frank two years earlier. Frank apparently admitted the sexual encounter during a taped interview at West Point, but alleged that Dir had forced him to have sex at gunpoint. Dir denied Frank's allegations regarding the use of force, and on January 7, 1956, he gave a handwritten, one-page, unsworn statement (Dir Statement) recounting his version of what occurred. In that statement, Dir wrote, "Afterwards we [Dir and Frank] talked about gay affairs that he [Frank] had had with [a classmate] and his cousin Fred Uranga." As a result of the investigation, Frank was kicked out of West Point.

In its "The Boy Most Likely" story, the Statesman printed a photographic representation of the Dir Statement, including the allegation regarding Uranga. In the body of the story, it summarized that portion of Dir's allegations as follows: "Afterward, they talked about sexual liaisons Frank had had with a high school classmate and with a cousin—both of whom Frank identified by name, according to Dir." The Statesman did not mention Uranga's name in the body of the story.

After the Statesman story was published, Uranga submitted a written request that it retract the sentence in the Dir Statement that implicated him in homosexual activity, claiming that the statement was libelous and invaded his privacy. The Statesman refused to do so, but offered to permit Uranga to submit a written response to be published in a "Speaker's Corner" feature to appear on the editorial page. If Uranga did not want to submit a written response, the Statesman offered to publish an explanation of its publication of the Dir Statement and to state that the Statesman does not have any opinion as to the veracity of Dir's written statement and did not intend to imply that it was truthful.

On October 14, 1997, Uranga filed a complaint against the Statesman _P, D_ alleging claims for invasion of privacy and intentional and/or reckless infliction of emotional distress. The Statesman filed an answer and then moved for summary judgment on the grounds that it was immune from liability under the First Amendment * * *.

The cause of action for public disclosure of embarrassing private facts "provides for tort liability involving a judgment for damages for publicity given to true statements of fact." RESTATEMENT (SECOND) OF TORTS § 652D special note (1976). The issue before us in this case is whether, consistently with the First and Fourteenth Amendments to the Constitution of the United States, a person can have a cause of action for invasion of privacy by public disclosure of embarrassing private facts caused by the accurate publication of information in a court record open to the public.

When the Statesman published a photographic reproduction of the Dir Statement, the Statement was a court record. * * * [I]t is undisputed that the Dir Statement was located in a court file when the Statesman photographed the Statement.

Court files are open to the public for examination, inspection, and copying unless the record is exempt from disclosure by statute, case law, or court rule. * * * The Statesman did not obtain a copy of the Statement by using any improper means.

In Cox Broadcasting Corporation v. Cohn, 420 U.S. 469 (1975), the United States Supreme Court addressed the issue of whether, consistently with the First and Fourteenth Amendments, a state may grant a cause of action for invasion of privacy caused by the publication of information obtained from a court record. * * *

The Court concluded, "Thus even the prevailing law of invasion of privacy generally recognizes that the interests in privacy fade when the information involved already appears on the public record." * * *

Uranga argues that the information published in Cox Broadcasting concerned a current criminal prosecution, while the Dir Statement was connected with a criminal prosecution that had occurred almost forty years earlier. There is no indication that the First Amendment provides less protection to historians than to those reporting current events. "No suggestion can be found in the Constitution that the freedom there guaranteed for speech and the press bears an inverse ratio to the timeliness and importance of the ideas seeking expression." Bridges v. California, 314 U.S. 252 (1941).

Uranga also contends that even if the story published by the Statesman concerned a matter of public significance, his name was not newsworthy. Therefore, the Statesman should have redacted his name before publishing a copy of the Dir Statement. In The Florida Star v. B.J.F. (1989), the Supreme Court addressed the issue of the public significance of publishing the name of the rape victim. * * * The Supreme Court indicated that whether or not the article is a matter of public concern is based upon the article generally. Each fact included within the article need not be a matter of public significance.

The instant case is not sufficiently distinguishable from Cox Broadcasting. The First and Fourteenth Amendments do not permit the Statesman to be held liable in damages for accurately publishing a document contained in a court record open to the public. Changing the cause of action from invasion of privacy to infliction of emotional distress does not circumvent the constitutional protection of the publication.

SIPPLE v. CHRONICLE PUBLISHING CO.

154 Cal.App.3d 1040 (Cal. Ct. App. 1984).

CALDECOTT, J.

On September 22, 1975, Sara Jane Moore attempted to assassinate President Gerald R. Ford while the latter was visiting San Francisco, California. Plaintiff Oliver W. Sipple (hereafter appellant or Sipple) who was in the crowd at Union Square, San Francisco, grabbed or struck Moore's arm as the latter was about to fire the gun and shoot at the President. Although no one can be certain whether or not Sipple actually saved the President's life, the assassination attempt did not succeed and Sipple was considered a hero for his selfless action and was subject to significant publicity throughout the nation following the assassination attempt.

Among the many articles concerning the event was a column written by Herb Caen and published by the San Francisco Chronicle on September 24, 1975. The article read in part as follows: "One of the heroes of the day, Oliver 'Bill' Sipple, the ex-Marine who grabbed Sara Jane Moore's arm just as her gun was fired and thereby may have saved the President's life, was the center of midnight attention at the Red Lantern, a Golden Gate Ave. bar he favors. The Rev. Ray Broshears, head of Helping Hands, and Gay Politico, Harvey Milk, who claim to be among Sipple's close friends, describe themselves as 'proud—maybe this will help break the stereotype'. Sipple is among the workers in Milk's campaign for Supervisor."

Thereafter, the Los Angeles Times and numerous out-of-state newspapers published articles which, referring to the primary source (i.e., the story published in the San Francisco Chronicle), mentioned both the heroic act shown by Sipple and the fact that he was a prominent member of the San Francisco gay community. Some of those articles speculated that President Ford's failure to promptly thank Sipple for his heroic act was a result of Sipple's sexual orientation.

Finding the articles offensive to his private life, on September 30, 1975, Sipple filed an action against the California defendants, the Chronicle Publishing Company, Charles de Young Thieriot, the publisher of the Chronicle, Herb Caen, a columnist for the Chronicle, the Times Mirror Company, the owner and publisher of the Los Angeles Times, and Otis Chandler (hereafter together respondents) and numerous out-of-state newspapers. The complaint was predicated upon the theory of invasion of privacy and alleged in essence that defendants without authorization and consent published private facts about plaintiff's life by disclosing that plaintiff was homosexual in his personal and private sexual orientation; that said publications were highly offensive to plaintiff inasmuch as his parents, brothers and sisters learned for the first time of his homosexual orientation; and that as a consequence of disclosure of private facts about his life plaintiff was abandoned by his family, exposed to contempt and ridicule causing him great mental anguish, embarrassment and humiliation. Plaintiff finally alleged that defendants' conduct amounted to malice and oppression calling for both compensatory and punitive damages. * * *

[A] crucial ingredient of the tort premised upon invasion of one's privacy is a public disclosure of private facts, that is, the unwarranted publication of intimate details of one's private life which are outside the realm of legitimate public interest * * *. In elaborating on the notion, the cases explain that there can be no privacy with respect to a matter which is already public * * *.

The undisputed facts reveal that prior to the publication of the newspaper articles in question appellant's homosexual orientation and participation in gay community activities had been known by hundreds of people in a variety of cities, including New York, Dallas, Houston, San Diego, Los Angeles and San Francisco. Thus, appellant's deposition shows that prior to the assassination attempt appellant spent a lot of time in "Tenderloin" and "Castro," the well-known gay sections of San Francisco; that he frequented gay bars and other homosexual gatherings in both San Francisco and other cities; that he marched in gay parades on several occasions; that he supported the campaign of Mike Caringi for the election of "Emperor"; that he participated in the coronation of the "Emperor" and sat at Caringi's table on that occasion; that his friendship with Harvey Milk, another prominent gay, was well-known and publicized in gay newspapers; and that his homosexual association and name had been reported in gay magazines (such as Data Boy, Pacific Coast Times, Male Express, etc.) several times before the publications in question. In fact, appellant quite candidly conceded that he did not make a secret of his being a homosexual and that if anyone would ask, he would frankly admit that he was gay. In short, since appellant's sexual orientation was already in public domain and since the articles in question did no more than to give further publicity to matters which appellant left open to the eye of the public, a vital element of the tort was missing rendering it vulnerable to summary disposal.

Although the conclusion reached above applies with equal force to all respondents, we cannot help observing that respondents Times Mirror and its editor are exempt from liability on the additional ground that the Los Angeles Times only republished the Chronicle article which implied that appellant was gay. It is, of course, axiomatic that no right of privacy attaches to a matter of general interest that has already been publicly released in a periodical or in a newspaper of local or regional circulation * * *.

But even aside from the aforegoing considerations, the summary judgment dismissing the action against respondents was justified on the additional, independent basis that the publication contained in the articles in dispute was newsworthy. * * *

In the case at bench the publication of appellant's homosexual orientation which had already been widely known by many people in a number of communities was not so offensive even at the time of the publication as to shock the community notions of decency. Moreover, and perhaps even more to the point, the record shows that the publications were not motivated by a morbid and sensational prying into appellant's private life but rather were prompted by legitimate political considerations, i.e., to dispel the false public opinion that gays were timid, weak and unheroic figures and to raise the equally important political question whether the President of the United States entertained a discriminatory attitude or bias against a minority group such as homosexuals. * * *

DAVID A. J. RICHARDS, PUBLIC AND PRIVATE IN THE DISCOURSE OF THE FIRST AMENDMENT

12 Cardozo Stud. L. & Literature 61, 90 (2000).

Consider the constitutional issues that would be raised by the use of a privacy action against the publication of the names of gays and lesbians who do not want the fact of their sexual orientations and lives to be a matter of public record. The right to conscience protects and justifies an expansive principle of free speech making possible the politics of gay and lesbian identity that advances the reasonable understanding and remedy of the structural injustice of homophobia. But, the same right protects the right of privacy of those gays and lesbians who choose to keep their sexual orientation and lives a private matter. The reasonable balance between these different aspects of the right to conscience is to immunize from the protection of free speech those true private facts, control of which is indispensable to the just ethical individuality of groups afflicted by structural injustice. There is, properly understood, no conflict between the right of free speech and of privacy, since they protect, in mutually complementary and supportive ways, aspects of the underlying human rights to live lives free of the unjust force of irrationalist stereotypes of gender and sexuality. Indeed, it would itself be unjustly stereotypical to suppose that all gays and lesbians must be publicly identified as such. For this reason, there should be no constitutional objection, in principle, to a privacy action brought against the media for the outing of one's homosexuality.

E.   THE FALSE LIGHT TORT

1.   AMERICAN LAW INSTITUTE, RESTATEMENT (SECOND) OF TORTS § 652E

§ 652E. Publicity Placing Person In False Light

One who gives publicity to a matter concerning another that places the other before the public in a false light is subject to liability to the other for invasion of his privacy, if

(a) the false light in which the other was placed would be highly offensive to a reasonable person, and

(b) the actor had knowledge of or acted in reckless disregard as to the falsity of the publicized matter and the false light in which the other would be placed.

2. LOOKING BAD IN THE PUBLIC EYE

LOVGREN v. CITIZENS FIRST NAT'L BANK

126 Ill. 2d 411 (Ill. 1989).

RYAN, J. * * *

In November 1985, advertisements were placed in local newspapers and handbills were circulated stating that the plaintiff was selling his farm at a public auction that would take place on November 25, 1985. No such sale, however, had been scheduled, and the placing of these advertisements was accomplished without the plaintiff's knowledge or consent. The advertisements did not mention the Bank's mortgage on the property, nor did they state that the public sale was being held to satisfy the plaintiff's financial obligations. Further, the act of placing the advertisements and circulating the handbills took place without the Bank's having instituted mortgage foreclosure proceedings on the property. * * *

We recognize that the facts alleged in the present case may constitute an invasion of privacy. This court recognized the right to privacy in Leopold v. Levin (1970), 45 Ill. 2d 434, where this court stated that "[p]rivacy is one of the sensitive and necessary human values and undeniably there are circumstances under which it should enjoy the protection of law." * * *

We first must decide whether the allegations show that the plaintiff was placed in a false light before the public as a result of the defendants' actions. After an examination of the advertisement placed in the local newspaper, we note that sufficient publicity was generated to satisfy this requirement. Further, because the advertisement stated that the farm was for sale by public auction, and named the plaintiff as seller—which was clearly untrue—the defendants' actions placed the plaintiff in a false light before the public.

Second, we must determine whether a finder of fact could decide that the false light in which the plaintiff was placed would be highly offensive to a reasonable person. The test articulated by the Restatement states that this element is met "when the defendant knows that the plaintiff, as a reasonable man, would be justified in the eyes of the community in feeling seriously offended and aggrieved by the publicity." (Restatement (Second) of Torts § 625E, comment c, at 396 (1977).) We caution, however, that minor mistakes in reporting, even if made deliberately, or false facts that offend a hypersensitive individual will not satisfy this element. * * *

PARNIGONI v. ST. COLUMBA'S NURSERY SCHOOL

681 F.Supp.2d 1 (D.D.C., 2010).

The plaintiffs in this civil lawsuit are Fiona Parnigoni, David Parnigoni, and Andrew Parnigoni ("the plaintiffs"), who are residents of Arlington, Virginia. Plaintiff Fiona Parnigoni is the wife of co-plaintiff David Parnigoni, and co-plaintiff Andrew Parnigoni is their three-year-old son. The dispute between the parties occurred during Fiona Parnigoni's employment as a teacher from 2001 to 2008 at St. Columba's Nursery School (the "Nursery School" or "School") located in the District of Columbia.

In 2004, while she was employed by the School, Mrs. Parnigoni's fiancé at that time, David Parnigoni, was charged with and ultimately convicted of indecently exposing himself to a minor. Mrs. Parnigoni had no involvement in that incident, but while the case was still pending resolution, Mrs. Parnigoni informed the Director of the School of the situation regarding her fiancé, and the Director in turn informed the Board of Governors of the Church (the "Board") and the Rector, Reverend James Donald, of David Parnigoni's situation. The defendants took no action at that time and Mrs. Parnigoni continued to work at the School without any further discussions about the matter. Sometime thereafter, David and Fiona Parnigoni married, and at no time did anyone associated with the School or Church Parish indicate that Mrs. Parnigoni's subsequent marriage to Mr. Parnigoni was or would be cause for concern or place her job in jeopardy.

Three years after Mr. Parnigoni's conviction, in 2007, the Parnigonis decided to enroll their son at the School as a student, and they were notified of his acceptance in March 2007. Neither before nor at the time of the son's acceptance was there any indication that the defendants would publicly disclose information regarding Mr. Parnigoni's conviction as a sex offender as a result of the child's enrollment in the school. However, in August of 2007, Julia Berry, who was named Director of the School in 2006, met with Mrs. Parnigoni and requested information from her regarding the details concerning Mr. Parnigoni's 2004 conviction. The Director stated that Mrs. Parnigoni was required to disclose the details of her husband's conviction so that the Director would be able to explain the circumstances to any parent who might inquire about the situation. Mrs. Parnigoni provided the Director with the requested information and offered the Director the opportunity to speak with her husband's lawyers, however, the record is unclear as to whether the Director accepted or declined the offer.

On "the first day of the 2007–2008 term for teachers, the Director informed Mrs. Parnigoni that the Board was 'nervous' about [Mr. Parnigoni's] 2004 conviction." The Board's apprehension apparently stemmed from the fact that "Mr. Parnigoni might [now] have reason to be on the School property to pick [ ] up [his son]." * * * The Board was allegedly "relieved" to learn of the Parnigonis' arrangements to take their son off campus when Mr. Parnigoni needed to pick him up from school; however, the Director still requested Mr. Parnigoni's "lawyer's contact information so that St. Columba's counsel could make a 'courtesy call' * * *". The Church's attorney then contacted Mr. Parnigoni's lawyer and informed him that the Church was satisfied with the arrangement of walking Andrew away from the school to meet Mr. Parnigoni and assured the lawyer that "everything is fine" and that the Parnigonis "would not hear from the Church again on this issue." *Id.* Andrew Parnigioni's first day as a student at the School was September 17, 2007.

On October 1, 2007, the Director of the School told Mrs. Parnigoni that the Rector of the Church, Janet Vincent, wished to "meet with her." The "meeting was held two days later on October 3, 2007," *id.,* and those in attendance included the Rector of the Church, the Director of the School, the Church's attorney, the Chairman of the Church's Board of Governors, Mrs. Parnigoni, and her attorney. During the meeting, the Rector announced "her decision to make a full public disclosure" of Mr. Parnigoni's 2004 conviction "to all parents of students [attending] the Nursery School and the entire Parish." It was also indicated that the Church planned to announce "the fact that Mrs. Parnigoni, a teacher at the school, was married to a convicted sex offender."

As noted earlier, the Church had not mentioned previously any concerns regarding Mrs. Parnigoni's marriage to Mr. Parnigoni; therefore, Mr. and Mrs Parnigoni surmised that the new concern was related "to her son's enrollment in the [S]chool." Accordingly, Mrs. Parnigoni offered to withdraw Andrew from the School to avoid any "embarrassment to her and her family," and the Church's attorney allegedly informed Mrs. Parnigoni that removing her son from the School would "certainly 'help' " the situation, and the attorney "encouraged" her to do so. Mrs. Parnigoni therefore removed her son from the School in early October 2007, and she also "offered to resign her position" as a teacher "in order to avert public disclosure" of her husband's conviction, but the School "rejected" her offer.

On October 12, 2007, the Director of the School "met with Mrs. Parnigoni's co-teacher and two other colleagues" to discuss the impending disclosures about Mr. Parnigoni. "[T]he Director stated that while she was sorry that this had happened to Mrs. Parnigoni, she put the blame for the entire situation on Mrs. Parnigoni, and declared that if Mrs. Parnigoni had not married [her husband], she 'would not be in this position.' " That same day, the Director emailed Mrs. Parnigoni asking her to remain at home on October 15, 2007, so that the Rector could inform the staff about the " 'disclosure' without her being present." When the Rector spoke to the School staff during the meeting, she apparently "made it clear" that the sole reason for the disclosure was due to Mrs. Parnigoni's " 'poor judgment in marrying David' " and denied that the disclosures were based on their son's "enrollment in the School." The Rector further stated that she would have made "the disclosure … even if [Mrs. Parnigoni] re-signed."

"On or about October 18, 2007, [the Rector] sent a letter (the "October 18th letter") to the parents of the students of the School and to all members of the Church's parish," which, *inter alia,* informed them of Mr. Parnigoni's registration "with the Virginia Sex Offenders and Crimes Against Minors Registry as a result of [his] July 3, 2004 conviction for indecent exposure to a minor." The letter identified David as Fiona's husband and indicated that "[u]ntil recently their son had attended the Nursery School." The letter went on to state that it had been issued to "enable [parents] to make informed decisions as to whom [they should] entrust the care and supervision of [their children]." It further stated that because the defendants lacked the ability "to anticipate every possible future scenario [they] believe[d their] best course of action [was] to give [the] parents the information they need[ed] to protect their children." Moreover, the letter stated that the "disclosures [were] necessary for the sake of our children" because the parents were "entitled to information that may impact the safety of [their children]." The Church sent the letter to "[o]ver 3,500 households in the D.C. metropolitan area," although the number of people who actually "read the letter" is unknown. "On the same day that the [October 18th letter] was sent to the parents and the entire parish," the Director sought suggestions and recommendations from other nursery school directors in "an email to the DC Directors' Exchange list-serve, a group consisting of approximately 37 nursery school directors in the Washington, D.C. area." The email included all of the details regarding the Parnigoni's situation and their relationship with the School without identifying them by name.

On October 31, 2007, the Parnigonis "received a letter from a parent" expressing the view that the School's "approach [was] totally unjustified," resulting in the Parnigoni "family's name and reputation [being] tarnished, [and their] personal affairs publicized, and [their] son [ ] taken out of the school." On that same day, the Parnigonis received a copy of another letter sent to the Rector from a parent of one of the children attending the school that expressed disappointment with the school's decision to embarrass Mrs. Parnigonis and her family. As had been announced in the October 18th letter, "on November 1, 2007[,] a meeting, open to the public, was held to address any questions or concerns that the [October 18th letter] might have raised." Some who attended "the meeting indicated that they believed the Rector's letter unfairly cast Mrs. Parnigoni as a threat to children."

"On or about November 9, 2007, [the Director] sent another letter (the "November 9th letter") to the parents of students who attended the nursery school and[, it is believed by the plaintiffs], the entire parish as well. Among other things, the letter stated "that the world can be a less-than safe place for our children." *Id.* According to the plaintiffs, the letter "reinforced" the notion that "Mrs. Parnigoni was a potential threat to the School's children * * *", despite there having been no previous incidents suggesting "that Mrs. Parnigoni, because of her marriage to Mr. Parnigoni[,] or for any other reason, endangered or posed a threat to any student of the School or member of St. Columba's parish".

Although the Director informed Mrs. Parnigoni "that the Board would renew her contract for the next [school] year and that her teaching position with the school was safe and that she need not worry as the 'storm would soon pass' " at a meeting held shortly after the October 18th letter was sent, Mrs. Parnigoni's contract was not renewed for the 2008–2009 school year despite her unblemished employment record. The plaintiffs assert that the Director told a parent that Mrs. Parnigoni's contract was not renewed "because of the disclosures contained in the [October 18th letter] and because current parents allegedly wanted to withdraw [their children] from Mrs. Parnigoni's class and prospective students did not want to be in her class [the following] year." 43.

* * *

As a result of the actions allegedly taken by the defendants, the plaintiffs seek compensatory and punitive damages, the costs of pursuing this action, and attorney's fees. The defendants now seek dismissal of this action under Rule 12(b)(6) for failure to state any claims upon which relief may be granted.

* * *

1. *Invasion of Privacy–False Light*

The defendants contend that the plaintiffs' invasion of privacy-false light claim fails because their communications were constitutionally protected. They also argue that none of the statements were false nor could the statements be understood by a reasonable person to imply that Andrew and Fiona Parnigoni presented threats to the safety of other children. *Id.* Specifically, defendants maintain that the statements made by Reverend Vincent about parents ensuring that their children not fall prey to sexual abusers were merely general reminders and in no way were meant to imply that Andrew Parnigoni, a three year old, or Fiona Parnigoni, a teacher employed by the school, were "threat[s] to [the] safety and well-being" of children. *Id.* (citation and internal quotation marks omitted). The defendants also assert that an invasion of privacy-false light claim is only actionable for statements that are false and cannot be based on opinions that do not convey a false inference.

The plaintiffs, on the other hand, argue that they have pled the elements of a false light claim with sufficient "specificity" in their Amended Complaint. They contend that the two letters (1) constitute publicity; (2) contained statements that falsely represented or imputed that Fiona and Andrew Parnigoni "were dangerous to children, a threat to their safety and well being, and that parents should take action to ensure that the children did not become victims of sexual abuse;" (3) included statements that "were directed to and concerned Fiona and Andrew Parnigoni;" and (4) "improperly atribut[ed] to [Fiona and Andrew Parnigoni] conduct and characteristics that were false [and] highly offensive to a reasonable person as demonstrated, in part, by the letter responses from the recipients of the letters at issue." The plaintiffs respond that rather than focusing on whether the elements of the claim have been adequately pled, the defendants have instead tried to argue the merits of their claim, which is improper in making a Rule 12(b)(6) challenge. *Id.* at 28. They also contend that the defendants "misunderstand or misconstrue the entire basis for [the plaintiffs'] false light claim" in arguing "that the 'expressed view that parents were entitled to know about David Parnigoni . . . [is] constitutionally protected opinion.'" *Id.* (quoting Defs.' Mem. at 22).

For the plaintiffs' claim for invasion of privacy-false light to defeat a Rule 12(b)(6) motion, their complaint must allege that the defendants' actions created "(1) publicity (2) about a false statement, representation or imputation (3) understood to be of and concerning the plaintiff[s], and (4) which places the plaintiff[s] in a false light that would be offensive to a reasonable person." *Washburn v. Lavoie,* 437 F.3d 84, 88 n. 3 (D.C.Cir. 2006) (quoting *Kitt v. Capital Concerts, Inc.,* 742 A.2d 856, 859 (D.C.1999)) (internal citations and quotations omitted). Because this tort is "so similar" to the tort of defamation, "[a] plaintiff may only recover on one of the two theories based on single publication, but is free to plead them in the alternative." *Weyrich v. New Republic, Inc.,* 235 F.3d 617, 628 (D.C.Cir.2001) (quoting *Moldea v. New York,* 15 F.3d 1137, 1151 (D.C.Cir. 1994)).

[handwritten: elements]

The plaintiffs' assertion that the defendants distributed the letters to over 3,500 households satisfies the publicity prong of the tort. The defendants' release of information about Mr. Parnigoni's conviction as a sex offender and statements about whom parents should trust with the care of their children reasonably created the false impression that Mrs. Parnigoni was a threat to the students simply because of her association with Mr. Parnigoni. Therefore, the second and third components of the tort have been sufficiently pled. However, even if the Court had found that the statements against Mrs. Parnigoni were incapable of a defamatory meaning, the Court would still be required to consider whether the statements or their imputations place the plaintiffs in a "highly offensive" light. *See Weyrich,* 235 F.3d at 628. Because the statements in the letters, which implied that Mrs. Parnigoni posed a risk of harm to the children at the school, were highly offensive, the plaintiffs have satisfied the third element of the tort. *See Benz v. Washington Publ'g Co.,* No. 05–1760(EGS), 2006 WL 2844896, at *6 (D.D.C. Sept. 29, 2006) (finding that false statements that sexually linked the plaintiff to a known "porn king" would be highly offensive to a reasonable person). In fact, Mrs. Parnigoni and the defendants received letters expressing outrage at the defendants' actions and their implication that she presented a risk to the safety of the students at the School. Therefore, the allegations in the complaint concerning Ms. Parnigoni are more than adequate to defeat the defendants' Rule 12(b)(6) motion to dismiss.

[handwritten: element 1]

However, the plaintiffs have not pled facts sufficient to support a claim of invasion of privacy-false light with respect to Andrew Parnigoni. The only statement the complaint asserts the defendants made in any of the communications about Andrew was that he no longer attended the School, which was obvious from his absence from the classroom. This in no way suggested anything negative about Andrew and therefore Andrew's invasion of privacy-false light claim cannot survive the defendants' Rule 12(b)(6) motion. The motion is therefore granted as to Andrew Parnigoni.

ABDELHAK v. THE JEWISH PRESS INC., ET AL.

411 N.J.Super. 211, 985 A.2d 197 (2009).

Plaintiff [Yaakov Abdelhak] is a physician specializing in high risk obstetrics, whose patients are, almost without exception, women of the Orthodox Jewish faith. Plaintiff is a practicing Orthodox Jew and was raised as such by his parents. * * *

In August 2004, defendant [Gabrielle] Tito, who was plaintiff's wife, instituted divorce proceedings and informed him that she would seek custody of their two daughters and did not intend to honor her earlier promise to raise the children as Orthodox Jews. Although Tito had renounced the tenets of Orthodox Judaism, she nonetheless demanded that plaintiff provide her with a *Get,* which is a religious divorce granted by a husband to a wife. Unless granted a *Get,* an observant Orthodox Jewish woman is not free to marry again; a civil divorce is not sufficient. Moreover, children born of any subsequent marriage are deemed to have been born out of wedlock and bear a considerable stigma among Orthodox Jews. Based on advice and counsel purportedly issued to plaintiff by his spiritual adviser, Rabbi Rudinsky, plaintiff took the position that so long as Tito continued to refuse to raise their children in the Orthodox tradition, he was not obliged to grant her a *Get.* * * *

Tito contacted *The Jewish Press,* a newspaper that bills itself as the "largest independent weekly Jewish newspaper in the United States." *The Jewish Press* champions the cause of women whose husbands refuse to provide a *Get* by listing such men's names on its *Seruv* list. The *Seruv* list is designed to publicly shame such recalcitrant husbands into providing the requested *Get.* * * *

[Plaintiff subsequently brought a lawsuit alleging, inter alia, false light invasion of privacy. The judge dismissed the false light claim and others.]

Last, we address plaintiff's claim that Judge Miller wrongly dismissed his cause of action for invasion of privacy/false light. To prevail on such claim, a plaintiff must demonstrate that a defendant interfered with the plaintiff's right to be left alone, and did so by portraying him in a false light in the public eye. Such depiction of a plaintiff "need not be defamatory, but must be something that would be objectionable to the ordinary reasonable person." *Rumbauskas v. Cantor,* 138 *N.J.* 173, 180, 649 *A.*2d 853 (1994). We need not tarry long on discussion of this claim because, like plaintiff's two other causes of action, a jury could not resolve this one without "delving dangerously" into issues of religious doctrine. A jury could not determine whether the accusation of withholding a *Get* would be objectionable to a person of the Orthodox Jewish faith without analyzing tenets of Orthodox Jewish doctrine. For that reason, this claim, like the other two, was properly dismissed on abstention grounds.

WEST v. MEDIA GEN. CONVERGENCE, INC.

53 S.W.3d 640 (Tenn. 2001).

DROWOTA, J. * * *

Plaintiffs operated a private probation services business, and were referred this business by the general sessions courts. Plaintiffs claim that WDEF–TV defamed them by broadcasting false statements that the plaintiffs' business is illegal. Plaintiff West, in particular, claims that the defendant invaded her privacy by implying that she had a sexual relationship with one of the general session judges; and that the general sessions judges and the plaintiffs otherwise had a "cozy," and hence improper, relationship.

Specifically at issue in this case is whether Tennessee recognizes the separate tort of false light invasion of privacy. Section 652E of the Restatement (Second) of Torts (1977) defines the tort of false light * * *.

After considering the relevant authorities, we agree with the majority of jurisdictions that false light should be recognized as a distinct, actionable tort. While the law of defamation and false light invasion of privacy conceivably overlap in some ways, we conclude that the differences between the two torts warrant their separate recognition. * * *

In defamation law only statements that are false are actionable; truth is, almost universally, a defense. In privacy law, other than in false light cases, the facts published are true; indeed it is the very truth of the facts that creates the claimed invasion of privacy. Secondly, in defamation cases the interest sought to be protected is the objective one of reputation, either economic, political, or personal, in the outside world. In privacy cases the interest affected is the subjective one of injury to [the] inner person. Thirdly, where the issue is truth or falsity, the marketplace of ideas furnishes a forum in which the battle can be fought. In privacy cases, resort to the marketplace simply accentuates the injury. * * *

In light of the uncertain position of the United States Supreme Court with respect to the constitutional standard for false light claims brought by private individuals about matters of private interest, many courts and Section 652E of the Restatement (Second) of Torts adopt actual malice as the standard for all false light claims. * * * We hold that actual malice is the appropriate standard for false light claims when the plaintiff is a public official or public figure, or when the claim is asserted by a private individual about a matter of public concern. We do not, however, adopt the actual malice standard for false light claims brought by private plaintiffs about matters of private concern. * * *

Consistent with defamation, we emphasize that plaintiffs seeking to recover on false light claims must specifically plead and prove damages allegedly suffered from the invasion of their privacy. See Memphis Publishing, 569 S.W.2d at 419. As with defamation, there must be proof of actual damages. See Myers v. Pickering Firm, Inc., 959 S.W.2d 152 (Tenn. Ct. App. 1997). The plaintiff need not prove special damages or out of pocket losses necessarily, as evidence of injury to standing in the community, humiliation, or emotional distress is sufficient.

In addition, for purposes of clarification, this Court adopts Section 652I of the Restatement (Second) of Torts (1977) which recognizes that the right to privacy is a personal right. As such, the right cannot attach to corporations or other business entities, may not be assigned to another, nor may it be asserted by a member of the individual's family, even if brought after the death of the individual. Restatement (Second) of Torts § 652I cmt. a–c (1977). Therefore, only those persons who have been placed in a false light may recover for invasion of their privacy.

Finally, we recognize that application of different statutes of limitation for false light and defamation cases could undermine the effectiveness of limitations on defamation claims. Therefore, we hold that false light claims are subject to the statutes of limitation that apply to libel and slander, as stated in Tenn. Code Ann. §§ 28–3–103 and 28–3–104(a)(1), depending on the form of the publicity, whether in spoken or fixed form. * * *

3. SOME COURTS REJECT THE FALSE LIGHT TORT

LAKE v. WAL–MART STORES, INC.

582 N.W.2d 231 (Minn. 1998).

BLATZ, CHIEF JUSTICE. * * *

Nineteen-year-old Elli Lake and 20–year–old Melissa Weber vacationed in Mexico in March 1995 with Weber's sister. During the vacation, Weber's sister took a photograph of Lake and Weber naked in the shower together. After their vacation, Lake and Weber brought five rolls of film to the Dilworth, Minnesota Wal–Mart store and photo lab. When they received their developed photographs along with the negatives, an enclosed written notice stated that one or more of the photographs had not been printed because of their "nature."

In July 1995, an acquaintance of Lake and Weber alluded to the photograph and questioned their sexual orientation. Again, in December 1995, another friend told Lake and Weber that a Wal–Mart employee had shown her a copy of the photograph. By February 1996, Lake was informed that one or more copies of the photograph were circulating in the community.

Lake and Weber filed a complaint against Wal–Mart Stores, Inc. and one or more as-yet unidentified Wal–Mart employees on February 23, 1996, alleging the four traditional invasion of privacy torts—intrusion upon seclusion, appropriation, publication of private facts, and false light publicity. Wal–Mart denied the allegations and made a motion to dismiss the complaint under Minn. R. Civ. P. 12.02, for failure to state a claim upon which relief may be granted. The district court granted Wal–Mart's motion to dismiss, explaining that Minnesota has not recognized any of the four invasion of privacy torts. The court of appeals affirmed. * * *

Today we join the majority of jurisdictions and recognize the tort of invasion of privacy. The right to privacy is an integral part of our humanity; one has a public persona, exposed and active, and a private persona, guarded and preserved. The heart of our liberty is choosing which parts of our lives shall become public and which parts we shall hold close.

Here Lake and Weber allege in their complaint that a photograph of their nude bodies has been publicized. One's naked body is a very private part of one's person and generally known to others only by choice. This is a type of privacy interest worthy of protection. Therefore, without consideration of the merits of Lake and Weber's claims, we recognize the torts of intrusion upon seclusion, appropriation, and publication of private facts. Accordingly, we reverse the court of appeals and the district court and hold that Lake and Weber have stated a claim upon which relief may be granted and their lawsuit may proceed. * * *

We decline to recognize the tort of false light publicity at this time. We are concerned that claims under false light are similar to claims of defamation, and to the extent that false light is more expansive than defamation, tension between this tort and the First Amendment is increased. * * *

Although there may be some untrue and hurtful publicity that should be actionable under false light, the risk of chilling speech is too great to justify protection for this small category of false publication not protected under defamation.

DENVER PUBL. CO. v. BUENO

54 P.3d 893 (Colo. 2002).

En banc

JUSTICE KOURLIS delivered the Opinion of the Court. * * *

The Denver Publishing Company, d/b/a/ Rocky Mountain News (the News), published a four-page, thirteen-column article with the bold headline: "Denver's Biggest Crime Family." Ann Carnahan, Denver's Biggest Crime Family, Rocky Mountain News, Aug. 28, 1994, at 20A. Bueno sued the News and Ann Carnahan, contending the story defamed him and invaded his privacy.

The story's first page depicted a "family tree," the center of which contained a photo of Della and Pete Bueno on their wedding day in 1937. Mug-shot style photos of their eighteen children encircled the parents' photo; captions summarized each of the Bueno siblings' misdeeds, misfortunes, and, where applicable, criminal records. * * *

Eddie Bueno, now fifty-five, left his home when he was thirteen years old and has had virtually no contact with other family members since then. He married his present wife at age twenty-one, and they have three children, all married with families of their own. Eddie Bueno served six years in the United States Army, departing with an Honorable Discharge. His current employment began twenty-five years ago with the City and County of Denver's vehicle maintenance department. He has worked his way up to the position he now holds, center supervisor. He had no involvement whatsoever in his siblings' criminal activities, nor did he seek publicity in his life generally. Quite the contrary, Eddie Bueno purposefully kept secret from most of his friends and family the fact that he was related to the other, more notorious, Bueno children.

The reporter for the News worked on the story for six months. She interviewed numerous law enforcement officials and reviewed court and police department records. She attempted to contact all surviving children, ultimately interviewing seven of them. Three times she attempted to contact Eddie Bueno, but he did not return her calls.

Carnahan and the News insist that the article makes no false statements about Bueno. First, they argue that he did not "stay out of trouble." For this, they point to an "arrest card" in their possession that appears to indicate Bueno had a run-in with police when he was a teenager. No charges, convictions, or other ramifications resulted from that incident and Bueno disputes the card's authenticity. At trial, the judge ruled the arrest card inadmissible for any purpose, and the court of appeals affirmed.

The News further points out a portion of the article it contends rectifies any possible misunderstanding vis-a-vis Eddie Bueno: "Freddie, the youngest, and Eddie, the oldest, are the only two Bueno boys who have stayed out of trouble." * * *

Both because it substantially overlaps with another tort, defamation, and because it is difficult to quantify, courts and legal scholars heartily debate whether false light invasion of privacy deserves a place among the recognized torts. "False light remains the least-recognized and most controversial aspect of invasion of privacy." * * *

Privacy torts protect one's right "to be let alone." Thomas M. Cooley, A Treatise on the Law of Torts, 29 (2d ed. 1888). In false light terms, Prosser describes such "right" as "a person's interest in being let alone" in instances where there "has been publicity of a kind that is highly offensive." Prosser and Keeton, Torts, § 117, at 864 (5th ed. 1984). "Highly offensive" is the element of false light that distinguishes it from defamation. A defamation claim requires a showing that the publication damaged the plaintiff's reputation in the community. False light requires no such showing. Rather, false light requires a showing that the publication is highly offensive, but need not have damaged that plaintiff's reputation in the community. The theory is that a publication could be highly offensive to an individual without meeting the standard of lowering that person's reputation in the community, a standard required by defamation law. Bolduc v. Bailey, 586 F. Supp. 896, 900 (D. Colo. 1984) ("The gravamen of an action for defamation is the damage to one's reputation in the community caused by the defamatory statement(s)."). If the statement did lower the person's reputation, it would clearly be actionable as defamation. If it did not, then, and only then, would there be a need for a false light tort that was not coextensive with defamation. In sum, defamation protects individuals from (public) offense, but only false light will serve where the offense does not lower that individual's reputation in the community.

The question then is what is the nature of the interest that the tort protects? Scholars writing on false light variously describe the protected interest as "peace of mind," "injury to the inner person," "freedom from scorn and ridicule, freedom from embarrassment, humiliation and harassment, freedom from personal outrage, freedom from injury to feelings, freedom from mental anguish, freedom from contempt and disgrace, and the right to be let alone." Lying at the core of all these "interests" are the personal feelings of the false light plaintiff. The issue is not whether others are given cause to change their perception of the plaintiff, but how the plaintiff himself responds to the publication. * * *

We believe that recognition of the different interests protected rests primarily on parsing a too subtle distinction between an individual's personal sensibilities and his or her reputation in the community. In fact, the United States Supreme Court trampled any such subtleties in Zacchini v. Scripps–Howard Broadcasting Co. " 'The interest protected' in permitting recovery for placing the plaintiff in a false light 'is clearly that of reputation, with the same overtones of mental distress as in defamation.' " Id. at 573 (quoting Prosser, supra, at 400.).

We agree. False statements that a plaintiff finds "highly offensive" will generally either portray that plaintiff negatively or attack his conduct or character. At the same time, publicized statements that are disparaging and false satisfy the elements of defamation. See Schwartz, supra, at 887. Thus, the same publications that defame are likely to offend, and publications that offend are likely to defame. For example, if the article here did indeed portray Eddie Bueno as a criminal, then that statement is defamatory and not merely offensive. Those cases in which offense is taken, although no damage is done to plaintiff's reputation, are few and far between. Because the likelihood of a chilling effect is much greater than the likelihood that an offended plaintiff will be left with no cause of action, we feel that defamation law will adequately and most appropriately protect the public. * * *

Our decision today to reject false light in Colorado reflects not only caution with respect to adopting new torts, but also our recognition that the tort implicates First Amendment principles. Freedom of the press is a critical part of our constitutional framework. * * *

CAIN v. HEARST CORP.

878 S.W.2d 577 (Tex. 1994).

GONZALEZ, J. delivered the opinion of the Court * * *

Clyde Cain is a prison inmate in the Texas Department of Corrections serving a life sentence for murder. He sued the Hearst Corporation, d/b/a the Houston Chronicle Publishing Company, claiming that a newspaper article invaded his privacy by placing him in a false light. The article, which appeared in the Chronicle on June 30, 1991, referred to Cain as a burglar, thief, pimp, and killer. In recounting Cain's criminal record the article, in summary, states that:

Cain is believed to have killed as many as eight people; Cain killed one of his lawyers in 1973 and married the lawyer's widow a few months later; Cain killed a 67 year old man in 1977; in 1983 he "bought" a prostitute from a friend to help finance his activities; Cain persuaded the prostitute to marry a trailer park owner named Anderson, so that Cain could kill Anderson and share the prostitute's inheritance from Anderson; when the prostitute balked, Cain threatened to kill her 5 year old daughter and "deliver her daughter's head in a wastepaper basket"; the prostitute married Anderson 3 days later, and on January 5, 1985 Cain killed Anderson.

Cain's sole complaint is that the article printed false information that he was a member of the "Dixie Mafia" and that he had killed as many as eight people. Cain asserted that these statements put him in a false light with the public. Suit was filed in state court one and one-half years after the article was published. * * *

We reject the false light invasion of privacy tort for two reasons: 1) it largely duplicates other rights of recovery, particularly defamation; and 2) it lacks many of the procedural limitations that accompany actions for defamation, thus unacceptably increasing the tension that already exists between free speech constitutional guarantees and tort law. * * *

JUSTICE HIGHTOWER, joined by JUSTICE DOGGETT, JUSTICE GAMMAGE and JUSTICE SPECTOR, dissenting. * * *

That the substance of communications constituting defamation will usually also constitute false light does not make the two torts coextensive. The scope of actionable conduct differs between the torts, and the torts are designed to protect different interests. First, the court rightly notes, as do many courts and commentators, that there are communications which,

based on their content, are not defamatory but may be false light violations of privacy because they are highly offensive. * * * For example, an
article which falsely reports that an individual suffers from a serious
disease such as cancer would not be defamatory but could comprise a
cause of action for false light. Gary T. Schwartz, Explaining and Justifying
A Limited Tort of False Light Invasion of Privacy, 41 Case W. Res. 885,
895 (1991).

Second, the torts protect different interests. Defamation preserves
individuals' reputation interests, but false light invasion of privacy, as the
other branches of the right of privacy, safeguards individuals' sensitivities
about what people know and believe about them. * * *

Furthermore, the scopes of the torts differ with respect to the level of
publicity required for the cause of action to arise. False light requires
significantly broader publication than does defamation. Defamation only
requires publication to a single individual, but false light requires widespread dissemination. * * *

The court's conclusion that many, if not all, of the injuries redressed
by the false light tort are redressed by defamation is plainly wrong as a
matter of logic. That false light covers some of the injuries covered by
defamation in no way leads to the conclusion that defamation covers most
of the injuries covered by false light.

Furthermore, overlap, by itself, is no reason to reject a cause of action
for false light invasion of privacy. For example, in Texas, a citizen who
feels cheated in a financial transaction has a variety of choices for a cause
of action, including a claim for fraud, violation of the Deceptive Trade
Practices Act, breach of warranty, or a combination of any and all of these
claims. Moreover, although traditional theories such as actions for eavesdropping and wiretapping protected individuals from invasions into their
private business and personal affairs, the availability of such actions did
not preclude the court from adopting the right of privacy in the wiretapping context.

The court's only explanation of why it will tolerate no overlap in this
arena is that free speech rights are implicated because the procedures
attending defamation are lacking. Rather than assess and weigh the
interests at stake in each right and add any procedures necessary to
effectuate an even balance of the rights, the court simply concludes that
false light invasion of privacy and free speech cannot coexist. * * *

4. ALTERNATIVE REMEDIES FOR UNFLATTERING DEPICTIONS— STRATEGIES AND DEFENSES

NOTE: DISTORTION

What are the best arguments for and against recognition of the false light
tort? The three cases in this section are not technically false light cases. The

plaintiffs—a senior citizen in a nursing home, a Steelers football fan, and a famous preacher—based their lawsuits on other privacy tort theories or on the tort known as intentional infliction of emotional distress. But the cases are included here to emphasize the common law options and defenses available when a plaintiff alleges that the defendant has published a distortion or an unflattering depiction of the plaintiff. Will the death of the plaintiff or his consent constitute a defense? What if the offending publication was intended as a parody of a public figure? The cases seek to answer these doctrinal questions.

WELLER v. HOME NEWS PUBLISHING CO.

112 N.J.Super. 502 (N.J. Super. Ct. 1970).

FURMAN, J. * * *

Mrs. Weller in 1967 was a paying patient in defendant hospital suffering from a heart affliction. Defendant Murray as its public relations director prepared a series of three articles dealing with charity patient care. Defendant newspaper published these articles. The second had as its central figure Prudence "Grandmom" Pickett, a charity patient not eligible for Medicare, cheerful, unselfish and destitute. "Grandmom" Pickett was fictitious, although the article, which was published on Sunday, December 10, 1967, did not so state. The accompanying photograph, captioned "Grandmom" Pickett, was that of Mrs. Weller in a walker in profile view.

A release entitled "Photographic Consent" is alleged but not relied upon by defendants on this motion. Plaintiffs deny such consent.

As to Mrs. Weller's causes of action for libel and invasion of privacy, defendants urge their abatement upon her death during the pendency of the litigation. The authority cited is Alpaugh v. Conkling, 88 N.J.L. 64 (Sup. Ct. 1915), which held that the survival statute (now N.J.S.A. 2A:15–4) did not apply to a cause of action for slander by the decedent, who died during the pendency of the litigation. Justice Parker stated broadly (that "the conclusion that the Legislature did not intend that libel or slander, considered purely as injurious to the feelings and reputation and apart from special damage, should survive to the personal representative.") * * *

All tort actions abated at [early] common law upon the death of a party.

The survival statute abrogating the common law rule preserved a decedent's cause of action for trespass to person or property and a cause of action against a decedent for trespass to person or property without stated exceptions. To construe trespass to person as not encompassing libel or invasion of the right of privacy is to import a limitation into the survival statute which is not expressed. The term "trespass" in the statute is equated with "tort." It should not be modified by implication to exclude torts in which damages for emotional distress, not physical injury, are sought. Any such distinction is arbitrary. Damages for mental suffering and nervous anguish without physical injury were recoverable at common law in several causes of action arising out of trespass on the case, e.g., libel, slander, malicious prosecution and alienation of affections. Nor is there any logical basis for Justice Parker's dictum in Alpaugh that defamation actions alleging special damages, that is, property or money losses, are within the survival statute, although defamation actions alleging general damages are not.

The survival statute is, therefore, construed to apply to the torts of libel and invasion of the right of privacy resulting in damage to reputation and emotional distress without special damages. Alpaugh is specifically not followed. The motion for summary judgment on the two counts brought by Mrs. Weller, now deceased, is denied. * * *

NEFF v. TIME, INC.

406 F.Supp. 858 (W.D. Pa. 1976).

MARSH, DISTRICT JUDGE.

The complaint was verified by [John W.] Neff and alleged that the ⌐P defendant is the owner of a magazine known as Sports Illustrated sold D weekly throughout Pennsylvania; that Neff is a private citizen employed in education; that in its issue of August 5, 1974, the defendant's magazine used Neff's picture without his prior knowledge and consent to illustrate an article entitled "A Strange Kind of Love;" that the photograph shows Neff with the front zipper of his trousers completely opened implying that he is a "crazy, drunken slob," and combined with the title of the article, "a sexual deviate." Neff alleges that the unauthorized publication and circulation of his picture to illustrate the article invaded his right of privacy and subjected him to public ridicule and contempt, injured his personal esteem and the esteem of his profession, reflected on his character, diminished his high standing reputation among his family, friends, neighbors and business associates, destroyed his peace of mind and caused him severe mental and emotional distress to his damage in excess of $5,000, amended to aver in excess of $10,000.

The affidavits establish that the photograph was taken about 1:00 o'clock P.M. November 25, 1973, while Neff was present on a dugout with a group of fans prior to a professional football game at Cleveland between the Cleveland Browns and the Pittsburgh Steelers. The photographer was on the field intending to take pictures of the Steeler players as they entered the field from the dugout. Neff and the others were jumping up and down in full view of the fans in the stadium; they were waving Steeler banners and drinking beer; they all seemed to be slightly inebriated. One of the group asked the photographer for whom he was working and was told Sports Illustrated, whereupon the group began to act as if a television camera had been put on them; as the pictures were taken they began to react even more, screaming and howling and imploring the photographer to take more pictures. The more pictures taken of the group, the more they hammed it up. All were aware that the photographer was covering the game for Sports Illustrated. There were no objections; they wanted to be photographed. Thirty pictures were taken of the group on the dugout from different angles.

During the period from July through December, 1973, this photographer took 7,200 pictures pursuant to his assignment to cover the Steelers. As part of his duty he edited the pictures and submitted one hundred to the magazine for selection by a committee of five employees. After several screenings of the thirty pictures of the group on the dugout, the committee selected Neff's picture with his fly open. Although Neff's fly was not open to the point of being revealing, the selection was deliberate and surely in utmost bad taste; subjectively, as to Neff, the published picture could have been embarrassing, humiliating and offensive to his sensibilities. Without doubt the magazine deliberately exhibited Neff in an embarrassing manner. * * *

It seems to us that art directors and editors should hesitate to deliberately publish a picture which most likely would be offensive and cause embarrassment to the subject when many other pictures of the same variety are available. Notwithstanding, "[the] courts are not concerned with establishing canons of good taste for the press or the public." Aquino v. Bulletin Company, 190 Pa.Super. 528, 154 A.2d 422, 425 (1959). * * *

The article about Pittsburgh Steeler fans was of legitimate public interest; the football game in Cleveland was of legitimate public interest; Neff's picture was taken in a public place with his knowledge and with his encouragement; he was catapulted into the news by his own actions; nothing was falsified; a photograph taken at a public event which everyone present could see, with the knowledge and implied consent of the subject, is not a matter concerning a private fact. A factually accurate public disclosure is not tortious when connected with a newsworthy event even though offensive to ordinary sensibilities. The constitutional privilege protects all truthful publications relevant to matters of public interest. * * *

Of course, we are concerned that Neff's picture was deliberately selected by an editorial committee from a number of similar pictures and segregated and published alone. If his picture had appeared as part of the general crowd scene of fans at a game, even though embarrassing, there would be no problem. Although we have some misgivings, it is our opinion that the publication of Neff's photograph taken with his active encouragement and participation, and with knowledge that the photographer was connected with a publication, even though taken without his express consent, is protected by the Constitution.

HUSTLER MAGAZINE v. FALWELL

485 U.S. 46 (1988).

CHIEF JUSTICE REHNQUIST delivered the opinion of the Court. * * *

The inside front cover of the November 1983 issue of Hustler Magazine featured a "parody" of an advertisement for Campari Liqueur that contained the name and picture of respondent and was entitled "Jerry Falwell talks about his first time." This parody was modeled after actual Campari ads that included interviews with various celebrities about their "first times." Although it was apparent by the end of each interview that this meant the first time they sampled Campari, the ads clearly played on the sexual double entendre of the general subject of "first times." Copying the form and layout of these Campari ads, Hustler's editors chose respondent as the featured celebrity and drafted an alleged "interview" with him in which he states that his "first time" was during a drunken incestuous rendezvous with his mother in an outhouse. The Hustler parody portrays respondent and his mother as drunk and immoral, and suggests that respondent is a hypocrite who preaches only when he is drunk. In small print at the bottom of the page, the ad contains the disclaimer, "ad parody—not to be taken seriously." The magazine's table of contents also lists the ad as "Fiction; Ad and Personality Parody." * * *

This case presents us with a novel question involving First Amendment limitations upon a State's authority to protect its citizens from the intentional infliction of emotional distress. We must decide whether a public figure may recover damages for emotional harm caused by the publication of an ad parody offensive to him, and doubtless gross and repugnant in the eyes of most. * * *

The sort of robust political debate encouraged by the First Amendment is bound to produce speech that is critical of those who hold public office or those public figures who are "intimately involved in the resolution of important public questions or, by reason of their fame, shape events in areas of concern to society at large."

Generally speaking the law does not regard the intent to inflict emotional distress as one which should receive much solicitude, and it is quite understandable that most if not all jurisdictions have chosen to make it civilly culpable where the conduct in question is sufficiently "outrageous." But in the world of debate about public affairs, many things done with motives that are less than admirable are protected by the First Amendment. * * *

We conclude that public figures and public officials may not recover for the tort of intentional infliction of emotional distress by reason of publications such as the one here at issue without showing in addition that the publication contains a false statement of fact which was made with "actual malice," i.e., with knowledge that the statement was false or with reckless disregard as to whether or not it was true. This is not merely a "blind application" of the New York Times standard, see Time, Inc. v. Hill, 385 U.S. 374, 390 (1967), it reflects our considered judgment that such a standard is necessary to give adequate "breathing space" to the freedoms protected by the First Amendment.

Here it is clear that respondent Falwell is a "public figure" for purposes of First Amendment law. The jury found against respondent on his libel claim when it decided that the Hustler ad parody could not "reasonably be understood as describing actual facts about [respondent] or actual events in which [he] participated." App. to Pet. for Cert. C1. The Court of Appeals interpreted the jury's finding to be that the ad parody "was not reasonably believable," 797 F.2d, at 1278, and in accordance with our custom we accept this finding. Respondent is thus relegated to his claim for damages awarded by the jury for the intentional infliction of emotional distress by "outrageous" conduct. But for reasons heretofore stated this claim cannot, consistently with the First Amendment, form a basis for the award of damages when the conduct in question is the publication of a caricature such as the ad parody involved here. The judgment of the Court of Appeals is accordingly. Reversed.

F. THE APPROPRIATION TORT

1. AMERICAN LAW INSTITUTE, RESTATEMENT (SECOND) OF TORTS § 652C

§ 652C, Appropriation Of Name Or Likeness

One who appropriates to his own use or benefit the name or likeness of another is subject to liability to the other for invasion of his privacy.

2. COMMON LAW LIABILITY FOR APPROPRIATION

CASTRO v. NYT TV

370 N.J.Super. 282 (N.J. Super. Ct. 2004).

SKILLMAN, P.J.A.D. * * *

While in the emergency room, plaintiffs were videotaped by the media defendants, with the permission of the medical defendants, for a television show called "Trauma: Life in the ER," which is shown on the Learning Channel. Plaintiffs signed forms consenting to this videotaping at some point during their hospitalizations. However, plaintiffs allege that they were not competent to give such consents due to the severity of their injuries or illnesses and the heavy medications they were receiving at the time. Plaintiffs also allege that the media defendants made various deceptive statements to induce them to sign the consents. * * *

The common law tort of commercial appropriation of a person's name or likeness is one of four torts set forth in Restatement (Second) of Torts § 652 (1977). * * *

The foundation for this tort is recognition that a person has an interest in their name or likeness "in the nature of a property right." Restatement (Second) of Torts, § 652C comment a. Its most common form consists of "the appropriation and use of the plaintiff's name or likeness to advertise the defendant's business or product." Id., comment b. Thus, the use of a person's name or likeness "for trade purposes" is an essential element of the tort.

The broadcast of videotape footage on a television show does not give a person who has been videotaped the right to maintain an action for appropriation of his or her likeness because no one has the right to object merely because his name or his appearance is brought before the public, since neither is in any way a private matter and both are open to public observation. It is only when the publicity is given for the purpose of appropriating to the defendants' benefit the commercial or other values associated with the name or the likeness that the right of privacy is invaded. The fact that the defendant is engaged in the business of publication, for example of a newspaper, out of which he makes or seeks to make a profit, is not enough to make the incidental publication a commercial use of the name or likeness. Thus a newspaper, although it is not a philanthropic institution, does not become liable under the rule stated in this Section to every person whose name or likeness it publishes. * * *

The privilege of enlightening the public [is] not, however, limited to the dissemination of news in the sense of current events. It extends also to information or education, or even entertainment and amusement, by books, articles, pictures, films and broadcasts concerning interesting phases of human activity in general, as well as the reproduction of the public scene in newsreels and travelogues. * * *

Plaintiffs' complaints do not allege that any of the videotape footage taken of them at Jersey Shore has been used for "trade purposes." * * * Their complaints simply assert that "defendants appropriated plaintiffs' likenesses, images and/or names for commercial profit and advantage." However, such an assertion is a conclusion of law, not an allegation of fact that could support this conclusion. Plaintiffs do not allege, for example, that any videotape footage of them was used for any specific promotional purpose * * *. Therefore, plaintiffs' complaints do not state causes of action for commercial appropriation of their likenesses.

NOTE: NO COMMON LAW PRIVACY FOR CORPORATIONS

The *Castro* case illustrates an important limitation on the common law appropriation tort. News-related depictions are fair game. The same limitation will apply to appropriation cases brought pursuant to the New York Civil Rights Law §§ 50 and 51, illustrated in Section 3 by *Time v. Hill, Friedan v. Friedan* and *Finger v. Omni Publ'ns Int'l.* The *Felsher* case, just below, raises novel questions about remedies against individuals who do mischief with false identities they create on internet webpages. It raises a more traditional question, too, about whether a corporation has a right to privacy. The rule of common law has been that a corporation may not assert a right to privacy, but must rely on the law of defamation, trade secrets, trademarks, copyright, and unfair trade practices to protect secrets and reputation. Why? The basis of the rule seems to be that the purpose of the privacy torts is to right wrongs that damage feelings and sensibilities. As legal persons only, corporations lack emotions. Is there any reason, in principle, why the reach of the privacy torts could not or should not be broadened to include protections for corporations?

FELSHER v. UNIVERSITY OF EVANSVILLE

755 N.E.2d 589 (Ind. 2001).

SHEPARD, CHIEF JUSTICE.

We live in an age when technology pushes us quickly ahead, and the law struggles to keep up. In this case, we encounter for the first time assumption of identity via the Internet. A number of existing statutes and common law precepts seem to serve surprisingly well in this dramatic new environment.

In 1997, [Dr. William] Felsher created Internet websites and electronic mail accounts containing portions of the names of Dr. James S. Vinson, President of the University; Dr. Stephen G. Greiner, Vice President for Academic Affairs; and Dr. Larry W. Colter, Dean of the College of Arts and Sciences. Each of these addresses also contained the letters UE, which is a common abbreviation for the University of Evansville.

Felsher featured articles that he had written on the websites he created. The articles alleged wrongdoings by Vinson and other University employees. One article alleged that President Vinson violated the University Faculty Manual. In another article Felsher stated that one UE professor had publicly declared himself unqualified to teach one of his courses. * * *

Using the e-mail accounts he created, Felsher sent mail to several universities nominating each of the University officials, in turn, for various academic positions. In his e-mail message, Felsher directed the reader to one of the web pages he had created as a reference for the nominee's activities.

The University, Vinson, Greiner and Colter filed this lawsuit alleging invasion of privacy, and Felsher then removed the e-mail addresses and the websites. Felsher later created another twelve websites containing roughly the same information as had appeared on the previously removed sites.

Pending resolution of the suit, the University sought and obtained a preliminary injunction prohibiting Felsher from engaging in certain Internet activities. * * *

Felsher first argues that the trial court erred because the University is not entitled to an invasion of privacy claim. * * * Felsher asserts that the right to privacy has an "intensely personal nature" and therefore applies to real persons and not to corporations. * * *

The issue of whether a corporate entity is entitled to an invasion of privacy claim is one of first impression in Indiana. We begin our analysis by acknowledging the position taken in the Restatement (Second) of Torts, § 652 A(1) (1977): "One who invades the right of privacy of another is subject to liability for the resulting harm to the interests of the other." * * *

The only injury at issue here is appropriation. The University argues that it may maintain an action for appropriation because the claim addresses a property interest rather than personal feelings. * * * The University also relies on Restatement § 652I, which says, "Except for the appropriation of one's name or likeness, an action for invasion of privacy can be maintained only by a living individual whose privacy is invaded." * * *

While we agree that an appropriation claim involves a privacy issue "in the nature of a property right," we think the University's reliance on the exception set forth in the Restatement is misplaced. Each of the comments to Restatement § 652I negates the inference that a corporation is entitled to an appropriation claim.

The first comment states that the privacy right is personal. The comment then states a rule: "The cause of action is not assignable, and it cannot be maintained by other persons * * *." Restatement (Second) of Torts, § 652I cmt. a (1977). The appropriation exception that follows addresses this rule, not the personal character of the right.

The second comment discusses the general requirement that "the action for the invasion of privacy cannot be maintained after the death of the individual whose privacy is invaded." Id., cmt. b. This comment states an exception for appropriation actions due to its "similarity to [an] impairment of a property right * * *." The exception is clarified as a recognition of survival rights in an appropriation action. *Not for a corp.*

Finally, the third comment declares, without exception, "A corporation, partnership or unincorporated association has no personal right of privacy." Id., cmt. c. The comment then states that a corporation has "no cause of action for any of the four forms of invasion covered by §§ 652B to 652E." Id. The following sentence in the comment indicates that although these sections (including § 652C) do not entitle a corporation claim, a corporation has "a limited right to the exclusive use of its own name or identity in so far as they are of use or benefit, and it receives protection from the law of unfair competition." Id. This comment suggests the existence of an analogous right that corporations may be afforded by the law of unfair competition. * * *

Therefore, we think these Restatement sections do not support the position that a corporation may bring an appropriation claim resting on notions of privacy.

Our assessment of the Second Restatement is consistent with an overwhelming majority of other states that have addressed the issue of corporate actions for invasion of privacy.

Among the most recent of these is Warner–Lambert Co. v. Execuquest Corp., 427 Mass. 46, 691 N.E.2d 545 (Mass. 1998). The Supreme Judicial Court noted that it had not previously been presented with the issue of "whether a corporation has a corporate right to privacy entitled to the protection of [Massachusetts privacy right law]." 691 N.E.2d at 548. The court held that because "[a] corporation is not an 'individual' with traits of a 'highly personal or intimate nature,' " its privacy law did not extend protection to the corporation. Id. Justice Margaret Marshall noted that other jurisdictions have "unanimously denied a right of privacy to corporations."

Although the Second Restatement suggests that unique circumstances may "give rise to the expansion of the four forms of tort liability for invasion of privacy," Restatement (Second) of Torts, § 652A cmt. c (1977), we decline to do so today. Instead, we explore the nature of relevant Internet activities and look to business law for protection against the misappropriation of a corporation's name. * * *

The Internet offers its subscribers access to a myriad of functions. These functions include the opportunity to communicate, share and even exploit intellectual property. As a prelude to our examination of business law provisions applicable to misappropriation on the Internet, we discuss the nature of the Internet and the deceptive activities that it confronts. * * *

[T]he Internet is an international aggregation of networks that connects numerous individual computer networks and computers. This system of networks, also called the World Wide Web (WWW), has been described as "a highly diffuse and complex system over which no entity has authority or control."

Most North American websites on the Internet register with an organization called InterNIC and receive a unique identifying number called an Internet Protocol (IP) address. For convenience, most of these numeric addresses are also assigned corresponding textual addresses. For example, Microsoft's IP address is 131.107.1.7, which can also be accessed by its textual address, microsoft.com. This textual address is referred to as the domain name. WWW registrants frequently select domain names that identify the registrant's name or interest, for the same reasons businesses and individuals have historically sought telephone numbers that were easy to remember. As visitors to websites delve further and further into a website beyond its home page, each web page is stored and accessed as a separate file located by a unique address called a Uniform Resource Locator (URL).

The last three letters of most domain names are the highest level domain reference and serve as the primary information Internet computers use to locate and identify the website sought. Current highest level domains include ".com" for businesses, ".net" for Internet services, ".edu" for educational institutions, ".gov" for government agencies, ".mil" for military connections, and ".org" for non-profit organizations.

Therefore, an Internet user can connect to the White House's website by typing in the address field the following: http://www.whitehouse.gov.

In addition to supporting the Web, the Internet also facilitates personalized communication through electronic mail (e-mail). The portion of e-mail addresses to the left of the "at" symbol is the user identification and typically identifies the account owner, while that portion of the address to the right of the "at" symbol is the domain name of the mail server. For example, a person can e-mail the President by addressing the message to president at whitehouse.gov.

Nearly anyone can create a website or an e-mail address. Using readily available software, the task requires little skill or investment. An individual can currently acquire and register a unique domain name (web address), a customizable website and a corresponding e-mail address for about $70 a year. Such ease and affordability have stimulated commercial businesses, educational institutions, organizations and individuals to participate in Internet communication.

People purchase websites, register domain names, and establish e-mail addresses to efficiently and effectively market and promote products, services and ideas to the literal "world" of the WWW. The ease of initiating these transactions also tempts the interests of wrongdoers, particularly in the context of domain name registrations.

As alluded to earlier, the organization in charge of maintaining the registration of North American domain names is InterNIC. Initially, registration of domain names occurred on a first-come, first-served basis. This policy was discontinued after more businesses began registering names and conflicts in requested names multiplied. The original policy permitted many enterprising individuals to attain domain names that were identical or significantly similar to trademarked names that had not yet been registered on the Internet. These individuals, sometimes referred to as "cyberpredators," may be further sub-categorized according to their purpose for registering a popular name.

"Cybersquatters" are individuals who register domain names that are well known, not to use the addresses, but to re-sell them at a profit. For example, the domain name "wallstreet.com" was sold for $1 million. Cybersquatters who register previously trademarked names rarely prevail in litigation between the squatter and the holder of the trademark.

Unlike cybersquatters, "copycats" register a domain name and use the address to operate a website that intentionally misleads users into believing they are doing business with someone else. Copycats either beat the legitimate organization to a domain name or register a close variation of an organization's domain name. The latter most frequently occurs when a unique spelling of an organization's name and/or domain name makes a close, but different spelling believable to a web user.

Copycat domain name use is "intentionally inimical to the trademark owner." For example, in Planned Parenthood Federation of America, Inc.

v. Bucci * * * defendant was enjoined from using the domain name "plannedparenthood.com," which he had previously registered and used to display anti-abortion material. Similarly, in Jews for Jesus v. Brodsky, 993 F. Supp. 282, 290–91, 313 (D.N.J. 1998), the defendant was enjoined from using the registered domain name "jewsforjesus.org," where he had previously created a website for the purpose of contradicting the teachings of the actual Jews for Jesus organization. Our previous example, white-house.gov, has also fallen prey to a notorious, though unlitigated, example of copycat use. * * *

Felsher's actions seem to fall in this second category of cyberpredators. He created the imposter websites and e-mail addresses for the sole purpose of harming the reputation of the University and its officials.

Thus, it might seem appropriate to grant the University the relief gained by the plaintiffs in * * * Jews for Jesus. These plaintiff organizations, however, based their claims on provisions of the Lanham Trade–Mark Act, 15 U.S.C. §§ 1114, 1125(a), (c) (trademark infringement, trademark dilution, unfair competition and false designation of origin). * * *

These trademark actions require commercial use of the domain name. See 15 U.S.C. § 1125(c)(4)(B) (1999) (noncommercial use of a mark is not actionable under this section). Courts have held, "The mere registration of a domain name, without more, is not a 'commercial use' of a trademark." Jews for Jesus, 993 F.Supp. at 307 (citations omitted). The Lanham Act does not include claims for non-commercial use of a trademark in order to "prevent courts from enjoining constitutionally protected speech." Id. (citing Panavision International, L.P. v. Toeppen, 945 F.Supp. 1296, 1303 (1996)).

In any event, the plaintiffs here do not assert a right to relief under the Lanham Act, so we need not debate whether the "commercial use" requirement for trademark actions is satisfied by domain name registration and corresponding presentation of information on a website. * * *

Amici curiae argue that an appropriate remedy for the misappropriation of a corporation name or likeness is found under the state unfair competition law and trademark statutes, as well as common law torts unrelated to notions of privacy, such as tortious interference with business relations. * * * We agree. * * *

The trial court based its decision to grant injunctive relief on its finding that Felsher composed and sent e-mail messages purposefully appearing to have been authored by either Vinson or Colter. * * *

The reasonable inference that may be drawn from these findings is that Felsher might well continue his retaliatory endeavors via the Internet if he is not enjoined from doing so. Felsher removed the objectionable e-mail accounts and websites only after he received notice of the plaintiffs' complaint. His assertion that this voluntary action, along with his promise, relieves any necessity for an injunction is unsupported. Removed e-mail accounts and websites are easily replaced. Felsher's actions are only facially remedial and provide no assurance that he will permanently discontinue his Internet activities against the University and its officers.

The trial court's findings and the reasonable inferences that they provide confirm that the trial court acted within its discretion when it enjoined Felsher. * * *

Concluding that the University itself has no claim in the nature of common law privacy, we reverse that portion of the injunction relating to the institution, noting that it may be entitled to similar relief under other law not so far pleaded.

AFL PHILADELPHIA LLC v. KRAUSE

639 F.Supp.2d 512 (E.D.Pa.,2009).

Baylson, District Judge.

In sports, as in legal battles, there are winners and there are losers, and the case before this Court tells the tale of both. In the instant matter, the local arena football team the Philadelphia Soul—partially owned by rock icon Jon Bongiovi (also known as Bon Jovi)—rose in a "Blaze of Glory" to win the 2008 national championship Arena Bowl and then was "Shot Through the Heart" when its 2009 season was cancelled by the League due to financial problems. The team and League remain "Living on a Prayer" that they will return in the 2010 season and beyond. In the meantime, the Philadelphia Soul and a former employee are trading accusations concerning the fall-out of the season's cancellation, in which they each experienced a taste of "Bad Medicine." * * *

Defendant Krause is the former Director of Sales for the Philadelphia Soul, which included responsibility for game and season ticket sales. Defendant alleges as follows: he was hired for the position because of his well-known and favorable reputation in the sports and entertainment business as an energetic personality and public relations specialist who brought ongoing personal and business relationships to his position; he utilized his solid reputation and ongoing relationships to promote the team in general and to sell game and season tickets, therefore enhancing his solid reputation in the industry amongst fans and season ticket holders; and the team's record-breaking ticket sales were due directly to his efforts.

In mid-December 2008, the Arena Football League suspended its 2009 season. Defendant and other employees were given a one-week notice of termination. Defendant claims that the decision to cancel the 2009 season was hugely unpopular among the team's fans, especially 2009 season ticket holders.

* * * Defendant further alleges the following: after his termination, the Philadelphia Soul sent an email to its fans about the season's cancellation that falsely designated the origin of the email as having been sent from Defendant's Philadelphia Soul email address; Defendant did not send the email, had no role in notifying fans of the season's cancellation, and

never authorized the Philadelphia Soul to use his name or email address for such a notification; by this false designation, the Philadelphia Soul sought to cause confusion amongst fans as to Defendant's association with the unpopular decision to cancel the 2009 season and the resulting controversy over season ticket refunds; and the Soul traded on his good name and reputation amongst the fan base. * * *

[The parties bring various claims and counterclaims. Defendant Krause counterclaims] invasion of privacy, specifically misappropriation of name. This tort is described in the Restatement as follows: "One who appropriates to his own use or benefit the name or likeness of another is subject to liability to the other for invasion of his privacy." Restatement (Second) of Torts § 652C (1977). * * * The Pennsylvania Supreme Court has expressly recognized a cause of action for "invasion of privacy" by "appropriation of name or likeness." * * * In an appropriation claim, the "use or benefit" at issue is typically a commercial use of one's name or likeness. *Fanelle v. LoJack Corp.,* 79 F.Supp.2d 558, 563–564 (E.D.Pa. 2000)

As federal district courts have noted, the law concerning the tort of appropriation in Pennsylvania is somewhat unsettled. *Fanelle,* 79 F.Supp.2d at 563; *Worthy v. Carroll,* 2003 WL 25706359, at *4 (E.D.Pa. 2003). In 1996, Judge Broderick predicted that the Pennsylvania Supreme Court would clarify the law of appropriation by adopting the Restatement (Third) of Unfair Competition. *Seale v. Gramercy Pictures,* 949 F.Supp. 331 (E.D.Pa.1996). However, the Pennsylvania Supreme Court has not done so; therefore the Second Restatement appropriation analysis applies. *Carroll,* 2003 WL 25706359, at *4; *Fanelle,* 79 F.Supp.2d at 564.

To be liable for appropriation under the Restatement (Second) of Torts, "defendant must have appropriated to his own use or benefit the reputation, prestige, social or commercial standing, public interest or other values of the plaintiff's name or likeness. . . . Until the value of the name has in some way been appropriated, there is no tort." § 652C cmt. c. In the instant case, Defendant has pled that the Philadelphia Soul falsely designated the email as originating from himself "as a way to trade upon his good name and reputation." In addition, Defendant pled that the Philadelphia Soul used his name "for the express purpose of appropriating the commercial benefit that is particularly associated with Krause's name; specifically the good will and reputation Krause developed with the Philadelphia Soul fan base." Therefore, Defendant has adequately pled that Plaintiffs sought to appropriate the value of Defendant's name by benefitting from Defendant's reputation and prestige.

Plaintiffs argue that Defendant has not alleged that his name was appropriated for a commercial purpose, and therefore Defendant has not alleged a proper appropriation claim. Despite the fact that Defendant did plead appropriation for "commercial benefit," Plaintiffs legal argument is mistaken. Plaintiffs cite to several cases that discuss the relationship between the misappropriation of name tort based in the right to privacy and the right to publicity: *World Wrestling Fed'n Entm't, Inc. v. Big Dog Holdings, Inc.,* 280 F.Supp.2d 413, 443–444 (W.D.Pa.2003); *Fanelle,* 79 F.Supp.2d 558; and *Eagle's Eye, Inc. v. Ambler Fashion Shop, Inc.,* 627 F.Supp. 856, 862 (E.D.Pa.1985). Using these cases, they argue that * * * the tort of misappropriation of name requires a showing that the name was appropriated for commercial advantage.

However, Plaintiffs are conflating two different, though similar, torts. *See Rose v. Triple Crown Nutrition, Inc.,* 2007 WL 707348, at *3 (M.D.Pa. 2007) ("[T]he right of publicity is not identical to invasion of privacy by appropriation of name or likeness. Invasion of privacy by appropriation of name or likeness does not require the appropriation to be done commercially." (citing Restatement (Second) of Torts § 652C cmt. b. (1977))); *Eagle's Eye,* 627 F.Supp. at 862 (quoting *Zacchini v. Scripps–Howard Broadcasting Co.,* 433 U.S. 562, 97 S.Ct. 2849, 53 L.Ed.2d 965 (1977) for the proposition that the Supreme Court has recognized the right of publicity as an entirely different tort than the traditional invasion of privacy); *Lewis,* 527 F.Supp.2d at 428–29 (analyzing the torts of misappropriation of publicity and invasion of privacy by misappropriation of identity as two separate and distinct torts). Comment (b) to the Restatement on the misappropriation of name tort clarifies that there is no "commercial benefit" requirement:

> "The common form of invasion of privacy under the rule here stated is the appropriation and use of the plaintiff's name or likeness to advertise the defendant's business or product, or for some similar commercial purpose.... however, the rule stated is not limited to commercial appropriation. It applies also when the defendant makes use of the plaintiff's name or likeness for his own purposes and benefit, even though the use is not a commercial one, and even though the benefit sought to be obtained is not a pecuniary one."

Restatement (Second) of Torts § 652C cmt. b. Comment (d) goes on to clarify that "incidental use," for example mere mention of the plaintiff's name or publication of the plaintiff's likeness without the purpose of taking advantage of its value, is not misappropriation. *Id.* at cmt. d. However, "when the publicity is given for the purpose of appropriating to the defendant's benefit the commercial or other values associated with the name or the likeness [ ] the right of privacy is invaded." *Id.*

Based on this Restatement commentary, Defendant has pled value in his name, specifically its reputation, prestige, and commercial standing in the sports and entertainment industry, as described in the secondary meaning analysis above. In addition, Defendant specifically pled that Plaintiffs falsely designated the origin of the contested email "to trade upon his good name and reputation" and "for the express purpose of appropriating [its] commercial benefit". Therefore, Defendant has alleged a valid claim for misappropriation of name. *Compare Lewis,* 527 F.Supp.2d at 429 n. 9 (finding that an esteemed former executive chef whose name continued to be advertised by his former employer in connection with its catering packages had adequately pled commercial value in his name to state a misappropriation of name claim) *and Fanelle,* 79 F.Supp.2d at 564 (finding that plaintiff's allegations that defendant used a newspaper article with his name and likeness in a promotional brochure were sufficient to state an misappropriation of name claim) *with Worthy,* 2003 WL 25706359, at *4 (dismissing a misappropriation of name claim by the plaintiff, who was mentioned in a chapter of defendant's book, because plaintiff had failed to allege that his name had any special reputation, prestige or commercial value or that defendants used it for commercial purposes).

Plaintiffs further argue that Eastern District decisions require that for a valid misappropriation claim, the name or likeness must have secondary meaning. However the case that Plaintiffs cite for this proposition, *Philadelphia Orchestra Ass'n v. Walt Disney Co.,* 821 F.Supp. 341, 349–350 (E.D.Pa.1993), analyzes a right to publicity claim, not a misappropriation of name claim. Since these claims are distinct, this Court finds that no pleading of secondary meaning is required to sustain Defendant's misappropriation of name claim. *See Lewis,* 527 F.Supp.2d at 429 (not performing a secondary meaning analysis to a misappropriation of name claim); *Fanelle,* 79 F.Supp.2d at 564 (same).

Based on the above discussion, Defendant's misappropriation of name claim has been adequately pled, and this Court will deny Plaintiffs' Motion to Dismiss the counterclaim.

NOTE: SECONDARY MEANING

"The Lanham Act does not create a right of publicity without either secondary meaning or likelihood of confusion, the essential elements of a trademark claim." See *Astaire v. McKenzie,* 2010 WL 2331524 (SDNY 2010) (Plaintiff widow of Fred Astaire denied restraining order because she has not shown that consumers will be deceived into believing that the late Fred Astaire endorsed defendants' awards, which are described as "in tribute" to Fred and sister Adele Astaire). Judge Bayleson maintained in *AFL Philadelphia LLC v. Krause* that the appropriation branch of the invasion of privacy tort does not require that a person's name have acquired "secondary meaning" before it can be appropriated. When does a name have secondary meaning? The name of a commodity has secondary meaning when it no longer merely refers to a generic type of good, but also signifies a specific set or attributes, such as a specific origin. "A name has acquired secondary meaning when the primary significance of the term in the minds of the consuming public is not the product but the producer." See *Welding Servs., Inc. v. Forman,* 509 F.3d 1351, 1358 (11th Cir.2007); *Coach House Rest.,* 934 F.2d at 1560. A person's first and last names can acquire secondary meaning beyond mere reference. "Names—both surnames and first names—are regarded as descriptive terms and therefore one who claims federal trademark rights in a name must prove that the name has acquired a secondary meaning." *Perini Corp. v. Perini Constr., Inc.,* 915 F.2d 121, 125 (4th Cir.1990); *815 Tonawanda St. Corp. v. Fay's Drug Co., Inc.,* 842 F.2d 643, 648 (2d Cir.1988) (same).

3. NEW YORK MISAPPROPRIATION STATUTE

NEW YORK PRIVACY STATUTE

NY CLS Civ R §§ 50, 51 (2007).

§ 50. Right of privacy

A person, firm or corporation that uses for advertising purposes, or for the purposes of trade, the name, portrait or picture of any living person without having first obtained the written consent of such person, or if a minor of his or her parent or guardian, is guilty of a misdemeanor.

§ 51. Action for injunction and for damages

Any person whose name, portrait, picture or voice is used within this state for advertising purposes or for the purposes of trade without the written consent first obtained as above provided may maintain an equitable action in the supreme court of this state against the person, firm or corporation so using his name, portrait, picture or voice, to prevent and restrain the use thereof; and may also sue and recover damages for any injuries sustained by reason of such use and if the defendant shall have knowingly used such person's name, portrait, picture or voice in such manner as is forbidden or declared to be unlawful by section fifty of this article, the jury, in its discretion, may award exemplary damages. But nothing contained in this article shall be so construed as to prevent any person, firm or corporation from selling or otherwise transferring any material containing such name, portrait, picture or voice in whatever medium to any user of such name, portrait, picture or voice, or to any third party for sale or transfer directly or indirectly to such a user, for use in a manner lawful under this article; nothing contained in this article shall be so construed as to prevent any person, firm or corporation, practicing the profession of photography, from exhibiting in or about his or its establishment specimens of the work of such establishment, unless the same is continued by such person, firm or corporation after written notice objecting thereto has been given by the person portrayed; and nothing contained in this article shall be so construed as to prevent any person, firm or corporation from using the name, portrait, picture or voice of any manufacturer or dealer in connection with the goods, wares and merchandise manufactured, produced or dealt in by him which he has sold or disposed of with such name, portrait, picture or voice used in connection therewith; or from using the name, portrait, picture or voice of any author, composer or artist in connection with his literary, musical or artistic productions which he has sold or disposed of with such name, portrait, picture or voice used in connection therewith. Nothing contained in this section shall be construed to prohibit the copyright owner of a sound recording from disposing of, dealing in, licensing or selling that sound recording to any party, if the right to dispose of, deal in, license or sell such sound recording has been conferred by contract or other written document by such living person or the holder of such right. Nothing contained in the foregoing sentence shall be deemed to abrogate or otherwise limit any rights or remedies otherwise conferred by federal law or state law.

TIME v. HILL

385 U.S. 374 (1967).

MR. JUSTICE BRENNAN delivered the opinion of the Court.

P

[James Hill] * * * his wife and five children involuntarily became the subjects of a front-page news story after being held hostage by three escaped convicts in their suburban, Whitemarsh, Pennsylvania, home for 19 hours on September 11–12, 1952. The family was released unharmed. In an interview with newsmen after the convicts departed, appellee stressed that the convicts had treated the family courteously, had not molested them, and had not been at all violent. The convicts were thereafter apprehended in a widely publicized encounter with the police which resulted in the killing of two of the convicts. Shortly thereafter the family moved to Connecticut. The appellee discouraged all efforts to keep them in the public spotlight through magazine articles or appearances on television.

D

In the spring of 1953, Joseph Hayes' novel, The Desperate Hours, was published. The story depicted the experience of a family of four held hostage by three escaped convicts in the family's suburban home. But, unlike Hill's experience, the family of the story suffer violence at the hands of the convicts; the father and son are beaten and the daughter subjected to a verbal sexual insult.

The book was made into a play, also entitled The Desperate Hours, and it is Life's article about the play which is the subject of appellee's action. The complaint sought damages under 50–51 on allegations that the Life article was intended to, and did, give the impression that the play mirrored the Hill family's experience, which, to the knowledge of defendant " * * * was false and untrue." Appellant's defense was that the article was "a subject of legitimate news interest," "a subject of general interest and of value and concern to the public" at the time of publication, and that it was "published in good faith without any malice whatsoever * * *." A motion to dismiss the complaint for substantially these reasons was made at the close of the case and was denied by the trial judge on the ground that the proofs presented a jury question as to the truth of the article.

PH

The jury awarded appellee $50,000 compensatory and $25,000 punitive damages. On appeal the Appellate Division of the Supreme Court ordered a new trial as to damages but sustained the jury verdict of liability. * * *

[W]e have had the advantage of an opinion of the Court of Appeals of New York which has materially aided us in our understanding of that court's construction of the statute * * *. The statute was enacted in 1903 following the decision of the Court of Appeals in 1902 in Roberson v. Rochester Folding Box Co., 171 N.Y. 538, 64 N.E. 442. * * *

[The New York's Civil Rights Law §§ 50 and 51 is not unconstitutional on its face. However, it must be interpreted, consistent with First Amendment principles, to bar press liability for false reports of newsworthy events, unless there is proof that the publisher knew of their falsity or acted in reckless disregard of the truth. See New York Times Co. v. Sullivan, 376 U.S. 254, 284–95 (1964).] * * *

The guarantees for speech and press are not the preserve of political expression or comment upon public affairs, essential as those are to healthy government. One need only pick up any newspaper or magazine to comprehend the vast range of published matter which exposes persons to public view, both private citizens and public officials. Exposure of the self to others in varying degrees is a concomitant of life in a civilized community. The risk of this exposure is an essential incident of life in a society which places a primary value on freedom of speech and of press.

FRIEDAN v. FRIEDAN

414 F.Supp. 77 (S.D.N.Y. 1976).

EDWARD WEINFELD, DISTRICT JUDGE.

Defendants move for summary judgment in this action brought under sections 50 and 51 of the Civil Rights Law of New York. Plaintiff seeks damages for the unauthorized use of his name and photograph in an article written by his former wife, Betty Friedan, and published in New York Magazine, both of whom are named as defendants with respect to that publication. He also seeks recovery of damages from three defendant broadcasting companies for the use of that photograph appearing on a page of the magazine broadcast in spot commercials on their television channels as part of an advertising campaign promoting the issue in which the article appeared.

The theme of the magazine issue was a twenty-five year throwback to the year 1949 described as "The Year We Entered Modern Times" with a series of articles. The Betty Friedan article, describing her life as a housewife in that year, was illustrated by the photograph, which pictured the author, her then husband, plaintiff Carl Friedan, and their son Danny in 1949.

Defendant Betty Friedan, as a leader of the feminist movement, is a public figure. All incidents of her life, including those which contrast with her present status and views, are significant in terms of the interest of the public in news. Thus, her connubial life and experience twenty-five years ago is a matter of public interest, and those who played a part in her life then may be referred to publicly.

Her former husband's right of privacy is subordinated to the public interest in news. In a family picture, which in a sense invades her then husband's privacy as one of the three shown in the picture, plaintiff cannot be separated from the other members of his family. As was put in Sidis v. F–R Pub. Corp.: "Everyone will agree that at some point the public interest in obtaining information becomes dominant over the individual's desire for privacy."

The picture of plaintiff together with his former wife and their child was related to and illustrative of the article describing her life twenty-five years ago, which was a matter of public interest. In this circumstance it cannot be considered used for the purpose of trade or advertising within the prohibition of the New York Civil Rights statute. "It has long been recognized that the use of name or picture in a newspaper, magazine, or newsreel, in connection with an item of news or one that is newsworthy, is not a use for purposes of trade within the meaning of the Civil Rights Law."

On the other hand, the use of plaintiff's photograph on television in commercials advertising the New York Magazine issue in which his former wife's article appeared was clearly "for advertising purposes." However, it has long been held that, under New York law, an advertisement, the purpose of which is to advertise the article, "shares the privilege enjoyed by the article" if the "article itself was unobjectionable."

Thus, although plaintiff alleges he has made every effort to disassociate himself from his former wife's public status to preserve his identity as a private person, he does not assert a cause of action under the New York Civil Rights Act. As the court held in Man v. Warner Bros., Inc., "[it] is plain that the restrictions on the application of Section 51 * * * are not limited to public figures." Matters of public interest may and often do involve wholly private individuals and may still be reported or depicted without entailing liability under section 51. While plaintiff here has not acted affirmatively to make himself newsworthy, within the limited context of his past relationship to defendant Betty Friedan, who is a public figure, such a role has been thrust upon him.

Since plaintiff has failed to state a claim under the New York Civil Rights Act upon which his complaint is exclusively grounded, the defendants' motion for summary judgment is granted.

FINGER v. OMNI PUBL'NS INT'L

77 N.Y.2d 138 (N.Y. 1990).

ALEXANDER, J.

Plaintiffs Joseph and Ida Finger commenced this action on behalf of themselves and their six children against defendant Omni Publications International, Ltd. seeking damages for the publication, without their consent, of a photograph of plaintiffs in conjunction with an article in Omni magazine discussing a research project relating to caffeine-aided fertilization.

The salient facts are uncontroverted. The June 1988 issue of Omni magazine included in its "Continuum" segment an article entitled "Caffeine and Fast Sperm", in which it was indicated that based on research conducted at the University of Pennsylvania School of Medicine, in vitro fertilization rates may be enhanced by exposing sperm to high concentrations of caffeine.

A photograph of plaintiffs depicting two adults surrounded by six attractive and apparently healthy children accompanied the article. The caption beneath the photograph read "Want a big family? Maybe your sperm needs a cup of Java in the morning. Tests reveal that caffeine-spritzed sperm swim faster, which may increase the chances for in vitro fertilization." Neither the article nor the caption mentioned plaintiffs' names or indicated in any fashion that the adult plaintiffs used caffeine or that the children were produced through in vitro fertilization.

Plaintiffs commenced this action alleging only violations of Civil Rights Law §§ 50 and 51. Defendant moved to dismiss the complaint, arguing that its use of the photograph in conjunction with the article did not violate Civil Rights Law §§ 50 and 51 because the picture was not used for trade or advertising but to illustrate a related news article on fertility. Defendant contended that because fertility is a topic of legitimate public interest, its use of the picture fit within the "newsworthiness exception" to the prohibitions of Civil Rights Law § 50. Supreme Court granted the motion on the authority of Arrington v New York Times (55 NY2d 433) and the Appellate Division affirmed. We granted leave to appeal and now affirm the Appellate Division.

Plaintiffs contend that defendant violated Civil Rights Law §§ 50 and 51 by using their photograph without their consent "for advertising purposes or for the purposes of trade."

We have repeatedly observed that the prohibitions of Civil Rights Law §§ 50 and 51 are to be strictly limited to nonconsensual commercial appropriations of the name, portrait or picture of a living person. These statutory provisions prohibit the use of pictures, names or portraits "for advertising purposes or for the purposes of trade" only, and nothing more * * *. The statute was a direct legislative response to our decision in Roberson v Rochester Folding Box Co. (171 NY 538) and was "drafted narrowly to encompass only the commercial use of an individual's name or likeness and no more." * * *

Although the statute does not define "purposes of trade" or "advertising," courts have consistently refused to construe these terms as encompassing publications concerning newsworthy events or matters of public interest * * *. [I]t is also well settled that " '[a] picture illustrating an article on a matter of public interest is not considered used for the purpose of trade or advertising within the prohibition of the statute * * * unless it has no real relationship to the article * * * or unless the article is an advertisement in disguise'." * * *

Plaintiffs do not contest the existence of this "newsworthiness exception" and concede that the discussion of in vitro fertilization and the use of caffeine to enhance sperm velocity and motility are newsworthy topics.

They contend, however, that their photograph bears "no real relationship" to the article, that none of plaintiffs' children were conceived by in vitro fertilization or any other artificial means, and that they never participated in the caffeine-enhanced reproductive research conducted at the University of Pennsylvania.

Consequently, according to plaintiffs, there was no "real relationship" between their photograph and the article, and any relationship that may exist is too tenuous to be considered a relationship at all. * * *

Plaintiffs misperceive the "newsworthy" theme of the article, which is fertility or increased fertility. Indeed, the article, in its opening sentences, observes that caffeine "can increase a man's fertility by boosting the performance of his sperm" and further indicates that "those who are looking for a fertility tonic shouldn't head for the nearest coffee pot" because the concentrations of caffeine used in the experiment "were so high [as to] be toxic."

The theme of fertility is reasonably reflected both in the caption beneath the picture, "Want a big family?", and the images used—six healthy and attractive children with their parents to whom each child bears a striking resemblance. Clearly then, there is a "real relationship" between the fertility theme of the article and the large family depicted in the photograph. That the article also discusses in vitro fertilization as being enhanced by "caffeine-spritzed sperm" does no more than discuss a specific aspect of fertilization and does not detract from the relationship between the photograph and the article.

As we have noted, the "newsworthiness exception" should be liberally applied * * *. The exception applies not only to reports of political happenings and social trends * * * and to news stories and articles of consumer interest such as developments in the fashion world * * * but to matters of scientific and biological interest such as enhanced fertility and in vitro fertilization as well. Moreover, questions of "newsworthiness" are better left to reasonable editorial judgment and discretion * * *; judicial intervention should occur only in those instances where there is " 'no real relationship' " between a photograph and an article or where the article is an " 'advertisement in disguise'."

We conclude here that it cannot be said, as a matter of law, that there is no "real relationship" between the content of the article and the photograph of plaintiffs. Thus the use of the photograph does not violate the prohibitions of Civil Rights Law §§ 50 and 51.

NOTE: USING PEOPLE

Explain the reasoning of the court in the *Finger* case. Compare it to the reasoning in the *Friedan* case. Is there a principled limit on the right of the media to "use" people for their own news or entertainment purposes? What do the *Friedan* case and the *Costanza* case, below, say about the risks of association with people who may someday become public figures?

COSTANZA v. SEINFELD

181 Misc. 2d 562 (N.Y. Sup. 1999).

HAROLD TOMPKINS, J.

A person is seeking an enormous sum of money for claims that the New York State courts have rejected for decades. This could be the plot for an episode in a situation comedy. Instead, it is the case brought by plaintiff Michael Costanza who is suing the comedian, Jerry Seinfeld, ~~P, Ds~~ Larry David (who was the cocreator of the television program Seinfeld), the National Broadcasting Company, Inc. and the production companies for $100 million. He is seeking relief for violation of New York's Civil Rights Law §§ 50 and 51, being cast in a false light, invasion of privacy and defamation. * * *

The substantive assertions of the complaint are that the defendants used the name and likeness of plaintiff Michael Costanza without his permission, that they invaded his privacy, that he was portrayed in a negative, humiliating light and that he was defamed by defendant Larry David when reports were published by a spokesman that plaintiff Michael Costanza had a tenuous connection and was a "flagrant opportunist" seeking to cash in when the hyperbole of the Seinfeld program's final episode was at its peak. Plaintiff Michael Costanza asserts that the fictional character of George Costanza in the television program Seinfeld is based upon him. In the show, George Costanza is a long-time friend of the lead character, Jerry Seinfeld. He is constantly having problems with poor employment situations, disastrous romantic relationships, conflicts with his parents and general self-absorption.

These aspects are part of the comedic interplay with Jerry Seinfeld and the other actors that lead to the great success of the television show Seinfeld. Plaintiff Michael Costanza points to various similarities between himself and the character George Costanza to bolster his claim that his name and likeness are being appropriated. He claims that, like him, George Costanza is short, fat, bald, that he knew Jerry Seinfeld from college purportedly as the character George Costanza did and they both came from Queens. Plaintiff Michael Costanza asserts that the self-centered nature and unreliability of the character George Costanza are attributed to him and this humiliates him. * * *

The issues in this case come before the court in the context of a preanswer motion to dismiss. At this stage of a legal proceeding, the court must read the allegations of the complaint as true and give them every favorable inference (see, Arrington v New York Times Co., 55 NY2d 433 [1982]). Even under this exceedingly favorable standard, plaintiff Michael Costanza's claims for being placed in a false light and invasion of privacy must be dismissed. They cannot stand because New York law does not and never has allowed a common-law claim for invasion of privacy * * *. In New York State, there is no common-law right to privacy * * * and any relief must be sought under the statute (Civil Rights Law §§ 50, 51).

The court now turns to the assertion that plaintiff Michael Costanza's name and likeness are being appropriated without his written consent. This claim faces several separate obstacles. First, defendants assert that plaintiff Michael Costanza has waived any claim by appearing on the show. * * * [Second,] [t]he Seinfeld television program was a fictional comedic presentation. It does not fall within the scope of trade or advertising * * *.

Plaintiff Michael Costanza's claim for violation of Civil Rights Law §§ 50 and 51 must be dismissed. Additionally, plaintiff Michael Costanza's claim under Civil Rights Law §§ 50 and 51 is barred by the Statute of Limitations. This type of case must be brought within one year of when a person learns of the improper use of his name or likeness * * *.

Finally, defendants seek sanctions against plaintiff for pursuing a frivolous lawsuit. A frivolous lawsuit is one for which there is no genuine basis either in law or fact, or good-faith argument for a change in the law * * *. In this regard, defendants placed plaintiff Michael Costanza on notice of the lack of any merit by writing to his lawyer citing the legal authority that barred this action prior to seeking dismissal of the lawsuit. At oral argument, the court also noted in particular the long-standing New York law that barred claims for invasion of privacy and being placed in a false light. * * * Essentially, plaintiff was informed that his case was based on nothing. While a program about nothing can be successful, a lawsuit must have more substance. The court awards sanctions in the sum of $2,500 each against plaintiff Michael Costanza and his attorney.

4. FLORIDA MISAPPROPRIATION STATUTE

NOTE: THE PERFECT STORM

In the *Tyne* case, excerpted below, the families of the Andrea Gail "Perfect Storm" victims unsuccessfully brought appropriation (and false light) claims against filmmakers. An entertainment or work of art, like a news story, is not a commercial appropriation of the identities of featured individuals, the court held. Do you agree? Is direct advertising the only sort of appropriation that should legally matter? *Pavesich* remains the paradigm.

TYNE v. TIME WARNER ENTM'T CO.

901 So.2d 802 (Fla. 2005).

WELLS, J. * * *

In October, 1991, a rare confluence of meteorological events led to a "massively powerful" weather system off the New England coast. The fishing vessel known as the Andrea Gail was caught in this storm and lost at sea. All six of the crewmembers on board the Andrea Gail, including Billy Tyne and Dale Murphy, Sr., were presumed to have been killed. Newspaper and television reports extensively chronicled the storm and its impact. Based on these reports, and personal interviews with meteorologists, local fisherman, and family members, Sebastian Junger penned a book, entitled The Perfect Storm: A True Story of Men Against the Sea, recounting the storm and the last voyage of the Andrea Gail and its crew. The book was published in 1997.

That same year, Warner Bros. purchased from Junger and his publisher the rights to produce a motion picture based on the book. Warner Bros. released the film, entitled The Perfect Storm, for public consumption in 2000. The Picture depicted the lives and deaths of Billy Tyne and Dale Murphy, Sr., who were the main characters in the film. It also included brief portrayals of each individual that is a party to this appeal. Nonetheless, Warner Bros. neither sought permission from the individuals depicted in the picture nor compensated them in any manner.

Unlike the book, the Picture presented a concededly dramatized account of both the storm and the crew of the Andrea Gail. For example, the main protagonist in the Picture, Billy Tyne, was portrayed as a down-and-out swordboat captain who was obsessed with the next big catch. In one scene, the Picture relates an admittedly fabricated depiction of Tyne berating his crew for wanting to return to port in Gloucester, Massachusetts. Warner Bros. took additional liberties with the land-based interpersonal relationships between the crewmembers and their families.

While the Picture did not hold itself out as factually accurate, it did indicate at the beginning of the film that "THIS FILM IS BASED ON A TRUE STORY." A disclaimer inserted during the closing credits elaborated on this point with the following statement: "This film is based on actual historical events contained in 'The Perfect Storm' by Sebastian Junger. Dialogue and certain events and characters in the film were created for the purpose of fictionalization."

On August 24, 2000, the Tyne and Murphy children * * * filed suit against Warner Bros. [in the United States District Court for the Middle District of Florida] seeking recompense under Florida's commercial misappropriation law [section 540.08, Florida Statutes (2000)] and for common law false light invasion of privacy. * * *

In Lane v. MRA Holdings, LLC, 242 F. Supp. 2d 1205 (M.D. Fla. 2002), the Middle District of Florida considered whether section 540.08 was violated by the defendants' display of the plaintiff exposing her breasts in a "Girls Gone Wild" video. The plaintiff had consented to being videotaped but was unaware that the video would be sold to the public.

The federal court rejected the plaintiff's section 540.08 argument, reasoning as follows:

Under Fla. Stat. § 540.08, the terms "trade," "commercial," or "advertising purpose" mean using a person's name or likeness to directly promote a product or service.

As a matter of law, this Court finds that Lane's image and likeness were not used to promote a product or service. In coming to this conclusion, this Court relies on section 47 of the Restatement (Third) of Unfair

Competition which defines "the purposes of trade" as follows: "The names, likeness, and other indicia of a person's identity are used 'for the purposes of trade' * * * if they are used in advertising the user's goods or services, or are placed on merchandise marketed by the user, or are used in connection with services rendered by the user." However, use "for the purpose of trade" does not ordinarily include the use of a person's identity in news reporting, commentary, entertainment, works of fiction or nonfiction, or in advertising incidental to such uses.

Therefore, under this definition, the "use of another's identity in a novel, play, or motion picture is * * * not ordinarily an infringement * * * [unless] the name or likeness is used solely to attract attention to a work that is not related to the identified person." Id. at comment c. * * *

[T]he Legislature enacted section 540.08 in 1967. Since that time, the only amendment to the statute was to rephrase it in gender neutral terms. The Legislature has not amended the statute in response to the decisions that have required that the statute apply to a use that directly promotes a product or service. This inaction may be viewed as legislative acceptance or approval of the judicial construction of the statute. Goldenberg v. Sawczak, 791 So. 2d 1078, 1083 (Fla. 2001).

For the foregoing reasons, we * * * hold that the term "commercial purpose" as used in section 540.08(1) does not apply to publications, including motion pictures, which do not directly promote a product or service.

G. THE RIGHT TO PUBLICITY TORT

1. RIGHTS IN A PERFORMANCE

ZACCHINI v. SCRIPPS–HOWARD BROADCASTING CO.

433 U.S. 562 (1977).

Mr. Justice White delivered the opinion of the Court.

Petitioner, Hugo Zacchini, is an entertainer. He performs a "human cannonball" act in which he is shot from a cannon into a net some 200 feet away. Each performance occupies some 15 seconds. In August and September 1972, petitioner was engaged to perform his act on a regular basis at the Geauga County Fair in Burton, Ohio. He performed in a fenced area, surrounded by grandstands, at the fair grounds. Members of the public attending the fair were not charged a separate admission fee to observe his act.

On August 30, a free-lance reporter for Scripps–Howard Broadcasting Co., the operator of a television broadcasting station and respondent in this case, attended the fair. He carried a small movie camera. Petitioner noticed the reporter and asked him not to film the performance. The reporter did not do so on that day; but on the instructions of the producer of respondent's daily newscast, he returned the following day and videotaped the entire act. This film clip, approximately 15 seconds in length, was shown on the 11 o'clock news program that night, together with favorable commentary.

Petitioner then brought this action for damages, alleging that he is "engaged in the entertainment business," that the act he performs is one "invented by his father and * * * performed only by his family for the last fifty years," that respondent "showed and commercialized the film of his act without his consent," and that such conduct was an "unlawful appropriation of plaintiff's professional property." * * *

We granted certiorari, 429 U.S. 1037 (1977), to consider an issue unresolved by this Court: whether the First and Fourteenth Amendments immunized respondent from damages for its alleged infringement of petitioner's state-law "right of publicity." * * *

There is no doubt that petitioner's complaint was grounded in state law and that the right of publicity which petitioner was held to possess was a right arising under Ohio law. * * *

The Ohio Supreme Court nevertheless held that the challenged invasion was privileged, saying that the press "must be accorded broad latitude in its choice of how much it presents of each story or incident, and of the emphasis to be given to such presentation." * * *

The Ohio Supreme Court relied heavily on Time, Inc. v. Hill, 385 U.S. 374 (1967), but that case does not mandate a media privilege to televise a performer's entire act without his consent. Involved in Time, Inc. v. Hill was a claim under the New York "Right of Privacy" statute that Life Magazine, in the course of reviewing a new play, had connected the play with a long-past incident involving petitioner and his family and had falsely described their experience and conduct at that time. * * *

The broadcast of a film of petitioner's entire act poses a substantial threat to the economic value of that performance. As the Ohio court recognized, this act is the product of petitioner's own talents and energy, the end result of much time, effort, and expense. Much of its economic value lies in the "right of exclusive control over the publicity given to his performance"; if the public can see the act free on television, it will be less willing to pay to see it at the fair. * * *

We conclude that although the State of Ohio may as a matter of its own law privilege the press in the circumstances of this case, the First and Fourteenth Amendments do not require it to do so.

NOTE: ONE SHOT DEAL

Why wasn't it just Zacchini's bad luck—or bad judgment—that he designed an act that could be easily captured in its entirety for broadcast on the evening news? Should public policy encourage the design of richer, more complex entertainments by not allowing plaintiffs like Zacchini to recover? Is it likely that a case like this case would come out differently today, in an age of personal video cameras, cell phone cameras and Youtube.com?

2.   RIGHTS IN A NAME

CARSON v. HERE'S JOHNNY PORTABLE TOILETS

698 F.2d 831 (6th Cir. 1983).

BROWN, J. * * *

Appellant, John W. Carson (Carson), is the host and star of "The Tonight Show," a well-known television program broadcast five nights a week by the National Broadcasting Company. Carson also appears as an entertainer in night clubs and theaters around the country. From the time he began hosting "The Tonight Show" in 1962, he has been introduced on the show each night with the phrase "Here's Johnny." This method of introduction was first used for Carson in 1957 when he hosted a daily television program for the American Broadcasting Company. The phrase "Here's Johnny" is generally associated with Carson by a substantial segment of the television viewing public. In 1967, Carson first authorized use of this phrase by an outside business venture, permitting it to be used by a chain of restaurants called "Here's Johnny Restaurants."

Appellant Johnny Carson Apparel, Inc. (Apparel), formed in 1970, manufactures and markets men's clothing to retail stores. Carson, the president of Apparel and owner of 20% of its stock, has licensed Apparel to use his name and picture, which appear on virtually all of Apparel's products and promotional material. Apparel has also used, with Carson's consent, the phrase "Here's Johnny" on labels for clothing and in advertising campaigns. In 1977, Apparel granted a license to Marcy Laboratories to use "Here's Johnny" as the name of a line of men's toiletries. The phrase "Here's Johnny" has never been registered by appellants as a trademark or service mark.

Appellee, Here's Johnny Portable Toilets, Inc., is a Michigan corporation engaged in the business of renting and selling "Here's Johnny" portable toilets. Appellee's founder was aware at the time he formed the corporation that "Here's Johnny" was the introductory slogan for Carson on "The Tonight Show." He indicated that he coupled the phrase with a second one, "The World's Foremost Commodian," to make "a good play on a phrase." * * *

The appellants also claim that the appellee's use of the phrase "Here's Johnny" violates the common law right of privacy and right of publicity. The confusion in this area of the law requires a brief analysis of the relationship between these two rights. * * *

We do not believe that Carson's claim that his right of privacy has been invaded is supported by the law or the facts. Apparently, the gist of this claim is that Carson is embarrassed by and considers it odious to be associated with the appellee's product. Clearly, the association does not appeal to Carson's sense of humor. But the facts here presented do not, it appears to us, amount to an invasion of any of the interests protected by the right of privacy. In any event, our disposition of the claim of an invasion of the right of publicity makes it unnecessary for us to accept or reject the claim of an invasion of the right of privacy.

The right of publicity has developed to protect the commercial interest of celebrities in their identities. The theory of the right is that a celebrity's identity can be valuable in the promotion of products, and the celebrity has an interest that may be protected from the unauthorized commercial exploitation of that identity. In Memphis Development Foundation v. Factors Etc., Inc., 616 F.2d 956 (6th Cir.), cert. denied, 449 U.S. 953 (1980), we stated: "The famous have an exclusive legal right during life to control and profit from the commercial use of their name and personality." * * *

Now, we've stipulated in this case that the public tends to associate the words "Johnny Carson", the words "Here's Johnny" with plaintiff, John Carson and, Mr. Braxton, in his deposition, admitted that he knew that and probably absent that identification, he would not have chosen it. * * *

That the "Here's Johnny" name was selected by Braxton because of its identification with Carson was the clear inference from Braxton's testimony irrespective of such admission in the opening statement.

We therefore conclude that, applying the correct legal standards, appellants are entitled to judgment. The proof showed without question that appellee had appropriated Carson's identity in connection with its corporate name and its product.

NOTE: HOW LONG?

Now deceased, Johnny Carson has been off the air for many years. Few young people remember him or his slogan. Should a new portable toilet company be able freely to use "Here's Johnny" as its brand name, now that the era of "The Tonight Show with Johnny Carson" has passed?

3. RIGHTS IN A FACIAL LIKENESS

MARTIN LUTHER KING, JR. CENTER FOR SOCIAL CHANGE v. AMERICAN HERITAGE PRODUCTS

250 Ga. 135 (Ga. 1982).

HILL, J. * * *

The plaintiffs are the Martin Luther King, Jr. Center for Social Change (the Center), Coretta Scott King, as administratrix of Dr. King's estate, and Motown Record Corporation, the assignee of the rights to several of Dr. King's copyrighted speeches. Defendant James F. Bolen is the sole proprietor of a business known as B & S Sales, which manufactures and sells various plastic products as funeral accessories. Defendant James E. Bolen, the son of James F. Bolen, developed the concept of marketing a plastic bust of Dr. Martin Luther King, Jr., and formed a company, B & S Enterprises, to sell the busts, which would be manufactured by B & S Sales. B & S Enterprises was later incorporated under the name of American Heritage Products, Inc.

Although Bolen sought the endorsement and participation of the Martin Luther King, Jr. Center for Social Change, Inc., in the marketing of the bust, the Center refused Bolen's offer. Bolen pursued the idea, nevertheless, hiring an artist to prepare a mold and an agent to handle the promotion of the product. Defendant took out two half-page advertisements in the November and December 1980 issues of Ebony magazine, which purported to offer the bust as "an exclusive memorial" and "an opportunity to support the Martin Luther King, Jr., Center for Social Change." The advertisement stated that "a contribution from your order goes to the King Center for Social Change." Out of the $29.95 purchase price, defendant Bolen testified he set aside 3% or $.90, as a contribution to the Center. The advertisement also offered "free" with the purchase of the bust a booklet about the life of Dr. King entitled "A Tribute to Dr. Martin Luther King, Jr."

In addition to the two advertisements in Ebony, defendant published a brochure or pamphlet which was inserted in 80,000 copies of newspapers across the country. The brochure reiterated what was stated in the magazine advertisements, and also contained photographs of Dr. King and excerpts from his copyrighted speeches. The brochure promised that each "memorial" (bust) is accompanied by a Certificate of Appreciation "testifying that a contribution has been made to the Martin Luther King, Jr., Center for Social Change."

Defendant James E. Bolen testified that he created a trust fund for that portion of the earnings which was to be contributed to the Center. The trust fund agreement, however, was never executed, and James E. Bolen testified that this was due to the plaintiffs' attorneys' request to cease and desist from all activities in issue. Testimony in the district court disclosed that money had been tendered to the Center, but was not accepted by its governing board. Also, the district court found that, as of the date of the preliminary injunction, the defendants had sold approximately 200 busts and had outstanding orders for 23 more.

On November 21, 1980, and December 19, 1980, the plaintiffs demanded that the Bolens cease and desist from further advertisements and sales of the bust, and on December 31, 1980, the plaintiffs filed a complaint in the United States District Court for the Northern District of Georgia. * * *

The right of publicity may be defined as a celebrity's right to the exclusive use of his or her name and likeness. * * * The right is most often asserted by or on behalf of professional athletes, comedians, actors and actresses, and other entertainers. This case involves none of those occupations. As is known to all, from 1955 until he was assassinated on April 4, 1968, Dr. King, a Baptist minister by profession, was the foremost leader of the civil rights movement in the United States. He was awarded the Nobel Prize for Peace in 1964. Although not a public official, Dr. King was a public figure, and we deal in this opinion with public figures who are neither public officials nor entertainers. Within this framework, we turn to the questions posed.

Georgia has long recognized the right of privacy. Following denial of the existence of the right of privacy in a controversial decision by the New York Court of Appeals in Roberson v. Rochester Folding Box Co., 171 N. Y. 538 (64 NE 442) (1902), the Georgia Supreme Court became the first such court to recognize the right of privacy in Pavesich v. New England Life Ins. Co., 122 Ga. 190 (50 SE 68) (1905). See Prosser, Law of Torts, pp. 802–804 (1971). * * *

Finding that Pavesich, although an artist, was not recognized as a public figure, the court said: "It is not necessary in this case to hold, nor are we prepared to do so, that the mere fact that a man has become what is called a public character, either by aspiring to public office, or by holding public office, or by exercising a profession which places him before the public, or by engaging in a business which has necessarily a public nature, gives to everyone the right to print and circulate his picture." 122 Ga. at 217–218 (50 SE at 79–80). Thus, although recognizing the right of privacy, the Pavesich court left open the question facing us involving the likeness of a public figure.

The "right of publicity" was first recognized in Haelan Laboratories v. Topps Chewing Gum, 202 F2d 866 (2d Cir. 1953). There plaintiff had acquired by contract the exclusive right to use certain ball players' photographs in connection with the sales of plaintiff's chewing gum. An independent publishing company acquired similar rights from some of the same ball players. Defendant, a chewing gum manufacturer competing with plaintiff and knowing of plaintiff's contracts, acquired the contracts from the publishing company. As to these contracts the court found that the defendant had violated the ball players' "right of publicity" acquired by the plaintiff * * *.

The right to publicity is not absolute. In Hicks v. Casablanca Records, 464 F.Supp. 426 (S.D.N.Y. 1978), the court held that a fictional novel and movie concerning an unexplained eleven-day disappearance by Agatha Christie, author of numerous mystery novels, were permissible under the first amendment. On the other hand, in Zacchini v. Scripps–Howard Broadcasting Co., 433 U.S. 562 (97 S.Ct. 2849, 53 L.Ed.2d 965) (1977), a television station broadcast on its news program plaintiff's 15–second "human cannonball" flight filmed at a local fair. The Supreme Court held that freedom of the press does not authorize the media to broadcast a performer's entire act without his consent, just as the media could not televise a stage play, prize fight or baseball game without consent. * * *

The right of publicity was first recognized in Georgia by the Court of Appeals in Cabaniss v. Hipsley, 114 Ga. App. 367 (151 SE2d 496) (1966). There the court held that the plaintiff, an exotic dancer, could recover from the owner of the Atlanta Playboy Club for the unauthorized use of the dancer's misnamed photograph in an entertainment magazine advertising the Playboy Club. Although plaintiff had had her picture taken to promote her performances, she was not performing at the Playboy Club. * * *

We know of no reason why a public figure prominent in religion and civil rights should be entitled to less protection than an exotic dancer or a movie actress. Therefore, we hold that the appropriation of another's name and likeness, whether such likeness be a photograph or sculpture, without consent and for the financial gain of the appropriator is a tort in Georgia, whether the person whose name and likeness is used is a private citizen, entertainer, or as here a public figure who is not a public official. * * *

[T]he right to privacy at least should be protectable after death. Pavesich, supra, 122 Ga. at 210 (50 SE at 76).

The right of publicity is assignable during the life of the celebrity, for without this characteristic, full commercial exploitation of one's name and likeness is practically impossible. * * *

In Factors Etc., Inc. v. Pro Arts, Inc., 579 F2d 215 (2d Cir. 1978), Elvis Presley had assigned his right of publicity to Boxcar Enterprises, which assigned that right to Factors after Presley's death. Defendant Pro Arts published a poster of Presley entitled "In Memory." In affirming the grant of injunction against Pro Arts, the Second Circuit Court of Appeals said (579 F2d at 221): "The identification of this exclusive right belonging to Boxcar as a transferable property right compels the conclusion that the right survives Presley's death. The death of Presley, who was merely the beneficiary of an income interest in Boxcar's exclusive right, should not in itself extinguish Boxcar's property right. Instead, the income interest, continually produced from Boxcar's exclusive right of commercial exploitation, should inure to Presley's estate at death like any other intangible property right. To hold that the right did not survive Presley's death, would be to grant competitors of Factors, such as Pro Arts, a windfall in the form of profits from the use of Presley's name and likeness. At the same time, the exclusive right purchased by Factors and the financial benefits accruing to the celebrity's heirs would be rendered virtually worthless." * * *

For the reasons which follow we hold that the right of publicity survives the death of its owner and is inheritable and devisable. Recognition of the right of publicity rewards and thereby encourages effort and creativity. If the right of publicity dies with the celebrity, the economic value of the right of publicity during life would be diminished because the celebrity's untimely death would seriously impair, if not destroy, the value of the right of continued commercial use. Conversely, those who would profit from the fame of a celebrity after his or her death for their own benefit and without authorization have failed to establish their claim that they should be the beneficiaries of the celebrity's death. Finally, the trend since the early common law has been to recognize survivability, notwithstanding the legal problems which may thereby arise. * * *

That we should single out for protection after death those entertainers and athletes who exploit their personae during life, and deny protection after death to those who enjoy public acclamation but did not exploit themselves during life, puts a premium on exploitation. Having found that there are valid reasons for recognizing the right of publicity during life, we find no reason to protect after death only those who took commercial advantage of their fame. * * *

Without doubt, Dr. King could have exploited his name and likeness during his lifetime. That this opportunity was not appealing to him does not mean that others have the right to use his name and likeness in ways he himself chose not to do. Nor does it strip his family and estate of the right to control, preserve and extend his status and memory and to prevent unauthorized exploitation thereof by others. Here, they seek to prevent the exploitation of his likeness in a manner they consider unflattering and unfitting. We cannot deny them this right merely because Dr. King chose not to exploit or commercialize himself during his lifetime.

NOTE: HONORING GIANTS

How does this case differ from *Schuyler v. Curtis*, 147 N.Y. 434 (1895), in which a family objected to the display of a statue in honor of a prominent New York woman?

Suppose the United States decided it wanted to mint a coin bearing the image of Dr. King. Would it be necessary to obtain permission from his heirs or estate? Does the fact that the government has created a national federal holiday honoring Dr. King have any bearing on the question?

DOE v. TCI CABLEVISION

110 S.W.3d 363 (Mo. 2003).

STEPHEN N. LIMBAUGH, JR. * * *

Tony Twist began his NHL career in 1988 playing for the St. Louis Blues, later to be transferred to the Quebec Nordiques, only to return to St. Louis where he finished his career in 1999, due to injuries suffered in a motorcycle accident. During his hockey career, Twist became the League's preeminent "enforcer," a player whose chief responsibility was to protect goal scorers from physical assaults by opponents. In that role, Twist was notorious for his violent tactics on the ice. * * *

Despite his well-deserved reputation as a tough-guy "enforcer," or perhaps because of that reputation, Twist was immensely popular with the hometown fans. He endorsed products, appeared on radio and television, hosted the "Tony Twist" television talk show for two years, and became actively involved with several children's charities. It is undisputed that Twist engaged in these activities to foster a positive image of himself in the community and to prepare for a career after hockey as a sports commentator and product endorser. * * *

Spawn is "a dark and surreal fantasy" [comic book created by Respondent Todd McFarlane] centered on a character named Al Simmons, a CIA assassin who was killed by the Mafia and descended to hell upon death. Simmons, having made a deal with the devil, was transformed into the creature Spawn and returned to earth to commit various violent and sexual acts on the devil's behalf. In 1993, a fictional character named "Anthony 'Tony Twist' Twistelli" was added to the Spawn storyline. The fictional "Tony Twist" is a Mafia don whose list of evil deeds includes multiple murders, abduction of children and sex with prostitutes. The fictional and real Tony Twist bear no physical resemblance to each other and, aside from the common nickname, are similar only in that each can be characterized as having an "enforcer" or tough-guy persona.

Each issue of the Spawn comic book contains a section entitled "Spawning Ground" in which fan letters are published and McFarlane responds to fan questions. In the September 1994 issue, McFarlane admitted that some of the Spawn characters were named after profession-al hockey players, including the "Tony Twist" character: "Antonio Twis-telli, a/k/a Tony Twist, is actually the name of a hockey player of the Quebec Nordiques." And, again, in the November 1994 issue, McFarlane stated that the name of the fictional character was based on Twist, a real hockey player, and further promised the readers that they "will continue to see current and past hockey players' names in my books." * * *

In October 1997, Twist filed suit against McFarlane and various companies associated with the Spawn comic book (collectively "respon-dents"), seeking an injunction and damages for, inter alia, misappropria-tion of name and defamation, the latter claim being later dismissed. McFarlane and the other defendants filed motions for summary judgment asserting First Amendment protection from a prosecution of the misappro-priation of name claim, but the motions were overruled. * * *

To establish the misappropriation tort, the plaintiff must prove that the defendant used the plaintiff's name without consent to obtain some advantage. Nemani v. St. Louis Univ., 33 S.W.3d 184, 185 (Mo. banc 2000); Haith, 704 S.W.2d at 687. In a right of publicity action, the plaintiff must prove the same elements as in a misappropriation suit, with the minor exception that the plaintiff must prove that the defendant used the name to obtain a commercial advantage. * * *

Here, all parties agree that the "Tony Twist" character is not "about" him, in that the character does not physically resemble Twist nor does the Spawn story line attempt to track Twist's real life. Instead, Twist maintains that the sharing of the same (and most unusual) name and the common persona of a tough-guy "enforcer" create an unmistakable corre-lation between Twist the hockey player and Twist the Mafia don that, when coupled with Twist's fame as a NHL star, conclusively establishes that respondents used his name and identity. This Court agrees. Indeed, respondent McFarlane appears to have conceded the point by informing his readers in separate issues of Spawn and in the Wizard article that the hockey player Tony Twist was the basis for the comic book character's name.

Arguably, without these concessions, some Spawn readers may not have made the connection between Twist and his fictional counterpart. However, other evidence at trial clearly demonstrated that, at some point, Spawn's readers did in fact make the connection, for both Twist and his mother were approached by young hockey fans under the belief that appellant was somehow affiliated with the Spawn character. * * *

Twist contends, and this Court again agrees, that the evidence admitted at trial was sufficient to establish respondents' intent to gain a commercial advantage by using Twist's name to attract consumer attention to Spawn comic books and related products. * * *

But this is not all. At trial, Twist introduced evidence that respondents marketed their products directly to hockey fans. For example, respondents produced and distributed Spawn hockey jerseys and pucks and sponsored a "Spawn Night" at a minor league hockey game where other Spawn products were distributed, including products featuring the character "Tony Twist." * * *

Having determined that Twist made a submissible case at trial, we next address whether the right of publicity claim is nevertheless prohibited by the First Amendment. * * *

Several approaches have been offered to distinguish between expressive speech and commercial speech. The Restatement, for example, employs a "relatedness" test that protects the use of another person's name or identity in a work that is "related to" that person. The catalogue of "related" uses includes "the use of a person's name or likeness in news reporting, whether in newspapers, magazines, or broadcast news * * * use in entertainment and other creative works, including both fiction and nonfiction * * * use as part of an article published in a fan magazine or in a feature story broadcast on an entertainment program * * * dissemination of an unauthorized print or broadcast biography, [and use] of another's identity in a novel, play, or motion picture * * *." Restatement (Third) of Unfair Competition sec. 47 cmt. c at 549. The proviso to that list, however, is that "if the name or likeness is used solely to attract attention to a work that is not related to the identified person, the user may be subject to liability for a use of the other's identity in advertising * * *."

California courts use a different approach, called the "transformative test," that was most recently invoked in Winters v. DC Comics, 30 Cal.4th 881, 69 P.3d 473 (Cal. 2003), a case with a remarkably similar fact situation. * * *

The weakness of the Restatement's "relatedness" test and California's "transformative" test is that they give too little consideration to the fact that many uses of a person's name and identity have both expressive and commercial components. These tests operate to preclude a cause of action whenever the use of the name and identity is in any way expressive, regardless of its commercial exploitation. * * *

[We find that if] * * * a product is being sold that predominantly exploits the commercial value of an individual's identity, that product should be held to violate the right of publicity and not be protected by the First Amendment, even if there is some "expressive" content in it that might qualify as "speech" in other circumstances. If, on the other hand, the predominant purpose of the product is to make an expressive comment on or about a celebrity, the expressive values could be given greater weight. * * *

The relative merit of these several tests can be seen when applied to the unusual circumstances of the case at hand. As discussed, Twist made a submissible case that respondents' use of his name and identity was for a commercial advantage. Nonetheless, there is still an expressive component in the use of his name and identity as a metaphorical reference to tough-guy "enforcers." And yet, respondents agree (perhaps to avoid a defamation claim) that the use was not a parody or other expressive comment or a fictionalized account of the real Twist. As such, the metaphorical reference to Twist, though a literary device, has very little literary value compared to its commercial value. On the record here, the use and identity of Twist's name has become predominantly a ploy to sell comic books and related products rather than an artistic or literary expression, and under these circumstances, free speech must give way to the right of publicity. * * *

In addition to the misappropriation of name claim, Twist sought equitable relief from the circuit court in the form of a permanent injunction prohibiting respondents from using his "name, commercial image, persona, autograph and/or likeness for any purpose without his consent." * * * The court denied equitable relief concluding, inter alia, that the injunction sought was overbroad because it could "interfere with legitimate and proper action by the defendants in the future." This Court holds that the circuit court was correct in doing so, because, as respondents state in their brief, the requested injunction attempted to prohibit respondents "from engaging in a variety of expressive activities unrelated to the subject matter of this lawsuit and undoubtedly protected by the First Amendment—e.g., a parody of plaintiff, a commentary on his fighting style, a factual report on this lawsuit." * * *

For the foregoing reasons, the circuit court's judgment notwithstanding the verdict is reversed, the judgment granting a new trial is affirmed, the judgment denying injunctive relief is affirmed, and the case is remanded.

4. CALIFORNIA RIGHT TO PUBLICITY STATUTE

CALIFORNIA PUBLICITY STATUTE STATE
SECTION 3344, SUBDIVISION (A)

"Any person who knowingly uses another's name, voice, signature, photograph, or likeness, in any manner, on or in products, merchandise, or goods, or for purposes of advertising or selling, or soliciting purchases of, products, merchandise, goods or services, without such person's prior consent * * * shall be liable for any damages sustained by the person or persons injured as a result thereof. In addition, in any action brought under this section, the person who violated the section shall be liable to the injured party or parties in an amount equal to the greater of seven hundred fifty dollars ($750) or the actual damages suffered by him or her as a result of the unauthorized use, and any profits from the unauthorized use that are attributable to the use and are not taken into account in computing the actual damages * * *."

MIDLER v. FORD MOTOR CO.

849 F.2d 460 (9th Cir. 1988).

JOHN T. NOONAN, CIRCUIT JUDGE:

This case centers on the protectability of the voice of a celebrated chanteuse from commercial exploitation without her consent. Ford Motor Company and its advertising agency, Young & Rubicam, Inc., in 1985 advertised the Ford Lincoln Mercury with a series of nineteen 30 or 60 second television commercials in what the agency called "The Yuppie Campaign." The aim was to make an emotional connection with Yuppies, bringing back memories of when they were in college. Different popular songs of the seventies were sung on each commercial. The agency tried to get "the original people," that is, the singers who had popularized the songs, to sing them. Failing in that endeavor in ten cases the agency had the songs sung by "sound alikes." Bette Midler, the plaintiff and appellant here, was done by a sound alike.

Midler is a nationally known actress and singer. She won a Grammy as early as 1973 as the Best New Artist of that year. Records made by her since then have gone Platinum and Gold. She was nominated in 1979 for an Academy award for Best Female Actress in The Rose, in which she portrayed a pop singer. Newsweek in its June 30, 1986 issue described her as an "outrageously original singer/comedian." Time hailed her in its March 2, 1987 issue as "a legend" and "the most dynamic and poignant singer-actress of her time."

When Young & Rubicam was preparing the Yuppie Campaign it presented the commercial to its client by playing an edited version of Midler singing "Do You Want To Dance," taken from the 1973 Midler album, "The Divine Miss M." After the client accepted the idea and form of the commercial, the agency contacted Midler's manager, Jerry Edelstein. The conversation went as follows: "Hello, I am Craig Hazen from

Young and Rubicam. I am calling you to find out if Bette Midler would be interested in doing * * *?'' Edelstein: "Is it a commercial?" "Yes." "We are not interested."

Undeterred, Young & Rubicam sought out Ula Hedwig whom it knew to have been one of "the Harlettes" a backup singer for Midler for ten years. Hedwig was told by Young & Rubicam that "they wanted someone who could sound like Bette Midler's recording of [Do You Want To Dance]." She was asked to make a "demo" tape of the song if she was interested. She made an a capella demo and got the job.

At the direction of Young & Rubicam, Hedwig then made a record for the commercial. The Midler record of "Do You Want To Dance" was first played to her. She was told to "sound as much as possible like the Bette Midler record," leaving out only a few "aahs" unsuitable for the commercial. Hedwig imitated Midler to the best of her ability.

After the commercial was aired Midler was told by "a number of people" that it "sounded exactly" like her record of "Do You Want To Dance." Hedwig was told by "many personal friends" that they thought it was Midler singing the commercial. Ken Fritz, a personal manager in the entertainment business not associated with Midler, declares by affidavit that he heard the commercial on more than one occasion and thought Midler was doing the singing.

Neither the name nor the picture of Midler was used in the commercial; Young & Rubicam had a license from the copyright holder to use the song. At issue in this case is only the protection of Midler's voice. The district court described the defendants' conduct as that "of the average thief." They decided, "If we can't buy it, we'll take it." The court nonetheless believed there was no legal principle preventing imitation of Midler's voice and so gave summary judgment for the defendants. Midler appeals.

The First Amendment protects much of what the media do in the reproduction of likenesses or sounds. A primary value is freedom of speech and press. Time, Inc. v. Hill, 385 U.S. 374 (1967). The purpose of the media's use of a person's identity is central. If the purpose is "informative or cultural" the use is immune; "if it serves no such function but merely exploits the individual portrayed, immunity will not be granted." Felcher and Rubin, "Privacy, Publicity and the Portrayal of Real People by the Media," 88 Yale L.J. 1577, 1596 (1979). Moreover, federal copyright law preempts much of the area. "Mere imitation of a recorded performance would not constitute a copyright infringement even where one performer deliberately sets out to simulate another's performance as exactly as possible." Notes of Committee on the Judiciary, 17 U.S.C.A. § 114(b). It is in the context of these First Amendment and federal copyright distinctions that we address the present appeal. * * *

California Civil Code section 3344 is also of no aid to Midler. The statute affords damages to a person injured by another who uses the person's "name, voice, signature, photograph or likeness, in any manner."

The defendants did not use Midler's name or anything else whose use is prohibited by the statute. The voice they used was Hedwig's, not hers. The term "likeness" refers to a visual image not a vocal imitation. The statute, however, does not preclude Midler from pursuing any cause of action she may have at common law; the statute itself implies that such common law causes of action do exist because it says its remedies are merely "cumulative." Id. § 3344(g).

The companion statute protecting the use of a deceased person's name, voice, signature, photograph or likeness states that the rights it recognizes are "property rights." Id. § 990(b). By analogy the common law rights are also property rights. Appropriation of such common law rights is a tort in California. * * *

Why did the defendants ask Midler to sing if her voice was not of value to them? Why did they studiously acquire the services of a sound-alike and instruct her to imitate Midler if Midler's voice was not of value to them? What they sought was an attribute of Midler's identity. Its value was what the market would have paid for Midler to have sung the commercial in person. * * *

A voice is as distinctive and personal as a face. The human voice is one of the most palpable ways identity is manifested. We are all aware that a friend is at once known by a few words on the phone. At a philosophical level it has been observed that with the sound of a voice, "the other stands before me." D. Ihde, Listening and Voice 77 (1976). A fortiori, these observations hold true of singing, especially singing by a singer of renown. The singer manifests herself in the song. To impersonate her voice is to pirate her identity. See W. Keeton, D. Dobbs, R. Keeton, D. Owen, Prosser & Keeton on Torts 852 (5th ed. 1984).

We need not and do not go so far as to hold that every imitation of a voice to advertise merchandise is actionable. We hold only that when a distinctive voice of a professional singer is widely known and is deliberately imitated in order to sell a product, the sellers have appropriated what is not theirs and have committed a tort in California. Midler has made a showing, sufficient to defeat summary judgment, that the defendants here for their own profit in selling their product did appropriate part of her identity.

DASTAR CORPORATION v. TWENTIETH CENTURY FOX FILM CORPORATION, ET AL.

539 U.S. 23 (2003).

SCALIA, JUSTICE

The Lanham Act was intended to make "actionable the deceptive and misleading use of marks," and "to protect persons engaged in ... commerce against unfair competition." 15 U.S.C. § 1127. While much of the Lanham Act addresses the registration, use, and infringement of trademarks and related marks, § 43(a), 15 U.S.C. § 1125(a) is one of the few provisions that goes beyond trademark protection. As originally enacted, § 43(a) created a federal remedy against a person who used in commerce either "a false designation of origin, or any false description or representation" in connection with "any goods or services." 60 Stat. 441. As the Second Circuit accurately observed with regard to the original enactment, however—and as remains true after the 1988 revision—§ 43(a) "does not have boundless application as a remedy for unfair trade practices," *Alfred Dunhill, Ltd. v. Interstate Cigar Co.,* 499 F.2d 232, 237 (C.A.2 1974). "[B]ecause of its inherently limited wording, § 43(a) can never be a federal 'codification' of the overall law of 'unfair competition,'" 4 J. McCarthy, Trademarks and Unfair Competition § 27:7, p. 27–14 (4th ed. 2002) (McCarthy), but can apply only to certain unfair trade practices prohibited by its text. * * *

Section 43(a) of the Lanham Act now provides:

"Any person who, on or in connection with any goods or services, or any container for goods, uses in commerce any word, term, name, symbol, or device, or any combination thereof, or any false designation of origin, false or misleading description of fact, or false or misleading representation of fact, which—

"(A) is likely to cause confusion, or to cause mistake, or to deceive as to the affiliation, connection, or association of such person with another person, or as to the origin, sponsorship, or approval of his or her goods, services, or commercial activities by another person, or

"(B) in commercial advertising or promotion, misrepresents the nature, characteristics, qualities, or geographic origin of his or her or another person's goods, services, or commercial activities,

shall be liable in a civil action by any person who believes that he or she is or is likely to be damaged by such act." 15 U.S.C. § 1125(a)(1).

WHITE v. SAMSUNG ELECTRONICS AMERICA, INC.

971 F.2d 1395 (9th Cir. 1992).

GOODWIN, CIRCUIT JUDGE * * *

Plaintiff Vanna White is the hostess of "Wheel of Fortune," one of the most popular game shows in television history. An estimated forty million people watch the program daily. Capitalizing on the fame which her participation in the show has bestowed on her, White markets her identity to various advertisers.

The dispute in this case arose out of a series of advertisements prepared for Samsung by Deutsch. The series ran in at least half a dozen publications with widespread, and in some cases national, circulation. Each of the advertisements in the series followed the same theme. Each depicted a current item from popular culture and a Samsung electronic product. Each was set in the twenty-first century and conveyed the message that the Samsung product would still be in use by that time. By hypothesizing outrageous future outcomes for the cultural items, the ads created humorous effects. For example, one lampooned current popular notions of an unhealthy diet by depicting a raw steak with the caption: "Revealed to be health food. 2010 A.D." Another depicted irreverent "news"—show host Morton Downey Jr. in front of an American flag with the caption: "Presidential candidate. 2008 A.D."

The advertisement which prompted the current dispute was for Samsung video-cassette recorders (VCRs). The ad depicted a robot, dressed in a wig, gown, and jewelry which Deutsch consciously selected to resemble White's hair and dress. The robot was posed next to a game board which is instantly recognizable as the Wheel of Fortune game show set, in a stance for which White is famous. The caption of the ad read: "Longest-running game show. 2012 A.D." Defendants referred to the ad as the "Vanna White" ad. Unlike the other celebrities used in the campaign, White neither consented to the ads nor was she paid.

Following the circulation of the robot ad, White sued Samsung and Deutsch in federal district court under: (1) California Civil Code § 3344; (2) the California common law right of publicity; and (3) § 43(a) of the Lanham Act, 15 U.S.C. § 1125(a). The district court granted summary judgment against White on each of her claims. White now appeals. * * *

White first argues that the district court erred in rejecting her claim under section 3344. Section 3344(a) provides, in pertinent part, that "any person who knowingly uses another's name, voice, signature, photograph, or likeness, in any manner, * * * for purposes of advertising or selling, * * * without such person's prior consent * * * shall be liable for any damages sustained by the person or persons injured as a result thereof."

In this case, Samsung and Deutsch used a robot with mechanical features, and not, for example, a manikin molded to White's precise features. Without deciding for all purposes when a caricature or impressionistic resemblance might become a "likeness," we agree with the district court that the robot at issue here was not White's "likeness" within the meaning of section 3344. Accordingly, we affirm the court's dismissal of White's section 3344 claim. * * *

White next argues that the district court erred in granting summary judgment to defendants on White's common law right of publicity claim. * * * The district court dismissed White's claim * * *, reasoning that defendants had not appropriated White's "name or likeness" with their robot ad. We agree that the robot ad did not make use of White's name or likeness. However, the common law right of publicity is not so confined. * * *

In Midler, this court held that, even though the defendants had not used Midler's name or likeness, Midler had stated a claim for violation of her California common law right of publicity because "the defendants * * * for their own profit in selling their product did appropriate part of her identity" by using a Midler sound-alike. Id. at 463–64.

In Carson v. Here's Johnny Portable Toilets, Inc., 698 F.2d 831 (6th Cir. 1983), the defendant had marketed portable toilets under the brand name "Here's Johnny"—Johnny Carson's signature "Tonight Show" introduction—without Carson's permission. The district court had dismissed Carson's Michigan common law right of publicity claim because the defendants had not used Carson's "name or likeness." Id. at 835. In reversing the district court, the sixth circuit found "the district court's conception of the right of publicity * * * too narrow" and held that the right was implicated because the defendant had appropriated Carson's identity by using, inter alia, the phrase "Here's Johnny." Id. at 835–37.

These cases teach not only that the common law right of publicity reaches means of appropriation other than name or likeness, but that the specific means of appropriation are relevant only for determining whether the defendant has in fact appropriated the plaintiff's identity. The right of publicity does not require that appropriations of identity be accomplished through particular means to be actionable. * * *

Indeed, if we treated the means of appropriation as dispositive in our analysis of the right of publicity, we would not only weaken the right but effectively eviscerate it. The right would fail to protect those plaintiffs most in need of its protection. Advertisers use celebrities to promote their products. The more popular the celebrity, the greater the number of people who recognize her, and the greater the visibility for the product. The identities of the most popular celebrities are not only the most attractive for advertisers, but also the easiest to evoke without resorting to obvious means such as name, likeness, or voice.

Consider a hypothetical advertisement which depicts a mechanical robot with male features, an African–American complexion, and a bald head. The robot is wearing black hightop Air Jordan basketball sneakers, and a red basketball uniform with black trim, baggy shorts, and the number 23 (though not revealing "Bulls" or "Jordan" lettering). The ad depicts the robot dunking a basketball one-handed, stiff-armed, legs extended like open scissors, and tongue hanging out. Now envision that this ad is run on television during professional basketball games. Considered individually, the robot's physical attributes, its dress, and its stance tell us little. Taken together, they lead to the only conclusion that any sports viewer who has registered a discernible pulse in the past five years would reach: the ad is about Michael Jordan.

Viewed separately, the individual aspects of the advertisement in the present case say little. Viewed together, they leave little doubt about the celebrity the ad is meant to depict. The female-shaped robot is wearing a long gown, blond wig, and large jewelry. Vanna White dresses exactly like this at times, but so do many other women. The robot is in the process of turning a block letter on a game-board. Vanna White dresses like this while turning letters on a game-board but perhaps similarly attired Scrabble-playing women do this as well. The robot is standing on what looks to be the Wheel of Fortune game show set. Vanna White dresses like this, turns letters, and does this on the Wheel of Fortune game show. She is the only one. Indeed, defendants themselves referred to their ad as the "Vanna White" ad. We are not surprised. * * *

In defense, defendants cite a number of cases for the proposition that their robot ad constituted protected speech. The only cases they cite which are even remotely relevant to this case are Hustler Magazine v. Falwell, 485 U.S. 46 (1988) and L.L. Bean, Inc. v. Drake Publishers, Inc., 811 F.2d 26 (1st Cir. 1987). Those cases involved parodies of advertisements run for the purpose of poking fun at Jerry Falwell and L.L. Bean, respectively. This case involves a true advertisement run for the purpose of selling Samsung VCRs. The ad's spoof of Vanna White and Wheel of Fortune is subservient and only tangentially related to the ad's primary message: "buy Samsung VCRs." Defendants' parody arguments are better addressed to non-commercial parodies. The difference between a "parody" and a "knock-off" is the difference between fun and profit. * * *

In remanding this case, we hold only that White has pleaded claims which can go to the jury for its decision.

HOFFMAN v. CAPITAL CITIES/ABC, INC.

33 F.Supp.2d 867 (C.D. Cal. 1999).

DICKRAN TEVRIZIAN, J. * * *

Plaintiff, Dustin Hoffman, is a highly successful and recognizable motion picture actor. For the past thirty years he has appeared in scores of motion pictures and has received numerous honors, including six Academy Award nominations and two Academy Awards. He has also been nominated and has been awarded a Golden Globe Award and an Emmy Award for his work. It can be said that Mr. Hoffman is truly one of our country's living treasures, joining the ranks of an exclusive handful of motion picture talent. * * *

Defendant, ABC, Inc. (formerly known as Capital Cities/ABC, Inc.), is owned by the Walt Disney Company. ABC, Inc. owns 100% of Defendant, Los Angeles Magazine, Inc., the publisher of Los Angeles Magazine. While many officers and corporate directors of ABC, Inc. serve on the Board of Directors of Los Angeles Magazine, Inc., insufficient evidence was presented to the Court to hold Defendant, ABC, Inc., liable on the theories of ratification and/or alter ego. In fact, the operative pleadings are silent as to these theories.

At Page 118 of its March 1997 issue [in conjunction with an article on shopping opportunities], Los Angeles Magazine published a photograph of Mr. Hoffman as he appeared to have appeared in the successful 1982 motion picture Tootsie, and through a process of technology employing computer imaging software, manipulated and altered the photograph to make it appear that Mr. Hoffman was wearing what appeared to be a contemporary silk gown designed by Richard Tyler and high-heel shoes designed by Ralph Lauren. Page 118 also contained the following text:

"Dustin Hoffman isn't a drag in a butter-colored silk gown by Richard Tyler and Ralph Lauren heels." * * *

Plaintiff's right of publicity claims proceed under the theory that Defendants' computerized manipulation of the Tootsie image and Defendants' publication of that manipulated image amount to an unauthorized use of Plaintiff's name and likeness. Plaintiff argues that his right to protect the use of his own name and image is separate from the copyrighted interest of Columbia in the motion picture Tootsie * * * This Court agrees. Plaintiff's own likeness and name cannot seriously be argued to constitute a "work of authorship" within the meaning of 17 U.S.C. § 102. Thus, copyright preemption does not apply. * * *

Plaintiff, Dustin Hoffman, has been damaged by Defendant, Los Angeles Magazine, Inc., for the unauthorized use of his name and likeness to endorse and promote articles of clothing designed by Richard Tyler and Ralph Lauren. In addition, Plaintiff, Mr. Hoffman, has been damaged by Defendant, Los Angeles Magazine, Inc., for the unauthorized use of his name and likeness as a "runway model."

The fair market value of Plaintiff's damages is the value that a celebrity of Mr. Hoffman's reputation, appeal, talent and fame would bring in the open market for this type of one-time use in a publication in a regional magazine, in the Los Angeles market area. The Court has considered the following five (5) factors in making its award:

1. Stature of Plaintiff in the motion picture industry for the past thirty (30) years;

2. The first-time use of Mr. Hoffman's name and likeness in a non-movie promotional context;

3. Self-perception by Plaintiff of what impact the commercial use of Plaintiff's name and likeness would have on executives in the motion picture industry as being less of a box office draw;

4. Uniqueness of opportunity in the role and character Plaintiff had created in the motion picture Tootsie; and,

5. The fact that the periodical involved was a regional periodical in the home town of the motion picture industry.

After considering these five (5) factors, this Court finds the Fair Market Value of Plaintiff's name and likeness used for endorsement purposes to be $1,500,000.

WINTER v. DC COMICS

30 Cal.4th 881 (Cal. 2003).

CHIN, J. * * *

Plaintiffs, Johnny and Edgar Winter, well-known performing and recording musicians originally from Texas, sued DC Comics and others alleging several causes of action including, as relevant here, appropriation of their names and likenesses under Civil Code section 3344. They alleged that the defendants selected the names Johnny and Edgar Autumn to signal readers the Winter brothers were being portrayed; that the Autumn brothers were drawn with long white hair and albino features similar to plaintiffs'; that the Johnny Autumn character was depicted as wearing a tall black top hat similar to the one Johnny Winter often wore; and that the title of volume 4, Autumns of Our Discontent, refers to the famous Shakespearian [sic] phrase, "the winter of our discontent." They also alleged that the comics falsely portrayed them as "vile, depraved, stupid, cowardly, subhuman individuals who engage in wanton acts of violence, murder and bestiality for pleasure and who should be killed." * * *

We have reviewed the comic books and attach a copy of a representative page. We can readily ascertain that they are not just conventional depictions of plaintiffs but contain significant expressive content other than plaintiffs' mere likenesses. Although the fictional characters Johnny and Edgar Autumn are less-than-subtle evocations of Johnny and Edgar Winter, the books do not depict plaintiffs literally. Instead, plaintiffs are merely part of the raw materials from which the comic books were synthesized. To the extent the drawings of the Autumn brothers resemble plaintiffs at all, they are distorted for purposes of lampoon, parody, or caricature. And the Autumn brothers are but cartoon characters—half-human and half-worm—in a larger story, which is itself quite expressive. The characters and their portrayals do not greatly threaten plaintiffs' right of publicity. Plaintiffs' fans who want to purchase pictures of them would find the drawings of the Autumn brothers unsatisfactory as a substitute for conventional depictions. * * *

NOTE: REPRODUCING CELEBRITIES

Why did the *Midler* court not go further and hold that all non-consensual imitations of a celebrity's voice in advertising is actionable? What did the defendants in *Midler* do that was distinctly wrong that other imitators might not do? In what respects did the robot ad at issue in *White* arguably violate Vanna White's publicity rights? Did Samsung view its robot as a substitute for the real Vanna White, the way Ford viewed the Midler sound-alike as a substitute for the real Bette Midler?

Judge Alex Kozinski vigorously dissented in the Vanna White case, urging that Samsung was engaged in constitutionally protected parody and asking "Where does White get this right to control our thoughts?" *White* at 1519. Kozinski summed up the problem in this way: "The panel's opinion is a classic case of overprotection. Concerned about what it sees as a wrong done to Vanna White, the panel majority erects a property right of remarkable and dangerous breadth: Under the majority's opinion, it's now a tort for advertisers to remind the public of a celebrity. Not to use a celebrity's name, voice, signature or likeness; not to imply the celebrity endorses a product; but simply to evoke the celebrity's image in the public's mind. This Orwellian notion withdraws far more from the public domain than prudence and common sense allow. It conflicts with the Copyright Act and the Copyright

Clause. It raises serious First Amendment problems. It's bad law, and it deserves a long, hard second look." *White* at 1514.

The Court in *Hoffman* awarded film star Dustin Hoffman, $1.5 million dollars because the defendant published a photo-collage of Hoffman made up as the character "Tootsie" and wearing a designer evening gown. Was Hoffman over-compensated? Was the photo-collage arguably a transformative work of art? Why does the court say that the computer manipulated image of Hoffman "cannot seriously be argued to constitute a work of authorship"? Johnny and Edgar Winter lost their case against D.C. Comics, whose artists evoked their identities in the character of "Johnny Autumn". The *Winter* court noted that fans wishing pictures of Johnny and Edgar would not purchase a D.C. Comics instead. One might ask, would a fan wanting a picture of Dustin Hoffman, find the computer-manipulated *Los Angeles Magazine* image an adequate substitute?

5. POSTHUMOUS PUBLICITY RIGHTS STATUTES

COMEDY III PRODS. v. GARY SADERUP

25 Cal.4th 387 (Cal. 2001).

Mosk, J.

A California statute grants the right of publicity to specified successors in interest of deceased celebrities, prohibiting any other person from using a celebrity's name, voice, signature, photograph, or likeness for commercial purposes without the consent of such successors.

In this state the right of publicity is both a statutory and a common law right. The statutory right originated in Civil Code section 3344 (hereafter section 3344), enacted in 1971, authorizing recovery of damages by any living person whose name, photograph, or likeness has been used for commercial purposes without his or her consent. Eight years later, in Lugosi v. Universal Pictures (1979) 25 Cal.3d 813 [160 Cal.Rptr. 323, 603 P.2d 425, 10 A.L.R.4th 1150] (Lugosi), we also recognized a common law right of publicity, which the statute was said to complement. * * * But because the common law right was derived from the law of privacy, we held in Lugosi that the cause of action did not survive the death of the person whose identity was exploited and was not descendible to his or her heirs or assignees. * * *

In 1984 the Legislature enacted an additional measure on the subject, creating a second statutory right of publicity that was descendible to the heirs and assignees of deceased persons. (Stats. 1984, ch. 1704, § 1, p. 6169.) The statute was evidently modeled on section 3344: many of the key provisions of the two statutory schemes were identical. The 1984 measure is the statute in issue in the case at bar. At the time of trial and while the appeal was pending before the Court of Appeal, the statute was numbered section 990 of the Civil Code.

Section 990 declares broadly that "Any person who uses a deceased personality's name, voice, signature, photograph, or likeness, in any manner, on or in products, merchandise, or goods, or for purposes of advertising or selling, or soliciting purchases of, products, merchandise, goods, or services, without prior consent from the person or persons specified in subdivision (c), shall be liable for any damages sustained by the person or persons injured as a result thereof. * * *'' The amount recoverable includes "any profits from the unauthorized use," as well as punitive damages, attorney fees, and costs. (Ibid.)

The statute defines "deceased personality" as a person "whose name, voice, signature, photograph, or likeness has commercial value at the time of his or her death," whether or not the person actually used any of those features for commercial purposes while alive.

The statute further declares that "The rights recognized under this section are property rights" that are transferable before or after the personality dies, by contract or by trust or will. Consent to use the deceased personality's name, voice, photograph, etc., must be obtained from such a transferee or, if there is none, from certain described survivors of the personality.

Any person claiming to be such a transferee or survivor must register the claim with the Secretary of State before recovering damages.

The right to require consent under the statute terminates if there is neither transferee nor survivor or 50 years after the personality dies.

The statute provides a number of exemptions from the requirement of consent to use. Thus a use "in connection with any news, public affairs, or sports broadcast or account, or any political campaign" does not require consent. * * *

Comedy III is the registered owner of all rights to the former comedy act known as The Three Stooges, who are deceased personalities within the meaning of the statute.

Saderup is an artist with over 25 years' experience in making charcoal drawings of celebrities. These drawings are used to create lithographic and silkscreen masters, which in turn are used to produce multiple reproductions in the form, respectively, of lithographic prints and silkscreened images on T-shirts. Saderup creates the original drawings and is actively involved in the ensuing lithographic and silkscreening processes.

Without securing Comedy III's consent, Saderup sold lithographs and T-shirts bearing a likeness of The Three Stooges reproduced from a charcoal drawing he had made. These lithographs and T-shirts did not constitute an advertisement, endorsement, or sponsorship of any product.

Saderup's profits from the sale of unlicensed lithographs and T-shirts bearing a likeness of The Three Stooges was $75,000 and Comedy III's reasonable attorney fees were $150,000. * * *

Saderup contends the statute applies only to uses of a deceased personality's name, voice, photograph, etc., for the purpose of advertising, selling, or soliciting the purchase of, products or services. He then stresses the stipulated fact (and subsequent finding) that the lithographs and T-shirts at issue in this case did not constitute an advertisement, endorsement, or sponsorship of any product. He concludes the statute therefore does not apply in the case at bar. As will appear, the major premise of his argument—his construction of the statute—is unpersuasive. * * *

Saderup's lithographic prints of The Three Stooges are themselves tangible personal property, consisting of paper and ink, made as products to be sold and displayed on walls like similar graphic art. Saderup's T-shirts are likewise tangible personal property, consisting of fabric and ink, made as products to be sold and worn on the body like similar garments. By producing and selling such lithographs and T-shirts, Saderup thus used the likeness of The Three Stooges "on * * * products, merchandise, or goods" within the meaning of the statute. * * *

Saderup next contends that enforcement of the judgment against him violates his right of free speech and expression under the First Amendment. He raises a difficult issue, which we address below. * * *

But having recognized the high degree of First Amendment protection for noncommercial speech about celebrities, we need not conclude that all expression that trenches on the right of publicity receives such protection. The right of publicity, like copyright, protects a form of intellectual property that society deems to have some social utility. "Often considerable money, time and energy are needed to develop one's prominence in a particular field." * * *

The present case exemplifies this kind of creative labor. Moe and Jerome (Curly) Howard and Larry Fein fashioned personae collectively known as The Three Stooges, first in vaudeville and later in movie shorts, over a period extending from the 1920's to the 1940's. * * * The three comic characters they created and whose names they shared—Larry, Moe, and Curly—possess a kind of mythic status in our culture. Their journey from ordinary vaudeville performers to the heights (or depths) of slapstick comic celebrity was long and arduous. * * * Through their talent and labor, they joined the relatively small group of actors who constructed identifiable, recurrent comic personalities that they brought to the many parts they were scripted to play. "Groucho Marx just being Groucho Marx, with his moustache, cigar, slouch and leer, cannot be exploited by others. Red Skelton's variety of self-devised roles would appear to be protectible, as would the unique personal creations of Abbott and Costello, Laurel and Hardy and others of that genre * * *. '[W]e deal here with actors portraying themselves and developing their own characters.' " * * *

In sum, society may recognize, as the Legislature has done here, that a celebrity's heirs and assigns have a legitimate protectible interest in exploiting the value to be obtained from merchandising the celebrity's image, whether that interest be conceived as a kind of natural property right or as an incentive for encouraging creative work. * * * Although critics have questioned whether the right of publicity truly serves any social purpose, there is no question that the Legislature has a rational basis for permitting celebrities and their heirs to control the commercial exploitation of the celebrity's likeness. * * *

[An] inquiry into whether a work is "transformative" appears to us to be necessarily at the heart of any judicial attempt to square the right of publicity with the First Amendment. * * * When artistic expression takes the form of a literal depiction or imitation of a celebrity for commercial gain, directly trespassing on the right of publicity without adding significant expression beyond that trespass, the state law interest in protecting the fruits of artistic labor outweighs the expressive interests of the imitative artist. * * *

On the other hand, when a work contains significant transformative elements, it is not only especially worthy of First Amendment protection, but it is also less likely to interfere with the economic interest protected by the right of publicity. * * *

In sum, when an artist is faced with a right of publicity challenge to his or her work, he or she may raise as affirmative defense that the work is protected by the First Amendment inasmuch as it contains significant transformative elements or that the value of the work does not derive primarily from the celebrity's fame. * * *

[W]e do not hold that all reproductions of celebrity portraits are unprotected by the First Amendment. The silkscreens of Andy Warhol, for example, have as their subjects the images of such celebrities as Marilyn Monroe, Elizabeth Taylor, and Elvis Presley. Through distortion and the careful manipulation of context, Warhol was able to convey a message that went beyond the commercial exploitation of celebrity images and became a form of ironic social comment on the dehumanization of celebrity itself. Such expression may well be entitled to First Amendment protection. * * *

Turning to Saderup's work, we can discern no significant transformative or creative contribution. His undeniable skill is manifestly subordinated to the overall goal of creating literal, conventional depictions of The Three Stooges so as to exploit their fame. Indeed, were we to decide that Saderup's depictions were protected by the First Amendment, we cannot perceive how the right of publicity would remain a viable right other than in cases of falsified celebrity endorsements.

Moreover, the marketability and economic value of Saderup's work derives primarily from the fame of the celebrities depicted. While that fact alone does not necessarily mean the work receives no First Amendment protection, we can perceive no transformative elements in Saderup's works that would require such protection. * * *

Thus, under section 990, if Saderup wishes to continue to depict The Three Stooges as he has done, he may do so only with the consent of the right of publicity holder.

MONTGOMERY v. MONTGOMERY

60 S.W.3d 524 (Ky. 2001).

JOHNSTONE, J.

Harold E. Montgomery was a musician in and around Garrard County in Central Kentucky. He wrote several songs that were recorded in small recording studios. Harold performed alone and with other musicians over a period of years at festivals in his local area. While he rarely appeared outside the Commonwealth of Kentucky, he did twice venture to Nashville, Tennessee, where he recorded a song entitled, "Let Me Be Young Again," and appeared on a local television show.

John Michael Montgomery, Harold's son by Harold's first wife, is a nationally-known country music star. With Harold's encouragement, John Michael took an early interest in country music. The two formed an extraordinary bond.

Harold married Barbara Rogers in 1988. * * *

Harold was diagnosed with cancer in 1993 and died in 1994. Barbara was the sole beneficiary of his estate under his will and was named as executrix thereof. She settled the estate informally and expeditiously.

In February 1997, John Michael released his fourth album, which contains the song entitled, "I Miss You a Little." The song is a tribute to [his father] Harold. Additionally, a music video of the song was released shortly afterwards. The video lies at the center of the controversy in this case. As found by the trial court, the music video is four minutes and twenty-seven seconds (4:27) long and Harold Montgomery's "likeness" appears in approximately thirty (30) seconds of the video as follows: (1) Harold is heard singing, "Let Me Be Young Again"; (2) Harold's gravestone appears; (3) a forty-five rpm record of "Let Me Be Young Again" bearing Harold's name appears; (4) a picture of Harold and John Michael performing together appears; (5) an article headed "John Michael is living out his father's dream" appears; (6) a picture of Harold performing appears; (7) Harold's gravestone appears a second time; (8) a second picture of John Michael and Harold performing together appears; and (9) the closing dedication states, "This song is written in memory of my father, Harold E. Montgomery." John Michael did not get permission from his father's estate to reproduce Harold's images or vocalizations contained in the music video.

The music video first aired nationally on or about March 3, 1997. Thereafter, Barbara, as executrix of Harold Montgomery's estate, filed suit claiming among other allegations that the use of Harold's likeness in the video violated his estate's common-law and statutory right of publicity. * * *

The only issue before us concerns the proper construction of KRS 391.170, which creates a posthumous right of publicity and provides:

(1) The General Assembly recognizes that a person has property rights in his name and likeness which are entitled to protection from commercial exploitation. The General Assembly further recognizes that although the traditional right of privacy terminates upon death of the person asserting it, the right of publicity, which is a right of protection from appropriation of some element of an individual's personality for commercial exploitation, does not terminate upon death.

(2) The name or likeness of a person who is a public figure shall not be used for commercial profit for a period of fifty (50) years from the date of his death without the written consent of the executor or administrator of his estate.

In this case, Harold's name, image, and voice were used in a music video. "Music, as a form of expression and communication, is protected under the First Amendment." Likewise, "entertainment * * * is protected; motion pictures, programs broadcast by radio and television, and live entertainment, such as musical and dramatic works, fall within the First Amendment guarantee." Therefore, we have little difficulty in concluding that the music video in question is protected free expression under the U.S. and Kentucky Constitutions. Thus, under the general rule, Barbara's right of publicity claim is not actionable. Like all rules, an exception exists, but it does not apply in this instance.

The use of a person's name or likeness or other interest protected by the right of publicity may be actionable when used within a work that enjoys First Amendment protection, if the use is not sufficiently related to the underlying work, or, if the otherwise constitutionally-protected work is "simply disguised commercial advertisement for the sale of goods or services." In this case, the use of Harold's likeness is intimately related to the underlying work (the song and music video are both a tribute to him) and the music video itself is not a disguised commercial advertisement for the sale of compact discs of either the single, "I Miss You A Little," or the album upon which it appears. This remains true even though music videos can be and are viewed as promotional films for the sale of music.

Most creative works are produced for sale and profit. This, of course, includes the songs that underlie music videos. While music videos are not produced primarily for the sale of the video but, rather, the underlying song, this does not strip them of their First Amendment protection. Music videos are in essence mini-movies that often require the same level of artistic and creative input from the performers, actors, and directors as is required in the making of motion pictures. Moreover, music videos are aired on television not as advertisements but as the main attraction, the airing of which, consequently, is supported by commercial advertisements. Simply put, the commercial nature of music videos does not deprive them of constitutional protection.

The fact that a person's likeness is used in a constitutionally-protected work to create or enhance profits does not make the use actionable.

Nor does the use of that person's name or likeness in an advertisement or promotion for the underlying work infringe upon a person's right of publicity. To put it another way, John Michael—without either the consent or approval of Harold's estate—could have produced a film biography of his father and promoted the film using Harold's name and likeness without violating Harold's estate's right of publicity (assuming it exists under the statute). He can do the same in a music video. Accord, Parks v. LaFace Records.

In Parks, the music group Outkast included a song entitled "Rosa Parks" on one of its albums, without Ms. Parks' permission. In 1955, Parks made a famous and heroic stance against racial inequality by refusing to give up her seat to a white person and move to the back of a bus. This single act of defiance sparked a bus boycott that ended segregation on public transportation in Montgomery, Alabama, which in turn was an important precursor to the Civil Rights Movement of the 1960s. Parks brought suit alleging inter alia that the use of her name violated her common-law right of publicity.

After concluding that both the song and the song's title were entitled to First Amendment protection, the district court stated, "The right of publicity is * * * inapplicable under the First Amendment if the content of an expressive work bears any relationship to the use of a celebrity's name." Upon review of the song, the district court found that there was an obvious metaphoric and symbolic relationship between the lyrics of the song, which contained numerous references to going to the back of the bus, and its title, "Rosa Parks." The district court then found, as a matter of law, that Parks' right of publicity claim was not applicable. The district court further concluded that the fact that Outkast profited from the sale of the song and album and heavily promoted the single, "Rosa Parks," did not affect this result.

Like the song title "Rosa Parks" and its lyrics, there exists a genuine connection between the use of Harold's name likeness in the music video "I Miss You a Little" and the song of the same name. Thus, we hold as a matter of law that Barbara Montgomery's right of publicity claim, which was brought under KRS 391.170 on behalf of Harold Montgomery's estate, is inapplicable in this case.

NOTE: POPULAR CULTURE

Is there an argument to be made that at some point popular culture belongs to the people—that the people should be able to exchange ideas and make products in response to visible personalities and achievements?

Should the law recognize differences between the publicity interests of people enjoying their first (and perhaps only) "fifteen minutes of fame" and enduring cultural icons? Who merits more protection, novices or icons?

6. EXTRATERRITORIAL PUBLICITY RIGHTS

LOVE v. ASSOCIATED NEWSPAPERS, LTD. ET AL.

611 F.3d 601 (C.A.9 (Cal.2010)).

THOMAS, CIRCUIT JUDGE:

This appeal presents the question, *inter alia,* of whether the Lanham Act and California's common law right of publicity apply extra-territorially to events occurring in Great Britain. Under the circumstances presented by this case, we conclude that such claims are not viable, and we affirm the judgments entered by the district court.

In 2004, founding Beach Boy member Brian Wilson, who had written (or co-written) most of the iconic Beach Boy hits, released a solo album called *Smile.* Wilson mounted a tour, with backup band, to support the album. It had been years since Brian Wilson had toured regularly with The Beach Boys. As part of settlement of earlier litigation, Mike Love, also a founding member of The Beach Boys, had acquired the right to use The Beach Boys trademark in live performances. He continued to tour as The Beach Boys with a varying lineup, playing hundreds of shows a year.

As part of a promotion campaign, the British newspaper the *Mail on Sunday* distributed a compact disc, consisting of Brian Wilson's solo versions of Beach Boy songs, along with his solo work, with approximately 2.6 million copies of the paper. The CDs were distributed in the United Kingdom and Ireland. Approximately 425 copies of that edition of the *Mail* were distributed in the United States without the CD, including 18 in California.

The cover of the distributed compact disc, entitled *Good Vibrations,* featured Brian Wilson, along with three smaller photographs of The Beach Boys. The small photographs of the group included a picture of Mike Love. The front page of the *Mail on Sunday* advertised the CD prominently, and included an image of the CD's cover. In addition to sound recordings, the CD contained two videos of live performances by Wilson's band.

Love was concerned that a second British invasion and Wilson's return to touring and recording would dampen ticket sales for the live performances of his touring group. Thus, in response to the English promotion, Love sued a variety of parties [including Wilson and his wife] for their involvement in the promotion campaign. * * *

The district court dismissed the complaint against [a number of the defendants]. * * *

The district court dismissed the claims for violation of California's statutory and common law rights of publicity after holding that English law, which does not recognize a right of publicity, governed. It dismissed three Lanham Act claims, two for lack of standing, and one after finding that the extra-territorial reach of the statute did not encompass the claims. * * *

The central issue before us is whether American claims for relief can be asserted on the basis of conduct that only occurred in Great Britain. The defendants think not. Love wishes they all could be California torts.

II

* * *

Although England does not recognize a right of publicity, it does provide celebrities with certain other limited protections against commercial misappropriation, including copyright, trademark, and the tort of "passing off." Alain J. Lapter, *How the Other Half Lives (Revisited): Twenty years since Midler v. Ford—A global perspective on the right of publicity,* 15 Tex. Intell. Prop. L.J. 239, 278–83 (2007). *See generally,* Julie King, *The Protection of Personality Rights for Athletes and Entertainers under English Intellectual Property Law: Practical difficulties in relying on an action of passing off,* 7 Sports Law. J. 351 (2000). Additionally, while England does not recognize a right to privacy as such, it does provide stronger protections against defamation than the United States. *See* J. Thomas McCarthy, 1 Rights of Publicity and Privacy § 6:155 (2d ed.) (explaining that England has never recognized a right to privacy); Raymond W. Beauchamp, Note, *England's Chilling Forecast: The case for granting declaratory relief to prevent English defamation actions from chilling American speech,* 74 Fordham L.Rev. 3073, 3077–91 (2006) (comparing American and English defamation law). Thus, we agree with the First Circuit that England has manifested "a policy choice favoring unrestricted competition in the area of commercial exploitation of names and likenesses." *Bi–Rite,* 757 F.2d at 445; *see also id.* ("In the area of publicity rights, as in the areas of trademark, patent, and copyright, the law must balance the competing goals, on the one hand, of facilitating public access to valuable images, inventions and ideas and, on the other, rewarding individual effort.").

Even if California has an interest in protecting the right of an entertainer with economic ties to the state to exploit his image overseas, that interest is not nearly as significant as England's interest in (not) regulating the distribution of millions of copies of a newspaper and millions of compact discs by a British paper primarily in the United Kingdom. * * *

* * * Love has the limited exclusive right to use The Beach Boys trademark in live performances. Love has alleged that the use of the mark "The Beach Boys" on and to promote *Good Vibrations,* in conjunction with the inclusion of video recordings of live performances on the disc, infringed upon and diluted his interests in the trademark, and competed with his live band unfairly. Sanctuary argues that because the creation, promotion, and distribution of *Good Vibrations* all occurred in Europe, the Lanham Act does not apply in this case. We agree with Sanctuary. * * *

We analyze the Lanham Act's coverage of foreign activities under a three-part test originally developed in the antitrust context. *See Star–Kist*

Foods, Inc. v. P.J. Rhodes & Co., 769 F.2d 1393, 1395 (9th Cir.1985) (citing *Timberlane Lumber Co. v. Bank of Am. Nat'l Trust & Sav. Ass'n,* 549 F.2d 597 (9th Cir.1976), *superseded by statute,* 15 U.S.C. § 6a). For the Lanham Act to apply extraterritorially: (1) the alleged violations must create some effect on American foreign commerce; (2) the effect must be sufficiently great to present a cognizable injury to the plaintiffs under the Lanham Act; and (3) the interests of and links to American foreign commerce must be sufficiently strong in relation to those of other nations to justify an assertion of extraterritorial authority. *Id.*

The first two criteria may be met even where all of the challenged transactions occurred abroad, and where "injury would seem to be limited to the deception of consumers" abroad, as long as "there is monetary injury in the United States" to an American plaintiff. * * *

Here, it is undisputed that all relevant acts occurred abroad. The idea for the CD originated with Ian Spero of BigTime.tv, who then approached ANL. BigTime.tv and ANL are both British entities. The CDs were physically manufactured by Optical Disc Services Limited, a company in Germany with offices in London. * * * The only CDs shown to have entered the United States never reached the market, as Wilson's attorney kept the CDs in his office until this litigation commenced. Although BigTime.tv did discuss the album with Wilson's attorney in California, it ignored the attorney's advice not to use the images of anyone other than Wilson, or at least to secure the permission of any other Beach Boy whose image would be used. * * *

Therefore, for the Lanham Act to apply, Love must have presented evidence that the complained of actions caused him monetary injury in the United States. Love' declaration—that his ticket sales in the United States were lower after the distribution of *Good Vibrations,* the release of *Smile,* and the U.S. tour embarked upon by Wilson—is insufficient. Even if, as Love argues, European purchasers of the *Mail of Sunday* would mistakenly associate the promotional CD with Love, *Smile,* and the official Beach Boys touring band, it is too great of a stretch to ask us, or a jury, to believe that such confusion overseas resulted in the decreased ticket sales in the United States.

Because Love failed to present any evidence that the alleged Lanham Act violations affected United States commerce in any way, we affirm dismissal * * * on that ground.

H. BREACH OF CONFIDENTIALITY

NOTE: TORTS, EVIDENTIARY PRIVILEGES AND PROFESSIONAL ETHICS

Confidentiality consists of limiting sensitive information to authorized recipients. People often feel that their privacy has been violated when the professionals with whom they deal reveal confidences. In this section, we take a look at the legal, personal and professional consequences of breaching confidences. The defendants in the excerpted cases include a physician, a hospital, a hospital worker, a rabbi, a priest and an attorney.

In some states, the invasion of privacy tort is a plausible civil remedy against a professional who breaches a confidence. In other states, a plaintiff may be able to rely on a state statute or a separate "breach of confidentiality" tort. What is the difference between publishing a private fact and breaching confidentiality?

The rules of civil and criminal procedure include evidentiary privileges that do not permit lawyers (and certain other professionals) to testify about matters revealed in confidence, unless their clients' consent. These rules of privilege are, in a sense, privacy laws. They protect the privacy of people who seek the professional help of attorneys and physicians, for example.

A client can sue her lawyer for malpractice for improperly revealing confidences. Moreover, a lawyer who reveals confidences can face disciplinary charges based on her state's adoption of American Bar Association Model Rules or Canons of Professional Conduct.

1. HEALTH PROVIDERS AND PATIENTS

HUMPHERS v. FIRST INTERSTATE BANK

298 Or. 706 (Or. 1985).

LINDE, J.

We are called upon to decide whether plaintiff has stated a claim for damages in alleging that her former physician revealed her identity to a daughter whom she had given up for adoption.

In 1959, according to the complaint, plaintiff, then known as Ramona Elwess or by her maiden name, Ramona Jean Peek, gave birth to a daughter in St. Charles Medical Center in Bend, Oregon. She was unmarried at the time, and her physician, Dr. Harry E. Mackey, registered her in the hospital as "Mrs. Jean Smith." The next day, Ramona consented to the child's adoption by Leslie and Shirley Swarens of Bend, who named her Leslie Dawn. The hospital's medical records concerning the birth were sealed and marked to show that they were not public. Ramona subsequently remarried and raised a family. Only Ramona's mother and husband and Dr. Mackey knew about the daughter she had given up for adoption.

Twenty-one years later the daughter, now known as Dawn Kastning, wished to establish contact with her biological mother. Unable to gain access to the confidential court file of her adoption (though apparently able to locate the attending physician), Dawn sought out Dr. Mackey, and he agreed to assist in her quest. Dr. Mackey gave Dawn a letter which stated that he had registered Ramona Jean Peek at the hospital, that although he could not locate his medical records, he remembered administering diethylstilbestrol to her, and that the possible consequences of this medication made it important for Dawn to find her biological mother. The latter statements were untrue and made only to help Dawn to breach the confidentiality of the records concerning her birth and adoption. In 1982, hospital personnel, relying on Dr. Mackey's letter, allowed Dawn to make copies of plaintiff's medical records, which enabled her to locate plaintiff, now Ramona Humphers.

Ramona Humphers was not pleased. The unexpected development upset her and caused her emotional distress, worry, sleeplessness, humiliation, embarrassment, and inability to function normally. She sought damages from the estate of Dr. Mackey, who had died, by this action against defendant as the personal representative. After alleging the facts recounted above, her complaint pleads for relief on five different theories. * * * We hold that if plaintiff has a claim, it arose from a breach by Dr. Mackey of a professional duty to keep plaintiff's secret rather than from a violation of plaintiff's privacy.

holding

Although claims of a breach of privacy and of wrongful disclosure of confidential information may seem very similar in a case like the present, which involves the disclosure of an intimate personal secret, the two claims depend on different premises and cover different ground. Their common denominator is that both assert a right to control information, but they differ in important respects. Not every secret concerns personal or private information; commercial secrets are not personal, and governmental secrets are neither personal nor private. Secrecy involves intentional concealment. "But privacy need not hide; and secrecy hides far more than what is private." Bok, Secrets 11 (1983).

For our immediate purpose, the most important distinction is that only one who holds information in confidence can be charged with a breach of confidence. If an act qualifies as a tortious invasion of privacy, it theoretically could be committed by anyone. In the present case, Dr. Mackey's professional role is relevant to a claim that he breached a duty of confidentiality, but he could be charged with an invasion of plaintiff's privacy only if anyone else who told Dawn Kastning the facts of her birth without a special privilege to do so would be liable in tort for invading the privacy of her mother.

Whether "privacy" is a usable legal category has been much debated in other English-speaking jurisdictions as well as in this country, especially since its use in tort law, to claim the protection of government against intrusions by others, became entangled with its use in constitutional law, to claim protection against rather different intrusions by government. No concept in modern law has unleashed a comparable flood of commentary, its defenders arguing that "privacy" encompasses related interests of personality and autonomy, while its critics say that these interests are properly identified, evaluated, and protected below that exalted philosophical level. * * *

A number of decisions have held that unauthorized and unprivileged disclosure of confidential information obtained in a confidential relationship can give rise to tort damages. * * *

One commentator, upon analyzing the cases allowing or denying recovery on a variety of theories, concluded that the tort consists in a breach of confidence in a "nonpersonal" confidential relationship, using the word "nonpersonal" to exclude liability for failing to keep secrets among members of a family or close friends. Note, Breach of Confidence: An Emerging Tort, 82 Colum. L. Rev. 1426 (1982). The problem with this formulation of civil liability lies in identifying the confidential relationships that carry a duty of keeping secrets. The writer suggests that the duty arises in all nonpersonal relationships "customarily understood" to carry such an obligation. * * *

A physician's duty to keep medical and related information about a patient in confidence is beyond question. It is imposed by statute. ORS 677.190(5) provides for disqualifying or otherwise disciplining a physician for "wilfully or negligently divulging a professional secret." The Court of Appeals thought that breach of this statutory provision could not lead to civil liability when such liability would be quite inappropriate to other provisions of ORS 677.190, but that misses the point. The actionable wrong is the breach of duty in a confidential relationship; ORS 677.190(5) only establishes the duty of secrecy in the medical relationship. See also ORS 192.525, ORS 192.530.

It is less obvious whether Dr. Mackey violated ORS 677.190(5) when he told Dawn Kastning what he knew of her birth. She was not, after all, a stranger to that proceeding. Lord Mansfield, in denying a common law privilege against testimony of the Duchess of Kingston's surgeon concerning the birth of her child, said that "[i]f a surgeon was voluntarily to reveal these secrets, to be sure he would be guilty of a breach of honor, and of great indiscretion;" but he was not speaking of revealing them to the child. If Ms. Kastning needed information about her natural mother for medical reasons, as Dr. Mackey pretended, the State Board of Medical Examiners likely would find the disclosure privileged against a charge under ORS 677.190(5); but the statement is alleged to have been a pretext designed to give her access to the hospital records. If only ORS 677.190(5) were involved, we do not know how the Board would judge a physician who assists at the birth of a child and decades later reveals to that person his or her parentage. But as already noted, other statutes specifically mandate the secrecy of adoption records. ORS 7.211 provides that court records in adoption cases may not be inspected or disclosed except upon court order, and ORS 432.420 requires a court order before sealed adoption records may be opened by the state registrar. Given these clear legal constraints, there is no privilege to disregard the professional duty imposed by ORS 677.190(5) solely in order to satisfy the curiosity of the person who was given up for adoption. See also ORS 192.525, ORS 192.530.

For these reasons, we agree with the Court of Appeals that plaintiff may proceed under her claim of breach of confidentiality in a confidential relationship. The decision of the Court of Appeals is reversed with respect to plaintiff's claim of invasion of privacy and affirmed with respect to her claim of breach of confidence in a confidential relationship, and the case is remanded to the circuit court for further proceedings on that claim.

MORRIS v. CONSOLIDATION COAL CO.

191 W.Va. 426 (W.Va. 1994).

McHUGH, JUSTICE: * * *

On July 10, 1991, Mr. Morris claims he was injured while working for Consolidation Coal Company when a board fell off a supply car and hit him on the left leg. He also claims that he sprained his back at work on the same date when a wheelbarrow he was pushing turned over. Mr. Morris states that he did not report to work on July 11 and 12, 1991, due to his injuries. Mr. Morris was examined by his physician. * * *

On September 16, 1991, Mark Hrutkay, a representative of Consolidation Coal Company, went to Dr. Schwarzenberg's office and asked to speak to the doctor about Mr. Morris. On that day, Mr. Hrutkay showed Dr. Schwarzenberg pictures and a video of Mr. Morris digging a trench for a water line on July 13, 15, and 16, 1991. Mr. Morris was not informed of the meeting until after it occurred. However, Mr. Morris has admitted that the photographs and video accurately depict him doing the work.

On that same day, Dr. Schwarzenberg wrote a letter to Workers' Compensation stating that he was unable to certify any disability for Mr. Morris from the July 10, 1991, injury based on the photographs and video. On September 23, 1991, Workers' Compensation sent a letter to Mr. Morris rejecting his application for temporary total disability (TTD) benefits based on a finding that Mr. Morris had not been injured in the course of employment.

Consolidation Coal Company suspended Mr. Morris from work on September 17, 1991. Pursuant to the collective bargaining agreement an arbitrator was appointed. The arbitrator upheld Consolidation Coal Company's decision to discharge Mr. Morris from work. Additionally, Mr. Morris attempted to obtain unemployment benefits; however, his application was rejected upon a finding of gross misconduct.

Eventually, Mr. Morris filed a civil action against Dr. Schwarzenberg for breaching his confidential physician-patient relationship by disclosing information to Consolidation Coal Company, and against Consolidation Coal Company for its willful, intentional and malicious interference with his "confidential relationship" with his treating physician. * * *

The defendants acknowledge that West Virginia has recognized a fiduciary relationship between a physician and patient. However, they argue that this relationship should not prohibit ex parte communication between the employer and the claimant's physician in a workers' compensation claim. * * *

As the defendants point out other jurisdictions have held that in the workers' compensation context, ex parte contacts with a claimant's treat-

ing physician are permissible in order to expeditiously resolve the claim.
* * *

Additionally, the defendants contend that even if a fiduciary relationship exists between a physician and the patient in a workers' compensation proceeding, this Court should conclude that the claimant waived this privilege by filing a claim. * * *

However, W. Va. Code, 23–4–7 [1991] does not specifically authorize oral discussions by an employer with a claimant's treating physician concerning a claimant's medical condition. In fact, W. Va. Code, 23–4–7 [1991], in part, specifically states that a physician may release to the claimant's employer "medical reports[.]" The term "medical reports" implies a written document. Moreover, we decline to follow the Supreme Court of Oregon's interpretation since that would circumvent the public policy principles behind recognizing a fiduciary relationship between a patient and a physician.

Although we decline to open the door to a free exchange of information between the treating physician and the employer, we recognize that in order to resolve a claim more expeditiously there may be times when the employer may need to verbally contact the treating physician. However, this oral ex parte communication is limited to the information contained in the written medical reports authorized by W. Va. Code, 23–4–7 [1991] or other routine inquiries which do not involve the exchange of confidential information. * **

The defendants also ask that this Court find that an employer's oral ex parte communication with the claimant's treating physician is allowed when the employer is investigating a possible fraud. * * *

Although we disapprove of any fraud and obviously agree that an alleged fraud should be investigated, we do not find that this is a sufficient reason to ignore the principles behind prohibiting unauthorized ex parte communication which involves the disclosure of confidential information between the employer and the claimant's treating physician. * * *

There are proper ways in which evidence of fraud can be submitted to the Workers' Compensation Fund without the physician having to participate in unauthorized ex parte communication. * * *

Accordingly, we hold that a fiduciary relationship exists between a treating physician and a claimant in a workers' compensation proceeding. This fiduciary relationship prohibits oral ex parte communication which involves providing confidential information and any other ex parte communication which involves providing confidential information which is not authorized under the statutes or procedural rules governing a workers' compensation claim between the treating physician and the adversarial party. When a claimant files a workers' compensation claim, he does consent to the release of written medical reports to the adversarial party pursuant to W. Va. Code, 23–4–7 [1991]; however, this consent does not waive the existing fiduciary relationship thereby permitting ex parte oral communication between the physician and the adversarial party which involves providing confidential information unrelated to the written medical reports authorized by W. Va. Code, 23–4–7 [1991]. * * *

The question now becomes what type of cause of action does the patient have against the treating physician for a breach of the fiduciary relationship. One writer notes that there are four theories upon which recovery may be based for a physician's wrongful disclosure: "(1) breach of the duty of confidentiality; (2) invasion of the right to privacy; (3) violation of statutes concerning physician conduct; and (4) breach of implied contract." Lonette E. Lamb, To Tell or Not to Tell: Physician's Liability for Disclosure of Confidential Information about a Patient, 13 Cumb. L. Rev. 617 (1983). See also Zelin, supra.

A review of the cases which have acknowledged the various causes of actions indicates that there has not been a universal acceptance by the courts of each of the four theories upon which recovery may be based for a physician's wrongful disclosure. We find that the more logical cause of action would be an action for the breach of the duty of confidentiality. After all, when a physician wrongfully discloses information, the right which is violated is the patient's right to have the information kept confidential. Additionally, the principle behind prohibiting unauthorized ex parte contacts between the adversary and the treating physician is to prevent the disclosure of irrelevant confidential information.

There are courts which have found that a cause of action for the breach of confidentiality exists when a physician wrongfully discloses patient information. * * * Accordingly, we hold that a patient does have a cause of action for the breach of the duty of confidentiality against a treating physician who wrongfully divulges confidential information. * * *

The last issue raised by the certified questions is whether a patient has a cause of action against a third party who induces the physician to breach his fiduciary relationship by disclosing confidential information. There are fewer cases on this issue than on the previous issue. However, there are courts which have recognized that patients have a cause of action against third parties who have induced a physician to release confidential information. * * *

Accordingly, we hold that a patient does have a cause of action against a third party who induces a physician to breach his fiduciary relationship if the following elements are met: (1) the third party knew or reasonably should have known of the existence of the physician-patient relationship; (2) the third party intended to induce the physician to wrongfully disclose information about the patient or the third party should have reasonably anticipated that his actions would induce the physician to wrongfully disclose such information; (3) the third party did not reasonably believe that the physician could disclose that information to the third party without violating the duty of confidentiality that the physician owed the patient; and (4) the physician wrongfully divulges confidential information to the third party.

BAGENT v. BLESSING CARE CORPORATION

862 N.E.2d 985 (Ill. 2007).

JUDGE FREEMAN * * *

In August 2001, Illini Hospital hired [Misty] Young as a phlebotomist, i.e., a person trained in drawing blood. In February 2003, the hospital required employees, including Young, to attend a training session regarding the Health Insurance Portability and Accountability Act of 1996 (HIPAA) (Pub. L. No. 104–191, 110 Stat. 1936) and its privacy provisions. Young attended the session and signed the hospital's confidentiality policy and code of conduct, acknowledging in each document that she understood and accepted its terms. Attendees at the training session received a motto to remember: "What you see here, and what you hear here, remains here." * * *

Young received a fax from a facility that performs tests for Illini Hospital. The fax contained results of plaintiff's blood test, which indicated to Young that plaintiff was pregnant. Young made two copies, one for plaintiff's physician and one for hospital records.

On a subsequent weekend night, Young and several of her friends visited a local tavern. Plaintiff's sister, Sarah Bagent, was a waitress there and happened to be one of Young's best friends. According to Young's deposition: "I didn't plan on going into the bar and trying to find Sarah, you know. The only thing I was thinking at the moment is, hi, Sarah, how are you, how is your sister doing?" Young further recounted her conversation with Sarah as follows:

"Little chitchat here and there, hi, how are you, what's going on, how have you been, who are you seeing, stuff like that. And then how is your sister, Suzanne, and how is she feeling? And she's [Sarah] like what do you mean? I'm like I thought she was pregnant, you know. And she's like no. And from there on out, I told her, I said I'm really sorry. Actually, I told her I was sorry. I said please don't tell Suzanne I said that I told you. Because she told me she's like how did you find this out? And she was just asking me more and more questions. And I'm like, well, I seen her result. I said that I could get fired for this, I'm really sorry, I didn't realize that you didn't know. I just assumed. And she's like, no, its okay, it's all right. She's like Suzanne won't care, blah, blah, blah."

Young explained that, as soon as she said it, she "instantly knew" that she had made a mistake.

Further, Young explained her disclosure as follows:

"[T]he only reason why I said something that evening was because [Sarah] was a friend of mine, and I was assuming that, one of my best friends and her twin and being sisters, that they would speak to each other about this. And I just assumed. And assuming makes an ass out of me."

That was the only conversation Young had with Sarah. Young testified in her deposition that they had subsequently avoided each other.

On October 13, 2003, plaintiff telephoned Connie Schroeder, chief executive officer of Illini Hospital, to complain that plaintiff's patient confidentiality had been violated. Upon investigation, Schroeder learned that Young had disclosed the information. On December 14, 2003, Young accepted the hospital's offer of resignation in lieu of termination.

Plaintiff timely filed a complaint, in which she pled separate counts not only against Young, but also against Illini Hospital under a theory of respondeat superior. Plaintiff alleged breach of health-care practitioner/patient confidentiality, invasion of privacy, negligent infliction of emotional distress and, against Young alone, intentional infliction of emotional distress * * *

In its answer, Illini Hospital admitted that Young discovered certain information about plaintiff from reviewing plaintiff's medical records and revealed that information to plaintiff's sister at a tavern. Illini Hospital further alleged, however, that when Young revealed the information, she was acting outside the scope of her employment with the hospital. * * *

The fact that Illini Hospital expressly forbade Young to reveal patient information bolsters our conclusion that Young's disclosure of plaintiff's medical records was not the kind of conduct she was employed to perform. Of course, an act of an employee, although forbidden, may be within the scope of employment. An employer cannot avoid vicarious liability for the misconduct of an employee by telling the employee to act carefully. Restatement (Second) of Agency § 230, Comment c, at 512 (1958). However, it must be remembered that an act is outside of the scope of employment if it has no connection with the conduct the employee is required to perform. Prohibition to perform acts, except those of a certain category, may indicate that the scope of employment extends only to acts of that category. Furthermore, the employer's prohibition may be a factor in determining, in an otherwise doubtful case, whether the act of the employee is incidental to the employment. The employer's prohibition accentuates the limits of the employee's permissible action and, hence, supports a finding that the prohibited act is entirely beyond the scope of employment. Restatement (Second) of Agency § 230, Comment c, at 512 (1958).

In the present case, not only was Young's disclosure of plaintiff's medical records not incidental to Young's employment, but the hospital plainly forbade Young from so doing. No reasonable person could conclude that Young's conduct was the kind she was employed to perform. * * *

Applying the correct legal standard to this case, there is no genuine issue of material fact as to Young's motivation for disclosing plaintiff's medical record. By her own candid admission, Young disclosed plaintiff's pregnancy to Sarah, plaintiff's sister, because Sarah was both plaintiff's sister and Young's friend. Young assumed, albeit incorrectly, that plaintiff had already related the information to Sarah. Young was in no way motivated to serve the hospital. As the dissent correctly reasoned, "nothing in the record supports an inference that Young was attempting to benefit or serve her employer when she divulged plaintiff's medical records. In fact, such disclosure was in direct contravention to the confidentiality agreements and did nothing to further the business of Illini Hospital." 363 Ill.App.3d at 925 (Turner, P.J., dissenting). We agree and so hold. See, e.g., Hentges v. Thomford, 569 N.W.2d 424, 427–29 (Minn. App. 1997) (holding that employee-minister was not motivated by purpose to serve employer-congregation when he accidentally shot parishioner during deer hunting). * * *

In the present case, * * * we uphold the circuit court's grant of summary judgment in favor of Illini Hospital.

SLOAN v. FARMER

217 S.W.3d 763 (Tex.App. 2007).

RICHTER, J. * * *

I. FACTUAL AND PROCEDURAL BACKGROUND.

Stephen Farmer suffered from chronic back pain, cervical disease, cervical facet arthoplasty, myfascial pain, and throracic outlet syndrome. Dr. Sloan is a pain management physician who was treating Farmer for his chronic pain syndrome. Pain Net Physicians Group, P.A. (Pain Net, P.A.) is Sloan's professional association. Pain Net of Texas, Inc. (Pain Net, Inc.) is the corporation that is alleged to have managed Sloan's practice.

Sloan prescribed a number of controlled substances during the course of Farmer's treatment, and required Farmer to execute a narcotic administration contract in connection with this treatment. Under the terms of the contract, Farmer agreed to only take medications prescribed by Sloan, and to submit to random urine and blood screen testing to detect the use of other medications. Failure to abide by the terms of the contract was a ground for terminating the patient-physician relationship.

Farmer was employed by TXU. In April 2003, Sloan determined that Farmer should be placed on light-duty work, and opined that Farmer was a good candidate for long-term disability. TXU removed Farmer from full-duty work with a continuation of his salary. Subsequently, TXU hired Concentra Integrated Services, Inc. to monitor Farmer's treatment with respect to the salary continuation program and the application for long-term disability. Naomi Garrett was the caseworker assigned to Farmer's case.

In August 2003, a random urine drug screen was performed by Sloan on Farmer, and he tested positive for a controlled substance that was not among the current medications Sloan had prescribed. Sloan concluded that Farmer had violated the narcotic contract. He reported his conclusion in a letter to Farmer that informed Farmer that he had tested positive for a substance not prescribed by him and terminated the patient-physician relationship. Sloan gave the letter to an employee at Pain Net, Inc., presumably for the purpose of filing with Farmer's patient records. The employee then provided a copy of the letter to Garrett, who in turn communicated the information to TXU. Farmer had not consented to the disclosure of this information. TXU confronted Farmer with the information before he had received Sloan's letter, and then terminated Farmer's benefits and employment.

On August 2, 2004, Farmer and his wife initiated this lawsuit, naming Sloan, Pain Net, Inc. and Pain Net, P.A. as defendants. The original petition asserted that the unauthorized disclosure of privileged medical information to Farmer's employer constituted slander and a violation of the physician-patient confidentiality privilege. Plaintiffs' original petition was later amended to include allegations that the disclosure also violated the Health Insurance Portability & Accountability Act (HIPPA), the Texas Medical Records Privacy Act (TMRPA), the Texas Rules of Evidence, and section 159.009 of the Texas Occupations Code. The amended petition acknowledges, however, that neither HIPPA nor the TMRPA provide a private remedy. In June 2005, plaintiffs' petition was amended for the second time to add Texas Pain Net, Inc. and Concentra as defendants and to assert an alleged violation of an additional federal statute.

Sloan and Pain Net, P.A. maintained that the Farmers' claims were health care liability claims and moved for dismissal with prejudice and an award of attorney's fees pursuant to section 74.351 of the civil practice and remedies code. The motions were based on the Farmers' failure to serve an expert report and curriculum vitae within the statutorily proscribed time. The Farmers responded that the claims were not medical negligence claims, and therefore no expert reports were required. The trial court granted the motions in part and denied them in part, dismissing all of the Farmers' claims "except for plaintiffs' claims and causes of action asserted for violation of the Texas Occupational Code § 159.09." This interlocutory appeal ensued.

II. MOTION TO DISMISS FOR FAILURE TO FILE EXPERT REPORT.

In a single issue, Sloan and Pain Net argue that the trial court erred in its partial denial of their motions to dismiss because the Farmers' claim for the unauthorized communication of confidential health care information is a health care liability claim subject to dismissal for noncompliance with the expert report requirement of the Texas Medical Liability and Insurance Improvement Act (the MLIIA). Based on our review of the record and the applicable law, we agree. * * *

C. The Farmers' Claim.

The Farmers' claim is based on Sloan's alleged breach of confidentiality. In this regard, the Farmers rely on the section of the occupations code that provides "[a] communication between a physician and a patient, relative to or in connection with any professional services as a physician to the patient, is confidential and privileged and may not be disclosed except as provided in this chapter." TEX. OCC.CODE ANN. § 159.002(a) (Vernon 2004). The statute further provides that a person aggrieved by the unauthorized release of confidential information may bring a cause of action for civil damages. *See* TEX. OCC.CODE ANN. § 159.009(b) (Vernon 2004).

Although the Farmers argue that their claim is not a health care liability claim, they concede in oral argument that Sloan did not intentionally communicate the confidential information to Farmer's employer, and that their claims sound in negligence. The essence of the claim is that Sloan breached his duty of confidentiality and the breach caused the Farmers to suffer damages. The question then becomes whether a physician's duty of confidentiality is an inseparable part of the rendition of health care services or based on a standard of care applicable to health care providers. Within the confines of the requisite analysis, we are constrained to conclude that the duty of confidentiality is inseparable from the health care services to be provided, and the claimed breach necessarily implicates the standard of care.

Maintaining the confidentiality of patient records is part of the core function of providing health care services. The patient's records reflect and memorialize the services that were rendered. The privilege between a physician and his patient is an expression of the standard in the health-care profession which recognizes the confidential nature of the scope of the relationship and the communications that occur within the context of that relationship. The letter from Sloan to Farmer concerned the terms of the relationship as defined in the narcotic administration contract. The urinalysis was part of Farmer's treatment. The Farmers' claim is based on an alleged departure from the standard of confidentiality applicable to this letter concerning the relationship and treatment.

Sloan and Pain Net argue that Sloan's decision to terminate the relationship also implicates the standard of care. We agree, but note that the reasons for termination exceed the scope of the underlying claim. The crux of the claim is not the termination of the relationship, but rather the allegedly careless manner in which the reasons for the decision were wrongfully communicated to a third party.

The statute that forms the basis of the Farmers' claim further illustrates the underlying nature of the claim. The types of communications that are privileged under the statute are those "relative to or in connection with any professional services as a physician to a patient." *See* TEX. OCC.CODE ANN. § 159.002(a) (Vernon 2004). The duty of confidentiality that arises under the statute results from the physician-patient relationship; the duty does not exist independent of the relationship. A party is aggrieved for purposes of recovering damages only if a physician-patient relationship exists. *Warnke v. Boone,* 4 S.W.3d 266, 268 (Tex.App.–Houston [14th Dist.] 1998, no pet.). We therefore conclude that any duty Sloan may have had to maintain the confidentiality of the health-care communication is inextricably intertwined with the physician-patient relationship and the health-care services to which the communication pertains.

The Farmers argue further that no medical expert testimony is required to set forth "the standard of patient-physician confidentiality" because the standard is set out in the statute. The expert report requirement, however, is a threshold requirement for the continuation of a lawsuit, not a requirement for recovery. *Murphy v. Russell,* 167 S.W.3d 835, 838 (Tex.2005). The fact that expert testimony may not be necessary to support a verdict does not mean the claim is not a health care liability claim. *Id.* In this case, the fact that expert *testimony* may or may not be required does not alter our conclusion about the claim.

Sloan and Pain Net also argue that the Farmers' claim is a health care liability claim because it involves an "administrative service." The Farmers respond that the claim can not be considered an administrative service because it does not involve physical injury or death. Because we have determined that the claimed breach of confidentiality involves a departure from accepted standards of medical or health care and is inseparable from the rendition of health care services, we need not decide whether the claim further comports with the definition of a health care liability claim.

III. CONCLUSION

We conclude that the Farmers' claim meets the statutory definition of a "health care liability claim" and is therefore subject to the expert report requirements of section 74.351(b). Because the Farmers failed to file an expert report, we reverse the portion of the trial court's order denying the motions to dismiss, render judgment in Sloan and Pain Net's favor dismissing the Farmers' claims with prejudice, and order that Sloan and Pain Net recover from the Farmers the costs of this appeal.

Sloan and Pain Net have also requested attorney's fees and costs incurred in the trial court, which are mandatory under the statute when a claimant fails to file an expert report in a health care liability claim. See TEX. CIV. PRAC. & REM.CODE ANN. § 74.351(b)(1). Accordingly, we remand this suit solely for a determination of costs and attorney's fees incurred by Sloan and Pain Net in the trial court.

2. PSYCHOTHERAPISTS AND PATIENTS

NOTE: THE TARASOFF RULE

Therapists are expected to keep their patients' secrets. They are not permitted to reveal secrets such as infidelity, closeted sexual orientation, or ruined finances. Therapists are required by state law to report child abuse and neglect about which they learn in the course of consultation. State law may also require that a therapist report to potential victims evidence that a patient has imminent plans to commit murder or other serious bodily harm.

This is the so-called Tarasoff rule from *Tarasoff v. Regents of the University of California*, 17 Cal.3d 425 (1976), imposing a duty on mental health-care providers to warn third parties of threats by their parents of serious bodily harm.

MORAVEK v. UNITED STATES

2008 WL 2383664.

[On November 10, 2004, plaintiff Steven G. Moravek, was indicted by a federal grand jury for violating 18 U.S.C. 471, Uttering Counterfeit Twenty–Dollar Federal Reserve Notes ($20.00 bills), in a case investigated by the United States Secret Service. On November 23, 2004, plaintiff was arraigned in U.S. District Court, entered a plea of not guilty and was placed on a personal recognizance bond.] * * *

On December 6, 2004 Plaintiff was seen pursuant to a pre-scheduled psychotherapy session by Dr. Carol Denier, a clinical psychologist licensed by the State of South Carolina. During that clinical visit, plaintiff made comments which Dr. Denier charted in the medical record relating to suicidal and homicidal ideations * * *:

> Pt reports another legal problem: was arrested for multiple charges of counterfeiting * * *. This has apparently exacerbated old fantasies of killing people because the 'system' is wrong. Denies intention or planning; reports thinking about 'taking people out as a statement,' or defending himself against agents who might come to the house with search warrants. Admits that 'innocent people' might suffer, but rationalizes this as it 'it must be part of God's plan—they were in that place for a reason.' * * *

* * * On December 7, 2004, Dr. Denier discussed the matter at length with Dr. Robert Rubey, the attending psychiatrist at the VA Medical Center–Charleston * * * Based on Dr. Denier's conversation with Dr. Rubey, she contacted attorney Reid Ellis, VA–Regional Counsel on December 7, 2004 by telephone, to discuss plaintiff's homicidal ideations and fantasies of going to the courthouse and "taking people out" and that plaintiff was actually scheduled to be at the federal courthouse approximately one week later. As a result of the telephone call, Mr. Ellis requested medical records relating to this issue. He received and reviewed said records.

On December 8, 2004, Mr. Ellis contacted the United States Attorney's Office–Charleston and confirmed that plaintiff was due in federal court on December 13, 2004. * * * As a result of the December 8, 2004 telephone conversation between the VA–Regional Counsel and the U.S. Attorney's Office, the United States Attorney's Office, on December 16, 2004, requested a copy of plaintiff's medical records * * *. * * *

On December 15, 2004, an Order was issued in plaintiff's criminal case for (1) plaintiff's personal recognizance bond to be revoked; (2) an arrest warrant was issued; and (3) an Order for plaintiff to undergo a psychiatric exam was issued.

On December 16, 2004, plaintiff was arrested by the US. Marshal Service; and on December 17, 2004, plaintiff appeared at his bond revocation hearing and was detained and transported to a federal facility to undergo a psychiatric examination to determine competency to stand trial on the criminal Indictment. [Plaintiff was found competent to stand trial, and on July 11, 2005 entered a guilty plea to the Indictment, and was sentenced on August 2, 2005.]

PLAINTIFF'S ALLEGATIONS AND CAUSES OF ACTION

Plaintiff's Complaint alleges that the VA Medical Center allowed the statements made by plaintiff during the December 6, 2004 clinical visit regarding the homicidal threats made against the federal law enforcement agents and others to be transmitted to the Assistant United States Attorney who was handling the criminal prosecution.

As a result of those allegations, plaintiff brings this cause of action under the [Federal Torts Claims Act, "FTCA"] for Breach of Privacy and Negligence. * * *

* * * The South Carolina Supreme Court ruled that physicians in South Carolina have a duty to maintain the confidentiality of doctor-patient communications. *South Carolina State Board of Medical Examiners v. Hedgepath,* 480 S.E. 2d 724, 726 (1997). The Court of Appeals followed by recognizing a cause of action in tort for breach of a physician's duty of confidentiality under the common law in the absence of a compelling public interest or other justification for the disclosure. *McCormick v. England,* 494 S.E. 2d 431, 437 (S.C. App. 1997). The tort of a physician's breach of confidentiality has been defined in general terms as the unconsented, unprivileged disclosure to a third party of nonpublic information that the defendant has learned within a confidential relationship. *Physician's Liability For Breach of Confidentiality: Beyond the Limitations Of The Privacy Tort* 49 S.C. Law Rev. 1271 (1997) citing Alan Vickery, *Breach of Confidence: An Emerging Tort,* 82 Colum. L. Rev. 1426, note 12, at 1455 (1982). * * *

The United States Supreme Court has recognized a "testimonial" psychotherapist-patient privilege, protecting confidential communications but identified an exception if a serious threat of harm to the patient or to others can be averted by means of a therapist. *Jaffee v. Redmond,* 116 S. Ct. 1923 (1996).

FIRST CAUSE OF ACTION: BREACH OF PRIVACY

Plaintiff alleges that he is entitled to recover damages for injuries under the theory of Breach of Privacy. Plaintiff sites S.C. Code Ann 44–20–90 and common law as providing the scheme for relief. His reliance is misplaced.

The tort of invasion of privacy (or breach of privacy as alleged by plaintiff) was first recognized in [South Carolina] *Holloman v. Life Insurance Co. Of Virginia,* 7 S.E. 2d 169 (1940). Then *Meetze v. Associated Press,* 95 S.E. 2d 606, 608 (1956) specified three distinct causes of action for invasion of privacy: (1) unwarranted appropriation of one's personality; (2) publicizing of one's private affairs with which the public has no legitimate interest; or (3) wrongful intrusion into one's private activities.

A communication to a single individual or to a small group of people will not give rise to an invasion (or breach) of privacy claim. This case involves a communication to an individual and not under any of the accepted causes of action for breach of privacy.

In the instant case, the confidential communication disclosed without consent went to the U.S. Attorney's Office. It was compelled. There was no publicity or publication. Therefore, there is no breach of privacy. * * *

SECOND CAUSE OF ACTION: NEGLIGENCE

* * * South Carolina recognizes a tortious recovery in common law for a psychotherapist's breach of confidential communications of a patient. However, South Carolina case law and statutory schemes prevent recovery in this case, and therefore, plaintiff failed to state a claim upon which relief can be granted, or in the alternative, no genuine issue of material fact exists and the defendant is entitled to judgment as a matter of law.

In this case, plaintiff communicated a homicidal and suicidal threat to his psychotherapist on December 6, 2004 relating to an identified Secret Service agent and other innocent persons that would be in the Courtroom at an upcoming scheduled hearing, stating that he would rather die than go to jail. At the time the threats were made, the possibility of plaintiff going to jail were real, in that he was formally charged by a federal Indictment. Based on the December 6, 2004 communication, in conjunction with Dr. Denier's knowledge of plaintiff, she was compelled to disclose.

The disclosure of the privileged communication by Dr. Denier to the U.S. Attorney's Office fits within the purview of the McCormick Court's exception to the common law tort of breach of confidentiality because the disclosure was compelled by law or was in the best interest of the patient and others. The disclosure by Dr. Denier was within the purview of the Privacy Act, 5 U.S.C. 522a. The disclosure by Dr. Denier was within the purview of the South Carolina confidentiality statute S.C. Code Ann. 19–11–95(C)(2). The disclosure by Dr. Denier was within the purview of HIPPA regulations.45 C.F.R. 164.512.

COMMON LAW DUTY TO WARN POTENTIAL VICTIMS

The seminal case on the liability of one treating a mentally afflicted patient for failure to warn or protect third persons threatened by a patient is *Tarasoff v. Regents of University of California,* 551 P.2d 334 (Ca. 1976). *Bishop v. South Carolina Department of Mental Health,* 502 S.E. 2d 78, 87

(S.C. 1998). When a defendant has the ability to monitor, supervise, and control an individual's conduct, a special relationship exists between the defendant and the individual, and the defendant may have a common law duty to warn potential victims of the individual's dangerous conduct. This duty to warn arises when the individual has made a specific threat of harm directed at a specific individual. *Bishop,* at 86.

The South Carolina Supreme Court has expanded *Bishop* by stating that the key is that there must be a specific threat made by the patient to harm a readily identifiable third party. *Doe v. Marion,* 645 S.E. 2d 245, 251 (S.C. 2007). In the instant case, we have a specific threat made against readily identifiable third parties. The threat was made which identified the place (The U.S. Courthouse), the time (Hearing set for December 13, 2004), the identifiable third parties (U.S. Secret Service agents that investigated his criminal case and innocent people specifically located at the U.S. Courthouse that were at that place for a reason that might suffer "as part of God's plan"), and a statement that plaintiff would rather die than go to jail (which was a very real possibility seeing that he was formally charged in a criminal indictment).

This court could easily determine from those facts that Dr. Denier had a common law duty to warn the federal authorities under the special relationship exception. * * *

SUMMARY JUDGMENT:

Summary judgment is appropriate only if there are no material facts in dispute and the moving party is entitled to judgment as a matter of law. * * *

In this case, the communications made by plaintiff are not in dispute. The dispute arises whether Dr. Denier breached her duty of confidentiality by disclosing privileged communications. There are no genuine issues of material fact in dispute that she was compelled by law and in the best interest of the patient and others to do so.

GRACEY v. EAKER

837 So. 2d 348 (Fla. 2002).

LEWIS, J.

[Donna and Joseph Gracey ("Graceys") sued their marriage counsel- P, D or, seeking to recover for emotional injuries. Each spouse alleges that psychotherapist Dr. Donald W. Eaker ("Eaker") revealed to the other spouse confidential information obtained in private individual therapy sessions, without consent.]

[T]he Graceys averred that Eaker is a licensed psychotherapist who, for profit, provided treatment to them in individual counseling sessions, ostensibly seeking to intervene in the most personal of matters directed to marital difficulties. They also alleged that Eaker, during individual thera- py sessions, would inquire about, and each of the [petitioners] would disclose to him, very sensitive and personal information that neither had disclosed to the other spouse at any time during their relationship. [Petitioners] would disclose this information because they were led to believe, by [Eaker], that such information was necessary for treatment purposes.

The petitioners further alleged that a direct violation of Florida law occurred in that despite being under a statutorily imposed duty to keep the disclosed information confidential, Eaker nevertheless unlawfully divulged to each of the petitioners "individual, confidential information which the other spouse had told him in their private sessions." Subsequent to these disclosures, the Graceys set forth that they realized that Eaker had devised "a plan of action * * * designed to get [them] to divorce each other." The Graceys claimed that such actions by Eaker constituted "breaches * * * of his fiduciary duty of confidentiality [that was] owed [individually] to [them]."

With regard to the damages resulting from Eaker's actions, the Graceys alleged that they have sustained severe mental anguish upon learning of [the] actions of the other spouse, of which they individually were not aware, and that [Eaker's] disclosure [of these actions] has caused irreparable damage to any trust that they would have had for each other * * *. [Moreover, they alleged that Eaker's] actions have caused great mental anguish for them individually in their personal relationships with others due to their inability to trust the others in those personal relationships. * * *

[W]e determine that the plaintiffs have presented a cognizable claim for recovery of emotional damages under the theory that there has been a breach of fiduciary duty arising from the very special psychotherapist-patient confidential relationship recognized and created under section 491.0147 of the Florida Statutes. * * *

In addition to our stated public policy and statutory structure of protection for certain confidential relationships, we have recently recognized the fiduciary duty generally arising in counseling relationships in Doe v. Evans, 814 So. 2d 370, 373–75 (Fla. 2002). There, one having marital difficulties alleged that a priest intervened in the situation and during counseling activities breached a duty of trust and confidence by becoming sexually involved with her. Recognizing the principles suggested in the Restatement (Second) of Torts, we noted that a fiduciary relationship does exist between persons when one is under a duty to act for or give advice for the benefit of another upon matters within the scope of the relationship. * * * Further, one in such a fiduciary relationship is subject to legal responsibility for harm flowing from a breach of fiduciary duty imposed by the relationship. See id.

With this backdrop of both common law and statutory protection the source of Eaker's duty to the petitioners is easily identified. The statutory scheme clearly mandated that the communications between the petitioners and Eaker "shall be confidential." § 491.0147, Fla. Stat. (1997). This created a clear statutory duty that, if violated, generated a viable cause of action in tort. * * *

The elements of a claim for breach of fiduciary duty are: the existence of a fiduciary duty, and the breach of that duty such that it is the proximate cause of the plaintiff's damages. Florida courts have previously recognized a cause of action for breach of fiduciary duty in different contexts when a fiduciary has allegedly disclosed confidential information to a third party. * * * Moreover, courts in other jurisdictions, along with legal commentators, have concluded that a fiduciary relationship exists between a mental health therapist and his patient. * * *

Clearly evident in the decisions of courts that have determined that a fiduciary relationship exists in the psychotherapist-patient and physician-patient contexts is the notion that a fiduciary has a duty not to disclose the confidences reposed in him by his patients. * * *

We emphasize that while we determine that a duty of confidentiality exists, it is not absolute. For instance, section 491.0147(1)–(3) of the Florida Statutes delineates three instances in which communications between patient and psychotherapist are not cloaked with confidentiality (none of which applies in the instant case). * * *

The "impact rule" requires that a plaintiff seeking to recover emotional distress damages in a negligence action prove that "the emotional distress * * * flows from physical injuries the plaintiff sustained in an impact [upon his person]." R.J. v. Humana of Florida, Inc., 652 So. 2d 360, 362 (Fla. 1995). Florida's version of the impact rule has more aptly been described as having a "hybrid" nature, requiring either impact upon one's person or, in certain situations, at a minimum the manifestation of emotional distress in the form of a discernible physical injury or illness. See Kush v. Lloyd, 616 So. 2d 415, 422 (Fla. 1992). We have stated that "the underlying basis for the [impact] rule is that allowing recovery for injuries resulting from purely emotional distress would open the floodgates for fictitious or speculative claims." R.J., 652 So. 2d at 362.

We have, however, in a limited number of instances either recognized an exception to the impact rule or found it to be inapplicable. In Kush v. Lloyd, we noted that the impact rule generally "is inapplicable to recognized torts in which damages often are predominately emotional." * * *

The emotional distress that the Graceys allege they have suffered is at least equal to that typically suffered by the victim of a defamation or an invasion of privacy. Indeed, we can envision few occurrences more likely to result in emotional distress than having one's psychotherapist reveal without authorization or justification the most confidential details of one's life. * * *

Therefore, we hold that the impact rule is inapplicable in cases in which a psychotherapist has created a fiduciary relationship and has breached a statutory duty of confidentiality to his or her patient. We therefore answer the rephrased certified question in the negative. We make no comment or determination regarding the merits of the instant case. * * *

We reaffirm * * * our conclusion that the impact rule continues to serve its purpose of assuring the validity of claims for emotional or psychic damages, and find that the impact rule should remain part of the law of this state.

Today we simply hold that the impact rule is inapplicable under the particular facts of the case before us.

NOTE: CONFIDENTIALITY IN HEALTH CARE

What harm can result from disclosing a medical confidence to someone's sister or adult child? Is it less acceptable to disclose an illness like cancer or AIDS than to disclose a pregnancy? Helen Nissenbaum maintains that norms of appropriateness "circumscribe the type and nature of information about various individuals that, within a given context, is allowable, expected, or even demanded to be revealed." Helen Nissenbaum, Privacy as Contextual Integrity, 79 *Wash. L. Rev.* 119, 136 (2004). Were norms of appropriateness implicated in *Bagent* and *Humphers*? Why or why not? Are norms of appropriateness also implicated by *Morris*?

Nissenbaum also maintains that norms of "information flow" govern disclosures. What norms concerning the proper distribution or flow of information were arguably violated in *Morris* and *Gracey*? Was the real error in Gracey the inherent conflict of interest involved in providing both individual and couples therapy to the parties in an ailing marriage?

In a different vein, philosopher Leslie Frances and a co-author have argued that enhancing patient and physician autonomy should be the goal of confidentiality in healthcare:

> The accepted rationale for health privacy and confidentiality is autonomy. [See Tom L. Beauchamp & James F. Childress, *Principles of Biomedical Ethics* 410 (4th ed. 1994).] A patient exercises his autonomy—based right of privacy when he shares (or declines to share) information with his healthcare provider or, for that matter, with anyone else. Any subsequent disclosure by the provider is policed by autonomy-based confidentiality. Constitutional and common law confidentiality protections suggested a rights-based approach to legal confidentiality that paralleled the autonomy principle. In contrast, the modern law of medical confidence (particularly the federal code) does not appear to be based on an autonomy model but on a more limited instrumental model.

> The simplest (and least corrosive) instrumental justification for medical confidentiality is that patients provide information to physicians to further their diagnosis with the correlate that physicians respect confidences in order to encourage patients to disclose personal and medical information that will make diagnosis and treatment more effective. This instrumental approach becomes dangerous when applied to institutional or industrial models of care. In such models, the notion too easily falls prey to arguments that see the generation, dispersal, and processing of

longitudinal patient health information primarily as a necessity to reduce overall healthcare costs and to minimize medical error. As the context changes, therefore, the simple and innocuous instrumental approach becomes increasingly problematic.

This movement to an instrumental rationale for protecting patient information was exacerbated by HIPAA [the central federal health privacy statute]. * * * [T]he federal standards have gutted the nascent rights-based approach to privacy and confidentiality, preferring an instrumental rationale that is almost totally focused on institutions and compliance.

See Leslie P. Francis and Nicolas Terry, Ensuring The Privacy and Confidentiality Electronic Health Records, 2007 *U. Ill. L.* Rev. 681, 699 (2007).

Traditionally, adoption records were sealed. The grounds for secrecy included allowing birth mothers to avoid stigma and get on with their lives; and enabling adopted children and their new families to lead normal lives. Prior to the 1980s, it was not uncommon for adoptive families to conceal the fact of adoption from their adopted children. In most instances of agency-facilitated adoption, families and birth mothers did not know one another's identities. The trend in recent years has been toward "open" adoptions in which birth families and adoptive families maintain a relationship. Many states have amended their laws to make it easier for adopted adults to learn the identities of their biological parents. Has adoption secrecy outlived its usefulness? See generally Sally Haslanger and Charlotte Witt (ed.), *Adoption Matters: Philosophical and Feminist Essays* (2005). Is a physician obligated to maintain birth parents' patient confidentiality respecting childbirth, even if adoption practices are open?

3. CLERGY AND CONGREGANTS

LIGHTMAN v. FLAUM

97 N.Y.2d 128 (N.Y. 2001).

GRAFFEO, J.

In this appeal, we must decide whether [state law] imposes a fiduciary duty of confidentiality upon members of the clergy that subjects them to civil liability for the disclosure of confidential communications. We hold that it does not.

After 15 years of marriage, plaintiff Chani Lightman initiated a divorce proceeding against her husband, Hylton Lightman, in February 1996. She also sought an order granting her temporary custody of the parties' four children. In opposition to plaintiff's application, her husband submitted, under seal, affirmations from two rabbis, apparently intending to show that his wife was jeopardizing the Orthodox Jewish upbringing of the children by not following religious law. Rabbi Tzvi Flaum, who was associated with the synagogue where the Lightmans were congregants, stated that plaintiff had advised him that she had stopped engaging in "religious purification laws" and was "seeing a man in a social setting." Similarly, Rabbi David Weinberger, an acquaintance of the Lightmans, in his affirmation indicated that plaintiff had acknowledged to him that "she freely stopped her religious bathing so [that] she did not have to engage in any sexual relations" with her husband, and he opined that plaintiff no longer wanted "to adhere to Jewish law despite the fact that she is an Orthodox Jew and her children are being raised Orthodox as well."

As a result of the rabbis' disclosures of those conversations, plaintiff commenced this action against them, asserting causes of action for breach of fiduciary duty in violation of the CPLR 4505 "clergy-penitent privilege" and intentional infliction of emotional distress against both rabbis and defamation against Rabbi Weinberger. * * *

Rabbi Flaum submitted two additional affirmations in which he expanded on the nature of his discussions with the Lightmans. He claimed that more than two years earlier Hylton Lightman first revealed marital problems to him. That conversation prompted plaintiff's mother to request that he speak with plaintiff. At the meeting, plaintiff and her mother berated him for discussing the marriage with plaintiff's husband and for giving advice without obtaining plaintiff's version of the situation. He alleged that plaintiff admitted to discontinuing her religious purification rituals and indicated she was socializing with men other than her husband. Rabbi Flaum further contended that these statements were not confidential because plaintiff never requested spiritual guidance and that, pursuant to Jewish law, he was obliged to relay this information to plaintiff's husband in order to prevent him from engaging in conjugal relations with his wife in violation of the Torah, as well as to shield the couple's children from exposure to plaintiff's improper conduct.

Rabbi Weinberger echoed this doctrinal explanation for the disclosures and alleged that he had met jointly, and separately, with the Lightmans. He claimed plaintiff was accompanied by a friend at these meetings on more than one occasion. Expressing surprise that plaintiff would have admitted her failure to follow religious laws of family purity while in the presence of a friend, Weinberger indicated that these revelations led him to believe the discussions were not confidential. Plaintiff disputed defendants' interpretation of religious law, and characterized her interactions with defendants as spiritual counseling received with the expectation that intimate information would remain confidential. * * *

The common law insulated certain confidential information from disclosure at trial, such as interspousal communications made during the course of a marriage (see, 1 McCormick, Evidence § 78, at 323–324 [5th ed 1999]). Eventually, special categories of confidential communications were deemed by statute to be entitled to a privilege against disclosure (see, Prince, Richardson on Evidence § 5–101, at 225 [Farrell 11th ed 1995]). CPLR article 45 codifies rules of evidence that restrict the admissibility of information obtained in specified confidential contexts, such as that which exists between spouses (CPLR 4502), attorney and client (CPLR 4503), physician and patient (CPLR 4504), psychologist and client (CPLR 4507) and social worker and client (CPLR 4508). In general, these statutes protect special relationships akin to fiduciary bonds, which operate and flourish "in an atmosphere of transcendent trust and confidence" (Aufrichtig v Lowell, 85 NY2d 540, 546).

The clergy-penitent privilege was unknown at common law (see, Matter of Keenan v Gigante, 47 NY2d 160, 166, cert denied sub nom. Gigante v Lankler, 444 US 887). It arose from the Roman Catholic sacrament of Penance, which requires sins to be disclosed to a priest who is prohibited by ecclesiastical law from revealing the substance of those disclosures even when the refusal to disclose results in imprisonment for contempt * * *.

Recognizing the value of extending the privilege to other religions (see, Second Prelim Rep of Advisory Comm on Prac & Pro, 1958 NY Legis Doc No. 13, at 93), the Legislature adopted CPLR 4505, which applies to confidential communications made by congregants to clerics of all religions (see, People v Carmona, 82 NY2d at 608–609). CPLR 4505 provides that unless "the person confessing or confiding waives the privilege, a clergyman, or other minister of any religion or duly accredited Christian Science practitioner, shall not be allowed [to] disclose a confession or confidence made to him in his professional character as spiritual advisor." A communication is not privileged merely because it is made to a cleric (see, Matter of Keenan v Gigante, 47 NY2d at 166). Rather, the statute's protection envelops only information imparted "in confidence and for the purpose of obtaining spiritual guidance" (People v Carmona, 82 NY2d at 609).

We find a distinction between confidential information under the rules and regulations that govern secular professionals and information cloaked by an evidentiary privilege under the CPLR. This difference demonstrates that statutory privileges are not themselves the sources of fiduciary duties but are merely reflections of the public policy of this State to proscribe the introduction into evidence of certain confidential information absent the permission of or waiver by a declarant. For example, in the attorney-client context, CPLR 4503 applies only to "confidential communication[s] made between the attorney or his employee and the client." The Code of Professional Responsibility, however, prohibits the disclosure not only of "confidences," defined as "information protected by the attorney-client privilege," but also of "secrets," described as "other information gained in the professional relationship that the client has requested be held inviolate or the disclosure of which would be embarrassing or would be likely to be detrimental to the client" (Code of Professional Responsibility DR 4–101 [a], [b] [22 NYCRR 1200.19 (a), (b)]). Thus, an attorney's duty of confidentiality is substantially broader than that reflected in CPLR 4503.

In fact, we have previously explained that a significant purpose of the Code of Professional Responsibility is to ensure "that attorneys remain faithful to the fiduciary duties of loyalty and confidentiality owed by attorneys to their clients" * * *.

A similar dichotomy between professional confidentiality obligations and evidentiary rules designed to preserve confidentiality exists for physicians and other health care professionals. CPLR 4504 prevents the disclosure of information "acquired in attending a patient in a professional capacity, and which was necessary to enable [the physician or other health care professional] to act in that capacity." Nevertheless, information obtained in a professional capacity but not necessary to enable the physician to fulfill his or her medical role is a protected confidence, the disclosure of which constitutes professional misconduct in the absence of patient consent or legal authorization (see, Education Law § 6530 [23]; see also, 8 NYCRR 29.1 [b] [8]). Thus, although the statutory privileges may in some instances overlap with the applicable fiduciary duties of confidentiality which have been defined elsewhere in the law, those evidentiary rules are not the sources of the underlying duties, and article 45 does not establish the parameters of those fiduciary relationships.

The clergy and the other classes of professionals specified in CPLR article 45 are also fundamentally different with respect to the extent of State regulation of their professional practices. Individuals employed in other fields subject to statutory privileges derive their authority to practice from the State, which conditions the issuance of a license on, among other requirements, the completion of formalized education and/or training * * *. In contrast, clerics are free to engage in religious activities without the State's permission, they are not subject to State-dictated educational prerequisites and, significantly, no comprehensive statutory scheme regulates the clergy-congregant spiritual counseling relationship. This explains plaintiff's inability to identify a source of defendants' alleged duty of confidentiality independent of CPLR 4505. * * *

The United States Constitution protects the right of individuals to "believe what they cannot prove. They may not be put to the proof of their religious doctrines or beliefs * * * If those doctrines are subject to trial before a jury charged with finding their truth or falsity, then the same can be done with the religious beliefs of any sect. When the triers of fact undertake that task, they enter a forbidden domain" (United States v Ballard, 322 US 78, 86–87). As we explained in a different context, "civil courts are forbidden from interfering in or determining religious disputes. Such rulings violate the First Amendment because they simultaneously establish one religious belief as correct * * * while interfering with the free exercise of the opposing faction's beliefs" * * *.

Guided by these well-settled principles and in the absence of a statute, regulation or other source delineating the scope and nature of the alleged fiduciary duty, we view the CPLR 4505 privilege in the manner intended by the Legislature—as a rule of evidence and not as the basis of a private cause of action. Although plaintiff understandably resents the disclosure of intimate information she claims she revealed to defendants in their role as spiritual counselors, we hold that, as a matter of law, CPLR 4505—directed at the admissibility of evidence—does not give rise to a cause of action for breach of a fiduciary duty involving the disclosure of oral communications between a congregant and a cleric. Remittal for factual determinations is thus unnecessary and defendants are entitled to summary judgment dismissing the first and second causes of action.

EX PARTE FATHER PAUL G. ZOGHBY

958 So.2d 314 (Ala. 2006).

STUART, JUSTICE.

Linda Ledet and her husband and children were parishioners at St. Mary's Catholic Church in Mobile from 1995 through 2001. During that time, Zoghby, who was an associate priest at St. Mary's at that time, developed a friendship with Ledet. According to Ledet, in late 1997 Zoghby began making improper and unwelcome advances toward her, including attempting to physically embrace her in an intimate or sexual manner, touching her on intimate parts of her body in a sexual manner, making lewd and sexually suggestive comments to her, exposing his genitalia to her, and attempting to force her, physically and by command as a priest, to engage in sexual relations with him.

During the summer of 2002, after attending a meeting described as an "open invitation to victims of abuse" sponsored by the Catholic Archdiocese of Mobile, Ledet filed a formal written complaint with the Archdiocese, asserting claims of sexual misconduct against Zoghby. This complaint was reviewed by Archbishop Oscar Lipscomb and Chancellor Michael Farmer. In his deposition testimony, Archbishop Lipscomb explained that when allegations of sexual misconduct are made, the Archbishop is responsible for directing the investigation into the alleged misconduct for the Archdiocese and for making a judgment and disposing of the complaint. He stated that because Ledet requested strict confidentiality in this matter, he investigated her claims himself.

Archbishop Lipscomb stated that when he began his investigation and confronted Zoghby about Ledet's allegations, Zoghby denied the alleged * * *. In September 2002, when Archbishop Lipscomb again confronted Zoghby about the allegations and his response, Zoghby recanted his false allegations against Ledet and admitted his misconduct.

After Zoghby admitted his misconduct, the Archdiocese, acting through Archbishop Lipscomb, attempted to resolve Ledet's complaint. Archbishop Lipscomb explained that in resolving an issue of sexual misconduct by a priest in his Archdiocese he first addressed the needs of the victim; he then tried to "deal with the perpetrator to see is he salvageable and what are the conditions under which you might approach a return to some kind of active ministry." * * *

In 2003 Ledet learned that Zoghby had returned to active ministry and that he had been "promoted" to the position of pastor over a parish in Foley. She also began "to question" whether Zoghby was actually receiving the therapy and counseling mandated by the agreement. According to Ledet, when she notified Archbishop Lipscomb that she believed the

Archdiocese had not fulfilled its part of the agreement, Archbishop Lipscomb threatened her, "stating that publicity surrounding Zoghby's actions would be harmful to her and to her husband and children and that it would destroy [her] reputation."

The revelations that Zoghby had not received treatment and that he had been promoted to the position of pastor of a parish triggered "emotional trauma" in Ledet. She underwent treatment for this trauma at several facilities. When she presented the bills for her treatment to the Archdiocese for payment, the Archdiocese refused to pay.

In 2004, Ledet sued the Archdiocese, Archbishop Lipscomb, and Chancellor Farmer, alleging breach of contract and the tort of outrage. Ledet did not name Zoghby as a defendant. As discovery progressed, Ledet learned that Zoghby had received some counseling under the supervision of Father Benedict Groeschel at Trinity Retreat, a Catholic counseling center in New York state that is connected with a psychiatric hospital, and that Zoghby had authorized the release of the records resulting from that counseling to Archbishop Lipscomb. Ledet requested that the Archdiocese produce all psychiatric records and reports relative to Zoghby's treatment, including "complete and correct" copies of all psychological and psychiatric testing. The defendants objected, alleging confidentiality and privilege. * * *

The trial court granted Ledet's motion to compel * * *.

Zoghby contends that the trial court exceeded the scope of its discretion in ordering the discovery of his psychiatric records and reports because, he says, the documents are privileged pursuant to Rules 503 and 505, Ala. R. Evid. According to Zoghby, the trial court's order ignores the fact that "the Alabama Rules of Civil Procedure recognize the importance of preserving confidential relationships and confidential information arising therefrom by providing that privileged matters are not subject to discovery." * * *

"The priest-penitent privilege recognizes the human need to disclose to a spiritual counselor, in total and absolute confidence, what are believed to be flawed acts or thoughts and to receive priestly consolation and guidance in return." Trammel v. United States, 445 U.S. 40, 51 (1980).

Rule 505(b), Ala. R. Evid., provides:

> "If any person shall communicate with a clergyman in the clergyman's professional capacity and in a confidential manner, then that person or the clergyman shall have a privilege to refuse to disclose, and to prevent another from disclosing, that confidential communication."

Thus, for a communication with a clergyman to be privileged, the communication must be made 1) to a clergyman 2) "in the clergyman's professional capacity" and 3) "in a confidential manner." Rule 505(b), Ala. R. Evid.

Clergyman is defined in Rule 505(a)(1) as

"any duly ordained, licensed, or commissioned minister, pastor, priest, rabbi, or practitioner of any bona fide established church or religious organization; the term 'clergyman' includes, and is limited to, any person who regularly, as a vocation, devotes a substantial portion of his or her time and abilities to the service of his or her church or religious organization."

Additionally, "[a] communication is 'confidential' if it is made privately and is not intended for further disclosure except to other persons present in furtherance of the purpose of the communication." Rule 505(a)(2), Ala. R. Evid.

Rule 505, however, does not define the phrase "in the clergyman's professional capacity." Before the promulgation of Rule 505, Ala. R. Evid., the clergyman privilege was limited in scope to communications made in a confessional or of marital nature. * * *

[W]e hold that the phrase means that the clergyman is serving in his professional capacity when he is serving as a specialist in the spiritual matters of his religious organization. In other words, the communication must be made to the clergyman in his role as a provider of spiritual care, guidance, or consolation to the individual making the communication. Whether a communication is made to a clergyman "in the clergyman's professional capacity" must be examined on a case-by-case basis. * * *

Here, the parties do not dispute that Archbishop Lipscomb is a clergyman, nor do they dispute that the disclosure to Archbishop Lipscomb of the documents Ledet seeks was made in a confidential manner. Therefore, our analysis focuses on whether the documents were disclosed to Archbishop Lipscomb while he was acting in his professional capacity as a spiritual advisor.

The facts before us establish that at the time Zoghby authorized the release of the documents to Archbishop Lipscomb, Archbishop Lipscomb had dual roles in the church—as a priest and as an administrator in the Archdiocese. Other jurisdictions have confronted situations similar to this one—a privilege is asserted when a communication is made to a clergyman who is serving both as a spiritual advisor and as an administrator. * * *

Here, the trial court was faced with the factual question of whether the documents were released to Archbishop Lipscomb in Archbishop Lipscomb's professional capacity as Zoghby's spiritual advisor or in the course of Archbishop Lipscomb's resolution of Ledet's complaint against Zoghby. Zoghby averred in his affidavit that he released the documents to Archbishop Lipscomb "to assist the Archbishop in giving [him] personal and spiritual guidance"; evidence offered by Ledet established otherwise. Archbishop Lipscomb's deposition testimony refutes Zoghby's statement. Archbishop Lipscomb's testimony established that before, during, and after the investigation into Ledet's complaint against Zoghby, he was not acting as Zoghby's spiritual advisor but as an investigator looking into Ledet's allegations and a resolver of her complaint. * * * Given the totality of the facts in this case, the trial court's conclusion that the privilege does not apply is supported by evidence indicating that the documents Ledet seeks were released by Zoghby to Archbishop Lipscomb not for the purpose of Zoghby's receiving spiritual advice from Archbishop Lipscomb, but for the purpose of Zoghby's establishing his compliance with the Archdiocese's agreement with Ledet and his readiness to return to active ministry. Thus, Zoghby has not established that the trial court exceeded the scope of its discretion in this matter and has not established that he has a clear legal right to the relief requested.

Zoghby further argues that, even if his records are not protected by the clergyman privilege, the documents remain protected the psychotherapist-patient privilege because, he says, he did not "objectively manifest a clear intent not to rely on the [psychotherapist-patient] privilege." Zoghby's argument, however, ignores the fact that he expressly released the documents to Archbishop Lipscomb. In his affidavit he admits that he signed "a release authorizing [his] counselor to send to and give the Archbishop access to [his] counseling records." As previously noted, nothing before us establishes that Zoghby did not intend for the documents to be used to assist in evaluating his readiness to return to active ministry. This express release, which the circumstances establish was for purposes other than counseling or treatment, objectively manifests Zoghby's clear intent not to rely on the psychotherapist-patient privilege. Therefore, Zoghby has not established that the trial court exceeded the scope of its discretion in holding that these documents are not protected from disclosure. * * *

PARKER, JUSTICE (dissenting). * * *

Because Archbishop Lipscomb acted in a "clergyman's professional capacity" and as Father Zoghby's "spiritual advisor in the broadest sense" and because Father Zoghby clearly and reasonably believed when he authorized the release of his records that these records were within the protection of the clergy-parishioner privilege, I believe the records are privileged under Rule 505(b). I further believe that, just as the attorney-client privilege is a deeply rooted common-law principle deemed essential to ensure the client's right to effective representation of counsel, so also is the clergy-parishioner privilege a deeply rooted common-law principle deemed essential to protect the right of penitents to seek spiritual help and to preserve the integrity of the Church.

NOTE: BOUNDS OF PROFESSIONALISM: MARKING PRIVATE SPHERES

What is the purpose of the clergy-penitent privilege? Lightman appears to hold that an Orthodox Jew (or other religious practitioner) has no private cause of action against a rabbi (or other clergy) for breaching her confidence in a manner that violates the clergy-penitent privilege. Although congregants are entitled to a clergy-penitent privilege under the rules of evidence, under *Lightman* New York clergy have no legally enforceable fiduciary obligation to maintain the secrecy of information provided in confidence. The First Amendment prohibits secular law from second-guessing clerical judgment about appropriate disclosure. Does this principle place organized religious groups in a sphere impenetrable by government? What does clergy autonomy mean for the privacy of individuals of faith? Does it mean they confide in clergy at their peril? Does clergy autonomy make sense in a world in which clergy play counseling roles analogous to those played by licensed psychologists and social workers? Is the professional licensing difference alluded to by the court an adequate justification for the denial of private rights of action?

Do you agree that Father Zoghby, a Catholic priest, should have lost the benefit of a psychotherapist-patient privilege concerning his medical records, because he voluntarily released them to the Archbishop investigating sexual harassment charges? What might have been Zoghby's actual subjective expectations? How could the holding of *Zoghby* adversely affect future such cases?

Is the *Holley* case, below, about protecting privacy as well as confidentiality? Can you think of an example in which a breach of confidence by a lawyer would clearly also constitute an invasion of someone's privacy? Suppose an attorney revealed her client's closeted sexual orientation to the media? What if an attorney revealed the contents of his living client's will and testament to a journalist?

4. LAWYERS AND CLIENTS

AMERICAN BAR ASSOCIATION MODEL RULES OF PROFESSIONAL CONDUCT RULE 1.6 CONFIDENTIALITY OF INFORMATION

(a) A lawyer shall not reveal information relating to the representation of a client unless the client gives informed consent, the disclosure is impliedly authorized in order to carry out the representation or the disclosure is permitted by paragraph (b).

(b) A lawyer may reveal information relating to the representation of a client to the extent the lawyer reasonably believes necessary:

    (1) to prevent reasonably certain death or substantial bodily harm;

    (2) to prevent the client from committing a crime or fraud that is reasonably certain to result in substantial injury to the financial interests or property of another and in furtherance of which the client has used or is using the lawyer's services;

    (3) to prevent, mitigate or rectify substantial injury to the financial interests or property of another that is reasonably certain to result or has resulted from the client's commission of a crime or fraud in furtherance of which the client has used the lawyer's services;

    (4) to secure legal advice about the lawyer's compliance with these Rules;

    (5) to establish a claim or defense on behalf of the lawyer in a controversy between the lawyer and the client, to establish a

defense to a criminal charge or civil claim against the lawyer based upon conduct in which the client was involved, or to respond to allegations in any proceeding concerning the lawyer's representation of the client; or

(6) to comply with other law or a court order.

AMERICAN BAR ASSOCIATION MODEL RULES OF PROFESSIONAL CONDUCT RULE 1.6 CONFIDENTIALITY OF INFORMATION, COMMENTS 16 AND 17

[16] A lawyer must act competently to safeguard information relating to the representation of a client against inadvertent or unauthorized disclosure by the lawyer or other persons who are participating in the representation of the client or who are subject to the lawyer's supervision. * * *

[17] When transmitting a communication that includes information relating to the representation of a client, the lawyer must take reasonable precautions to prevent the information from coming into the hands of unintended recipients. This duty, however, does not require that the lawyer use special security measures if the method of communication affords a reasonable expectation of privacy. Special circumstances, however, may warrant special precautions. Factors to be considered in determining the reasonableness of the lawyer's expectation of confidentiality include the sensitivity of the information and the extent to which the privacy of the communication is protected by law or by a confidentiality agreement.

IN THE MATTER OF STEVEN L. HOLLEY

285 A.D.2d 216, 729 N.Y.S.2d 128 (N.Y. App. Div. 2001).

PER CURIAM * * *

[Steven L. Holley was a prominent antitrust litigator, a partner at Sullivan & Cromwell. He had represented Microsoft and the rock band Pearl Jam. Holley provided *Business Week* with a copy of sealed court documents from a case involving his firm's corporate client, Bankers Trust Co. When he got caught, he initially lied. He claimed he had not learned the documents were sealed until a week after getting them from an associate and releasing them to a *Business Week* writer with whom he was friendly. The writer wrote a story based on the sealed documents, and the story was eventually published. Although use of the original documents Holley provided was enjoined by the court, the judge permitted *Business Week* to use another copy of the same documents, which were made public after Holley's error.]

On or about January 27, 1998, respondent [attorney Steven L. Holley] was served with a notice and statement of charges which alleged that he violated several Disciplinary Rules. Respondent was charged with engaging in professional misconduct by improperly disclosing a sealed court document to the legal affairs editor of Business Week magazine and then falsely denying at an evidentiary hearing before a Federal judge, and later at a deposition before the Departmental Disciplinary Committee (DDC) [of the First Judicial Department], that the journalist had alerted him to the fact that the documents he sent her the previous day had been sealed. * * *

A Hearing Panel, by a report dated January 18, 2001 * * * recommended a sanction of public censure. [The Panel did not recommend the harsher sanctions of suspension or disbarment.] The Panel noted, by way of mitigation, that respondent has had an unblemished career, enjoys a good reputation for his legal skill and honesty, and has suffered as a result of his conduct in having been the subject of adverse publicity and having been financially sanctioned by his law firm. * * *

The [Disciplinary] Committee argues that public [censure] was appropriate in this case where respondent, in violation of his firm's internal policy and in his duty to his client, did not take ordinary precautions to determine if he was acting in the best interest of his client when he turned over the document without any inquiry.

Respondent argues that this Court should disaffirm the recommendation of the Referee and Hearing Panel and impose no sanction at all. Respondent suggests that under all of the circumstances including: the absence of any aggravating factors; the presence of "numerous" mitigating circumstances; the lack of potential or actual injury to his firm, the client or the Federal court; the lack of case precedent; and that his due process rights were violated, this Court should refrain from imposing any sanction, let alone a public censure.

While it is true that the Referee found respondent behaved recklessly * * * and the Hearing Panel disagreed, finding instead that he had behaved negligently, a prudent and reasonable attorney would have, at a minimum, made some kind of inquiry * * *. Indeed, whether he acted recklessly or negligently does not matter since, either way, respondent's failure to take adequate precautions to safeguard confidential materials of a client, even if considered unintentional, was careless conduct that reflects adversely on his fitness to practice law * * *.

Nor is the recommended sanction punitive, as respondent urges. Respondent complains that, as a litigator who practices nationally, he will be severely prejudiced by a sanction that impairs his ability to secure admission pro hac vice in numerous State and Federal jurisdictions. In some of these jurisdictions, the pro hac vice requirements call for disclosure of, or are affected by, discipline less than suspension or disbarment. While this collateral consequence may prove embarrassing to respondent, it is certainly not unduly harsh, as claimed. Moreover, the Hearing Panel specifically took this factor into consideration when determining its recommended sanction. With regard to his character evidence, respondent makes much of the testimony concerning his carefulness as an attorney and his professionalism. While this may be true, the fact remains that his lack of diligence in this instance resulted in his turning over a sealed document to a journalist without even asking why she wanted it or why she did not get it from the Federal court. * * *

Finally, given that this case is one of first impression, respondent urges the Court to publish its opinion on an anonymous basis. However, the Court sees no reason to grant anonymity to this opinion. Respondent's act of casually turning over a document to a journalist without first determining whether it was restricted or not and knowing that it would be subject to the possibility of widespread dissemination, was a critical lapse in professional and moral responsibility.

Accordingly, the Committee's motion to confirm should be granted, and respondent publicly censured. Respondent's request for a stay pending appeal to the Court of Appeals and for publication of the opinion on an anonymous basis should be denied.

NOTE: CARELESS DISCLOSURE AND ATTORNEY DISQUALIFICATION

In what ways did attorney Holley violate the ABA Model Rules of Professional Responsibility? The ABA confidentiality rules make no distinction between clients who may be individuals and clients who are corporations. Should they? Accountants who represent corporate entities are held to rules of confidentiality, of course. See United States v. Deloitte LLP, 2010 WL 2572965 (C.A.D.C. 2010) ("We conclude that Dow had a reasonable expectation of confidentiality because Deloitte, as an independent auditor, has an obligation to refrain from disclosing confidential client information. Rule 301 of the American Institute of Certified Public Accountants (AICPA) Code of Professional Conduct provides: 'A member in public practice shall not disclose any confidential client information without the specific consent of the client.' * * * ").

Holley inadvertently caused a client's secrets to be disclosed to a third party. In theory a lawyer could disclose client confidences intentionally for personal gain or to help another client. For this reason, the principle that lawyers must preserve client secrets obtained in the course of confidential communications has been interpreted also to mean that a lawyer may be unable to represent a party in a matter concerning which he or she has previously represented an adverse party. The purpose of this restriction is to prevent lawyers from using one client's confidences to benefit an adverse concurrent or future client. Motions to disqualify are commonplace procedural mechanisms for asking courts to bar lawyers from representing particular clients, where doing so would compromise confidentiality.

IN RE TXU U.S. HOLDINGS CO.

110 S.W.3d 62 (Ct. App. TX. 2002).

REX D. DAVIS, CHIEF JUSTICE.

TXU U.S. Holdings Company d/b/a TU Electric ("TXU") seeks a writ of mandamus compelling Respondent, the Honorable Alan Mayfield, Judge of the 74th District Court of McLennan County, to grant TXU's motion to disqualify the firm of Waters & Kraus, L.L.P. from representing the plaintiffs in the underlying suit.

BACKGROUND

Joe and Carol Mitcham filed suit against TXU and others for injuries Joe allegedly sustained as a result of asbestos exposure on premises owned by TXU. Waters & Kraus represents the Mitchams in this lawsuit. The firm of Burford & Ryburn, L.L.P. represents TXU. The alleged disqualification in this proceeding arises from the fact that a former employee of Burford & Ryburn worked for a period of time as an attorney with Waters & Kraus. She is no longer employed with Waters & Kraus.

Gayle Mortola–Strasser worked for Burford & Ryburn as a legal assistant while attending law school. During her employment with the firm, she provided substantial assistance in the firm's representation of TXU as a defendant in asbestos suits. She conducted research, collected and reviewed confidential documents, conferred with TXU representatives, and assisted in formulating defense strategies for current and future asbestos litigation.

After Mortola–Strasser graduated from law school and obtained her law license, Waters & Kraus hired her. As a result of negotiations with Burford & Ryburn, Andrew Waters and Mortola–Strasser signed an "Agreement Regarding Conflicts of Interest" in which they agreed that neither they nor any attorneys at Waters & Kraus would participate in any claims or suits against TXU involving asbestos exposure.

Mortola–Strasser left the employment of Waters & Kraus in January 2002. Waters & Krause filed the underlying suit against TXU on January 23, 2002. Burford & Ryburn filed the motion to disqualify on March 11. After an April 10 hearing, Respondent signed an order denying the motion on June 19.

APPLICABLE LAW

Mandamus will issue to correct a clear abuse of discretion when there is no other adequate remedy at law. * * * Mandamus will issue when a trial court abuses its discretion in determining whether counsel is disqualified because the relator has no adequate remedy by appeal.

Although the Disciplinary Rules of Professional Conduct do not determine disqualification issues, they do provide guidance. * * * Disciplinary Rule 1.09 is the pertinent rule here:

Rule 1.09. Conflict of Interest: Former Client

(a) Without prior consent, a lawyer who personally has formerly represented a client in a matter shall not thereafter represent another person in a matter adverse to the former client:

(1) in which such other person questions the validity of the lawyer's services or work product for the former client; or

(2) if the representation in reasonable probability will involve a violation of Rule 1.05.

(3) if it is the same or a substantially related matter.

(b) Except to the extent authorized by Rule 1.10, when lawyers are or have become members of or associated with a firm, none of them shall knowingly represent a client if any one of them practicing alone would be prohibited from doing so by paragraph (a).

(c) When the association of a lawyer with a firm has terminated, the lawyers who were then associated with that lawyer shall not knowingly represent a client if the lawyer whose association with that firm has terminated would be prohibited from doing so by paragraph (a)(1) or if the representation in reasonable probability will involve a violation of Rule 1.05.

Tex. Disciplinary R. Prof'l Conduct 1.09, Reprinted In Tex. Gov.Code. Ann., Tit. 2, Subtit. G App. A (Vernon 1998) (Tex. State Bar R. Art. X, § 9).

Disciplinary Rule 1.05 is also implicated. Rule 1.05 prohibits an attorney from disclosing confidential client information. *Id.* 1.05. Rule 1.05 provides several exceptions under which an attorney may disclose confidential information. However, none of these exceptions applies to the present case.

An attorney is disqualified from undertaking representation of an interest which is adverse to that of a former client and which involves a matter "substantially related" to the subject matter of the former client's representation. * * * If an attorney is disqualified in this manner, any firm with which the attorney is associated is likewise disqualified. * * *

In this situation, the Supreme Court has determined that an irrebuttable presumption exists that the other attorneys in the firm have access to the confidences of the former clients of the attorney who is disqualified. * * * The Supreme Court set out the reasons for this presumption:

One reason for this presumption is that it would always be virtually impossible for a former client to prove that attorneys in the same firm had not shared confidences. Another reason for the presumption is that it helps clients feel more secure. Also, the presumption helps guard the integrity of the legal practice by removing undue suspicion that clients' interests are not being fully protected. * * * (citations omitted).

According to Rule 1.09(c), the firm will continue to be disqualified even after the attorney who previously represented the adverse client departs "if the representation in reasonable probability will involve a violation of Rule 1.05." *Tex. Disciplinary R. Prof'l Conduct 1.09(c)*

A different rule applies to a firm which hires a nonlawyer who previously worked for opposing counsel. * * * If the former client establishes that the nonlawyer worked on its case, a conclusive presumption exists that the client's confidences were imparted to the nonlawyer. * * *

Unlike the irrebuttable presumption which exists for a disqualified attorney however, a rebuttable presumption exists that a nonlawyer has shared the confidences of a former client with his new employer. * * * The presumption may be rebutted "only by establishing that 'sufficient precautions have been taken to guard against any disclosure of confidences.' " * * *

As the Supreme Court explained: *"the only way* the rebuttable presumption can be overcome is: (1) to instruct the legal assistant "not to work on any matter on which the paralegal worked during the prior employment, or regarding which the paralegal has information relating to the former employer's representation," and (2) to "take other reasonable steps to ensure that the paralegal does not work in connection with matters on which the paralegal worked during the prior employment, absent client consent." *Id.* (citing *Phoenix Founders,* 887 S.W.2d at 835).

The Court explained that nonlawyers are treated differently because of "a concern that the mobility of a nonlawyer could be unduly restricted." *Am. Home Prods.,* 985 S.W.2d at 75; *Phoenix Founders,* 887 S.W.2d at 835.

APPLICATION

Because Mortola–Strasser worked as a nonlawyer for Burford & Ryburn and as an attorney for Waters & Kraus, we must first determine whether the rebuttable presumption for nonlawyers enunciated in *American Home Products* and *Phoenix Founders* or the irrebuttable presumption for attorneys enunciated in *National Medical Enterprises* applies. Mortola–Strasser is an attorney. Thus, the concern of restricted mobility noted above does not apply to her.

For this reason, we conclude that the irrebuttable presumption of *National Medical Enterprises* applies. Thus, an irrebuttable presumption existed that the other attorneys at Waters & Kraus had access to the confidences of TXU while Mortola–Strasser was employed with that firm. *Nat'l Med. Enters.,* 924 S.W.2d at 131. The issue we must decide is whether that irrebuttable presumption continued after Mortola–Strasser left the firm. Consideration of the reasons for which the Supreme Court enunciated this irrebuttable presumption leads us to conclude that the presumption does continue.

As the Court explained, the presumption is irrebuttable because "it would *always* be virtually impossible for a former client to prove that attorneys in the same firm had not shared confidences." *Id.* (emphasis added). Additionally, the irrebuttable presumption serves to help the former client feel more secure and to protect the integrity of the legal profession. *Id.*

TXU is not in an appreciably better position now to prove that Mortola–Strasser and other attorneys at Waters & Kraus had not shared confidential information about TXU than when Mortola–Strasser was employed at that firm. Nor should TXU have any reason to feel more secure now than it did when Mortola–Strasser worked for opposing counsel. In conclusion, a requirement that the irrebuttable presumption continues to apply after the disqualified attorney leaves the firm serves to uphold the integrity of the legal profession.

Waters & Kraus argues that, under Disciplinary Rule 1.09(c), it should not be disqualified unless TXU establishes a "reasonable probability" that Mortola–Strasser shared confidential information regarding TXU to other attorneys at the firm. However, the Disciplinary Rules do not determine disqualification issues; they only provide guidance. * * * As we have already observed, TXU is not in an appreciably better position now to establish such a "reasonable probability" than before. Thus, we conclude that the better approach is to maintain the irrebuttable presumption recognized in *National Medical Enterprises*.

In sum, we hold that an irrebuttable presumption exists that Mortola–Strasser shared the confidences of TXU with other attorneys at Waters & Kraus during her employ with that firm. Thus, Waters & Kraus is disqualified from representing the Mitchams in the suit against TXU. Accordingly, Respondent abused his discretion by denying TXU's motion to disqualify Waters & Kraus.

For the foregoing reasons, we conditionally grant the requested writ.

5. POLICE AND CITIZENS

DOE v. BARRINGTON

729 F. Supp. 376 (D.N.J. 1990)..

STANLEY S. BROTMAN, US DISTRICT JUDGE * * *

On March 25, 1987, Jane Doe, her husband, and their friend James Tarvis were traveling in the Doe's pickup truck through the Borough of Barrington ("Barrington"). At approximately 9:00 a.m., a Barrington police officer stopped the truck and questioned the occupants. As a result of the vehicle stop, Barrington officers arrested Jane Doe's husband and impounded the pickup truck. Barrington officers escorted Jane Doe, her husband, and James Tarvis to the Barrington Police Station.

When he was initially arrested, Jane Doe's husband told the police officers that he had tested HIV positive and that the officers should be careful in searching him because he had "weeping lesions." There is some dispute over the exact words used by Jane Doe's husband and about the number of persons present when Jane Doe's husband revealed the information. These disputed facts do not change the outcome here. Barrington police released Jane Doe and James Tarvis from custody, but detained Jane Doe's husband on charges of unlawful possession of a hypodermic needle and a burglary detainer entered by Essex County.

Sometime in the late afternoon of the same day, Jane Doe and James Tarvis drove Tarvis's car to the Doe residence in the Borough of Runnemede ("Runnemede"). The car engine was left running, and the car apparently slipped into gear, rolling down the driveway into a neighbor's fence. The neighbors owning the fence are Michael DiAngelo and defendant Rita DiAngelo. Rita DiAngelo is an employee in the school district in Runnemede.

Two Runnemede police officers, Steven Van Camp and defendant Russell Smith, responded to the radio call about the incident. While they were at the scene, Detective Preen of the Barrington police arrived and, in a private conversation with Van Camp, revealed that Jane Doe's husband had been arrested earlier in the day and had told Barrington police officers that he had AIDS. Van Camp then told defendant Smith.

After Jane Doe and Tarvis left the immediate vicinity, defendant Smith told the DiAngelos that Jane Doe's husband had AIDS and that, to protect herself, Rita DiAngelo should wash with disinfectant. There is some dispute about Smith's exact words to the DiAngelos, however this dispute does not change the outcome here. Defendant Rita DiAngelo became upset upon hearing this information. Knowing that the four Doe children attended the Downing School in Runnemede, the school that her own daughter attended, DiAngelo contacted other parents with children in the school. She also contacted the media. The next day, eleven parents removed nineteen children from the Downing School due to a panic over the Doe children's attending the school. The media was present, and the story was covered in the local newspapers and on television. At least one of the reports mentioned the name of the Doe family. Plaintiffs allege that as a result of the disclosure, they have suffered harassment, discrimination, and humiliation. They allege they have been shunned by the community.

Plaintiffs brought this civil rights action against the police officer Smith and the municipalities of Barrington and Runnemede for violations of their federal constitutional rights pursuant to 42 U.S.C. § 1983 (1982). The federal constitutional right is their right to privacy under the fourteenth amendment. The suit contains pendent state claims against defendant DiAngelo for invasion of privacy and intentional infliction of emotional distress. The plaintiffs' motion for summary judgment seeks judgment against only defendants Runnemede and Smith; these defendants filed a cross-motion for summary judgment with their response to plaintiffs' motion. * * *

This court finds that the Constitution protects plaintiffs from governmental disclosure of their husband's and father's infection with the AIDS virus. The United States Supreme Court has recognized that the fourteenth amendment protects two types of privacy interests. "One is the individual interest in avoiding disclosure of personal matters, and another is the interest in independence in making certain kinds of important decisions." Whalen v. Roe, 429 U.S. 589, 599–600 (1977) (footnotes omitted). Disclosure of a family member's medical condition, especially exposure to or infection with the AIDS virus, is a disclosure of a "personal matter."

The Third Circuit recognizes a privacy right in medical records and medical information. United States v. Westinghouse, 638 F.2d 570, 577 (3d Cir. 1980) (employee medical records clearly within zone of privacy protection). See also In re Search Warrant (Sealed), 810 F.2d 67, 71 (3d Cir.), cert. denied, 483 U.S. 1007 (1987) (medical records clearly within constitutional sphere of right of privacy); Trade Waste Management Ass'n, Inc. v. Hughey, 780 F.2d 221, 234 (3d Cir. 1985) (personal medical history protected from random governmental intrusion). * * *

At least one court has addressed disclosure of a patient's condition with AIDS. In Woods v. White, 689 F. Supp. 874, 876 (W.D.Wis. 1988), the court held that prison officials who discussed the fact that plaintiff had tested positive for AIDS with nonmedical prison personnel and with other inmates violated the inmate's constitutional rights and could be held liable under section 1983. The court recognized plaintiff's privacy interest in the information. * * *

This court finds the reasoning employed by [other] courts persuasive. The sensitive nature of medical information about AIDS makes a compelling argument for keeping this information confidential. Society's moral judgments about the high-risk activities associated with the disease, including sexual relations and drug use, make the information of the most personal kind. Also, the privacy interest in one's exposure to the AIDS virus is even greater than one's privacy interest in ordinary medical records because of the stigma that attaches with the disease. The potential for harm in the event of a nonconsensual disclosure is substantial; plaintiff's brief details the stigma and harassment that comes with public knowledge of one's affliction with AIDS.

The hysteria surrounding AIDS extends beyond those who have the disease. The stigma attaches not only to the AIDS victim, but to those in contact with AIDS patients, see N.Y. Times, Sept. 8, 1985, at A1, col. 1 (doctor of gay patients threatened with eviction), and to those in high risk groups who do not have the disease. See Poff v. Caro, 228 N.J.Super. 370, 374, 549 A.2d 900, 903 (N.J.Super.Law Div. 1987) (landlord refused to rent to three gay men for fear of AIDS); Newsweek, July 1, 1985, at 61 (healthy gay men fired because of AIDS phobia); Nat'l L.J., July 25, 1983, at 3, 11 (California police demand masks and rubber gloves be used when dealing with gays); N.Y. Times, June 28, 1983, at A18, col. 1, 4 (Haitians denied employment because of fear of AIDS). Revealing that one's family or household member has AIDS causes the entire family to be ostracized. The right to privacy in this information extends to members of the AIDS patient's immediate family. Those sharing a household with an infected person suffer from disclosure just as the victim does. Family members, therefore, have a substantial interest in keeping this information confidential. Disclosures about AIDS cause a violation of the family's privacy much greater than simply revealing any other aspect of their family medical history.

The government's interest in disclosure here does not outweigh the substantial privacy interest involved. The government has not shown a compelling state interest in breaching the Does' privacy. The government contends that Officer Smith advised the DiAngelos to wash with disinfectant because of his concern for the prevention and avoidance of AIDS, an incurable and contagious disease. While prevention of this deadly disease is clearly an appropriate state objective, this objective was not served by Smith's statement that the DiAngelos should wash with disinfectant. Disclosure of the Does' confidential information did not advance a compelling governmental interest in preventing the spread of the disease because there was no risk that Mr. or Mrs. DiAngelo might be exposed to the HIV virus through casual contact with Jane Doe. The state of medical knowledge at the time of this incident established that AIDS is not transmitted by casual contact. Smith's statement could not prevent the transmission of AIDS because there was no threat of transmission present.

This court concludes that the Does have a constitutional right of privacy in the information disclosed by Smith and the state had no *holding* compelling interest in revealing that information. As such, the disclosure violated the Does' constitutional rights. This conclusion is consistent with the United States Supreme Court's discussion in Whalen v. Roe, 429 U.S. 589, 605 (1977) that the government may have a duty to avoid disclosure of personal information. Although sidestepping the question of whether the government had the duty to protect confidential information it lawfully obtains, the Court suggested that such a duty exists. See id. at 605–06. * * *

Smith asserts that, because Jane Doe's husband told police that he had AIDS, the husband "published" the information, giving up any right to privacy in the information. Defendants do not cite any authority for this premise, but ask the court to use its "common sense." Defendant confuses a federal cause of action under section 1983 for violation of plaintiffs' constitutional right to privacy with a state tort claim for invasion of privacy. The court has found no authority that publication by plaintiff eliminates a cause of action against the government for a federal constitutional violation of one's right to privacy. Additionally, "common sense" requires analysis of the underlying policy supporting Jane Doe's husband's selective disclosure of his condition to police. * * *

In light of the duties assigned to police officers, the need for police training about AIDS is obvious. Officers frequently come into contact with members of high risk populations, such as intravenous drug users, therefore, police must understand the disease and its transmission to protect themselves and the public. The nature of an officer's duties may bring him or her into contact with bodily fluids, particularly blood, or with nonsterile hypodermic needles.

Additionally, the need for police training to keep confidential one's infection with the AIDS virus is obvious. With the hysteria that surrounds AIDS victims and their families, disclosure clearly has a devastating effect that is easily anticipated. The panic sparked by AIDS was widely known in 1987. The failure to instruct officers to keep information about AIDS carriers confidential was likely to result in disclosure and fan the flames of hysteria. Runnemede's failure to train officers, therefore, was likely to result in a violation of constitutional rights.

The absence of training here is also a deliberate and conscious choice by the municipality. Police Chief James M. Leason testified in his deposition that he knew AIDS was a serious disease, almost always fatal, and prevalent within a population that was a prime target of police operations, that is, intravenous drug users. He also testified in his deposition that, prior to the incident, he had heard from other police chiefs in the county about various precautions being taken to protect police officers from AIDS. Yet, the Borough of Runnemede did not train any officers about AIDS prevention and control. The Borough did not provide an operating procedure or policy to guide officers. * * *

An officer trained as to the facts about AIDS would have known that no hazard of transmission of the virus existed under the circumstances, whether or not Jane Doe came into physical contact with the DiAngelos. Failure to train officers on the basic facts about AIDS assured that officers coming into contact with AIDS carriers would be ill-equipped to evaluate the risk of transmission present. * * *

This court notes that it does not decide whether a municipality may reveal one's affliction with AIDS to those actually at risk of contracting the disease from a known AIDS carrier. Likewise, municipal liability is restricted to failure to train about the disease AIDS. The need for training about AIDS and the need to keep the identity of AIDS carriers confidential satisfies the Supreme Court's standard that the need for training be so obvious that failure to do so amounts to deliberate indifference; training about other confidential matters or their disclosure may not be so obvious. No other disease in recent history has sparked such widespread and publicized panic and hysteria. One's condition with AIDS is a unique personal matter; its disclosure provokes a regrettable, but predictable, response from the community that disclosure of other personal matters would not provoke. Thus, municipal liability for disclosure of this personal matter is appropriate.

This court finds that plaintiffs have established that defendants Smith and Runnemede violated their constitutional right to privacy and that defendants are liable under section 1983. Plaintiffs' motion for summary judgment on the issue of liability with respect to defendants Smith and Runnemede will be granted.

U.S. CODE, TITLE 42, SECTION 1983 CIVIL ACTION FOR DEPRIVATION OF RIGHTS

Every person who, under color of any statute, ordinance, regulation, custom, or usage, of any State or Territory or the District of Columbia, subjects, or causes to be subjected, any citizen of the United States or other person within the jurisdiction thereof to the deprivation of any rights, privileges, or immunities secured by the Constitution and laws, shall be liable to the party injured in an action at law, suit in equity, or other proper proceeding for redress, except that in any action brought against a judicial officer for an act or omission taken in such officer's judicial capacity, injunctive relief shall not be granted unless a declaratory decree was violated or declaratory relief was unavailable. For the purposes of this section, any Act of Congress applicable exclusively to the District of Columbia shall be considered to be a statute of the District of Columbia.

NOTE: SECTION *1983*

The *Doe v. Barrington* plaintiffs sued local police after officers disclosed family medical information related to HIV/AIDS to neighbors. To get into federal district court, the plaintiffs relied on a federal statute, 42 U.S.C. § 1983, and asserted violations of a federal right. Specifically, the plaintiffs alleged violations of their right to privacy protected by the Fourteenth Amendment of the U.S. Constitution. Plaintiffs also alleged invasion of privacy and infliction of emotional distress, state tort claims. Purely state claims of this sort may be heard in federal court in a "diversity case" (a case involving parties from different state jurisdictions); or, as in *Doe v. Barrington*, AS "pendent" state claims alongside appropriate federal claims. Section 1983 claims may also be brought in state court.

Originally enacted after the Civil War to protect African Americans from racially motivated violence, 42 U.S.C. § 1983 gives individuals the right to sue police and other non-judicial officers or individuals acting "under color of" authority. Despite its beginnings in Reconstruction, Section 1983 is by no means used only in cases of alleged racial injustice. Leading Supreme Court cases interpreting the broader relevance of 1983 include *Monroe v. Pape*, 365 U.S. 167 (1961), and *Monell v. Department of Social Services*, 436 U.S. 658 (1978).

A great many Section 1983 claims are brought each year alleging police misconduct, law enforcement negligence, prisoner mistreatment, and wrongs by public employers. A percentage of these claims allege violations of federally protected privacy interests. See, e.g., *Wilson v. Layne*, 525 U.S. 981 (1998), aff'd 526 U.S. 603 (1999) (officers who brought news media into private home in violation of the Fourth Amendment entitled to qualified immunity defense); cf. *Bivens v. Six Unknown Named Agents of Federal Bureau of Narcotics*, 403 U.S. 388 (1971) (federal officials liable for damages for violations of Fourth Amendment).

Officials who are sued under Section 1983 may have defenses available to them, including immunity and qualified immunity defenses. See Note, 42 U.S.C. § 1983. Qualified Immunity of Police Officers—Eighth Circuit Finds No Clearly Established Right to Be Free from Police–Authorized Media Coverage of Searches—*Parker v. Boyer*, 93 F.3d 445 (8th Cir. 1996), 110 *Harvard Law Review* 1340 (1997).

CHAPTER 2

CONSTITUTIONAL PRIVACY

■ ■ ■

Introduction

The United States Constitution protects privacy interests. No provision contains the word "privacy." However, the U.S. Supreme Court has held that the Bill of Rights and the Fourteenth Amendment protect privacy interests relating to a host of core concerns: religion; thought and opinion; political, social and civic association; and decision-making about education, child-bearing and rearing, marriage, health and sexuality.

Chapter 1 demonstrated that law protects privacy interests through the recognition of the four invasion of privacy torts, the publicity tort, and rules of professional confidentiality. Physical, informational and proprietary modes of privacy are the common law's main province. Constitutional law, by contrast, protects privacy interests through a number of the Constitution's original and post-Civil war amendments. As you will see, physical, informational, associational, intellectual, but, especially, decisional modes of privacy are constitutional law's crucial domain.

Like the common law doctrines introduced in Chapter 1, the constitutional doctrines introduced here in Chapter 2 strongly presuppose political liberty, that is, a political system premised on a set of entitlements to lives shaped substantially by persons' own identities, traditions, principles and preferences. The problem of undue private-sector interference loomed large in Chapter 1: fellow citizens, employers, professionals and the media were often the unwanted privacy invaders. Now, in Chapter 2, government and government-facilitated interference is the predominate concern. State, local and federal governments are the unwelcome intruders. Indeed, "state action" is required to bring a valid case to court premised on alleged infringement of a constitutional privacy right.

The organization of this chapter follows the organization of the U.S. Constitution itself. A section is devoted to each of nine amendments, starting with the First Amendment and concluding with the Twenty-first. But we begin by identifying conceptions of political liberty and legitimate coercive limitations on liberty that arise in connection with constitutional privacy claims.

The breadth of constitutional privacy has been tested in the U.S. through distinctly contemporary debates—about abortion, sexual orientation, the right to die, and the use of surveillance technology, for example. Yet privacy is not a wholly novel or recent constitutional concern.

NOTE: THE FEDERALIST PAPERS

A case can be made that the *Federalist Papers* (1788) implicitly embraced decisional privacy as a principle of good government. See Jacob Cooke, ed., *The Federalist* (1961, first published 1788). Under the pseudonym "Publius," Alexander Hamilton, James Madison, and John Jay addressed the *Federalist* to the people of New York to muster support for the federal Constitution. The authors endorsed the concept of a strong central government and sovereign states, presupposing a division between a politically prior "private" people and a created "public" government. The *Federalist* makes frequent reference to the people as the "ultimate authority" and as the "only legitimate fountain of power." The papers depict the Constitution as creating a national government with specific, limited powers: "the people surrender nothing and as they retain everything, they have no need of particular reservations [of rights]." The *Federalist* essays do not enumerate specific rights of privacy, but mention "private rights of particular classes of citizens" and "certain immunities and modes of proceeding, which are relative to personal and private concerns." *Id.* at 528 and 581. The United States wound up with a federal constitution, a robust Bill of Rights, and an array of additional Amendments beyond the first ten. These protect privacy interests of nearly every recognized sort.

NOTE: THE TEXTUAL BASES OF CONSTITUTIONAL PRIVACY

It is easy to make too much of the fact that the word "privacy" does not appear in the text of the federal Constitution. The word and the concept are pervasive in the case law interpreting the Constitution, especially after the middle of the 20th century. Courts and litigants have marshaled the First Amendment guarantee of religion, free expression and free association on behalf of interests in spiritual life, private thought, and exclusive group association. The Third Amendment guarantee of freedom from state appropriation of private homes has been used to protect interests in possessing a residence of one's own. The Fourth Amendment guarantee of freedom from arbitrary search and seizure has been recruited to secure expectations of privacy, in homes, possessions, and the human body.

As the courts have frequently observed, the Fifth Amendment guarantee of freedom from compulsory self-incrimination advances interests in silence and mental reserve. The cruel and unusual punishment requirements of the Eight Amendment bear on just how much our jails and prisons can deny inmates desired forms of modesty, private communication, confidentiality and religion. The Ninth Amendment guarantee of unenumerated rights acknowledges deeply rooted traditions of non-interference with decision-making about personal life. While federal courts have not much invited such an interpretation, enterprising litigants have occasionally turned to the Second Amendment as a further source of legal protection of privacy within the Bill of

Rights, namely, the privacy of personal firearm possession. Recent Supreme Court cases directly tie personal gun ownership to the sanctity and security of the home.

After the Civil War, the federal Constitution was amended to reflect the abolition of slavery. The new provisions included the Fourteenth Amendment, which limited the ability of government to deprive persons of equality, life, liberty and property. The general language of the Fourteenth Amendment has proven to be an important source of protection for substantive liberties and equalities related to privacy and private life. In more than a century of Fourteenth Amendment cases, the Supreme Court has frequently declared that privacy is an important interest, even a fundamental right. The Fourteenth Amendment broadly limits state and federal regulation of health care, marriage, procreation, education, and sexuality.

Privacy protections may subsist elsewhere among the amendments. The Twenty-first Amendment arguably protects the "privacy" of the evening cocktail as a personal choice barred by formal prohibition of alcoholic beverages. For the most part, however, lifestyle choices, such as clothing and hairstyle preferences, receive whatever formal privacy protection the Constitution affords, as First or Fourteenth Amendment liberties.

NOTE: STATE CONSTITUTIONS

In addition to a voluminous and controversial jurisprudence of privacy premised on the provisions of the federal Constitution, the United States boasts a strikingly protective jurisprudence of privacy based on provisions of its states' constitutions. Most state constitutions have provisions that mirror the Bill of Rights and the Fourteenth Amendment. Interestingly, ten state constitutions contain provisions, without analogue in the federal constitution, expressly embracing the right to privacy: Alaska, Arizona, California, Florida, Hawaii, Illinois, Louisiana, Montana, South Carolina, and Washington. *See* National Conference of State Legislatures, http://www.ncsl.org/Issues Research/TelecommunicationsInformationTechnology/PrivacyProtectionsin StateConstitutions/tabid/13467/Default.aspx. Criminal defendants seeking to suppress evidence may find that their states' search and seizure law provides stronger protections for privacy expectations than federal search and seizure law. State courts have held that their states' constitutions dictate abortion rights and civil same-sex marriage rights as strong or stronger than any recognized under the federal Constitution. Protections for the right to die, surrogate parenting arrangements, and homosexuality were first granted, not by the federal courts applying the federal Constitution, but by state courts interpreting state constitutions.

NOTE: LIMITS ON COERCION

In the U.S., the moral and political case for constitutional privacy protection commonly appeals to ideals of liberty and associated notions of autonomy, moral pluralism, tolerance, state neutrality, and limited government. It goes without saying that a good government—even a liberal democratic government committed to tolerating moral, political and religious diversity—cannot allow everyone to do just as they please. Some choices must be respected, but others need not be. The problem is how to choose which is which.

Is there a category of choices that should be categorically immune from state interference? We might label such a category the "private sphere"—a sphere of personal liberty that is off-limits to government.

There are at least two ways one might seek to characterize an ideal private sphere. The first way would be to make a wish list of choices that should be left to individuals. One might put sex, marriage and having babies on such a list. Anyone who chooses the wish list approach will have to face the task of explaining why particular choices, even some that have been traditionally regarded as private, should be left to individuals. Why abortion? Why not taxes? Why heterosexual marriage? Why not polygamous unions? Why religion? Why not secular philosophies? The decision to place an item into a private sphere rather than a public sphere will require justification.

A second way to decide what choices belong in a private sphere would be to defend a general principle for categorizing choices as properly private or properly public. The general principle would become the justification for ascribing specific privacy rights. Philosophers have undertaken to come up with just such a sorting principle, perhaps none more debated than the principle devised by the 19th century British utilitarian philosopher, John Stuart Mill.

JOHN STUART MILL, On Liberty (1859)

The object of this Essay is to assert one very simple principle, as entitled to govern absolutely the dealings of society with the individual in the way of compulsion and control, whether the means used be physical force in the form of legal penalties, or the moral coercion of public opinion. That principle is, that the sole end for which mankind are warranted, individually or collectively in interfering with the liberty of action of any of their number, is self-protection. That the only purpose for which power can be rightfully exercised over any member of a civilized community, against his will, is to prevent harm to others. His own good, either physical or moral, is not a sufficient warrant. He cannot rightfully be compelled to do or forbear because it will be better for him to do so, because it will make him happier, because, in the opinions of others, to do so would be wise, or even right. These are good reasons for remonstrating with him, or reasoning with him, or persuading him, or entreating him, but not for compelling him, or visiting him with any evil, in case he do otherwise. To justify that, the conduct from which it is desired to deter him must be calculated to produce evil to some one else. The only part of the conduct of any one, for which he is amenable to society, is that which concerns others. In the part which merely concerns himself, his independence is, of right, absolute. Over himself, over his own body and mind, the individual is sovereign.

It is, perhaps, hardly necessary to say that this doctrine is meant to apply only to human beings in the maturity of their faculties. We are not speaking of children, or of young persons below the age which the law may fix as that of manhood or womanhood. Those who are still in a state to require being taken care of by others, must be protected against their own actions as well as against external injury. For the same reason, we may leave out of consideration those backward states of society in which the race itself may be considered as in its nonage. * * *

The objections to government interference, when it is not such as to involve infringement of liberty, may be of three kinds * * *. The first is, when the thing to be done is likely to be better done by individuals than by the government. Speaking generally, there is no one so fit to conduct any business, or to determine how or by whom it shall be conducted, as those who are personally interested in it. This principle condemns the interferences, once so common, of the legislature, or the officers of government, with the ordinary processes of industry * * *. The second objection is [this]. In many cases, though individuals may not do the particular thing so well, on the average, as the officers of government, it is nevertheless desirable that it should be done by them, rather than by the government, as a means to their own mental education—a mode of strengthening their active faculties, exercising their judgment, and giving them a familiar knowledge of the subjects with which they are thus left to deal. * * * The third, and most cogent reason for restricting the interference of government, is the great evil of adding unnecessarily to its power.

NOTE: MILL'S HARM PRINCIPLE AND ITS CRITICS

In his elegantly written essay *On Liberty* (1859), Mill suggested we draw a line between what is properly public and properly private by appeal to a principle of "other-regarding" harms: if a choice is harmless or only harmful to the chooser, it goes into the properly private pile; but if a choice is seriously harmful to others, it goes into the public pile.

More fully, Mill urged that the individual should be let alone by government to make his or her own choices on two conditions: first, on the condition that the individual's choices are self-regarding, meaning that they pertain primarily and essentially to the individual himself or herself; and second, on the condition that the individual's choices do not significantly harm or injure the legitimate interests of others. Self-regarding conduct is conduct that "neither violates any specific duty to the public, nor occasions perceptible hurt to any assignable individual except himself." Phrased differently, an individual's conduct is self-regarding when it "affects the interests of no persons besides himself, or need not affect them unless they like." Mill believed government should be bound by his famous Harm Principle, even though some citizens are likely to use their freedom to commit acts of immorality and self-injury. As explained by Mill: "No one pretends that actions should be as free as opinions. The liberty of the individual must be thus far limited; he must not make himself a nuisance to other people. But if he refrains from molesting others in what concerns them, and merely acts according to his own inclination and judgment in things which concern himself * * * [then] the same reasons which show that opinion should be free, prove also that he should be allowed, without molestation, to carry his opinions into practice at his own cost."

Mill argued that each individual is ultimately the best judge of his or her own utility or interest. Consequently, "[t]he strongest of all the arguments against the interference of the public with purely personal conduct is that, when it does interfere, the odds are that it interferes wrongly and in the wrong place." This is because, with respect to his own feelings and circumstances, the most ordinary man or woman has means of knowledge immeasurably surpassing those that can be possessed by anyone else, contended Mill. Was he right about this?

Using these simple arguments, Mill drew a line between appropriately public and private realms. However, Mill's simple solution seems to have been too simple. Is it possible to apply the "Harm Principle" in a way that avoids intractable disagreements over what is "harmful" and/or "self-regarding"?

The realm of privacy Mill marked by appeal to the Harm Principle has parameters many in the U.S. would reject. Mill believed government should take a more active role in regulating marriage, childbearing and education, than most Americans think appropriate. In the U.S., marriage, childbearing and childrearing are often regarded as quintessentially private matters. Mill saw the matter differently. He did not consider behavior respecting one's own children "self-regarding" behavior. Mill thought government ought to regulate marriage and childbearing heavily: "[t]he laws which * * * forbid marriage unless the parties can show that they have the means of supporting a family do not exceed the legitimate powers of the State * * * [and] are not objectionable" as violations of liberty. Mill observed that "to bestow a life which may be either a curse or a blessing[,] unless the being on whom it is to be bestowed will have at least the ordinary chances of a desirable existence, is a crime against that being." In an overpopulated or potentially overpopulated country, "to produce children, beyond a very small number, with the effect of reducing the reward of labor by their competition is a serious offense against all who live by the remuneration of their labor."

Mill was criticized in his own time, and continues to be criticized today. Some reject the individualism of his stance. Others see his view that government should not protect people from harming themselves as excessively libertarian. Still others reject the implication that government cannot ban or punish deeply offensive, but not harmful behavior, such as insults and hate speech aimed at Jews, racial minorities or gay, lesbian and transgender Americans. His strongly anti-paternalistic beliefs led Mill to oppose drug, alcohol and gambling prohibitions aimed at avoiding self-abuse or intemperance. But if the best medical and social science are in agreement that a certain form of conduct is harmful to people, should the community stand by and watch its members destroy themselves? In a related vein, Mill is also criticized for his view that government should not prohibit what a majority believes is immoral conduct. A critic of Mill and defender of what is often termed "legal moralism," James Fitzjames Stephen wrote a book-length attack on Mill, defending the idea that regulation of and by morals is both legitimate and inevitable. The timeless flavor of the Mill–Stephen debate can be gleaned from the excerpts that follow. What did Stephen mean by "privacy," and "morals"? Note Stephen's interesting observation that it can be an invasion of privacy to compel or persuade a person "to direct too much attention to his own feelings and to attach too much importance to their analysis."

JAMES FITZJAMES STEPHEN, *LIBERTY, EQUALITY, FRATERNITY (1873)*

As to Mr. Mill's doctrine that the coercive influence of public opinion ought to be exercised only for self-protective purposes, it seems to me a paradox so startling that it is almost impossible to argue against it. A single consideration on the subject is sufficient to prove this. The principle is one which it is simply impossible to carry out. It is like telling a rose that it ought to smell sweet only for the purpose of affording pleasure to the owner of the ground in which it grows. People form and express their opinions on each other, which, collectively, form public opinion, for a thousand reasons; to amuse themselves; for the sake of something to talk about; to gratify this or that momentary feeling; but the effect of such opinions, when formed, is quite independent of the grounds of their formation. A man is tried for murder, and just escapes conviction. People read the trial from curiosity; they discuss it for the sake of the discussion; but if, by whatever means, they are brought to think that the man was in all probability guilty, they shun his society as they would shun any other hateful thing. The opinion produces its effect in precisely the same way whatever was its origin.

The result of these observations is that both law and public opinion do in many cases exercise a powerful coercive influence on morals, for objects which are good in the sense explained above, and by means well calculated to attain those objects, to a greater or less extent at a not inadequate expense. If this is so, I say law and public opinion do well, and I do not see how either the premises or the conclusion are to be disproved.

Of course there are limits to the possibility of useful interference with morals, either by law or by public opinion; and it is of the highest practical importance that these limits should be carefully observed. The great leading principles on the subject are few and simple, though they cannot be stated with any great precision. It will be enough to mention the following:

1.   Neither legislation nor public opinion ought to be meddlesome. A very large proportion of the matters upon which people wish to interfere with their neighbours are trumpery little things which are of no real importance at all. The busybody and world-betterer who will never let things alone, or trust people to take care of themselves, is a common and a contemptible character. The commonplaces directed against these small creatures are perfectly just, but to try to put them

down by denying the connection between law and morals is like shutting all light and air out of a house in order to keep out gnats and blue-bottle flies.

2.   Both legislation and public opinion, but especially the latter, are apt to be most mischievous and cruelly unjust if they proceed upon imperfect evidence. To form and express strong opinions about the wickedness of a man whom you do not know, the immorality or impiety of a book you have not read, the merits of a question on which you are uninformed, is to run a great risk of inflicting a great wrong. It is hanging first and trying afterwards, or more frequently not trying at all. This, however, is no argument against hanging after a fair trial.

3.   Legislation ought in all cases to be graduated to the existing level of morals in the time and country in which it is employed. You cannot punish anything which public opinion, as expressed in the common practice of society, does not strenuously and unequivocally condemn. To try to do so is a sure way to produce gross hypocrisy and furious reaction. To be able to punish, a moral majority must be overwhelming. Law cannot be better than the nation in which it exists, though it may and can protect an acknowledged moral standard, and may gradually be increased in strictness as the standard rises. We punish, with the utmost severity, practices which in Greece and Rome went almost uncensored. It is possible that a time may come when it may appear natural and right to punish adultery, seduction, or possibly even fornication, but the prospect is, in the eyes of all reasonable people, indefinitely remote, and it may be doubted whether we are moving in that direction.

4.   Legislation and public opinion ought in all cases whatever scrupulously to respect privacy. To define the province of privacy distinctly is impossible, but it can be described in general terms. All the more intimate and delicate relations of life are of such a nature that to submit them to unsympathetic observation, or to observation which is sympathetic in the wrong way, inflicts great pain, and may inflict lasting moral injury. Privacy may be violated not only by the intrusion of a stranger, but by compelling or persuading a person to direct too much attention to his own feelings and to attach too much importance to their analysis. The common usage of language affords a practical test which is almost perfect upon this subject. Conduct which can be described as indecent is always in one way or another a violation of privacy. * * *

[It] may perhaps be said that the principal importance of [regulating vice] by criminal law is that in extreme cases it brands gross acts of vice with the deepest mark of infamy which can be impressed upon them, and that in this manner it protects the public and accepted standard of morals from being grossly and openly violated. In short, it affirms in a singularly emphatic manner a principle which is absolutely inconsistent with and contradictory to Mr. Mill's—the principle, namely, that there are acts of wickedness so gross and outrageous that, self-protection apart, they must be prevented as far as possible at any cost to the offender, and punished, if they occur, with exemplary severity. * * *

If people neither formed nor expressed any opinions on their neighbours' conduct except in so far as that conduct affected them personally, one of the principal motives to do well and one of the principal restraints from doing ill would be withdrawn from the world.

NOTE: MODERN REPLAYS

Philosophers and constitutional theorists continue to debate the normative questions posed by Mill and Stephen. What is harm? What is "self-regarding"? Should government regulate morals? Should government concern itself with people bent on their own self-destruction? Are there certain categories of choices that surely belong in a protected, hands-off private sphere—religion perhaps, reproduction, consensual adult sex? Should government have a hand in reinforcing both personal commitments and cultural traditions, communities and identities not of our own choosing?

Philosopher Joel Feinberg reframed the debate that Mill started over the legitimacy of government interference. Feinberg endorsed a presumption in favor of liberty. Such a presumption places the burden of proof on government to justify any interference with liberty. Accordingly, the question of justice is not, why privacy, but rather why not? Everything belongs in the category of the private until the government comes up with a good reason to take something out. Coercion, not privacy or private choice, needs legitimizing.

Bernard Harcourt explains the famous Hart–Devlin debate of the 1950's as a replay of the Mill–Stephen debate of a hundred years prior. He then persuasively argues that the terms of debate have shifted in the U.S. We do not debate the propriety of regulating morals, as much as we debate whether and how immoralities are sufficiently harmful to merit criminal regulation. Robert George is a contemporary scholar who takes us back to the original terms of debate, defending head-on the practice of regulating to protect and improve public morals. His language though, is calculated to resonate with 21st century audiences—we ought to regulate morals to safeguard society's "moral ecology".

JOEL FEINBERG, *HARM TO OTHERS*
(1984) pp. 9–13

While it is easy to overemphasize the value of liberty, there is no denying its necessity, and for that reason most writers on our subject have endorsed a kind of "presumption in favor of liberty" requiring that whenever a legislator is faced with a choice between imposing a legal duty on citizens or leaving them at liberty, other things being equal, he should leave individuals free to make their own choices. Liberty should be the norm; coercion always needs some special justification. * * * [T]he person deprived of a liberty will think of its absence as a genuine personal loss, and when we put ourselves in his shoes we naturally share his assessment. Moreover, loss of liberty both in individuals and societies entails loss of flexibility and greater vulnerability to unforeseen contingencies. Finally, free citizens are likelier to be highly capable and creative persons through the constant exercise of their capacities to choose, make decisions and assume responsibilities. Perhaps these simple truisms, by no means the whole of the case for liberty, are nevertheless sufficient to establish some presumption in liberty's favor, and transfer the burden of argument to the shoulders of the advocate of coercion who must, in particular instances, show that the standing case for liberty can be overridden by even weightier reasons on the side of the scales. * * *

[W]hat kinds of reasons can have weight when balanced against the presumptive case for liberty? Answers to this question take the form of what I shall call "liberty-limiting principles" (or equivalently, "coercion-legitimizing principles"). A liberty-limiting principle is one which states that a given type of consideration is always a morally relevant reason in support of * * * legislation even if other reasons may in the circumstances outweigh it. * * *

About one class of crimes there can be no controversy. [Crimes against the person, such as rape and murder are crimes everywhere in the world.] Almost as noncontroversial as these serious "crimes against the person" are various serious "crimes against property": burglary, grand larceny, and various offenses involving fraud and misrepresentation. The common element in crimes of these two categories is the direct production of serious harm to individual persons and groups. Other kinds of properly prohibited behavior, like reckless driving and discharging of lethal weapons, are banned not because they necessarily cause harm in every case, but rather because they create unreasonable risks of harm to other persons.

Still other crimes that have an unquestioned place in our penal codes are kinds of conduct that rarely cause clear and substantial harm to any specific person or group, but are said to cause harm to "the public," "society," "the state," public institutions or practices, the general ambience of neighborhoods, the economy, the climate, or the environment. Typical crimes in this general category are counterfeiting, smuggling, income tax evasion, contempt of court, and violation of zoning and antipollution ordinances. * * *

Generalizing then from the clearest cases we can assert tentatively that it is legitimate for the state to prohibit conduct that causes serious private harm, or the unreasonable risk of such harm, or harm to important public institutions and practices * * *. [C]oncisely, the need to prevent harm (private or public) to parties other than the actor is always an appropriate reason for legal coercion. This principle * * * can be called "the harm principle" for short * * *. John Stuart Mill argued in effect that the harm principle is the only valid principle for determining legitimate invasions of liberty * * *.

The harm principle * * * is a useful starting place * * *. Clearly not every kind of act that causes harm to others can be rightly prohibited, but only those that cause avoidable and substantial harm. * * * So the harm principle must be made sufficiently precise to permit the formulation of a criterion of "seriousness" * * * [f]or virtually every kind of human conduct can affect the interests of others for better or worse to some degree. * * *

The more radical view of Mill's that such considerations are the only relevant reasons cannot be evaluated until the classes of reasons put forth by other candidate principles have been examined. Most writers would accept at least some additional kinds of reasons as equally legitimate. Three others have won widespread support. It has been held (but not always by the same person) that: (1) it is reasonably necessary to prevent hurt * * * or offense (as oppose to injury or harm) to others (the offense principle); (2) it is reasonably necessary to prevent harm to the very person it prohibits from acting, as opposed to "others" (legal paternalism); (3) it is reasonably necessary to prevent inherently immoral conduct whether or not such conduct is harmful or offensive to anyone (legal moralism). An especially interesting [fourth] position * * * holds that a good reason for restricting a person's liberty is that it is reasonably necessary to prevent moral * * * harm to the person himself. This view, which provides one of the leading rationales for the prohibition of pornography, can be labeled moralistic paternalism.

BERNARD E. HARCOURT, CRIMINAL LAW: THE COLLAPSE OF THE HARM PRINCIPLE

90 J. Crim. L. & Criminology 109 (1999).

The harm principle traces back to John Stuart Mill's essay On Liberty. * * *

Beginning at least in the 1950s, liberal theorists, most prominently Professors H.L.A. Hart and Joel Feinberg, returned to Mill's original, simple statement of the harm principle. The context was the debate over the legal enforcement of morality. In England, this debate was reignited by the recommendation of the Committee on Homosexual Offences and Prostitution (the "Wolfenden Report") that private homosexual acts between consenting adults no longer be criminalized. In the United States, the debate was reignited by the Supreme Court's struggle over the definition and treatment of obscenity and the drafting of the Model Penal Code. In both countries, the debate was fueled by the perception among liberal theorists that legal moralist principles were experiencing a rejuvenation and were threatening to encroach on liberalism.

More than anyone else, Lord Patrick Devlin catalyzed this perceived threat. In his Maccabaean Lecture, delivered to the British Academy in

1959, Lord Devlin argued that purportedly immoral activities, like homosexuality and prostitution, should remain criminal offenses. Lord Devlin published his lecture and other essays under the title The Enforcement of Morals, and Devlin soon became associated with the principle of legal moralism—the principle that moral offenses should be regulated because they are immoral.

The Hart–Devlin exchange structured the debate over the legal enforcement of morality, and thus there emerged, in the 1960s, a pairing of two familiar arguments—the harm principle and legal moralism. All the participants at the time recognized, naturally, that this structure was a recurrence of a very similar pairing of arguments that had set the contours of the debate a hundred years earlier. The Hart–Devlin debate replicated, in many ways, the earlier debate between Mill and another famous British jurist, Lord James Fitzjames Stephen. * * *

Though the paired structure of arguments was similar, it was not exactly the same. In contrast to Stephen's straightforward legal moralist argument, Lord Devlin's argument in The Enforcement of Morality was ambiguous and susceptible to competing interpretations. Devlin's argument played on the ambivalence in the notion of harm—at times courting the idea of social harm, at other times aligning more closely with the legal moralism of his predecessor. As a result, the conservative position began to fragment and there developed at least two interpretations of Devlin's argument: the first relied on public harm, the second on legal moralism. Professors Hart and Feinberg labeled these two versions, respectively, the moderate thesis and the extreme thesis.

A * * * shift in justification is evident in a wide range of debates over the regulation or prohibition of activities that have traditionally been associated with moral offense—from prostitution and pornography, to loitering and drug use, to homosexual and heterosexual conduct. In a wide array of contexts, the proponents of regulation and prohibition have turned away from arguments based on morality, and turned instead to harm arguments * * *.

Similarly, in the pornography debate, Professor Catharine MacKinnon has proposed influential administrative and judicial measures to regulate pornographic material. Her enforcement proposals, again, are not based on the immorality of pornography. Instead, the principal justification is the multiple harms that pornography and commercial sex cause women. "The evidence of the harm of such material," MacKinnon explains, "shows that these materials change attitudes and impel behaviors in ways that are unique in their extent and devastating in their consequences." MacKinnon's provocative discourse, and her vivid descriptions of injury, violence, and rape, are all about harm. In a similar vein, the recent crackdown on commercial sex establishments—peep shows, strip clubs, adult book and video stores—in New York City has been justified in the name of tourism, crime rates, and property value, not morality.

A similar development has taken place in the debate over homosexuality. In the 1980s, the AIDS epidemic became the harm that justified legal intervention. When San Francisco and New York City moved to close gay bathhouses in the mid–1980s, the argument was not about the immorality of homosexual conduct. Instead, the debate was about the harm associated with the potential spread of AIDS at gay bathhouses * * *.

This is illustrated also in the ongoing controversy over the legalization of marijuana and other psychoactive drugs. In response to a wave of enforcement of anti-drug policies in the 1980s—a wave of enforcement that was justified because of the harms associated with drug use and the illicit drug trade—the movement for drug policy reform has increasingly turned to the argument of "harm reduction." Whereas thirty years ago the opponents of criminalization talked about marijuana use as a "victimless crime"—as not causing harm to others—the opponents of criminalization now emphasize the harms associated with the war on drugs. * * *

The shift has had a dramatic effect on the structure of the debate. It has, in effect, undermined the structure itself. In contrast to the earlier pairing of harm and legal moralist arguments, or even to the later dominance of the harm argument over legal moralism, today the debate is no longer structured. It is, instead, a harm free-for-all: a cacophony of competing harm arguments without any way to resolve them. There is no argument within the structure of the debate to resolve the competing claims of harm. The only real contender would have been the harm principle. But that principle provides no guidance to compare harm arguments. Once a non-trivial harm argument has been made and the necessary condition of harm has been satisfied, the harm principle has exhausted its purpose. The triumph and universalization of harm has collapsed the very structure of the debate.

ROBERT P. GEORGE, FORUM ON PUBLIC MORALITY: THE CONCEPT OF PUBLIC MORALITY

45 Am. J. Juris. 17 (2000).

Public morality, like public health and safety, is a concern that goes beyond considerations of law and public policy. Public morals are affected, for good or ill, by the activities of private (in the sense of "nongovernmental") parties, and such parties have obligations in respect to it. The acts of private parties—indeed, sometimes even the apparently private acts of private parties—can and do have public consequences. And choices to do things that one knows will bring about these consequences, whether directly or indirectly (in any of the relevant senses of "directly" and "indirectly") are governed by moral norms, including, above all, norms of justice. Such norms will often constitute conclusive reasons for private parties to refrain from actions that produce harmful public consequences.

Let us for just a moment lay aside the issue of public morality and focus instead on matters of public health and safety. Even apart from laws prohibiting the creation of fire hazards, for example, individuals have an obligation to avoid placing persons and property in jeopardy of fire. Similarly, even apart from legal liability in tort for unreasonably subjecting people to toxic pollutants, companies are under an obligation in justice to avoid freely spewing forth, say, carcinogenic smoke from their factories. Concerns for public health and safety are, to be sure, justificatory grounds of criminal and civil laws; but they also ground moral obligations that obtain even apart from laws or in their absence.

What is true of public health and safety is equally true of public morals. Take, as an example, the problem of pornography. Material designed to appeal to the prurient interest in sex by arousing carnal desire unintegrated with the procreative and unitive goods of marriage, where it flourishes, damages a community's moral ecology in ways analogous to those in which carcinogenic smoke spewing from a factory's stacks damages the community's physical ecology.

NOTE: APPROACHING THE CONSTITUTION

Now we begin at the beginning, with the First Amendment. The relevance of the Mill–Stephen and the Hart–Devlin normative debates become clear as we see the federal courts struggling with the question of where to draw the line between public regulation and private choice. Can government outlaw polygamy? Can it mandate attending school? But the Mill–Stephen, Hart/Devlin debates do not exhaust the philosophical dilemmas posed in the First Amendment privacy cases. We face dilemmas, too, of how to situate individuals within families and social groups that claim power over them.

The courts are guided by the text of the First Amendment and precedent. But like philosophers interpreting the abstract demands of "justice," judges interpreting the demands of "free exercise" and "freedom" are impelled by their own values and those embodied in the history and traditions of the communities they serve.

A. FIRST AMENDMENT PRIVACY

1. THE FIRST AMENDMENT

"Congress shall make no law respecting an establishment of religion, or prohibiting the free exercise thereof; or abridging the freedom of speech, or of the press; or the right of the people peaceably to assemble, and to petition the Government for a redress of grievances."

2. EXERCISING RELIGIOUS FREEDOM

NOTE: TOLERATION

The First Amendment of the U.S. Constitution calls for religious freedom and tolerance. Government is not generally entitled to dictate or forbid a system of spiritual beliefs and practices. Minority and unpopular religions are supposed to be tolerated, majority and popular religions held at bay. Religion is, in this respect, private.

Does the privacy of religion mean that anything goes, if it is pursued on the basis of sincerely held religious belief? Under the First Amendment, the privacy of religion is not absolute. Religion is not license, for example, to break the criminal law or the child labor laws. See *Prince v. Massachusetts*, 321 U.S. 158 (1944), in which the Court acknowledged "the private realm of family life which the state cannot enter," but upheld child labor laws that prohibited the children of Jehovah's Witnesses from distributing religious literature to the public.

The landmark cases excerpted in this section consider whether government may ban polygamy dictated by the Mormon religion, compel compulsory secondary education rejected by the Amish, or deny government unemployment benefits to former employees who lost their jobs because they consumed peyote in a Native American church sacrament. The cases make it plain that the government may interfere with religious free exercise when its interest in doing so is seemingly compelling. Is it fair to say, though, that religious belief and exercise are presumptive liberties, in the strong sense articulated by Joel Feinberg, above?

REYNOLDS v. UNITED STATES

98 U.S. 145 (1878).

MR. CHIEF JUSTICE WAITE delivered the opinion of the court. * * *

[Congress enacted a statute prohibiting polygamy in the U.S. territories. Mr. Reynolds, a Mormon took a second wife in violation of the law.] On the trial, the plaintiff in error, the accused, proved that at the time of his alleged second marriage he was, and for many years before had been, a member of the Church of Jesus Christ of Latter–Day Saints, commonly called the Mormon Church, and a believer in its doctrines; that it was an accepted doctrine of that church "that it was the duty of male members of said church, circumstances permitting, to practise polygamy; * * * that this duty was enjoined by different books which the members of said church believed to be to divine origin, and among others the Holy Bible, and also that the members of the church believed that the practice of polygamy was directly enjoined upon the male members thereof by the Almighty God, in a revelation to Joseph Smith, the founder and prophet of said church; that the failing or refusing to practise polygamy by such male members of said church, when circumstances would admit, would be punished, and that the penalty for such failure and refusal would be damnation in the life to come." He also proved "that he had received permission from the recognized authorities in said church to enter into polygamous marriage; * * * that Daniel H. Wells, one having authority in said church to perform the marriage ceremony, married the said defendant on or about the time the crime is alleged to have been committed, to some woman by the name of Schofield, and that such marriage ceremony was performed under and pursuant to the doctrines of said church." * * *

Congress cannot pass a law for the government of the Territories which shall prohibit the free exercise of religion. The first amendment to the Constitution expressly forbids such legislation. Religious freedom is guaranteed everywhere throughout the United States * * *.

Polygamy has always been odious among the northern and western nations of Europe, and, until the establishment of the Mormon Church, was almost exclusively a feature of the life of Asiatic and of African people. At common law, the second marriage was always void (2 Kent, Com. 79), and from the earliest history of England polygamy has been treated as an [offense] against society. * * *

In our opinion, the statute immediately under consideration is within the legislative power of Congress. It is constitutional and valid as prescribing a rule of action for all those residing in the Territories, and in places over which the United States have exclusive control. This being so, the only question which remains is, whether those who make polygamy a part of their religion are excepted from the operation of the statute. * * * Laws are made for the government of actions, and while they cannot interfere with mere religious belief and opinions, they may with practices. Suppose one believed that human sacrifices were a necessary part of religious worship, would it be seriously contended that the civil government under which he lived could not interfere to prevent a sacrifice? Or if a wife religiously believed it was her duty to burn herself upon the funeral pile of her dead husband, would it be beyond the power of the civil government to prevent her carrying her belief into practice?

So here, as a law of the organization of society under the exclusive dominion of the United States, it is provided that plural marriages shall not be allowed. Can a man excuse his practices to the contrary because of his religious belief? The permit this would be to make the professed doctrines of religious belief superior to the law of the land, and in effect to permit every citizen to become a law unto himself. Government could exist only in name under such circumstances.

WISCONSIN v. YODER

406 U.S. 205 (1972).

Mr. Chief Justice Burger delivered the opinion of the Court. * * *

Respondents Jonas Yoder and Wallace Miller are members of the Old Order Amish religion, and respondent Adin Yutzy is a member of the Conservative Amish Mennonite Church. They and their families are residents of Green County, Wisconsin. Wisconsin's compulsory school-attendance law required them to cause their children to attend public or private school until reaching age 16 but the respondents declined to send their children, ages 14 and 15, to public school after they completed the eighth grade. The children were not enrolled in any private school, or within any recognized exception to the compulsory-attendance law, and they are conceded to be subject to the Wisconsin statute.

On complaint of the school district administrator for the public schools, respondents were charged, tried, and convicted of violating the compulsory-attendance law in Green County Court and were fined the sum of $5 each. Respondents defended on the ground that the application of the compulsory-attendance law violated their rights under the First and Fourteenth Amendments. * * *

Formal high school education beyond the eighth grade is contrary to Amish beliefs, not only because it places Amish children in an environment hostile to Amish beliefs with increasing emphasis on competition in class work and sports and with pressure to conform to the styles, manners, and ways of the peer group, but also because it takes them away from their community, physically and emotionally, during the crucial and formative adolescent period of life. During this period, the children must acquire Amish attitudes favoring manual work and self-reliance and the specific skills needed to perform the adult role of an Amish farmer or housewife. They must learn to enjoy physical labor. Once a child has learned basic reading, writing, and elementary mathematics, these traits, skills, and attitudes admittedly fall within the category of those best learned through example and "doing" rather than in a classroom. And, at this time in life, the Amish child must also grow in his faith and his relationship to the Amish community if he is to be prepared to accept the heavy obligations imposed by adult baptism. In short, high school attendance with teachers who are not of the Amish faith—and may even be hostile to it—interposes a serious barrier to the integration of the Amish child into the Amish religious community. * * *

[T]he record in this case abundantly supports the claim that the traditional way of life of the Amish is not merely a matter of personal preference, but one of deep religious conviction, shared by an organized group, and intimately related to daily living. That the Old Order Amish daily life and religious practice stem from their faith is shown by the fact that it is in response to their literal interpretation of the Biblical injunction from the Epistle of Paul to the Romans, "be not conformed to this world * * *." This command is fundamental to the Amish faith. Moreover, for the Old Order Amish, religion is not simply a matter of theocratic belief. As the expert witnesses explained, the Old Order Amish religion pervades and determines virtually their entire way of life, regulating it with the detail of the Talmudic diet through the strictly enforced rules of the church community. * * *

Their rejection of telephones, automobiles, radios, and television, their mode of dress, of speech, their habits of manual work do indeed set them apart from much of contemporary society; these customs are both symbolic and practical.

As the society around the Amish has become more populous, urban, industrialized, and complex, particularly in this century, government regulation of human affairs has correspondingly become more detailed and pervasive. The Amish mode of life has thus come into conflict increasingly with requirements of contemporary society exerting a hydraulic insistence on conformity to majoritarian standards. * * * As the record so strongly shows, the values and programs of the modern secondary school are in sharp conflict with the fundamental mode of life mandated by the Amish religion; modern laws requiring compulsory secondary education have accordingly engendered great concern and conflict. * * *

As the record shows, compulsory school attendance to age 16 for Amish children carries with it a very real threat of undermining the Amish community and religious practice as they exist today; they must either abandon belief and be assimilated into society at large, or be forced to migrate to some other and more tolerant region. * * *

The State advances two primary arguments in support of its system of compulsory education. It notes, as Thomas Jefferson pointed out early in our history, that some degree of education is necessary to prepare citizens to participate effectively and intelligently in our open political system if we are to preserve freedom and independence. Further, education prepares individuals to be self-reliant and self-sufficient participants in society. We accept these propositions.

However, the evidence adduced by the Amish in this case is persuasively to the effect that an additional one or two years of formal high school for Amish children in place of their long-established program of informal vocational education would do little to serve those interests. * * *

[O]ur holding today in no degree depends on the assertion of the religious interest of the child as contrasted with that of the parents. It is the parents who are subject to prosecution here for failing to cause their children to attend school, and it is their right of free exercise, not that of their children, that must determine Wisconsin's power to impose criminal penalties on the parent. The dissent argues that a child who expresses a desire to attend public high school in conflict with the wishes of his parents should not be prevented from doing so. There is no reason for the Court to consider that point since it is not an issue in the case. * * *

The State's argument proceeds without reliance on any actual conflict between the wishes of parents and children. It appears to rest on the potential that exemption of Amish parents from the requirements of the compulsory-education law might allow some parents to act contrary to the best interests of their children by foreclosing their opportunity to make an intelligent choice between the Amish way of life and that of the outside world. The same argument could, of course, be made with respect to all church schools short of college. There is nothing in the record or in the ordinary course of human experience to suggest that non-Amish parents generally consult with children of ages 14–16 if they are placed in a church school of the parents' faith. * * *

For the reasons stated we hold, with the Supreme Court of Wisconsin, that the First and Fourteenth Amendments prevent the State from compelling respondents to cause their children to attend formal high school to age 16. * * *

Nothing we hold is intended to undermine the general applicability of the State's compulsory school-attendance statutes or to limit the power of the State to promulgate reasonable standards that, while not impairing the free exercise of religion, provide for continuing agricultural vocational education under parental and church guidance by the Old Order Amish or others similarly situated. * * * Affirmed.

MR. JUSTICE DOUGLAS, dissenting in part. * * *

I agree with the Court that the religious scruples of the Amish are opposed to the education of their children beyond the grade schools, yet I disagree with the Court's conclusion that the matter is within the dispensation of parents alone. The Court's analysis assumes that the only interests at stake in the case are those of the Amish parents on the one hand, and those of the State on the other. The difficulty with this approach is that, despite the Court's claim, the parents are seeking to vindicate not only their own free exercise claims, but also those of their high-school-age children. * * *

Religion is an individual experience. It is not necessary, nor even appropriate, for every Amish child to express his views on the subject in a prosecution of a single adult. Crucial, however, are the views of the child whose parent is the subject of the suit. Frieda Yoder has in fact testified that her own religious views are opposed to high-school education. I therefore join the judgment of the Court as to respondent Jonas Yoder. But Frieda Yoder's views may not be those of Vernon Yutzy or Barbara Miller. I must dissent, therefore, as to respondents Adin Yutzy and Wallace Miller as their motion to dismiss also raised the question of their children's religious liberty. * * *

I think the emphasis of the Court on the "law and order" record of this Amish group of people is quite irrelevant. A religion is a religion irrespective of what the misdemeanor or felony records of its members might be.

EMPLOYMENT DIV., DEPT. HUM. RES. OF OREGON v. SMITH

494 U.S. 872 (1990).

JUSTICE SCALIA delivered the opinion of the Court.

This case requires us to decide whether the Free Exercise Clause of the First Amendment permits the State of Oregon to include religiously inspired peyote use within the reach of its general criminal prohibition on use of that drug, and thus permits the State to deny unemployment benefits to persons dismissed from their jobs because of such religiously inspired use. * * *

[T]he "exercise of religion" often involves not only belief and profession but the performance of (or abstention from) physical acts: assembling with others for a worship service, participating in sacramental use of bread and wine, proselytizing, abstaining from certain foods or certain modes of transportation. It would be true, we think (though no case of ours has involved the point), that a State would be "prohibiting the free exercise [of religion]" if it sought to ban such acts or abstentions only when they are engaged in for religious reasons, or only because of the religious belief that they display. It would doubtless be unconstitutional, for example, to ban the casting of "statues that are to be used for worship purposes," or to prohibit bowing down before a golden calf.

Respondents in the present case, however, seek to carry the meaning of "prohibiting the free exercise [of religion]" one large step further. They contend that their religious motivation for using peyote places them beyond the reach of a criminal law that is not specifically directed at their religious practice, and that is concededly constitutional as applied to those who use the drug for other reasons. * * *

We have never held that an individual's religious beliefs excuse him from compliance with an otherwise valid law prohibiting conduct that the State is free to regulate. On the contrary, the record of more than a century of our free exercise jurisprudence contradicts that proposition. * * * We first had occasion to assert that principle in Reynolds v. United States, 98 U.S. 145 (1879), where we rejected the claim that criminal laws against polygamy could not be constitutionally applied to those whose religion commanded the practice. "Laws," we said, "are made for the government of actions, and while they cannot interfere with mere religious belief and opinions, they may with practices. * * * Can a man excuse his practices to the contrary because of his religious belief? To permit this would be to make the professed doctrines of religious belief superior to the law of the land, and in effect to permit every citizen to become a law unto himself." * * *

Our most recent decision involving a neutral, generally applicable regulatory law that compelled activity forbidden by an individual's religion was United States v. Lee, 455 U.S., at 258–261. There, an Amish employer, on behalf of himself and his employees, sought exemption from collection and payment of Social Security taxes on the ground that the Amish faith prohibited participation in governmental support programs. We rejected the claim that an exemption was constitutionally required. There would be no way, we observed, to distinguish the Amish believer's objection to Social Security taxes from the religious objections that others might have to the collection or use of other taxes. * * *

The only decisions in which we have held that the First Amendment bars application of a neutral, generally applicable law to religiously motivated action have involved not the Free Exercise Clause alone, but the Free Exercise Clause in conjunction with other constitutional protections, such as freedom of speech and of the press * * * or the right of parents, acknowledged in Pierce v. Society of Sisters * * *, to direct the education of their children, see Wisconsin v. Yoder, * * * (invalidating compulsory school-attendance laws as applied to Amish parents who refused on religious grounds to send their children to school). * * *

The present case does not present such a hybrid situation, but a free exercise claim unconnected with any communicative activity or parental right. Respondents urge us to hold, quite simply, that when otherwise prohibitable conduct is accompanied by religious convictions, not only the convictions but the conduct itself must be free from governmental regulation. We have never held that, and decline to do so now. * * *

holding

Because respondents' ingestion of peyote was prohibited under Oregon law, and because that prohibition is constitutional, Oregon may, consistent with the Free Exercise Clause, deny respondents unemployment compensation when their dismissal results from use of the drug. The decision of the Oregon Supreme Court is accordingly reversed.

NOTE: DISCRIMINATION AND DIFFERENCE

Congress enacted the Religious Freedom Restoration Act (1993) in response to *Smith*. See 42 U.S.C. § 2000bb (1993). However, a few years later the Supreme Court found that the statute was unconstitutional as applied to state and local authorities. See *City of Boerne, Texas v. Flores* 521 U.S. 507 (1997). A number of states have enacted their own versions of the RFRA. See, e.g., Fla. Stat. Ann. §§ 761.01–761.05 (1998). Cf. *Freeman v. State*, 2003 WL 21338619 (Fla.Cir.Ct. Jun 06, 2003) (NO. 2002–CA–2828); affirmed by *Freeman v. Department of Highway Safety and Motor Vehicles*, 924 So.2d 48, 31 Fla. L. Weekly D537 (Fla.App. 5 Dist. Feb. 13, 2006) (NO. 5D03–2296), rehearing denied (Mar 29, 2006). In the *Freeman* case a religious Muslim unsuccessfully alleged that state officials violated the Florida Constitution and the Florida Religious Freedom Restoration Act (FRFRA) when they revoked her driver's license because she refused to be photographed without her niqab. The niqab is a modesty head covering that leaves only a woman's eyes uncovered.

Did the Court in *Yoder* award the Amish too much control over the fates of their children? Did the holding of *Reynolds* benefit Mormon women? Criminal laws prohibiting polygamy and peyote may be enforced against persons of faith, but not mandatory secondary school-attendance laws. Why? Does the difference have anything to do with the harmfulness of the conduct involved? Is using sacramental peyote more harmful than not attending high school? Why is it important that the Amish pay social security taxes, see *United States v. Lee*, cited in *Smith*, but not that they send their children to high school? Reconcile *Yoder* and *Reynolds*. Why did the ways of the Amish merit protection but the ways of the Mormons did not?

JOHN STUART MILL, *ON LIBERTY* (1859)

I cannot refrain from adding to these examples of the little account commonly made of human liberty, the language of downright persecution which breaks out from the press of this country, whenever it feels called on to notice the remarkable phenomenon of Mormonism. Much might be said on the unexpected and instructive fact, that an alleged new revelation, and a religion, founded on it, the product of palpable imposture, not even supported by the prestige of extraordinary qualities in its founder, is believed by hundreds of thousands, and has been made the foundation of a society, in the age of newspapers, railways, and the electric telegraph. What here concerns us is, that this religion, like other and better religions, has its martyrs; that its prophet and founder was, for his teaching, put to death by a mob; that others of its adherents lost their lives by the same lawless violence; that they were forcibly expelled, in a body, from the country in which they first grew up; while, now that they have been chased into a solitary recess in the midst of a desert, many in this country openly declare that it would be right (only that it is not convenient) to send an expedition against them, and compel them by force to conform to the opinions of other people. The article of the Mormonite doctrine which is the chief provocative to the antipathy which thus breaks through the ordinary restraints of religious tolerance, is its sanction of polygamy; which, though permitted to Mahomedans, and Hindoos, and Chinese, seems to excite unquenchable animosity when practised by persons who speak English, and profess to be a kind of Christians. No one has a deeper disapprobation than I have of this Mormon institution; both for other reasons, and because, far from being in any way countenanced by the principle of liberty, it is a direct infraction of that principle, being a mere riveting of the chains of one half of the community, and an emancipation of the other from reciprocity of obligation towards them. Still, it must be remembered that this relation is as much voluntary on the part of the women concerned in it, and who may be deemed the sufferers by it, as is the case with any other form of the marriage institution; and however surprising this fact may appear, it has its explanation in the common ideas and customs of the world, which teaching women to think marriage the one thing needful, make it intelligible that many a woman should prefer being one of several wives, to not being a wife at all. Other countries are not asked to recognize such unions, or release any portion of their inhabitants from their own laws on the score of Mormonite opinions. But when the dissentients have conceded to the hostile sentiments of others, far more than could justly be demanded; when they have left the countries to which their doctrines were unacceptable, and established themselves in a remote corner of the earth, which they have been the first to render habitable to human beings; it is difficult to see on what principles but those of tyranny they can be prevented from living there under what laws they please, provided they commit no aggression on other nations, and allow perfect freedom of departure to those who are dissatisfied with their ways. A recent writer, in some respects of considerable merit, proposes (to use his own words,) not a crusade, but a civilizade, against this polygamous community, to put an end to what seems to him a retrograde step in civilization. It also appears so to me, but I am not aware that any community has a right to force another to be civilized. So long as the sufferers by the bad law do not invoke assistance from other communities,

I cannot admit that persons entirely unconnected with them ought to step in and require that a condition of things with which all who are directly interested appear to be satisfied, should be put an end to because it is a scandal to persons some thousands of miles distant, who have no part or concern in it. Let them send missionaries, if they please, to preach against it; and let them, by any fair means, (of which silencing the teachers is not one,) oppose the progress of similar doctrines among their own people. If civilization has got the better of barbarism when barbarism had the world to itself, it is too much to profess to be afraid lest barbarism, after having been fairly got under, should revive and conquer civilization. A civilization that can thus succumb to its vanquished enemy must first have become so degenerate, that neither its appointed priests and teachers, nor anybody else, has the capacity, or will take the trouble, to stand up for it. If this be so, the sooner such a civilization receives notice to quit, the better. It can only go on from bad to worse, until destroyed and regenerated (like the Western Empire) by energetic barbarians.

3. PRIVATE ASSOCIATION AND RACE POLITICS

NOTE: PRIVACY AS A DOUBLE-EDGED SWORD

The First Amendment cases in this next section tell a story of American race and politics. The cases also shine a light on the ironic role that the legal concept of privacy played both in promoting and frustrating the goals of the civil rights movement.

The NAACP (in one case) and the Black Muslims (in another) promoted desegregation and demanded to be treated as private associations entitled to confidential membership lists. A private club and private school (in a third and fourth case) sought the right to continue exclusive, whites-only enclaves. They demanded private association status, too. Is what's good for the goose not good for the gander? The Supreme Court has taken the position that truly private social clubs are permitted to have discriminatory membership criteria, and that private schools may teach racial segregation, so long as they keep their doors open to all.

We begin with *NAACP v. State of Alabama*. The case has enjoyed a lively afterlife. Although the resolution of the case was partly premised on Fourteenth Amendment due process, the Court stressed the importance of freedom of association, associational privacy and anonymity, themes picked up in First Amendment cases that would later cite *NAACP* as precedent.

NAACP v. ALABAMA

357 U.S. 449 (1958).

MR. JUSTICE HARLAN delivered the opinion of the Court. * * *

Alabama has a statute similar to those of many other States which requires a foreign corporation * * * to qualify before doing business by filing its corporate charter with the Secretary of State and designating a place of business and an agent to receive service of process. The statute imposes a fine on a corporation transacting intrastate business before qualifying and provides for criminal prosecution * * *. The National Association for the Advancement of Colored People is a nonprofit membership corporation organized under the laws of New York. * * * The first Alabama affiliates were chartered in 1918. Since that time the aims of the Association have been advanced through activities of its affiliates, and in 1951 the Association itself opened a regional office in Alabama, at which it employed two supervisory persons and one clerical worker. The Association has never complied with the qualification statute, from which it considered itself exempt.

In 1956 the Attorney General of Alabama brought an equity suit in the State Circuit Court, Montgomery County, to enjoin the Association from conducting further activities within, and to oust it from, the State. Among other things the bill in equity alleged that the Association had opened a regional office and had organized various affiliates in Alabama; had recruited members and solicited contributions within the State; had given financial support and furnished legal assistance to Negro students seeking admission to the state university; and had supported a Negro boycott of the bus lines in Montgomery to compel the seating of passengers without regard to race. The bill recited that the Association, by continuing to do business in Alabama without complying with the qualification statute, was " * * * causing irreparable injury to the property and civil rights of the residents and citizens of the State of Alabama for which criminal prosecution and civil actions at law afford no adequate relief * * *." On the day the complaint was filed, the Circuit Court issued ex parte an order restraining the Association, pendente lite, from engaging in further activities within the State and forbidding it to take any steps to qualify itself to do business therein. * * *

We thus reach petitioner's claim that the production order in the state litigation trespasses upon fundamental freedoms protected by the Due Process Clause of the Fourteenth Amendment. Petitioner argues that in view of the facts and circumstances shown in the record, the effect of compelled disclosure of the membership lists will be to abridge the rights of its rank-and-file members to engage in lawful association in support of their common beliefs. It contends that governmental action which, although not directly suppressing association, nevertheless carries this consequence, can be justified only upon some overriding valid interest of the State. * * *

It is hardly a novel perception that compelled disclosure of affiliation with groups engaged in advocacy may constitute as effective a restraint on freedom of association as the forms of governmental action in the cases above were thought likely to produce upon the particular constitutional rights there involved. This Court has recognized the vital relationship between freedom to associate and privacy in one's associations. * * * Compelled disclosure of membership in an organization engaged in advocacy of particular beliefs is of the same order. Inviolability of privacy in group association may in many circumstances be indispensable to preservation of freedom of association, particularly where a group espouses dissident beliefs. * * *

We think that the production order, in the respects here drawn in question, must be regarded as entailing the likelihood of a substantial restraint upon the exercise by petitioner's members of their right to freedom of association. Petitioner has made an uncontroverted showing that on past occasions revelation of the identity of its rank-and-file members has exposed these members to economic reprisal, loss of employment, threat of physical coercion, and other manifestations of public hostility. Under these circumstances, we think it apparent that compelled disclosure of petitioner's Alabama membership is likely to affect adversely the ability of petitioner and its members to pursue their collective effort to foster beliefs which they admittedly have the right to advocate, in that it may induce members to withdraw from the Association and dissuade others from joining it because of fear of exposure of their beliefs shown through their associations and of the consequences of this exposure.

It is not sufficient to answer, as the State does here, that whatever repressive effect compulsory disclosure of names of petitioner's members may have upon participation by Alabama citizens in petitioner's activities follows not from state action but from private community pressures. The crucial factor is the interplay of governmental and private action, for it is only after the initial exertion of state power represented by the production order that private action takes hold. * * *

It is important to bear in mind that petitioner asserts no right to absolute immunity from state investigation, and no right to disregard Alabama's laws. As shown by its substantial compliance with the production order, petitioner does not deny Alabama's right to obtain from it such information as the State desires concerning the purposes of the Association and its activities within the State. Petitioner has not objected to divulging the identity of its members who are employed by or hold official positions with it. It has urged the rights solely of its ordinary rank-and-file members * * *.

We hold that the immunity from state scrutiny of membership lists which the Association claims on behalf of its members is here so related to the right of the members to pursue their lawful private interests privately and to associate freely with others in so doing as to come within the protection of the Fourteenth Amendment. And we conclude that Alabama has fallen short of showing a controlling justification for the deterrent effect on the free enjoyment of the right to associate which disclosure of membership lists is likely to have. Accordingly, the judgment of civil contempt and the $100,000 fine which resulted from petitioner's refusal to comply with the production order in this respect must fall. * * *

For the reasons stated, the judgment of the Supreme Court of Alabama must be reversed and the case remanded for proceedings not inconsistent with this opinion.

Note: The Remarkable Legacy of *NAACP* v. *Alabama*

Bates v. City of Little Rock, 361 U.S. 516 (1960), upheld the NAACP's refusal to provide the names of its members to city tax revenue officials. A number of lower courts have followed the *NAACP* decision. In *Wallace v. Brewer*, 315 F. Supp. 431 (M.D. Ala. 1970), Alabama lost its bid to obtain the membership list of a group of Black Muslims who purchased land with the intent to settle in the state.

The *NAACP* decision has not always protected individuals seeking to remain anonymous. The courts have sometimes found that the state's interest in the accountability of potential wrong-doers outweighs the privacy interest in confidential group association or individual expression. In *Uphaus v. Wyman*, 360 U.S. 72 (1959), the Court upheld the right of the state of New Hampshire to order a group with ties to known communists to turn over a list of individuals who had been guests at one of its camps. It also observed that failure to comply with a bureaucratic state law was the rationale Alabama gave for seeking the NAACP's membership list, whereas New Hampshire's aim was a good faith investigation of subversives. The Court argued that the state of New Hampshire's approach to investigating "subversive" activity was narrowly tailored to further a compelling state interest. In Church of the American Knights of the *Ku Klux Klan v. Kerik* (2004) the Second Circuit Court of Appeals held that hooded masks worn by KKK members did not constitute expressive conduct entitled to First Amendment protection, and that New York's anti-mask statute was not facially unconstitutional. The KKK, an infamous unincorporated political group, sometimes styled a church, that advocates on behalf of white Christians, has a history of vigilante violence against African Americans, Catholics, Asians, Jews and other minority groups. Although the Court of Appeals cited *NAACP*, it found that KKK members' interest in anonymity was not sufficiently strong to invalidate the New York rule: "[T]he Supreme Court has never held that freedom of association or the right to engage in anonymous speech entails a right to conceal one's appearance in a public demonstration."

Less predictably, the NAACP case has played a role in the Supreme Court's decisional privacy cases. It was cited toward recognition of a free standing right to constitutional privacy in *Griswold v. Connecticut*, 381 U.S. 479 (1965). In *Griswold* Justice Douglas argued that a right to privacy had been implicit in great precedents of the Court interpreting the Bills of Rights and the Fourteenth Amendment, including *NAACP*. On the surface, the right to access to birth control, at issue in *Griswold*, and the right to private group membership, at issue in *NAACP* are very different sorts of rights. But they have in a common a basis in a broad and critical liberal ideal: every autonomous citizen having an individual right of privacy to be free from unwanted monitoring and interference by the government. Both *Roe v. Wade*, 410 U.S. 113 (1973), the landmark case striking down laws categorically criminalizing abortion, and *Lawrence v. Texas*, 539 U.S. 558 (2003), the landmark in which the Court struck down laws criminalizing homosexual sodomy, are heirs of *Griswold* with a debt to *NAACP v. Alabama*'s vigorous defense of freedom from state interference.

WALLACE v. BREWER

315 F.Supp. 431 (M.D. Ala. 1970).

PER CURIAM * * *

The Black Muslims made their first purchase of land in St. Clair County [Alabama] in July 1969 under the name Progressive Land Developers, Inc. (PLD). The 376–acre farm in north St. Clair County was purchased for $115,105 from Ray Wyatt, a resident of St. Clair County. In May 1969, Wyatt and Robert McClung bought a 541–acre farm, Big Beaver Ranch, * * * and then resold the farm to PLD for $80,646.11. * * *

Early in November the citizens of St. Clair County became aware of the purchases of land by the Black Muslims. * * * [A] series of activities, both legal and extralegal, were instituted to prevent the establishment of these farms. On November 11 defendant John Golden, under the claim of a lease with option to purchase the 376–acre farm in north St. Clair County, swore to a warrant for the arrest of plaintiff Holmes on a charge of trespass after warning * * *. On the same day a warrant charging Holmes with "Failure to Register as a Muslim" in violation of Title 14, § 97(4a), was sworn to by defendant Bishop.

On November 19, 1969, a warrant was sworn to by defendant Bishop and issued for the arrest of plaintiff Billingsley, a Negro attorney. The warrant * * * charged Billingsley with acting as an agent for "a foreign corporation which was without a license authorizing it to do business in the State." The specific act was the filing of a deed, which conveyed land to PLD, with the Judge of Probate in Pell City, Alabama. * * *

On November 21, 1969, defendants Wyatt, Bishop and Golden organized and conducted a meeting attended by approximately 2000 residents of St. Clair County. The meeting organized for the purpose of rallying public support for a "Stop the Muslims" movement was attended by defendant Strickland who spoke on behalf of the Alabama Legislative Commission to Preserve the Peace. Strickland warned that the Muslims "don't respect our flag and they support communist positions in many ways while they regard Christianity as the enemy," noted that violence initiated by whites could be a natural outgrowth of attempts by "black people" to buy land in St. Clair County, and stated that Attorney General Gallion intended to aid the white citizens of St. Clair County.

Defendant Gallion issued a statement (1) warning that "the so-called farms can easily be used for storage of weapons and training in guerrilla warfare," (2) warning the public not to sell land to Muslims "who engage in every type of subversive activity," and (3) pledging full support of his office to the white citizens of St. Clair County. * * *

Initially, it should be pointed out that the [Alabama] statutory scheme, Title 14, §§ 97(1)–(8), pertains to the communist party, members of the communist party, communist front organizations, and members of communist front organizations. The one exception is section 97(4a) which requires the registration of communists, nazis, muslims and members of communist front organizations. The statutory scheme is thus applicable to plaintiffs only insofar as section 97(4a) requires them to register as muslims. * * *

Plaintiffs challenge the constitutionality of section 97(4a), both on its face and as applied [on a number of grounds] * * *. [W]e find section 97(4a) unconstitutional on first amendment grounds * * *.

There are two approaches in examining the statute's effect on first amendment rights: (1) Whether the Black Muslims and the Lost Found Nation of Islam constitute a religion, and, if so, whether section 97(4a) intrudes upon their freedom of religion (and thus violates the free exercise clause of the first amendment); or (2) whether the statute constitutes a vague and overbroad condemnation of political association, thus infringing upon plaintiffs' freedom of association. Our analysis of the statute is limited to the second approach. * * *

Where a state attempts regulation in the first amendment area, "[p]recision of regulation must be the touchstone in an area so closely touching our most precious freedoms." NAACP v. Button, 371 U.S. 415 (1963). Here, the statute closely touches the freedom of association guaranteed by the first amendment. * * * Section 97(4a) does not withstand * * * [the] required close scrutiny and is impermissibly vague and overbroad in several aspects.

In subsections 2 and 3 of section 97(4a), a registrant and a member of a muslim organization registering his organization are required to give "any other information requested by the department of public safety which is relevant to the purposes of this section." With emphasis on precision in statutory regulation in the first amendment area, this requirement is obviously vague and overbroad.

In subsection 1, all "muslims" who remain in Alabama for one day must register with the department of public safety. No definition of muslim is included in the statute. * * * In requiring all muslims to register, whether or not they are members of an organization in which the state has a legitimate interest, the statute is susceptible to constitutional attack on grounds of overbreadth. * * * When registering the muslim organization, a member is required by subsection 3 to list all members in the organization. * * *

[T]he statute suffers the constitutional infirmity of vagueness and overbreadth. Even if these defects are removed and the statute is construed to apply only to Black Muslims, it is doubtful whether their registration is constitutionally permissible. * * *

[T]he first amendment reasoning of the Supreme Court in the production of membership list cases is equally applicable where the statute requires registration of individual members. * * * This reasoning was best exemplified in NAACP v. Alabama ex rel. Patterson, supra, 357 U.S. at 462, 78 S.Ct. at 1171–1172: "This Court has recognized the vital relationship between freedom to associate and privacy in one's associations. When referring to the varied forms of governmental action which might interfere with freedom of assembly, it said in American Communications Ass'n v. Douds, supra (339 U.S. 382) at 402. A requirement that adherents of particular religious faiths or political parties wear identifying arm-bands, for example, is obviously of this nature.'' Compelled disclosure of membership in an organization engaged in advocacy of particular beliefs is of the same order. Inviolability of privacy in group association may in many circumstances be indispensable to preservation of freedom of association, particularly where a group espouses dissident beliefs. * * *

The defendants argue that the State of Alabama had a legitimate interest and purpose in requiring muslims to register. Although the question of legitimate state purpose remains a pertinent inquiry, the cases in which the Supreme Court has found a legitimate and substantial governmental interest are clearly distinguishable * * *.

For the above reasons, we conclude that section 97(4a) is an unconstitutional abridgement upon the first amendment right of freedom of association. * * *

[W]e do not intend to "tie the hands" of local law enforcement officials or state courts. Federal courts will not interfere with state criminal prosecutions instituted pursuant to a valid state statute and not for the sole purpose of harassing and intimidating individuals in the lawful exercise of their first amendment rights.

WRIGHT v. CORK CLUB

315 F.Supp. 1143 (S.D. Tex. 1970).

SINGLETON, DISTRICT JUDGE.

Plaintiff, Mrs. Noah Wright, was denied membership in the Cork Club and the use of its facilities because she is a Negro. * * *

In May, 1967, Ethel Banks, a Negro and a member of the Gamma Omega Chapter of the predominantly Negro Zeta Phi Sorority talked by telephone to defendant, Al Uhlenhoff, resident auditor of the Cork Club, regarding the possibility of the sorority's having a luncheon and style show at the Cork Club in October, 1967. * * * Uhlenhoff was unaware of Mrs. Banks' race or the race of most Zeta Phi Beta members. She was assured by Mr. Uhlenhoff that membership was not necessary for use of the Cork Club's facilities and that the sorority members could be guests of defendant, Glenn H. McCarthy, president of the Cork Club. Mr. Uhlenhoff inquired whether any member of the sorority would like to become a member of the Club and volunteered to send Mrs. Banks application forms for that purpose. On May 29, 1967, Mr. Uhlenhoff mailed to Mrs. Banks a letter confirming the arrangements for the October luncheon and style show and enclosed several membership applications. Plaintiff [Wright] filled out one of these applications * * * and duly received her membership card.

On June 9, 1967, Mrs. Wright and Mr. and Mrs. Banks went to the Club for drinks. They were served. Mrs. Wright used her membership card and Mr. and Mrs. Banks were treated as guests of Mr. McCarthy. On June 14, 1967, Mrs. Wright and a friend were again served at the Club.

By a letter dated June 14, 1967, Mr. Uhlenhoff advised Mrs. Wright that "the matter of integration has never come before the membership of the Cork Club;" that the question of integration would be brought up at the next stated meeting in January, 1968; and that her membership card would not be active until the question was settled; Mr. Uhlenhoff also advised Mrs. Banks that the sorority's plans for a luncheon and style show at the Cork Club were cancelled. * * *

At a special meeting * * * on September 28, 1967, called for the single purpose of securing a vote on integration of the Club, 352 members voted against integration; 34 voted for integration; 8 were neutral.

The Cork Club is located on two floors of an office building on the edge of downtown Houston. The thirteenth floor, known as the Century Room, consists of a large dining room with a capacity of six hundred, where a fourteen piece orchestra appears regularly and "name" floor shows appear regularly. There are two facilities on the fourteenth floor— the Clover Room and the Brass Rail. The Brass Rail is promoted as a luncheon facility for businessmen.

The Cork Club came into being in 1949, when its initial charter was filed with the Secretary of State of the State of Texas. In 1966 the charter was amended and a Certificate of Restated Articles of Incorporation under the Texas Non–Profit Corporation Act was issued. * * *

The financial statements of the Cork Club reflect that it has made no net profit * * * for * * * [several] years. The Club has been exempted from the Federal income tax by virtue of the "Social Club" exemption, Int. Rev. Code § 501(c)(7), by determination letter from the District Director, Internal Revenue Service, effective June 8, 1966 and dated May 19, 1967. In addition, the Club holds Private Club Registration Permit No. 33743 issued by the Texas Liquor Control Board under article 666–15(e), Vernon's Texas Penal Code Annotated. * * *

Initially, plaintiff contends that the Cork Club is a place of public accommodations subject to the provisions of Title II of the Civil Rights Act of 1964, 42 U.S.C. § 2000a et seq. * * *

The agreed statement of facts reflects that a substantial amount of the food served at the Cork Club has moved in interstate commerce; that any food sold by the Cork Club is only for consumption on the Club's premises; that the Cork Club serves food to members or guests, some of whom are interstate travelers; that a number of the members of the Cork Club are not residents of the State of Texas; and, that the majority of the entertainers appearing at the Cork Club are from outside the State of Texas. These facts indicate a substantial effect on interstate commerce which would subject the Cork Club to the coverage of the public accommodations provisions of the Civil Rights Act of 1964. * * *

The Cork Club falls within the strictures of the Civil Rights Act of 1964, unless, as defendant contends, the Club is excluded from the Act's coverage by subsection (e). 42 U.S.C. Sec. 2000a(e) (1964). Subsection (e) provides:

> "(e) The provisions of this subchapter shall not apply to a private club or other establishment not in fact open to the public, except to the extent that the facilities of such establishment are made available to the customers or patrons of an establishment within the scope of subsection (b) of this section."

Thus, the applicability of the Civil Rights Act to defendant hinges upon a determination of whether defendant qualifies for private club status. The burden of proof is on defendant to substantiate its claim to private club status. * * *

The Civil Rights Act, itself, is of little value as a guide for determining whether a particular establishment qualifies as a private club. The statute sets forth a factual test of sorts—"not in fact open to the public," but it does not define "private club." The general intent and purpose of the Act was "to end discrimination in certain facilities open to the general public," and "to eliminate the inconvenience, unfairness and humiliation of racial discrimination." * * * This is the extent of the guidance provided by the statute.

It is necessary to consult case law to resolve the question of what is a private club. The cases reveal that there is no single definition of "private club." Courts consider a multitude of factors, no one of which is dispositive. * * *

Although it seems clear that each case within this area must be decided in its own particular setting and factual background and within the context of the entire record before the Court, still this Court believes it helpful to enumerate certain minimum standards that should be met by any organization to come within private club exemption provided for in 42 U.S.C. § 2000a(e). Such minimum standards would be as follows:

> (1) An organization which has permanent machinery established to carefully screen applicants for membership and who selects or rejects such applicants on any basis or no basis at all; (2) which limits the use of the facilities and the services of the organization strictly to members and bona fide guests of members in good standing; (3) which organization is controlled by the membership either in the form of general meetings or in some organizational form that would and does permit the members to select and elect those member officers who control and direct the organization; (4) which organization is non-profit and operated solely for the benefit and pleasure of the members; and (5) whose publicity, if any, is directed solely and only to members for their information and guidance.

This Court adopts the above definition as setting forth in a comprehensive manner the factors determinative of "private club" status. Having reviewed the facts of the present case, in light of these enumerated minimum standards, this Court can reach no conclusion other than that the Cork Club does not meet any one, much less all, of these enumerated minimum standards and therefore falls short of being afforded private club status.

The fact that the Cork Club has been exempted from the Federal Income tax by virtue of the "Social Club" exemption is of little evidentiary value in this matter * * *.

In a similar vein, the fact that the Cork Club qualifies as a "private club" under the Texas Liquor Control Act, Tex. Penal Code Ann., art. 666–15(e), is not persuasive. This Court is familiar with the hypocrisy of the Texas liquor laws, and knows that often what are termed "private clubs" under these laws are nothing more than commercial ventures. Texans are forbidden by their state constitution to operate "open saloons." Thus, so-called "private clubs" have been established to dispense liquor-by-the-drink to Texans. Some of these establishments may qualify as "private clubs" under the Civil Rights Act, others may not * * *.

Admittedly, the Cork Club was formed to comply with the requirements of the Texas Liquor Control Act. It was not designed to evade the proscriptions of the Civil Rights Act. In Texas, in 1949, segregation of public accommodations was the rule. There was no need to form a private club in order to avoid integration. However, the fact that the Cork Club has been in operation for many years prior to the passage of the Civil Rights Act will not foreclose an inquiry into its "private club" status. * * *

The lax membership policies of the Cork Club provide further evidence of this lack of selectivity of its members. While the Cork Club has some of the trappings of a "private club," it is in fact open to white people generally and only occasionally are good credit and good character required. The Cork Club does not carefully screen applications for membership * * *.

Further evidencing this lack of selectivity on the part of the Cork Club is the wholesale solicitation of applications from groups such as teachers and the sending of form letters to other individuals soliciting applications. * * *

The Cork Club is not an organization which limits the use of its facilities or services strictly to members and bona fide guests. The Cork Club's facilities are regularly used by nonmembers who are not bona fide guests of members. * * *

Further illustrating the commercial nature of the Cork Club is the publicity the Cork Club has sought in the usual advertising media. Performers appearing at the Cork Club promote club shows on local radio and television programs. The Cork Club buys ads in the Houston and

Dallas newspapers. These ads are placed on the entertainment pages of the newspapers. They constitute a general invitation to the public to attend the Cork Club * * *.

When considered individually no one of the above factors may be persuasive as to the Cork Club's status, but when the status of the Cork Club is viewed within its own particular setting and the factual background surrounding its creation and its continued operation and viewed within the context of the entire record before this Court, there can be no doubt but that the Cork Club does not qualify for the private club exemption provided for in 42 U.S.C. Sec. 2000a(e). The Cork Club is a place of public accommodation described in 42 U.S.C. Sec. 2000a(b)(2) and (3) and (c)(2) and (3).

The only purpose of the "private club" format when it was adopted by the Cork Club was to enable it to sell mixed drinks. Thus, the Cork Club has characterized itself as a "private club" as an accommodation to the outmoded hypocritical liquor laws of the State of Texas. The Cork Club now seeks to further this perversion of the term "private club" by using it as a device to prevent integration of facilities which are for all legal and practical purposes open to the public.

If this Court were not completely convinced from the record before it of the Cork Club's status as a place of public accommodation this Court would uphold the racial restrictions involved, because this Court agrees with Justice Goldberg when he said:

> "Prejudice and bigotry in any form are regrettable, but it is the constitutional right of every person to close his home or club to any person or to choose his social intimates and business partners solely on the basis of his personal prejudices including race. These and other rights pertaining to privacy and private association are themselves constitutionally protected liberties." Bell v. Maryland, 378 U.S. 226, 313 (1964) (concurring opinion).

However, the Cork Club is a place of public accommodation, a commercial venture, and is generally open to the white public and its form is dictated by the requirements of the Texas Liquor Control Act rather than any passion for privacy.

In conclusion, to make it perfectly clear, the Court wishes to reiterate that any truly private organization or association, such as a country club, a social club, a business partnership, or a political association would be beyond the bounds of government regulation with regard to membership. More often than not the resolution of constitutional disputes is accomplished, not by the application of absolute rules, but by a balancing process. The cause of racial integration is a laudable one indeed. But to allow the government to intrude into the essentially private affairs of men, even in the name of integration, would work a greater injustice to all citizens, no matter what may be their race, creed, or religion.

To allow such a governmental intrusion would violate not only the First Amendment, but the very essence of the Bill of Rights. The Bill of Rights stands for the proposition that there are bounds beyond which the government cannot go in interfering with individual rights. The Supreme Court in numerous past decisions has drawn the lines establishing the metes and bounds of governmental authority. See, e.g., * * * N.A.A.C.P. v. Alabama, 357 U.S. 449 * * * (1958) (privacy of association). Foremost among the protected areas is the privacy of the individual, in his home, in his private associations, and even in the very words which he utters in private. The Bill of Rights, though it does not say it in so many words, guarantees to every individual the basic right of privacy. In essence, when the courts protect the individual from governmental interference with his right of assembly or freedom of speech and press, protect him from unreasonable searches and seizures or from being forced to incriminate himself, they are protecting his integrity and privacy as an individual. * * *

In this Court's view, governmental regulation of the membership of private clubs is beyond the pale of governmental authority. If the government were allowed to regulate the membership of truly private clubs, private organizations, or private associations, then it could determine for each citizen who would be his personal friends and what would be his private associations, and the Bill of Rights would be for naught.

HANNAH ARENDT, REFLECTIONS ON LITTLE ROCK

6 Dissent 45–56 (1959).

[There are political realms and social realms.] In order to illustrate this distinction between the political and the social, I shall give two examples of discrimination, one in my opinion entirely justified and outside the scope of government intervention, the other scandalously unjustified and positively harmful to the political realm.

It is common knowledge that vacation resorts in this country are frequently "restricted" according to ethnic origin. There are many people who object to this practice; nevertheless it is only an extension of the right to free association. If as a Jew I wish to spend my vacations only in the company of Jews, I cannot see how anyone can reasonably prevent my doing so; just as I see no reason why other resorts should not cater to a clientele that wishes not to see Jews while on a holiday. There cannot be a "right to go into any hotel or recreation area or place of amusement," because many of these are in the realm of the purely social where the right to free association, and therefore to discrimination, has greater validity than the principle of equality. * * *

It is, however, another matter altogether when we come to "the right to sit where one pleases in a bus" or a railroad car or station, as well as the right to enter hotels and restaurants in business districts, in short, when we are dealing with services which, whether privately or publicly owned, are in fact public services that everyone needs in order to pursue his business and lead his life. Though not strictly in the political realm, such services are clearly in the public domain where all men are equal; and discrimination in Southern railroads and buses is as scandalous as discrimination in hotels and restaurants throughout the country. Obviously the situation is far worse in the South because segregation in public services is enforced by law and plainly visible to all. It is unfortunate indeed that the first steps toward clearing up the segregation situation in the South after so many decades of complete neglect did not begin with its most inhuman and its most conspicuous aspects.

The third realm, finally, in which we move and live together with other people—the realm of privacy—is ruled neither by equality nor by discrimination, but by exclusiveness. Here we choose those with whom we wish to spend our lives, personal friends and those we love; and our choice is guided not by likeness or qualities shared by a group of people—it is not guided, indeed, by any objective standards or rules—but strikes, inexplicably and unerringly, at one person in his uniqueness, his unlikeness to all other people we know. The rules of uniqueness and exclusiveness are, and always will be, in conflict with the standards of society precisely because social discrimination violates the principle, and lacks validity for the conduct, of private life. Thus every mixed marriage constitutes a challenge to society and means that the partners to such a marriage have so far preferred personal happiness to social adjustment that they are willing to bear the burden of discrimination. This is and must remain their private business. The scandal begins only when their challenge to society and prevailing customs, to which every citizen has a right, is interpreted as a criminal offense so that by stepping outside the social realm they find themselves in conflict with the law as well. Social standards are not legal standards and if legislature follows social prejudice, society has become tyrannical.

For reasons too complicated to discuss here, the power of society in our time is greater than it ever was before, and not many people are left who know the rules of and live a private life. But this provides the body politic with no excuse for forgetting the rights of privacy, for failing to understand that the rights of privacy are grossly violated whenever legislation begins to enforce social discrimination. While the government has no right to interfere with the prejudices and discriminatory practices of society, it has not only the right but the duty to make sure that these practices are not legally enforced.

Just as the government has to ensure that social discrimination never curtails political equality, it must also safeguard the rights of every person to do as he pleases within the four walls of his own home. The moment social discrimination is legally enforced, it becomes persecution, and of this crime many Southern states have been guilty. The moment social discrimination is legally abolished, the freedom of society is violated, and the danger is that thoughtless handling of the civil rights issue by the Federal government will result in such a violation. The government can legitimately take no steps against social discrimination because government can act only in the name of equality—a principle which does not obtain in the social sphere. The only public force that can fight social prejudice is the churches, and they can do so in the name of the uniqueness of the person, for it is on the principle of the uniqueness of souls that religion (and especially the Christian faith) is based. The churches are indeed the only communal and public place where appearances do not count, and if discrimination creeps into the houses of worship, this is an infallible sign of their religious failing. They then have become social and are no longer religious institutions. * * *

Parents' rights over their children are legally restricted by compulsory education and nothing else. The state has the unchallengeable right to prescribe minimum requirements for future citizenship and beyond that to further and support the teaching of subjects and professions which are felt to be desirable and necessary to the nation as a whole. All this involves, however, only the content of the child's education, not the context of association and social life which invariably develops out of his attendance at school; otherwise one would have to challenge the right of private schools to exist. For the child himself, school is the first place away from home where he establishes contact with the public world that surrounds him and his family. This public world is not political but social, and the school is to the child what a job is to an adult. The only difference is that the element of free choice which, in a free society, exists at least in principle in the choosing of jobs and the associations connected with them, is not yet at the disposal of the child but rests with his parents.

To force parents to send their children to an integrated school against their will means to deprive them of rights which clearly belong to them in all free societies—the private right over their children and the social right to free association. As for the children, forced integration means a very serious conflict between home and school, between their private and their social life, and while such conflicts are common in adult life, children cannot be expected to handle them and therefore should not be exposed to them. It has often been remarked that man is never so much of a conformer—that is, a purely social being as in childhood. The reason is that every child instinctively seeks authorities to guide it into the world in which he is still a stranger, in which he cannot orient himself by his own judgment. To the extent that parents and teachers fail him as authorities, the child will conform more strongly to his own group, and under certain conditions the peer group will become his supreme authority. The result can only be a rise of mob and gang rule, as the news photograph [of a schoolgirl escorted by the federal officers] so eloquently demonstrate. The conflict between a segregated home and a desegregated school, between family prejudice and school demands, abolishes at one stroke both the teachers' and the parents' authority, replacing it with the rule of public opinion among children * * *.

Because the many different factors involved in public education can quickly be set to work at cross purposes, government intervention, even at its best, will always be rather controversial. Hence it seems highly questionable whether it was wise to begin enforcement of civil rights in a domain where no basic human and no basic political right is at stake, and where other rights—social and private—whose protection is no less vital, can so easily be hurt. * * *

NOTE: PRIVACY RIGHTS AND SEGREGATION

Must a "right to privacy" include a right to exclude people of other races from your "social" life? What does Arendt mean by "social" as opposed to "political" life? "Public" as opposed to "private"? How, according to Arendt, were African American children harmed by government mandated school desegregation? How were unwilling white Southerners harmed, too, in her view? What would you expect Arendt to say about the wisdom of the Civil Rights Act of 1866 and the Court's decision in *Runyon v. McCrary*, below?

CIVIL RIGHTS ACT OF 1866
42 U.S.C. Section 1981.

Section 1981. Equal rights under the law.

(a) Statement of equal rights

All persons within the jurisdiction of the United States shall have the same right in every State and Territory to make and enforce contracts, to sue, be parties, give evidence, and to the full and equal benefit of all laws and proceedings for the security of persons and property as is enjoyed by white citizens, and shall be subject to like punishment, pains, penalties, taxes, licenses, and exactions of every kind, and to no other.

(b) "Make and enforce contracts" defined

For purposes of this section, the term "make and enforce contracts" includes the making, performance, modification, and termination of contracts, and the enjoyment of all benefits, privileges, terms, and conditions of the contractual relationship.

(c) Protection against impairment

The rights protected by this section are protected against impairment by nongovernmental discrimination and impairment under color of State law.

RUNYON v. McCRARY
427 U.S. 160 (1976).

MR. JUSTICE STEWART delivered the opinion of the Court.

The principal issue presented by these consolidated cases is whether a federal law, namely 42 U.S.C. § 1981, prohibits private schools from excluding qualified children solely because they are Negroes. * * *

The parents of Colin Gonzales and Michael McCrary sought to enter into contractual relationships with Bobbe's School for educational services. Colin Gonzales' parents sought to enter into a similar relationship with the Fairfax–Brewster School. Under those contractual relationships, the schools would have received payments for services rendered, and the prospective students would have received instruction in return for those payments. The educational services of Bobbe's School and the Fairfax–Brewster School were advertised and offered to members of the general public. But neither school offered services on an equal basis to white and nonwhite students. * * *

In NAACP v. Alabama, 357 U.S. 449, and similar decisions, the Court has recognized a First Amendment right "to engage in association for the advancement of beliefs and ideas * * *." That right is protected because it promotes and may well be essential to the "[effective] advocacy of both public and private points of view, particularly controversial ones" that the First Amendment is designed to foster. * * *

From this principle it may be assumed that parents have a First Amendment right to send their children to educational institutions that promote the belief that racial segregation is desirable, and that the children have an equal right to attend such institutions. But it does not follow that the practice of excluding racial minorities from such institutions is also protected by the same principle. As the Court stated in Norwood v. Harrison, "the Constitution * * * places no value on discrimination," * * * and while "[invidious] private discrimination may be characterized as a form of exercising freedom of association protected by the First Amendment * * * it has never been accorded affirmative constitutional protections. And even some private discrimination is subject to special remedial legislation in certain circumstances under § 2 of the Thirteenth Amendment; Congress has made such discrimination unlawful in other significant contexts." * * * In any event, as the Court of Appeals noted, "there is no showing that discontinuance of [the] discriminatory admission practices would inhibit in any way the teaching in these schools of any ideas or dogma." * * *

In Meyer v. Nebraska, 262 U.S. 390, the Court held that the liberty protected by the Due Process Clause of the Fourteenth Amendment includes the right "to acquire useful knowledge, to marry, establish a home and bring up children," * * * and, concomitantly, the right to send one's children to a private school that offers specialized training—in that case, instruction in the German language. In Pierce v. Society of Sisters, 268 U.S. 510, the Court applied "the doctrine of Meyer v. Nebraska," * * * to hold unconstitutional an Oregon law requiring the parent, guardian, or other person having custody of a child between 8 and 16 years of age to send that child to public school on pain of criminal liability. The Court thought it "entirely plain that the [statute] unreasonably interferes with the liberty of parents and guardians to direct the upbringing and education of children under their control." * * *

No challenge is made to the petitioner schools' right to operate or the right of parents to send their children to a particular private school rather than a public school. Nor do these cases involve a challenge to the subject matter which is taught at any private school. Thus, the Fairfax–Brewster School and Bobbe's School and members of the intervenor association remain presumptively free to inculcate whatever values and standards they deem desirable. Meyer and its progeny entitle them to no more. * * *

The Court has held that in some situations the Constitution confers a right of privacy. * * * While the application of § 1981 to the conduct at issue here—a private school's adherence to a racially discriminatory admissions policy—does not represent governmental intrusion into the privacy of the home or a similarly intimate setting, it does implicate parental interests. * * *

The Court has repeatedly stressed that while parents have a constitutional right to send their children to private schools and a constitutional right to select private schools that offer specialized instruction, they have no constitutional right to provide their children with private school education unfettered by reasonable government regulation. * * * Indeed, the Court in Pierce expressly acknowledged "the power of the State reasonably to regulate all schools, to inspect, supervise and examine them, their teachers and pupils * * *." 268 U.S., at 534. See also Prince v. Massachusetts, 321 U.S. 158, 166.

Section 1981, as applied to the conduct at issue here, constitutes an exercise of federal legislative power under § 2 of the Thirteenth Amendment [prohibiting involuntary servitude]. * * * The prohibition of racial discrimination that interferes with the making and enforcement of contracts for private educational services furthers goals closely analogous to those served by § 1981's elimination of racial discrimination in the making of private employment contracts and, more generally, by § 1982's guarantee that "a dollar in the hands of a Negro will purchase the same thing as a dollar in the hands of a white man." * * *

NOTE: MAKING SENSE OF THE SEGREGATION CASES

Did the Black Muslims in *Wallace* have a stronger right to keep their membership lists confidential than the NAACP had had, given that the former, but not the latter, is a religious group? Why did the court skirt the issue of whether the Black Muslims "constitute a religion"?

How did the Cork Club court find that the Constitution requires tolerating discriminatory private clubs? Is that perspective beyond cavil?

Did the Supreme Court in *Runyon* take seriously the desire of the schools at issue to teach segregationist values? Would African–American or Hispanic parents want to send their children to a school that was open to people of color but that sought to inculcate a belief in racial segregation or white superiority?

4. SENSITIVE DATA

NOTE: *NAACP* AND SENSITIVE DATA

Construed broadly, *NAACP* held that individuals have a strong, constitutional interest in the protection of sensitive data. The case was thus cited in *Whalen v. Roe*, 429 U.S. 589 (1977), which recognized the sensitivity of medical information and elevated informational privacy to the status of an independent constitutional guarantee. Cf. *Nelson v. National Aeronautics and Space Admin.*, 568 F.3d 1028 (9th Cir. 2009) (Kozinski, J., dissenting), cert. granted 2010 (pursuant to post 9/11 policies, government may seek additional personal and medical information from employees of its contractors). In *NAACP*, the demands of the protection of sensitive data and the demands of the First Amendment were consistent. But sometimes the First Amendment is held to require the disclosure of highly sensitive information individuals and the state might wish to conceal, as in *Ostergren v. Cuccinelli*. Cf. *IMS Health Incorporated v. Mills*, WL 2010 3025496 (CA 1 (Me.)), holding over First Amendment and Commerce Clause objections that the state may restrict access to prescription drug prescriber information.

OSTERGREN v. CUCCINELLI

2010 WL 2891576 (C.A.4 (Va.)).

Betty Ostergren resides in Hanover County, Virginia, and advocates for information privacy across the country. Calling attention to Virginia's practice of placing land records on the Internet without first redacting SSNs, she displayed copies of Virginia land records containing unredacted SSNs on her website. * * *

Virginia argues that the unredacted SSNs on Ostergren's website should not be protected under the First Amendment because they facilitate identity theft and are no essential part of any exposition of ideas. *See* Eugene Volokh, *Crime-Facilitating Speech*, 57 Stan. L.Rev. 1095, 1146–47 (2005) (arguing that SSNs and computer passwords are "categories of speech that are likely to have virtually no noncriminal uses" and that "[r]estricting the publication of full social security numbers or passwords ... will not materially interfere with valuable speech"). Although these observations might be true under certain circumstances, we cannot agree with Virginia's argument here. The unredacted SSNs on Virginia land records that Ostergren has posted online are integral to her message. Indeed, they *are* her message. Displaying them proves Virginia's failure to safeguard private information and powerfully demonstrates why Virginia citizens should be concerned. *Cf. United States v. Hubbell*, 530 U.S. 27, 36–37, 120 S.Ct. 2037, 147 L.Ed.2d 24 (2000) (noting that "the act of producing documents in response to a subpoena ... may implicitly communicate statements of fact" because "[b]y producing documents ... the witness would admit that the papers existed, were in his possession or control, and were authentic" (internal quotations omitted)).

We find particularly significant just how Ostergren communicates SSNs. She does not simply list them beside people's names but rather provides copies of entire documents maintained by government officials. Given her criticism about how public records are managed, we cannot see how drawing attention to the problem by displaying those very documents could be considered unprotected speech. Indeed, the Supreme Court has deemed such speech particularly valuable within our society:

> Public records by their very nature are of interest to those concerned with the administration of government, and a public benefit is performed by the reporting of the true contents of the records by the media. The freedom of the press to publish that information appears to us to be of critical importance to our type of government in which the citizenry is the final judge of the proper conduct of public business.

Cox Broad. Corp. v. Cohn, 420 U.S. 469, 495, 95 S.Ct. 1029, 43 L.Ed.2d 328 (1975). Thus, although we do not foreclose the possibility that communicating SSNs might be found unprotected in other situations, we conclude, on these facts, that the First Amendment does reach Ostergren's publication of Virginia land records containing unredacted SSNs.

IMS HEALTH INCORPORATED v. MILLS

2010 WL 3025496 (CA 1 (Me.)).

LYNCH, CHIEF JUDGE.

This case involves constitutional challenges to a Maine statute enacted to reduce health care costs and protect prescribers' data privacy. In Maine and elsewhere, each time a prescription from a physician or other licensed prescriber is given to a pharmacy, the pharmacy obtains a number of facts that identify the prescriber. Data put together from multiple transactions involving the same prescriber reveal certain patterns and preferences, including her prescribing history, her choice of particular brand-name drugs versus their generic equivalents, and the likelihood she will adopt new brand-name drugs.

Plaintiffs challenge the constitutionality of 22 Me. Rev. Stat. Ann. tit. 22, § 1711–E(2–A), which allows prescribers licensed in Maine to choose not to make this identifying information available for use in marketing prescription drugs to them. Section 1711–E(2–A) does not directly prohibit any marketing practices. Rather, it prohibits certain entities from licensing, using, selling, transferring, or exchanging this information for a marketing purpose if the prescriber has opted to protect the confidentiality of her prescribing data. Me. Rev. Stat. Ann. tit. 22, § 1711–E(2–A).

Plaintiffs, companies that collect vast amounts of identifying data about individual prescribers and aggregate the data into reports and databases for use when marketing pharmaceutical products, are covered in the text of the law, as are others. See id. § 1711–E(1)(A)(I). Immediately after section 1711–E(2–A)'s enactment in 2008, and before its enforcement, plaintiffs sued Maine's attorney general in the federal district court of Maine under 42 U.S.C. § 1983, claiming that section 1711–E(2–A)'s restrictions on the licensing, use, sale, transfer, or exchange of Maine prescribers' identifying data for a marketing purpose are unconstitutional limitations on protected speech under the First Amendment; that these restrictions are unconstitutionally vague and overbroad under the First and Fourteenth Amendments; and that the law also regulates transactions outside of Maine in violation of the dormant Commerce Clause. On December 21, 2007, the district court granted plaintiffs a preliminary injunction and prohibited Maine from enforcing section 1711–E(2–A) on the basis of plaintiffs' First Amendment claims. See IMS Health Corp. v. Rowe, 532 F. Supp. 2d 153, 183 (D. Me. 2007).

P lf

The district court also enjoined Maine from enforcing parts of section 1711–E implementing section 1171–E(2–A). See Rowe, 532 F. Supp. 2d at 183.

This case comes to us in an unusual posture. Maine is not the only state to have restricted plaintiffs' use of prescriber-identifying data, and this is not the first time plaintiffs have made these constitutional claims. On November 18, 2008, after the district court granted plaintiffs a preliminary injunction in this case, this court upheld a similar, but not identical, New Hampshire statute against plaintiffs' constitutional challenges, a ruling that binds this panel. See IMS Health Inc. v. Ayotte, 550 F.3d 42 (1st Cir. 2008), cert. denied, 129 S. Ct. 2864 (2009). In the meantime, the district court's injunction has remained in effect during this appeal, and Maine has never implemented section 1711–E(2–A).

We reject all of plaintiffs' constitutional challenges to section 1711–E(2–A). Plaintiffs' First Amendment challenges fail for the reasons stated in Ayotte: the statute regulates conduct, not speech, and even if it regulates commercial speech, that regulation satisfies constitutional standards. They also fail for reasons not present in Ayotte. The Maine statute constitutionally protects Maine prescribers' choice to opt in to confidentiality protection to avoid being subjected to unwanted solicitations based on their identifying data. We also reject the argument that the statute is void for vagueness.

H o l D i n G

Plaintiffs' argument that section 1711–E(2–A) is unconstitutional under the dormant Commerce Clause if applied to plaintiffs' out-of-state use or sale of opted-in Maine prescribers' identifying data also fails. We interpret the Maine statute using Maine's principles of statutory construction and hold that section 1711–E(2–A) regulates prescription drug information intermediaries' out-of-state use or sale of opted-in Maine prescribers' data. We hold that this interpretation does not raise constitutional concerns under the dormant Commerce Clause, which might necessitate a narrower reading of the statute under the doctrine of constitutional avoidance.

The Supreme Court's current dormant Commerce Clause jurisprudence does not leave Maine powerless to protect Maine prescribers who have sought to prevent the use of their identifying data in transactions that also cause substantial in-state harms, including increased health care costs. The statute constitutionally reaches plaintiffs' out-of-state transactions as a necessary incident of Maine's strong interest in protecting opted-in Maine prescribers from unwanted solicitations, a policy that Maine also rationally believes will lower its health care costs. Nor, we hold, would section 1711–E(2–A)'s regulation of prescription drug information intermediaries' out-of-state use or sale of opted-in Maine prescribers' identifying data raise constitutional concerns as a disproportionate burden on interstate commerce under Pike v. Bruce Church, Inc., 397 U.S. 137 (1970). * * *

5. ANONYMOUS SPEECH

NOTE: *NAACP* AND ANONYMOUS SPEECH

The Court's subsequent decisions regarding anonymous speech rights owe a debt to *NAACP v. Alabama*. In *Talley v. California*, 362 U.S. 60 (1960), the Court invalidated a Los Angeles ordinance banning distribution of leaflets that did not bear the names and addresses of the people responsible for their distribution. In *McIntyre v. Ohio Elections Comm'n*, 514 U.S. 334 (1995) the Court struck down an Ohio law prohibiting distribution of anonymous campaign materials. In *Buckley v. American Constitutional Law Foundation, Inc.*, 525 U.S. 182 (1999), the court found that a Colorado statute requiring that door-to-door solicitors wear identification badges violated the First Amendment. In *Watchtower Bible, & Tract Soc'y of N.Y., Inc. v. Village of Stratton*, 536 U.S. 150 (2002), the Court struck down an ordinance requiring individuals to obtain a permit prior to engaging in door-to-door advocacy and to display the permit upon demand. But see *Doe v. Reed*, 130 S.Ct. 2811 (2010), below.

Several cases have accorded anonymous speech rights on the internet. See, e.g., *Doe v. 2TheMart.com, Inc.*, 140 F.Supp.2d 1088, 1092 (W.D.Wash. 2001) (individuals should be allowed to participate in online forums without fear their identity will be exposed); *American Civil Liberties Union v. Johnson*, 4 F.Supp.2d 1029 (D.N.M.1998), aff'd 194 F.3d 1149 (10th Cir.1999) (state statute requiring age verification before web access to speech on internet violates First and Fourteenth Amendments); *American Civil Liberties Union of Georgia, et al. v. Miller, et al.*, 977 F.Supp. 1228, 1230 (N.D.Ga.1997) (state statute prohibiting use of false names on the internet "impos[ed] unconstitutional content-based restrictions on . . . right to communicate anonymously and pseudo-anonymously over the internet." Cf. *In re Anonymous Online Speakers*, 611 F.3d 653 C.A.9 (Nev. 2010).

DOE v. REED

130 S.Ct. 2811 (2010).

CHIEF JUSTICE ROBERTS delivered the opinion of the Court.

The State of Washington allows its citizens to challenge state laws by referendum. Roughly four percent of Washington voters must sign a petition to place such a referendum on the ballot. That petition, which by law must include the names and addresses of the signers, is then submitted to the government for verification and canvassing, to ensure that only lawful signatures are counted. The Washington Public Records Act (PRA) authorizes private parties to obtain copies of government documents, and the State construes the PRA to cover submitted referendum petitions.

This case arises out of a state law extending certain benefits to same-sex couples, and a corresponding referendum petition to put that law to a popular vote. Respondent intervenors invoked the PRA to obtain copies of the petition, with the names and addresses of the signers. Certain petition signers and the petition sponsor objected, arguing that such public disclosure would violate their rights under the First Amendment.

The course of this litigation, however, has framed the legal question before us more broadly. The issue at this stage of the case is not whether disclosure of this particular petition would violate the First Amendment, but whether disclosure of referendum petitions in general would do so. We conclude that such disclosure does not as a general matter violate the First Amendment, and we therefore affirm the judgment of the Court of Appeals. We leave it to the lower courts to consider in the first instance the signers' more focused claim concerning disclosure of the information on this particular petition, which is pending before the District Court. * * *

We have a series of precedents considering First Amendment challenges to disclosure requirements in the electoral context. These precedents have reviewed such challenges under what has been termed "exacting scrutiny." See, *e.g., Buckley* v. *Valeo,* 424 U. S. 1, 64 (1976) (*per curiam*) ("Since *NAACP* v. *Alabama* [357 U. S. 449 (1958),] we have required that the subordinating interests of the State [offered to justify compelled disclosure] survive exacting scrutiny") * * *.

That standard "requires a 'substantial relation' between the disclosure requirement and a 'sufficiently important' governmental interest." * * * To withstand this scrutiny, "the strength of the governmental interest must reflect the seriousness of the actual burden on First Amendment rights." * * *

[Plaintiff's] argue that disclosure is not necessary because the secretary of state is already charged with verifying and canvassing the names on a petition, advocates and opponents of a measure can observe that process, and any citizen can challenge the secretary's actions in court. * * *

But the secretary's verification and canvassing will not catch all invalid signatures: The job is large and difficult (the secretary ordinarily checks "only 3 to 5% of signatures," Brief for Respondent WFST 54), and the secretary can make mistakes, too, see Brief for Respondent Reed 42. Public disclosure can help cure the inadequacies of the verification and canvassing process.

Disclosure also helps prevent certain types of petition fraud otherwise difficult to detect, such as outright forgery and "bait and switch" fraud, in which an individual signs the petition based on a misrepresentation of the underlying issue. See Brief for Respondent WFST 9–11, 53–54; cf. Brief for Massachusetts Gay and Lesbian Political Caucus et al. as *Amici Curiae* 18–22 (detailing "bait and switch" fraud in a petition drive in Massachusetts). The signer is in the best position to detect these types of fraud, and public disclosure can bring the issue to the signer's attention.

Public disclosure thus helps ensure that the only signatures counted are those that should be, and that the only referenda placed on the ballot are those that garner enough valid signatures. Public disclosure also promotes transparency and accountability in the electoral process to an extent other measures cannot. In light of the foregoing, we reject plaintiffs' argument and conclude that public disclosure of referendum petitions in general is substantially related to the important interest of preserving the integrity of the electoral process. * * *

[Taking another tact] Plaintiffs explain that once on the Internet, the petition signers' names and addresses "can be combined with publicly available phone numbers and maps," in what will effectively become a blueprint for harassment and intimidation. *Id.*, at 46. To support their claim that they will be subject to reprisals, plaintiffs cite examples from the history of a similar proposition in California, see, *e.g.*, *id.*, at 2–6, 31–32, and from the experience of one of the petition sponsors in this case, see App. 9. * * *

The problem for plaintiffs is that their argument rests almost entirely on the specific harm they say would attend disclosure of the information on the R–71 petition, or on similarly controversial ones. See, *e.g.*, Brief for Petitioners 10, 26–29, 46, 56. But typical referendum petitions "concern tax policy, revenue, budget, or other state law issues." * * *

Faced with the State's unrebutted arguments that only modest burdens attend the disclosure of a typical petition, we must reject plaintiffs' broad challenge to the PRA.

NOTE: POLITICS AND THE FIRST AMENDMENT

Should states be permitted to require voters to identify themselves using state-issued identification? *See Crawford v. Marion*, 553 U.S. 181 (2008), holding that, consistent with the Fourteenth Amendment right to vote and the Voting Rights Act, a state may require voters to present government-issued identification at the polls. Does *Crawford* make it harder for poor voters to participate in elections, at a time when the courts have made it easier for the rich to exert political influence? A number of recent cases reflect a broadening of rights to use private monies to support political campaigns. *See Citizens United v. Federal Election*, 130 S.Ct. 876 (2010), holding that suppression of political speech on the basis of the speaker's corporate identity and barring independent corporate expenditures for electioneering communications violate the First Amendment, and overruling *Austin v. Michigan Chamber of Commerce*, 494 U.S. 652 (1990) and *McConnell v. Federal Election Com'n*, 540 U.S. 93 (2003). See *Davis v. Federal Election* 128 S.Ct. 2759 (2008), holding that federal election law provisions, that under certain circumstances impose different campaign contribution limits on candidates competing for the same congressional seat, violate of the constitution.

DOE I AND DOE II v. INDIVIDUALS, WHOSE TRUE NAMES ARE UNKNOWN

561 F.Supp.2d 249 (D. Ct. 2008).

CHRISTOPHER F. DRONEY, DISTRICT JUDGE.

On February 1, 2008, the plaintiffs, Jane Doe I and Jane Doe II (the "Does") issued a subpoena *duces tecum* to SBC Internet Services, Inc., now known as AT&T Internet Services ("AT&T"), the internet service provider, for information relating to the identity of the person assigned to the Internet Protocol ("IP") address from which an individual using the pseudonym "AK47" posted comments on a website. The individual whose internet account is associated with the IP address at issue, referring to himself as John Doe 21, has moved to quash that subpoena. John Doe 21 has also moved for permission to proceed anonymously in this matter.

I. *Background*

This action was brought by Doe I and Doe II, both female students at Yale Law School, against unknown individuals using thirty-nine different pseudonymous names to post on a law school admissions website named AutoAdmit.com ("AutoAdmit"). The plaintiffs allege that they were the targets of defamatory, threatening, and harassing statements posted on AutoAdmit from 2005 to 2007.

AutoAdmit is an internet discussion board on which participants post and review comments and information about undergraduate colleges, graduate schools, and law schools. It draws between 800,000 and one million visitors per month. Anyone who can access the internet can access AutoAdmit and view the messages posted on its discussion boards. Individuals who register with AutoAdmit, which can be done under real or assumed names, may post new messages and respond to the messages of other registered users. When a participant posts a new message, any further comments or responses to that message are collected as a "thread." Messages and threads containing certain words or subject matter can be found by searching for those words using an internet search engine.

The first message about Doe II that appeared on AutoAdmit was posted on January 31, 2007, by an anonymous poster. The message linked to a photograph of Doe II and encouraged others to "Rate this HUGE breasted cheerful big tit girl from YLS." After this message was posted, dozens of additional messages about Doe II appeared in the thread. These messages contained comments on Doe II's breasts and the posters' desire to engage in sexual relations with her. Certain of the posters appeared to be Doe II's classmates at Yale Law School because of personal information they revealed. The posts regarding Doe II continued throughout the winter and spring of 2007, and included statements, for example, that she fantasized about being raped by her father, that she enjoyed having sex while family members watched, that she encouraged others to punch her in the stomach while seven months pregnant, that she had a sexually transmitted disease, that she had abused heroin, and that a poster "hope[s] she gets raped and dies." On March 9, 2007, a poster sent an email directly to Doe II and at least one member of the Yale Law School faculty describing the alleged criminal history of Doe II's father. This message was also posted on AutoAdmit.

By March, nearly two hundred threads had been posted about Doe II on AutoAdmit. It is in this context that an anonymous poster under the moniker "AK47," known on AutoAdmit for posting threatening and derogatory comments about minority groups, posted a message falsely stating "Alex Atkind, Stephen Reynolds, [Doe II], and me: GAY LOVERS."

The posting of comments regarding Doe II continued into April and May of 2007, including one message which the poster claimed had also been sent to Doe II's future employer which recounted some of the claims made about Doe II on AutoAdmit. On June 8, 2007, Doe II, along with Doe I, filed the complaint in the instant action, alleging libel, invasion of privacy, negligent and intentional infliction of emotional distress, and copyright violations. Doe II's complaint described the harm and results she experienced because of the comments about her on AutoAdmit, including treatment for severe emotional distress, interference with her educational progress, reputational harm, and pecuniary harm.

The news of the filing of the Does' complaint quickly became a subject of discussion on AutoAdmit. AK47, for example, wrote a post concerning his opinion on the merits of the plaintiffs' case, and wondered whether posters were "allowed to use [Doe II's] name in thread's anymore." Subsequently, on June 17, 2007, AK47 posted the statement "Women named Jill and Doe II should be raped." On June 24, 2007, AK47 started a thread entitled "Inflicting emotional distress on cheerful girls named [Doe II]."

On February 1, 2008, the plaintiffs issued a subpoena *duces tecum* to AT&T for information relating to the identity of the person assigned to the IP address from which an individual using the pseudonym "AK47" posted comments on AutoAdmit about Doe II. This subpoena was issued in accordance with this Court's order of January 29, 2008, which granted the Does' motion to engage in limited, expedited discovery to uncover the identities of the defendants in this case. On February 7, 2008, AT&T sent a letter to the person whose internet account corresponded with the IP address at issue, John Doe 21 ("Doe 21"), notifying Doe 21 that it had received a subpoena ordering it to produce certain information relating to

Doe 21's internet account. The letter stated that Doe 21 could file a motion to quash or for a protective order before the date of production, which was February 25, 2008, and that AT&T must receive a copy of such a motion prior to that date. Doe 21 filed the instant motion to quash on February 25, 2008, and on February 26, 2008, AT&T complied with the subpoena. On March 12, 2008, Doe 21 filed his motion to proceed anonymously.

Because Doe 21 does not have counsel and his true identity is yet unknown to the Court, the Court appointed pro bono counsel to represent the interests of Doe 21 at oral argument on the instant motions, which took place on May 5, 2008.

II. *Motion to Quash*

* * *

B. Merits of the Motion to Quash

A subpoena shall be quashed if it "requires disclosure of privileged or other protected matter and no exception or waiver applies." Fed.R.Civ.P. 45(c)(3)(A)(iii). Doe 21 moves to quash the subpoena because he claims disclosure of his identity would be a violation of his First Amendment right to engage in anonymous speech.

The First Amendment generally protects anonymous speech. *Buckley v. American Constitutional Law Found.*, 525 U.S. 182, 199–200, 119 S.Ct. 636, 142 L.Ed.2d 599 (1999) (invalidating statute requiring initiative petitioners to wear identification badges as violation First Amendment); *McIntyre v. Ohio Elections Comm'n*, 514 U.S. 334, 357, 115 S.Ct. 1511, 131 L.Ed.2d 426 (1995) (overturning state statute that prohibited dissemination of campaign literature that did not list name and address of person issuing literature on First Amendment grounds); *Talley v. California*, 362 U.S. 60, 65, 80 S.Ct. 536, 4 L.Ed.2d 559 (invalidating statute that prohibited distribution of handbills without the name and address of preparer). The United States Supreme Court has also made clear that the First Amendment's protection extends to speech on the internet. *See Reno v. ACLU*, 521 U.S. 844, 870–71, 117 S.Ct. 2329, 138 L.Ed.2d 874 (1997) (applying First Amendment analysis to online speech, noting "[t]hrough the use of chat rooms, any person with a phone line can become a town crier with a voice that resonates farther than it could from any soapbox. Through the use of Web pages, mail exploders and newsgroups, the same individual can become a pamphleteer."). Courts also recognize that anonymity is a particularly important component of Internet speech. "Internet anonymity facilitates the rich, diverse, and far ranging exchange of ideas [;] ... the constitutional rights of Internet users, including the First Amendment right to speak anonymously, must be carefully safeguarded." *Doe v. 2TheMart.com Inc.*, 140 F.Supp.2d 1088, 1092, 1097 (W.D.Wash. 2001). However, the right to speak anonymously, on the internet or otherwise, is not absolute and does not protect speech that otherwise would be unprotected. *See, e.g., McIntyre,* 514 U.S. at 353, 115 S.Ct. 1511 ("We recognize that a State's enforcement interest might justify a more limited identification requirement."); *Harper & Row Publishers, Inc. v. Nation Enters.,* 471 U.S. 539, 555–56, 105 S.Ct. 2218, 85 L.Ed.2d 588 (1985) (First Amendment does not protect copyright infringement); *In re Subpoena Duces Tecum to America Online, Inc.,* No. 40570, 2000 WL 1210372, at *6 (Va.Cir.Ct.2000) ("Those who suffer damages as a result of tortious or other actionable communications on the Internet should be able to seek appropriate redress by preventing the wrongdoers from hiding behind an illusory shield of purported First Amendment rights.").

Courts have held that subpoenas seeking information regarding anonymous individuals raise First Amendment concerns; *see NAACP v. Alabama ex rel. Patterson,* 357 U.S. 449, 462, 78 S.Ct. 1163, 2 L.Ed.2d 1488 (1958) (holding that discovery order requiring NAACP to disclose its membership list violated First Amendment); and have addressed motions to quash subpoenas that, like the one at issue here, seek identifying subscriber information from ISPs. *See, e.g., Sony Music,* 326 F.Supp.2d at 567 ("[D]efendants' First Amendment right to remain anonymous must give way to plaintiffs' right to use the judicial process to pursue what appear to be meritorious copyright infringement claims").

The forgoing principles and decisions make clear that Doe 21 has a First Amendment right to anonymous Internet speech, but that the right is not absolute and must be weighed against Doe II's need for discovery to redress alleged wrongs. Courts have considered a number of factors in balancing these two competing interests. This balancing analysis ensures that the First Amendment rights of anonymous Internet speakers are not lost unnecessarily, and that plaintiffs do not use discovery to "harass, intimidate or silence critics in the public forum opportunities presented by the Internet." *Dendrite Intern. Inc. v. Doe No. 3,* 342 N.J.Super. 134, 775 A.2d 756, 771 (2001). The Court will address each factor in turn.

First, the Court should consider whether the plaintiff has undertaken efforts to notify the anonymous posters that they are the subject of a subpoena and withheld action to afford the fictitiously named defendants a reasonable opportunity to file and serve opposition to the application. See *Krinsky v. Doe 6,* 159 Cal.App.4th 1154, 72 Cal.Rptr.3d 231 (2008); *Dendrite Intern. Inc. v. Doe No. 3,* 342 N.J.Super. 134, 775 A.2d 756, 760 (2001). In this case, the plaintiffs have satisfied this factor by posting notice regarding the subpoenas on AutoAdmit in January of 2008, which allowed the posters ample time to respond, as evidenced by Doe 21's activity in this action.

Second, the Court should consider whether the plaintiff has identified and set forth the exact statements purportedly made by each anonymous poster that the plaintiff alleges constitutes actionable speech. *Dendrite,* 775 A.2d at 760. Doe II has identified the allegedly actionable statements by AK47/Doe 21: the first such statement is "Alex Atkind, Stephen Reynolds, [Doe II], and me: GAY LOVERS;" and the second such statement is "Women named Jill and Doe II should be raped." The potential liability for at least the first statement is more fully discussed below.

The Court should also consider the specificity of the discovery request and whether there is an alternative means of obtaining the information called for in the subpoena. *Sony Music,* 326 F.Supp.2d at 565; *Columbia Inc. v. seescandy.com,* 185 F.R.D. 573, 578, 580 (N.D.Cal.1999). Here, the subpoena sought, and AT&T provided, only the name, address, telephone number, and email address of the person believed to have posted defamatory or otherwise tortious content about Doe II on AutoAdmit, and is thus sufficiently specific. Furthermore, there are no other adequate means of obtaining the information because AT&T's subscriber data is the plaintiffs' only source regarding the identity of AK47.

Similarly, the Court should consider whether there is a central need for the subpoenaed information to advance the plaintiffs' claims. *America Online, Inc.,* 2000 WL 1210372 at *7; *Dendrite,* 775 A.2d at 760–61. Here, clearly the defendant's identity is central to Doe II's pursuit of her claims against him.

Next, the Court should consider the subpoenaed party's expectation of privacy at the time the online material was posted. *Sony Music,* 326 F.Supp.2d at 566–67; *Verizon Internet Services,* 257 F.Supp.2d 244, 267–68 (D.D.C.2003), *rev'd on other grounds,* 351 F.3d 1229 (D.C.Cir.2003). Doe 21's expectation of privacy here was minimal because AT&T's Internet Services Privacy Policy states, in pertinent part: "We may, where permitted or required by law, provide personal identifying information to third parties ... without your consent ... To comply with court orders, subpoenas, or other legal or regulatory requirements." Thus, Doe 21 has little expectation of privacy in using AT&T's service to engage in tortious conduct that would subject him to discovery under the federal rules.

Finally, and most importantly, the Court must consider whether the plaintiffs have made an adequate showing as to their claims against the anonymous defendant. Courts have differed on what constitutes such an adequate showing. Several courts have employed standards fairly deferential to the plaintiff, requiring that the plaintiff show a "good faith basis" to contend it may be the victim of conduct actionable in the jurisdiction where the suit was filed; *America Online,* 2000 WL 1210372, at *8; or to show that there is probable cause for a claim against the anonymous defendant; *La Societe Metro Cash & Carry France v. Time Warner Cable,* No. 030197400, 2003 WL 22962857, *7 (Conn.Super.2003). The Court finds these standards set the threshold for disclosure too low to adequately protect the First Amendment rights of anonymous defendants, and thus declines to follow these approaches.

Other courts have required that a plaintiff show its claims can withstand a motion to dismiss. *seescandy.com,* 185 F.R.D. at 579; *Lassa v. Rongstad,* 294 Wis.2d 187, 718 N.W.2d 673, 687 (2006). However, other courts have rejected this procedural label as potentially confusing because of the variations in the motion to dismiss standard in different jurisdictions. *See Krinsky,* 72 Cal.Rptr.3d at 244. Similarly, but more burdensome, some courts have used a standard which required plaintiffs to show their claims could withstand a motion for summary judgment. *Best Western Intern., Inc. v. Doe,* No. CV–06–1537, 2006 WL 2091695, *4 (D.Ariz. 2006); *Doe v. Cahill,* 884 A.2d 451, 461 (Del.Supr.2005). The Court finds this standard to be both potentially confusing and also difficult for a plaintiff to satisfy when she has been unable to conduct any discovery at this juncture. Indeed, it would be impossible to meet this standard for any cause of action which required evidence within the control of the defendant.

Several courts have required that a plaintiff make a concrete showing as to each element of a prima facie case against the defendant. *Highfields Capital Management L.P. v. Doe,* 385 F.Supp.2d 969, 976 (N.D.Cal.2005); *Sony Music,* 326 F.Supp.2d at 565; *Krinsky v. Doe 6,* 72 Cal.Rptr.3d at 245; *Dendrite,* 775 A.2d at 760–61. Under such a standard, "[w]hen there is a factual and legal basis for believing [actionable speech] has occurred, the writer's message will not be protected by the First Amendment." *Krinsky,* 72 Cal.Rptr.3d at 245. The Court finds such a standard strikes the most appropriate balance between the First Amendment rights of the defendant and the interest in the plaintiffs of pursuing their claims, ensuring that the plaintiff "is not merely seeking to harass or embarrass the speaker or stifle legitimate criticism." *Id.* at 244.

Doe II has presented evidence constituting a concrete showing as to each element of a prima facie case of libel against Doe 21. Libel is written defamation. To establish a prima facie case of defamation under Connecticut law, the Doe II must demonstrate that: (1) Doe 21 published a defamatory statement; (2) the defamatory statement identified the plaintiff to a third person; (3) the defamatory statement was published to a third person; and (4) the plaintiff's reputation suffered injury as a result of the statement. *Cweklinsky v. Mobil Chem. Co.,* 267 Conn. 210, 837 A.2d 759, 763–64 (2004), *citing QSP, Inc. v. Aetna Casualty & Surety Co.,* 256 Conn. 343, 773 A.2d 906, 916 (2001); 3 Restatement (Second), Torts § 558, 580B, at 155, 221–22 (1977); W. Prosser & W. Keeton, Torts (5th Ed.1984) § 113, at 802.

A defamatory statement is defined as a communication that tends to "harm the reputation of another as to lower him in the reputation of the community or to deter third persons from associating or dealing with him ..." *QSP, Inc.,* 773 A.2d at 916 (internal quotation marks omitted). Doe II alleges, and has presented evidence tending to show that, AK47's statement, "Alex Atkind, Stephen Reynolds, [Doe II], and me: GAY LOVERS," is defamatory, because any discussion of Doe II's sexual behavior on the internet tends to lower her reputation in the community, particular in the case of any potential employers who might search for her name online. In fact, in the similar context of slander (spoken defamation), any statement that imputes "serious sexual misconduct" to a person subjects the publisher to liability, without any need to prove the special harms required for other slanderous speech. *See* 3 Restatement (Second), Torts § 574, at 195–96.

Doe II has also alleged and presented evidence that Doe 21's statement clearly identified Doe II by name and was available to a large number of third persons (peers, colleagues, potential employers), whether they were on Autoadmit for their own purposes, or searched for Doe II via a search engine. Finally, Doe II has alleged and provided evidence that her reputation did suffer injury because of this comment. In her interviews with potential employers in the Fall of 2007, Doe II felt she needed to disclose that existence of this and other such comments on AutoAdmit and explain that she had been targeted by pseudonymous online posters. In addition, this statement has contributed to difficulties in Doe II's relationships with her family, friends, and classmates at Yale Law School.

Thus, the plaintiff has shown sufficient evidence supporting a prima facie case for libel, and thus the balancing test of the plaintiff's interest in pursuing discovery in this case outweighs the defendant's First Amendment right to speak anonymously. The defendant's motion to quash is denied.

III. *Defendant's Motion to Proceed Anonymously*

Parties to a lawsuit must generally identify themselves. Fed.R.Civ.P. 10(a) (complaint must "include the names of all the parties"). This rule protects the public's legitimate interest in knowing all of the facts involved, including the identities of the parties. *K.D. v. City of Norwalk*, 2006 WL 1662905, at *1 (D.Conn.2006). Thus, "[c]ourts should not permit parties to proceed pseudonymously just to protect the parties' professional or economic life." *Doe v. United Services Life Ins. Co.*, 123 F.R.D. 437, 439 n. 1 (S.D.N.Y.1988). A party may proceed anonymously only after demonstrating "a substantial privacy right which outweighs the customary and constitutionally embedded presumption of openness in judicial proceedings." *K.D. v. City of Norwalk*, 2006 WL 1662905, at *1 (citing Fed. R.Civ.P. 10(a); *Doe v. Stegall*, 653 F.2d 180 (5th Cir.1981)).

Doe 21 has not made a showing of any substantial privacy right or of any potential physical or mental harm as a result of being a named party to this litigation. He argues that other named defendants have been subjected to ridicule on AutoAdmit or lost employment. However, even if Doe 21 could show he was likely to receive the same alleged treatment, which he has not, these harms are not the special harms required in order to proceed anonymously, but rather social stigma, embarrassment, and economic harm, none of which are grounds for proceeding anonymously. *See James v. Jacobson*, 6 F.3d 233, 238–39 (4th Cir.1993) (citing cases); *Doe v. Frank*, 951 F.2d 320, 324 (11 Cir.1992); *Guerrilla Girls Inc. v. Kaz*, 224 F.R.D. 571, 573 (S.D.N.Y.2004). In addition, Doe 21's argument that he should be allowed to proceed anonymously because the plaintiffs have been allowed to do so is also without merit and irrelevant to the defendant's status.

Thus, the defendant's motion to proceed anonymously is denied.

IV. *Conclusion*

The motion of the defendant, identifying himself as Doe 21, to quash plaintiff's subpoena * * * is DENIED. The defendant's motion to proceed anonymously * * * is DENIED.

6. FREEDOM OF IDEAS

INTELLECTUAL PRIVACY

Neil M. Richards
87 Tex. L. Rev. 387, 389, 403 (2008).

Intellectual privacy is the ability, whether protected by law or social circumstances, to develop ideas and beliefs away from the unwanted gaze or interference of others. Surveillance or interference can warp the integrity of our freedom of thought and can skew the way we think, with clear repercussions for the content of our subsequent speech or writing. The ability to freely make up our minds and to develop new ideas thus depends upon a substantial measure of intellectual privacy. In this way, intellectual privacy is a cornerstone of meaningful First Amendment liberties. * * *

It is unfortunate that the principal theories of the First Amendment have failed to treat intellectual privacy as an important First Amendment value. This deficiency is a critical one, because meaningful freedom of speech requires meaningful intellectual privacy. To illustrate this point, imagine a system of free speech law that is deeply protective of the act of speaking, but which has little protection for the act of thinking. Under a system like this, people could speak freely on a whole host of controversial issues, and could engage in widespread obscene, racist, libelous, or inciting speech. Current theory would consider such a regime to be deeply speech-protective.

But if this system had little protection for intellectual privacy, the government would be free to secretly monitor phone calls, Internet usage, and the movements and associations of individuals. Private industry would also be relatively unconstrained in its ability to participate in a market for the same information. Such a world would have plenty of speech but little privacy; indeed, some observers have predicted that this is the future of our online world and, by extension, the expressive topography of our society as a whole.

A regime that protected speech but not thoughts would be deeply problematic, to say the least. In a world of widespread public and private scrutiny, novel but unpopular ideas would have little room to breathe. Much could be said, but it would rarely be new, because original ideas would have no refuge in which to develop, save perhaps in the minds of hermits. Such a world has in the past been the domain of writers of speculative and science fiction, but it should be no less familiar as a result.

Indeed, the word "Orwellian" strikes with deep resonance in this context. Moreover, as many scholars have argued, surveillance has a deep effect on the actions of the subject. The knowledge that others are watching (or may be watching) tends the preference of the individual towards the bland and the mainstream. Thoroughgoing surveillance, whether by public or private actors, has a normalizing and stifling effect.

Intellectual privacy creates a screen against such surveillance. As the English philosopher Timothy Macklem has argued, "The isolating shield of privacy enables people to develop and exchange ideas, or to foster and share activities, that the presence or even awareness of other people might stifle. For better and for worse, then, privacy is sponsor and guardian to the creative and subversive." When there is protection from surveillance, new ideas can be entertained, even when they might be deeply subversive or threatening to conventional or orthodox views. If we value a pluralistic society or the cognitive processes that produce new ideas, then some measure of intellectual privacy, some respite from cognitive surveillance, is essential. Any meaningful freedom of speech requires an underlying culture of vibrant intellectual innovation. Intellectual privacy nurtures that innovation, protecting the engine of expression—the imagination of the human mind. To the extent that orthodox First Amendment theory is underprotective of intellectual privacy, we must rehabilitate it to take account of these vital norms.

NOTE: PORNOGRAPHY AND ADULTERY

The First Amendment protects the mind's encounters with the sacred and the profane. The next pair of cases illustrates respects in which using obscene materials in the privacy of one's own home, and engaging in heterosexual adultery in the privacy of one's own home are constitutionally protected First Amendment freedoms. But is sexuality (e.g., masturbation or adultery) the freedom protected at bottom or is "intellectual privacy" what these cases are all about? Is a person's sexuality an aspect of her intellectual life?

STANLEY v. GEORGIA

394 U.S. 557 (1969).

Mr. Justice Marshall delivered the opinion of the Court.

An investigation of appellant's alleged bookmaking activities led to the issuance of a search warrant for appellant's home. Under authority of this warrant, federal and state agents secured entrance. They found very little evidence of bookmaking activity, but while looking through a desk drawer in an upstairs bedroom, one of the federal agents, accompanied by a state officer, found three reels of eight-millimeter film. Using a projector and screen found in an upstairs living room, they viewed the films. The state officer concluded that they were obscene and seized them. Since a further examination of the bedroom indicated that appellant occupied it, he was charged with possession of obscene matter and placed under

PH

arrest. He was later indicted for "knowingly hav[ing] possession of * * * obscene matter" in violation of Georgia law. Appellant was tried before a jury and convicted. The Supreme Court of Georgia affirmed. [We reverse.]

Appellant raises several challenges to the validity of his conviction. We find it necessary to consider only one. Appellant argues here, and argued below, that the Georgia obscenity statute, insofar as it punishes mere private possession of obscene matter, violates the First Amendment, as made applicable to the States by the Fourteenth Amendment. For reasons set forth below, we agree that the mere private possession of obscene matter cannot constitutionally be made a crime. * * *

holding

Th[e] right to receive information and ideas, regardless of their social worth, is fundamental to our free society. Moreover, in the context of this case—a prosecution for mere possession of printed or filmed matter in the privacy of a person's own home—that right takes on an added dimension. For also fundamental is the right to be free, except in very limited circumstances, from unwanted governmental intrusions into one's privacy. * * *

These are the rights that appellant is asserting in the case before us. He is asserting the right to read or observe what he pleases—the right to satisfy his intellectual and emotional needs in the privacy of his own home. He is asserting the right to be free from state inquiry into the contents of his library. Georgia contends that appellant does not have these rights, that there are certain types of materials that the individual may not read or even possess. Georgia justifies this assertion by arguing that the films in the present case are obscene. But we think that mere categorization of these films as "obscene" is insufficient justification for such a drastic invasion of personal liberties guaranteed by the First and Fourteenth Amendments. Whatever may be the justifications for other statutes regulating obscenity, we do not think they reach into the privacy of one's own home. If the First Amendment means anything, it means that a State has no business telling a man, sitting alone in his own house, what books he may read or what films he may watch. Our whole constitutional heritage rebels at the thought of giving government the power to control men's minds.

And yet, in the face of these traditional notions of individual liberty, Georgia asserts the right to protect the individual's mind from the effects of obscenity. We are not certain that this argument amounts to anything more than the assertion that the State has the right to control the moral content of a person's thoughts. To some, this may be a noble purpose, but it is wholly inconsistent with the philosophy of the First Amendment. * * *

Perhaps recognizing this, Georgia asserts that exposure to obscene materials may lead to deviant sexual behavior or crimes of sexual violence. There appears to be little empirical basis for that assertion. But more important, if the State is only concerned about printed or filmed materials inducing antisocial conduct, we believe that in the context of private consumption of ideas and information we should adhere to the view that "among free men, the deterrents ordinarily to be applied to prevent crime are education and punishment for violations of the law * * *." Whitney v. California, 274 U.S. 357, 378 (1927) (Brandeis, J., concurring). * * *

Finally, we are faced with the argument that prohibition of possession of obscene materials is a necessary incident to statutory schemes prohibiting distribution. That argument is based on alleged difficulties of proving an intent to distribute or in producing evidence of actual distribution. We are not convinced that such difficulties exist, but even if they did we do not think that they would justify infringement of the individual's right to read or observe what he pleases. Because that right is so fundamental to our scheme of individual liberty, its restriction may not be justified by the need to ease the administration of otherwise valid criminal laws. See Smith v. California, 361 U.S. 147 (1959).

We hold that the First and Fourteenth Amendments prohibit making mere private possession of obscene material a crime. * * * As we have said, the States retain broad power to regulate obscenity; that power simply does not extend to mere possession by the individual in the privacy of his own home. Accordingly, the judgment of the court below is reversed and the case is remanded for proceedings not inconsistent with this opinion. * * *

MR. JUSTICE STEWART, with whom MR. JUSTICE BRENNAN and MR. JUSTICE WHITE join, concurring in the result.

Before the commencement of the trial in this case, the appellant filed a motion to suppress the films as evidence upon the ground that they had been seized in violation of the Fourth and Fourteenth Amendments. The motion was denied, and the films were admitted in evidence at the trial. In affirming the appellant's conviction, the Georgia Supreme Court specifically determined that the films had been lawfully seized. The appellant correctly contends that this determination was clearly wrong under established principles of constitutional law. But the Court today disregards this preliminary issue in its hurry to move on to newer constitutional frontiers. I cannot so readily overlook the serious inroads upon Fourth Amendment guarantees countenanced in this case by the Georgia courts. * * *

There can be no doubt, therefore, that the agents were lawfully present in the appellant's house, lawfully authorized to search for any and all of the items specified in the warrant, and lawfully empowered to seize any such items they might find. It follows, therefore, that the agents were acting within the authority of the warrant when they proceeded to the appellant's upstairs bedroom and pulled open the drawers of his desk. But when they found in one of those drawers not gambling material but moving picture films, the warrant gave them no authority to seize the films. * * *

This is not a case where agents in the course of a lawful search came upon contraband, criminal activity, or criminal evidence in plain view. For the record makes clear that the contents of the films could not be determined by mere inspection. And this is not a case that presents any questions as to the permissible scope of a search made incident to a lawful arrest. For the appellant had not been arrested when the agents found the films. After finding them, the agents spent some 50 minutes exhibiting them by means of the appellant's projector in another upstairs room. Only then did the agents return downstairs and arrest the appellant. * * *

Because the films were seized in violation of the Fourth and Fourteenth Amendments, they were inadmissible in evidence at the appellant's trial.

NOTE: "INTELLECTUAL PRIVACY"

Does the Supreme Court get off base by linking the right to a stash of adult movies to the "right to receive information and ideas," or is its highbrow framing of the issue exactly right? Is *Stanley* an instance of the Court showing respect for what Professor Neil Richards, above, calls "intellectual privacy"? Cf. Reliable Consultants v. Earle, 517 F.3d 738 (5th 2008).

Mr. Stanley got away with breaking the law against possessing obscenity. Was it because police found the films in his *home*? What if the police had found obscenity in his office or in his car? Did the state of Georgia have no interest in regulating Stanley's morals despite his possession of pornography in his *home*? The Texas law at issue in *Earle* banned sales of "sex toys."

Was Mr. Stanley hurting anyone by collecting legally obscene adult movies? Catherine MacKinnon and other lawyers opposed to pornography have argued that the creation, distribution and use of some "hard core" sexually explicit materials can be harmful to women. Does "intellectual privacy" trump concerns about harm to women? Cf. Catharine A. MacKinnon, *Only Words* (1993) (discussing conflict between protecting speech and preventing harm).

Many animal lovers balked at *United States v. Stevens*, 130 S.Ct. 1577 (2010) (Roberts, CJ), holding that a statute criminalizing the commercial creation, sale, or possession of depictions of animal cruelty was overbroad and facially invalid under the First Amendment free speech provisions. Is *Stevens* an intellectual privacy decision?

Justice Alito dissented from the majority opinion in *Stevens*: "The Court strikes down in its entirety a valuable statute, 18 U.S.C. § 48, that was enacted not to suppress speech, but to prevent horrific acts of animal cruelty—in particular, the creation and commercial exploitation of 'crush videos,' a form of depraved entertainment that has no social value. The Court's approach, which has the practical effect of legalizing the sale of such videos and is thus likely to spur a resumption of their production, is unwarranted. Respondent was convicted under § 48 for selling videos depicting dogfights. On appeal, he argued, among other things, that § 48 is unconstitutional as applied to the facts of this case, and he highlighted features of those videos that might distinguish them from other dogfight videos brought to our attention. The Court of Appeals—incorrectly, in my view—declined to decide whether § 48 is unconstitutional as applied to respondent's videos and instead reached out to hold that the statute is facially invalid. Today's decision does not endorse the Court of Appeals' reasoning, but it nevertheless strikes down § 48 using what has been aptly termed the "strong medicine" of the overbreadth doctrine, *United States v. Williams,* 553 U.S. 285, 293, 128 S.Ct. 1830, 170 L.Ed.2d 650 (2008) (internal quotation marks omitted), a potion that generally should be administered only as 'a last resort.' *Los Angeles Police Dept. v. United Reporting Publishing Corp.,* 528 U.S. 32, 39, 120 S.Ct. 483, 145 L.Ed.2d 451 (1999) (internal quotation marks omitted)."

KRAUS v. VILLAGE OF BARRINGTON HILLS

571 F.Supp. 538 (N.D. Ill. 1982).

GRADY, DISTRICT JUDGE * * *

Plaintiff lives with his wife, Gigi, in a home they own in Barrington Hills, Illinois. He and his wife have organized "an association of heterosexual couples, both married and unmarried, who come together periodically for the purpose of discussion, association, and experimentation relative to sexual mores and activities and who do also engage in sexual activities with each others' partners on a consentual [sic] basis." The organization is called "The Happy Medium Unlimited," and plaintiff refers to its members' practice of exchanging sexual partners as "swinging." * * *

In November 1981, plaintiff conferred with the Commander of the P Cook County Vice Squad and informed him fully of the organization's swinging activities. The Commander decided that swinging was legal so long as it was consensual and private. On November 26, 1981, the Barrington Courier published a lengthy expose of The Happy Medium. Two reporters, posing as a potential swinging couple, gained admission to the plaintiff's home during an organizational meeting and published a detailed account of the members' actions. Four days later the Barrington Hills Village Trustees met to consider whether action should be taken D against The Happy Medium. A newspaper quoted Trustee Louis Klein as saying, "Let's do everything to get rid of it." Similar comments were made by other defendants.

The Police Chief of Barrington Hills and the County Vice Squad Sargeant reported to the Board that they could do nothing about plaintiff's activities in his home. Nevertheless, the Board at the November 30, 1981, meeting voted to take whatever action was necessary to stop the activities of The Happy Medium.

On December 1, 1981, Mary C. Marre, the Building/Enforcement Officer of Barrington Hills, wrote to plaintiff informing him that operation of a private club in his home was a violation of § 5–5–2(A) of Barrington Hills' zoning ordinance. Section 5–11–12(B) of the ordinance provides that each day a violation continues is a separate offense. Section 1–4–1 provides for a fine of $500.00 for each offense. Plaintiff's residence is zoned R–1 Residential. Plaintiff contends that Barrington Hills allows other persons owning property zoned R–1 Residential to engage in commercial ventures, such as the practice of law, running a printing shop, and breeding and trading horses.

Barrington Hills has also employed its police in an attempt to end the activities at plaintiff's home. Police officers have been instructed to stop and ticket for the most trivial of violations all cars turning into plaintiff's property. Squad cars are stationed near the entrance to plaintiff's property on Saturday nights during meetings of The Happy Medium. Cars entering and leaving the property are surveilled and their license plate numbers recorded.

Plaintiff contends that Barrington Hills is applying its zoning ordinances arbitrarily, capriciously and selectively against him in order to end the activities of The Happy Medium. Barrington Hills' actions have allegedly violated plaintiff's First, Fourth and Fourteenth Amendment rights. Plaintiff asks that the court enjoin Barrington Hills and its agents from continuing their actions against plaintiff, his guests, and The Happy Medium. Plaintiff also asks for $1 million in compensatory and punitive damages. * * *

To support a Section 1983 claim [alleging that officials caused him a "deprivation of any rights, privileges, or immunities secured by the Constitution and laws"], plaintiff must allege that a constitutional right has been violated. Plaintiff claims the activities on his premises are protected by the guarantees of freedom of speech, assembly and association, and the right to privacy.

Defendants, in their brief, argue that the club is commercial in nature and therefore has no fundamental constitutional privacy or associational rights. They claim that the size of The Happy Medium, its weekly meetings, and the fact that couples come from at least three states rebuts any claim that a purely personal or friendship relationship is involved. * * * [The case law] does not support the proposition that a club which accepts a small donation from its members is thereby transformed into a commercial enterprise. Consequently, we reject this argument.

Next, defendants argue that even if The Happy Medium is a noncommercial organization, its activities—consensual exchange of sexual partners—are not protected by the Constitution.

The First Amendment contemplates freedom of speech, press, assembly and petition. By implication, it also contemplates freedom of association—a derivative of the specified freedoms. NAACP v. Alabama * * * (1958). Plaintiff contends that his right to association with others in the way he desires is at stake in this case. In cases involving freedom of speech, the Supreme Court has protected advocacy which was not "directed to inciting or producing imminent lawless action" or "likely to incite or produce such action." Brandenburg v. Ohio, 395 U.S. 444 * * * (1969). We believe this same principle applies to the derivative freedom of association. Absent associational activities which are illegal or would incite illegal actions, the freedom of association is inviolate. Here, the members of The Happy Medium participate in sexual activities—including adultery—which many would consider immoral. The Illinois statutes, however, only prohibit sexual activities that are "open and notorious." * * * One of the four basic premises underlying the Act was "protection of the public from open and notorious conduct which disturbs the peace, tends to promote breaches of the peace, or openly flouts accepted standards of morality in the community." Ill. Rev. Stats. ch. 38, para. 11–8 (Smith–Hurd Committee Comments—1961). The Happy Medium conducts its meetings and activities entirely within the residence of plaintiff. We do not believe that sexual activities behind closed doors jeopardize the public peace; nor does it appear at this stage of the proceeding that the activity is "open" within the meaning of the criminal statutes.

The litmus test of constitutionality is not whether conduct is distasteful. Advocating adultery has long been protected under the First Amendment. * * *

Having said all this, it does not avail the plaintiff Kraus that the conduct of the members of The Happy Medium is protected by freedom of association. Kraus has failed to allege sufficient injury to support his claim that his own freedom of association has been infringed. * * *

Of the * * * alleged injuries, only the prosecution of Kraus for zoning ordinance violations directly injures him. Neither the stationing of the police cars on the public street near the entrance to Kraus' property, nor the harassment or surveillance of the cars entering or leaving the property, appear to affect Kraus' associational rights in a direct way. That police cars surveil the property apparently has not forced a cessation of the meetings of The Happy Medium. Nor have members been deterred from attending because police have stopped them for minor violations. Plaintiff does not allege that his guests were innocent of the violations for which they were stopped. License plate numbers are public information and not protected from the eyes of the police. Plaintiff does not allege that by taking down the numbers the police have successfully dissuaded members of The Happy Medium from attending meetings.

This police conduct also does not injure whatever privacy rights plaintiff may have to engage in sexual activities behind the closed doors of his home. By stopping cars for violating traffic laws, taking down license plate numbers and surveilling those entering plaintiff's property, the police have not halted the activities of The Happy Medium. Here, the facts are quite different from cases involving prosecution of persons for using contraceptives, * * * or for private possession of obscene material, * * * or even for sodomy * * *. Plaintiff is not being prosecuted for anything but a zoning ordinance violation. His privacy is unaffected by the acts of the police—he need only close the door and pull the drapes. * * *

Plaintiff has failed to allege facts sufficient to support his claims of abridgement of his freedom of speech, assembly and association or his right to privacy. * * * We stay the proceedings herein regarding the application of the Barrington Hills' zoning ordinance to plaintiff while the parties pursue appropriate state court remedies.

NOTE: "SWINGING"

Does the First Amendment right to associate with other adulterers recognized by the district court in *Krause* entail a right to engage in adulterous sex? Group sex? Only in private homes?

7. FREEDOM OF ASSOCIATION AND THE EXCLUSION OF LESBIANS, GAYS AND BISEXUALS

NOTE: THE SEXUAL ORIENTATION CASES

Do any of the First Amendment associational privacy cases examined thus far trade on the notion that privacy "amounts to the state of the agent having control over decisions concerning matters that draw their meaning and value from the agent's love, caring and liking"? See Julie Inness, *Privacy, Intimacy and Isolation 91* (1992). Is the crucial point of freedom of association that government cannot tell us whom to "like"?

The First Amendment protects "truly private clubs" that discriminate on the basis of race. It also protects discrimination on the basis of sexual orientation, according to the Supreme Court. *But see Christian Legal Society v. Martinez*, 130 S.Ct. 2971 (2010) (law school's policy of requiring all officially recognized student groups to comply with school's nondiscrimination policy prohibiting discrimination on the basis of sexual orientation was reasonable and content neutral, and did not violate the organization's First and Fourteenth Amendment rights to free speech, expressive association, and free exercise of religion.) The Court has held that heterosexuals' freedom of association means that they may exclude homosexuals from a parade held in a public place (*Hurley v. Irish–American Gay, Lesbian and Bisexual Group of Boston*) and a youth organization advertised to the public (*Boy Scouts v. Dale*). Would Hannah Arendt agree?

Note that the LGB parties in these constitutional cases (filed in the 1990's) wanted to be "out" and included. As the privacy tort cases in Chapter 1 of this textbook reflect, some LGB plaintiffs have sued because they preferred to be let alone, closeted, or only selectively "out."

HURLEY v. IRISH–AMERICAN GAY, LESBIAN AND BISEXUAL GROUP OF BOSTON
515 U.S. 557 (1995).

JUSTICE SOUTER delivered the opinion of the Court.

March 17 is set aside for two celebrations in South Boston. As early as 1737, some people in Boston observed the feast of the apostle to Ireland, and since 1776 the day has marked the evacuation of royal troops and Loyalists from the city, prompted by the guns captured at Ticonderoga and set up on Dorchester Heights under General Washington's command. Washington himself reportedly drew on the earlier tradition in choosing "St. Patrick" as the response to "Boston," the password used in the colonial lines on evacuation day. * * *

The tradition of formal sponsorship by the city came to an end in 1947, however, when Mayor James Michael Curley himself granted authority to organize and conduct the St. Patrick's Day–Evacuation Day Parade to the petitioner South Boston Allied War Veterans Council, an unincorporated association of individuals elected from various South Boston veterans groups. Every year since that time, the Council has applied for and received a permit for the parade, which at times has included as many as 20,000 marchers and drawn up to 1 million watchers. No other applicant has ever applied for that permit. * * * Through 1992, the city allowed the Council to use the city's official seal, and provided printing services as well as direct funding.

In 1992, a number of gay, lesbian, and bisexual descendants of the Irish immigrants joined together with other supporters to form the respondent organization, GLIB, to march in the parade as a way to express pride in their Irish heritage as openly gay, lesbian, and bisexual individuals, to demonstrate that there are such men and women among those so descended, and to express their solidarity with like individuals who sought to march in New York's St. Patrick's Day Parade. * * * Although the Council denied GLIB's application to take part in the 1992 parade, GLIB obtained a state-court order to include its contingent, which marched "uneventfully" among that year's 10,000 participants and 750,-000 spectators. * * *

In 1993, after the Council had again refused to admit GLIB to the upcoming parade, the organization and some of its members filed this suit against the Council, the individual petitioner John J. "Wacko" Hurley, and the city of Boston, alleging violations of the State and Federal Constitutions and of the state public accommodations law, which prohibits "any distinction, discrimination or restriction on account of * * * sexual orientation * * * relative to the admission of any person to, or treatment in any place of public accommodation, resort or amusement." Mass. Gen. Laws Section 272:98 (1992). After finding that "for at least the past 47 years, the Parade has traveled the same basic route along the public streets of South Boston, providing entertainment, amusement, and recreation to participants and spectators alike," * * * the state trial court ruled that the parade fell within the statutory definition of a public accommodation, which includes "any place * * * which is open to and accepts or solicits the patronage of the general public * * * ".

Accordingly, [the trial court] ruled that "GLIB is entitled to participate in the Parade on the same terms and conditions as other participants." * * *

The Supreme Judicial Court of Massachusetts affirmed. * * *

We granted certiorari to determine whether the requirement to admit a parade contingent expressing a message not of the private organizers' own choosing violates the First Amendment. We hold that it does and reverse. * * *

If there were no reason for a group of people to march from here to there except to reach a destination, they could make the trip without expressing any message beyond the fact of the march itself. Some people might call such a procession a parade, but it would not be much of one. Real "parades are public dramas of social relations, and in them performers define who can be a social actor and what subjects and ideas are available for communication and consideration." * * * Parades are thus a form of expression, not just motion, and the inherent expressiveness of marching to make a point explains our cases involving protest marches. * * *

The protected expression that inheres in a parade is not limited to its banners and songs, however, for the Constitution looks beyond written or spoken words as mediums of expression. Noting that "symbolism is a primitive but effective way of communicating ideas," our cases have recognized that the First Amendment shields such acts as saluting a flag (and refusing to do so), wearing an armband to protest a war, displaying a red flag, and even "marching, walking or parading" in uniforms "displaying the swastika". As some of these examples show, a narrow, succinctly articulable message is not a condition of constitutional protection, which if confined to expressions conveying a "particularized message," would never reach the unquestionably shielded painting of Jackson Pollock, music of Arnold Schoenberg, or Jabberwocky verse of Lewis Carroll.

Not many marches, then, are beyond the realm of expressive parades, and the South Boston celebration is not one of them. Spectators line the streets; people march in costumes and uniforms, carrying flags and banners with all sorts of messages (e.g., "England get out of Ireland," "Say no to drugs"); marching bands and pipers play; floats are pulled along; and the whole show is broadcast over Boston television. * * * To be sure, we agree with the state courts that in spite of excluding some applicants, the Council is rather lenient in admitting participants. But a private speaker does not forfeit constitutional protection simply by combining multifarious voices, or by failing to edit their themes to isolate an exact message as the exclusive subject matter of the speech. Nor, under our precedent, does First Amendment protection require a speaker to generate, as an original matter, each item featured in the communication * * *.

Respondents' participation as a unit in the parade was equally expressive. * * * In 1993, members of GLIB marched behind a shamrock-strewn banner with the simple inscription "Irish American Gay, Lesbian and Bisexual Group of Boston." GLIB understandably seeks to communicate its ideas as part of the existing parade, rather than staging one of its own. * * *

The Massachusetts public accommodations law under which respondents brought suit has a venerable history. At common law, innkeepers, smiths, and others who "made profession of a public employment," were prohibited from refusing, without good reason, to serve a customer. * * *

After the Civil War, the Commonwealth of Massachusetts was the first State to codify this principle to ensure access to public accommodations regardless of race. * * * As with many public accommodations statutes across the Nation, the legislature continued to broaden the scope of legislation, to the point that the law today prohibits discrimination on the basis of "race, color, religious creed, national origin, sex, sexual orientation * * *, deafness, blindness or any physical or mental disability or ancestry" in "the admission of any person to, or treatment in any place of public accommodation, resort or amusement." Mass. Gen. Laws Sec. 272:98 (1992). Provisions like these are well within the State's usual power to enact when a legislature has reason to believe that a given group is the target of discrimination, and they do not, as a general matter, violate the First or Fourteenth Amendments. * * *

In the case before us, however, the Massachusetts law has been applied in a peculiar way. Its enforcement does not address any dispute about the participation of openly gay, lesbian, or bisexual individuals in various units admitted to the parade. Petitioners disclaim any intent to exclude homosexuals as such, and no individual member of GLIB claims to have been excluded from parading as a member of any group that the Council has approved to march. Instead, the disagreement goes to the admission of GLIB as its own parade unit carrying its own banner. * * * Since every participating unit affects the message conveyed by the private organizers, the state courts' application of the statute produced an order essentially requiring petitioners to alter the expressive content of their parade. * * *

"Since all speech inherently involves choices of what to say and what to leave unsaid," Pacific Gas & Electric Co. v. Public Utilities Comm'n of Cal., 475 U.S. 1, 11 (1986) (plurality opinion) * * *, one important manifestation of the principle of free speech is that one who chooses to speak may also decide "what not to say" * * *.

Petitioners' claim to the benefit of this principle of autonomy to control one's own speech is as sound as the South Boston parade is expressive. Rather like a composer, the Council selects the expressive units of the parade from potential participants, and though the score may not produce a particularized message, each contingent's expression in the Council's eyes comports with what merits celebration on that day. * * * The parade's organizers may object to unqualified social acceptance of gays and lesbians or have some other reason for wishing to keep GLIB's message out of the parade. But whatever the reason, it boils down to the choice of a speaker not to propound a particular point of view, and that choice is presumed to lie beyond the government's power to control.

Respondents contend * * * that admission of GLIB to the parade would not threaten the core principle of speaker's autonomy because the Council, like a cable operator, is merely "a conduit" for the speech of participants in the parade "rather than itself a speaker." * * * But this metaphor is not apt here, because GLIB's participation would likely be perceived as having resulted from the Council's customary determination about a unit admitted to the parade, that its message was worthy of presentation and quite possibly of support as well. A newspaper, similarly, "is more than a passive receptacle or conduit for news, comment, and advertising," and we have held that "the choice of material * * * and the decisions made as to limitations on the size and content * * * and treatment of public issues * * *—whether fair or unfair—constitute the exercise of editorial control and judgment" upon which the State can not intrude.

Unlike the programming offered on various channels by a cable network, the parade does not consist of individual, unrelated segments that happen to be transmitted together for individual selection by members of the audience. Although each parade unit generally identifies itself, each is understood to contribute something to a common theme, and accordingly there is no customary practice whereby private sponsors disavow "any identity of viewpoint" between themselves and the selected participants * * *.

Our holding today rests not on any particular view about the Council's message but on the Nation's commitment to protect freedom of speech. Disapproval of a private speaker's statement does not legitimize use of the Commonwealth's power to compel the speaker to alter the message by including one more acceptable to others. Accordingly, the judgment of the Supreme Judicial Court is reversed and the case remanded for proceedings not inconsistent with this opinion.

BOY SCOUTS OF AMERICA v. DALE

530 U.S. 640 (2000).

CHIEF JUSTICE REHNQUIST delivered the opinion of the Court.

Petitioners are the Boy Scouts of America and the Monmouth Council, a division of the Boy Scouts of America (collectively, Boy Scouts). The Boy Scouts is a private, not-for-profit organization engaged in instilling its system of values in young people. The Boy Scouts asserts that homosexual conduct is inconsistent with the values it seeks to instill. Respondent is James Dale, a former Eagle Scout whose adult membership in the Boy Scouts was revoked when the Boy Scouts learned that he is an avowed homosexual and gay rights activist. The New Jersey Supreme Court held that New Jersey's public accommodations law requires that the Boy Scouts admit Dale. This case presents the question whether applying New Jersey's public accommodations law in this way violates the Boy Scouts' First Amendment right of expressive association. We hold that it does. * * *

James Dale entered scouting in 1978 at the age of eight by joining Monmouth Council's Cub Scout Pack 142. Dale became a Boy Scout in 1981 and remained a Scout until he turned 18. By all accounts, Dale was an exemplary Scout. In 1988, he achieved the rank of Eagle Scout, one of Scouting's highest honors.

Dale applied for adult membership in the Boy Scouts in 1989. The Boy Scouts approved his application for the position of assistant scoutmaster of Troop 73. Around the same time, Dale left home to attend Rutgers University. After arriving at Rutgers, Dale first acknowledged to himself and others that he is gay. He quickly became involved with, and eventually became the copresident of, the Rutgers University Lesbian/Gay Alliance. In 1990, Dale attended a seminar addressing the psychological and health needs of lesbian and gay teenagers. A newspaper covering the event interviewed Dale about his advocacy of homosexual teenagers' need for gay role models. In early July 1990, the newspaper published the interview and Dale's photograph over a caption identifying him as the copresident of the Lesbian/Gay Alliance.

Later that month, Dale received a letter from Monmouth Council Executive James Kay revoking his adult membership. Dale wrote to Kay requesting the reason for Monmouth Council's decision. Kay responded by letter that the Boy Scouts "specifically forbid membership to homosexuals."

In 1992, Dale filed a complaint against the Boy Scouts in the New Jersey Superior Court. The complaint alleged that the Boy Scouts had violated New Jersey's public accommodations statute and its common law by revoking Dale's membership based solely on his sexual orientation. New Jersey's public accommodations statute prohibits, among other things, discrimination on the basis of sexual orientation in places of public accommodation. N. J. Stat. Ann. Sections 10:5–4 and 10:5–5 (West Supp. 2000) * * *.

The New Jersey Superior Court's Chancery Division granted summary judgment in favor of the Boy Scouts.

The New Jersey Superior Court's Appellate Division * * * held that New Jersey's public accommodations law applied to the Boy Scouts and that the Boy Scouts violated it. The Appellate Division rejected the Boy Scouts' federal constitutional claims.

The New Jersey Supreme Court affirmed the judgment of the Appellate Division. It held that the Boy Scouts was a place of public accommodation subject to the public accommodations law, that the organization was not exempt from the law under any of its express exceptions, and that the Boy Scouts violated the law by revoking Dale's membership based on his avowed homosexuality. * * *

We granted the Boy Scouts' petition for certiorari to determine whether the application of New Jersey's public accommodations law violated the First Amendment. * * *

In Roberts v. United States Jaycees, 468 U.S. 609 (1984), we observed that "implicit in the right to engage in activities protected by the First Amendment" is "a corresponding right to associate with others in pursuit of a wide variety of political, social, economic, educational, religious, and cultural ends." This right is crucial in preventing the majority from imposing its views on groups that would rather express other, perhaps unpopular, ideas. Forcing a group to accept certain members may impair the ability of the group to express those views, and only those views, that it intends to express. Thus, "[f]reedom of association * * * plainly presupposes a freedom not to associate." * * *

The forced inclusion of an unwanted person in a group infringes the group's freedom of expressive association if the presence of that person affects in a significant way the group's ability to advocate public or private viewpoints. * * * But the freedom of expressive association, like many freedoms, is not absolute. We have held that the freedom could be overridden "by regulations adopted to serve compelling state interests, unrelated to the suppression of ideas, that cannot be achieved through means significantly less restrictive of associational freedoms." * * *

To determine whether a group is protected by the First Amendment's expressive associational right, we must determine whether the group engages in "expressive association." The First Amendment's protection of expressive association is not reserved for advocacy groups. But to come within its ambit, a group must engage in some form of expression, whether it be public or private.

Because this is a First Amendment case where the ultimate conclusions of law are virtually inseparable from findings of fact, we are obligated to independently review the factual record to ensure that the state court's judgment does not unlawfully intrude on free expression. * * * The Boy Scouts is a private, nonprofit organization. According to its mission statement: "It is the mission of the Boy Scouts of America to serve others by helping to instill values in young people and, in other ways, to prepare them to make ethical choices over their lifetime in achieving their full potential." * * *

Thus, the general mission of the Boy Scouts is clear: "To instill values in young people." * * * The Boy Scouts seeks to instill these values by having its adult leaders spend time with the youth members, instructing and engaging them in activities like camping, archery, and fishing. During the time spent with the youth members, the scoutmasters and assistant scoutmasters inculcate them with the Boy Scouts' values—both expressly and by example. It seems indisputable that an association that seeks to transmit such a system of values engages in expressive activity. * * *

The values the Boy Scouts seeks to instill are "based on" those listed in the Scout Oath and Law. App. 184. The Boy Scouts explains that the Scout Oath and Law provide "a positive moral code for living; they are a list of 'do's' rather than 'don'ts.' " Brief for Petitioners 3. The Boy Scouts asserts that homosexual conduct is inconsistent with the values embodied in the Scout Oath and Law, particularly with the values represented by the terms "morally straight" and "clean."

Obviously, the Scout Oath and Law do not expressly mention sexuality or sexual orientation. * * * And the terms "morally straight" and "clean" are by no means self-defining. Different people would attribute to those terms very different meanings. For example, some people may believe that engaging in homosexual conduct is not at odds with being "morally straight" and "clean." And others may believe that engaging in homosexual conduct is contrary to being "morally straight" and "clean." The Boy Scouts says it falls within the latter category. * * *

The Boy Scouts asserts that it "teaches that homosexual conduct is not morally straight," Brief for Petitioners 39, and that it does "not want to promote homosexual conduct as a legitimate form of behavior," Reply Brief for Petitioners 5. We accept the Boy Scouts' assertion. We need not inquire further to determine the nature of the Boy Scouts' expression with respect to homosexuality. But because the record before us contains written evidence of the Boy Scouts' viewpoint, we look to it as instructive, if only on the question of the sincerity of the professed beliefs.

A 1978 position statement to the Boy Scouts' Executive Committee, signed by Downing B. Jenks, the President of the Boy Scouts, and Harvey L. Price, the Chief Scout Executive, expresses the Boy Scouts' "official position" with regard to "homosexuality and Scouting":

"Q. May an individual who openly declares himself to be a homosexual be a volunteer Scout leader?

"A. No. The Boy Scouts of America is a private, membership organization and leadership therein is a privilege and not a right. We do not believe that homosexuality and leadership in Scouting are appropriate. We will continue to select only those who in our judgment meet our standards and qualifications for leadership." App. 453–454.

Thus, at least as of 1978—the year James Dale entered Scouting—the official position of the Boy Scouts was that avowed homosexuals were not to be Scout leaders.

A position statement promulgated by the Boy Scouts in 1991 (after Dale's membership was revoked but before this litigation was filed) also supports its current view:

"We believe that homosexual conduct is inconsistent with the requirement in the Scout Oath that a Scout be morally straight and in the Scout Law that a Scout be clean in word and deed, and that homosexuals do not provide a desirable role model for Scouts." Id. at 457.

This position statement was redrafted numerous times but its core message remained consistent. For example, a 1993 position statement, the most recent in the record, reads, in part:

"The Boy Scouts of America has always reflected the expectations that Scouting families have had for the organization. We do not believe that homosexuals provide a role model consistent with these expectations. Accordingly, we do not allow for the registration of avowed homosexuals as members or as leaders of the BSA." Id. at 461.

The Boy Scouts publicly expressed its views with respect to homosexual conduct by its assertions in prior litigation. For example, throughout a California case with similar facts filed in the early 1980's, the Boy Scouts consistently asserted the same position with respect to homosexuality that it asserts today. * * * We cannot doubt that the Boy Scouts sincerely holds this view. * * *

We must then determine whether Dale's presence as an assistant scoutmaster would significantly burden the Boy Scouts' desire to not "promote homosexual conduct as a legitimate form of behavior." Reply Brief for Petitioners 5. As we give deference to an association's assertions regarding the nature of its expression, we must also give deference to an association's view of what would impair its expression. * * *

Here, we have found that the Boy Scouts believes that homosexual conduct is inconsistent with the values it seeks to instill in its youth members; it will not "promote homosexual conduct as a legitimate form of behavior." * * * As the presence of GLIB in Boston's St. Patrick's Day parade would have interfered with the parade organizers' choice not to propound a particular point of view, the presence of Dale as an assistant scoutmaster would just as surely interfere with the Boy Scout's choice not to propound a point of view contrary to its beliefs. * * *

Having determined that the Boy Scouts is an expressive association and that the forced inclusion of Dale would significantly affect its expression, we inquire whether the application of New Jersey's public accommodations law to require that the Boy Scouts accept Dale as an assistant scoutmaster runs afoul of the Scouts' freedom of expressive association. We conclude that it does. * * *

We are not, as we must not be, guided by our views of whether the Boy Scouts' teachings with respect to homosexual conduct are right or wrong; public or judicial disapproval of a tenet of an organization's expression does not justify the State's effort to compel the organization to accept members where such acceptance would derogate from the organization's expressive message. "While the law is free to promote all sorts of conduct in place of harmful behavior, it is not free to interfere with speech for no better reason than promoting an approved message or discouraging a disfavored one, however enlightened either purpose may strike the government." Hurley, 515 U.S. at 579.

The judgment of the New Jersey Supreme Court is reversed, and the cause remanded for further proceedings not inconsistent with this opinion. * * * It is so ordered.

JUSTICE STEVENS, with whom JUSTICE SOUTER, JUSTICE GINSBURG and JUSTICE BREYER join, dissenting. * * *

Surely there are instances in which an organization that truly aims to foster a belief at odds with the purposes of a State's antidiscrimination laws will have a First Amendment right to association that precludes forced compliance with those laws. But that right is not a freedom to discriminate at will, nor is it a right to maintain an exclusionary membership policy simply out of fear of what the public reaction would be if the group's membership were opened up. It is an implicit right designed to protect the enumerated rights of the First Amendment, not a license to act on any discriminatory impulse. To prevail in asserting a right of expressive association as a defense to a charge of violating an antidiscrimination law, the organization must at least show it has adopted and advocated an unequivocal position inconsistent with a position advocated or epitomized by the person whom the organization seeks to exclude. If this Court were to defer to whatever position an organization is prepared to assert in its briefs, there would be no way to mark the proper boundary between genuine exercises of the right to associate, on the one hand, and sham claims that are simply attempts to insulate nonexpressive private discrimination, on the other hand. Shielding a litigant's claim from judicial scrutiny would, in turn, render civil rights legislation a nullity, and turn this important constitutional right into a farce. Accordingly, the Court's prescription of total deference will not do. * * *

Even if BSA's right to associate argument fails, it nonetheless might have a First Amendment right to refrain from including debate and dialogue about homosexuality as part of its mission to instill values in Scouts. It can, for example, advise Scouts who are entering adulthood and have questions about sex to talk "with your parents, religious leaders, teachers, or Scoutmaster," and, in turn, it can direct Scoutmasters who are asked such questions "not undertake to instruct Scouts, in any formalized manner, in the subject of sex and family life" because "it is not construed to be Scouting's proper area." * * * Dale's right to advocate certain beliefs in a public forum or in a private debate does not include a right to advocate these ideas when he is working as a Scoutmaster. And BSA cannot be compelled to include a message about homosexuality among the values it actually chooses to teach its Scouts, if it would prefer to remain silent on that subject. * * *

BSA has not contended, nor does the record support, that Dale had ever advocated a view on homosexuality to his troop before his membership was revoked. Accordingly, BSA's revocation could only have been based on an assumption that he would do so in the future. * * *

The Scoutmaster Handbook instructs Dale, like all Scoutmasters, that sexual issues are not their "proper area," and there is no evidence that Dale had any intention of violating this rule. Indeed, from all accounts Dale was a model Boy Scout and Assistant Scoutmaster up until the day his membership was revoked, and there is no reason to believe that he would suddenly disobey the directives of BSA because of anything he said in the newspaper article. * * *

The only apparent explanation for the majority's holding, then, is that homosexuals are simply so different from the rest of society that their presence alone—unlike any other individual's—should be singled out for special First Amendment treatment. Under the majority's reasoning, an openly gay male is irreversibly affixed with the label "homosexual." That label, even though unseen, communicates a message that permits his exclusion wherever he goes. His openness is the sole and sufficient justification for his ostracism. * * *

If we would guide by the light of reason, we must let our minds be bold. I respectfully dissent.

NOTE: HETEROSEXUAL RIGHTS

First, what was the "state action" at issue in the *Boy Scouts* case? What "state action" gave the disappointed Irish–American Gay, Lesbian and Bisexual group a colorable First Amendment claim in *Hurley*?

Second, the Boston parade organizers argued that they had an "autonomy" interest in controlling the content of the speech implicit in their festivities. Would autonomy entail that they could lawfully both exclude a group planning to march under the banner of sexuality difference *and* (if they choose to) ask all parade participants to sign a statement attesting to their heterosexual sexual orientation? What exactly is "autonomy"? How does it relate to the associational privacy protected by the First Amendment? The concept of "autonomy" appears in connection with First and Fourteenth Amendment decisional privacy cases, too.

NOTE: AUTONOMY AND ITS ALTERNATIVES

Autonomy can be defined as the capacity to make independent, rational decisions and then to act on them. Influenced by Immanuel Kant and the 18th Century European Enlightenment, many modern philosophers have argued that individual autonomy is the essence of human personality and the ethical basis of moral accountability. See J.B. Schneewind, *The Invention of Autonomy: A History of Modern Moral Philosophy* (1998).

Philosopher Gerald Dworkin explained that: "The central idea that underlines the concept of autonomy is indicated by the etymology of the terms: autos (self) and nomos (rule or law)." See Gerald Dworkin, *The Theory and Practice of Autonomy* (1988) 12–13. According to Dworkin: "The most general formulation of moral autonomy is: A person is morally autonomous if and only if his [or her] moral principles are his [or her] own." *Id*. at 34. Moral principles tend to be shared and learned. Recognizing that, strictly speaking, individuals are not sole authors of their moral principles, Dworkin argued that "What is valuable about autonomy is that the commitments and promises a person makes be ones he [or she] views as his [or hers], as part of the person he [or she] wants to be * * *." Id. at 37. So conceived, "[a]n autonomous person is not necessarily a saint or a sinner, a rugged individualist or champion of fraternity, a leader or a follower." Id. Collecting obscene films can be autonomous conduct, as can discriminating on the basis of sexual orientation.

Autonomy is thus self-rule or self-sovereignty. It is self-determination and self-government. See Joel Feinberg, Autonomy, Sovereignty and Privacy: Moral Ideals in the Constitution?, 58 *Notre Dame L. Rev.* 445 (1983).

Which comes first, autonomy or privacy rights? Moral autonomy has been defended as requiring legal privacy rights for its protection; and legal privacy rights have been defended as necessary to foster the development of moral autonomy. Perhaps only by being treated through consistent social practices as if one is autonomous, can one develop a subjective sense of moral autonomy. See Joseph Kupfer, Privacy, Autonomy, and Self Concept, 24 *Philosophical Quarterly* 81, 82 (1987).

Is there a moral difference between individual and organizational discrimination? Do organizations have the same entitlement to respect for their autonomy as individuals? Is an individual's choosing only to date persons of their same race more defensible than an organization's establishing racial criteria for membership? Could the Boy Scouts legally refuse to admit both homosexuals and Asian–Americans? Are capricious and bigoted but deeply felt criteria of exclusion deserving of constitutional protection on autonomy grounds?

Autonomy is not a popular concept with legal scholars who prefer to emphasize the socially interdependent character of human existence. An autonomous existence is a lonely, alienated one, according to Anthony Cook. See Anthony Cook, Beyond Critical Legal Studies: The Reconstructive Theology of Dr. Martin Luther King, Jr., 103 *Harv. L. Rev.* 985 (1990). Autonomy is arguably blemished by inherently masculine connotations, to the extent that "women's existential state * * * is grounded in women's potential for physical, material connection to human life." See Robin West, Jurisprudence and Gender, 55 *U. Chi. L. Rev.* 1 (1988).

Was the Court primarily trying to determine the just limits of legal autonomy when it adjudicated disputes about the Amish and the Boy Scouts? In his book, *Democracy's Discontent* (1996), Michael Sandel contrasted "republican" and "voluntarist" strands in the constitutional privacy cases. The voluntarist strand stresses "the ability independently to define one's identity." The republican strand stresses the ability to partake of traditions that are constitutive of an identity that is not solely of one's own choosing: "[a]s the Court has sometimes acknowledged, 'certain kinds of personal bonds have played a critical role in the culture and traditions of the Nation by cultivating and transmitting shared ideals and beliefs; they thereby foster diversity and act as critical buffers between the individual and the power of the state.' " *Id.* at 93. Does the holding of the *Hurley* case foster either republican identity or voluntarist autonomy?

Jed Rubenfeld has defended an analysis of privacy that rejects the idea of government properly giving maximal sway to the vicissitudes of individual autonomy; but on quite different grounds than Sandel. Rubenfeld argued that the main function of constitutional privacy is to prevent government from becoming repressive or "totalitarian." "Privacy," he says, "takes a stand at the outer boundaries of the legitimate exercise of state power. It is to be invoked only where the government threatens to take over or occupy our lives—to exert power in some way over the totality of our lives." Jed Rubenfeld, The Right of Privacy, 102 *Harv. L. Rev* 737, 740–47 (1989). On this understanding of privacy, was the *Hurley* case correctly decided? Would being forced to march in a parade that also included homosexuals amount to the government taking over the totality of anyone's life? Does the *Yoder* case seem correctly decided from Rubenfeld's point of view? For a criticism of Rubenfeld from a liberal rights perspective in the tradition of John Stuart Mill, see Karen Struening, Privacy and Sexuality in a Society Divided Over Moral Culture, 49 *Political Research Quarterly* 505 (1996).

Are "privacy" and "autonomy" synonyms? Some commentators have resisted the tendency to construe privacy as synonymous with autonomy, freedom, or liberty, arguing that doing so makes the right to privacy too expansive. See, e.g., Raymond Wacks, The Poverty of Privacy, 96 *Law Quarterly Review*, 73, 78–81 (1980). A number of writers have argued that we should define privacy narrowly so that informational and physical intrusions are invasions of "privacy" but interference with personal choices are not. See, e.g., Ruth Gavison, Privacy and the Limits of Law, 89 *Yale L. J.* 421 (1980). Although these linguistic purists may have a point, the legal rodeo has begun and the bulls are already out of the gate. The word "privacy" is used in many senses, including a now well-established decisional sense in which it refers or is identified with "autonomy." Privacy is protected through the "freedom" language of the First Amendment and the "liberty," "equality" and "due process" language of the Fourteenth Amendment.

This is not to say that the public should eagerly embrace any and all applications of the concept of privacy. The politics of "privacy" rhetoric are none too subtle. The growing, established presence of "privacy" discourse in constitutional law invites new applications of the term by groups trying to win controversial new freedoms. Would you advise enthusiastic gun owners seeking expanded rights to freely purchase and possess firearms to adopt the rhetoric of privacy rights for interpreting their perceived entitlements under the Second Amendment? How successful could they be?

B. SECOND AMENDMENT PRIVACY

1. THE SECOND AMENDMENT

"A well regulated militia, being necessary to the security of a free state, the right of the people to keep and bear arms, shall not be infringed."

2. UNDERSTANDING "THE RIGHT TO KEEP AND BEAR ARMS"

The belief that private citizens have a common law right to bear arms—independent of any statute or provision of a constitution—has been around for a long time. Cf. *United States v. Cruikshank*, 92 U.S. 542 (1875), in which defendants accused of a racially motivated assault alleged the right to possess guns. Moreover, the belief that private citizens have a federal constitutional right to weapons of their own has had a long and interesting life, too. *United States v. Miller* permitted limitations on the possession of guns; but on Second Amendment grounds, *District of Columbia v. Heller* strongly chastised the District of Columbia's efforts to restrict the possession of readily operable handguns in private homes.

UNITED STATES v. MILLER
307 U.S. 174 (1939).

MR. JUSTICE McREYNOLDS delivered the opinion of the Court.

[An indictment in the District Court Western District Arkansas charged that Jack Miller and Frank Layton transported an unregistered double barrel 12–gauge Stevens shotgun with a barrel less that 18 inches long from Oklahoma to Arkansas in violation of the federal "National Firearms Act" of 1934. Miller and Layton alleged in their defense that: "The National Firearms Act is * * * an attempt to usurp police power reserved to the States, and is therefore unconstitutional." Also, it offends the inhibition of the Second Amendment to the Constitution—"A well regulated Militia, being necessary to the security of a free State, the right of people to keep and bear Arms, shall not be infringed."] * * *

[T]he objection that the Act usurps police power reserved to the States is plainly untenable.

In the absence of any evidence tending to show that possession or use of a "shotgun having a barrel of less than eighteen inches in length" at this time has some reasonable relationship to the preservation or efficiency of a well regulated militia, we cannot say that the Second Amendment guarantees the right to keep and bear such an instrument. Certainly it is not within judicial notice that this weapon is any part of the ordinary military equipment or that its use could contribute to the common defense. * * *

The Constitution as originally adopted granted to the Congress power—"To provide for calling forth the Militia to execute the Laws of the Union, suppress Insurrections and repel Invasions; To provide for organizing, arming, and disciplining, the Militia, and for governing such Part of them as may be employed in the Service of the United States, reserving to the States respectively, the Appointment of the Officers, and the Authority of training the Militia according to the discipline prescribed by Congress." With obvious purpose to assure the continuation and render possible the effectiveness of such forces the declaration and guarantee of the Second Amendment were made. It must be interpreted and applied with that end in view.

The Militia which the States were expected to maintain and train is set in contrast with Troops which they were forbidden to keep without the consent of Congress. The sentiment of the time strongly disfavored standing armies; the common view was that adequate defense of country and laws could be secured through the Militia—civilians primarily, soldiers on occasion.

The signification attributed to the term Militia appears from the debates in the Convention, the history and legislation of Colonies and States, and the writings of approved commentators. These show plainly enough that the Militia comprised all males physically capable of acting in concert for the common defense. "A body of citizens enrolled for military discipline." And further, that ordinarily when called for service these men were expected to appear bearing arms supplied by themselves and of the kind in common use at the time. * * *

Most if not all of the States have adopted provisions touching the right to keep and bear arms. Differences in the language employed in these have naturally led to somewhat variant conclusions concerning the scope of the right guaranteed. But none of them seem to afford any material support for the challenged ruling of the court below.

We are unable to accept the conclusion of the court below and the challenged judgment must be reversed. The cause will be remanded for further proceedings.

3. PRIVATE OWNERSHIP OF FIREARMS

STATE v. WILLIAMS

158 Wn.2d 904, 148 P.3d 993 (Wash. 2006).

JUDGE BARBARA A. MADSEN

In April 2003, Mr. Williams was helping his grandmother move out of her house and into another residence. While he was cleaning out his grandmother's garage he came across his deceased grandfather's shotgun. Mr. Williams took the shotgun and placed it in the bathroom that was inside the back bedroom—the bedroom that had been his grandmother's—because there was a lock on that door and the garage did not have a lock. He then locked the door to the bedroom to prevent others from stumbling upon the gun and hurting themselves.

The following week, Mr. Williams was leaving his grandmother's house to run some errands when Deputy Sheriff Mark Malloque approached him and inquired about a certain juvenile suspect for whom Malloque was looking. Mr. Williams said that the juvenile was not at his grandmother's house. At Deputy Malloque's request Mr. Williams allowed him to search the house for the juvenile. He unlocked the bedroom door to allow Deputy Malloque to look for the juvenile. Inside the bathroom Malloque saw the shotgun sitting on top of the toilet tank and noticed that the barrel was shorter than allowed by law. When asked about the weapon Williams initially denied knowing anything about the gun. Upon further inquiry, he said the gun came from the garage. Deputy Malloque arrested Mr. Williams. Williams said he did not understand why he was being arrested until Deputy Malloque informed him that the gun was too short.

The barrel on the shotgun measured 13 1/8 inches with an overall length of 24 3/8 inches. The State charged Mr. Williams with one count of possession of an unlawful firearm pursuant to RCW 9.41.190(1). * * *

The jury found Mr. Williams guilty, and the court sentenced him to 45 days in jail (with possibility of jail alternatives). Williams appealed his conviction, arguing that the State needed to prove that he knew the facts that made the firearm illegal. The Court of Appeals disagreed, holding that the State need only prove that a defendant knowingly possessed the unlawful firearm.

[P]ossessing a firearm can be innocent conduct. Citizens have a constitutional right to bear arms under both the federal and state constitutions. U.S. CONST. amend. II; WASH. CONST. art. I, § 24. A person may lawfully own a shotgun so long as the barrel length is more than 18 inches in length and has an overall length of less than 26 inches. RCW 9.41.190 precludes possession of a short-barreled shotgun. Moreover, the statute also criminalizes possession of a short-barreled rifle and a machine gun. The factor concerned with innocent conduct is particularly important in the case of a machine gun, which can be altered in ways not easily observable. If strict liability is imposed, a person could innocently come into the possession of a shotgun, rifle, or weapon meeting the definition of a machine gun but then be subject to imprisonment, despite ignorance of the gun's characteristics, if the barrel turns out to be shorter than allowed by law or the weapon has been altered, making it a machine gun. The legislature likely did not intend to imprison persons for such seemingly innocent conduct. * * *

We think the jury was more than justified in finding that he knew or should have known that the barrel of his shotgun was less than 18 inches (5 inches shorter than the law permits) and thus met the legal definition of a short-barreled shotgun. Accordingly, we find that any error in this case was harmless.

The Court of Appeals is affirmed.

J.M. JOHNSON, J. (Dissenting)

The majority recognizes the high standard before possession of certain firearms may be held criminal: "the legislature intended that the State prove that a person knew, or should have known, the characteristics that make a firearm illegal to be convicted under RCW 9.41.190." Majority at 14. While the majority aptly states the law, it immediately misapplies it. I must disagree with the conclusion that an admittedly "potentially ambiguous" and "deficient" * * * jury instruction, which here implicates constitutionally protected rights, amounts to harmless error. * * * Thus, I dissent.

DISTRICT OF COLUMBIA v. HELLER
128 S.Ct. 2783 (2008).

SCALIA, J.

Respondent Dick Heller is a D. C. special police officer authorized to carry a handgun while on duty at the Federal Judicial Center. He applied for a registration certificate for a handgun that he wished to keep at home, but the District refused. He thereafter filed a lawsuit in the Federal District Court for the District of Columbia seeking, on Second Amendment grounds, to enjoin the city from enforcing the bar on the registration of handguns, the licensing requirement insofar as it prohibits the carrying of a firearm in the home without a license, and the trigger-lock requirement insofar as it prohibits the use of "functional firearms within the home." The District Court dismissed respondent's complaint, see *Parker* v. *District of Columbia*, 311 F. Supp. 2d 103, 109 (2004). The Court of Appeals for the District of Columbia Circuit, construing his complaint as seeking the right to render a firearm operable and carry it about his home in that condition only when necessary for self-defense, reversed, see *Parker* v. *District of Columbia*, 478 F. 3d 370, 401 (2007). It held that the Second Amendment protects an individual right to possess firearms and that the city's total ban on handguns, as well as its requirement that firearms in the home be kept nonfunctional even when necessary for self-defense, violated that right. The Court of Appeals directed the District Court to enter summary judgment for respondent. * * *

Putting all of the[ ] textual elements together, we find that they guarantee the individual right to possess and carry weapons in case of confrontation. This meaning is strongly confirmed by the historical background of the Second Amendment. * * * [T]he inherent right of self-defense has been central to the Second Amendment right. The handgun ban amounts to a prohibition of an entire class of "arms" that is overwhelmingly chosen by American society for that lawful purpose. The prohibition extends, moreover, to the home, where the need for defense of self, family, and property is most acute. Under any of the standards of scrutiny that we have applied to enumerated constitutional rights, banning from the home "the most preferred firearm in the nation to 'keep' and use for protection of one's home and family," 478 F. 3d, at 400, would fail constitutional muster. * * *

Few laws in the history of our Nation have come close to the severe restriction of the District's handgun ban. * * *

There are many reasons that a citizen may prefer a handgun for home defense: It is easier to store in a location that is readily accessible in an emergency; it cannot easily be redirected or wrestled away by an attacker; it is easier to use for those without the upper-body strength to lift and aim a long gun; it can be pointed at a burglar with one hand while the other hand dials the police. Whatever the reason, handguns are the most popular weapon chosen by Americans for self-defense in the home, and a complete prohibition of their use is invalid. * * *

We must also address the District's requirement (as applied to respondent's handgun) that firearms in the home be rendered and kept inoperable at all times. This makes it impossible for citizens to use them for the core lawful purpose of self-defense and is hence unconstitutional. * * *

We are aware of the problem of handgun violence in this country, and we take seriously the concerns raised by the many *amici* who believe that prohibition of handgun ownership is a solution. The Constitution leaves the District of Columbia a variety of tools for combating that problem, including some measures regulating handguns, see *supra,* at 54–55, and n. 26. But the enshrinement of constitutional rights necessarily takes certain policy choices off the table. These include the absolute prohibition of handguns held and used for self-defense in the home. Undoubtedly some think that the Second Amendment is outmoded in a society where our standing army is the pride of our Nation, where well-trained police forces provide personal security, and where gun violence is a serious problem. That is perhaps debatable, but what is not debatable is that it is not the role of this Court to pronounce the Second Amendment extinct.

We affirm the judgment of the Court of Appeals.

Breyer, joined by Stevens, Souter and Ginsburg, dissenting.

* * *

The majority's conclusion is wrong for two independent reasons. The first reason is that set forth by Justice Stevens—namely, that the Second Amendment protects militia-related, not self-defense-related, interests. These two interests are sometimes intertwined. To assure 18th-century citizens that they could keep arms for militia purposes would necessarily have allowed them to keep arms that they could have used for self-defense as well. But self-defense alone, detached from any militia-related objective, is not the Amendment's concern.

The second independent reason is that the protection the Amendment provides is not absolute. The Amendment permits government to regulate the interests that it serves. Thus, irrespective of what those interests are—whether they do or do not include an independent interest in self-defense—the majority's view cannot be correct unless it can show that the District's regulation is unreasonable or inappropriate in Second Amendment terms. This the majority cannot do. * * *

* * * Given the purposes for which the Framers enacted the Second Amendment, how should it be applied to modern-day circumstances that they could not have anticipated? Assume, for argument's sake, that the Framers did intend the Amendment to offer a degree of self-defense protection. Does that mean that the Framers also intended to guarantee a right to possess a loaded gun near swimming pools, parks, and playgrounds? That they would not have cared about the children who might pick up a loaded gun on their parents' bedside table? That they (who certainly showed concern for the risk of fire, see *supra*, at 5–7) would have lacked concern for the risk of accidental deaths or suicides that readily accessible loaded handguns in urban areas might bring? Unless we believe that they intended future generations to ignore such matters, answering questions such as the questions in this case requires judgment—judicial judgment exercised within a framework for constitutional analysis that guides that judgment and which makes its exercise transparent. One cannot answer those questions by combining inconclusive historical research with judicial *ipse dixit*.

NOTE: GUNS AT HOME

In *McDonald v. Chicago*, 130 S.Ct. 3020 (2010) (Alito, J.), the Supreme Court held that the 14th Amendment makes the Second Amendment right to bear arms as articulated in *Heller* fully applicable to the States. *State v. Williams*, above, upheld the conviction of a man who placed an old shotgun in a locked room of a private home. Did *U.S. v. Miller* support the conviction or was the conviction the result of over-regulation of firearm possession? Does *Heller*, in combination with *McDonald v. Chicago*, entail that *State v. Williams* ought to have come out differently? Is a sawed off shotgun kept in the home a constitutionally protected private possession, assuming Justice Scalia's assertion in *Heller* that the Second Amendment elevates "above all other interests the right of law-abiding, responsible citizens to use arms in defense of hearth and home."

Whether held for self-defense or recreation, guns in homes sometimes contribute to family tragedies. On February 20, 2009, an 11–year–old fifth grader named Jordan Anthony Brown shot his father's pregnant fiancé, Kenzie Marie Houk, with a hunting rifle he had gotten for Christmas. Jordan then hopped on a school bus and went to school. The boy was apparently jealous of the woman and her two young daughters, whom had recently moved in with the boy and his father. See http://www.cbc.ca/world/story/2010/03/29/ shotgun-youth-fiancee-pregnant.html. Lawrence County, Pennsylvania charged Jordan with two counts of first-degree murder and initially placed the fifth grader in an adult jail. Lawrence County Judge Dominick Motto decided that the boy should be tried as an adult rather than as a juvenile: "This offence was an execution-style killing of a defenseless pregnant young mother. A more horrific crime is difficult to imagine."

NOTE: GUNS AT WORK

The plaintiffs in *Bastible v. Weyerhaeuser*, 437 F.3d 999 (10th Cir. 2006), were former paper mill workers. They alleged invasions of privacy and violation of the Oklahoma constitution's right to bear arms provision, Okla. Const. art. 2, § 26, after they lost their jobs for keeping guns in their cars. Their cars were lawfully parked in a designated workplace lot. The weapons were discovered by accident. Weyerhaeuser's management had called in the local sheriff when it came to suspect substance abuse among its employees. The sheriff's department physically searched cars parked in the company lot, after trained sniffing dogs deployed by company security agents "alerted" to drugs and/or firearms. Plaintiffs' cars contained guns in violation of an explicit, well-publicized workplace rule banning firearms on the site. Plaintiffs lost their jobs. Affirming a motion of summary judgment on behalf of defendant employer, the Tenth Circuit held that the plaintiffs had "no absolute common-law or constitutional right to carry loaded weapons at all times and under all circumstances" and could be terminated.

4. ANONYMOUS GUN OWNERSHIP

ELECTRONIC PRIVACY INFORMATION CENTER, GUN OWNERS' PRIVACY

http://epic.org/privacy/firearms/#introduction.

Most often debates concerning firearms center around who has the right to acquire a firearm. However, more recently, the debate has focused on the right of legal gun purchasers to maintain their anonymity. Some gun-control lobbyists argue that if records of gun owners were made available, then this increased regulation of weapons would decrease potentially violent crimes. Taking the opposite view, other advocates believe it is their legal right to own and use a firearm, and that anonymity is critically linked this ownership. They assert that the disclosure of gun ownership records could provide a potential road map for criminals in search of firearms, as well as potential for neighborhood gossip. Gun ownership organizations, such as the Texas State Rifle Association and the National Rifle Association, argue that the release of information about licensed concealed handgun holders may create a larger illegal secondary market for gun resale, which in turn would create a more dangerous society.

NATIONAL RIFLE ASSOCIATION, A "PILLAR" OF THE FIRST AMENDMENT DISCRIMINATES AGAINST THE SECOND

Friday, October 26, 2007
http://www.nraila.org/Legislation/Read.aspx?id=3273.

Earlier this year, Virginia's *Roanoke Times* newspaper came under intense scrutiny and near-universal condemnation after its editors made the irresponsible and dangerous choice to post a searchable database of Virginia's Right-to-Carry permit holders on its website. In doing so, the paper provided anyone with access to the internet (including criminals) the name, home address, and permit issuance and expiration date of more than 135,000 Virginia permit holders.

Thankfully, after hearing from outraged, law-abiding gun owners and non-gun owners alike, the paper prudently decided to remove the database from its website and not repost it, citing a "concern for public safety."

Now, after igniting and enduring that firestorm of criticism, the *Roanoke Times* is once again up to its anti-gun antics.

Local gun show promoter "Showmasters" recently contacted the paper to advertise for its upcoming Roanoke Valley Gun Show and was told in no uncertain terms that the *Roanoke Times* would no longer accept advertising for gun shows. Specifically, Mary Whelchel, the Retail Advertising Manager for the paper said in an e-mail to Annette Elliott of Showmasters, "The *Roanoke Times* has amended their policy after the Virginia Tech massacre. It was initiated in the advertising department *to be more in line with our editorial stance* [emphasis added] and I think you know what that is. I have nothing good to tell you. We will no longer accept advertising from The Roanoke Valley Gun Show." In a subsequent e-mail, Welchel qualified the paper's stance, saying "To restate our policy, we only accept advertising for firearms and accessories *from licensed dealers* [emphasis added]."

In the first place, the horrible murders at Virginia Tech had nothing to do with gun shows whatsoever. * * * Secondly, the paper's decision to accept advertising for firearms and accessories *only from licensed dealers* is blatantly discriminatory. If an auto show were coming to town, would the *Roanoke Times* demand the licenses of every car dealer and individual vendor displaying at the show before the editorial department would grant permission to advertise the event in its paper? Of course not. That would be an arbitrary and absurd reaction. And that's the point.

C. THIRD AMENDMENT PRIVACY

1. THIRD AMENDMENT

"No soldier shall, in time of peace be quartered in any house, without the consent of the owner, nor in time of war, but in a manner to be prescribed by law."

2. THE LITTLE USED AMENDMENT, USED

ENGBLOM v. CAREY

677 F.2d 957 (2d Cir. 1982).

WALTER R. MANSFIELD, JUDGE

In this action, * * * plaintiffs-appellants contend that their due process and Third Amendment rights were violated during a statewide strike of correction officers in April and May of 1979 when they were evicted from their facility-residences without notice or hearing and their residences were used to house members of the National Guard without their consent. For the first time a federal court is asked to invalidate as violative of the Third Amendment the peacetime quartering of troops "in any house, without the consent of the Owner." District Judge Robert W. Sweet granted defendants' motion for summary judgment dismissing the complaint on the ground that appellants did not have a sufficient possessory interest in their facility-residences to entitle them to protection under the Third Amendment and the Due Process clause of the Fourteenth Amendment. We affirm the dismissal of the due process claim on the ground that adequate post-deprivation procedures were afforded to protect appellants' rights. We reverse the dismissal of the Third Amendment claim on the ground that issues as to material facts rendered summary judgment inappropriate. * * *

At the time of the strike appellants had worked at Mid–Orange for nearly two years and were residing in housing located on the grounds of the facility. Of the total staff of some 210, approximately 36–45 officers resided in the "Upper and Lower Staff Buildings" located at Mid–Orange. Although only employees were eligible to live there, such residence was optional on the employee's part and not a condition of employment.

The Upper Staff Building was appellants' sole residence. The building, located about a quarter mile from the prison, consists of a layout of living facilities, each comprising a room with semi-private or private bath, and sharing common kitchens. Aside from the fixtures and a bed and dresser, the occupants of each facility supplied all other furnishings and accessories. The occupancy or "tenancy" was governed by two Correction Department documents. One was entitled "Facility Housing–Rules and Regulations" ("Rules"), signed by the occupants and Superintendent Joseph C. Snow, setting forth various conditions. The other, a "Department Directive" dated January 29, 1976 ("Directive"), set forth the procedure for selecting occupants and additional conditions of the occupancy. These documents throughout refer to the occupants as "tenants" and to the $36 deducted monthly from the payroll of each occupant as "rent" or "rental cost." The Directive made clear that the rent was not to be treated as a mere business expense; it specified that the rental cost could not be deducted by a resident-officer from his salary for income tax purposes. The Directive also obligated Mid–Orange to repair and maintain the rooms "in accordance with normal 'landlord-tenant' responsibilities and practices."

These documents placed various restrictions on the occupants. For example, overnight and long-term guests were prohibited, the rooms could be opened by a master key, personally owned firearms were not permitted to be stored in the rooms, and the rooms were subject to inspection. There was no evidence, however, concerning the extent to which these restrictions were enforced. The documents also provided that an occupant could be evicted on designated grounds but only after an investigation and a six-month written notice to vacate. In an emergency the Superintendent was empowered to "suspend such portions of any or all rules which might impede proper emergency action."

On April 18, 1979, a statewide strike was called by the Security and Law Enforcement Employees Council 82, AFL–CIO. On that day Governor Hugh L. Carey issued a Proclamation and Executive Order activating the National Guard. On April 19 most of the officers at Mid–Orange joined the strike. Either on that day or the following day Superintendent Snow because of the strike issued an order barring striking employees from the facility grounds unless they obtained his permission. At 12:10 A.M. on April 21 Snow finally declared an emergency at Mid–Orange. Beginning around April 19, National Guardsmen had begun arriving at Mid–Orange, eventually reaching a maximum force of 260.

As a result of these developments, from April 19 to April 25 appellants and other employees believed to be on strike were repeatedly denied access to the administration building. Striking officers who lived in staff housing were thus also denied access to their apartments, with one exception on April 20 when appellant Engblom was permitted to retrieve some personal items. The payroll rental deductions were cancelled effective April 19, 1979. Some time before April 25 a decision was made by Mid–Orange to clear the rooms that had been leased to the striking officers so that the rooms could be used to house National Guardsmen, who until then had been housed in the school and administration buildings. On April 25 officer-tenants were permitted to enter and remove and store their belongings in a locked storage area in the building, and appellants did so. Their rooms had been ransacked and personal property was found to be missing or destroyed. Beginning at the same time Guardsmen were housed in these rooms and remained until the end of the strike on May 5. It is undisputed that Palmer's room was so used. While Snow's affidavit states that Engblom's room was never occupied by Guardsmen, this was disputed by Engblom's affidavit.

Participation in the strike was the sole reason for evicting resident staff-tenants and using their rooms to house the Guard. However, at no time prior to the evictions did Mid–Orange provide notice or undertake investigations in accordance with its own regulations. Palmer joined the strike on April 19 and remained on strike through May 3. However, there is a dispute concerning Engblom's alleged participation. Snow stated in his affidavit that he had received second-hand reports that Engblom had been seen on the picket lines and engaging in vandalism. Engblom's affidavit, however, stated that April 18 and 19 were her scheduled days off and that thereafter she was absent from work for medical reasons.

When the strike was over on May 5, appellants were made an offer to resume residence in their staff housing, which they declined. Neither was terminated and both continue to work as correction officers at Mid–Orange. * * *

The Third Amendment was designed to assure a fundamental right to privacy. Griswold v. Connecticut, 381 U.S. 479 (1965); Poe v. Ullman, 367 U.S. 497(1961), at 552 (Douglas, J., dissenting), at 549 (Harlan, J., dissenting). Since the privacy interest arises out of the use and enjoyment of property, compare Griswold, supra (privacy in marital relationship), an inquiry into the nature of the property-based privacy interest seeking protection becomes necessary. In closely analogous contexts rigid notions of ownership are not prerequisites to constitutional protections. When determining whether a legitimate expectation of privacy exists for the purposes of the Fourth Amendment, for instance, the Supreme Court has rejected the notion that a protected privacy interest in a place must be "based on a common-law interest in real or personal property." Rakas v.

Illinois, 439 U.S. 128 (1978). Rather, the Court stated that "one who owns or lawfully possesses or controls property will in all likelihood have a legitimate expectation of privacy." Id. Similarly, in applying the due process clause, the Court has extended its procedural protection "well beyond actual ownership of real estate, chattels, or money," Board of Regents v. Roth, 408 U.S. 564 (1972) * * *. A rigid reading of the word "Owner" in the Third Amendment would be wholly anomalous when viewed, for example, alongside established Fourth Amendment doctrine, since it would lead to an apartment tenant's being denied a privacy right against the forced quartering of troops, while that same tenant, or his guest, or even a hotel visitor, would have a legitimate privacy interest protected against unreasonable searches and seizures. See, e.g., Jones v. United States, 362 U.S. 257 (1960) (friend's apartment); United States v. Agapito, 620 F.2d 324, 333–35 (2d Cir.) (hotel room), cert. denied, 449 U.S. 834 (1980); United States v. Bell, 488 F. Supp. 371 (D.D.C.1980) (apartment tenant).

Accordingly we hold that property-based privacy interests protected by the Third Amendment are not limited solely to those arising out of fee simple ownership but extend to those recognized and permitted by society as founded on lawful occupation or possession with a legal right to exclude others. * * *

Applying these principles, as a matter of state law appellants throughout the strike had a lawful interest in their living quarters sufficient to entitle them to exclude others. * * *

On this record we cannot agree with the district court's finding that appellants' occupancy was more analogous to a possession incident to employment, which under New York law does not constitute a landlord-tenant relationship. Snow's affidavit stating that employees were housed on the premises for the purpose of having personnel close at hand at all times is contradicted by the written Rules and Directive governing the relationship. In addition, the Directive's priority list for selecting housing applications contains two categories of employees, only one of which is designated "Facility employees whose presence is desired near the institution;" the other employee category contains no such restriction. Thus not only does Mid–Orange's selection procedure specifically contemplate housing some employees whose presence is not for the facility's benefit, but there is also no record information as to the employee category from which appellants were chosen. Finally appellants' jobs were not conditioned on their living in staff housing; nor was staff housing provided as a form of remuneration for their employment. It was only after appellants had been on their jobs as correction officers that they became eligible to apply for staff housing. Thus New York decisions relied upon by the district court are not on point, since they all involve apartment superintendents whose jobs required occupancy on the premises.

We conclude, therefore, that in the context of a motion for summary judgment the record, viewed most favorably to appellants, does not preclude a finding that they had a substantial tenancy interest in their staff housing, and that they enjoyed significant privacy due to their right to exclude others from what were functionally their homes. * * *

Accordingly, we * * * remand the dismissal of the Third Amendment claim for proceedings not inconsistent with this opinion.

IRVING R. KAUFMAN, CIRCUIT JUDGE, concurring in part and dissenting in part: * * *

Although a man's home is his castle under the Third Amendment, it is not the case, as Gertrude Stein might say, that a house is a house is a house. A reasonable analysis of Engblom's and Palmer's possessory interest in their rooms at the Mid–Orange Correctional Facility, the relationship between their possession of the rooms and their employment as correction officers, and a realistic acknowledgment that the physical context of their possessory interest was a prison, support the district court's conclusion that Engblom and Palmer did not have the kind of property right that warrants protection under the Third Amendment. While technical ownership has not been deemed a prerequisite for a constitutionally protected property interest in other contexts, see e.g., Katz v. United States, 389 U.S. 347 (1967); United States v. Agapito, 620 F.2d 324, 333–35 (2d Cir.), cert. denied, 449 U.S. 834 (1980), it does not follow that the Third Amendment's protection covers every conceivable type of possessory interest, from full ownership to the rights enjoyed by the casual visitor.

NOTE: NO PLACE LIKE THE HOME

The circumstances that gave rise to the *Engblom* case are extremely unusual. But could something similar happen again? What if there were riots on a state university campus, administrators forced students to leave their dormitories, and then stationed national guardsmen in the dormitories as officials sought to restore order?

It is not the Third Amendment that is the central locus of privacy protection for the home. It is rather the intrusion tort (Chapter 1) and the Fourth Amendment. And yet the broad proscriptions against unreasonable search and seizure contained in the Fourth Amendment have been held since the 1960's to protect people, not places. The Fourth Amendment now extends to reasonable expectations of physical and informational privacy from the bathtub to the iconic phone booth.

D. FOURTH AMENDMENT PRIVACY

1. THE FOURTH AMENDMENT

"The right of the people to be secure in their persons, houses, papers, and effects, against unreasonable searches and seizures, shall not be violated, and no warrants shall issue, but upon probable cause, supported by oath or affirmation, and particularly describing the place to be searched, and the persons or things to be seized."

2. THE EXPECTATION OF PRIVACY PRINCIPLE

OLMSTEAD v. UNITED STATES

277 U.S. 438 (1928).

MR. JUSTICE BRANDEIS, dissenting.

The defendants were convicted of conspiring to violate the National Prohibition Act. Before any of the persons now charged had been arrested or indicted, the telephones by means of which they habitually communicated with one another and with others had been tapped by federal officers. To this end, a lineman of long experience in wire-tapping was employed, on behalf of the Government and at its expense. He tapped eight telephones, some in the homes of the persons charged, some in their offices. Acting on behalf of the Government and in their official capacity, at least six other prohibition agents listened over the tapped wires and reported the messages taken. Their operations extended over a period of nearly five months. The type-written record of the notes of conversations overheard occupies 775 typewritten pages. By objections seasonably made and persistently renewed, the defendants objected to the admission of the evidence obtained by wire-tapping, on the ground that the Government's wire-tapping constituted an unreasonable search and seizure, in violation of the Fourth Amendment; and that the use as evidence of the conversations overheard compelled the defendants to be witnesses against themselves, in violation of the Fifth Amendment. * * *

In Ex parte Jackson, 96 U.S. 727, it was held that a sealed letter entrusted to the mail is protected by the Amendments. The mail is a public service furnished by the Government. The telephone is a public service furnished by its authority. There is, in essence, no difference between the sealed letter and the private telephone message. As Judge Rudkin said below: "True the one is visible, the other invisible; the one is tangible, the other intangible; the one is sealed and the other unsealed, but these are distinctions without a difference." The evil incident to invasion of the privacy of the telephone is far greater than that involved in tampering with the mails. Whenever a telephone line is tapped, the privacy of the persons at both ends of the line is invaded and all conversations between them upon any subject, and although proper, confidential and privileged, may be overheard. Moreover, the tapping of one man's telephone line involves the tapping of the telephone of every other person whom he may call or who may call him. As a means of espionage, writs of assistance and general warrants are but puny instruments of tyranny and oppression when compared with wire-tapping.

The makers of our Constitution undertook to secure conditions favorable to the pursuit of happiness. They recognized the significance of man's spiritual nature, of his feelings and of his intellect. They knew that only a part of the pain, pleasure and satisfactions of life are to be found in material things. They sought to protect Americans in their beliefs, their thoughts, their emotions and their sensations. They conferred, as against the Government, the right to be let alone—the most comprehensive of rights and the right most valued by civilized men. To protect that right, every unjustifiable intrusion by the Government upon the privacy of the individual, whatever the means employed, must be deemed a violation of the Fourth Amendment. And the use, as evidence in a criminal proceeding, of facts ascertained by such intrusion must be deemed a violation of the Fifth.

Applying to the Fourth and Fifth Amendments the established rule of construction, the defendants' objections to the evidence obtained by wiretapping must, in my opinion, be sustained. It is, of course, immaterial where the physical connection with the telephone wires leading into the defendants' premises was made. And it is also immaterial that the intrusion was in aid of law enforcement. Experience should teach us to be most on our guard to protect liberty when the Government's purposes are beneficent. Men born to freedom are naturally alert to repel invasion of their liberty by evil-minded rulers. The greatest dangers to liberty lurk in insidious encroachment by men of zeal, well-meaning but without understanding. * * *

The door of a court is not barred because the plaintiff has committed a crime. The confirmed criminal is as much entitled to redress as his most virtuous fellow citizen; no record of crime, however long, makes one an outlaw. * * *

Decency, security and liberty alike demand that government officials shall be subjected to the same rules of conduct that are commands to the citizen. In a government of laws, existence of the government will be imperilled if it fails to observe the law scrupulously. Our Government is the potent, the omnipresent teacher. For good or for ill, it teaches the whole people by its example. Crime is contagious. If the Government becomes a lawbreaker, it breeds contempt for law; it invites every man to become a law unto himself; it invites anarchy. To declare that in the administration of the criminal law the end justifies the means—to declare that the Government may commit crimes in order to secure the conviction of a private criminal—would bring terrible retribution. Against that pernicious doctrine this Court should resolutely set its face.

NOTE: JUSTICE BRANDEIS AND THE RIGHT TO PRIVACY—A FAMOUS REPRISE

The language Justice Brandeis used to describe privacy as a constitutional value in his oft-cited *Olmstead* dissent strongly echoes the language he used to describe privacy as a common law value in the opening paragraphs of Samuel D. Warren and Louis D. Brandeis, "The Right to Privacy," *Harvard Law Review* (1890). In both places he speaks of the importance of "man's spiritual nature" and of regard for "his feelings and his intellect". Moreover, in both places he characterizes privacy protections as an inevitable development and a requirement of civilized society.

In *Herring v. United States*, 129 S. Ct. 695 (2009) (Roberts, J.), a man was arrested by police who had been told by law enforcement in a nearby county that there was a warrant out for his arrest. In truth the warrant had been recalled. Based on the faulty information, the arrestee's vehicle was searched and guns and illegal drugs were found. The Supreme Court held that the "exclusionary rule," which bars unlawfully obtained evidence from use in criminal trials, did not apply where the evidence leading to an arrest was obtained as the result of an administrative error. County officials had failed to update records, which ought to have shown that a prior arrest warrant had been recalled. Is *Herring* consistent with Justice Brandeis remark in *Olmstead* that "every unjustifiable intrusion by the Government upon the privacy of the individual, whatever the means employed, must be deemed a violation of the Fourth Amendment. And the use, as evidence in a criminal proceeding, of facts ascertained by such intrusion must be deemed a violation of the Fifth."?

KATZ v. UNITED STATES

389 U.S. 347 (1967).

MR. JUSTICE STEWART delivered the opinion of the Court.

The petitioner was convicted in the District Court for the Southern District of California under an eight-count indictment charging him with transmitting wagering information by telephone from Los Angeles to Miami and Boston, in violation of a federal statute. At trial the Government was permitted, over the petitioner's objection, to introduce evidence of the petitioner's end of telephone conversations, overheard by FBI agents who had attached an electronic listening and recording device to the outside of the public telephone booth from which he had placed his calls. In affirming his conviction, the Court of Appeals rejected the contention that the recordings had been obtained in violation of the Fourth Amendment, because "there was no physical entrance into the area occupied by [the petitioner]." We granted certiorari in order to consider the constitutional questions thus presented. * * *

The Government stresses the fact that the telephone booth from which the petitioner made his calls was constructed partly of glass, so that he was as visible after he entered it as he would have been if he had remained outside. But what he sought to exclude when he entered the booth was not the intruding eye—it was the uninvited ear. He did not shed his right to do so simply because he made his calls from a place where he might be seen. No less than an individual in a business office, in a friend's apartment, or in a taxicab, a person in a telephone booth may rely upon the protection of the Fourth Amendment. One who occupies it, shuts the door behind him, and pays the toll that permits him to place a call is surely entitled to assume that the words he utters into the mouthpiece will not be broadcast to the world. To read the Constitution more narrowly is to ignore the vital role that the public telephone has come to play in private communication.

The Government contends, however, that the activities of its agents in this case should not be tested by Fourth Amendment requirements, for the surveillance technique they employed involved no physical penetration of the telephone booth from which the petitioner placed his calls. It is true that the absence of such penetration was at one time thought to foreclose further Fourth Amendment inquiry, Olmstead v. United States * * *.

We conclude that the underpinnings of Olmstead [and similar cases] have been so eroded by our subsequent decisions that the "trespass" doctrine there enunciated can no longer be regarded as controlling. The Government's activities in electronically listening to and recording the petitioner's words violated the privacy upon which he justifiably relied while using the telephone booth and thus constituted a "search and seizure" within the meaning of the Fourth Amendment. The fact that the electronic device employed to achieve that end did not happen to penetrate the wall of the booth can have no constitutional significance.

The question remaining for decision, then, is whether the search and seizure conducted in this case complied with constitutional standards. In that regard, the Government's position is that its agents acted in an entirely defensible manner: They did not begin their electronic surveillance until investigation of the petitioner's activities had established a strong probability that he was using the telephone in question to transmit gambling information to persons in other States, in violation of federal law. Moreover, the surveillance was limited, both in scope and in duration, to the specific purpose of establishing the contents of the petitioner's unlawful telephonic communications. The agents confined their surveillance to the brief periods during which he used the telephone booth, and they took great care to overhear only the conversations of the petitioner himself.

Accepting this account of the Government's actions as accurate, it is clear that this surveillance was so narrowly circumscribed that a duly authorized magistrate, properly notified of the need for such investigation, specifically informed of the basis on which it was to proceed, and clearly apprised of the precise intrusion it would entail, could constitutionally have authorized, with appropriate safeguards, the very limited search and seizure that the Government asserts in fact took place.

The Government * * * urges the creation of a new exception to cover this case. It argues that surveillance of a telephone booth should be exempted from the usual requirement of advance authorization by a magistrate upon a showing of probable cause. We cannot agree. Omission of such authorization "bypasses the safeguards provided by an objective predetermination of probable cause, and substitutes instead the far less reliable procedure of an after-the-event justification for the * * * search, too likely to be subtly influenced by the familiar shortcomings of hindsight judgment." Beck v. Ohio, 379 U.S. 89, 96. * * *

These considerations do not vanish when the search in question is transferred from the setting of a home, an office, or a hotel room to that of a telephone booth. Wherever a man may be, he is entitled to know that he will remain free from unreasonable searches and seizures. The government agents here ignored "the procedure of antecedent justification * * * that is central to the Fourth Amendment," a procedure that we hold to be a constitutional precondition of the kind of electronic surveillance involved in this case. Because the surveillance here failed to meet that condition, and because it led to the petitioner's conviction, the judgment must be reversed. * * *

MR. JUSTICE HARLAN, concurring.

I join the opinion of the Court, which I read to hold only (a) that an enclosed telephone booth is an area where, like a home, * * * a person has a constitutionally protected reasonable expectation of privacy; (b) that electronic, as well as physical, intrusion into a place that is in this sense private may constitute a violation of the Fourth Amendment, and (c) that the invasion of a constitutionally protected area by federal authorities is, as the Court has long held, presumptively unreasonable in the absence of a search warrant.

As the Court's opinion states, "the Fourth Amendment protects people, not places." The question, however, is what protection it affords to those people. Generally, as here, the answer to that question requires reference to a "place." My understanding of the rule that has emerged from prior decisions is that there is a twofold requirement, first that a person have exhibited an actual (subjective) expectation of privacy and, second, that the expectation be one that society is prepared to recognize as "reasonable." Thus, a man's home is, for most purposes, a place where he expects privacy, but objects, activities, or statements that he exposes to the "plain view" of outsiders are not "protected," because no intention to keep them to himself has been exhibited. On the other hand, conversations in the open would not be protected against being overheard, for the expectation of privacy under the circumstances would be unreasonable.

MR. JUSTICE WHITE, concurring. * * *

I agree that the official surveillance of petitioner's telephone conversations in a public booth must be subjected to the test of reasonableness under the Fourth Amendment and that on the record now before us the particular surveillance undertaken was unreasonable absent a warrant properly authorizing it. This application of the Fourth Amendment need not interfere with legitimate needs of law enforcement.

In joining the Court's opinion, I note the Court's acknowledgment that there are circumstances in which it is reasonable to search without a warrant. In this connection, * * * the Court points out that today's decision does not reach national security cases. Wiretapping to protect the security of the Nation has been authorized by successive Presidents. The present Administration would apparently save national security cases from restrictions against wiretapping. See Berger v. New York, 388 U.S. 41, 112–118 (1967) (White, J., dissenting). We should not require the warrant procedure and the magistrate's judgment if the President of the United States or his chief legal officer, the Attorney General, has considered the requirements of national security and authorized electronic surveillance as reasonable.

NOTE: DARK CORNERS MADE VISIBLE

The *Katz* decision restrains the power of government to keep an eye on its citizens, even when they have left their homes and entered the public streets to make use of a commercial utility. However, with a valid warrant or court order, the government gets the go-ahead to listen in on otherwise private conversations.

Recall Robert Post's conception of "civility" rules or Helen Nissenbaum's conception of "appropriateness" and "distribution" norms, introduced in Chapter 1 in connection with the intrusion tort. Do they illuminate the values at stake in Fourth Amendment privacy cases? What of dignity, respect for personal autonomy or liberty—are they underlying values in Fourth Amendment jurisprudence?

Ken I. Kersch has argued that "[t]he Fourth Amendment's protection against unreasonable search and seizures and the Fifth Amendment's self incrimination privilege stood as potentially crippling limitations on the line of sight of the new American State, which needed to render many formerly dark corners of civil society visible in order to control and manipulate them." Ken I. Kersch, The Reconstruction of Constitutional Privacy Rights and the New American State, 16 *Studies in American Political Development* 61, 62 (2002). The "new" American state differs from the old American state, which was "rural and agricultural" and then "urban and industrial." *Id.* at 61. The new state is a corporate-administrative capitalist state whose success depends on detailed knowledge of who and what it must manage and control. The state's imposing necessity for management and control will often dwarf the asserted importance of individual privacy. Citizens' subjective expectations of privacy in the new American state can easily seem unreasonable, indeed. As you go through the Fourth and Fifth Amendment cases, gather evidence for and against Kersch's thesis. Have the courts interpreted the constitution's search, seizure and self-incrimination rules to foster the corporate-administrative state rather than to protect individual rights? Do the exceptions to the warrant requirement and the "government special needs" doctrine, introduced below, neatly prove Kersch's point? Will the surveillance law cases in Chapter 4 tend to support Kersch's perspective?

a. Misplaced Trust

UNITED STATES v. WHITE
401 U.S. 745 (1971).

MR. JUSTICE WHITE announced the judgment of the Court * * *.

The issue before us is whether the Fourth Amendment bars from evidence the testimony of governmental agents who related certain conversations which had occurred between defendant White and a government informant, Harvey Jackson, and which the agents overheard by monitoring the frequency of a radio transmitter carried by Jackson and concealed on his person. * * *

The Court of Appeals understood Katz to render inadmissible against White the agents' testimony concerning conversations that Jackson broadcast to them. We cannot agree. * * *

Hoffa v. United States, 385 U.S. 293 (1966), which was left undisturbed by Katz, held that however strongly a defendant may trust an apparent colleague, his expectations in this respect are not protected by the Fourth Amendment when it turns out that the colleague is a government agent regularly communicating with the authorities. In these circumstances, "no interest legitimately protected by the Fourth Amendment is involved," for that amendment affords no protection to "a wrongdoer's misplaced belief that a person to whom he voluntarily confides his wrongdoing will not reveal it." Hoffa v. United States, at 302. No warrant to "search and seize" is required in such circumstances, nor is it when the Government sends to defendant's home a secret agent who conceals his identity and makes a purchase of narcotics from the accused, Lewis v. United States, 385 U.S. 206 (1966), or when the same agent, unbeknown to the defendant, carries electronic equipment to record the defendant's words and the evidence so gathered is later offered in evidence. Lopez v. United States, 373 U.S. 427 (1963). * * *

If the law gives no protection to the wrongdoer whose trusted accomplice is or becomes a police agent, neither should it protect him when that same agent has recorded or transmitted the conversations which are later offered in evidence to prove the State's case. * * *

Inescapably, one contemplating illegal activities must realize and risk that his companions may be reporting to the police. If he sufficiently doubts their trustworthiness, the association will very probably end or never materialize. But if he has no doubts, or allays them, or risks what doubt he has, the risk is his. In terms of what his course will be, what he will or will not do or say, we are unpersuaded that he would distinguish between probable informers on the one hand and probable informers with transmitters on the other. Given the possibility or probability that one of his colleagues is cooperating with the police, it is only speculation to assert that the defendant's utterances would be substantially different or his sense of security any less if he also thought it possible that the suspected colleague is wired for sound. At least there is no persuasive evidence that the difference in this respect between the electronically equipped and the unequipped agent is substantial enough to require discrete constitutional recognition, particularly under the Fourth Amendment which is ruled by fluid concepts of "reasonableness."

Nor should we be too ready to erect constitutional barriers to relevant and probative evidence which is also accurate and reliable. An electronic recording will many times produce a more reliable rendition of what a defendant has said than will the unaided memory of a police agent. It may also be that with the recording in existence it is less likely that the informant will change his mind, less chance that threat or injury will suppress unfavorable evidence and less chance that cross-examination will confound the testimony. Considerations like these obviously do not favor the defendant, but we are not prepared to hold that a defendant who has no constitutional right to exclude the informer's unaided testimony nevertheless has a Fourth Amendment privilege against a more accurate version of the events in question. It is thus untenable to consider the activities and reports of the police agent himself, though acting without a warrant, to be a "reasonable" investigative effort and lawful under the Fourth Amendment but to view the same agent with a recorder or transmitter as conducting an "unreasonable" and unconstitutional search and seizure. * * *

b.   Terrorism Surveillance—An Earlier Era

UNITED STATES v. UNITED STATES DISTRICT COURT
407 U.S. 297 (1972).

MR. JUSTICE POWELL delivered the opinion of the Court.

The issue before us is an important one for the people of our country and their Government. It involves the delicate question of the President's power, acting through the Attorney General, to authorize electronic surveillance in internal security matters without prior judicial approval. Successive Presidents for more than one-quarter of a century have authorized such surveillance in varying degrees, without guidance from the Congress or a definitive decision of this Court. This case brings the issue here for the first time. Its resolution is a matter of national concern, requiring sensitivity both to the Government's right to protect itself from unlawful subversion and attack and to the citizen's right to be secure in his privacy against unreasonable Government intrusion.

This case arises from a criminal proceeding in the United States District Court for the Eastern District of Michigan, in which the United States charged three defendants with conspiracy to destroy Government property * * *. One of the defendants, Plamondon, was charged with the dynamite bombing of an office of the Central Intelligence Agency in Ann Arbor, Michigan.

During pretrial proceedings, the defendants moved to compel the United States to disclose certain electronic surveillance information and to conduct a hearing to determine whether this information "tainted" the evidence on which the indictment was based or which the Government intended to offer at trial. In response, the Government filed an affidavit of the Attorney General, acknowledging that its agents had overheard conversations in which Plamondon had participated. The affidavit also stated that the Attorney General approved the wiretaps "to gather intelligence information deemed necessary to protect the nation from attempts of domestic organizations to attack and subvert the existing structure of the Government." * * *

[T]he Government asserted that the surveillance was lawful, though conducted without prior judicial approval, as a reasonable exercise of the President's power (exercised through the Attorney General) to protect the national security. The District Court held that the surveillance violated the Fourth Amendment, and ordered the Government to make full disclosure to Plamondon of his overheard conversations. * * * [The Court of Appeals] held that the surveillance was unlawful and that the District Court had properly required disclosure of the overheard conversations * * *. We granted certiorari * * *.

Though the Government and respondents debate their seriousness and magnitude, threats and acts of sabotage against the Government exist in sufficient number to justify investigative powers with respect to them. The covertness and complexity of potential unlawful conduct against the Government and the necessary dependency of many conspirators upon the telephone make electronic surveillance an effective investigatory instrument in certain circumstances. The marked acceleration in technological developments and sophistication in their use have resulted in new techniques for the planning, commission, and concealment of criminal activities. It would be contrary to the public interest for Government to deny to itself the prudent and lawful employment of those very techniques which are employed against the Government and its law-abiding citizens. * * *

The price of lawful public dissent must not be a dread of subjection to an unchecked surveillance power. Nor must the fear of unauthorized official eavesdropping deter vigorous citizen dissent and discussion of Government action in private conversation. For private dissent, no less than open public discourse, is essential to our free society. * * *

As the Fourth Amendment is not absolute in its terms, our task is to examine and balance the basic values at stake in this case: the duty of Government to protect the domestic security, and the potential danger posed by unreasonable surveillance to individual privacy and free expression. If the legitimate need of Government to safeguard domestic security requires the use of electronic surveillance, the question is whether the needs of citizens for privacy and free expression may not be better protected by requiring a warrant before such surveillance is undertaken. We must also ask whether a warrant requirement would unduly frustrate the efforts of Government to protect itself from acts of subversion and overthrow directed against it. * * *

Fourth Amendment freedoms cannot properly be guaranteed if domestic security surveillances may be conducted solely within the discretion of the Branch. The Fourth Amendment does not contemplate the executive officers of Government as neutral and disinterested magistrates. Their duty and responsibility are to enforce the laws, to investigate, and to prosecute. * * * But those charged with this investigative and prosecutorial duty should not be the sole judges of when to utilize constitutionally sensitive means in pursuing their tasks. The historical judgment, which the Fourth Amendment accepts, is that unreviewed executive discretion may yield too readily to pressures to obtain incriminating evidence and overlook potential invasions of privacy and protected speech. * * *

The Government argues that the special circumstances applicable to domestic security surveillances necessitate a further exception to the warrant requirement. It is urged that the requirement of prior judicial review would obstruct the President in the discharge of his constitutional duty to protect domestic security. * * *

The Government further insists that courts "as a practical matter would have neither the knowledge nor the techniques necessary to determine whether there was probable cause to believe that surveillance was necessary to protect national security." These security problems, the Government contends, involve "a large number of complex and subtle factors" beyond the competence of courts to evaluate. * * *

As a final reason for exemption from a warrant requirement, the Government believes that disclosure to a magistrate of all or even a significant portion of the information involved in domestic security surveillances "would create serious potential dangers to the national security and to the lives of informants and agents * * *. Secrecy is the essential ingredient in intelligence gathering; requiring prior judicial authorization would create a greater 'danger of leaks * * *, because in addition to the judge, you have the clerk, the stenographer and some other officer like a law assistant or bailiff who may be apprised of the nature' of the surveillance." * * *.

These contentions on behalf of a complete exemption from the warrant requirement, when urged on behalf of the President and the national security in its domestic implications, merit the most careful consideration. * * *

But we do not think a case has been made for the requested departure from Fourth Amendment standards. The circumstances described do not justify complete exemption of domestic security surveillance from prior judicial scrutiny. Official surveillance, whether its purpose be criminal investigation or ongoing intelligence gathering, risks infringement of constitutionally protected privacy of speech. * * *

We cannot accept the Government's argument that internal security matters are too subtle and complex for judicial evaluation. Courts regularly deal with the most difficult issues of our society. * * *

Nor do we believe prior judicial approval will fracture the secrecy essential to official intelligence gathering. * * *

Thus, we conclude that the Government's concerns do not justify departure in this case from the customary Fourth Amendment requirement of judicial approval prior to initiation of a search or surveillance. Although some added burden will be imposed upon the Attorney General, this inconvenience is justified in a free society to protect constitutional values. * * *

We emphasize, before concluding this opinion, the scope of our decision. As stated at the outset, this case involves only the domestic aspects of national security. We have not addressed, and express no opinion as to, the issues which may be involved with respect to activities of foreign powers or their agents.

3.   HOUSE AND CURTILAGE

EDWIN GODKIN, THE RIGHTS OF THE CITIZEN TO HIS REPUTATION

8 Scribner's Mag. 58, 65 (1890).

To have a house of one's own is the ambition of nearly all civilized men and women, and the reason which most makes them enjoy it is the opportunity it affords to deciding for themselves how much or how little publicity should surround their daily lives.

The right to decide how much knowledge of * * * personal thought and feeling, and how much knowledge, therefore, of his tastes, and habits, of his own private doings and affairs, and those of his family living under his roof, the public at large shall have is as much one of his natural rights as his right to decide how he shall eat and drink, what he shall wear, and in what manner he shall pass his leisure hours.

UNITED STATES v. KARO

468 U.S. 705 (1984).

JUSTICE WHITE delivered the opinion of the Court.

This case * * * presents the question whether the monitoring of a beeper in a private residence, a location not open to visual surveillance, violates the Fourth Amendment rights of those who have a justifiable interest in the privacy of the residence. Contrary to the submission of the United States, we think that it does.

At the risk of belaboring the obvious, private residences are places in which the individual normally expects privacy free of governmental intrusion not authorized by a warrant, and that expectation is plainly one that society is prepared to recognize as justifiable. Our cases have not deviated from this basic Fourth Amendment principle. Searches and seizures inside a home without a warrant are presumptively unreasonable absent exigent circumstances.

The monitoring of an electronic device such as a beeper is, of course, less intrusive than a full-scale search, but it does reveal a critical fact about the interior of the premises that the Government is extremely interested in knowing and that it could not have otherwise obtained without a warrant. * * *

We cannot accept the Government's contention that it should be completely free from the constraints of the Fourth Amendment to determine by means of an electronic device, without a warrant and without probable cause or reasonable suspicion, whether a particular article—or a person, for that matter—is in an individual's home at a particular time. Indiscriminate monitoring of property that has been withdrawn from public view would present far too serious a threat to privacy interests in the home to escape entirely some sort of Fourth Amendment oversight.

We also reject the Government's contention that it should be able to monitor beepers in private residences without a warrant if there is the requisite justification in the facts for believing that a crime is being or will be committed and that monitoring the beeper wherever it goes is likely to produce evidence of criminal activity. Warrantless searches are presumptively unreasonable, though the Court has recognized a few limited exceptions to this general rule.

If agents are required to obtain warrants prior to monitoring a beeper when it has been withdrawn from public view, the Government argues, for all practical purposes they will be forced to obtain warrants in every case in which they seek to use a beeper, because they have no way of knowing in advance whether the beeper will be transmitting its signals from inside private premises. The argument that a warrant requirement would oblige the Government to obtain warrants in a large number of cases is hardly a compelling argument against the requirement. It is worthy of note that, in any event, this is not a particularly attractive case in which to argue that it is impractical to obtain a warrant, since a warrant was in fact obtained in this case, seemingly on probable cause.

We are also unpersuaded by the argument that a warrant should not be required because of the difficulty in satisfying the particularity requirement of the Fourth Amendment. The Government contends that it would be impossible to describe the "place" to be searched, because the location of the place is precisely what is sought to be discovered through the search. However true that may be, it will still be possible to describe the object into which the beeper is to be placed, the circumstances that led agents to wish to install the beeper, and the length of time for which beeper surveillance is requested. In our view, this information will suffice to permit issuance of a warrant authorizing beeper installation and surveillance.

In sum, we discern no reason for deviating from the general rule that a search of a house should be conducted pursuant to a warrant.

NOTE: WARRANTLESS HOME ENTRY PERMITTED IN EXIGENT CIRCUMSTANCES

Law enforcement may enter a private home in an emergency. *See Michigan v. Fisher*, 130 S.Ct. 546 (2009). Police went to Jeremy Fisher's home after neighbors reported someone was "going crazy" at that location. When they arrived at the scene the officers found:

"a pickup truck in the driveway with its front smashed, damaged fenceposts along the side of the property, and three broken house windows, the glass still on the ground outside. The officers also noticed blood on the hood of the pickup and on clothes inside of it, as well as on one of the doors to the house. * * * Through a window, the officers could see respondent, Jeremy Fisher, inside the house, screaming and throwing things. The back door was locked, and a couch had been placed to block the front door. The officers knocked, but Fisher refused to answer. They saw that Fisher had a cut on his hand, and they asked him whether he needed medical attention. Fisher ignored these questions and demanded, with accompanying profanity, that the officers go to get a search warrant. Officer Goolsby then pushed the front door partway open and ventured into the house. Through the window of the open door he saw Fisher pointing a long gun at him. Officer Goolsby withdrew. *Id.* at 547

Fisher was arrested and charged with assault with a dangerous weapon and possession of a firearm during the commission of a felony. The trial court concluded that when an officer entered Fisher's house, he violated Fisher's Fourth Amendment right. Fisher won a motion to suppress the evidence obtained as a result of the illegal search of his home, and a subsequent appeal. But the Supreme Court found that "It sufficed to invoke the emergency aid exception that it was reasonable to believe that Fisher had hurt himself (albeit nonfatally) and needed treatment that in his rage he was unable to provide, or that Fisher was about to hurt, or had already hurt, someone else." *Id.* at 549.

CALIFORNIA v. CIRAOLO

476 U.S. 207 (1986).

CHIEF JUSTICE BURGER delivered the opinion of the Court.

We granted certiorari to determine whether the Fourth Amendment is violated by aerial observation without a warrant from an altitude of 1,000 feet of a fenced-in backyard within the curtilage of a home. * * *

On September 2, 1982, Santa Clara Police received an anonymous telephone tip that marijuana was growing in respondent's backyard. Police were unable to observe the contents of respondent's yard from ground level because of a 6–foot outer fence and a 10–foot inner fence completely enclosing the yard. Later that day, Officer Shutz, who was assigned to investigate, secured a private plane and flew over respondent's house at an altitude of 1,000 feet, within navigable airspace; he was accompanied by Officer Rodriguez. Both officers were trained in marijuana identification. From the overflight, the officers readily identified marijuana plants 8 feet to 10 feet in height growing in a 15–by 25–foot plot in respondent's yard; they photographed the area with a standard 35mm camera.

On September 8, 1982, Officer Shutz obtained a search warrant on the basis of an affidavit describing the anonymous tip and their observations; a photograph depicting respondent's house, the backyard, and neighboring homes was attached to the affidavit as an exhibit. The warrant was executed the next day and 73 plants were seized; it is not disputed that these were marijuana. * * *

The touchstone of Fourth Amendment analysis is whether a person has a "constitutionally protected reasonable expectation of privacy." Katz v. United States, 389 U.S. 347, 360 (1967) (Harlan, J., concurring). Katz posits a two-part inquiry: first, has the individual manifested a subjective expectation of privacy in the object of the challenged search? Second, is society willing to recognize that expectation as reasonable? See Smith v. Maryland, 442 U.S. 735, 740 (1979).

Clearly—and understandably—respondent has met the test of manifesting his own subjective intent and desire to maintain privacy as to his unlawful agricultural pursuits. * * * It can reasonably be assumed that the 10–foot fence was placed to conceal the marijuana crop from at least street-level views. So far as the normal sidewalk traffic was concerned, this fence served that purpose, because respondent "took normal precautions to maintain his privacy." Rawlings v. Kentucky, 448 U.S. 98, 105 (1980).

Yet a 10–foot fence might not shield these plants from the eyes of a citizen or a policeman perched on the top of a truck or a two-level bus. Whether respondent therefore manifested a subjective expectation of privacy from all observations of his backyard, or whether instead he manifested merely a hope that no one would observe his unlawful gardening pursuits, is not entirely clear in these circumstances. Respondent appears to challenge the authority of government to observe his activity from any vantage point or place if the viewing is motivated by a law enforcement purpose, and not the result of a casual, accidental observation.

We turn, therefore, to the second inquiry under Katz, i. e., whether that expectation is reasonable. In pursuing this inquiry, we must keep in mind that "[the] test of legitimacy is not whether the individual chooses to conceal assertedly 'private' activity," but instead "whether the government's intrusion infringes upon the personal and societal values protected by the Fourth Amendment." Oliver, supra, at 181–183.

Respondent argues that because his yard was in the curtilage of his home, no governmental aerial observation is permissible under the Fourth Amendment without a warrant. The history and genesis of the curtilage doctrine are instructive. "At common law, the curtilage is the area to which extends the intimate activity associated with the 'sanctity of a man's home and the privacies of life.' " * * * (quoting Boyd v. United States, 116 U.S. 616, 630 (1886) * * *). The protection afforded the curtilage is essentially a protection of families and personal privacy in an area intimately linked to the home, both physically and psychologically, where privacy expectations are most heightened. The claimed area here was immediately adjacent to a suburban home, surrounded by high double fences. * * *

That the area is within the curtilage does not itself bar all police observation. The Fourth Amendment protection of the home has never been extended to require law enforcement officers to shield their eyes when passing by a home on public thoroughfares. Nor does the mere fact that an individual has taken measures to restrict some views of his activities preclude an officer's observations from a public vantage point where he has a right to be and which renders the activities clearly visible. * * *

The observations by Officers Shutz and Rodriguez in this case took place within public navigable airspace * * * in a physically nonintrusive manner; from this point they were able to observe plants readily discernible to the naked eye as marijuana. That the observation from aircraft was directed at identifying the plants and the officers were trained to recognize marijuana is irrelevant. Such observation is precisely what a judicial officer needs to provide a basis for a warrant. Any member of the public flying in this airspace who glanced down could have seen everything that these officers observed. On this record, we readily conclude that respondent's expectation that his garden was protected from such observation is unreasonable and is not an expectation that society is prepared to honor. * * * Reversed.

JUSTICE POWELL, with whom JUSTICE BRENNAN, JUSTICE MARSHALL, and JUSTICE BLACKMUN join, dissenting. * * *

The Court begins its analysis of the Fourth Amendment issue posed here by deciding that respondent had an expectation of privacy in his backyard. * * *

The Court concludes, nevertheless, that Shutz could use an airplane—a product of modern technology—to intrude visually into respondent's yard. The Court argues that respondent had no reasonable expectation of privacy from aerial observation. * * *

This line of reasoning is flawed. First, the actual risk to privacy from commercial or pleasure aircraft is virtually nonexistent. Travelers on commercial flights, as well as private planes used for business or personal reasons, normally obtain at most a fleeting, anonymous, and nondiscriminating glimpse of the landscape and buildings over which they pass. The risk that a passenger on such a plane might observe private activities, and might connect those activities with particular people, is simply too trivial to protect against. It is no accident that, as a matter of common experience, many people build fences around their residential areas, but few build roofs over their backyards. Therefore, contrary to the Court's suggestion, * * * people do not " 'knowingly [expose]' " their residential yards " 'to the public' " merely by failing to build barriers that prevent aerial surveillance.

KYLLO v. UNITED STATES

533 U.S. 27 (2001).

JUSTICE SCALIA delivered the opinion of the Court.

This case presents the question whether the use of a thermal-imaging device aimed at a private home from a public street to detect relative amounts of heat within the home constitutes a "search" within the meaning of the Fourth Amendment. * * *

In 1991 Agent William Elliott of the United States Department of the Interior came to suspect that marijuana was being grown in the home belonging to petitioner Danny Kyllo, part of a triplex on Rhododendron Drive in Florence, Oregon. Indoor marijuana growth typically requires high-intensity lamps. In order to determine whether an amount of heat was emanating from petitioner's home consistent with the use of such lamps, at 3:20 a.m. on January 16, 1992, Agent Elliott and Dan Haas used an Agema Thermovision 210 thermal imager to scan the triplex. Thermal imagers detect infrared radiation, which virtually all objects emit but which is not visible to the naked eye. The imager converts radiation into images based on relative warmth—black is cool, white is hot, shades of gray connote relative differences; in that respect, it operates somewhat like a video camera showing heat images. The scan of Kyllo's home took only a few minutes and was performed from the passenger seat of Agent Elliott's vehicle across the street from the front of the house and also from the street in back of the house. The scan showed that the roof over the garage and a side wall of petitioner's home were relatively hot compared to the rest of the home and substantially warmer than neighboring homes in the triplex. Agent Elliott concluded that petitioner was using halide lights to grow marijuana in his house, which indeed he was. Based on tips from informants, utility bills, and the thermal imaging, a Federal Magistrate Judge issued a warrant authorizing a search of petitioner's home, and the agents found an indoor growing operation involving more than 100 plants. Petitioner was indicted on one count of manufacturing marijuana. * * * He unsuccessfully moved to suppress the evidence seized from his home and then entered a conditional guilty plea. * * *

The Government maintains * * * that the thermal imaging must be upheld because it detected "only heat radiating from the external surface of the house," * * * But just as a thermal imager captures only heat emanating from a house, so also a powerful directional microphone picks up only sound emanating from a house—and a satellite capable of scanning from many miles away would pick up only visible light emanating from a house. * * *

The Government also contends that the thermal imaging was constitutional because it did not "detect private activities occurring in private areas," * * * The Fourth Amendment's protection of the home has never been tied to measurement of the quality or quantity of information obtained. * * * [T]here is certainly no exception to the warrant requirement for the officer who barely cracks open the front door and sees nothing but the nonintimate rug on the vestibule floor. In the home, our cases show, all details are intimate details, because the entire area is held safe from prying government eyes. * * *

Limiting the prohibition of thermal imaging to "intimate details" would not only be wrong in principle; it would be impractical in application, failing to provide "a workable accommodation between the needs of law enforcement and the interests protected by the Fourth Amendment," Oliver v. United States, 466 U.S. 170. To begin with, there is no necessary connection between the sophistication of the surveillance equipment and the "intimacy" of the details that it observes—which means that one cannot say (and the police cannot be assured) that use of the relatively crude equipment at issue here will always be lawful. The Agema Thermovision 210 might disclose, for example, at what hour each night the lady of the house takes her daily sauna and bath—a detail that many would consider "intimate"; and a much more sophisticated system might detect nothing more intimate than the fact that someone left a closet light on. * * *

We have said that the Fourth Amendment draws "a firm line at the entrance to the house," Payton, 445 U.S. at 590. That line, we think, must be not only firm but also bright—which requires clear specification of those methods of surveillance that require a warrant. While it is certainly possible to conclude from the videotape of the thermal imaging that occurred in this case that no "significant" compromise of the homeowner's privacy has occurred, we must take the long view, from the original meaning of the Fourth Amendment forward. * * *

Where, as here, the Government uses a device that is not in general public use, to explore details of the home that would previously have been unknowable without physical intrusion, the surveillance is a "search" and is presumptively unreasonable without a warrant.

Since we hold the Thermovision imaging to have been an unlawful search, it will remain for the District Court to determine whether, without the evidence it provided, the search warrant issued in this case was supported by probable cause—and if not, whether there is any other basis for supporting admission of the evidence that the search pursuant to the warrant produced.

The judgment of the Court of Appeals is reversed; the case is remanded for further proceedings consistent with this opinion.

JUSTICE STEVENS, with whom the CHIEF JUSTICE, JUSTICE O'CONNOR, and JUSTICE KENNEDY join, dissenting.

There is, in my judgment, a distinction of constitutional magnitude between "through-the-wall surveillance" that gives the observer or listener direct access to information in a private area, on the one hand, and the thought processes used to draw inferences from information in the public domain, on the other hand. The Court has crafted a rule that purports to deal with direct observations of the inside of the home, but the case before us merely involves indirect deductions from "off-the-wall" surveillance, that is, observations of the exterior of the home * * *.

NOTE: ROK LAMPE, PROTECTION OF THE HOME IN EUROPEAN LAW

As in the US, in Europe, "a man's home is a man's castle". In the case law of the European Court of Human Rights the term "home" applies to houses, apartments and other residences. For example in *Buckley v. UK,* the Court recognized the mobile trailer of a Roma family as a "home" protected under Article 8 of the European Convention on Human Rights: "Everyone has the right to respect for his private and family life, his home and his correspondence."

In *Camenzind v. Switzerland,* 136/1996/755/954 (16 December 1997), a leading case concerning search and seizure, the European Court of Human Rights considered whether the Swiss legal framework governing home searches provided adequate protection of the applicant's rights. The right to the privacy of the home is subject to the Article 8 limitation that: "There shall be no interference by a public authority with the exercise of this right except such as is in accordance with the law and is necessary in a democratic society in the interests of national security, public safety or the economic well-being of the country, for the prevention of disorder or crime, for the protection of health or morals, or for the protection of the rights and freedoms of others." The Court thus weighed whether the interference in question was "in accordance with the law" and pursued aims consistent with Convention's tolerance of measures necessary for "prevention of disorder or crime". Finding that the search was limited in scope, the Court concluded that the interference with the complainant's right to respect for his home had been proportionate and necessary within the terms of Article 8. Consequently, there had been no a violation of Article 8. An important precedent, *Camenzind v. Switzerland* established the criteria each European State must meet within its sovereign jurisdiction in regulating searches and seizures of premises:

- A search may only be effected under a written warrant issued by a limited number of designated senior public servants and carried out by officials specially trained for the purpose.

- These officials each have an obligation to stand down if circumstances exist which could affect their impartiality.

- Searches can only be carried out in dwellings and other premises if it is likely that a suspect is in hiding there or if objects or valuables liable to seizure or evidence of the commission of an offence are to be found there.

- They cannot be conducted on Sundays, public holidays or at night "except in important cases or where there is imminent danger".

- At the beginning of a search the investigating official must produce evidence of identity and inform the occupier of the premises of the purpose of the search and that person or a relative or other household member must be asked to attend.

- In principle, there will also be a public officer present to ensure that the search does not deviate from its purpose.

- A record of the search is drawn up immediately in the presence of the persons who attended and if they so request, they must be provided with a copy of the search warrant and of the record.

- Searches for documents are subject to special restrictions.

- Suspects are entitled to representation whatever the circumstances.

- Anyone affected by an "investigative measure" who has "an interest worthy of protection in having the measure . . . quashed or varied" may complain to the court.

- A "suspect" who is found to have no case to answer may seek compensation for any loss sustained.

The case law of the European Court of Human Rights has continuously demanded a judicial warrant in order for the public authority to comply with demands of Article 8. But, is a judicial warrant always sufficient to comply with Article 8? In a significant search and seizure case, the Court found that the fact that a judicial warrant has been obtained will not always be sufficient. In *Niemietz v. Germany* (1992), the law offices of the applicant were searched by the Public Prosecutors' office and the police, who were looking for documents which could reveal the identity of the person who had insulted a certain other individual. The Court found that a search of the premises of a lawyer in pursuit of documents to be used in criminal proceedings was disproportionate to its purposes of preventing disorder and crime and protecting the rights of others, notwithstanding the prior judicial approval. The Court held that the warrant was drawn in terms which were too broad and the search impinged on the professional secrecy of some of the materials which had been inspected. As a result, and because German law did not provide for any special procedural safeguards relating to the exercise of search powers, it was disproportionate to the aim which it pursued and was found to violate the applicant's right to privacy grounded in the Article 8.

In a surprising judgment, the European Court of Human Rights in *Lopez Ostra v. Spain* (1994) extended the right to the privacy of the home to freedom from environmental pollution. The essence of the judgment is that severe environmental pollution may affect individuals' well-being and prevent them from enjoying their homes in such a way as to affect their private and family health adversely without, however, seriously endangering their health. The applicant had complained about smells, noise and polluting fumes caused by a waste treatment plant situated a few meters from her home. These nuisances, she argued, infringed her right to respect for her home, privacy and family life. Even taking the State's interest ("margin of appreciation") into account, however, it held that the State did not succeed in striking a fair balance between the interest of the town's economic well-being—that of having a waste treatment plant—and the applicant's effective enjoyment for her right to respect for her home and family life.

4. SCHOOL SEARCHES

NOTE: CHILDREN'S PRIVACY

Does the warrant requirement apply to children, no less than to adults? Should the subjective expectations of minors matter less, given their lack of experience and judgment, when compared to typical adults? The Supreme Court has been generous in granting the state warrantless access to school children, based on the asserted special needs of educators to monitor and discipline. Schools may search students for contraband without probable cause and without a warrant. In addition, schools may randomly test students participating in extracurricular activities and sports for evidence of substance abuse. What remains of pupil privacy after the Court's decision in *Board of Education v. Earls*? Is Justice Ginsburg's dissent in *Earls* on point?

NEW JERSEY v. T. L. O.
469 U.S. 325 (1985).

JUSTICE WHITE delivered the opinion of the Court.

We granted certiorari in this case to examine the appropriateness of the exclusionary rule as a remedy for searches carried out in violation of the Fourth Amendment by public school authorities. Our consideration of the proper application of the Fourth Amendment to the public schools, however, has led us to conclude that the search that gave rise to the case now before us did not violate the Fourth Amendment. Accordingly, we here address only the questions of the proper standard for assessing the legality of searches conducted by public school officials and the application of that standard to the facts of this case. * * *

On March 7, 1980, a teacher at Piscataway High School in Middlesex County, N. J., discovered two girls smoking in a lavatory. One of the two girls was the respondent T. L. O., who at that time was a 14–year–old high school freshman. Because smoking in the lavatory was a violation of a school rule, the teacher took the two girls to the Principal's office, where they met with Assistant Vice Principal Theodore Choplick. In response to questioning by Mr. Choplick, T. L. O.'s companion admitted that she had violated the rule. T. L. O., however, denied that she had been smoking in the lavatory and claimed that she did not smoke at all.

Mr. Choplick asked T. L. O. to come into his private office and demanded to see her purse. Opening the purse, he found a pack of cigarettes, which he removed from the purse and held before T. L. O. as he accused her of having lied to him. As he reached into the purse for the cigarettes, Mr. Choplick also noticed a package of cigarette rolling papers. In his experience, possession of rolling papers by high school students was closely associated with the use of marihuana. Suspecting that a closer examination of the purse might yield further evidence of drug use, Mr. Choplick proceeded to search the purse thoroughly. The search revealed a small amount of marihuana, a pipe, a number of empty plastic bags, a substantial quantity of money in one-dollar bills, an index card that appeared to be a list of students who owed T. L. O. money, and two letters that implicated T. L. O. in marihuana dealing.

Mr. Choplick notified T. L. O.'s mother and the police, and turned the evidence of drug dealing over to the police. At the request of the police, T. L. O.'s mother took her daughter to police headquarters, where T. L. O. confessed that she had been selling marihuana at the high school. On the basis of the confession and the evidence seized by Mr. Choplick, the State brought delinquency charges against T. L. O. in the Juvenile and Domestic Relations Court of Middlesex County. Contending that Mr. Choplick's search of her purse violated the Fourth Amendment, T. L. O. moved to suppress the evidence found in her purse as well as her confession, which, she argued, was tainted by the allegedly unlawful search. The Juvenile Court denied the motion to suppress. State ex rel. T. L. O., 178 N. J. Super. 329, 428 A. 2d 1327 (1980). Although the court concluded that the Fourth Amendment did apply to searches carried out by school officials, it held that "a school official may properly conduct a search of a student's person if the official has a reasonable suspicion that a crime has been or is in the process of being committed, or reasonable cause to believe that the search is necessary to maintain school discipline or enforce school policies." Id., at 341, 428 A. 2d, at 1333.

Applying this standard, the court concluded that the search conducted by Mr. Choplick was a reasonable one. The initial decision to open the purse was justified by Mr. Choplick's well-founded suspicion that T. L. O. had violated the rule forbidding smoking in the lavatory. Once the purse was open, evidence of marihuana violations was in plain view, and Mr. Choplick was entitled to conduct a thorough search to determine the nature and extent of T. L. O.'s drug-related activities. Id., at 343, 428 A. 2d, at 1334. Having denied the motion to suppress, the court on March 23, 1981, found T. L. O. to be a delinquent and on January 8, 1982, sentenced her to a year's probation. * * *

It may well be true that the evil toward which the Fourth Amendment was primarily directed was the resurrection of the pre-Revolutionary practice of using general warrants or "writs of assistance" to authorize searches for contraband by officers of the Crown. See United States v. Chadwick, 433 U.S. 1, 7–8 (1977); Boyd v. United States, 116 U.S. 616, 624–629 (1886). But this Court has never limited the Amendment's prohibition on unreasonable searches and seizures to operations conducted by the police. Rather, the Court has long spoken of the Fourth Amendment's strictures as restraints imposed upon "governmental action"—that is, "upon the activities of sovereign authority." Burdeau v. McDowell, 256 U.S. 465, 475 (1921). Accordingly, we have held the Fourth Amendment applicable to the activities of civil as well as criminal authorities * * *.

In carrying out searches and other disciplinary functions pursuant to such policies, school officials act as representatives of the State, not merely as surrogates for the parents, and they cannot claim the parents' immunity from the strictures of the Fourth Amendment. * * *

We have recognized that even a limited search of the person is a substantial invasion of privacy. Terry v. Ohio, 392 U.S. 1, 24–25 (1967). We have also recognized that searches of closed items of personal luggage are intrusions on protected privacy interests, for "the Fourth Amendment provides protection to the owner of every container that conceals its contents from plain view." * * * A search of a child's person or of a closed purse or other bag carried on her person, no less than a similar search carried out on an adult, is undoubtedly a severe violation of subjective expectations of privacy.

Of course, the Fourth Amendment does not protect subjective expectations of privacy that are unreasonable or otherwise "illegitimate." * * * The State of New Jersey has argued that because of the pervasive supervision to which children in the schools are necessarily subject, a child has virtually no legitimate expectation of privacy in articles of personal property "unnecessarily" carried into a school. This argument has two factual premises: (1) the fundamental incompatibility of expectations of privacy with the maintenance of a sound educational environment; and (2) the minimal interest of the child in bringing any items of personal property into the school. Both premises are severely flawed.

Although this Court may take notice of the difficulty of maintaining discipline in the public schools today, the situation is not so dire that students in the schools may claim no legitimate expectations of privacy. We have recently recognized that the need to maintain order in a prison is such that prisoners retain no legitimate expectations of privacy in their cells, but it goes almost without saying that "[the] prisoner and the schoolchild stand in wholly different circumstances, separated by the harsh facts of criminal conviction and incarceration." * * * We are not yet ready to hold that the schools and the prisons need be equated for purposes of the Fourth Amendment.

Nor does the State's suggestion that children have no legitimate need to bring personal property into the schools seem well anchored in reality. Students at a minimum must bring to school not only the supplies needed for their studies, but also keys, money, and the necessaries of personal hygiene and grooming. In addition, students may carry on their persons or in purses or wallets such nondisruptive yet highly personal items as photographs, letters, and diaries. Finally, students may have perfectly legitimate reasons to carry with them articles of property needed in connection with extracurricular or recreational activities. In short, schoolchildren may find it necessary to carry with them a variety of legitimate, noncontraband items, and there is no reason to conclude that they have necessarily waived all rights to privacy in such items merely by bringing them onto school grounds.

Against the child's interest in privacy must be set the substantial interest of teachers and administrators in maintaining discipline in the classroom and on school grounds. Maintaining order in the classroom has never been easy, but in recent years, school disorder has often taken particularly ugly forms: drug use and violent crime in the schools have become major social problems. * * *

The school setting also requires some modification of the level of suspicion of illicit activity needed to justify a search. Ordinarily, a search—even one that may permissibly be carried out without a warrant—must be based upon "probable cause" to believe that a violation of the law has occurred. * * * Where a careful balancing of governmental and private interests suggests that the public interest is best served by a Fourth Amendment standard of reasonableness that stops short of probable cause, we have not hesitated to adopt such a standard.

We join the majority of courts that have examined this issue in concluding that the accommodation of the privacy interests of schoolchildren with the substantial need of teachers and administrators for freedom to maintain order in the schools does not require strict adherence to the requirement that searches be based on probable cause to believe that the subject of the search has violated or is violating the law. Rather, the legality of a search of a student should depend simply on the reasonableness, under all the circumstances, of the search. * * * Such a search will be permissible in its scope when the measures adopted are reasonably related to the objectives of the search and not excessively intrusive in light of the age and sex of the student and the nature of the infraction.

This standard will, we trust, neither unduly burden the efforts of school authorities to maintain order in their schools nor authorize unrestrained intrusions upon the privacy of schoolchildren. By focusing attention on the question of reasonableness, the standard will spare teachers and school administrators the necessity of schooling themselves in the niceties of probable cause and permit them to regulate their conduct according to the dictates of reason and common sense. At the same time, the reasonableness standard should ensure that the interests of students will be invaded no more than is necessary to achieve the legitimate end of preserving order in the schools. * * *

SAFFORD UNIFIED SCHOOL DISTRICT v. REDDING
129 S.Ct. 2633 (2009).

JUSTICE SOUTER delivered the opinion of the Court.

The issue here is whether a 13–year–old student's Fourth Amendment right was violated when she was subjected to a search of her bra and underpants by school officials acting on reasonable suspicion that she had brought forbidden prescription and over-the-counter drugs to school. Because there were no reasons to suspect the drugs presented a danger or were concealed in her underwear, we hold that the search did violate the Constitution, but because there is reason to question the clarity with which the right was established, the official who ordered the unconstitutional search is entitled to qualified immunity from liability. * * *

The events immediately prior to the search in question began in 13–year–old Savana Redding's math class at Safford Middle School one

October day in 2003. The assistant principal of the school, Kerry Wilson, came into the room and asked Savana to go to his office. There, he showed her a day planner, unzipped and open flat on his desk, in which there were several knives, lighters, a permanent marker, and a cigarette. Wilson asked Savana whether the planner was hers; she said it was, but that a few days before she had lent it to her friend, Marissa Glines. Savana stated that none of the items in the planner belonged to her.

Wilson then showed Savana four white prescription-strength ibuprofen 400–mg pills, and one over-the-counter blue naproxen 200–mg pill, all used for pain and inflammation but banned under school rules without advance permission. He asked Savana if she knew anything about the pills. Savana answered that she did not. Wilson then told Savana that he had received a report that she was giving these pills to fellow students; Savana denied it and agreed to let Wilson search her belongings. Helen Romero, an administrative assistant, came into the office, and together with Wilson they searched Savana's backpack, finding nothing.

At that point, Wilson instructed Romero to take Savana to the school nurse's office to search her clothes for pills. Romero and the nurse, Peggy Schwallier, asked Savana to remove her jacket, socks, and shoes, leaving her in stretch pants and a T-shirt (both without pockets), which she was then asked to remove. Finally, Savana was told to pull her bra out and to the side and shake it, and to pull out the elastic on her underpants, thus exposing her breasts and pelvic area to some degree. No pills were found.

Savana's mother filed suit against Safford Unified School District #1, Wilson, Romero, and Schwallier for conducting a strip search in violation of Savana's Fourth Amendment rights. * * *

[Searching Savana's book bag and outer clothing was reasonable, but the additional search of her undergarments was not.] The very fact of Savana's pulling her underwear away from her body in the presence of the two officials who were able to see her necessarily exposed her breasts and pelvic area to some degree, and both subjective and reasonable societal expectations of personal privacy support the treatment of such a search as categorically distinct, requiring distinct elements of justification on the part of school authorities for going beyond a search of outer clothing and belongings.

Savana's subjective expectation of privacy against such a search is inherent in her account of it as embarrassing, frightening, and humiliating. The reasonableness of her expectation (required by the Fourth Amendment standard) is indicated by the consistent experiences of other young people similarly searched, whose adolescent vulnerability intensifies the patent intrusiveness of the exposure. See Brief for National Association of Social Workers et al. as *Amici Curiae* 6–14; Hyman & Perone, The Other Side of School Violence: Educator Policies and Practices that may Contribute to Student Misbehavior, 36 J. School Psychology 7, 13 (1998) (strip search can "result in serious emotional damage"). * * *

The indignity of the search does not, of course, outlaw it, but it does implicate the rule of reasonableness as stated in *T.L.O.,* that "the search as actually conducted [be] reasonably related in scope to the circumstances which justified the interference in the first place." 469 U.S., at 341, 105 S.Ct. 733 (internal quotation marks omitted). The scope will be permissible, that is, when it is "not excessively intrusive in light of the age and sex of the student and the nature of the infraction." *Id.,* at 342, 105 S.Ct. 733.

Here, the content of the suspicion failed to match the degree of intrusion.

VERNONIA SCHOOL DISTRICT v. ACTON
515 U.S. 646 (1995).

JUSTICE SCALIA delivered the opinion of the Court.

The Student Athlete Drug Policy adopted by School District 47J in the town of Vernonia, Oregon, authorizes random urinalysis drug testing of students who participate in the District's school athletics programs. We granted certiorari to decide whether this violates the Fourth and Fourteenth Amendments to the United States Constitution. * * *

The Policy applies to all students participating in interscholastic athletics. Students wishing to play sports must sign a form consenting to the testing and must obtain the written consent of their parents. Athletes are tested at the beginning of the season for their sport. In addition, once each week of the season the names of the athletes are placed in a "pool" from which a student, with the supervision of two adults, blindly draws the names of 10% of the athletes for random testing. Those selected are notified and tested that same day, if possible.

In the fall of 1991, respondent James Acton, then a seventh grader, signed up to play football at one of the District's grade schools. He was denied participation, however, because he and his parents refused to sign the testing consent forms. The Actons filed suit, seeking declaratory and injunctive relief from enforcement of the Policy on the grounds that it violated the Fourth and Fourteenth Amendments to the United States Constitution and Article I, Section 9, of the Oregon Constitution. After a bench trial, the District Court entered an order denying the claims on the merits and dismissing the action. 796 F. Supp. at 1355. The United States Court of Appeals for the Ninth Circuit reversed, holding that the Policy violated both the Fourth and Fourteenth Amendments and Article I, Section 9, of the Oregon Constitution. 23 F.3d 1514 (1994). We granted certiorari. 513 U.S. 1013 (1994). * * *

Fourth Amendment rights, no less than First and Fourteenth Amendment rights, are different in public schools than elsewhere; the "reasonableness" inquiry cannot disregard the schools' custodial and tutelary responsibility for children. For their own good and that of their classmates, public school children are routinely required to submit to various physical examinations, and to be vaccinated against various diseases. According to the American Academy of Pediatrics, most public schools "provide vision and hearing screening and dental and dermatological checks * * *. Others also mandate scoliosis screening at appropriate grade levels." * * * Particularly with regard to medical examinations and procedures, therefore, "students within the school environment have a lesser expectation of privacy than members of the population generally." T. L. O., supra, at 348 (Powell, J., concurring).

Legitimate privacy expectations are even less with regard to student athletes. School sports are not for the bashful. They require "suiting up" before each practice or event, and showering and changing afterwards. Public school locker rooms, the usual sites for these activities, are not notable for the privacy they afford. The locker rooms in Vernonia are typical: No individual dressing rooms are provided; shower heads are lined up along a wall, unseparated by any sort of partition or curtain; not even all the toilet stalls have doors. As the United States Court of Appeals for the Seventh Circuit has noted, there is "an element of 'communal undress' inherent in athletic participation," * * *.

There is an additional respect in which school athletes have a reduced expectation of privacy. By choosing to "go out for the team," they voluntarily subject themselves to a degree of regulation even higher than that imposed on students generally. In Vernonia's public schools, they must submit to a preseason physical exam (James testified that his included the giving of a urine sample, App. 17), they must acquire adequate insurance coverage or sign an insurance waiver, maintain a minimum grade point average, and comply with any "rules of conduct, dress, training hours and related matters as may be established for each sport by the head coach and athletic director with the principal's approval." * * * Somewhat like adults who choose to participate in a "closely regulated industry," students who voluntarily participate in school athletics have reason to expect intrusions upon normal rights and privileges, including privacy.

Having considered the scope of the legitimate expectation of privacy at issue here, we turn next to the character of the intrusion that is complained of. * * * Under the District's Policy, male students produce samples at a urinal along a wall. They remain fully clothed and are only observed from behind, if at all. Female students produce samples in an enclosed stall, with a female monitor standing outside listening only for sounds of tampering. These conditions are nearly identical to those typically encountered in public restrooms, which men, women, and especially school children use daily. Under such conditions, the privacy interests compromised by the process of obtaining the urine sample are in our view negligible. * * *

Finally, we turn to consider the nature and immediacy of the governmental concern at issue here, and the efficacy of this means for meeting it. * * *

That the nature of the concern is important—indeed, perhaps compelling—can hardly be doubted. Deterring drug use by our Nation's schoolchildren is at least as important as enhancing efficient enforcement of the Nation's laws against the importation of drugs, * * * or deterring drug use by engineers and trainmen * * *. School years are the time when the physical, psychological, and addictive effects of drugs are most severe. "Maturing nervous systems are more critically impaired by intoxicants than mature ones are; childhood losses in learning are lifelong and profound"; "children grow chemically dependent more quickly than adults, and their record of recovery is depressingly poor." * * * And of course the effects of a drug-infested school are visited not just upon the users, but upon the entire student body and faculty, as the educational process is disrupted. In the present case, moreover, the necessity for the State to act is magnified by the fact that this evil is being visited not just upon individuals at large, but upon children for whom it has undertaken a special responsibility of care and direction. Finally, it must not be lost sight of that this program is directed more narrowly to drug use by school athletes, where the risk of immediate physical harm to the drug user or those with whom he is playing his sport is particularly high. Apart from psychological effects, which include impairment of judgment, slow reaction time, and a lessening of the perception of pain, the particular drugs screened by the District's Policy [amphetamines, marijuana and cocaine] have been demonstrated to pose substantial physical risks to athletes. * * *

As to the efficacy of this means for addressing the problem: It seems to us self-evident that a drug problem largely fueled by the "role model" effect of athletes' drug use, and of particular danger to athletes, is effectively addressed by making sure that athletes do not use drugs. Respondents argue that a "less intrusive means to the same end" was available, namely, "drug testing on suspicion of drug use." * * * We have repeatedly refused to declare that only the "least intrusive" search practicable can be reasonable under the Fourth Amendment. * * *

Taking into account all the factors we have considered above—the decreased expectation of privacy, the relative unobtrusiveness of the search, and the severity of the need met by the search—we conclude Vernonia's Policy is reasonable and hence constitutional.

We caution against the assumption that suspicionless drug testing will readily pass constitutional muster in other contexts. The most significant element in this case is the first we discussed: that the Policy was undertaken in furtherance of the government's responsibilities, under a public school system, as guardian and tutor of children entrusted to its care. * * * It is so ordered.

JUSTICE O'CONNOR, with whom JUSTICE STEVENS and JUSTICE SOUTER join, dissenting.

The population of our Nation's public schools, grades 7 through 12, numbers around 18 million. * * *

Blanket searches, because they can involve "thousands or millions" of searches, "pose a greater threat to liberty" than do suspicion-based ones, which "affect one person at a time," Illinois v. Krull, 480 U.S. 340, 365 (1987) (O'Connor, J., dissenting).

It cannot be too often stated that the greatest threats to our constitutional freedoms come in times of crisis. But we must also stay mindful that not all government responses to such times are hysterical overreactions; some crises are quite real, and when they are, they serve precisely as the compelling state interest that we have said may justify a measured intrusion on constitutional rights. The only way for judges to mediate these conflicting impulses is to do what they should do anyway: stay close to the record in each case that appears before them, and make their judgments based on that alone. Having reviewed the record here, I cannot avoid the conclusion that the District's suspicionless policy of testing all student athletes sweeps too broadly, and too imprecisely, to be reasonable under the Fourth Amendment.

BOARD OF EDUCATION v. EARLS

536 U.S. 822 (2002).

JUSTICE THOMAS delivered the opinion of the Court.

The city of Tecumseh, Oklahoma, is a rural community located approximately 40 miles southeast of Oklahoma City. The School District administers all Tecumseh public schools. In the fall of 1998, the School District adopted the Student Activities Drug Testing Policy (Policy), which requires all middle and high school students to consent to drug testing in order to participate in any extracurricular activity. In practice, the Policy has been applied only to competitive extracurricular activities sanctioned by the Oklahoma Secondary Schools Activities Association, such as the Academic Team, Future Farmers of America, Future Homemakers of America, band, choir, pom pom, cheerleading, and athletics. Under the Policy, students are required to take a drug test before participating in an extracurricular activity, must submit to random drug testing while participating in that activity, and must agree to be tested at any time upon reasonable suspicion. The urinalysis tests are designed to detect only the use of illegal drugs, including amphetamines, marijuana, cocaine, opiates, and barbituates, not medical conditions or the presence of authorized prescription medications.

At the time of their suit, both respondents attended Tecumseh High School. Respondent Lindsay Earls was a member of the show choir, the marching band, the Academic Team, and the National Honor Society. Respondent Daniel James sought to participate in the Academic Team. * * * They alleged that the Policy violates the Fourth Amendment as incorporated by the Fourteenth Amendment and requested injunctive and declarative relief. They also argued that the School District failed to identify a special need for testing students who participate in extracurricular activities, and that the "Drug Testing Policy neither addresses a proven problem nor promises to bring any benefit to students or the school." * * *

[S]tudents who participate in competitive extracurricular activities voluntarily subject themselves to many of the same intrusions on their privacy as do athletes. Some of these clubs and activities require occasional off-campus travel and communal undress. All of them have their own rules and requirements for participating students that do not apply to the student body as a whole. * * * For example, each of the competitive extracurricular activities governed by the Policy must abide by the rules of the Oklahoma Secondary Schools Activities Association, and a faculty sponsor monitors the students for compliance with the various rules dictated by the clubs and activities. * * * This regulation of extracurricular activities further diminishes the expectation of privacy among schoolchildren. * * * We therefore conclude that the students affected by this Policy have a limited expectation of privacy. * * *

Under the Policy, a faculty monitor waits outside the closed restroom stall for the student to produce a sample and must "listen for the normal sounds of urination in order to guard against tampered specimens and to insure an accurate chain of custody." The monitor then pours the sample into two bottles that are sealed and placed into a mailing pouch along with a consent form signed by the student.

In addition, the Policy clearly requires that the test results be kept in confidential files separate from a student's other educational records and released to school personnel only on a "need to know" basis. * * *

Moreover, the test results are not turned over to any law enforcement authority. Nor do the test results here lead to the imposition of discipline or have any academic consequences. * * * Rather, the only consequence of a failed drug test is to limit the student's privilege of participating in extracurricular activities. Indeed, a student may test positive for drugs twice and still be allowed to participate in extracurricular activities. After the first positive test, the school contacts the student's parent or guardian for a meeting. The student may continue to participate in the activity if within five days of the meeting the student shows proof of receiving drug counseling and submits to a second drug test in two weeks. * * *

Given the minimally intrusive nature of the sample collection and the limited uses to which the test results are put, we conclude that the invasion of students' privacy is not significant. * * *

Finally, this Court must consider the nature and immediacy of the government's concerns and the efficacy of the Policy in meeting them. * * * The health and safety risks identified in Vernonia apply with equal force to Tecumseh's children. Indeed, the nationwide drug epidemic makes the war against drugs a pressing concern in every school.

Additionally, the School District in this case has presented specific evidence of drug use at Tecumseh schools. Teachers testified that they had seen students who appeared to be under the influence of drugs and that they had heard students speaking openly about using drugs. * * * The School District has provided sufficient evidence to shore up the need for its drug testing program. * * *

Finally, we find that testing students who participate in extracurricular activities is a reasonably effective means of addressing the School District's legitimate concerns in preventing, deterring, and detecting drug use. While in Vernonia there might have been a closer fit between the testing of athletes and the trial court's finding that the drug problem was "fueled by the 'role model' effect of athletes' drug use," such a finding was not essential to the holding. * * * Vernonia did not require the school to test the group of students most likely to use drugs, but rather considered the constitutionality of the program in the context of the public school's custodial responsibilities. Evaluating the Policy in this context, we conclude that the drug testing of Tecumseh students who participate in extracurricular activities effectively serves the School District's interest in protecting the safety and health of its students.

JUSTICE GINSBURG, with whom JUSTICE STEVENS, JUSTICE O'CONNOR, and JUSTICE SOUTER join, dissenting. * * *

Nationwide, students who participate in extracurricular activities are significantly less likely to develop substance abuse problems than are their less-involved peers * * *. Even if students might be deterred from drug use in order to preserve their extracurricular eligibility, it is at least as likely that other students might forgo their extracurricular involvement in order to avoid detection of their drug use. Tecumseh's policy thus falls short doubly if deterrence is its aim: It invades the privacy of students who need deterrence least, and risks steering students at greatest risk for substance abuse away from extracurricular involvement that potentially may palliate drug problems.

To summarize, this case resembles Vernonia only in that the School Districts in both cases conditioned engagement in activities outside the obligatory curriculum on random subjection to urinalysis. The defining characteristics of the two programs, however, are entirely dissimilar. The Vernonia district sought to test a subpopulation of students distinguished by their reduced expectation of privacy, their special susceptibility to drug-related injury, and their heavy involvement with drug use. The Tecumseh district seeks to test a much larger population associated with none of these factors. * * * A program so sweeping not sheltered by Vernonia; its unreasonable reach renders it impermissible under the Fourth Amendment.

5. WORKPLACE SEARCHES

NOTE: CITY OF ONTARIO 130 S.CT. 2619 (2010)

The city of Ontario, California issued pagers to police officers in its police department. Petitioner Jeff Quon was a police officer for the city and was issued a pager through which he could receive text messages. Officer Quon and several other employees exceeded the monthly alphanumeric character limit provided in the contract between Ontario and its service provider, Arch Wireless, resulting in higher fees for the city. When Arch Wireless provided the city with transcripts of the employees' August and September 2002 text messages, it was discovered that many of the messages were not work-related and some were sexually explicit.

Officer Quon and other employees of the department brought a lawsuit alleging that by obtaining and reviewing the transcripts of their pager text messages, the city violated the Fourth Amendment; and that by giving the city the transcript of their messages, Arch Wireless violated the federal Stored Communications Act, Title II of the Electronic Communications Privacy Act (1986). The Stored Communications Act, which will be introduced in Chapter 4 of this textbook, prohibits unauthorized access to certain electronic communications and places restrictions on the service providers' disclosure of certain communications. The Stored Communications Act also permits a governmental entity to compel a service provider to disclose the contents of communications in certain circumstances. See *Warshak v. United States*, 532 F.3d 521, 523 (2008) (petitioner alleged that the government's compelled disclosure of his e-mail without a warrant violated the Fourth Amendment and the Stored Communications Act) (claim dismissed for lack of ripeness).

In *City of Ontario*, the Court emphasized past decisions holding that "operational realities" could reduce employees' privacy expectations and that these could be taken into account when considering whether a workplace search was constitutionally reasonable. The court further cautioned: "Prudence counsels caution before the facts in the instant case are used to establish far-reaching premises that define the existence, and extent, of privacy expectations enjoyed by employees when using employer-provided communication devices. Rapid changes in the dynamics of communication and information transmission are evident not just in the technology itself but in what society accepts as proper behavior."

The court concluded that even assuming the officer had a reasonable expectation of privacy in the text messages sent on the pager provided to him by the city and even assuming that requesting and reviewing the transcripts constituted a search for purposes of the Fourth Amendment, the search was reasonable. The court determined that because the search was motivated by a legitimate work-related purpose, and because it was not excessive in scope, the search was reasonable, consistent with the Court's prior workplace search ruling, *O'Connor v. Ortega*, 480 US 709 (1987). Neither officer Quon nor the individuals with whom he communicated by means of his pager had valid Fourth Amendment claims against the city. The Court did not address the petitioners' Stored Communications Act claims.

O'CONNOR v. ORTEGA

480 U.S. 709 (1987).

JUSTICE O'CONNOR announced the judgment of the Court and delivered an opinion in which the CHIEF JUSTICE, JUSTICE WHITE, and JUSTICE POWELL join.

This suit under 42 U. S. C. § 1983 presents two issues concerning the Fourth Amendment rights of public employees. First, we must determine whether the respondent, a public employee, had a reasonable expectation of privacy in his office, desk, and file cabinets at his place of work. Second, we must address the appropriate Fourth Amendment standard for a search conducted by a public employer in areas in which a public employee is found to have a reasonable expectation of privacy. * * *

Dr. Magno Ortega, a physician and psychiatrist, held the position of Chief of Professional Education at Napa State Hospital (Hospital) for 17 years, until his dismissal from that position in 1981. As Chief of Professional Education, Dr. Ortega had primary responsibility for training young physicians in psychiatric residency programs.

In July 1981, Hospital officials, including Dr. Dennis O'Connor, the Executive Director of the Hospital, became concerned about possible improprieties in Dr. Ortega's management of the residency program. In particular, the Hospital officials were concerned with Dr. Ortega's acquisition of an Apple II computer for use in the residency program. The officials thought that Dr. Ortega may have misled Dr. O'Connor into believing that the computer had been donated, when in fact the computer had been financed by the possibly coerced contributions of residents. Additionally, the Hospital officials were concerned with charges that Dr. Ortega had sexually harassed two female Hospital employees, and had taken inappropriate disciplinary action against a resident.

On July 30, 1981, Dr. O'Connor requested that Dr. Ortega take paid administrative leave during an investigation of these charges. At Dr. Ortega's request, Dr. O'Connor agreed to allow Dr. Ortega to take two weeks' vacation instead of administrative leave. Dr. Ortega, however, was requested to stay off Hospital grounds for the duration of the investigation. On August 14, 1981, Dr. O'Connor informed Dr. Ortega that the investigation had not yet been completed, and that he was being placed on paid administrative leave. Dr. Ortega remained on administrative leave until the Hospital terminated his employment on September 22, 1981.

Dr. O'Connor selected several Hospital personnel to conduct the investigation, including an accountant, a physician, and a Hospital security officer. Richard Friday, the Hospital Administrator, led this "investigative team." At some point during the investigation, Mr. Friday made the decision to enter Dr. Ortega's office. The specific reason for the entry into Dr. Ortega's office is unclear from the record. The petitioners claim that the search was conducted to secure state property. Initially, petitioners contended that such a search was pursuant to a Hospital policy of conducting a routine inventory of state property in the office of a terminated employee. At the time of the search, however, the Hospital had not yet terminated Dr. Ortega's employment; Dr. Ortega was still on administrative leave. Apparently, there was no policy of inventorying the offices of those on administrative leave. Before the search had been initiated, however, petitioners had become aware that Dr. Ortega had taken the computer to his home. Dr. Ortega contends that the purpose of the search was to secure evidence for use against him in administrative disciplinary proceedings.

The resulting search of Dr. Ortega's office was quite thorough. The investigators entered the office a number of times and seized several items from Dr. Ortega's desk and file cabinets, including a Valentine's Day card, a photograph, and a book of poetry all sent to Dr. Ortega by a former resident physician. These items were later used in a proceeding before a hearing officer of the California State Personnel Board to impeach the credibility of the former resident, who testified on Dr. Ortega's behalf. The investigators also seized billing documentation of one of Dr. Ortega's private patients under the California Medicaid program. The investigators did not otherwise separate Dr. Ortega's property from state property because, as one investigator testified, "[trying] to sort State from non-State, it was too much to do, so I gave it up and boxed it up." App. 62. Thus, no formal inventory of the property in the office was ever made. Instead, all the papers in Dr. Ortega's office were merely placed in boxes, and put in storage for Dr. Ortega to retrieve. * * *

The Fourth Amendment protects the "right of the people to be secure in their persons, houses, papers, and effects, against unreasonable searches and seizures * * *." Our cases establish that Dr. Ortega's Fourth Amendment rights are implicated only if the conduct of the Hospital officials at issue in this case infringed "an expectation of privacy that society is prepared to consider reasonable." United States v. Jacobsen, 466 U.S. 109, 113 (1984). * * *

Within the workplace context, this Court has recognized that employees may have a reasonable expectation of privacy against intrusions by police. See Mancusi v. DeForte, 392 U.S. 364 (1968). As with the expectation of privacy in one's home, such an expectation in one's place of work is "based upon societal expectations that have deep roots in the history of the Amendment." * * *

Given the societal expectations of privacy in one's place of work expressed in * * * Mancusi, we reject the contention made by the Solicitor General and petitioners that public employees can never have a reasonable expectation of privacy in their place of work. Individuals do not lose Fourth Amendment rights merely because they work for the government instead of a private employer. The operational realities of the workplace, however, may make some employees' expectations of privacy unreasonable when an intrusion is by a supervisor rather than a law enforcement official. Public employees' expectations of privacy in their offices, desks, and file cabinets, like similar expectations of employees in the private sector, may be reduced by virtue of actual office practices and procedures, or by legitimate regulation. Indeed, in Mancusi itself, the Court suggested that the union employee did not have a reasonable expectation of privacy against his union supervisors. 392 U.S., at 369. The employee's expectation of privacy must be assessed in the context of the employment relation. An office is seldom a private enclave free from entry by supervisors, other employees, and business and personal invitees. Instead, in many cases offices are continually entered by fellow employees and other visitors during the workday for conferences, consultations, and other work-related visits. Simply put, it is the nature of government offices that others—such as fellow employees, supervisors, consensual visitors, and the general public—may have frequent access to an individual's office. * * *

On the basis of this undisputed evidence, we accept the conclusion of the Court of Appeals that Dr. Ortega had a reasonable expectation of privacy at least in his desk and file cabinets.

Having determined that Dr. Ortega had a reasonable expectation of privacy in his office, the Court of Appeals simply concluded without discussion that the "search * * * was not a reasonable search under the fourth amendment." * * *

There is surprisingly little case law on the appropriate Fourth Amendment standard of reasonableness for a public employer's work-related search of its employee's offices, desks, or file cabinets. Generally, however, the lower courts have held that any "work-related" search by an employer satisfies the Fourth Amendment reasonableness requirement. * * *

The legitimate privacy interests of public employees in the private objects they bring to the workplace may be substantial. Against these privacy interests, however, must be balanced the realities of the work-place, which strongly suggest that a warrant requirement would be unworkable. While police, and even administrative enforcement personnel, conduct searches for the primary purpose of obtaining evidence for use in criminal or other enforcement proceedings, employers most frequently need to enter the offices and desks of their employees for legitimate work-related reasons wholly unrelated to illegal conduct. Employers and super-visors are focused primarily on the need to complete the government agency's work in a prompt and efficient manner. An employer may have need for correspondence, or a file or report available only in an employee's office while the employee is away from the office. Or, as is alleged to have been the case here, employers may need to safeguard or identify state property or records in an office in connection with a pending investigation into suspected employee misfeasance.

In our view, requiring an employer to obtain a warrant whenever the employer wished to enter an employee's office, desk, or file cabinets for a work-related purpose would seriously disrupt the routine conduct of business and would be unduly burdensome. Imposing unwieldy warrant procedures in such cases upon supervisors, who would otherwise have no reason to be familiar with such procedures, is simply unreasonable. In contrast to other circumstances in which we have required warrants, supervisors in offices such as at the Hospital are hardly in the business of investigating the violation of criminal laws. Rather, work-related searches are merely incident to the primary business of the agency. Under these circumstances, the imposition of a warrant requirement would conflict with "the common-sense realization that government offices could not function if every employment decision became a constitutional matter." Connick v. Myers, 461 U.S. 138, 143 (1983).

Whether probable cause is an inappropriate standard for public employer searches of their employees' offices presents a more difficult issue. For the most part, we have required that a search be based upon probable cause, but as we noted in New Jersey v. T. L. O., "[the] fundamental command of the Fourth Amendment is that searches and seizures be reasonable, and although 'both the concept of probable cause and the requirement of a warrant bear on the reasonableness of a search, * * * in certain limited circumstances neither is required.' " 469 U.S., at 340 (quoting Almeida–Sanchez v. United States, 413 U.S. 266, 277 (1973) (POWELL, J., concurring)). Thus, "[where] a careful balancing of governmental and private interests suggests that the public interest is best served by a Fourth Amendment standard of reasonableness that stops short of probable cause, we have not hesitated to adopt such a standard." 469 U.S., at 341. We have concluded, for example, that the appropriate standard for administrative searches is not probable cause in its traditional meaning. Instead, an administrative warrant can be obtained if there is a showing that reasonable legislative or administrative standards for conducting an inspection are satisfied. See Marshall v. Barlow's, Inc., 436 U.S., at 320; Camara v. Municipal Court, 387 U.S., at 538. * * *

To ensure the efficient and proper operation of the agency, therefore, public employers must be given wide latitude to enter employee offices for work-related, noninvestigatory reasons.

We come to a similar conclusion for searches conducted pursuant to an investigation of work-related employee misconduct. Even when employers conduct an investigation, they have an interest substantially different from "the normal need for law enforcement." New Jersey v. T. L. O., supra, at 351 (Blackmun, J., concurring in judgment). Public employers have an interest in ensuring that their agencies operate in an effective and efficient manner, and the work of these agencies inevitably suffers from the inefficiency, incompetence, mismanagement, or other work-related misfeasance of its employees. Indeed, in many cases, public employees are entrusted with tremendous responsibility, and the consequences of their misconduct or incompetence to both the agency and the public interest can be severe. * * *

Balanced against the substantial government interests in the efficient and proper operation of the workplace are the privacy interests of government employees in their place of work which, while not insubstantial, are far less than those found at home or in some other contexts. As with the building inspections in Camara, the employer intrusions at issue here "involve a relatively limited invasion" of employee privacy. 387 U.S., at 537. Government offices are provided to employees for the sole purpose of facilitating the work of an agency. The employee may avoid exposing personal belongings at work by simply leaving them at home.

In sum, we conclude that the "special needs, beyond the normal need for law enforcement make the * * * probable-cause requirement impracticable," 469 U.S., at 351 (Blackmun, J., concurring in judgment), for legitimate work-related, noninvestigatory intrusions as well as investigations of work-related misconduct. A standard of reasonableness will neither unduly burden the efforts of government employers to ensure the efficient and proper operation of the workplace, nor authorize arbitrary intrusions upon the privacy of public employees. We hold, therefore, that public employer intrusions on the constitutionally protected privacy interests of government employees for noninvestigatory, work-related purposes, as well as for investigations of work-related misconduct, should be judged by the standard of reasonableness under all the circumstances. Under this reasonableness standard, both the inception and the scope of the intrusion must be reasonable: "Determining the reasonableness of any search involves a twofold inquiry: first, one must consider 'whether the * * * action was justified at its inception,' Terry v. Ohio, 392 U.S., at 20; second, one must determine whether the search as actually conducted 'was reasonably related in scope to the circumstances which justified the interference in the first place,' ibid." New Jersey v. T. L. O., supra, at 341.

Ordinarily, a search of an employee's office by a supervisor will be "justified at its inception" when there are reasonable grounds for suspecting that the search will turn up evidence that the employee is guilty of work-related misconduct, or that the search is necessary for a noninvestigatory work-related purpose such as to retrieve a needed file. Because petitioners had an "individualized suspicion" of misconduct by Dr. Ortega, we need not decide whether individualized suspicion is an essential element of the standard of reasonableness that we adopt today. See New Jersey v. T. L. O., supra, at 342, n. 8. The search will be permissible in its scope when "the measures adopted are reasonably related to the objectives of the search and not excessively intrusive in light of * * * the nature of the [misconduct]." 469 U.S., at 342. * * *

We believe that both the District Court and the Court of Appeals were in error because summary judgment was inappropriate. The parties were in dispute about the actual justification for the search, and the record was inadequate for a determination on motion for summary judgment of the reasonableness of the search and seizure. * * *

Under these circumstances, the District Court was in error in granting petitioners summary judgment. There was a dispute of fact about the character of the search, and the District Court acted under the erroneous assumption that the search was conducted pursuant to a Hospital policy. Moreover, no findings were made as to the scope of the search that was undertaken.

The Court of Appeals concluded that Dr. Ortega was entitled to partial summary judgment on liability. It noted that the Hospital had no policy of inventorying the property of employees on administrative leave, but it did not consider whether the search was otherwise reasonable. Under the standard of reasonableness articulated in this case, however, the absence of a Hospital policy did not necessarily make the search unlawful. A search to secure state property is valid as long as petitioners had a reasonable belief that there was government property in Dr. Ortega's office which needed to be secured, and the scope of the intrusion was itself reasonable in light of this justification. Indeed, petitioners have put forward evidence that they had such a reasonable belief; at the time of the search, petitioners knew that Dr. Ortega had removed the computer from the Hospital. The removal of the computer—together with the allegations of mismanagement of the residency program and sexual harassment—may have made the search reasonable at its inception under the standard we have put forth in this case. As with the District Court order, therefore, the Court of Appeals conclusion that summary judgment was appropriate cannot stand.

On remand, therefore, the District Court must determine the justification for the search and seizure, and evaluate the reasonableness of both the inception of the search and its scope.

6. ALCOHOL, DRUG, DISEASE AND DNA TESTING

a. Alcohol and Drugs

SCHMERBER v. CALIFORNIA

384 U.S. 757 (1966).

MR. JUSTICE BRENNAN delivered the opinion of the Court.

Petitioner was convicted in Los Angeles Municipal Court of the criminal offense of driving an automobile while under the influence of intoxicating liquor. He had been arrested at a hospital while receiving treatment for injuries suffered in an accident involving the automobile that he had apparently been driving. At the direction of a police officer, a blood sample was then withdrawn from petitioner's body by a physician at the hospital. The chemical analysis of this sample revealed a percent by weight of alcohol in his blood at the time of the offense which indicated intoxication, and the report of this analysis was admitted in evidence at the trial. Petitioner objected to receipt of this evidence of the analysis on the ground that the blood had been withdrawn despite his refusal, on the advice of his counsel, to consent to the test. He contended that in that circumstance the withdrawal of the blood and the admission of the analysis in evidence denied him [rights including] his right not to be subjected to unreasonable searches and seizures in violation of the Fourth Amendment. * * *

The overriding function of the Fourth Amendment is to protect personal privacy and dignity against unwarranted intrusion by the State. * * *

The values protected by the Fourth Amendment thus substantially overlap those the Fifth Amendment helps to protect. * * * [C]ompulsory administration of a blood test * * * plainly involves the broadly conceived reach of a search and seizure under the Fourth Amendment. * * * It could not reasonably be argued, and indeed respondent does not argue, that the administration of the blood test in this case was free of the constraints of the Fourth Amendment. Such testing procedures plainly constitute searches of "persons," and depend antecedently upon seizures of "persons," within the meaning of that Amendment.

Because we are dealing with intrusions into the human body rather than with state interferences with property relationships or private papers—"houses, papers, and effects"—we write on a clean slate. * * *

In this case, as will often be true when charges of driving under the influence of alcohol are pressed, these questions arise in the context of an arrest made by an officer without a warrant. Here, there was plainly probable cause for the officer to arrest petitioner and charge him with driving an automobile while under the influence of intoxicating liquor. The police officer who arrived at the scene shortly after the accident smelled liquor on petitioner's breath, and testified that petitioner's eyes were "bloodshot, watery, sort of a glassy appearance." The officer saw petitioner again at the hospital, within two hours of the accident. There he noticed similar symptoms of drunkenness. He thereupon informed petitioner "that he was under arrest and that he was entitled to the services of an attorney, and that he could remain silent, and that anything that he told me would be used against him in evidence." * * *

The interests in human dignity and privacy which the Fourth Amendment protects forbid any such intrusions on the mere chance that desired evidence might be obtained. In the absence of a clear indication that in fact such evidence will be found, these fundamental human interests require law officers to suffer the risk that such evidence may disappear unless there is an immediate search.

Although the facts which established probable cause to arrest in this case also suggested the required relevance and likely success of a test of petitioner's blood for alcohol, the question remains whether the arresting officer was permitted to draw these inferences himself, or was required instead to procure a warrant before proceeding with the test. Search warrants are ordinarily required for searches of dwellings, and, absent an emergency, no less could be required where intrusions into the human body are concerned. * * *

The officer in the present case, however, might reasonably have believed that he was confronted with an emergency, in which the delay necessary to obtain a warrant, under the circumstances, threatened "the destruction of evidence," Preston v. United States, 376 U.S. 364, 367. We are told that the percentage of alcohol in the blood begins to diminish shortly after drinking stops, as the body functions to eliminate it from the system. Particularly in a case such as this, where time had to be taken to bring the accused to a hospital and to investigate the scene of the accident, there was no time to seek out a magistrate and secure a warrant. Given these special facts, we conclude that the attempt to secure evidence of blood-alcohol content in this case was an appropriate incident to petitioner's arrest.

Similarly, we are satisfied that the test chosen to measure petitioner's blood-alcohol level was a reasonable one. Extraction of blood samples for testing is a highly effective means of determining the degree to which a person is under the influence of alcohol. * * * Such tests are a commonplace in these days of periodic physical examinations and experience with them teaches that the quantity of blood extracted is minimal, and that for most people the procedure involves virtually no risk, trauma, or pain. * * *

Finally, the record shows that the test was performed in a reasonable manner. Petitioner's blood was taken by a physician in a hospital environment according to accepted medical practices. * * *

We thus conclude that the present record shows no violation of petitioner's right under the Fourth and Fourteenth Amendments to be free of unreasonable searches and seizures. It bears repeating, however, that we reach this judgment only on the facts of the present record. The integrity of an individual's person is a cherished value of our society. That we today hold that the Constitution does not forbid the States minor intrusions into an individual's body under stringently limited conditions in no way indicates that it permits more substantial intrusions, or intrusions under other conditions. * * * Affirmed. * * *

MR. JUSTICE BLACK with whom MR. JUSTICE DOUGLAS joins, dissenting.

I would reverse petitioner's conviction. I agree with the Court that the Fourteenth Amendment made applicable to the States the Fifth Amendment's provision that "No person * * * shall be compelled in any criminal case to be a witness against himself * * *." But I disagree with the Court's holding that California did not violate petitioner's constitutional right against self-incrimination when it compelled him, against his will, to allow a doctor to puncture his blood vessels in order to extract a sample of blood and analyze it for alcoholic content, and then used that analysis as evidence to convict petitioner of a crime.

The Court admits that "the State compelled [petitioner] to submit to an attempt to discover evidence [in his blood] that might be [and was] used to prosecute him for a criminal offense." To reach the conclusion that compelling a person to give his blood to help the State convict him is not equivalent to compelling him to be a witness against himself strikes me as quite an extraordinary feat.

SKINNER v. RAILWAY LABOR EXECUTIVES' ASSOC.
489 U.S. 602 (1989).

JUSTICE KENNEDY delivered the opinion of the Court.

The Federal Railroad Safety Act of 1970 authorizes the Secretary of Transportation to "prescribe, as necessary, appropriate rules, regulations, orders, and standards for all areas of railroad safety." 84 Stat. 971, 45 U. S. C. § 431(a). Finding that alcohol and drug abuse by railroad employees poses a serious threat to safety, the Federal Railroad Administration (FRA) has promulgated regulations that mandate blood and urine tests of employees who are involved in certain train accidents. The FRA also has adopted regulations that do not require, but do authorize, railroads to administer breath and urine tests to employees who violate certain safety rules. The question presented by this case is whether these regulations violate the Fourth Amendment. * * *

The problem of alcohol use on American railroads is as old as the industry itself, and efforts to deter it by carrier rules began at least a century ago. For many years, railroads have prohibited operating employees from possessing alcohol or being intoxicated while on duty and from consuming alcoholic beverages while subject to being called for duty. More recently, these proscriptions have been expanded to forbid possession or use of certain drugs. * * *

In July 1983, the FRA expressed concern that these industry efforts were not adequate to curb alcohol and drug abuse by railroad employees. The FRA pointed to evidence indicating that on-the-job intoxication was a significant problem in the railroad industry. The FRA also found, after a review of accident investigation reports, that from 1972 to 1983 "the nation's railroads experienced at least 21 significant train accidents involving alcohol or drug use as a probable cause or contributing factor," and that these accidents "resulted in 25 fatalities, 61 non-fatal injuries, and property damage estimated at $19 million (approximately $27 million in 1982 dollars)." 48 Fed. Reg. 30726 (1983). The FRA further identified "an additional 17 fatalities to operating employees working on or around rail rolling stock that involved alcohol or drugs as a contributing factor." Ibid. In light of these problems, the FRA solicited comments from interested parties on a various regulatory approaches to the problems of alcohol and drug abuse throughout the Nation's railroad system. * * *

[T]he FRA, in 1985, promulgated regulations addressing the problem of alcohol and drugs on the railroads. * * * The regulations prohibit covered employees from using or possessing alcohol or any controlled substance. * * * The regulations further prohibit those employees from reporting for covered service while under the influence of, or impaired by, alcohol, while having a blood alcohol concentration of 0.04 or more, or while under the influence of, or impaired by, any controlled substance. * * *

[T]wo subparts of the regulations relate to testing. Subpart C, which is entitled "Post–Accident Toxicological Testing," is mandatory. It provides that railroads "shall take all practicable steps to assure that all covered employees of the railroad directly involved * * * provide blood and urine samples for toxicological testing by FRA," * * * upon the occurrence of certain specified events. Toxicological testing is required following a "major train accident," * * * after an "impact accident,"

[and] * * * after "[a]ny train incident that involves a fatality to any on duty railroad employee." * * *

Subpart D of the regulations, which is entitled "Authorization to Test for Cause," is permissive. It authorizes railroads to require covered employees to submit to breath or urine tests in certain circumstances not addressed by Subpart C. Breath or urine tests, or both, may be ordered (1) after a reportable accident or incident, where a supervisor has a "reasonable suspicion" that an employee's acts or omissions contributed to the occurrence or severity of the accident or incident, * * *; or (2) in the event of certain specific rule violations, including noncompliance with a signal and excessive speeding, * * *. A railroad also may require breath tests where a supervisor has a "reasonable suspicion" that an employee is under the influence of alcohol, based upon specific, personal observations concerning the appearance, behavior, speech, or body odors of the employee. * * * Where impairment is suspected, a railroad, in addition, may require urine tests, but only if two supervisors make the appropriate determination, * * * and, where the supervisors suspect impairment due to a substance other than alcohol, at least one of those supervisors must have received specialized training in detecting the signs of drug intoxication * * *.

Respondents, the Railway Labor Executives' Association and various of its member labor organizations, brought the instant suit in the United States District Court for the Northern District of California * * *. The court concluded that railroad employees "have a valid interest in the integrity of their own bodies" that deserved protection under the Fourth Amendment. * * * The court held, however, that this interest was outweighed by the competing "public and governmental interest in the * * * promotion of * * * railway safety, safety for employees, and safety for the general public that is involved with the transportation." * * *

A divided panel of the Court of Appeals for the Ninth Circuit reversed. * * *

We granted the federal parties' petition for a writ of certiorari, 486 U.S. 1042 (1988), to consider whether the regulations invalidated by the Court of Appeals violate the Fourth Amendment. We now reverse. * * *

The Fourth Amendment provides that "[t]he right of the people to be secure in their persons, houses, papers, and effects, against unreasonable searches and seizures, shall not be violated * * *." The Amendment guarantees the privacy, dignity, and security of persons against certain arbitrary and invasive acts by officers of the Government or those acting at their direction. * * *

Although the Fourth Amendment does not apply to a search or seizure, even an arbitrary one, effected by a private party on his own initiative, the Amendment protects against such intrusions if the private party acted as an instrument or agent of the Government. * * *

Whether a private party should be deemed an agent or instrument of the Government for Fourth Amendment purposes necessarily turns on the degree of [official control]. The fact that the Government has not compelled a private party to perform a search does not, by itself, establish that the search is a private one. Here, specific features of the regulations combine to convince us that the Government did more than adopt a passive position toward the underlying private conduct. * * *

Our precedents teach that where, as here, the Government seeks to obtain physical evidence from a person, the Fourth Amendment may be relevant at several levels. * * *

We have long recognized that a "compelled intrusio[n] into the body for blood to be analyzed for alcohol content" must be deemed a Fourth Amendment search. See Schmerber v. California, 384 U.S. 757, 767–768 (1966). * * *

Unlike the blood-testing procedure at issue in Schmerber, the procedures prescribed by the FRA regulations for collecting and testing urine samples do not entail a surgical intrusion into the body. It is not disputed, however, that chemical analysis of urine, like that of blood, can reveal a host of private medical facts about an employee, including whether he or she is epileptic, pregnant, or diabetic. Nor can it be disputed that the process of collecting the sample to be tested, which may in some cases involve visual or aural monitoring of the act of urination, itself implicates privacy interests. * * *

Because it is clear that the collection and testing of urine intrudes upon expectations of privacy that society has long recognized as reasonable, the Federal Courts of Appeals have concluded unanimously, and we agree, that these intrusions must be deemed searches under the Fourth Amendment. * * *

To hold that the Fourth Amendment is applicable to the drug and alcohol testing prescribed by the FRA regulations is only to begin the inquiry into the standards governing such intrusions. * * * For the Fourth Amendment does not proscribe all searches and seizures, but only those that are unreasonable. * * * [T]he permissibility of a particular practice "is judged by balancing its intrusion on the individual's Fourth Amendment interests against its promotion of legitimate governmental interests."

In most criminal cases, we strike this balance in favor of the procedures described by the Warrant Clause of the Fourth Amendment. * * * We have recognized exceptions to this rule, however, "when 'special needs, beyond the normal need for law enforcement, make the warrant and probable-cause requirement impracticable.'" * * * When faced with such special needs, we have not hesitated to balance the governmental and privacy interests to assess the practicality of the warrant and probable-cause requirements in the particular context. See, e.g., * * * New Jersey v. T. L. O., supra, at 337–342 (search of student's property by school officials); Bell v. Wolfish, 441 U.S. 520, 558–560 (1979) (body cavity searches of prison inmates). * * *

We have recognized * * * that the government's interest in dispensing with the warrant requirement is at its strongest when, as here, "the burden of obtaining a warrant is likely to frustrate the governmental purpose behind the search." * * * As the FRA recognized, alcohol and other drugs are eliminated from the bloodstream at a constant rate, * * * and blood and breath samples taken to measure whether these substances were in the bloodstream when a triggering event occurred must be obtained as soon as possible. See Schmerber v. California, 384 U.S., at 770–771. Although the metabolites of some drugs remain in the urine for longer periods of time and may enable the FRA to estimate whether the employee was impaired by those drugs at the time of a covered accident, incident, or rule violation, 49 Fed. Reg. 24291 (1984), the delay necessary to procure a warrant nevertheless may result in the destruction of valuable evidence. * * *

In sum, imposing a warrant requirement in the present context would add little to the assurances of certainty and regularity already afforded by the regulations, while significantly hindering, and in many cases frustrating, the objectives of the Government's testing program. We do not believe that a warrant is essential to render the intrusions here at issue reasonable under the Fourth Amendment. * * *

Our cases indicate that even a search that may be performed without a warrant must be based, as a general matter, on probable cause to believe that the person to be searched has violated the law. See New Jersey v. T. L. O., supra, at 340. When the balance of interests precludes insistence on a showing of probable cause, we have usually required "some quantum of individualized suspicion" before concluding that a search is reasonable. * * * In limited circumstances, where the privacy interests implicated by the search are minimal, and where an important governmental interest furthered by the intrusion would be placed in jeopardy by a requirement of individualized suspicion, a search may be reasonable despite the absence of such suspicion. We believe this is true of the intrusions in question here. * * *

Our * * * decision in Schmerber v. California, * * * held that a State could direct that a blood sample be withdrawn from a motorist suspected of driving while intoxicated, despite his refusal to consent to the intrusion. We noted that the test was performed in a reasonable manner, as the motorist's "blood was taken by a physician in a hospital environment according to accepted medical practices." * * * We said also that the intrusion occasioned by a blood test is not significant, since such "tests are a commonplace in these days of periodic physical examinations and experience with them teaches that the quantity of blood extracted is minimal, and that for most people the procedure involves virtually no risk, trauma, or pain." Ibid. Schmerber thus confirmed "society's judgment that blood tests do not constitute an unduly extensive imposition on an individual's privacy and bodily integrity.''

The breath tests authorized by Subpart D of the regulations are even less intrusive than the blood tests prescribed by Subpart C. Unlike blood tests, breath tests do not require piercing the skin and may be conducted safely outside a hospital environment and with a minimum of inconvenience or embarrassment. Further, breath tests reveal the level of alcohol in the employee's bloodstream and nothing more. * * * In all the circumstances, we cannot conclude that the administration of a breath test implicates significant privacy concerns.

A more difficult question is presented by urine tests. Like breath tests, urine tests are not invasive of the body and, under the regulations, may not be used as an occasion for inquiring into private facts unrelated to alcohol or drug use. * * * We recognize, however, that the procedures for collecting the necessary samples, which require employees to perform an excretory function traditionally shielded by great privacy, raise concerns not implicated by blood or breath tests. While we would not characterize these additional privacy concerns as minimal in most contexts, we note that the regulations endeavor to reduce the intrusiveness of the collection process. The regulations do not require that samples be furnished under the direct observation of a monitor, despite the desirability of such a procedure to ensure the integrity of the sample. * * * The sample is also collected in a medical environment, by personnel unrelated to the railroad employer, and is thus not unlike similar procedures encountered often in the context of a regular physical examination.

More importantly, the expectations of privacy of covered employees are diminished by reason of their participation in an industry that is regulated pervasively to ensure safety, a goal dependent, in substantial part, on the health and fitness of covered employees. * * *

We do not suggest, of course, that the interest in bodily security enjoyed by those employed in a regulated industry must always be considered minimal. * * * We conclude * * * that the testing procedures contemplated by Subparts C and D pose only limited threats to the justifiable expectations of privacy of covered employees.

By contrast, the Government interest in testing without a showing of individualized suspicion is compelling. Employees subject to the tests discharge duties fraught with such risks of injury to others that even a momentary lapse of attention can have disastrous consequences. Much like persons who have routine access to dangerous nuclear power facilities, see, e. g., Rushton v. Nebraska Public Power Dist., 844 F. 2d 562, 566 (CA8 1988); Alverado v. Washington Public Power Supply System, 111 Wash. 2d 424, 436, 759 P. 2d 427, 433–434 (1988), cert. pending, No. 88–645, employees who are subject to testing under the FRA regulations can cause great human loss before any signs of impairment become noticeable to supervisors or others. * * *

A requirement of particularized suspicion of drug or alcohol use would seriously impede an employer's ability to obtain this information, despite its obvious importance. Experience confirms the FRA's judgment that the scene of a serious rail accident is chaotic. Investigators who arrive at the scene shortly after a major accident has occurred may find it difficult to determine which members of a train crew contributed to its occurrence. Obtaining evidence that might give rise to the suspicion that a particular employee is impaired, a difficult endeavor in the best of circumstances, is most impracticable in the aftermath of a serious accident. While events following the rule violations that activate the testing authority of Subpart D may be less chaotic, objective indicia of impairment are absent in these instances as well. Indeed, any attempt to gather evidence relating to the possible impairment of particular employees likely would result in the loss or deterioration of the evidence furnished by the tests. * * *

We conclude that the compelling Government interests served by the FRA's regulations would be significantly hindered if railroads were required to point to specific facts giving rise to a reasonable suspicion of impairment before testing a given employee. In view of our conclusion that, on the present record, the toxicological testing contemplated by the regulations is not an undue infringement on the justifiable expectations of privacy of covered employees, the Government's compelling interests outweigh privacy concerns. * * *

JUSTICE MARSHALL, with whom JUSTICE BRENNAN joins, dissenting.

The issue in this case is not whether declaring a war on illegal drugs is good public policy. The importance of ridding our society of such drugs is, by now, apparent to all. Rather, the issue here is whether the Government's deployment in that war of a particularly Draconian weapon—the compulsory collection and chemical testing of railroad workers' blood and urine—comports with the Fourth Amendment. Precisely because the need for action against the drug scourge is manifest, the need for vigilance against unconstitutional excess is great. History teaches that grave threats to liberty often come in times of urgency, when constitutional rights seem too extravagant to endure. The World War II relocation-camp cases, Hirabayashi v. United States, 320 U.S. 81 (1943); Korematsu v. United States, 323 U.S. 214 (1944), and the Red scare and McCarthy-era internal subversion cases, Schenck v. United States, 249 U.S. 47 (1919); Dennis v. United States, 341 U.S. 494 (1951), are only the most extreme reminders that when we allow fundamental freedoms to be sacrificed in the name of real or perceived exigency, we invariably come to regret it.

In permitting the Government to force entire railroad crews to submit to invasive blood and urine tests, even when it lacks any evidence of drug or alcohol use or other wrongdoing, the majority today joins those short-sighted courts which have allowed basic constitutional rights to fall prey to momentary emergencies. * * *

I believe the Framers would be appalled by the vision of mass governmental intrusions upon the integrity of the human body that the majority allows to become reality. The immediate victims of the majority's constitutional timorousness will be those railroad workers whose bodily fluids the Government may now forcibly collect and analyze. But ultimately, today's decision will reduce the privacy all citizens may enjoy, for, as Justice Holmes understood, principles of law, once bent, do not snap back easily. I dissent.

NATIONAL TREASURY EMPLOYEES UNION v. VON RAAB

489 U.S. 656 (1989).

JUSTICE KENNEDY delivered the opinion of the Court.

We granted certiorari to decide whether it violates the Fourth Amendment for the United States Customs Service to require a urinalysis test from employees who seek transfer or promotion to certain positions. * * *

The United States Customs Service, a bureau of the Department of the Treasury, is the federal agency responsible for processing persons, carriers, cargo, and mail into the United States, collecting revenue from imports, and enforcing customs and related laws * * *. In 1987 alone, Customs agents seized drugs with a retail value of nearly $9 billion. * * *

In May 1986, the Commissioner [of Customs] announced implementation of the drug-testing program. Drug tests were made a condition of placement or employment for positions that meet one or more of three criteria. The first is direct involvement in drug interdiction or enforcement of related laws, an activity the Commissioner deemed fraught with obvious dangers to the mission of the agency and the lives of Customs agents. * * * The second criterion is a requirement that the incumbent carry firearms, as the Commissioner concluded that "public safety demands that employees who carry deadly arms and are prepared to make instant life or death decisions be drug free." * * *. The third criterion is a requirement for the incumbent to handle "classified" material, which the Commissioner determined might fall into the hands of smugglers if accessible to employees who, by reason of their own illegal drug use, are susceptible to bribery or blackmail.

After an employee qualifies for a position covered by the Customs testing program, the Service advises him by letter that his final selection is contingent upon successful completion of drug screening. An independent contractor contacts the employee to fix the time and place for collecting the sample. On reporting for the test, the employee must produce photographic identification and remove any outer garments, such as a coat or a jacket, and personal belongings. The employee may produce the sample behind a partition, or in the privacy of a bathroom stall if he so chooses. To ensure against adulteration of the specimen, or substitution of a sample from another person, a monitor of the same sex as the employee remains close at hand to listen for the normal sounds of urination. Dye is added to the toilet water to prevent the employee from using the water to adulterate the sample.

Upon receiving the specimen, the monitor inspects it to ensure its proper temperature and color, places a tamper-proof custody seal over the container, and affixes an identification label indicating the date and the individual's specimen number. The employee signs a chain-of-custody form, which is initialed by the monitor, and the urine sample is placed in a plastic bag, sealed, and submitted to a laboratory. * * *

Customs employees who test positive for drugs and who can offer no satisfactory explanation are subject to dismissal from the Service. Test results may not, however, be turned over to any other agency, including criminal prosecutors, without the employee's written consent. * * *

Petitioners, a union of federal employees and a union official, commenced this suit in the United States District Court for the Eastern District of Louisiana on behalf of current Customs Service employees who seek covered positions. Petitioners alleged that the Custom Service drug-testing program violated, inter alia, the Fourth Amendment. * * *

In Skinner v. Railway Labor Executives' Assn, decided today, we held that federal regulations requiring employees of private railroads to produce urine samples for chemical testing implicate the Fourth Amendment, as those tests invade reasonable expectations of privacy. Our earlier cases have settled that the Fourth Amendment protects individuals from unreasonable searches conducted by the Government, even when the Government acts as an employer * * *. [I]n view of our holding in Railway Labor Executives that urine tests are searches, it follows that the Customs Service's drug-testing program must meet the reasonableness requirement of the Fourth Amendment. * * *

It is clear that the Customs Service's drug-testing program is not designed to serve the ordinary needs of law enforcement. Test results may not be used in a criminal prosecution of the employee without the employee's consent. The purposes of the program are to deter drug use among those eligible for promotion to sensitive positions within the Service and to prevent the promotion of drug users to those positions. These substantial interests, no less than the Government's concern for safe rail transportation at issue in Railway Labor Executives, present a special need that may justify departure from the ordinary warrant and probable-cause requirements. * * *

We have recognized before that requiring the Government to procure a warrant for every work-related intrusion "would conflict with 'the common-sense realization that government offices could not function if every employment decision became a constitutional matter.'" * * * New Jersey v. T. L. O. * * * (noting that "the warrant requirement * * * is unsuited to the school environment: requiring a teacher to obtain a warrant before searching a child suspected of an infraction of school rules (or of the criminal law) would unduly interfere with the maintenance of the swift and informal disciplinary procedures needed in the schools").

Even if Customs Service employees are more likely to be familiar with the procedures required to obtain a warrant than most other Government workers, requiring a warrant in this context would serve only to divert valuable agency resources from the Service's primary mission. The Customs Service has been entrusted with pressing responsibilities, and its mission would be compromised if it were required to seek search warrants in connection with routine, yet sensitive, employment decisions.

Furthermore, a warrant would provide little or nothing in the way of additional protection of personal privacy. * * * Under the Customs program, every employee who seeks a transfer to a covered position knows that he must take a drug test, and is likewise aware of the procedures the Service must follow in administering the test. * * * The process becomes automatic when the employee elects to apply for, and thereafter pursue, a covered position. Because the Service does not make a discretionary determination to search based on a judgment that certain conditions are present, there are simply "no special facts for a neutral magistrate to evaluate." * * *

Even where it is reasonable to dispense with the warrant requirement in the particular circumstances, a search ordinarily must be based on probable cause. * * * Our cases teach, however, that the probable-cause standard " 'is peculiarly related to criminal investigations.' " * * * In particular, the traditional probable-cause standard may be unhelpful in analyzing the reasonableness of routine administrative functions, * * * where the Government seeks to prevent the development of hazardous conditions or to detect violations that rarely generate articulable grounds for searching any particular place or person. * * * We think the Government's need to conduct the suspicionless searches required by the Customs program outweighs the privacy interests of employees engaged directly in drug interdiction, and of those who otherwise are required to carry firearms.

The Customs Service is our Nation's first line of defense against one of the greatest problems affecting the health and welfare of our population. We have adverted before to "the veritable national crisis in law enforcement caused by smuggling of illicit narcotics." * * *

Many of the Service's employees are often exposed to this criminal element and to the controlled substances it seeks to smuggle into the country. * * * The physical safety of these employees may be threatened, and many may be tempted not only by bribes from the traffickers with whom they deal, but also by their own access to vast sources of valuable contraband seized and controlled by the Service. The Commissioner indicated below that "Customs officers have been shot, stabbed, run over, dragged by automobiles, and assaulted with blunt objects while performing their duties." * * * He also noted that Customs officers have been the targets of bribery by drug smugglers on numerous occasions, and several have been removed from the Service for accepting bribes and for other integrity violations. * * *

It is readily apparent that the Government has a compelling interest in ensuring that front-line interdiction personnel are physically fit, and have unimpeachable integrity and judgment. Indeed, the Government's interest here is at least as important as its interest in searching travelers entering the country. We have long held that travelers seeking to enter the country may be stopped and required to submit to a routine search without probable cause, or even founded suspicion, "because of national self protection reasonably requiring one entering the country to identify himself as entitled to come in, and his belongings as effects which may be lawfully brought in." * * * The public interest likewise demands effective measures to prevent the promotion of drug users to positions that require the incumbent to carry a firearm, even if the incumbent is not engaged directly in the interdiction of drugs. Customs employees who may use deadly force plainly "discharge duties fraught with such risks of injury to others that even a momentary lapse of attention can have disastrous consequences." We agree with the Government that the public should not bear the risk that employees who may suffer from impaired perception and judgment will be promoted to positions where they may need to employ deadly force. Indeed, ensuring against the creation of this danger-ous risk will itself further Fourth Amendment values, as the use of deadly force may violate the Fourth Amendment in certain circumstances. * * *

We think Customs employees who are directly involved in the inter-diction of illegal drugs or who are required to carry firearms in the line of duty likewise have a diminished expectation of privacy in respect to the intrusions occasioned by a urine test. Unlike most private citizens or government employees in general, employees involved in drug interdiction reasonably should expect effective inquiry into their fitness and probity. Much the same is true of employees who are required to carry firearms. Because successful performance of their duties depends uniquely on their judgment and dexterity, these employees cannot reasonably expect to keep from the Service personal information that bears directly on their fitness. * * *

Without disparaging the importance of the governmental interests that support the suspicionless searches of these employees, petitioners nevertheless contend that the Service's drug-testing program is unreason-able in two particulars. First, petitioners argue that the program is unjustified because it is not based on a belief that testing will reveal any drug use by covered employees. In pressing this argument, petitioners point out that the Service's testing scheme was not implemented in response to any perceived drug problem among Customs employees, and that the program actually has not led to the discovery of a significant number of drug users. * * * Counsel for petitioners informed us at oral argument that no more than 5 employees out of 3,600 have tested positive for drugs. * * * Second, petitioners contend that the Service's scheme is not a "sufficiently productive mechanism to justify [its] intrusion upon Fourth Amendment interests," Delaware v. Prouse, 440 U.S. 648, 658–659 (1979), because illegal drug users can avoid detection with ease by temporary abstinence or by surreptitious adulteration of their urine specimens. * * *

Petitioners' first contention evinces an unduly narrow view of the context in which the Service's testing program was implemented. Petitioners do not dispute, nor can there be doubt, that drug abuse is one of the most serious problems confronting our society today. There is little reason to believe that American workplaces are immune from this pervasive social problem, as is amply illustrated by our decision in Railway Labor Executives. * * *

We think petitioners' second argument—that the Service's testing program is ineffective because employees may attempt to deceive the test by a brief abstention before the test date, or by adulterating their urine specimens—overstates the case. As the Court of Appeals noted, addicts may be unable to abstain even for a limited period of time, or may be unaware of the "fade-away effect" of certain drugs. * * *

In sum, we believe the Government has demonstrated that its compelling interests in safeguarding our borders and the public safety outweigh the privacy expectations of employees who seek to be promoted to positions that directly involve the interdiction of illegal drugs or that require the incumbent to carry a firearm. We hold that the testing of these employees is reasonable under the Fourth Amendment. * * *

We are unable, on the present record, to assess the reasonableness of the Government's testing program insofar as it covers employees who are required "to handle classified material." * * *

We * * * think it is appropriate to remand the case to the Court of Appeals for such proceedings as may be necessary to clarify the scope of this category of employees subject to testing. Upon remand the Court of Appeals should examine the criteria used by the Service in determining what materials are classified and in deciding whom to test under this rubric. In assessing the reasonableness of requiring tests of these employees, the court should also consider pertinent information bearing upon the employees' privacy expectations, as well as the supervision to which these employees are already subject. * * *

We hold that the suspicionless testing of employees who apply for promotion to positions directly involving the interdiction of illegal drugs, or to positions that require the incumbent to carry a firearm, is reasonable. The Government's compelling interests in preventing the promotion of drug users to positions where they might endanger the integrity of our Nation's borders or the life of the citizenry outweigh the privacy interests of those who seek promotion to these positions, who enjoy a diminished expectation of privacy by virtue of the special, and obvious, physical and ethical demands of those positions. We do not decide whether testing those who apply for promotion to positions where they would handle "classified" information is reasonable because we find the record inadequate for this purpose.

The judgment of the Court of Appeals for the Fifth Circuit is affirmed in part and vacated in part, and the case is remanded for further proceedings consistent with this opinion. * * * It is so ordered. * * *

JUSTICE SCALIA, with whom JUSTICE STEVENS joins, dissenting.

The issue in this case is not whether Customs Service employees can constitutionally be denied promotion, or even dismissed, for a single instance of unlawful drug use, at home or at work. They assuredly can. The issue here is what steps can constitutionally be taken to detect such drug use. The Government asserts it can demand that employees perform "an excretory function traditionally shielded by great privacy," Skinner v. Railway Labor Executives' Assn., * * * while "a monitor of the same sex * * * remains close at hand to listen for the normal sounds," * * * and that the excretion thus produced be turned over to the Government for chemical analysis. The Court agrees that this constitutes a search for purposes of the Fourth Amendment—and I think it obvious that it is a type of search particularly destructive of privacy and offensive to personal dignity. * * *

What is absent in the Government's justifications—notably absent, revealingly absent, and as far as I am concerned dispositively absent—is the recitation of even a single instance in which any of the speculated horribles actually occurred: an instance, that is, in which the cause of bribetaking, or of poor aim, or of unsympathetic law enforcement, or of compromise of classified information, was drug use. Although the Court points out that several employees have in the past been removed from the Service for accepting bribes and other integrity violations, and that at least nine officers have died in the line of duty since 1974, * * * there is no indication whatever that these incidents were related to drug use by Service employees. Perhaps concrete evidence of the severity of a problem is unnecessary when it is so well known that courts can almost take judicial notice of it; but that is surely not the case here. The Commissioner of Customs himself has stated that he "believe[s] that Customs is largely drug-free," that "the extent of illegal drug use by Customs employees was not the reason for establishing this program," and that he "hope[s] and expect[s] to receive reports of very few positive findings through drug screening."

CHANDLER v. MILLER

520 U.S. 305 (1997).

JUSTICE GINSBURG delivered the opinion of the Court.

Georgia requires candidates for designated state offices to certify that they have taken a drug test and that the test result was negative. * * * We confront in this case the question whether that requirement ranks among the limited circumstances in which suspicionless searches are warranted. Relying on this Court's precedents sustaining drug-testing programs for student athletes, customs employees, and railway employees, see Vernonia School Dist. 47J v. Acton, 515 U.S. 646 (1995) * * * (random drug testing of students who participate in interscholastic sports); Von Raab, 489 U.S. at 659 (drug tests for United States Customs Service employees who seek transfer or promotion to certain positions); Skinner v. Railway Labor Executives' Assn., 489 U.S. 602 * * * (1989) (drug and alcohol tests for railway employees involved in train accidents and for those who violate particular safety rules), the United States Court of Appeals for the Eleventh Circuit judged Georgia's law constitutional. We reverse that judgment. Georgia's requirement that candidates for state office pass a drug test, we hold, does not fit within the closely guarded category of constitutionally permissible suspicionless searches. * * *

Under the Georgia statute, to qualify for a place on the ballot, a candidate must present a certificate from a state-approved laboratory, in a form approved by the Secretary of State, reporting that the candidate submitted to a urinalysis drug test within 30 days prior to qualifying for nomination or election and that the results were negative. * * * The statute lists as "illegal drugs": marijuana, cocaine, opiates, amphetamines, and phencyclidines. * * *

Petitioners were Libertarian Party nominees in 1994 for state offices subject to the requirements of Section 21–2–140. The Party nominated Walker L. Chandler for the office of Lieutenant Governor, Sharon T. Harris for the office of Commissioner of Agriculture, and James D. Walker for the office of member of the General Assembly. In May 1994, about one month before the deadline for submission of the certificates required by Section 21–2–140, petitioners Chandler, Harris, and Walker filed this action in the United States District Court for the Northern District of Georgia. They asserted, inter alia, that the drug tests required by [state law] violated their rights under the First, Fourth, and Fourteenth Amendments to the United States Constitution. * * *

We begin our discussion of this case with an uncontested point: Georgia's drug-testing requirement, imposed by law and enforced by state officials, effects a search within the meaning of the Fourth and Fourteenth Amendments. * * * Because "these intrusions [are] searches under the Fourth Amendment," * * * we focus on the question: Are the searches reasonable?

To be reasonable under the Fourth Amendment, a search ordinarily must be based on individualized suspicion of wrongdoing. See Vernonia, 515 U.S. at 664–667. But particularized exceptions to the main rule are sometimes warranted based on "special needs, beyond the normal need for law enforcement." Skinner, 489 U.S. at 619 (internal quotation marks omitted). When such "special needs"—concerns other than crime detection—are alleged in justification of a Fourth Amendment intrusion, courts must undertake a context-specific inquiry, examining closely the competing private and public interests advanced by the parties. See Von Raab, 489 U.S. at 665–666; see also id., at 668. * * *

In evaluating Georgia's ballot-access, drug-testing statute—a measure plainly not tied to individualized suspicion—the Eleventh Circuit sought to " 'balance the individual's privacy expectations against the [State's] interests,' " 73 F.3d at 1545 (quoting Von Raab, 489 U.S. at 665), in line with our precedents most immediately in point: Skinner, Von Raab, and Vernonia. * * *

Respondents urge that the precedents just examined are not the sole guides for assessing the constitutional validity of the Georgia statute. The "special needs" analysis, they contend, must be viewed through a different lens because [the state law in question] implicates Georgia's sovereign power, reserved to it under the Tenth Amendment, to establish qualifications for those who seek state office. * * * We are aware of no precedent suggesting that a State's power to establish qualifications for state offices—any more than its sovereign power to prosecute crime—diminishes the constraints on state action imposed by the Fourth Amendment. We therefore reject respondents' invitation to apply in this case a framework extraordinarily deferential to state measures setting conditions of candidacy for state office. Our guides remain Skinner, Von Raab, and Vernonia.

Turning to those guides, we note, first, that the testing method the Georgia statute describes is relatively noninvasive; therefore, if the "special need" showing had been made, the State could not be faulted for excessive intrusion. * * * Because the State has effectively limited the invasiveness of the testing procedure, we concentrate on the core issue: Is the certification requirement warranted by a special need?

Our precedents establish that the proffered special need for drug testing must be substantial—important enough to override the individual's acknowledged privacy interest, sufficiently vital to suppress the Fourth Amendment's normal requirement of individualized suspicion. * * * Georgia has failed to show * * * a special need of that kind.

Respondents' defense of the statute rests primarily on the incompatibility of unlawful drug use with holding high state office. The statute is justified, respondents contend, because the use of illegal drugs draws into question an official's judgment and integrity; jeopardizes the discharge of public functions, including antidrug law enforcement efforts; and undermines public confidence and trust in elected officials * * *. Notably lacking in respondents' presentation is any indication of a concrete danger demanding departure from the Fourth Amendment's main rule.

Nothing in the record hints that the hazards respondents broadly describe are real and not simply hypothetical for Georgia's polity. The statute was not enacted, as counsel for respondents readily acknowledged at oral argument, in response to any fear or suspicion of drug use by state officials. * * *

In contrast to the effective testing regimes upheld in Skinner, Von Raab, and Vernonia, Georgia's certification requirement is not well designed to identify candidates who violate antidrug laws. Nor is the scheme a credible means to deter illicit drug users from seeking election to state office. The test date—to be scheduled by the candidate anytime within 30 days prior to qualifying for a place on the ballot—is no secret. As counsel for respondents acknowledged at oral argument, users of illegal drugs, save for those prohibitively addicted, could abstain for a pretest period sufficient to avoid detection. * * *

What is left, after close review of Georgia's scheme, is the image the State seeks to project. By requiring candidates for public office to submit to drug testing, Georgia displays its commitment to the struggle against drug abuse. The suspicionless tests, according to respondents, signify that candidates, if elected, will be fit to serve their constituents free from the influence of illegal drugs. But Georgia asserts no evidence of a drug problem among the State's elected officials, those officials typically do not perform high-risk, safety-sensitive tasks, and the required certification immediately aids no interdiction effort. The need revealed, in short, is symbolic, not "special," as that term draws meaning from our case law. * * *

We note, finally, matters this opinion does not treat. Georgia's singular drug test for candidates is not part of a medical examination designed to provide certification of a candidate's general health, and we express no opinion on such examinations. Nor do we touch on financial disclosure requirements, which implicate different concerns and procedures. * * * And we do not speak to drug testing in the private sector, a domain unguarded by Fourth Amendment constraints.

For the reasons stated, the judgment of the Court of Appeals for the Eleventh Circuit is [reversed].

CHIEF JUSTICE REHNQUIST, dissenting.

I fear that the novelty of this Georgia law has led the Court to distort Fourth Amendment doctrine in order to strike it down. * * *

Few would doubt that the use of illegal drugs and abuse of legal drugs is one of the major problems of our society. Cases before this Court involving drug use extend to numerous occupations * * *. It would take a bolder person than I to say that such widespread drug usage could never extend to candidates for public office such as Governor of Georgia. The Court says that "nothing in the record hints that the hazards respondents broadly describe are real and not simply hypothetical for Georgia's polity." But surely the State need not wait for a drug addict, or one inclined to use drugs illegally, to run for or actually become Governor before it installs a prophylactic mechanism. We held as much in Von Raab * * *.

FERGUSON v. CITY OF CHARLESTON

532 U.S. 67 (2001).

JUSTICE STEVENS delivered the opinion of the Court.

In this case, we must decide whether a state hospital's performance of a diagnostic test to obtain evidence of a patient's criminal conduct for law enforcement purposes is an unreasonable search if the patient has not consented to the procedure. More narrowly, the question is whether the interest in using the threat of criminal sanctions to deter pregnant women from using cocaine can justify a departure from the general rule that an official nonconsensual search is unconstitutional if not authorized by a valid warrant. * * *

In the fall of 1988, staff members at the public hospital operated in the city of Charleston by the Medical University of South Carolina (MUSC) became concerned about an apparent increase in the use of cocaine by patients who were receiving prenatal treatment. In response to this perceived increase, as of April 1989, MUSC began to order drug screens to be performed on urine samples from maternity patients who were suspected of using cocaine. If a patient tested positive, she was then referred by MUSC staff to the county substance abuse commission for counseling and treatment. However, despite the referrals, the incidence of cocaine use among the patients at MUSC did not appear to change.

Some four months later, Nurse Shirley Brown, the case manager for the MUSC obstetrics department, heard a news broadcast reporting that the police in Greenville, South Carolina, were arresting pregnant users of cocaine on the theory that such use harmed the fetus and was therefore child abuse. Nurse Brown discussed the story with MUSC's general counsel, Joseph C. Good, Jr., who then contacted Charleston Solicitor Charles Condon in order to offer MUSC's cooperation in prosecuting mothers whose children tested positive for drugs at birth.

After receiving Good's letter, Solicitor Condon took the first steps in developing the policy at issue in this case. He organized the initial meetings, decided who would participate, and issued the invitations, in which he described his plan to prosecute women who tested positive for cocaine while pregnant. The task force that Condon formed included representatives of MUSC, the police, the County Substance Abuse Commission and the Department of Social Services. Their deliberations led to MUSC's adoption of a 12–page document entitled "POLICY M–7," dealing with the subject of "Management of Drug Abuse During Pregnancy." * * *

The first three pages of Policy M–7 set forth the procedure to be followed by the hospital staff to "identify/assist pregnant patients suspected of drug abuse." * * * The first section, entitled the "Identification of Drug Abusers," provided that a patient should be tested for cocaine through a urine drug screen if she met one or more of nine criteria. It also stated that a chain of custody should be followed when obtaining and testing urine samples, presumably to make sure that the results could be used in subsequent criminal proceedings. The policy also provided for education and referral to a substance abuse clinic for patients who tested positive. Most important, it added the threat of law enforcement intervention that "provided the necessary 'leverage' to make the policy effective." * * * That threat was, as respondents candidly acknowledge, essential to the program's success in getting women into treatment and keeping them there.

The threat of law enforcement involvement was set forth in two protocols, the first dealing with the identification of drug use during pregnancy, and the second with identification of drug use after labor. Under the latter protocol, the police were to be notified without delay and the patient promptly arrested. Under the former, after the initial positive drug test, the police were to be notified (and the patient arrested) only if the patient tested positive for cocaine a second time or if she missed an appointment with a substance abuse counselor. * * * In 1990, however, the policy was modified at the behest of the solicitor's office to give the patient who tested positive during labor, like the patient who tested positive during a prenatal care visit, an opportunity to avoid arrest by consenting to substance abuse treatment.

The last six pages of the policy contained forms for the patients to sign, as well as procedures for the police to follow when a patient was arrested. The policy also prescribed in detail the precise offenses with which a woman could be charged, depending on the stage of her pregnancy. If the pregnancy was 27 weeks or less, the patient was to be charged with simple possession. If it was 28 weeks or more, she was to be charged with possession and distribution to a person under the age of 18—in this case, the fetus. If she delivered "while testing positive for illegal drugs," she was also to be charged with unlawful neglect of a child. * * * Under the policy, the police were instructed to interrogate the arrestee in order "to ascertain the identity of the subject who provided illegal drugs to the suspect." * * * Other than the provisions describing the substance abuse treatment to be offered to women who tested positive, the policy made no mention of any change in the prenatal care of such patients, nor did it prescribe any special treatment for the newborns. * * *

Petitioners are 10 women who received obstetrical care at MUSC and who were arrested after testing positive for cocaine. Four of them were arrested during the initial implementation of the policy; they were not offered the opportunity to receive drug treatment as an alternative to arrest. The others were arrested after the policy was modified in 1990; they either failed to comply with the terms of the drug treatment program or tested positive for a second time. Respondents include the city of Charleston, law enforcement officials who helped develop and enforce the policy, and representatives of MUSC.

Petitioners' complaint challenged the validity of the policy under various theories, including the claim that warrantless and nonconsensual drug tests conducted for criminal investigatory purposes were unconstitutional searches. * * *

We granted certiorari, 528 U.S. 1187 (2000), to review the appellate court's holding on the "special needs" issue. Because we do not reach the question of the sufficiency of the evidence with respect to consent, we necessarily assume for purposes of our decision—as did the Court of

Appeals—that the searches were conducted without the informed consent of the patients. We conclude that the judgment should be reversed and the case remanded for a decision on the consent issue. * * *

Because MUSC is a state hospital, the members of its staff are government actors, subject to the strictures of the Fourth Amendment. * * * Moreover, the urine tests conducted by those staff members were indisputably searches within the meaning of the Fourth Amendment. * * * [G]iven the posture in which the case comes to us, we must assume for purposes of our decision that the tests were performed without the informed consent of the patients.

Because the hospital seeks to justify its authority to conduct drug tests and to turn the results over to law enforcement agents without the knowledge or consent of the patients, this case differs from the four previous cases in which we have considered whether comparable drug tests "fit within the closely guarded category of constitutionally permissible suspicionless searches." * * *

The critical difference between [previous] drug-testing cases and this one, however, lies in the nature of the "special need" asserted as justification for the warrantless searches. In each of those earlier cases, the "special need" that was advanced as a justification for the absence of a warrant or individualized suspicion was one divorced from the State's general interest in law enforcement. * * * In this case, however, the central and indispensable feature of the policy from its inception was the use of law enforcement to coerce the patients into substance abuse treatment. This fact distinguishes this case from circumstances in which physicians or psychologists, in the * * * course of ordinary medical procedures aimed at helping the patient herself, come across information that under rules of law or ethics is subject to reporting requirements, which no one has challenged here. * * *

Respondents argue in essence that their ultimate purpose—namely, protecting the health of both mother and child—is a beneficent one. In Chandler, however, we did not simply accept the State's invocation of a "special need." Instead, we carried out a "close review" of the scheme at issue before concluding that the need in question was not "special," as that term has been defined in our cases. * * *

[T]hroughout the development and application of the policy, the Charleston prosecutors and police were extensively involved in the day-to-day administration of the policy. Police and prosecutors decided who would receive the reports of positive drug screens and what information would be included with those reports. Law enforcement officials also helped determine the procedures to be followed when performing the screens * * *. In the course of the policy's administration, they had access to * * * medical files on the women who tested positive, routinely attended the substance abuse team's meetings, and regularly received copies of team documents discussing the women's progress. Police took pains to coordinate the timing and circumstances of the arrests with MUSC staff * * *.

While the ultimate goal of the program may well have been to get the women in question into substance abuse treatment and off of drugs, the immediate objective of the searches was to generate evidence for law enforcement purposes in order to reach that goal. * * * The threat of law enforcement may ultimately have been intended as a means to an end, but the direct and primary purpose of MUSC's policy was to ensure the use of those means. In our opinion, this distinction is critical. Because law enforcement involvement always serves some broader social purpose or objective, under respondents' view, virtually any nonconsensual suspicion-less search could be immunized under the special needs doctrine by defining the search solely in terms of its ultimate, rather than immediate, purpose. * * * Such an approach is inconsistent with the Fourth Amendment. Given the primary purpose of the Charleston program, which was to use the threat of arrest and prosecution in order to force women into treatment, and given the extensive involvement of law enforcement officials at every stage of the policy, this case simply does not fit within the closely guarded category of "special needs." * * *

Accordingly, the judgment of the Court of Appeals is reversed, and the case is remanded for further proceedings consistent with this opinion. * * * It is so ordered.

JUSTICE SCALIA, with whom the CHIEF JUSTICE and JUSTICE THOMAS join as to Part II, dissenting. * * *

It is rudimentary Fourth Amendment law that a search which has been consented to is not unreasonable. There is no contention in the present case that the urine samples were extracted forcibly. * * *

Until today, we have never held—or even suggested—that material which a person voluntarily entrusts to someone else cannot be given by that person to the police, and used for whatever evidence it may contain. Without so much as discussing the point, the Court today opens a hole in our Fourth Amendment jurisprudence, the size and shape of which is entirely indeterminate. Today's holding would be remarkable enough if the confidential relationship violated by the police conduct were at least one protected by state law. It would be surprising to learn, for example, that in a State which recognizes a spousal evidentiary privilege the police cannot use evidence obtained from a cooperating husband or wife. But today's holding goes even beyond that, since there does not exist any physician-patient privilege in South Carolina. See, e.g., Peagler v. Atlantic Coast R. R. Co., 232 S.C. 274 (1958).

UNITED STATES v. COMPREHENSIVE DRUG TESTING, INC.

579 F.3d 989 (C.A.9 (Cal.), 2009).

KOZINSKI, CHIEF JUDGE:

* * *

In 2002, the federal government commenced an investigation into the Bay Area Lab Cooperative (Balco), which it suspected of providing steroids to professional baseball players. That year, the Major League Baseball Players Association (the Players) also entered into a collective bargaining agreement with Major League Baseball providing for suspicionless drug testing of all players. Urine samples were to be collected during the first year of the agreement and each sample was to be tested for banned substances. The players were assured that the results would remain anonymous and confidential; the purpose of the testing was solely to determine whether more than five percent of players tested positive, in which case there would be additional testing in future seasons.

Comprehensive Drug Testing, Inc. (CDT), an independent business, administered the program and collected the specimens from the players; the actual tests were performed by Quest Diagnostics, Inc., a laboratory. CDT maintained the list of players and their respective test results; Quest kept the actual specimens on which the tests were conducted.

During the Balco investigation, federal authorities learned of ten players who had tested positive in the CDT program. The government secured a grand jury subpoena in the Northern District of California seeking *all* "drug testing records and specimens" pertaining to Major League Baseball in CDT's possession. CDT and the Players tried to negotiate a compliance agreement with the government but, when negotiations failed, moved to quash the subpoena.

The day that the motion to quash was filed, the government obtained a warrant in the Central District of California authorizing the search of CDT's facilities in Long Beach. Unlike the subpoena, the warrant was limited to the records of the ten players as to whom the government had probable cause. When the warrant was executed, however, the government seized and promptly reviewed the drug testing records for hundreds of players in Major League Baseball (and a great many other people).

The government also obtained a warrant from the District of Nevada for the urine samples on which the drug tests had been performed. These were kept at Quest's facilities in Las Vegas. Subsequently, the government obtained additional warrants for records at CDT's facilities in Long Beach and Quest's lab in Las Vegas. Finally, the government served CDT and Quest with new subpoenas in the Northern District of California, demanding production of the same records it had just seized.

CDT and the Players moved in the Central District of California, pursuant to Federal Rule of Criminal Procedure 41(g), for return of the property seized there. Judge Cooper found that the government had failed to comply with the procedures specified in the warrant and, on that basis and others, ordered the property returned. We will refer to this as the Cooper Order.

CDT and the Players subsequently moved in the District of Nevada, pursuant to Federal Rule of Criminal Procedure 41(g), for return of the property seized under the warrants issued by that court. The matter came before Judge Mahan, who granted the motion and ordered the government to return the property it had seized, with the exception of materials pertaining to the ten identified baseball players. We will refer to this as the Mahan Order.

CDT and the Players finally moved in the Northern District of California, pursuant to Federal Rule of Criminal Procedure 17(c), to quash the latest round of subpoenas and the matter was heard by Judge Illston. (The original subpoena, and the motion to quash it that was filed in 2003, aren't before us.) In an oral ruling, Judge Illston quashed the subpoenas. We will refer to this as the Illston Quashal. *See* Bryan A. Garner, *A Dictionary of Modern American Legal Usage* 725 (2d ed.1995).

* * *

Concluding Thoughts

This case well illustrates both the challenges faced by modern law enforcement in retrieving information it needs to pursue and prosecute wrongdoers, and the threat to the privacy of innocent parties from a vigorous criminal investigation. At the time of *Tamura* [United States v. Tamura, 694 F.2d 591 (9th Cir. 1982)], most individuals and enterprises kept records in their file cabinets or similar physical facilities. Today, the same kind of data is usually stored electronically, often far from the premises. Electronic storage facilities intermingle data, making them difficult to retrieve without a thorough understanding of the filing and classification systems used—something that can often only be determined by closely analyzing the data in a controlled environment. *Tamura* involved a few dozen boxes and was considered a broad seizure; but even inexpensive electronic storage media today can store the equivalent of millions of pages of information.

Wrongdoers and their collaborators have obvious incentives to make data difficult to find, but parties involved in lawful activities may also encrypt or compress data for entirely legitimate reasons: protection of privacy, preservation of privileged communications, warding off industrial espionage or preventing general mischief such as identity theft. Law enforcement today thus has a far more difficult, exacting and sensitive task in pursuing evidence of criminal activities than even in the relatively recent past. The legitimate need to scoop up large quantities of data, and sift through it carefully for concealed or disguised pieces of evidence, is one we've often recognized. *See, e.g., United States v. Hill,* 459 F.3d 966 (9th Cir.2006).

This pressing need of law enforcement for broad authorization to examine electronic records, so persuasively demonstrated in the introduction to the original warrant in this case, * * * creates a serious risk that every warrant for electronic information will become, in effect, a general warrant, rendering the Fourth Amendment irrelevant. The problem can be stated very simply: There is no way to be sure exactly what an electronic file contains without somehow examining its contents—either by opening it and looking, using specialized forensic software, keyword searching or some other such technique. But electronic files are generally found on media that also contain thousands or millions of other files among which the sought-after data may be stored or concealed. By necessity, government efforts to locate particular files will require examining a great many other files to exclude the possibility that the sought-after data are concealed there.

Once a file is examined, however, the government may claim (as it did in this case) that its contents are in plain view and, if incriminating, the government can keep it. Authorization to search *some* computer files therefore automatically becomes authorization to search all files in the same subdirectory, and all files in an enveloping directory, a neighboring hard drive, a nearby computer or nearby storage media. Where computers are not near each other, but are connected electronically, the original search might justify examining files in computers many miles away, on a theory that incriminating electronic data could have been shuttled and concealed there.

The advent of fast, cheap networking has made it possible to store information at remote third-party locations, where it is intermingled with that of other users. For example, many people no longer keep their email primarily on their personal computer, and instead use a web-based email provider, which stores their messages along with billions of messages from and to millions of other people. Similar services exist for photographs, slide shows, computer code and many other types of data. As a result, people now have personal data that are stored with that of innumerable strangers. Seizure of, for example, Google's email servers to look for a few incriminating messages could jeopardize the privacy of millions.

It's no answer to suggest, as did the majority of the three-judge panel, that people can avoid these hazards by not storing their data electronically. To begin with, the choice about how information is stored is often made by someone other than the individuals whose privacy would be invaded by the search. Most people have no idea whether their doctor, lawyer or accountant maintains records in paper or electronic format, whether they are stored on the premises or on a server farm in Rancho Cucamonga, whether they are commingled with those of many other professionals or kept entirely separate. Here, for example, the Tracey Directory contained a huge number of drug testing records, not only of the ten players for whom the government had probable cause but hundreds of other professional baseball players, thirteen other sports organizations, three unrelated sporting competitions, and a non-sports business entity-thousands of files in all, reflecting the test results of an unknown number of people, most having no relationship to professional baseball except that they had the bad luck of having their test results stored on the same computer as the baseball players.

Second, there are very important benefits to storing data electronically. Being able to back up the data and avoid the loss by fire, flood or earthquake is one of them. Ease of access from remote locations while traveling is another. The ability to swiftly share the data among professionals, such as sending MRIs for examination by a cancer specialist halfway around the world, can mean the difference between death and a full recovery. Electronic storage and transmission of data is no longer a peculiarity or a luxury of the very rich; it's a way of life. Government intrusions into large private databases thus have the potential to expose exceedingly sensitive information about countless individuals not implicated in any criminal activity, who might not even know that the information about them has been seized and thus can do nothing to protect their privacy.

It is not surprising, then, that all three of the district judges below were severely troubled by the government's conduct in this case. Judge Mahan, for example, asked "what ever happened to the Fourth Amendment? Was it ... repealed somehow?" Judge Cooper referred to "the image of quickly and skillfully moving the cup so no one can find the pea." And Judge Illston regarded the government's tactics as "unreasonable" and found that they constituted "harassment." Judge Thomas, too, in his panel dissent, expressed frustration with the government's conduct and position, calling it a "breathtaking expansion of the 'plain view' doctrine, which clearly has no application to intermingled private electronic data." *Comprehensive Drug Testing*, 513 F.3d at 1117.

Everyone's interests are best served if there are clear rules to follow that strike a fair balance between the legitimate needs of law enforcement and the right of individuals and enterprises to the privacy that is at the heart of the Fourth Amendment. *Tamura* has provided a workable framework for almost three decades, and might well have sufficed in this case had its teachings been followed. We believe it is useful, therefore, to update *Tamura* to apply to the daunting realities of electronic searches which will nearly always present the kind of situation that *Tamura* believed would be rare and exceptional—the inability of government agents to segregate seizable from non-seizable materials at the scene of the search, and thus the necessity to seize far more than is actually authorized.

We accept the reality that such over-seizing is an inherent part of the electronic search process and proceed on the assumption that, when it comes to the seizure of electronic records, this will be far more common than in the days of paper records. This calls for greater vigilance on the part of judicial officers in striking the right balance between the government's interest in law enforcement and the right of individuals to be free from unreasonable searches and seizures. The process of segregating electronic data that is seizable from that which is not must not become a vehicle for the government to gain access to data which it has no probable cause to collect. In general, we adopt *Tamura*'s solution to the problem of necessary over-seizing of evidence: When the government wishes to obtain a warrant to examine a computer hard drive or electronic storage medium in searching for certain incriminating files, or when a search for evidence could result in the seizure of a computer, *see, e.g., United States v. Giberson,* 527 F.3d 882 (9th Cir.2008), magistrate judges must be vigilant in observing the guidance we have set out throughout our opinion, which can be summed up as follows:

1.   Magistrates should insist that the government waive reliance upon the plain view doctrine in digital evidence cases. * * *

2.   Segregation and redaction must be either done by specialized personnel or an independent third party. * * * If the segregation is to be done by government computer personnel, it must agree in the warrant application that the computer personnel will not disclose to the investigators any information other than that which is the target of the warrant.

3.   Warrants and subpoenas must disclose the actual risks of destruction of information as well as prior efforts to seize that information in other judicial fora. * * *

4.   The government's search protocol must be designed to uncover only the information for which it has probable cause, and only that information may be examined by the case agents. * * *

5.   The government must destroy or, if the recipient may lawfully possess it, return non-responsive data, keeping the issuing magistrate informed about when it has done so and what it has kept. * * *

Just as *Tamura* [*United States v. Tamura,* 694 F.2d 591 (9th Cir. 1982)] has served as a guidepost for decades, we trust that the procedures we have outlined above will prove a useful tool for the future. In the end, however, we must rely on the good sense and vigilance of our magistrate judges, who are in the front line of preserving the constitutional freedoms of our citizens while assisting the government in its legitimate efforts to prosecute criminal activity. Nothing we could say would substitute for the sound judgment that judicial officers must exercise in striking this delicate balance. * * *

b.   HIV/AIDS and Hepatitis

GLOVER v. EASTERN NEBRASKA COMMUNITY OFFICE OF RETARDATION

686 F.Supp. 243 (D. Neb. 1988).

LYLE E. STROM, CHIEF UNITED STATES DISTRICT JUDGE * * *

The controversy in this case surrounds the Chronic Infectious Disease Policy No. 8.85 (the policy) adopted by the governing board of defendant Eastern Nebraska Human Services Agency (ENHSA) which requires certain employees to submit to mandatory testing for tuberculosis (TB), hepatitis B (HBV), and human immunodeficiency virus (HIV). * * *

In September of 1987, an ENCOR employee * * * died from AIDS. At this point, the ENHSA governing board instructed Executive Director

Donald Moray to develop a policy for mandatory AIDS testing of employees. The original policy was announced and challenged by the ENCOR employees. After this Court restrained the policy, and pending the trial on the merits, the policy was reviewed and some aspects were changed. The new policy, effective January 20, 1988, states that the persons holding or applying for the following titles must undergo testing: home teacher, residential associate, residential assistant, vocational program manager, vocational production manager, registered nurse, and licensed practical nurse. The policy also states that new positions may be added to the list. The rationale behind testing staff members in the identified positions is that these positions involve extensive contact with clients. The evidence in this case, however, shows that staff members who hold non-test positions have also been the recipients of bites and scratches from ENCOR clients.

The evidence shows that the ENCOR staff member who died from AIDS was involved in numerous incidents where he was bitten, scratched, pinched, kicked and hit by clients. When this staff member died from AIDS, however, ENCOR did not follow up on the clients involved in any of these incidents, nor did they notify these clients or their guardians that ENCOR believed they were potentially at risk of contracting the AIDS virus because of the contact with this staff member.

There is some evidence of sexual abuse of clients at ENCOR. These incidents, however, are not limited to staff/client contacts, of which there are few reported incidents. The testimony of the ENCOR staff members, Executive Director Moray, and Deputy Director Brinker are all in agreement and establish that there is not a sexual abuse problem at ENCOR.

The AIDS virus may be detected by two medical tests, the enzyme-linked immunoassay test (ELISA) or the confirmatory test, the Western blot. Both of these tests are blood tests which determine the presence of antibodies to the AIDS virus. * * *

The medically indicated reasons for HIV testing are: (a) as an adjunct to the medical workup of a patient who may be infected, (b) for epidemiological purposes to establish the level of infection in a community, and (c) as a device used in conjunction with counseling those in high risk groups to stimulate them to change their high-risk behaviors. Testing in isolation as provided in ENCOR's policy does not serve these purposes. * * *

A positive report of an HIV test is a "very foreboding kind of message." (Testimony of Dr. Goldsmith). The reaction of patients to this news is devastation. If not handled properly, it can lead to disastrous results, including suicide. Because of the foreboding message that accompanies a positive HIV test result, some people simply do not want to know if they are infected.

In this case, the ENCOR employees who test positive would receive this devastating message from Curtis Starks, the affirmative action and employee relations officer at ENHSA. If Mr. Starks is unavailable, the personnel director will deliver the test results to employees. In addition, tested employees will not have the option of not being told of their test results.

There is no known cure for AIDS. Experimental studies are now under way searching for a cure for this disease. * * * Until a cure is found, education about the prevention of the disease is the best available route to deal with AIDS. * * *

According to the Morbidity and Mortality Weekly Report (MMWR) of May 22, 1987, there have been five reports of HIV infection by non-needle stick exposure of health care workers who denied other risk factors. Two of these cases resulted from providing nursing care to HIV infected persons. These cases involved people who had daily, repeated contact with blood or body fluids of an infected patient over an extended period of time and who did not follow any routinely recommended barrier precautions.

Three additional health care workers have become infected with HIV following non-needle stick exposures to blood from infected patients. Two of these exposures involved prolonged contact with infected blood and with neither of the workers wearing gloves. The other exposure was the result of a blood splatter, with blood splashing into the mouth of the health care worker. * * *

The evidence establishes that the risk of transmission of the AIDS virus from staff to client, assuming a staff member is infected with HIV, in the ENCOR environment is extremely low, approaching zero. The medical evidence is undisputed that the disease is not contracted by casual contact. The risk of transmission of the disease to clients as a result of a client biting or scratching a staff member, and potentially drawing blood, is extraordinarily low, also approaching zero. The risk of transmission of the virus from staff to client due to the staff member attending to a client's personal hygiene needs is zero. Further, there is absolutely no evidence of drug use or needle sharing at ENCOR, nor is there a problem of sexual abuse of clients by staff.

In short, the evidence in this case establishes that the risk of transmission of the HIV virus at ENCOR is minuscule at best and will have little, if any, effect in preventing the spread of HIV or in protecting the clients. Further, from a medical viewpoint, this policy is not necessary to protect clients from any medical risks.

This case raises issues involving the Fourth Amendment rights of public employees. The Fourth Amendment to the United States Constitution protects the "right of the people to be secure in their persons, houses, papers, and effects, against unreasonable searches and seizures * * *," rights which are implicated only if the conduct at issue infringes "an expectation of privacy that society is prepared to consider reasonable." * * * The Fourth Amendment is enforceable against the states through the Fourteenth amendment and seeks to "safeguard the privacy and security of individuals against arbitrary invasions by governmental officials." * * *

Individuals have a reasonable expectation of privacy in the personal information their body fluids contain. Compulsory administration of a blood test "plainly involves the broadly conceived reach of a search and seizure under the Fourth Amendment." Schmerber v. California, 384 U.S. 757 (1966). The mandatory testing required by the policy involves an involuntary intrusion into the body by the State for the purposes of withdrawing blood and constitutes a search and seizure for purposes of the Fourth Amendment. * * * Having determined that the mandatory blood tests required by the policy constitutes a search and seizure, this Court must then determine whether the search meets the Fourth Amendment test of reasonableness.

To determine the appropriate standard of reasonableness in this matter, this Court must balance the "nature and quality of the intrusion on the individual's Fourth Amendment interests against the importance of the governmental interests alleged to justify the intrusion. * * * " In this matter, the Court must balance the ENCOR employees' reasonable expectations of privacy with ENCOR's interest in a safe training and living environment for all developmentally disabled persons receiving services from the agency. * * *

Although the pursuit of a safe work environment for employees and a safe training and living environment for all clients is a worthy one, the policy does not reasonably serve that purpose. There is simply no real basis to be concerned that clients are at risk of contracting the AIDS virus at the work place. These clients are not in danger of contracting the AIDS virus from staff members and such an unreasonable fear cannot justify a policy which intrudes on staff members' constitutionally protected rights. * * *

The Court is convinced that the evidence, considered in its entirety, leads to the conclusion that the policy was prompted by concerns about the AIDS virus, formulated with little or erroneous medical knowledge, and is a constitutionally impermissible reaction to a devastating disease with no known cure. The risk of transmission of the disease from the staff to the clients at ENCOR is minuscule, trivial, extremely low, extraordinarily low, theoretical, and approaches zero. Such a risk does not justify the implementation of such a sweeping policy which ignores and violates the staff members' constitutional rights.

Likewise, the mandatory testing of staff members for HBV is not justified at its inception. There is no evidence in this case that the clients are at risk of contracting HBV from staff members. Even if there were evidence of such a risk, the policy would not be justified as other measures exist to promote ENCOR's interests in protecting its clients. Specifically, ENCOR could administer the HBV immunization to its clients, and be prepared to administer the hepatitis B immune globulin to an unimmunized client who was exposed to the disease. In addition, unlike testing, these measures are effective in preventing the spread of HBV and protecting the health of ENCOR's clients.

Accordingly, a separate order will be issued this date in conformity with this opinion enjoining the defendant from implementing ENHSA policy 8.85, the chronic infectious disease policy, in regard to hepatitis B and human immunodeficiency virus.

c. DNA

MAYFIELD v. DALTON

109 F.3d 1423 (9th Cir. 1997).

SCHROEDER, CIRCUIT JUDGE:

The plaintiffs-appellants in this case, John C. Mayfield and Joseph Vlacovsky, filed this action when they were on active duty in the Marine Corps. They challenged the constitutionality of a Department of Defense program to collect and store blood and tissue samples from all members of the armed forces for future DNA analysis (the "repository"). Mayfield and Vlacovsky argued that the compulsory taking of specimens without proper safeguards to maintain the privacy of the donor was a violation of the Fourth Amendment prohibition against unreasonable searches and sei- zures. * * * In addition, they feared that information obtained from the repository samples, regarding the donors' propensities for hereditary diseases and genetic disorders, might be used to discriminate against applicants for jobs, insurance or benefit programs. Id. at 304. * * *

We agree with the government that Mayfield and Vlacovsky's chal- lenge is moot because they are no longer subject to the DNA collection program, and face only a remote possibility that they may ever be subject to the repository policies they seek to challenge. * * *

Moreover, in the intervening time * * * the military changed the repository in ways that appear to respond to some of plaintiffs-appellants' main concerns. As of April 1996, for example, the maximum length of time that the specimens will now be retained has been shortened from the originally challenged duration of 75 years to 50 years. In addition, upon the request of the donor, the military will now destroy individual specimen samples following the conclusion of the service member's military obli- gation. * * *

Having determined that Mayfield and Vlacovsky's separation from active duty has mooted this appeal, we * * * vacate the judgment of the district court and remand with instructions to dismiss the case as moot.

NOTE: MANDATORY DNA TESTING FOR CRIMINAL JUSTICE

The DNA Analysis Backlog Elimination Act of 2000 ("DNA Act"), Pub. L. No. 106–546, 114 Stat. 2726 (2000), requires persons convicted of certain federal crimes and incarcerated, on parole, on probation, or on supervised release to provide federal authorities with a DNA sample. The FBI prefers DNA derived from blood for its Combined DNA Index System. A proposed Sexual Assault Forensic Evidence Registry Act of 2010 would amend the DNA Act to facilitate testing of DNA "Rape Kit" evidence.

United States v. Kincade, 379 F.3d 813 (9th Cir. 2004) considered whether conditionally released felons can be required to submit DNA samples, even in the absence of grounds to believe they would commit future crimes. The court concluded that "suspicionless searches of * * * person and property even in the absence of some non-law enforcement 'special need' " are permissible "where such searches meet the Fourth Amendment touchstone of reasonableness as gauged by the totality of the circumstances." Conditional released persons have "diminished expectations of privacy." The court concluded that: "As currently structured and implemented * * * the DNA Act's compulsory profiling of qualified federal offenders can only be described as minimally invasive—both in terms of the bodily intrusion it occasions, and the information it lawfully produces." On the other hand, "the interests furthered by the federal DNA Act are undeniably compelling." Through "establishing a means of identification that can be used to link conditional releasees to crimes committed while they are at large, compulsory DNA profiling serves society's 'overwhelming interest' in ensuring that a parolee complies with the requirements [of his release] and is returned to prison if he fails to do so."

7. TRAFFIC AND IDENTITY STOPS

a. Sobriety Checkpoints

MICHIGAN DEPT. OF STATE POLICE v. SITZ

496 U.S. 444 (1990).

JUSTICE REHNQUIST

This case poses the question whether a State's use of highway sobriety checkpoints violates the Fourth and Fourteenth Amendments to the United States Constitution. We hold that it does not and therefore reverse the contrary holding of the Court of Appeals of Michigan.

Petitioners, the Michigan Department of State Police and its Director, established a sobriety checkpoint pilot program in early 1986. * * *

Under the [program] guidelines, checkpoints would be set up at selected sites along state roads. All vehicles passing through a checkpoint would be stopped and their drivers briefly examined for signs of intoxication. In cases where a checkpoint officer detected signs of intoxication, the motorist would be directed to a location out of the traffic flow where an officer would check the motorist's driver's license and car registration and, if warranted, conduct further sobriety tests. Should the field tests and the officer's observations suggest that the driver was intoxicated, an arrest would be made. All other drivers would be permitted to resume their journey immediately.

The first—and to date the only—sobriety checkpoint operated under the program was conducted in Saginaw County with the assistance of the Saginaw County Sheriff's Department. During the hour-and-fifteen-minute duration of the checkpoint's operation, 126 vehicles passed through the checkpoint. The average delay for each vehicle was approximately 25 seconds. Two drivers were detained for field sobriety testing, and one of the two was arrested for driving under the influence of alcohol. A third driver * * * was pulled over by an officer in an observation vehicle and arrested for driving under the influence.

On the day before the operation of the Saginaw County checkpoint, respondents filed a compliant in the Circuit Court of Wayne County seeking declaratory and injunctive relief from potential subjection to the checkpoints. Each of the respondents "is a licensed driver in the State of Michigan * * * who regularly travels throughout the State in his automobile." * * * During pretrial proceedings, petitioners agreed to delay further implementation of the checkpoint program pending the outcome of this litigation. * * *

No one can seriously dispute the magnitude of the drunken driving problem or the States' interest in eradicating it. Media reports of alcohol-related death and mutilation on the Nation's roads are legion. The anecdotal is confirmed by the statistical. "Drunk drivers cause an annual death toll of over 25,000 and in the same time span cause nearly one million personal injuries and more than five billion dollars in property damage." * * *

Conversely, the weight bearing on the other scale—the measure of the intrusion on motorists stopped briefly at sobriety checkpoints—is slight. We reached a similar conclusion as to the intrusion on motorists subjected to a brief stop at a highway checkpoint for detecting illegal aliens. We see virtually no difference between the levels of intrusion on law-abiding motorists from the brief stops necessary to the effectuation of these two types of checkpoints, which to the average motorist would seem identical save for the nature of the questions the checkpoint officers might ask. The trial court and the Court of Appeals, thus, accurately gauged the "objective" intrusion, measured by the duration of the seizure and the intensity of the investigation, as minimal. * * * With respect to what it perceived to be the "subjective" intrusion on motorists, however, the Court of Appeals found such intrusion substantial. * * *

The Court of Appeals went on to consider as part of the balancing analysis the "effectiveness" of the proposed checkpoint program. Based on extensive testimony in the trial record, the court concluded that the checkpoint program failed the "effectiveness" part of the test, and that this failure materially discounted petitioners' strong interest in implementing the program. We think the Court of Appeals was wrong on this point * * *.

The actual language from Brown v. Texas, upon which the Michigan courts based their evaluation of "effectiveness," describes the balancing factor as "the degree to which the seizure advances the public interest." * * * This passage from Brown was not meant to transfer from politically accountable officials to the courts the decision as to which among reasonable alternative law enforcement techniques should be employed to deal with a serious public danger. Experts in police science might disagree over which of several methods of apprehending drunken drivers is preferable as an ideal. But for purposes of Fourth Amendment analysis, the choice among such reasonable alternatives remains with the governmental officials who have a unique understanding of, and a responsibility for, limited public resources, including a finite number of police officers. * * *

In Delaware v. Prouse * * * we disapproved random stops made by Delaware Highway Patrol officers in an effort to apprehend unlicensed drivers and unsafe vehicles. We observed that no empirical evidence indicated that such stops would be an effective means of promoting roadway safety and said that "it seems common sense that the percentage of all drivers on the road who are driving without a license is very small and that the number of licensed drivers who will be stopped in order to find one unlicensed operator will be large indeed." * * * We observed that the random stops involved the "kind of standardless and unconstrained discretion [which] is the evil the Court has discerned when in previous cases it has insisted that the discretion of the official in the field be circumscribed, at least to some extent." * * * We went on to state that our holding did not "cast doubt on the permissibility of roadside truck weigh-stations and inspection checkpoints, at which some vehicles may be subject to further detention for safety and regulatory inspection than are others." * * *

Unlike Prouse, this case involves neither a complete absence of empirical data nor a challenge to random highway stops. During the operation of the Saginaw County checkpoint, the detention of each of the 126 vehicles that entered the checkpoint resulted in the arrest of two drunken drivers. Stated as a percentage, approximately 1.5 percent of the drivers passing through the checkpoint were arrested for alcohol impairment. In addition, an expert witness testified at the trial that experience in other States demonstrated that, on the whole, sobriety checkpoints resulted in drunken driving arrests of around 1 percent of all motorists stopped. * * * By way of comparison, the record from one of the consolidated cases in Martinez–Fuerte, showed that in the associated checkpoint, illegal aliens were found in only 0.12 percent of the vehicles passing through the checkpoint. See 428 U.S., at 554. The ratio of illegal aliens detected to vehicles stopped (considering that on occasion two or more illegal aliens were found in a single vehicle) was approximately 0.5 percent. * * * We concluded that this "record * * * provides a rather complete picture of the effectiveness of the San Clemente checkpoint", ibid., and we sustained its constitutionality. We see no justification for a different conclusion here.

In sum, the balance of the State's interest in preventing drunken driving, the extent to which this system can reasonably be said to advance that interest, and the degree of intrusion upon individual motorists who are briefly stopped, weighs in favor of the state program. We therefore hold that it is consistent with the Fourth Amendment. The judgment of the Michigan Court of Appeals is accordingly reversed, and the cause is remanded for further proceedings not inconsistent with this opinion. Reversed. * * *

JUSTICE BRENNAN, with whom JUSTICE MARSHALL joins, dissenting.

I do not dispute the immense social cost caused by drunken drivers, nor do I slight the government's efforts to prevent such tragic losses. Indeed, I would hazard a guess that today's opinion will be received favorably by a majority of our society, who would willingly suffer the minimal intrusion of a sobriety checkpoint stop in order to prevent drunken driving. But consensus that a particular law enforcement technique serves a laudable purpose has never been the touchstone of constitutional analysis.

"The Fourth Amendment was designed not merely to protect against official intrusions whose social utility was less as measured by some 'balancing test' than its intrusion on individual privacy; it was designed in addition to grant the individual a zone of privacy whose protections could be breached only where the 'reasonable' requirements of the probable cause standard were met. Moved by whatever momentary evil has aroused their fears, officials—perhaps even supported by a majority of citizens— may be tempted to conduct searches that sacrifice the liberty of each citizen to assuage the perceived evil. But the Fourth Amendment rests on the principle that a true balance between the individual and society depends on the recognition of 'the right to be let alone—the most comprehensive of rights and the right most valued by civilized men.' Olmstead v. United States, 277 U.S. 438, 478 (1928) (Brandeis, J., dissenting)." * * *

In the face of the "momentary evil" of drunken driving, the Court today abdicates its role as the protector of that fundamental right. I respectfully dissent.

JUSTICE STEVENS, with whom JUSTICE BRENNAN and JUSTICE MARSHALL join as to Parts I and II, dissenting. * * *

There is a critical difference between a seizure that is preceded by fair notice and one that is effected by surprise. * * * That is one reason why a border search, or indeed any search at a permanent and fixed checkpoint, is much less intrusive than a random stop. A motorist with advance notice of the location of a permanent checkpoint has an opportunity to avoid the search entirely, or at least to prepare for, and limit, the intrusion on her privacy.

No such opportunity is available in the case of a random stop or a temporary checkpoint, which both depend for their effectiveness on the element of surprise. A driver who discovers an unexpected checkpoint on a familiar local road will be startled and distressed. She may infer, correctly, that the checkpoint is not simply "business as usual," and may likewise infer, again correctly, that the police have made a discretionary decision to focus their law enforcement efforts upon her and others who pass the chosen point.

This element of surprise is the most obvious distinction between the sobriety checkpoints permitted by today's majority and the interior border checkpoints approved by this Court in Martinez–Fuerte. The distinction casts immediate doubt upon the majority's argument, for Martinez–Fuerte is the only case in which we have upheld suspicionless seizures of motorists. But the difference between notice and surprise is only one of the important reasons for distinguishing between permanent and mobile checkpoints. With respect to the former, there is no room for discretion in either the timing or the location of the stop—it is a permanent part of the landscape. In the latter case, however, although the checkpoint is most frequently employed during the hours of darkness on weekends (because that is when drivers with alcohol in their blood are most apt to be found on the road), the police have extremely broad discretion in determining the exact timing and placement of the roadblock.

b. Narcotics Interdiction Checkpoints

CITY OF INDIANAPOLIS v. EDMOND

531 U.S. 32 (2000).

JUSTICE O'CONNOR delivered the opinion of the Court.

In Michigan Dept. of State Police v. Sitz, 496 U.S. 444 (1990), and United States v. Martinez–Fuerte, 428 U.S. 543 (1976), we held that brief, suspicionless seizures at highway checkpoints for the purposes of combating drunk driving and intercepting illegal immigrants were constitutional. We now consider the constitutionality of a highway checkpoint program whose primary purpose is the discovery and interdiction of illegal narcotics. * * *

In August 1998, the city of Indianapolis began to operate vehicle checkpoints on Indianapolis roads in an effort to interdict unlawful drugs. The city conducted six such roadblocks between August and November that year, stopping 1,161 vehicles and arresting 104 motorists. Fifty-five arrests were for drug-related crimes, while 49 were for offenses unrelated to drugs. Edmond v. Goldsmith, 183 F.3d 659, 661 (CA7 1999). The overall "hit rate" of the program was thus approximately nine percent.

The parties stipulated to the facts concerning the operation of the checkpoints by the Indianapolis Police Department (IPD) for purposes of the preliminary injunction proceedings instituted below. At each checkpoint location, the police stop a predetermined number of vehicles. Approximately 30 officers are stationed at the checkpoint. Pursuant to written directives issued by the chief of police, at least one officer approaches the vehicle, advises the driver that he or she is being stopped briefly at a drug checkpoint, and asks the driver to produce a license and registration. The officer also looks for signs of impairment and conducts an open-view examination of the vehicle from the outside. A narcotics-detection dog walks around the outside of each stopped vehicle.

The directives instruct the officers that they may conduct a search only by consent or based on the appropriate quantum of particularized suspicion. The officers must conduct each stop in the same manner until particularized suspicion develops, and the officers have no discretion to stop any vehicle out of sequence. The city agreed in the stipulation to operate the checkpoints in such a way as to ensure that the total duration of each stop, absent reasonable suspicion or probable cause, would be five minutes or less.

The affidavit of Indianapolis Police Sergeant Marshall DePew, although it is technically outside the parties' stipulation, provides further insight concerning the operation of the checkpoints. According to Sergeant DePew, checkpoint locations are selected weeks in advance based on such considerations as area crime statistics and traffic flow. The checkpoints are generally operated during daylight hours and are identified with lighted signs reading, "NARCOTICS CHECKPOINT MILE AHEAD, NARCOTICS K–9 IN USE, BE PREPARED TO STOP." App. to Pet. for Cert. 57a. Once a group of cars has been stopped, other traffic proceeds without interruption until all the stopped cars have been processed or diverted for further processing. Sergeant DePew also stated that the average stop for a vehicle not subject to further processing lasts two to three minutes or less.

Respondents James Edmond and Joell Palmer were each stopped at a narcotics checkpoint in late September 1998. Respondents then filed a lawsuit on behalf of themselves and the class of all motorists who had been stopped or were subject to being stopped in the future at the Indianapolis drug checkpoints. Respondents claimed that the roadblocks violated the Fourth Amendment of the United States Constitution and the search and seizure provision of the Indiana Constitution. Respondents requested declaratory and injunctive relief for the class, as well as damages and attorney's fees for themselves.

Respondents then moved for a preliminary injunction. Although respondents alleged that the officers who stopped them did not follow the written directives, they agreed to the stipulation concerning the operation of the checkpoints for purposes of the preliminary injunction proceedings. The parties also stipulated to certification of the plaintiff class. The United States District Court for the Southern District of Indiana agreed to class certification and denied the motion for a preliminary injunction, holding that the checkpoint program did not violate the Fourth Amendment. Edmond v. Goldsmith, 38 F. Supp. 2d 1016 (1998). A divided panel of the United States Court of Appeals for the Seventh Circuit reversed, holding that the checkpoints contravened the Fourth Amendment. 183 F.3d 659 (1999). The panel denied rehearing. We granted certiorari, 528 U.S. 1153 (2000), and now affirm. * * *

It is well established that a vehicle stop at a highway checkpoint effectuates a seizure within the meaning of the Fourth Amendment. * * *

As petitioners concede, the Indianapolis checkpoint program unquestionably has the primary purpose of interdicting illegal narcotics. * * *

We have never approved a checkpoint program whose primary purpose was to detect evidence of ordinary criminal wrongdoing. Rather, our checkpoint cases have recognized only limited exceptions to the general rule that a seizure must be accompanied by some measure of individualized suspicion. * * *

Petitioners propose several ways in which the narcotics-detection purpose of the instant checkpoint program may instead resemble the primary purposes of the checkpoints [the Court has upheld]. Petitioners state that the checkpoints in those cases had the same ultimate purpose of arresting those suspected of committing crimes. * * * Securing the border and apprehending drunk drivers are, of course, law enforcement activities, and law enforcement officers employ arrests and criminal prosecutions in pursuit of these goals. * * * If we were to rest the case at this high level of generality, there would be little check on the ability of the authorities to construct roadblocks for almost any conceivable law enforcement purpose. Without drawing the line at roadblocks designed primarily to serve the general interest in crime control, the Fourth Amendment would do little to prevent such intrusions from becoming a routine part of American life.

Petitioners also emphasize the severe and intractable nature of the drug problem as justification for the checkpoint program. * * * We are particularly reluctant to recognize exceptions to the general rule of individualized suspicion where governmental authorities primarily pursue their general crime control ends.

Nor can the narcotics-interdiction purpose of the checkpoints be rationalized in terms of a highway safety concern. * * * The detection and punishment of almost any criminal offense serves broadly the safety of the community, and our streets would no doubt be safer but for the scourge of illegal drugs. Only with respect to a smaller class of offenses, however, is society confronted with the type of immediate, vehicle-bound threat to life and limb that the sobriety checkpoint [is] * * * designed to eliminate.

The primary purpose of the Indianapolis narcotics checkpoints is in the end to advance "the general interest in crime control," Prouse, 440 U.S. at 659, n. 18. We decline to suspend the usual requirement of individualized suspicion where the police seek to employ a checkpoint primarily for the ordinary enterprise of investigating crimes. We cannot sanction stops justified only by the generalized and ever-present possibility that interrogation and inspection may reveal that any given motorist has committed some crime. * * *

It goes without saying that our holding today does nothing to alter the constitutional status of the sobriety and border checkpoints * * * or of the type of traffic checkpoint that we [have upheld in previous cases]. The constitutionality of such checkpoint programs still depends on a balancing of the competing interests at stake and the effectiveness of the program. When law enforcement authorities pursue primarily general crime control purposes at checkpoints such as here, however, stops can only be justified by some quantum of individualized suspicion.

Because the primary purpose of the Indianapolis checkpoint program is ultimately indistinguishable from the general interest in crime control, the checkpoints violate the Fourth Amendment. The judgment of the Court of Appeals is accordingly affirmed. * * * It is so ordered.

CHIEF JUSTICE REHNQUIST, with whom JUSTICE THOMAS joins, and with whom JUSTICE SCALIA joins as to Part I, dissenting.

The State's use of a drug-sniffing dog, according to the Court's holding, annuls what is otherwise plainly constitutional under our Fourth Amendment jurisprudence: brief, standardized, discretionless, roadblock seizures of automobiles, seizures which effectively serve a weighty state interest with only minimal intrusion on the privacy of their occupants. Because these seizures serve the State's accepted and significant interests of preventing drunken driving and checking for driver's licenses and vehicle registrations, and because there is nothing in the record to indicate that the addition of the dog sniff lengthens these otherwise legitimate seizures, I dissent. * * *

JUSTICE THOMAS, dissenting.

Taken together, our decisions in Michigan Dept. of State Police v. Sitz, 496 U.S. 444 (1990), and United States v. Martinez–Fuerte, 428 U.S. 543 (1976), stand for the proposition that suspicionless roadblock seizures are constitutionally permissible if conducted according to a plan that limits the discretion of the officers conducting the stops. I am not convinced that Sitz and Martinez–Fuerte were correctly decided. Indeed, I rather doubt that the Framers of the Fourth Amendment would have considered "reasonable" a program of indiscriminate stops of individuals not suspected of wrongdoing.

Respondents did not, however, advocate the overruling of Sitz and Martinez–Fuerte, and I am reluctant to consider such a step without the benefit of briefing and argument. For the reasons given by the Chief Justice, I believe that those cases compel upholding the program at issue here. I, therefore, join his opinion.

c. Stop and Identify

HIIBEL v. SIXTH JUDICIAL DISTRICT COURT

542 U.S. 177 (2004).

JUSTICE KENNEDY delivered the opinion of the Court.

The petitioner was arrested and convicted for refusing to identify himself during a stop allowed by Terry v. Ohio, 392 U.S. 1 (1968). He challenges his conviction under the Fourth and Fifth Amendments to the United States Constitution, applicable to the States through the Fourteenth Amendment. * * *

The sheriff's department in Humboldt County, Nevada, received an afternoon telephone call reporting an assault. The caller reported seeing a man assault a woman in a red and silver GMC truck on Grass Valley Road. Deputy Sheriff Lee Dove was dispatched to investigate. When the officer arrived at the scene, he found the truck parked on the side of the road. A man was standing by the truck, and a young woman was sitting inside it. The officer observed skid marks in the gravel behind the vehicle, leading him to believe it had come to a sudden stop.

The officer approached the man and explained that he was investigating a report of a fight. The man appeared to be intoxicated. The officer asked him if he had "any identification on [him]," which we understand as a request to produce a driver's license or some other form of written identification. The man refused and asked why the officer wanted to see identification. The officer responded that he was conducting an investigation and needed to see some identification. The unidentified man became agitated and insisted he had done nothing wrong. The officer explained that he wanted to find out who the man was and what he was doing there. After continued refusals to comply with the officer's request for identification, the man began to taunt the officer by placing his hands behind his back and telling the officer to arrest him and take him to jail. This routine kept up for several minutes: the officer asked for identification 11 times and was refused each time. After warning the man that he would be arrested if he continued to refuse to comply, the officer placed him under arrest.

We now know that the man arrested on Grass Valley Road is Larry Dudley Hiibel. Hiibel was charged with "willfully resist[ing], delay[ing], or obstruct[ing] a public officer in discharging or attempting to discharge any legal duty of his office" in violation of Nev. Rev. Stat. (NRS) Section 199.280 (2003). The government reasoned that Hiibel had obstructed the officer in carrying out his duties under Section 171.123, a Nevada statute that defines the legal rights and duties of a police officer in the context of an investigative stop. * * *

 Hiibel was tried in the Justice Court of Union Township. * * * Hiibel was convicted and fined $250. * * *

Stop and identify statutes [on the books in Nevada and many other states] often combine elements of traditional vagrancy laws with provisions intended to regulate police behavior in the course of investigatory stops. The statutes vary from State to State, but all permit an officer to ask or require a suspect to disclose his identity. A few States model their statutes on the Uniform Arrest Act, a model code that permits an officer to stop a person reasonably suspected of committing a crime and "demand of him his name, address, business abroad and whither he is going." Warner, The Uniform Arrest Act, 28 Va. L. Rev. 315, 344 (1942). Other statutes are based on the text proposed by the American Law Institute as part of the Institute's Model Penal Code. See ALI, Model Penal Code, Section 250.6, Comment 4, pp 392–393 (1980). The provision * * * provides that a person who is loitering "under circumstances which justify suspicion that he may be engaged or about to engage in crime commits a violation if he refuses the request of a peace officer that he identify himself and give a reasonably credible account of the lawfulness of his conduct and purposes." In some States, a suspect's refusal to identify himself is a misdemeanor offense or civil violation; in others, it is a factor to be considered in whether the suspect has violated loitering laws. In other States, a suspect may decline to identify himself without penalty.

Stop and identify statutes have their roots in early English vagrancy laws that required suspected vagrants to face arrest unless they gave "a good Account of themselves," 15 Geo. 2, ch. 5, § 2 (1744), a power that itself reflected common-law rights of private persons to "arrest any suspicious night-walker, and detain him till he give a good account of himself * * *." 2 W. Hawkins, Pleas of the Crown, ch 13, § 6, p 130. (6th ed. 1787). In recent decades, the Court has found constitutional infirmity in traditional vagrancy laws. In Papachristou v. Jacksonville, 405 U.S. 156 (1972), the Court held that a traditional vagrancy law was void for vagueness. Its broad scope and imprecise terms denied proper notice to potential offenders and permitted police officers to exercise unfettered discretion in the enforcement of the law. * * *

The Court has recognized similar constitutional limitations on the scope and operation of stop and identify statutes. In Brown v. Texas, 443 U.S. 47, 52 (1979), the Court invalidated a conviction for violating a Texas stop and identify statute on Fourth Amendment grounds. The Court ruled that the initial stop was not based on specific, objective facts establishing reasonable suspicion to believe the suspect was involved in criminal activity. * * * Absent that factual basis for detaining the defendant, the Court held, the risk of "arbitrary and abusive police practices" was too great and the stop was impermissible.

The present case begins where our prior cases left off. Here there is no question that the initial stop was based on reasonable suspicion, satisfying the Fourth Amendment requirements noted in Brown. Further, the petitioner has not alleged that the statute is unconstitutionally vague. * * *

Hiibel argues that his conviction cannot stand because the officer's conduct violated his Fourth Amendment rights. We disagree.

Asking questions is an essential part of police investigations. In the ordinary course a police officer is free to ask a person for identification without implicating the Fourth Amendment. "[I]nterrogation relating to one's identity or a request for identification by the police does not, by itself, constitute a Fourth Amendment seizure." INS v. Delgado, 466 U.S. 210, 216 (1984). * * *

Our decisions make clear that questions concerning a suspect's identity are a routine and accepted part of many Terry stops. * * *

Although it is well established that an officer may ask a suspect to identify himself in the course of a Terry stop, it has been an open question whether the suspect can be arrested and prosecuted for refusal to answer. See Brown, 443 U.S., at 53, n. 3. Petitioner draws our attention to statements in prior opinions that, according to him, answer the question in his favor. * * * In the course of explaining why Terry stops have not been subject to Miranda, the Court suggested reasons why Terry stops have a "nonthreatening character," among them the fact that a suspect detained during a Terry stop "is not obliged to respond" to questions. * * * According to petitioner, these statements establish a right to refuse to answer questions during a Terry stop.

We do not read these statements as controlling. The passages recognize that the Fourth Amendment does not impose obligations on the citizen but instead provides rights against the government. As a result, the Fourth Amendment itself cannot require a suspect to answer questions. This case concerns a different issue, however. Here, the source of the legal obligation arises from Nevada state law, not the Fourth Amendment. Further, the statutory obligation does not go beyond answering an officer's request to disclose a name. * * * ("Any person so detained shall identify himself, but may not be compelled to answer any other inquiry of any peace officer"). As a result, we cannot view dicta * * * or Justice White's concurrence in Terry as answering the question whether a State can compel a suspect to disclose his name during a Terry stop.

The principles of Terry permit a State to require a suspect to disclose his name in the course of a Terry stop. The reasonableness of a seizure under the Fourth Amendment is determined "by balancing its intrusion on the individual's Fourth Amendment interests against its promotion of legitimate government interests." Delaware v. Prouse, 440 U.S. 648, 654 (1979). The Nevada statute satisfies that standard. The request for identity has an immediate relation to the purpose, rationale, and practical demands of a Terry stop. The threat of criminal sanction helps ensure that the request for identity does not become a legal nullity. * * * A state law requiring a suspect to disclose his name in the course of a valid Terry stop is consistent with Fourth Amendment prohibitions against unreasonable searches and seizures.

8. AIRPORT SEARCHES

UNITED STATES v. ARNOLD

523 F.3d 941 (2008).

O'SCANNLAIN, CIRCUIT JUDGE:

We must decide whether customs officers at Los Angeles International Airport may examine the electronic contents of a passenger's laptop computer without reasonable suspicion. * * *

On July 17, 2005, forty-three-year-old Michael Arnold arrived at Los Angeles International Airport ("LAX") after a nearly twenty-hour flight from the Philippines. After retrieving his luggage from the baggage claim, Arnold proceeded to customs. U.S. Customs and Border Patrol ("CBP") Officer Laura Peng first saw Arnold while he was in line waiting to go through the checkpoint and selected him for secondary questioning. She asked Arnold where he had traveled, the purpose of his travel, and the length of his trip. Arnold stated that he had been on vacation for three weeks visiting friends in the Philippines.

Peng then inspected Arnold's luggage, which contained his laptop computer, a separate hard drive, a computer memory stick (also called a flash drive or USB drive), and six compact discs. Peng instructed Arnold to turn on the computer so she could see if it was functioning. While the computer was booting up, Peng turned it over to her colleague, CBP Officer John Roberts, and continued to inspect Arnold's luggage.

When the computer had booted up, its desktop displayed numerous icons and folders. Two folders were entitled "Kodak Pictures" and one was entitled "Kodak Memories." Peng and Roberts clicked on the Kodak folders, opened the files, and viewed the photos on Arnold's computer including one that depicted two nude women. Roberts called in supervisors, who in turn called in special agents with the United States Department of Homeland Security, Immigration and Customs Enforcement ("ICE"). The ICE agents questioned Arnold about the contents of his computer and detained him for several hours. They examined the computer equipment and found numerous images depicting what they believed to be child pornography. The officers seized the computer and storage devices but released Arnold. Two weeks later, federal agents obtained a warrant.

A grand jury charged Arnold with: (1) "knowingly transport[ing] child pornography, as defined in[18 U.S.C. § 2256(8)(A)], in interstate and foreign commerce, by any means, including by computer, knowing that the images were child pornography"; (2) "knowingly possess[ing] a computer hard drive and compact discs which both contained more than one image of child pornography, as defined in [18 U.S.C. § 2256(8)(A)], that had been shipped and transported in interstate and foreign commerce by any means, including by computer, knowing that the images were child pornography"; and (3) "knowingly and intentionally travel[ing] in foreign commerce and attempt[ing] to engage in illicit sexual conduct, as defined in [18 U.S.C. § 2423(f)], in a foreign place, namely, the Philippines, with a person under 18 years of age, in violation of [18 U.S.C. § 2423(c)]."

Arnold filed a motion to suppress arguing that the government conducted the search without reasonable suspicion. The government countered that: (1) reasonable suspicion was not required under the Fourth Amendment because of the border-search doctrine; and (2) if reasonable suspicion were necessary, that it was present in this case.

The district court granted Arnold's motion to suppress finding that: (1) reasonable suspicion was indeed necessary to search the laptop; and (2) the government had failed to meet the burden of showing that the CBP officers had reasonable suspicion to search.

The government timely appealed the district court's order granting the motion to suppress. * * *

The Supreme Court has stated that:

The authority of the United States to search the baggage of arriving international travelers is based on its inherent sovereign authority to protect its territorial integrity. By reason of that authority, it is entitled to require that whoever seeks entry must establish the right to enter and to bring into the country whatever he may carry. * * *

Courts have long held that searches of closed containers and their contents can be conducted at the border without particularized suspicion under the Fourth Amendment. Searches of the following specific items have been upheld without particularized suspicion: (1) the contents of a traveler's briefcase and luggage; (2) a traveler's "purse, wallet, or pockets;" (3) papers found in containers such as pockets * * *; and (4) pictures, films and other graphic materials. [citations omitted]

Nevertheless, the Supreme Court has drawn some limits on the border search power. Specifically, the Supreme Court has held that reasonable suspicion is required to search a traveler's "alimentary canal," *United States v. Montoya de Hernandez,* 473 U.S. 531, 541, 105 S.Ct. 3304, 87 L.Ed.2d 381 (1985), because " '[t]he interests in human dignity and privacy which the Fourth Amendment protects forbid any such intrusion [beyond the body's surface] on the mere chance that desired evidence might be obtained.' " *Id.* at 540 n. 3, 105 S.Ct. 3304 (quoting *Schmerber v. California,* 384 U.S. 757, 769, 86 S.Ct. 1826, 16 L.Ed.2d 908 (1966)). However, it has expressly declined to decide "what level of suspicion, *if any,* is required for non-routine border searches such as strip, body cavity, or involuntary x-ray searches." *Id.* at 541 n. 4, 105 S.Ct. 3304 (emphasis added). Furthermore, the Supreme Court has rejected creating a balancing test based on a "routine" and "non-routine" search framework, and has treated the terms as purely descriptive. *See United States v. Cortez–Rocha,* 394 F.3d 1115, 1122 (9th Cir.2005).

Other than when "intrusive searches of *the person*" are at issue, *Flores–Montano,* 541 U.S. at 152, 124 S.Ct. 1582 (emphasis added), the Supreme Court has held open the possibility, "that some searches of *property* are so destructive as to require" particularized suspicion. *Id.* at 155–56, 124 S.Ct. 1582 (emphasis added) (holding that complete disassembly and reassembly of a car gas tank did not require particularized suspicion). Indeed, the Supreme Court has left open the question of " 'whether, and under what circumstances, a border search might be deemed 'unreasonable' because of the particularly offensive manner in which it is carried out.' " *Id.* at 155 n. 2, 124 S.Ct. 1582 (quoting *Ramsey,* 431 U.S. at 618 n. 13, 97 S.Ct. 1972). * * *

In any event, the district court's holding that particularized suspicion is required to search a laptop, based on cases involving the search of the person, was erroneous. * * *

The Supreme Court has stated that "[c]omplex balancing tests to determine what is a 'routine' search of a vehicle, as opposed to a more 'intrusive' search of a person, have no place in border searches of vehicles." *Flores–Montano,* 541 U.S. at 152, 124 S.Ct. 1582. * * *

* * * [W]e are satisfied that reasonable suspicion is not needed for customs officials to search a laptop or other personal electronic storage devices at the border. * * *

* * * Arnold has never claimed that the government's search of his laptop damaged it in any way; therefore, we need not consider whether "exceptional damage to property" applies. Arnold does raise the "particularly offensive manner" exception to the government's broad border search powers. But, there is nothing in the record to indicate that the manner in which the CBP officers conducted the search was "particularly offensive" in comparison with other lawful border searches. According to Arnold, the CBP officers simply "had me boot [the laptop] up, and looked at what I had inside. . . ."

Whatever "particularly offensive manner" might mean, this search certainly does not meet that test. Arnold has failed to distinguish how the search of his laptop and its electronic contents is logically any different from the suspicionless border searches of travelers' luggage that the Supreme Court and we have allowed. *See Ross,* 456 U.S. at 823, 102 S.Ct. 2157; *see also Vance,* 62 F.3d at 1156 ("In a border search, a person is subject to search of luggage, contents of pockets and purse without any suspicion at all.").

With respect to these searches, the Supreme Court has refused to draw distinctions between containers of information and contraband with respect to their quality or nature for purposes of determining the appropriate level of Fourth Amendment protection. Arnold's analogy to a search of a home based on a laptop's storage capacity is without merit. The Supreme Court has expressly rejected applying the Fourth Amendment protections afforded to homes to property which is *"capable of functioning as a home"* simply due to its size, or, distinguishing between "worthy and 'unworthy' containers." *California v. Carney,* 471 U.S. 386, 393–94, 105 S.Ct. 2066, 85 L.Ed.2d 406 (1985).

In *Carney,* the Supreme Court rejected the argument that evidence obtained from a warrantless search of a mobile home should be suppressed because it was *"capable of functioning as a home." Id.* at 387–88, 393–94, 105 S.Ct. 2066. The Supreme Court refused to treat a mobile home differently from other vehicles just because it could be used as a home. *Id.* at 394–95, 105 S.Ct. 2066. The two main reasons that the Court gave in support of its holding, were: (1) that a mobile home is "readily movable," and (2) that "the expectation [of privacy] with respect to one's automobile is significantly less than that relating to one's home or office." *Id.* at 391, 105 S.Ct. 2066 (quotation marks omitted).

Here, beyond the simple fact that one cannot live in a laptop, *Carney* militates against the proposition that a laptop is a home. First, as Arnold himself admits, a laptop goes with the person, and, therefore is "readily mobile." *Carney,* 471 U.S. at 391, 105 S.Ct. 2066. Second, one's "expectation of privacy [at the border] . . . is significantly less than that relating to one's home or office." *Id.*

Moreover, case law does not support a finding that a search which occurs in an otherwise ordinary manner, is "particularly offensive" simply due to the storage capacity of the object being searched. *See California v. Acevedo,* 500 U.S. 565, 576, 111 S.Ct. 1982, 114 L.Ed.2d 619 (1991) (refusing to find that "looking inside a closed container" when already properly searching a car was unreasonable when the Court had previously found "destroying the interior of an automobile" to be reasonable in *Carroll v. United States,* 267 U.S. 132, 45 S.Ct. 280, 69 L.Ed. 543 (1925)).

Because there is no basis in the record to support the contention that the manner in which the search occurred was "particularly offensive" in light of other searches allowed by the Supreme Court and our precedents, the district court's judgment cannot be sustained.

Finally, despite Arnold's arguments to the contrary we are unpersuaded that we should create a split with the Fourth Circuit's decision in *Ickes.* In that case, the defendant was stopped by Customs agents as he attempted to drive his van from Canada into the United States. 393 F.3d at 502. Upon a "cursory search" of defendant's van, the inspecting agent discovered a video camera containing a tape of a tennis match which "focused excessively on a young ball boy." *Id.* This prompted a more thorough examination of the vehicle, which uncovered several photograph albums depicting provocatively-posed prepubescent boys, most nude or semi-nude. *Id.* at 503.

The Fourth Circuit held that the warrantless search of defendant's van was permissible under the border search doctrine. The court refused to carve out a First Amendment exception to that doctrine because such a rule would: (1) protect terrorist communications "which are inherently 'expressive' "; (2) create an unworkable standard for government agents who "would have to decide—on their feet—which expressive material is covered by the First Amendment"; and (3) contravene the weight of Supreme Court precedent refusing to subject government action to greater scrutiny with respect to the Fourth Amendment when an alleged First Amendment interest is also at stake. *See id.* at 506–08 (citing *New York v. P.J. Video,* 475 U.S. 868, 874, 106 S.Ct. 1610, 89 L.Ed.2d 871 (1986) (refusing to require a higher standard of probable cause for warrant applications when expressive material is involved)).

We are persuaded by the analysis of our sister circuit and will follow the reasoning of *Ickes* in this case.

UNITED STATES v. PLACE

462 U.S. 696 (1983).

JUSTICE O'CONNOR delivered the opinion of the Court. * * *

Raymond J. Place's behavior aroused the suspicions of law enforcement officers as he waited in line at the Miami International Airport to purchase a ticket to New York's La Guardia Airport. As Place proceeded to the gate for his flight, the agents approached him and requested his airline ticket and some identification. Place complied with the request and consented to a search of the two suitcases he had checked. Because his flight was about to depart, however, the agents decided not to search the luggage.

Prompted by Place's parting remark that he had recognized that they were police, the agents inspected the address tags on the checked luggage and noted discrepancies in the two street addresses. Further investigation revealed that neither address existed and that the telephone number Place had given the airline belonged to a third address on the same street. On the basis of their encounter with Place and this information, the Miami agents called Drug Enforcement Administration (DEA) authorities in New York to relay their information about Place.

Two DEA agents waited for Place at the arrival gate at La Guardia Airport in New York. There again, his behavior aroused the suspicion of the agents. After he had claimed his two bags and called a limousine, the agents decided to approach him. They identified themselves as federal narcotics agents, to which Place responded that he knew they were "cops" and had spotted them as soon as he had deplaned. One of the agents informed Place that, based on their own observations and information obtained from the Miami authorities, they believed that he might be carrying narcotics. * * * When Place refused to consent to a search of his luggage, one of the agents told him that they were going to take the luggage to a federal judge to try to obtain a search warrant and that Place was free to accompany them. Place declined, but obtained from one of the agents telephone numbers at which the agents could be reached.

The agents then took the bags to Kennedy Airport, where they subjected the bags to a "sniff test" by a trained narcotics detection dog. The dog reacted positively to the smaller of the two bags but ambiguously to the larger bag. Approximately 90 minutes had elapsed since the seizure of respondent's luggage. Because it was late on a Friday afternoon, the agents retained the luggage until Monday morning, when they secured a search warrant from a Magistrate for the smaller bag. Upon opening that bag, the agents discovered 1,125 grams of cocaine. * * *

In this case, the Government asks us to recognize the reasonableness under the Fourth Amendment of warrantless seizures of personal luggage from the custody of the owner on the basis of less than probable cause, for the purpose of pursuing a limited course of investigation, short of opening the luggage, that would quickly confirm or dispel the authorities' suspicion. Specifically, we are asked to * * * permit such seizures on the basis of reasonable, articulable suspicion, premised on objective facts, that the luggage contains contraband or evidence of a crime. * * *

In Terry [v. Ohio] the Court first recognized "the narrow authority of police officers who suspect criminal activity to make limited intrusions on an individual's personal security based on less than probable cause." * * *

[W]e conclude that when an officer's observations lead him reasonably to believe that a traveler is carrying luggage that contains narcotics, the principles of Terry and its progeny would permit the officer to detain the luggage briefly to investigate the circumstances that aroused his suspicion, provided that the investigative detention is properly limited in scope.

The purpose for which respondent's luggage was seized, of course, was to arrange its exposure to a narcotics detection dog. Obviously, if this investigative procedure is itself a search requiring probable cause, the initial seizure of respondent's luggage for the purpose of subjecting it to the sniff test—no matter how brief—could not be justified on less than probable cause. * * *

The Fourth Amendment "protects people from unreasonable government intrusions into their legitimate expectations of privacy." United States v. Chadwick, 433 U.S., at 7. We have affirmed that a person possesses a privacy interest in the contents of personal luggage that is protected by the Fourth Amendment. Id., at 13. A "canine sniff" by a well-trained narcotics detection dog, however, does not require opening the luggage. It does not expose noncontraband items that otherwise would remain hidden from public view, as does, for example, an officer's rummaging through the contents of the luggage. Thus, the manner in which information is obtained through this investigative technique is much less intrusive than a typical search. Moreover, the sniff discloses only the presence or absence of narcotics, a contraband item. Thus, despite the fact that the sniff tells the authorities something about the contents of the luggage, the information obtained is limited. This limited disclosure also ensures that the owner of the property is not subjected to the embarrassment and inconvenience entailed in less discriminate and more intrusive investigative methods.

In these respects, the canine sniff is sui generis. We are aware of no other investigative procedure that is so limited both in the manner in which the information is obtained and in the content of the information revealed by the procedure. Therefore, we conclude that the particular course of investigation that the agents intended to pursue here—exposure of respondent's luggage, which was located in a public place, to a trained canine—did not constitute a "search" within the meaning of the Fourth Amendment. * * *

There is no doubt that the agents made a "seizure" of Place's luggage for purposes of the Fourth Amendment when, following his refusal to consent to a search, the agent told Place that he was going to take the luggage to a federal judge to secure issuance of a warrant. As we observed in Terry, "[the] manner in which the seizure * * * [was] conducted is, of course, as vital a part of the inquiry as whether [it was] warranted at all." 392 U.S., at 28. We therefore examine whether the agents' conduct in this case was such as to place the seizure within the general rule requiring probable cause for a seizure or within Terry's exception to that rule. * * *

The person whose luggage is detained is technically still free to continue his travels or carry out other personal activities pending release of the luggage. Moreover, he is not subjected to the coercive atmosphere of a custodial confinement or to the public indignity of being personally detained. Nevertheless, such a seizure can effectively restrain the person since he is subjected to the possible disruption of his travel plans in order to remain with his luggage or to arrange for its return. Therefore, when the police seize luggage from the suspect's custody, we think the limitations applicable to investigative detentions of the person should define the permissible scope of an investigative detention of the person's luggage on less than probable cause. Under this standard, it is clear that the police conduct here exceeded the permissible limits of a Terry-type investigative stop.

The length of the detention of respondent's luggage alone precludes the conclusion that the seizure was reasonable in the absence of probable cause. [I]n assessing the effect of the length of the detention, we take into account whether the police diligently pursue their investigation. We note that here the New York agents knew the time of Place's scheduled arrival at La Guardia, had ample time to arrange for their additional investigation at that location, and thereby could have minimized the intrusion on respondent's Fourth Amendment interests. Thus, although we decline to adopt any outside time limitation for a permissible Terry stop, we have never approved a seizure of the person for the prolonged 90–minute period involved here and cannot do so on the facts presented by this case.

Although the 90–minute detention of respondent's luggage is sufficient to render the seizure unreasonable, the violation was exacerbated by the failure of the agents to accurately inform respondent of the place to which they were transporting his luggage, of the length of time he might be dispossessed, and of what arrangements would be made for return of the luggage if the investigation dispelled the suspicion. In short, we hold that the detention of respondent's luggage in this case went beyond the narrow authority possessed by police to detain briefly luggage reasonably suspected to contain narcotics. * * *

We conclude that, under all of the circumstances of this case, the seizure of respondent's luggage was unreasonable under the Fourth Amendment. Consequently, the evidence obtained from the subsequent search of his luggage was inadmissible, and Place's conviction must be reversed. The judgment of the Court of Appeals, accordingly, is affirmed.

UNITED STATES v. AUKAI

440 F.3d 1168 (9th Cir. 2006).

BEA, CIRCUIT JUDGE:

We must decide whether a prospective commercial airline passenger, who presented no identification at check-in, and who voluntarily walked through a metal detector without setting off an alarm, can then prevent a government-ordered secondary screening search by stating he has decided not to fly and wants to leave the terminal. We hold that such passenger cannot prevent the secondary search * * *.

On February 1, 2003, Defendant–Appellant Daniel Kuualoha Aukai arrived at the Honolulu International Airport intending to take a Hawaiian Airlines flight from Honolulu, Hawaii to Kona, Hawaii. He proceeded to check in at the ticket counter, but did not produce a government-issued picture identification. Accordingly, the ticket agent wrote the phrase "No ID" on Aukai's boarding pass.

Aukai then proceeded to the security checkpoint, where signs were posted advising prospective passengers that they and their carry-on baggage were subject to search. He entered the security checkpoint at approximately 9:00 a.m., placed his shoes and a few other items into a plastic bin, and then voluntarily walked through the metal detector or magnetometer. The parties agree that the magnetometer did not signal the presence of metal as Aukai walked through it. Nor did his belongings trigger an alarm or otherwise raise suspicion as they passed through the x-ray machine. After walking through the magnetometer, Aukai presented his boarding pass to Transportation Security Administration ("TSA") Officer Corrine Motonaga.

Pursuant to TSA procedures, a passenger who presents a boarding pass on which "No ID" has been written is subject to secondary screening even if he or she has passed through the initial screening without triggering an alarm or otherwise raising suspicion. * * *

Because Aukai's boarding pass had the "No ID" notation, Motonaga directed Aukai to a nearby, roped-off area for secondary screening. Aukai initially complied, but complained that he was in a hurry to catch his flight, which, according to the boarding pass, was scheduled to leave at 9:05 a.m. Although Aukai went to the roped-off area as directed, he did not stay there. When Motonaga noticed that Aukai had left the area and was gathering his belongings from the plastic bin, she instructed Aukai that he was not allowed to retrieve his property and that he had to stay in the roped-off area.

Aukai then appealed to TSA Officer Andrew Misajon, who was to perform the secondary screening, explaining again that he was in a hurry to catch his flight. Misajon nonetheless had Aukai sit in a chair, and thereafter proceeded to use the wand to detect metal objects. At some point, Misajon had Aukai stand, and when Misajon passed the wand across the front of Aukai's body, the wand alarm was triggered at Aukai's front right pants pocket. Misajon asked Aukai if he had anything in his pocket, and Aukai responded that he did not. Misajon passed the wand over the pocket a second time; again the wand alarm was triggered. Misajon again inquired whether Aukai had anything in his pocket; again Aukai said he did not. Misajon then felt the outside of Aukai's pocket and concluded that something was inside the pocket. Misajon could also see the outline of an unknown object in Aukai's pocket. At some point during this screening process, Aukai informed Misajon that he wanted to leave the airport.

At this point, TSA Supervisor Joseph Vizcarra approached Misajon and asked whether he needed assistance. Misajon related the events; Vizcarra asked Misajon to pass the wand over Aukai's pocket again. When the wand alarm again was triggered, Vizcarra directed Aukai to empty his pocket. Aukai again protested that he had nothing in his pocket. Using the back of his hand, Vizcarra touched the outside of Aukai's pocket and felt something in the pocket. He again directed Aukai to empty his pocket. This time Aukai reached into his pocket and removed either his keys or change, but a bulge was still visible in his pocket. Vizcarra directed Aukai to remove all contents from his pocket. After claiming at first that there was nothing more, Aukai finally removed an object wrapped in some form of tissue paper and placed it on a tray in front of him.

Suspecting that the item might be a weapon, Vizcarra summoned a nearby law enforcement officer. Vizcarra then unwrapped it and discovered a glass pipe used to smoke methamphetamine. The law enforcement officer took control and escorted Aukai to a small office near the security checkpoint. Aukai was placed under arrest and was searched incident to his arrest. During the search, the police discovered in Aukai's front pants pockets several transparent bags containing a white crystal substance. Aukai eventually was taken into federal custody, where he was advised of and waived his Miranda rights, and then gave a statement in which he inculpated himself in the possession of methamphetamine. * * *

Five days later, Aukai was indicted for knowingly and intentionally possessing, with the intent to distribute, 50 grams or more of methamphetamine, its salts, isomers, and salts of its isomers, a Schedule II controlled substance * * *. Aukai filed a motion to suppress the evidence found incident to his arrest at the airport and the statement he later made, which motion the district court denied. Aukai then pleaded guilty pursuant to a written plea agreement that preserved his right to appeal the denial of his suppression motion. The district court sentenced Aukai to a term of imprisonment of 70 months and a term of supervised release of 5 years, and Aukai timely appealed. We have jurisdiction * * * and affirm Aukai's conviction. * * *

Federal law mandates that commercial airlines must refuse to transport any prospective passengers who do not submit to a search of their persons and possessions for dangerous weapons, explosives and other destructive devices prior to boarding an aircraft. 49 U.S.C. Section 44902. In United States v. Davis, 482 F.2d 893 (9th Cir. 1973), we held that such "nationwide anti-hijacking program[s,] conceived, directed, and implemented by federal officials in cooperation with air carriers," are [administrative searches] * * * "permissible under the Fourth Amendment though not supported by a showing of probable cause directed to a particular place or person," * * *. Finally, we concluded that an airport security screening process satisfies [the] reasonableness standard provided "[1] that [it] is no more extensive nor intensive than necessary, in the light of current technology, to detect the presence of weapons or explosives, [2] that it is confined in good faith to that purpose, and [3] that potential passengers may avoid the search by electing not to fly." Id. at 913.

At issue here is only the third element of the Davis test: "That potential passengers may avoid the search by electing not to fly." * * * [W]e assume, as Aukai represents and as the government concedes, that Aukai declared his election not to fly and his desire to leave the airport before the wanding procedure. Our task, to which we now turn, is to determine whether that election was valid. * * *

Although we held in Davis that "airport screening searches are valid only if they recognize the right of a person to avoid [the] search by electing not to board the aircraft," 482 F.2d at 910–11, we did not address when such a choice must be made—that is, whether there is some stage during or after which a prospective passenger may not withdraw his implied consent to a search of his person or carry-on baggage by electing not to fly. * * * Following Davis, however, we have addressed this question a number of times. * * *

On the one hand, we have implied in a number of cases that a prospective passenger may elect not to fly so as to avoid a search at any time. * * *

Despite these cases and the rather sweeping language in [one case] that "Davis strongly indicates * * * that a party may revoke his consent to be searched any time prior to boarding the plane * * * if he agrees to leave the boarding area" and "that a passenger always maintains the option of leaving," Homburg, 546 F.2d at 1352, we nonetheless have held that under certain circumstances a prospective passenger may not revoke his consent even by electing not to fly. * * *

Recently, in Torbet v. United Airlines, Inc., 298 F.3d 1087 (9th Cir. 2002), we [reconsidered the issue of the right of a prospective airline passenger to revoke consent to search]. Torbet walked through the magnetometer at a security checkpoint, and his carry-on bag passed through the x-ray machine, all apparently without triggering an alarm or otherwise arousing suspicion. * * * Nevertheless, acting pursuant to a policy of randomly searching bags, even without the slightest suspicion that a particular bag contained weapons or explosives, airport security personnel selected Torbet's bag for such a random search. * * * He refused to consent to the secondary search of his bag, stating instead that he wished simply to leave the airport. * * * Torbet was nevertheless detained, and his bag was searched. * * * The search revealed nothing of note. * * * Torbet then sued the airline, airport, and police officer that conducted the search, alleging in relevant part that the random search to which he had not consented violated his Fourth Amendment right against unreasonable searches insofar as the initial screening did not arouse suspicion that his bag contained weapons or explosives. The defendants moved for judgment on the pleadings, which the district court granted. * * *

We affirmed and held that a potential passenger irrevocably consents to a secondary screening when he voluntarily submits to an initial screening that is "inconclusive" as to the presence of weapons or explosives. * * * We then interpreted the term "inconclusive" broadly:

> An x-ray scan may be deemed inconclusive, justifying further search, even when it doesn't affirmatively reveal anything suspicious. "Firearms and explosives can be small and easily concealed." Consequently, any x-ray scan that doesn't rule out every possibility of dangerous contents is, of necessity, inconclusive.

Therefore, even when a secondary screening is triggered solely as part of a systemized random search policy—the initial screening "doesn't affirmatively reveal anything suspicious"—the initial screening prohibits the potential passenger from revoking his implied consent for the secondary screening if there still is a chance the passenger may be carrying as-yet-undetected weapons or explosives. In other words, the "inconclusive" nature of a proper initial screening, by itself, establishes that the potential passenger has impliedly consented to a secondary screening. * * *

Having now surveyed our relevant precedent, we conclude that the secondary screening at issue here is most akin to that which we held reasonable in Torbet. Both here and in Torbet, the contested search occurred at the security checkpoint, but after the prospective passenger had voluntarily passed through initial screening, which, although it did not "affirmatively reveal anything suspicious," was nonetheless "inconclusive" insofar as it did not "rule out every possibility of dangerous contents." Torbet, 298 F.3d at 1089–90. Accordingly, we follow the reasoning underlying Torbet in holding that Aukai impliedly consented to a secondary search of his person by walking through the magnetometer, and that he could not subsequently revoke his consent to the secondary screening. We recognize, of course, that the screening here was different from that in Torbet in three respects: (1) whereas the initial screening here was conducted by a magnetometer, the initial screening in Torbet was conducted by an x-ray machine; (2) whereas the contested search here was of Aukai himself, the contested search in Torbet was of the prospective passenger's carry-on baggage rather than his person; and (3) whereas the contested search here was triggered by Aukai's failure to present identification when checking in, the contested search in Torbet was the product of random selection. Nonetheless, * * * we find none of these differences of distinguishing significance. * * *

9. STATE CONSTITUTIONS' FOURTH AMENDMENT ANALOGS

a. Bank Records

BURROWS v. SUPERIOR COURT OF SAN BERNADINO

13 Cal.3d 238, 529 P.2d 590, 118 Cal.Rptr. 166 (Cal. 1974).

JUDGE MOSK

Petitioner is an attorney suspected of having misappropriated the funds of a client. Respondent court issued a warrant authorizing the search of his office; pursuant thereto, the police conducted a search of his office files as well as his automobile, and seized a large number of documents. Thereafter a detective contacted several banks in which petitioner maintained accounts, and without a warrant or any court process obtained from at least one bank photostatic copies of petitioner's financial statements. Ultimately petitioner was charged with grand theft. He moved to suppress the evidence obtained from his office, automobile and the bank. (Pen. Code, § 1538.5.) The motion was denied, and in this proceeding he seeks a statutory writ of mandate to annul the court's order and to compel it to grant the motion. * * *

Initially, we discuss the most significant and novel issue in this case: whether the police violated petitioner's rights under the California Constitution, article I, section in obtaining, without benefit of legal process, copies of statements from a bank in which he maintained an account. [Article I, section 13, of the California Constitution provides, in part: "The right of the people to be secure in their persons, houses, papers, and effects against unreasonable seizures and searches may not be violated * * *."] We have held, consonant with Katz v. United States (1967) * * * that, in determining whether an illegal search has occurred under the provisions of our Constitution, the appropriate test is whether a person has exhibited a reasonable expectation of privacy and, if so, whether that expectation has been violated by unreasonable governmental intrusion. * * *

It cannot be gainsaid that the customer of a bank expects that the documents, such as checks, which he transmits to the bank in the course of his business operations, will remain private, and that such an expectation is reasonable. The prosecution concedes as much, although it asserts that this expectation is not constitutionally cognizable. Representatives of several banks testified at the suppression hearing that information in their possession regarding a customer's account is deemed by them to be confidential.

In the present case, although the record establishes that copies of petitioner's bank statements rather than of his checks were provided to the officer, the distinction is not significant with relation to petitioner's expectation of privacy. That the bank alters the form in which it records the information transmitted to it by the depositor to show the receipt and disbursement of money on a bank statement does not diminish the depositor's anticipation of privacy in the matters which he confides to the bank. A bank customer's reasonable expectation is that, absent compulsion by legal process, the matters he reveals to the bank will be utilized by the bank only for internal banking purposes. Thus, we hold petitioner had a reasonable expectation that the bank would maintain the confidentiality of those papers which originated with him in check form and of the bank statements into which a record of those same checks had been transformed pursuant to internal bank practice.

We next determine whether the police unreasonably interfered with petitioner's expectation of privacy. It is significant in this connection that the bank provided the statements to the police in response to an informal oral request for information about all of petitioner's accounts. Thus, the character, scope, and relevancy of the material obtained were determined entirely by the exercise of the unbridled discretion of the police. If this search may be deemed reasonable, nothing could prevent any law enforcement officer from informally requesting and obtaining all of a person's or business entity's records which had been confided to a bank, though such records might have no relevance to a crime, if any, under investigation; and those records could be introduced into evidence in any subsequent criminal prosecution.

The People advance no governmental justification for such a sweeping exploratory invasion into an individual's privacy. Their primary assertion is not that it is essential to effective law enforcement to obtain bank records without judicial process, or even that the interests of a person in the confidentiality of his financial affairs is outweighed by the advantages to society in disclosure of the information. Instead, it is argued, banks have an independent interest in voluntarily cooperating with law enforcement officers because financial institutions desire to foster a favorable public image, and like any good citizen, to assist in the detection of crime. However laudable these motives may be, we are not here concerned with the conduct or reputation of banks, but with whether the police violated petitioner's rights by obtaining from banks, without legal process, documents in which petitioner had a reasonable expectation of privacy. * * *

It is not the right of privacy of the bank but of the petitioner which is at issue, and thus it would be untenable to conclude that the bank, a neutral entity with no significant interest in the matter, may validly consent to an invasion of its depositors' rights. However, if the bank is not neutral, as for example where it is itself a victim of the defendant's suspected wrongdoing, the depositor's right of privacy will not prevail. * * *

We hold that any bank statements or copies thereof obtained by the sheriff and prosecutor without the benefit of legal process were acquired as the result of an illegal search and seizure (Cal. Const., art. I, § 13), and that the trial court should have granted the motion to suppress such documents. * * *

Since we have concluded that petitioner's motion to suppress should have been granted on the basis of the provisions of the California Constitution, it is not necessary to consider his rights under the Fourth Amendment to the United States Constitution.

SUBURBAN TRUST v. WALLER

44 Md.App. 335, 408 A.2d 758 (Ct. Sp. App. Md. 1979).

CHIEF JUSTICE GILBERT * * *

Waller, in February 1976, opened an account at the Bank's Langley Park branch. About a month later, March 16, 1976, he attempted to have an income tax refund check cashed there, but that attempt was rebuffed because the balance in his account was insufficient to "cover" the check. He, along with Marvin Turner, a fellow employee of Waller who also wanted a check cashed, went to the United States Treasury Department in the District of Columbia. The checks were cashed, and Waller and his companion returned to the Bank, where Waller made a deposit of $800. Simultaneously, Turner deposited an identical amount in a new account. The money was in fifty and one hundred dollar bills, and the serial numbers printed thereon were sequential.

The employee who handled Waller's deposit was a teller-trainee. Believing the transaction involving large sequentially numbered bills to be of an unusual nature, he called the matter to the attention of Mrs. Bane, who, together with her duties at her own teller station, was charged with supervising the trainees' work. Mrs. Bane, in turn, notified the assistant manager, James Jones, who contacted the security department. Jones spoke to William Brandt, an assistant security officer for the Bank. Brandt was asked if the serial numbers on the bills were on any of the "warning lists that the Bank receives periodically." The security officer told Jones that he would check out the matter. Pending information from Brandt, Assistant Manager Jones instructed Mrs. Bane to withhold the bills from circulation.

Brandt first contacted the Federal Bureau of Investigation in order to ascertain whether the serial numbers had appeared on that agency's "N.C.I. register." The reply, we infer, was in the negative. Brandt, seemingly unsatisfied with stopping at that point, began to call the local law enforcement agencies. When he contacted the Montgomery County Police Department, he spoke to Corporal Howell. The police officer testified that Brandt asked him if there had been any large cash robberies recently. Howell replied that in a recent "residential robbery" $3,000 in fifty and one hundred dollar bills had been taken. He then read the descriptions of the suspects to Brandt, who replied that they were "similar to two individuals who had come in the Suburban Trust Bank, the branch at Langley Park." Brandt then disclosed to Howell Waller's name, address, description, and employment, as well as the information concerning his deposit of that morning. Subsequently, the Bank's surveillance photographs were also made available to the police.

Howell turned over the information that had been furnished by Brandt to Detective Ingels, who was the person who obtained Waller's photographs from Brandt. The pictures were shown to the victim of the residential robbery, one Brody, who tentatively identified Waller as one of the perpetrators of the crime. The police then acquired a different photograph from Waller's employer. Brody then positively identified Waller as one of the robbers. Waller was arrested and criminally processed. Ultimately, the victim retracted the identification, and the charges against Waller were dropped.

He then filed suit alleging that the bank had (1) invaded his privacy and (2) breached an implied condition of their contract, i.e., the obligation of confidentiality. The case proceeded to trial, where, at the close of Waller's evidence, the trial judge directed a verdict against him on the count for invasion of privacy and on the matter of punitive damages. Following the presentation of the Bank's defense, the court directed a verdict in favor of Waller on the issue of liability, leaving the assessment of damages to the jury. * * *

At common law, the relationship of a bank to its customer was not considered to be fiduciary in nature, but rather as that of a debtor and his creditor * * *

Modern society virtually demands that one maintain a bank account of some sort. "In a sense a person is defined by the checks he writes. By examining them * * * [one] get[s] to know his doctors, lawyers, creditors, political allies, social connections, religious affiliation, educational interests, the papers and magazines he reads, and so on ad infinitum." California Bankers Association v. Shultz, 416 U.S. 21, 85 (1974) (Douglas, J., dissenting). * * *

Courts have recognized the special considerations inherent in the bank-depositor relationship and have not hesitated to find that a bank implicitly warrants to maintain, in strict confidence, information regarding its depositor's affairs. * * *

Although the courts, without exception, have implied a warranty of confidentiality they have diverged in their outlook as to the circumstances under which the bank is released from its obligation. * * *

We think that a bank depositor in this State has a right to expect that the bank will, to the extent permitted by law, treat as confidential, all information regarding his account and any transaction relating thereto. Accordingly, we hold that, absent compulsion by law, a bank may not make any disclosures concerning a depositor's account without the express or implied consent of the depositor.

b. Telephone Records

NEW JERSEY v. HUNT

91 N.J. 338, 450 A.2d 952 (N.J. 1982).

JUDGE SCHREIBER

Merrell Hunt and Ralph Pirillo, Sr. were indicted for bookmaking, N.J.S.A. 2A:112–3, maintaining a place for gambling, N.J.S.A. 2A:112–3, conspiracy to commit bookmaking, N.J.S.A. 2A:98–1, and aiding and abetting bookmaking, N.J.S.A. 2A:85–14. After the defendants' motions to suppress evidence because of allegedly unlawful searches and seizures by the police were denied, the defendants pursuant to a plea bargain pled guilty to conspiracy and bookmaking. The remaining counts were dismissed. Hunt was sentenced to four months in the Atlantic County jail, placed on probation for three years, and fined $1,000. Pirillo was sentenced to 75 days in the Atlantic County jail, placed on probation for two years, and fined $500.

The defendants appealed to the Appellate Division, raising eight separate issues relating to their suppression motions. The convictions were summarily affirmed. We granted defendants' joint petition for certification, 89 N.J. 413 (1982), primarily to consider the constitutionality of the warrantless search and seizure of defendants' telephone toll billing records. We have considered the other issues raised by the defendants and find no merit in them. Accordingly, our discussion will be primarily directed to the disclosure of the telephone records.

The late Judge George Schoch, then Assignment Judge of Mercer County, authorized the wiretapping of the telephone of Robert A. Notaro, who was engaged in an illegal sports bookmaking enterprise. At least three telephone conversations between Notaro and the defendant Hunt relating to betting were overheard. The State police, having been alerted by one of the conversations, also observed Notaro meet with Hunt and Pirillo in Atlantic City on December 1, 1977 to discuss some gambling business. At about the same time a reliable informant advised the State police that Pirillo was a bookmaker with whom he had previously placed wagers on sporting events.

On September 18, 1978, another reliable informant advised Detective M. Robert Warner of the State police that defendant Hunt was conducting a gambling business daily between 11:00 a.m. and 9:00 p.m. over two telephones with different numbers. One of these numbers had already been revealed during the 1977 investigation. The two telephone numbers were listed in defendant Hunt's name at 17 North Hartford Ave., Apt. 5, Atlantic City. Detective Warner next went to the offices of the New Jersey Bell Telephone Company and obtained Hunt's home toll billing records for both telephone numbers for the two month period between June 23 and August 23, 1978. These records indicated frequent calls to Sports Phone

Service, which furnishes up-to-the-minute data on results of sporting events. * * *

As indicated at the outset, our concern is with the toll billing records. The key questions are whether an individual has a protectible interest in those records under the Fourth Amendment to the federal Constitution or Article I, par. 7 of the New Jersey Constitution. Both constitutional provisions acknowledge the "right of the people to be secure in their persons, houses, papers, and effects, against unreasonable searches and seizures." The historical roots of the Fourth Amendment centered about protection from unwarranted intrusions into the home. This privacy interest in the home and place of business has continued unabated throughout our judicial history. Indeed, as the telephone has taken its place in the home and at business, the privacy interest has expanded to include telephone conversations.

The United States Supreme Court has protected a telephone conversation from governmental eavesdropping by an electronic recording device. Katz v. United States, 389 U.S. 347 (1967). That Court has also indicated that it will not protect information or material beyond the conversation itself. We surmise as much because of its decision in Smith v. Maryland, 442 U.S. 735 (1979). In that case, without a warrant or court order, the police placed a pen register on the defendant's telephone. On the basis of information obtained from the pen register and other evidence, the police obtained a warrant to search the defendant's home. The defendant sought to suppress the evidence obtained. The Supreme Court rejected the motion.

Justice Blackmun, writing for the majority of five, stated that two discrete questions were involved. The first was whether the "individual, by his conduct, has 'exhibited an actual (subjective) expectation of privacy' * * *." He answered this in the negative, holding that people do not generally entertain any actual expectation of privacy in the numbers dialed because the telephone company must be made aware of the number in order to effectuate the call, bill the caller, and use the information for other legitimate reasons. The second question was whether, irrespective of the individual's expectation of privacy, society was prepared to recognize such an expectation as reasonable. * * * Justice Blackmun also answered this question in the negative because a person has no legitimate expectation of privacy in information voluntarily turned over to third parties. He analogized the telephone caller to a bank depositor who has no legitimate expectation of privacy in financial information transmitted to banks and exposed to their employees.

The expectation of privacy in a pen register, both subjectively and objectively, is substantially similar to that in toll billing records. The difference between toll billing records, which reflect long distance completed calls, and the pen register, which identifies all local and long distance numbers dialed, whether completed or not, does not have any impact upon

Justice Blackmun's analysis. His rationale places the toll billing record into the pen register mold. This conclusion is borne out by the federal courts that have passed on this question and have concluded that toll billing records are not entitled to Fourth Amendment protection. Reporters Committee v. American Telephone & Telegraph Co., 593 F.2d 1030 (D.C.Cir.1978), cert. denied, 440 U.S. 949 (1979). * * *

Our inquiry does not end at this point, for we must consider the application of the search and seizure safeguard in the New Jersey Constitution. This Court has seen fit to hold that the search and seizure provisions in the federal and New Jersey Constitutions are not always coterminous, despite the congruity of the language. * * * Though notions of federalism may seem to justify this difference, enforcement of criminal laws in federal and state courts, sometimes involving the identical episodes, encourages application of uniform rules governing search and seizure. Divergent interpretations are unsatisfactory from the public perspective, particularly where the historical roots and purposes of the federal and state provisions are the same.

Sound policy reasons, however, may justify a departure. New Jersey has had an established policy of providing the utmost protection for telephonic communications. Long before the Supreme Court's opinion in Katz v. United States, supra, the New Jersey Legislature had in a 1930 statute made it a misdemeanor to tap a telephone line. * * *

In addition to the legislative restrictions on wiretaps, our case law has adopted a policy of protecting the privacy of telephonic communications. In In re Wire Communication, we held that "[s]tatutes that directly impinge on the individual's right to be free from unwarranted governmental intrusion into privacy should be construed narrowly." 76 N.J. at 268. See also State v. Catania, 85 N.J. 418 (1981) (interpretation of wiretap minimization provision); State v. Cerbo, 78 N.J. 595 (1979) (State must seal tapes of completed wiretap immediately upon expiration of the tap).

In this case we are persuaded that the equities so strongly favor protection of a person's privacy interest that we should apply our own standard rather than defer to the federal provision. We do so in the spirit announced in a recent comment, "The Interpretation of State Constitutional Rights," 95 Harv.L.Rev. 1324, 1367 (1982):

> In our federal system, state constitutions have a significant role to play as protectors of individual rights and liberties. This role derives its character from the freedom of state courts to move beyond the protections provided by federal doctrine and from the distinctive character of state courts and state constitutions. But the state constitutional role is also shaped by the emergence of the federal Bill of Rights in recent decades as the primary constitutional shield against intrusions by all levels of government. The present function of state constitutions is as a second line of defense for those rights protected

by the federal Constitution and as an independent source of supplemental rights unrecognized by federal law.

Technological developments have enlarged our conception of what constitutes the home. The telephone has become an essential instrument in carrying on our personal affairs. It has become part and parcel of the home. When a telephone call is made, it is as if two people are having a private conversation in the sanctity of their living room. It is generally understood to consist of a conversation between two persons, no third person being privy to it in the absence of consent. It is well settled that telephone conversations carried on by people in their homes or offices are fully protected from governmental intrusions. Katz v. United States * * *.

Not all telephone conversations enjoy the same privacy. If one party makes the conversation available to others, such as through the use of a speaker phone or by permitting someone else to hear, as was done on occasion in this case when the informant permitted the detective to listen to the conversation, the privacy interest does not remain the same. However, when neither party permits any interference with the call and only the telephone company in the course of its operations is privy to any information, the question remains whether the company's participation destroys the sanctity of the call, which comprises data as to both who was contacted and what message was conveyed, so as to permit unauthorized governmental intrusion.

The telephone caller is "entitled to assume that the words he utters into the mouthpiece will not be broadcast to the world." * * * The call is made from a person's home or office, locations entitled to protection under the Fourth Amendment and Article I, par. 7 of the New Jersey Constitution. * * *

Allowing such seizures without warrants can pose significant dangers to political liberty. * * *

It is unrealistic to say that the cloak of privacy has been shed because the telephone company and some of its employees are aware of this information. Telephone calls cannot be made except through the telephone company's property and without payment to it for the service. This disclosure has been necessitated because of the nature of the instrumentality, but more significantly the disclosure has been made for a limited business purpose and not for release to other persons for other reasons. The toll billing record is a part of the privacy package.

We realize that some state courts have followed the reasoning of Smith, holding there is no expectation of privacy in long distance call records of the telephone company * * * However, this view has been sharply criticized * * *. Thus we are satisfied that the police wrongfully obtained the toll billing records of the defendant Hunt in that they were procured without any judicial sanction or proceeding.

c. Business Premises

COMMONWEALTH v. SELL

504 Pa. 46, 470 A.2d 457 (Pa. 1983).

JUDGE NIX, opinion of the court

In this appeal we have agreed to decide whether, under Article I, section 8 of the Pennsylvania Constitution, which guarantees the citizens of this Commonwealth protection against unreasonable governmental searches and seizures, a defendant accused of a possessory crime will continue to have "automatic standing" to challenge the admissibility of evidence alleged to be the fruit of an illegal search and seizure. The United States Supreme Court has abolished "automatic standing" under the Fourth Amendment to the federal Constitution. United States v. Salvucci, 448 U.S. 83, (1980). In interpreting Article I, section 8, therefore, we must decide whether to retain the "automatic standing" principle as a matter of state constitutional law, or to embrace the reasoning and conclusions of the United States Supreme Court and eliminate that concept. * * *

On December 11, 1978 the Allentown Police Department executed a search warrant at an amusement arcade known as Games Galore located in the city of Allentown. The items set forth in the search warrant included firearms stolen in a recent burglary. As a result of the search, the police retrieved a number of firearms. These firearms were located on open shelves beneath the counter in the arcade. It was later established that this area was one to which all of the employees had access.

Appellant, who was a partner in the business, was not present at the time that the search was conducted. Subsequent to the search appellant was arrested and charged with the crimes of receiving stolen property and criminal conspiracy. The firearms recovered during the search formed the basis for the charge of receiving stolen property. Appellant, through his counsel in a pre-trial motion, sought to suppress the use of the fruits derived from the search, contending that the search warrant was defective. The court of common pleas determined that appellant had "automatic standing" to assert the illegality of the search and, further concluding that the warrant was defective because the reliability of the informant had not been properly established, suppressed the seized evidence. The Superior Court * * * disagreed and held that appellant did not have standing. That court concluded that the concept of "automatic" standing had been overruled and was no longer viable and further that the appellant was unable to establish "actual" standing. We permitted review and are now being called upon to determine whether appellant was entitled to "automatic standing" under Article I, Section 8, of the Pennsylvania Constitution. * * *

Preliminarily, we note that constitutional protection against unreasonable searches and seizures existed in Pennsylvania more than a decade before the adoption of the federal Constitution, and fifteen years prior to the promulgation of the Fourth Amendment. Clause 10 of the Pennsylvania Constitution of 1776 afforded such a guarantee. Our present Constitution, in section 8 of Article I, the Declaration of Rights, states: The people shall be secure in their persons, houses, papers and possessions from unreasonable searches and seizures, and no warrant to search any place or to seize any person or things shall issue without describing them as nearly as may be, nor without probable cause, supported by oath or affirmation subscribed to by the affiant. Pa. Const. Art. I, § 8.

While minimum federal constitutional guarantees are "equally applicable to the [analogous] state constitutional provision," see, e.g., Commonwealth v. Platou, 455 Pa. 258, 260 n. 2, 312 A.2d 29, 31 n. 2 (1973), the state has the power to provide broader standards than those mandated by the federal Constitution * * *.

This Court has not hesitated to interpret the Pennsylvania Constitution as affording greater protection to defendants than the federal Constitution. * * * In Commonwealth v. DeJohn, 486 Pa. 32, 403 A.2d 1283 (1979), cert. denied, 444 U.S. 1032 * * * (1980), this Court declined to follow the United States Supreme Court's Fourth Amendment decision in United States v. Miller, 425 U.S. 435 * * * (1976), in construing Article I, section 8's protection against unreasonable searches and seizures. The DeJohn majority, concluding that under Article 1, section 8, bank customers have a legitimate expectation of privacy in records kept at a bank pertaining to their affairs, agreed that the appellant, whose records had been seized by the police, had standing to challenge their admissibility.

In construing Article I, section 8, we find it highly significant that the language employed in that provision does not vary in any significant respect from the words of its counterpart in our first constitution. The text of Article I, section 8 thus provides no basis for the conclusion that the philosophy and purpose it embodies today differs from those which first prompted the Commonwealth to guarantee protection from unreasonable governmental intrusion. Rather, the survival of the language now employed in Article I, section 8 through over 200 years of profound change in other areas demonstrates that the paramount concern for privacy first adopted as a part of our organic law in 1776 continues to enjoy the mandate of the people of this Commonwealth. Our task of interpretation is further facilitated by the existence of prior decisions of this Court construing the protection afforded by Article I, section 8, including a case embracing the concept of "automatic standing" as a matter of state constitutional law. * * *

Like the Supreme Court of our sister state, New Jersey, we find the United States Supreme Court's grounds for abandoning the Jones "automatic standing" rule unpersuasive. See State v. Alston, 88 N.J. 211, 440 A.2d 1311 (1981). Rather we are convinced, as is the New Jersey Supreme Court, that: [t]he automatic standing rule is a salutary one which protects the rights of defendants and eliminates the wasteful requirement of making a preliminary showing of standing in pretrial proceedings involving possessory offenses, where the charge itself alleges an interest sufficient to support a Fourth Amendment claim.

We decline to undermine the clear language of Article I, section 8 by making the Fourth Amendment's amorphous "legitimate expectation of privacy" standard a part of our state guarantee against unreasonable searches and seizures. We * * * believe the United States Supreme Court's current use of the "legitimate expectation of privacy" concept needlessly detracts from the critical element of unreasonable governmental intrusion.

Article I, section 8 of the Pennsylvania Constitution, as consistently interpreted by this Court, mandates greater recognition of the need for protection from illegal governmental conduct offensive to the right of privacy. * * *

Moreover, we have held that personal possessions remain constitutionally protected under Article I, section 8 until their owner meaningfully abdicates his control, ownership or possessory interest therein. * * * We remain convinced that ownership or possession of the seized property is adequate to entitle the owner or possessor thereof to invoke the constitutional protection of Article I, section 8 by way of a motion to suppress its use as evidence. * * *

Since we regard ownership or possession of the seized property as sufficient to confer standing to challenge a search and seizure under Article I, section 8, it necessarily follows that a person charged with a possessory offense must be accorded "automatic standing" adopted by this Court in Commonwealth v. Knowles. * * *

In the instant case, appellant was charged with receiving stolen property * * *. From the definition of "receiving" in section 3925(b), it is clear that possession is an essential element of the crime charged herein. * * *

We therefore conclude that appellant is entitled to "automatic standing" under Article I, section 8 of the Pennsylvania Constitution to maintain a motion to suppress. The Order of the Superior Court must therefore be reversed and the matter remanded for consideration of the merits of appellant's claim.

d. Sex Videotape

COMMONWEALTH v. KEAN

382 Pa.Super. 587 (Pa. Super. 1989).

JUDGE BECK * * *

The appellants, Daniel and Lucile Kean, are husband and wife. They are nearly sixty years of age and for many years they were highly respected members of the community. In 1986, Lucile Kean began to have sexual relations with two male juveniles with her husband's knowledge and approval. The juveniles, Alan and Steve, lived in the same neighborhood as the appellants and were under sixteen years of age when sexual contact was initiated. Alan lived next door to the appellants and resided with his half-sister and her husband, Kevin Kean; Kevin Kean was both Alan's brother-in-law and the appellants' son. Steve lived in a separate residence with his step-father and his mother. On several occasions, Alan and Steve arrived together at the appellants' house and proceeded to have sex with Lucile Kean while Daniel Kean watched.

Eventually, relations between the juveniles and the appellants took a turn for the worse. Alan and Steve borrowed the Keans' car without their permission and then became concerned that the Keans might notify the police. Alan and Steve were also afraid that Lucile Kean might falsely claim that the boys had forced her to participate in their sexual activities. Sometime during the summer of 1986, the boys decided to videotape one of their sexual encounters with the Keans. In this way, they hoped to gather evidence that Mrs. Kean's participation was consensual. They also reasoned that they could use the tape to blackmail the Keans into not reporting the unauthorized use of their vehicle.

In order to accomplish their objective, the boys removed a videocamera equipped with videotape from Kevin Kean's home. The camera and tape belonged to Kevin and were taken without his knowledge or permission. The boys then broke into the appellants' house when no one was home and planted the videocamera in the bedroom. They carefully concealed the camera under a pile of clothing so that only the lens protruded, and they focused the lens on appellants' bed. At midnight, the boys returned and were admitted into the house by the appellants. When the boys entered the bedroom, they secretly triggered the camera's recording mechanism before performing sexual acts with Mrs. Kean.

The following day, the boys once again broke into the appellants' home, this time to retrieve the camera. They took the camera back to Kevin's house where they watched the tape and made a duplicate by recording over another videotape which belonged to Kevin. The tape was approximately forty minutes long and showed Mr. Kean lying in bed next to Mrs. Kean while Mrs. Kean had sexual intercourse and oral sex with both Alan and Steve. Alan kept one copy of the tape for himself; this copy was later found by Kevin and erased. Alan gave the other copy to Steve who took it back to his own home.

Alan could not resist screening his copy of the videotape for two of his friends before his copy was erased. Perhaps as a result of this exposure, rumors concerning the existence of the tape began to circulate in the community. Steve's mother, Cherelynn, heard about the tape. When she asked Steve about it, Steve admitted without hesitation that he had his own copy. Cherelynn could not bear to watch the tape herself, so she asked her father Arthur to view the tape and tell her what was on it. Steve, without protest, handed the tape over to Arthur. Arthur took the tape to his house and viewed it on his own videorecorder. He then returned the tape to Cherelynn and informed her of its contents. Cherelynn then contacted a district justice who told her that the matter was outside his jurisdiction. At this point, Cherelynn placed the tape in her attic where it remained for the next several weeks. She later stated at the suppression hearing: "I wanted to make sure [the tape] got in the right hands, and I didn't know who to turn to." R.R. at 121.

Meanwhile, the Crawford County Children and Youth Services had received an anonymous report concerning the sexual activities of the appellants. The agency referred the matter to Officer Lloyd of the Pennsylvania State Police who interviewed Alan and Steve. Alan and Steve told Officer Lloyd about the tape. On October 24, 1986, Officer Lloyd came to Cherelynn's home and asked her if he could have the tape. Cherelynn voluntarily handed the tape over to Officer Lloyd. At this time, the tape contained no outer markings or labels and it was not possible to examine the contents of the tape with the naked eye. Without first securing a search warrant, Lloyd took the tape to the office of the district attorney where he and the district attorney played it on a videorecorder. After viewing the contents, Lloyd swore out a criminal complaint against the appellants.

Lucile Kean was charged with two counts of involuntary deviate sexual intercourse. In addition, Lucile Kean and Daniel Kean were each charged with two counts of conspiracy to commit involuntary deviate sexual intercourse and two counts of corruption of minors. Defense counsel for the Keans filed a pretrial motion to suppress the videotape which was denied. The Keans were jointly tried before a jury. Alan and Steve testified as Commonwealth witnesses, and the videotape was introduced into evidence and played at trial. On March 17, 1987, appellants were found guilty on all counts. Following the denial of post-trial motions, Lucile Kean was sentenced to a total of five to fifteen years imprisonment and Daniel Kean was sentenced to a total of twenty-three to seventy-two months imprisonment. Both parties filed timely notices of appeal from their judgments of sentence and the appeals were consolidated for review by this court. * * *

Appellants base their challenge to the admission of the videotape on both the fourth amendment of the United States Constitution and on article 1, section 8 of the Pennsylvania Constitution. We begin our analysis by reviewing the scope of these provisions, especially insofar as they relate to the conduct of private citizens. * * *

In his influential concurring opinion in Katz v. United States, 389 U.S. 347 (1967), Justice Harlan interpreted the amendment as prohibiting unreasonable searches of areas and objects in which a defendant manifests a "reasonable expectation of privacy." Harlan defined this phrase with reference to a two-part standard: 1) whether the individual, by his conduct, has "exhibited an actual (subjective) expectation of privacy" and 2) whether this subjective expectation is "one that society is prepared to recognize as 'reasonable' ''. Id. at 361. This standard was later explicitly adopted by the United States Supreme Court and is now recognized as the central concept in federal search and seizure jurisprudence. See, e.g., Smith v. Maryland, 442 U.S. 735, 740 (1979).

Article I, section 8 of the Pennsylvania Constitution provides:

The people shall be secure in their persons, houses, papers and possessions from unreasonable searches and seizures, and no warrant to search any person or things shall issue without describing them as nearly as may be, nor without probable cause, supported by oath or affirmation subscribed to by the affiant.

Like the fourth amendment, this provision has been interpreted as protecting "those zones where one has a reasonable expectation of privacy." Commonwealth v. DeJohn, 486 Pa. 32, 403 A.2d 1283 (1979), cert. denied, 444 U.S. 1032 (1980). See also Commonwealth v. Blystone, 519 Pa. 450, 463, 549 A.2d 81, 87 (1988). n2 This court, however, is not bound by fourth amendment precedents when construing claims raised under article 1, section 8. The Pennsylvania Constitution provides broader coverage than its federal counterpart, and an expectation of privacy which is deemed unreasonable by federal courts may be recognized as legitimate in this jurisdiction. See Commonwealth v. Johnston, 515 Pa. 454, 530 A.2d 74 (1987); Commonwealth v. Sell, supra n. 2; Commonwealth v. DeJohn, supra; Commonwealth v. Beauford, 327 Pa.Super. 253, 475 A.2d 783 (1984) (extending protection afforded under article 1, section 8 beyond limits of fourth amendment).

Nevertheless, both the fourth amendment and article 1, section 8 were designed to serve the same vital function—to prevent government officials from unjustifiably invading the privacy of individuals. Thus, both state and federal constitutional limitations on "unreasonable searches and seizures" apply exclusively to the conduct of persons who are acting as instruments or agents of the state. Commonwealth v. Goldhammer, 322 Pa.Super. 242, 469 A.2d 601 (1983), aff'd 507 Pa. 236, 489 A.2d 1307, rev'd sub nom. on other grounds, Pennsylvania v. Goldhammer, 474 U.S. 28 (1985). The federal courts have clearly established that the fourth amendment does not provide a remedy for the victims of unreasonable private searches. See, e.g., Coolidge v. New Hampshire, 403 U.S. 443 (1971); Burdeau v. McDowell, 256 U.S. 465 (1921). Similarly, we have held that article I, section 8 does not require the exclusion of evidence wrongfully obtained by a private party. Commonwealth v. Dingfelt, 227 Pa.Super. 380, 323 A.2d 145 (1974). See also Simpson v. Unemployment Compensation Board, 69 Pa.Commw. 120, 450 A.2d 305 (1982), 3 cert. denied, 464 U.S. 822 (1983).

In the case sub judice, the Commonwealth's chief exhibit was a videotape which would never have been created if not for an extraordinary invasion of the appellants' privacy. This invasion, however, was carried out by two juveniles who were clearly not acting at the behest of any government authority. We conclude that no constitutional violation occurred when Alan and Steve broke into appellants' home and concealed a video camera in the bedroom. Although we in no way condone the juveniles' actions, this private misconduct did not render the evidence inadmissible.

Appellants, however, maintain that their constitutional rights were infringed by Officer Lloyd, while Lloyd was acting in his official capacity as a police investigator. In their motion to suppress, in post-trial motions, and on appeal to this court, appellants have specifically argued that Lloyd conducted an unreasonable search when he played the videotape on a videorecorder in the District Attorney's Office. This visual inspection of the film was a form of state action and as such was subject to constitutional constraints. We must therefore proceed to determine if this inspection was prohibited by the federal or state constitutions. * * *

Appellants concede that Lloyd had probable cause to believe that the tape would reveal that appellants had committed several criminal offenses. They claim that Lloyd should have obtained a search warrant before viewing any images on the videotape which could not be seen with the naked eye. In support of this claim, they primarily rely on Walter v. United States, 447 U.S. 649 (1980). * * *

We agree with appellants that if they had a constitutionally protected privacy interest in the videotape, an examination of the videotape by the police with the aid of a videorecorder would have been a search subject to the warrant requirement. However, we must determine at the outset whether appellants had a privacy interest in the videotape at the time it was viewed by Officer Lloyd. As to this issue, Walter offers limited guidance since Walter addressed the privacy rights of a film owner. It is undisputed that appellants neither owned the videotape nor were aware of its existence until after it had been removed from their home and repeatedly viewed by private parties.

We shall explore the nature of appellant's privacy interest in the videotape by adopting a three part analysis. In subsection A, we find that appellants had a reasonable expectation of privacy in the place which was videotaped—the bedroom of their home. In subsection B, we find that this expectation of privacy was transferred to the videotape itself at the time of its creation. In subsection C, we consider whether this expectation of privacy was frustrated by events which occurred between the time the tape was created and the time that the tape was examined by the police. We find that appellants' privacy interest in the tape was not substantially eroded when the tape was viewed by private parties before coming into police custody. We conclude, however, that appellants' privacy interest in the tape was extinguished when the mother of one of the juveniles handed the tape over to the police.

A.

A videotape is a precise visual recreation of events in particular locations. We will consider at the outset whether the location depicted on the videotape which appellants sought to suppress merits constitutional protection.

Although a wide variety of locations may qualify as private for constitutional purposes, including offices and places of business, hotel rooms, telephone booths, and public bathrooms, nowhere is the right to privacy more firmly established than in a private residence. * * * At the risk of belaboring the obvious, men and women are ordinarily justified in assuming that what happens in the bedroom will not be observed by uninvited spectators. The Commonwealth argues, however, that in the instant case, appellants forfeited their right to privacy when they admitted Alan and Steve into their home. The Commonwealth maintains that "[o]nce [the Keans] engaged in illegal sexual activities with the victims, they had no right to believe the boys would not tell someone what they were doing, or record their activities." * * * We can readily agree that appellants assumed the risk that the juveniles might talk about their sexual experiences. Whether appellants also assumed the risk that the juveniles would plant a videocamera in the bedroom and create a permanent record of these experiences is a far different question. * * *

The Commonwealth position is supported to some extent by the recent decision of the Pennsylvania Supreme Court in Commonwealth v. Blystone * * *. In Blystone, the defendant discussed the details of a murder he had committed with a police informant who had been equipped with a hidden tape recorder. Prior to trial, the defendant unsuccessfully sought to suppress the tape on the grounds that the warrantless recording of his conversation violated the federal and state constitutions. On appeal to the Pennsylvania Supreme Court, five of the seven Justices voted to affirm the judgment of sentence. * * *

We find, however, that the case sub judice differ significantly from Blystone * * *. The Pennsylvania Supreme Court has not previously considered whether the same policies which relate to the interception of conversations apply with equal force to the secret filming of events. The Commonwealth argues that there is no relevant distinction between the covert use of audiotape and the covert use of videotape. We cannot agree. * * *

The uniquely invasive nature of surreptitious videotaping is particularly well illustrated by the facts of the instant case. Appellants were videotaped while nude and in bed and while Mrs. Kean engaged in sexual intercourse and oral sex. One can imagine the sense of violation and outrage which appellants must have felt when they learned that the videotape existed. There is something deep in the roots of our civilization which leads us to associate nudity with privacy and to shield our bodies from the uninvited eye. Even many who feel comfortable with openly discussing the details of their sex lives would rebel at the thought of having sex while being watched by a hidden intruder. One cannot pretend that the Keans would have suffered as great an invasion of their privacy if the juveniles had merely bragged about their exploits. We believe that the

Keans expected that whatever else might come to pass, they would not be videotaped in bed, and we believe that society is prepared to recognize that expectation as reasonable.

We need express no opinion regarding the impact of the fourth amendment on the present case. We conclude that under article I, section 8 of the Pennsylvania Constitution, a citizen of this Commonwealth may maintain a legitimate expectation of privacy in the home notwithstanding the fact that the interior of the home is secretly videotaped by a guest. We therefore find that the Keans did not waive their constitutionally protected interest in privacy when they admitted Alan and Steve into their bedroom.

B.

We must next determine whether the appellants' legitimate expectation of privacy in their home attached to the videotape of their home which was introduced into evidence against them. The Commonwealth notes that appellants did not own the videotape they sought to suppress. The Commonwealth also 6 emphasizes that appellants were not even aware that the videotape existed until sometime after it had been removed from their bedroom by Alan and Steve. The Commonwealth would therefore have us conclude, as the suppression court concluded, that appellants had no legal interest in the videotape itself. We could subscribe to this reasoning if the videotape were nothing more than a blank strip of celluloid wound tightly about a plastic reel. Yet, we cannot overlook the fact that the videotape has a content, and that this content was a visual recreation of one of the most private things imaginable: appellants' naked bodies in the bedroom of their own home.

As we have already noted, a legitimate expectation of privacy ordinarily requires both a subjective expectation of privacy and a societal recognition that this subjective expectation is justifiable. See Katz v. United States, supra. The Commonwealth forcefully asserts that appellants could not have expected that the videotape would remain private since they were not aware that they had been videotaped. To say this is to look only at the surface of things. The value of 7 the videotape as a prosecution exhibit was that it embodied images of and information concerning what went on inside the appellants' residence and it was these images and this information that the appellants sought to keep private when they excluded the general public from their home. Moreover, the very nature of the videotape was such that a screening of the tape was a visual inspection of the home—a visual inspection which was at least as revealing as an actual entry into the home on the night of appellants' crime would have been. For purposes of the law of search and seizure, the videotape cannot be considered wholly apart from the place whose imprint it bears; an examination of the videotape was a search of the home. Since appellants had a constitutionally protected privacy interest in the home, we think it follows that this privacy interest could have been infringed upon when the police peered into the recesses of their home by means of playing the videotape.

In urging a contrary conclusion, the Commonwealth relies heavily on the fact that appellants had no proprietary interest in the videotape cassette. Yet, the issue of whether an illegal search has taken place is distinct from the issue of whether the government has interfered with the defendant's right to control his own property. Cf. United States v. Karo, 468 U.S. 705 (1984) (common law trespass neither necessary nor sufficient to establish fourth amendment violation). In the landmark case of Katz v. United States, supra, FBI agents investigating an illegal gambling operation monitored a phone conversation by placing a recording device on the outside of a public telephone booth. Mr. Katz owned neither the phone booth, nor the phone, nor the telephone company's transmission wires, yet the Court held that by listening in on his conversation, the government exceeded the limits of the fourth amendment. If a legitimate expectation of privacy can exist in a conversation conducted over a third party's wires, we see no reason why a legitimate expectation of privacy cannot exist in an image projected from a third party's videotape. To require that the defendant own the videotape which bears the image of her naked body in order to assert a privacy claim would be to treat privacy as a commodity that must be purchased, rather than as a central aspect of liberty.

The Commonwealth also stresses that appellants had no idea that they were being videotaped while they were in bed with the juveniles. This is true, but we can safely assume that Mr. Katz had no idea that he was being tape recorded when he placed bets over the public telephone. There is no requirement that in order to demonstrate a legitimate expectation of privacy, a defendant must consciously guard against the precise threat to privacy which materialized. When Katz closed the door of the telephone booth and picked up the phone, he had the right to assume that the police would not later listen to his words on a tape recorder. When appellants admitted the juveniles to their home and closed the door behind them, they had the right to assume that the police would not later watch their images on a videotape. * * * Finally, although we are aware of no precise analogy to the facts of the case sub judice, we note that the Pennsylvania Supreme Court has implicitly recognized that a defendant may have a legitimate expectation of privacy in an object which is created by a private party and later obtained by the police. * * *

If a depositor has a protected privacy interest in the image of a financial record which a private bank imprints on microfilm, we believe that a home owner can have a protected privacy interest in an image of herself engaging in sexual activities which a private party records on videotape. Today, we heed the * * * call to keep pace with the threat to privacy engendered by new electronic devices; we act with awareness of the dangers posed by the increasingly widespread dissemination of video-cameras and videorecorders among the general public. We hold that appellants had a legitimate expectation of privacy not only in their home, but also in the reflection of their home that the videotape captured and preserved.

C.

We next consider whether appellants' legitimate expectation of privacy in the videotape was frustrated by the events which occurred between the time that the tape was created and the time that the tape was viewed by the police. As we have noted, Alan and Steve broke into appellants' home and stole the tape. Alan then copied the tape for Steve, and this copy of the tape passed from Steve to his grandfather Arthur, and then to his mother Cherelynn. Cherelynn later voluntarily relinquished possession of the tape to Officer Lloyd. During the time that the tape was in private hands, it was viewed: 1) by Alan and Steve on the videorecorder in Steve's house; 2) by Steve and two friends on the videorecorder in Steve's house; and 3) by Arthur on a videorecorder in his own residence.

The Commonwealth argues that Officer Lloyd did not need to obtain a warrant before playing the tape because the tape had previously been viewed by various private parties. The trial court apparently agreed that the examination of a videotape by a private citizen is sufficient to destroy a constitutionally protected privacy interest. We agree with the trial court's ultimate conclusion that under all the circumstances of this case, Officer Lloyd did not violate the appellants' constitutional rights. However, we base that conclusion on reasoning which differs from the position that was advocated by the Commonwealth and adopted by the suppression court. * * *

[T]he police did not violate appellants' constitutional rights when they examined the videotape without first securing a warrant. We reach this conclusion by focusing on the manner in which the tape passed from private hands into the custody of state officials.

After Steve brought the videotape into his parents' home, the tape passed into the sole possession of his mother Cherelynn who stored it in her attic for several weeks. She later made what the trial court described as a free and voluntary decision to turn the tape over to the police investigator. * * * Although Cherelynn did not specifically direct the police to screen the tape, she was clearly aware that the police intended to view its contents when she willingly and unconditionally relinquished possession of the tape to Officer Lloyd. Viewed in the light most favorable to the Commonwealth, the prevailing party at the suppression hearing, the record indicates that Cherelynn implicitly consented to Officer Lloyd's subsequent viewing of the videotape. * * *

Cherelynn discovered the videotape in her home and had sole possession of the videotape for several weeks. Moreover, she clearly did not violate any duty to the appellants when she gave the videotape to the police; appellants could not reasonably expect that Cherelynn would harbor the videotape indefinitely. This is not to deny that appellants had a reasonable expectation of privacy in the videotape. However, * * * this reasonable expectation of privacy was destroyed when a third party with whom the appellants did not have contact agreed to turn over evidence to the police. * * *

In summary, under the Pennsylvania Constitution, appellants had a legitimate expectation of privacy both in their home and in the images on the videotape which was surreptitiously recorded in their home. This privacy interest did not disappear when the videotape was viewed by private parties. However, the subsequent warrantless viewing of the videotape by the police may be justified as a valid third party consent search. Therefore, appellants' constitutional rights were not violated.

e. Misplaced Trust—State Law

COMMONWEALTH v. BLOOD

400 Mass. 61, 507 N.E.2d 1029 (Mass. 1987).

HENNESSEY, C.J., WILKINS, LIACOS, NOLAN, LYNCH, & O'CONNOR, JJ. NOLAN, J., dissenting, with whom LYNCH, J., joins.

The defendants, James Blood and Ernest Lorenzen, were found guilty of conspiracy to break and enter a building and conspiracy to commit larceny. They assign as error the denial of their motions to suppress evidence gathered through warrantless electronic surveillance. They argue * * * that * * * suppression was * * * required by art. 14 of the Massachusetts Declaration of Rights. We agree with the latter contention. Therefore we reverse the convictions.

These convictions arise out of an alleged conspiracy to break into a building of the Eastern Smelting & Refining Corporation (Eastern) in Lynn. The object of this scheme was a cache of gold bars stored on Eastern's premises and valued at approximately $3,000,000. The object was not achieved, however, because one of the alleged conspirators, Charles Hudson, was a police informant. * * * Hudson ultimately transmitted seven conversations, three of which were used by the prosecution at the trial of Blood and Lorenzen. * * *

At issue in this appeal is the sufficiency, in light of art. 14, of that portion of the statutory design which renders admissible the evidentiary fruits of warrantless electronic surveillance of organized crime where police have obtained the consent of at least one, but not each, party to a conversation. * * *

We have often recognized that art. 14 of the Declaration of Rights does, or may, afford more substantive protection to individuals than that which prevails under the Constitution of the United States. * * *

We consider whether society at large would think it reasonable for the defendants to expect that, in normal course, conversations held in private homes will not be broadcast and recorded surreptitiously. At common law "[i]t is certain every man has a right to keep his own sentiments, if he pleases. He has certainly a right to judge whether he will make them public, or commit them only to the sight of his friends." * * * Warren & Brandeis, The Right to Privacy, 4 Harv. L. Rev. 193, 198 n.2 (1890). The Legislature also has recognized the reasonableness, within limits, of every person's claim to control the flow of personal information. * * * Thus, it has long been thought reasonable to expect that what is supposedly said only to friends or close associates will not become generally, indiscriminately known or "etched in stone" without the speaker's consent.

Article 14, like the Fourth Amendment, was intended by its drafters not merely to protect the citizen against "the breaking of his doors, and the rummaging of his drawers," Boyd v. United States, 116 U.S. 616, 630 (1886); but also "to protect Americans in their beliefs, their thoughts, their emotions and their sensations" by conferring, "as against the government, the right to be let alone—the most comprehensive of rights and the right most valued by civilized men." Olmstead v. United States, 277 U.S. 438, 478 (1928) (Brandeis, J., dissenting). But it is not just the right to a silent, solitary autonomy which is threatened by electronic surveillance: It is the right to bring thoughts and emotions forth from the self in company with others doing likewise, the right to be known to others and to know them, and thus to be whole as a free member of a free society. * * *

The instruments of electronic eavesdropping are peculiarly adapted to search our thoughts and emotions. Thus, these devices are peculiarly valuable to those charged with policing crimes, such as the crime of conspiracy at issue here. Indeed, the modern art of eavesdropping may be invaluable in the multitude of situations where specific intent must be proved. But, because the peculiar virtues of these techniques are ones which threaten the privacy of our most cherished possessions, our thoughts and emotions, these techniques are peculiarly intrusive upon that sense of personal security which art. 14 commands us to protect.

Therefore, in circumstances not disclosing any speaker's intent to cast words beyond a narrow compass of known listeners, we conclude that it is objectively reasonable to expect that conversational interchange in a private home will not be invaded surreptitiously by warrantless electronic transmission or recording. The remaining question is whether "one party consent" so alters the balance as to obviate the need for a warrant requirement. It does not. Such consent only affords the State a person willing to transport the invisible instruments of eavesdropping into "earshot." * * *

The vice of the consent exception is that it institutionalizes the historic danger that art. 14 was adopted to guard against. * * * * "[T]he colonists' memory of the use and abuse of the writs was one of the reasons for the adoption, by several colonies, of constitutional safeguards regulating searches. In 1780 Massachusetts enacted art. 14 of the Massachusetts Declaration of Rights, specifically condemning 'unreasonable searches, and seizures.' * * * The antipathy of Massachusetts colonists to the writs of assistance was forcefully expressed by James Otis in the Massachusetts Superior Court in 1761. * * * Otis is said to have stated in his argument that the writ of assistance was 'the worst instrument of arbitrary power, the most destructive of English liberty, and the fundamental principles of the constitution, that ever was found in an English lawbook. * * * It is a power that places the liberty of every man in the hands of every petty officer.' " (Citations omitted.) Id. at 144. In like manner, the consent exception puts the conversational liberty of every person in the hands of any officer lucky enough to find a consenting informant. What was intolerable in 1780 remains so today.

E. FIFTH AMENDMENT PRIVACY

1. THE FIFTH AMENDMENT

"No person shall be held to answer for a capital, or otherwise infamous crime, unless on a presentment or indictment of a grand jury, except in cases arising in the land or naval forces, or in the militia, when in actual service in time of war or public danger; nor shall any person be subject for the same offense to be twice put in jeopardy of life or limb; nor shall be compelled in any criminal case to be a witness against himself, nor be deprived of life, liberty, or property, without due process of law; nor shall private property be taken for public use, without just compensation."

2. "TESTIMONIAL" AND "INCRIMINATING"

NOTE: HEAD GAMES

As observed by James Fitzjames Stephen in *Liberty, Equality, Fraternity (1873)*, the sense of "Privacy may be violated * * * by compelling or persuading a person to direct too much attention to his own feelings * * * ". This observation illuminates the claim made by murder suspect Van Chester Thompkins that his Fifth Amendment right against self incrimination was violated by an interrogation in which police officers asked about his religious beliefs.

BERGHUIS v. THOMPKINS

130 S.Ct. 2250 (2010).

KENNEDY, J., delivered the opinion of the Court, in which ROBERTS, C.J., and SCALIA, THOMAS, and ALITO, JJ., joined. SOTOMAYOR, J., filed a dissenting opinion, in which STEVENS, GINSBURG, and BREYER, JJ., joined.

On January 10, 2000, a shooting occurred outside a mall in Southfield, Michigan. Among the victims was Samuel Morris, who died from multiple gunshot wounds. The other victim, Frederick France, recovered from his injuries and later testified. [Van Chester] Thompkins, who was a suspect, fled. About one year later he was found in Ohio and arrested there. * * *

Two Southfield police officers traveled to Ohio to interrogate Thompkins, then awaiting transfer to Michigan. * * * About 2 hours and 45 minutes into the interrogation [during which Thompkins was mostly silent], Helgert asked Thompkins, "Do you believe in God?" Thompkins made eye contact with Helgert and said "Yes," as his eyes "well[ed] up with tears." Helgert asked, "Do you pray to God?" Thompkins said "Yes." Helgert asked, "Do you pray to God to forgive you for shooting that boy down?" Thompkins answered "Yes" and looked away. *Ibid.* Thompkins refused to make a written confession, and the interrogation ended about 15 minutes later. * * * [citations omitted].

Thompkins was charged with first-degree murder, assault with intent to commit murder, and certain firearms-related offenses. He moved to suppress the statements made during the interrogation. He argued that he had invoked his Fifth Amendment right to remain silent [by remaining mostly silent], requiring police to end the interrogation at once, see *Michigan v. Mosley,* 423 U.S. 96, 103, 96 S.Ct. 321, 46 L.Ed.2d 313 (1975) (citing *Miranda,* 384 U.S., at 474, 86 S.Ct. 1602), that he had not waived his right to remain silent, and that his inculpatory statements were involuntary. The trial court denied the motion. [Appeals followed] * * *

[T]here is no evidence that Thompkins's statement was coerced. * * * Thompkins does not claim that police threatened or injured him during the interrogation or that he was in any way fearful. The interrogation was conducted in a standard-sized room in the middle of the afternoon. It is true that apparently he was in a straight-backed chair for three hours, but there is no authority for the proposition that an interrogation of this length is inherently coercive. Indeed, even where interrogations of greater duration were held to be improper, they were accompanied, as this one was not, by other facts indicating coercion, such as an incapacitated and sedated suspect, sleep and food deprivation, and threats. Cf. *Connelly,* 479 U.S., at 163–164, n. 1, 107 S.Ct. 515. The fact that Helgert's question referred to Thompkins's religious beliefs also did not render Thompkins's statement involuntary. "[T]he Fifth Amendment privilege is not concerned 'with moral and psychological pressures to confess emanating from sources other than official coercion.'" *Id.,* at 170, 107 S.Ct. 515 (quoting *Oregon v. Elstad,* 470 U.S. 298, 305, 105 S.Ct. 1285, 84 L.Ed.2d 222 (1985)). In these circumstances, Thompkins knowingly and voluntarily made a statement to police, so he waived his right to remain silent.

NOTE: *A RIGHT TO MENTAL RESERVE*

In the early 1960s the Supreme Court ruled that the Fifth Amendment bars adverse comments by the government about a criminal defendant's decision not to testify. In *Tehan v. United States,* 382 U.S. 406 (1966), a defendant who had declined to testify at his trial sought retrospective application of the ruling. In their closing statements prosecutors had made much of the defendant's silence, and the jury had found the defendant guilty. The Court declined to apply the new rule to cases that occurred prior to the rule's adoption, but acknowledged the importance of the Fifth Amendment to the individual's sense of privacy. Justice Stewart, writing for the Court, argued that protecting privacy is a purpose of the Fifth Amendment: "the federal privilege against self-incrimination reflects the Constitution's concern for the essential values represented by our respect for the inviolability of the human personality and of the right of each individual to a private enclave where he may lead a private life." Yet [t]he federal standard cannot now be remedied. As we pointed out in [another case] with respect to the Fourth Amendment rights there in question, "the ruptured privacy * * * cannot be restored."

In criminal cases defendants will sometimes claim that authorities have violated both their Fourth and Fifth Amendment rights. The next two cases appear in this textbook for a second time, now to highlight the Supreme Court's treatment of Fifth Amendment claims. To qualify for Fifth Amendment protection, the Court has held that evidence extracted from a defendant must be, not only compulsory, but both "testimonial" and "incriminating."

SCHMERBER v. CALIFORNIA

384 U.S. 757 (1966).

MR. JUSTICE BRENNAN delivered the opinion of the Court.

[A man convicted of drunk driving on the evidence of a non-consensual blood alcohol test, alleged violation of rights, including those created by the Fifth Amendment.]

We hold that the privilege [against self-incrimination] protects an accused only from being compelled to testify against himself, or otherwise provide the State with evidence of a testimonial or communicative nature, and that the withdrawal of blood and use of the analysis in question in this case did not involve compulsion to these ends.

It could not be denied that in requiring petitioner to submit to the withdrawal and chemical analysis of his blood the State compelled him to submit to an attempt to discover evidence that might be used to prosecute him for a criminal offense. He submitted only after the police officer rejected his objection and directed the physician to proceed. The officer's direction to the physician to administer the test over petitioner's objection constituted compulsion for the purposes of the privilege. The critical question, then, is whether petitioner was thus compelled "to be a witness against himself." * * *

Not even a shadow of testimonial compulsion upon or enforced communication by the accused was involved either in the extraction or in the chemical analysis. Petitioner's testimonial capacities were in no way implicated; indeed, his participation, except as a donor, was irrelevant to the results of the test, which depend on chemical analysis and on that alone. Since the blood test evidence, although an incriminating product of compulsion, was neither petitioner's testimony nor evidence relating to some communicative act or writing by the petitioner, it was not inadmissible on privilege grounds.

HIIBEL v. SIXTH JUDICIAL DISTRICT COURT

542 U.S. 177 (2004).

JUSTICE KENNEDY delivered the opinion of the Court.

Petitioner [who had been arrested and convicted for refusing to identify himself to police during a lawful stop] contends that his conviction violates the Fifth Amendment's prohibition on compelled self-incrimination. * * * To qualify for the Fifth Amendment privilege, a communication must be testimonial, incriminating, and compelled. See United States v. Hubbell, 530 U.S. 27 (2000). * * *

As we stated in Kastigar v. United States, 406 U.S. 441 (1972), the Fifth Amendment privilege against compulsory self-incrimination "protects against any disclosures that the witness reasonably believes could be used in a criminal prosecution or could lead to other evidence that might be so used." Suspects who have been granted immunity from prosecution may, therefore, be compelled to answer; with the threat of prosecution removed, there can be no reasonable belief that the evidence will be used against them. * * *

In this case petitioner's refusal to disclose his name was not based on any articulated real and appreciable fear that his name would be used to incriminate him, or that it "would furnish a link in the chain of evidence needed to prosecute" him. Hoffman v. United States, 341 U.S. 479, 486 (1951). As best we can tell, petitioner refused to identify himself only because he thought his name was none of the officer's business. Even today, petitioner does not explain how the disclosure of his name could have been used against him in a criminal case. * * *

One's identity is, by definition, unique; yet it is, in another sense, a universal characteristic. Answering a request to disclose a name is likely to be so insignificant in the scheme of things as to be incriminating only in unusual circumstances. * * * [A] case may arise where there is a substantial allegation that furnishing identity at the time of a stop would have given the police a link in the chain of evidence needed to convict the individual of a separate offense. In that case, the court can then consider whether the privilege applies, and, if the Fifth Amendment has been violated, what remedy must follow. We need not resolve those questions here.

The judgment of the Nevada Supreme Court is affirmed.

JUSTICE STEVENS, dissenting. * * *

Given a proper understanding of the category of "incriminating" communications that fall within the Fifth Amendment privilege, it is clear that the disclosure of petitioner's identity is protected. The Court reasons that we should not assume that the disclosure of petitioner's name would be used to incriminate him or that it would furnish a link in a chain of evidence needed to prosecute him. But why else would an officer ask for it? And why else would the Nevada Legislature require its disclosure only when circumstances "reasonably indicate that the person has committed, is committing or is about to commit a crime"? If the Court is correct, then petitioner's refusal to cooperate did not impede the police investigation. Indeed, if we accept the predicate for the Court's holding, the statute requires nothing more than a useless invasion of privacy. I think that, on the contrary, the Nevada Legislature intended to provide its police officers with a useful law enforcement tool, and that the very existence of the statute demonstrates the value of the information it demands.

A person's identity obviously bears informational and incriminating worth, "even if the [name] itself is not inculpatory." Hubbell, 530 U.S., at 38. A name can provide the key to a broad array of information about the person, particularly in the hands of a police officer with access to a range of law enforcement databases. And that information, in turn, can be tremendously useful in a criminal prosecution. It is therefore quite wrong to suggest that a person's identity provides a link in the chain to incriminating evidence "only in unusual circumstances."

F. EIGHTH AMENDMENT PRIVACY

1. THE EIGHTH AMENDMENT

"Excessive bail shall not be required, nor excessive fines imposed, nor cruel and unusual punishments inflicted."

2. PRIVACY RIGHTS IN PRISON

JOHNSON v. PHELAN

69 F.3d 144 (7th Cir. 1995).

EASTERBROOK, CIRCUIT JUDGE.

Albert Johnson brought this suit under 42 U.S.C. Section 1983. According to his complaint, which the district court dismissed for failure to state a claim on which relief may be granted, female guards at the Cook County Jail are assigned to monitor male prisoners' movements and can see men naked in their cells, the shower, and the toilet. Johnson sought damages. * * *

[H]is argument that cross-sex monitoring in the Jail violates the due process clause requires additional discussion in light of Canedy v. Boardman, 16 F.3d 183 (7th Cir. 1994), which holds that a right of privacy limits the ability of wardens to subject men to body searches by women, or the reverse. Our case involves visual rather than tactile inspections, and we must decide whether male prisoners are entitled to prevent female guards from watching them while undressed.

Observation is a form of search, and the initial question therefore is whether monitoring is "unreasonable" under the fourth amendment. So the Supreme Court conceived the issue in Bell v. Wolfish, 441 U.S. 520 (1979), where a pretrial detainee argued that routine inspections of his body cavities violated the Constitution. (Johnson also was a pretrial detainee at the time of the events covered in his complaint, but in light of Wolfish he does not argue that detainees have rights exceeding those of prisoners following conviction.) The Court held that these searches are "reasonable" because they are prudent precautions against smuggling drugs and other contraband into prison. 441 U.S. at 558–60. Prisoners argued that metal detectors plus supervision of inmates' contacts with outsiders would be superior to body-cavity inspections. The Court replied that prisons need not adopt the best alternatives. 441 U.S. at 559–60 n.40. Less-restrictive alternative arguments are too powerful: a prison always can do something, at some cost, to make prisons more habitable, but if courts assess and compare these costs and benefits then judges rather than wardens are the real prison administrators. Wolfish emphasized what is the animating theme of the Court's prison jurisprudence for the last 20 years: the requirement that judges respect hard choices made by prison administrators. * * *

Wolfish assumed without deciding that prisoners retain some right of privacy under the fourth amendment. Five years later the Court held that they do not. Hudson v. Palmer, 468 U.S. 517 (1984), observes that privacy is the thing most surely extinguished by a judgment committing someone to prison. Guards take control of where and how prisoners live; they do not retain any right of seclusion or secrecy against their captors, who are entitled to watch and regulate every detail of daily life. After Wolfish and Hudson monitoring of naked prisoners is not only permissible—wardens are entitled to take precautions against drugs and weapons (which can be passed through the alimentary canal or hidden in the rectal cavity and collected from a toilet bowl)—but also sometimes mandatory. Inter-prisoner violence is endemic, so constant vigilance without regard to the state of the prisoners' dress is essential. Vigilance over showers, vigilance over cells—vigilance everywhere, which means that guards gaze upon naked inmates.

Johnson mentions the fourth amendment but ignores Wolfish and Hudson. * * * "Privacy" has too many other connotations—from the right of reproductive autonomy that has nothing to do with searches and seizures to the common law right to control the publication of certain facts about oneself, including the depiction of one's naked body, see Haynes v. Alfred A. Knopf, Inc., 8 F.3d 1222, 1229–30 (7th Cir. 1993)—to be a useful substitute for the fourth amendment (or, as we discuss below, the eighth). * * *

After holding in Hudson that prisoners lack any reasonable expectation of privacy under the fourth amendment, the Court remarked that a prisoner could use the eighth amendment to overcome "calculated harassment unrelated to prison needs." 468 U.S. at 530. Similarly, the Court observed in Graham that the eighth amendment offers some protection supplementary to the fourth. 490 U.S. at 392, 394. We therefore think it best to understand the references to "privacy" in [the precedents] * * * as invocations of the eighth amendment's ban on cruel and unusual punishments. See Jordan v. Gardner, 986 F.2d 1521 (9th Cir. 1993) (en banc), which makes explicit the role of that provision. * * *

One who makes a claim under the cruel and unusual punishments clause must show that the state has created risk or inflicted pain pointlessly. "After incarceration, only the unnecessary and wanton infliction of pain * * * constitutes cruel and unusual punishment forbidden by the Eighth Amendment." Whitley v. Albers, 475 U.S. 312 (1986) (internal quotations omitted). * * * Does cross-sex monitoring serve a function beyond the infliction of pain? Monitoring is vital, but how about the cross-sex part? For this there are two justifications.

First, it makes good use of the staff. It is more expensive for a prison to have a group of guards dedicated to shower and toilet monitoring (equivalently, a group that can do every function except this) than to have guards all of whom can serve each role in the prison. If only men can monitor showers, then female guards are less useful to the prison; if female guards can't perform this task, the prison must have more guards on hand to cover for them. It is a form of featherbedding. * * * There are too many permutations to place guards and prisoners into multiple classes by sex, sexual orientation, and perhaps other criteria, allowing each group to be observed only by the corresponding groups that occasion the least unhappiness.

Second, cross-sex monitoring reduces the need for prisons to make sex a criterion of employment, and therefore reduces the potential for conflict with Title VII and the equal protection clause. Cells and showers are designed so that guards can see in, to prevent violence and other offenses. Prisoners dress, undress, and bathe under watchful eyes. Guards roaming the corridors are bound to see naked prisoners. * * *

To the riposte that Title VII and the equal protection clause can't authorize a violation of the eighth amendment, we rejoin: True enough, but not pertinent. A warden must accommodate conflicting interests—the embarrassment of reticent prisoners, the entitlement of women to equal treatment in the workplace. A state may reject the prisoner's claim if it has a reason, as Wolfish establishes for a substantially greater intrusion. The interest of women in equal treatment is a solid reason, with more secure footing in American law than prisoners' modesty, leading to the conclusion that there is no violation of the eighth amendment. * * * When interests clash, a judge must prefer those based on legislative decisions over those that reflect their own views of sound policy. The premise of judicial review is that the Constitution is an authoritative decision binding on all branches of government; when it has only such substance as judges pour into it themselves, the decisions of the elected branches prevail. * * *

How odd it would be to find in the eighth amendment a right not to be seen by the other sex. Physicians and nurses of one sex routinely examine the other. In exotic places such as California people regularly sit in saunas and hot tubs with unclothed strangers. Cf. Miller v. South Bend,

904 F.2d 1081 (7th Cir. 1990) (en banc) (holding that there is a constitutional right to dance nude in public), reversed under the name Barnes v. Glen Theatre, Inc., 501 U.S. 560 (1991). Most persons' aversion to public nudity pales compared with the taboo against detailed inspections of body cavities, yet the Court found no constitutional obstacle to these in Wolfish; the Constitution does not require prison managers to respect the social conventions of free society. Drug testing is common, although this often requires observation of urination. Vernonia School District 47J v. Acton (1995) (drug testing of seventh grade boy as condition of participation in sports is "reasonable" under the fourth amendment); see also Dimeo v. Griffin, 943 F.2d 679, 682–83 (7th Cir. 1991) (en banc), in which this court treated the imposition on privacy as slight. More to the point, the clash between modesty and equal employment opportunities has been played out in sports. Women reporters routinely enter locker rooms after games. How could an imposition that male athletes tolerate be deemed cruel and unusual punishment? * * *

Any practice allowed under the due process [clause] * * * is acceptable under the eighth amendment too—not only because the objective component of cruel and unusual punishment is more tolerant toward wardens, but also because the eighth amendment has a demanding mental state component. [T]he standard is criminal recklessness. The guard or warden must want to injure the prisoner or must know of and disregard a substantial risk that harm will befall the prisoner. Johnson does not allege that any of the defendants sought to humiliate him. * * *

Where does this leave us? The fourth amendment does not protect privacy interests within prisons. Moving to other amendments does not change the outcome. Cross-sex monitoring is not a senseless imposition. * * * It cannot be called "inhumane" and therefore does not fall below the floor set by the objective component of the eighth amendment. And Johnson does not contend that his captors adopted their monitoring patterns because of, rather than in spite of, the embarrassment it causes some prisoners. He does not submit that the warden ignored his sensibilities; he argues only that they received too little weight in the felicific calculus. Like the district court, therefore, we conclude that the complaint fails to state a claim on which relief may be granted. Affirmed

POSNER, CHIEF JUDGE, concurring and dissenting. * * *

The cruel and unusual punishments clause of the Eighth Amendment to the United States Constitution, like so much in the Bill of Rights, is a Rohrschach test. What the judge sees in it is the reflection of his or her own values, values shaped by personal experience and temperament as well as by historical reflection, public opinion, and other sources of moral judgment. * * *

The nudity taboo retains great strength in the United States. It should not be confused with prudery. It is a taboo against being seen in the nude by strangers, not by one's intimates. Ours is a morally diverse populace and the nudity taboo is not of uniform strength across it. It is strongest among professing Christians, because of the historical antipathy of the Church to nudity; and as it happens the plaintiff alleges that his right "to practice Christian modesty is being violated." The taboo is particularly strong when the stranger belongs to the opposite sex. There are radical feminists who regard "sex" as a social construction and the very concept of "the opposite sex," implying as it does the dichotomization of the "sexes" (the "genders," as we are being taught to say), as a sign of patriarchy. For these feminists the surveillance of naked male prisoners by female guards and naked female prisoners by male guards are way stations on the road to sexual equality. If prisoners have no rights, the reconceptualization of the prison as a site of progressive social engineering should give us no qualms. Animals have no right to wear clothing. Why prisoners, if they are no better than animals? There is no answer, if the premise is accepted. But it should be rejected, and if it is rejected, and the duty of a society that would like to think of itself as civilized to treat its prisoners humanely therefore acknowledged, then I think that the interest of a prisoner in being free from unnecessary cross-sex surveillance has priority over the unisex-bathroom movement and requires us to reverse the judgment of the district court throwing out this lawsuit.

I have been painting in broad strokes, and it is time to consider the particulars of this case and the state of the precedents. * * *

The parties have confused the first issue by describing it as the extent of a prisoner's "right of privacy." They cannot be criticized too harshly for this. Countless cases, including our own Canedy v. Boardman, 16 F.3d 183 (7th Cir. 1994), have done the same thing. E.g., Cornwell v. Dahlberg, 963 F.2d 912, 916–17 (6th Cir. 1992); Cookish v. Powell, 945 F.2d 441, 446 (1st Cir. 1991) (per curiam); Cumbey v. Meachum, 684 F.2d 712 (10th Cir. 1982) (per curiam). The problem is that the term "right of privacy" bears meanings in law that are remote from its primary ordinary-language meaning, which happens to be the meaning that a suit of this sort invokes. One thing it means in law is the right to reproductive autonomy; another is a congeries of tort rights only one of which relates to the naked body; still another is the right to maintain the confidentiality of certain documents and conversations. Another and overlapping meaning is the set of interests protected by the Fourth Amendment, which prohibits unreasonable searches and seizures. It has been held to be inapplicable to searches and seizures within prisons, Hudson v. Palmer, 468 U.S. 517 (1984), and if applicable to jails housing pretrial detainees as distinct from convicted defendants—an unsettled question—is only tenuously so, Bell v. Wolfish, 441 U.S. 520 (1979) * * *.

One part of the tort right of privacy is the right to prevent the publicizing of intimate facts, including the sight of the naked body. Haynes v. Alfred A. Knopf, Inc., 8 F.3d 1222, 1229–30 (7th Cir. 1993). Even this right is not the basis of Johnson's suit. This is not a common law tort suit, and anyway the sight of his naked body was not "publicized" in the sense that this term bears in the law of torts.

Whalen v. Roe, 429 U.S. 589 (1977), while holding that a statute which required keeping a record of the names of people for whom physicians prescribed certain dangerous though lawful drugs did not invade any constitutional right of privacy, can be read to imply that the disclosure by or under the compulsion of the government of a person's medical records might invade a constitutional right of privacy, presumably a "substantive due process" right. "Disclosure" of the person's naked body might be argued to violate a cognate right to the concealment of the body. In this way a right to "privacy" in the rather literal sense in which it is invoked here might laboriously be extracted from constitutional precedent.

I consider this too tortuous and uncertain a route to follow in the quest for constitutional limitations on the infliction of humiliation on prison inmates. The Eighth Amendment forbids the federal government (and by an interpretation of the due process clause of the Fourteenth Amendment the states as well) to inflict cruel and unusual punishments. The due process clause has been interpreted to lay a similar prohibition on the infliction of cruel and unusual punishments on pretrial detainees who, like Johnson, not having been convicted, are not formally being "punished." * * * I take it that purely psychological punishments can sometimes be deemed cruel and unusual * * *. The question is then whether exposing naked prisoners to guards of the opposite sex can ever be deemed one of these cruel and unusual psychological punishments. * * *

I have no patience with the suggestion that Title VII of the Civil Right Act of 1964 forbids a prison or jail to impede, however slightly, the career opportunities of female guards by shielding naked male prisoners from their eyes. It is true that since the male prison population is vastly greater than the female, female guards would gain no corresponding advantage from being allowed to monopolize the surveillance of naked female prisoners. But Title VII cannot override the Constitution. There cannot be a right to inflict cruel and unusual punishments in order to secure a merely statutory entitlement to equal opportunities for women in the field of corrections. * * *

This is not to say that exposing the naked male body to women's eyes constitutes cruel and unusual punishment in all circumstances. A male prisoner has no constitutional right to be treated by a male doctor. * * * Even the "right of privacy" cases reject the suggestion that any time a female guard glimpses a naked male prisoner his rights have been invaded. See, e.g., Michenfelder v. Sumner, 860 F.2d 328, 335 (9th Cir. 1988); Grummett v. Rushen, 779 F.2d 491, 494–95 (9th Cir. 1985). Not only is the injury from an occasional glimpse slight; but in addition, as we can see when the "right of privacy" cases are reclassified under the proper constitutional rubrics, neither the Eighth Amendment nor the counterpart protections of pretrial detainees under the due process clauses extend to unintentional wrongs. * * * Deliberately to place male prisoners under continuous visual surveillance by female guards, however, so that whenever the prisoner dresses or undresses, takes a shower, or uses the toilet, a woman is watching him, gives even my colleagues pause.

Ours is the intermediate case, where the prison or jail makes no effort, or a patently inadequate effort, to shield the male prisoners from the gaze of female guards when the prisoners are nude. * * * What is in question is the right of prison officials to entrust the surveillance of naked prisoners to guards of the opposite sex from the prisoners. * * *

The Eighth Amendment requires in my view that reasonable efforts be made to prevent frequent, deliberate, gratuitous exposure of nude prisoners of one sex to guards of the other sex. I doubt that any more precise statement of the proper constitutional test is feasible. It is precise enough to show that my colleagues indulge in hyperbole when they say that a decision for Johnson would mean that "female guards are shuffled off to back office jobs." They would not be, but that is not the most important point. The most important point is that sexual equality may not be pursued with no regard to competing interests, and with an eye blind to reality. * * *

I turn now to the question whether the complaint states a claim for the infringement of the right that I have sketched. * * *

My colleagues say that we must respect "the hard choices made by prison administrators." I agree. There is no basis in the record, however, for supposing that such a choice was made here, or for believing that an effort to limit cross-sex surveillance would involve an inefficient use of staff—"featherbedding," as my colleagues put it. There is no record. The case was dismissed on the complaint. We do not know whether the Cook County Jail cannot afford a thicker [shower curtain] or, more to the point, cannot feasibly confine the surveillance of naked male prisoners to male guards and naked female prisoners to female guards. We do not even know what crime Anderson is charged with. My colleagues urge deference to prison administrators, but at the same time speak confidently about the costs of redeploying staff to protect Johnson's rights. It would be nice to know a little more about the facts before making a judgment that condones barbarism.

NOTE: JUDGE POSNER ON CHRISTIANITY AND NUDITY

In his dissenting opinion in *Johnson v. Phelan*, Chief Judge Richard Posner asserts that a taboo against nudity is "strongest among professing Christians, because of the historical antipathy of the Church to nudity; and as it happens the plaintiff alleges that his right 'to practice Christian modesty is being violated.'" It is not self-evidently correct that, of all the world religions, Christianity contains the strongest modesty norms. But, passages from the Christian Bible reflect of the taboo about which Posner speculated. Cf. Milton R. Konvitz, Privacy and the Law: A Philosophical Prelude, 31 *Law and Contemp. Probs.* 272, 272–76 (1966).

THE JUDEO–CHRISTIAN NUDITY TABOO, BIBLE (REVISED STANDARD VERSION)

Genesis, Chapter 3: 1–24; Chapter 9: 18–29.

Chapter 3: Adam and Eve Cover Up

1: Now the serpent was more subtle than any other wild creature that the LORD God had made. He said to the woman, "Did God say, 'You shall not eat of any tree of the garden'?"

2: And the woman said to the serpent, "We may eat of the fruit of the trees of the garden;

3: but God said, 'You shall not eat of the fruit of the tree which is in the midst of the garden, neither shall you touch it, lest you die.'"

4: But the serpent said to the woman, "You will not die.

5: For God knows that when you eat of it your eyes will be opened, and you will be like God, knowing good and evil."

6: So when the woman saw that the tree was good for food, and that it was a delight to the eyes, and that the tree was to be desired to make one wise, she took of its fruit and ate; and she also gave some to her husband, and he ate.

7: Then the eyes of both were opened, and they knew that they were naked; and they sewed fig leaves together and made themselves aprons.

8: And they heard the sound of the LORD God walking in the garden in the cool of the day, and the man and his wife hid themselves from the presence of the LORD God among the trees of the garden.

9: But the LORD God called to the man, and said to him, "Where are you?"

10: And he said, "I heard the sound of thee in the garden, and I was afraid, because I was naked; and I hid myself."

11: He said, "Who told you that you were naked? Have you eaten of the tree of which I commanded you not to eat?"

12: The man said, "The woman whom thou gavest to be with me, she gave me fruit of the tree, and I ate."

13: Then the LORD God said to the woman, "What is this that you have done?" The woman said, "The serpent beguiled me, and I ate."

14: The LORD God said to the serpent, "Because you have done this, cursed are you above all cattle, and above all wild animals; upon your belly you shall go, and dust you shall eat all the days of your life.

15: I will put enmity between you and the woman, and between your seed and her seed; he shall bruise your head, and you shall bruise his heel."

16: To the woman he said, "I will greatly multiply your pain in childbearing; in pain you shall bring forth children, yet your desire shall be for your husband, and he shall rule over you."

17: And to Adam he said, "Because you have listened to the voice of your wife, and have eaten of the tree of which I commanded you, 'You shall not eat of it,' cursed is the ground because of you; in toil you shall eat of it all the days of your life;

18: thorns and thistles it shall bring forth to you; and you shall eat the plants of the field.

19: In the sweat of your face you shall eat bread till you return to the ground, for out of it you were taken; you are dust, and to dust you shall return."

20: The man called his wife's name Eve, because she was the mother of all living.

21: And the LORD God made for Adam and for his wife garments of skins, and clothed them.

22: Then the LORD God said, "Behold, the man has become like one of us, knowing good and evil; and now, lest he put forth his hand and take also of the tree of life, and eat, and live for ever"—

23: therefore the LORD God sent him forth from the garden of Eden, to till the ground from which he was taken.

24: He drove out the man; and at the east of the garden of Eden he placed the cherubim, and a flaming sword which turned every way, to guard the way to the tree of life.

Chapter 9: Noah Gets Covered

18: The sons of Noah who went forth from the ark were Shem, Ham, and Japheth. Ham was the father of Canaan.

19: These three were the sons of Noah; and from these the whole earth was peopled.

20: Noah was the first tiller of the soil. He planted a vineyard;

21: and he drank of the wine, and became drunk, and lay uncovered in his tent.

22: And Ham, the father of Canaan, saw the nakedness of his father, and told his two brothers outside.

23: Then Shem and Japheth took a garment, laid it upon both their shoulders, and walked backward and covered the nakedness of their father; their faces were turned away, and they did not see their father's nakedness.

24: When Noah awoke from his wine and knew what his youngest son had done to him,

25: he said, "Cursed be Canaan; a slave of slaves shall he be to his brothers."

26: He also said, "Blessed by the LORD my God be Shem; and let Canaan be his slave."

27: God enlarge Japheth, and let him dwell in the tents of Shem; and let Canaan be his slave."

28: After the flood Noah lived three hundred and fifty years.

29: All the days of Noah were nine hundred and fifty years; and he died.

3. ISOLATION, MODESTY AND SECURITY

MERIWETHER v. FAULKNER

821 F.2d 408 (7th Cir. 1987).

CUMMINGS, CIRCUIT JUDGE.

Since May 1982, plaintiff has been serving a thirty-five year sentence for murder. She is a pre-operative transsexual suffering from gender dysphoria, a medically recognized psychological disorder. She has been chemically (although not surgically) castrated as a result of approximately nine years of estrogen therapy under the supervision of physicians and has undergone surgical augmentation of her facial structure, breasts, and hips so as to alter her body shape to resemble that of a biological female. She has feminine mannerisms, wears makeup and feminine clothing and undergarments when permitted, considers herself to be a female, and in fact has been living as a female since the age of fourteen. * * *

Since the inception of her incarceration, plaintiff has been denied all medical treatment—chemical, psychiatric, or otherwise—for her gender dysphoria and related medical needs. The Medical Director at the Pendleton institution, Dr. Choi, has allegedly made humiliating remarks about plaintiff's need for estrogen and apparently once told her that "as long as she was in the Department of Corrections she would never receive the medication [estrogen] and that he would make sure of this." * * * Plaintiff has suffered severe withdrawal symptoms as a result of the termination of estrogen therapy after nine years and has failed to receive any treatment for problems associated with silicone surgical implants. * * *

Plaintiff initially contends that the defendants' failure to provide any medical treatment for her gender dysphoria constitutes a violation of her right under the Eighth Amendment to adequate medical care. * * *

A state has an affirmative obligation under the Eighth Amendment "to provide persons in its custody with a medical care system that meets minimal standards of adequacy." * * *

Courts have repeatedly held that treatment of a psychiatric or psychological condition may present a "serious medical need" * * *. * * * There is no reason to treat transsexualism differently than any other psychiatric disorder. Thus contrary to the district court's determination, plaintiff's complaint does state a "serious medical need." * * *

We therefore conclude that plaintiff has stated a valid claim under the Eighth Amendment which, if proven, would entitle her to some kind of medical treatment. * * * While we can and will not prescribe any overall plan of treatment, the plaintiff has stated a claim under the Eighth Amendment entitling her to some kind of medical care. * * *

The complaint raises a number of issues concerning the conditions of plaintiff's confinement. * * * [W]hile plaintiff's prolonged confinement in administrative segregation does not constitute a violation of due process, it may constitute cruel and unusual punishment in violation of the Eighth Amendment.

The Eighth Amendment prohibits punishments which involve the unnecessary and wanton infliction of pain, are grossly disproportionate to the severity of the crime for which an inmate was imprisoned, or are totally without penological justification. * * * Conditions of confinement, being "part of the penalty that criminal offenders pay for their offenses against society," fall within the ambit of the Eighth Amendment. * * *

In addition to her claim challenging her indefinite confinement in administrative segregation, plaintiff's complaint raises several other challenges to the conditions of her confinement. Specifically plaintiff alleges that she has been the victim of frequent sexual assaults and other acts of violence. She also alleges that prison guards have repeatedly and unnecessarily required her to strip in front of inmates and other correctional officers solely so that they might view her unique physical characteristics. The district court did not mention either of these claims in dismissing plaintiff's lawsuit. In view of our disposition of the claims concerning medical care and administrative segregation the district court should consider these latter two claims in the first instance.

This Court has repeatedly recognized that the failure of prison officials to protect an inmate from assaults by other inmates may rise to the level of an Eighth Amendment violation if the officials were "deliberately indifferent" to the strong likelihood of an attack. * * *

Plaintiff's claim that the defendants have deliberately failed to protect her from sexual assault is somewhat in conflict with her desire not to remain in administrative segregation indefinitely. As suggested above, however, placing the plaintiff in a general population cell appears to be an unacceptable and impractical solution. The complaint alleges that the assaults have continued while plaintiff has been confined in administrative segregation, and she certainly has a right under the Eighth Amendment to be protected from those assaults which occur as a result of the defendants' "deliberate indifference."

With respect to plaintiff's claim that she is regularly forced to strip before guards and other inmates, it should be noted that while a prisoner's expectation of privacy is extremely limited in light of the overriding need to maintain institutional order and security, see Bell v. Wolfish, 441 U.S. 520, the Supreme Court has recognized that a prisoner retains a remedy for "calculated harassment unrelated to prison needs." Hudson v.

Palmer, 468 U.S. 517. The Eighth Amendment's prohibition against cruel and unusual punishment stands as a protection from bodily searches which are maliciously motivated, unrelated to institutional security, and hence "totally without penological justification."

4.   THE PANOPTICON AND THE SUPERMAX

Note: The Panopticon

Would the "inspection house" designed by the philosopher Jeremy Bentham pass muster with the Eighth Amendment, if used as the basis of prison design? Are the essential characteristics of the Panopticon, in fact, a part of the design of contemporary maximum security and "supermax" prisons in the United States?

Bentham described the layout of his "inspection house" in a series of letters to a friend. The letters were published in 1787 as *Panopticon*. Bentham suggested his design would be suitable for any institution in which a large number of people needed to be under close, constant surveillance, such as, "penitentiary houses, prisons, houses of industry, work-houses, lazarettos, manufactories, hospitals, mad-houses and schools."

The basic plan of Bentham's penitentiary-house appeared in Letter III: "The building is circular. The apartments of the prisoners occupy the circumference. You may call them, if you please, the cells. These cells are divided from one another, and the prisoners by that means secluded from all communication with each other, by partitions in the form of radii issuing from the circumference towards the centre, and extending as many feet as shall be thought necessary to form the largest dimension of the cell. The apartment of the inspector occupies the centre; you may call it if you please the inspector's lodge. It will be convenient in most, if not in all cases, to have a vacant space or area all round, between such centre and such circumference. You may call it if you please the intermediate or annular area. About the width of a cell may be sufficient for a passage from the outside of the building to the lodge. Each cell has in the outward circumference, a window, large enough, not only to light the cell, but, through the cell, to afford light enough to the correspondent part of the lodge. The inner circumference of the cell is formed by an iron grating, so light as not to screen any part of the cell from the inspector's view. Of this grating, a part sufficiently large opens, in form of a door, to admit the prisoner at his first entrance; and to give admission at any time to the inspector or any of his attendants. To cut off from each prisoner the view of every other, the partitions are carried on a few feet beyond the grating * * *."

JEREMY BENTHAM, THE PANOPTICON (1787)

It may be of use, that among all the particulars you have seen, it should be clearly understood what circumstances are, and what are not, essential to the plan. The essence of it consists, then, in the centrality of the inspector's situation, combined with the well-known and most effectual contrivances for seeing without being seen. As to the general form of the building, the most commodious for most purposes seems to be the circular: but this is not an absolutely essential circumstance. Of all figures, however, this, you will observe, is the only one that affords a perfect view, and the same view, of an indefinite number of apartments of the same dimensions: that affords a spot from which, without any change of situation, a man may survey, in the same perfection, the whole number, and without so much as a change of posture, the half of the whole number, at the same time: that, within a boundary of a given extent, contains the greatest quantity of room:—that places the centre at the least distance from the light:—that gives the cells most width, at the part where, on account of the light, most light may, for the purposes of work, be wanted:—and that reduces to the greatest possible shortness the path taken by the inspector, in passing from each part of the field of inspection to every other.

You will please to observe, that though perhaps it is the most important point, that the persons to be inspected should always feel themselves as if under inspection, at least as standing a great chance of being so, yet it is not by any means the only one. If it were, the same advantage might be given to buildings of almost any form. What is also of importance is, that for the greatest proportion of time possible, each man should actually be under inspection. This is material in all cases, that the inspector may have the satisfaction of knowing, that the discipline actually has the effect which it is designed to have: and it is more particularly material in such cases where the inspector, besides seeing that they conform to such standing rules as are prescribed, has more or less frequent occasion to give them such transient and incidental directions as will require to be given and enforced, at the commencement at least of every course of industry. And I think, it needs not much argument to prove, that the business of inspection, like every other, will be performed to a greater degree of perfection, the less trouble the performance of it requires.

Not only so, but the greater chance there is, of a given person's being at a given time actually under inspection, the more strong will be the persuasion—the more intense, if I may say so, the feeling, he has of his being so. How little turn so ever the greater number of persons so circumstanced may be supposed to have for calculation, some rough sort of calculation can scarcely, under such circumstances, avoid forcing itself upon the rudest mind. Experiment, venturing first upon slight transgressions, and so on, in proportion to success, upon more and more considerable ones, will not fail to teach him the difference between a loose inspection and a strict one.

It is for these reasons, that I cannot help looking upon every form as less and less eligible, in proportion as it deviates from the circular.

A very material point is, that room be allotted to the lodge, sufficient to adapt it to the purpose of a complete and constant habitation for the principal inspector or head-keeper, and his family. The more numerous also the family, the better; since, by this means, there will in fact be as many inspectors, as the family consists of persons, though only one be paid for it. Neither the orders of the inspector himself, nor any interest which they may feel, or not feel, in the regular performance of his duty, would be requisite to find them motives adequate to the purpose. Secluded oftentimes, by their situation, from every other object, they will naturally, and in a manner unavoidably, give their eyes a direction conformable to that purpose, in every momentary interval of their ordinary occupations. It will supply in their instance the place of that great and constant fund of entertainment to the sedentary and vacant in towns—the looking out of the window. The scene, though a confined, would be a very various, and therefore, perhaps, not altogether an unamusing one.

CHERRY v. LITSCHER

2002 WL 32350051 (W.D. Wis. 2002).

BARBARA B. CRABB

Petitioner Eugene L. Cherry, who is presently confined at the Super-max Correctional Institution in Boscobel, Wisconsin, contends that respondents violated [constitutional provisions including the Fourth and Eighth Amendment] * * *.

Petitioner's request for leave to proceed on his Eighth Amendment [claims] will be granted. * * * His request for leave to proceed on his claims of due process, equal protection and right to privacy will be denied because the claims are legally frivolous. * * *

Supermax is an extended control facility in which inmates are isolated from contact with other human beings. Human contact is limited to instances when medical staff, clergy or a counselor stops at the inmate's cell front during rounds. Physical contact is limited to being touched through a security door by a correctional officer while being placed in restraints or having restraints removed. The bulk of verbal communication with staff occurs through an intercom system and inmates talk to each other through the prison's ventilation system. Further minimization of human contact results from the use of technologies, such as cameras, remote listening devices and control devices for televisions, water and lights. * * *

Petitioner is subjected to the destruction of the normal functioning of his brain, which depends on constant sensory bombardment. Sensory stimuli have the general function of maintaining the brain. When a person is restricted under isolating conditions for long periods of time like petitioner, the brain loses its power of arousal.

In order to receive meals, clothing, medication, mail and other items, respondent Berge requires inmates to dress in full prison garb, turn on the bright light and stand in the middle of the cell with palms exposed. This policy is meant to humiliate and degrade petitioner.

On October 24, 2001, third-shift officers refused to open petitioner's trap door and allow the nurse to give petitioner his medication because he refused to take his t-shirt off his head. * * *

On December 14, 2001, second-shift unit staff refused to give petitioner hygiene supplies and his meal for refusing to take his t-shirt off his head. Petitioner was hungry all night and suffered stomach cramps. Petitioner had no soap or toothpaste, so he had a foul body odor for three days. Staff refused to give petitioner toilet tissue for three days, so he had to wipe himself with a face cloth, which sat in a corner until staff issued a new one.

Respondents Apple and Cullen are psychologists at Supermax who have the authority to order petitioner to be transferred to an inpatient facility if he shows signs of a serious mental illness. Petitioner has numerous entries in his clinical file that show that he suffers from several mental illnesses that the staff at Supermax cannot address. From July 2000, to September 2001, petitioner made numerous requests to respondents Apple and Cullen, asking to discuss his suicidal thoughts and unreported suicide attempts. Respondent Apple "turned a blind eye." Respondent Cullen refused to speak with petitioner about his mental illness and instead sent an officer to petitioner's cell to deliver a packet on depression, without instructions on what petitioner was to do with the packet. * * *

Petitioner's cell is equipped with showers and cameras. Respondent Berge does not allow staff to shut off cameras during showers, when petitioner is using the facilities or washing himself, but he allows staff to give petitioner warnings and conduct reports for exposing himself to staff if staff are doing rounds and see petitioner naked and washing himself. Respondent Berge does not provide robes or allow petitioner or other inmates to purchase them to maintain their modesty on shower and clothing exchange days, causing petitioner to expose himself to female staff when the towel falls off. Respondent Berge does not provide an inexpensive shower or privacy curtain to petitioner. Respondent Berge allows petitioner to be subjected to opposite sex surveillance.

Petitioner is often subjected to body cavity and cell searches in the total absence of security and penological justification. These searches are meant to harass petitioner. * * *

Respondent Berge does not allow level one inmates to possess books, magazines, newspapers, pamphlets or typed and photocopied materials. Respondent Berge does not allow inmates on levels two through five to keep magazines, newspapers, pamphlets or photocopied materials and he limits them to five soft covered books. Under the level system, respondent Berge prohibits legal books and journals. Wis. Admin. Code allows inmates to retain property purchased by the inmate amounting to 8000 cubic inches. Wis. Admin. Code allows inmates to keep religious materials, prayer sheets, prayer schedules, pamphlets, books and magazines that do not cause a disruption. Respondent Berge's level system infringes on these rights. Respondent Berge has no security or penological reasons to deny petitioner his photographs on level one, limit petitioner's photographs to 12 on other levels or deny petitioner correspondence courses or photocopied material.

Petitioner alleges that he was transferred to Supermax, where the conditions are severe, after a classification hearing, the outcome of which was not approved by the chief of the bureau of offenders classification. However, the placement decision about which petitioner complains does not implicate a liberty interest. Prisoners do not have a liberty interest in not being transferred from one institution to another. Meachum v. Fano, 427 U.S. 215 (1976) (due process clause does not limit interprison transfer even when new institution is much more disagreeable).

Petitioner also alleges that he does not meet the mandatory criteria for placement at Supermax. Although respondents may not be following a Department of Corrections policy, regulation or even a Wisconsin statute, their failure to do so does not infringe upon a liberty interest of petitioner. At most, the allegation supports a claim that petitioner's rights under state law may have been violated, but such a claim must be raised in state court. Because petitioner has not alleged facts sufficient to establish that remaining out of Supermax implicates a liberty interest [recognized by the constitution], his request for leave to proceed on this claim will be denied as legally frivolous.

Petitioner alleges that the level system at Supermax violates his right to due process. In Sandin, 515 U.S. at 483–484, the Supreme Court held that liberty interests "will be generally limited to freedom from restraint which * * * imposes [an] atypical and significant hardship on the inmate in relation to the ordinary incidents of prison life." After Sandin, in the prison context, protected liberty interests are limited essentially to the loss of good time credits because the loss of such credit affects the duration of an inmate's sentence. * * * Petitioner's request for leave to proceed on his claim that the level system violates due process will be denied because the claim is legally frivolous. * * *

Petitioner alleges that several of the conditions at Supermax violate his right to be free from cruel and unusual punishment: isolation from contact with other human beings; the intercom system; constant monitoring; constant lighting; lack of sunshine; constant boom of cell doors; remote listening devices; and remote control devices for televisions, water and lights. Petitioner alleges that he has suffered physically and mentally as a result of the totality of these conditions. * * *

Prisoners are entitled to "the minimal civilized measure of life's necessities." Rhodes v. Chapman, 452 U.S. 337 (1981). Regardless of the merit of petitioner's claims individually, the determination whether prison conditions violate the Eighth Amendment requires a court to consider the totality of the conditions of confinement, considering things such as security and feasibility as well as the length of confinement. See Gutierrez v. Peters, 111 F.3d 1364, 1374 (7th Cir. 1997); DeMallory v. Cullen, 855

F.2d 442, 445 (7th Cir. 1988). The rationale for examining the prisoner's conditions as a whole is that "some conditions of confinement may establish an Eighth Amendment violation 'in combination' when each would not do so alone, but only when they have a mutually enforcing effect that produces the deprivation of a single identifiable human need such as food, warmth or exercise—for example, a low cell temperature at night combined with a failure to issue blankets." Wilson v. Seiter, 501 U.S. 294 (1991).

Because petitioner's allegations of total isolation and sensory deprivation coupled with inadequate physical activity may violate "contemporary standards of decency," Caldwell v. Miller, 790 F.2d 589, 600 (7th Cir. 1986), petitioner may proceed in forma pauperis on a totality of the circumstances claim against respondents Litscher and Berge. As Secretary of the Department of Corrections and warden of Supermax, respondents Litscher and Berge are presumed to be aware of the conditions of confinement at Supermax. * * *

I understand petitioner to contend that respondents are violating his right to privacy under the Fourth Amendment by monitoring him constantly and by assigning female guards to his unit where they were likely to see male inmates such as plaintiff undressing, showering and using their cell toilets. The Fourth Amendment is not triggered unless the state intrudes into an area "in which there is a 'constitutionally protected reasonable expectation of privacy.'" New York v. Class, 475 U.S. 106 (1986) (citing Katz v. United States, 389 U.S. 347 (1967) (Harlan, J., concurring)). Although prisoners do not forfeit all of their rights to privacy, these rights are severely curtailed. Hudson v. Palmer, 468 U.S. 517 (1984) (prisoner had no reasonable expectation of privacy in his prison cell); Lanza v. New York, 370 U.S. 139 (1962) (prisoner had no reasonable expectation of privacy in jail visiting rooms). Pretrial detainees are subject to the same diminished expectations of privacy. Bell v. Wolfish, 441 U.S. 520, 546, (1979).

In Johnson v. Phelan, 69 F.3d 144, 145 (7th Cir. 1995), the Court of Appeals for the Seventh Circuit held that the Cook County jail did not violate the Fourth Amendment by assigning female guards to monitor a male pretrial detainee, even though such monitoring meant that these guards would observe the inmate naked in his cell, taking a shower or using the toilet. The court explained that inmates "do not retain any right of seclusion or secrecy against their captors, who are entitled to watch and regulate every detail of daily life." Id. at 146. In light of Johnson, it is clear that any female guards who observe petitioner undressing, showering or using his cell toilet are not violating his right to privacy. Petitioner's request for leave to proceed will be denied on this claim because it is legally frivolous.

Petitioner alleges that he is subjected to body cavity and cell searches for no legitimate reason. In Bell v. Wolfish, 441 U.S. 520 (1979), pretrial detainees at a New York City facility alleged that the policy of conducting body cavity searches following visits from outsiders violated their Fourth Amendment rights. On the merits, the Supreme Court found that the searches were reasonable in light of the circumstances. Id. at 558–60. The Court held that reasonableness must be determined by balancing the need for the search against the invasion of personal rights, as revealed by four factors: "the scope of the particular intrusion, the manner in which it is conducted, the justification for initiating it, and the place in which it is conducted." Id. at 559. The court held that the danger of contraband entering the facility was so significant that it outweighed the intrusive nature of the search. Id. at 560. It may be that petitioner has been searched following visits with visitors or visits to the law library or recreation area. However, from the allegations in petitioner's complaint, I cannot determine whether the cell and strip searches are reasonable. Petitioner's request for leave to proceed on this claim against respondents Berge and Litscher will be granted.

In his motion for appointment of counsel, petitioner asserts that he has contacted several lawyers in an attempt to find representation. * * * At this time I do not believe that the presence of counsel would make a difference in the outcome of petitioner's case. For this reason, I will deny petitioner's motion for appointment of counsel without prejudice.

NOTE: LIBERTY INTEREST AGAINST SUPERMAX ISOLATION

In 2005 the Supreme Court held that inmates have a liberty interest in not being placed in supermax accommodations. But an inmate's liberty interest must be balanced against the needs and resources of the correctional system.

WILKINSON v. AUSTIN

545 U.S. 209 (2005).

JUSTICE KENNEDY delivered the opinion of the Court.

This case involves the process by which Ohio classifies prisoners for placement at its highest security prison, known as a "Supermax" facility. Supermax facilities are maximum-security prisons with highly restrictive conditions, designed to segregate the most dangerous prisoners from the general prison population. We must consider what process the Fourteenth Amendment to the United States Constitution requires Ohio to afford to inmates before assigning them to Supermax. We hold that the procedures Ohio has adopted provide sufficient procedural protection to comply with due process requirements.

I

The use of Supermax prisons has increased over the last 20 years, in part as a response to the rise in prison gangs and prison violence. See generally U.S. Dept. of Justice, National Institute of Corrections, C. Riveland, Supermax Prisons: Overview and General Considerations 1

(1999), http://www.nicic.org/pubs/1999/014937.pdf (as visited June 29, 2005, and available in Clerk of Court's case file). About 30 States now operate Supermax prisons, in addition to the two somewhat comparable facilities operated by the Federal Government. See Brief for United States as *Amicus Curiae* 2. In 1998, Ohio opened its only Supermax facility, the Ohio State Penitentiary (OSP), after a riot in one of its maximum-security prisons. OSP has the capacity to house up to 504 inmates in single-inmate cells and is designed to " 'separate the most predatory and dangerous prisoners from the rest of the . . . general [prison] population.' " See 189 F.Supp.2d 719, 723 (N.D.Ohio 2002) *(Austin I)* (quoting deposition of R. Wilkinson, pp. 24–25).

Conditions at OSP are more restrictive than any other form of incarceration in Ohio, including conditions on its death row or in its administrative control units. The latter are themselves a highly restrictive form of solitary confinement. * * * In OSP almost every aspect of an inmate's life is controlled and monitored. Inmates must remain in their cells, which measure 7 by 14 feet, for 23 hours per day. A light remains on in the cell at all times, though it is sometimes dimmed, and an inmate who attempts to shield the light to sleep is subject to further discipline. During the one hour per day that an inmate may leave his cell, access is limited to one of two indoor recreation cells.

Incarceration at OSP is synonymous with extreme isolation. In contrast to any other Ohio prison, including any segregation unit, OSP cells have solid metal doors with metal strips along their sides and bottoms which prevent conversation or communication with other inmates. All meals are taken alone in the inmate's cell instead of in a common eating area. Opportunities for visitation are rare and in all events are conducted through glass walls. It is fair to say OSP inmates are deprived of almost any environmental or sensory stimuli and of almost all human contact.

Aside from the severity of the conditions, placement at OSP is for an indefinite period of time, limited only by an inmate's sentence. For an inmate serving a life sentence, there is no indication how long he may be incarcerated at OSP once assigned there. * * * Inmates otherwise eligible for parole lose their eligibility while incarcerated at OSP. * * *

Placement at OSP is determined in the following manner: Upon entering the prison system, all Ohio inmates are assigned a numerical security classification from level 1 through level 5, with 1 the lowest security risk and 5 the highest. The initial security classification is based on numerous factors (*e.g.,* the nature of the underlying offense, criminal history, or gang affiliation) but is subject to modification at any time during the inmate's prison term if, for instance, he engages in misconduct or is deemed a security risk. Level 5 inmates are placed in OSP, and levels 1 through 4 inmates are placed at lower security facilities throughout the State.

Ohio concedes that when OSP first became operational, the procedures used to assign inmates to the facility were inconsistent and undefined. For a time, no official policy governing placement was in effect. * * * Haphazard placements were not uncommon, and some individuals who did not pose high-security risks were designated, nonetheless, for OSP. In an effort to establish guidelines for the selection and classification of inmates suitable for OSP, Ohio issued Department of Rehabilitation and Correction Policy 111–07 (Aug. 31, 1998). This policy has been revised at various points but relevant here are two versions: the "Old Policy" and the "New Policy." The Old Policy took effect on January 28, 1999, but problems with assignment appear to have persisted even under this written set of standards. * * * After forming a committee to study the matter and retaining a national expert in prison security, Ohio promulgated the New Policy in early 2002. The New Policy provided more guidance regarding the factors to be considered in placement decisions and afforded inmates more procedural protection against erroneous placement at OSP.

Although the record is not altogether clear regarding the precise manner in which the New Policy operates, we construe it based on the policy's text, the accompanying forms, and the parties' representations at oral argument and in their briefs. The New Policy appears to operate as follows: A classification review for OSP placement can occur either (1) upon entry into the prison system if the inmate was convicted of certain offenses, *e.g.,* organized crime, or (2) during the term of incarceration if an inmate engages in specified conduct, *e.g.,* leads a prison gang. The review process begins when a prison official prepares a "Security Designation Long Form" (Long Form). This three-page form details matters such as the inmate's recent violence, escape attempts, gang affiliation, underlying offense, and other pertinent details.

A three-member Classification Committee (Committee) convenes to review the proposed classification and to hold a hearing. At least 48 hours before the hearing, the inmate is provided with written notice summarizing the conduct or offense triggering the review. At the time of notice, the inmate also has access to the Long Form, which details why the review was initiated. The inmate may attend the hearing, may "offer any pertinent information, explanation and/or objections to [OSP] placement," and may submit a written statement. He may not call witnesses.

If the Committee does not recommend OSP placement, the process terminates. If the Committee does recommend OSP placement, it documents the decision on a "Classification Committee Report" (CCR), setting forth "the nature of the threat the inmate presents and the committee's reasons for the recommendation," * * *. The Committee sends the completed CCR to the warden of the prison where the inmate is housed or, in the case of an inmate just entering the prison system, to another designated official.

If, after reviewing the CCR, the warden (or the designated official) disagrees and concludes that OSP is inappropriate, the process terminates and the inmate is not placed in OSP. If the warden agrees, he indicates his approval on the CCR, provides his reasons, and forwards the annotated

CCR to the Bureau of Classification (Bureau) for a final decision. (The Bureau is a body of Ohio prison officials vested with final decisionmaking authority over all Ohio inmate assignments.) The annotated CCR is served upon the inmate, notifying him of the Committee's and warden's recommendations and reasons. The inmate has 15 days to file any objections with the Bureau.

After the 15–day period, the Bureau reviews the CCR and makes a final determination. If it concludes OSP placement is inappropriate, the process terminates. If the Bureau approves the warden's recommendation, the inmate is transferred to OSP. The Bureau's chief notes the reasons for the decision on the CCR, and the CCR is again provided to the inmate.

Inmates assigned to OSP receive another review within 30 days of their arrival. That review is conducted by a designated OSP staff member, who examines the inmate's file. If the OSP staff member deems the inmate inappropriately placed, he prepares a written recommendation to the OSP warden that the inmate be transferred to a lower security institution. If the OSP warden concurs, he forwards that transfer recommendation to the Bureau for appropriate action. If the inmate is deemed properly placed, he remains in OSP and his placement is reviewed on at least an annual basis according to the initial three-tier classification review process outlined above. * * *

For an inmate placed in OSP, almost all human contact is prohibited, even to the point that conversation is not permitted from cell to cell; the light, though it may be dimmed, is on for 24 hours; exercise is for 1 hour per day, but only in a small indoor room. Save perhaps for the especially severe limitations on all human contact, these conditions likely would apply to most solitary confinement facilities, but here there are two added components. First is the duration. Unlike the 30–day placement in *Sandin,* placement at OSP is indefinite and, after an initial 30–day review, is reviewed just annually. Second is that placement disqualifies an otherwise eligible inmate for parole consideration. *Austin I,* 189 F.Supp.2d, at 728. While any of these conditions standing alone might not be sufficient to create a liberty interest, taken together they impose an atypical and significant hardship within the correctional context. It follows that respondents have a liberty interest in avoiding assignment to OSP. *Sandin, supra,* at 483, 115 S.Ct. 2293.

OSP's harsh conditions may well be necessary and appropriate in light of the danger that high-risk inmates pose both to prison officials and to other prisoners. See *infra,* at 2396–2397. That necessity, however, does not diminish our conclusion that the conditions give rise to a liberty interest in their avoidance. * * *

Prolonged confinement in Supermax may be the State's only option for the control of some inmates, and claims alleging violation of the Eighth Amendment's prohibition of cruel and unusual punishments were resolved, or withdrawn, by settlement in an early phase of this case. Here, any claim of excessive punishment in individual circumstances is not before us.

The complaint challenged OSP assignments under the Old Policy, and the unwritten policies that preceded it, and alleged injuries resulting from those systems. Ohio conceded that assignments made under the Old Policy were, to say the least, imprecise. The District Court found constitutional violations had arisen under those earlier versions, and held that the New Policy would produce many of the same constitutional problems. *Austin I*, 189 F.Supp.2d, at 749–754. We now hold that the New Policy as described in this opinion strikes a constitutionally permissible balance between the factors of the *Mathews* framework. If an inmate were to demonstrate that the New Policy did not in practice operate in this fashion, resulting in a cognizable injury, that could be the subject of an appropriate future challenge. On remand, the Court of Appeals, or the District Court, may consider in the first instance what, if any, prospective relief is still a necessary and appropriate remedy for due process violations under Ohio's previous policies. Any such relief must, of course, satisfy the conditions set forth in 18 U.S.C. § 3626(a)(1)(A).

* * *

The Court of Appeals was correct to find the inmates possess a liberty interest in avoiding assignment at OSP. The Court of Appeals was incorrect, however, to sustain the procedural modifications ordered by the District Court. The portion of the Court of Appeals' opinion reversing the District Court's substantive modifications was not the subject of review upon certiorari and is unaltered by our decision.

The judgment of the Court of Appeals is affirmed in part and reversed in part, and the case is remanded for further proceedings consistent with this opinion.

G.   NINTH AMENDMENT PRIVACY

1.   THE NINTH AMENDMENT

"The enumeration in the Constitution, of certain rights, shall not be construed to deny or disparage others retained by the people."

2.   JUSTICE GOLDBERG'S FIND

GRISWOLD v. CONNECTICUT
381 U.S. 479 (1965), Goldberg, J., concurring.

MR. JUSTICE GOLDBERG, whom the CHIEF JUSTICE and MR. JUSTICE BRENNAN join, concurring.

[Appellants were a Planned Parenthood director and a physician convicted and fined under a Connecticut statute criminalizing birth control. They appealed their convictions asserting that the statute violated the privacy rights of married persons wishing to obtain birth control.]

I agree with the Court that Connecticut's birth-control law unconstitutionally intrudes upon the right of marital privacy, and I join in its opinion and judgment. * * * I add these words to emphasize the relevance of that Amendment to the Court's holding. * * *

The Ninth Amendment * * * is almost entirely the work of James Madison. It was introduced in Congress by him and passed the House and Senate with little or no debate and virtually no change in language. It was proffered to quiet expressed fears that a bill of specifically enumerated rights could not be sufficiently broad to cover all essential rights and that the specific mention of certain rights would be interpreted as a denial that others were protected. * * *

While this Court has had little occasion to interpret the Ninth Amendment, "it cannot be presumed that any clause in the constitution is intended to be without effect." Marbury v. Madison, 1 Cranch 137, 174. In interpreting the Constitution, "real effect should be given to all the words it uses." * * * The Ninth Amendment to the Constitution may be regarded by some as a recent discovery and may be forgotten by others, but since 1791 it has been a basic part of the Constitution which we are sworn to uphold. To hold that a right so basic and fundamental and so deep-rooted in our society as the right of privacy in marriage may be infringed because that right is not guaranteed in so many words by the first eight amendments to the Constitution is to ignore the Ninth Amendment and to give it no effect whatsoever. Moreover, a judicial construction that this fundamental right is not protected by the Constitution because it is not mentioned in explicit terms by one of the first eight amendments or elsewhere in the Constitution would violate the Ninth Amendment, which specifically states that "the enumeration in the Constitution, of certain rights, shall not be construed to deny or disparage others retained by the people."

A dissenting opinion suggests that my interpretation of the Ninth Amendment somehow "broaden[s] the powers of this Court." * * * With all due respect, I believe that it misses the import of what I am saying. I do not take the position of my Brother BLACK in his dissent in Adamson v. California, 332 U.S. 46, 68, that the entire Bill of Rights is incorporated in the Fourteenth Amendment, and I do not mean to imply that the Ninth Amendment is applied against the States by the Fourteenth. Nor do I mean to state that the Ninth Amendment constitutes an independent source of rights protected from infringement by either the States or the Federal Government. Rather, the Ninth Amendment shows a belief of the Constitution's authors that fundamental rights exist that are not expressly enumerated in the first eight amendments and an intent that the list of rights included there not be deemed exhaustive. * * * The Ninth Amendment simply shows the intent of the Constitution's authors that other fundamental personal rights should not be denied such protection or disparaged in any other way simply because they are not specifically listed in the first eight constitutional amendments. I do not see how this broadens the authority of the Court; rather it serves to support what this Court has been doing in protecting fundamental rights.

Nor am I turning somersaults with history in arguing that the Ninth Amendment is relevant in a case dealing with a State's infringement of a fundamental right. While the Ninth Amendment—and indeed the entire Bill of Rights—originally concerned restrictions upon federal power, the subsequently enacted Fourteenth Amendment prohibits the States as well from abridging fundamental personal liberties. And, the Ninth Amendment, in indicating that not all such liberties are specifically mentioned in the first eight amendments, is surely relevant in showing the existence of other fundamental personal rights, now protected from state, as well as federal, infringement. In sum, the Ninth Amendment simply lends strong support to the view that the "liberty" protected by the Fifth and Fourteenth Amendments from infringement by the Federal Government or the States is not restricted to rights specifically mentioned in the first eight amendments. * * *

In determining which rights are fundamental, judges are not left at large to decide cases in light of their personal and private notions. Rather, they must look to the "traditions and [collective] conscience of our people" to determine whether a principle is "so rooted [there] * * * as to be ranked as fundamental." Snyder v. Massachusetts, 291 U.S. 97, 105. The inquiry is whether a right involved "is of such a character that it cannot be denied without violating those 'fundamental principles of liberty and which lie at the base of all our civil and political institutions' * * *." Powell v. Alabama, 287 U.S. 45, 67. "Liberty" also "gains content from the emanations of * * * specific [constitutional] guarantees" and "from experience with the requirements of a free society." Poe v. Ullman, 367 U.S. 497, 517 (dissenting opinion of Mr. Justice Douglas). * * *

Finally, it should be said of the Court's holding today that it in no way interferes with a State's proper regulation of sexual promiscuity or misconduct. As my Brother Harlan so well stated in his dissenting opinion in Poe v. Ullman, supra, at 553.

"Adultery, homosexuality and the like are sexual intimacies which the State forbids * * * but the intimacy of husband and wife is necessarily an essential and accepted feature of the institution of marriage, an institution which the State not only must allow, but which always and in every age it has fostered and protected. It is one thing when the State exerts its power either to forbid extra-marital sexuality * * * or to say who may marry, but it is quite another when, having acknowledged a marriage and the intimacies inherent in it, it undertakes to regulate by means of the criminal law the details of that intimacy."

In sum, I believe that the right of privacy in the marital relation is fundamental and basic—a personal right "retained by the people" within the meaning of the Ninth Amendment. Connecticut cannot constitutionally abridge this fundamental right, which is protected by the Fourteenth

Amendment from infringement by the States. I agree with the Court that petitioners' convictions must therefore be reversed. * * *

H.　FOURTEENTH AMENDMENT PRIVACY

1.　THE FOURTEENTH AMENDMENT

"Section 1. All persons born or naturalized in the United States, and subject to the jurisdiction thereof, are citizens of the United States and of the state wherein they reside. No state shall make or enforce any law which shall abridge the privileges or immunities of citizens of the United States; nor shall any state deprive any person of life, liberty, or property, without due process of law; nor deny to any person within its jurisdiction the equal protection of the laws."

NOTE: THE MAIN SOURCE

The Fourteenth Amendment's due process and equal protection clauses have emerged as the main sources of privacy protection in constitutional law. The due process clause, with its language of "liberty", has proven especially important. The cases collected in this lengthy section tell the complete story of "the right to privacy," beloved and belittled.

2.　PRIVATE LIVES, PRIVATE CHOICES

MEYER v. NEBRASKA

262 U.S. 390 (1923).

MR. JUSTICE MCREYNOLDS delivered the opinion of the Court. * * *

[In 1920, while an instructor at the Zion Parochial School, plaintiff began teaching a ten year old boy how to read German. For his effort, he was convicted of violating a statute passed in 1919, "An act relating to the teaching of foreign languages in the State of Nebraska." The statute provided that teaching in any "denominational, parochial or public school" be conducted in the English language, that teaching of foreign languages not commence until after the eighth grade, and that violators "shall be subject to a fine of not less than twenty-five dollars ($25), nor more than one hundred dollars ($100) or be confined in the county jail for any period not exceeding thirty days for each offense."]

The American people have always regarded education and acquisition of knowledge as matters of supreme importance which should be diligently promoted. The Ordinance of 1787 declares, "Religion, morality, and knowledge being necessary to good government and the happiness of mankind, schools and the means of education shall forever be encouraged." Corresponding to the right of control, it is the natural duty of the parent to give his children education suitable to their station in life; and nearly all the States, including Nebraska, enforce this obligation by compulsory laws.

Practically, education of the young is only possible in schools conducted by especially qualified persons who devote themselves thereto. The calling always has been regarded as useful and honorable, essential, indeed, to the public welfare. Mere knowledge of the German language cannot reasonable be regarded as harmful. Heretofore it has been commonly looked upon as helpful and desirable. Plaintiff in error taught this language in school as part of his occupation. His right thus to teach and the right of parents to engage him so to instruct their children, we think, are within the liberty of the Amendment.

The challenged statute forbids the teaching in school of any subject except in English; also the teaching of any other language until the pupil has attained and successfully passed the eighth grade, which is not usually accomplished before the age of twelve. The Supreme Court of the State has held that "the so-called ancient or dead languages" are not "within the spirit or the purpose of the act." Nebraska District of Evangelical Lutheran Synod v. McKelvie, 187 N.W.927. Latin, Greek, Hebrew are not proscribed; but German, French, Spanish, Italian and every other alien speech are within the ban. Evidently the legislature has attempted materially to interfere with the calling of modern language teachers, with the opportunities of pupils to acquire knowledge, and with the power of parents to control the education of their own.

It is said the purpose of the legislation was to promote civic development by inhibiting training and education of the immature in foreign tongues and ideals before they could learn English and acquire American ideals; and "that the English language should be and become the mother tongue of all children reared in this State." It is also affirmed that the foreign born population is very large, that certain communities commonly use foreign words, follow foreign leaders, move in a foreign atmosphere, and that the children are thereby hindered from becoming citizens of the most useful type and the public safety is imperiled.

That the State may do much, go very far, indeed, in order to improve the quality of its citizens, physically, mentally and morally, is clear; but the individual has certain fundamental rights which must be respected. The protection of the Constitution extends to all, to those who speak other languages as well as to those born with English on the tongue. Perhaps it would be highly advantageous if all had ready understanding of our ordinary speech, but this cannot be coerced by methods which conflict with the Constitution—a desirable end cannot be promoted by prohibited means.

For the welfare of his Ideal Commonwealth, Plato suggested a law which should provide: "That the wives of our guardians are to be common, and their children are to be common, and no parent is to know his own child, nor any child his parent * * *. The proper officers will take the offspring of the goods parents to the pen or fold, and there they will deposit them with certain nurses who dwell in a separate quarter; but the offspring of the inferior, or of the better when they chance to be deformed, will be put away in some mysterious, unknown place, as they should be." In order to submerge the individual and develop ideal citizens, Sparta assembled the males at seven into barracks and intrusted their subsequent education and training to official guardians. Although such measures have been deliberately approved by men of great genius, their ideas touching the relation between individual and State were wholly different from those upon which our institutions rest; and it hardly will be affirmed that any legislature could impose such restrictions upon the people of a State without doing violence to both letter and spirit of the Constitution.

The desire of the legislature to foster a homogeneous people with American ideals prepared readily to understand current discussions of civic matters is easy to appreciate. Unfortunate experiences during the late war and aversion toward every characteristic of truculent adversaries were certainly enough to quicken that aspiration. But the means adopted, we think, exceed the limitations upon the power of the State and conflict with rights assured to plaintiff in error. The interference is plain enough and no adequate reason therefore in time of peace and domestic tranquility has been shown.

The power of the State to compel attendance at some school and to make reasonable regulations for all schools, including a requirement that they shall give instructions in English, is not questioned. Nor has challenge been made of the State's power to prescribe a curriculum for institutions which it supports. * * * No emergency has arisen which renders knowledge by a child of some language other than English so clearly harmful as to justify its inhibition with the consequent infringement of rights long freely enjoyed. We are constrained to conclude that the statute as applied is arbitrary and without reasonable relation to any end within the competency of the State.

As the statute undertakes to interfere only with teaching which involves a modern language, leaving complete freedom as to other matters, there seems no adequate foundation for the suggestion that the purpose was to protect the child's health by limiting his mental activities. It is well known that proficiency in a foreign language seldom comes to one not instructed at an early age, and experience shows that this is not injurious to the health, morals or understanding of the ordinary child.

The judgment of the court below must be reversed and the cause remanded for further proceedings not inconsistent with this opinion.

YORK v. STORY

324 F.2d 450 (9th Cir. 1963).

JUDGE HAMLEY

This action was brought by Angelynn York against three officers of the Police Department of the City of Chino, California, to recover damages for taking and distributing photographs of her in the nude. District court jurisdiction was asserted * * * it being alleged that the claim arises under

Rev.Stat. § 1979 (1875), 42 U.S.C. § 1983 (1958). The action was dismissed on motion. Plaintiff appeals.

We first state the allegations of the amended complaint. In October, 1958, appellant went to the police department of Chino for the purpose of filing charges in connection with an assault upon her. Appellee Ron Story, an officer of that police department, then acting under color of his authority as such, advised appellant that it was necessary to take photographs of her. Story then took appellant to a room in the police station, locked the door, and directed her to undress, which she did. Story then directed appellant to assume various indecent positions, and photographed her in those positions. These photographs were not made for any lawful or legitimate purpose. * * * [Officer Story and another officer later distributed the lewd photographs of Ms. York to others.]

The alleged act of Story in taking photographs of appellant in the nude, if proved, may or may not constitute an unreasonable search in the Fourth Amendment sense. But if we should hold that it does, this would not dispose of the whole case for the alleged subsequent acts of * * * distributing prints of these photographs, of which appellant also complains, could hardly be characterized as unreasonable searches.

It is therefore necessary, in any event, to reach appellant's * * * argument * * * relating to invasions of privacy. Accordingly, we turn at once to appellant's * * * contention—that all of these acts constituted such invasions of her privacy as to amount to deprivations of liberty without due process of law, guaranteed to her by the Due Process Clause of the Fourteenth Amendment.

We are not called upon to decide as an original proposition whether "privacy," as such, is comprehended within the "liberty" of which one may not be deprived without due process of law, as used in the Due Process Clause of the Fourteenth Amendment. For it has already been declared by the Supreme Court that the security of one's privacy against arbitrary intrusion by the police is basic to a free society and is therefore "implicit in the concept of ordered liberty," embraced within the Due Process Clause of the Fourteenth Amendment.

What we must decide, however, is whether the acts of the police, as here alleged, constitute an arbitrary invasion upon the security of one's privacy in upon Due Process sense.

We cannot conceive of a more basic subject of privacy than the naked body. The desire to shield one's unclothed figured from view of strangers, and particularly strangers of the opposite sex, is impelled by elementary self-respect and personal dignity. A search of one's home has been established to be an invasion of one's privacy against intrusion by the police, which, if "unreasonable," is arbitrary and therefore banned under the Fourth Amendment. We do not see how it can be argued that the searching of one's home deprives him of privacy, but the photographing of one's nude body, and the distribution of such photographs to strangers does not.

Nor can we imagine a more arbitrary police intrusion upon the security of that privacy than for a male police officer to unnecessarily photograph the nude body of a female citizen who has made complaint of an assault upon her, over her protest that the photographs would show no injuries, and at a time when a female police officer could have been, but was not, called in for this purpose, and to distribute those photographs to other personnel of the police department despite the fact that such distribution of the photographs could not have aided in apprehending the person who perpetrated the assault.

But granting all of that, must it still be held that the particular intrusions here alleged are not secured against by the Due Process Clause of the Fourteenth Amendment because they are not expressly proscribed in the Bill of Rights?

We think not. In the field of civil rights litigation the cases are not infrequent in which law enforcement action not banned in terms by any provision of the Bill of Rights had been made the subject of a successful claim.

All of the cases just cited involved persons who were in police custody at the time of the incident complained of. This circumstance, however, is indicative only of the infrequency of a case such as this, in which one not in custody is the alleged victim of arbitrary police action. No statute, decision or principle that we know of makes the Civil Rights Act available to those in the toils of the law, but closes the federal courthouse to law abiding citizens who have suffered just as grievous a deprivation of constitutional rights.

This case is novel not only in the respect just mentioned, but also with regard to the precise nature of the arbitrary police action complained of. But, as Justice Brandeis, dissenting in Olmstead v. United States, 277 U.S. 438 * * *, long ago made clear, the Constitution is capable of meeting new problems.

The fact that this is the first such case to reach a court of appeals indicates that civil rights actions of this kind are not likely to swamp the federal courts. * * *

Appellees assert that appellant has a civil remedy in the courts of California. But it is immaterial, insofar as the right to pursue remedies under the Civil Rights Act is concerned, that state remedies may also be available. * * *

We therefore conclude that, under the allegations of the amended complaint, appellant has laid a foundation for proving, if she can, not only that appellees were acting under color of local authority at the times in question, but that such acts constituted an arbitrary intrusion upon the security of her privacy, as guaranteed to her by the Due Process Clause of the Fourteenth Amendment. It was therefore error to dismiss the action on the ground that the amended complaint did not state a claim upon which relief can be granted.

a. Sterilization, Birth Control and Abortion

NOTE: COMSTOCK, SANGER AND A PACKAGE OF PESSARIES

In 1872, a former dry goods salesman by the name of Anthony Comstock became the "point man for purity reform" for the recently established New York Society for the Suppression of Vice. See Michael Grossberg, *Governing the Hearth: Law and Family in Nineteenth Century America* (1985), pp. 157–159. With the blessings of the Society, Comstock went to Washington to lobby Congress for the passage of national laws to combat vice and obscenity.

Under the tutelage of Vice President Henry Wilson and Supreme Court Justice William Strong, Comstock drafted what came to be known as the federal "Comstock Law", "An Act for the Suppression of Trade in, and Circulation of, Obscene Literature and Articles of Immoral Use", 17 Stat. 598–99 (1873), amended as 19 Stat. 90 (1876).

The Comstock Law criminalized using the mails to circulate indecent materials and materials relating to birth control and abortion: "Every obscene, lewd, or lascivious book pamphlet, picture, paper, writing, print, or other publication of an indecent character, and every article or thing designed or intended for the prevention of conception or procuring of abortion, and every article or thing intended or adapted for any indecent or immoral use, and every written or printed card, circular, book, pamphlet, advertisement, or notice of any kind giving information, directly or indirectly, where, or how, or of whom, or by what means, any of the hereinbefore mentioned matters, articles or things may be obtained or made * * * are hereby declared to be non-mailable matter, and shall not be conveyed in the mails, nor delivered from any post office or by any letter carrier. * * *" The punishment for violating the Comstock Law was serious: "he shall be imprisoned at hard labor in the penitentiary for not less than six months nor more than five years for each offense, or fined not less than one hundred dollars nor more than two thousand dollars, with costs of court." Comstock's influential 1873 Act led to the Tariff Act of 1930's restrictions prohibiting the mailing, importing or transporting in interstate commerce of articles "designed, adapted, or intended for preventing conception, or producing abortion."

Did Congress intend with its passage of the Comstock Law to ban the use of birth control and abortion implements outright? Aiming to clamp down on the use of birth control and abortion within their borders, many states adopted Comstock-style criminal laws of their own.

Famous birth control activist Margaret Sanger challenged New York's Comstock law, Penal Law Section 1142. The law made it a "misdemeanor for a person to sell, or give away, or to advertise or offer for sale, any instrument or article, drug or medicine, for the prevention of conception; or to give information orally, stating when, where or how such an instrument, article or medicine can be purchased or obtained." The law contained an exception for physicians. See *People v. Sanger*, 222 N.Y. 192, 193, 118 N.E. 637 (1918). Sanger, who was not a physician, deliberately violated the statute by distributing information about contraception to members of the general public in a "clinic" setting. Sanger was charged, convicted and sentenced to thirty days in a work house. Although her conviction was affirmed, the court found that birth control devices or information circulated to married persons by physicians or vendors for the purpose of preventing or curing disease fell within the exception to the law. *People v. Sanger*, 222 N.Y. 192, 118 N.E. 637 (1918).

In 1932 Sanger won an even larger victory for her movement. At Sanger's request, a New York gynecologist accepted a shipment of birth control devices from Japan in flagrant violation of federal law. Customs officials confiscated Dr. Stone's shipment. In *United States v. One Package of Japanese Pessaries*, 86 F.2d 737 (2d Cir. 1936), the court determined that the federal government lacked authority to bar physicians from prescribing birth control for their patients. Dr. Stone had testified in the case that "she prescribes the use of pessaries in cases where it would not be desirable for a patient to undertake a pregnancy." Circuit Judge Augustus Hand reasoned that the mail and import prohibitions "embraced only such articles as Congress would have denounced as immoral if it had understood all the conditions under which they were to be used." Hand wrote that the law's "design, in our opinion, was not to prevent the importation, sale, or carriage by mail of things which might intelligently be employed by conscientious and competent physicians for the purpose of saving life or promoting the well being of their patients."

NOTE: EQUAL PROTECTION

Skinner v. Oklahoma, 316 U.S. 535 (1942), is cited as precedent for constitutional privacy rights, most notably, the right to control procreation implicated in sterilization, contraception and abortion statutes. It is one of a handful of leading Fourteenth Amendment "privacy" cases decided on the basis of the Equal Protection Clause, rather than a substantive reading of the Due Process Clause. See also *Loving v. Virginia* (striking down laws prohibiting interracial marriages) and *Eisenstadt v. Baird* (striking down laws denying unmarried persons access to birth control), defending private choice on equal protection grounds.

SKINNER v. OKLAHOMA

316 U.S. 535 (1942).

MR. JUSTICE DOUGLAS delivered the opinion of the Court.

This case touches a sensitive and important area of human rights. Oklahoma deprives certain individuals of a right which is basic to the perpetuation of a race—the right to have offspring. Oklahoma has decreed the enforcement of its law against petitioner, overruling his claim that it violated the Fourteenth Amendment. Because that decision raised grave and substantial constitutional questions, we granted the petition for certiorari.

The statute involved is Oklahoma's Habitual Criminal Sterilization Act. Okla. Stat. Ann. Tit. 57, Sections 171, et seq.; L. 1935, pp. 94 et seq. That Act defines an "habitual criminal" as a person who, having been convicted two or more times for crimes "amounting to felonies involving moral turpitude," either in an Oklahoma court or in a court of any other

State, is thereafter convicted of such a felony in Oklahoma and is sentenced to a term of imprisonment in an Oklahoma penal institution. * * * Machinery is provided for the institution by the Attorney General of a proceeding against such a person in the Oklahoma courts for a judgment that such person shall be rendered sexually sterile. * * * Notice, an opportunity to be heard, and the right to a jury trial are provided. * * * The issues triable in such a proceeding are narrow and confined. If the court or jury finds that the defendant is an "habitual criminal" and that he "may be rendered sexually sterile without detriment to his or her general health," then the court "shall render judgment to the effect that said defendant be rendered sexually sterile" * * * by the operation of vasectomy in case of a male, and of salpingectomy in case of a female. * * * Only one other provision of the Act is material here, * * * which provides that "offenses arising out of the violation of the prohibitory laws, revenue acts, embezzlement, or political offenses, shall not come or be considered within the terms of this Act."

Petitioner was convicted in 1926 of the crime of stealing chickens, and was sentenced to the Oklahoma State Reformatory. In 1929 he was convicted of the crime of robbery with firearms, and was sentenced to the reformatory. In 1934 he was convicted again of robbery with firearms, and was sentenced to the penitentiary. He was confined there in 1935 when the Act was passed. In 1936 the Attorney General instituted proceedings against him. Petitioner in his answer challenged the Act as unconstitutional by reason of the Fourteenth Amendment. A jury trial was had. The court instructed the jury that the crimes of which petitioner had been convicted were felonies involving moral turpitude, and that the only question for the jury was whether the operation of vasectomy could be performed on petitioner without detriment to his general health. The jury found that it could be. A judgment directing that the operation of vasectomy be performed on petitioner was affirmed by the Supreme Court of Oklahoma by a five to four decision. 189 Okla. 235, 115 P. 2d 123.

Several objections to the constitutionality of the Act have been pressed upon us. * * * We pass those points without intimating an opinion on them, for there is a feature of the Act which clearly condemns it. That is, its failure to meet the requirements of the equal protection clause of the Fourteenth Amendment.

We do not stop to point out all of the inequalities in this Act. A few examples will suffice. In Oklahoma, grand larceny is a felony. * * * Larceny is grand larceny when the property taken exceeds $20 in value. * * * Embezzlement is punishable "in the manner prescribed for feloniously stealing property of the value of that embezzled." * * * Hence, he who embezzles property worth more than $20 is guilty of a felony. A clerk who appropriates over $20 from his employer's till * * * and a stranger who steals the same amount are thus both guilty of felonies. If the latter repeats his act and is convicted three times, he may be sterilized. But the clerk is not subject to the pains and penalties of the Act no matter how large his embezzlements nor how frequent his convictions. A person who enters a chicken coop and steals chickens commits a felony; and he may be sterilized if he is thrice convicted. If, however, he is a bailee of the property and fraudulently appropriates it, he is an embezzler. * * * Hence, no matter how habitual his proclivities for embezzlement are and no matter how often his conviction, he may not be sterilized.

It was stated in Buck v. Bell, supra, that the claim that state legislation violates the equal protection clause of the Fourteenth Amendment is "the usual last resort of constitutional arguments." 274 U.S. p. 208. Under our constitutional system the States in determining the reach and scope of particular legislation need not provide "abstract symmetry." * * *

But the instant legislation runs afoul of the equal protection clause, though we give Oklahoma that large deference which the rule of the foregoing cases requires. We are dealing here with legislation which involves one of the basic civil rights of man. Marriage and procreation are fundamental to the very existence and survival of the race. The power to sterilize, if exercised, may have subtle, far-reaching and devastating effects. In evil or reckless hands it can cause races or types which are inimical to the dominant group to wither and disappear. There is no redemption for the individual whom the law touches. Any experiment which the State conducts is to his irreparable injury. He is forever deprived of a basic liberty. We mention these matters not to reexamine the scope of the police power of the States. We advert to them merely in emphasis of our view that strict scrutiny of the classification which a State makes in a sterilization law is essential, lest unwittingly, or otherwise, invidious discriminations are made against groups or types of individuals in violation of the constitutional guaranty of just and equal laws. The guaranty of "equal protection of the laws is a pledge of the protection of equal laws." Yick Wo v. Hopkins, 118 U.S. 356, 369. When the law lays an unequal hand on those who have committed intrinsically the same quality of offense and sterilizes one and not the other, it has made as invidious a discrimination as if it had selected a particular race or nationality for oppressive treatment. Yick Wo v. Hopkins, supra; Gaines v. Canada, 305 U.S. 337. Sterilization of those who have thrice committed grand larceny, with immunity for those who are embezzlers, is a clear, pointed, unmistakable discrimination. Oklahoma makes no attempt to say that he who commits larceny by trespass or trick or fraud has biologically inheritable traits which he who commits embezzlement lacks. * * *

Note: "Pro-Life" v. "Pro-Choice"

Margaret Sanger's efforts assured that Comstock's vice campaign would not long shape the entire nation's reproductive health policy. But statutes of one sort or another criminalizing contraception were to remain on the books until the 1960's. Statutes criminalizing the prescription and use of contraception were declared unconstitutional on privacy grounds in *Griswold v. Connecticut*, 381 U.S. 479 (1965) (married persons) and *Eisenstadt v. Baird*, 405

U.S. 438 (1972) (married or single persons). Laws categorically criminalizing abortion were struck down in *Roe v. Wade*, 410 U.S. 113 (1973) and *Doe v. Bolton*, 410 U.S. 179 (1973).

The legal battles over access to birth control and abortion have continued. Can the state mandate particular "informed consent" procedures and ultrasound imaging to deter abortion? Questions remain over the extent to which pharmacists may refuse to fill prescriptions for birth control. Numerous Food and Drug Administration approved birth control pills, patches, implants, injections and devices are sold in the United States. Some pharmacists decline to fill doctor's prescriptions for any of them. Cf. *Noesen v. Medical Staffing Network, Inc.*, 2006 WL 1529664 (W.D. Wis. 2006). In the Noesen case, a Catholic pharmacist who refused to fill contraception prescriptions sued after losing his job at Wal–Mart for treating customers and co-workers with disrespect. The pharmacist sued, unsuccessfully, maintaining that he was a victim of discrimination on the basis of his religious beliefs. Interestingly, the plaintiff was hired by Wal–Mart as a pharmacist even though he had been disciplined by the State of Wisconsin Pharmacy Examining Board because he "refused to process or refer a young woman's contraceptive prescriptions." On April 13, 2005 the Board found that the man had endangered the "health, welfare or safety of a patient."

The constitutionality of state and federal laws banning the dilation and evacuation and dilation and extraction ("partial birth") abortion methods for second and third trimester pregnancies went before the Supreme Court twice in a half dozen years. See *Stenberg v. Carhart*, 530 U.S. 914 (2000), striking down a Nebraska law outlawing "partial birth" abortions. A constitutional challenge to the federal Partial–Birth Abortion Ban Act of 2003, Pub. L. No. 108–105, 117 Stat. 1201 (to be codified at 18 U.S.C. 1531) went before the Supreme Court in 2006–2007, in two cases, *Planned Parenthood v. Gonzales*, 435 F.3d 1163 (9th Cir. 2006) and *Carhart v. Gonzales*, 413 F.3d 791 (8th Cir. 2005). The Court upheld the federal ban in *Gonzales v. Carhart*, 127 S.Ct. 1610 (2007).

The cases that follow trace the history of legal protection for decision-making about birth control and abortion.

POE v. ULLMAN

367 U.S. 497 (1961), Douglas, J., dissenting.

MR. JUSTICE DOUGLAS, dissenting. * * *

For years the Court struck down social legislation when a particular law did not fit the notions of a majority of Justices as to legislation appropriate for a free enterprise system. Mr. Justice Holmes, dissenting, rightly said that "a constitution is not intended to embody a particular economic theory, whether of paternalism and the organic relation of the citizen to the State or of laissez faire. It is made for people of fundamentally differing views, and the accident of our finding certain opinions natural and familiar or novel and even shocking ought not to conclude our judgment upon the question whether statutes embodying them conflict with the Constitution of the United States." Lochner v. New York, 198 U.S. 45, 75–76.

The error of the old Court, as I see it, was not in entertaining inquiries concerning the constitutionality of social legislation but in applying the standards that it did. * * *

The regime of a free society needs room for vast experimentation. Crises, emergencies, experience at the individual and community levels produce new insights; problems emerge in new dimensions; needs, once never imagined, appear. To stop experimentation and the testing of new decrees and controls is to deprive society of a needed versatility. Yet to say that a legislature may do anything not within a specific guarantee of the Constitution may be as crippling to a free society as to allow it to override specific guarantees so long as what it does fails to shock the sensibilities of a majority of the Court. * * *

The regulation as applied in this case touches the relationship between man and wife. It reaches into the intimacies of the marriage relationship. If we imagine a regime of full enforcement of the law in the manner of an Anthony Comstock, we would reach the point where search warrants issued and officers appeared in bedrooms to find out what went on. It is said that this is not that case. And so it is not. But when the State makes "use" a crime and applies the criminal sanction to man and wife, the State has entered the innermost sanctum of the home. If it can make this law, it can enforce it. And proof of its violation necessarily involves an inquiry into the relations between man and wife.

That is an invasion of the privacy that is implicit in a free society. A noted theologian who conceives of the use of a contraceptive as a "sin" nonetheless admits that a "use" statute such as this enters a forbidden domain. * * *

This notion of privacy is not drawn from the blue. It emanates from the totality of the constitutional scheme under which we live.

"One of the earmarks of the totalitarian understanding of society is that it seeks to make all subcommunities—family, school, business, press, church—completely subject to control by the State. The State then is not one vital institution among others: a policeman, a referee, and a source of initiative for the common good. Instead, it seeks to be coextensive with family and school, press, business community, and the Church, so that all of these component interest groups are, in principle, reduced to organs and agencies of the State. In a democratic political order, this megatherian concept is expressly rejected as out of accord with the democratic understanding of social good, and with the actual make-up of the human community."

I dissent from a dismissal of these cases and our refusal to strike down this law.

GRISWOLD v. CONNECTICUT

381 U.S. 479 (1965).

MR. JUSTICE DOUGLAS delivered the opinion of the Court.

Appellant Griswold is Executive Director of the Planned Parenthood League of Connecticut. Appellant Buxton is a licensed physician and a professor at the Yale Medical School who served as Medical Director for the League at its Center in New Haven—a center open and operating from November 1 to November 10, 1961, when appellants were arrested.

They gave information, instruction, and medical advice to married persons as to the means of preventing conception. They examined the wife and prescribed the best contraceptive device or material for her use. Fees were usually charged, although some couples were serviced free.

The statutes whose constitutionality is involved in this appeal are Sections 53–32 and 54–196 of the General Statutes of Connecticut (1958 rev.). The former provides:

"Any person who uses any drug, medicinal article or instrument for the purpose of preventing conception shall be fined not less than fifty dollars or imprisoned not less than sixty days nor more than one year or be both fined and imprisoned."

Section 54–196 provides:

"Any person who assists, abets, counsels, causes, hires or commands another to commit any offense may be prosecuted and punished as if he were the principal offender."

The appellants were found guilty as accessories and fined $100 each, against the claim that the accessory statute as so applied violated the Fourteenth Amendment. The Appellate Division of the Circuit Court affirmed. The Supreme Court of Errors affirmed that judgment. 151 Conn. 544, 200 A. 2d 479. We noted probable jurisdiction. 379 U.S. 926.

We think that appellants have standing to raise the constitutional rights of the married people with whom they had a professional relationship. * * *

Coming to the merits, we are met with a wide range of questions that implicate the Due Process Clause of the Fourteenth Amendment. Overtones of some arguments suggest that Lochner v. New York, 198 U.S. 45, should be our guide. But we decline that invitation * * *. We do not sit as a super-legislature to determine the wisdom, need, and propriety of laws that touch economic problems, business affairs, or social conditions. This law, however, operates directly on an intimate relation of husband and wife and their physician's role in one aspect of that relation.

The association of people is not mentioned in the Constitution nor in the Bill of Rights. The right to educate a child in a school of the parents' choice—whether public or private or parochial—is also not mentioned. Nor is the right to study any particular subject or any foreign language.

Yet the First Amendment has been construed to include certain of those rights.

By Pierce v. Society of Sisters, supra, the right to educate one's children as one chooses is made applicable to the States by the force of the First and Fourteenth Amendments. By Meyer v. Nebraska, supra, the same dignity is given the right to study the German language in a private school. In other words, the State may not, consistently with the spirit of the First Amendment, contract the spectrum of available knowledge. The right of freedom of speech and press includes not only the right to utter or to print, but the right to distribute, the right to receive, the right to read * * * and freedom of inquiry, freedom of thought, and freedom to teach * * * indeed the freedom of the entire university community. * * * Without those peripheral rights the specific rights would be less secure. And so we reaffirm the principle of the Pierce and the Meyer cases.

In NAACP v. Alabama, 357 U.S. 449, 462, we protected the "freedom to associate and privacy in one's associations," noting that freedom of association was a peripheral First Amendment right. Disclosure of membership lists of a constitutionally valid association, we held, was invalid "as entailing the likelihood of a substantial restraint upon the exercise by petitioner's members of their right to freedom of association." Ibid. In other words, the First Amendment has a penumbra where privacy is protected from governmental intrusion. In like context, we have protected forms of "association" that are not political in the customary sense but pertain to the social, legal, and economic benefit of the members. NAACP v. Button, 371 U.S. 415, 430–431. In Schware v. Board of Bar Examiners, 353 U.S. 232, we held it not permissible to bar a lawyer from practice, because he had once been a member of the Communist Party. The man's "association with that Party" was not shown to be "anything more than a political faith in a political party" (id., at 244) and was not action of a kind proving bad moral character. Id., at 245–246.

Those cases involved more than the "right of assembly"—a right that extends to all irrespective of their race or ideology. De Jonge v. Oregon, 299 U.S. 353. The right of "association," like the right of belief (Board of Education v. Barnette, 319 U.S. 624), is more than the right to attend a meeting; it includes the right to express one's attitudes or philosophies by membership in a group or by affiliation with it or by other lawful means. Association in that context is a form of expression of opinion; and while it is not expressly included in the First Amendment its existence is necessary in making the express guarantees fully meaningful.

The foregoing cases suggest that specific guarantees in the Bill of Rights have penumbras, formed by emanations from those guarantees that help give them life and substance. See Poe v. Ullman, 367 U.S. 497, 516–522 (dissenting opinion). Various guarantees create zones of privacy. The right of association contained in the penumbra of the First Amendment is one, as we have seen. The Third Amendment in its prohibition against the quartering of soldiers "in any house" in time of peace without the consent of the owner is another facet of that privacy. The Fourth Amendment explicitly affirms the "right of the people to be secure in their persons, houses, papers, and effects, against unreasonable searches and seizures." The Fifth Amendment in its Self–Incrimination Clause enables the citizen to create a zone of privacy which government may not force him to surrender to his detriment. The Ninth Amendment provides: "The enumeration in the Constitution, of certain rights, shall not be construed to deny or disparage others retained by the people."

The Fourth and Fifth Amendments were described in Boyd v. United States, 116 U.S. 616, 630, as protection against all governmental invasions "of the sanctity of a man's home and the privacies of life." We recently referred in Mapp v. Ohio, 367 U.S. 643, 656, to the Fourth Amendment as creating a "right to privacy, no less important than any other right carefully and particularly reserved to the people." * * *

We have had many controversies over these penumbral rights of "privacy and repose." * * * These cases bear witness that the right of privacy which presses for recognition here is a legitimate one.

The present case, then, concerns a relationship lying within the zone of privacy created by several fundamental constitutional guarantees. And it concerns a law which, in forbidding the use of contraceptives rather than regulating their manufacture or sale, seeks to achieve its goals by means having a maximum destructive impact upon that relationship. Such a law cannot stand in light of the familiar principle, so often applied by this Court, that a "governmental purpose to control or prevent activities constitutionally subject to state regulation may not be achieved by means which sweep unnecessarily broadly and thereby invade the area of protected freedoms." NAACP v. Alabama, 377 U.S. 288, 307. Would we allow the police to search the sacred precincts of marital bedrooms for telltale signs of the use of contraceptives? The very idea is repulsive to the notions of privacy surrounding the marriage relationship.

We deal with a right of privacy older than the Bill of Rights—older than our political parties, older than our school system. Marriage is a coming together for better or for worse, hopefully enduring, and intimate to the degree of being sacred. It is an association that promotes a way of life, not causes; a harmony in living, not political faiths; a bilateral loyalty, not commercial or social projects. Yet it is an association for as noble a purpose as any involved in our prior decisions. * * * Reversed.

MR. JUSTICE WHITE, concurring in the judgment.

In my view this Connecticut law as applied to married couples deprives them of "liberty" without due process of law, as that concept is used in the Fourteenth Amendment. * * * Suffice it to say that this is not the first time this Court has had occasion to articulate that the liberty entitled to protection under the Fourteenth Amendment includes the right "to marry, establish a home and bring up children," Meyer v. Nebraska * * * and "the liberty * * * to direct the upbringing and education of children," Pierce v. Society of Sisters, 268 U.S. 510, 534–535, and that these are among "the basic civil rights of man." Skinner v. Oklahoma [infra]. These decisions affirm that there is a "realm of family life which the state cannot enter" without substantial justification. Prince v. Massachusetts, 321 U.S. 158, 166. Surely the right invoked in this case, to be free of regulation of the intimacies of the marriage relationship, "come[s] to this Court with a momentum for respect lacking when appeal is made to liberties which derive merely from shifting economic arrangements." * * *

MR. JUSTICE BLACK, with whom MR. JUSTICE STEWART joins, dissenting. * * *

The Court talks about a constitutional "right of privacy" as though there is some constitutional provision or provisions forbidding any law ever to be passed which might abridge the "privacy" of individuals. But there is not. There are, of course, guarantees in certain specific constitutional provisions which are designed in part to protect privacy at certain times and places with respect to certain activities. * * *

I get nowhere in this case by talk about a constitutional "right of privacy" as an emanation from one or more constitutional provisions. I like my privacy as well as the next one, but I am nevertheless compelled to admit that government has a right to invade it unless prohibited by some specific constitutional provision. For these reasons I cannot agree with the Court's judgment and the reasons it gives for holding this Connecticut law unconstitutional. * * *

MR. JUSTICE STEWART, whom MR. JUSTICE BLACK joins, dissenting.

Since 1879 Connecticut has had on its books a law which forbids the use of contraceptives by anyone. I think this is an uncommonly silly law. As a practical matter, the law is obviously unenforceable, except in the oblique context of the present case. As a philosophical matter, I believe the use of contraceptives in the relationship of marriage should be left to personal and private choice, based upon each individual's moral, ethical, and religious beliefs. As a matter of social policy, I think professional counsel about methods of birth control should be available to all, so that each individual's choice can be meaningfully made. But we are not asked in this case to say whether we think this law is unwise, or even asinine. We are asked to hold that it violates the United States Constitution. And that I cannot do. * * *

As to the First, Third, Fourth, and Fifth Amendments, I can find nothing in any of them to invalidate this Connecticut law, even assuming that all those Amendments are fully applicable against the States. It has not even been argued that this is a law "respecting an establishment of religion, or prohibiting the free exercise thereof." And surely, unless the solemn process of constitutional adjudication is to descend to the level of a play on words, there is not involved here any abridgment of "the freedom of speech, or of the press; or the right of the people peaceably to assemble, and to petition the Government for a redress of grievances." No soldier has been quartered in any house. There has been no search, and no seizure. Nobody has been compelled to be a witness against himself.

The Court also quotes the Ninth Amendment, and my Brother Goldberg's concurring opinion relies heavily upon it. But to say that the Ninth Amendment has anything to do with this case is to turn somersaults with history. The Ninth Amendment, like its companion the Tenth, which this Court held "states but a truism that all is retained which has not been surrendered," United States v. Darby, 312 U.S. 100, 124, was framed by James Madison and adopted by the States simply to make clear that the adoption of the Bill of Rights did not alter the plan that the Federal Government was to be a government of express and limited powers, and that all rights and powers not delegated to it were retained by the people and the individual States. * * * What provision of the Constitution, then, does make this state law invalid? The Court says it is the right of privacy "created by several fundamental constitutional guarantees." With all deference, I can find no such general right of privacy in the Bill of Rights, in any other part of the Constitution, or in any case ever before decided by this Court. * * *

EISENSTADT v. BAIRD

405 U.S. 438 (1972).

MR. JUSTICE BRENNAN delivered the opinion of the Court.

Appellee William Baird was convicted at a bench trial in the Massachusetts Superior Court under Massachusetts General Laws Ann., c. 272, Sec. 21, first, for exhibiting contraceptive articles in the course of delivering a lecture on contraception to a group of students at Boston University and, second, for giving a young woman a package of Emko vaginal foam at the close of his address. The Massachusetts Supreme Judicial Court unanimously set aside the conviction for exhibiting contraceptives on the ground that it violated Baird's First Amendment rights, but by a four-to-three vote sustained the conviction for giving away the foam. * * * Baird subsequently filed a petition for a federal writ of habeas corpus, which the District Court dismissed. On appeal, however, the Court of Appeals for the First Circuit vacated the dismissal and remanded the action with directions to grant the writ discharging Baird. * * * We affirm.

Massachusetts General Laws Ann., c. 272, Section 21, under which Baird was convicted, provides a maximum five-year term of imprisonment for "whoever * * * gives away * * * any drug, medicine, instrument or article whatever for the prevention of conception," except as authorized in Section 21A. Under Section 21A, "[a] registered physician may administer to or prescribe for any married person drugs or articles intended for the prevention of pregnancy or conception. [And a] registered pharmacist actually engaged in the business of pharmacy may furnish such drugs or articles to any married person presenting a prescription from a registered physician." * * *

[We hold] that the statute, viewed as a prohibition on contraception per se, violates the rights of single persons under the Equal Protection Clause of the Fourteenth Amendment. * * *

The basic principles governing application of the Equal Protection Clause of the Fourteenth Amendment are familiar. As the Chief Justice only recently explained in Reed v. Reed, 404 U.S. 71, 75–76 (1971):

"In applying that clause, this Court has consistently recognized that the Fourteenth Amendment does not deny to States the power to treat different classes of persons in different ways. Barbier v. Connolly, 113 U.S. 27 (1885); Lindsley v. Natural Carbonic Gas Co., 220 U.S. 61 (1911); Railway Express Agency v. New York, 336 U.S. 106 (1949); McDonald v. Board of Election Commissioners, 394 U.S. 802 (1969). The Equal Protection Clause of that amendment does, however, deny to States the power to legislate that different treatment be accorded to persons placed by a statute into different classes on the basis of criteria wholly unrelated to the objective of that statute. A classification 'must be reasonable, not arbitrary, and must rest upon some ground of difference having a fair and substantial relation to the object of the legislation, so that all persons similarly circumstanced shall be treated alike.' Royster Guano Co. v. Virginia, 253 U.S. 412, 415 (1920)."

The question for our determination in this case is whether there is some ground of difference that rationally explains the different treatment accorded married and unmarried persons under [the] Massachusetts [birth control law]. [W]e conclude that no such ground exists. * * *

[T]he object of the legislation is to discourage premarital sexual intercourse. Conceding that the State could, consistently with the Equal Protection Clause, regard the problems of extramarital and premarital sexual relations as "evils * * * of different dimensions and proportions, requiring different remedies," Williamson v. Lee Optical Inc., 348 U.S. 483, 489 (1955), we cannot agree that the deterrence of premarital sex may reasonably be regarded as the purpose of the Massachusetts law.

It would be plainly unreasonable to assume that Massachusetts has prescribed pregnancy and the birth of an unwanted child as punishment for fornication, which is a misdemeanor under Massachusetts [law] * * *. Aside from the scheme of values that assumption would attribute to the State, it is abundantly clear that the effect of the ban on distribution of contraceptives to unmarried persons has at best a marginal relation to the proffered objective. * * *

Moreover, Sections 21 and 21A on their face have a dubious relation to the State's criminal prohibition on fornication. As the Court of Appeals explained, "Fornication is a misdemeanor [in Massachusetts], entailing a thirty dollar fine, or three months in jail. * * * Violation of the present statute is a felony, punishable by five years in prison. We find it hard to believe that the legislature adopted a statute carrying a five-year penalty for its possible, obviously by no means fully effective, deterrence of the commission of a ninety-day misdemeanor."

Second. * * * Again, we must agree with the Court of Appeals. If health were the rationale of § 21A, the statute would be both discriminatory and overbroad. * * * If there is need to have a physician prescribe (and a pharmacist dispense) contraceptives, that need is as great for unmarried persons as for married persons." * * *

Third. If the Massachusetts statute cannot be upheld as a deterrent to fornication or as a health measure, may it, nevertheless, be sustained simply as a prohibition on contraception? * * *

We need not and do not, however, decide that important question in this case because, whatever the rights of the individual to access to contraceptives may be, the rights must be the same for the unmarried and the married alike.

If under Griswold the distribution of contraceptives to married persons cannot be prohibited, a ban on distribution to unmarried persons would be equally impermissible. It is true that in Griswold the right of privacy in question inhered in the marital relationship. Yet the marital couple is not an independent entity with a mind and heart of its own, but an association of two individuals each with a separate intellectual and emotional makeup. If the right of privacy means anything, it is the right of the individual, married or single, to be free from unwarranted governmental intrusion into matters so fundamentally affecting a person as the decision whether to bear or beget a child. See Stanley v. Georgia, 394 U.S. 557 (1969). * * *

We hold that by providing dissimilar treatment for married and unmarried persons who are similarly situated, Massachusetts General Laws Ann., c. 272, Sections 21 and 21A, violate the Equal Protection Clause. The judgment of the Court of Appeals is Affirmed.

ROE v. WADE
410 U.S. 113 (1973).

MR. JUSTICE BLACKMUN delivered the opinion of the Court. * * *

The Texas statutes that concern us here are Arts. 1191–1194 and 1196 of the State's Penal Code. These make it a crime to "procure an abortion," as therein defined, or to attempt one, except with respect to "an abortion procured or attempted by medical advice for the purpose of saving the life of the mother." Similar statutes are in existence in a majority of the States.

Texas first enacted a criminal abortion statute in 1854. * * * This was soon modified into language that has remained substantially unchanged to the present time. * * *

Jane Roe, a single woman who was residing in Dallas County, Texas, instituted this federal action in March 1970 against the District Attorney of the county. She sought a declaratory judgment that the Texas criminal abortion statutes were unconstitutional on their face, and an injunction restraining the defendant from enforcing the statutes.

Roe alleged that she was unmarried and pregnant; that she wished to terminate her pregnancy by an abortion "performed by a competent, licensed physician, under safe, clinical conditions"; that she was unable to get a "legal" abortion in Texas because her life did not appear to be threatened by the continuation of her pregnancy; and that she could not afford to travel to another jurisdiction in order to secure a legal abortion under safe conditions. She claimed that the Texas statutes were unconstitutionally vague and that they abridged her right of personal privacy * * *. By an amendment to her complaint Roe purported to sue "on behalf of herself and all other women" similarly situated. * * *

It perhaps is not generally appreciated that the restrictive criminal abortion laws in effect in a majority of States today are of relatively recent vintage. Those laws, generally proscribing abortion or its attempt at any time during pregnancy except when necessary to preserve the pregnant woman's life, are not of ancient or even of common-law origin. Instead, they derive from statutory changes effected, for the most part, in the latter half of the 19th century. * * *

Connecticut, the first State to enact abortion legislation, adopted in 1821 that part of Lord Ellenborough's Act that related to a woman "quick with child." The death penalty was not imposed. Abortion before quickening [i.e., fetal movement] was made a crime in that State only in 1860. In 1828, New York enacted legislation that, in two respects, was to serve as a model for early anti-abortion statutes. First, while barring destruction of an unquickened fetus as well as a quick fetus, it made the former only a misdemeanor, but the latter second-degree manslaughter. Second, it incorporated a concept of therapeutic abortion by providing that an abortion was excused if it "shall have been necessary to preserve the life of such mother, or shall have been advised by two physicians to be necessary for such purpose." By 1840, when Texas had received the common law, only eight American States had statutes dealing with abortion. It was not until after the War Between the States that legislation began generally to replace the common law. Most of these initial statutes dealt severely with abortion after quickening but were lenient with it before quickening. Most punished attempts equally with completed abortions. While many statutes included the exception for an abortion thought by one or more physicians to be necessary to save the mother's life, that provision soon disappeared and the typical law required that the procedure actually be necessary for that purpose.

Gradually, in the middle and late 19th century the quickening distinction disappeared from the statutory law of most States and the degree of the offense and the penalties were increased. By the end of the 1950's, a large majority of the jurisdictions banned abortion, however and whenever performed, unless done to save or preserve the life of the mother. The exceptions, Alabama and the District of Columbia, permitted abortion to preserve the mother's health. Three States permitted abortions that were not "unlawfully" performed or that were not "without lawful justification," leaving interpretation of those standards to the courts. In the past several years, however, a trend toward liberalization of abortion statutes has resulted in adoption, by about one-third of the States, of less stringent laws, most of them patterned after the ALI Model Penal Code, Section 230.3 * * *.

It is thus apparent that at common law, at the time of the adoption of our Constitution, and throughout the major portion of the 19th century, abortion was viewed with less disfavor than under most American statutes currently in effect. Phrasing it another way, a woman enjoyed a substantially broader right to terminate a pregnancy than she does in most States today. At least with respect to the early stage of pregnancy, and very possibly without such a limitation, the opportunity to make this choice was present in this country well into the 19th century. Even later, the law continued for some time to treat less punitively an abortion procured in early pregnancy. * * *

The anti-abortion mood prevalent in this country in the late 19th century was shared by the medical profession. Indeed, the attitude of the profession may have played a significant role in the enactment of stringent criminal abortion legislation during that period. * * *

Three reasons have been advanced to explain historically the enactment of criminal abortion laws in the 19th century and to justify their continued existence.

It has been argued occasionally that these laws were the product of a Victorian social concern to discourage illicit sexual conduct. Texas, however, does not advance this justification in the present case, and it appears that no court or commentator has taken the argument seriously. * * *

A second reason is concerned with abortion as a medical procedure. When most criminal abortion laws were first enacted, the procedure was a hazardous one for the woman. This was particularly true prior to the development of antisepsis. Antiseptic techniques, of course, were based on discoveries by Lister, Pasteur, and others first announced in 1867, but were not generally accepted and employed until about the turn of the century. * * * Thus, it has been argued that a State's real concern in enacting a criminal abortion law was to protect the pregnant woman, that is, to restrain her from submitting to a procedure that placed her life in serious jeopardy. * * *

The third reason is the State's interest—some phrase it in terms of duty—in protecting prenatal life. Some of the argument for this justification rests on the theory that a new human life is present from the moment of conception. The State's interest and general obligation to protect life then extends, it is argued, to prenatal life. Only when the life of the pregnant mother herself is at stake, balanced against the life she carries within her, should the interest of the embryo or fetus not prevail. Logically, of course, a legitimate state interest in this area need not stand or fall on acceptance of the belief that life begins at conception or at some other point prior to live birth. In assessing the State's interest, recognition may be given to the less rigid claim that as long as at least potential life is involved, the State may assert interests beyond the protection of the pregnant woman alone. * * *

The Constitution does not explicitly mention any right of privacy. In a line of decisions, however, going back perhaps as far as Union Pacific R. Co. v. Botsford * * * (1891), the Court has recognized that a right of personal privacy, or a guarantee of certain areas or zones of privacy, does exist under the Constitution. In varying contexts, the Court or individual Justices have, indeed, found at least the roots of that right in the First Amendment, Stanley v. Georgia, 394 U.S. 557, 564 (1969); in the Fourth and Fifth Amendments, Terry v. Ohio, 392 U.S. 1, 8–9 (1968), Katz v. United States, 389 U.S. 347, 350 (1967), Boyd v. United States, 116 U.S. 616 (1886), see Olmstead v. United States, 277 U.S. 438, 478 (1928) (Brandeis, J., dissenting); in the penumbras of the Bill of Rights, Griswold v. Connecticut, 381 U.S., at 484–485; in the Ninth Amendment, id., at 486 (Goldberg, J., concurring); or in the concept of liberty guaranteed by the first section of the Fourteenth Amendment, see Meyer v. Nebraska, 262 U.S. 390, 399 (1923). These decisions make it clear that only personal rights that can be deemed "fundamental" or "implicit in the concept of ordered liberty," Palko v. Connecticut, 302 U.S. 319, 325 (1937), are included in this guarantee of personal privacy. They also make it clear that the right has some extension to activities relating to marriage, Loving v. Virginia, 388 U.S. 1, 12 (1967); procreation, Skinner v. Oklahoma, 316 U.S. 535, 541–542 (1942); contraception, Eisenstadt v. Baird, 405 U.S., at 453–454; id., at 460, 463–465 (WHITE, J., concurring in result); family relationships, Prince v. Massachusetts, 321 U.S. 158, 166 (1944); and child rearing and education, Pierce v. Society of Sisters, 268 U.S. 510, 535 (1925), Meyer v. Nebraska * * *.

This right of privacy, whether it be founded in the Fourteenth Amendment's concept of personal liberty and restrictions upon state action, as we feel it is, or, as the District Court determined, in the Ninth Amendment's reservation of rights to the people, is broad enough to encompass a woman's decision whether or not to terminate her pregnancy. The detriment that the State would impose upon the pregnant woman by denying this choice altogether is apparent. Specific and direct harm medically diagnosable even in early pregnancy may be involved. Maternity, or additional offspring, may force upon the woman a distressful life and future. Psychological harm may be imminent. Mental and physical health may be taxed by child care. There is also the distress, for all concerned, associated with the unwanted child, and there is the problem of bringing a child into a family already unable, psychologically and otherwise, to care for it. In other cases, as in this one, the additional difficulties and continuing stigma of unwed motherhood may be involved. All these are factors the woman and her responsible physician necessarily will consider in consultation.

On the basis of elements such as these, appellant and some amici argue that the woman's right is absolute and that she is entitled to terminate her pregnancy at whatever time, in whatever way, and for whatever reason she alone chooses. With this we do not agree. Appellant's arguments that Texas either has no valid interest at all in regulating the abortion decision, or no interest strong enough to support any limitation upon the woman's sole determination, are unpersuasive. The Court's decisions recognizing a right of privacy also acknowledge that some state regulation in areas protected by that right is appropriate. As noted above, a State may properly assert important interests in safeguarding health, in maintaining medical standards, and in protecting potential life. At some point in pregnancy, these respective interests become sufficiently compelling to sustain regulation of the factors that govern the abortion decision. The privacy right involved, therefore, cannot be said to be absolute. * * *

We, therefore, conclude that the right of personal privacy includes the abortion decision, but that this right is not unqualified and must be considered against important state interests in regulation. * * *

The appellee and certain amici argue that the fetus is a "person" within the language and meaning of the Fourteenth Amendment. In support of this, they outline at length and in detail the well-known facts of fetal development. If this suggestion of personhood is established, the appellant's case, of course, collapses, for the fetus' right to life would then be guaranteed specifically by the Amendment. * * *

The Constitution does not define "person" in so many words. Section 1 of the Fourteenth Amendment contains three references to "person." The first, in defining "citizens," speaks of "persons born or naturalized in the United States." The word also appears both in the Due Process Clause and in the Equal Protection Clause. "Person" is used in other places in the Constitution * * *. But in nearly all these instances, the use of the word is such that it has application only postnatally. None indicates, with any assurance, that it has any possible pre-natal application.

All this, together with our observation, supra, that throughout the major portion of the 19th century prevailing legal abortion practices were far freer than they are today, persuades us that the word "person," as used in the Fourteenth Amendment, does not include the unborn. This is in accord with the results reached in those few cases where the issue has been squarely presented. * * *

The pregnant woman cannot be isolated in her privacy. She carries an embryo and, later, a fetus, if one accepts the medical definitions of the developing young in the human uterus. * * * The situation therefore is inherently different from marital intimacy, or bedroom possession of obscene material, or marriage, or procreation, or education, with which Eisenstadt and Griswold, Stanley, Loving, Skinner, and Pierce and Meyer were respectively concerned. As we have intimated above, it is reasonable and appropriate for a State to decide that at some point in time another interest, that of health of the mother or that of potential human life, becomes significantly involved. The woman's privacy is no longer sole and any right of privacy she possesses must be measured accordingly.

Texas urges that, apart from the Fourteenth Amendment, life begins at conception and is present throughout pregnancy, and that, therefore, the State has a compelling interest in protecting that life from and after conception. We need not resolve the difficult question of when life begins. When those trained in the respective disciplines of medicine, philosophy, and theology are unable to arrive at any consensus, the judiciary, at this point in the development of man's knowledge, is not in a position to speculate as to the answer.

It should be sufficient to note briefly the wide divergence of thinking on this most sensitive and difficult question. There has always been strong support for the view that life does not begin until live birth. * * *

In areas other than criminal abortion, the law has been reluctant to endorse any theory that life, as we recognize it, begins before live birth or to accord legal rights to the unborn except in narrowly defined situations and except when the rights are contingent upon live birth. For example, the traditional rule of tort law denied recovery for prenatal injuries even though the child was born alive. That rule has been changed in almost every jurisdiction. [But] the unborn have never been recognized in the law as persons in the whole sense. * * *

In view of all this, we do not agree that, by adopting one theory of life, Texas may override the rights of the pregnant woman that are at stake. We repeat, however, that the State does have an important and legitimate interest in preserving and protecting the health of the pregnant woman, whether she be a resident of the State or a nonresident who seeks medical consultation and treatment there, and that it has still another important and legitimate interest in protecting the potentiality of human life. These interests are separate and distinct. Each grows in substantiality as the woman approaches term and, at a point during pregnancy, each becomes ''compelling.''

With respect to the State's important and legitimate interest in the health of the mother, the ''compelling'' point, in the light of present medical knowledge, is at approximately the end of the first trimester. This is so because of the now-established medical fact, referred to above at 149, that until the end of the first trimester mortality in abortion may be less than mortality in normal childbirth. It follows that, from and after this point, a State may regulate the abortion procedure to the extent that the regulation reasonably relates to the preservation and protection of maternal health. Examples of permissible state regulation in this area are requirements as to the qualifications of the person who is to perform the abortion; as to the licensure of that person; as to the facility in which the procedure is to be performed, that is, whether it must be a hospital or may be a clinic or some other place of less-than-hospital status; as to the licensing of the facility; and the like.

This means, on the other hand, that, for the period of pregnancy prior to this ''compelling'' point, the attending physician, in consultation with his patient, is free to determine, without regulation by the State, that, in his medical judgment, the patient's pregnancy should be terminated. If that decision is reached, the judgment may be effectuated by an abortion free of interference by the State.

With respect to the State's important and legitimate interest in potential life, the "compelling" point is at viability. This is so because the fetus then presumably has the capability of meaningful life outside the mother's womb. State regulation protective of fetal life after viability thus has both logical and biological justifications. If the State is interested in protecting fetal life after viability, it may go so far as to proscribe abortion during that period, except when it is necessary to preserve the life or health of the mother.

Measured against these standards, Art. 1196 of the Texas Penal Code, in restricting legal abortions to those "procured or attempted by medical advice for the purpose of saving the life of the mother," sweeps too broadly. The statute makes no distinction between abortions performed early in pregnancy and those performed later, and it limits to a single reason, "saving" the mother's life, the legal justification for the procedure. The statute, therefore, cannot survive the constitutional attack made upon it here. * * *

To summarize and to repeat:

1. A state criminal abortion statute of the current Texas type, that excepts from criminality only a lifesaving procedure on behalf of the mother, without regard to pregnancy stage and without recognition of the other interests involved, is violative of the Due Process Clause of the Fourteenth Amendment.

(a) For the stage prior to approximately the end of the first trimester, the abortion decision and its effectuation must be left to the medical judgment of the pregnant woman's attending physician.

(b) For the stage subsequent to approximately the end of the first trimester, the State, in promoting its interest in the health of the mother, may, if it chooses, regulate the abortion procedure in ways that are reasonably related to maternal health.

(c) For the stage subsequent to viability, the State in promoting its interest in the potentiality of human life may, if it chooses, regulate, and even proscribe, abortion except where it is necessary, in appropriate medical judgment, for the preservation of the life or health of the mother.

2. The state may define the term "physician," as it has been employed in the preceding paragraphs of this Part XI of this opinion, to mean only a physician currently licensed by the State, and may proscribe any abortion by a person who is not a physician as so defined.

In Doe v. Bolton, [Roe's companion case], procedural requirements contained in one of the modern abortion statutes are considered. That opinion and this one, of course, are to be read together.

This holding, we feel, is consistent with the relative weights of the respective interests involved, with the lessons and examples of medical and legal history, with the lenity of the common law, and with the demands of the profound problems of the present day. The decision leaves the State free to place increasing restrictions on abortion as the period of pregnancy lengthens, so long as those restrictions are tailored to the recognized state interests. The decision vindicates the right of the physician to administer medical treatment according to his professional judgment up to the points where important state interests provide compelling justifications for intervention. Up to those points, the abortion decision in all its aspects is inherently, and primarily, a medical decision, and basic responsibility for it must rest with the physician. If an individual practitioner abuses the privilege of exercising proper medical judgment, the usual remedies, judicial and intra-professional, are available. * * * It is so ordered.

MR. JUSTICE REHNQUIST, dissenting. * * *

The Court's opinion decides that a State may impose virtually no restriction on the performance of abortions during the first trimester of pregnancy. * * *

I would reach a conclusion opposite to that reached by the Court. I have difficulty in concluding, as the Court does, that the right of "privacy" is involved in this case. Texas, by the statute here challenged, bars the performance of a medical abortion by a licensed physician on a plaintiff such as Roe. A transaction resulting in an operation such as this is not "private" in the ordinary usage of that word. Nor is the "privacy" that the Court finds here even a distant relative of the freedom from searches and seizures protected by the Fourth Amendment to the Constitution, which the Court has referred to as embodying a right to privacy. Katz v. United States, 389 U.S. 347 (1967).

If the Court means by the term "privacy" no more than that the claim of a person to be free from unwanted state regulation of consensual transactions may be a form of "liberty" protected by the Fourteenth Amendment, there is no doubt that similar claims have been upheld in our earlier decisions on the basis of that liberty. * * * The test traditionally applied in the area of social and economic legislation is whether or not a law such as that challenged has a rational relation to a valid state objective. Williamson v. Lee Optical Inc., 348 U.S. 483, 491 (1955). * * * If the Texas statute were to prohibit an abortion even where the mother's life is in jeopardy, I have little doubt that such a statute would lack a rational relation to a valid state objective under the test stated in Williamson, supra. But the Court's sweeping invalidation of any restrictions on abortion during the first trimester is impossible to justify under that standard, and the conscious weighing of competing factors that the Court's opinion apparently substitutes for the established test is far more appropriate to a legislative judgment than to a judicial one.

While the Court's opinion quotes from the dissent of Mr. Justice Holmes in Lochner v. New York, 198 U.S. 45, 74 (1905), the result it reaches is more closely attuned to the majority opinion of Mr. Justice Peckham in that case. As in Lochner and similar cases applying substantive due process standards to economic and social welfare legislation, the adoption of the compelling state interest standard will inevitably require this Court to examine the legislative policies and pass on the wisdom of these policies in the very process of deciding whether a particular state interest put forward may or may not be "compelling." The decision here to break pregnancy into three distinct terms and to outline the permissible restrictions the State may impose in each one, for example, partakes more of judicial legislation than it does of a determination of the intent of the drafters of the Fourteenth Amendment.

The fact that a majority of the States reflecting, after all, the majority sentiment in those States, have had restrictions on abortions for at least a century is a strong indication, it seems to me, that the asserted right to an abortion is not "so rooted in the traditions and conscience of our people as to be ranked as fundamental," Snyder v. Massachusetts, 291 U.S. 97, 105 (1934). Even today, when society's views on abortion are changing, the very existence of the debate is evidence that the "right" to an abortion is not so universally accepted as the appellant would have us believe.

To reach its result, the Court necessarily has had to find within the scope of the Fourteenth Amendment a right that was apparently completely unknown to the drafters of the Amendment. * * *

There apparently was no question concerning the validity of this provision or of any of the other state statutes when the Fourteenth Amendment was adopted. The only conclusion possible from this history is that the drafters did not intend to have the Fourteenth Amendment withdraw from the States the power to legislate with respect to this matter. * * *

Even if one were to agree that the case that the Court decides were here, and that the enunciation of the substantive constitutional law in the Court's opinion were proper, the actual disposition of the case by the Court is still difficult to justify. The Texas statute is struck down in toto, even though the Court apparently concedes that at later periods of pregnancy Texas might impose these selfsame statutory limitations on abortion. My understanding of past practice is that a statute found to be invalid as applied to a particular plaintiff, but not unconstitutional as a whole, is not simply "struck down" but is, instead, declared unconstitutional as applied to the fact situation before the Court. * * *

For all of the foregoing reasons, I respectfully dissent.

NOTE: PERIOD PIECES

Is *Roe v. Wade* well-reasoned? Poorly reasoned? Nearly everyone agrees it could have been better reasoned, see Jack Balkin (ed.), *What Roe v. Wade*

Should Have Said: The Nation's Top Legal Experts Rewrite America's Most Controversial Decision (2005). What role did *Griswold* play in the decision? The two excerpts that follow are from law review articles that appeared soon after *Roe. v. Wade*. In one, John Hart Ely questioned the reasoning of *Roe*, contending that it was a resurrection of a discredited, "substantive due process", jurisprudence. The *Roe* Court illegitimately struck down laws it considered bad social policy, Ely suggested. In the other, Philip B. Heymann and Douglas E. Barzelay make the case for *Roe*'s legitimacy. They argued that the decision flows easily from the Court's respected precedents.

JOHN HART ELY, THE WAGES OF CRYING WOLF: A COMMENT ON ROE v. WADE

82 Yale L.J. 920 (1973).

Let us not underestimate what is at stake: Having an unwanted child can go a long way toward ruining a woman's life. And at bottom Roe signals the Court's judgment that this result cannot be justified by any good that anti-abortion legislation accomplishes. This surely is an understandable conclusion—indeed it is one with which I agree—but ordinarily the Court claims no mandate to second-guess legislative balances, at least not when the Constitution has designated neither of the values in conflict as entitled to special protection. * * *

Were I a legislator I would vote for a statute very much like the one the court ends up drafting. I hope this reaction reflects more than the psychological phenomenon that keeps bombardiers sane—the fact that it is somehow easier to "terminate" those you cannot see—and I am inclined to think it does: that the mother, unlike the unborn child, has begun to imagine a future for herself strikes me as morally quite significant. But God knows I'm not happy with that resolution. Abortion is too much like infanticide on the one hand, and too much like contraception on the other, to leave one comfortable with any answer; and the moral issue it poses is as fiendish as any philosopher's hypothetical. * * *

From its 1905 decision in Lochner v. New York into the 1930's the Court, frequently though not always under the rubric of "liberty of contract," employed the Due Process Clauses of the Fourteenth and Fifth Amendments to invalidate a good deal of legislation. * * *

It may be, however—at least it is not the sort of claim one can disprove—that the "right to an abortion," or noneconomic rights generally, accord more closely with "this generation's idealization of America" than the "rights" asserted in either Lochner or Dandridge. But that attitude, of course, is precisely the point of the Lochner philosophy, which would grant unusual protection to those "rights" that somehow seem most pressing, regardless of whether the Constitution suggests any special solicitude for them. The Constitution has little say about contract, less about abortion, and those who would speculate about which the framers would have been more likely to protect may not be pleased with the answer. The Court continues to disavow the philosophy of Lochner. Yet as

Justice Stewart's concurrence admits, it is impossible candidly to regard Roe as the product of anything else.

That alone should be enough to damn it. Criticism of the Lochner philosophy has been virtually universal and will not be rehearsed here. I would, however, like to suggest briefly that although Lochner and Roe are twins to be sure, they are not identical. While I would hesitate to argue the one is more defensible than the other in terms of judicial style, there are differences in that regard that suggest Roe may turn out to be the more dangerous precedent.

All the "superimposition of the Court's own value choice" talk is, of course, the characterization of others and not the language of Lochner or its progeny. Indeed, those cases did not argue that "liberty of contract" was a preferred constitutional freedom, but rather represented it as merely one among the numerous aspects of "liberty" the Fourteenth Amendment protects, therefore requiring of its inhibitors a "rational" defense. * * *

Thus the test Lochner and its progeny purported to apply is that which would theoretically control the same questions today: whether a plausible argument can be made that the legislative action furthers some permissible governmental goal. The trouble, of course, is they misapplied it. Roe, on the other had, is quite explicit that the right to an abortion is a "fundamental" one, requiring not merely a "rational" defense for its inhibition but rather a "compelling" one. * * *

I do wish "Wolf!" hadn't been cried so often. When I suggest to my students that Roe lacks even colorable support in the constitutional text, history, or any other appropriate source of constitutional doctrine, they tell me they've heard all that before. When I point out they haven't heard it before from me, I can't really blame them for smiling.

But at least crying "Wolf!" doesn't influence the wolves; crying "Lochner!" may. Of course the Warren Court was aggressive in enforcing its ideals of liberty and equality. But by and large, it attempted to defend its decisions in terms of inferences from values the Constitution marks as special. Its inferences were often controversial, but just as often our profession's prominent criticism deigned not to address them on their terms and contented itself with assertions that the Court was indulging in sheer acts of will, ramming its personal preferences down the country's throat—that it was, in a word, Lochnering. One possible judicial response to this style of criticism would be to conclude that one might as well be hanged for a sheep as a goat: So long as you're going to be told, no matter what you say, that all you do is Lochner, you might as well Lochner. Another, perhaps more likely in a new appointee, might be to reason that since Lochnering has so long been standard procedure, "just one more" (in a good cause, of course) can hardly matter. Actual reactions, of course, are not likely to be this self-conscious, but the critical style of offhand dismissal may have taken its toll nonetheless. * * *

PHILIP B. HEYMANN AND DOUGLAS E. BARZELAY, THE FOREST AND THE TREES: ROE v. WADE AND ITS CRITICS

53 B.U.L. Rev. 775 (1973).

The thesis of this article is that the Court's opinion in Roe is amply justified both by precedent and by those principles that have long guided the Court in making the ever-delicate determination of when it must tell a state that it may not pursue certain measures, because to do so would impinge on those rights of individuals that the Constitution explicitly or implicitly protects. The language of the Court's opinion in Roe too often obscures the full strength of the four-step argument that underlies its decision.

(1) Under the fourteenth amendment to the Constitution, there are certain interests of individuals, long called "fundamental" in judicial decisions, that a state cannot abridge without a very good reason.

(2) The Court has never limited this set of "fundamental" interests to those explicitly mentioned elsewhere in the Constitution.

(3) One set of nonenumerated but fundamental rights, which the Court has recognized for 50 years but has only more recently begun calling aspects of "privacy," includes rights of individual choice as to marriage, procreation and child rearing.

(4) Since the issue of a right to terminate a pregnancy falls squarely within this long-established area of special judicial concern, the Court was obligated to determine in Roe whether the states did in fact have a sufficiently compelling reason for abridging the individual's freedom of choice as to abortion. * * *

The specific protection afforded particular rights has gone far beyond the explicit provisions of the first eight amendments. The right of association is not mentioned in the first amendment, but the Court has deemed its protection implicit in the several guarantees of that amendment. The Court has also treated the right to travel as fundamental, requiring a showing of a compelling interest to support a state's burdening of the right. Yet no such right is specified in the Constitution; it is apparently enough that it has come to be recognized in a series of cases as "fundamental to the concept of our Federal Union." Indeed, the Court went even further in the instance of voting rights. While acknowledging that there is no constitutional right, explicit or implicit, to vote in state elections, it nonetheless found a constitutionally protected right "to participate in elections on an equal basis with other citizens in the jurisdiction" against which state interference must be strictly scrutinized. This is so, apparently, because the question of distribution of the franchise goes to the heart of the legitimacy of government, posing "the danger of denying, some citizens any effective voice in the governmental affairs which substantially affect their lives."

In short, the criticism that has been directed at the Court's opinion in Roe is not and could hardly be addressed to the first two steps of its argument. It is generally conceded that there are certain interests of individuals that a state cannot abridge without very good reason and the these interests have not been limited to those that were stated explicitly by the Framers of the fourteenth amendment nor even to this category as supplemented by a judicial power to incorporate some of the first eight amendments. What was said by Justice Harlan in his dissent in Poe v. Ullman remains true a dozen years later. * * *

Skinner v. Oklahoma involved a state law compelling sterilization of "habitual criminals." While framing the case in equal protection terms, the Court recognized the presence of an interest that calls for a much stricter scrutiny than that normally given in equal protection cases: "We are dealing here with legislation which involves one of the basic civil rights of man. Marriage and procreation are fundamental to the very existence and survival of the race." This sentiment was echoed in Griswold v. Connecticut, where the Court noted that "[w]e deal with a right of privacy older than the Bill of Rights * * *." In Griswold, statutes that forbade the use of contraceptives by married couples, and the giving of advice as to such use, were struck down as a violation of the marital right to privacy. While seven of the Justices agreed as to the existence of such a right, they divided as to its source. Nonetheless it is apparent that, whatever the source, the right of a married couple to make its own decisions about contraception was clearly linked with the zone of protection from unwarranted government intrusion in familial and procreative affairs established by Meyer, Pierce, Prince and Skinner.

Two years later, in Loving v. Virginia, the Court reaffirmed the protected status of marital interests under the due process clause, noting that "[t]he freedom to marry has long been recognized as one of the vital personal rights essential to the orderly pursuit of happiness by free men." Marriage interests were also at the core of the due process protection in Boddie v. Connecticut, in which the Court held that access to the courts in a divorce case could not, in contrast to such access in an ordinary civil suit, be conditioned on the payment of fees by an indigent.

Contraception was again a central issue in Eisenstadt v. Baird, in which a number of the questions left open in Griswold were raised. The Massachusetts statutes, unlike those considered in Griswold, proscribed distribution of contraceptives, although not in all circumstances. The decision purported to find the statutes in violation of the equal protection clause, thereby leaving open the issue of whether states could totally forbid distribution of contraceptives. In fact the opinion made it clear that any regulation of contraception would be very strictly scrutinized. * * *

In this light, the long line of precedent in this area under the fourteenth amendment is entirely principled. For the Court to have declined strict review of state legislation that limits the private right to choose whom to marry and whether to raise a family, or decide within wide bounds how to rear one's children, would have been to leave the most basic substructure of our society and government subject to change at political whim. To have treated these matters as rather remote emanations of protections found in the first amendment or elsewhere in the Bill of Rights would have been disingenuous at best, ineffective at worst.

The similarity of the protected rights in the areas of marriage, procreation and child rearing to the expressly protected rights in the area of religion is striking. Like religious beliefs, beliefs in these areas are often deeply held, involving loyalties fully as powerful as those that bind the citizen to the state. Decisions on these matters tend to affect the quality of an entire lifetime, and may not easily be reversed. The choice of whom to marry or whether or not to have a child, once taken, will have as strong an impact on the life patterns of the individuals involved for years to come as any adoption of a religious belief or viewpoint. Decisions of families in the area of "privacy" like decisions of individuals in the area of religion, cannot easily be controlled by the state; and the devices needed for effective enforcement of state policy may themselves be so intrusive as to be deeply offensive. At the same time, the impact of an individual's decisions on questions of marriage, procreation and child rearing diminishes greatly beyond the setting of the family itself, just as most religious practices affect primarily those who adopt and engage in them. In other words, the impact on such decisions falls largely within one of the basic units of our society and thus does not involve the powerful interest of society in regulating the relationships among its familial and individual units.

PLANNED PARENTHOOD OF CENTRAL MISSOURI v. DANFORTH

428 U.S. 52 (1976).

MR. JUSTICE BLACKMUN delivered the opinion of the Court. * * *

In Roe and Doe we specifically reserved decision on the question whether a requirement for consent by the father of the fetus, by the spouse, or by the parents, or a parent, of an unmarried minor, may be constitutionally imposed. 410 U.S., at 165 n. 67. We now hold that the State may not constitutionally require the consent of the spouse.

Clearly, since the State cannot regulate or proscribe abortion during the first stage, when the physician and his patient make that decision, the State cannot delegate authority to any particular person, even the spouse, to prevent abortion during that same period.

We are not unaware of the deep and proper concern and interest that a devoted and protective husband has in his wife's pregnancy and in the growth and development of the fetus she is carrying. Neither has this Court failed to appreciate the importance of the marital relationship in our society.

It seems manifest that, ideally, the decision to terminate a pregnancy should be one concurred in by both the wife and her husband. No marriage may be viewed as harmonious or successful if the marriage partners are fundamentally divided on so important and vital an issue. But it is difficult to believe that the goal of fostering mutuality and trust in a marriage, and of strengthening the marital relationship and the marriage institution, will be achieved by giving the husband a veto power exercisable for any reason whatsoever or for no reason at all. * * *

We recognize, of course, that when a woman, with the approval of her physician but without the approval of her husband, decides to terminate her pregnancy, it could be said that she is acting unilaterally. The obvious fact is that when the wife and the husband disagree on this decision, the view of only one of the two marriage partners can prevail. Inasmuch as it is the woman who physically bears the child and who is the more directly and immediately affected by the pregnancy, as between the two, the balance weighs in her favor. * * *

[Parents of minors may not be given the power to veto an abortion.] * * * Just as with the requirement of consent from the spouse, so here, the State does not have the constitutional authority to give a third party an absolute, and possibly arbitrary, veto over the decision of the physician and his patient to terminate the patient's pregnancy, regardless of the reason for withholding the consent.

Constitutional rights do not mature and come into being magically only when one attains the state-defined age of majority. Minors, as well as adults, are protected by the Constitution and possess constitutional rights.

One suggested interest is the safeguarding of the family unit and of parental authority. * * * It is difficult, however, to conclude that providing a parent with absolute power to overrule a determination, made by the physician and his minor patient, to terminate the patient's pregnancy will serve to strengthen the family unit. Neither is it likely that such veto power will enhance parental authority or control where the minor and the nonconsenting parent are so fundamentally in conflict and the very existence of the pregnancy already has fractured the family structure. Any independent interest the parent may have in the termination of the minor daughter's pregnancy is no more weighty than the right of privacy of the competent minor mature enough to have become pregnant.

MAHER v. ROE

432 U.S. 464 (1977).

MR. JUSTICE POWELL delivered the opinion of the Court.

[A Connecticut statute provided state medical assistance for poor women's pregnancies, but not their abortions. The Court holds that a state need not pay for nontherapeutic abortions when it pays for childbirth].

The Constitution imposes no obligation on the States to pay the pregnancy-related medical expenses of indigent women, or indeed to pay any of the medical expenses of indigents. * * * This challenge to the classifications established by the Connecticut regulation presents a question arising under the Equal Protection Clause of the Fourteenth Amendment. The basic framework of analysis of such a claim is well settled: "We must decide, first, whether [state legislation] operates to the disadvantage of some suspect class or impinges upon a fundamental right explicitly or implicitly protected by the Constitution, thereby requiring strict judicial scrutiny * * *. If not, the [legislative] scheme must still be examined to determine whether it rationally furthers some legitimate, articulated state purpose and therefore does not constitute an invidious discrimination * * *." San Antonio School Dist. v. Rodriguez, 411 U.S. 1, 17 (1973). * * *

This case involves no discrimination against a suspect class. An indigent woman desiring an abortion does not come within the limited category of disadvantaged classes so recognized by our cases. Nor does the fact that the impact of the regulation falls upon those who cannot pay lead to a different conclusion. * * *

Our conclusion signals no retreat from Roe or the cases applying it. There is a basic difference between direct state interference with a protected activity and state encouragement of an alternative activity consonant with legislative policy. Constitutional concerns are greatest when the State attempts to impose its will by force of law; the State's power to encourage actions deemed to be in the public interest is necessarily far broader. * * *

MR. JUSTICE BRENNAN, with whom MR. JUSTICE MARSHALL and MR. JUSTICE BLACKMUN join, dissenting. * * *

[A] distressing insensitivity to the plight of impoverished pregnant women is inherent in the Court's analysis. The stark reality for too many, not just "some," indigent pregnant women is that indigency makes access to competent licensed physicians not merely "difficult" but "impossible." As a practical matter, many indigent women will feel they have no choice but to carry their pregnancies to term because the State will pay for the associated medical services, even though they would have chosen to have abortions if the State had also provided funds for that procedure, or indeed if the State had provided funds for neither procedure. This disparity in funding by the State clearly operates to coerce indigent pregnant women to bear children they would not otherwise choose to have, and just as clearly, this coercion can only operate upon the poor, who are uniquely the victims of this form of financial pressure. * * *

The Court's premise is that only an equal protection claim is presented here. Claims of interference with enjoyment of fundamental rights have, however, occupied a rather protean position in our constitutional jurisprudence. Whether or not the Court's analysis may reasonably proceed under the Equal Protection Clause, the Court plainly errs in ignoring, as it does, the unanswerable argument of appellees, and the holding of the District Court, that the regulation unconstitutionally impinges upon their claim of privacy derived from the Due Process Clause.

HARRIS v. McRAE
448 U.S. 297 (1980).

MR. JUSTICE STEWART delivered the opinion of the Court.

This case presents statutory and constitutional questions concerning the public funding of abortions under Title XIX of the Social Security Act, commonly known as the "Medicaid" Act, and * * * the so-called "Hyde Amendment." The statutory question is whether Title XIX requires a State that participates in the Medicaid program to fund the cost of medically necessary abortions for which federal reimbursement is unavailable under the Hyde Amendment. * * *

In Maher v. Roe, 432 U.S. 464, the Court was presented with the question whether the scope of personal constitutional freedom recognized in Roe v. Wade included an entitlement to Medicaid payments for abortions that are not medically necessary. At issue in Maher was a Connecticut welfare regulation under which Medicaid recipients received payments for medical services incident to childbirth, but not for medical services incident to nontherapeutic abortions. * * *

The Hyde Amendment, like the Connecticut welfare regulation at issue in Maher, places no governmental obstacle in the path of a woman who chooses to terminate her pregnancy, but rather, by means of unequal subsidization of abortion and other medical services, encourages alternative activity deemed in the public interest.

[I]t simply does not follow that a woman's freedom of choice carries with it a constitutional entitlement to the financial resources to avail herself of the full range of protected choices. * * * We are thus not persuaded that the Hyde Amendment impinges on the constitutionally protected freedom of choice recognized in Wade.

THORNBURGH v. AMERICAN COLLEGE
476 U.S. 747 (1986), White, J., dissenting.

JUSTICE WHITE, with whom JUSTICE REHNQUIST joins, dissenting.

In my view, the time has come to recognize that Roe v. Wade * * * "departs from a proper understanding" of the Constitution and to overrule it. I do not claim that the arguments in support of this proposition are new ones or that they were not considered by the Court in Roe or in the cases that succeeded it. * * * But if an argument that a constitutional decision is erroneous must be novel in order to justify overruling that precedent, the Court's decisions in Lochner v. New York, 198 U.S. 45 (1905), and Plessy v. Ferguson, 163 U.S. 537 (1896), would remain the law * * *.

The Court has justified the recognition of a woman's fundamental right to terminate her pregnancy by invoking decisions upholding claims of personal autonomy in connection with the conduct of family life, the rearing of children, marital privacy, the use of contraceptives, and the preservation of the individual's capacity to procreate. See Carey v. Population Services International, 431 U.S. 678 (1977); Moore v. East Cleveland, supra; Eisenstadt v. Baird, 405 U.S. 438 (1972); Griswold v. Connecticut, supra; Skinner v. Oklahoma, 316 U.S. 535 (1942); Pierce v. Society of Sisters, 268 U.S. 510 (1925); Meyer v. Nebraska, 262 U.S. 390 (1923). Even if each of these cases was correctly decided and could be properly grounded in rights that are "implicit in the concept of ordered liberty" or "deeply rooted in this Nation's history and tradition," the issues in the cases cited differ from those at stake where abortion is concerned. As the Court appropriately recognized in Roe v. Wade, "[the] pregnant woman cannot be isolated in her privacy," 410 U.S., at 159; the termination of a pregnancy typically involves the destruction of another entity: the fetus. However one answers the metaphysical or theological question whether the fetus is a "human being" or the legal question whether it is a "person" as that term is used in the Constitution, one must at least recognize, first, that the fetus is an entity that bears in its cells all the genetic information that characterizes a member of the species homo sapiens and distinguishes an individual member of that species from all others, and second, that there is no nonarbitrary line separating a fetus from a child or, indeed, an adult human being. Given that the continued existence and development—that is to say, the life—of such an entity are so directly at stake in the woman's decision whether or not to terminate her pregnancy, that decision must be recognized as sui generis, different in kind from the others that the Court has protected under the rubric of personal or family privacy and autonomy. * * *

If the woman's liberty to choose an abortion is fundamental, then, it is not because any of our precedents (aside from Roe itself) command or justify that result; it can only be because protection for this unique choice is itself "implicit in the concept of ordered liberty" or, perhaps, "deeply rooted in this Nation's history and tradition." It seems clear to me that it is neither. The Court's opinion in Roe itself convincingly refutes the notion that the abortion liberty is deeply rooted in the history or tradition of our people, as does the continuing and deep division of the people themselves over the question of abortion. As for the notion that choice in the matter of abortion is implicit in the concept of ordered liberty, it seems apparent to me that a free, egalitarian, and democratic society does not presuppose any particular rule or set of rules with respect to abortion. And again, the fact that many men and women of good will and high commitment to constitutional government place themselves on both sides of the abortion controversy strengthens my own conviction that the values animating the Constitution do not compel recognition of the abortion liberty as fundamental. In so denominating that liberty, the Court engages not in constitutional interpretation, but in the unrestrained imposition of its own, extraconstitutional value preferences. * * *

A second, equally basic error infects the Court's decision in Roe v. Wade. * * *

The governmental interest at issue is in protecting those who will be citizens if their lives are not ended in the womb. The substantiality of this interest is in no way dependent on the probability that the fetus may be capable of surviving outside the womb at any given point in its development, as the possibility of fetal survival is contingent on the state of medical practice and technology, factors that are in essence morally and constitutionally irrelevant. The State's interest is in the fetus as an entity in itself, and the character of this entity does not change at the point of viability under conventional medical wisdom. Accordingly, the State's interest, if compelling after viability, is equally compelling before viability.

Further, it is self-evident that neither the legislative decision to assert a state interest in fetal life before viability nor the judicial decision to recognize that interest as compelling constitutes an impermissible "religious" decision merely because it coincides with the belief of one or more religions. Certainly the fact that the prohibition of murder coincides with one of the Ten Commandments does not render a State's interest in its murder statutes less than compelling, nor are legislative and judicial decisions concerning the use of the death penalty tainted by their correspondence to varying religious views on that subject. The simple, and perhaps unfortunate, fact of the matter is that in determining whether to assert an interest in fetal life, a State cannot avoid taking a position that will correspond to some religious beliefs and contradict others. * * * Faced with such a decision, the most appropriate course of action for the Court is to defer to a legislative resolution of the issue: in other words, if a state legislature asserts an interest in protecting fetal life, I can see no satisfactory basis for denying that it is compelling. * * *

Both the characterization of the abortion liberty as fundamental and the denigration of the State's interest in preserving the lives of nonviable fetuses are essential to the detailed set of constitutional rules devised by the Court to limit the States' power to regulate abortion. If either or both of these facets of Roe v. Wade were rejected, a broad range of limitations on abortion (including outright prohibition) that are now unavailable to the States would again become constitutional possibilities. * * *

I would return the issue to the people by overruling Roe v. Wade.

WEBSTER v. REPRODUCTIVE HEALTH SERVICES

492 U.S. 490 (1989).

CHIEF JUSTICE REHNQUIST * * *

This appeal concerns the constitutionality of a Missouri statute regulating the performance of abortions. The United States Court of Appeals for the Eighth Circuit struck down several provisions of the statute on the ground that they violated this Court's decision in Roe v. Wade, 410 U.S. 113 (1973), and cases following it. [We now reverse.]

The Act's preamble, as noted, sets forth "findings" by the Missouri Legislature that "[t]he life of each human being begins at conception," and that "[u]nborn children have protectable interests in life, health, and well-being." Mo. Rev. Stat. §§ 1.205.1(1), (2) (1986). * * * The Court has emphasized that Roe v. Wade "implies no limitation on the authority of a State to make a value judgment favoring childbirth over abortion." Maher v. Roe, 432 U.S., at 474. The preamble can be read simply to express that sort of value judgment. * * *

Missouri's refusal to allow public employees to perform abortions in public hospitals leaves a pregnant woman with the same choices as if the State had chosen not to operate any public hospitals at all. The challenged provisions only restrict a woman's ability to obtain an abortion to the extent that she chooses to use a physician affiliated with a public hospital. * * *

The viability-testing provision of the Missouri Act is concerned with promoting the State's interest in potential human life rather than in maternal health. Section 188.029 creates what is essentially a presumption of viability at 20 weeks, which the physician must rebut with tests indicating that the fetus is not viable prior to performing an abortion. * * *

We think that the doubt cast upon the Missouri statute * * * is not so much a flaw in the statute as it is a reflection of the fact that the rigid trimester analysis of the course of a pregnancy enunciated in Roe has resulted in subsequent cases * * * making constitutional law in this area a virtual Procrustean bed. * * *

Because none of the challenged provisions of the Missouri Act properly before us conflict with the Constitution, the judgment of the Court of Appeals is Reversed.

NOTE: GOVERNMENT NEUTRALITY, POSITIVE AND NEGATIVE LIBERTIES

Does the government have an obligation to remain neutral on controversial moral issues? *Maher, Harris* and *Webster* say "no". How can government non-neutrality be defended?

The Supreme Court characterizes the right to privacy as a negative liberty in the abortion cases. That is, the right is delineated as a right not to be interfered with, rather than as a right to the provision of a service. If abortion rights were "positive" liberties in the eyes of the Court, the state and federal government would presumably have an affirmative duty to secure poor women's access to abortions preferred over childbirth. A first trimester abortion cost $300–$400 in 2007; a second trimester abortions could cost as much as $2,000. Although clinics subsidize poor women's abortions, many low income women go into debt to obtain abortions. See website of the Women's Medical Fund, http://www.womensmedicalfund.org/ (citing H. Boonstra and A. Sonfield, Rights Without Access: Revisiting Public Funding of Abortion for Poor Women, Guttmacher Report on Public Policy (April, 2000), contending that "[o]ne third of pregnant women choose abortion but are forced to carry to term due to lack of funds").

HODGSON v. MINNESOTA

497 U.S. 417 (1990).

JUSTICE STEVENS announced the judgment of the Court * * *

The Minnesota parental notice statute was enacted in 1981 as an amendment to the Minors' Consent to Health Services Act. * * *

The 1981 amendment qualified the authority of an "unemancipated minor" to give effective consent to an abortion by requiring that either her physician or an agent notify "the parent" personally or by certified mail at least 48 hours before the procedure is performed. * * *

A natural parent who has demonstrated sufficient commitment to his or her children is thereafter entitled to raise the children free from undue state interference. * * *

We think it is clear that a requirement that a minor wait 48 hours after notifying a single parent of her intention to get an abortion would reasonably further the legitimate state interest in ensuring that the minor's decision is knowing and intelligent. We have held that when a parent or another person has assumed "primary responsibility" for a minor's well-being, the State may properly enact "laws designed to aid discharge of that responsibility." Ginsberg v. New York, 390 U.S. 629 (1968). To the extent that subdivision 2 of the Minnesota statute requires notification of only one parent, it does just that. The brief waiting period provides the parent the opportunity to consult with his or her spouse and a family physician, and it permits the parent to inquire into the competency of the doctor performing the abortion, discuss the religious or moral implications of the abortion decision, and provide the daughter needed guidance and counsel in evaluating the impact of the decision on her future. * * *

The 48–hour delay imposes only a minimal burden on the right of the minor to decide whether or not to terminate her pregnancy. Although the District Court found that scheduling factors, weather, and the minor's school and work commitments may combine, in many cases, to create a delay of a week or longer between the initiation of notification and the abortion, 648 F. Supp. at 765, there is no evidence that the 48–hour period itself is unreasonable or longer than appropriate for adequate consultation between parent and child. * * *

It is equally clear that the requirement that both parents be notified, whether or not both wish to be notified or have assumed responsibility for the upbringing of the child, does not reasonably further any legitimate state interest. * * *

Not only does two-parent notification fail to serve any state interest with respect to functioning families, it disserves the state interest in protecting and assisting the minor with respect to dysfunctional families.

The record reveals that in the thousands of dysfunctional families affected by this statute, the two-parent notice requirement proved positively harmful to the minor and her family. * * *

Unsurprisingly, the Minnesota two-parent notification requirement is an oddity among state and federal consent provisions governing the health, welfare, and education of children. A minor desiring to enlist in the armed services or the Reserve Officers' Training Corps (ROTC) need only obtain the consent of "his parent or guardian." 10 U. S. C. Sections 505(a), 2104(b)(4), 2107(b)(4). * * * We therefore hold that this requirement violates the Constitution.

JUSTICE O'CONNOR, concurring in part and concurring in the judgment in part. * * *

It has been my understanding in this area that "if the particular regulation does not 'unduly burden' the fundamental right, * * * then our evaluation of that regulation is limited to our determination that the regulation rationally relates to a legitimate state purpose." Akron v. Akron Center for Reproductive Health, Inc., 462 U.S. 416 (1983) (O'Connor, J., dissenting); see also Webster v. Reproductive Health Services, 492 U.S. 490, 530 (1989) (O'Connor, J., concurring in part and concurring in judgment). It is with that understanding that I agree with Justice Stevens' statement that the "statute cannot be sustained if the obstacles it imposes are not reasonably related to legitimate state interests." * * *

RUST v. SULLIVAN

500 U.S. 173 (1991).

CHIEF JUSTICE REHNQUIST delivered the opinion of the Court.

These cases concern a facial challenge to Department of Health and Human Services (HHS) regulations which limit ability of Title X fund recipients to engage in abortion-related activities. * * *

Petitioners contend that the regulations violate the First Amendment by impermissibly discriminating based on viewpoint because they prohibit "all discussion about abortion as a lawful option—including counseling, referral, and the provision of neutral and accurate information about ending a pregnancy—while compelling the clinic or counselor to provide information that promotes continuing a pregnancy to term." * * * They assert that the regulations violate the "free speech rights of private health care organizations that receive Title X funds, of their staff, and of their patients" by impermissibly imposing "viewpoint-discriminatory conditions on government subsidies" and thus "penalize speech funded with non-Title X monies." * * * Because "Title X continues to fund speech ancillary to pregnancy testing in a manner that is not evenhanded with respect to views and information about abortion, it invidiously discriminates on the basis of viewpoint." * * *

The challenged regulations implement the statutory prohibition by prohibiting counseling, referral, and the provision of information regarding abortion as a method of family planning. They are designed to ensure that the limits of the federal program are observed. The Title X program is designed not for prenatal care, but to encourage family planning. A doctor who wished to offer prenatal care to a project patient who became pregnant could properly be prohibited from doing so because such service is outside the scope of the federally funded program. The regulations prohibiting abortion counseling and referral are of the same ilk; "no funds appropriated for the project may be used in programs where abortion is a method of family planning," and a doctor employed by the project may be prohibited in the course of his project duties from counseling abortion or referring for abortion. This is not a case of the Government "suppressing a dangerous idea," but of a prohibition on a project grantee or its employees from engaging in activities outside of the project's scope.

To hold that the Government unconstitutionally discriminates on the basis of viewpoint when it chooses to fund a program dedicated to advance certain permissible goals, because the program in advancing those goals necessarily discourages alternative goals, would render numerous Government programs constitutionally suspect.

PLANNED PARENTHOOD v. CASEY
505 U.S. 833 (1992).

JUSTICE O'CONNOR, JUSTICE KENNEDY, and JUSTICE SOUTER announced the judgment of the Court. * * *

Liberty finds no refuge in a jurisprudence of doubt. Yet 19 years after our holding that the Constitution protects a woman's right to terminate her pregnancy in its early stages, Roe v. Wade, 410 U.S. 113 (1973), that definition of liberty is still questioned. * * *

At issue in these cases are five provisions of the Pennsylvania Abortion Control Act of 1982, as amended in 1988 and 1989. 18 Pa. Cons. Stat. Sections 3203–3220 (1990). * * *

[W]e are led to conclude this: the essential holding of Roe v. Wade should be retained and once again reaffirmed.

It must be stated at the outset and with clarity that Roe's essential holding, the holding we reaffirm, has three parts. First is a recognition of the right of the woman to choose to have an abortion before viability and to obtain it without undue interference from the State. Before viability, the State's interests are not strong enough to support a prohibition of abortion or the imposition of a substantial obstacle to the woman's effective right to elect the procedure. Second is a confirmation of the State's power to restrict abortions after fetal viability, if the law contains exceptions for pregnancies which endanger the woman's life or health. And third is the principle that the State has legitimate interests from the outset of the pregnancy in protecting the health of the woman and the life of the fetus that may become a child. These principles do not contradict one another; and we adhere to each. * * *

Although Roe has engendered opposition, it has in no sense proven "unworkable," see Garcia v. San Antonio Metropolitan Transit Authority, 469 U.S. 528, 546 (1985), representing as it does a simple limitation beyond which a state law is unenforceable. While Roe has, of course, required judicial assessment of state laws affecting the exercise of the choice guaranteed against government infringement, and although the need for such review will remain as a consequence of today's decision, the required determinations fall within judicial competence. * * *

We have seen how time has overtaken some of Roe's factual assumptions: advances in maternal health care allow for abortions safe to the mother later in pregnancy than was true in 1973, * * * and advances in neonatal care have advanced viability to a point somewhat earlier. * * * But these facts go only to the scheme of time limits on the realization of competing interests, and the divergences from the factual premises of 1973 have no bearing on the validity of Roe's central holding, that viability marks the earliest point at which the State's interest in fetal life is constitutionally adequate to justify a legislative ban on nontherapeutic abortions. * * *

An entire generation has come of age free to assume Roe's concept of liberty in defining the capacity of women to act in society, and to make reproductive decisions; no erosion of principle going to liberty or personal autonomy has left Roe's central holding a doctrinal remnant; Roe portends no developments at odds with other precedent for the analysis of personal liberty; and no changes of fact have rendered viability more or less appropriate as the point at which the balance of interests tips. Within the bounds of normal stare decisis analysis, then, and subject to the considerations on which it customarily turns, the stronger argument is for affirming Roe's central holding, with whatever degree of personal reluctance any of us may have, not for overruling it. * * *

From what we have said so far it follows that it is a constitutional liberty of the woman to have some freedom to terminate her pregnancy. We conclude that the basic decision in Roe was based on a constitutional analysis which we cannot now repudiate. The woman's liberty is not so unlimited, however, that from the outset the State cannot show its concern for the life of the unborn, and at a later point in fetal development the State's interest in life has sufficient force so that the right of the woman to terminate the pregnancy can be restricted. * * *

Liberty must not be extinguished for want of a line that is clear. And it falls to us to give some real substance to the woman's liberty to determine whether to carry her pregnancy to full term.

We conclude the line should be drawn at viability, so that before that time the woman has a right to choose to terminate her pregnancy.

The woman's right to terminate her pregnancy before viability is the most central principle of Roe v. Wade. It is a rule of law and a component of liberty we cannot renounce. * * *

Roe established a trimester framework to govern abortion regulations. * * *

The trimester framework no doubt was erected to ensure that the woman's right to choose not become so subordinate to the State's interest in promoting fetal life that her choice exists in theory but not in fact. We do not agree, however, that the trimester approach is necessary to accomplish this objective. A framework of this rigidity was unnecessary and in its later interpretation sometimes contradicted the State's permissible exercise of its powers. * * *

We reject the trimester framework, which we do not consider to be part of the essential holding of Roe. * * * The trimester framework suffers from these basic flaws: in its formulation it misconceives the nature of the pregnant woman's interest; and in practice it undervalues the State's interest in potential life, as recognized in Roe. * * *

(a) To protect the central right recognized by Roe v. Wade while at the same time accommodating the State's profound interest in potential life, we will employ the undue burden analysis as explained in this opinion. An undue burden exists, and therefore a provision of law is invalid, if its purpose or effect is to place a substantial obstacle in the path of a woman seeking an abortion before the fetus attains viability.

(b) We reject the rigid trimester framework of Roe v. Wade. To promote the State's profound interest in potential life, throughout pregnancy the State may take measures to ensure that the woman's choice is informed, and measures designed to advance this interest will not be invalidated as long as their purpose is to persuade the woman to choose childbirth over abortion. These measures must not be an undue burden on the right.

(c) As with any medical procedure, the State may enact regulations to further the health or safety of a woman seeking an abortion. Unnecessary health regulations that have the purpose or effect of presenting a substantial obstacle to a woman seeking an abortion impose an undue burden on the right.

(d) Our adoption of the undue burden analysis does not disturb the central holding of Roe v. Wade, and we reaffirm that holding. Regardless of whether exceptions are made for particular circumstances, a State may not prohibit any woman from making the ultimate decision to terminate her pregnancy before viability.

(e) We also reaffirm Roe's holding that "subsequent to viability, the State in promoting its interest in the potentiality of human life may, if it chooses, regulate, and even proscribe, abortion except where it is necessary, in appropriate medical judgment, for the preservation of the life or health of the mother." Roe v. Wade, 410 U.S. at 164–165.

These principles control our assessment of the Pennsylvania statute, and we now turn to the issue of the validity of its challenged provisions. * * *

The Court of Appeals applied what it believed to be the undue burden standard and upheld each of the provisions except for the husband notification requirement. We agree generally with this conclusion * * *.

Section 3209 of Pennsylvania's abortion law provides, except in cases of medical emergency, that no physician shall perform an abortion on a married woman without receiving a signed statement from the woman that she has notified her spouse that she is about to undergo an abortion. The woman has the option of providing an alternative signed statement certifying that her husband is not the man who impregnated her; that her husband could not be located; that the pregnancy is the result of spousal sexual assault which she has reported; or that the woman believes that notifying her husband will cause him or someone else to inflict bodily injury upon her. A physician who performs an abortion on a married woman without receiving the appropriate signed statement will have his or her license revoked, and is liable to the husband for damages. * * *

The American Medical Association (AMA) has published a summary of the recent research in this field, which indicates that in an average 12–month period in this country, approximately two million women are the victims of severe assaults by their male partners. In a 1985 survey, women reported that nearly one of every eight husbands had assaulted their wives during the past year. The AMA views these figures as "marked underestimates," because the nature of these incidents discourages women from reporting them, and because surveys typically exclude the very poor, those who do not speak English well, and women who are homeless or in institutions or hospitals when the survey is conducted. According to the AMA, "researchers on family violence agree that the true incidence of partner violence is probably double the above estimates; or four million severely assaulted women per year. Studies on prevalence suggest that from one-fifth to one-third of all women will be physically assaulted by a partner or ex-partner during their lifetime." AMA Council on Scientific Affairs, Violence Against Women 7 (1991). Thus on an average day in the United States, nearly 11,000 women are severely assaulted by their male partners. Many of these incidents involve sexual assault. * * * In families where wifebeating takes place, moreover, child abuse is often present as well. * * *

Other studies fill in the rest of this troubling picture. Physical violence is only the most visible form of abuse. Psychological abuse, particularly forced social and economic isolation of women, is also common. * * *

The spousal notification requirement is thus likely to prevent a significant number of women from obtaining an abortion. It does not merely make abortions a little more difficult or expensive to obtain; for many women, it will impose a substantial obstacle. We must not blind ourselves to the fact that the significant number of women who fear for their safety and the safety of their children are likely to be deterred from procuring an abortion as surely as if the Commonwealth had outlawed abortion in all cases. * * *

This conclusion is in no way inconsistent with our decisions upholding parental notification or consent requirements. * * * Those enactments, and our judgment that they are constitutional, are based on the quite reasonable assumption that minors will benefit from consultation with their parents and that children will often not realize that their parents have their best interests at heart. We cannot adopt a parallel assumption about adult women. * * *

It is an inescapable biological fact that state regulation with respect to the child a woman is carrying will have a far greater impact on the mother's liberty than on the father's. * * * The Court has held that "when the wife and the husband disagree on this decision, the view of only one of the two marriage partners can prevail. Inasmuch as it is the woman who physically bears the child and who is the more directly and immediately affected by the pregnancy, as between the two, the balance weighs in her favor." * * *

There was a time, not so long ago, when a different understanding of the family and of the Constitution prevailed. In Bradwell v. State, 83 U.S. (16 Wall.) 130, three Members of this Court reaffirmed the common-law principle that "a woman had no legal existence separate from her husband, who was regarded as her head and representative in the social state; and, notwithstanding some recent modifications of this civil status, many of the special rules of law flowing from and dependent upon this cardinal principle still exist in full force in most States." * * * Only one generation has passed since this Court observed that "woman is still regarded as the center of home and family life," with attendant "special responsibilities" that precluded full and independent legal status under the Constitution. * * * These views, of course, are no longer consistent with our understanding of the family, the individual, or the Constitution. * * *

Our Constitution is a covenant running from the first generation of Americans to us and then to future generations. It is a coherent succession. Each generation must learn anew that the Constitution's written terms embody ideas and aspirations that must survive more ages than one. We accept our responsibility not to retreat from interpreting the full meaning of the covenant in light of all of our precedents. We invoke it once again to define the freedom guaranteed by the Constitution's own promise, the promise of liberty. * * *

JUSTICE STEVENS, concurring in part and dissenting in part. * * *

The Court is unquestionably correct in concluding that the doctrine of stare decisis has controlling significance in a case of this kind, notwithstanding an individual Justice's concerns about the merits. * * * The societal costs of overruling Roe at this late date would be enormous. Roe is an integral part of a correct understanding of both the concept of liberty and the basic equality of men and women. * * *

JUSTICE BLACKMUN, concurring in part, concurring in the judgment in part, and dissenting in part. * * *

Three years ago, in Webster v. Reproductive Health Services, 492 U.S. 490 (1989), four Members of this Court appeared poised to "cast into darkness the hopes and visions of every woman in this country" who had come to believe that the Constitution guaranteed her the right to reproductive choice. * * * But now, just when so many expected the darkness to fall, the flame has grown bright. * * *

And I fear for the darkness as four Justices anxiously await the single vote necessary to extinguish the light. * * *

[W]hile I believe that the joint opinion errs in failing to invalidate [all of the Pennsylvania] * * * regulations, I am pleased that the joint opinion has not ruled out the possibility that these regulations may be shown to impose an unconstitutional burden. The joint opinion makes clear that its specific holdings are based on the insufficiency of the record before it. * * * I am confident that in the future evidence will be produced to show that "in a large fraction of the cases in which [these regulations are] relevant, [they] will operate as a substantial obstacle to a woman's choice to undergo an abortion." * * *

I am 83 years old. I cannot remain on this Court forever, and when I do step down, the confirmation process for my successor well may focus on the issue before us today. That, I regret, may be exactly where the choice between the two worlds will be made.

CHIEF JUSTICE REHNQUIST, with whom JUSTICE WHITE, JUSTICE SCALIA, and JUSTICE THOMAS join, concurring in the judgment in part and dissenting in part. * * *

The joint opinion, following its newly minted variation on stare decisis, retains the outer shell of Roe v. Wade, 410 U.S. 113 (1973), but beats a wholesale retreat from the substance of that case. We believe that Roe was wrongly decided, and that it can and should be overruled consistently with our traditional approach to stare decisis in constitutional cases. We would adopt the approach of the plurality in Webster v. Reproductive Health Services, 492 U.S. 490 (1989), and uphold the challenged provisions of the Pennsylvania statute in their entirety. * * *

In our view, authentic principles of stare decisis do not require that any portion of the reasoning in Roe be kept intact. "Stare decisis is not * * * a universal, inexorable command," especially in cases involving the interpretation of the Federal Constitution. * * * Erroneous decisions in such constitutional cases are uniquely durable, because correction through legislative action, save for constitutional amendment, is impossible. It is therefore our duty to reconsider constitutional interpretations that "depart from a proper understanding" of the Constitution. * * * Our constitutional watch does not cease merely because we have spoken before on an issue; when it becomes clear that a prior constitutional interpretation is unsound we are obliged to reexamine the question. * * *

STENBERG v. CARHART

530 U.S. 914 (2000).

JUSTICE BREYER delivered the opinion of the Court. * * *

Dr. Leroy Carhart is a Nebraska physician who performs abortions in a clinical setting. He brought this lawsuit in Federal District Court seeking a declaration that the Nebraska ["partial-birth" abortion] statute violates the Federal Constitution, and asking for an injunction forbidding its enforcement. After a trial on the merits, during which both sides presented several expert witnesses, the District Court held the statute unconstitutional. * * * On appeal, the Eighth Circuit affirmed. We granted certiorari to consider the matter. [We affirm.] * * *

Approximately 10% of all abortions are performed during the second trimester of pregnancy (12 to 24 weeks). Abortion Surveillance 41. In the early 1970's, inducing labor through the injection of saline into the uterus was the predominant method of second trimester abortion. * * * Today, however, the medical profession has switched from medical induction of labor to surgical procedures for most second trimester abortions. The most commonly used procedure is called "dilation and evacuation" (D & E). That procedure (together with a modified form of vacuum aspiration used in the early second trimester) accounts for about 95% of all abortions performed from 12 to 20 weeks of gestational age. * * *

"D & E is similar to vacuum aspiration except that the cervix must be dilated more widely because surgical instruments are used to remove larger pieces of tissue. Osmotic dilators are usually used. Intravenous fluids and an analgesic or sedative may be administered. A local anesthetic such as a paracervical block may be administered, dilating agents, if used, are removed and instruments are inserted through the cervix into the uterus to removal fetal and placental tissue. Because fetal tissue is friable and easily broken, the fetus may not be removed intact. The walls of the uterus are scraped with a curette to ensure that no tissue remains." * * *

At trial, Dr. Carhart and Dr. Stubblefield described a variation of the D & E procedure, which they referred to as an "intact D & E." * * * The procedure * * * involves removing the fetus from the uterus through the cervix "intact," i.e., in one pass, rather than in several passes. * * * It is used after 16 weeks at the earliest, as vacuum aspiration becomes ineffective and the fetal skull becomes too large to pass through the cervix. * * *

Dr. Carhart testified he attempts to use the intact D & E procedure [also called D & X] during weeks 16 to 20 because (1) it reduces the dangers from sharp bone fragments passing through the cervix, (2) minimizes the number of instrument passes needed for extraction and lessens the likelihood of uterine perforations caused by those instruments, (3) reduces the likelihood of leaving infection-causing fetal and placental tissue in the uterus, and (4) could help to prevent potentially fatal absorption of fetal tissue into the maternal circulation. * * *

There are no reliable data on the number of D & X abortions performed annually. Estimates have ranged between 640 and 5,000 per year.

The question before us is whether Nebraska's statute, making criminal the performance of a "partial birth abortion," violates the Federal Constitution. We conclude that it does for at least two independent reasons. First, the law lacks any exception " 'for the preservation of the * * * health of the mother.' " Casey, 505 U.S. at 879. Second, it "imposes an undue burden on a woman's ability" to choose a D & E abortion, thereby unduly burdening the right to choose abortion itself. 505 U.S. at 874. * * *

The Casey joint opinion reiterated what the Court held in Roe; that " 'subsequent to viability, the State in promoting its interest in the potentiality of human life may, if it chooses, regulate, and even proscribe, abortion except where it is necessary, in appropriate medical judgment, for the preservation of the life or health of the mother.' " 505 U.S. at 879 (quoting Roe, 410 U.S. at 164–165).

The fact that Nebraska's law applies both pre- and postviability aggravates the constitutional problem presented. The State's interest in regulating abortion previability is considerably weaker than postviability. * * *

Nebraska has not convinced us that a health exception is "never necessary to preserve the health of women." * * * [W]here substantial medical authority supports the proposition that banning a particular abortion procedure could endanger women's health, Casey requires the statute to include a health exception when the procedure is " 'necessary, in appropriate medical judgment, for the preservation of the life or health of the mother.' " 505 U.S. at 879. * * *

[S]ome present prosecutors and future Attorneys General may choose to pursue physicians who use D & E procedures, the most commonly used method for performing previability second trimester abortions. All those who perform abortion procedures using that method must fear prosecution, conviction, and imprisonment. The result is an undue burden upon a woman's right to make an abortion decision. We must consequently find the statute unconstitutional.

NOTE: GONZALES V. CARHART AND PLANNED PARENTHOOD

The United States Congress enacted a Partial–Birth Abortion Ban Act, signed into law by President George W. Bush in 2003. As its name suggests, the Act bans "partial birth abortions". But what is a "partial-birth" abortion?

The term "partial-birth abortion" is colloquial rather than medical or scientific. It refers to a type of abortion in which a fetus is killed after partial extraction from the womb through a medically dilated cervix. To understand what is banned, one must look to the definition Congress included in the Act. Under the Act "the term 'partial-birth abortion' means an abortion in which—(A) the person performing the abortion deliberately and intentionally vaginally delivers a (B) living fetus until, in the case of a head-first presentation, the entire fetal head is outside the body of the mother, or, in the case of breech presentation, any part of the fetal trunk past the navel is outside the body of the mother, for the purpose of performing an overt act that the person knows will kill the partially delivered living fetus; and performs the overt act, other than completion of (B) delivery, that kills the partially delivered living fetus * * *." The Act thus criminalizes abortions in which a living viable or non-viable fetus is killed after its head or navel passes from the womb through the cervix. The Act includes an exception for abortions necessary to save the life of the pregnant woman, but no exception for the woman's health.

Abortion providers and abortion-rights advocacy groups went to court to oppose the Act. See *Gonzales v. Carhart* and *Gonzales v. Planned Parenthood*, joined as *Gonzales v. Carhart*, 127 S.Ct. 1610 (2007). Cf. *Northwestern Memorial Hospital v. Ashcroft*, 362 F.3d 923 (7th Cir. 2004). Providers and advocates believed the Act would and could be interpreted to prohibit a medically safe and recommended abortion technique commonly used to terminate second trimester pregnancies, the dilation and evacuation ("D & E") procedure. In this procedure, the (typically non-viable) fetus is killed before, as, or after it passes through the birth canal. Most abortions are performed during the first trimester, and are not "partial-birth" abortions. Some second and third trimester abortions do not use "partial-birth" methods.

Providers and advocates maintained before the Supreme Court that the Act was unconstitutionally vague, just like the Nebraska law the Court struck down a few years earlier in Stenberg v. Carhart. These opponents of the Act also argued that by proscribing medically safe and popular D & E abortions of non-viable fetuses, and by not including a maternal health exception, the Act imposed an undue burden on the woman's right to choose, in violation of *Roe v. Wade* and *Planned Parenthood v. Casey*.

Applying the logic of *Planned Parenthood v. Casey* to the case at hand, the Court held 5 to 4 that the Partial–Birth Abortion Ban Act is constitutionally valid. The Court acknowledged the holding of *Casey* that: "Before viability, a State 'may not prohibit any woman from making the ultimate decision to terminate her pregnancy.'" And that: "It also may not impose upon this right an undue burden, which exists if a regulation's 'purpose or effect is to place a substantial obstacle in the path of a woman seeking an abortion before the fetus attains viability.'" Yet, under the holding of *Casey*, "[r]egulations which do no more than create a structural mechanism by which the State, or the parent or guardian of a minor, may express profound respect for the life of the unborn are permitted, if they are not a substantial obstacle to the woman's exercise of the right to choose."

In an opinion by Justice Kennedy, the Court reasoned that the Act is not unconstitutionally vague and does not unduly burden the woman's right to choose.

First, reasoned Justice Kennedy, the Act is not vague: "Doctors performing D & E will know that if they do not deliver a living fetus to an anatomical landmark they will not face criminal liability." Moreover, the Act requires knowing conduct and in its precedent: "The Court has made clear that scienter requirements alleviate vagueness concerns."

Second, the Act is not unduly burdensome. It does not prohibit most or all abortions. Nor does the Act ban D & E procedures as such, the Court said. The Court read the Act to only and specifically ban the "intact" D & E procedure. In the words of the Court: "In an intact D & E procedure the doctor extracts the fetus in a way conducive to pulling out its entire body, instead of ripping it apart." The Act proscribes only those D & E abortions performed both intentionally (not accidentally) and by killing an intact fetus whose head (or abdomen) has been delivered past the cervix.

Justice Kennedy argued that the Act does not require a health exception because there are alternatives to the banned procedure. Physicians can offer women medically safe alternatives for termination of pregnancy. The Court noted that neither an injection to induce vaginal expulsion of a non-viable living fetus, nor surgery to remove the non-viable fetus is banned by the Act. Opponents challenging the Act thus failed to "demonstrate[] that the Act would be unconstitutional in a large fraction of relevant cases."

The majority defended the Act as a constitutional expression of respect for life and concern about the ethics of the medical professional, public regard for physicians and women's psychological well-being. In a dissenting opinion, Justice Ruth Bader Ginsburg argued that the majority wrongfully embraces governmental efforts to take moral control of women's lives. Is Justice Ginsburg right that the Court's concern about the impact of fetal dismemberment on women's psychological health is veiled sex discrimination? Does the holding of this case make it more likely that *Roe v. Wade* will eventually be overruled?

Initially, anti-abortion activists emphasized the welfare and humanity of the fetus in calling for overruling *Roe*. In the 1990's their strategy shifted to also stressing the needs of teenagers affected by pregnancy and the rights of parents to be involved in teen health. In recent years activists opposing abortion rights have focused on women's psychological health. Are all three strategies equally well grounded in moral values, medical science and public policy? Is the women's health strategy problematically paternalistic?

GONZALES v. CARHART

127 S.Ct. 1610 (2007), Ginsburg dissenting.

JUSTICE GINSBURG, * * * dissenting. * * *

Delivery of an intact, albeit nonviable, fetus warrants special condemnation, the Court maintains, because a fetus that is not dismembered resembles an infant. But so, too, does a fetus delivered intact after it is terminated by injection a day or two before the surgical evacuation, or a fetus delivered through medical induction or cesarean. Yet, the availability of those procedures—along with D & E by dismemberment—the Court says, saves the ban on intact D & E from a declaration of unconstitutionality. Never mind that the procedures deemed acceptable might put a woman's health at greater risk.

Ultimately, the Court admits that "moral concerns" are at work, concerns that could yield prohibitions on any abortion. ("Congress could * * * conclude that the type of abortion proscribed by the Act requires specific regulation because it implicates additional ethical and moral concerns that justify a special prohibition."). Notably, the concerns expressed are untethered to any ground genuinely serving the Government's interest in preserving life. By allowing such concerns to carry the day and case, overriding fundamental rights, the Court dishonors our precedent. See, e.g., Casey, 505 U.S., at 850 ("Some of us as individuals find abortion offensive to our most basic principles of morality, but that cannot control our decision. Our obligation is to define the liberty of all, not to mandate our own moral code."); Lawrence v. Texas, 539 U.S. 558, 571 (2003) (Though "[f]or many persons [objections to homosexual conduct] are not trivial concerns but profound and deep convictions accepted as ethical and moral principles," the power of the State may not be used "to enforce these views on the whole society through operation of the criminal law." (citing Casey, 505 U.S., at 850)).

Revealing in this regard, the Court invokes an antiabortion shibboleth for which it concededly has no reliable evidence: Women who have abortions come to regret their choices, and consequently suffer from "[s]evere depression and loss of esteem." Ante, at 29.7. Because of women's fragile emotional state and because of the "bond of love the mother has for her child," the Court worries, doctors may withhold information about the nature of the intact D & E procedure. The solution the Court approves, then, is not to require doctors to inform women, accurately and adequately, of the different procedures and their attendant risks. Cf. Casey, 505 U.S., at 873 (plurality opinion) ("States are free to enact laws to provide a reasonable framework for a woman to make a decision that has such profound and lasting meaning."). Instead, the Court deprives women of the right to make an autonomous choice, even at the expense of their safety

This way of thinking reflects ancient notions about women's place in the family and under the Constitution—ideas that have long since been discredited. Compare, e.g., Muller v. Oregon, 208 U.S. 412, 422–423 (1908) ("protective" legislation imposing hours-of-work limitations on women only held permissible in view of women's "physical structure and a proper discharge of her maternal funct[ion]"); Bradwell v. State, 16 Wall. 130, 141 (1873) (Bradley, J., concurring) ("Man is, or should be, woman's protector and defender. The natural and proper timidity and delicacy which belongs to the female sex evidently unfits it for many of the occupations of civil life. * * * The paramount destiny and mission of woman are to fulfil[l] the noble and benign offices of wife and mother."), with United States v. Virginia, 518 U.S. 515, n.12 (1996) (State may not rely on "overbroad generalizations" about the "talents, capacities, or preferences" of women; "[s]uch judgments have * * * impeded * * * women's progress toward full citizenship stature throughout our Nation's history"); Califano v. Goldfarb, 430 U.S. 199, 207 (1977) (gender-based

Social Security classification rejected because it rested on "archaic and overbroad generalizations" "such as assumptions as to [women's] dependency" (internal quotation marks omitted)).

Though today's majority may regard women's feelings on the matter as "self-evident," this Court has repeatedly confirmed that "[t]he destiny of the woman must be shaped * * * on her own conception of her spiritual imperatives and her place in society." Casey, 505 U.S., at 852. See also id., at 877 (plurality opinion) ("[M]eans chosen by the State to further the interest in potential life must be calculated to inform the woman's free choice, not hinder it.") * * *.

NOTE: HOW FAR SHOULD REPRODUCTIVE FREEDOM GO?

A pregnant woman is nearing death from cancer. She is expected to die within two weeks. Physicians treating her believe her fetus of 30 weeks gestational age is fully viable and could be delivered safely via caesarian section if delivered as soon as possible and before the woman's death. However, the woman refuses to give permission for a caesarian section. She does not want the pain of surgery added to the pain of her cancer. Should physicians be permitted to perform the operation over the woman's objections? See *In Re A.C.*, 573 A.2d 1235 (D.C. Ct. App. 1990).

Should the sperm of a deceased person ever be used to create a child? Imagine that a young man dies suddenly and unexpectedly? Should his wife, girlfriend or parent be permitted to harvest sperm from his corpse for later use to produce a child or grandchild? Do constitutional rights of procreation extend that far? What about the rights of the dead man to reproductive autonomy? See Tom Plohetski, "Dead Man's Sperm to be Taken by Court Order," *Austin Legal*, Stateman.com, April 7, 2009.

Despite federal funding bans currently in place for human reproductive cloning research, someday it will be possible to produce human children by cloning. (Sheep, dogs and other large mammals are already being cloned). Once the technology is available, a woman will be able to have a child without sperm or other biological material from a man. A man could produce sons who would be his genetic identical. Would laws banning cloning for reproductive purposes be constitutional? Do autonomy interests argue in favor of ascribing adults who wish to reproduce the right to clone, or do future persons have autonomy interests in not coming into being as a result of cloning? See Elizabeth Price Foley, The Constitutional Implications of Human Cloning, 42 *Ariz. L. Rev.* 647 (2000) ("Another objection voiced by opponents of human cloning is that a child born by cloning inherently would be deprived of the kind of personal autonomy and privacy enjoyed by other persons. * * * Philosopher * * * Joel Feinberg labeled it a 'right to an open future.' * * * The genome of the child created by cloning, being a known quantity, is ineluctably denied a full opportunity for individuality because he is burdened with the foreknowledge of himself.").

M. CATHLEEN KAVENY, CLONING AND POSITIVE LIBERTY

13 Notre Dame J.L. Ethics & Pub. Pol'y 15 (1999).

But what does proper respect for human freedom actually require of the law in the case of human cloning? Whose freedom is at stake? That of the parents or that of the child? The stance adopted by the United States toward regulation of reproductive technologies thus far has protected a nearly absolute negative freedom of adults to have their "own" child (i.e., a child biologically related to oneself or one's partner), virtually unimpeded by anything but the limits of science. It has not, however, paid much attention to the positive freedom of the child to come into existence under conditions that will enable her to become an autonomous person of equal dignity with her parents, capable of deliberating upon and choosing a life-plan for herself. Nor has it paid sufficient attention to the fact that freedom has a social dimension; a culture which truly values autonomy must insure that the conditions of freedom are protected, promoted, and passed down to the next generation. * * *

I would like to suggest that the laissez-faire American attitude toward emerging reproductive technologies provides us with an inadequate model for regulating human cloning, precisely because it fails to attend to the developing autonomy of the child and the importance of a culture that supports autonomy. Far from requiring us to refrain from imposing any restrictions upon human cloning, proper respect for human freedom may require us to set stringent legal limitations upon its use, perhaps even to ban it entirely. * * *

[T]he advent of human cloning will exacerbate some of the problems already created by [new] * * * technologies. * * * [C]loning undermines the positive freedom of the children whom it brings into being. Furthermore, permitting the practice of human cloning, even on a comparatively limited basis, will erode essential cultural supports for the value of autonomy. * * * Liberal legal theory, properly understood, justifies measures designed to restrict or even to prevent the practice of human cloning, despite their interference with the negative liberty of those persons who wish to produce a child through somatic cell nuclear transfer.

b. Marriage and Divorce

LOVING v. VIRGINIA

388 U.S. 1 (1967).

MR. CHIEF JUSTICE WARREN delivered the opinion of the Court.

This case presents a constitutional question never addressed by this Court: whether a statutory scheme adopted by the State of Virginia to prevent marriages between persons solely on the basis of racial classifications violates the Equal Protection and Due Process Clauses of the Fourteenth Amendment. For reasons which seem to us to reflect the central meaning of those constitutional commands, we conclude that these statutes cannot stand consistently with the Fourteenth Amendment.

In June 1958, two residents of Virginia, Mildred Jeter, a Negro woman, and Richard Loving, a white man, were married in the District of Columbia pursuant to its laws. Shortly after their marriage, the Lovings returned to Virginia and established their marital abode in Caroline County. At the October Term, 1958, of the Circuit Court of Caroline County, a grand jury issued an indictment charging the Lovings with violating Virginia's ban on interracial marriages. On January 6, 1959, the Lovings pleaded guilty to the charge and were sentenced to one year in jail; however, the trial judge suspended the sentence for a period of 25 years on the condition that the Lovings leave the State and not return to Virginia together for 25 years. He stated in an opinion that:

"Almighty God created the races white, black, yellow, malay and red, and he placed them on separate continents. And but for the interference with his arrangement there would be no cause for such marriages. The fact that he separated the races shows that he did not intend for the races to mix."

After their convictions, the Lovings took up residence in the District of Columbia. On November 6, 1963, they filed a motion in the state trial court to vacate the judgment and set aside the sentence on the ground that the statutes which they had violated were repugnant to the Fourteenth Amendment. The motion not having been decided by October 28, 1964, the Lovings instituted a class action in the United States District Court for the Eastern District of Virginia requesting that a three-judge court be convened to declare the Virginia antimiscegenation statutes unconstitutional and to enjoin state officials from enforcing their convictions. On January 22, 1965, the state trial judge denied the motion to vacate the sentences, and the Lovings perfected an appeal to the Supreme Court of Appeals of Virginia. On February 11, 1965, the three-judge District Court continued the case to allow the Lovings to present their constitutional claims to the highest state court.

The Supreme Court of Appeals upheld the constitutionality of the antimiscegenation statutes and, after modifying the sentence, affirmed the convictions. The Lovings appealed this decision, and we noted probable jurisdiction on December 12, 1966, 385 U.S. 986.

The two statutes under which appellants were convicted and sentenced are part of a comprehensive statutory scheme aimed at prohibiting and punishing interracial marriages. The Lovings were convicted of violating Section 20–58 of the Virginia Code:

"Leaving State to evade law.—If any white person and colored person shall go out of this State, for the purpose of being married, and with the intention of returning, and be married out of it, and afterwards return to and reside in it, cohabiting as man and wife, they shall be punished as provided in Section 20–59, and the marriage shall be governed by the same law as if it had been solemnized in this State. The fact of their cohabitation here as man and wife shall be evidence of their marriage."

Section 20–59, which defines the penalty for miscegenation, provides:

"Punishment for marriage.—If any white person intermarry with a colored person, or any colored person intermarry with a white person, he shall be guilty of a felony and shall be punished by confinement in the penitentiary for not less than one nor more than five years."

Other central provisions in the Virginia statutory scheme [void] all marriages between "a white person and a colored person" without any judicial proceeding, and [define] "white persons" and "colored persons and Indians" for purposes of the statutory prohibitions. The Lovings have never disputed in the course of this litigation that Mrs. Loving is a "colored person" or that Mr. Loving is a "white person" within the meanings given those terms by the Virginia statutes.

Virginia is now one of 16 States which prohibit and punish marriages on the basis of racial classifications. Penalties for miscegenation arose as an incident to slavery and have been common in Virginia since the colonial period. The present statutory scheme dates from the adoption of the Racial Integrity Act of 1924, passed during the period of extreme nativism which followed the end of the First World War. The central features of this Act, and current Virginia law, are the absolute prohibition of a "white person" marrying other than another "white person," a prohibition against issuing marriage licenses until the issuing official is satisfied that the applicants' statements as to their race are correct, certificates of "racial composition" to be kept by both local and state registrars, and the carrying forward of earlier prohibitions against racial intermarriage. * * *

In upholding the constitutionality of these provisions in the decision below, the Supreme Court of Appeals of Virginia referred to its 1955 decision in Naim v. Naim, 197 Va. 80, 87 S. E. 2d 749, as stating the reasons supporting the validity of these laws. In Naim, the state court concluded that the State's legitimate purposes were "to preserve the racial integrity of its citizens," and to prevent "the corruption of blood," "a mongrel breed of citizens," and "the obliteration of racial pride," obviously an endorsement of the doctrine of White Supremacy. Id., at 90, 87 S. E. 2d, at 756. The court also reasoned that marriage has traditionally been subject to state regulation without federal intervention, and, consequently, the regulation of marriage should be left to exclusive state control by the Tenth Amendment.

While the state court is no doubt correct in asserting that marriage is a social relation subject to the State's police power, Maynard v. Hill, 125 U.S. 190 (1888), the State does not contend in its argument before this Court that its powers to regulate marriage are unlimited notwithstanding the commands of the Fourteenth Amendment. Nor could it do so in light of Meyer v. Nebraska, 262 U.S. 390 (1923), and Skinner v. Oklahoma, 316 U.S. 535 (1942). Instead, the State argues that the meaning of the Equal

Protection Clause, as illuminated by the statements of the Framers, is only that state penal laws containing an interracial element as part of the definition of the offense must apply equally to whites and Negroes in the sense that members of each race are punished to the same degree. * * *

Because we reject the notion that the mere "equal application" of a statute containing racial classifications is enough to remove the classifications from the Fourteenth Amendment's proscription of all invidious racial discriminations, we do not accept the State's contention that these statutes should be upheld if there is any possible basis for concluding that they serve a rational purpose. The mere fact of equal application does not mean that our analysis of these statutes should follow the approach we have taken in cases involving no racial discrimination where the Equal Protection Clause has been arrayed against a statute discriminating between the kinds of advertising which may be displayed on trucks in New York City, Railway Express Agency, Inc. v. New York, 336 U.S. 106 (1949), or an exemption in Ohio's ad valorem tax for merchandise owned by a nonresident in a storage warehouse, Allied Stores of Ohio, [*9] Inc. v. Bowers, 358 U.S. 522 (1959). In these cases, involving distinctions not drawn according to race, the Court has merely asked whether there is any rational foundation for the discriminations, and has deferred to the wisdom of the state legislatures. In the case at bar, however, we deal with statutes containing racial classifications, and the fact of equal application does not immunize the statute from the very heavy burden of justification which the Fourteenth Amendment has traditionally required of state statutes drawn according to race.

The State argues that statements in the Thirty-ninth Congress about the time of the passage of the Fourteenth Amendment indicate that the Framers did not intend the Amendment to make unconstitutional state miscegenation laws. * * *

The clear and central purpose of the Fourteenth Amendment was to eliminate all official state sources of invidious racial discrimination in the States. Slaughter–House Cases, 16 Wall. 36, 71 (1873); Strauder v. West Virginia, 100 U.S. 303, 307–308 (1880); Ex parte Virginia, 100 U.S. 339, 344–345 (1880); Shelley v. Kraemer, 334 U.S. 1 (1948); Burton v. Wilmington Parking Authority, 365 U.S. 715 (1961).

There can be no question but that Virginia's miscegenation statutes rest solely upon distinctions drawn according to race. The statutes proscribe generally accepted conduct if engaged in by members of different races. Over the years, this Court has consistently repudiated "distinctions between citizens solely because of their ancestry" as being "odious to a free people whose institutions are founded upon the doctrine of equality." Hirabayashi v. United States, 320 U.S. 81, 100 (1943). At the very least, the Equal Protection Clause demands that racial classifications, especially suspect in criminal statutes, be subjected to the "most rigid scrutiny," Korematsu v. United States, 323 U.S. 214, 216 (1944), and, if they are ever to be upheld, they must be shown to be necessary to the accomplishment of some permissible state objective, independent of the racial discrimination which it was the object of the Fourteenth Amendment to eliminate. Indeed, two members of this Court have already stated that they "cannot conceive of a valid legislative purpose * * * which makes the color of a person's skin the test of whether his conduct is a criminal offense." * * *

There is patently no legitimate overriding purpose independent of invidious racial discrimination which justifies this classification. The fact that Virginia prohibits only interracial marriages involving white persons demonstrates that the racial classifications must stand on their own justification, as measures designed to maintain White Supremacy. We have consistently denied the constitutionality of measures which restrict the rights of citizens on account of race. There can be no doubt that restricting the freedom to marry solely because of racial classifications violates the central meaning of the Equal Protection Clause. * * *

These statutes also deprive the Lovings of liberty without due process of law in violation of the Due Process Clause of the Fourteenth Amendment. The freedom to marry has long been recognized as one of the vital personal rights essential to the orderly pursuit of happiness by free men.

Marriage is one of the "basic civil rights of man," fundamental to our very existence and survival. Skinner v. Oklahoma, 316 U.S. 535, 541 (1942). See also Maynard v. Hill, 125 U.S. 190 (1888). To deny this fundamental freedom on so unsupportable a basis as the racial classifications embodied in these statutes, classifications so directly subversive of the principle of equality at the heart of the Fourteenth Amendment, is surely to deprive all the State's citizens of liberty without due process of law. The Fourteenth Amendment requires that the freedom of choice to marry not be restricted by invidious racial discriminations. Under our Constitution, the freedom to marry, or not marry, a person of another race resides with the individual and cannot be infringed by the State. * * * These convictions must be reversed.

PALMORE v. SIDOTI

466 U.S. 429 (1984).

CHIEF JUSTICE BURGER delivered the opinion of the Court.

We granted certiorari to review a judgment of a state court divesting a natural mother of the custody of her infant child because of her remarriage to a person of a different race. * * *

When petitioner Linda Sidoti Palmore and respondent Anthony J. Sidoti, both Caucasians, were divorced in May 1980 in Florida, the mother was awarded custody of their 3–year–old daughter.

In September 1981 the father sought custody of the child by filing a petition to modify the prior judgment because of changed conditions. The change was that the child's mother was then cohabiting with a Negro,

Clarence Palmore, Jr., whom she married two months later. Additionally, the father made several allegations of instances in which the mother had not properly cared for the child. * * *

It would ignore reality to suggest that racial and ethnic prejudices do not exist or that all manifestations of those prejudices have been eliminated. There is a risk that a child living with a stepparent of a different race may be subject to a variety of pressures and stresses not present if the child were living with parents of the same racial or ethnic origin.

The question, however, is whether the reality of private biases and the possible injury they might inflict are permissible considerations for removal of an infant child from the custody of its natural mother. We have little difficulty concluding that they are not. The Constitution cannot control such prejudices but neither can it tolerate them. Private biases may be outside the reach of the law, but the law cannot, directly or indirectly, give them effect. "Public officials sworn to uphold the Constitution may not avoid a constitutional duty by bowing to the hypothetical effects of private racial prejudice that they assume to be both widely and deeply held." * * *

Whatever problems racially mixed households may pose for children in 1984 can no more support a denial of constitutional rights [under the Equal Protection Clause] than could the stresses that residential integration was thought to entail in 1917. The effects of racial prejudice, however real, cannot justify a racial classification removing an infant child from the custody of its natural mother found to be an appropriate person to have such custody.

c. Parenting

SMITH v. ORGANIZATION OF FOSTER FAMILIES
431 U.S. 816 (1977).

Mr. Justice Brennan delivered the opinion of the Court.

Appellees, individual foster parents and an organization of foster parents, brought this civil rights class action pursuant to 42 U.S.C. § 1983 in the United States District Court for the Southern District of New York, on their own behalf and on behalf of children for whom they have provided homes for a year or more. They sought declaratory and injunctive relief against New York State and New York City officials, alleging that the procedures governing the removal of foster children from foster homes provided in [New York] * * * violated the Due Process and Equal Protection Clauses of the Fourteenth Amendment. * * *

Foster care of children is a sensitive and emotion-laden subject, and foster-care programs consequently stir strong controversy. The New York regulatory scheme is no exception. * * *

Our first inquiry is whether appellees have asserted interests within the Fourteenth Amendment's protection of "liberty" and "property." Board of Regents v. Roth, 408 U.S. 564, 571 (1972).

The appellees' basic contention is that when a child has lived in a foster home for a year or more, a psychological tie is created between the child and the foster parents which constitutes the foster family the true "psychological family" of the child. See J. Goldstein, A. Freud, & A. Solnit, Beyond the Best Interests of the Child (1973). That family, they argue, has a "liberty interest" in its survival as a family protected by the Fourteenth Amendment. Cf. Moore v. East Cleveland, ante, p. 494. Upon this premise they conclude that the foster child cannot be removed without a prior hearing satisfying due process their rights to their children before the children could be returned to them. * * *

We therefore turn to appellees' assertion that they have a constitutionally protected liberty interest—in the words of the District Court, a "right to familial privacy," 418 F.Supp., at 279—in the integrity of their family unit. This assertion clearly presents difficulties. * * *

It is, of course, true that "freedom of personal choice in matters of * * * family life is one of the liberties protected by the Due Process Clause of the Fourteenth Amendment." Cleveland Board of Education v. LaFleur, 414 U.S. 632, 639–640 (1974). There does exist a "private realm of family life which the state cannot enter," Prince v. Massachusetts, 321 U.S. 158, 166 (1944), that has been afforded both substantive and procedural protection. But is the relation of foster parent to foster child sufficiently akin to the concept of "family" recognized in our precedents to merit similar protection? Although considerable difficulty has attended the task of defining "family" for purposes of the Due Process Clause * * * we are not without guides to some of the elements that define the concept of "family" and contribute to its place in our society.

First, the usual understanding of "family" implies biological relationships, and most decisions treating the relation between parent and child have stressed this element. Stanley v. Illinois, 405 U.S. 645, 651 (1972), for example, spoke of "[t]he rights to conceive and to raise one's children" as essential rights. * * *

A biological relationship is not present in the case of the usual foster family. But biological relationships are not exclusive determination of the existence of a family. The basic foundation of the family in our society, the marriage relationship, is of course not a matter of blood relation. * * *

But there are also important distinctions between the foster family and the natural family. First, unlike the earlier cases recognizing a right to family privacy, the State here seeks to interfere, not with a relationship having its origins entirely apart from the power of the State, but rather with a foster family which has its source in state law and contractual arrangements. The individual's freedom to marry and reproduce is "older than the Bill of Rights," Griswold v. Connecticut, supra, at 486. Accordingly, unlike the property interests that are also protected by the Fourteenth Amendment, cf. Board of Regents v. Roth, 408 U.S., at 577, the liberty interest in family privacy has its source, and its contours are ordinarily to be sought, not in state law, but in intrinsic human rights, as they have been understood in "this Nation's history and tradition." Moore v. East Cleveland, ante, at 503. * * * Here, however, whatever emotional ties may develop between foster parent and foster child have their origins in an arrangement in which the State has been a partner from the outset. While the Court has recognized that liberty interests may in some cases arise from positive-law sources, see, e.g., Wolff v. McDonnell, 418 U.S. 539, 557 (1974), in such a case, and particularly where, as here, the claimed interest derives from a knowingly assumed contractual relation with the State, it is appropriate to ascertain from state law the expectations and entitlements of the parties. In this case, the limited recognition accorded to the foster family by the New York statutes and the contracts executed by the foster parents argue against any but the most limited constitutional "liberty" in the foster family. * * *

Where procedural due process must be afforded because a "liberty" or "property" interest is within the Fourteenth Amendment's protection, there must be determined "what process is due" in the particular context. * * *

It is true that "[b]efore a person is deprived of a protected interest, he must be afforded opportunity for some kind of a hearing, 'except for extraordinary situations where some valid governmental interest is at stake that justifies postponing the hearing until after the event.' " * * * But the hearing required is only one "appropriate to the nature of the case." Mullane v. Central Hanover Bank & Trust Co., 339 U.S. 306, 313 (1950). * * *

Turning first to the procedure applicable in New York City * * * [which] provides that before a child is removed from a foster home for transfer to another foster home, the foster parents may request an "independent review." * * * Such a procedure would appear to give a more elaborate trial-type hearing to foster families than this Court has found required in other contexts of administrative determinations. Cf. Goldberg v. Kelly, supra, at 266–271. * * *

Outside New York City, where only the statewide procedures apply, foster parents are provided not only with the procedures of a preremoval conference and postremoval hearing * * * but also with the preremoval judicial hearing available on request to foster parents who have in their care children who have been in foster care for 18 months or more * * *. [A] foster parent in such case may obtain an order that the child remain in his care. * * *

We deal here with issues of unusual delicacy, in an area where professional judgments regarding desirable procedures are constantly and rapidly changing. In such a context, restraint is appropriate on the part of courts called upon to adjudicate whether a particular procedural scheme is adequate under the Constitution. Since we hold that the procedures provided by New York State * * * and by New York [City] are adequate to protect whatever liberty interests appellees may have, the judgment of the District Court is Reversed.

NOTE: FATHERS' RIGHTS

A pair of noteworthy Supreme Court decisions detail the nature of a man's right to rear his biological children. In *Stanley v. Illinois*, 405 U.S. 645 (1972), a man who had lived with the mother of his three children intermittently for 18 years, but never married her, lost custody of their children when the mother died. Because Mr. Stanley was unmarried, his minor children were declared wards of the state and placed with court-appointed guardians. Had he been an unmarried mother rather than an unmarried father, the state would have assumed custody only after a hearing and proof of neglect. The Court held on equal protection grounds that, like any similarly situated woman in the state of Illinois, Mr. Stanley was entitled to a "hearing on his parental qualifications."

Michael H. v. Gerald D., 491 U.S. 110 (1989) was bad news for biological fathers. In this case the lover (Michael H.) of a married woman fathered a child by her and sought the rights of a father in California. A California statute defined a married woman's husband as the conclusively presumptive father of any child she bore. On that basis Michael was denied an opportunity to demonstrate paternity in an evidentiary proceeding. Michael brought suit claiming a liberty interest protected by the Fourteenth Amendment in an opportunity to establish the basis for a right to a parental relationship with his daughter. His case was especially strong since the child's mother had lived with him for a while, had admitted his paternity publicly, and had for a time allowed him to have a live-in relationship with the child. The Supreme Court nonetheless upheld the California statute and denied that a biological father has a constitutional right to a relationship with a child born out of wedlock to a married woman.

X, Y AND Z v. THE UNITED KINGDOM

(European Court of Human Rights Nr. 75/1995/581/667) 22/04/1997.

AS TO THE FACTS

I. Circumstances of the case

12. The applicants are British citizens, resident in Manchester, England.

The first applicant, "X", was born in 1955 and works as a college lecturer. X is a female-to-male transsexual and will be referred to throughout this judgment using the male personal pronouns "he", "him" and "his".

Since 1979 he has lived in a permanent and stable union with the second applicant, "Y", a woman born in 1959. The third applicant, "Z", was born in 1992 to the second applicant as a result of artificial insemination by donor ("AID"). Y has subsequently given birth to a second child by the same method.

13. X was born with a female body. However, from the age of four he felt himself to be a sexual misfit and was drawn to "masculine" roles

of behaviour. This discrepancy caused him to suffer suicidal depression during adolescence.

In 1975, he started to take hormone treatment and to live and work as a man. In 1979, he began living with Y and later that year he underwent gender reassignment surgery, having been accepted for treatment after counselling and psychological testing.

14. In 1990, X and Y applied through their general practitioner ("GP") for AID. They were interviewed by a specialist in January 1991 with a view to obtaining treatment and their application was referred to a hospital ethics committee, supported by two references and a letter from their GP. It was, however, refused.

15. They appealed, making representations which included reference to a research study in which it was reported that in a study of thirty-seven children raised by transsexual or homosexual parents or carers, there was no evidence of abnormal sexual orientation or any other adverse effect (R. Green, "Sexual identity of 37 children raised by homosexual or transsexual parents", American Journal of Psychiatry, 1978, vol. 135, pp. 692–97).

In November 1991, the hospital ethics committee agreed to provide treatment as requested by the applicants. They asked X to acknowledge himself to be the father of the child within the meaning of the Human Fertility and Embryology Act 1990.

16. On 30 January 1992, Y was impregnated through AID treatment with sperm from an anonymous donor. X was present throughout the process. Z was born on 13 October 1992.

17. In February 1992, X had enquired of the Registrar General whether there was an objection to his being registered as the father of Y's child. In a reply dated 4 June 1992 to X's Member of Parliament, the Minister of Health replied that, having taken legal advice, the Registrar General was of the view that only a biological man could be regarded as a father for the purposes of registration. It was pointed out that the child could lawfully bear X's surname and, subject to the relevant conditions, X would be entitled to an additional personal tax allowance if he could show that he provided financial support to the child.

18. Nonetheless, following Z's birth, X and Y attempted to register the child in their joint names as mother and father. However, X was not permitted to be registered as the child's father and that part of the register was left blank. Z was given X's surname in the register.

19. In November 1995, X's existing job contract came to an end and he applied for approximately thirty posts. The only job offer which he received was from a university in Botswana. The conditions of service included accommodation and free education for the dependants of the employee. However, X decided not to accept the job when he was informed by a Botswanan official that only spouses and biological or

adopted children would qualify as "dependants". He subsequently obtained another job in Manchester where he continues to work.

AS TO THE LAW

I. ALLEGED VIOLATION OF ARTICLE 8 OF THE CONVENTION (art. 8)

32. The applicants, with whom the Commission agreed, submitted that the lack of legal recognition of the relationship between X and Z amounted to a violation of Article 8 of the Convention. * * * The Government denied that Article 8 was applicable and, in the alternative, claimed that there had been no violation.

A. The existence of "family life"

33. The applicants submitted that they had shared a "family life" within the meaning of Article 8 since Z's birth. They emphasised that, according to the jurisprudence of the Commission and the Court, social reality, rather than formal legal status, was decisive. Thus, it was important to note that X had irrevocably changed many of his physical characteristics and provided financial and emotional support to Y and Z. To all appearances, the applicants lived as a traditional family.

34. The Government did not accept that the concept of "family life" applied to the relationships between X and Y or X and Z. They reasoned that X and Y had to be treated as two women living together, because X was still regarded as female under domestic law and a complete change of sex was not medically possible. Case-law of the Commission indicated that a "family" could not be based on two unrelated persons of the same sex, including a lesbian couple (see the Commission's decisions on admissibility in X and Y v. the United Kingdom, application no. 9369/81, Decisions and Reports 32, p. 220, and Kerkhoven and Others v. the Netherlands, application no. 15666/89). Nor could X be said to enjoy "family life" with Z since he was not related to the child by blood, marriage or adoption.

At the hearing before the Court, counsel for the Government accepted that if X and Y applied for and were granted a joint residence order in respect of Z (see paragraph 27 above), it would be difficult to maintain that there was no "family life" for the purposes of Article 8.

35. The Commission considered that the relationship between X and Y could not be equated with that of a lesbian couple, since X was living in society as a man, having undergone gender reassignment surgery. Aside from the fact that X was registered at birth as a woman and was therefore under a legal incapacity to marry Y or be registered as Z's father, the applicants' situation was indistinguishable from the traditional notion of "family life".

36. The Court recalls that the notion of "family life" in Article 8 is not confined solely to families based on marriage and may encompass other de facto relationships (see the Marckx v. Belgium judgment of

13 June 1979, Series A no. 31, p. 14, para. 31; the Keegan v. Ireland judgment of 26 May 1994, Series A no. 290, p. 17, para. 44; and the Kroon and Others v. the Netherlands judgment of 27 October 1994, Series A no. 297–C, pp. 55–56, para. 30). When deciding whether a relationship can be said to amount to "family life", a number of factors may be relevant, including whether the couple live together, the length of their relationship and whether they have demonstrated their commitment to each other by having children together or by any other means (see, for example, the above-mentioned Kroon and Others judgment, loc. cit.).

37.   In the present case, the Court notes that X is a transsexual who has undergone gender reassignment surgery. He has lived with Y, to all appearances as her male partner, since 1979. The couple applied jointly for, and were granted, treatment by AID to allow Y to have a child. X was involved throughout that process and has acted as Z's "father" in every respect since the birth (see paragraphs 14–16 above). In these circumstances, the Court considers that de facto family ties link the three applicants.

It follows that Article 8 is applicable.

B.   Compliance with Article 8

1.   The arguments as to the applicable general principles

38.   The applicants pointed out that the Court had recognised in its Rees v. the United Kingdom judgment (17 October 1986, Series A no. 106, p. 19, para. 47), that the need for appropriate legal measures affecting transsexuals should be kept under review having regard in particular to scientific and societal developments. They maintained that there had been significant development since that decision: in particular, the European Parliament and the Parliamentary Assembly of the Council of Europe had called for comprehensive recognition of transsexual identity (Resolution OJ 1989 C256 and Recommendation 1117 of 29 September 1989 respectively); the Court of Justice of the European Communities had decided that the dismissal of a transsexual for a reason related to gender reassignment amounted to discrimination contrary to Community Directive 76/207 (P. v. S. and Cornwall County Council, C–13/94, 30 April 1996); and scientific research had been published which suggested that transsexuality was not merely a psychological disorder, but had a physiological basis in the structure of the brain (see, for example, "Biological Aspects of Transsexualism" by Professor L.J.G. Gooren, Council of Europe document no. CJ–DE/XXIII (93) 5, and Zhou, Hofman, Gooren and Swaab, "A sex difference in the human brain and its relation to transsexuality", Nature, 2 November 1995, vol. 378, p. 68). These developments made it appropriate for the Court to re-examine the principles underlying its decisions in the above-mentioned Rees case and in Cossey v. the United Kingdom (27 September 1990, Series A no. 184), in so far as they had an impact on the present problem. The Court should now

hold that the notion of respect for family and/or private life required States to recognise the present sexual identity of post-operative transsexuals for legal purposes, including parental rights.

However, they also emphasised that the issue in their case was very different from that in Rees and Cossey, since X was not seeking to amend his own birth certificate but rather to be named in Z's birth certificate as her father. They submitted that the margin of appreciation afforded to the respondent State should be narrower in such a case and the need for positive action to ensure respect much stronger, having regard to the interests of the child in having her social father recognised as such by law.

39. The Government contended that Contracting States enjoyed a wide margin of appreciation in relation to the complex issues raised by transsexuality, in view of the lack of a uniform approach to the problem and the transitional state of the law. They denied that there had been any significant change in the scientific or legal position with regard to transsexuals: despite recent research, there still remained uncertainty as to the essential nature of the condition and there was not yet any sufficiently broad consensus between the member States of the Council of Europe (see, for example, the Report of the Proceedings of the XXIIIrd Colloquy on European Law, Transsexualism, Medicine and the Law, Council of Europe, 1993, and S.M. Breedlove, "Another Important Organ", Nature, 2 November 1995, vol. 378, p. 15). The judgment of the Court of Justice of the European Communities in P. v. S. and Cornwall County Council (cited at paragraph 38 above) did not assist the applicants because it was notconcerned with the extent to which a State was obliged to recognise a person's change of sex for legal purposes.

Like the applicants, the Government stressed that the present case was not merely concerned with transsexuality. Since it also raised difficult and novel questions relating to the treatment of children born by AID, the State should enjoy a very broad margin of appreciation.

40. The Commission referred to a clear trend within the Contracting States towards the legal recognition of gender reassignment. It took the view that, in the case of a transsexual who had undergone gender reassignment surgery in the Contracting State and who lived there as part of a family relationship, there had to be a presumption in favour of legal recognition of that relationship, the denial of which required special justification.

2. The Court's general approach

41. The Court reiterates that, although the essential object of Article 8 is to protect the individual against arbitrary interferences by the public authorities, there may in addition be positive obligations inherent in an effective respect for private or family life. The boundaries between the State's positive and negative obligations under this

provision do not always lend themselves to precise definition; none-theless, the applicable principles are similar. In both contexts, regard must be had to the fair balance that has to be struck between the competing interests of the individual and of the community as a whole, and in both cases the State enjoys a certain margin of appreci-ation (see, for example, the above-mentioned Rees judgment, p. 14, para. 35, and the above-mentioned Kroon and Others judgment, p. 56, para. 31).

42. The present case is distinguishable from the previous cases concerning transsexuals which have been brought before the Court (see the above-mentioned Rees judgment, the above-mentioned Cossey judgment and the B. v. France judgment of 25 March 1992, Series A no. 232–C), because here the applicants' complaint is not that the domestic law makes no provision for the recognition of the transsexu-al's change of identity, but rather that it is not possible for such a person to be registered as the father of a child; indeed, it is for this reason that the Court is examining this case in relation to family, rather than private, life (see paragraph 37 above).

43. It is true that the Court has held in the past that where the existence of a family tie with a child has been established, the State must act in a manner calculated to enable that tie to be developed and legal safeguards must be established that render possible, from the moment of birth or as soon as practicable thereafter, the child's integration in his family (see for example the above-mentioned Marckx judgment, p. 15, para. 31; the Johnston and Others v. Ireland judgment of 18 December 1986, Series A no. 112, p. 29, para. 72; the above-mentioned Keegan judgment, p. 19, para. 50; and the above-mentioned Kroon and Others judgment, p. 56, para. 32). However, hitherto in this context it has been called upon to consider only family ties existing between biological parents and their offspring. The present case raises different issues, since Z was conceived by AID and is not related, in the biological sense, to X, who is a transsexual.

44. The Court observes that there is no common European standard with regard to the granting of parental rights to transsexuals. In addition, it has not been established before the Court that there exists any generally shared approach amongst the High Contracting Parties with regard to the manner in which the social relationship between a child conceived by AID and the person who performs the role of father should be reflected in law. Indeed, according to the information available to the Court, although the technology of medically assisted procreation has been available in Europe for several decades, many of the issues to which it gives rise, particularly with regard to the question of filiation, remain the subject of debate. For example, there is no consensus amongst the member States of the Council of Europe on the question whether the interests of a child conceived in such a way are best served by preserving the anonymity of the donor of the

sperm or whether the child should have the right to know the donor's identity.

Since the issues in the case, therefore, touch on areas where there is little common ground amongst the member States of the Council of Europe and, generally speaking, the law appears to be in a transitional stage, the respondent State must be afforded a wide margin of appreciation (see, mutatis mutandis, the above mentioned Rees judgment, p. 15, para. 37, and the above-mentioned Cossey judgment, p. 16, para. 40).

3.   Whether a fair balance was struck in the instant case

45.   The applicants, with whom the Commission agreed, argued that a number of consequences flowed from the lack of legal recognition of X's role as father. Perhaps most importantly, the child's sense of security within the family might be undermined. Furthermore, the absence of X's name on her birth certificate might cause distress on those occasions when a full-length certificate had to be produced, for example on registration with a doctor or school, if an insurance policy was taken out on her life or when she applied for a passport. Although Z was a British citizen by birth and could trace connection through her mother in immigration and nationality matters, problems could still arise if X sought to work abroad. For example, he had already had to turn down an offer of employment in Botswana because he had been informed that Y and Z would not have been recognised as his "dependants" and would not, therefore, have been entitled to receive certain benefits (see paragraph 19 above). Moreover, in contrast to the position where a parent-child relationship was recognised by law, Z could not inherit from X on intestacy or succeed to certain tenancies on X's death. The possibility of X obtaining a residence order in respect of Z (see paragraph 27 above) did not satisfy the requirement of respect, since this would entail the incurring of legal expense and an investigation by a court welfare officer which might distress the child.

In their submission, it was apparent that the legal recognition sought would not interfere with the rights of others or require any fundamental reorganisation of the United Kingdom system of registration of births, since the Human Fertility and Embryology Act 1990 allowed a man who was not a transsexual to be registered as the father of a child born to his female partner by AID (see paragraph 21 above).

46.   The Government pointed out that the applicants were not restrained in any way from living together as a "family" and they asserted that the concerns expressed by them were highly theoretical. Furthermore, X and Y could jointly apply for a residence order, conferring on them parental rights and duties in relation to Z.

47.   First, the Court observes that the community as a whole has an interest in maintaining a coherent system of family law which places

the best interests of the child at the forefront. In this respect, the Court notes that, whilst it has not been suggested that the amendment to the law sought by the applicants would be harmful to the interests of Z or of children conceived by AID in general, it is not clear that it would necessarily be to the advantage of such children.

In these circumstances, the Court considers that the State may justifiably be cautious in changing the law, since it is possible that the amendment sought might have undesirable or unforeseen ramifications for children in Z's position. Furthermore, such an amendment might have implications in other areas of family law. For example, the law might be open to criticism on the ground of inconsistency if a female-to-male transsexual were granted the possibility of becoming a "father" in law while still being treated for other legal purposes as female and capable of contracting marriage to a man.

48. Against these general interests, the Court must weigh the disadvantages suffered by the applicants as a result of the refusal to recognise X in law as Z's "father".

The applicants identify a number of legal consequences flowing from this lack of recognition (see paragraph 45 above). For example, they point to the fact that if X were to die intestate, Z would have no automatic right of inheritance. The Court notes, however, that the problem could be solved in practice if X were to make a will. No evidence has been adduced to show that X is the beneficiary of any transmissible tenancies of the type referred to; similarly, since Z is a British citizen by birth and can trace connection through her mother in immigration and nationality matters, she will not be disadvantaged in this respect by the lack of a legal relationship with X.

The Court considers, therefore, that these legal consequences would be unlikely to cause undue hardship given the facts of the present case.

49. In addition, the applicants claimed that Z might suffer various social or developmental difficulties. Thus, it was argued that she would be caused distress on those occasions when it was necessary to produce her birth certificate.

In relation to the absence of X's name on the birth certificate, the Court notes, first, that unless X and Y choose to make such information public, neither the child nor any third party will know that this absence is a consequence of the fact that X was born female. It follows that the applicants are in a similar position to any other family where, for whatever reason, the person who performs the role of the child's "father" is not registered as such. The Court does not find it established that any particular stigma still attaches to children or families in such circumstances.

Secondly, the Court recalls that in the United Kingdom a birth certificate is not in common use for administrative or identification purposes and that there are few occasions when it is necessary to produce a full length certificate.

50.   The applicants were also concerned, more generally, that Z's sense of personal identity and security within her family would be affected by the lack of legal recognition of X as father.

In this respect, the Court notes that X is not prevented in any way from acting as Z's father in the social sense. Thus, for example, he lives with her, providing emotional and financial support to her and Y, and he is free to describe himself to her and others as her "father" and to give her his surname (see paragraph 24 above). Furthermore, together with Y, he could apply for a joint residence order in respect of Z, which would automatically confer on them full parental responsibility for her in English law.

51.   It is impossible to predict the extent to which the absence of a legal connection between X and Z will affect the latter's development. As previously mentioned, at the present time there is uncertainty with regard to how the interests of children in Z's position can best be protected and the Court should not adopt or impose any single viewpoint.

52.   In conclusion, given that transsexuality raises complex scientific, legal, moral and social issues, in respect of which there is no generally shared approach among the Contracting States, the Court is of the opinion that Article 8 cannot, in this context, be taken to imply an obligation for the respondent State formally to recognise as the father of a child a person who is not the biological father. That being so, the fact that the law of the United Kingdom does not allow special legal recognition of the relationship between X and Z does not amount to a failure to respect family life within the meaning of that provision.

It follows that there has been no violation of Article 8 of the Convention.

* * *

FOR THESE REASONS, THE COURT

1.   Holds unanimously that Article 8 of the Convention (art. 8) is applicable in the present case;

2.   Holds by fourteen votes to six that there has been no violation of Article 8 * * *.

NOTE: GRANDPARENTS' RIGHTS

In *Troxel v. Granville*, 530 U.S. 57 (2000), the paternal grandparents of two minor children whose father had committed suicide sought visitation rights over the objection of the children's mother. The grandparents relied on a state law granting "any person" the right to petition the court for visitation "at any time" and the courts the right to grant such a petition when it was in the "best interests of the child." The mother believed the grandparents wanted too much time with her children. The Court held that the judgment of fit parents to determine their children's best interest demanded deference. Justice Steven's argued in dissent that children have a liberty interest in relationships with third-parties, such as their grandparents. When children's and parents' interests clash, Stevens argued, government need not defer to an exercise of authority by a parent. Is Steven's perspective workable?

NOTE: FAMILIES BEHIND BARS

The men and women who wind up in prison often leave families behind. Is there a fundamental right to maintain a relationship with a parent, spouse, or child, despite incarceration? Cf. *Williamson v. Nuttall*, 35 A.D.3d 926 (N.Y.A.D. 2006). Should women jailed for non-violent crimes be permitted to care for their infants? Family visits are an option for most prisoners, and some prisons even allow conjugal visits on grounds. Courts have held that men and women in prison may marry. How should prisons approach requests for same-sex marriages or civil unions between inmates?

d. Informational Privacy

NOTE: THE WHALEN DOCTRINE

Whalen v. Roe is an unusual 14th Amendment privacy case. The privacy interests under consideration are mostly informational not decisional in character. When you are reading *Whalen*, consider the role the state's promise of data security and confidentiality play in the outcome of the case. Are concerns about data breaches more numerous today than in the 1970's? How have things changed?

Is the 14th Amendment a general constraint on collecting and passing on sensitive information? Decades after *Whalen v. Roe*, the contours of a constitutional right of information privacy remain vague. See *Nelson v. National Aeronautics and Space Admin.*, 568 F.3d 1028 (9th Cir. 2009) (Kozinski, dissenting), cert. granted by National Aeronautics and Space Admin. v. Nelson, 130 S.Ct. 1755, 176 L.Ed.2d 211, 78 USLW 3272, 78 USLW 3517, 78 USLW 3521 (U.S. Mar 08, 2010) (NO. 09–530). At least two federal circuits have held that prisoners have an informational privacy right in medical information protected by the Fourteenth Amendment.

WHALEN v. ROE
429 U.S. 589 (1977).

MR. JUSTICE STEVENS delivered the opinion of the Court.

The constitutional question presented is whether the State of New York may record, in a centralized computer file, the names and addresses of all persons who have obtained, pursuant to a doctor's prescription, certain drugs for which there is both a lawful and an unlawful market.

The District Court enjoined enforcement of the portions of the New York State Controlled Substances Act of 1972 which require such recording on the ground that they violate appellees' constitutionally protected rights of privacy. We * * * now reverse. * * *

Many drugs have both legitimate and illegitimate uses. In response to a concern that such drugs were being diverted into unlawful channels, in 1970 the New York Legislature created a special commission to evaluate the State's drug control laws. The commission found the existing laws deficient in several respects. There was no effective way to prevent the use of stolen or revised prescriptions, to prevent unscrupulous pharmacists from repeatedly refilling prescriptions, to prevent users from obtaining prescriptions from more than one doctor, or to prevent doctors from overprescribing, either by authorizing an excessive amount in one prescription or by giving one patient multiple prescriptions. In drafting new legislation to correct such defects, the commission consulted with enforcement officials in California and Illinois where central reporting systems were being used effectively. * * *

Appellees contend that the statute invades a constitutionally protected "zone of privacy." The cases sometimes characterized as protecting "privacy" have in fact involved at least two different kinds of interests. One is the individual interest in avoiding disclosure of personal matters, and another is the interest in independence in making certain kinds of important decisions. Appellees argue that both of these interests are impaired by statute. The mere existence in readily available form of the information about patients' use of * * * [certain] drugs creates a genuine concern that the information will become publicly known and that it will adversely affect their reputations. This concern makes some patients reluctant to use, and some doctors reluctant to prescribe, such drugs even when their use is medically indicated. It follows, they argue, that the making of decisions about matters vital to the care of their health is inevitably affected by the statute. Thus, the statute threatens to impair both their interest in the nondisclosure of private information and also their interest in making important decisions independently.

We are persuaded, however, that the New York program does not, on its face, pose a sufficiently grievous threat to either interest to establish a constitutional violation.

Public disclosure of patient information can come about in three ways. Health Department employees may violate the statute by failing, either deliberately or negligently, to maintain proper security. A patient or a doctor may be accused of a violation and the stored data may be offered in evidence in a judicial proceeding. Or, thirdly, a doctor, a pharmacist, or the patient may voluntarily reveal information on a prescription form.

The third possibility existed under the prior law and is entirely unrelated to the existence of the computerized data bank. Neither of the other two possibilities provides a proper ground for attacking the statute as invalid on its face. There is no support in the record, or in the experience of the two States that New York has emulated, for an assumption that the security provisions of the statute will be administered improperly. And the remote possibility that judicial supervision of the evidentiary use of particular items of stored information will provide inadequate protection against unwarranted disclosures is surely not a sufficient reason for invalidating the entire patient-identification program.

Even without public disclosure, it is, of course, true that private information must be disclosed to the authorized employees of the New York Department of Health. Such disclosures, however, are not significantly different from those that were required under the prior law. Nor are they meaningfully distinguishable from a host of other unpleasant invasions of privacy that are associated with many facets of health care. Unquestionably, some individuals' concern for their own privacy may lead them to avoid or to postpone needed medical attention. Nevertheless, disclosures of private medical information to doctors, to hospital personnel, to insurance companies, and to public health agencies are often an essential part of modern medical practice even when the disclosure may reflect unfavorably on the character of the patient. Requiring such disclosures to representatives of the State having responsibility for the health of the community, does not automatically amount to an impermissible invasion of privacy.

Appellees also argue, however, that even if unwarranted disclosures do not actually occur, the knowledge that the information is readily available in a computerized file creates a genuine concern that causes some persons to decline medication. The record supports the conclusion that some use of [certain] * * * drugs has been discouraged by that concern; it also is clear, however, that about 100,000 prescriptions for such drugs were being filled each month prior to the entry of the District Court's injunction. Clearly, therefore, the statute did not deprive the public of access to the drugs.

Nor can it be said that any individual has been deprived of the right to decide independently, with the advice of his physician, to acquire and to use needed medication. Although the State no doubt could prohibit entirely the use of particular Schedule II drugs, it has not done so. This case is therefore unlike those in which the Court held that a total prohibition of certain conduct was an impermissible deprivation of liberty. Nor does the State require access to these drugs to be conditioned on the consent of any state official or other third party. Within dosage limits which appellees do not challenge, the decision to prescribe, or to use, is left entirely to the physician and the patient.

We hold that neither the immediate nor the threatened impact of the patient-identification requirements in the New York State Controlled Substances Act of 1972 on either the reputation or the independence of patients for whom Schedule II drugs are medically indicated is sufficient to constitute an invasion of any right or liberty protected by the Fourteenth Amendment. * * *

MOORE v. PREVO

2010 WL 1849208 (C.A.6 (Mich.)).

This is a prisoner civil rights action filed pursuant to 42 U.S.C. § 1983. Tyrone Moore was a prisoner at the Riverside Correctional Facility in Ionia, Michigan. He alleges that, on July 2, 2007, Nurse Prevo and two correction officers, Simmons and Doe, informed fellow-prisoner Franks, that Moore is HIV positive. Moore also alleges that Inspector L. Brown asked prisoner Henton if he knew that Moore had a sexually transmitted disease, and that Officer Satterlee was "involved." * * *

On August 4, 2008, Moore filed a pro se complaint and application to proceed *in forma pauperis* in the United States District Court for the Western District of Michigan, alleging that Prevo, Simmons, Doe, Satterlee, and Brown, in their individual and official capacities, had violated his Fourth Amendment right to privacy when they disclosed his HIV-positive status to other officers and inmates. * * *

It is beyond question that information about one's HIV-positive status is information of the most personal kind and that an individual has an interest in protecting against the dissemination of such information. *See Doe v. [Southeastern Pa. Transp. Autho.]*, 72 F.3d [1133,] 1140 [(3d Cir.1995)]; *Westinghouse*, 638 F.2d at 577. Moreover, a prisoner's right to privacy in this medical information is not fundamentally inconsistent with incarceration. Therefore, we join the Second Circuit in recognizing that the constitutional right to privacy in one's medical information exists in prison. *See Powell*, 175 F.3d at 112.

We acknowledge, however, that a prisoner does not enjoy a right of privacy in his medical information to the same extent as a free citizen. We do not suggest that [the appellant] has a right to conceal this diagnosed medical condition from everyone in the corrections system. [The appellant's] constitutional right is subject to substantial restrictions and limitations in order for correctional officials to achieve legitimate correctional goals and maintain institutional security.

Delie, 257 F.3d at 317 (finding that prison officials who disclosed an inmate's HIV-positive status to officers, guards, and inmates had violated the inmate's constitutionally protected privacy right). The Second Circuit also has held that "prison officials can impinge upon [the right to maintain the confidentiality of previously undisclosed medical information] only to the extent that their actions are 'reasonably related to legitimate penological interests.'" *Powell*, 175 F.3d at 112 (finding that a prisoner had a privacy interest in keeping his transsexual status from other inmates).

We join our sister circuits in finding that, as a matter of law, inmates have a Fourteenth Amendment privacy interest in guarding against disclosure of sensitive medical information from other inmates subject to legitimate penological interests. Accordingly, the district court erred in finding that Moore's privacy claims failed as a matter of law. It remains to be seen if Moore's allegations have any factual support.

NELSON v. NATIONAL AERONAUTICS AND SPACE ADMIN.

568 F.3d 1028 (9th Cir. 2009).

WARDLAW, CIRCUIT JUDGE, concurring in the denial of rehearing en banc, joined by PREGERSON, REINHARDT, W. FLETCHER, FISHER, PAEZ, and BERZON CIRCUIT JUDGES:

This is an interlocutory appeal from the denial of a preliminary injunction sought by a class of long-term California Institute of Technology ("Caltech") employees, including scientists, engineers, and administrative support personnel—all classified by the National Aeronautics and Space Administration ("NASA") as low risk employees. They oppose implementation of a new, wide-ranging, and highly intrusive background check imposed as a condition of their continued employment at Jet Propulsion Laboratory ("JPL"). Caltech itself objected to the new requirement as "inappropriate." Reversing the district court's denial of the preliminary injunction, we concluded that, as to the constitutional right of privacy claim, "serious questions going to the merits were raised and the balance of harms tips sharply in[the plaintiff-class's] favor," *Walczak v. EPL Prolong, Inc.*, 198 F.3d 725, 731 (9th Cir.1999), where the class faced the Hobson's choice of losing their jobs or submitting to an unprecedented intrusion into their private lives for which the government failed to advance a legitimate state interest. *Nelson v. NASA* (*Nelson II*), 530 F.3d 865, 883 (9th Cir.2008). * * *

The 9/11 Commission found that "[a]ll but one of the 9/11 hijackers acquired some form of U.S. identification document, some by fraud," and recommended that the federal government set standards for the issuance of identification because identification fraud is a concern at "vulnerable facilities." THE 9/11 COMMISSION REPORT 390 (2004). On August 27, 2004, the President of the United States issued Homeland Security Presidential Directive 12 ("HSPD–12") in response to security concerns identified by the 9/11 Commission Report and mandated that the Commerce Department develop a uniform federal standard, applicable to federal employees and contractors alike, for secure and reliable forms of identification. The order emphasized that the Commerce Department should act to eliminate the "[w]ide variations in the quality and security of forms of identification used to gain access to secure Federal and other facilities where there is potential for terrorist attacks...."

Acting pursuant to this directive, the Commerce Department promulgated Federal Information Processing Standards ("FIPS") 201 and 201–1, which required security measures for contract employees commensurate with those applicable to comparable federal employees. FIPS 201–1 sets forth a standard for "identification issued by Federal departments and agencies to Federal employees and contractors (including contractor employees) for gaining physical access to federally-controlled facilities and logical access to Federally controlled information systems." * * *

Meanwhile, on August 5, 2005, the Office of Management and Budget ("OMB") provided guidance on the implementation of HSPD–12, requiring agencies "develop a plan and begin the required background investigations for all current contractors who do not have a successfully adjudicated investigation on record ... no later than October 27, 2007." Memorandum from OMB on Implementation of Homeland Sec. Presidential Directive (HSPD) 12–Policy for a Common Identification Standard for Fed. Employees and Contractors 6 (Aug. 5, 2005). OMB stated that the completion of a NACI would be a prerequisite to the issuance of any identification. *Id.* at 5. Across all NASA facilities, over 57,000 individuals are subject to these new requirements, over 46,000 had applied as of August 31, 2007, and approximately 39,000 NASA contractors had completed the background investigation as of September 21, 2007.

CHIEF JUDGE KOZINSKI, with whom JUDGES KLEINFELD and BEA join, dissenting from the denial of rehearing en banc:

Is there a constitutional right to informational privacy? Thirty-two Terms ago, the Supreme Court hinted that there might be and has never said another word about it. *See Whalen v. Roe,* 429 U.S. 589, 599, 97 S.Ct. 869, 51 L.Ed.2d 64 (1977) (alluding to "the individual interest in avoiding disclosure of personal matters"), and *Nixon v. Administrator of General Services,* 433 U.S. 425, 457, 97 S.Ct. 2777, 53 L.Ed.2d 867 (1977) (quoting the above phrase from *Whalen*). With no Supreme Court guidance except this opaque fragment, the courts of appeals have been left to develop the contours of this free-floating privacy guarantee on their own. It's a bit like building a dinosaur from a jawbone or a skull fragment, and the result looks more like a turducken. We have a grab-bag of cases on specific issues, but no theory as to what this right (if it exists) is all about. The result in each case seems to turn more on instinct than on any overarching principle.

One important function of the en banc process is to synthesize the accumulated experience of panels into firmer guideposts. We ought to have taken this case en banc for precisely that reason. Unless and until the Supreme Court again weighs in on this topic, only an en banc court can trim the hedges, correct what now appear to be missteps and give the force of law to those distinctions that experience has revealed to be important.

1. One such distinction is between mere government *collection* of information and the government's *disclosure* of private information to the public. *Whalen* involved the latter: patients who feared public disclosure of their prescription records. Many of the cases in our circuit fall into this mold. In *Tucson Woman's Clinic v. Eden,* we held that women had a right not to have the government disclose their pregnancy records to a third-party contractor. 379 F.3d 531, 553 (9th Cir.2004). *In re Crawford* featured a bankruptcy preparer who didn't want his Social Security

number published. 194 F.3d 954 (9th Cir.1999). But in other cases, such as the one now before us, we have sustained informational privacy claims without any allegations that the government might publish what it learned. *See, e.g., Norman–Bloodsaw v. Lawrence Berkeley Laboratory,* 135 F.3d 1260 (9th Cir.1998).

The distinction matters. Government acquisition of information is already regulated by express constitutional provisions, particularly those in the Fourth, Fifth and Sixth Amendments. How can the creation of new constitutional constraints be squared with the teachings of *Medina v. California,* which cautioned against discovering protections in the Due Process Clause in areas where the "Bill of Rights speaks in explicit terms"? 505 U.S. 437, 443, 112 S.Ct. 2572, 120 L.Ed.2d 353 (1992). Our cases, including this one, neither address nor acknowledge this problem. Yet limiting the government's ability to gather information has very serious implications, as Judge Callahan's dissent illustrates.

2.   There's also an important distinction between disclosures that the target may refuse and those imposed regardless of his consent. The latter is inherently more invasive. *Nixon* is instructive: There, the former president was required by law to submit his papers for screening by the National Archives. This requirement wasn't imposed as a condition on some benefit or job opportunity; rather, it was imposed outright under penalty of law. 433 U.S. at 429, 97 S.Ct. 2777. Though Nixon was unsuccessful, it wasn't because his claim wasn't found to be cognizable; the public interest was held to outweigh his privacy. In *Whalen,* the only way for the patients to avoid having their prescription records turned over was to give up needed pharmaceuticals. Our cases sometimes fit comfortably in this mold: What was so creepy about the medical tests in *Norman–Bloodsaw,* for example, was the sneaky way they were done without the subjects' knowledge or consent. 135 F.3d at 1269.

It strikes me as quite a different case when the government seeks to collect information directly from persons who are free to say no. The plaintiffs here had a simple way to keep their private dealings private: They could have declined to fill out the forms, provided no references and sought other employment. Does being asked to disclose information one would prefer to keep private, in order to keep a government job to which one has no particular entitlement, amount to a constitutional violation? If the answer is yes, then the government commits all manner of constitutional violations on tax returns, government contract bids, loan qualification forms and thousands of job applications that are routinely filled out every day.

3.   There is also a distinction, recognized by some of our sister circuits, between information that pertains to a fundamental right, such as the right to an abortion or contraception, *see, e.g., Bloch v. Ribar,* 156 F.3d 673, 684 (6th Cir.1998), and a free-standing right not to have the world know bad things about you. The former kind of right seems to stand on far sounder constitutional footing than the latter.

4. Consider also the contrast between investigating a subject by digging through his bank records or medical files, and contacting third parties to find out what they know about him. One's pregnancy status (perhaps known to no one), as in *Norman–Bloodsaw,* or the need for certain pharmaceuticals, as in *Whalen,* is private precisely because one has been careful not to disclose it. But one's privacy interest ought to wane the more widely the information is known. The Supreme Court has made a related point about the Fourth Amendment: Individuals lack a reasonable expectation of privacy in information that they share voluntarily with others. *See United States v. Miller,* 425 U.S. 435, 443, 96 S.Ct. 1619, 48 L.Ed.2d 71 (1976).

Does one really have a free-standing constitutional right to withhold from the government information that others in the community are aware of? I don't think so. How then can it be constitutionally impermissible for the government to ask a subject's friends, family and neighbors what they know about him? Surely there's no constitutional right to have the state be the last to know.

5. A final distinction that emerges from the cases is between the government's different functions as enforcer of the laws and as employer. In *Whalen,* the government was acting as the former, collecting prescription records to aid later investigation of unlawful distribution. 429 U.S. at 591–92, 97 S.Ct. 869. Similarly, in *Tucson Woman's Clinic,* the government was ostensibly scooping up patient information to protect the public health. 379 F.3d at 536–37. Here, as Judge Kleinfeld illustrates in his dissent, the government is simply acting as any other employer might: collecting information for its own purposes to make employment decisions.

If a right to informational privacy exists at all, *but see American Federation of Government Emp., AFL–CIO v. Department of Housing and Urban Development,* 118 F.3d 786, 791, 793 (D.C.Cir.1997), it would be far more likely to apply when the government is exercising its sovereign authority than when it is monitoring its own employees.

While I can think of many reasons to worry when the government seeks to uncover private information using the special powers that private entities lack, it's far less obvious why it should be hamstrung in ensuring the security and integrity of its operations in ways that private employers are not. The delicate knowledge handled by thousands of federal employees seems as worthy of protection as the formula for Coca–Cola.

* * *

As we have recognized elsewhere, there are circumstances when a well-worn doctrine can grow into "a vexing thicket of precedent" that then becomes "difficult for litigants to follow and for district courts—and ourselves—to apply with consistency." *United States v. Heredia,* 483 F.3d 913, 919 (9th Cir.2007) (en banc). The back-and-forth between the panel and my dissenting colleagues illustrates that we have reached this point with the doctrine of informational privacy. Though I am sympathetic to the arguments of my dissenting colleagues, it's not clear that the panel has misapplied circuit law; when the law is so subjective and amorphous, it's difficult to know exactly what a misapplication might look like.

It's time to clear the brush. An en banc court is the only practical way we have to do it. We didn't undertake that chore today, but we'll have to sooner or later, unless the Supreme Court should intervene.

SEATON v. MAYBERG

610 F.3d 530 (9th Cir. 2010).

[Michael Leon] Seaton was convicted in 1986 of two counts each of forcible rape and forcible oral copulation, and one count of kidnaping for the purpose of committing rape. He had two prior serious felony convictions, and was sentenced to 42 years in state prison, later reduced to 37 and then 31 years. After 16 years, apparently because he was approaching early release, the county sheriff's department had him transferred to a state hospital for evaluation for possible civil commitment.

He sued the Director of the California Department of Mental Health, the Administrator of Atascadero State Hospital, and the two psychologists who examined him and gave their opinions to the county district attorney's office. Though he raises several theories, the most substantial is that the defendants violated his constitutional right to privacy by allowing the psychologists to look at his records and to communicate their opinions and supporting data to the district attorney's office. This case is his section 1983 claim, not his habeas corpus case.

Seaton's medical records were being examined to decide whether to seek his commitment under California's Sexually Violent Predator Act. The Act enables the state to commit some sex offenders civilly for indeterminate terms subject to yearly evaluations. A "sexually violent predator" under the statute is one who (1) has been convicted of a sexually violent offense, (2) has a diagnosed mental disorder, (3) that makes him a danger to the health and safety of others, (4) the danger being "that it is likely that he or she will engage in sexually violent criminal behavior." The prior offense may be evidence, but is not conclusive. A mental disorder "that predisposes the person to the commission of criminal sexual acts in a degree constituting the person a menace" is a *sine qua non*. Thus the statute provides for the civil commitment of persons whose mental disease predisposes them to crime and whose criminal history gives weight to the predictive judgment.

The statute provides for the Secretary of the Department of Corrections and Rehabilitation to refer for evaluation, at least six months before release, prisoners who may be sexually violent predators if they are serving a determinate sentence or their parole has been revoked. The Department of Corrections first screens the prisoners with a screening instrument developed by the State Department of Mental Health, considering their "social, criminal and institutional history." If it appears that they are indeed sexually violent predators, then they are referred to the State Department of Mental Health for a full evaluation, in accord with a standardized assessment protocol, including "diagnosable mental disorders" and "factors known to be associated with the risk of reoffense" including "criminal and psychosexual history, type degree and duration of sexual deviance, and severity of mental disorder." The Director of Mental Health designates two practicing psychiatrists or psychologists to do the evaluation, and if they agree, the Director of Mental Health requests a petition from the county. The "evaluation reports and any other supporting documents" are made available to "the attorney designated by the county," and if that attorney agrees with the recommendation, he files a petition for commitment in superior court. The person gets a hearing before a judge to determine whether there is probable cause, and if there is, a jury trial at the prisoner's election with the assistance of counsel and proof beyond a reasonable doubt.

Two psychologists reviewed Seaton's medical records from prison and recommended that he be civilly committed. They forwarded their evaluations and the supporting documents to the county district attorney, who then filed a petition to commit Seaton. The Santa Barbara County Superior Court found probable cause to detain Seaton. He was transferred to the Santa Barbara County Jail and, subsequently, the Atascadero State Hospital, pending a civil commitment trial.

* * *

We have found only one Supreme Court decision addressing whether the constitution protects medical privacy, *Whalen v. Roe.* The case for privacy was considerably stronger in *Whalen,* because the state law at issue invaded the medical privacy of people who had not been convicted of any crimes, and any prediction of possible criminality did not have a history of past criminality to support the prediction. Under New York law, a physician could not prescribe opiates and other drugs subject to criminal abuse without sending a form to the state giving the name, address and age of the patient. About 100,000 such forms per month were collected by the state and the information was stored on computers. Physicians claimed in the lawsuit that the law deterred them from providing medically desirable prescriptions, and patients that they feared stigmatization as drug addicts, both claiming that the statute invaded constitutionally protected privacy.

The doctors and patients lost their case. The Court distinguished such cases as *Roe v. Wade* limiting government power to regulate "marriage, procreation, contraception, family relationships, and child rearing and education," and held that the compelled disclosure of prescriptions did not "pose a sufficiently grievous threat" to patients' interest in making important medical decisions or keeping them private "to establish a constitutional violation." Though the Court appeared to leave the door open to some sort of constitutional protection of privacy in another case, it did not hold that there was one. The holding in *Whalen* was that the New

York law did not violate any constitutional rights of the patients whose prescriptions were revealed to the government. In so holding, the Court acknowledged that some patients might avoid medicine they ought to have, and some physicians might avoid prescribing it, but said that the New York law did not pose a "sufficiently grievous" threat to these medical concerns to establish a constitutional violation, and the security provisions of the New York law appeared sufficient to guard against public disclosure. As for disclosure to the state employees who would administer the program, the Court characterized it as but one of the "unpleasant invasions of privacy that are associated with many facets of health care," such as those disclosures to physicians, hospital personnel, insurance companies and public health agencies. The closest *Whalen* comes to recognizing any constitutional right to privacy of medical information is its acknowledgment that "the accumulation of vast amounts of personal information" by the government is typically accompanied by a statutory or regulatory duty to avoid unwarranted disclosures, and that duty "arguably" has some constitutional basis. Some of our sister circuits recognize a constitutional right to privacy in medical records, though the Supreme Court has never so held.

Seaton argues that *Hydrick v. Hunter* requires factual development before his case can be dismissed, but *Hydrick* is not on point and has since been vacated by the Supreme Court Although eight constitutional violations were claimed by the *Hydrick* prisoners relating to the California sexually violent predator procedures, the prisoners did not claim that communication of their medical and psychological information was among the eight violations, so we had no occasion to consider the claim Seaton raises.

We have recognized a constitutional right to the privacy of medical information that *Whalen* did not, but in contexts different from this case. We held in *Tucson Woman's Clinic v. Eden,* that there was such a right, but the context was burdening of abortion, which *Whalen* expressly distinguished. Arizona required physicians who performed abortions to allow warrantless, unbounded inspections of their office and access by the state to their patient records. Physicians also had to send to a state contractor copies of fetal ultrasounds of subsequently aborted fetuses. We held that summary judgment was precluded because there was a genuine issue of material fact as to "whether the scheme creates an undue burden on the right to seek an abortion." We held in this context that there was "a constitutionally protected interest in avoiding disclosure of personal matters including medical information" and offered a list of five factors to be considered among others to decide "whether the governmental interest in obtaining information outweighs the individual's privacy interest." We commented that disclosure of the abortion information to government employees might violate individuals' rights even without public disclosure. We have held that the constitutional right to medical privacy "is a conditional right which may be infringed upon a showing of proper governmental interest." In aid of determining when a proper governmental interest trumps a right to medical privacy, we stated that the five factors articulated in *Tucson Woman's Clinic* are "not exhaustive, and the relevant considerations will necessarily vary from case to case. . . . In most cases, it will be the overall context, rather than the particular item of information, that will dictate the tipping of the scales."

It is not entirely clear yet whether the constitutional right we have recognized falls entirely within the class *Whalen* carves out, for disclosure that burdens "matters relating to marriage, procreation, contraception, family relationships, and child rearing and education." We recognized a much broader right to informational privacy in *Nelson v. NASA,* but the Supreme Court has granted certiorari in that case so it is not yet final, and *Nelson* involved employment applications, not civil commitment. In the context of evidentiary privilege rather than a constitutional right to privacy, we held in *United States v. Chase* that medical information may be privileged from introduction as evidence even when there is a duty to disclose it to the state.

Whatever constitutional right to privacy of medical information may exist, the California civil commitment procedure for sexually violent predators falls outside it. Assuming for purposes of discussion that Seaton has such a constitutional right and that the five-factor balancing test from *Tucson Women's Clinic* applies, Seaton's information falls on the unprotected side of the test. The test is to "balance the following factors to determine whether the governmental interest in obtaining information outweighs the individual's privacy interest: (1) the type of information requested, (2) the potential for harm in any subsequent non-consensual disclosure, (3) the adequacy of safeguards to prevent unauthorized disclosure, (4) the degree of need for access, and (5) whether there is an express statutory mandate, articulated public policy, or other recognizable public interest militating toward access."

The "type of information requested" does not have any possibility of burdening a constitutional right to abortion or any other right other than the putative right to privacy of the information itself. No serious potential for harm from the disclosure, such as discouraging people from obtaining medical assistance, has been pleaded or argued. Disclosure is limited to the parties and the court, and the psychological reports remain confidential for all other purposes. The need for access to the information to protect the public is substantial, because the persons subject to it have shown by their history that concern about the risk of sexual predation is not a chimera. There is an express statutory mandate to protect the public from persons whose mental illness causes them to be sexually violent predators.

Analogy to medical privacy in other contexts shows that the reasons for it do not apply in this context. Confidentiality of communications to physicians, and the evidentiary privilege to prevent disclosure, exist for a purpose-enabling patients to disclose what may be highly personal or embarrassing conditions to physicians so that they may obtain treatment, serving both their private interest in and the public interest in their health. Those purposes do not apply to this case. A person referred for evaluation for civil commitment as a possible sexually violent predator has not sought out the evaluation so that he may be treated. Medical evaluation is imposed, not sought, so there can be no concern that the person might avoid treatment needed for his health.

Nor is there any need, out of more general concerns of privacy, propriety, and decency, to protect the criminal from the disclosures. The public record of his conviction for the crimes discloses his conduct. He has already lost his privacy to the laws requiring registration on publicly available lists of his name and address as a sex offender. And the disclosure is far more limited than either, being only to the person in the district attorney's office designated by the county for the disclosures, unless a decision is made to proceed with civil commitment proceedings.

Sexually violent predator evaluation falls within two long established exceptions to the confidentiality of medical communications. One is public health and safety requirements. "A person sought to be restrained as *insane* is customarily subject to medical inspection by order of the court.... This principle has received further extension, by modern public health statutes, to persons believed to be suffering from *contagious diseases*—in particular *leprosy* and *venereal disease*." Physicians typically are required to disclose to the state, despite patient objections, various medical matters of public concern, such as possible domestic abuse of children and gunshot wounds. Even where a patient seeks curative treatment and volunteers information to his own physician, the physician may be required to breach his patient's confidence.

The second exception is for communications made to a physician for a potential adversary's purpose and not for curative treatment. That is why examination of a plaintiff by a physician hired by the defendant in a personal injury case, examination of an injured employee by a physician designated by the employer or a workers compensation board, and examination of a veteran by a physician evaluating him for veterans' disability, may be disclosed over his objection. A person communicating with a psychiatrist or psychologist for sexually violent predator evaluation likewise is being examined by a potential adversary's doctor for the potential adversary's purpose.

Sexually violent predators are involuntarily committed because their mental disease makes them dangerous to others. Neither the commitment nor the evaluation proceeding is something they themselves seek in order to obtain a cure. The state evaluates and commits to protect others from them. All the jurisdictions in our circuit have some sort of nonconfidential civil commitment evaluations, and they impinge on privacy interests much more substantial than the sexually violent predator statute. For most civil commitments, a history of criminality is not an essential predicate, and commitment may be imposed on innocent people. Were we to treat a sexually violent predator evaluation as constitutionally secret, we would be hard put to distinguish civil commitments of people who are sick but have not committed serious crimes. Congress in protecting the secrecy of medical information in HIPAA expressly provided that "[n]othing in this part shall be construed to invalidate or limit the authority, power, or procedures established under any law providing for ... public health investigation or intervention," evidently recognizing the well-established need for disclosure for these reasons.

One who goes to a physician in order to obtain medical benefit to himself or his family has substantial privacy interests that may or may not be constitutionally protected. One who is compelled to submit to medical examination for the benefit of the public, to determine whether because of mental disease he is likely to engage in sexually predatory behavior, does not.

NOTE: ROK LAMPE, INFORMATION PRIVACY AS A HUMAN RIGHT AND FUNDAMENTAL FREEDOM

The European Court of Human Rights has held that information relating to sex-reassignment is protected from disclosure under Article 8 of the European Convention on Human Rights. The Court no longer views states as having a strong interest ("margin of appreciation") that would inevitably trump respect for individuals' privacy. In *Christine Goodwin v. United Kingdom*, the plaintiff alleged that mistreatment with respect to employment, social security, pensions and marriage violated rights guaranteed by the European Convention for the Protection of Human Rights and Fundamental Freedoms. Pay particular notice to the information privacy claims she asserted with respect to medical matters and state identifiers.

CHRISTINE GOODWIN v. THE UNITED KINGDOM

(European Court of Human Rights, No. 28957/95, 11 July 2002).

I. THE CIRCUMSTANCES OF THE CASE

* * *

12. The applicant is a United Kingdom citizen born in 1937 and is a post-operative male to female transsexual.

13. The applicant had a tendency to dress as a woman from early childhood and underwent aversion therapy in 1963–64. In the mid–1960s, she was diagnosed as a transsexual. Though she married a woman and they had four children, her conviction was that her "brain sex" did not fit her body. From that time until 1984 she dressed as a man for work but as a woman in her free time. In January 1985, the applicant began treatment in earnest, attending appointments once every three months at the Gender Identity Clinic at the Charing Cross Hospital, which included regular consultations with a psychiatrist as well as on occasion a psychologist. She was prescribed hormone therapy, began attending grooming classes and voice training. Since this time, she has lived fully as a woman.

In October 1986, she underwent surgery to shorten her vocal chords. In August 1987, she was accepted on the waiting list for gender re-assignment surgery. In 1990, she underwent gender re-assignment surgery at a National Health Service hospital. Her treatment and surgery was provided for and paid for by the National Health Service.

14. The applicant divorced from her former wife on a date unspecified but continued to enjoy the love and support of her children.

15. The applicant claims that between 1990 and 1992 she was sexually harassed by colleagues at work. She attempted to pursue a case of sexual harassment in the Industrial Tribunal but claimed that she was unsuccessful because she was considered in law to be a man. She did not challenge this decision by appealing to the Employment Appeal Tribunal. The applicant was subsequently dismissed from her employment for reasons connected with her health, but alleges that the real reason was that she was a transsexual.

16. In 1996, the applicant started work with a new employer and was required to provide her National Insurance ("NI") number. She was concerned that the new employer would be in a position to trace her details as once in the possession of the number it would have been possible to find out about her previous employers and obtain information from them. Although she requested the allocation of a new NI number from the Department of Social Security ("DSS"), this was rejected and she eventually gave the new employer her NI number. The applicant claims that the new employer has now traced back her identity as she began experiencing problems at work. Colleagues stopped speaking to her and she was told that everyone was talking about her behind her back.

17. The DSS Contributions Agency informed the applicant that she would be ineligible for a State pension at the age of 60, the age of entitlement for women in the United Kingdom. In April 1997, the DSS informed the applicant that her pension contributions would have to be continued until the date at which she reached the age of 65, being the age of entitlement for men, namely April 2002. On 23 April 1997, she therefore entered into an undertaking with the DSS to pay direct the NI contributions which would otherwise be deducted by her employer as for all male employees. In the light of this undertaking, on 2 May 1997, the DSS Contributions Agency issued the applicant with a Form CF 384 Age Exemption Certificate (see Relevant domestic law and practice below).

18. The applicant's files at the DSS were marked "sensitive" to ensure that only an employee of a particular grade had access to her files. This meant in practice that the applicant had to make special appointments for even the most trivial matters and could not deal directly with the local office or deal with queries over the telephone. Her record continues to state her sex as male and despite the "special procedures" she has received letters from the DSS addressed to the male name which she was given at birth.

19. In a number of instances, the applicant stated that she has had to choose between revealing her birth certificate and foregoing certain advantages which were conditional upon her producing her birth certificate. In particular, she has not followed through a loan conditional upon life insurance, a re-mortgage offer and an entitlement to winter fuel allowance from the DSS. Similarly, the applicant remains obliged to pay the higher motor insurance premiums applicable to men. Nor did she feel able to report a theft of 200 pounds sterling to the police, for fear that the investigation would require her to reveal her identity.

. . .

I. ALLEGED VIOLATION OF ARTICLE 8 OF THE CONVENTION

* * *

59. The applicant claims a violation of Article 8 of the Convention, the relevant part of which provides as follows:

> 1. Everyone has the right to respect for his private . . . life . . .
>
> 2. There shall be no interference by a public authority with the exercise of this right except such as is in accordance with the law and is necessary in a democratic society in the interests of national security, public safety or the economic well-being of the country, for the prevention of disorder or crime, for the protection of health or morals, or for the protection of the rights and freedoms of others.

B. The Court's assessment

1. Preliminary considerations

* * *

71. This case raises the issue whether or not the respondent State has failed to comply with a positive obligation to ensure the right of the applicant, a post-operative male to female transsexual, to respect for her private life, in particular through the lack of legal recognition given to her gender re-assignment.

72. The Court recalls that the notion of "respect" as understood in Article 8 is not clear cut, especially as far as the positive obligations inherent in that concept are concerned: having regard to the diversity of practices followed and the situations obtaining in the Contracting States, the notion's requirements will vary considerably from case to case and the margin of appreciation to be accorded to the authorities may be wider than that applied in other areas under the Convention. In determining whether or not a positive obligation exists, regard must also be had to the fair balance that has to be struck between the general interest of the community and the interests of the individual, the search for which balance is inherent in the whole of the Convention (Cossey v. the United Kingdom judgment of 27 September 1990, Series A no. 184, p. 15, § 37).

73. The Court recalls that it has already examined complaints about the position of transsexuals in the United Kingdom (see the Rees v. the

United Kingdom judgment of 17 October 1986, Series A no. 106, the Cossey v. the United Kingdom judgment, cited above; the X., Y. and Z. v. the United Kingdom judgment of 22 April 1997, Reports of Judgments and Decisions 1997–II, and the Sheffield and Horsham v. the United Kingdom judgment of 30 July 1998, Reports 1998–V, p. 2011). In those cases, it held that the refusal of the United Kingdom Government to alter the register of births or to issue birth certificates whose contents and nature differed from those of the original entries concerning the recorded gender of the individual could not be considered as an interference with the right to respect for private life (the above-mentioned Rees judgment, p. 14, § 35, and Cossey judgment, p. 15, § 36). It also held that there was no positive obligation on the Government to alter their existing system for the registration of births by establishing a new system or type of documentation to provide proof of current civil status. Similarly, there was no duty on the Government to permit annotations to the existing register of births, or to keep any such annotation secret from third parties (the above-mentioned Rees judgment, p. 17, § 42, and Cossey judgment, p. 15, §§ 38–39). It was found in those cases that the authorities had taken steps to minimise intrusive enquiries (for example, by allowing transsexuals to be issued with driving licences, passports and other types of documents in their new name and gender). Nor had it been shown that the failure to accord general legal recognition of the change of gender had given rise in the applicants' own case histories to detriment of sufficient seriousness to override the respondent State's margin of appreciation in this area (the Sheffield and Horsham judgment cited above, p. 2028–29, § 59).

· · ·

75. The Court proposes therefore to look at the situation within and outside the Contracting State to assess "in the light of present-day conditions" what is now the appropriate interpretation and application of the Convention (see the Tyrer v. the United Kingdom judgment of 25 April 1978, Series A no. 26, § 31, and subsequent case-law).

   2.   *The applicant's situation as a transsexual*

76. The Court observes that the applicant, registered at birth as male, has undergone gender re-assignment surgery and lives in society as a female. Nonetheless, the applicant remains, for legal purposes, a male. This has had, and continues to have, effects on the applicant's life where sex is of legal relevance and distinctions are made between men and women, as, inter alia, in the area of pensions and retirement age. For example, the applicant must continue to pay national insurance contributions until the age of 65 due to her legal status as male. However as she is employed in her gender identity as a female, she has had to obtain an exemption certificate which allows the payments from her employer to stop while she continues to make such payments herself. Though the Government submitted that this made due allowance for the difficulties of her position, the Court would note that she nonetheless has to make use of a special procedure that might in itself call attention to her status.

77. It must also be recognised that serious interference with private life can arise where the state of domestic law conflicts with an important aspect of personal identity (see, mutatis mutandis, Dudgeon v. the United Kingdom judgment of 22 October 1981, Series A no. 45, § 41). The stress and alienation arising from a discordance between the position in society assumed by a post-operative transsexual and the status imposed by law which refuses to recognise the change of gender cannot, in the Court's view, be regarded as a minor inconvenience arising from a formality. A conflict between social reality and law arises which places the transsexual in an anomalous position, in which he or she may experience feelings of vulnerability, humiliation and anxiety.

78. In this case, as in many others, the applicant's gender re-assignment was carried out by the national health service, which recognises the condition of gender dysphoria and provides, inter alia, re-assignment by surgery, with a view to achieving as one of its principal purposes as close an assimilation as possible to the gender in which the transsexual perceives that he or she properly belongs. The Court is struck by the fact that nonetheless the gender re-assignment which is lawfully provided is not met with full recognition in law, which might be regarded as the final and culminating step in the long and difficult process of transformation which the transsexual has undergone. The coherence of the administrative and legal practices within the domestic system must be regarded as an important factor in the assessment carried out under Article 8 of the Convention. Where a State has authorised the treatment and surgery alleviating the condition of a transsexual, financed or assisted in financing the operations and indeed permits the artificial insemination of a woman living with a female-to-male transsexual (as demonstrated in the case of X., Y. and Z. v. the United Kingdom, cited above), it appears illogical to refuse to recognise the legal implications of the result to which the treatment leads.

79. The Court notes that the unsatisfactory nature of the current position and plight of transsexuals in the United Kingdom has been acknowledged in the domestic courts (see Bellinger v. Bellinger, cited above, paragraph 52) and by the Interdepartmental Working Group which surveyed the situation in the United Kingdom and concluded that, notwithstanding the accommodations reached in practice, transsexual people were conscious of certain problems which did not have to be faced by the majority of the population (paragraph 50 above).

80. Against these considerations, the Court has examined the countervailing arguments of a public interest nature put forward as justifying the continuation of the present situation. It observes that in the previous United Kingdom cases weight was given to medical and scientific considerations, the state of any European and international consensus and the impact of any changes to the current birth register system.

   3. Medical and scientific considerations

81. It remains the case that there are no conclusive findings as to the cause of transsexualism and, in particular, whether it is wholly psychologi-

cal or associated with physical differentiation in the brain. The expert evidence in the domestic case of Bellinger v. Bellinger was found to indicate a growing acceptance of findings of sexual differences in the brain that are determined pre-natally, though scientific proof for the theory was far from complete. The Court considers it more significant however that transsexualism has wide international recognition as a medical condition for which treatment is provided in order to afford relief (for example, the Diagnostic and Statistical Manual fourth edition (DSM–IV) replaced the diagnosis of transsexualism with "gender identity disorder"; see also the International Classification of Diseases, tenth edition (ICD–10)). The United Kingdom national health service, in common with the vast majority of Contracting States, acknowledges the existence of the condition and provides or permits treatment, including irreversible surgery. The medical and surgical acts which in this case rendered the gender re-assignment possible were indeed carried out under the supervision of the national health authorities. Nor, given the numerous and painful interventions involved in such surgery and the level of commitment and conviction required to achieve a change in social gender role, can it be suggested that there is anything arbitrary or capricious in the decision taken by a person to undergo gender re-assignment. In those circumstances, the ongoing scientific and medical debate as to the exact causes of the condition is of diminished relevance.

82.   While it also remains the case that a transsexual cannot acquire all the biological characteristics of the assigned sex (Sheffield and Horsham, cited above, p. 2028, § 56), the Court notes that with increasingly sophisticated surgery and types of hormonal treatments, the principal unchanging biological aspect of gender identity is the chromosomal element. It is known however that chromosomal anomalies may arise naturally (for example, in cases of intersex conditions where the biological criteria at birth are not congruent) and in those cases, some persons have to be assigned to one sex or the other as seems most appropriate in the circumstances of the individual case. It is not apparent to the Court that the chromosomal element, amongst all the others, must inevitably take on decisive significance for the purposes of legal attribution of gender identity for transsexuals (see the dissenting opinion of Thorpe LJ in Bellinger v. Bellinger cited in paragraph 52 above; and the judgment of Chisholm J in the Australian case, Re Kevin, cited in paragraph 55 above).

83.   The Court is not persuaded therefore that the state of medical science or scientific knowledge provides any determining argument as regards the legal recognition of transsexuals.

   4. *The state of any European and international consensus*

84.   Already at the time of the Sheffield and Horsham case, there was an emerging consensus within Contracting States in the Council of Europe on providing legal recognition following gender re-assignment (see § 35 of that judgment). The latest survey submitted by Liberty in the present case shows a continuing international trend towards legal recognition (see

paragraphs 55–56 above). In Australia and New Zealand, it appears that the courts are moving away from the biological birth view of sex (as set out in the United Kingdom case of Corbett v. Corbett) and taking the view that sex, in the context of a transsexual wishing to marry, should depend on a multitude of factors to be assessed at the time of the marriage.

85. The Court observes that in the case of Rees in 1986 it had noted that little common ground existed between States, some of which did permit change of gender and some of which did not and that generally speaking the law seemed to be in a state of transition (see § 37). In the later case of Sheffield and Horsham, the Court's judgment laid emphasis on the lack of a common European approach as to how to address the repercussions which the legal recognition of a change of sex may entail for other areas of law such as marriage, filiation, privacy or data protection. While this would appear to remain the case, the lack of such a common approach among forty-three Contracting States with widely diverse legal systems and traditions is hardly surprising. In accordance with the principle of subsidiarity, it is indeed primarily for the Contracting States to decide on the measures necessary to secure Convention rights within their jurisdiction and, in resolving within their domestic legal systems the practical problems created by the legal recognition of post-operative gender status, the Contracting States must enjoy a wide margin of appreciation. The Court accordingly attaches less importance to the lack of evidence of a common European approach to the resolution of the legal and practical problems posed, than to the clear and uncontested evidence of a continuing international trend in favour not only of increased social acceptance of transsexuals but of legal recognition of the new sexual identity of post-operative transsexuals.

* * *

6. *Striking a balance in the present case*

89. The Court has noted above (paragraphs 76–79) the difficulties and anomalies of the applicant's situation as a post-operative transsexual. It must be acknowledged that the level of daily interference suffered by the applicant in B. v. France (judgment of 25 March 1992, Series A no. 232) has not been attained in this case and that on certain points the risk of difficulties or embarrassment faced by the present applicant may be avoided or minimised by the practices adopted by the authorities.

90. Nonetheless, the very essence of the Convention is respect for human dignity and human freedom. Under Article 8 of the Convention in particular, where the notion of personal autonomy is an important principle underlying the interpretation of its guarantees, protection is given to the personal sphere of each individual, including the right to establish details of their identity as individual human beings (see, inter alia, Pretty v. the United Kingdom, no. 2346/02, judgment of 29 April 2002, § 62, and Mikulić v. Croatia, no. 53176/99, judgment of 7 February 2002, § 53, both to be published in ECHR 2002–. . .). In the twenty first century the right of transsexuals to personal development and to physical and moral securi-

ty in the full sense enjoyed by others in society cannot be regarded as a matter of controversy requiring the lapse of time to cast clearer light on the issues involved. In short, the unsatisfactory situation in which post-operative transsexuals live in an intermediate zone as not quite one gender or the other is no longer sustainable. Domestic recognition of this evaluation may be found in the report of the Interdepartmental Working Group and the Court of Appeal's judgment of Bellinger v. Bellinger (see paragraphs 50, 52–53).

91. The Court does not underestimate the difficulties posed or the important repercussions which any major change in the system will inevitably have, not only in the field of birth registration, but also in the areas of access to records, family law, affiliation, inheritance, criminal justice, employment, social security and insurance. However, as is made clear by the report of the Interdepartmental Working Group, these problems are far from insuperable, to the extent that the Working Group felt able to propose as one of the options full legal recognition of the new gender, subject to certain criteria and procedures. As Lord Justice Thorpe observed in the Bellinger case, any "spectral difficulties", particularly in the field of family law, are both manageable and acceptable if confined to the case of fully achieved and post-operative transsexuals. Nor is the Court convinced by arguments that allowing the applicant to fall under the rules applicable to women, which would also change the date of eligibility for her state pension, would cause any injustice to others in the national insurance and state pension systems as alleged by the Government. No concrete or substantial hardship or detriment to the public interest has indeed been demonstrated as likely to flow from any change to the status of transsexuals and, as regards other possible consequences, the Court considers that society may reasonably be expected to tolerate a certain inconvenience to enable individuals to live in dignity and worth in accordance with the sexual identity chosen by them at great personal cost.

92. In the previous cases from the United Kingdom, this Court has since 1986 emphasised the importance of keeping the need for appropriate legal measures under review having regard to scientific and societal developments (see references at paragraph 73). Most recently in the Sheffield and Horsham case in 1998, it observed that the respondent State had not yet taken any steps to do so despite an increase in the social acceptance of the phenomenon of transsexualism and a growing recognition of the problems with which transsexuals are confronted (cited above, paragraph 60). Even though it found no violation in that case, the need to keep this area under review was expressly re-iterated. Since then, a report has been issued in April 2000 by the Interdepartmental Working Group which set out a survey of the current position of transsexuals in inter alia criminal law, family and employment matters and identified various options for reform. Nothing has effectively been done to further these proposals and in July 2001 the Court of Appeal noted that there were no plans to do so (see paragraphs 52–53). It may be observed that the only legislative reform of note, applying certain non-discrimination provisions to transsexuals,

flowed from a decision of the European Court of Justice of 30 April 1996 which held that discrimination based on a change of gender was equivalent to discrimination on grounds of sex (see paragraphs 43–45 above).

93. Having regard to the above considerations, the Court finds that the respondent Government can no longer claim that the matter falls within their margin of appreciation, save as regards the appropriate means of achieving recognition of the right protected under the Convention. Since there are no significant factors of public interest to weigh against the interest of this individual applicant in obtaining legal recognition of her gender re-assignment, it reaches the conclusion that the fair balance that is inherent in the Convention now tilts decisively in favour of the applicant. There has, accordingly, been a failure to respect her right to private life in breach of Article 8 of the Convention.

* * *

FOR THESE REASONS, THE COURT

1. Holds unanimously that there has been a violation of Article 8 of the Convention; The Court also held unanimously that there has been a violation of Article 12, 14, 13 of the Convention; that the finding of violation constitutes in itself sufficient just satisfaction for the non-pecuniary damage sustained by the applicant; that the respondent State is to pay the applicant, within three months, EUR 39,000 (thirty nine thousand euros) in respect of costs and expenses, together with any value-added tax that may be chargeable, to be converted into pounds sterling at the date of settlement; dismissed unanimously the remainder of the applicant's claim for just satisfaction.

e. The Right to Death and Suicide

CRUZAN v. DIRECTOR, MISSOURI DEPARTMENT OF HEALTH

497 U.S. 261 (1990).

CHIEF JUSTICE REHNQUIST delivered the opinion of the Court.

Petitioner Nancy Beth Cruzan was rendered incompetent as a result of severe injuries sustained during an automobile accident. Copetitioners Lester and Joyce Cruzan, Nancy's parents and coguardians, sought a court order directing the withdrawal of their daughter's artificial feeding and hydration equipment after it became apparent that she had virtually no chance of recovering her cognitive faculties. The Supreme Court of Missouri held that because there was no clear and convincing evidence of Nancy's desire to have life-sustaining treatment withdrawn under such circumstances, her parents lacked authority to effectuate such a request. We granted certiorari, 492 U.S. 917 (1989), and now affirm.

On the night of January 11, 1983, Nancy Cruzan lost control of her car as she traveled down Elm Road in Jasper County, Missouri. The vehicle overturned, and Cruzan was discovered lying face down in a ditch without detectable respiratory or cardiac function. Paramedics were able to restore her breathing and heartbeat at the accident site, and she was transported to a hospital in an unconscious state. An attending neurosurgeon diagnosed her as having sustained probable cerebral contusions compounded by significant anoxia (lack of oxygen). The Missouri trial court in this case found that permanent brain damage generally results after 6 minutes in an anoxic state; it was estimated that Cruzan was deprived of oxygen from 12 to 14 minutes. She remained in a coma for approximately three weeks and then progressed to an unconscious state in which she was able to orally ingest some nutrition. In order to ease feeding and further the recovery, surgeons implanted a gastrostomy feeding and hydration tube in Cruzan with the consent of her then husband. Subsequent rehabilitative efforts proved unavailing. She now lies in a Missouri state hospital in what is commonly referred to as a persistent vegetative state: generally, a condition in which a person exhibits motor reflexes but evinces no indications of significant cognitive function. The State of Missouri is bearing the cost of her care.

After it had become apparent that Nancy Cruzan had virtually no chance of regaining her mental faculties, her parents asked hospital employees to terminate the artificial nutrition and hydration procedures. All agree that such a removal would cause her death. The employees refused to honor the request without court approval. The parents then sought and received authorization from the state trial court for termination. The court found that a person in Nancy's condition had a fundamental right under the State and Federal Constitutions to refuse or direct the withdrawal of "death prolonging procedures." * * * The court also found that Nancy's "expressed thoughts at age twenty-five in somewhat serious conversation with a housemate friend that if sick or injured she would not wish to continue her life unless she could live at least halfway normally suggests that given her present condition she would not wish to continue on with her nutrition and hydration." * * *

The Supreme Court of Missouri reversed by a divided vote. The court recognized a right to refuse treatment embodied in the common-law doctrine of informed consent, but expressed skepticism about the application of that doctrine in the circumstances of this case * * *. The court also declined to read a broad right of privacy into the State Constitution which would "support the right of a person to refuse medical treatment in every circumstance," and expressed doubt as to whether such a right existed under the United States Constitution. * * * The court found that Cruzan's statements to her roommate regarding her desire to live or die under certain conditions were "unreliable for the purpose of determining her intent," id., at 424, "and thus insufficient to support the co-guardians['] claim to exercise substituted judgment on Nancy's behalf." Id., at 426. It rejected the argument that Cruzan's parents were entitled to order the termination of her medical treatment, concluding that "no person can assume that choice for an incompetent in the absence of the formalities required under Missouri's Living Will statutes or the clear and convincing, inherently reliable evidence absent here." Id., at 425. The court also expressed its view that "broad policy questions bearing on life and death are more properly addressed by representative assemblies" than judicial bodies. Id., at 426.

We granted certiorari to consider the question whether Cruzan has a right under the United States Constitution which would require the hospital to withdraw life-sustaining treatment from her under these circumstances. * * *

The Fourteenth Amendment provides that no State shall "deprive any person of life, liberty, or property, without due process of law." The principle that a competent person has a constitutionally protected liberty interest in refusing unwanted medical treatment may be inferred from our prior decisions. In Jacobson v. Massachusetts, 197 U.S. 11, 24–30 (1905), for instance, the Court balanced an individual's liberty interest in declining an unwanted smallpox vaccine against the State's interest in preventing disease. Decisions prior to the incorporation of the Fourth Amendment into the Fourteenth Amendment analyzed searches and seizures involving the body under the Due Process Clause and were thought to implicate substantial liberty interests. See, e.g., Breithaupt v. Abram, 352 U.S. 432, 439 (1957) ("As against the right of an individual that his person be held inviolable * * * must be set the interests of society * * * ").

Just this Term, in the course of holding that a State's procedures for administering antipsychotic medication to prisoners were sufficient to satisfy due process concerns, we recognized that prisoners possess "a significant liberty interest in avoiding the unwanted administration of antipsychotic drugs under the Due Process Clause of the Fourteenth Amendment." Washington v. Harper, 494 U.S. 210, 221–222 (1990); see also id., at 229 ("The forcible injection of medication into a nonconsenting person's body represents a substantial interference with that person's liberty"). Still other cases support the recognition of a general liberty interest in refusing medical treatment. Vitek v. Jones, 445 U.S. 480 (1980) (transfer to mental hospital coupled with mandatory behavior modification treatment implicated liberty interests); Parham v. J. R., 442 U.S. 584, 600, (1979) ("[A] child, in common with adults, has a substantial liberty interest in not being confined unnecessarily for medical treatment"). * * *

But determining that a person has a "liberty interest" under the Due Process Clause does not end the inquiry; "whether respondent's constitutional rights have been violated must be determined by balancing his liberty interests against the relevant state interests." * * *

Petitioners insist that under the general holdings of our cases, the forced administration of life-sustaining medical treatment, and even of artificially delivered food and water essential to life, would implicate a competent person's liberty interest. Although we think the logic of the cases discussed above would embrace such a liberty interest, the dramatic consequences involved in refusal of such treatment would inform the inquiry as to whether the deprivation of that interest is constitutionally permissible. But for purposes of this case, we assume that the United States Constitution would grant a competent person a constitutionally protected right to refuse lifesaving hydration and nutrition.

Petitioners go on to assert that an incompetent person should possess the same right in this respect as is possessed by a competent person. * * *

The difficulty with petitioners' claim is that in a sense it begs the question: An incompetent person is not able to make an informed and voluntary choice to exercise a hypothetical right to refuse treatment or any other right. Such a "right" must be exercised for her, if at all, by some sort of surrogate * * *. Missouri requires that evidence of the incompetent's wishes as to the withdrawal of treatment be proved by clear and convincing evidence. The question, then, is whether the United States Constitution forbids the establishment of this procedural requirement by the State. We hold that it does not. * * *

[W]e conclude that a State may apply a clear and convincing evidence standard in proceedings where a guardian seeks to discontinue nutrition and hydration of a person diagnosed to be in a persistent vegetative state. We note that many courts which have adopted some sort of substituted judgment procedure in situations like this, whether they limit consideration of evidence to the prior expressed wishes of the incompetent individual, or whether they allow more general proof of what the individual's decision would have been, require a clear and convincing standard of proof for such evidence.

The Supreme Court of Missouri held that in this case the testimony adduced at trial did not amount to clear and convincing proof of the patient's desire to have hydration and nutrition withdrawn. In so doing, it reversed a decision of the Missouri trial court which had found that the evidence "suggested" Nancy Cruzan would not have desired to continue such measures, App. to Pet. for Cert. A98, but which had not adopted the standard of "clear and convincing evidence" enunciated by the Supreme Court. The testimony adduced at trial consisted primarily of Nancy Cruzan's statements made to a housemate about a year before her accident that she would not want to live should she face life as a "vegetable," and other observations to the same effect. The observations did not deal in terms with withdrawal of medical treatment or of hydration and nutrition. We cannot say that the Supreme Court of Missouri committed constitutional error in reaching the conclusion that it did. * * *

JUSTICE SCALIA, concurring. * * *

I would have preferred that we announce, clearly and promptly, that the federal courts have no business in this field; that American law has always accorded the State the power to prevent, by force if necessary, suicide—including suicide by refusing to take appropriate measures necessary to preserve one's life; that the point at which life becomes "worthless," and the point at which the means necessary to preserve it become "extraordinary" or "inappropriate," are neither set forth in the Constitution nor known to the nine Justices of this Court any better than they are known to nine people picked at random from the Kansas City telephone directory; and hence, that even when it is demonstrated by clear and convincing evidence that a patient no longer wishes certain measures to be taken to preserve his or her life, it is up to the citizens of Missouri to decide, through their elected representatives, whether that wish will be honored. It is quite impossible (because the Constitution says nothing about the matter) that those citizens will decide upon a line less lawful than the one we would choose; and it is unlikely (because we know no more about "life and death" than they do) that they will decide upon a line less reasonable. * * *

But to return to the principal point for present purposes: the irrelevance of the action-inaction distinction. Starving oneself to death is no different from putting a gun to one's temple as far as the common-law definition of suicide is concerned; the cause of death in both cases is the suicide's conscious decision to "put an end to his own existence." * * * Of course the common law rejected the action-inaction distinction in other contexts involving the taking of human life as well. In the prosecution of a parent for the starvation death of her infant, it was no defense that the infant's death was "caused" by no action of the parent but by the natural process of starvation, or by the infant's natural inability to provide for itself. * * * It is not surprising, therefore, that the early cases considering the claimed right to refuse medical treatment dismissed as specious the nice distinction between "passively submitting to death and actively seeking it. The distinction may be merely verbal, as it would be if an adult sought death by starvation instead of a drug. If the State may interrupt one mode of self-destruction, it may with equal authority interfere with the other." * * *

JUSTICE BRENNAN, with whom JUSTICE MARSHALL and JUSTICE BLACKMUN join, dissenting. * * *

[I]f a competent person has a liberty interest to be free of unwanted medical treatment, as both the majority and Justice O'Connor's concede, it must be fundamental. "We are dealing here with [a decision] which involves one of the basic civil rights of man." Skinner v. Oklahoma ex rel. Williamson, 316 U.S. 535 * * * (1942) (invalidating a statute authorizing sterilization of certain felons). Whatever other liberties protected by the Due Process Clause are fundamental, "those liberties that are 'deeply rooted in this Nation's history and tradition'" are among them. * * *

The right to be free from medical attention without consent, to determine what shall be done with one's own body, is deeply rooted in this Nation's traditions, as the majority acknowledges. * * * This right has long been "firmly entrenched in American tort law" and is securely grounded in the earliest common law. * * * "The inviolability of the person" has been held as "sacred" and "carefully guarded" as any common-law right. Union Pacific R. Co. v. Botsford * * * (1891). Thus, freedom from unwanted medical attention is unquestionably among those principles "so rooted in the traditions and conscience of our people as to be ranked as fundamental." Snyder v. Massachusetts, 291 U.S. 97 * * * (1934). * * *

Although the right to be free of unwanted medical intervention, like other constitutionally protected interests, may not be absolute, no state interest could outweigh the rights of an individual in Nancy Cruzan's position. Whatever a State's possible interests in mandating life-support treatment under other circumstances, there is no good to be obtained here by Missouri's insistence that Nancy Cruzan remain on life-support systems if it is indeed her wish not to do so. Missouri does not claim, nor could it, that society as a whole will be benefited by Nancy's receiving medical treatment. * * *

Too few people execute living wills or equivalently formal directives for such an evidentiary rule to ensure adequately that the wishes of incompetent persons will be honored. While it might be a wise social policy to encourage people to furnish such instructions, no general conclusion about a patient's choice can be drawn from the absence of formalities. The probability of becoming irreversibly vegetative is so low that many people may not feel an urgency to marshal formal evidence of their preferences. Some may not wish to dwell on their own physical deterioration and mortality. Even someone with a resolute determination to avoid life support under circumstances such as Nancy's would still need to know that such things as living wills exist and how to execute one. Often legal help would be necessary, especially given the majority's apparent willingness to permit States to insist that a person's wishes are not truly known unless the particular medical treatment is specified. * * *

The testimony of close friends and family members, on the other hand, may often be the best evidence available of what the patient's choice would be. It is they with whom the patient most likely will have discussed such questions and they who know the patient best. "Family members have a unique knowledge of the patient which is vital to any decision on his or her behalf." * * *

WASHINGTON v. GLUCKSBERG

521 U.S. 702 (1997).

CHIEF JUSTICE REHNQUIST delivered the opinion of the Court.

The question presented in this case is whether Washington's prohibition against "causing" or "aiding" a suicide offends the Fourteenth Amendment to the United States Constitution. We hold that it does not. * * *

The plaintiffs asserted "the existence of a liberty interest protected by the Fourteenth Amendment which extends to a personal choice by a mentally competent, terminally ill adult to commit physician-assisted suicide." * * * Relying primarily on Planned Parenthood v. Casey * * * (1992), and Cruzan v. Director, Missouri Dept. of Health * * * (1990), the District Court agreed * * * and concluded that Washington's assisted-suicide ban is unconstitutional because it "places an undue burden on the exercise of [that] constitutionally protected liberty interest." * * * The District Court also decided that the Washington statute violated the Equal Protection Clause's requirement that " 'all persons similarly situated * * * be treated alike.' " * * *

A panel of the Court of Appeals for the Ninth Circuit reversed, emphasizing that "in the two hundred and five years of our existence no constitutional right to aid in killing oneself has ever been asserted and upheld by a court of final jurisdiction." * * * The Ninth Circuit reheard the case en banc, reversed the panel's decision, and affirmed the District Court. We * * * now reverse. * * *

We begin, as we do in all due-process cases, by examining our Nation's history, legal traditions, and practices. * * * In almost every State—indeed, in almost every western democracy—it is a crime to assist a suicide. The States' assisted-suicide bans are not innovations. Rather, they are longstanding expressions of the States' commitment to the protection and preservation of all human life. * * * Indeed, opposition to and condemnation of suicide—and, therefore, of assisting suicide—are consistent and enduring themes of our philosophical, legal, and cultural heritages. * * *

More specifically, for over 700 years, the Anglo–American common-law tradition has punished or otherwise disapproved of both suicide and assisting suicide. * * *

For the most part, the early American colonies adopted the common-law approach. * * *

The earliest American statute explicitly to outlaw assisting suicide was enacted in New York in 1828 * * * and many of the new States and Territories followed New York's example. Marzen 73–74. Between 1857 and 1865, a New York commission led by Dudley Field drafted a criminal code that prohibited "aiding" a suicide and, specifically, "furnishing another person with any deadly weapon or poisonous drug, knowing that such person intends to use such weapon or drug in taking his own life." * * * By the time the Fourteenth Amendment was ratified, it was a crime in most States to assist a suicide. * * *

Though deeply rooted, the States' assisted-suicide bans have in recent years been reexamined and, generally, reaffirmed. Because of advances in medicine and technology, Americans today are increasingly likely to die in institutions, from chronic illnesses. * * * Many States, for example, now permit "living wills," surrogate health-care decisionmaking, and the withdrawal or refusal of life-sustaining medical treatment. * * * At the same time, however, voters and legislators continue for the most part to reaffirm their States' prohibitions on assisting suicide.

The Washington statute at issue in this case * * * was enacted in 1975 as part of a revision of that State's criminal code. Four years later, Washington passed its Natural Death Act, which specifically stated that the "withholding or withdrawal of life-sustaining treatment * * * shall not, for any purpose, constitute a suicide" and that "nothing in this chapter shall be construed to condone, authorize, or approve mercy killing * * *." In 1991, Washington voters rejected a ballot initiative which, had it passed, would have permitted a form of physician-assisted suicide. Washington then added a provision to the Natural Death Act expressly excluding physician-assisted suicide. * * *

The Due Process Clause guarantees more than fair process, and the "liberty" it protects includes more than the absence of physical restraint. * * * We have also assumed, and strongly suggested, that the Due Process Clause protects the traditional right to refuse unwanted lifesaving medical treatment. Cruzan, 497 U.S. at 278–279. * * *

Our established method of substantive-due-process analysis has two primary features: First, we have regularly observed that the Due Process Clause specially protects those fundamental rights and liberties which are, objectively, "deeply rooted in this Nation's history and tradition," id., at 503 (plurality opinion); Snyder v. Massachusetts, 291 U.S. 97, 105 (1934) ("so rooted in the traditions and conscience of our people as to be ranked as fundamental"), and "implicit in the concept of ordered liberty," such that "neither liberty nor Justice would exist if they were sacrificed," Palko v. Connecticut, 302 U.S. 319, 325, 326 (1937). Second, we have required in substantive-due-process cases a "careful description" of the asserted fundamental liberty interest. Flores, supra, at 302; Collins, supra, at 125; Cruzan, supra, at 277–278. Our Nation's history, legal traditions, and practices thus provide the crucial "guideposts for responsible decision-making," Collins, supra, at 125, that direct and restrain our exposition of the Due Process Clause. As we stated recently in Flores, the Fourteenth Amendment "forbids the government to infringe * * * 'fundamental' liberty interests at all, no matter what process is provided, unless the infringement is narrowly tailored to serve a compelling state interest." 507 U.S. at 302.

The Washington statute at issue in this case prohibits "aiding another person to attempt suicide," * * * and, thus, the question before us is whether the "liberty" specially protected by the Due Process Clause includes a right to commit suicide which itself includes a right to assistance in doing so.

We now inquire whether this asserted right has any place in our Nation's traditions. Here, as discussed above, supra, at 4–15, we are confronted with a consistent and almost universal tradition that has long rejected the asserted right, and continues explicitly to reject it today, even for terminally ill, mentally competent adults. To hold for respondents, we would have to reverse centuries of legal doctrine and practice, and strike down the considered policy choice of almost every State. * * *

The history of the law's treatment of assisted suicide in this country has been and continues to be one of the rejection of nearly all efforts to permit it. That being the case, our decisions lead us to conclude that the asserted "right" to assistance in committing suicide is not a fundamental liberty interest protected by the Due Process Clause. The Constitution also requires, however, that Washington's assisted-suicide ban be rationally related to legitimate government interests. * * * This requirement is unquestionably met here. * * *

First, Washington has an "unqualified interest in the preservation of human life." Cruzan, 497 U.S. at 282. The State's prohibition on assisted suicide, like all homicide laws, both reflects and advances its commitment to this interest. * * * This interest is symbolic and aspirational as well as practical * * *.

Relatedly, all admit that suicide is a serious public-health problem, especially among persons in otherwise vulnerable groups. * * * The State has an interest in preventing suicide, and in studying, identifying, and treating its causes.

Those who attempt suicide—terminally ill or not—often suffer from depression or other mental disorders. * * * Research indicates, however, that many people who request physician-assisted suicide withdraw that request if their depression and pain are treated.

The State also has an interest in protecting the integrity and ethics of the medical profession. * * * And physician-assisted suicide could, it is argued, undermine the trust that is essential to the doctor-patient relationship by blurring the time-honored line between healing and harming. * * *

Next, the State has an interest in protecting vulnerable groups—including the poor, the elderly, and disabled persons—from abuse, neglect, and mistakes. * * * The risk of harm is greatest for the many individuals in our society whose autonomy and well-being are already compromised by poverty, lack of access to good medical care, advanced age, or membership in a stigmatized social group. * * * If physician-assisted suicide were permitted, many might resort to it to spare their families the substantial financial burden of end-of-life health-care costs.

The State's interest here goes beyond protecting the vulnerable from coercion; it extends to protecting disabled and terminally ill people from prejudice, negative and inaccurate stereotypes, and "societal indifference." * * * The State's assisted-suicide ban reflects and reinforces its policy that the lives of terminally ill, disabled, and elderly people must be no less valued than the lives of the young and healthy, and that a seriously disabled person's suicidal impulses should be interpreted and treated the same way as anyone else's. * * *

Finally, the State may fear that permitting assisted suicide will start it down the path to voluntary and perhaps even involuntary euthanasia. * * * [W]hat is couched as a limited right to "physician-assisted suicide" is likely, in effect, a much broader license, which could prove extremely difficult to police and contain. Washington's ban on assisting suicide prevents such erosion. * * *

Throughout the Nation, Americans are engaged in an earnest and profound debate about the morality, legality, and practicality of physician-assisted suicide. Our holding permits this debate to continue, as it should in a democratic society. The decision of the en banc Court of Appeals is reversed, and the case is remanded for further proceedings consistent with this opinion.

VACCO v. QUILL

521 U.S. 793 (1997).

CHIEF JUSTICE REHNQUIST delivered the opinion of the Court.

In New York, as in most States, it is a crime to aid another to commit or attempt suicide, but patients may refuse even lifesaving medical treatment. The question presented by this case is whether New York's prohibition on assisting suicide therefore violates the Equal Protection Clause of the Fourteenth Amendment. We hold that it does not.

Petitioners are various New York public officials. Respondents Timothy E. Quill, Samuel C. Klagsbrun, and Howard A. Grossman are physicians who practice in New York. They assert that although it would be "consistent with the standards of [their] medical practices" to prescribe lethal medication for "mentally competent, terminally ill patients" who are suffering great pain and desire a doctor's help in taking their own lives, they are deterred from doing so by New York's ban on assisting suicide. App. 25–26. Respondents, and three gravely ill patients who have since died, sued the State's Attorney General in the United States District Court. They urged that because New York permits a competent person to refuse life-sustaining medical treatment, and because the refusal of such treatment is "essentially the same thing" as physician-assisted suicide, New York's assisted-suicide ban violates the Equal Protection Clause. Quill v. Koppell, 870 F. Supp. 78, 84–85 (SDNY 1994). * * *

The Equal Protection Clause commands that no State shall "deny to any person within its jurisdiction the equal protection of the laws." This provision creates no substantive rights. * * * Instead, it embodies a general rule that States must treat like cases alike but may treat unlike cases accordingly. * * * If a legislative classification or distinction "neither burdens a fundamental right nor targets a suspect class, we will uphold [it] so long as it bears a rational relation to some legitimate end."

New York's statutes outlawing assisting suicide affect and address matters of profound significance to all New Yorkers alike. They neither infringe fundamental rights nor involve suspect classifications. * * * These laws are therefore entitled to a "strong presumption of validity." Heller v. Doe, 509 U.S. 312, 319 (1993).

On their faces, neither New York's ban on assisting suicide nor its statutes permitting patients to refuse medical treatment treat anyone differently than anyone else or draw any distinctions between persons. Everyone, regardless of physical condition, is entitled, if competent, to refuse unwanted lifesaving medical treatment; no one is permitted to assist a suicide. Generally speaking, laws that apply evenhandedly to all "unquestionably comply" with the Equal Protection Clause.

The Court of Appeals, however, concluded that some terminally ill people—those who are on life-support systems—are treated differently than those who are not, in that the former may "hasten death" by ending treatment, but the latter may not "hasten death" through physician-assisted suicide. * * * This conclusion depends on the submission that ending or refusing lifesaving medical treatment "is nothing more nor less than assisted suicide." * * * Unlike the Court of Appeals, we think the distinction between assisting suicide and withdrawing life-sustaining treatment, a distinction widely recognized and endorsed in the medical profession and in our legal traditions, is both important and logical; it is certainly rational. * * *

The distinction comports with fundamental legal principles of causation and intent. First, when a patient refuses life-sustaining medical treatment, he dies from an underlying fatal disease or pathology; but if a patient ingests lethal medication prescribed by a physician, he is killed by that medication. * * *

The law has long used actors' intent or purpose to distinguish between two acts that may have the same result. * * * Put differently, the law distinguishes actions taken "because of" a given end from actions taken "in spite of" their unintended but foreseen consequences. * * *

Given these general principles, it is not surprising that many courts, including New York courts, have carefully distinguished refusing life-sustaining treatment from suicide. * * * And recently, the Michigan Supreme Court also rejected the argument that the distinction "between acts that artificially sustain life and acts that artificially curtail life" is merely a "distinction without constitutional significance—a meaningless exercise in semantic gymnastics," insisting that "the Cruzan majority disagreed and so do we." Kevorkian, 447 Mich., at 471, 527 N. W. 2d, at 728. n8

Similarly, the overwhelming majority of state legislatures have drawn a clear line between assisting suicide and withdrawing or permitting the refusal of unwanted lifesaving medical treatment by prohibiting the former and permitting the latter. * * *

New York is a case in point. The State enacted its current assisted-suicide statutes in 1965. Since then, New York has acted several times to protect patients' common-law right to refuse treatment. * * *

This Court has also recognized, at least implicitly, the distinction between letting a patient die and making that patient die. In Cruzan v.

Director, Mo. Dept. of Health, 497 U.S. 261, 278 (1990), we concluded that "the principle that a competent person has a constitutionally protected liberty interest in refusing unwanted medical treatment may be inferred from our prior decisions," and we assumed the existence of such a right for purposes of that case, id., at 279. But our assumption of a right to refuse treatment was grounded not, as the Court of Appeals supposed, on the proposition that patients have a general and abstract "right to hasten death," 80 F.3d at 727–728, but on well established, traditional rights to bodily integrity and freedom from unwanted touching * * *. In fact, we observed that "the majority of States in this country have laws imposing criminal penalties on one who assists another to commit suicide." Id., at 280. Cruzan therefore provides no support for the notion that refusing life-sustaining medical treatment is "nothing more nor less than suicide."

For all these reasons, we disagree with respondents' claim that the distinction between refusing lifesaving medical treatment and assisted suicide is "arbitrary" and "irrational." * * *

New York's reasons for recognizing and acting on this distinction—including prohibiting intentional killing and preserving life; preventing suicide; maintaining physicians' role as their patients' healers; protecting vulnerable people from indifference, prejudice, and psychological and financial pressure to end their lives; and avoiding a possible slide towards euthanasia—are discussed in greater detail in [Glucksberg]. These valid and important public interests easily satisfy the constitutional requirement that a legislative classification bear a rational relation to some legitimate end.

NOTE: THE ETHICS OF SUICIDE

Is ending one's own life a legitimate exercise of liberty? In the *Metaphysics of Morals* the philosopher Immanuel Kant described suicide as self-murder, an ethical wrong, inconsistent with genuine rational autonomy: "[T]o dispose of one's life for some fancied end, is to degrade the humanity subsisting in his person and entrusted to him to the end that he might uphold and preserve it." Some contemporary philosophers argue that suicide can be a moral duty of individuals anticipating a loss of effective moral agency due to, for example, dementia. Cf. Felicia Ackerman, "For now I have my Death": The "Duty to Die" versus the Duty to Help the Ill Stay Alive, 24 *Midwest Studies in Philosophy* 172 (2000).

Does it matter whether the right to physician-assisted suicide is framed in terms of privacy, autonomy or dignity? Could appeal to the concepts of privacy, autonomy and human dignity result in rather different arguments for a right to end one's own life?

PENNY LEWIS, RIGHTS DISCOURSE AND ASSISTED SUICIDE

27 Am. J.L. and Med. 45 (2001).

Right-based arguments in favor of assisted suicide are generally derived from some combination of the interrelated rights of self-determination, autonomy, privacy and liberty. Other such arguments include: the right to suicide or assisted suicide as one element of a fundamental right to dignity; the right to assisted suicide as a part of a commitment to equality rights; the right to suicide or assisted suicide as implicit in the right to freedom of conscience and religion; and the right to suicide as a necessary concomitant of the individual's property rights in her body or her life * * *. Arguments in favor of a right to suicide or assisted suicide derived from the right to privacy are closely related to [but not identical to] those derived from the rights to autonomy and liberty. Suicide has been described as "the ultimate exercise of one's right to privacy * * *."

A right to suicide derived from a right to dignity is a more limited creature than the expansive rights derived from autonomy, liberty or privacy discussed above. Such a right to suicide would be overridden in cases where the suicide does not promote dignity, on the grounds of the individual's lack of competence to exercise the right in a way designed to attain its end. A central problem with a "right to dignity" approach to suicide or assisted suicide would undoubtedly be the difficulty of distinguishing dignity-constitutive suicides (or proposed suicides) from those which do not promote the individual's dignity.

NOTE: ROK LAMPE, ASSISTED SUICIDE IN THE UNITED KINGDOM AND EUROPE

One of the leading cases of the European Court of Human Rights addressing the issue of assisted suicide was decided in 2001. The decision was in accord with the US Supreme Court's decisions in *Glucksberg* and *Vacco* in the United States: states may prohibit assisted suicide. This case was brought against Great Britain and Northern Ireland by a United Kingdom national, Mrs. Diane Pretty.

The applicant (plaintiff) was a 43-year-old woman who suffered from motor neurone disease ("MND"). This is a progressive neuro-degenerative disease of motor cells within the central nervous system. The disease is associated with progressive muscle weakness affecting the voluntary muscles of the body. As a result of the progression of the disease, severe weakness of the arms and legs and the muscles involved in the control of breathing are affected. Death usually occurs as a result of weakness of the breathing muscles, in association with weakness of the muscles controlling speaking and swallowing, leading to respiratory failure and pneumonia. No treatment can prevent the progression of the disease.

Mrs. Pretty who was paralysed and suffering from a degenerative and incurable illness, alleged that (1) the refusal of the Director of Public Prosecutions to grant an immunity from prosecution to her husband if he assisted her in committing suicide and (2) the prohibition in domestic law on assisting suicide infringed her rights under Article 2 (right to life), Article 3 (prohibition against inhuman or degrading treatment) and Article 8 (right to privacy) of the Convention for the Protection of Human Rights and Fundamental Freedoms.

PRETTY v. THE UNITED KINGDOM

(European Court of Human Rights Application No. 2346/02) 29 April 2002.

I. THE CIRCUMSTANCES OF THE CASE

1. The applicant's condition has deteriorated rapidly since MND was diagnosed in November 1999. The disease is now at an advanced stage. She is essentially paralysed from the neck down, has virtually no decipherable speech and is fed through a tube. Her life expectancy is very poor, measurable only in weeks or months. However, her intellect and capacity to make decisions are unimpaired. The final stages of the disease are exceedingly distressing and undignified. As she is frightened and distressed at the suffering and indignity that she will endure if the disease runs its course, she very strongly wishes to be able to control how and when she dies and thereby be spared that suffering and indignity.

2. Although it is not a crime to commit suicide under English law, the applicant is prevented by her disease from taking such a step without assistance. It is however a crime to assist another to commit suicide (section 2(1) of the Suicide Act 1961).

3. Intending that she might commit suicide with the assistance of her husband, the applicant's solicitor asked the Director of Public Prosecutions (DPP), in a letter dated 27 July 2001 written on her behalf, to give an undertaking not to prosecute the applicant's husband should he assist her to commit suicide in accordance with her wishes.

4. In a letter dated 8 August 2001, the DPP refused to give the undertaking:

> "Successive Directors—and Attorneys General—have explained that they will not grant immunities that condone, require, or purport to authorise or permit the future commission of any criminal offence, no matter how exceptional the circumstances. * * *."

5. On 20 August 2001 the applicant applied for judicial review of the DPP's decision and the following relief which was refused and consequently applied to the House of Lords.

> [The judgment of the House of Lords can be summarized through the Lord Hope concurred opinion regarding Article 8 of the Convention:
>
> "100. . . . Respect for a person's 'private life', which is the only part of Article 8 which is in play here, relates to the way a person lives. The way she chooses to pass the closing moments of her life is part of the act of living, and she has a right to ask that this too must be respected. In that respect Mrs Pretty has the right of self-determination. In that sense, her private life is engaged even where in the face

of terminal illness she seeks to choose death rather than life. But it is an entirely different thing to imply into these words a positive obligation to give effect to her wish to end her own life by means of an assisted suicide. I think that to do so would be to stretch the meaning of the words too far."]

* * *

II. RELEVANT DOMESTIC LAW

A. Suicide, assisted suicide and consensual killing

6. Suicide ceased to be a crime in England and Wales by virtue of the Suicide Act 1961. However, section 2(1) of the Act provides:

> "A person who aids, abets, counsels or procures the suicide of another, or an attempt by another to commit suicide, shall be liable on conviction on indictment to imprisonment for a term not exceeding fourteen years."

Section 2(4) provides:

> "No proceedings shall be instituted for an offence under this section except by or with the consent of the Director of Public Prosecutions."

7. Case-law has established that an individual may refuse to accept life-prolonging or life-preserving treatment:

> "First it is established that the principle of self-determination requires that respect must be given to the wishes of the patient, so that if an adult patient of sound mind refuses, however unreasonably, to consent to treatment or care by which his life would or might be prolonged, the doctors responsible for his care must give effect to his wishes, even though they do not consider it to be in his best interests to do so ... To this extent, the principle of the sanctity of human life must yield to the principle of self-determination ..." (Lord Goff in Airedale NHS Trust v. Bland [1993] AC 789, at p. 864)

8. This principle has been most recently affirmed in Ms B. v. an NHS Hospital, Court of Appeal judgment of 22 March 2002. It has also been recognised that "dual effect" treatment can be lawfully administered, that is treatment calculated to ease a patient's pain and suffering which might also, as a side-effect, shorten their life expectancy (see, for example, Re J [1991] Fam 3).

* * *

III. RELEVANT INTERNATIONAL MATERIALS

9. Recommendation 1418 (1999) of the Parliamentary Assembly of the Council of Europe recommended, inter alia, as follows (paragraph 9):

> "... that the Committee of Ministers encourage the member States of the Council of Europe to respect and protect the dignity of terminally ill or dying persons in all respects:

* * *

c. by upholding the prohibition against intentionally taking the life of terminally ill or dying persons, while:

> i. recognising that the right to life, especially with regard to a terminally ill or dying person, is guaranteed by the member States, in accordance with Article 2 of the European Convention on Human Rights which states that 'no one shall be deprived of his life intentionally';

> ii. recognising that a terminally ill or dying person's wish to die never constitutes any legal claim to die at the hand of another person;

> recognising that a terminally ill or dying person's wish to die cannot of itself constitute a legal justification to carry out actions intended to bring about death."

* * *

THE LAW

* * *

II. ALLEGED VIOLATION OF ARTICLE 2 OF THE CONVENTION

10. The relevant parts of Article 2 of the Convention provide:

> "1. Everyone's right to life shall be protected by law. No one shall be deprived of his life intentionally save in the execution of a sentence of a court following his conviction of a crime for which this penalty is provided by law.

* * *

A. Submissions of the parties

1. The applicant

11. The applicant submitted that permitting her to be assisted in committing suicide would not be in conflict with Article 2 of the Convention, otherwise those countries in which assisted suicide was not unlawful would be in breach of this provision. Furthermore, Article 2 protected not only the right to life but also the right to choose whether or not to go on living. It protected the right to life and not life itself, while the sentence concerning deprivation of life was directed towards protecting individuals from third parties, namely the State and public authorities, not from themselves. Article 2 therefore acknowledged that it was for the individual to choose whether or not to go on living and protected her right to die to avoid inevitable suffering and indignity as the corollary of the right to life. In so far as the Keenan case referred to by the Government indicated that an obligation could arise for prison authorities to protect a prisoner who tried to take his own life, the obligation only arose because he was a prisoner and lacked, due to his mental illness, the capacity to take a rational decision to end his life (see Keenan v. the United Kingdom, no. 27229/95, ECHR 2001–III).

2. The Government

12. The Government submitted that the applicant's reliance on Article 2 was misconceived, being unsupported by direct authority and being inconsistent with existing authority and with the language of the provision. Article 2, guaranteeing one of the most fundamental rights, imposed primarily a negative obligation. Although it had in some cases been found to impose positive obligations, this concerned steps appropriate to safeguard life. In previous cases the State's responsibility under Article 2 to protect a prisoner had not been affected by the fact that he committed suicide (see Keenan, cited above) and it had also been recognised that the State was entitled to force-feed a prisoner on hunger strike (see X v. Germany, no. 10565/83, Commission decision of 9 May 1984, unreported). The wording of Article 2 expressly provided that no one should be deprived of their life intentionally, save in strictly limited circumstances which did not apply in the present case. The right to die was not the corollary, but the antithesis of the right to life.

B. The Court's assessment

13. The Court's case-law accords pre-eminence to Article 2 as one of the most fundamental provisions of the Convention (see McCann and Others v. the United Kingdom, judgment of 27 September 1995, Series A no. 324, pp. 45–46, §§ 146–47). It safeguards the right to life, without which enjoyment of any of the other rights and freedoms in the Convention is rendered nugatory. It sets out the limited circumstances when deprivation of life may be justified and the Court has applied a strict scrutiny when those exceptions have been relied on by the respondent States (ibid., p. 46, §§ 149–50).

14. The text of Article 2 expressly regulates the deliberate or intended use of lethal force by State agents. However, it has been interpreted as covering not only intentional killing but also the situations where it is permitted to 'use force' which may result, as an unintended outcome, in the deprivation of life (ibid., p. 46, § 148). Furthermore, the Court has held that the first sentence of Article 2 § 1 enjoins the State not only to refrain from the intentional and unlawful taking of life, but also to take appropriate steps to safeguard the lives of those within its jurisdiction (see L.C.B. v. the United Kingdom, judgment of 9 June 1998, Reports of Judgments and Decisions 1998–III, p. 1403, § 36). This obligation extends beyond a primary duty to secure the right to life by putting in place effective criminal-law provisions to deter the commission of offences against the person backed up by law-enforcement machinery for the prevention, suppression and sanctioning of breaches of such provisions; it may also imply in certain well-defined circumstances a positive obligation on the authorities to take preventive operational measures to protect an individual whose life is at risk from the criminal acts of another individual (see Osman v. the United Kingdom, judgment of 28 October 1998, Reports 1998–VIII, p. 3159, § 115, and Kılıç v. Turkey, no. 22492/93, §§ 62 and 76, ECHR 2000–III). More recently, in Keenan, Article 2 was found to apply

to the situation of a mentally ill prisoner who disclosed signs of being a suicide risk (see Keenan, cited above, § 91).

15.   The consistent emphasis in all the cases before the Court has been the obligation of the State to protect life. The Court is not persuaded that 'the right to life' guaranteed in Article 2 can be interpreted as involving a negative aspect. While, for example in the context of Article 11 of the Convention, the freedom of association has been found to involve not only a right to join an association but a corresponding right not to be forced to join an association, the Court observes that the notion of a freedom implies some measure of choice as to its exercise (see Young, James and Webster v. the United Kingdom, judgment of 13 August 1981, Series A no. 44, pp. 21–22, § 52, and Sigurður A. Sigurjónsson v. Iceland, judgment of 30 June 1993, Series A no. 264, pp. 15–16, § 35). Article 2 of the Convention is phrased in different terms. It is unconcerned with issues to do with the quality of living or what a person chooses to do with his or her life. To the extent that these aspects are recognised as so fundamental to the human condition that they require protection from State interference, they may be reflected in the rights guaranteed by other Articles of the Convention, or in other international human rights instruments. Article 2 cannot, without a distortion of language, be interpreted as conferring the diametrically opposite right, namely a right to die; nor can it create a right to self-determination in the sense of conferring on an individual the entitlement to choose death rather than life.

16.   The Court accordingly finds that no right to die, whether at the hands of a third person or with the assistance of a public authority, can be derived from Article 2 of the Convention. It is confirmed in this view by the recent Recommendation 1418 (1999) of the Parliamentary Assembly of the Council of Europe (see paragraph 24 above).

17.   The applicant has argued that a failure to acknowledge a right to die under the Convention would place those countries which do permit assisted suicide in breach of the Convention. It is not for the Court in this case to attempt to assess whether or not the state of law in any other country fails to protect the right to life. As it recognised in Keenan, the measures which may reasonably be taken to protect a prisoner from self-harm will be subject to the restraints imposed by other provisions of the Convention, such as Articles 5 and 8, as well as more general principles of personal autonomy (see Keenan, cited above, § 92). Similarly, the extent to which a State permits, or seeks to regulate, the possibility for the infliction of harm on individuals at liberty, by their own or another's hand, may raise conflicting considerations of personal freedom and the public interest that can only be resolved on examination of the concrete circumstances of the case (see, mutatis mutandis, Laskey, Jaggard and Brown v. the United Kingdom, judgment of 19 February 1997, Reports 1997–I). However, even if circumstances prevailing in a particular country which permitted assisted suicide were found not to infringe Article 2 of the Convention, that would not assist the applicant in this case, where the very different proposition—that the United Kingdom would be in breach

of its obligations under Article 2 if it did not allow assisted suicide—has not been established.

18. The Court finds that there has been no violation of Article 2 of the Convention.

* * *

IV. ALLEGED VIOLATION OF ARTICLE 8 OF THE CONVENTION

19. Article 8 of the Convention provides as relevant:

"1. Everyone has the right to respect for his private and family life . . .

2. There shall be no interference by a public authority with the exercise of this right except such as is in accordance with the law and is necessary in a democratic society in the interests of national security, public safety or the economic well-being of the country, for the prevention of disorder or crime, for the protection of health or morals, or for the protection of the rights and freedoms of others."

A. Submissions of the parties

1. The applicant

20. The applicant argued that, while the right to self-determination ran like a thread through the Convention as a whole, it was Article 8 in which that right was most explicitly recognised and guaranteed. It was clear that the right to self-determination encompassed the right to make decisions about one's body and what happened to it. She submitted that this included the right to choose when and how to die and that nothing could be more intimately connected to the manner in which a person conducted her life than the manner and timing of her death. It followed that the DPP's refusal to give an undertaking and the State's blanket ban on assisted suicide interfered with her rights under Article 8 § 1.

21. The applicant argued that there must be particularly serious reasons for interfering with such an intimate part of her private life. However, the Government had failed to show that the interference was justified as no consideration had been given to her individual circumstances. She referred here to the arguments also raised in the context of Article 3 of the Convention (see paragraphs 45–46 above).

2. The Government

22. The Government argued that the rights under Article 8 were not engaged as the right to private life did not include a right to die. It covered the manner in which a person conducted her life, not the manner in which she departed from it. Otherwise, the alleged right would extinguish the very benefit on which it was based. Even if they were wrong on this, any interference with rights under Article 8 would be fully justified. The State was entitled, within its margin of appreciation, to determine the extent to which individuals could consent to the infliction of injuries on themselves and so was even more clearly entitled to determine whether a person could consent to being killed.

B. The Court's assessment

1. Applicability of Article 8 § 1 of the Convention

23. As the Court has had previous occasion to remark, the concept of "private life" is a broad term not susceptible to exhaustive definition. It covers the physical and psychological integrity of a person (see X and Y v. the Netherlands, judgment of 26 March 1985, Series A no. 91, p. 11, § 22). It can sometimes embrace aspects of an individual's physical and social identity (see Mikulić v. Croatia, no. 53176/99, § 53, ECHR 2002–I). Elements such as, for example, gender identification, name and sexual orientation and sexual life fall within the personal sphere protected by Article 8 (see, for example, B. v. France, judgment of 25 March 1992, Series A no. 232–C, pp. 53–54, § 63; Burghartz v. Switzerland, judgment of 22 February 1994, Series A no. 280–B, p. 28, § 24; Dudgeon v. the United Kingdom, judgment of 22 October 1981, Series A no. 45, pp. 18–19, § 41; and Laskey, Jaggard and Brown, cited above, p. 131, § 36). Article 8 also protects a right to personal development, and the right to establish and develop relationships with other human beings and the outside world (see, for example, Burghartz, cited above, opinion of the Commission, p. 37, § 47, and Friedl v. Austria, judgment of 31 January 1995, Series A no. 305–B, opinion of the Commission, p. 20, § 45). Although no previous case has established as such any right to self-determination as being contained in Article 8 of the Convention, the Court considers that the notion of personal autonomy is an important principle underlying the interpretation of its guarantees.

24. The Government have argued that the right to private life cannot encapsulate a right to die with assistance, such being a negation of the protection that the Convention was intended to provide. The Court would observe that the ability to conduct one's life in a manner of one's own choosing may also include the opportunity to pursue activities perceived to be of a physically or morally harmful or dangerous nature for the individual concerned. The extent to which a State can use compulsory powers or the criminal law to protect people from the consequences of their chosen lifestyle has long been a topic of moral and jurisprudential discussion, the fact that the interference is often viewed as trespassing on the private and personal sphere adding to the vigour of the debate. However, even where the conduct poses a danger to health or, arguably, where it is of a life-threatening nature, the case-law of the Convention institutions has regarded the State's imposition of compulsory or criminal measures as impinging on the private life of the applicant within the meaning of Article 8 § 1 and requiring justification in terms of the second paragraph (see, for example, concerning involvement in consensual sado-masochistic activities which amounted to assault and wounding, Laskey, Jaggard and Brown, cited above, and concerning refusal of medical treatment, Acmanne and Others v. Belgium, no. 10435/83, Commission decision of 10 December 1984, Decisions and Reports (DR) 40, p. 251).

25. While it might be pointed out that death was not the intended consequence of the applicants' conduct in the above situations, the Court does not consider that this can be a decisive factor. In the sphere of medical treatment, the refusal to accept a particular treatment might, inevitably, lead to a fatal outcome, yet the imposition of medical treatment, without the consent of a mentally competent adult patient, would interfere with a person's physical integrity in a manner capable of engaging the rights protected under Article 8 § 1 of the Convention. As recognised in domestic case-law, a person may claim to exercise a choice to die by declining to consent to treatment which might have the effect of prolonging his life (see paragraphs 17–18 above).

26. In the present case, although medical treatment is not an issue, the applicant is suffering from the devastating effects of a degenerative disease which will cause her condition to deteriorate further and increase her physical and mental suffering. She wishes to mitigate that suffering by exercising a choice to end her life with the assistance of her husband. As stated by Lord Hope, the way she chooses to pass the closing moments of her life is part of the act of living, and she has a right to ask that this too must be respected.

27. The very essence of the Convention is respect for human dignity and human freedom. Without in any way negating the principle of sanctity of life protected under the Convention, the Court considers that it is under Article 8 that notions of the quality of life take on significance. In an era of growing medical sophistication combined with longer life expectancies, many people are concerned that they should not be forced to linger on in old age or in states of advanced physical or mental decrepitude which conflict with strongly held ideas of self and personal identity.

28. In Rodriguez v. the Attorney General of Canada ([1994] 2 Law Reports of Canada 136), which concerned a not dissimilar situation to the present, the majority opinion of the Supreme Court considered that the prohibition on the appellant in that case receiving assistance in suicide contributed to her distress and prevented her from managing her death. This deprived her of autonomy and required justification under principles of fundamental justice. Although the Canadian court was considering a provision of the Canadian Charter framed in different terms from those of Article 8 of the Convention, comparable concerns arose regarding the principle of personal autonomy in the sense of the right to make choices about one's own body.

29. The applicant in this case is prevented by law from exercising her choice to avoid what she considers will be an undignified and distressing end to her life. The Court is not prepared to exclude that this constitutes an interference with her right to respect for private life as guaranteed under Article 8 § 1 of the Convention. It considers below whether this interference conforms with the requirements of the second paragraph of Article 8.

2. Compliance with Article 8 § 2 of the Convention

30. An interference with the exercise of an Article 8 right will not be compatible with Article 8 § 2 unless it is "in accordance with the law", has an aim or aims that is or are legitimate under that paragraph and is "necessary in a democratic society" for the aforesaid aim or aims (see Dudgeon, cited above, p. 19, § 43).

31. The only issue arising from the arguments of the parties is the necessity of any interference, it being common ground that the restriction on assisted suicide in this case was imposed by law and in pursuit of the legitimate aim of safeguarding life and thereby protecting the rights of others.

32. According to the Court's established case-law, the notion of necessity implies that the interference corresponds to a pressing social need and, in particular, that it is proportionate to the legitimate aim pursued; in determining whether an interference is "necessary in a democratic society", the Court will take into account that a margin of appreciation is left to the national authorities, whose decision remains subject to review by the Court for conformity with the requirements of the Convention. The margin of appreciation to be accorded to the competent national authorities will vary in accordance with the nature of the issues and the importance of the interests at stake.

33. The Court recalls that the margin of appreciation has been found to be narrow as regards interferences in the intimate area of an individual's sexual life (see Dudgeon, cited above, p. 21, § 52, and A.D.T. v. the United Kingdom, no. 35765/97, § 37, ECHR 2000–IX). Although the applicant has argued that there must therefore be particularly compelling reasons for the interference in her case, the Court does not find that the matter under consideration in this case can be regarded as of the same nature, or as attracting the same reasoning.

34. The parties' arguments have focused on the proportionality of the interference as disclosed in the applicant's case. The applicant attacked in particular the blanket nature of the ban on assisted suicide as failing to take into account her situation as a mentally competent adult who knows her own mind, who is free from pressure and who has made a fully informed and voluntary decision, and therefore cannot be regarded as vulnerable and requiring protection. This inflexibility means, in her submission, that she will be compelled to endure the consequences of her incurable and distressing illness, at a very high personal cost.

35. The Court would note that although the Government argued that the applicant, as a person who is both contemplating suicide and severely disabled, must be regarded as vulnerable, this assertion is not supported by the evidence before the domestic courts or by the judgments of the House of Lords which, while emphasising that the law in the United Kingdom was there to protect the vulnerable, did not find that the applicant was in that category.

36. Nonetheless, the Court finds, in agreement with the House of Lords and the majority of the Canadian Supreme Court in Rodriguez, that States are entitled to regulate through the operation of the general criminal law activities which are detrimental to the life and safety of other individuals (see also Laskey, Jaggard and Brown, cited above, pp. 132–33, § 43). The more serious the harm involved the more heavily will weigh in the balance considerations of public health and safety against the countervailing principle of personal autonomy. The law in issue in this case, section 2 of the 1961 Act, was designed to safeguard life by protecting the weak and vulnerable and especially those who are not in a condition to take informed decisions against acts intended to end life or to assist in ending life. Doubtless the condition of terminally ill individuals will vary. But many will be vulnerable and it is the vulnerability of the class which provides the rationale for the law in question. It is primarily for States to assess the risk and the likely incidence of abuse if the general prohibition on assisted suicides were relaxed or if exceptions were to be created. Clear risks of abuse do exist, notwithstanding arguments as to the possibility of safeguards and protective procedures.

37. The applicant's counsel attempted to persuade the Court that a finding of a violation in this case would not create a general precedent or any risk to others. It is true that it is not this Court's role under Article 34 of the Convention to issue opinions in the abstract but to apply the Convention to the concrete facts of the individual case. However, judgments issued in individual cases establish precedents albeit to a greater or lesser extent and a decision in this case could not, either in theory or practice, be framed in such a way as to prevent application in later cases.

38. The Court does not consider therefore that the blanket nature of the ban on assisted suicide is disproportionate. The Government have stated that flexibility is provided for in individual cases by the fact that consent is needed from the DPP to bring a prosecution and by the fact that a maximum sentence is provided, allowing lesser penalties to be imposed as appropriate. The Select Committee report indicated that between 1981 and 1992 in twenty-two cases in which "mercy killing" was an issue, there was only one conviction for murder, with a sentence of life imprisonment, while lesser offences were substituted in the others and most resulted in probation or suspended sentences (paragraph 128 of the report cited at paragraph 21 above). It does not appear to be arbitrary to the Court for the law to reflect the importance of the right to life, by prohibiting assisted suicide while providing for a system of enforcement and adjudication which allows due regard to be given in each particular case to the public interest in bringing a prosecution, as well as to the fair and proper requirements of retribution and deterrence.

39. Nor in the circumstances is there anything disproportionate in the refusal of the DPP to give an advance undertaking that no prosecution would be brought against the applicant's husband. Strong arguments based on the rule of law could be raised against any claim by the executive to exempt individuals or classes of individuals from the operation of the

law. In any event, the seriousness of the act for which immunity was claimed was such that the decision of the DPP to refuse the undertaking sought in the present case cannot be said to be arbitrary or unreasonable.

40. The Court concludes that the interference in this case may be justified as "necessary in a democratic society" for the protection of the rights of others and, accordingly, that there has been no violation of Article 8 of the Convention.

FOR THESE REASONS, THE COURT UNANIMOUSLY

1. Declares the application admissible;

2. Holds that there has been no violation of Article 2 of the Convention;

3. Holds that there has been no violation of Article 8 of the Convention;

* * *

NOTE: ROK LAMPE, PHYSICIAN ASSISTED SUICIDE IN THE NETHERLANDS

It is well-known that some European countries permit voluntary termination of life on request, through formal procedures regulated by law. In the Netherlands, euthanasia is understood to mean the termination of life by a doctor at the patient's request, with the aim of putting an end to unbearable suffering with no prospect of improvement. It includes suicide with the assistance of a doctor. The voluntary nature of the patient's request is crucial: euthanasia may only take place at the explicit request of the patient.

The Dutch definition of euthanasia contrasts with definitions used elsewhere, where the term refers to termination of life by a doctor without the consent of the patient.

In the past 30 years, the question whether euthanasia should remain a punishable offence has been the subject of debate in the Netherlands. Under a new law introduced on April 1, 2002, doctors who perform euthanasia are no longer punishable provided they have followed the prescribed procedures and reported death by non-natural causes to the regional euthanasia review committee. The Criminal Code was amended to include grounds for immunity from criminal liability.

A physician who helps a patient to die must comply with two conditions to remain exempt from punishment:

1. He must practice due care as set forth in a separate law, the Termination of Life on Request and Assisted Suicide (Review Procedures) Act;

2. He must report the cause of death to the municipal coroner in accordance with the relevant provisions of the Burial and Cremation Act.

The incorporation of a special provision on exemption from punishment in the Criminal Code (Article 293, paragraph two, and in Article 294, paragraph two, sentence two), does not decriminalise other forms of euthanasia and assisted suicide. Therefore, to say that euthanasia and assisted suicide are no longer punishable is not a technically correct presentation of the Dutch legislation.

The Termination of Life on Request Act contains provisions governing requests for termination of life or assisted suicide by minors, and recognizes the validity of written living wills. Doctors may grant both oral and written requests for euthanasia, but are never obliged to do so. Under Dutch legislation, termination of life on request is punishable but will not be prosecuted if due care requirements have been complied with. The due care requirements stipulate, among other things, that the patient's request to die must be voluntary and well-considered, that his condition is hopeless and his pain unbearable, that a second doctor must be consulted and that the euthanasia or assisted suicide is performed with due medical care. Furthermore, the physician is obliged to report that the cause of death is euthanasia or assisted suicide. The physician's action is then examined by a regional review committee to determine whether it was performed with due care. The judgment of the review committee is then sent to the Public Prosecution Service, which uses it as a major argument to decide whether or not to institute proceedings against the physician in question.

The due care requirements are formulated extensively in Criminal Code Article 293, paragraph two. They stipulate that the physician:

— must be convinced that the patient has made a voluntary and well-considered request to die;

— must be convinced that the patient's is facing interminable and unendurable suffering;

— has informed the patient about his situation and his prospects;

— together with the patient, must be convinced that there is no other reasonable solution;

— has consulted at least one other independent doctor of the patient;

— has seen and given his written assessment of the due care requirements as referred to in points 1 to 4;

— has helped the patient to die with due medical care.

NOTE: UNORTHODOX TREATMENTS

Is there a "privacy" right to use unorthodox, unapproved medical treatments? See *Rutherford v. United States*, 438 F.Supp. 1287 (W.D. Okla. 1977) and *Suenram v. Society of Valley Hospital*, 155 N.J. Super. 593, 383 A.2d 143 (Law Div. 1977). The cases concern a cancer treatment called "laetrile," but similar arguments were made about experimental medications for AIDS in the 1980's and 1990's. The Supreme Court of California has held that the right of privacy does not include a right to use unproven cancer drugs or to escape punishment for peddling them. *People v. Privitera*, 23 Cal.3d 697, 591 P.2d 919, 153 Cal.Rptr. 431 (en banc 1979). Cf. *Citizens for Implementing Medical Marijuana v. Anchorage*, 129 P.3d 898 (Alaska 2006).

f. Sexual Orientation and Sodomy Laws

NOTE: SHIFTING CONSENSUS

Homosexuality was once a crime in many European countries, as well as in the United States. Homosexuality was decriminalized in Europe—through case law of the European Court of Human Rights applying the right to privacy guaranteed in Article 8 of the Convention for the Protection of Human Rights and Fundamental Freedoms—before it was decriminalized in the United States. *Dudgeon v. United Kingdom* (1981), below, preceded *Bowers v. Hardwick* (1986), below, which held that states of the United States were free to criminalize homosexual sodomy between consenting adults.

DUDGEON v. UNITED KINGDOM

Series A, No. 45 Before the European Court of Human Rights.
23 September 1981.

Summary

In Northern Ireland, the commission of an act of buggery and an attempt to commit buggery are offences under sections 61 and 62 of the Offences against the Person Act 1861. * * *

Held, by 15 votes to four, that there had been a breach of Article 8 in regard to the existing law in relation to men aged over 21; but that it was for countries to fix for themselves, in the first instance, any appropriate extension of the age of consent in relation to such conduct.

Facts

13. Mr. Jeffrey Dudgeon, who is 35 years of age, is a shipping clerk resident in Belfast, Northern Ireland.

Mr. Dudgeon is a homosexual and his complaints are directed primarily against the existence in Northern Ireland of laws which have the effect of making certain homosexual acts between consenting adult males criminal offences.

14. The relevant provisions currently in force in Northern Ireland are contained in the Offences against the Person Act 1861 ('the 1861 Act'), the Criminal Law Amendment Act 1885 ('the 1885 Act') and the common law.

Under sections 61 and 62 of the 1861 Act, committing and attempting to commit buggery are made offences punishable with maximum sentences of life imprisonment and 10 years' imprisonment, respectively. Buggery consists of sexual intercourse *per anum* by a man with a man or a woman, or *per anum* or *per vaginam* by a man or a woman with an animal.

By section 11 of the 1885 Act, it is an offence, punishable with a maximum of two years' imprisonment, for any male person, in public or in private, to commit an act of 'gross indecency' with another male. 'Gross indecency' is not statutorily defined but relates to any act involving sexual indecency between male persons; according to the evidence submitted to the Wolfenden Committee (see para. 17, below), it usually takes the form of mutual masturbation, inter-crural contact or oral-genital contact. At common law, an attempt to commit an offence is itself an offence and, accordingly, it is an offence to attempt to commit an act proscribed by section 11 of the 1885 Act. An attempt is in theory punishable in Northern Ireland by an unlimited sentence (but as to this, see para. 31, below).

Consent is no defence to any of these offences and no distinction regarding age is made in the text of the Acts.

An account of how the law is applied in practice is given below at paragraphs 29 to 31.

15.   Acts of homosexuality between females are not, and have never been, criminal offences, although the offence of indecent assault may be committed by one woman on another under the age of 17. * * * [discussion of arguments against reform of relevant laws in Northern Ireland] In brief, there are two differing viewpoints. One, based on an interpretation of religious principles, holds that homosexual acts under any circumstances are immoral and that the criminal law should be used, by treating them as crimes, to enforce moral behaviour. The other view distinguishes between, on the one hand that area of private morality within which a homosexual individual can (as a matter of civil liberty) exercise his private right of conscience and, on the other hand, the area of public concern where the State ought and must use the law for the protection of society and in particular for the protection of children, those who are mentally retarded and others who are incapable of valid personal consent.

32.   The applicant has, on his own evidence, been consciously homosexual from the age of 14. For some time he and others have been conducting a campaign aimed at bringing the law in Northern Ireland into line with that in force in England and Wales and, if possible, achieving a minimum age of consent lower than 21 years.

33.   On 21 January 1976, the police went to Mr. Dudgeon's address to execute a warrant under the Misuse of Drugs Act 1971. During the search of the house a quantity of cannabis was found which subsequently led to another person being charged with drug offences. Personal papers, including correspondence and diaries, belonging to the applicant in which were described homosexual activities were also found and seized. As a result, he was asked to go to a police station where for about four-and-a-half hours he was questioned, on the basis of these papers, about his sexual life. The police investigation file was sent to the Director of Public Prosecutions. It was considered with a view to instituting proceedings for the offence of gross indecency between males. The Director, in consultation with the Attorney–General, decided that it would not be in the public interest for proceedings to be brought. Mr. Dudgeon was so informed in February 1977 and his papers, with annotations marked over them, were returned to him.

I.　THE ALLEGED BREACH OF ARTICLE 8

37.　The applicant complained that under the law in force in Northern Ireland he is liable to criminal prosecution on account of his homosexual conduct and that he has experienced fear, suffering and psychological distress directly caused by the very existence of the laws in question, including fear of harassment and blackmail. He further complained that, following the search of his house in January 1976, he was questioned by the police about certain homosexual activities and that personal papers belonging to him were seized during the search and not returned until more than a year later. He alleged that, in breach of Article 8 of the Convention, he has thereby suffered, and continues to suffer, an unjustified interference with his right to respect for his private life.

38.　Article 8 provides as follows:

1.　Everyone has the right to respect for his private and family life, his home and his correspondence.

2.　There shall be no interference by a public authority with the exercise of this right except such as is in accordance with the law and is necessary in a democratic society in the interests of national security, public safety or the economic well-being of the country, for the prevention of disorder or crime, for the protection of health or morals, or for the protection of the rights and freedoms of others.

39.　Although it is not homosexuality itself which is prohibited but the particular acts of gross indecency between males and buggery there can be no doubt but that male homosexual practices whose prohibition is the subject of the applicant's complaints come within the scope of the offences punishable under the impugned legislation; it is on that basis that the case has been argued by the Government, the applicant and the Commission. Furthermore, the offences are committed whether the act takes place in public or in private, whatever the age or relationship of the participants involved, and whether or not the participants are consenting. It is evident from Mr. Dudgeon's submissions, however, that his complaint was in essence directed against the fact that homosexual acts which he might commit in private with other males capable of valid consent are criminal offences under the law of Northern Ireland.

40.　* * * The Commission unanimously concluded that the legislation complained of interferes with the applicant's right to respect for his private life guaranteed by Article 8 (1), in so far as it prohibits homosexual acts committed in private between consenting males.

41.　The Court sees no reason to differ from the views of the Commission: the maintenance in force of the impugned legislation constitutes a continuing interference with the applicant's right to respect for his private life (which includes his sexual life) within the meaning of Article 8 (1). In the personal circumstances of the applicant, the very existence of this legislation continuously and directly affects his private life either he respects the law and refrains from engaging (even in private with consenting male partners) in prohibited sexual acts to which he is disposed by reason of his homosexual tendencies, or he commits such acts and thereby becomes liable to criminal prosecution.

49.   There can be no denial that some degree of regulation of male homosexual conduct, as indeed of other forms of sexual conduct, by means of the criminal law can be justified as 'necessary in a democratic society'. The overall function served by the criminal law in this field is, in the words of the Wolfenden report 'to preserve public order and decency [and] to protect the citizen from what is offensive or injurious'. Furthermore, this necessity for some degree of control may even extend to consensual acts committed in private, notably where there is call (to quote the Wolfenden report once more) to provide sufficient safeguards against exploitation and corruption of others, particularly those who are specially vulnerable because they are young, weak in body or mind, inexperienced, or in a state of special physical, official or economic dependence.

In practice there is legislation on the matter in all the member States of the Council of Europe, but what distinguishes the law in Northern Ireland from that existing in the great majority of the member-States is that it prohibits generally gross indecency between males and buggery whatever the circumstances. It being accepted that some form of legislation is 'necessary' to protect particular sections of society as well as the moral ethos of society as a whole, the question in the present case is whether the contested provisions of the law of Northern Ireland and their enforcement remain within the bounds of what, in a democratic society, may be regarded as necessary in order to accomplish those aims.

50.   A number of principles relevant to the assessment of the 'necessity', 'in a democratic society', of a measure taken in furtherance of an aim that is legitimate under the Convention have been stated by the Court in previous judgments.

51.   First, 'necessary' in this context does not have the flexibility of such expressions as 'useful', 'reasonable', or 'desirable', but implies the existence of a 'pressing social need' for the interference in question.

52.   In the second place, it is for the national authorities to make the initial assessment of the pressing social need in each case; accordingly, a margin of appreciation is left to them. However, their decision remains subject to review by the Court... However, not only the nature of the aim of the restriction but also the nature of the activities involved will affect the scope of the margin of appreciation. The present case concerns a most intimate aspect of private life. Accordingly, there must exist particularly serious reasons before interferences on the part of the public authorities can be legitimate for the purposes of Article 8 (2).

54.   The Court's task is to determine on the basis of the afore-stated principles whether the reasons purporting to justify the 'interference' in question are relevant and sufficient under Article 8 (2). The Court is not concerned with making any value-judgment as to the morality of homosexual relations between adult males.

55. It is convenient to begin by examining the reasons set out by the Government in their arguments contesting the Commission's conclusion that the penal prohibition of private consensual homosexual acts involving male persons over 21 years of age is not justified under Article 8 (2)

56. In the first place, the Government drew attention to what they described as profound differences of attitude and public opinion between Northern Ireland and Great Britain in relation to questions of morality. Northern Ireland society was said to be more conservative and to place greater emphasis on religious factors, as was illustrated by more restrictive laws even in the field of heterosexual conduct.

* * * As the Government and the Commission both emphasised, in assessing the requirements of the protection of morals in Northern Ireland, the contested measures must be seen in the context of Northern Ireland society.

The fact that similar measures are not considered necessary in other parts of the United Kingdom or in other member-States of the Council of Europe does not mean that they cannot be necessary in Northern Ireland. Where there are disparate cultural communities residing within the same State, it may well be that different requirements, both moral and social, will face the governing authorities.

57. As the Government correctly submitted, it follows that the moral climate in Northern Ireland in sexual matters, in particular as evidenced by the opposition to the proposed legislative change, is one of the matters which the national authorities may legitimately take into account in exercising their discretion. There is, the Court accepts, a strong body of opposition stemming from a genuine and sincere conviction shared by a large number of responsible members of the Northern Ireland community that a change in the law would be seriously damaging to the moral fabric of society. This opposition reflects (as do in another way the recommendations made in 1977 by the Advisory Commission (see para. 23, above)) a view both of the requirements of morals in Northern Ireland and of the measures thought within the community to be necessary to preserve prevailing moral standards.

Whether this point of view be right or wrong, and although it may be out of line with current attitudes in other communities, its existence among an important sector of Northern Ireland society is certainly relevant for the purposes of Article 8 (2).

58. * * * In the present circumstances of direct rule, the need for caution and for sensitivity to public opinion in Northern Ireland is evident. However, the Court does not consider it conclusive in assessing the 'necessity', for the purposes of the Convention, of maintaining the impugned legislation that the decision was taken, not by the former Northern Ireland Government and Parliament, but by the United Kingdom authorities during what they hope to be an interim period of direct rule.

60. * * * In Northern Ireland itself, the authorities have refrained in recent years from enforcing the law in respect of private homosexual acts between consenting males over the age of 21 years capable of valid consent (see para. 30, above). No evidence has been adduced to show that this has been injurious to moral standards in Northern Ireland or that there has been any public demand for stricter enforcement of the law.

It cannot be maintained in these circumstances that there is a 'pressing social need' to make such acts criminal offences, there being no sufficient justification provided by the risk of harm to vulnerable sections of society requiring protection or by the effects on the public. On the issue of proportionality, the Court considers that such justifications as there are for retaining the law in force unamended are outweighed by the detrimental effects which the very existence of the legislative provisions in question can have on the life of a person of homosexual orientation like the applicant. Although members of the public who regard homosexuality as immoral may be shocked, offended or disturbed by the commission by others of private homosexual acts, this cannot on its own warrant the application of penal sanctions when it is consenting adults alone who are involved.

61. Accordingly, the reasons given by the Government, although relevant, are not sufficient to justify the maintenance in force of the impugned legislation in so far as it has the general effect of criminalising private homosexual relations between adult males capable of valid consent. In particular, the moral attitudes towards male homosexuality in Northern Ireland and the concern that any relaxation in the law would tend to erode existing moral standards cannot, without more, warrant interfering with the applicant's private life to such an extent. 'Decriminalisation' does not imply approval, and a fear that some sectors of the population might draw misguided conclusions in this respect from reform of the legislation does not afford a good ground for maintaining it in force with all its unjustifiable features.

To sum up, the restriction imposed on Mr. Dudgeon under Northern Ireland law, by reason of its breadth and absolute character, is, quite apart from the severity of the possible penalties provided for, disproportionate to the aims sought to be achieved.

The Court has already acknowledged the legitimate necessity in a democratic society for some degree of control over homosexual conduct notably in order to provide safeguards against the exploitation and corruption of those who are specially vulnerable by reason, for example, of their youth (see para. 49, above). However, it falls in the first instance to the national authorities to decide on the appropriate safeguards of this kind required for the defence of morals in their society and, in particular, to fix the age under which young people should have the protection of the criminal law

D. *Conclusion*

63. Mr. Dudgeon has suffered and continues to suffer an unjustified interference with his right to respect for his private life. There is accordingly a breach of Article 8.

[The Court deems it necessary to examine the case under Article 14 as well.]

Dissenting Opinion of JUDGE ZEKIA

I am dealing only with the crucial point which led the Court to find a breach of Article 8 (1) of the Convention by the respondent Government.

The Acts of 1861 and 1885 still in force in Northern Ireland prohibit gross indecency between males and buggery. These enactments in their un-amended form are found to interfere with the right to respect for the private life of the applicant, admittedly a homosexual.

The decisive central issue in this case is therefore whether the provisions of the aforesaid laws criminalising homosexual relations *were necessary* in a democratic society for the protection of morals and for the protection of the rights and freedoms of others, such a necessity being a prerequisite for the validity of the enactment under Article 8 (2) of the Convention.

* * * I proceed to give my reasons as briefly as possible for finding no violation on the part of the respondent Government in this case.

1.   Christian and Moslem religions are all united in the condemnation of homosexual relations and of sodomy. Moral conceptions to a great degree are rooted in religious beliefs.

2.   All civilised countries until recent years penalised sodomy and buggery and similar unnatural practices.

In Cyprus, criminal provisions similar to those embodied in the Acts of 1861 and 1885 in the North of Ireland are in force. Section 171 of the Cyprus Criminal Code, which was enacted in 1929, reads

Any person who

(a) has carnal knowledge of any person against the order of nature, or

(b) permits a male person to have carnal knowledge of him against the order of nature is guilty of a felony and is liable to imprisonment for five years.

Under section 173 anyone who attempts to commit such an offence is liable to three years' imprisonment.

While on the one hand I may be thought biased for being a Cypriot judge, on the other hand I may be considered to be in a better position in forecasting the public outcry and the turmoil which would ensue if such laws are repealed or amended in favour of homosexuals either in Cyprus or in Northern Ireland. Both countries are religious-minded and adhere to moral standards which are centuries old.

3.   While considering the respect due to the private life of a homosexual under Article 8 (1), we must not forget and must bear in mind that respect is also due to the people holding the opposite view, especially in a country populated by a great majority of such people who are completely against unnatural immoral practices. Surely the majority in a democratic society are also entitled under Articles 8, 9 and 10 of the Convention and Article 2

of Protocol No. 1 to respect for their religious and moral beliefs and entitled to teach and bring up their children consistently with their own religious and philosophical convictions.

A democratic society is governed by the rule of the majority. It seems to me somewhat odd and perplexing, in considering the necessity of respect for one's private life, to underestimate the necessity of keeping a law in force for the protection of morals held in high esteem by the majority of people.

A change of the law so as to legalise homosexual activities in private by adults is very likely to cause many disturbances in the country in question. The respondent Government were justified in finding it necessary to keep the relevant Acts on the statute book for the protection of morals as well as for the preservation of public peace.

4. If a homosexual claims to be a sufferer because of physiological, psychological or other reasons and the law ignores such circumstances, his case might then be one of exculpation or mitigation if his tendencies are curable or incurable. Neither of these arguments has been put forward or contested. Had the applicant done so, then his domestic remedies ought to have been exhausted. In fact he has not been prosecuted for any offence. * * *

Much has been said about the scarcity of cases coming to court under the prohibitive provisions of the Acts we are discussing. It was contended that this fact indicates the indifference of the people in Northern Ireland to the non-prosecution of homosexual offences committed. The same fact, however, might indicate the rarity of homosexual offences having been perpetrated and also the unnecessariness and the inexpediency of changing the law.

BOWERS v. HARDWICK

478 U.S. 186 (1986), overruled.

JUSTICE WHITE delivered the opinion of the Court.

In August 1982, respondent Hardwick (hereafter respondent) was charged with violating the Georgia statute criminalizing sodomy by committing that act with another adult male in the bedroom of respondent's home. After a preliminary hearing, the District Attorney decided not to present the matter to the grand jury unless further evidence developed.

Respondent then brought suit in the Federal District Court, challenging the constitutionality of the statute insofar as it criminalized consensual sodomy. He asserted that he was a practicing homosexual, that the Georgia sodomy statute, as administered by the defendants, placed him in imminent danger of arrest, and that the statute for several reasons violates the Federal Constitution. * * *

We first register our disagreement with the Court of Appeals and with respondent that the Court's prior cases have construed the Constitution to confer a right of privacy that extends to homosexual sodomy and for all intents and purposes have decided this case. * * *

No connection between family, marriage, or procreation on the one hand and homosexual activity on the other has been demonstrated, either by the Court of Appeals or by respondent. Moreover, any claim that [prior privacy cases] nevertheless stand for the proposition that any kind of private sexual conduct between consenting adults is constitutionally insulated from state proscription is unsupportable. Indeed, the Court's opinion in Carey twice asserted that the privacy right, which the Griswold line of cases found to be one of the protections provided by the Due Process Clause, did not reach so far. * * *

Precedent aside, however, respondent would have us announce, as the Court of Appeals did, a fundamental right to engage in homosexual sodomy. This we are quite unwilling to do. * * *

Striving to assure itself and the public that announcing rights not readily identifiable in the Constitution's text involves much more than the imposition of the Justices' own choice of values on the States and the Federal Government, the Court has sought to identify the nature of the rights qualifying for heightened judicial protection. In Palko v. Connecticut, 302 U.S. 319, 325, 326 (1937), it was said that this category includes those fundamental liberties that are "implicit in the concept of ordered liberty," such that "neither liberty nor justice would exist if [they] were sacrificed." A different description of fundamental liberties appeared in Moore v. East Cleveland, 431 U.S. 494, 503 (1977) (opinion of Powell, J.), where they are characterized as those liberties that are "deeply rooted in this Nation's history and tradition." Id., at 503 (Powell, J.). See also Griswold v. Connecticut, 381 U.S., at 506.

It is obvious to us that neither of these formulations would extend a fundamental right to homosexuals to engage in acts of consensual sodomy. Proscriptions against that conduct have ancient roots. * * * [Twenty four] States and the District of Columbia continue to provide criminal penalties for sodomy performed in private and between consenting adults. * * * Against this background, to claim that a right to engage in such conduct is "deeply rooted in this Nation's history and tradition" or "implicit in the concept of ordered liberty" is, at best, facetious.

Nor are we inclined to take a more expansive view of our authority to discover new fundamental rights imbedded in the Due Process Clause. The Court is most vulnerable and comes nearest to illegitimacy when it deals with judge-made constitutional law having little or no cognizable roots in the language or design of the Constitution. * * *

Respondent, however, asserts that the result should be different where the homosexual conduct occurs in the privacy of the home. He relies on Stanley v. Georgia, 394 U.S. 557 (1969), where the Court held that the First Amendment prevents conviction for possessing and reading obscene material in the privacy of one's home: "If the First Amendment means anything, it means that a State has no business telling a man, sitting alone in his house, what books he may read or what films he may watch." Id., at 565.

Stanley did protect conduct that would not have been protected outside the home, and it partially prevented the enforcement of state obscenity laws; but the decision was firmly grounded in the First Amendment. The right pressed upon us here has no similar support in the text of the Constitution, and it does not qualify for recognition under the prevailing principles for construing the Fourteenth Amendment. Its limits are also difficult to discern. Plainly enough, otherwise illegal conduct is not always immunized whenever it occurs in the home. Victimless crimes, such as the possession and use of illegal drugs, do not escape the law where they are committed at home. Stanley itself recognized that its holding offered no protection for the possession in the home of drugs, firearms, or stolen goods. * * *

Even if the conduct at issue here is not a fundamental right, respondent asserts that there must be a rational basis for the law and that there is none in this case other than the presumed belief of a majority of the electorate in Georgia that homosexual sodomy is immoral and unacceptable. This is said to be an inadequate rationale to support the law. The law, however, is constantly based on notions of morality, and if all laws representing essentially moral choices are to be invalidated under the Due Process Clause, the courts will be very busy indeed. Even respondent makes no such claim, but insists that majority sentiments about the morality of homosexuality should be declared inadequate. We do not agree, and are unpersuaded that the sodomy laws of some 25 States should be invalidated on this basis. * * *

CHIEF JUSTICE BURGER, concurring.

I join the Court's opinion, but I write separately to underscore my view that in constitutional terms there is no such thing as a fundamental right to commit homosexual sodomy. * * *

To hold that the act of homosexual sodomy is somehow protected as a fundamental right would be to cast aside millennia of moral teaching.

This is essentially not a question of personal "preferences" but rather of the legislative authority of the State. I find nothing in the Constitution depriving a State of the power to enact the statute challenged here.

JUSTICE BLACKMUN, with whom JUSTICE BRENNAN, JUSTICE MARSHALL and JUSTICE STEVENS join, dissenting.

This case is no more about "a fundamental right to engage in homosexual sodomy," as the Court purports to declare, ante, at 191, than Stanley v. Georgia, 394 U.S. 557 (1969), was about a fundamental right to watch obscene movies, or Katz v. United States, 389 U.S. 347 (1967), was about a fundamental right to place interstate bets from a telephone booth. Rather, this case is about "the most comprehensive of rights and the right most valued by civilized men," namely, "the right to be let alone."

Olmstead v. United States, 277 U.S. 438, 478 (1928) (Brandeis, J., dissenting).

CLAIRE FINKELSTEIN, POSITIVISM AND THE NOTION OF AN OFFENSE

88 Calif. L. Rev. 335 (2000).

While the point is not entirely beyond argument, a legislature ought not to be able to forbid consensual intercourse between adults. We can put the point in general, jurisprudential terms by suggesting that sexual intercourse between consenting adults is not a harm or evil that could justify the use of the criminal sanction. Under the harm principle, a criminal offense whose purpose it is to prohibit immoral but nonharmful conduct is not justifiable as a valid infringement of liberty. A court could thus find that the proposed rape statute failed to meet its burden of justification.

But what about the Georgia anti-sodomy law the court upheld in Bowers v. Hardwick? If the Court is predominantly concerned with harm, and the harm the Georgia legislature sought to avert by criminalizing sodomy was sufficient to justify the significant infringement of the liberty interest citizens have in sexual autonomy, arguably the more serious harm of rape could justify vastly greater infringements on that same interest. Would the harm principle help to supply a theory of offense definition in this case?

Bowers, however, is a rather stunning illustration of why a harm-based theory of justified criminalization is to be preferred to both positivism and legal moralism. Had the Court recognized a harm-based account of offense definition as a legitimate way of protecting individual liberty it probably would have found the use of the criminal sanction in Bowers unjustified. At the very least, adopting a harm-based theory in the place of either a morality-based theory (legal moralism) or no theory at all (positivism) would focus debate about such statutes in the right place. The question would become whether forbidding consensual sodomy was sufficiently important to public welfare to justify the extensive infringement of liberty involved.

VINCENT J. SAMAR, GAY–RIGHTS AS A PARTICULAR INSTANTIATION OF HUMAN RIGHTS

64 Alb. L. Rev. 983, 1011–1015 (2001).

[W]e can derive a definition for what a private act is, which I take to be central to the law of privacy. That definition is: "An action is self-regarding (private) with respect to a group of other actors if and only if the consequences of the act impinge in the first instance on the basic interests of the actor and not on the interests of the specified class of actors." The definition derives from the two common strands of privacy law insofar as it provides a theoretical definition of what self-regarding-ness means and a rationale for understanding why one would claim to be left alone. * * *

[T]here is a sense in which any act (by the mere fact of its being known) can affect another person. A fundamentalist Christian, for example, may feel disgust living in a state that allows abortion or same-sex sexual relationships. Thus, to avoid the problem of having no act ever be private, I understand the phrase in the first instance to mean that a mere description of the act without the inclusion of any additional facts or causal theories suggests a conflict with another's interest. * * *

Another issue concerning the definition of a private act is the difference between the basic interest of the actor and the interest of the specified class of actors. The point is not to undo, by an overly broad sense of the word "interest," what the specification of "in the first instance" achieves. To prevent this from happening, one must understand a basic interest as an interest that does not presuppose any institutional or factual conception. Any other interest is a derivative interest, as it would include such institutional or factual conceptions. So, for example, the category "freedom" subsumes such basic interests as expression, privacy, thought, and worship. The category of well-being subsumes such basic interests as health, physical integrity, and mental equilibrium. By contrast, the right to marry is derivative of the basic interest in freedom combined with the institutional arrangement of marriage, and the right to a primary education is derivative of the basic interest in well-being combined with the factual conception that a primary education advances one's well-being.

However, the definition of a private act does not capture why private information and states of affairs are protected. For that a separate, but related, definition of a private state of affairs is needed. "A state of affairs is private with respect to a group of other actors if and only if there is a convention, recognized by the members of the group, that defines, protects, preserves, or guards that state of affairs for the performance of private acts." The first definition works to define what a private act is. The second works to identify the privacy interest at stake where information and places are causally connected to private acts. The two definitions are related because what other people know or can find out about another may inhibit a person from the performance of private acts. They are also related because people sometimes need a private space to feel the personal satisfaction that makes worthwhile the performance of private acts. Thus, while the first definition is part of what is meant by privacy, the second definition comes about because of the psychological/causal connection between private acts and what others can find about them.

A justification for the right to privacy begins with autonomy as a value. Properly understood, autonomy, in the sense meant here, refers to the conditions under which one acts, as opposed to privacy, which involves the nature of one's action. The conditions under which one acts, if autonomous, should follow out of the nature of the action itself and not from any outside forces. So, for example, if individuals play the stock market, their choices are autonomous even when limited by the economic laws of supply and demand, but they are less autonomous when SEC regulations mandate additional, non-market rules. Understood in this way, the value associated with autonomy is the value associated with self-rule, in which the individual is free to act unless doing so would jeopardize the equal autonomy of others. That said, one could use this notion of justified autonomy itself as a justification for privacy rights.

The justification works as follows. If autonomy is a value, then the most idealized instance of autonomy must also be a value. Since privacy, according to our definition, involves only actions that do not affect others in the first instance, it must be a value if autonomy is valued. One often wants to say that autonomy is limited only when another's interest is at stake. However, since privacy, by definition, involves only those actions where another's interests are not at stake, at least not in the first instance, to value autonomy at all, * * * is to value privacy.

Beyond protecting private acts, this notion of autonomy also justifies democratic government and private states of affairs. Where the former justification of private acts is a priori, the latter two are a posteriori. That is to say, where, in the former situation, the value of private acts follows out of what it means to value autonomy at all, in the latter situation the value of private information and states of affairs derive from the causal connection autonomy has to both democracy and private states of affairs. That connection is that protecting these latter two ends preserves autonomy generally. Promoting democracy protects autonomy by ensuring that everyone can engage in self-rule; protecting private states of affairs guarantees autonomy by providing individuals with the opportunity to perform private acts. Interestingly, democracy and the protection of private states of affairs are inter-justificationally related because, if one has the opportunity to engage in private acts or to discover information about them, one can be a more informed voter. And if one is an informed voter, one will seek to protect private states of affairs as a condition under which that information is obtained unless there would be some harm caused to others in the process. So, even from a minimal understanding of autonomy, such as involving the idealized protection of private acts, one can derive safeguards for the protection of private places and private information. * * *

[Basic human rights include a right to privacy. What does the human right to privacy mean specifically for gay-rights? It means that laws, which prohibit adult consensual same-sex activities in the home, are morally illicit and should be held unconstitutional if the constitution is to be interpreted as affording basic human rights protections.]

NOTE: ROK LAMPE, PRIVACY AS A HUMAN RIGHT

United Nations, Article 12, Universal Declaration of Human Rights (1948) provides that: "No one shall be subjected to arbitrary interference with his privacy, family, home or correspondence, nor to attacks upon his honour and reputation. Everyone has the right to the protection of the law against such interference or attacks." One of the main objectives of international law is to protect, promote and to assure human rights for all. This noble idea—"to reaffirm faith in fundamental human rights, in the dignity and worth of the human person, in the equal rights of men and women and of nations large and small"—is set in the preamble to the Charter of the United Nations (1945). It is premised on a belief that, first, all human beings are endowed with rights; and second, that the State is obliged to assure and to protect these rights.

1. Universal Declaration of Human Rights

The United Nations Charter did not define the fundamental human rights. However, in 1948 the United Nations General Assembly adopted the Universal Declaration of Human Rights. Formulated against the background of the horrors of the Second World War, the Declaration was the first attempt by modern States to agree, in a single document, on a comprehensive catalogue of the rights of the human person. As its name suggests, the Declaration was not conceived of as a treaty, but rather a proclamation of basic rights and freedoms, bearing the moral force of universal agreement. Its purpose has thus been described as setting "a common standard of achievement for all peoples in all nations".

The Universal Declaration of Human Rights, see http://www.un.org/Overview/rights.html, includes a general right to privacy. Article 12 states that: "No one shall be subjected to arbitrary interference with his privacy, family, home or correspondence, nor to attacks upon his honour and reputation. Everyone has the right to the protection of the law against such interference or attacks." Article 12 serves as a general guideline, circumscribing a private sphere distinct from the public realm. States are exhorted to refrain from arbitrary interference. States are called upon to offer adequate legal protection in the form of rights and remedies. Indeed, Article 12 must be read in parallel with Article 29, paragraph 2: "In the exercise of his rights and freedoms, everyone shall be subject only to such limitations as are determined by law solely for the purpose of securing due recognition and respect for the rights and freedoms of others and of meeting the just requirements of morality, public order and the general welfare in a democratic society".

This general rule—the proportionality principle—is the key in understanding the logic of privacy law in international and European perspectives. Struggling to balance protection of the right to privacy on the one hand and of the various conflicting interests of the community on the other hand, the Universal Declaration demands that limitations and interference with the right to privacy must be determined by law (legality criteria) only for legitimate aims (legitimate aim criteria) and necessary in a democratic society (democracy criteria). Legitimate aims are limited to protecting the rights and freedoms of others and to just requirements of morality, public order and the general welfare of a society.

The general guideline that the Universal Declaration offers for the protection of privacy can be summed up in this way. Privacy rights should be accorded to all, and should protect individuals against arbitrary State interference in the private sphere, which includes personal and family life, the home and correspondence. The State is obliged not only to refrain from arbitrary interference, but also to shape a legal environment in which individuals can enjoy privacy. Privacy is thus a negative and a positive liberty—freedom from something (interference) and freedom to something (the legal conditions necessary for the enjoyment of privacy).

2.   International Covenant on Civil and Political Rights

Although the Universal Declaration is one of the main political authorities in the international human rights system, it is not a legally binding instrument. Already at the time of the adoption of the Universal Declaration, there was a broad agreement that human rights should be translated into legal form as a treaty, which would be directly binding on the States that agreed to be bound by its terms.

In 1966, the General Assembly adopted the International Covenant on Civil and Political Rights ("Covenant") which is the core binding general treaty covering a wide variety of issues in the field of human rights. See http://www.unhchr.ch/html/menu3/b/a_ccpr.htm. Other subsequent specialized conventions, declarations, sets of rules and principles owe a debt to the International Covenant on Civil and Political Rights, including the International Convention on the Elimination of All Forms of Racial Discrimination (1965); the Convention on the Elimination of All Forms of Discrimination against Women (1979); the Convention against Torture and Other Cruel, Inhuman or Degrading Treatment or Punishment (1984); and the Convention on the Rights of the Child (1989).

3.   The Right to Privacy Under the Covenant on Civil and Political Rights

In 1966, the United Nations General Assembly adopted the International Covenant on Civil and Political Rights ("Covenant") which is the core binding general treaty covering a wide variety of issues in the field of human rights. See http://www.unhchr.ch/html/menu3/b/a_ccpr.htm. The aim of the Covenant is to build "rules concerning the basic rights of the human person" which are *erga omnes* obligations, binding on every State which is a party to the treaty. According to international treaty law, a State party to the Covenant must fulfill all the existing international obligations set down in a treaty.

The Covenant incorporates the definition of the right to privacy found in the Universal Declaration on Human Rights. Parties must refrain from arbitrary interference with individuals' privacy (negative obligation) and to assure all necessary legal tools for protecting the enjoyment of privacy (positive obligation). Article 17 of the Covenant is divided in two paragraphs, which read: "1. No one shall be subjected to arbitrary or unlawful interference with his privacy, family, home or correspondence, nor to unlawful attacks on his honour and reputation. 2. Everyone has the right to the protection of the law against such interference or attacks".

A Human Rights Committee was formed pursuant to the Covenant on Civil and Political Rights to hear complaints brought by party states or by individuals claiming human rights violations. The Human Rights Committee adopts "Views" on the substance, or merits, of the complaint it hears. If the Human Rights Committee finds a violation in a particular case, the State party is requested to remedy that violation, pursuant to the obligation—in article 2, paragraph 3, of the Covenant—to provide an effective remedy for Covenant violations. The recommended remedy may take specific form, such as repeal or amendment of legislation or payment of compensation.

In 1988 the Human Rights Committee published its general comments on the right to privacy founded in article 17 of the Covenant.

HUMAN RIGHTS COMMITTEE

General Comment No. 16: The right to respect of privacy,
family, home and correspondence, and protection of
honour and reputation (Art. 17): 08/04/88.
(Thirty-second session, 1988).

1. Article 17 provides for the right of every person to be protected against arbitrary or unlawful interference with his privacy, family, home or correspondence as well as against unlawful attacks on his honour and reputation. In the view of the Committee this right is required to be guaranteed against all such interferences and attacks whether they emanate from State authorities or from natural or legal persons. The obligations imposed by this article require the State to adopt legislative and other measures to give effect to the prohibition against such interferences and attacks as well as to the protection of this right.

2. In this connection, the Committee wishes to point out that in the reports of States parties to the Covenant the necessary attention is not being given to information concerning the manner in which respect for this right is guaranteed by legislative, administrative or judicial authorities, and in general by the competent organs established in the State. In particular, insufficient attention is paid to the fact that article 17 of the Covenant deals with protection against both unlawful and arbitrary interference. That means that it is precisely in State legislation above all that provision must be made for the protection of the right set forth in that article. At present the reports either say nothing about such legislation or provide insufficient information on the subject.

3. The term "unlawful" means that no interference can take place except in cases envisaged by the law. Interference authorized by States can only take place on the basis of law, which itself must comply with the provisions, aims and objectives of the Covenant.

4. The expression "arbitrary interference" is also relevant to the protection of the right provided for in article 17. In the Committee's view the expression "arbitrary interference" can also extend to interference provided for under the law. The introduction of the concept of arbitrariness is intended to guarantee that even interference provided for by law should be in accordance with the provisions, aims and objectives of the Covenant and should be, in any event, reasonable in the particular circumstances.

5. Regarding the term "family", the objectives of the Covenant require that for purposes of article 17 this term be given a broad interpretation to include all those comprising the family as understood in the society of the

State party concerned. The term "home" in English ... as used in article 17 of the Covenant, is to be understood to indicate the place where a person resides or carries out his usual occupation. In this connection, the Committee invites States to indicate in their reports the meaning given in their society to the terms "family" and "home".

6. The Committee considers that the reports should include information on the authorities and organs set up within the legal system of the State which are competent to authorize interference allowed by the law. It is also indispensable to have information on the authorities which are entitled to exercise control over such interference with strict regard for the law, and to know in what manner and through which organs persons concerned may complain of a violation of the right provided for in article 17 of the Covenant. States should in their reports make clear the extent to which actual practice conforms to the law. State party reports should also contain information on complaints lodged in respect of arbitrary or unlawful interference, and the number of any findings in that regard, as well as the remedies provided in such cases.

7. As all persons live in society, the protection of privacy is necessarily relative. However, the competent public authorities should only be able to call for such information relating to an individual's private life the knowledge of which is essential in the interests of society as understood under the Covenant. Accordingly, the Committee recommends that States should indicate in their reports the laws and regulations that govern authorized interferences with private life.

8. Even with regard to interferences that conform to the Covenant, relevant legislation must specify in detail the precise circumstances in which such interferences may be permitted. A decision to make use of such authorized interference must be made only by the authority designated under the law, and on a case-by-case basis. Compliance with article 17 requires that the integrity and confidentiality of correspondence should be guaranteed de jure and de facto. Correspondence should be delivered to the addressee without interception and without being opened or otherwise read. Surveillance, whether electronic or otherwise, interceptions of telephonic, telegraphic and other forms of communication, wire-tapping and recording of conversations should be prohibited. Searches of a person's home should be restricted to a search for necessary evidence and should not be allowed to amount to harassment. So far as personal and body search is concerned, effective measures should ensure that such searches are carried out in a manner consistent with the dignity of the person who is being searched. Persons being subjected to body search by State officials, or medical personnel acting at the request of the State, should only be examined by persons of the same sex.

9. States parties are under a duty themselves not to engage in interferences inconsistent with article 17 of the Covenant and to provide the legislative framework prohibiting such acts by natural or legal persons.

10. The gathering and holding of personal information on computers, data banks and other devices, whether by public authorities or private individuals or bodies, must be regulated by law. Effective measures have to be taken by States to ensure that information concerning a person's private life does not reach the hands of persons who are not authorized by law to receive, process and use it, and is never used for purposes incompatible with the Covenant. In order to have the most effective protection of his private life, every individual should have the right to ascertain in an intelligible form, whether, and if so, what personal data is stored in automatic data files, and for what purposes. Every individual should also be able to ascertain which public authorises or private individuals or bodies control or may control their files. If such files contain incorrect personal data or have been collected or processed contrary to the provisions of the law, every individual should have the right to request rectification or elimination.

11. Article 17 affords protection to personal honour and reputation and States are under an obligation to provide adequate legislation to that end. Provision must also be made for everyone effectively to be able to protect himself against any unlawful attacks that do occur and to have an effective remedy against those responsible. States parties should indicate in their reports to what extent the honour or reputation of individuals is protected by law and how this protection is achieved according to their legal system.

NOTE: ROK LAMPE, RIGHTS FOR HOMOSEXUALS UNDER THE COVENANT ON CIVIL AND POLITICAL RIGHTS

The first privacy decision of the Human Rights Committee was the result of an individual complaint ("communication") under the Optional Protocol to the International Covenant on Civil and Political Rights. It is one of the leading decisions based on the Article 17 of the Covenant. It was submitted in 1991 by Nicholas Toonen, an Australian citizen born in 1964, residing in Hobart in the state of Tasmania, Australia. He was a leading member of the Tasmanian Gay Law Reform Group and claimed to be a victim of privacy and equality violations by the government of Australia.

HUMAN RIGHTS COMMITTEE

Communication No. 488/1992: Australia. 04/04/94.
CCPR/C/50/D/488/1992.

* * * The facts as submitted by the author

2.1   The author is an activist for the promotion of the rights of homosexuals in Tasmania, one of Australia's six constitutive states. He challenges two provisions of the Tasmanian Criminal Code, namely, sections 122 (a) and (c) and 123, which criminalize various forms of sexual contact between men, including all forms of sexual contact between consenting adult homosexual men in private.

2.2   The author observes that the above sections of the Tasmanian Criminal Code empower Tasmanian police officers to investigate intimate aspects of his private life and to detain him, if they have reason to believe that he is involved in sexual activities which contravene the above sections. He adds that the Director of Public Prosecutions announced, in August 1988, that proceedings pursuant to sections 122 (a) and (c) and 123 would be initiated if there was sufficient evidence of the commission of a crime.

2.3   Although in practice the Tasmanian police has not charged anyone either with "unnatural sexual intercourse" or "intercourse against nature" (section 122) nor with "indecent practice between male persons" (section 123) for several years, the author argues that because of his long-term relationship with another man, his active lobbying of Tasmanian politicians and the reports about his activities in the local media, and because of his activities as a gay rights activist and gay HIV/AIDS worker, his private life and his liberty are threatened by the continued existence of sections 122 (a) and (c) and 123 of the Criminal Code.

2.4   Mr. Toonen further argues that the criminalization of homosexuality in private has not permitted him to expose openly his sexuality and to publicize his views on reform of the relevant laws on sexual matters, as he felt that this would have been extremely prejudicial to his employment. In this context, he contends that sections 122 (a) and (c) and 123 have created the conditions for discrimination in employment, constant stigmatization, vilification, threats of physical violence and the violation of basic democratic rights.

2.5   The author observes that numerous "figures of authority" in Tasmania have made either derogatory or downright insulting remarks about homosexual men and women over the past few years. These include statements made by members of the Lower House of Parliament, municipal councillors (such as "representatives of the gay community are no better than Saddam Hussein" and "the act of homosexuality is unacceptable in any society, let alone a civilized society"), of the church and of members of the general public, whose statements have been directed against the integrity and welfare of homosexual men and women in Tasmania (such as "[g]ays want to lower society to their level" and "You are 15 times more likely to be murdered by a homosexual than a heterosexual ..."). In some public meetings, it has been suggested that all Tasmanian homosexuals should be rounded up and "dumped" on an uninhabited island, or be subjected to compulsory sterilization. Remarks such as these, the author affirms, have had the effect of creating constant stress and suspicion in what ought to be routine contacts with the authorities in Tasmania.

2.6   The author further argues that Tasmania has witnessed, and continues to witness, a "campaign of official and unofficial hatred" against homosexuals and lesbians. This campaign has made it difficult for the Tasmanian Gay Law Reform Group to disseminate information about its activities and advocate the decriminalization of homosexuality. Thus, in September 1988, for example, the Group was refused permission to put up a stand in a public square in the city of Hobart, and the author claims that he, as a leading protester against the ban, was subjected to police intimidation.

2.7   Finally, the author argues that the continued existence of sections 122 (a) and (c) and 123 of the Criminal Code of Tasmania continue to have profound and harmful impacts on many people in Tasmania, including himself, in that it fuels discrimination and violence against and harassment of the homosexual community of Tasmania.

   The complaint

3.1   The author affirms that sections 122 and 123 of the Tasmanian Criminal Code violate articles 2, paragraph 1; 17; and 26 of the Covenant because:

(a) They do not distinguish between sexual activity in private and sexual activity in public and bring private activity into the public domain. In their enforcement, these provisions result in a violation of the right to privacy, since they enable the police to enter a household on the mere suspicion that two consenting adult homosexual men may be committing a criminal offence. Given the stigma attached to homosexuality in Australian society (and especially in Tasmania), the violation of the right to privacy may lead to unlawful attacks on the honour and the reputation of the individuals concerned;

(b) They distinguish between individuals in the exercise of their right to privacy on the basis of sexual activity, sexual orientation and sexual identity;

(c) The Tasmanian Criminal Code does not outlaw any form of homosexual activity between consenting homosexual women in private and only some forms of consenting heterosexual activity between adult men and women in private. That the laws in question are not currently enforced by the judicial authorities of Tasmania should not be taken to mean that homosexual men in Tasmania enjoy effective equality under the law.

3.2   For the author, the only remedy for the rights infringed by sections 122 (a) and (c) and 123 of the Criminal Code through the criminalization of all forms of sexual activity between consenting adult homosexual men in private would be the repeal of these provisions.

3.3   The author submits that no effective remedies are available against sections 122 (a) and (c) and 123. At the legislative level, state jurisdictions have primary responsibility for the enactment and enforcement of criminal law. As the Upper and Lower Houses of the Tasmanian Parliament have been deeply divided over the decriminalization of homosexual activities and reform of the Criminal Code, this potential avenue of redress is said to be ineffective. The author further observes that effective administrative remedies are not available, as they would depend on the support of a majority of members of both Houses of Parliament, support which is lacking. Finally, the author contends that no judicial remedies for a violation of the Covenant are available, as the Covenant has not been incorporated into Australian law, and Australian courts have been unwilling to apply treaties not incorporated into domestic law.

The State party's information and observations

4.1 The State party did not challenge the admissibility of the communication on any grounds, while reserving its position on the substance of the author's claims.

4.2 The State party notes that the laws challenged by Mr. Toonen are those of the state of Tasmania and only apply within the jurisdiction of that state. Laws similar to those challenged by the author once applied in other Australian jurisdictions but have since been repealed.

[* * *]

The State party's observations on the merits and author's comments thereon

6.1 In its submission under article 4, paragraph 2, of the Optional Protocol, dated 15 September 1993, the State party concedes that the author has been a victim of arbitrary interference with his privacy, and that the legislative provisions challenged by him cannot be justified on public health or moral grounds. It incorporates into its submission the observations of the government of Tasmania, which denies that the author has been the victim of a violation of the Covenant.

6.2 With regard to article 17, the Federal Government notes that the Tasmanian government submits that article 17 does not create a "right to privacy" but only a right to freedom from arbitrary or unlawful interference with privacy, and that as the challenged laws were enacted by democratic process, they cannot be an unlawful interference with privacy. The Federal Government, after reviewing the travaux préparatoires of article 17, subscribes to the following definition of "private": "matters which are individual, personal, or confidential, or which are kept or removed from public observation". The State party acknowledges that based on this definition, consensual sexual activity in private is encompassed by the concept of "privacy" in article 17.

[* * *]

6.4 As to whether the interference with the author's privacy was arbitrary or unlawful, the State party refers to the travaux préparatoires of article 17 and observes that the drafting history of the provision in the Commission on Human Rights appears to indicate that the term "arbitrary" was meant to cover interferences which, under Australian law, would be covered by the concept of "unreasonableness". Furthermore, the Human Rights Committee, in its general comment 16 (32) on article 17, states that the "concept of arbitrariness is intended to guarantee that even interference provided for by law should be in accordance with the provisions, aims and objectives of the Covenant and should be ... reasonable in the particular circumstances". a/ On the basis of this and the

Committee's jurisprudence on the concept of "reasonableness", the State party interprets "reasonable" interferences with privacy as measures which are based on reasonable and objective criteria and which are proportional to the purpose for which they are adopted.

[* * *]

6.7   On the basis of the above, the State party contends that there is now a general Australian acceptance that no individual should be disadvantaged on the basis of his or her sexual orientation. Given the legal and social situation in all of Australia except Tasmania, the State party acknowledges that a complete prohibition on sexual activity between men is unnecessary to sustain the moral fabric of Australian society. On balance, the State party "does not seek to claim that the challenged laws are based on reasonable and objective criteria".

6.8   Finally, the State party examines, in the context of article 17, whether the challenged laws are a proportional response to the aim sought. It does not accept the argument of the Tasmanian authorities that the extent of interference with personal privacy occasioned by sections 122 and 123 of the Tasmanian Criminal Code is a proportional response to the perceived threat to the moral standards of Tasmanian society. In this context, it notes that the very fact that the laws are not enforced against individuals engaging in private, consensual sexual activity indicates that the laws are not essential to the protection of that society's moral standards. In the light of all the above, the State party concludes that the challenged laws are not reasonable in the circumstances, and that their interference with privacy is arbitrary. It notes that the repeal of the laws has been proposed at various times in the recent past by Tasmanian governments.

[* * *]

Examination of the merits

8.1   The Committee is called upon to determine whether Mr. Toonen has been the victim of an unlawful or arbitrary interference with his privacy, contrary to article 17, paragraph 1, and whether he has been discriminated against in his right to equal protection of the law, contrary to article 26.

8.2   In so far as article 17 is concerned, it is undisputed that adult consensual sexual activity in private is covered by the concept of "privacy", and that Mr. Toonen is actually and currently affected by the continued existence of the Tasmanian laws. The Committee considers that sections 122 (a) and (c) and 123 of the Tasmanian Criminal Code "interfere" with the author's privacy, even if these provisions have not been enforced for a decade. In this context, it notes that the policy of the Department of Public Prosecutions not to initiate criminal proceedings in respect of private homosexual conduct does not amount to a guarantee that no actions will be brought against homosexuals in the future, particularly in the light of undisputed statements of the Director of Public

Prosecutions of Tasmania in 1988 and those of members of the Tasmanian Parliament. The continued existence of the challenged provisions therefore continuously and directly "interferes" with the author's privacy.

8.3 The prohibition against private homosexual behaviour is provided for by law, namely, sections 122 and 123 of the Tasmanian Criminal Code. As to whether it may be deemed arbitrary, the Committee recalls that pursuant to its general comment 16 (32) on article 17, the "introduction of the concept of arbitrariness is intended to guarantee that even interference provided for by the law should be in accordance with the provisions, aims and objectives of the Covenant and should be, in any event, reasonable in the circumstances". The Committee interprets the requirement of reasonableness to imply that any interference with privacy must be proportional to the end sought and be necessary in the circumstances of any given case.

8.4 While the State party acknowledges that the impugned provisions constitute an arbitrary interference with Mr. Toonen's privacy, the Tasmanian authorities submit that the challenged laws are justified on public health and moral grounds, as they are intended in part to prevent the spread of HIV/AIDS in Tasmania, and because, in the absence of specific limitation clauses in article 17, moral issues must be deemed a matter for domestic decision.

8.5 As far as the public health argument of the Tasmanian authorities is concerned, the Committee notes that the criminalization of homosexual practices cannot be considered a reasonable means or proportionate measure to achieve the aim of preventing the spread of AIDS/HIV. The Government of Australia observes that statutes criminalizing homosexual activity tend to impede public health programmes "by driving underground many of the people at the risk of infection". Criminalization of homosexual activity thus would appear to run counter to the implementation of effective education programmes in respect of the HIV/AIDS prevention. Secondly, the Committee notes that no link has been shown between the continued criminalization of homosexual activity and the effective control of the spread of the HIV/AIDS virus.

8.6 The Committee cannot accept either that for the purposes of article 17 of the Covenant, moral issues are exclusively a matter of domestic concern, as this would open the door to withdrawing from the Committee's scrutiny a potentially large number of statutes interfering with privacy. It further notes that with the exception of Tasmania, all laws criminalizing homosexuality have been repealed throughout Australia and that, even in Tasmania, it is apparent that there is no consensus as to whether sections 122 and 123 should not also be repealed. Considering further that these provisions are not currently enforced, which implies that they are not deemed essential to the protection of morals in Tasmania, the Committee concludes that the provisions do not meet the "reasonableness" test in the circumstances of the case, and that they arbitrarily interfere with Mr. Toonen's right under article 17, paragraph 1.

8.7   The State party has sought the Committee's guidance as to whether sexual orientation may be considered an "other status" for the purposes of article 26. The same issue could arise under article 2, paragraph 1, of the Covenant. The Committee confines itself to noting, however, that in its view, the reference to "sex" in articles 2, paragraph 1, and 26 is to be taken as including sexual orientation.

9.   The Human Rights Committee, acting under article 5, paragraph 4, of the Optional Protocol to the International Covenant on Civil and Political Rights, is of the view that the facts before it reveal a violation of articles 17, paragraph 1, juncto 2, paragraph 1, of the Covenant.

10.   Under article 2, paragraph 3 (a), of the Covenant, the author, as a victim of a violation of articles 17, paragraph 1, juncto 2, paragraph 1, of the Covenant, is entitled to a remedy. In the opinion of the Committee, an effective remedy would be the repeal of sections 122 (a) and (c) and 123 of the Tasmanian Criminal Code.

11.   Since the Committee has found a violation of Mr. Toonen's rights under articles 17, paragraph 1, and 2, paragraph 1, of the Covenant requiring the repeal of the offending law, the Committee does not consider it necessary to consider whether there has also been a violation of article 26 of the Covenant.

12.   The Committee would wish to receive, within 90 days of the date of the transmittal of its views, information from the State party on the measures taken to give effect to the views.

LAWRENCE v. TEXAS

539 U.S. 558 (2003).

JUSTICE KENNEDY delivered the opinion of the Court.

Liberty protects the person from unwarranted government intrusions into a dwelling or other private places. In our tradition the State is not omnipresent in the home. And there are other spheres of our lives and existence, outside the home, where the State should not be a dominant presence. Freedom extends beyond spatial bounds. Liberty presumes an autonomy of self that includes freedom of thought, belief, expression, and certain intimate conduct. The instant case involves liberty of the person both in its spatial and more transcendent dimensions. * * *

The question before the Court is the validity of a Texas statute making it a crime for two persons of the same sex to engage in certain intimate sexual conduct.

In Houston, Texas, officers of the Harris County Police Department were dispatched to a private residence in response to a reported weapons disturbance. They entered an apartment where one of the petitioners, John Geddes Lawrence, resided. The right of the police to enter does not seem to have been questioned. The officers observed Lawrence and another man, Tyron Garner, engaging in a sexual act. The two petitioners were arrested, held in custody over night, and charged and convicted before a Justice of the Peace.

The complaints described their crime as "deviate sexual intercourse, namely anal sex, with a member of the same sex (man)." * * * The applicable state law is Tex. Penal Code Ann. Section 21.06(a) (2003). It provides: "A person commits an offense if he engages in deviate sexual intercourse with another individual of the same sex." The statute defines "deviate sexual intercourse" as follows:

"(A) any contact between any part of the genitals of one person and the mouth or anus of another person; or

"(B) the penetration of the genitals or the anus of another person with an object." * * *

The petitioners were adults at the time of the alleged offense. Their conduct was in private and consensual. * * *

We conclude the case should be resolved by determining whether the petitioners were free as adults to engage in the private conduct in the exercise of their liberty under the Due Process Clause of the Fourteenth Amendment to the Constitution. For this inquiry we deem it necessary to reconsider the Court's holding in Bowers. * * *

The facts in Bowers had some similarities to the instant case. A police officer, whose right to enter seems not to have been in question, observed Hardwick, in his own bedroom, engaging in intimate sexual conduct with another adult male. The conduct was in violation of a Georgia statute making it a criminal offense to engage in sodomy. One difference between the two cases is that the Georgia statute prohibited the conduct whether or not the participants were of the same sex, while the Texas statute, as we have seen, applies only to participants of the same sex. Hardwick was not prosecuted, but he brought an action in federal court to declare the state statute invalid. He alleged he was a practicing homosexual and that the criminal prohibition violated rights guaranteed to him by the Constitution. The Court, in an opinion by Justice White, sustained the Georgia law. * * *

The Court began its substantive discussion in Bowers as follows: "The issue presented is whether the Federal Constitution confers a fundamental right upon homosexuals to engage in sodomy and hence invalidates the laws of the many States that still make such conduct illegal and have done so for a very long time." Id., at 190, 92 L. Ed. 2d 140, 106 S. Ct. 2841. That statement, we now conclude, discloses the Court's own failure to appreciate the extent of the liberty at stake. To say that the issue in Bowers was simply the right to engage in certain sexual conduct demeans the claim the individual put forward, just as it would demean a married couple were it to be said marriage is simply about the right to have sexual intercourse. The laws involved in Bowers and here are, to be sure, statutes that purport to do no more than prohibit a particular sexual act. Their penalties and purposes, though, have more far-reaching consequences, touching upon the most private human conduct, sexual behavior, and in the most private of places, the home. The statutes do seek to control a personal relationship that, whether or not entitled to formal recognition in the law, is within the liberty of persons to choose without being punished as criminals.

At the outset it should be noted that there is no longstanding history in this country of laws directed at homosexual conduct as a distinct matter. * * * This does not suggest approval of homosexual conduct. It does tend to show that this particular form of conduct was not thought of as a separate category from like conduct between heterosexual persons.

Laws prohibiting sodomy do not seem to have been enforced against consenting adults acting in private. A substantial number of sodomy prosecutions and convictions for which there are surviving records were for predatory acts against those who could not or did not consent, as in the case of a minor or the victim of an assault. As to these, one purpose for the prohibitions was to ensure there would be no lack of coverage if a predator committed a sexual assault that did not constitute rape as defined by the criminal law. Thus the model sodomy indictments presented in a 19th-century treatise * * * addressed the predatory acts of an adult man against a minor girl or minor boy. Instead of targeting relations between consenting adults in private, 19th-century sodomy prosecutions typically involved relations between men and minor girls or minor boys, relations between adults involving force, relations between adults implicating disparity in status, or relations between men and animals. * * *

The policy of punishing consenting adults for private acts was not much discussed in the early legal literature. We can infer that one reason for this was the very private nature of the conduct. Despite the absence of prosecutions, there may have been periods in which there was public criticism of homosexuals as such and an insistence that the criminal laws be enforced to discourage their practices. But far from possessing "ancient roots," Bowers, 478 U.S., at 192, American laws targeting same-sex couples did not develop until the last third of the 20th century. The reported decisions concerning the prosecution of consensual, homosexual sodomy between adults for the years 1880–1995 are not always clear in the details, but a significant number involved conduct in a public place. See Brief for American Civil Liberties Union et al. as Amici Curiae 14–15, and n 18.

It was not until the 1970's that any State singled out same-sex relations for criminal prosecution, and only nine States have done so. Post–Bowers even some of these States did not adhere to the policy of suppressing homosexual conduct. Over the course of the last decades, States with same-sex prohibitions have moved toward abolishing them. * * *

In summary, the historical grounds relied upon in Bowers are more complex than the majority opinion and the concurring opinion by Chief

Justice Burger indicate. Their historical premises are not without doubt and, at the very least, are overstated.

It must be acknowledged, of course, that the Court in Bowers was making the broader point that for centuries there have been powerful voices to condemn homosexual conduct as immoral. The condemnation has been shaped by religious beliefs, conceptions of right and acceptable behavior, and respect for the traditional family. For many persons these are not trivial concerns but profound and deep convictions accepted as ethical and moral principles to which they aspire and which thus determine the course of their lives. These considerations do not answer the question before us, however. The issue is whether the majority may use the power of the State to enforce these views on the whole society through operation of the criminal law. "Our obligation is to define the liberty of all, not to mandate our own moral code." Planned Parenthood of Southeastern Pa. v. Casey * * *.

In our own constitutional system the deficiencies in Bowers became even more apparent in the years following its announcement. The 25 States with laws prohibiting the relevant conduct referenced in the Bowers decision are reduced now to 13, of which 4 enforce their laws only against homosexual conduct. In those States where sodomy is still proscribed, whether for same-sex or heterosexual conduct, there is a pattern of nonenforcement with respect to consenting adults acting in private. The State of Texas admitted in 1994 that as of that date it had not prosecuted anyone under those circumstances.

[In] the post-Bowers case, Romer v. Evans, 517 U.S. 620 * * * (1996) * * * the Court struck down class-based legislation directed at homosexuals as a violation of the Equal Protection Clause. Romer invalidated an amendment to Colorado's constitution which named as a solitary class persons who were homosexuals, lesbians, or bisexual either by "orientation, conduct, practices or relationships," id., at 624, 134 L. Ed. 2d 855, 116 S. Ct. 1620 (internal quotation marks omitted), and deprived them of protection under state antidiscrimination laws. We concluded that the provision was "born of animosity toward the class of persons affected" and further that it had no rational relation to a legitimate governmental purpose. * * *

As an alternative argument in this case, counsel for the petitioners and some amici contend that Romer provides the basis for declaring the Texas statute invalid under the Equal Protection Clause. That is a tenable argument, but we conclude the instant case requires us to address whether Bowers itself has continuing validity. Were we to hold the statute invalid under the Equal Protection Clause some might question whether a prohibition would be valid if drawn differently, say, to prohibit the conduct both between same-sex and different-sex participants.

Equality of treatment and the due process right to demand respect for conduct protected by the substantive guarantee of liberty are linked in important respects, and a decision on the latter point advances both interests. If protected conduct is made criminal and the law which does so remains unexamined for its substantive validity, its stigma might remain even if it were not enforceable as drawn for equal protection reasons. When homosexual conduct is made criminal by the law of the State, that declaration in and of itself is an invitation to subject homosexual persons to discrimination both in the public and in the private spheres. The central holding of Bowers has been brought in question by this case, and it should be addressed. Its continuance as precedent demeans the lives of homosexual persons.

The stigma this criminal statute imposes, moreover, is not trivial. The offense, to be sure, is but a class C misdemeanor, a minor offense in the Texas legal system. Still, it remains a criminal offense with all that imports for the dignity of the persons charged. The petitioners will bear on their record the history of their criminal convictions. * * * We are advised that if Texas convicted an adult for private, consensual homosexual conduct under the statute here in question the convicted person would come within the registration laws of at least four States were he or she to be subject to their jurisdiction. * * * This underscores the consequential nature of the punishment and the state-sponsored condemnation attendant to the criminal prohibition. Furthermore, the Texas criminal conviction carries with it the other collateral consequences always following a conviction, such as notations on job application forms, to mention but one example.

The foundations of Bowers have sustained serious erosion from our recent decisions in Casey and Romer. When our precedent has been thus weakened, criticism from other sources is of greater significance * * *.

The doctrine of stare decisis is essential to the respect accorded to the judgments of the Court and to the stability of the law. It is not, however, an inexorable command. Payne v. Tennessee, 501 U.S. 808(1991) ("Stare decisis is not an inexorable command; rather, it 'is a principle of policy and not a mechanical formula of adherence to the latest decision' "). In Casey we noted that when a Court is asked to overrule a precedent recognizing a constitutional liberty interest, individual or societal reliance on the existence of that liberty cautions with particular strength against reversing course. * * * The holding in Bowers, however, has not induced detrimental reliance comparable to some instances where recognized individual rights are involved. Indeed, there has been no individual or societal reliance on Bowers of the sort that could counsel against overturning its holding once there are compelling reasons to do so. Bowers itself causes uncertainty, for the precedents before and after its issuance contradict its central holding.

Bowers was not correct when it was decided, and it is not correct today. It ought not to remain binding precedent. Bowers v. Hardwick should be and now is overruled.

The present case does not involve minors. It does not involve persons who might be injured or coerced or who are situated in relationships where consent might not easily be refused. It does not involve public conduct or prostitution. It does not involve whether the government must give formal recognition to any relationship that homosexual persons seek to enter. The case does involve two adults who, with full and mutual consent from each other, engaged in sexual practices common to a homosexual lifestyle. The petitioners are entitled to respect for their private lives. The State cannot demean their existence or control their destiny by making their private sexual conduct a crime. Their right to liberty under the Due Process Clause gives them the full right to engage in their conduct without intervention of the government. "It is a promise of the Constitution that there is a realm of personal liberty which the government may not enter." Casey, supra, at 847. The Texas statute furthers no legitimate state interest which can justify its intrusion into the personal and private life of the individual.

Had those who drew and ratified the Due Process Clauses of the Fifth Amendment or the Fourteenth Amendment known the components of liberty in its manifold possibilities, they might have been more specific. They did not presume to have this insight. They knew times can blind us to certain truths and later generations can see that laws once thought necessary and proper in fact serve only to oppress. As the Constitution endures, persons in every generation can invoke its principles in their own search for greater freedom.

The judgment of the Court of Appeals for the Texas Fourteenth District is reversed, and the case is remanded for further proceedings not inconsistent with this opinion. * * * It is so ordered.

JUSTICE SCALIA, with whom the CHIEF JUSTICE and JUSTICE THOMAS join, dissenting. * * *

I begin with the Court's surprising readiness to reconsider a decision rendered a mere 17 years ago in Bowers v. Hardwick. I do not myself believe in rigid adherence to stare decisis in constitutional cases; but I do believe that we should be consistent rather than manipulative in invoking the doctrine. Today's opinions in support of reversal do not bother to distinguish—or indeed, even bother to mention—the paean to stare decisis coauthored by three Members of today's majority in Planned Parenthood v. Casey. * * *

To tell the truth, it does not surprise me, and should surprise no one, that the Court has chosen today to revise the standards of stare decisis set forth in Casey. It has thereby exposed Casey's extraordinary deference to precedent for the result-oriented expedient that it is. * * *

Today's opinion is the product of a Court, which is the product of a law-profession culture, that has largely signed on to the so-called homosexual agenda, by which I mean the agenda promoted by some homosexual activists directed at eliminating the moral opprobrium that has traditionally attached to homosexual conduct. I noted in an earlier opinion the fact that the American Association of Law Schools (to which any reputable law school must seek to belong) excludes from membership any school that refuses to ban from its job-interview facilities a law firm (no matter how small) that does not wish to hire as a prospective partner a person who openly engages in homosexual conduct. * * *

Let me be clear that I have nothing against homosexuals, or any other group, promoting their agenda through normal democratic means. Social perceptions of sexual and other morality change over time, and every group has the right to persuade its fellow citizens that its view of such matters is the best. That homosexuals have achieved some success in that enterprise is attested to by the fact that Texas is one of the few remaining States that criminalize private, consensual homosexual acts. But persuading one's fellow citizens is one thing, and imposing one's views in absence of democratic majority will is something else. I would no more require a State to criminalize homosexual acts—or, for that matter, display any moral disapprobation of them—than I would forbid it to do so. What Texas has chosen to do is well within the range of traditional democratic action, and its hand should not be stayed through the invention of a brand-new "constitutional right" by a Court that is impatient of democratic change. * * *

PATRICK M. GARRY, A DIFFERENT MODEL FOR THE RIGHT TO PRIVACY: THE POLITICAL QUESTION DOCTRINE AS A SUBSTITUTE FOR SUBSTANTIVE DUE PROCESS

61 U. Miami L. Rev. 169, 188 (2006).

The Court's privacy rulings presume that judges have the ability and duty to determine those personal choices that define human life and sustain personal dignity. These rulings presume that courts can adequately draw the fine lines between individual privacy, democratic values, and social policies. The constitutional doctrines on privacy further presume that a centralized judiciary can better determine the parameters of individual autonomy than can any democratically-elected legislature.

In its privacy decisions, the Court has not only used a right not mentioned in the Constitution to dictate policy choices and social values uniformly to every community in the nation, but in doing so it has defined what constitutes the vital ingredients of personal dignity and autonomy for all Americans. Moreover, as the privacy cases show, the Supreme Court has decided that constitutional privacy is to be defined almost exclusively in terms of sexual activity freedoms. * * *

The irony of the constitutional right of privacy is that it exists in a society where every aspect of personal privacy other than sexual conduct is being eroded. Sexual privacy is constitutionally protected, even though identity and informational privacy is under increasing assault from new technologies. * * *

Another paradox in the Court's privacy rulings is that, as it has been developing a right to privacy, the Court has continued to downplay or ignore property rights, which for a century and a half were an explicit and primary focus of constitutional law. In fact, only after the Court stopped treating property rights as fundamental rights, requiring a substantive due process analysis, did it begin to adopt a substantive due process analysis for issues involving non-economic individual rights. * * *

Due to the way privacy has evolved as a court-created right, there is an arbitrariness to the current constitutional doctrines. Why, for instance, did the Court pick sexual activity as the area covered by privacy rights? What if there are many people who define themselves not through their sexual activities, but through some other activity? Who is to say that the only real measure of privacy is in sexual relations, as the Court has suggested? Is sexual privacy so much more important to human autonomy and dignity than informational privacy? Why is there not a constitutional right of privacy against media disclosure of private information, which seems far more violative of privacy rights than restrictions on abortion? * * *

Through its information privacy laws, America has often preferred the free flow of information over individual privacy rights. For instance, although the Privacy Act of 1974 applied the fair information practices to the federal public sector, there is no comprehensive information privacy law applying information privacy principles to the private sector. Furthermore, information privacy laws have been enacted on a piecemeal basis to deal with specific problems in isolated sectors, such as in relation to credit information and financial institutions. Thus, the political process has balanced America's need for privacy with its desire for public openness of information. As a reflection of this balancing, and because indications exist that the public is becoming more concerned about the technological assault on privacy, Congress has become far more active in its legislative agenda on privacy. * * *

Since Griswold, the Due Process Clause of the Fourteenth Amendment has served as the Court's "chosen vessel" for the protection of unenumerated rights. Under a substantive due process approach, the Court recognizes a right as fundamental when it can be shown that the right is grounded in tradition. However, tradition can be a highly subjective concept. John Hart Ely states that "people have come to understand that tradition can be invoked in support of almost any cause." Consequently, the substantive due process approach has been criticized as allowing judges to impose their own personal views at the expense of the democratic process. According to Chief Justice Rehnquist, judges can use substantive due process to effectively rob the legislatures of their ability to consider important issues of self-governance. * * *

There seems to be little logic in determining what qualifies as a fundamental freedom, unless one simply concludes that anything connected with sexual activity has a much greater chance of receiving fundamental rights status than does any other human act or decision.

In Washington v. Glucksberg, which declined to hold physician-assisted suicide a fundamental right, the Court emphasized the need to resist expanding the scope of substantive due process. * * *

A comparison of Glucksberg with Casey and Lawrence suggests that substantive due process permits, and perhaps requires, a continually fluid approach to constitutional interpretations, in which each generation will read its own cultural practices into the Constitution. A comparison of the cases also indicates the heightened status given to sex by substantive due process. According to the Court, a person's destiny and meaning of life is uniquely tied to her sexual orientation and activities. Sexual activity thus becomes the key component of personal dignity, which under the Lawrence analysis seems to be more important than either history or tradition in determining fundamental rights status.

The subjectivity and unpredictability inherent in the substantive due process approach can also be seen in Lawrence's overruling of Bowers. * * * In Bowers, the Court found no constitutional basis for "a fundamental right to engage in homosexual sodomy." After examining whether American history and tradition had in effect created such a fundamental right, the Bowers Court concluded that prohibitions against sodomy "have ancient roots" in history and that the act of sodomy had been criminalized by many states since the colonial era.

Seventeen years later, however, the Court reversed itself. In Lawrence, Justice Kennedy conducted the same kind of historical examination that swayed the Court's decision in Bowers, but this time found no national history or tradition of condemning homosexual sodomy. * * *

Aside from the Bowers reversal, substantive due process has historically proved to be unreliable. The first era of substantive due process took place from the latter part of the nineteenth century to the 1930s. During this era, defined by the Court's decision in Lochner v. New York, property and economic rights were protected under a substantive due process approach. Lochner rested on the Court's assertion that liberty of contract was a fundamental right protected by the Due Process Clause. * * *

During the Lochner era, the Court struck down nearly two hundred state laws for violating the liberty of contract inherent in the Due Process Clause. But the constitutional revolution of the New Deal brought an end to this era. Under pressure from President Roosevelt's court-packing plan, the Court ceased using substantive due process to strike down New Deal economic legislation. Lochner was not only abandoned, it was roundly criticized as being "not merely a wrong decision, but a very bad one, as well." Critics have since condemned Lochner as a result of individual Justices injecting their personal views into the Constitution. Others have argued that the Due Process Clause should address only procedural and not substantive matters. Still others have argued that the Fourteenth Amendment was aimed solely at eliminating racial inequity in the aftermath of the Civil War.

Despite this criticism of substantive due process as a means to protect the liberty of contract during the pre-New Deal period, it has nonetheless been embraced as a source of protection for another judicially-created fundamental right: the right of privacy. The Court in Planned Parenthood of Southeastern Pennsylvania v. Casey, in language reminiscent of the Lochner era, ruled that substantive due process protects those matters and choices "central to personal dignity and autonomy." * * *

The modern Court's use of substantive due process renders uncertain the proper balance between legislative and judicial power. In 1824, Chief Justice John Marshall expressed the prevailing view of the Court's role: "Judicial power is never exercised for the purpose of giving effect to the will of the judge; always for the purpose of giving effect . . . to the will of the legislature." Marshall also suggested that, on doubtful questions of constitutionality, the judgments of the political branches "ought to receive a considerable impression."

The weakness of the substantive due process approach is that it places before the Court issues that should be addressed in the democratic arena. Through this approach, the Court seals off the democratic process from addressing the matter at issue; but in doing so, as shown by the abortion decisions, the Court only intensifies and prolongs the political and legal anguish over the issue. As John Hart Ely theorized, an overactive judiciary exerts a suffocating influence on the democratic process. Justice Kennedy repeated this theme when he said that " '[s]ociety has to recognize that it has to confront hard decisions in neutral, rational, dispassionate debate * * * [a]nd not just leave it to the courts * * * [because it's] a weak society that leaves it to courts.' " * * *

Privacy rights activists see the individual ideal as being in a state of nature. But this is not how the Constitution sees individuals, especially individuals who are members of a democratic society. The Constitution is primarily concerned with the workings of the democratic community, not with trying to return individuals to some imaginary state of nature. The Framers did not see human beings as solitary creatures, with no relationships or obligations to society. Indeed, by joining democratic society, the individual is no longer in a state of nature. Therefore, laws should not be crafted as if individuals lived separate from society, disconnected from its democratic process. According to William Blackstone, when society was formed, individuals gave up the liberty they enjoyed in the state of nature and exchanged it for a more limited set of liberties and rights under civil society. However, the Court's privacy rulings seem to presume that individual freedom cannot truly exist within majoritarian rule, as if majoritarian rule is inherently oppressive.

NOTE: DON'T ASK, DON'T TELL

The *Lawrence* decision decriminalized homosexual sex, but left intact the "Don't Ask, Don't Tell" policy of the U.S. military, codified as 10 U.S.C. § 654(b): "Policy. A member of the armed forces shall be separated from the armed forces under regulations prescribed by the Secretary of Defense if one or more of the following findings is made and approved in accordance with procedures set forth in such regulations: * * *

(1) That the member has engaged in, attempted to engage in, or solicited another to engage in a homosexual act or acts * * *

(2) That the member has stated that he or she is a homosexual or bisexual, or words to that effect, unless there is a further finding, made and approved in accordance with procedures set forth in the regulations, that the member has demonstrated that he or she is not a person who engages in, attempts to engage in, has a propensity to engage in, or intends to engage in homosexual acts.

(3) That the member has married or attempted to marry a person known to be of the same biological sex.''

A member of the armed forces faces discharge if he or she discloses a homosexual or bisexual orientation. The policy demands secrecy of homosexual or bisexual service members who wish to remain in service. The government has cited the privacy interests of heterosexuals as among the reasons to ban professed non-heterosexuals from the military. See *Able v. United States*, 155 F.3d 628 (2d Cir.1998) ("the United States has justified § 654's prohibition on homosexual conduct on the basis that it promotes unit cohesion, enhances privacy and reduces sexual tension.")

President Barack Obama expressed opposition to and a desire to repeal the military policy known as Don't Ask Don't Tell [DADT]. Repealing DADT was also part of the Democratic Party National Platform for the first time in the 2008 elections. Popular support of the American people for allowing openly gay people to serve in the military is increasing. For example, a 2010 CNN poll indicates that 78 percent of Americans are in favor of repeal of DADT in comparison with only 44 percent in 1993. Military officials, too, have expressed their support for the repeal of DADT (e.g., Admiral Mullen and the Defense Secretary Robert Gates). President Obama asserted, however, that such a policy change should be achieved through consensus and with congressional and military cooperation. While the Pentagon examined the mechanisms by which DADT might be repealed, in March 2010, Defense Secretary Robert Gates announced new guidelines that make it more difficult to discharge LGB soldiers. The guidelines require that information provided by a third party must be given under oath. The approval of a general or an admiral is needed to initiate a discharge process. In May 2010, the House adopted the National Defense Authorization Act for Fiscal Year 2011, which includes a provision that allows the Defense Department to repeal DADT. In July 2010, as part of the preparation process for repeal, the military surveyed the attitudes of 400,000 American soldiers toward LGB service people. In September 2010, a Senate vote on lifting the ban fell short of passage by four votes.

While the White House was in the process of attaining majority support in Congress for repeal of the act, two important court cases called DADT into question. In the first case, *Witt v. Air Force*, 527 F.3d 806 (2008), the Ninth Circuit ruled that in every discharge of an LGB soldier, the US army must prove that the individual soldier caused actual harm to unit cohesion. This is a very high burden of proof to meet, one that makes it almost impossible for the military to secure lawful discharges. This case was returned to the district court to examine whether such proof existed. The US Justice Department did not seek certiorari in the US Supreme Court. In a second case, a district court judge in California declared DADT unconstitutional because it violates both the First and Fifth Amendments of the US constitution, and the government failed to show that these infringements serve a compelling interest (*Log Cabin Republicans v. U.S.*, 2010 WL 3526272 (C.D.Cal.)).

JEAN L. COHEN, IS THERE A DUTY OF PRIVACY?

6 Texas Journal of Women and the Law 47, 59–64 (1996).

The new military policy is a textbook example of the conception of privacy appropriately described as the "epistemology of closet" and of the sham of a purportedly liberal and tolerant public policy that forces privatization and secrecy onto certain groups. The operative conception of privacy here is that of secrecy about what one does at home, self-effacement ("discretion") in public. But, * * * these dynamics come into play precisely in a context in which the privacy rights (along with certain speech, associational, and equality rights) of gays and lesbians have been denied constitutional protection. The military policy does not concede such rights, rather it offers an exchange: we won't pursue you into your bedrooms on the condition of silence and concealment of your sexuality. This (rather disingenuous) offer of non-interrogation and non-harassment is made conditional on acceptance of a duty of privacy; rights have nothing to do with it.

Indeed, what I am calling the "duty of privacy" is not the correlative of the right to privacy in the usual sense. Rather, the form it has taken ("don't tell") is predicated precisely on the absence of key privacy rights for those on whom it is imposed. Under constitutional privacy doctrine, to say that a matter is private means that it is presumptively immune from legal prohibition and that the decisional autonomy of the individual in the matter is protected. This also means that the decision whether or not to reveal one's private affairs in public is protected. The concept of a right to privacy securing decisional autonomy thus includes—along with the right to associate intimately and sexually with partners of your choice—the right to say and be who you are in public without risking either your dispositional control over information—access to the self and speech—or the claim to have your individual integrity respected and recognized. In other words, if certain conduct, information, or relationships are constitutionally protected as private, it does not follow that society may mandate that they be kept secret! On the contrary, if the relevant intimate relationships, sexual acts, object choices, bedrooms, etc. of gays and lesbians were protected by constitutionalized privacy rights, government would be powerless to impose special requirements of secrecy or silence about them.

This becomes obvious so soon as one reflects upon what it is precisely that the obligation of privacy conceptualized as silence and secrecy entailed in the "don't ask, don't tell, don't pursue" policy involves. Let us be very clear. The duty at stake here is not that one refrain, out of mutual consideration for each other's "privacy," from engaging in sexual intercourse or sexual acts visibly and openly in public. Since sex acts are coded as intimate in our society and since we have cultural taboos on nudity, everyone is presumed to owe everyone else a duty of civility which involves refraining from violating these taboos. That is what strictures about public decency supposedly enforce.

Whatever we might think of such rules of civility, they are not at issue here. But then, what is? The obligation of privacy imposed in the "don't ask, don't tell" policy explicitly enjoins speech and expression about sex acts, and, despite disclaimers, insists upon discretion regarding sexual orientation and desire—a duty imposed selectively and exclusively on homosexuals and lesbians. To be more specific, people are required to refrain from indicating in any way that one has, does, or might engage in acts of sexual intimacy with others of the same sex. The duty of privacy here refers to speech about acts when linked to homosexual orientation, not to the public or private performance of the acts.

The new policy makes no distinction at all between public and private conduct, between acts engaged in on or off duty, on or off base. It is one thing to forbid genital sexual activity between any one on base or on duty, something apparently well within the province of military authority. It is quite another to attempt to regulate speech about what one does in private or off base, especially when such regulations are applied only to a particular group. No such obligation of secrecy, no such duty of privacy is imposed on heterosexuals. So far as I am aware there has never been a case in which a legal duty to be discrete about legal action has been selectively imposed by regulatory action on any group.

The question to ask in this context is, of course, how the administrative imposition of such an obviously discriminatory obligation onto a minority is legally possible? One would think that in addition to the violation of personal autonomy there are obvious First Amendment issues involved here, not to mention anti-discrimination principles. Indeed, two recent Court rulings, Watkins v. United States Army and Meinhold v. United States Department of Defense, have held that homosexuals as persons are entitled to Constitutional protection under the Equal Protection Clause, and that the former policy of the U.S. Army and the Department of Defense—of discharging service members merely for admitting that they are homosexual—violates Constitutional principles. Hence the new military policy no longer cites homosexual status as a reason for interrogation, investigation, or discharge. What then, does it cite? We already have the answer: "conduct" and its voluntary disclosure. * * *

Insisting on privacy rights for gays and lesbians is thus not a matter of getting sex back into the impermeable space of the bedroom, but of challenging the role that sex law plays in regulating all individuals, in privileging certain forms of intimate association, and in oppressing specific categories of people without even naming the categories. The decriminalization of sodomy won't yield the full panoply of rights that gays and lesbians need, but it would pull the rug out from under the rhetorical and legal construction of gays and lesbians as a tendentially criminal population undeserving of the equivalent rights that others enjoy. The current military policy ostensibly focusing on conduct rather than status would thereby lose its raison d'etre. Affording privacy protection to cover the consensual sexual choices and intimate associations of gays and lesbians would abolish many of the inequalities established and reinforced by sex law, including gender hierarchies. Moreover, it would constitute an enormous symbolic victory, for it would indicate that the law no longer construes homosexuals as so different (i.e., inferior) that they may be denied basic rights and be subject to a degree of surveillance and administrative or police intrusion in their personal lives which would not be tolerated if imposed on, say, heterosexual men.

Accordingly, the privacy argument for striking down statutes involves far more than the protection of idiosyncratic sexual tastes. It does not ignore the political stakes of the issue. On the contrary, it is one of the stakes, because it is aimed at abolishing the pretext for the denial of liberty and equality to individuals on the basis of their sexual behavior and orientation. Creating a legal context in which gays and lesbians enjoy full privacy rights would thus be an important step towards undermining the epistemology of the closet which is based on denial of such rights. It would also help to expand and ensure the privacy rights of everyone.

CARLOS A. BALL, COMMUNITARIANISM AND GAY RIGHTS

85 Cornell L. Rev. 443 (2000).

Peter Nardi published a book in which he explores the influence that gay men's friendships, as a form of community, have on the development and maintenance of gay men's identities. Nardi asserts that "friendship among gay men is a means toward learning about one's gay identity and a source of freedom from the limitations imposed by the culture on being able to live a gay life." Moreover, Nardi states that gay friendships, as well as, participation in the gay communities' institutions (bars, baths, restaurants, book stores, media, political and social organizations, etc.) contributes to gay identity achievement, and gay identity leads to the creation and maintenance of gay communities which, in an ongoing dialectic, provide a context for reproducing identity in a newer generation of people searching for meaning and friendship.

Liberals generally pay insufficient attention to the role of communities in helping marginalized individuals such as gay men and lesbians attain personal freedom. In the specific context of sexual orientation, many liberals believe that privacy is the most important value for protecting gay men and lesbians from the rest of society. The protection of privacy has an intuitive appeal for liberals because it grants the individual a zone of personal freedom with which the state may not interfere. The liberal can advocate the protection of this zone without addressing the social or moral effects of the acts that take place behind "closed doors." In fact, a primary purpose of privacy doctrine is to separate the value (or lack thereof) of conduct that occurs in private from the right of the individual to engage in such conduct.

While the liberal privacy model has some obvious benefits for gay rights positions, it also has limitations. The privacy model "presumes nothing about the primacy of sexual orientation for the political identity of individual gay men and women and nothing about belonging to an actual 'gay community,' whose distinctive neighborhoods, norms, culture, and social relations are structured around sexual practices and erotic ties." The model does not take into account those identities, social relationships, and communities that emanate directly from the private expression of sexuality and whose effects go far beyond what transpires behind closed doors. As Shane Phelan points out, the liberal attempt to make sexuality simply a matter of what people do in bed does not have the force of intuition behind it * * *. The fundamental insight of both gay liberation and lesbian feminism has been the need for counterexplanations of the role of sexuality in personality organization as well as social structure.

By focusing on the right to engage in acts behind the veil of privacy and by ignoring the consequences, including the community-building consequences, of those acts, liberals blind themselves to the role of "interconnections and interdependencies" in people's lives. As Robin West notes, in the context of Supreme Court opinions, "privacy cases, liberal rhetoric to the contrary notwithstanding, do not by any stretch protect the isolated liberty right of individuals 'to be left alone.' They protect the right of individuals to form independent societies of interaction with select others, within which the state will not intrude." Many gay men and lesbians, then, can attest to [Michael] Sandel's view that communities assist individuals in forming identities and play a vital role in the development of individual character and sense of self-worth. As Sandel explains, community * * * describes not just a feeling but a mode of self-understanding partly constitutive of the agent's identity * * *. To say that [individuals] are bound by a sense of community is not simply to say that a great many of them profess communitarian sentiments and pursue communitarian aims, but rather that they conceive their identity * * * as defined to some extent by the community of which they are a part.

g. Lifestyles: Choosing an Image

NOTE: NO "PROPER VISAGE"

In this section we consider what are sometimes termed "life-style" choices that could be left to personal discretion. The section opens with a famous declaration of the individual's God-given capacity for self-design. Rather than having a "proper visage" human beings gets to paint their own faces. Mirandola's humanistic vision could be offered as the grounds for rights to a life style as well as a right to make important decisions about one's own life.

GIOVANNI PICO DELLA MIRANDOLA, ON THE DIGNITY OF MAN (1486)

http://www.cscs.umich.edu/?crshalizi/Mirandola/.

At last, the Supreme Maker decreed that this creature, to whom He could give nothing wholly his own, should have a share in the particular endowment of every other creature. Taking man, therefore, this creature of indeterminate image, He set him in the middle of the world and thus spoke to him:

"We have given you, O Adam, no visage proper to yourself, nor endowment properly your own, in order that whatever place, whatever form, whatever gifts you may, with premeditation, select, these same you may have and possess through your own judgment and decision. The nature of all other creatures is defined and restricted within laws which We have laid down; you, by contrast, impeded by no such restrictions, may, by your own free will, to whose custody We have assigned you, trace for yourself the lineaments of your own nature. I have placed you at the very center of the world, so that from that vantage point you may with greater ease glance round about you on all that the world contains. We have made you a creature neither of heaven nor of earth, neither mortal nor immortal, in order that you may, as the free and proud shaper of your own being, fashion yourself in the form you may prefer. It will be in your power to descend to the lower, brutish forms of life; you will be able, through your own decision, to rise again to the superior orders whose life is divine."

NOTE: HAIRSTYLES AND CLOTHING UNDER THE 14TH AMENDMENT

Can employers or schools dictate clothing and hairstyles? Are these precisely the sorts of trivial decisions about lifestyle over which other people and the state should have no say?

In *Kelley v. Johnson*, 425 U.S. 238 (1976), the Supreme Court refused to invalidate a hair-length regulation promulgated by a Police Department. Justice Rehnquist argued for the majority that: "Choice of organization, dress, and equipment for law enforcement personnel is a decision entitled to the same sort of presumption of legislative validity as are state choices designed to promote other aims within the cognizance of the State's police power * * *." In a dissent joined by Justice Brennan, Justice Marshall made the case for individuality: "An individual's personal appearance may reflect, sustain, and nourish his personality and may well be used as a means of expressing his attitude and lifestyle. In taking control over a citizen's personal appearance, the government forces him to sacrifice substantial elements of his integrity and identity as well. To say that the liberty guarantee of the Fourteenth Amendment does not encompass matters of personal appearance would be fundamentally inconsistent with the values of privacy, self-identity, autonomy, and personal integrity that I have always assumed the Constitution was designed to protect."

In *Stull v. School Board of Western Beaver Jr–Sr High School*, 459 F.2d 339 (3d Cir. 1972), the Court of Appeals recognized that "the length and style of one's hair is implicit in the liberty assurance of the Due Process Clause of the Fourteenth Amendment." A fifteen year old male student had refused to comply with his school's policy that boys' hair not cover their ears or fall below their collar lines. The court held the policy invalid and unenforceable, "except as applied to shop classes," where safety was an apparent issue.

NOTE: WHAT'S IN A NAME?

There is no fundamental privacy right to give a child a surname other than that of one of his or her parents. This was the finding of the court in *Henne v. Wright*, 904 F.2d 1208 (8th Cir. 1990), upholding a Nebraska statute limiting the ability of parents to name their own children in the interests of promoting child welfare, deterring the misappropriation of names, and in efficient record-keeping. But see *Jech v. Burch*, 466 F.Supp. 714 (D.C. Hawaii 1979) (parents need not assign newborn their surnames).

NOTE: MORE THAN A LIFESTYLE: MARRIAGE AND DIVORCE

A Milwaukee man was denied a marriage license because he had failed to fulfill his child support obligations for a child fathered out of wedlock. He owed $3,700. The Supreme Court invalidated the statute under which the marriage license application was denied, on the ground that the rule needlessly burdened the fundamental right to marry. "As the facts of this case illustrate," Justice Marshall wrote, "it would make little sense to recognize a right of privacy with respect to matters of family life and not with respect to the decision to enter the relationship that is the foundation of the family in our society." *Zablocki v. Redhail*, 434 U.S. 374 (1978). "When a statutory classification significantly interferes with the exercise of a fundamental right, it cannot be upheld unless it is supported by sufficiently important state interests and is closely tailored to effectuate only those interests," Marshall argued. And "the means selected by the State for achieving * * * [its interests in having fathers take responsibility for their children] unnecessarily impinge on the right to marry * * *."

Fourteenth Amendment due process prohibits states from erecting financial barriers to divorce, "given the basic position of the marriage relationship in this society's hierarchy of values and the concomitant state monopolization of the means for legally dissolving their relationship * * *". *Boddie v. Connecticut*, 401 U.S. 371 (1971).

NOTE: NO RIGHT TO DOMESTIC VIOLENCE

A Pennsylvania man convicted of raping his wife appealed his 18 month jail sentence, arguing that the Pennsylvania Spousal Sexual Assault Statute violated his constitutional right to privacy. The assault took place after a heated argument over custody arrangements for their child, in which the couple pushed and shoved one another. The husband grabbed a sharp knife and forced his wife to have vaginal and oral intercourse. In *Commonwealth v. Shoemaker*, 359 Pa.Super. 111, 518 A.2d 591 (Pa. Super. 1986), the court found that marital rape and involuntary sex are crimes of violence the Constitution does not protect as an incidence of marriage.

NOTE: PROSTITUTION, DRUGS, AND SMOKING

Is what we do at home a matter of lifestyle that the state should not criminalize or penalize? In *Skinner v. Oklahoma*, the Supreme Court held that a man cannot be prosecuted for enjoying obscene materials in the privacy of his home, even if the materials could not be lawfully purchased or sold. Can a woman engage in prostitution with consenting adult customers, as long as she confines her work to her own house or apartment? Can a man use illegal drugs, as long as he does not sell drugs and only uses them in his own home? Can a woman who smokes cigarettes be denied a job as a civil servant, even if she would not smoke at work? In the next section, you will learn the outcome of cases in which people who wanted to do these things—prostitute (*Mueller v. Hawaii*), use illegal drugs (*Ravin v. State*) and remain a tobacco smoker (City of *North Miami v. Kurtz*)—appealed to state courts and state constitutions for relief. State law often affords more privacy protection to lifestyle, parenting choices, intimate partnerships and to life-and-death decision-making.

3. STATE CONSTITUTIONS' FOURTEENTH AMENDMENT ANALOGS

a. New Jersey Right to Die

IN THE MATTER OF KAREN QUINLAN

70 N.J. 10, 355 A.2d 647 (N.J. 1976).

HUGHES, C.J. * * *

On the night of April 15, 1975, for reasons still unclear, Karen Quinlan ceased breathing for at least two 15 minute periods. She received some ineffectual mouth-to-mouth resuscitation from friends. She was taken by ambulance to Newton Memorial Hospital. There she had a temperature of 100 degrees, her pupils were unreactive and she was unresponsive even to deep pain. The history at the time of her admission to that hospital was essentially incomplete and uninformative.

Dr. Morse and other expert physicians who examined her characterized Karen as being in a "chronic persistent vegetative state." Dr. Fred Plum, one of such expert witnesses, defined this as a "subject who remains with the capacity to maintain the vegetative parts of neurological function but who * * * no longer has any cognitive function."

The experts believe that Karen cannot now survive without the assistance of the respirator; that exactly how long she would live without it is unknown; that the strong likelihood is that death would follow soon after its removal, and that removal would also risk further brain damage and would curtail the assistance the respirator presently provides in warding off infection.

It seemed to be the consensus not only of the treating physicians but also of the several qualified experts who testified in the case, that removal from the respirator would not conform to medical practices, standards and traditions. * * *

Karen remains in the intensive care unit at Saint Clare's Hospital, receiving 24–hour care by a team of four nurses characterized, as was the medical attention, as "excellent." She is nourished by feeding by way of a nasal-gastro tube and is routinely examined for infection, which under these circumstances is a serious life threat. The result is that her condition is considered remarkable under the unhappy circumstances involved.

Karen is described as emaciated, having suffered a weight loss of at least 40 pounds, and undergoing a continuing deteriorative process. Her posture is described as fetal-like and grotesque; there is extreme flexion-rigidity of the arms, legs and related muscles and her joints are severely rigid and deformed. * * *

We turn to that branch of the factual case pertaining to the application for guardianship, as distinguished from the nature of the authorization sought by the applicant. The character and general suitability of Joseph Quinlan as guardian for his daughter, in ordinary circumstances, could not be doubted. The record bespeaks the high degree of familial love which pervaded the home of Joseph Quinlan and reached out fully to embrace Karen, although she was living elsewhere at the time of her collapse. The proofs showed him to be deeply religious, imbued with a morality so sensitive that months of tortured indecision preceded his belated conclusion (despite earlier moral judgments reached by the other family members, but unexpressed to him in order not to influence him) to seek the termination of life-supportive measures sustaining Karen. A communicant of the Roman Catholic Church, as were other family members, he first sought solace in private prayer looking with confidence, as he says, to the Creator, first for the recovery of Karen and then, if that were not possible, for guidance with respect to the awesome decision confronting him. * * *

At the outset we note the dual role in which plaintiff comes before the Court. He not only raises, derivatively, what he perceives to be the constitutional and legal rights of his daughter Karen, but he also claims certain rights independently as parent. * * *

The Court in Griswold found the unwritten constitutional right of privacy to exist in the penumbra of specific guarantees of the Bill of Rights "formed by emanations from those guarantees that help give them life and substance." * * * Presumably this right is broad enough to encompass a patient's decision to decline medical treatment under certain circumstances, in much the same way as it is broad enough to encompass a woman's decision to terminate pregnancy under certain conditions. Roe v. Wade, 410 U.S. 113 * * * (1973).

Nor is such right of privacy forgotten in the New Jersey Constitution. N.J. Const. (1947), Art. I, par. 1. * * *

Our affirmation of Karen's independent right of choice, however, would ordinarily be based upon her competency to assert it. The sad truth, however, is that she is grossly incompetent and we cannot discern her supposed choice based on the testimony of her previous conversations with friends, where such testimony is without sufficient probative weight. 137 N.J. Super. at 260. Nevertheless we have concluded that Karen's right of privacy may be asserted on her behalf by her guardian under the peculiar circumstances here present.

If a putative decision by Karen to permit this non-cognitive, vegetative existence to terminate by natural forces is regarded as a valuable incident of her right of privacy, as we believe it to be, then it should not be discarded solely on the basis that her condition prevents her conscious exercise of the choice. The only practical way to prevent destruction of the right is to permit the guardian and family of Karen to render their best judgment, subject to the qualifications hereinafter stated, as to whether she would exercise it in these circumstances. If their conclusion is in the affirmative this decision should be accepted by a society the overwhelming majority of whose members would, we think, in similar circumstances, exercise such a choice in the same way for themselves or for those closest to them. It is for this reason that we determine that Karen's right of privacy may be asserted in her behalf, in this respect, by her guardian and family under the particular circumstances presented by this record.

Regarding Mr. Quinlan's right of privacy * * * there is no parental constitutional right that would entitle him to a grant of relief * * *.

We thus arrive at the formulation of the declaratory relief which we have concluded is appropriate to this case. * * * Upon the concurrence of the guardian and family of Karen, should the responsible attending physicians conclude that there is no reasonable possibility of Karen's ever emerging from her present comatose condition to a cognitive, sapient state and that the life-support apparatus now being administered to Karen should be discontinued, they shall consult with the hospital "Ethics Committee" or like body of the institution in which Karen is then hospitalized. If that consultative body agrees that there is no reasonable possibility of Karen's ever emerging from her present comatose condition to a cognitive, sapient state, the present life-support system may be withdrawn and said action shall be without any civil or criminal liability therefor on the part of any participant, whether guardian, physician, hospital or others. We herewith specifically so hold.

b. New Jersey and California Surrogate Parenting Rules

IN THE MATTER OF BABY M

109 N.J. 396, 537 A.2d 1227 (N.J. 1988).

WILENTZ

In this matter the Court is asked to determine the validity of a contract that purports to provide a new way of bringing children into a family. For a fee of $10,000, a woman agrees to be artificially inseminated with the semen of another woman's husband; she is to conceive a child, carry it to term, and after its birth surrender it to the natural father and his wife. * * *

We invalidate the surrogacy contract because it conflicts with the law and public policy of this State. While we recognize the depth of the yearning of infertile couples to have their own children, we find the payment of money to a "surrogate" mother illegal, perhaps criminal, and potentially degrading to women. Although in this case we grant custody to the natural father, the evidence having clearly proved such custody to be in the best interests of the infant, we void both the termination of the surrogate mother's parental rights and the adoption of the child by the wife/stepparent. We thus restore the "surrogate" as the mother of the child. We remand the issue of the natural mother's visitation rights to the trial court, since that issue was not reached below and the record before us is not sufficient to permit us to decide it de novo. * * *

In February 1985, William Stern and Mary Beth Whitehead entered into a surrogacy contract. It recited that Stern's wife, Elizabeth, was infertile, that they wanted a child, and that Mrs. Whitehead was willing to provide that child as the mother with Mr. Stern as the father.

Mrs. Whitehead realized, almost from the moment of birth, that she could not part with this child. She had felt a bond with it even during pregnancy. * * *

The Sterns were thrilled with their new child. They had planned extensively for its arrival, far beyond the practical furnishing of a room for her. It was a time of joyful celebration—not just for them but for their friends as well. The Sterns looked forward to raising their daughter, whom they named Melissa. While aware by then that Mrs. Whitehead was undergoing an emotional crisis, they were as yet not cognizant of the depth of that crisis and its implications for their newly-enlarged family. * * *

The depth of Mrs. Whitehead's despair surprised and frightened the Sterns. She told them that she could not live without her baby, that she must have her, even if only for one week, that thereafter she would surrender her child. The Sterns, concerned that Mrs. Whitehead might indeed commit suicide, not wanting under any circumstances to risk that, and in any event believing that Mrs. Whitehead would keep her word, turned the child over to her. * * *

The struggle over Baby M began when it became apparent that Mrs. Whitehead could not return the child to Mr. Stern. Due to Mrs. Whitehead's refusal to relinquish the baby, Mr. Stern filed a complaint seeking enforcement of the surrogacy contract. * * *

Both parties argue that the Constitutions—state and federal—mandate approval of their basic claims. The source of their constitutional arguments is essentially the same: the right of privacy, the right to procreate, the right to the companionship of one's child, those rights flowing either directly from the fourteenth amendment or by its incorporation of the Bill of Rights, or from the ninth amendment, or through the penumbra surrounding all of the Bill of Rights. * * *

The right to procreate, as protected by the Constitution, has been ruled on directly only once by the United States Supreme Court. See Skinner v. Oklahoma * * * (forced sterilization of habitual criminals violates equal protection clause of fourteenth amendment). * * * To assert that Mr. Stern's right of procreation gives him the right to the custody of Baby M would be to assert that Mrs. Whitehead's right of procreation does not give her the right to the custody of Baby M; it would be to assert that the constitutional right of procreation includes within it a constitutionally protected contractual right to destroy someone else's right of procreation.

We conclude that the right of procreation is best understood and protected if confined to its essentials, and that when dealing with rights concerning the resulting child, different interests come into play. There is nothing in our culture or society that even begins to suggest a fundamental right on the part of the father to the custody of the child as part of his right to procreate when opposed by the claim of the mother to the same child. We therefore disagree with the trial court: there is no constitutional basis whatsoever requiring that Mr. Stern's claim to the custody of Baby M be sustained. Our conclusion may thus be understood as illustrating that a person's rights of privacy and self-determination are qualified by the effect on innocent third persons of the exercise of those rights. * * *

Having decided that the surrogacy contract is illegal and unenforceable, we now must decide the custody question without regard to the provisions of the surrogacy contract that would give Mr. Stern sole and permanent custody. * * * With the surrogacy contract disposed of, the legal framework becomes a dispute between two couples over the custody of a child produced by the artificial insemination of one couple's wife by the other's husband. Under the Parentage Act the claims of the natural father and the natural mother are entitled to equal weight, i.e., one is not preferred over the other solely because he or she is the father or the mother. N.J.S.A. 9:17–40. The applicable rule given these circumstances is clear: the child's best interests determine custody. * * *

The Sterns have no other children, but all indications are that their household and their personalities promise a much more likely foundation for Melissa to grow and thrive. There is a track record of sorts—during the one-and-a-half years of custody Baby M has done very well, and the relationship between both Mr. and Mrs. Stern and the baby has become very strong. The household is stable, and likely to remain so. Their finances are more than adequate, their circle of friends supportive, and their marriage happy. Most important, they are loving, giving, nurturing, and open-minded people. They have demonstrated the wish and ability to nurture and protect Melissa, yet at the same time to encourage her independence. * * *

Based on all of this we have concluded, independent of the trial court's identical conclusion, that Melissa's best interests call for custody in the Sterns. * * *

We have decided that Mrs. Whitehead is entitled to visitation at some point, and that question is not open to the trial court on this remand. The trial court will determine what kind of visitation shall be granted to her, with or without conditions, and when and under what circumstances it should commence. It also should be noted that the guardian's recommendation of a five-year delay is most unusual—one might argue that it begins to border on termination. * * *

If the Legislature decides to address surrogacy, consideration of this case will highlight many of its potential harms. We do not underestimate the difficulties of legislating on this subject. * * *

The judgment is affirmed in part, reversed in part, and remanded for further proceedings consistent with this opinion.

JOHNSON v. CALVERT

5 Cal.4th 84, 851 P.2d 776, 19 Cal.Rptr.2d 494 (Cal. 1993).

PANELLI, J. * * *

On January 15, 1990, Mark, Crispina, and Anna signed a contract providing that an embryo created by the sperm of Mark and the egg of Crispina would be implanted in Anna and the child born would be taken into Mark and Crispina's home "as their child." Anna agreed she would relinquish "all parental rights" to the child in favor of Mark and Crispina. In return, Mark and Crispina would pay Anna $10,000 in a series of installments, the last to be paid six weeks after the child's birth. Mark and Crispina were also to pay for a $200,000 life insurance policy on Anna's life.

The zygote was implanted on January 19, 1990. Less than a month later, an ultrasound test confirmed Anna was pregnant.

Unfortunately, relations deteriorated between the two sides. Mark learned that Anna had not disclosed she had suffered several stillbirths and miscarriages. Anna felt Mark and Crispina did not do enough to obtain the required insurance policy. She also felt abandoned during an onset of premature labor in June.

In July 1990, Anna sent Mark and Crispina a letter demanding the balance of the payments due her or else she would refuse to give up the child. The following month, Mark and Crispina responded with a lawsuit, seeking a declaration they were the legal parents of the unborn child. Anna filed her own action to be declared the mother of the child, and the two cases were eventually consolidated. The parties agreed to an independent guardian ad litem for the purposes of the suit.

* * * The parties agreed to a court order providing that the child would remain with Mark and Crispina on a temporary basis with visits by Anna.

At trial in October 1990, the parties stipulated that Mark and Crispina were the child's genetic parents. After hearing evidence and arguments, the trial court ruled that Mark and Crispina were the child's "genetic, biological and natural" father and mother, that Anna had no "parental" rights to the child, and that the surrogacy contract was legal and enforceable against Anna's claims. The court also terminated the order allowing visitation. Anna appealed from the trial court's judgment. The Court of Appeal for the Fourth District, Division Three, affirmed. We granted review [and affirm]. * * *

Anna relies mainly on theories of substantive due process, privacy, and procreative freedom, citing a number of decisions recognizing the fundamental liberty interest of natural parents in the custody and care of their children. * * * Most of the cases Anna cites deal with the rights of unwed fathers in the face of attempts to terminate their parental relationship to their children. * * * These cases do not support recognition of parental rights for a gestational surrogate. * * *

Anna relies principally on the decision of the United States Supreme Court in Michael H. v. Gerald D. (1989) 491 U.S. 110, to support her claim to a constitutionally protected liberty interest in the companionship of the child, based on her status as "birth mother." In that case, a plurality of the court held that a state may constitutionally deny a man parental rights with respect to a child he fathered during a liaison with the wife of another man, since it is the marital family that traditionally has been accorded a protected liberty interest, as reflected in the historic presumption of legitimacy of a child born into such a family. * * * The reasoning of the plurality in Michael H. does not assist Anna. Society has not traditionally protected the right of a woman who gestates and delivers a baby pursuant to an agreement with a couple who supply the zygote from which the baby develops and who intend to raise the child as their own; such arrangements are of too recent an origin to claim the protection of tradition. To the extent that tradition has a bearing on the present case, we believe it supports the claim of the couple who exercise their right to procreate in order to form a family of their own, albeit through novel medical procedures. * * *

Amicus curiae ACLU urges that Anna's right of privacy, embodied in the California Constitution (Cal. Const., art. I, Section 1), requires recognition and protection of her status as "birth mother." We cannot agree. Certainly it is true that our state Constitution has been construed to provide California citizens with privacy protections encompassing procreative decisionmaking—broader, indeed, than those recognized by the federal Constitution. * * * [Contrary to the U.S. Supreme Court interpreting the U.S. Constitution, the California court interpreting state law has determined that it is unconstitutional to permit legislative denial of funding for abortions for indigent women.] However, amicus curiae fails to articulate persuasively how Anna's claim falls within even the broad parameters of the state right of privacy. Amicus curiae appears to assume that the choice to gestate and deliver a baby for its genetic parents pursuant to a surrogacy agreement is the equivalent, in constitutional weight, of the decision whether to bear a child of one's own. We disagree. A woman who enters into a gestational surrogacy arrangement is not exercising her own right to make procreative choices; she is agreeing to provide a necessary and profoundly important service without (by definition) any expectation that she will raise the resulting child as her own.

Drawing an analogy to artificial insemination, Anna argues that Mark and Crispina were mere genetic donors who are entitled to no constitutional protection. That characterization of the facts is, however, inaccurate. Mark and Crispina never intended to "donate" genetic material to anyone. Rather, they intended to procreate a child genetically related to them by the only available means. Civil Code section 7005, governing artificial insemination, has no application here. * * *

It is not the role of the judiciary to inhibit the use of reproductive technology when the Legislature has not seen fit to do so; any such effort would raise serious questions in light of the fundamental nature of the rights of procreation and privacy. Rather, our task has been to resolve the dispute before us, interpreting the Act's use of the term "natural mother" (Civ. Code, § 7003, subd. (1)) when the biological functions essential to bringing a child into the world have been allocated between two women. * * *

K ENNARD, J USTICE, Dissenting. * * *

It requires little imagination to foresee cases in which the genetic mothers are, for example, unstable or substance abusers, or in which the genetic mothers' life circumstances change dramatically during the gestational mothers' pregnancies, while the gestational mothers, though of a less advantaged socioeconomic class, are stable, mature, capable and willing to provide a loving family environment in which the child will flourish. Under those circumstances, the majority's rigid reliance on the intent of the genetic mother will not serve the best interests of the child.

c. Florida's Heightened Privacy Right: Abortion and Smoking

IN RE T.W.
551 So.2d 1186 (Fla. 1989).

P ER C URIAM * * *

The procedure that a minor must follow to obtain an abortion in Florida is set out in the parental consent statute and related rules. Prior to undergoing an abortion, a minor must obtain parental consent or, alternatively, must convince a court that she is sufficiently mature to make the decision herself or that, if she is immature, the abortion nevertheless is in her best interests. Pursuant to this procedure, T.W., a pregnant, unmarried, fifteen-year-old, petitioned for a waiver of parental consent under the judicial bypass provision on the alternative grounds that (1) she was sufficiently mature to give an informed consent to the abortion, (2) she had a justified fear of physical or emotional abuse if her parents were requested to consent, and (3) her mother was seriously ill and informing her of the pregnancy would be an added burden. The trial court, after appointing counsel for T.W. and separate counsel as guardian ad litem for the fetus, conducted a hearing within twenty-four hours of the filing of the petition.

The relevant portions of the hearing consisted of T.W.'s uncontroverted testimony that she was a high-school student, participated in band and flag corps, worked twenty hours a week, baby-sat for her mother and neighbors, planned on finishing high school and attending vocational school or community college, had observed an instructional film on abortion, had taken a sex education course at school, would not put her child up for adoption, and had discussed her plans with the child's father and obtained his approval. She informed the court that due to her mother's illness, she had assumed extra duties at home caring for her sibling and that if she told her mother about the abortion, "it would kill her." Evidence was introduced showing that the pregnancy was in the first trimester. * * *

The district court found that the statute's judicial alternative to parental consent was unconstitutionally vague, permitting arbitrary denial of a petition, and noted the following defects: failure to provide for a record hearing, lack of guidelines relative to admissible evidence, a brief forty-eight-hour time limit, and failure to provide for appointed counsel for an indigent minor. The court declared the entire statute invalid, quashed the trial court's order requiring parental consent, and ordered the petition dismissed. The guardian ad litem appealed * * * [and] filed a number of motions to block the abortion but was unsuccessful and T.W. lawfully ended her pregnancy, which would normally moot the issue of parental consent.

Because the questions raised are of great public importance and are likely to recur, we accept jurisdiction despite T.W.'s abortion [making the matter seemingly moot]. * * * Preliminarily, we find that the appointment of a guardian ad litem for the fetus was clearly improper. * * *

In 1980, Florida voters by general election amended our state constitution to provide:

Section 23. Right of privacy.—Every natural person has the right to be let alone and free from governmental intrusion into his private life except as otherwise provided herein. This section shall not be construed to limit the public's right of access to public records and meetings as provided by law.

Art. I, Section 23, Fla. Const. This Court in Winfield described the far-reaching impact of the Florida amendment:

> The citizens of Florida opted for more protection from governmental intrusion when they approved article I, section 23, of the Florida Constitution. This amendment is an independent, freestanding constitutional provision which declares the fundamental right to privacy. Article I, section 23, was intentionally phrased in strong terms. The drafters of the amendment rejected the use of the words "unreasonable" or "unwarranted" before the phrase "governmental intrusion" in order to make the privacy right as strong as possible. Since the people of this state exercised their prerogative and enacted an amendment to the Florida Constitution which expressly and succinctly provides for a strong right of privacy not found in the United States Constitution, it can only be concluded that the right is much broader in scope than that of the Federal Constitution. * * *

In other words, the amendment embraces more privacy interests, and extends more protection to the individual in those interests, than does the federal Constitution.

Consistent with this analysis, we have said that the amendment provides "an explicit textual foundation for those privacy interests inherent in the concept of liberty which may not otherwise be protected by specific constitutional provisions." Rasmussen v. South Fla. Blood Serv., 500 So.2d 533, 536 (Fla. 1987) (footnote omitted). We have found the right implicated in a wide range of activities dealing with the public disclosure of personal matters. See Barron v. Florida Freedom Newspapers, 531 So.2d 113 (Fla. 1988) (closure of court proceedings and records); Rasmussen (confidential donor information concerning AIDS-tainted blood supply); Winfield (banking records); Florida Bd. of Bar Examiners re: Applicant, 443 So.2d 71 (Fla. 1983) (bar application questions concerning disclosure of psychiatric counselling). Florida courts have also found the right involved in a number of cases dealing with personal decisionmaking. See Public Health Trust v. Wons, 541 So.2d 96 (Fla. 1989) (refusal of blood transfusion that is necessary to sustain life); Corbett v. D'Alessandro, 487 So.2d 368 (Fla. 2d DCA), review denied, 492 So.2d 1331 (Fla. 1986) (removal of nasogastric feeding tube from adult in permanent vegetative state); In re Guardianship of Barry, 445 So.2d 365 (Fla. 2d DCA 1984) (removal of life support system from brain-dead infant); see also Satz v. Perlmutter, 379 So.2d 359 (Fla. 1980) (removal of respirator from competent adult, decided prior to passage of privacy amendment under general right of privacy).

The privacy section contains no express standard of review for evaluating the lawfulness of a government intrusion into one's private life, and this Court when called upon, adopted the following standard:

> Since the privacy section as adopted contains no textual standard of review, it is important for us to identify an explicit standard to be applied in order to give proper force and effect to the amendment. The right of privacy is a fundamental right which we believe demands the compelling state interest standard. This test shifts the burden of proof to the state to justify an intrusion on privacy. The burden can be met by demonstrating that the challenged regulation serves a compelling state interest and accomplishes its goal through the use of the least intrusive means.

Winfield, 477 So.2d at 547. When this standard was applied in disclosural cases, government intrusion generally was upheld as sufficiently compelling to overcome the individual's right to privacy. We reaffirm, however, that this is a highly stringent standard, emphasized by the fact that no government intrusion in the personal decisionmaking cases cited above has survived. * * *

The Florida Constitution embodies the principle that "few decisions are more personal and intimate, more properly private, or more basic to individual dignity and autonomy, than a woman's decision * * * whether to end her pregnancy. A woman's right to make that choice freely is fundamental." * * *

Based on the foregoing analysis of our state law, we hold that section 390.001(4)(a), Florida Statutes (Supp. 1988), violates the Florida Constitution. Accordingly, no further analysis under federal law is required. We expressly decide this case on state law grounds and cite federal precedent only to the extent that it illuminates Florida law. We approve the district court's decision.

CITY OF NORTH MIAMI v. KURTZ

653 So.2d 1025 (Fla. 1995).

OVERTON, J. * * *

To reduce costs and to increase productivity, the City of North Miami adopted an employment policy designed to reduce the number of employees who smoke tobacco. In accordance with that policy decision, the City issued Administrative Regulation 1–46, which requires all job applicants to sign an affidavit stating that they have not used tobacco or tobacco products for at least one year immediately preceding their application for employment. The intent of the regulation is to gradually reduce the number of smokers in the City's work force by means of natural attrition. Consequently, the regulation only applies to job applicants and does not affect current employees. Once an applicant has been hired, the applicant is free to start or resume smoking at any time. Evidence in the record, however, reflects that a high percentage of smokers who have adhered to the one year cessation requirement are unlikely to resume smoking.

Additional evidence submitted by the City indicates that each smoking employee costs the City as much as $4,611 per year in 1981 dollars over what it incurs for non-smoking employees. The City is a self-insurer and its taxpayers pay for 100% of its employees' medical expenses. In enacting the regulation, the City made a policy decision to reduce costs and increase productivity by eventually eliminating a substantial number of smokers from its work force. Evidence presented to the trial court indicated that the regulation would accomplish these goals.

The respondent in this case, Arlene Kurtz, applied for a clerk-typist position with the City. When she was interviewed for the position, she was informed of Regulation 1–46. She told the interviewer that she was a smoker and could not truthfully sign an affidavit to comply with the regulation. The interviewer then informed Kurtz that she would not be considered for employment until she was smoke-free for one year. There-after, Kurtz filed this action seeking to enjoin enforcement of the regula-tion and asking for a declaratory judgment finding the regulation to be unconstitutional.

[T]he district court concluded that the regulation violated Kurtz's privacy rights under article I, section 23, of the Florida Constitution. We disagree.

Florida's constitutional privacy provision, which is contained in article I, section 23, provides as follows:

> Right of privacy.—Every natural person has the right to be let alone and free from governmental intrusion into his private life except as otherwise provided herein. This section shall not be construed to limit the public's right of access to public records and meetings as provided by law.

This right to privacy protects Florida's citizens from the government's uninvited observation of or interference in those areas that fall within the ambit of the zone of privacy afforded under this provision. * * *

Although Florida's privacy right provides greater protection than the federal constitution, it was not intended to be a guarantee against all intrusion into the life of an individual. *Florida Bd. of Bar Examiners re Applicant*, 443 So. 2d 71 (Fla. 1983). * * *

In this case, we find that the City's action does not intrude into an aspect of Kurtz' life in which she has a legitimate expectation of privacy. In today's society, smokers are constantly required to reveal whether they smoke. When individuals are seated in a restaurant, they are asked whether they want a table in a smoking or non-smoking section. When individuals rent hotel or motel rooms, they are asked if they smoke so that management may ensure that certain rooms remain free from the smell of smoke odors. Likewise, when individuals rent cars, they are asked if they smoke so that rental agencies can make proper accommodations to main-tain vehicles for non-smokers. Further, employers generally provide smoke-free areas for non-smokers, and employees are often prohibited from smoking in certain areas. Given that individuals must reveal wheth-er they smoke in almost every aspect of life in today's society, we conclude that individuals have no reasonable expectation of privacy in the disclosure of that information when applying for a government job and, consequently, that Florida's right of privacy is not implicated under these unique circumstances.

In reaching the conclusion that the right to privacy is not implicated in this case, however, we emphasize that our holding is limited to the narrow issue presented. Notably, we are not addressing the issue of whether an applicant, once hired, could be compelled by a government agency to stop smoking. Equally as important, neither are we holding today that a governmental entity can ask any type of information it chooses of prospective job applicants.

Having determined that Kurtz has no legitimate expectation of privacy in revealing that she is a smoker under the Florida constitution, we turn now to her claim that the regulation violates her rights under the federal constitution. As noted, the federal constitution's implicit privacy provision extends only to such fundamental interests as marriage, procreation, contraception, family relationships, and the rearing and educating of children. * * * [We find] the regulation to be constitutional under both the federal and Florida constitutions.

KOGAN, J., dissenting.

The privacy issue is more troublesome, to my mind. There is a "slippery-slope" problem here because, if governmental employers can inquire too extensively into off-job-site behavior, a point eventually will be reached at which the right of privacy under article I, section 23 clearly will be breached. An obvious example would be an inquiry into the lawful sexual behavior of job applicants in an effort to identify those with the "most desirable" lifestyles. Such an effort easily could become the pretext for a constitutional violation. The time has not yet fully passed, for example, when women job applicants have been questioned about their plans for procreation in an effort to eliminate those who may be absent on family leave. I cannot conceive that such an act is anything other than a violation of the right of privacy when done by a governmental unit. * * *

While legal, tobacco use nevertheless is an activity increasingly regulated by the law. If the federal government, for instance, chose to regulate tobacco as a controlled substance, I have no trouble saying that this act alone does not undermine anyone's privacy right. However, regulation is not the issue here because tobacco use today remains legal. The sole question is whether the government may inquire into off-job-site behavior that is legal, however unhealthy it might be. In light of the inherently poor fit between the governmental objective and the ends actually achieved, I am more inclined to agree with the district court that the right of privacy has been violated here. I might reach a different result if the objective were better served by the means chosen.

d. Marriage and Civil Union Rights

GOODRIDGE v. DEPARTMENT OF PUBLIC HEALTH

440 Mass. 309, 798 N.E.2d 941 (2003).

MARSHALL, C.J. * * *

The plaintiffs include business executives, lawyers, an investment banker, educators, therapists, and a computer engineer. Many are active in church, community, and school groups. They have employed such legal means as are available to them—for example, joint adoption, powers of attorney, and joint ownership of real property—to secure aspects of their relationships. Each plaintiff attests a desire to marry his or her partner in order to affirm publicly their commitment to each other and to secure the legal protections and benefits afforded to married couples and their children. * * *

In March and April, 2001, each of the plaintiff couples attempted to obtain a marriage license from a city or town clerk's office. As required under G. L. c. 207, they completed notices of intention to marry on forms provided by the registry and presented these forms to a Massachusetts town or city clerk, together with the required health forms and marriage license fees * * *. In each case, the clerk either refused to accept the notice of intention to marry or denied a marriage license to the couple on the ground that Massachusetts does not recognize same-sex marriage. Because obtaining a marriage license is a necessary prerequisite to civil marriage in Massachusetts, denying marriage licenses to the plaintiffs was tantamount to denying them access to civil marriage itself, with its appurtenant social and legal protections, benefits, and obligations. * * *

Although the plaintiffs refer in passing to "the marriage statutes," they focus, quite properly, on G. L. c. 207, the marriage licensing statute, which controls entry into civil marriage. As a preliminary matter, we summarize the provisions of that law.

General Laws c. 207 is both a gatekeeping and a public records statute. It sets minimum qualifications for obtaining a marriage license and directs city and town clerks, the registrar, and the department to keep and maintain certain "vital records" of civil marriages. The gatekeeping provisions of G. L. c. 207 are minimal. They forbid marriage of individuals within certain degrees of consanguinity, * * * and polygamous marriages. * * * The statute requires that civil marriage be solemnized only by those so authorized. * * *

In short, for all the joy and solemnity that normally attend a marriage, G. L. c. 207, governing entrance to marriage, is a licensing law. The plaintiffs argue that because nothing in that licensing law specifically prohibits marriages between persons of the same sex, we may interpret the statute to permit "qualified same sex couples" to obtain marriage licenses, thereby avoiding the question whether the law is constitutional. * * *

The * * * question is whether, as the department claims, government action that bars same-sex couples from civil marriage constitutes a legitimate exercise of the State's authority to regulate conduct, or whether, as the plaintiffs claim, this categorical marriage exclusion violates the Massachusetts Constitution. We have recognized the long-standing statutory understanding, derived from the common law, that "marriage" means the lawful union of a woman and a man. But that history cannot and does not foreclose the constitutional question. * * *

The benefits accessible only by way of a marriage license are enormous, touching nearly every aspect of life and death. The department states that "hundreds of statutes" are related to marriage and to marital benefits. With no attempt to be comprehensive, we note that some of the statutory benefits conferred by the Legislature on those who enter into civil marriage include, as to property: joint Massachusetts income tax filing; tenancy by the entirety (a form of ownership that provides certain protections against creditors and allows for the automatic descent of property to the surviving spouse without probate); extension of the benefit of the homestead protection (securing up to $300,000 in equity from creditors) to one's spouse and children; automatic rights to inherit the property of a deceased spouse who does not leave a will; the rights of elective share and of dower (which allow surviving spouses certain property rights where the decedent spouse has not made adequate provision for the survivor in a will); entitlement to wages owed to a deceased employee; eligibility to continue certain businesses of a deceased spouse; the right to share the medical policy of one's spouse; preferential options under the Commonwealth's pension system; preferential benefits in the Commonwealth's medical program, MassHealth; access to veterans' spousal benefits and preferences; financial protections for spouses of certain Commonwealth employees; the equitable division of marital property on divorce; the right to separate support on separation of the parties that does not result in divorce; and the right to bring claims for wrongful death and loss of consortium, and for funeral and burial expenses and punitive damages resulting from tort actions.

Exclusive marital benefits that are not directly tied to property rights include the presumptions of legitimacy and parentage of children born to a married couple; and evidentiary rights, such as the prohibition against spouses testifying against one another about their private conversations, applicable in both civil and criminal cases. Other statutory benefits of a personal nature available only to married individuals include qualification for bereavement or medical leave to care for individuals related by blood or marriage; an automatic "family member" preference to make medical decisions for an incompetent or disabled spouse who does not have a contrary health care proxy; the application of predictable rules of child custody, visitation, support, and removal out-of-State when married parents divorce; priority rights to administer the estate of a deceased spouse who dies without a will, and requirement that surviving spouse must consent to the appointment of any other person as administrator; and the right to interment in the lot or tomb owned by one's deceased spouse.

Where a married couple has children, their children are also directly or indirectly, but no less auspiciously, the recipients of the special legal and economic protections obtained by civil marriage. Notwithstanding the Commonwealth's strong public policy to abolish legal distinctions between marital and nonmarital children in providing for the support and care of minors * * * the fact remains that marital children reap a measure of family stability and economic security based on their parents' legally privileged status that is largely inaccessible, or not as readily accessible, to nonmarital children. Some of these benefits are social, such as the enhanced approval that still attends the status of being a marital child. Others are material, such as the greater ease of access to family-based State and Federal benefits that attend the presumptions of one's parentage.

It is undoubtedly for these concrete reasons, as well as for its intimately personal significance, that civil marriage has long been termed a "civil right." * * *

Without the right to marry—or more properly, the right to choose to marry—one is excluded from the full range of human experience and denied full protection of the laws for one's "avowed commitment to an intimate and lasting human relationship." * * * Because civil marriage is central to the lives of individuals and the welfare of the community, our laws assiduously protect the individual's right to marry against undue government incursion. Laws may not "interfere directly and substantially with the right to marry." * * *

The Massachusetts Constitution protects matters of personal liberty against government incursion as zealously, and often more so, than does the Federal Constitution, even where both Constitutions employ essentially the same language. See Planned Parenthood League of Mass., Inc. v. Attorney Gen., 424 Mass. 586, 590, 677 N.E.2d 101 (1997); Corning Glass Works v. Ann & Hope, Inc. of Danvers, 363 Mass. 409, 416, 294 N.E.2d 354 (1973). That the Massachusetts Constitution is in some instances more protective of individual liberty interests than is the Federal Constitution is not surprising. Fundamental to the vigor of our Federal system of government is that "state courts are absolutely free to interpret state constitutional provisions to accord greater protection to individual rights than do similar provisions of the United States Constitution." * * *

The plaintiffs challenge the marriage statute on both equal protection and due process grounds. With respect to each such claim, we must first determine the appropriate standard of review. Where a statute implicates a fundamental right or uses a suspect classification, we employ "strict judicial scrutiny." Lowell v. Kowalski, 380 Mass. 663, 666, 405 N.E.2d 135 (1980). For all other statutes, we employ the " 'rational basis' test." English v. New England Med. Ctr., 405 Mass. 423, 428, 541 N.E.2d 329 (1989). For due process claims, rational basis analysis requires that statutes "bear[] a real and substantial relation to the public health, safety, morals, or some other phase of the general welfare." Coffee–Rich, Inc. v. Commissioner of Pub. Health, supra, quoting Sperry & Hutchinson Co. v. Director of the Div. on the Necessaries of Life, 307 Mass. 408, 418, 30 N.E.2d 269 (1940). For equal protection challenges, the rational basis test requires that "an impartial lawmaker could logically believe that the classification would serve a legitimate public purpose that transcends the harm to the members of the disadvantaged class." * * * Cleburne v. Cleburne Living Ctr., Inc., 473 U.S. 432, * * * (1985) (Stevens, J., concurring). * * *

The marriage ban works a deep and scarring hardship on a very real segment of the community for no rational reason. The absence of any reasonable relationship between, on the one hand, an absolute disqualification of same-sex couples who wish to enter into civil marriage and, on the other, protection of public health, safety, or general welfare, suggests that the marriage restriction is rooted in persistent prejudices against persons who are (or who are believed to be) homosexual. "The Constitution cannot control such prejudices but neither can it tolerate them. Private biases may be outside the reach of the law, but the law cannot, directly or indirectly, give them effect." Palmore v. Sidoti, 466 U.S. 429, 433, (1984) (construing Fourteenth Amendment). Limiting the protections, benefits, and obligations of civil marriage to opposite-sex couples violates the basic premises of individual liberty and equality under law protected by the Massachusetts Constitution. * * *

We consider next the plaintiffs' request for relief. * * * Here, no one argues that striking down the marriage laws is an appropriate form of relief.

Eliminating civil marriage would be wholly inconsistent with the Legislature's deep commitment to fostering stable families and would dismantle a vital organizing principle of our society. We face a problem similar to one that recently confronted the Court of Appeal for Ontario, the highest court of that Canadian province, when it considered the constitutionality of the same-sex marriage ban under Canada's Federal Constitution, the Charter of Rights and Freedoms (Charter). See Halpern v. Toronto (City), 172 O.A.C. 276 (2003). Canada, like the United States, adopted the common law of England that civil marriage is "the voluntary union for life of one man and one woman, to the exclusion of all others." Id. at par. (36), quoting Hyde v. Hyde, [1861–1873] All E.R. 175 (1866). In holding that the limitation of civil marriage to opposite-sex couples violated the Charter, the Court of Appeal refined the common-law meaning of marriage. We concur with this remedy, which is entirely consonant with established principles of jurisprudence empowering a court to refine a common-law principle in light of evolving constitutional standards. See Powers v. Wilkinson, 399 Mass. 650, 661–662, 506 N.E.2d 842 (1987) (reforming common-law rule of construction of "issue"); Lewis v. Lewis, 370 Mass. 619, 629, 351 N.E.2d 526 (1976) (abolishing common-law rule of certain interspousal immunity).

We construe civil marriage to mean the voluntary union of two persons as spouses, to the exclusion of all others. This reformulation redresses the plaintiffs' constitutional injury and furthers the aim of marriage to promote stable, exclusive relationships. It advances the two legitimate State interests the department has identified: providing a stable setting for child rearing and conserving State resources. It leaves intact the Legislature's broad discretion to regulate marriage. See Commonwealth v. Stowell, 389 Mass. 171, 175, 449 N.E.2d 357 (1983).

PERRY v. SCHWARZENEGGER

2010 WL 3025614 (N.D.Cal.).

WALKER, CJ

Plaintiffs challenge a November 2008 voter-enacted amendment to the California Constitution ("Proposition 8" or "Prop 8"). Cal. Const. Art. I, § 7.5. In its entirety, Proposition 8 provides: "Only marriage between a man and a woman is valid or recognized in California." Plaintiffs allege that Proposition 8 deprives them of due process and of equal protection of the laws contrary to the Fourteenth Amendment and that its enforcement by state officials violates 42 USC § 1983.

Plaintiffs are two couples. Kristin Perry and Sandra Stier reside in Berkeley, California and raise four children together. Jeffrey Zarrillo and Paul Katami reside in Burbank, California. Plaintiffs seek to marry their partners and have been denied marriage licenses by their respective county authorities on the basis of Proposition 8. No party contended, and no evidence at trial suggested, that the county authorities had any ground to deny marriage licenses to plaintiffs other than Proposition 8.

Having considered the trial evidence and the arguments of counsel, the court pursuant to FRCP 52(a) finds that Proposition 8 is unconstitutional and that its enforcement must be enjoined. * * *

The evidence at trial shows that marriage in the United States traditionally has not been open to same-sex couples. The evidence suggests many reasons for this tradition of exclusion, including gender roles mandated through coverture, social disapproval of same-sex relationships, and the reality that the vast majority of people are heterosexual and have had no reason to challenge the restriction. The evidence shows that the movement of marriage away from a gendered institution and toward an institution free from state-mandated gender roles reflects an evolution in the understanding of gender rather than a change in marriage. The evidence did not show any historical purpose for excluding same-sex couples from marriage, as states have never required spouses to have an ability or willingness to procreate in order to marry. Rather, the exclusion exists as an artifact of a time when the genders were seen as having distinct roles in society and in marriage. That time has passed.

The right to marry has been historically and remains the right to choose a spouse and, with mutual consent, join together and form a household. Race and gender restrictions shaped marriage during eras of race and gender inequality, but such restrictions were never part of the historical core of the institution of marriage. Today, gender is not relevant to the state in determining spouses' obligations to each other and to their dependents. Relative gender composition aside, same-sex couples are situated identically to opposite-sex couples in terms of their ability to perform the rights and obligations of marriage under California law. Gender no longer forms an essential part of marriage; marriage under law is a union of equals.

Plaintiffs seek to have the state recognize their committed relationships, and plaintiffs' relationships are consistent with the core of the history, tradition and practice of marriage in the United States. Perry and Stier seek to be spouses; they seek the mutual obligation and honor that attend marriage. Zarrillo and Katami seek recognition from the state that their union is "a coming together for better or for worse, hopefully enduring, and intimate to the degree of being sacred." *Griswold,* 381 U.S. at 486. Plaintiffs' unions encompass the historical purpose and form of marriage. Only the plaintiffs' genders relative to one another prevent California from giving their relationships due recognition.

Plaintiffs do not seek recognition of a new right. To characterize plaintiffs' objective as "the right to same-sex marriage" would suggest that plaintiffs seek something different from what opposite-sex couples across the state enjoy—namely, marriage. Rather, plaintiffs ask California to recognize their relationships for what they are: marriages.

HERNANDEZ v. ROBLES

7 N.Y.3d 338, 855 N.E.2d 1, 821 N.Y.S.2d 770 (N.Y. 2006).

R. S. SMITH, J.

New York's statutory law clearly limits marriage to opposite-sex couples. The more serious question is whether that limitation is consistent with the New York Constitution. * * *

New York is one of many states in which supporters of same-sex marriage have asserted it as a state constitutional right. Several other state courts have decided such cases, under various state constitutional provisions and with divergent. * * *

It is undisputed that the benefits of marriage are many. The diligence of counsel has identified 316 such benefits in New York law, of which it is enough to summarize some of the most important: Married people receive significant tax advantages, rights in probate and intestacy proceedings, rights to support from their spouses both during the marriage and after it is dissolved, and rights to be treated as family members in obtaining insurance coverage and making health care decisions. Beyond this, they receive the symbolic benefit, or moral satisfaction, of seeing their relationships recognized by the State.

The critical question is whether a rational legislature could decide that these benefits should be given to members of opposite-sex couples, but not same-sex couples. * * * We conclude * * * that there are at least two grounds that rationally support the limitation on marriage that the Legislature has enacted * * * both of which are derived from the undisputed assumption that marriage is important to the welfare of children.

First, the Legislature could rationally decide that, for the welfare of children, it is more important to promote stability, and to avoid instability, in opposite-sex than in same-sex relationships. Heterosexual intercourse has a natural tendency to lead to the birth of children; homosexual intercourse does not. Despite the advances of science, it remains true that the vast majority of children are born as a result of a sexual relationship between a man and a woman, and the Legislature could find that this will continue to be true. The Legislature could also find that such relationships are all too often casual or temporary. It could find that an important function of marriage is to create more stability and permanence in the relationships that cause children to be born. It thus could choose to offer an inducement—in the form of marriage and its attendant benefits—to opposite-sex couples who make a solemn, long-term commitment to each other.

The Legislature could find that this rationale for marriage does not apply with comparable force to same-sex couples. These couples can become parents by adoption, or by artificial insemination or other technological marvels, but they do not become parents as a result of accident or impulse. The Legislature could find that unstable relationships between people of the opposite sex present a greater danger that children will be born into or grow up in unstable homes than is the case with same-sex couples, and thus that promoting stability in opposite-sex relationships will help children more. This is one reason why the Legislature could rationally offer the benefits of marriage to opposite-sex couples only.

There is a second reason: The Legislature could rationally believe that it is better, other things being equal, for children to grow up with both a mother and a father. Intuition and experience suggest that a child benefits from having before his or her eyes, every day, living models of what both a man and a woman are like. It is obvious that there are exceptions to this general rule—some children who never know their fathers, or their mothers, do far better than some who grow up with parents of both sexes—but the Legislature could find that the general rule will usually hold. * * *

Plaintiffs seem to assume that they have demonstrated the irrationality of the view that opposite-sex marriages offer advantages to children by showing there is no scientific evidence to support it. Even assuming no such evidence exists, this reasoning is flawed. In the absence of conclusive scientific evidence, the Legislature could rationally proceed on the common-sense premise that children will do best with a mother and father in the home. * * *

If we were convinced that the restriction plaintiffs attack were founded on nothing but prejudice—if we agreed with the plaintiffs that it is comparable to the restriction in Loving v. Virginia, a prohibition on interracial marriage that was plainly "designed to maintain White Supremacy" * * * we would hold it invalid, no matter how long its history. As the dissent points out, a long and shameful history of racism lay behind the kind of statute invalidated in Loving.

But the historical background of Loving is different from the history underlying this case. Racism has been recognized for centuries—at first by a few people, and later by many more—as a revolting moral evil. This country fought a civil war to eliminate racism's worst manifestation, slavery, and passed three constitutional amendments to eliminate that curse and its vestiges. Loving was part of the civil rights revolution of the 1950's and 1960's, the triumph of a cause for which many heroes and many ordinary people had struggled since our nation began.

It is true that there has been serious injustice in the treatment of homosexuals also, a wrong that has been widely recognized only in the relatively recent past, and one our Legislature tried to address when it enacted the Sexual Orientation Non–Discrimination Act four years ago * * *. But the traditional definition of marriage is not merely a by-product of historical injustice. Its history is of a different kind. * * *

Our conclusion that there is a rational basis for limiting marriage to opposite-sex couples leads us to hold that that limitation is valid under the New York Due Process and Equal Protection Clauses, and that any expansion of the traditional definition of marriage should come from the Legislature. * * *

KAYE, CHIEF JUDGE (dissenting): * * *

Solely because of their sexual orientation, however—that is, because of who they love—plaintiffs are denied the rights and responsibilities of civil marriage. This State has a proud tradition of affording equal rights to all New Yorkers. Sadly, the Court today retreats from that proud tradition. * * *

Lawrence overruled Bowers v. Hardwick, which had upheld a Georgia statute criminalizing sodomy. In so doing, the Lawrence Court criticized Bowers for framing the issue presented too narrowly. Declaring that "Bowers was not correct when it was decided, and it is not correct today" * * *.

The same failure is evident here. An asserted liberty interest is not to be characterized so narrowly as to make inevitable the conclusion that the claimed right could not be fundamental because historically it has been denied to those who now seek to exercise it * * *

Simply put, fundamental rights are fundamental rights. They are not defined in terms of who is entitled to exercise them. * * *

I am confident that future generations will look back on today's decision as an unfortunate misstep.

LEWIS v. HARRIS

188 N.J. 415, 908 A.2d 196 (N.J. 2006).

JUSTIN ALBIN delivered the opinion of the Court.

The statutory and decisional laws of this State protect individuals from discrimination based on sexual orientation. When those individuals are gays and lesbians who follow the inclination of their sexual orientation and enter into a committed relationship with someone of the same sex, our laws treat them, as couples, differently than heterosexual couples. As committed same-sex partners, they are not permitted to marry or to enjoy the multitude of social and financial benefits and privileges conferred on opposite-sex married couples.

In this case, we must decide whether persons of the same sex have a fundamental right to marry that is encompassed within the concept of liberty guaranteed by Article I, Paragraph 1 of the New Jersey Constitution. Alternatively, we must decide whether Article I, Paragraph 1's equal protection guarantee requires that committed same-sex couples be given on equal terms the legal benefits and privileges awarded to married heterosexual couples and, if so, whether that guarantee also requires that the title of marriage, as opposed to some other term, define the committed same-sex legal relationship.

Only rights that are deeply rooted in the traditions, history, and conscience of the people are deemed to be fundamental. Although we cannot find that a fundamental right to same-sex marriage exists in this State, the unequal dispensation of rights and benefits to committed same-sex partners can no longer be tolerated under our State Constitution. With this State's legislative and judicial commitment to eradicating sexual orientation discrimination as our backdrop, we now hold that denying rights and benefits to committed same-sex couples that are statutorily given to their heterosexual counterparts violates the equal protection guarantee of Article I, Paragraph 1. To comply with this constitutional mandate, the Legislature must either amend the marriage statutes to include same-sex couples or create a parallel statutory structure, which will provide for, on equal terms, the rights and benefits enjoyed and burdens and obligations borne by married couples. We will not presume that a separate statutory scheme, which uses a title other than marriage, contravenes equal protection principles, so long as the rights and benefits of civil marriage are made equally available to same-sex couples. The name to be given to the statutory scheme that provides full rights and benefits to same-sex couples, whether marriage or some other term, is a matter left to the democratic process. * * *

Plaintiffs are seven same-sex couples who claim that New Jersey's laws, which restrict civil marriage to the union of a man and a woman, violate the liberty and equal protection guarantees of the New Jersey Constitution. Each plaintiff has been in a "permanent committed relationship" for more than ten years and each seeks to marry his or her partner and to enjoy the legal, financial, and social benefits that are afforded by marriage. * * * Plaintiffs contend that the right to marry a person of the same sex is a fundamental right secured by the liberty guarantee of Article I, Paragraph 1 of the New Jersey Constitution. Plaintiffs maintain that the liberty interest at stake is "the right of every adult to choose whom to marry without intervention of government." Plaintiffs do not profess a desire to overthrow all state regulation of marriage, such as the prohibition on polygamy and restrictions based on consanguinity and age. They therefore accept some limitations on "the exercise of personal choice in marriage." They do claim, however, that the State cannot regulate marriage by defining it as the union between a man and a woman without offending our State Constitution.

In assessing their liberty claim, we must determine whether the right of a person to marry someone of the same sex is so deeply rooted in the traditions and collective conscience of our people that it must be deemed fundamental under Article I, Paragraph 1. We thus begin with the text of Article I, Paragraph 1, which provides:

> All persons are by nature free and independent, and have certain natural and unalienable rights, among which are those of enjoying and defending life and liberty, of acquiring, possessing, and protecting property, and of pursuing and obtaining safety and happiness. [N.J. Const. art. I, P1.]

The origins of Article I, Paragraph 1 date back to New Jersey's 1844 Constitution. That first paragraph of our Constitution is, in part, "a 'general recognition of those absolute rights of the citizen which were a part of the common law.' " King v. S. Jersey Nat'l Bank, 66 N.J. 161, 178, 330 A.2d 1 (1974) (quoting Ransom v. Black, 54 N.J.L. 446, 448, 24 A. 489 (Sup. Ct. 1892), aff'd per curiam, 65 N.J.L. 688, 51 A. 1109 (E. & A. 1893)). In attempting to discern those substantive rights that are fundamental under Article I, Paragraph 1, we have adopted the general standard followed by the United States Supreme Court in construing the Due Process Clause of the Fourteenth Amendment of the Federal Constitution. * * *

Under Article I, Paragraph 1, as under the Fourteenth Amendment's substantive due process analysis, determining whether a fundamental right exists involves a two-step inquiry. First, the asserted fundamental liberty interest must be clearly identified. See Washington v. Glucksberg, 521 U.S. 702, 721. Second, that liberty interest must be objectively and deeply rooted in the traditions, history, and conscience of the people of this State. See King, supra, 66 N.J. at 178, 330 A.2d 1; see also Glucksberg * * * * * * .

The right to marriage is recognized as fundamental by both our Federal and State Constitutions. See, e.g., Zablocki v. Redhail, 434 U.S. 374 * * * (1978); J.B. v. M.B., 170 N.J. 9, 23–24, 783 A.2d 707 (2001). That broadly stated right, however, is "subject to reasonable state regulation." Greenberg, supra, 99 N.J. at 572, 494 A.2d 294. Although the fundamental right to marriage extends even to those imprisoned and those in noncompliance with their child support obligations, it does not extend to polygamous, incestuous, and adolescent marriages, N.J.S.A. 2C:24–1; N.J.S.A. 37:1–1, –6. In this case, the liberty interest at stake is not some undifferentiated, abstract right to marriage, but rather the right of people of the same sex to marry. Thus, we are concerned only with the question of whether the right to same-sex marriage is deeply rooted in this State's history and its people's collective conscience. * * *

In answering that question, we are not bound by the nation's experience or the precedents of other states, although they may provide guideposts and persuasive authority. * * * Our starting point is the State's marriage laws.

Plaintiffs do not dispute that New Jersey's civil marriage statutes, N.J.S.A. 37:1–1 to 37:2–41, which were first enacted in 1912, limit marriage to heterosexual couples. That limitation is clear from the use of gender-specific language in the text of various statutes. See, e.g., N.J.S.A. 37:1–1 (describing prohibited marriages in terms of opposite-sex relatives); N.J.S.A. 37:2–10 (providing that "husband" is not liable for debts of "wife" incurred before or after marriage); N.J.S.A. 37:2–18.1 (providing release [*437] rights of curtesy and dower for "husband" and "wife"). More recently, in passing the Domestic Partnership Act to ameliorate some of the economic and social disparities between committed same-sex couples and married heterosexual couples, the Legislature explicitly acknowledged that same-sex couples cannot marry. See N.J.S.A. 26:8A–2(e). * * *

Although today there is a nationwide public debate raging over whether same-sex marriage should be authorized under the laws or constitutions of the various states, the framers of the 1947 New Jersey Constitution, much less the drafters of our marriage statutes, could not have imagined that the liberty right protected by Article I, Paragraph 1 embraced the right of a person to marry someone of his or her own sex. * * *

Times and attitudes have changed, and there has been a developing understanding that discrimination against gays and lesbians is no longer acceptable in this State, as is evidenced by various laws and judicial decisions prohibiting differential treatment based on sexual orientation. See, e.g., N.J.S.A. 10:5–4 (prohibiting discrimination on basis of sexual orientation); N.J.S.A. 26:8A–1 to–13 (affording various rights to same-sex couples under Domestic Partnership Act); In re Adoption of a Child by J.M.G., 267 N.J. Super. 622, 623, 625, 632 A.2d 550 (Ch. Div. 1993) (determining that lesbian partner was entitled to adopt biological child of partner). See generally Joshua Kaplan, Unmasking the Federal Marriage Amendment: The Status of Sexuality, 6 Geo. J. Gender & L. 105, 123–24 (2005) (noting that "1969 is widely recognized as the beginning of the gay rights movement," which is considered "relatively new to the national agenda"). On the federal level, moreover, the United States Supreme

Court has struck down laws that have unconstitutionally targeted gays and lesbians for disparate treatment.

In Romer v. Evans Colorado passed an amendment to its constitution that prohibited all legislative, executive, or judicial action designed to afford homosexuals protection from discrimination based on sexual orientation. 517 U.S. 620 * * * (1996). The Supreme Court declared that Colorado's constitutional provision violated the Fourteenth Amendment's Equal Protection Clause because it "impos[ed] a broad and undifferentiated disability on a single named group" and appeared to be motivated by an "animus toward" gays and lesbians.

More recently, in Lawrence v. Texas, the Court invalidated on Fourteenth Amendment due process grounds Texas's sodomy statute, which made it a crime for homosexuals "to engage in certain intimate sexual conduct." * * * The Court held that the "liberty" protected by the Due Process Clause prevented Texas from controlling the destiny of homosexuals "by making their private sexual conduct a crime." * * * The Lawrence Court, however, pointedly noted that the case did "not involve whether the government must give formal recognition to any relationship that homosexual persons seek to enter." Ibid. In a concurring opinion, Justice O'Connor concluded that the Texas law, as applied to the private, consensual conduct of homosexuals, violated the Equal Protection Clause, but strongly suggested that a state's legitimate interest in "preserving the traditional institution of marriage" would allow for distinguishing between heterosexuals and homosexuals without offending equal protection principles. * * *

Plaintiffs rely on the Romer and Lawrence cases to argue that they have a fundamental right to marry under the New Jersey Constitution, not that they have such a right under the Federal Constitution. Although those recent cases openly advance the civil rights of gays and lesbians, they fall far short of establishing a right to same-sex marriage deeply rooted in the traditions, history, and conscience of the people of this State.

Plaintiffs also rely on Loving v. Virginia, 388 U.S. 1 * * * (1967), to support their claim that the right to same-sex marriage is fundamental. In Loving, the United States Supreme Court held that Virginia's antimiscegenation statutes, which prohibited and criminalized interracial marriages, violated the Equal Protection and Due Process Clauses of the Fourteenth Amendment. * * * Although the Court reaffirmed the fundamental right of marriage, the heart of the case was invidious discrimination based on race, the very evil that motivated passage of the Fourteenth Amendment. * * * The Court stated that "[t]he clear and central purpose of the Fourteenth Amendment was to eliminate all official state sources of invidious racial discrimination in the States." * * * We add that all of the United States Supreme Court cases cited by plaintiffs, Loving, Turner, and Zablocki, involved heterosexual couples seeking access to the right to marriage and did not implicate directly the primary question to be answered in this case.

Within the concept of liberty protected by Article I, Paragraph 1 of the New Jersey Constitution are core rights of such overriding value that we consider them to be fundamental. Determining whether a particular claimed right is fundamental is a task that requires both caution and foresight. * * * In searching for the meaning of "liberty" under Article I, Paragraph 1, we must resist the temptation of seeing in the majesty of that word only a mirror image of our own strongly felt opinions and beliefs. Under the guise of newly found rights, we must be careful not to impose our personal value system on eight-and-one-half million people, thus bypassing the democratic process as the primary means of effecting social change in this State. That being said, this Court will never abandon its responsibility to protect the fundamental rights of all of our citizens, even the most alienated and disfavored, no matter how strong the winds of popular opinion may blow.

Despite the rich diversity of this State, the tolerance and goodness of its people, and the many recent advances made by gays and lesbians toward achieving social acceptance and equality under the law, we cannot find that a right to same-sex marriage is so deeply rooted in the traditions, history, and conscience of the people of this State that it ranks as a fundamental right. When looking for the source of our rights under the New Jersey Constitution, we need not look beyond our borders. Nevertheless, we do take note that no jurisdiction, not even Massachusetts, has declared that there is a fundamental right to same-sex marriage under the federal or its own constitution. * * *

Having decided that there is no fundamental right to same-sex marriage does not end our inquiry. * * * We now must examine whether those laws that deny to committed same-sex couples both the right to and the rights of marriage afforded to heterosexual couples offend the equal protection principles of our State Constitution. [The New Jersey constitution indeed requires that homosexuals couples be afforded the rights of marriage enjoyed by heterosexual couples, though not necessarily the right to marry.]

NOTE: TRANSGENDER SPOUSES—NEW JERSEY

In *M.T. v. J.T.*, 140 N.J.Super. 77, 355 A.2d 204 (App. Div. 1976), a state court faced the problem of "how to tell the sex of a person for marital purposes". Plaintiff M.T., a postoperative transgender woman went to court seeking support and maintenance from the man she had married. Her husband J.T. claimed he did not have to provide for M.T. because "M.T. was a male and that their marriage was void." A trial court "determined that plaintiff was a female and that defendant was her husband, and there being no fraud, ordered defendant to pay plaintiff $50 a week support."

On appeal the court affirmed the trial court's ruling, concluding that the plaintiff transgender woman had been a female when J.T. married her, and that J.T. had known about her male birth sex. The court observed: "In so ruling we do no more than give legal effect to a fait accompli, based upon medical judgment and action which are irreversible. Such recognition will promote the individual's quest for inner peace and personal happiness, while in no way disserving any societal interest, principle of public order or precept of morality."

e. Commercial Sex

NOTE: PROSTITUTION AT HOME—HAWAII

Prostitution is a form of consensual adult sex that is criminalized in most states and highly regulated elsewhere. In *State v. Mueller*, 66 Haw. 616, 671 P.2d 1351 (Hawaii 1983), a woman who had engaged in prostitution behind closed doors at her residence alleged that she had a "constitutional right to privacy for activities that were conducted in the privacy of her own home." She relied unsuccessfully on the federal constitution and the Hawaii state constitution, Art. I, § 6., which provides that: "The right of the people to privacy is recognized and shall not be infringed without the showing of a compelling state interest. The legislature shall take affirmative steps to implement this right." Finding against her, the court cited morals: "A large segment of society undoubtedly regards prostitution as immoral and degrading, and the self-destructive or debilitating nature of the practice, at least for the prostitute, is often given as a reason for outlawing it. We could not deem these views irrational * * *."

f. Illegal Drug Possession

NOTE: ILLEGAL DRUG POSSESSION AT HOME—ALASKA

In the 1970s an Alaska man was arrested for possession of marijuana. He attacked statutes criminalizing the drug as violative of his right to privacy under the federal constitution and the Alaska Constitution, Art. I, Sec. 22. The Alaska Supreme Court agreed, holding that a basic right to privacy in the home encompasses the possession and ingestion of substances such as marijuana in a purely personal, non-commercial context by an adult. *Ravin v. State*, 537 P.2d 494 (Alaska 1975). In the case of an Alaska man and juvenile who sold two pounds of marijuana to an undercover agent, the Alaska court rejected the constitutional privacy defense. *Belgarde v. State*, 543 P.2d 206 (Alaska 1975). The U.S. Supreme Court decided *Morse v. Frederick*, 551 U.S. 393 (2007), the case of an Alaskan who, when he a was fourteen year old boy unfurled a banner at his public school bearing the message "Bong Hits 4 Jesus." The Court sided with Principal Morse: "The First Amendment does not require schools to tolerate * * * student expression that contributes to [the dangers of illegal drug use]."

I. 21st AMENDMENT PRIVACY

1. THE TWENTY–FIRST AMENDMENT

"Section 1. The eighteenth article of amendment to the Constitution of the United States is hereby repealed.

Section 2. The transportation or importation into any state, territory, or possession of the United States for delivery or use therein of intoxicating liquors, in violation of the laws thereof, is hereby prohibited.

Section 3. This article shall be inoperative unless it shall have been ratified as an amendment to the Constitution by conventions in the several States, as provided in the Constitution, within seven years from the date of the submission hereof to the States by the Congress.''

NOTE: PROHIBITION AND MODERN PATERNALISM

Alcoholic beverages are popular consumer goods. Beer and wine are routinely enjoyed with meals. For a time, the sale or transport of "intoxicating" beverages was a crime. The Eighteenth Amendment created the era of alcohol prohibition that the Twenty-first Amendment abolished. The Eighteenth Amendment was ratified in 1919 after being approved by 36 states. During the Act's short life span, many people were prosecuted for its violation. The National Prohibition Act of 1920 (Volstead Act) was passed to enforce the Eighteenth Amendment.

In *Carroll v. United States*, 267 U.S. 132 (1925), two men were arrested and charged with violations of the Volstead Act. Federal and state prohibition agents found 68 bottles of whisky and gin in their automobile during a search conducted without a warrant. The Court upheld the search as consistent with the Fourth Amendment. The well-known "bootleggers" had been driving a car in a neighborhood into which the arresting officers knew they had previously transported illegal alcohol. The strong likelihood that a crime was being committed, plus the impracticality of obtaining a warrant for an automobile search under exigent circumstances meant the search was lawful: "it is clear the officers here had justification for the search and seizure. This is to say that the facts and circumstances within their knowledge and of which they had reasonably trustworthy information were sufficient in themselves to warrant a man of reasonable caution in the belief that intoxicating liquor was being transported in the automobile which they stopped and searched." Id. at 163.

The 21st Amendment restored a popular pleasure but its real purpose related to restoring power to the states, not conferring individual liberties on the people. See *Granholm v. Heald*, 544 U.S. 460 (2005): "The aim of the Twenty-first Amendment was to allow States to maintain an effective and uniform system for controlling liquor by regulating its transportation, importation, and use. The Amendment did not give States the authority to pass nonuniform laws in order to discriminate against out-of-state goods, a privilege they had not enjoyed at any earlier time."

State and local officials may regulate the sale and consumption of alcoholic beverages lightly or extensively, to protect the health and welfare of the community:

> The justification for the exercise of the police power in restraining or prohibiting the sale of intoxicating liquors has been stated and restated by the courts time and again. It may be summed up as resting upon the fundamental principle that society has an inherent right to protect itself;

that the preservation of law and order is paramount to the rights of individuals or property in manufacturing or selling intoxicating liquors; that the sobriety, health, peace, comfort, and happiness of society demand reasonable regulation, if not entire prohibition, of the liquor traffic. Unrestricted, it leads to drunkenness, poverty, lawlessness, vice, and crime of almost every description. Against this result society has the inherent right to protect itself—a right which antedates all constitutions and written laws—a right which springs out of the very foundations upon which the social organism rests; a right which needs no other justification for its existence or exercise than that it is reasonably necessary in order to promote the general welfare of the state. *Odelberg v. City of Kenosha,* 20 Wis.2d 346, 122 N.W.2d 435 (1963), *Id.* at 350, 122 N.W.2d 435 (quoting *Zodrow v. State,* 154 Wis. 551, 555, 143 N.W. 693 (1913)).

For a recent example how localities struggle over the public welfare implications of access to intoxicants, see *Eichenseer v. Madison–Dane County Tavern League*, 308 Wis.2d 684, 748 N.W.2d 154 (2008), an unsuccessful bid to end city-wide rules disallowing price breaks on drinks in college town taverns near the University of Wisconsin, where underage and binge drinking were rampant.

2. LEGISLATING TEMPERANCE

JOHN STUART MILL, ON LIBERTY (1859)

[T]here are, in our own day, gross usurpations upon the liberty of private life actually practised, and still greater ones threatened with some expectation of success, and opinions propounded which assert an unlimited right in the public not only to prohibit by law everything which it thinks wrong, but in order to get at what it thinks wrong, to prohibit any number of things which it admits to be innocent.

Under the name of preventing intemperance, the people of one English colony, and of nearly half the United States, have been interdicted by law from making any use whatever of fermented drinks, except for medical purposes: for prohibition of their sale is in fact, as it is intended to be, prohibition of their use. And though the impracticability of executing the law has caused its repeal in several of the States which had adopted it, * * * an attempt has notwithstanding been commenced, and is prosecuted with considerable zeal by many of the professed philanthropists, to agitate for a similar law in this country [England]. The association, or "Alliance" as it terms itself, which has been formed for this purpose, has acquired some notoriety * * *.

The organ of the Alliance, who would "deeply deplore the recognition of any principle which could be wrested to justify bigotry and persecution," undertakes to point out the "broad and impassable barrier" which divides such principles from those of the association. "All matters relating to thought, opinion, conscience, appear to me," he says, "to be without the sphere of legislation; all pertaining to social act, habit, relation, subject only to a discretionary power vested in the State itself, and not in the individual, to be within it."

No mention is made of a third class, different from either of these, viz. acts and habits which are not social, but individual; although it is to this class, surely, that the act of drinking fermented liquors belongs. Selling fermented liquors, however, is trading, and trading is a social act. But the infringement complained of is not on the liberty of the seller, but on that of the buyer and consumer; since the State might just as well forbid him to drink wine, as purposely make it impossible for him to obtain it. * * *

NOTE: PRIVACY'S DOMAIN

The "Alliance" argued that matters of opinion and thought are properly immune from state regulation, but that social *acts* are properly regulated. Mill countered that some acts are not social but individual, including consumption of intoxicants. Based on the materials covered in Chapter 2 are you now prepared to say when an act is properly social (public) and when it is properly individual (private)? Do the materials suggest alternative ways to frame the question?

CHAPTER 3

FEDERAL PRIVACY STATUTES

■ ■ ■

Introduction

This chapter and the next focus on federal information law—the regulation of data protection practices by the United States Congress and federal administrative agencies, through general statutes and specific rules. The character of a nation's information law may be the best single measure of its commitment to freedom and personal privacy.

The study of information law helps to answer three central questions. How does the U.S. regulate access to personal and commercial communication? How does the U.S. address problems of data protection and data security? How does the U.S. govern public and private surveillance?

These questions are arising in a complex geo-political context. Many believe technology is eroding important traditional privacies, see Fred H. Cate, "Government Data Mining: The Need for a Legal Framework," 43 *Harvard Civil Rights–Civil Liberties Law Review* 435 (2008). Many believe the North American business sector has not done all it can to safeguard consumer privacy, see Ann Cavoukian and Tyler J. Hamilton, "Privacy Is Good for Business," in *Privacy Payoff, How Successful Businesses Build Customer Trust* (2002) And many believe the threat of catastrophic acts of terrorism require increased monitoring and surveillance. In the words of federal Judge Richard Posner: "Privacy is the terrorist's best friend," see Privacy, Surveillance and Law, 75 *University of Chicago Law Review* 245 (2008).

(1) Major Acts of Congress—An Overview

In 1968, Congress passed a comprehensive statute governing wiretaps and other surveillance of telephone calls, Title III of the Omnibus Crime Control and Safe Streets Act. Since then, by enacting new statutes and amending old ones, Congress has expanded its reach beyond hard-wired telephones to encompass digital, electronic, radio and cable communications.

Important acts of Congress that relate directly to communications and surveillance include: the Foreign Intelligence Surveillance Act (1978), setting the ground rules for top-secret government intelligence gathering;

the Electronic Communications Privacy Act (1986), amending Title III to broadly regulate access to wire, oral and electronic communications; and the Telephone Consumer Protection Act (1991), regulating telemarketing and amended to create the National Do–Not–Call Registry. They also include: the Communications Assistance for Law Enforcement Act (1994), preserving the capacity of law enforcement to conduct surveillance of electronic communications; the Telecommunications Act (1996), mandating the confidentiality of "customer proprietary network information"; the Identity Theft and Assumption Deterrence Act (1998), criminalizing identity theft; the Children's Online Privacy Protection Act (1998), limiting website operators' access to children's personal information; and the Uniting and Strengthening America by Providing Appropriate Tools Required to Intercept and Obstruct Terrorism Act (2001), extensively amending and supplementing federal information laws to facilitate investigations of terrorism.

Through data protection and public records laws, Congress regulates the collection and management of school, business, health, and public records containing personal information about individuals. The most significant such laws are the Fair Credit Reporting Act (1970), regulating bank credit reports; the Privacy and Freedom of Information Acts (1974), regulating federal record-keeping; the Family Educational Rights and Privacy Act (1974), regulating access to school records; the Right to Financial Privacy Act (1978), regulating access to bank records; the Privacy Protection Act (1980), regulating the search and seizure of work products protected by the First Amendment; and the Video Privacy Protection Act (1988), regulating access to video rental records. They further include: the Employee Polygraph Protection Act (1988), prohibiting employee lie-detection testing; the Driver's Privacy Protection Act (1994), regulating access to motor vehicle records; the Health Insurance Portability and Accountability Act (1996), regulating the privacy and security of medical information; Title V of the Gramm–Leach–Bliley Act (1999), regulating disclosures of financial information; and the CAN–SPAM Act (2003), prohibiting certain unsolicited email.

(2) Agency Rule-making and Enforcement

Congress has delegated some of its privacy-related rulemaking authority to federal agencies. For example, the Department of Health and Human Services was given primary responsibility for fashioning medical privacy rules under the Health Insurance Portability and Accountability Act (1996).

Congress relies on federal agencies to enforce privacy rules, too. The Department of Education has the power to enforce the confidentiality requirements of the Family Educational Rights and Privacy Act (1974). The Federal Trade Commission has the authority to bring enforcement actions seeking to restrain and punish non-compliance with federal internet, telecommunications and consumer finance privacy rules, including the Children's Online Privacy Protection Act (1998) and Title V of the

Gramm–Leach–Bliley Act (1999). See Joseph Turow, Chris J. Hoofnagle, Deirdre K. Mulligan, Nathaniel Good and Jens Grossklags, The Federal Trade Commission and Consumer Privacy in the Coming Decade, *3 I/S: A Journal of Law and Policy for the Information Society* 723 (2007).

(3) Fair Information Practices Principles

Originally developed in the early 1970's with the backing of Congress, exacting "fair information practice" principles have often guided the hands of Washington policy-makers. Fair information practice principles are standards for collecting, maintaining and disclosing personal information about individuals. Fair information practice ideals are evident in the Generally Accepted Privacy Principles developed by a Privacy Task Force convened jointly by the American Institute of Certified Public Accountants and the Canadian Institute of Chartered Accountants in 2001. See, Marilyn Prosch, "Protecting Personal Information Using Generally Accepted Privacy Principles (GAPP) and Continuous Controls Monitoring to Enhance Corporate Governance," *5 International Journal of Disclosure and Governance 153* (2008). Generally accepted privacy principles comprise a "comprehensive framework that provides specific criteria that [corporate chief privacy officers] and other privacy and security experts can use to assess, build, and monitor privacy programs." *Id.* at 153.

Yet the adequacy of U.S. privacy rules and the strength of the U.S. commitment to fair information practice principles is a matter of controversy. One point of controversy is the simple fact that Congress has not followed the lead of the multinational European Union to enact an overall data-protection statute incorporating fair information practice standards. Congress has debated the possibility of a national omnibus data-protection statute. But, so far, United States policy-makers have favored a combination of multiple, limited-purpose public laws and industry self-regulation. Government encouragement, the desire to comply with European standards and domestic market pressures have prompted the U.S. business sector voluntarily to adopt at least some privacy policies and fair information practices.

Over the years, Congress has enacted numerous privacy-protection statutes, resulting in a patchwork quilt of special-purpose rules. Is the exceptional U.S. approach inferior, or simply different? Privacy advocates at home and around the world have at times disparaged the U.S. sector-by-sector approach both as unduly ad hoc and as disrespectful of privacy when viewed as a human right. As the examination of European privacy protection which rounds off this Chapter demonstrates, the European privacy protection regimes—deeply rooted in admirable traditions of human rights—would be far from easy to transplant. *Cf.* Fred Cate, Some Essential Components of Privacy Regulation, *Privacy in the Information Age 116–132* (1997), arguing that the level of protection provided in the EU is unworkable and undesirable in the U.S. context; Paul Schwartz, Privacy and Preemption, 118 *Yale L.J.* 902 (2009), explaining the continuing US/EU differences as benign consequences of path dependency and elaborating the usefulness of omnibus laws in multi-nation systems that wish to harmonize their regulations.

Critics contend that U.S. privacy laws fail to take fair information practice standards seriously. In keeping with fair information practice standards, U.S. rules typically prohibit disclosing individuals' personal data to third-parties without notice and consent. However, U.S. rules generally count as notice and consent, the mere failure affirmatively to opt-out of disclosures data-holders describe in written notices that few consumers take the time to read. Arguably, stronger privacy laws would require notice and consent on an informed "opt in" basis, and forbid certain disclosures altogether.

(4) Litigating Legitimacy and Interpretation

Opinion polls suggest that the general public applauds recent efforts by Congress to expand privacy protections in response to new technologies, crime and terrorism. Yet neither consumers, business, nor government officials have been without complaint. Consumers complain that U.S. privacy rules contain self-defeating exceptions, and deny individuals standing to sue when things go wrong. For example, patients have no private right of action against physicians under the nation's major health confidentiality and data security statute, the Health Insurance Portability and Accountability Act (HIPAA). The corporate sector complains that privacy statutes aimed at consumer protection are onerous, expensive, and bad for business. Government officials complain, too, when privacy rules seem to stand in the way of efficient law enforcement or national security. All of these constituencies have resorted to federal litigation challenging the adequacy, and the very legitimacy, of the nation's privacy statutes and agency rules.

The federal courts have thus been called upon to interpret the rule-making authority of government entities. The courts have also been asked to interpret the particular requirements of statutes and agency rules when their requirements are vague, conflicting or ambiguous; or when a rule or statute is silent on matters about which the litigants disagree. The federal courts apply the same methods and philosophies of statutory interpretation to privacy laws that they apply to other substantive laws. The plain meaning of a text, its intent, its purposes and the needs of society—all of these potentially come into play in interpreting privacy rules and statutes

(5) Learning Information Law

The United States protects the privacy of its residents through a network of sectoral regulations rather than an omnibus, general-purpose privacy law. For students of privacy law, the volume and complexity of the regulations pose a special challenge.

There is perhaps no better way to learn federal statutory information law than by examining the difference the statutes and associated regulations have made in daily life, discernible through the problems and controversies that they have spawned. Here we approach the law one statute—and the cases and commentary interpreting it—at a time. This chapter is organized to make it easy to see the history and purposes of each of the major statutes covered.

The chapter begins with a group of statutes that regulate government record keeping; and a second group that regulate school, health, financial and video records. The chapter concludes with statutes that govern computers, the internet, telephones and cable services, followed by an overview of EU data protection laws. Chapter 4 rounds out our study of federal privacy statutes with a group of statutes that set the legal parameters for communications and for private, law enforcement and national security surveillance.

A. FEDERAL GOVERNMENT RECORD-KEEPING

In 1974, Congress enacted the Privacy Act, along with the Freedom of Information Act privacy exemptions, to regulate federal record-keeping. The new privacy laws were drafted in the spirit of the "fair information practice" standards they helped to popularize.

Section (a) of the Privacy Act, 93 P.L. 579, 88 Stat. 1896, sets out the findings of Congress that prompted legislation, including increased use of computers and sophisticated information technology. Section (a)(4) finds that privacy is a "personal and fundamental right protected by the Constitution". Was the Privacy Act influenced by *Katz v. U.S.* (1967) and *Roe v. Wade* (1973), chronicled in Chapter 2? Section (b) sets out the fair information practice principles according to which Congress intended federal record-keeping practices to be governed.

WHY CONGRESS UNDERTOOK REGULATION OF GOVERNMENT RECORD-KEEPING

Privacy Act of 1974, 93 P.L. 579; 88 Stat. 1896.

(a) The Congress finds that—

(1) the privacy of an individual is directly affected by the collection, maintenance, use, and dissemination of personal information by Federal agencies;

(2) the increasing use of computers and sophisticated information technology, while essential to the efficient operations of the Government, has greatly magnified the harm to individual privacy that can occur from any collection, maintenance, use, or dissemination of personal information;

(3) the opportunities for an individual to secure employment, insurance, and credit, and his right to due process, and other legal protections are endangered by the misuse of certain information systems;

(4) the right to privacy is a personal and fundamental right protected by the Constitution of the United States; and

(5) in order to protect the privacy of individuals identified in information systems maintained by Federal agencies, it is necessary and proper for the Congress to regulate the collection, maintenance, use, and dissemination of information by such agencies.

(b) The purpose of this Act * * * is to provide certain safeguards for an individual against an invasion of personal privacy by requiring Federal agencies, except as otherwise provided by law, to—

(1) permit an individual to determine what records pertaining to him are collected, maintained, used, or disseminated by such agencies;

(2) permit an individual to prevent records pertaining to him obtained by such agencies for a particular purpose from being used or made available for another purpose without his consent;

(3) permit an individual to gain access to information pertaining to him in Federal agency records, to have a copy made of all or any portion thereof, and to correct or amend such records;

(4) collect, maintain, use, or disseminate any record of identifiable personal information in a manner that assures that such action is for a necessary and lawful purpose, that the information is current and accurate for its intended use, and that adequate safeguards are provided to prevent misuse of such information;

(5) permit exemptions from the requirements with respect to records provided in this Act * * * and

(6) be subject to civil suit for any damages which occur as a result of willful or intentional action which violates any individual's rights under this Act * * *.

1. FAIR INFORMATION PRACTICES

THE ORIGIN OF FAIR INFORMATION PRACTICES

www.ftc.gov/reports/privacy3/fairinfo.htm.

Fair information practice principles were first articulated in a comprehensive manner in the United States Department of Health, Education and Welfare's seminal 1973 report entitled *Records, Computers and the Rights of Citizens* (1973). [A] canon of fair information practice principles has been developed by a variety of governmental and inter-governmental agencies. In addition to the HEW Report, the major reports setting forth the core fair information practice principles are: The Privacy Protection Study Commission, *Personal Privacy in an Information Society* (1977); Organization for Economic Cooperation and Development, *OECD Guidelines on the Protection of Privacy and Transborder Flows of Personal Data* (1980); Information Infrastructure Task Force, Information Policy Committee, Privacy Working Group, *Privacy and the National Information Infrastructure: Principles for Providing and Using Personal Information* (1995); [and the] U.S. Dept. of Commerce, *Privacy and the NII: Safe-*

guarding Telecommunications–Related Personal Information (1995). [Fair information practice principles are also embodied in the requirements of *the European Union Directive on the Protection of Personal Data* (1995) and the Canadian Standards Association, *Model Code for the Protection of Personal Information: A National Standard of Canada* (1996).]

AN EXPLANATION OF CORE FAIR INFORMATION PRACTICE PRINCIPLES

www.ftc.gov/reports/privacy3/fairinfo.htm.

Common to "fair information practice codes" are five core principles of privacy protection: (1) Notice/Awareness; (2) Choice/Consent; (3) Access/Participation; (4) Integrity/Security; and (5) Enforcement/Redress.

(1) Notice/Awareness. The most fundamental principle is notice. Consumers should be given notice of an entity's information practices before any personal information is collected from them. Without notice, a consumer cannot make an informed decision as to whether and to what extent to disclose personal information. Moreover, three of the other principles discussed below—choice/consent, access/participation, and enforcement/redress—are only meaningful when a consumer has notice of an entity's policies, and his or her rights with respect thereto.

While the scope and content of notice will depend on the entity's substantive information practices, notice of some or all of the following have been recognized as essential to ensuring that consumers are properly informed before divulging personal information:

- identification of the entity collecting the data;
- identification of the uses to which the data will be put;
- identification of any potential recipients of the data;
- the nature of the data collected and the means by which it is collected if not obvious (passively, by means of electronic monitoring, or actively, by asking the consumer to provide the information);
- whether the provision of the requested data is voluntary or required, and the consequences of a refusal to provide the requested information; and
- the steps taken by the data collector to ensure the confidentiality, integrity and quality of the data.

Some information practice codes state that the notice should also identify any available consumer rights, including: any choice respecting the use of the data; whether the consumer has been given a right of access to the data; the ability of the consumer to contest inaccuracies; the availability of redress for violations of the practice code; and how such rights can be exercised.

In the Internet context, notice can be accomplished easily by the posting of an information practice disclosure describing an entity's information practices on a company's site on the Web. To be effective, such a disclosure should be clear and conspicuous, posted in a prominent location, and readily accessible from both the site's home page and any Web page where information is collected from the consumer. It should also be unavoidable and understandable so that it gives consumers meaningful and effective notice of what will happen to the personal information they are asked to divulge.

(2) Choice/Consent. The second widely-accepted core principle of fair information practice is consumer choice or consent. At its simplest, choice means giving consumers options as to how any personal information collected from them may be used. Specifically, choice relates to secondary uses of information—*i.e.*, uses beyond those necessary to complete the contemplated transaction. Such secondary uses can be internal, such as placing the consumer on the collecting company's mailing list in order to market additional products or promotions, or external, such as the transfer of information to third parties.

Traditionally, two types of choice/consent regimes have been considered: opt-in or opt-out. Opt-in regimes require affirmative steps by the consumer to allow the collection and/or use of information; opt-out regimes require affirmative steps to prevent the collection and/or use of such information. The distinction lies in the default rule when no affirmative steps are taken by the consumer. Choice can also involve more than a binary yes/no option. Entities can, and do, allow consumers to tailor the nature of the information they reveal and the uses to which it will be put. Thus, for example, consumers can be provided separate choices as to whether they wish to be on a company's general internal mailing list or a marketing list sold to third parties. In order to be effective, any choice regime should provide a simple and easily-accessible way for consumers to exercise their choice.

In the online environment, choice easily can be exercised by simply clicking a box on the computer screen that indicates a user's decision with respect to the use and/or dissemination of the information being collected. The online environment also presents new possibilities to move beyond the opt-in/opt-out paradigm. For example, consumers could be required to specify their preferences regarding information use before entering a Web site, thus effectively eliminating any need for default rules.

(3) Access/Participation. Access is the third core principle. It refers to an individual's ability both to access data about him or herself—*i.e.*, to view the data in an entity's files—and to contest that data's accuracy and completeness. Both are essential to ensuring that data are accurate and complete. To be meaningful, access must encompass timely and inexpensive access to data, a simple means for contesting inaccurate or incomplete data, a mechanism by which the data collector can verify the information, and the means by which corrections and/or consumer objections can be added to the data file and sent to all data recipients.

(4) Integrity/Security. The fourth widely accepted principle is that data be accurate and secure. To assure data integrity, collectors must take reasonable steps, such as using only reputable sources of data and cross-referencing data against multiple sources, providing consumer access to data, and destroying untimely data or converting it to anonymous form.

Security involves both managerial and technical measures to protect against loss and the unauthorized access, destruction, use, or disclosure of the data. Managerial measures include internal organizational measures that limit access to data and ensure that those individuals with access do not utilize the data for unauthorized purposes. Technical security measures to prevent unauthorized access include encryption in the transmission and storage of data; limits on access through use of passwords; and the storage of data on secure servers or computers that are inaccessible by modem.

(5) Enforcement/Redress. It is generally agreed that the core principles of privacy protection can only be effective if there is a mechanism in place to enforce them. Absent an enforcement and redress mechanism, a fair information practice code is merely suggestive rather than prescriptive, and does not ensure compliance with core fair information practice principles. Among the alternative enforcement approaches are (a) industry self-regulation; (b) legislation that would create private remedies for consumers; and/or (c) regulatory schemes enforceable through civil and criminal sanctions.

(a) Self–Regulation. To be effective, self-regulatory regimes should include both mechanisms to ensure compliance (enforcement) and appropriate means of recourse by injured parties (redress). Mechanisms to ensure compliance include making acceptance of and compliance with a code of fair information practices a condition of membership in an industry association; external audits to verify compliance; and certification of entities that have adopted and comply with the code at issue. A self-regulatory regime with many of these principles has recently been adopted by the individual reference services industry.

Appropriate means of individual redress include, at a minimum, institutional mechanisms to ensure that consumers have a simple and effective way to have their concerns addressed. Thus, a self-regulatory system should provide a means to investigate complaints from individual consumers and ensure that consumers are aware of how to access such a system. If the self-regulatory code has been breached, consumers should have a remedy for the violation. Such a remedy can include both the righting of the wrong (*e.g.*, correction of any misinformation, cessation of unfair practices) and compensation for any harm suffered by the consumer. Monetary sanctions would serve both to compensate the victim of unfair practices and as an incentive for industry compliance. Industry codes can provide for alternative dispute resolution mechanisms to provide appropriate compensation.

(b) Private Remedies. A statutory scheme could create private rights of action for consumers harmed by an entity's unfair information practices. Several of the major information practice codes, including the seminal 1973 HEW Report, call for implementing legislation. The creation of private remedies would help create strong incentives for entities to adopt and implement fair information practices and ensure compensation for individuals harmed by misuse of their personal information. Important questions would need to be addressed in such legislation, *e.g.*, the definition of unfair information practices; the availability of compensatory, liquidated and/or punitive damages; and the elements of any such cause of action.

(c) Government Enforcement. Finally, government enforcement of fair information practices, by means of civil or criminal penalties, is a third means of enforcement. Fair information practice codes have called for some government enforcement, leaving open the question of the scope and extent of such powers. Whether enforcement is civil or criminal likely will depend on the nature of the data at issue and the violation committed.

Note: Generally Accepted Privacy Principles

Do businesses and governments have distinctly different information practice concerns? The Privacy Task Force of the American Institute of Certified Public Accountants and the Canadian Institute of Chartered Accountants' developed a set of 10 Generally Accepted Privacy Principles (GAPP) in the early 2000s, refreshed in 2009.

The GAPP were: "developed from a business perspective, referencing some, but by no means all, significant local, national and international privacy regulations. GAPP operationalizes complex privacy requirements into a single privacy objective that is supported by 10 privacy principles. Each principle is supported by objective, measurable criteria that form the basis for effective management of privacy risk and compliance in an organization. Illustrative policy requirements, communications and controls, including monitoring controls, are provided as support for the criteria." See generally http://www.aicpa. org/InterestAreas/InformationTechnology/Resources/Privacy/Generally AcceptedPrivacyPrinciples, describing the history of the GAPP and the purposes each principle was designed to serve.

How similar are the GAPP, which were designed to support the interests of large businesses, to the "fair information practice principles" outlined above? The GAPP are:

1. Management. The entity defines, documents, communicates and assigns accountability for its privacy policies and procedures.

2. Notice. The entity provides notice about its privacy policies and procedures and identifies the purposes for which personal information is collected, used, retained and disclosed.

3. Choice and consent. The entity describes the choices available to the individual and obtains implicit or explicit consent with respect to the collection, use and disclosure of personal information.

4. Collection. The entity collects personal information only for the purposes identified in the notice.

5. Use, retention and disposal. The entity limits the use of personal information to the purposes identified in the notice and for which the individual has provided implicit or explicit consent. The entity retains personal information for only as long as necessary to fulfill the stated purposes or as required by law or regulation and thereafter appropriately dispose of such information.

6. Access. The agency provides individuals with access to their personal information for review and update.

7. Disclosure to third parties. The entity discloses personal information to third parties only for the purposes identified in the notice and with the implicit or explicit consent of the individual.

8. Security for privacy. The entity protects personal information against unauthorized access (both physical and logical).

9. Quality. The agency maintains accurate, complete and relevant personal information for purposes identified in the notice. 10. Monitoring and enforcement. The entity monitors compliance with its privacy policies and procedures and has procedures to address privacy-related complaints and disputes.

10. Monitoring and Enforcement. The entity monitors compliance with its privacy policies and procedures and has procedures to address privacy-related complaints and disputes.

2. THE FEDERAL PRIVACY ACT

Inspired by "the increasing use of computers and sophisticated information technology," the Privacy Act (1974), 5 U.S.C. § 552a, establishes a statutory scheme to control the management of personal information held in records maintained by federal agencies. The Act regulates the manner in which agencies may release information to the general public and to other agencies. It also sets guidelines for the collection of personal information. The Act provides, for example, that information may only be collected for valid agency purposes; and that no record may be maintained regarding the manner in which individuals exercise their First Amendment rights.

The Privacy Act applies only to information about individuals that is part of a federal "record" that is "maintained" in a "system of records." In accord with fair information practice principles, the Act allows individuals to see, review and challenge the accuracy of records about them.

An agency's refusal to grant a request under the Privacy Act is subject both to administrative agency review and judicial review. After exhausting administrative remedies provided by a federal agency believed to have violated the statute, individuals may bring a suit in federal district court to recover provable "damages" they have suffered. An agency's "willful or intentional" violation of the Privacy Act opens the door to liability for monetary and injunctive relief. In addition, courts may impose criminal penalties on agency officers or employees who violate the Act's disclosure limitations, as well as on individuals who request information under false pretenses.

THE PRIVACY ACT OF 1974

5 U.S.C. § 552a, as amended.

§ 552a. Records maintained on individuals * * *

(b) Conditions of disclosure

No agency shall disclose any record which is contained in a system of records by any means of communication to any person, or to another agency, except pursuant to a written request by, or with the prior written consent of, the individual to whom the record pertains, unless [an exception provided in this section applies]. * * *

(d) Access to records

Each agency that maintains a system of records shall—(1) upon request by any individual to gain access to his record or to any information pertaining to him which is contained in the system, permit him and upon his request, a person of his own choosing to accompany him, to review the record and have a copy made of all or any portion thereof in a form comprehensible to him, except that the agency may require the individual to furnish a written statement authorizing discussion of that individual's record in the accompanying person's presence; (2) permit the individual to request amendment of a record pertaining to him * * *; (3) permit the individual who disagrees with the refusal of the agency to amend his record to request a review of such refusal * * *; (5) nothing in this section shall allow an individual access to any information compiled in reasonable anticipation of a civil action or proceeding.

(e) Agency requirements

Each agency that maintains a system of records shall—(1) maintain in its records only such information about an individual as is relevant and necessary to accomplish a purpose of the agency required to be accomplished by statute or by Executive order of the President; (2) collect information to the greatest extent practicable directly from the subject individual when the information may result in adverse determinations about an individual's rights, benefits, and privileges under Federal programs; (3) inform each individual whom it asks to supply information, on the form which it uses to collect the information or on a separate form that can be retained by the individual [the authority, purpose and effects of the information request]. * * *

(f) Agency rules

In order to carry out the provisions of this section, each agency that maintains a system of records shall promulgate rules [and procedures for complying with the Act].

(g) Civil remedies * * *

(1) Whenever any agency [violates the Act] * * * the individual may bring a civil action against the agency, and the district courts of the United States shall have jurisdiction * * *. The court may assess against the United States reasonable attorney fees and other litigation costs * * *. [T]he court may enjoin the agency from withholding the records and order the production to the complainant of any agency records improperly withheld from him. In such a case the court shall determine the matter de novo * * *. (4) In any suit * * * in which the court determines that the agency acted in a manner which was intentional or willful, the United States shall be liable to the individual in an amount equal to the sum of—(A) actual damages sustained by the individual as a result of the refusal or failure, but in no case shall a person entitled to recovery receive less than the sum of $1,000; and (B) the costs of the action together with reasonable attorney fees as determined by the court. * * *

(i) Criminal penalties * * *

(1) Any officer or employee of an agency, * * * who * * * willfully discloses * * * material in any manner to any person or agency not entitled to receive it, shall be guilty of a misdemeanor and fined not more than $5,000. (2) Any officer or employee of any agency who willfully maintains a system of records without meeting the notice requirements of subsection (e)(4) of this section shall be guilty of a misdemeanor and fined not more than $5,000. (3) Any person who knowingly and willfully requests or obtains any record concerning an individual from an agency under false pretenses shall be guilty of a misdemeanor and fined not more than $5,000.

(j) General exemptions * * *

(1) [Records maintained by the Central Intelligence Agency are exempt from disclosure].

(2) [Records maintained primarily for law enforcement purposes are exempt from disclosure].

NOTE: INTERPRETING THE PRIVACY ACT

What type of information is protected from disclosure under the Privacy Act? The Act protects "records" and defines a record as "any item, collection, or grouping of information about an individual that is maintained by an agency, including, but not limited to, his education, financial transactions, medical history, and criminal or employment history and that contains his name, or the identifying number, symbol, or other identifying particular assigned to the individual, such as a finger or voice print or a photograph." § 552a(a)(4).

Is the home address of a federal employee a "record"? The Supreme Could has held so, and it appears that a federal agency may withhold the home addresses of its employees, even from a bona fide labor union. See *U.S. Department of Defense v. Federal Labor Relations Authority*, 510 U.S. 487 (1994). Does the Privacy Act prohibit a federal employer from making a photograph of its employees? Can a federal employer make a tape recording of a meeting with its employees? See *Albright v. United States*, 203 U.S. App. D.C. 333 (D.C. Cir. 1980), below.

In practice, how much trouble do agencies and courts face interpreting the requirements of the Privacy Act? Do you detect a note of exasperation in the Justice Department's perspective on the Privacy Act, which follows?

U.S. DEPARTMENT OF JUSTICE

www.usdoj.gov/foia/privstat.htm.

The Privacy Act of 1974, 5 U.S.C. § 552a (2000), which has been in effect since September 27, 1975, can generally be characterized as an omnibus "code of fair information practices" that attempts to regulate the collection, maintenance, use, and dissemination of personal information by federal executive branch agencies. However, the Act's imprecise language, limited legislative history, and somewhat outdated regulatory guidelines have rendered it a difficult statute to decipher and apply. Moreover, even after more than twenty-five years of administrative and judicial analysis, numerous Privacy Act issues remain unresolved or unexplored. Adding to these interpretational difficulties is the fact that many Privacy Act cases are unpublished district court decisions.

a. Rule Against "Maintaining" a "Record" of Individual's Exercising First Amendment Rights

ALBRIGHT v. UNITED STATES

203 U.S. App. D.C. 333 (D.C. Cir. 1980).

Jᴜᴅɢᴇ Mɪᴋᴠᴀ

The Privacy Act forbids any government agency that "maintains a system of records" from maintaining, collecting, using, or disseminating any record of the exercise of an individual's First Amendment rights. This case raises the issue whether an agency may make and keep such a record even if it is not subsequently incorporated into the agency's system of records. The district court held that incorporation is necessary to trigger the applicability of the Act. We hold that the district court erred in its reading of the Act, and consequently we reverse. * * *

Appellants are career Hearing and Appeal Analysts with the Bureau of Hearings and Appeal, Social Security Administration, United States Department of Health, Education and Welfare. In the spring of 1977, several analysts were recommended for promotion to the GS–301 Grade, level 13. However, a subsequent classification determination by the Bureau's personnel division resulted in the downgrading of the GS–13 level positions to the GS–12 level. As a result, twenty-four analysts were denied the recommended promotions.

In order to explain the reclassification decision, R. Brian Makoff, the personnel officer responsible for the decision, called a meeting with the affected analysts. At the meeting, held in the Bureau's offices during business hours, there was a presentation by Makoff, followed by questions and answers and what has been described as a "heated exchange" between the analysts and Makoff. Although not announced to those present, the room in which the meeting was conducted contained videotaping equipment which was used to record the meeting. Afterwards the videotape was labeled "9/23/77, Brian Makoff Classification Address to Analysts" and placed in a locked file in the Bureau's office.

Having learned that the meeting had been videotaped, the analysts' union brought an unfair labor practice charge, and thereafter the tape was removed to a security branch office in Baltimore, Maryland. It is presently kept in a locked filing cabinet in a sealed envelope addressed to the chief of the security branch and marked "Confidential, Open by Addressee Only." The videotape has since been viewed on limited occasions in connection with this and the unfair labor practice proceeding.

The analysts, after exhausting their administrative remedies, brought an action in the district court for monetary, declaratory, and injunctive relief, alleging a violation of subsection (e)(7) of the Privacy Act of 1974, 5 U.S.C. § 552a(e)(7) (1976), and violations of the First and Fourth Amendments * * *.

Subsection (e)(7) of the Privacy Act, under which the claim in this case was filed, provides in pertinent part: " * * * Each agency that maintains a system of records shall * * * maintain no record describing how any individual exercises rights guaranteed by the First Amendment unless expressly authorized by statute or by the individual about whom the record is maintained or unless pertinent to and within the scope of an authorized law enforcement activity."

The Act defines a "record" as any item, collection, or grouping of information about an individual that is maintained by an agency, including, but not limited to, his education, financial transactions, medical history, and criminal or employment history and that contains his name, or the identifying number, symbol, or other identifying particular assigned to the individual, such as a finger or voice print or a photograph. 5 U.S.C. § 552a(a)(4).

A "system of records" is defined as a group of any records under the control of any agency from which information is retrieved by the name of the individual or by some identifying number, symbol, or other identifying particular assigned to the individual. 5 U.S.C. § 552a(a)(5).

"Maintain" is defined to include "maintain, collect, use, or disseminate." 5 U.S.C. § 552a(a)(3). * * *

The district court found that the videotape in this case was not, and was never intended to be, indexed according to the name or other identifying symbol of any of the analysts filmed. The court thus concluded that the record was not incorporated into the agency's system of records and consequently that the actions of the Bureau and Makoff in making the videotape did not fall within the subsection (e)(7) prohibition.

We do not agree with the district court's reading of the statute. The meaning of a statute must, in the first instance, be sought in the language of the statute itself. If the language is clear and unambiguous, a court must give effect to its plain meaning. The definition of "maintain" is the dispositive factor here. Subsection (e)(7) provides that any agency that maintains a system of records shall not "maintain (collect, use, or disseminate any) record describing how any individual exercises rights guaranteed by the First Amendment." When so read, the Act clearly prohibits even the mere collection of such a record, independent of the agency's maintenance, use, or dissemination of it thereafter. The district court's interpretation is thus inconsistent with the plain meaning of the language of the Act. * * *

The legislative history also reveals a concern for unwarranted collection of information as a distinct harm in and of itself. "(T)he section is directed to inquiries made for research or statistical purposes which, even though they may be accompanied by sincere pledges of confidentiality are, by the very fact that government make (sic) the inquiry, infringing on zones of personal privacy which should be exempted from unwarranted Federal inquiry." * * *

Similarly, although not expressly provided for in the Constitution, courts have long recognized that "the First Amendment has a penumbra where privacy is protected from governmental intrusion." Griswold v. Connecticut, 381 U.S. 479, 483, 85 S. Ct. 1678, 1681(1965). This penumbra of privacy can be invaded, under certain circumstances, by the mere inquiry of government into an individual's exercise of First Amendment rights. * * * Thus it is not surprising that Congress would have provided in this Act, dedicated to the protection of privacy, that an agency may not so much as collect information about an individual's exercise of First Amendment rights except under very circumscribed conditions. * * *

[W]e must turn to an examination of whether the agency violated the Act by making the videotape of the meeting with the analysts. The threshold issue in this regard is whether the videotape is a record of the exercise of First Amendment rights. We do not think the fact that the means of storing information in this case was a videotape makes it any less a record for purposes of the Act. * * * As long as the tape contains a means of identifying an individual by picture or voice, it falls within the definition of a "record" under the Privacy Act. * * *

The agency concedes that no statute expressly authorizes the making of the videotape. It is also undisputed that the participants in the meeting did not expressly consent to the videotaping, nor is there any assertion by the agency that the record was made in connection with an authorized law enforcement activity. Thus, it would appear that the analysts do state a viable claim of a violation of subsection (e)(7).

This does not mean that the analysts must necessarily prevail on their claim below. First, there is some disagreement between the parties as to which, if any, of the analysts participating in this appeal were depicted by voice or picture in the videotape. Although we hold that if the voices or pictures were depicted, the videotape would constitute a record under the Act, we cannot, on the facts presented, determine whether such was the case.

Second, in order to establish jurisdiction in the district court, the analysts would have to show that the making of this record had an adverse effect on them as required by subsection (g)(1)(D) of the Act. The analysts argue that they "properly alleged the adverse effect to them (in their complaint) since among other things * * * (they) have been identified as malcontents within the Agency. Accordingly, their promotion, transfer and assignment opportunities have been adversely affected." * * *

Finally, in order to be entitled to the damage remedy they seek, the analysts must establish that "the agency acted in a manner which was intentional or willful." 5 U.S.C. § 552a(g)(4). The agency argues that its action was based on its desire to preserve a record of the meeting for other analysts affected by the classification decision who were unable to attend. The agency asserts that the idea to record the meeting actually came initially from one such analyst. The agency points out that it volunteered to destroy the tape when it became aware that the analysts were upset about its having been made, but the offer was refused by the analysts' union.

If these assertions are found to be true, we have serious doubts whether the agency action was a willful and intentional violation of the Act which would justify the assessment of damages. However, we are not in a position to decide this question. The factual disputes existing in this case must be decided by the district court on remand. * * *

b. White House Not a Privacy Act "Agency"

FALWELL v. EXECUTIVE OFFICE OF THE PRESIDENT

113 F. Supp. 2d 967 (W.D. Va. 2000).

WILSON, CHIEF JUDGE * * *

On August 26, 1999, plaintiff Dr. Jerry Falwell made written requests to the EOP [Executive Office of the President] and FBI [Federal Bureau of Investigation] under the FOIA [Freedom of Information Act] and the Privacy Act for any documents that might pertain to him or any of the other named plaintiffs [who are numerous religious, social service, educational and broadcast media organizations with which Dr. Falwell was affiliated]. * * * His request to the EOP was directed to 1600 Pennsylvania Avenue, Washington, D.C., and Falwell admitted in oral argument that the only documents held by the EOP in which he is interested are those held by the Office of the President, which is a subset or component of the EOP. * * * The Office of the President responded on October 6, 1999, by denying Falwell's request * * *.

On January 20, 2000, Falwell filed suit in this court, against the EOP and the FBI. Falwell claims that the EOP and FBI violated the Privacy Act, that the FBI violated the FOIA, and that both defendants conspired to accomplish these violations * * *.

"Agency" is defined in the Act by expressly adopting the FOIA's definition of agency, which specifically includes the Executive Office of the President. 5 U.S.C. §§ 552a(a)(1), 552(f)(1). However, in interpreting the FOIA's definition of agency, the United States Supreme Court has held that, "the 'Executive Office' does not include the Office of the President." Kissinger v. Reporters Committee for Freedom of the Press, 445 U.S. 136 (1980). Citing legislative history, the Court recognized that " 'the President's immediate personal staff or units in the Executive Office whose sole function is to advise and assist the President' are not included within the term 'agency' under the FOIA." * * *

The Privacy Act clearly and expressly adopts the FOIA's definition of agency. This definition has been interpreted by the Supreme Court as excluding the Office of the President, a component of the EOP. Consequently, the FOIA's definition of agency and its judicial interpretation control the outcome of this case. Therefore, the court finds as a matter of law that the Office of the President is not subject to the Privacy Act and, therefore, is not required to comply with Falwell's request for information. Because Falwell concedes that the only documents held by the EOP in which he is interested are those held by the Office of the President component, this court need not consider Falwell's claim as to the other components of the EOP.

c.   Meeting the "Actual Damages" Requirement

DOE v. CHAO

306 F.3d 170 (4th Cir. 2002).

WILLIAMS, CIRCUIT JUDGE

[A coal miner using the pseudonym Buck Doe seeks recovery against the Secretary of Labor under the Privacy Act for the disclosure of his Social Security number (SSN). His SSN and the SSNs of hundreds of thousands of other coal miners were disclosed to the public through court documents and public reports in the course of adjudication of black lung-related workers compensation claims.] * * *

The question we must decide is whether a person must suffer "actual damages" in order to be considered "a person entitled to recovery" within the meaning of section 552a(g)(4)(A), and therefore entitled to the statutory minimum of $1,000 under that section. We hold that a person must sustain actual damages to be entitled to the statutory minimum damages award. * * *

Having determined that the district court correctly ruled that proven "actual damages" are a precondition to recovery of § 552a(g)(4)(A)'s statutory minimum damages award, we now turn to the merits of the district court's ruling that Buck Doe succeeded in proving "actual damages" and was entitled to summary judgment in the amount of the Act's $1,000 statutory damages award. The district court held that proven emotional distress constitutes "actual damages" under § 552a(g)(4)(A) and that Buck Doe introduced uncontroverted evidence of such damages, sufficient to entitle him to summary judgment. On appeal, Appellants defend this ruling, while the Government argues that Buck Doe failed to introduce sufficient evidence of compensable emotional distress and that, in the alternative, the term "actual damages" as used in the Act does not include damages for emotional distress. * * *

In determining whether sufficient evidence exists to support an award of more than nominal damages for emotional distress, we examine factors such as the need for medical, psychological, or psychiatric treatment, the presence of physical symptoms, loss of income, and impact on the plaintiff's conduct and lifestyle. [F]ailure to establish emotional distress with sufficient evidence will result in the award of only nominal damages. Id. Nominal damages, when available, are designed to vindicate legal rights "without proof of actual injury." Carey v. Piphus, 435 U.S. 247, 266 (1978). An award of merely nominal damages means that a plaintiff has not shown "actual injury." Thus, if Buck Doe's emotional distress evidence would entitle him only to nominal damages under the Price framework, he has shown no "actual injury," in other words, no "actual damages sustained."

Buck Doe's evidence of emotional distress in this case falls far below the level which our precedent demands before the issue of compensatory damages for emotional distress may be submitted to the finder of fact. He testified that he was "greatly concerned and worried" about the disclosure of his SSN; that he felt his privacy had been violated in "words he cannot describe"; that he felt the consequences of the disclosure of his SSN could be "devastating" for himself and his wife, and that the disclosure of his SSN had "torn [him] all to pieces," in a manner that "no amount of money" could ever compensate. * * * Buck Doe did not produce any evidence of tangible consequences stemming from his alleged angst over the disclosure of his SSN. He claimed no medical or psychological treatment, no purchase of medications (prescription or over-the-counter), no impact on his behavior, and no physical consequences. Further, no evidence of any kind corroborates the conclusory allegations in Buck Doe's affidavit. Under these circumstances, we need not reach the issue of whether the term "actual damages" as used in the Act encompasses damages for nonpecuniary emotional distress because, regardless of the disposition of that issue, Buck Doe's claims fail for lack of evidentiary support. In turn, because we have concluded that "actual damages" are a prerequisite to the recovery of statutory minimum damages, and because Buck Doe utterly failed to produce evidence sufficient to permit a rational trier of fact to conclude that he suffered any "actual damages," the district court's entry of summary judgment in Buck Doe's favor as to his entitlement to a statutory "actual damages" award must be reversed, and we must remand with instructions to enter summary judgment in favor of the Government on his claim.

NOTE: SOCIAL SECURITY NUMBERS

The Privacy Act of 1974 contained a proscription against coercive disclosure of social security numbers. The rule, currently found in a note to the Act as codified at § 552a, reads as follows: "It shall be unlawful for any Federal, State or local government agency to deny to any individual any right, benefit, or privilege provided by law because of such individual's refusal to disclose his social security account number." Did this proscription ever curb the widespread use of social security numbers as personal identifiers? In *Remsburg v. Docusearch*, 149 N.H. 148 (N.H. 2003), an online-based private investigation firm obtained a woman's social security number from a credit reporting agency and gave it to a man who later stalked and murdered her. In 2010, the Fourth court affirmed a District Court determination that the state of Virginia could not stop a privacy advocate from publishing state public records with unredacted SSNs on the internet to prove a point. See *Ostergren v. Cuccinelli*, 615 F.3d 263 (4th Cir. 2010).

d. Matching Rules Governing Interagency Disclosures

NOTE: COMPUTER MATCHING AND PRIVACY PROTECTION ACT OF 1988

The Privacy Act regulates the manner in which a federal agency may disclose private information about an individual to the general public. Importantly, it also regulates interagency information sharing.

The Computer Matching and Privacy Protection Act of 1988 (CMPPA), Public Law 100–503, amended the Privacy Act of 1974. The CMPPA was intended to standardize procedures governing the disclosure of personal information in any computer "matching programs." The law requires that each agency engaging in matching establish a Data Integrity Board to monitor the agency's matching activity: "Every agency conducting or participating in a matching program shall establish a Data Integrity Board to oversee and coordinate among the various components of such agency the agency's implementation of this section." 5 U.S.C. § 552a (u)(1).

The CMPPA defines a computer "matching program" as "any computerized comparison of—(i) two or more automated systems of records or a system of records with non-Federal records for the purpose of—(I) establishing or verifying the eligibility of, or continuing compliance with statutory and regulatory requirements by, applicants for, recipients or beneficiaries of, participants in, or providers of services with respect to, cash or in-kind assistance or payments under Federal benefit programs, or (II) recouping payments or delinquent debts under such Federal benefit programs, or (ii) two or more automated Federal personnel or payroll systems of records or a system of Federal personnel or payroll records with non-Federal records."

The CMPPA calls for written matching agreements between any federal agency providing records contained in a system of records (such as the IRS or the Labor Department) and the Federal or non-federal agency receiving records contained in a system of records for use in the matching program. Agreements must indicate the purpose, nature and anticipated results of matching procedures, along with intent to comply with fair information practice standards such as notice to record subjects, data verification, and security. Guidance for agencies implementing the CMPPA requirements has been issued by the federal Office of Management and Budget (OMB).

Suppose a federal agency discloses sensitive personal information about an individual to another federal agency, in a manner that violates the Privacy Act. May federal law enforcement authorities turn around and use the improperly disclosed information in a criminal proceeding against the individual? Should the information instead be suppressed—precluded from use by prosecutors?

UNITED STATES v. COOPER

2005 WL 3555713 (N.D.Cal.).

JUDGE VAUGHN R. WALKER

Defendant Stanmore Cawthon Cooper is charged with three counts of making false statements to a government agency in violation of 18 USC § 1001. Cooper moves to suppress evidence. For reasons discussed below, Cooper's motion is denied. * * *

The Federal Aviation Administration (FAA) licenses civilian pilots in the United States. Private pilots licensed by the FAA must pass a medical examination every two years in order to obtain or renew their medical certificate from the FAA, which is a precondition to continued licensure. FAA Form 8500–8 must be completed as part of the application for a medical certificate. The examinee completes the first part of the form; the examining physician completes the remainder of the form. Question 18 asks examinees to indicate whether they have been diagnosed with various medical conditions [and] inquires about "[o]ther illness, disability, or surgery."

Cooper obtained a private pilot license in 1964. In 1985, Cooper was diagnosed with the HIV virus. Because the FAA was not at that time issuing medical certificates to persons with HIV, Cooper did not renew his medical certificate. By 1995, Cooper's health had deteriorated and he applied for and obtained disability benefits from the Social Security Administration (SSA). New drug treatments allowed Cooper to terminate his disability benefits and return to work in 1996. In 1998, Cooper learned that the FAA had begun issuing medical certificates to eligible HIV-infected persons. Unable to find any guidance regarding eligibility, and for fear of being disqualified, Cooper applied for a medical certificate in 1998 without disclosing his HIV condition. In 2000, Cooper discovered the criteria governing special issuance of medical certificates to persons with HIV. Cooper verified for himself that he met the criteria but nevertheless did not disclose his condition in 2000, 2002 and 2004, fearing possible punitive repercussions for his failure to disclose his condition in 1998. * * *

The Office of the Inspector General of the Department of Transportation (DOT–OIG) and the Office of the Inspector General of the Social Security Administration (SSA–OIG) each have the responsibility of investigating crimes related to information gathered by their respective agencies. * * * In the aftermath of the terrorist attacks of September 11, 2001, SSA–OIG and DOT–OIG undertook a project known as "Operation Safe Pilot," whereby SSA–OIG reviewed information submitted by licensed pilots to the FAA. * * * The purpose of Operation Safe Pilot "was to identify any active FAA-licensed pilot who had obtained a license through misrepresentation, generally of an SSN, on an FAA application." * * * According to SSA Special Agent Robb Stickley, Operation Safe Pilot proceeded as follows: "DOT–OIG provided SSA–OIG with each pilot's name and SSN, as provided to the FAA by the pilot. SSA–OIG then compared that information to SSA databases. During the course of that comparison, SSA–OIG discovered that certain pilots were receiving or had received disability payments while simultaneously claiming to the FAA that they were medically fit to pilot an aircraft." * * * Although "these discoveries were ancillary to" the original purpose of Operation Safe Pilot, * * * they nonetheless prompted fraud investigations, whereby the SSA–OIG disclosed information to the DOT–OIG. Cooper was the subject of one such investigation.

Based on non-disclosure of his HIV condition on the applications for a medical certificate in 2000, 2002 and 2004, the indictment charges Cooper with three counts of making false statements to a government agency in violation of 18 USC § 1001. Cooper moves to suppress the records shared by the FAA and the SSA and all other evidence obtained as a result of the exchange of those records.

Cooper initially advanced three legal grounds for suppression: the agencies' sharing of his medical information violated (1) the Fourth Amendment; (2) the Privacy Act of 1974, 5 USC § 552a; and (3) the Computer Matching and Privacy Protection Act of 1988 (CMPPA). Cooper has since conceded that the CMPPA does not apply to the facts of this case. * * * Accordingly, the court confines its discussion to the first two claims, but in reverse order.

The Privacy Act provides: "No agency shall disclose any record which is contained in a system of records by any means of communication to any other person, or to another agency, except pursuant to a written request by, or with the prior written consent of, the individual to whom the record pertains." 5 USC § 552a(b). Significantly, however, this general prohibition is subject to twelve exceptions, including disclosures made pursuant to a "routine use." Id. § 552a(b)(3). The Act defines "routine use" as "the use of such record for a purpose which is compatible with the purpose for which it was collected." Agencies are required to publish routine uses in the Federal Register. * * *

It is doubtful whether disclosure of Cooper's SSA records to the FAA for the purpose of determining whether Cooper was entitled to a medical certificate from the FAA is "compatible with" the purpose for which Cooper's information was collected by the SSA. * * * These uncertainties aside, the court concludes that a violation of the Privacy Act does not, by itself, justify exclusion of evidence in a criminal proceeding. * * *

[J]udicially implied exclusionary remedies for statutory violations are disfavored, particularly when Congress has specified other remedies. Cooper overlooks these principles and does nothing more than argue that suppression is an appropriate remedy because the Privacy Act does not explicitly provide that its remedies are exclusive. The court is unpersuaded and declines to exercise its supervisory power to fashion an exclusionary remedy in this case. Accordingly, Cooper must show that his constitutional rights have been violated to obtain exclusion. * * *

[T]he protection of the Fourth Amendment is not without limits. * * * United States v. Miller, 425 U.S. 435 (1976). [W]hen a defendant transmits information with the knowledge that it may be recorded and used by a third party for certain purposes unrelated to law enforcement, there can be no legitimate expectation of privacy notwithstanding that the defendant did not actually anticipate that the information might be shared with law enforcement. * * *

Relying primarily upon the Privacy Act, Cooper contends he had a legitimate expectation that the medical records he submitted to the FAA and the SSA would be kept confidential. Although there is surprisingly little case law addressing whether the Privacy Act may give rise to a legitimate expectation of privacy in information provided to government agencies, courts have not been unreceptive to claims of a legitimate expectation of privacy predicated on the Privacy Act. * * * The court finds that the Privacy Act, although not necessarily dispositive, could properly bear on a defendant's subjective expectation of privacy or on society's preparedness to accept an expectation of privacy as reasonable. * * *

With regard to Cooper's subjective expectation of privacy in the information submitted to the FAA and the SSA, the Privacy Act statements printed on the forms completed by Cooper are the proper starting point. Form SSA–3368–BK, which Cooper completed as part of his application for disability benefits, states that information furnished "on this form is almost never used for any purpose other than making a determination on your disability claim." But the form goes on to provide that "such information may be disclosed by the [SSA] as follows: (1) To enable a third party or agency to assist [the SSA] in establishing rights to Social Security benefits and/or coverage; (2) to comply with Federal laws requiring the release of information from Social Security records (e.g., to the General Accounting Office and the Veterans Administration); and (3) to facilitate statistical research and audit activities necessary to assure the integrity and improvement of the Social Security programs." * * * Similarly, although FAA Form 8500–8, which Cooper completed in connection with his application for a medical certificate, states that "the purpose of the information is to determine whether you meet [FAA] medical requirements," it further provides: "These records and information in these records may be used (a) to provide basic airman certification and qualification information to the public upon request; (b) to disclose information to the National Transportation Safety Board (NTSB) in connection with its investigation responsibilities; (c) to provide information about airmen to Federal, state, and local law enforcement agencies when engaged in the investigation and apprehension of drug law violators; (d) to provide information about enforcement actions arising out of violations of the Federal Aviation Regulations to government agencies, the aviation industry, and the public upon request; (e) to disclose information to another Federal agency, or to a court or an administrative tribunal, when the Government or one of its agencies is a party to a [judicial or administrative proceeding]; and (f) to comply with the Prefatory Statement of General Routine Uses for the Department of Transportation."

Cooper argues that the disclosures were not made pursuant to any of the specific routine uses described on the forms. For Fourth Amendment purposes, Cooper's argument misses the mark. The question to be decided is whether Cooper had a subjective expectation of privacy, not whether the SSA and the FAA acted in conformance with the Privacy Act. And based on these two Privacy Act statements, Cooper could not have expected that his medical information would be held in a level of confidence that would implicate the protection of the Fourth Amendment.

According to Cooper, other considerations shaped his subjective expectation. * * * Cooper refers to a public policy known as "HIV Exceptionalism" described on the website of the Department of Health and Human Services, Health Resources and Services Administration. According to Cooper, "one of the purposes of this policy was to provide extra statutory privacy protections to persons infected with HIV." * * *

With regard to "HIV exceptionalism," there is no evidence that this rather vague "policy" was incorporated by statute or regulations of the SSA or the FAA. More importantly, Cooper does not—and likely cannot—state that this actually shaped his expectation of privacy when he submitted his medical information to the SSA or the FAA. * * *

Even if the court were to accept that Cooper harbored an expectation of privacy, the court finds that Cooper's expectation is not one that society is prepared to accept as reasonable. * * * Specifically, § 552a(b)(7) provides that agencies may disclose records "to another agency * * * for a civil or criminal law enforcement activity if the activity is authorized by law, and if the head of the agency has made a written request to the agency which maintains the record specifying the particular portion desired and the law enforcement activity for which the record is sought."

Again, although it does not appear that the FAA or the SSA acted pursuant to this exception when they exchanged Cooper's records, * * * that is of no import. What matters is that this exception reflects a societal determination that records containing information knowingly and voluntarily submitted to one agency are not protected from disclosure to another agency without a warrant or consent when such disclosure is made for purposes of law enforcement. * * * Consequently, the conduct of the FAA and the SSA does not implicate the Fourth Amendment.

NOTE: DATA SHARING REMEDIES

The aircraft pilot in *U.S. v. Cooper*, whose deception was uncovered when the FAA and the SSA compared their files, dropped a claim against the government for violation of the federal Computer Matching and Privacy Protection Act of 1988 (CMPPA). Why did he elect to rely solely on the Privacy Act and the Fourth Amendment? Does the CMPPA provide for a private remedy? Take a look at the text of the law, below, and see if it answers the question. What sanctions are authorized in section (q)? Who is entitled to notice of a matching program under section (r)?

COMPUTER MATCHING AND PRIVACY PROTECTION ACT OF 1988

5 U.S.C. § 552a(*o*) et seq.

(*o*) Matching agreements.—

(1) No record which is contained in a system of records may be disclosed to a recipient agency or non-Federal agency for use in a computer matching program except pursuant to a written agreement between the source agency and the recipient agency or non-Federal agency specifying—

> (A) the purpose and legal authority for conducting the program;

> (B) the justification for the program and the anticipated results, including a specific estimate of any savings;

> (C) a description of the records that will be matched, including each data element that will be used, the approximate number of records that will be matched, and the projected starting and completion dates of the matching program;

> (D) procedures for providing individualized notice * * *

(q) Sanctions.—

(1) Notwithstanding any other provision of law, no source agency may disclose any record which is contained in a system of records to a recipient agency or non-Federal agency for a matching program if such source agency has reason to believe that the requirements of [this Act], or

any matching agreement entered into pursuant to [this Act], or both, are not being met by such recipient agency.

    (2) No source agency may renew a matching agreement unless—

        (A) the recipient agency or non-Federal agency has certified that it has complied with the provisions of that agreement; and

        (B) the source agency has no reason to believe that the certification is inaccurate.

(r) Report on new systems and matching programs.—Each agency that proposes to establish or make a significant change in a system of records or a matching program shall provide adequate advance notice of any such proposal (in duplicate) to the Committee on Government Operations of the House of Representatives, the Committee on Governmental Affairs of the Senate, and the Office of Management and Budget in order to permit an evaluation of the probable or potential effect of such proposal on the privacy or other rights of individuals.

3. THE FREEDOM OF INFORMATION ACT OF 1974 ("FOIA") PRIVACY EXEMPTIONS

The Freedom of Information Act (FOIA), 5 U.S.C. § 552, is an open government statute. A version of the Act was on the books as part of administrative procedures law in the 1960's; but the current Act became law along with the Privacy Act in 1974. All federal agencies are required under FOIA to disclose records requested in writing by any person. FOIA applies only to federal agencies, and excludes records held by Congress, the courts and (according to the Supreme Court) the White House. Because some government records contain sensitive personal information about individuals, The Privacy Act and nine FOIA exemptions limit disclosures under the Act. Federal agencies are separately responsible for meeting their own FOIA responsibilities. Requests for records must be addressed to the appropriate agencies for processing. Individuals who believe they have been improperly denied a FOIA request and have exhausted their administrative remedies may sue in federal district court.

Using FOIA, the media, public interest groups and the general public can keep track of what the federal government is up to. Why might the accountability imposed by FOIA strike federal agency employees as a burden? How eager is the federal government to make disclosures under FOIA?

THE PRIVACY EXEMPTIONS, FREEDOM OF INFORMATION ACT
5 USCS § 552(b)(1)–(9).

(b) This section does not apply to matters that are—

    (1)(A) specifically authorized under criteria established by an Executive order to be kept secret in the interest of national defense or foreign policy and (B) are in fact properly classified pursuant to such Executive order;

(2) related solely to the internal personnel rules and practices of an agency;

(3) specifically exempted from disclosure by statute (other than section 552b of this title) provided that such statute (A) requires that the matters be withheld from the public in such a manner as to leave no discretion on the issue, or (B) establishes particular criteria for withholding or refers to particular types of matters to be withheld;

(4) trade secrets and commercial or financial information obtained from a person and privileged or confidential;

(5) inter-agency or intra-agency memorandums or letters which would not be available by law to a party other than an agency in litigation with the agency;

(6) personnel and medical files and similar files the disclosure of which would constitute a clearly unwarranted invasion of personal privacy;

(7) records or information compiled for law enforcement purposes, but only to the extent that the production of such law enforcement records or information (A) could reasonably be expected to interfere with enforcement proceedings, (B) would deprive a person of a right to a fair trial or an impartial adjudication, (C) could reasonably be expected to constitute an unwarranted invasion of personal privacy, (D) could reasonably be expected to disclose the identity of a confidential source, including a State, local, or foreign agency or authority or any private institution which furnished information on a confidential basis, and, in the case of a record or information compiled by criminal law enforcement authority in the course of a criminal investigation or by an agency conducting a lawful national security intelligence investigation, information furnished by a confidential source, (E) would disclose techniques and procedures for law enforcement investigations or prosecutions, or would disclose guidelines for law enforcement investigations or prosecutions if such disclosure could reasonably be expected to risk circumvention of the law, or (F) could reasonably be expected to endanger the life or physical safety of any individual;

(8) contained in or related to examination, operating, or condition reports prepared by, on behalf of, or for the use of an agency responsible for the regulation or supervision of financial institutions; or

(9) geological or geophysical information and data, including maps, concerning wells.

a. White House Not a FOIA "Agency"

KISSINGER v. REPORTERS COMM.
FOR FREEDOM OF PRESS

445 U.S. 136 (1980).

MR. JUSTICE REHNQUIST delivered the opinion of the Court.

Henry Kissinger served in the Nixon and Ford administrations for eight years. He assumed the position of Assistant to the President for National Security Affairs in January 1969. In September 1973, Kissinger was appointed to the office of Secretary of State, but retained his National Security Affairs advisory position until November 3, 1975. After his resignation from the latter position, Kissinger continued to serve as Secretary of State until January 20, 1977. Throughout this period of Government service, Kissinger's secretaries generally monitored his telephone conversations and recorded their contents either by shorthand or on tape. The stenographic notes or tapes were used to prepare detailed summaries, and sometimes verbatim transcripts, of Kissinger's conversations. Since Kissinger's secretaries generally monitored all of his conversations, the summaries discussed official business as well as personal matters. The summaries and transcripts prepared from the electronic or stenographic recording of his telephone conversations throughout his entire tenure in Government service were stored in his office at the State Department in personal files.

On October 29, 1976, while still Secretary of State, Kissinger arranged to move the telephone notes from his office in the State Department to the New York estate of Nelson Rockefeller. Before removing the notes, Kissinger did not consult the State Department's Foreign Affairs Document and Reference Center (FADRC), the center responsible for implementing the State Department's record maintenance and disposal program. Nor did he consult the National Archives and Records Service (NARS), a branch of the General Services Administration (GSA) which is responsible for records preservation throughout the Federal Government. Kissinger had obtained an opinion from the Legal Adviser of the Department of State, however, advising him that the telephone summaries were not agency records but were his personal papers which he would be free to take when he left office. * * *

Three separate FOIA requests form the basis of this litigation. All three requests were filed while Kissinger was Secretary of State, but only one request was filed prior to the removal of the telephone notes from the premises of the State Department. This first request was filed by William Safire, a New York Times columnist, on January 14, 1976. Safire requested the Department of State to produce any transcripts of Kissinger's telephone conversations between January 21, 1969, and February 12, 1971, in which (1) Safire's name appeared or (2) Kissinger discussed the subject of information "leaks" with certain named White House officials. The Department denied Safire's FOIA request by letter of February 11,

1976. The Department letter reasoned that the requested notes had been made while Kissinger was National Security Adviser and therefore were not agency records subject to FOIA disclosure.

The second FOIA request was filed on December 28 and 29, 1976, by the Military Audit Project (MAP) after Kissinger publicly announced the gift of his telephone notes to the United States and their placement in the Library of Congress. * * *

The third FOIA request was filed on January 13, 1977, by the Reporters Committee for Freedom of the Press (RCFP), the American Historical Association, the American Political Science Association, and a number of other journalists (collectively referred to as the RCFP requesters). This request also sought production of the telephone notes made by Kissinger both while he was National Security Adviser and Secretary of State. * * *

The United States has taken some action to seek recovery of the notes for record processing. On January 4, 1977, the Government Archivist wrote to Kissinger, requesting that he be permitted to inspect the telephone notes so that he could determine whether they were Department records, and to determine whether Kissinger had authority to remove them from Department custody. * * * On January 18, 1977, Kissinger replied to the Archivist, declining to permit access.

The Archivist renewed his request for an inspection on February 11, 1977, by which time Kissinger was no longer Secretary of State. With the request, he enclosed a memorandum of law prepared by the General Counsel of the GSA concluding that the materials in question might well be records rather than personal files and that the Archivist was entitled to inspect them under the Federal Records and Records Disposal Acts. Kissinger did not respond to the Archivist's second request. * * *

The FOIA represents a carefully balanced scheme of public rights and agency obligations designed to foster greater access to agency records than existed prior to its enactment. That statutory scheme authorizes federal courts to ensure private access to requested materials when three requirements have been met. Under 5 U.S.C. § 552 (a)(4)(B) federal jurisdiction is dependent upon a showing that an agency has (1) "improperly"; (2) "withheld"; (3) "agency records." Judicial authority to devise remedies and enjoin agencies can only be invoked, under the jurisdictional grant conferred by § 552, if the agency has contravened all three components of this obligation. We find it unnecessary to decide whether the telephone notes were "agency records" since we conclude that a covered agency— here the State Department—has not "withheld" those documents from the plaintiffs. We also need not decide the full contours of a prohibited "withholding." We do decide, however, that Congress did not mean that an agency improperly withholds a document which has been removed from the possession of the agency prior to the filing of the FOIA request. In such a case, the agency has neither the custody nor control necessary to enable it to withhold. * * *

The conclusion that possession or control is a prerequisite to FOIA disclosure duties is reinforced by an examination of the purposes of the Act. The Act does not obligate agencies to create or retain documents; it only obligates them to provide access to those which it in fact has created and retained. It has been settled by decision of this Court that only the Federal Records Act, and not the FOIA, requires an agency to actually create records, even though the agency's failure to do so deprives the public of information which might have otherwise been available to it.

If the agency is not required to create or to retain records under the FOIA, it is somewhat difficult to determine why the agency is nevertheless required to retrieve documents which have escaped its possession, but which it has not endeavored to recover. If the document is of so little interest to the agency that it does not believe the retrieval effort to be justified, the effect of this judgment on an FOIA request seems little different from the effect of an agency determination that a record should never be created, or should be discarded. * * *

The Safire request raises a separate question. At the time when Safire submitted his request for certain notes of Kissinger's telephone conversations, all the notes were still located in Kissinger's office at the State Department. For this reason, we do not rest our resolution of his claim on the grounds that there was no withholding by the State Department. As outlined above, the Act only prohibits the withholding of "agency records." We conclude that the Safire request sought disclosure of documents which were not "agency records" within the meaning of the FOIA.

Safire's request sought only a limited category of documents. He requested the Department to produce all transcripts of telephone conversations made by Kissinger from his White House office between January 21, 1969, and February 12, 1971, in which (1) Safire's name appeared; or (2) in which Kissinger discussed the subject of information "leaks" with General Alexander Haig, Attorney General John Mitchell, President Richard Nixon, J. Edgar Hoover, or any other official of the FBI.

The FOIA does render the "Executive Office of the President" an agency subject to the Act. 5 U.S.C. § 552(e). The legislative history is unambiguous, however, in explaining that the "Executive Office" does not include the Office of the President. The Conference Report for the 1974 FOIA Amendments indicates that "the President's immediate personal staff or units in the Executive Office whose sole function is to advise and assist the President" are not included within the term "agency" under the FOIA. H. R. Conf. Rep. No. 93–1380, p. 15 (1974), reprinted in Source Book II, p. 232. Safire's request was limited to a period of time in which Kissinger was serving as Assistant to the President. Thus these telephone notes were not "agency records" when they were made.

Accordingly, we reverse the order of the Court of Appeals compelling production of the telephone manuscripts made by Kissinger while Secretary of State and affirm the order denying the requests for transcripts produced while Kissinger served as National Security Adviser.

MARTIN E. HALSTUK, SHIELDING PRIVATE LIVES FROM PRYING EYES: THE ESCALATING CONFLICT BETWEEN CONSTITUTIONAL PRIVACY AND THE ACCOUNTABILITY PRINCIPLE OF DEMOCRACY

11 Commlaw Conspectus 71, 78–80 (2003).

[T]he Bush Administration has established a new Freedom of Information Act policy that urges the executive branch federal agencies to use the Act's privacy exemptions to resist disclosure of agency records. In a memorandum issued on October 12, 2001, Attorney General John Ashcroft rescinded the previous standard set by former Attorney General Janet Reno. The Reno FOIA policy emphasized "maximum responsible disclosure of government information" unless "disclosure would be harmful." Ashcroft replaced Reno's foreseeable-harm standard with a test that encourages withholding based on a "sound legal basis." Although shifts in FOIA policy are traditional whenever a President from a different party is elected, Ashcroft's approach represents a significant restriction even by Republican standards, which are typically less FOIA-friendly than those of Democratic administrations. For comparison, during the Reagan Administration, Attorney General William French Smith established a "substantial legal basis" test to withhold records. Ashcroft's "sound legal basis" test suggests an even lower hurdle than a "substantial legal basis" to justify withholding records.

The new Department of Justice policy has sparked concern among journalists, legislators and open-government advocates who fear the administration's new direction may mark the beginning of "a new era of governmental secrecy under the guise of protecting [personal] privacy." Implicit in Ashcroft's memorandum were concerns over national security and law enforcement in the aftermath of the September 11, 2001 terrorist attacks on Washington, D.C. and New York City. Yet, the policy's focus on privacy exemptions extends beyond matters related to national security and law enforcement. "The mere mention of a name in a record now * * * can be used to deny a FOIA request on the ground that it would violate someone's privacy," warned Lucy Dalglish, executive director of the Reporters Committee for Freedom of the Press. Senator Patrick Leahy of Vermont criticized the new FOIA policy as "contrary to the spirit of the FOIA, [which is] intended to give Americans answers to questions they believe are important, not just the information the government wants them to believe."

The use of FOIA privacy exemptions to restrict access to agency records was already a common practice even before the Ashcroft memorandum, according to the Department of Justice. In a 2002 analysis of recent agency annual reports, the Department of Justice reported that the general privacy exemption, Exemption 6, was the most commonly used of all the FOIA's nine statutory exemptions. Indeed, the history of FOIA privacy disputes that have reached the Supreme Court over the years shows that the Department of Justice has been extremely effective in defending agency decisions to withhold records; the Court has heard seven FOIA privacy cases since 1976, and it ruled in favor of agency decisions to withhold records in all but one of these cases.

In another move that fosters government secrecy by the Executive Branch, President George W. Bush has issued an executive order that conflicts with the 1978 Presidential Records Act, which had provided that presidential papers may be made public 12 years after a President leaves office. Bush's order gives the sitting President, as well as former Presidents, the right to withhold presidential papers. Bush's executive order takes control of presidential papers away from the National Archives of the United States.

Under Bush's order, journalists, historians, scholars, public citizens' groups and the general public now must demonstrate a specific need in order to obtain the presidential documents of Presidents Reagan, George Bush, Sr. and William Jefferson Clinton. The Presidential Records Act, which went into effect in 1981, would have made Reagan's papers available after the current President Bush was elected. However, those papers were not released because the current Bush Administration undertook a review of the policy shortly after Bush was elected. As a result, 68,000 pages of communications between President Reagan and his advisers were withheld even though officials at the National Archives, including the Reagan Library, wanted them made public. The White House defended the decision, saying that premature disclosure of confidential decision memos could stifle candid conversations among presidential advisers and the President. * * *

Finally, and remarkably, in 2002, the National Zoo in Washington, D.C., denied The Washington Post access to the medical records of a giraffe that had died, on the grounds that disclosure would violate the dead animal's privacy rights. Zoo Director Lucy Spelman told The Post that "privacy rules that apply to human medical records, and the physician-patient relationship, do not apply in precisely the same way to animal medicine at a public institution like the National Zoo. But we believe they do in principle."

NOTE: PRESIDENT BARACK OBAMA RESETS POLICY

On January 21, 2009, soon after he took office, President Obama ordered all covered federal agencies to adopt a "presumption" toward disclosure when responding to FIOA requests. According to the White House: "A democracy requires accountability, and accountability requires transparency."

b. FOIA Exemption 1: "National Security"—Access to Information About Use of USA Patriot Act Powers

ACLU v. UNITED STATES DOJ

321 F. Supp. 2d 24 (D.D.C. 2004).

JUDGE ELLEN SEGAL HUVELLE

This lawsuit represents plaintiffs' second attempt to obtain information under the Freedom of Information Act, 5 U.S.C. § 552 ("FOIA"), regarding the Department of Justice's (DOJ) use of the USA Patriot Act. Plaintiffs' first request concerned the number of times DOJ had used various surveillance and investigatory tools authorized by the Patriot Act, which gives federal officials greater authority to conduct surveillance within the United States to monitor the activity of foreign intelligence agents. In that case, the Court granted summary judgment to the government, upholding the government's withholding under Exemption 1 of FOIA. See ACLU v. DOJ, 265 F. Supp. 2d 20, 34 (D.D.C. 2003) ("ACLU I").

The section of the Patriot Act at issue here is section 215, which was also one of the provisions at issue in ACLU I. As explained in that case, section 215 substantially expands the powers of the FBI under the Foreign Intelligence Surveillance Act of 1978, 50 U.S.C. § 1801 et seq. ("FISA"), to "make an application for an order requiring the production of any tangible things (including books, records, papers, documents, and other items) for an investigation to obtain foreign intelligence information * * * or to protect against international terrorism or clandestine intelligence activities * * *." Patriot Act § 215, codified at 50 U.S.C. § 1861(a)(1). Before the amendment, the FBI could compel only the disclosure of certain business records (rather than "any tangible things") in the possession a "common carrier, public accommodation facility, physical storage facility, or vehicle rental facility," and could only exercise its authority when it had "specific and articulable facts giving reason to believe that the person to whom the records pertain is a foreign power or an agent of a foreign power." Pub. L. No. 105–272, 112 Stat. 2396 § 602 (Oct. 20, 1998). Now, the FBI need only specify in a FISA request that the "records concerned are sought for an authorized investigation" consistent with the purposes of *section 215.* 50 U.S.C. § 1861(b)(2).

Since its implementation, the government has provided limited information to the public regarding its use of section 215. The provision itself contains a subsection prohibiting anyone served with a section 215 order from disclosing that the FBI sought or obtained information under the provision. Id. § 1861(d). And, although the total number of secret surveillance warrants sought and issued under the Patriot Act is required to be disclosed annually, the number of applications submitted and approved under each provision is only shared with designated congressional oversight committees—in classified form. * * *

After the Court issued its opinion in ACLU I, the Attorney General, in order to address the "troubling amount of public distortion and misinformation in connection with Section 215," issued a memorandum declassifying "the number of times to date that the Department of Justice, including the Federal Bureau of Investigation (FBI), has utilized Section 215 of the USA Patriot Act relating to the production of business records. The number of times Section 215 has been used to date is zero (0)." In other words, the declassified statistic "represents the number of times a Section 215 FISA application has been approved by the FISA court and then implemented by the FBI."

The Attorney General's declassification decision prompted plaintiffs to renew their prior request, but this time focusing only on section 215. Currently, plaintiffs seek two categories of information pertaining to that provision. First, they have requested "the total number of Section 215 requests received by the FBI's National Security Law Unit" (at FBI headquarters) from FBI field offices between October 26, 2001 and February 7, 2003, and second, they seek "any and all records relating to Section 215 of the Patriot Act" on an expedited schedule. * * *

Plaintiffs have requested expedited processing of their request for "all records relating to *Section 215*." FOIA provides for expedited processing of requests for agency records, directing agencies to "process as soon as practicable any request for records to which [they have] granted expedited processing." 5 U.S.C. § 552(a)(6)(E)(iii). Expedition is available for requests "(I) in cases in which the person requesting the records demonstrates a compelling need; and (II) in other cases determined by the agency." Id. § 552(a)(6)(E)(i). * * *

[T]he record before the Court indicates that skepticism regarding government integrity with respect to the Patriot Act has not subsided since plaintiffs' first Patriot Act FOIA request. Therefore, the Court finds the government's decision to be unreasonable and orders expedited processing of plaintiffs' FOIA request. * * *

[P]laintiffs' claim for the information * * * still must overcome the formidable hurdle erected by Exemption 1, FOIA's national security exemption. The law relating to this exemption was set forth in this Court's prior opinion (see ACLU I, 265 F. Supp. 2d at 27–28) and need not be repeated here * * *. In ACLU I, the government successfully argued that the "Section 215 List" falls within Executive Order 12,958 and was properly classified because it contains information related to "intelligence activities * * *, sources or methods" that, if disclosed, " 'reasonably could be expected to result in damage to national security.' " 265 F. Supp. 2d at 28 (quoting Exec. Order No. 12,958 §§ 1.2, 1.5). There, the Court found that the government had satisfactorily explained that revealing information regarding the focus of the FBI's counterintelligence efforts could enable our adversaries to avoid or defeat such efforts, and in particular with respect to section 215, that "disclosing the number of FISA applications made for the production of tangible things could enable adversaries to discern whether and to what extent business records and other items in the possession of third parties offered a safe harbor from the FBI." Id. (citing Decl. of James A. Baker P17). Thus, the issue now before the Court is whether the Attorney General's September 2003 decision to declassify the number of section 215 applications granted by the FISA court means that the information that plaintiffs seek can no longer be withheld under Exemption 1.

While the resolution of this issue is hardly free from doubt, the Court will uphold the government's claim of exemption because it is mindful of the "long-recognized deference to the executive on national security issues," and the need to accord "substantial weight" to an agency's affidavit attesting to the classified status of documents implicating security issues. * * *

[I]t is not a question of whether the Court agrees with the defendant's assessment of the danger, but rather, "whether on the whole record the Agency's judgment objectively survives the test of reasonableness, good faith, specificity, and plausibility in this field of foreign intelligence in which the [agency] is expert and given by Congress a special role." *Gardels v. CIA*, 223 U.S. App. D.C. 88, 689 F.2d 1100, 1105 (D.C. Cir. 1982). The declarations of David M. Hardy, the Section Chief of the FBI's Record/Information Dissemination Section, satisfy this standard. They describe how the release of the number of section 215 field office requests poses the continuing potential to "harm our national security by enabling our adversaries to conduct their intelligence or international terrorist activities more securely." * * *

This Circuit's law constrains the Court to conclude that the government's explanation is sufficiently detailed and persuasive to justify the continued withholding under Exemption 1 of the number of section 215 applications submitted by FBI field offices.

c. FOIA Exemption 2: Internal Agency Records

MILNER v. DEPARTMENT OF NAVY

575 F.3d 959 (2009), cert. granted, 130 S.Ct. 3505 (2010).

This appeal highlights the tension between the public's right of access to government files under the Freedom of Information Act and the countervailing need to preserve sensitive information for efficient and effective government operations. Glen Scott Milner appeals the denial of a request he filed pursuant to the Freedom of Information Act ("FOIA"), 5 U.S.C. § 552. He sought information that would identify the locations and potential blast ranges of explosive ordnance stored at Washington's Naval Magazine Indian Island ("NMII"). The district court granted summary judgment in favor of the Navy. We have jurisdiction under 28 U.S.C. § 1291, and we affirm.

I

Indian Island is a small island strategically located in Puget Sound near the towns of Port Hadlock and Port Townsend, Washington. The island is used to store and transship munitions, weapons, weapon components, and explosives for the Navy, U.S. Joint Forces, Department of Homeland Security, and other federal agencies and allied forces. The Navy is responsible for all operations on NMII.

Magazine management and safety operations are conducted pursuant to a Navy manual entitled *Ammunition and Explosives Ashore Safety Regulations for Handling, Storing, and Production Renovation and Shipping* ("OP–5 manual"). Though the Navy considers the OP–5 manual to be restricted information, Milner managed to purchase one section of the manual on the Internet. * * *

The OP–5 manual also calls for development of technical drawings and specifications, which "should be consulted for additional, detailed requirements."

The technical information developed pursuant to the OP–5 manual includes Explosive Safety Quantity Distance ("ESQD") data. The ESQD calculations measure the effects of an explosion at a particular location. The information is expressed either as a mathematical formula or as an arc map, where the center of the arc is the source of an explosion and the arc's periphery is the maximum area over which the force of the explosion would reach. The Navy uses this information to design and construct NMII ammunition storage facilities in compliance with the safety guidelines spelled out in OP–5. The ESQD arcs indicate the maximum amounts of explosives that should be stored in any one storage facility, and minimum distances that various explosives should be stored from one another. This aids the Navy in storing ordnance in such a way that the risk of chain reactions, or "sympathetic detonations," is minimized if one storage facility suffers an attack or accident. The ESQD arcs are "designed to be a long term planning tool for the Navy."

Milner is a Puget Sound resident and a member of the Ground Zero Center for Nonviolent Action, an organization dedicated to raising community awareness of the dangers of the Navy's activities. On December 7, 2003, and January 29, 2004, he submitted two FOIA requests to the Navy. He requested three types of documents:

1. [A]ll documents on file regarding [ESQD] arcs or explosive handling zones at the ammunition depot at Indian Island. This would include all documents showing impacts or potential impacts of activities in the explosive handling zones to the ammunition depot and the surrounding areas;

2. [A]ll maps and diagrams of the ammunition depot at Indian Island which show ESQD arcs or explosive handling zones; and

3. [D]ocuments regarding any safety instructions or operating procedures for Navy or civilian maritime traffic within or near the explo-

sive handling zones or ESQD arcs at the ammunition depot at Indian Island.

The Navy identified 17 document packages totaling about 1,000 pages that met these parameters. The Navy compiled a thorough index of the relevant documents and disclosed most of them to Milner. It withheld only 81 documents, claiming that their disclosure could threaten the security of NMII and the surrounding community.

* * *

FOIA reflects "a general philosophy of full agency disclosure unless information is exempted under clearly delineated statutory language." *Dep't of the Air Force v. Rose,* 425 U.S. 352, 360–61, 96 S.Ct. 1592, 48 L.Ed.2d 11 (1976) (quoting S.Rep. No. 813–89, at 3 (1965)). An agency may withhold a document, or portions thereof, only if the material falls into one of the nine statutory exemptions delineated by Congress in § 552(b). *Id.* at 361, 96 S.Ct. 1592. These nine exemptions are "explicitly exclusive." *U.S. Dep't of Justice v. Tax Analysts,* 492 U.S. 136, 151, 109 S.Ct. 2841, 106 L.Ed.2d 112 (1989) (quoting *Adm'r FAA v. Robertson,* 422 U.S. 255, 262, 95 S.Ct. 2140, 45 L.Ed.2d 164 (1975)). The delineated exemptions "are to be interpreted narrowly." *Lahr v. NTSB,* 569 F.3d 964, 973 (9th Cir.2009) (quotation omitted).

Our concern in this case is the scope of Exemption 2. That section exempts from disclosure matters that are "related solely to the internal personnel rules and practices of an agency." 5 U.S.C. § 552(b)(2). There are two categories of information that may fall within Exemption 2's ambit—"Low 2" and "High 2." Low 2 materials include rules and practices regarding mundane employment matters such as parking facilities, lunch hours, and sick leave, which are not of "genuine and significant public interest." *See Rose,* 425 U.S. at 363, 96 S.Ct. 1592 (citing S.Rep. No. 813–89, at 8 (1965)); *id.* at 369, 96 S.Ct. 1592; *Hardy v. Bureau of Alcohol, Tobacco & Firearms,* 631 F.2d 653, 655 (9th Cir.1980).

The High 2 exemption protects more sensitive government information. This category applies to "internal personnel rules and practices," disclosure of which "may risk circumvention of agency regulation." *Rose,* 425 U.S. at 369, 96 S.Ct. 1592; *see, e.g., Schiller v. NLRB,* 964 F.2d 1205, 1208 (D.C.Cir.1992) (holding an agency's litigation strategy "does qualify as 'high 2' material because its disclosure would risk circumvention of statutes or agency regulations"). Only the High 2 category is at issue here.

* * *

Information may be exempted as High 2 if it (1) fits within the statutory language and (2) would present a risk of circumvention if disclosed. *See Morley v. CIA,* 508 F.3d 1108, 1124 (D.C.Cir.2007) (citing *Schwaner v. Dep't of Air Force,* 898 F.2d 793, 794 (D.C.Cir.1990)). The essential question in this case is what standard we employ to determine whether the requested information relates sufficiently to the "internal personnel rules and practices" of the agency, as required by the statute.

The Navy argues we should apply the "predominantly internal" standard employed by the D.C. Circuit. Milner argues our prior caselaw forecloses this approach, and that our inquiry is limited to whether the information at issue is "law enforcement material." * * *

We adopt the "predominantly internal" standard for several reasons. First, limiting Exemption 2 to "law enforcement" materials has no basis in either Supreme Court precedent or the statute. The Supreme Court in *Rose* does not use the phrase except in a footnote relating to a different FOIA exemption. Nor does the phrase "law enforcement" appear in the text of § 552(b)(2), which exempts matters "related solely to the internal personnel rules and practices of an agency." A proper standard would combine Congress's requirement that the material be related to "internal personnel rules and practices" and the Supreme Court's focus on the risk of circumvention of the law. *Crooker*'s standard properly reflects both.

As a matter of statutory interpretation, a definition of "internal personnel rules and practices" that rests solely on whether the information is "law enforcement" material makes little sense in light of the entire list of FOIA exemptions. "Under accepted canons of statutory interpretation, we must interpret statutes as a whole, giving effect to each word and making every effort not to interpret a provision in a manner that renders other provisions of the same statute inconsistent, meaningless or superfluous." *Boise Cascade Corp. v. EPA,* 942 F.2d 1427, 1432 (9th Cir.1991).

First, other provisions of FOIA indicate Congress was concerned with the disclosure of sensitive materials. Such materials will usually be, by their nature, predominantly internal. Exemption 1 covers information with a particular legal status—classified information. 5 U.S.C. § 552(b)(1). Exemptions 7(e) and (f) exempt law enforcement materials that, if disclosed, would risk circumvention of the law or place individuals in danger. *Id.* § 552(b)(7). These exemptions reflect a concern that much of an agency's internal information could be used by individuals with ill intent. It would be incongruent if FOIA protected sensitive information when it is contained in a classified or law enforcement document, but not when it is contained in a document developed predominantly for use by agency personnel. *Cf. Crooker,* 670 F.2d at 1065 ("It would be inconsistent to no small degree to hold that Exemption 2 would not bar the disclosure of investigatory techniques when contained in a manual restricted to internal use, but that Exemption 7(E) would exempt the release of such techniques if contained in an 'investigatory record.' ").

Second, Exemption 7 protects "records or information compiled for law enforcement purposes." 5 U.S.C. § 552(b)(7). If Exemption 2 also covers *only* "law enforcement" materials, Exemption 7 is redundant. *See, e.g., Gordon v. FBI,* 388 F.Supp.2d 1028, 1036 (N.D.Cal.2005) (discussing Exemptions 2 and 7 together, applying the same standards and reasoning to both). Moreover, Exemption 7 contains meaningful limitations on the use of law enforcement materials which are not present in Exemption 2. Exemption 7 protects "records or information compiled for law enforcement purposes," but only in certain situations, such as when disclosure would be expected to interfere with enforcement proceedings, deprive someone of a fair trial, or expose a confidential source. 5 U.S.C. § 552(b)(7). Applying a general "law enforcement materials" test under Exemption 2 renders meaningless the conditions that Congress has placed on non-disclosure of law enforcement materials under Exemption 7.

* * *

Finally, we note two practical considerations that favor adoption of the "predominantly internal" test. First, narrowing Exemption 2 to only "law enforcement" materials forces our courts to strain the term "law enforcement." * * *

Our second practical concern stems from a preference for national uniformity. *Crooker* has become the authoritative case on Exemption 2. It presents an extraordinarily comprehensive analysis of the statutory language, legislative history, and caselaw. At least four of our sister circuits have adopted or relied on *Crooker. See Abraham & Rose, PLC v. United States,* 138 F.3d 1075, 1080 (6th Cir.1998); *Audubon Soc.,* 104 F.3d at 1204; *Massey v. FBI,* 3 F.3d 620, 622 (2d Cir.1993); *Kaganove,* 856 F.2d at 889. Bringing our circuit into alignment with the D.C. Circuit would create a more uniform standard for national agencies like the U.S. Navy. It would also allow our district courts to seek guidance from the D.C. Circuit's extensive case law in applying Exemption 2, in the absence of authoritative Ninth Circuit or Supreme Court rulings. * * *

In conclusion, we reiterate our approach to Exemption 2. First, the material withheld must fall within the terms of the statutory language. To determine whether a personnel document falls within the statutory language, we inquire whether it is "predominantly internal." Law enforcement material * * * qualifies as predominantly internal, but it is not the only category of materials that may meet this test. Second, if the material is predominantly internal, the agency may defeat disclosure by proving that disclosure may risk circumvention of the law. The ESQD arcs requested here are predominantly internal personnel materials, and if disclosed would present a serious risk of circumvention of the law. The district court properly ruled that the information sought is exempt from FOIA disclosure.

d. FOIA Exemption 4: "Trade Secrets and Commercial or Financial Information"—Corporate "Reverse FOIA" Actions—"Virtual Representation" in FOIA Cases

CHRYSLER CORP. v. BROWN
441 U.S. 281 (1979).

MR. JUSTICE REHNQUIST delivered the opinion of the Court. * * *

This case belongs to a class that has been popularly denominated "reverse-FOIA" suits. The Chrysler Corp. (hereinafter Chrysler) seeks to enjoin agency disclosure on the grounds that it is inconsistent with the FOIA [and other laws]. * * *

The Defense Logistics Agency (DLA) (formerly the Defense Supply Agency) of the Department of Defense is the designated compliance agency responsible for monitoring Chrysler's employment practices. * * *

This controversy began on May 14, 1975, when the DLA informed Chrysler that third parties had made an FOIA request for disclosure of the 1974 AAP [affirmative action plan] for Chrysler's Newark, Del., assembly plant and an October 1974 CIR for the same facility. Nine days later, Chrysler objected to release of the requested information, relying on OFCCP's disclosure regulations and on exemptions to the FOIA. Chrysler also requested a copy of the CIR, since it had never seen it. DLA responded the following week that it had determined that the requested material was subject to disclosure under the FOIA and the OFCCP disclosure rules, and that both documents would be released five days later.

On the day the documents were to be released, Chrysler filed a complaint in the United States District Court for Delaware seeking to enjoin release of the Newark documents. The District Court granted a temporary restraining order barring disclosure of the Newark documents and requiring that DLA give five days' notice to Chrysler before releasing any similar documents. Pursuant to this order, Chrysler was informed on July 1, 1975, that DLA had received a similar request for information about Chrysler's Hamtramck, Mich., plant. Chrysler amended its complaint and obtained a restraining order with regard to the Hamtramck disclosure as well. * * *

We have decided a number of FOIA cases in the last few years. Although we have not had to face squarely the question whether the FOIA ex proprio vigore forbids governmental agencies from disclosing certain classes of information to the public, we have in the course of at least one opinion intimated an answer. We have, moreover, consistently recognized that the basic objective of the Act is disclosure.

In contending that the FOIA bars disclosure of the requested equal employment opportunity information, Chrysler relies on the Act's nine exemptions and argues that they require an agency to withhold exempted material. In this case it relies specifically on Exemption 4: "(b) [FOIA] does not apply to matters that are—* * * trade secrets and commercial or financial information obtained from a person and privileged or confidential * * *."

Chrysler contends that the nine exemptions in general, and Exemption 4 in particular, reflect a sensitivity to the privacy interests of private individuals and nongovernmental entities. That contention may be conceded without inexorably requiring the conclusion that the exemptions impose affirmative duties on an agency to withhold information sought. In fact, that conclusion is not supported by the language, logic, or history of the Act. * * *

We therefore conclude that Congress did not limit an agency's discretion to disclose information when it enacted the FOIA. It necessarily follows that the Act does not afford Chrysler any right to enjoin agency disclosure. * * *

TAYLOR v. STURGELL
553 U.S. 880 (2008).

GINSBRUG, J.

The virtual representation question we examine in this opinion arises in the following context. Petitioner Brent Taylor filed a lawsuit under the Freedom of Information Act seeking certain documents from the Federal Aviation Administration. Greg Herrick, Taylor's friend, had previously brought an unsuccessful suit seeking the same records. The two men have no legal relationship, and there is no evidence that Taylor controlled, financed, participated in, or even had notice of Herrick's earlier suit. Nevertheless, the D.C. Circuit held Taylor's suit precluded by the judgment against Herrick because, in that court's assessment, Herrick qualified as Taylor's "virtual representative."

We disapprove the doctrine of preclusion by "virtual representation," and hold, based on the record as it now stands, that the judgment against Herrick does not bar Taylor from maintaining this suit. * * *

The Freedom of Information Act (FOIA) accords "any person" a right to request any records held by a federal agency. 5 U.S.C. § 552(a)(3)(A) (2006 ed.). No reason need be given for a FOIA request, and unless the requested materials fall within one of the Act's enumerated exemptions, see § 552(a)(3)(E), (b), the agency must "make the records promptly available" to the requester, § 552(a)(3)(A). If an agency refuses to furnish the requested records, the requester may file suit in federal court and obtain an injunction "order[ing] the production of any agency records improperly withheld." § 552(a)(4)(B).

The courts below held the instant FOIA suit barred by the judgment in earlier litigation seeking the same records. Because the lower courts' decisions turned on the connection between the two lawsuits, we begin with a full account of each action.

A

The first suit was filed by Greg Herrick, an antique aircraft enthusiast and the owner of an F–45 airplane, a vintage model manufactured by the Fairchild Engine and Airplane Corporation (FEAC) in the 1930's. In 1997, seeking information that would help him restore his plane to its original condition, Herrick filed a FOIA request asking the Federal Aviation Administration (FAA) for copies of any technical documents about the F–45 contained in the agency's records.

To gain a certificate authorizing the manufacture and sale of the F–45, FEAC had submitted to the FAA's predecessor, the Civil Aeronautics

Authority, detailed specifications and other technical data about the plane. Hundreds of pages of documents produced by FEAC in the certification process remain in the FAA's records. The FAA denied Herrick's request, however, upon finding that the documents he sought are subject to FOIA's exemption for "trade secrets and commercial or financial information obtained from a person and privileged or confidential," § 552(b)(4). In an administrative appeal, Herrick urged that FEAC and its successors had waived any trade-secret protection. The FAA thereupon contacted FEAC's corporate successor, respondent Fairchild Corporation (Fairchild). Because Fairchild objected to release of the documents, the agency adhered to its original decision.

Herrick then filed suit in the U.S. District Court for the District of Wyoming. Challenging the FAA's invocation of the trade-secret exemption, Herrick placed heavy weight on a 1955 letter from FEAC to the Civil Aeronautics Authority. The letter authorized the agency to lend any documents in its files to the public "for use in making repairs or replacement parts for aircraft produced by Fairchild." *Herrick v. Garvey,* 298 F.3d 1184, 1193 (C.A.10 2002) (internal quotation marks omitted). This broad authorization, Herrick maintained, showed that the F–45 certification records held by the FAA could not be regarded as "secre[t]" or "confidential" within the meaning of § 552(b)(4).

Rejecting Herrick's argument, the District Court granted summary judgment to the FAA. *Herrick v. Garvey,* 200 F.Supp.2d 1321, 1328–1329 (D.Wyo.2000). The 1955 letter, the court reasoned, did not deprive the F–45 certification documents of trade-secret status, for those documents were never in fact released pursuant to the letter's blanket authorization. See *id.,* at 1329. The court also stated that even if the 1955 letter had waived trade-secret protection, Fairchild had successfully "reversed" the waiver by objecting to the FAA's release of the records to Herrick. *Ibid.*

On appeal, the Tenth Circuit agreed with Herrick that the 1955 letter had stripped the requested documents of trade-secret protection. See *Herrick,* 298 F.3d, at 1194. But the Court of Appeals upheld the District Court's alternative determination—*i.e.,* that Fairchild had restored trade-secret status by objecting to Herrick's FOIA request. *Id.,* at 1195. On that ground, the appeals court affirmed the entry of summary judgment for the FAA.

In so ruling, the Tenth Circuit noted that Herrick had failed to challenge two suppositions underlying the District Court's decision. First, the District Court assumed trade-secret status could be "restored" to documents that had lost protection. *Id.,* at 1194, n. 10. Second, the District Court also assumed that Fairchild had regained trade-secret status for the documents even though the company claimed that status only "*after* Herrick had initiated his request" for the F–45 records. *Ibid.* The Court of Appeals expressed no opinion on the validity of these suppositions. See *id.,* at 1194–1195, n. 10.

B

The Tenth Circuit's decision issued on July 24, 2002. Less than a month later, on August 22, petitioner Brent Taylor—a friend of Herrick's and an antique aircraft enthusiast in his own right—submitted a FOIA request seeking the same documents Herrick had unsuccessfully sued to obtain. When the FAA failed to respond, Taylor filed a complaint in the U.S. District Court for the District of Columbia. Like Herrick, Taylor argued that FEAC's 1955 letter had stripped the records of their trade-secret status. But Taylor also sought to litigate the two issues concerning recapture of protected status that Herrick had failed to raise in his appeal to the Tenth Circuit.

After Fairchild intervened as a defendant, the District Court in D.C. concluded that Taylor's suit was barred by claim preclusion; accordingly, it granted summary judgment to Fairchild and the FAA. The court acknowledged that Taylor was not a party to Herrick's suit. Relying on the Eighth Circuit's decision in *Tyus v. Schoemehl,* 93 F.3d 449 (1996), however, it held that a nonparty may be bound by a judgment if she was "virtually represented" by a party. App. to Pet. for Cert. 30a–31a.

* * *

[First, our] decisions emphasize the fundamental nature of the general rule that a litigant is not bound by a judgment to which she was not a party. See, *e.g., Richards,* 517 U.S., at 798–799, 116 S.Ct. 1761; *Martin,* 490 U.S., at 761–762, 109 S.Ct. 2180. Accordingly, we have endeavored to delineate discrete exceptions that apply in "limited circumstances." *Id.,* at 762, n. 2, 109 S.Ct. 2180. * * *

[Second, an] expansive doctrine of virtual representation * * * would "recogniz[e], in effect, a common-law kind of class action." * * * That is, virtual representation would authorize preclusion based on identity of interests and some kind of relationship between parties and nonparties, shorn of the procedural protections prescribed in [case law and federal rules of procedure]. These protections, grounded in due process, could be circumvented were we to approve a virtual representation doctrine that allowed courts to "create *de facto* class actions at will."

Third, a diffuse balancing approach to nonparty preclusion would likely create more headaches than it relieves. Most obviously, it could significantly complicate the task of district courts faced in the first instance with preclusion questions. An all-things-considered balancing approach might spark wide-ranging, time-consuming, and expensive discovery tracking factors potentially relevant under seven-or five-prong tests. And after the relevant facts are established, district judges would be called upon to evaluate them under a standard that provides no firm guidance. * * * Preclusion doctrine, it should be recalled, is intended to reduce the burden of litigation on courts and parties. Cf. *Montana,* 440 U.S., at 153–154, 99 S.Ct. 970. "In this area of the law," we agree, " 'crisp rules with sharp corners' are preferable to a round-about doctrine of opaque standards." *Bittinger v. Tecumseh Products Co.*, 123 F.3d 877, 881 (C.A.6 1997).

C

Finally, relying on the Eighth Circuit's decision in *Tyus*, 93 F.3d, at 456, the FAA maintains that nonparty preclusion should apply more broadly in "public law" litigation than in "private law" controversies. * * *

The Act, however, instructs agencies receiving FOIA requests to make the information available not to the public at large, but rather to the "person" making the request. § 552(a)(3)(A). * * * Thus, * * * a successful FOIA action results in a grant of relief to the individual plaintiff, not a decree benefiting the public at large. * * *

The FAA next argues that "the threat of vexatious litigation is heightened" in public-law cases because "the number of plaintiffs with standing is potentially limitless." * * * Thus it is theoretically possible that several persons could coordinate to mount a series of repetitive lawsuits.

But we are not convinced that this risk justifies departure from the usual rules governing nonparty preclusion. First, *stare decisis* will allow courts swiftly to dispose of repetitive suits brought in the same circuit. Second, even when *stare decisis* is not dispositive, "the human tendency not to waste money will deter the bringing of suits based on claims or issues that have already been adversely determined against others." * * * This intuition seems to be borne out by experience: The FAA has not called our attention to any instances of abusive FOIA suits in the Circuits that reject the virtual representation theory respondents advocate here.

* * *

For the foregoing reasons, we disapprove the theory of virtual representation on which the decision below rested.

PUBLIC INTEREST FOIA LITIGATION: ELECTRONIC PRIVACY INFORMATION CENTER BODY SCANNER LITIGATION

Epic.org, last visited August 4, 2010.

On July 20, 2010, the Department of Homeland Security announced a substantial change in the deployment of body scanners in US airports. According to the DHS Secretrary, the devices, which had once been part of a pilot program for secondary screening, will now be deployed in 28 additional airports. The devices are designed to capture and store photographic images of naked air travelers. EPIC has filed an emergency motion in federal court, urging the suspension of the program and citing violations of several federal statutes and the Fourth Amendment.

* * *

EPIC filed a Freedom of Information Act (FOIA) request with the United States Marshals Service, a component of the Department of Justice, to obtain information about the agency's use of full body scanners for courthouse security. EPIC pursued the case in federal court, and has obtained acknowledgement by the agency that a single machine has stored "approximately 35,314 images" of the full body scans of courthouse visitors over a six month period. EPIC also obtained a representative sample of the images stored by the devices.

* * *

In an open government lawsuit against the United States Marshals Service, EPIC has obtained more than one hundred images of undressed individuals entering federal courthouses. The images, which are routinely captured by the federal agency, prove that body scanning devices store and record images of individuals stripped naked. The 100 images are a small sample of more than 35,000 at issue in the EPIC lawsuit. EPIC has also filed suit to stop the deployment of the machines in US airports.

e. FOIA Exemption 6: "Personnel, Medical or Similar Files"—Winemakers and Passport Records

WINE HOBBY v. U.S. INTERNAL REVENUE SERVICE

502 F.2d 133 (3d Cir. 1974).

ROSENN, CIRCUIT JUDGE

This appeal requires us to consider the "invasion of privacy" exemption to the Freedom of Information Act, 5 U.S.C. § 552. Plaintiff, Wine Hobby USA, Inc. (Wine Hobby), a Pennsylvania corporation, brought suit to obtain the names and addresses of all persons who have registered with the United States Bureau of Alcohol, Tobacco and Firearms to produce wine for family use in the Mid–Atlantic region. * * *

Wine Hobby is engaged in the business of selling and distributing amateur winemaking equipment and supplies to amateur winemakers through franchises, wholly owned retail stores, and by mail order. Wine Hobby has stipulated in the district court that its purpose in obtaining the names and addresses of the * * * registrants is "to enable plaintiff to forward catalogues and other announcements to these persons regarding equipment and supplies that the plaintiff offers for sale."

We begin with the recognition that the Freedom of Information Act, enacted to remedy the inadequacies of its predecessor, section 3 of the Administrative Procedure Act, 5 U.S.C. § 1002 (1964): "is broadly conceived. It seeks to permit access to official information long shielded unnecessarily from public view and attempts to create a judicially enforceable public right to secure such information from possibly unwilling official hands." * * *

The Government relies on Exemption (6) as the basis for refusing to supply the information requested by Wine Hobby. The district court reluctantly concluded that despite the potential for abuse, the names and addresses sought here were not subject to this exemption as an invasion of privacy. The court also held that it had no power to exercise its equitable discretion to withhold and no alternative but to grant the request. We hold that the names and addresses sought are within the exemption and we therefore reverse.

To qualify under Exemption (6), the requested information must consist of "personnel, medical or similar files," and the disclosure of the material must constitute a "clearly unwarranted invasion of personal privacy."

We believe that the list of names and addresses is a "file" within the meaning of Exemption (6). A broad interpretation of the statutory term to include names and addresses is necessary to avoid a denial of statutory protection in a case where release of requested materials would result in a clearly unwarranted invasion of personal privacy. Since the thrust of the exemption is to avoid unwarranted invasions of privacy, the term "files" should not be given an interpretation that would often preclude inquiry into this more crucial question.

Furthermore, we believe the list of names and addresses is a file "similar" to the personnel and medical files specifically referred to in the exemption. The common denominator in "personnel and medical and similar files" is the personal quality of information in the file, the disclosure of which may constitute a clearly unwarranted invasion of personal privacy. We do not believe that the use of the term "similar" was intended to narrow the exemption from disclosure and permit the release of files which would otherwise be exempt because of the resultant invasion of privacy.

We now turn to the Government's contention that disclosure of the names and addresses to Wine Hobby would result in a "clearly unwarranted invasion of personal privacy." Because of an apparent conflict in the circuits, we must first consider whether the statutory language, which clearly demands an examination of the invasion of privacy, also requires inquiry into the interest in disclosure.

Our examination of the statute and its legislative history leads us to conclude, in the language of the District of Columbia Circuit, that "Exemption (6) necessarily requires the court to balance a public interest purpose for disclosure of personal information against the potential invasion of individual privacy." Getman v. N.L.R.B., 450 F.2d at 677 n. 24 (1971). On its face, the statute, by the use of term "unwarranted," compels a balancing of interests. * * *

Disclosure of the requested lists would involve a release of each registrant's home address, information that the individual may fervently wish to remain confidential or only selectively released. One consequence of this disclosure is that a registrant will be subjected to unsolicited and possibly unwanted mail from Wine Hobby and perhaps offensive mail from others. Moreover, information concerning personal activities within the home, namely wine-making, is revealed by disclosure. Similarly, disclosure reveals information concerning the family status of the registrant, including the fact that he is not living alone and that he exercises family control or responsibility in the household. Disclosure of these facts concerning the home and private activities within it constitutes an "invasion of personal privacy."

We must now balance the seriousness of this invasion of privacy against the public interest purpose asserted by the plaintiff. As noted, the sole purpose for which Wine Hobby has stipulated that it seeks the information is for private commercial exploitation. Wine Hobby advanced no direct or indirect public interest purpose in disclosure of these lists and indeed, we can conceive of none. The disclosure of names of potential customers for commercial business is wholly unrelated to the purposes behind the Freedom of Information Act and was never contemplated by Congress in enacting the Act. In light of this failure by Wine Hobby to assert a public interest purpose for disclosure, we conclude that the invasion of privacy caused by disclosure would be "clearly unwarranted," even though the invasion of privacy in this case is not as serious as that considered by the court in other cases. On balance, therefore, we believe that the list of names and addresses of the Form 1541 registrants is exempted from disclosure under § 552(b)(6) in the circumstances of this case.

U.S. DEP'T OF STATE v. WASHINGTON POST CO.

456 U.S. 595 (1982).

JUSTICE REHNQUIST delivered the opinion of the Court.

In September 1979, respondent Washington Post Co. filed a request under the Freedom of Information Act (FOIA), 5 U.S.C. § 552, requesting certain documents from petitioner United States Department of State. The subject of the request was defined as "documents indicating whether Dr. Ali Behzadnia and Dr. Ibrahim Yazdi * * * hold valid U.S. passports." The request indicated that respondent would "accept any record held by the Passport Office indicating whether either of these persons is an American citizen." Ibid. At the time of the request, both Behzadnia and Yazdi were Iranian nationals living in Iran.

The State Department denied respondent's request the following month, stating that release of the requested information "would be 'a clearly unwarranted invasion of [the] personal privacy' of these persons," and therefore was exempt from disclosure under Exemption 6 of the FOIA. Denial of respondent's request was affirmed on appeal by the Department's Council on Classification Policy, which concluded that "the privacy interests to be protected are not incidental ones, but rather are such that they clearly outweigh any public interests which might be served by release of the requested information." * * *

The language of Exemption 6 sheds little light on what Congress meant by "similar files." Fortunately, the legislative history is somewhat more illuminating. The House and Senate Reports, although not defining the phrase "similar files," suggest that Congress' primary purpose in enacting Exemption 6 was to protect individuals from the injury and embarrassment that can result from the unnecessary disclosure of personal information. * * *

Respondent relies upon passing references in the legislative history to argue that the phrase "similar files" does not include all files which contain information about particular individuals, but instead is limited to files containing "intimate details" and "highly personal" information. We disagree. Passing references and isolated phrases are not controlling when analyzing a legislative history. * * *

A proper analysis of the exemption must also take into account the fact that "personnel and medical files," the two benchmarks for measuring the term "similar files," are likely to contain much information about a particular individual that is not intimate. Information such as place of birth, date of birth, date of marriage, employment history, and comparable data is not normally regarded as highly personal, and yet respondent does not disagree that such information, if contained in a "personnel" or "medical" file, would be exempt from any disclosure that would constitute a clearly unwarranted invasion of personal privacy. The passport information here requested, if it exists, presumably would be found in files containing much of the same kind of information. Such files would contain at least the information that normally is required from a passport applicant. *See* 22 U.S.C. § 213. It strains the normal meaning of the word to say that such files are not "similar" to personnel or medical files. * * *

In sum, we do not think that Congress meant to limit Exemption 6 to a narrow class of files containing only a discrete kind of personal information. Rather, "[the] exemption [was] intended to cover detailed Government records on an individual which can be identified as applying to that individual." When disclosure of information which applies to a particular individual is sought from Government records, courts must determine whether release of the information would constitute a clearly unwarranted invasion of that person's privacy.

The citizenship information sought by respondent satisfies the "similar files" requirement of Exemption 6, and petitioners' denial of the request should have been sustained upon a showing by the Government that release of the information would constitute a clearly unwarranted invasion of personal privacy. The Court of Appeals expressly declined to consider the effect of disclosure upon the privacy interests of Behzadnia and Yazdi, and we think that such balancing should be left to the Court of Appeals or to the District Court on remand. The judgment of the Court of Appeals is reversed, and the case is remanded for further proceedings consistent with this opinion.

NOTE: GHOST DETAINEES

In *Amnesty International USA v. Central Intelligence Agency*, 2010 WL 3033822 (S.D.N.Y. 2010), the Southern District of New York denied plaintiffs' bid to compel the CIA to disclose certain records "relating to the identity of, transport and location(s) of, authority over, and treatment of all unregistered, CIA, and 'ghost' detainees interdicted, interrogated, and detained by any agency or department of the United States." *Id.* So called "ghost" detainees and prisoners are those believed to be held by the United States, but concerning whom the United States has declined to provide information to the press, civil liberties groups, or human rights groups.

The CIA produced some documents in the matter but withheld 131 documents under Exemption 6 and 61 documents under Exemption 7(C): "The CIA has withheld the names and email addresses of DOD personnel below the office-director level, or officers below the rank of Colonel; the names of OLC line attorneys, persons interviewed by the CIA OIG, and one detainee; and personal identifying information such as dates of birth, social security numbers, and biographical information."*Id.*

After weighing "the privacy concerns of the individuals whose information appears in the withheld documents against the public's interest in disclosure of alleged government misconduct," the district court found that the factors weighed in favor of nondisclosure: "It is clear from the CIA's declarations that the privacy concerns of releasing the personal information of agency employees is (sic) not overridden by any public interest in releasing the information. Plaintiffs have not provided the Court with any paramount public interest concerns, and the Court finds none after searching the record. Therefore, the Court finds that it was proper for the CIA to withhold the requested information pursuant to Exemptions 6 and 7(C)." *Id.*

f. FOIA Exemption 7: Law Enforcement Records—Access by Media to FBI "Rap Sheets"

U.S. DEP'T OF JUSTICE v. REPORTERS COMMITTEE FOR FREEDOM OF PRESS

489 U.S. 749 (1989).

JUSTICE STEVENS delivered the opinion of the Court.

The Federal Bureau of Investigation (FBI) has accumulated and maintains criminal identification records, sometimes referred to as "rap sheets," on over 24 million persons. The question presented by this case is whether the disclosure of the contents of such a file to a third party "could reasonably be expected to constitute an unwarranted invasion of personal privacy" within the meaning of the Freedom of Information Act (FOIA), 5 U.S.C. § 552(b)(7)(C) * * *.

In 1924 Congress appropriated funds to enable the Department of Justice (Department) to establish a program to collect and preserve fingerprints and other criminal identification records. That statute authorized the Department to exchange such information with "officials of

States, cities and other institutions." Ibid. Six years later Congress created the FBI's identification division, and gave it responsibility for "acquiring, collecting, classifying, and preserving criminal identification and other crime records and the exchanging of said criminal identification records with the duly authorized officials of governmental agencies, of States, cities, and penal institutions." * * * Rap sheets compiled pursuant to such authority contain certain descriptive information, such as date of birth and physical characteristics, as well as a history of arrests, charges, convictions, and incarcerations of the subject. Normally a rap sheet is preserved until its subject attains age 80. Because of the volume of rap sheets, they are sometimes incorrect or incomplete and sometimes contain information about other persons with similar names.

The local, state, and federal law enforcement agencies throughout the Nation that exchange rap-sheet data with the FBI do so on a voluntary basis. The principal use of the information is to assist in the detection and prosecution of offenders; it is also used by courts and corrections officials in connection with sentencing and parole decisions. As a matter of executive policy, the Department has generally treated rap sheets as confidential and, with certain exceptions, has restricted their use to governmental purposes. Consistent with the Department's basic policy of treating these records as confidential, Congress in 1957 amended the basic statute to provide that the FBI's exchange of rap-sheet information with any other agency is subject to cancellation "if dissemination is made outside the receiving departments or related agencies." * * *

As a matter of Department policy, the FBI has made two exceptions to its general practice of prohibiting unofficial access to rap sheets. First, it allows the subject of a rap sheet to obtain a copy, and second, it occasionally allows rap sheets to be used in the preparation of press releases and publicity designed to assist in the apprehension of wanted persons or fugitives.

In addition, on three separate occasions Congress has expressly authorized the release of rap sheets for other limited purposes. In 1972 it provided for such release to officials of federally chartered or insured banking institutions and "if authorized by State statute and approved by the Attorney General, to officials of State and local governments for purposes of employment and licensing * * *." In 1975, in an amendment to the Securities Exchange Act of 1934, Congress permitted the Attorney General to release rap sheets to self-regulatory organizations in the securities industry. * * * And finally, in 1986 Congress authorized release of criminal-history information to licensees or applicants before the Nuclear Regulatory Commission. These three targeted enactments—all adopted after the FOIA was passed in 1966—are consistent with the view that Congress understood and did not disapprove the FBI's general policy of treating rap sheets as nonpublic documents. * * *

Congress exempted nine categories of documents from the FOIA's broad disclosure requirements. Three of those exemptions are arguably relevant to this case. Exemption 3 applies to documents that are specifically exempted from disclosure by another statute. § 552(b)(3). Exemption 6 protects "personnel and medical files and similar files the disclosure of which would constitute a clearly unwarranted invasion of personal privacy." § 552(b)(6). Exemption 7(C) excludes records or information compiled for law enforcement purposes, "but only to the extent that the production of such [materials] * * * could reasonably be expected to constitute an unwarranted invasion of personal privacy." § 552(b)(7)(C). * * *

This case arises out of requests made by a CBS news correspondent and the Reporters Committee for Freedom of the Press (respondents) for information concerning the criminal records of four members of the Medico family. The Pennsylvania Crime Commission had identified the family's company, Medico Industries, as a legitimate business dominated by organized crime figures. Moreover, the company allegedly had obtained a number of defense contracts as a result of an improper arrangement with a corrupt Congressman.

The FOIA requests sought disclosure of any arrests, indictments, acquittals, convictions, and sentences of any of the four Medicos. Although the FBI originally denied the requests, it provided the requested data concerning three of the Medicos after their deaths. In their complaint in the District Court, respondents sought the rap sheet for the fourth, Charles Medico (Medico), insofar as it contained "matters of public record." App. 33. * * *

Exemption 7(C) requires us to balance the privacy interest in maintaining, as the Government puts it, the "practical obscurity" of the rap sheets against the public interest in their release.

The preliminary question is whether Medico's interest in the nondisclosure of any rap sheet the FBI might have on him is the sort of "personal privacy" interest that Congress intended Exemption 7(C) to protect. As we have pointed out before, "[t]he cases sometimes characterized as protecting 'privacy' have in fact involved at least two different kinds of interests. One is the individual interest in avoiding disclosure of personal matters, and another is the interest in independence in making certain kinds of important decisions." *Whalen v. Roe*, 429 U.S. 589, 598–600 (1977). Here, the former interest, "in avoiding disclosure of personal matters," is implicated. Because events summarized in a rap sheet have been previously disclosed to the public, respondents contend that Medico's privacy interest in avoiding disclosure of a federal compilation of these events approaches zero. We reject respondents' cramped notion of personal privacy.

To begin with, both the common law and the literal understandings of privacy encompass the individual's control of information concerning his or her person. In an organized society, there are few facts that are not at one time or another divulged to another. Thus the extent of the protection accorded a privacy right at common law rested in part on the degree of dissemination of the allegedly private fact and the extent to which the passage of time rendered it private. According to Webster's initial definition, information may be classified as "private" if it is "intended for or restricted to the use of a particular person or group or class of persons: not freely available to the public." Recognition of this attribute of a privacy interest supports the distinction, in terms of personal privacy, between scattered disclosure of the bits of information contained in a rap sheet and revelation of the rap sheet as a whole. The very fact that federal funds have been spent to prepare, index, and maintain these criminal-history files demonstrates that the individual items of information in the summaries would not otherwise be "freely available" either to the officials who have access to the underlying files or to the general public. Indeed, if the summaries were "freely available," there would be no reason to invoke the FOIA to obtain access to the information they contain. Granted, in many contexts the fact that information is not freely available is no reason to exempt that information from a statute generally requiring its dissemination. But the issue here is whether the compilation of otherwise hard-to-obtain information alters the privacy interest implicated by disclosure of that information. Plainly there is a vast difference between the public records that might be found after a diligent search of courthouse files, county archives, and local police stations throughout the country and a computerized summary located in a single clearinghouse of information. * * *

In sum, the fact that "an event is not wholly 'private' does not mean that an individual has no interest in limiting disclosure or dissemination of the information." Rehnquist, Is an Expanded Right of Privacy Consistent with Fair and Effective Law Enforcement?, Nelson Timothy Stephens Lectures, University of Kansas Law School, pt. 1, p. 13 (Sept. 26–27, 1974). The privacy interest in a rap sheet is substantial. The substantial character of that interest is affected by the fact that in today's society the computer can accumulate and store information that would otherwise have surely been forgotten long before a person attains age 80, when the FBI's rap sheets are discarded. * * *

Exemption 7(C), by its terms, permits an agency to withhold a document only when revelation "could reasonably be expected to constitute an unwarranted invasion of personal privacy." * * *

Thus whether disclosure of a private document under Exemption 7(C) is warranted must turn on the nature of the requested document and its relationship to "the basic purpose of the Freedom of Information Act 'to open agency action to the light of public scrutiny,' " rather than on the particular purpose for which the document is being requested. * * * Official information that sheds light on an agency's performance of its statutory duties falls squarely within that statutory purpose. That purpose, however, is not fostered by disclosure of information about private citizens that is accumulated in various governmental files but that reveals little or nothing about an agency's own conduct. In this case—and presumably in the typical case in which one private citizen is seeking information about another—the requester does not intend to discover anything about the conduct of the agency that has possession of the requested records. Indeed, response to this request would not shed any light on the conduct of any Government agency or official. * * *

[A] court must balance the public interest in disclosure against the interest Congress intended the Exemption to protect. Although both sides agree that such a balance must be undertaken, how such a balance should be done is in dispute. The Court of Appeals majority expressed concern about assigning federal judges the task of striking a proper case-by-case, or ad hoc, balance between individual privacy interests and the public interest in the disclosure of criminal-history information without providing those judges standards to assist in performing that task. Our cases provide support for the proposition that categorical decisions may be appropriate and individual circumstances disregarded when a case fits into a genus in which the balance characteristically tips in one direction. * * *

[W]e conclude today, upon closer inspection of Exemption 7(c), that for an appropriate class of law-enforcement records or information a categorical balance may be undertaken there as well. * * *

The privacy interest in maintaining the practical obscurity of rap-sheet information will always be high. When the subject of such a rap sheet is a private citizen and when the information is in the Government's control as a compilation, rather than as a record of "what the Government is up to," the privacy interest protected by Exemption 7(C) is in fact at its apex while the FOIA-based public interest in disclosure is at its nadir. See Parts IV and V, supra. Such a disparity on the scales of Justice holds for a class of cases without regard to individual circumstances; the standard virtues of bright-line rules are thus present, and the difficulties attendant to ad hoc adjudication may be avoided. Accordingly, we hold as a categorical matter that a third party's request for law enforcement records or information about a private citizen can reasonably be expected to invade that citizen's privacy, and that when the request seeks no "official information" about a Government agency, but merely records that the Government happens to be storing, the invasion of privacy is "unwarranted."

AT&T INC. v. FEDERAL COMMUNICATIONS COMMISSION

582 F.3d 490 (2009) cert. granted, 2010.

CHAGARES, CIRCUIT JUDGE.

The Freedom of Information Act ("FOIA"), 5 U.S.C. §§ 551–59, requires a federal agency to disclose certain documents within its possession. But FOIA exempts from mandatory disclosure "records or information compiled for law enforcement purposes * * * to the extent that the production of such law enforcement records or information * * * could reasonably be expected to constitute an unwarranted invasion of personal privacy," § 552(b)(7)(C) ("Exemption 7(C)"), and defines "person" to

"include an individual, partnership, corporation, association, or public or private organization other than an agency," § 551(2). Human beings have such "personal privacy." This case requires us to determine whether corporations do, as well.

AT&T, Inc. ("AT&T") argued that the Federal Communications Commission ("FCC") could not lawfully release documents obtained during the course of an investigation into an alleged overcharging on the ground that disclosure would likely invade the company's "personal privacy." The FCC rejected AT&T's argument and held that a corporation, as a matter of law, has no "personal privacy" in the first place. AT&T filed a petition for review. We will grant the petition and remand to the FCC for further proceedings. * * *

AT&T argues that the FCC incorrectly interpreted Exemption 7(C) when it held that a corporation lacks the "personal privacy" protected by that exemption. We agree with AT&T. * * *

The FCC's interpretation of Exemption 7(C) is not entitled to deference under *Chevron U.S.A., Inc. v. Natural Res. Def. Council, Inc.,* 467 U.S. 837, 104 S.Ct. 2778, 81 L.Ed.2d 694 (1984), because FOIA applies government-wide, and no one agency is charged with enforcing it. *ACLU v. Dep't of Def.,* 543 F.3d 59, 66 (2d Cir.2008) (declining to accord deference to Department of Defense interpretation of FOIA). Thus, we exercise plenary review of the FCC's interpretation of FOIA, and will set aside the FCC's decision if it is "arbitrary, capricious, an abuse of discretion, or otherwise not in accordance with law." *See* 5 U.S.C. § 706(2)(A). * * *

This case concerns the so-called law enforcement exemption, Exemption 7(C), which shields from mandatory disclosure "records or information compiled for law enforcement purposes, but only to the extent that the production of such law enforcement records or information * * * could reasonably be expected to constitute an unwarranted invasion of personal privacy." 5 U.S.C. § 552(b)(7)(C). FOIA's Exemption 6 also uses the phrase "personal privacy," shielding from compulsory disclosure "personnel and medical files and similar files the disclosure of which would constitute a clearly unwarranted invasion of personal privacy." § 552(b)(6). FOIA does not define "personal," but it does define "person" to "include[ ] an individual, partnership, corporation, association, or public or private organization other than an agency." § 551(2).

Neither the Supreme Court nor this Court has ever squarely rejected a proffered personal privacy interest of a corporation. The most that can be said of the Supreme Court's cases and of our cases is that they suggest that Exemptions 7(C) and 6 frequently and primarily protect—and that Congress may have intended them to protect—the privacy of individuals. *See, e.g., Reporters Comm.,* 489 U.S. at 764 n. 16, 109 S.Ct. 1468. * * *

B.

As the Supreme Court has held, a court must "begin by looking at the language of the [statute] * * *. When [the court] find[s] the terms of a statute unambiguous, judicial inquiry is complete, except 'in rare and exceptional circumstances.' " *Rubin v. United States,* 449 U.S. 424, 429–30, 101 S.Ct. 698, 66 L.Ed.2d 633 (1981) (quoting *TVA v. Hill,* 437 U.S. 153, 187 n. 33, 98 S.Ct. 2279, 57 L.Ed.2d 117 (1978) (quotation marks and citation omitted)).

AT&T argues that the plain text of Exemption 7(C) indicates that it applies to corporations. After all, "personal" is the adjectival form of "person," and FOIA defines "person" to include a corporation. We agree. It would be very odd indeed for an adjectival form of a defined term not to refer back to that defined term. See *Del. River Stevedores v. DiFidelto,* 440 F.3d 615, 623 (3d Cir.2006) (Fisher, J., concurring) (stating that it is a "grammatical imperative[ ]" that "a statute which defines a noun has thereby defined the adjectival form of that noun"). Further, FOIA's exemptions indicate that Congress knew how to refer solely to human beings (to the exclusion of corporations and other legal entities) when it wanted to. Exemption 7(F), for example, protects information gathered pursuant to a law enforcement investigation that, if released, "could reasonably be expected to endanger the life or physical safety of any *individual.*" 5 U.S.C. § 552(b)(7)(F) (emphasis added). Yet, Congress, in Exemption 7(C), did not refer to "the privacy of any individual" or some variant thereof; it used the phrase "personal privacy."

The FCC and CompTel's text-based arguments to the contrary are unconvincing. They cite Supreme Court case law for the proposition that, whenever possible, statutory words should be interpreted "in their ordinary, everyday senses." *Malat v. Riddell,* 383 U.S. 569, 571, 86 S.Ct. 1030, 16 L.Ed.2d 102 (1966). The ordinary meaning of "person" is human being, so, the argument concludes, "personal" must incorporate this ordinary meaning. This argument is unpersuasive. It fails to take into account that "person"—the root from which the statutory word at issue is derived—is a defined term. See *Biskupski v. Att'y Gen.,* 503 F.3d 274, 280 (3d Cir.2007) ("If, as here, 'a statute includes an explicit definition, we must follow that definition, even if it varies from that term's ordinary meaning.' " (quoting *Stenberg v. Carhart,* 530 U.S. 914, 942, 120 S.Ct. 2597, 147 L.Ed.2d 743 (2000))).

The FCC and CompTel next argue that FOIA's other uses of the phrase "personal privacy" indicate that the phrase does not encompass corporations. They point to Exemption 6, which shields from mandatory disclosure "personnel and medical files and similar files the disclosure of which would constitute a clearly unwarranted invasion of personal privacy," 5 U.S.C. § 552(b)(6), and observe that courts have held that this exemption applies only to individuals and not to corporations. Thus, the FCC and CompTel argue, the phrase "personal privacy" in Exemption 6 applies only to individuals, and therefore "personal privacy" in Exemption 7(C) applies only to individuals, as well. This argument is flawed. Suppose (though we express no opinion on the issue) that Exemption 6 applies only to individuals (and not to corporations). This does not mean that *each and every component phrase* in that exemption, taken on its own, limits

Exemption 6 to individuals. It means only that *some* language in that exemption does so. The phrase "personnel and medical files" serves this function. It limits Exemption 6 to individuals because only individuals (and not corporations) may be the subjects of such files. Therefore, nothing necessarily can be gleaned about the scope of "personal privacy," because Exemption 6 would apply only to individuals even if "personal privacy," taken on its own, encompasses corporations.

Thus, we hold that FOIA's text unambiguously indicates that a corporation may have a "personal privacy" interest within the meaning of Exemption 7(C). This, for us, ends the matter.

4. INTERNAL REVENUE SERVICE AND TAX RECORDS

Among the records held by federal agencies are federal income tax returns and related agency paperwork. Both the tax laws and the open records laws bear on information disclosures by the Internal Revenue Service (IRS). The two cases in this section deal with the problem of IRS agency disclosures to third parties and IRS handling of information requests submitted by tax protesters. How would you characterize the way the IRS treats taxpayers if all you knew was what could be discerned from these two cases? Rigorous or bureaucratic?

a. IRS Disclosure of Taxpayer Information to Third–Parties

PAYNE v. UNITED STATES
289 F.3d 377 (5th Cir. 2002).

KAZEN, CHIEF DISTRICT JUDGE * * *

In the fall of 1989, the Internal Revenue Service began a civil audit of 2618, Inc., a Texas corporation that operated a topless dance club under the name Caligula XXI. Jerry Payne, an attorney, became the owner of 2618, Inc. in 1988 as compensation for legal services for the then-owner, Gerhard Helmle. The IRS agent conducting the audit, Colin Levy, suspected fraud and referred the case to the IRS Criminal Investigation Division. The investigation of Payne was assigned to Special Agent Batista.

In October 1991, Batista and Levy arrived unannounced at Payne's law offices to inform Payne of the initiation of the investigation. At that time, Batista produced a summons for business and financial records associated with 2618, Inc. In response, Payne declared his willingness to cooperate fully and to provide the requested information in a timely manner. Batista was satisfied with the sincerity of Payne's stated intent to cooperate.

In December 1991, Batista began to contact third-parties seeking information regarding payments to Payne. For example, on December 19, 1991, Batista contacted the Texas Lawyers Insurance Exchange to inquire about a $36.00 payment it had made to Payne. Batista conceded that he could have obtained this information from Payne and that doing so would not have prejudiced his investigation. At trial, Batista admitted to making other third-party contacts as early as December 1991, and that he began to inquire into allegations of Payne's involvement with illegal drugs. * * *

By March of 1992, Batista apparently decided that Payne did not sincerely intend to cooperate with the investigation. * * * In any event, Batista accelerated the pace of his investigation during and after March 1992. In that month, Batista sent out ten summonses to various corporations and banks seeking bank statements, canceled checks, deposit slips and deposited items, loan applications/agreements and related records. During and after that month, Batista interviewed employees and officers of 2618, Inc. in person, introducing himself as a criminal investigator with the IRS who was investigating Payne's possible violation of criminal revenue laws. Batista asked some of the employees and some of Payne's relatives if they knew whether Payne used or sold illegal drugs. Batista contacted Payne's clients and former clients mostly by mail, issuing summonses for copies of any retainer agreements, expense reimbursement statements, or cancelled checks of payment. Batista also spoke with some of these clients over the telephone and interviewed some in person. During the course of the investigation, Batista issued a large number of summonses and letters to third-parties that disclosed on their face that Payne was under criminal investigation, and he revealed that fact during his in-person interviews.

In March of 1993, Batista terminated his investigation of Payne and recommended the case to the Justice Department for criminal prosecution. For the first time, an attorney for the Justice Department informed Payne of particular issues of concern, and in response Payne provided information that led the United States to conclude that criminal prosecution was not warranted for all the matters recommended by Batista. In 1995 Payne was indicted on two counts of violating I.R.C. § 7206 relating to tax fraud and three counts of violating I.R.C. § 7203 relating to failure to file tax returns. The trial court dismissed the § 7206 charges, and a jury acquitted Payne of the § 7203 charges.

Following the criminal trial, the IRS completed its civil examination and issued Payne a notice of deficiency for 1987 and 1988 individual income taxes and civil fraud penalties. The United States Tax Court entered a decision determining Payne's individual income tax for those years, and sustaining the fraud penalties. This court reversed. The panel found that the tax court erred in ruling that the United States had proven fraud by "clear and convincing" evidence and thus erroneously relied on the statutory fraud exception to prevail over the applicable statute of limitations.

Payne then filed this suit in the district court, seeking damages from the United States and several IRS agents for their actions in conducting the investigation. * * *

I.R.C. § 7431(a) creates a right of action against the United States if a federal employee or official knowingly or negligently violates the confidentiality provisions of § 6103. Section 6103 states in relevant part:

> Returns and return information shall be confidential, and except as authorized by [the Internal Revenue Code], no officer or employee of the United States * * * shall disclose any return or return information obtained by him in any manner in connection with his service as such an officer or an employee or otherwise under the provisions of this section.

I.R.C. § 6103(a). "Return information" is defined broadly, to include in relevant part, "a taxpayer's identity * * * [and] whether the taxpayer's return was, is being, or will be examined or subject to investigation * * *." I.R.C. § 6103(b)(2)(A). The United States concedes that Batista disclosed "return information." The United States does not incur liability for a violation of § 6103, however, if the violation "results from a good faith, but erroneous, interpretation of Section 6103." I.R.C. § 7431(b). In the case of a finding of liability, I.R.C. § 7431(c) Provides for the award of statutory or actual damages, punitive damages, and attorneys fees.

I.R.C. § 6103(k)(6) creates a safe harbor for IRS agents carrying out certain investigative duties, and allows for [certain] disclosures * * *.

As § 6103(k)(6) has been construed by case law, an IRS agent may disclose return information during an investigation in order to obtain information, provided three requirements are met: (1) the information sought is "with respect to the correct determination of tax, liability for tax, or the amount to be collected or with respect to the enforcement of any other provision of the [Internal Revenue Code]." (2) the information sought is "not otherwise reasonably available"; and (3) it is "necessary to make disclosures of return information in order to obtain the additional information sought." * * *

The United States argues that IRS special agents need never consider the taxpayer under investigation as a source from whom information is "reasonably available." Reviewing the statute and regulations promulgated under its authority, as well as the court decisions construing § 6103(k)(6), we find no convincing authority for this rigid proposition.

According to the regulations, disclosures are authorized only when the necessary information cannot be reasonably obtained in "accurate and sufficiently probative form" or in a "timely manner," and "without impairing the proper performance of * * * official duties." 26 C.F.R. § 301.6103(k)(6)–1(a) & (b). Whether a disclosure is authorized depends upon the "facts and circumstances of the particular case." Id. Rather than foreclosing the possibility that the taxpayer could ever be a source from whom necessary information may "reasonably be obtained," the regulations reflect the fact-intensive nature of the inquiry. * * *

The United States argues that it has the duty to corroborate a taxpayer's admissions and to investigate all reasonable leads to eliminate non-taxable deposits. Both of these tasks, the United States asserts, may only be accomplished through third-party contacts. To the extent that necessary evidence, corroborating or otherwise, is not reasonably available from sources provided by the taxpayer, § 6103(k)(6) obviously authorizes third-party contacts. However, even corroborating evidence might be available from bank or other records to which a taxpayer voluntarily grants access, thus negating the necessity of contacting third-parties. At any rate, in this case Batista was not merely corroborating information previously provided by Payne. Further, we find no contradiction between the need to eliminate nontaxable sources of income while still considering the taxpayer an "available source" of information, because "in the typical case, the taxpayer gives the IRS 'leads' to possible nontaxable sources."

We do not hold that the taxpayer is always such a fruitful and reliable source of information that IRS agents may never approach third-parties for necessary information. We hold only that such a determination must be made in light of the "facts and circumstances of the case," and that the taxpayer's cooperation legitimately forms part of the inquiry.

b. Request for Data by Tax Protesters

MAXWELL v. SNOW

409 F.3d 354 (DC Cir. 2005).

SENTELLE, CIRCUIT JUDGE

Appellant Lawrence S. Maxwell and approximately 562 other individuals and entities filed this action in the United States District Court for the District of Columbia seeking, inter alia, tax return information * * *. The District Court granted the government's motion to dismiss most of the claims, ruling that Appellants' requests had not complied with Freedom of Information Act ("FOIA") requirements * * *. Appellants contended that 26 U.S.C. § 6103 provides a basis to request "return information" not subject to FOIA; * * * and furthermore, that their claims were not frivolous. For the reasons more fully set forth below, we conclude that the District Court was correct and affirm its dismissal of Appellants' claims. * * *

In June of 2000, Appellant Lawrence S. Maxwell sent a ten-page letter to the National Office of the Internal Revenue Service ("IRS") Disclosure Unit seeking tax-related information for the tax years 1987–2000. He sought disclosure of at least nineteen types of information pertaining to himself including (1) "return information" as described in the Internal Revenue Code, 26 U.S.C. § 6103(b)(2), (2) records showing how his "taxable income" was determined, (3) records showing that he was given notice of a duty to file a tax, (4) records identifying him as an individual subject to taxation, (5) records indicating his citizenship and residency, purportedly because as a citizen and resident of the U.S. he would not be liable for income tax, (6) records showing that he "resided or worked within one of the specified areas of federal jurisdiction of the United

States government," purportedly because only such records would establish federal jurisdiction to tax him, and (7) records indicating the specific code sections showing him liable for a particular tax or requiring him to fill out certain forms. Maxwell cited the provisions of § 6103, relying on this Court's decision in Lake v. Rubin, 333 U.S. App. D.C. 223, 162 F.3d 113 (D.C. Cir. 1998), a case in which he was a party, for the proposition that "individuals seeking 'return information' * * * must do so pursuant to § 6103 * * * rather than the Privacy Act." Id. at 116. The other Appellants sent letters to the IRS that were identical to Maxwell's in all relevant respects. The IRS did not grant or deny the requests, but informed Appellants by letters that their "Freedom of Information/Privacy Act" requests did not comply with the "published procedures for making a request under the Privacy Act," advising them how to cure the error.

FOIA outlines procedures for agencies to make information available to the public under certain conditions. 5 U.S.C. § 552. Subsection (b)(3) provides that information need not be given out when it is specifically exempted from disclosure by another statute ("Exemption 3"). Id. § 552(b)(3). Section 6103 of the Internal Revenue Code specifically exempts tax returns from disclosure except in specified circumstances. For example, an individual may request inspection of his tax return or "return information," 26 U.S.C. § 6103(e)(1), (7) * * *. Section 6103 thus "does not supersede FOIA but rather gives rise to an exemption under Exemption 3" and FOIA procedures must still be followed in applying § 6103. Church of Scientology of California v. IRS, 253 U.S. App. D.C. 78, 792 F.2d 146, 149–50 (D.C. Cir. 1986).

Appellants disputed the IRS requirement that they must follow FOIA or Privacy Act procedures, and filed suit against the Secretary of the Treasury, seeking access to the requested information under § 6103, as well as fees, costs, and money damages. Appellants also requested declarations by the court that, among other things, Appellants are not citizens, that Texas is not a part of the United States, and that the United States itself is unconstitutional because it is not a republican form of government. The United States moved to dismiss the cases, arguing lack of subject matter jurisdiction under § 6103 and that Appellants had failed to make a proper FOIA request to exhaust their administrative remedies. Appellants responded that, under Lake, § 6103 provides jurisdiction independent of FOIA.

The District Court, * * * found that while § 6103 may supercede the Privacy Act, it does not supercede the procedural provisions in FOIA. It ruled that, while Appellants had failed to send their requests to the proper local bureau under FOIA, that error only tolled the Government's time to respond while the request was transferred to the correct bureau. It also found that the Appellants may have failed to "reasonably describe the records" sought, but that the IRS could not simply dismiss the entire request because some of the nineteen requests were incomplete or consisted of "pseudo-requests" attempting to challenge tax laws rather than seek information. It then reviewed the requests and found all to be overly broad or burdensome with the exception of the portion seeking "return information" as described in 26 U.S.C. § 6103. The District Court thus directed the IRS to process the portion of Appellants' requests for "return information" according to FOIA, granting the motion to dismiss as to the other requests. The other claims for declaratory and injunctive relief were dismissed as frivolous. Appellants filed this present appeal. * * *

Appellants first challenge the District Court's determination that their requests for "return information" under 26 U.S.C. § 6103 should be processed according to FOIA procedures. They argue that the Lake holding made § 6103 the exclusive statutory route to seek this information. They characterize the government's desire to follow FOIA procedures as a "deceptive shell game" in which the IRS throws up successive procedural barriers on shifting and "revisionist" legal theories to avoid answering Appellants' requests. Appellants also claim, without citing any support, that FOIA requirements cannot be applicable to their requests for personal information, but only to requests for public information. All of these arguments fail * * *.

The Appellants misread Lake by taking it out of the context of Circuit precedent and therefore their only legal argument is without merit. In 1986 this Court decided Church of Scientology, holding that FOIA is intended as an "across-the-board" statute covering all requests for information unless specifically exempted in a later statute. 792 F.2d at 149. Because § 6103 contains no such exemption and has no procedures or rules of its own implying an exception to FOIA, the court held that FOIA procedures apply to § 6103 requests. The Lake court decided in 1998 that 26 U.S.C. § 6103 was the proper vehicle for requesting information rather than the Privacy Act because 26 U.S.C. § 7852(e) withdrew the power of the federal courts to force the IRS to comply with the Privacy Act. It did not, as Appellants assume, make § 6103 the exclusive statute governing requests for information from the IRS, but only said that § 6103 must be used instead of the Privacy Act.

As the District Court notes, we must read Lake and Church of Scientology together and not assume with Appellants that Lake overruled Church of Scientology * * * The District Court was thus correct in holding that FOIA still applies to § 6103 claims.

5. THE FEDERAL CENSUS

NOTE: COLLECTING AND PROTECTING PERSONAL INFORMATION

Every ten years, the United States takes a population census. Although an "actual enumeration" is required by the Constitution, the 2000 census involved sophisticated statistical estimation, as well as actual head-counting.

The 2000 census was conducted by "short" and "long" questionnaires sent through the mail, and by face-to-face interviews. Each adult was asked to provide detailed information about his or her name, age, birth, race, sex, income, marital status, housing and health. Parents were asked to answer on behalf of minor children. Refusal to participate in the census was, as usual, a criminal offense.

The 2000 census was loudly criticized for requiring people to identify themselves by race and ethnicity, and for relying on population estimates. The 2000 census was also criticized for forcing people to answer detailed personal questions.

The 2010 census was no less demanding of self-classification and personal disclosure than the 2000 census. Is the modern census too invasive? Why must the census delve so deeply into personal lives? How does the government insure the confidentiality of the census data it collects? In upholding the constitutionality of the 2000 census, does the court in *Morales v. Daley*, below, take adequate notice of the plaintiffs' privacy concerns?

MORALES v. DALEY

116 F.Supp.2d 801 (S.D.Tex. 2000).

HARMON, DISTRICT JUDGE. * * *

Introduction

[Article I, Section 2, Clause 3 of the Constitution of the United States provides that an "actual Enumeration" of the population of each state, a census, shall be made every ten years in a manner Congress shall "by Law direct." The same provision directs that the census be the basis for an apportionment of representatives to the House of Representatives. Pursuant to constitutional authority to direct the manner in which the "actual Enumeration" of the population shall be made, Congress enacted the Census Act, 13 U.S.C. § 1 et seq. The Act delegated to the Secretary of Commerce authority to conduct the decennial census. The Census Bureau, acting under the Secretary of Commerce, conducts the census.]

Plaintiffs Edgar Morales, Laique Rehman, Nouhad K. Bassila, George Breckenridge, and William Jeffrey Van Fleet have brought a number of challenges to the constitutionality of Census 2000 and have asked for a permanent injunction of their obligation to answer the census questions asked of them. [All but Van Fleet were asked to answer questions on the "short form" census. Van Fleet was asked to answer questions on the "long form" census.]

A. Short Form

The first question asks how many people were living or staying in the house, apartment, or mobile home on April 1, 2000. This is the only question mandated by Article I, Section 2, Clause 3.

Question two asks if the house, apartment, or mobile home is owned, with a mortgage, owned free and clear, rented for cash, or lived in without payment of rent. A question concerning "tenure," that is, whether the housing is owned or rented, has been asked in some form since 1890.

Question three asks the name of a person who owns, is buying, or rents the home, apartment, or mobile home or any adult living or staying there. This person is then referred to as "person one."

Question four asks person one's telephone number.

Question five asks person one's sex. A question concerning the sex of individuals has been asked in the census since 1790.

Question six asks the age of person one and his date of birth. A question concerning the individual's age has been asked since 1790.

Question seven asks if person one is of Spanish, Hispanic, or Latino heritage. A question concerning Hispanic ethnicity has been asked on the census since 1970.

Question eight asks what is person one's race and directs person one to mark the block which he considers himself to be. These blocks are:

1. white,

2. black, African American, or Negro,

3. American Indian or Alaska native, with space to provide the name of the enrolled or principal tribe,

4. Asian Indian,

5. Chinese,

6. Filipino,

7. other Asian, with a space to print the race,

8. Japanese,

9. Korean,

10. Vietnamese,

11. Native Hawaiian,

12. Guamanian or Chamorro,

13. Samoan,

14. Other Pacific Islander, and a space to print in the race.

15. A block which reads "some other race," and a space in which person one is to print the name of the race.

A question concerning race has been asked on the census form since 1790, although certainly not in the detail called for in the Year 2000 census form.

After the first eight questions have been asked, the questionnaire goes on to ask about each of the other persons living in the house, apartment, or mobile home. These persons are designated as person two, person three, and so on. For each of these persons in addition to person one, the questionnaire in the first question asks that person's name.

Question two asks how the person is related to person one. The choices are

1. husband/wife,

2. natural born son/daughter,

3. adopted son/daughter,

4. stepson/stepdaughter,

5. brother/sister,

6. father/mother,

7. grandchild,

8. parent-in-law,

9. son-in-law/daughter-in-law,

10. "other relative," with a space provided in which the person is to print the exact relationship.

Question two also allows answers for non-related persons, and the choices are

1. roomer, boarder,

2. housemate, roommate,

3. unmarried partner,

4. foster child,

5. other non-relatives.

A question concerning the relationships the persons who live in the home have to one another has been on the census form since 1880.

Question three for the additional persons asks each person's sex.

Question four asks each person's age and date of birth.

Questions five and six for the additional persons repeat the race questions set out above, that is, questions seven and eight, asked of person one.

B. The Long Form

The long form has a format different from the short form. The first question asks how many people are living or staying in the house, apartment, or mobile home on April 1, 2000. The second question asks the names of all the persons who are living in the house. Then the census form addresses each person in turn. Person one answers a series of thirty-two questions beginning with his name (question one), telephone number (question two), sex (question three), age and date of birth (question four), whether the person is Spanish, Hispanic, or Latino (question five), and what is this person's race (question six).

Questions five and six on the long form are identical to questions seven and eight on the short form for person one, and questions five and six for the additional persons.

The long form then asks person one, in question seven, his marital status. A question on marital status has been asked in the census since 1880.

Question eight (a) asks, "At any time since February 1, 2000, has this person attended regular school or college?" Question eight (b) asks what grade or level was this person attending. A question concerning education enrollment has been asked on the census form since 1850.

Question nine asks what the highest degree or level of school was completed by the person answering. A question on education attainment has been asked on the census form since 1940.

Question ten asks, "What is this person's ancestry or ethnic origin?" It leaves a space in which the person can record his ethnic origin or ancestry, and suggests examples of Italian, Jamaican, African American, Cambodian, Cape Verdean, Norwegian, Dominican, French Canadian, Haitian, Korean, Lebanese, Polish, Nigerian, Mexican, Taiwanese, Ukranian, etc. A question on ancestry or ethnic origin has been asked on the census form since 1980.

Question eleven (a) asks if person one speaks a language other than English at home, and eleven (b) asks what that language is, giving examples of Korean, Italian, Spanish, and Vietnamese. Question eleven (c) asks how well the person speaks English and gives a choice between very well to not at all. A question concerning the language spoken at home was on the census form from 1890 through 1940, and has reappeared on the census forms from 1960 through the 1990 census.

Question twelve asks where the person was born and gives a space for the name of the state in which the person was born if the person was born in the United States, or a place for the name of the country if the person was born outside the United States. A question concerning place of birth has been asked on the census form since 1850.

Question thirteen asks if the person is a citizen of the United States and gives the choice of "yes," born in the United States, born in Puerto Rico, Guam, the U.S. Virgin Islands, or Northern Marianas, born abroad of American parent or parents, a U.S. citizen by naturalization, or of "no," not a citizen of the United States. A question of citizenship was asked on the census form from 1820 through 1830, again in 1870, and then from 1890 through 1990.

Question fourteen asks when did the person answering the question come to live in the United States, and gives boxes for printing the year. A question on the year of entry was asked on the census from 1890 through 1930 and then again from 1970 through 1990.

Question fifteen (a) asks if the person answering lived "in this house or apartment five years ago (on April 1, 1995)." The choices for this question are "Person is under 5 years old," "Yes, this house," "No, outside the United States," with a space for writing in the name of the foreign country, and "No, different house in the United States." Question fifteen (b) asks where the person lived five years ago and gives a space for the city, town, or post office. Question fifteen (b) further asks did this person live inside the limits of the city or town, and gives a block for yes or no. It further asks the name of the county in which the person lived, the name of the state, and the zip code. A question on "migration," that is, residence five years ago, has been on the census form since 1940.

Question sixteen asks, with blocks for "yes" or "no," "Does this person have any of the following long-lasting conditions, (a) Blindness, deafness, or a severe vision or hearing impairment? (b) A condition that substantially limits one or more basic physical activities such as walking, climbing stairs, reaching, lifting, or carrying?" Question seventeen asks, "Because of a physical, mental or emotional condition lasting 6 months or more, does this person have any difficulty in doing any of the following activities?" The choices given, with blocks for "yes" or "no," are "(a) Learning, remembering, or concentrating? (b) Dressing, bathing, or getting around inside the home? (c) (Answer if this person is 16 YEARS OLD OR OVER) going outside the home alone to shop or visit a doctor's office? [and] (d) (Answer if this person is 16 YEARS OLD OR OVER) working at a job or business?" Questions concerning disability were asked from 1830 through 1930, and again from 1970 through 1990.

Question eighteen asks if the person answering the questionnaire is under fifteen years of age on April 1, 2000. Again, a question on age has been asked on each census since the first one in 1790.

Question nineteen (a) asks if person one has any of his grandchildren under the age of eighteen living in the house or apartment. Question nineteen (b) asks if the grandparent is currently responsible for most of the basic needs of any grandchild under the age of eighteen who lives in the house or apartment. Question nineteen (c) asks how long the grandparent has been responsible for the grandchildren, and gives choices of less than six months, six to eleven months, one or two years, three or four years, five years or more. This question is the only question that has never before been asked on the census in some form.

Question twenty (a) asks if the person has ever served on active duty in the United States armed forces, military reserves, or national guard. Question twenty (b) asks when the person served on active duty in the armed forces, and gives choices of dates and wars in which the person served. Question twenty (c) asks in total how many years of active duty military service has this person had and gives choices for various periods of time. Questions on veteran status were asked in 1840, 1890, 1910, and from 1930 through 1990.

Question twenty-one asks, "Last week, did this person do any work for either pay or profit?" and gives a choice of "yes" or "no." A question on labor force status has been asked on the census form since 1930.

Question twenty-two asks at what location did this person work last week, with a space in subpart (a) for writing in the address (number and street name). The question also suggests that if the exact address is not known, a description of the location, such as the building name or the nearest street or intersection may be provided as an answer to this subpart. Subpart (b) of Question twenty-two asks the name of the city, town, or post office. Subpart (c) of Question twenty-two asks if the work location is inside the limits of that city or town. Subpart (d) of Question twenty-two asks the name of the county. Subpart (e) of Question twenty-two asks the name of the state or foreign country. Subpart (f) of the same question asks for the zip code. A question on the place of work has been asked since 1960 on the census form.

Question twenty-three (a) asks how person one usually got to work last week and gives a number of choices: car, truck, or van; bus or trolley bus; streetcar or trolley car; subway or elevated; railroad; ferry boat; taxi cab; motorcycle; bicycle; walked; worked at home; other method. The question then indicates that if "car, truck or van" is marked in twenty-three (a), the person responding to twenty-three (a) is to answer question twenty-three (b). If not, the person responding is to skip to twenty-four (a). Question twenty-three (b) asks how many people including person one usually rode to work in the car, truck, or van last week. Question twenty-three (b) gives the choices of drove alone, two people, three people, four people, five or six people, and seven or more people. Question twenty-four (a) asks at what time of day person one usually left home to go to work last week. Question twenty-four (b) asks how many miles that it usually takes person one to get from home to work last week with a space for writing in the minutes. A question about the journey to work has been asked on the census since 1960.

Questions twenty-five and twenty-six are for persons who did not work for pay or profit last week. Question twenty-five (a) asks if last week the responding person was on layoff from a job. Question twenty-five (b) asks if the person temporarily was absent from a job or business. Question twenty-five (c) asks if the person had been informed that he will be recalled to work within the next six months or been given a date to return to work. Question twenty-five (d) asks if person one has been looking for work during the last four weeks, and Question twenty-five (e) asks last week could the person have started a job if one was offered or returned to work if recalled. Question twenty-six asks when did person one last work even for a few days and gives two choices, either "1995 to 2000" or "1994 or earlier or never worked." Questions on labor force status have been on the census form since 1930.

Question twenty-seven concerns the industry or employer and asks person one to "describe this person's chief job or business last week. If this person had more than one job, describe the one at which this person worked the most hours. If this person had no job or business last week, give the information for his/her last job or business since 1995." Question twenty-seven (a) asks for whom the person worked. Question twenty-seven (b) asks about the kind of business or industry worked for, and suggests the activities (for example, hospital, newspaper publishing, mail order house, auto repair shop, bank). Question twenty-seven (c) asks if the job is mainly manufacturing, wholesale trade, retail trade, or other, with suggestions of agriculture, construction, service, and government. Questions about the industry for which a person worked has been asked on the census form beginning in 1820. Such questions were asked again in 1840, and have been asked in each census from 1910 through 1990.

Question twenty-eight asks about occupation. Question twenty-eight (a) asks "what kind of work was this person doing?" It gives the examples of registered nurse, personnel manager, supervisor of order department, auto mechanic, accountant. Question twenty-eight (b) asks what were this person's most important activities or duties, and suggests patient care, directing hiring policies, supervising order clerks, repairing automobiles, reconciling financial records. Questions on occupation have been asked on the census form since 1850.

Question twenty-nine asks what kind of enterprise the person was working in, and gives choices of employee of a private for profit company or business or of an individual for wages, salary or commissions; employee of a private not-for-profit tax exempt or charitable organization; local government employee; state government employee; federal government employee; self-employed in own not incorporated business, professional practice, or farm; self-employed in own incorporated business, professional practice, or farm; working without pay in family business or farm. Questions on the class of worker, that is, type of employment, whether private, governmental, self employed, or working as an unpaid family worker, have appeared on the census form since 1910.

Question thirty (a) asks "Last year, 1999, did this person work at a job or business at any time?" Blocks for "yes" or "no" are provided. Question thirty (b) asks how many weeks did this person work in 1999. Question thirty (c) asks, "During the weeks worked in 1999 how many hours did this person usually work each week?" Questions on work status last year have been on the census form since 1940.

Question thirty-one asks about income in 1999. Question thirty-one (a) asks about wages, salaries, commissions, bonuses, or tips from all jobs. Question thirty-one (b) asks about amount earned from self employment income from owned non-farm business or farm businesses, including proprietorships and partnerships. Question thirty-one (c) asks about interest, dividends, net original income, royalty income, or income from estates and trusts. Question thirty-one (d) asks about social security or railroad retirement. Question thirty-one (e) asks about supplemental security income. Question thirty-one (f) asks about any public assistance or welfare payments from the state or local welfare office. Question thirty-one (g) asks about retirement, survivor, or disability pensions. Question thirty-one (h) asks about any other sources of income received regularly such as veterans payments, unemployment compensation, child support, or alimony. Each of these subparts of question thirty-one asks person one to write out the annual amount in dollars. Question thirty-two asks what was this person's total income in 1999. Questions on amount of income have been on the census form since 1940.

Questions thirty-three through fifty-three ask person one a series of detailed questions concerning the house, apartment, or mobile home in which person one is living. In 1890 the persons were first asked if the home was rented or owned. Questions concerning the value of the home and the rent paid have been asked on the census form since 1930. Questions concerning the year the home structure was built, number of units in the structure, number of rooms in the structure, plumbing facilities, and house heating fuel have been asked on the census form since 1940. Since 1960, the census form has contained questions concerning number of bedrooms, kitchen facilities, and the year the person moved into the unit. Whether the home is a farm residence has been asked since 1970. Questions concerning whether telephone service is available and selected monthly owner costs were added in 1980.

Persons two through infinity are not asked on the long form about housing, but they are asked in question one their name, and in question two how the person is related to person one. Persons two through infinity are then asked questions three through thirty-two that are asked of person one.

Plaintiffs are complaining, in particular, about the questions on the short form that ask a resident of the United States if he is Hispanic and what kind of Hispanic he is. Plaintiffs also object to the question which asks the resident what race he would self categorize himself to be. They also object to the question asking how a person is related to the other persons who live in the house with him.

On the long form they object to these questions and a number of others. Specifically, they object to the question concerning marital status (7), educational background (8–10), ancestry and ethnic origin (10), whether the person speaks a language other than English, and, if so, which one, and how well the person speaks English (11), length of residence in the dwelling (15), medical conditions or problems (16 and 17), where the person worked "last week" (22), how the person got to work (23), when the person left home for work and how long it took to get there (24), work/layoff/absence history (25 and 26), occupation and employer (27–30), income and source of income (31 and 32), the nature of the housing, including the number of rooms and bedrooms in the house (37 and 38), plumbing, kitchen, and phone service (39 to 41), information about rent, mortgage, insurance, and home value (46–53). Plaintiffs also object to the fact that stated prominently on the envelope in which the census forms are mailed are the words, "You are required by law to answer these questions."

Title 13 U.S.C. § 221(a) and (b) provides that if a person fails to respond to an answer he can be fined up to $100 for each unanswered question. If an answer is incorrect, the person is subject to a fine of up to $500 for each incorrect answer. Plaintiffs contend that the questions on the long and short forms, beyond the questions dealing with the number of residents in the dwelling, are intrusive, objectionable, and invade their privacy. They do not want to answer them. They feel intimidated by the threat of criminal sanctions if they fail to answer the questions, and they feel that if they protect their privacy and refuse to answer that they will be exposing themselves to hundreds or, if they were unlucky and received the long form, thousands of dollars in fines. * * *

IV. First Amendment

The plaintiffs argue that by requiring them to classify and categorize themselves by race, the Bureau violates their rights under the First Amendment by forcing them to engage in speech which is abhorrent and contrary to their beliefs. * * *

Plaintiffs' argument is that they do not wish to categorize themselves by race and do not think of themselves in those terms. Nor do they think of themselves in terms of ethnicity or ethnic origin, and they find such classification and categorization by race "deeply offensive and abhorrent, personally, ethically and politically." They prefer to describe themselves merely as "Americans." The government, however, on the long and short form, requires the plaintiffs to classify, categorize, and describe themselves in terms of race and ethnicity. Failure to do so subjects them to criminal sanction and a fine of up to $100 for each question they fail to answer or up to $500 for each question they answer incorrectly. * * *

In United States v. Sindel, 53 F.3d 874 (8th Cir. 1995), the court rejected a claim that compelled disclosure of information on an Internal Revenue Service form was unlawful compelled speech. The Eighth Circuit held, "There is no right to refrain from speaking when 'essential operations of government require it for the preservation of an orderly society— as in the case of compulsion to give evidence in court.' " West Virginia Bd. of Educ. v. Barnette, 319 U.S. 624, 645 (Murphy, J., concurring). * * *

The government seeks from all residents of the United States certain demographic information from which it compiles statistics. It is these compiled statistics that are used for governmental purposes. Congress has decided that it needs this data. It has expressed, through the Census Bureau, its justification for the need. Plaintiffs may believe the justification is trivial; they may object to its use on political or moral grounds, but, as in Sindel, Congress has enacted a statute requiring all residents to provide the information. Since it is only information being sought, and plaintiffs are not being asked "to disseminate publicly a message with which [they] disagree [ ]," the First Amendment protection against compelled speech does not prevent the government from requiring the plaintiffs to answer these questions. Sindel, 53 F.3d at 878.

V. Fourth Amendment

Finally, plaintiff Van Fleet argues that the long form questionnaire, as presently constituted, violates his rights under the Fourth Amendment.

He argues that the numerous and intrusive questions that he is required to answer on the long form constitute an unreasonable and illegal search under the Fourth Amendment. Van Fleet argues that the Fourth Amendment, as interpreted in modern cases, protects privacy. He cites Katz v. United States, 389 U.S. 347 (1967), and United States v. Janik, 723 F.2d 537, 547–48 (7th Cir.1983). * * *

Van Fleet argues that the questions posed to him on the long form constitute a gross invasion of his privacy. He is required to disclose information about his medical history and condition, his ancestry and ethnic background, his income, his work habits, including how long it takes him to drive to work, and detailed information about his home, including the number of bedrooms, the nature of his plumbing, whether he owns or rents, even whether he pays his rent in cash. For all these matters, Van Fleet argues that he has a reasonable expectation of privacy, and cites Yin v. State of California, 95 F.3d 864, 868 (9th Cir.1996).

Van Fleet focuses on the questions concerning his medical condition, namely, question sixteen which asks about definite conditions and question seventeen which asks if he has difficulty because of his medical condition in doing a list of activities. He points out that "many if not all of these questions are matters a person would normally discuss only with his doctor or family member." A person has a reasonable expectation of privacy with respect to information regarding his medical condition. Cf. id. at 870; Terry v. Ohio, 392 U.S. 1, 9 (1968) (holding that society is concerned for the security of one's person).

Van Fleet argues that to compel him to answer questions about his medical condition under threat of criminal sanctions compels him to submit to a medical examination against his will and that such a medical examination clearly is a search that implicates the Fourth Amendment. Vernonia Sch. Dist. v. Acton (1995) (finding that high school drug testing is not an unreasonable search and seizure). In order to invade such privacy in a non-criminal context, the government must show "special needs" for the information, beyond the normal need for law enforcement. * * *

The Census Bureau points out that from the very first census, performed in 1790, Congress authorized questions pertaining to age, gender, and race. It also points out that the Supreme Court defers to the statutes of the First Congress because so many Framers of the Constitution were members of that congress. The fact that the First Congress included questions in addition to the head count is strong support for the constitutionality of additional questions as a general proposition. Thus, using the first step in the Supreme Court's Wyoming v. Houghton analysis, it is clear that asking personal questions of residents of the United States in the census was not regarded as an unlawful search. Of course, the Census 2000 goes beyond mere questions of sex, race, and age. Questions about the medical conditions of the members of Van Fleet's household would, in other contexts, be considered private, but Census

2000 is the not the first census to ask such questions. Inquiries on disability and health have been asked on the census since the fifth census in 1830. For example, that census asked if members of the household were "deaf," "dumb," or "blind." 4 Stat. 383 (1830). The sixth census for 1840 collected data on "idiots" and the "insane." 5 Stat. 331 (1839). Of course the mere fact that these inquiries were not challenged at the time does not prove that they were not unreasonable searches in violation of the Fourth Amendment, but it does give an historical perspective of the attitude of the Congress forty plus years after the framing of the Constitution. In 1850 the census asked additional information, including occupation or trade, place of birth, school attendance, literacy, and criminal records. Asking questions well beyond the constitutionally mandated headcount is far from a novel idea of twentieth century big government bureaucrats.
* * *

The Census Bureau cites a number of reasons why the questions on disability (16 and 17) are asked. For example, it states that the questions are "[u]sed to distribute funds and develop programs for people with disabilities and the elderly under the Rehabilitation Act * * * [and that they are] [n]eeded under the Americans with Disabilities Act to ensure that comparable public transportation services are available for all segments of the population, etc." * * * The Census Bureau has asked these private questions to obtain demographic data to be used for articulated reasons.

Although Van Fleet is required to answer these very private questions, the Census Bureau assures him and the court that the law forbids the Bureau from attributing Van Fleet's answers to Van Fleet. Rather, the Bureau is collecting this data merely for demographic purposes to inform the governing body of statistical facts so that they may better govern. The law requires that the census data on individuals is to be maintained in strict confidence. The census returns may only be viewed by sworn employees of the Bureau and the Department. 13 U.S.C. § 9(a)(3). Copying of individual returns is proscribed. Id. § 9(a). Census returns cannot be subpoenaed and may not be used as evidence in any proceeding without the consent of the individual. Section 9(a)(2) provides that the compilation cannot be released with information "whereby the data furnished by any particular establishment or individual can be identified * * *." Id. § 9(a)(2). The United States argues that the census is not in any real sense a "search and seizure" because it does not involve physical intrusion into the home, touching of the body, or seizure of property. The census consists merely of a mailing to the home of a series of questions, to which the government requires answers. The government cites United States v. Rickenbacker, 309 F.2d 462, 463 (2nd Cir.1962), which found the census to be reasonably related to government purposes and functions. Rickenbacker was convicted of refusing to answer a schedule entitled "Household Questionnaire for the 1960 Census of Population and Housing," in violation of 13 U.S.C. § 221(a). This questionnaire was sent to every fourth household in the United States. Rickenbacker told the census enumerator that he did not intend to answer the questionnaire, and he told the Grand Jury that indicted him that the questionnaire represented "an unnecessary invasion of my privacy" and that he desired to "maintain liberties in this country as a constitutional philosophical question." Id. He also told the grand jury that he did not base his failure to respond upon any fear of self-incrimination. Id. The Second Circuit found that "The authority to gather reliable statistical data reasonably related to governmental purposes and functions is a necessity if modern government is to legislate intelligently and effectively." Id. * * *

In reviewing a challenge to the government's collection of racial and ethnic information in the employment context, the Second Circuit in Caulfield v. Bd. of Educ. of the City of New York, 583 F.2d 605 (2nd Cir.1978), held that "there is no search or seizure" in the context of such a census and labeled the Fourth Amendment challenge as "frivolous" Id. at 612. The government reasons that the court was able to dismiss this claim easily because there was neither an entrance into the home nor interference with property interests, nor a seizure as contemplated by the Fourth Amendment. Cf. United States v. Jacobsen, 466 U.S. 109, 113 (1984) (stating that "[a] 'seizure' of property occurs when there is some meaningful interference with an individual's possessory interests in that property"). * * *

[I]t is clear that the degree to which these questions intrude upon an individual's privacy is limited, given the methods used to collect the census data and the statutory assurance that the answers and attribution to an individual will remain confidential. The degree to which the information is needed for the promotion of legitimate governmental interests has been found to be significant. A census of the type of Census 2000 has been taken every ten years since the first census in 1790. Such a census has been thought to be necessary for over two hundred years. There is no basis for holding that it is not necessary in the year 2000.

B. FEDERAL GOVERNANCE OF STATE RECORD–KEEPING

The federal statutes we have examined thus far govern access to federal records. Federal statutes also regulate access to state records. Where does recently asserted federal authority to regulate the privacy of state-held record data originate? Why has federal governance of state privacy practices proven controversial and led the states to sue?

1. DRIVER'S PRIVACY PROTECTION ACT OF 1994 (DPPA)

a. The DPPA

DRIVER'S PRIVACY PROTECTION ACT

18 U.S.C. § 2721.

§ 2721. Prohibition on release and use of certain personal information from State motor vehicle records

(a) In general. A State department of motor vehicles, and any officer, employee, or contractor thereof, shall not knowingly disclose or otherwise make available to any person or entity:

(1) personal information, as defined in 18 U.S.C. 2725(3), about any individual obtained by the department in connection with a motor vehicle record, except as provided in subsection (b) of this section; or

(2) highly restricted personal information, as defined in 18 U.S.C. 2725(4), about any individual obtained by the department in connection with a motor vehicle record, without the express consent of the person to whom such information applies, except uses permitted in subsections (b)(1), (b)(4), (b)(6), and (b)(9): Provided, That subsection (a)(2) shall not in any way affect the use of organ donation information on an individual's driver's license or affect the administration of organ donation initiatives in the States. * * *

(d) Waiver procedures. A State motor vehicle department may establish and carry out procedures under which the department or its agents, upon receiving a request for personal information that does not fall within one of the exceptions * * *, may mail a copy of the request to the individual about whom the information was requested, informing such individual of the request, together with a statement to the effect that the information will not be released unless the individual waives such individual's right to privacy under this section.

b. Constitutionality of the DPPA

PRYOR v. RENO

171 F.3d 1281 (11th Cir. 1999), overruled, 528 U.S. 141 (2000).

HILL, SENIOR CIRCUIT JUDGE * * *

[The] Driver's Privacy and Protection Act of 1994 ("DPPA" or "the Act"), 18 U.S.C. §§ 2721, et seq., regulates the sale, dissemination and use by the State and private individuals of personal information contained in the State's motor vehicle records. * * *

Alabama asserts that the DPPA violates the Tenth Amendment in two ways. First, Alabama contends that the Commerce Clause does not authorize Congress to invade the Tenth Amendment by regulating the

States' dissemination of motor vehicle information. Second, Alabama contends that the Tenth Amendment prohibits Congress from requiring it to administer a federal program.

The Supreme Court has recently made clear that the federal government may not command the States to administer or enforce a federal regulatory program. Printz v. United States, 521 U.S. 898 * * *.

No one disputes that Congress, through the DPPA, has enacted a federal regulatory program to control the dissemination and cloaking of the States' motor vehicle information. * * *

Furthermore, the Act is neither self-administering nor self-enforcing. State officers are directed to administer and enforce these rules. They must insure that protected information is disclosed only for the designated purposes specified by the federal rules. * * * Thus, we conclude the DPPA is a federal regulatory program which Congress has directed state officers to administer. Congress may not enlist state officers in this way. * * *

The United States argues that it is permissible for Congress to command state officers to assist in the implementation of federal law so long as Congress itself devises a clear legislative program that regulates the States directly rather than requiring them to regulate third parties. The DPPA, it is said, is constitutional because it directly regulates state activities and neither directs the States or their officials to regulate their citizens, nor to construct any regulatory regime. * * *

Instead of bringing the States within the scope of an otherwise generally applicable law, Congress passed the DPPA specifically to regulate the States' control of the States' own property—the motor vehicle records. * * *

When States are forced to administer federal programs, a fundamental attribute of State sovereignty is threatened: democratic accountability. It is this basic principle upon which the Supreme Court rested its holdings in New York and Printz * * *. * * *

This Act cannot be saved by the argument that it simply regulates a realm of national economic activity—the buying and selling of personal information—whether or not the economic actors happen to be State or citizens. The DPPA is not a law of general applicability. Only States collect driver's license and motor vehicle information. This is an exercise of sovereignty.

Thus, we conclude that the DPPA is a federal program which Congress has commanded the States to administer. As such, it offends the Tenth Amendment.

RENO v. CONDON

528 U.S. 141 (2000).

CHIEF JUSTICE REHNQUIST delivered the opinion of the Court.

The Driver's Privacy Protection Act of 1994 (DPPA or Act), 18 U.S.C. §§ 2721–2725 (1994 ed. and Supp. III), regulates the disclosure of personal information contained in the records of state motor vehicle departments (DMVs). We hold that in enacting this statute Congress did not run afoul of the federalism principles enunciated in New York v. United States, 505 U.S. 144 (1992), and Printz v. United States, 521 U.S. 898 (1997).

The DPPA regulates the disclosure and resale of personal information contained in the records of state DMVs. State DMVs require drivers and automobile owners to provide personal information, which may include a person's name, address, telephone number, vehicle description, Social Security number, medical information, and photograph, as a condition of obtaining a driver's license or registering an automobile. Congress found that many States, in turn, sell this personal information to individuals and businesses. * * *

The DPPA establishes a regulatory scheme that restricts the States' ability to disclose a driver's personal information without the driver's consent. The DPPA generally prohibits any state DMV, or officer, employee, or contractor thereof, from "knowingly disclosing or otherwise making available to any person or entity personal information about any individual obtained by the department in connection with a motor vehicle record." 18 U.S.C. § 2721(a). The DPPA defines "personal information" as any information "that identifies an individual, including an individual's photograph, social security number, driver identification number, name, address (but not the 5–digit zip code), telephone number, and medical or disability information," but not including "information on vehicular accidents, driving violations, and driver's status." § 2725(3). A "motor vehicle record" is defined as "any record that pertains to a motor vehicle operator's permit, motor vehicle title, motor vehicle registration, or identification card issued by a department of motor vehicles." § 2725(1).

The DPPA's ban on disclosure of personal information does not apply if drivers have consented to the release of their data. Under the amended DPPA, States may not imply consent from a driver's failure to take advantage of a state-afforded opportunity to block disclosure [opt-out], but must rather obtain a driver's affirmative consent to disclose the driver's personal information for use in surveys, marketing, solicitations, and other restricted purposes [opt-in].

The DPPA's prohibition of nonconsensual disclosures is also subject to a number of statutory exceptions. For example, the DPPA requires disclosure of personal information "for use in connection with matters of motor vehicle or driver safety and theft, motor vehicle emissions, motor vehicle product alterations, recalls, or advisories, performance monitoring of motor vehicles and dealers by motor vehicle manufacturers, and removal of non-owner records from the original owner records of motor vehicle manufacturers to carry out the purposes of [various federal laws]. The DPPA permits DMVs to disclose personal information from motor vehicle records for a number of purposes.

The DPPA's provisions do not apply solely to States. The Act also regulates the resale and redisclosure of drivers' personal information by private persons who have obtained that information from a state DMV. * * * If a State has obtained drivers' consent to disclose their personal information to private persons generally and a private person has obtained that information, the private person may redisclose the information for any purpose. Ibid. Additionally, a private actor who has obtained drivers' information from DMV records specifically for direct-marketing purposes may resell that information for other direct-marketing uses, but not otherwise. Any person who rediscloses or resells personal information from DMV records must, for five years, maintain records identifying to whom the records were disclosed and the permitted purpose for the resale or redisclosure.

The DPPA establishes several penalties to be imposed on States and private actors that fail to comply with its requirements. The Act makes it unlawful for any "person" knowingly to obtain or disclose any record for a use that is not permitted under its provisions, or to make a false representation in order to obtain personal information from a motor vehicle record. §§ 2722(a) and (b). Any person who knowingly violates the DPPA may be subject to a criminal fine, §§ 2723(a), 2725(2). Additionally, any person who knowingly obtains, discloses, or uses information from a state motor vehicle record for a use other than those specifically permitted by the DPPA may be subject to liability in a civil action brought by the driver to whom the information pertains. § 2724. While the DPPA defines "person" to exclude States and state agencies, § 2725(2), a state agency that maintains a "policy or practice of substantial noncompliance" with the Act maybe subject to a civil penalty imposed by the United States Attorney General of not more than $5,000 per day of substantial noncompliance. § 2723(b).

South Carolina law conflicts with the DPPA's provisions. Under that law, the information contained in the State's DMV records is available to any person or entity that fills out a form listing the requester's name and address and stating that the information will not be used for telephone solicitation. * * *

Following the DPPA's enactment, South Carolina and its Attorney General, respondent Condon, filed suit in the United States District Court for the District of South Carolina, alleging that the DPPA violates the Tenth and Eleventh Amendments to the United States Constitution. The District Court concluded that the Act is incompatible with the principles of federalism inherent in the Constitution's division of power between the States and the Federal Government. The court accordingly granted summary judgment for the State and permanently enjoined the Act's enforcement against the State and its officers. See 972 F. Supp. 977, 979 (1997). The Court of Appeals for the Fourth Circuit affirmed, concluding that the Act violates constitutional principles of federalism. See 155 F.3d 453 (1998). We granted certiorari, 526 U.S. 1111 (1999), and now reverse.

We of course begin with the time-honored presumption that the DPPA is a "constitutional exercise of legislative power." Close v. Glenwood Cemetery, 107 U.S. 466 (1883); see also INS v. Chadha, 462 U.S. 919 (1983).

The United States asserts that the DPPA is a proper exercise of Congress' authority to regulate interstate commerce under the Commerce Clause, U.S. Const., Art. I, § 8, cl. 3. The United States bases its Commerce Clause argument on the fact that the personal, identifying information that the DPPA regulates is a "thing in interstate commerce," and that the sale or release of that information in interstate commerce is therefore a proper subject of congressional regulation. United States v. Lopez, 514 U.S. 549, 558–559 (1995). We agree with the United States' contention. The motor vehicle information which the States have historically sold is used by insurers, manufacturers, direct marketers, and others engaged in interstate commerce to contact drivers with customized solicitations. The information is also used in the stream of interstate commerce by various public and private entities for matters related to interstate motoring. Because drivers' information is, in this context, an article of commerce, its sale or release into the interstate stream of business is sufficient to support congressional regulation. We therefore need not address the Government's alternative argument that the States' individual, intrastate activities in gathering, maintaining, and distributing drivers' personal information has a sufficiently substantial impact on interstate commerce to create a constitutional base for federal legislation.

But the fact that drivers' personal information is, in the context of this case, an article in interstate commerce does not conclusively resolve the constitutionality of the DPPA. In New York and Printz, we held federal statutes invalid, not because Congress lacked legislative authority over the subject matter, but because those statutes violated the principles of federalism contained in the Tenth Amendment. In New York, Congress commandeered the state legislative process by requiring a state legislature to enact a particular kind of law. We said: "While Congress has substantial powers to govern the Nation directly, including in areas of intimate concern to the States, the Constitution has never been understood to confer upon Congress the ability to require the States to govern according to Congress' instructions."

In Printz, we invalidated a provision of the Brady Act which commanded "state and local enforcement officers to conduct background check on prospective handgun purchasers," We said: "We held in New York that Congress cannot compel the States to enact or enforce a federal regulatory program. Today we hold that Congress cannot circumvent that prohibition by conscripting the States' officers directly. The Federal Government may neither issue directives requiring the States to address particular problems, nor command the States' officers, or those of their political subdivisions, to administer or enforce a federal regulatory program."

South Carolina contends that the DPPA violates the Tenth Amendment because it "thrusts upon the States all of the day-to-day responsibility for administering its complex provisions" * * *. South Carolina emphasizes that the DPPA requires the State's employees to learn and apply the Act's substantive restrictions, which are summarized above, and notes that these activities will consume the employees' time and thus the State's resources. South Carolina further notes that the DPPA's penalty provisions hang over the States as a potential punishment should they fail to comply with the Act.

We agree with South Carolina's assertion that the DPPA's provisions will require time and effort on the part of state employees, but reject the State's argument that the DPPA violates the principles laid down in either New York or Printz. We think, instead, that this case is governed by our decision in South Carolina v. Baker, 485 U.S. 505 (1988). In Baker, we upheld a statute that prohibited States from issuing unregistered bonds because the law "regulated state activities," rather than "seeking to control or influence the manner in which States regulate private parties." * * *

Like the statute at issue in Baker, the DPPA does not require the States in their sovereign capacity to regulate their own citizens. The DPPA regulates the States as the owners of databases. It does not require the South Carolina Legislature to enact any laws or regulations, and it does not require state officials to assist in the enforcement of federal statutes regulating private individuals. We accordingly conclude that the DPPA is consistent with the constitutional principles enunciated in New York and Printz.

As a final matter, we turn to South Carolina's argument that the DPPA is unconstitutional because it regulates the States exclusively. The essence of South Carolina's argument is that Congress may only regulate the States by means of "generally applicable" laws, or laws that apply to individuals as well as States. But we need not address the question whether general applicability is a constitutional requirement for federal regulation of the States, because the DPPA is generally applicable. The DPPA regulates the universe of entities that participate as suppliers to the market for motor vehicle information—the States as initial suppliers of the information in interstate commerce and private resellers or redisclosers of that information in commerce.

c. "Permissible Use" of Drivers' Data

RUSSELL v. CHOICEPOINT SERVICES, INC.

302 F. Supp. 2d 654 (E.D. La. 2004).

JUDGE STANWOOD R. DUVAL, JR.

Plaintiffs Betty D. Russell and Yvonne Morse brought the instant suit against defendant Reed Elsevier Services, Inc. ("Reed Elsevier") in July of 2003, claiming, inter alia, that defendant violated the Driver's Privacy Protection Act ("DPPA" or the "Act"), 18 U.S.C. § 2721, et seq. The

Complaint alleges that defendant illegally obtained plaintiffs' and other proposed class members' personal information from the Louisiana Department of Motor Vehicles ("DMV") for the impermissible purpose of disclosure and distribution by resale to Reed Elsevier customers. Plaintiffs further allege that defendant disclosed and distributed said information without any purpose permissible under the DPPA. The DMV disclosed said information to Reed Elsevier who, doing business as LexisNexis, redistributed the information to plaintiffs' legal counsel and possibly to others as well. Plaintiffs claim to have sustained injury as contemplated by the DPPA as a result of defendant obtaining and disclosing said information and they seek relief and damages under 18 U.S.C. § 2721, et seq.
* * *

State DMVs obtain personal information by requiring drivers and automobile owners to provide an address, telephone number, vehicle description, Social Security number, medical information, and photograph as a condition of obtaining a driver's license or registering an automobile. Reno v. Condon, 528 U.S. 141, 143 (2000). Largely in response to mounting public safety concerns over stalkers' and other criminals' access to the personal information maintained in state DMV records, Congress enacted the Driver's Privacy Protection Act of 1994, 18 U.S.C. § 2721–2725, to regulate the disclosure of such information. The DPPA's regulatory scheme restricts the States' ability to disclose a driver's personal information without the driver's consent. Reno, 528 U.S. at 144. * * *

The DPPA's ban on obtainment and disclosure of personal information is subject to a number of statutory exceptions. Personal information disclosure is permitted (or mandated) for a number of authorized purposes. "Permissible uses" of personal information are listed in 18 U.S.C. § 2721(b):

> Permissible uses—Personal information referred to in subsection (a) shall be disclosed for use in connection with matters of motor vehicle or driver safety and theft, motor vehicle emissions, motor vehicle product alterations, recalls, or advisories, performance monitoring of motor vehicles and dealers by motor vehicle manufacturers, and removal of non-owner records from the original owner records of motor vehicle manufacturers to carry out the purposes of titles I and IV of the Anti Car Theft Act of 1992, the Automobile Information Disclosure Act (15 U.S.C. 1231 et seq.), the Clean Air Act (42 U.S.C. 7401 et seq.), and chapters 301, 305, and 321–331 of title 49, and, subject to subsection (a)(2), may be disclosed as follows:

> (1) For use by any government agency, including any court or law enforcement agency, in carrying out its functions, or any private person or entity acting on behalf of a Federal, State, or local agency in carrying out its functions.

> (2) For use in connection with matters of motor vehicle or driver safety and theft; motor vehicle emissions; motor vehicle product alterations, recalls, or advisories; performance monitoring of motor

vehicles, motor vehicle parts and dealers; motor vehicle market research activities, including survey research; and removal of non-owner records from the original owner records of motor vehicle manufacturers.

(3) For use in the normal course of business by a legitimate business or its agents, employees, or contractors, but only—

(A) to verify the accuracy of personal information submitted by the individual to the business or its agents, employees, or contractors; and

(B) if such information as so submitted is not correct or is no longer correct, to obtain the correct information, but only for the purposes of preventing fraud by, pursuing legal remedies against, or recovering on a debt or security interest against, the individual.

(4) For use in connection with any civil, criminal, administrative, or arbitral proceeding in any Federal, State, or local court or agency or before any self-regulatory body, including the service of process, investigation in anticipation of litigation, and the execution or enforcement of judgments and orders, or pursuant to an order of a Federal, State, or local court.

(5) For use in research activities, and for use in producing statistical reports, so long as the personal information is not published, redisclosed, or used to contact individuals.

(6) For use by any insurer or insurance support organization, or by a self-insured entity, or its agents, employees, or contractors, in connection with claims investigation activities, antifraud activities, rating or underwriting.

(7) For use in providing notice to the owners of towed or impounded vehicles.

(8) For use by any licensed private investigative agency or licensed security service for any purpose permitted under this subsection.

(9) For use by an employer or its agent or insurer to obtain or verify information relating to a holder of a commercial driver's license that is required under chapter 313 of title 49.

(10) For use in connection with the operation of private toll transportation facilities.

(11) For any other use in response to requests for individual motor vehicle records if the State has obtained the express consent of the person to whom such personal information pertains.

(12) For bulk distribution for surveys, marketing or solicitations if the State has obtained the express consent of the person to whom such personal information pertains.

(13) For use by any requester, if the requester demonstrates it has obtained the written consent of the individual to whom the information pertains.

(14) For any other use specifically authorized under the law of the State that holds the record, if such use is related to the operation of a motor vehicle or public safety.

18 U.S.C. § 2721(b)

In addition to state DMV actions, the provisions of the DPPA apply to the further disclosure of drivers' personal information by private citizens who have obtained that information from a DMV. 18 U.S.C. § 2721(c) provides for the resale and redisclosure of personal information obtained by "authorized recipients":

> Resale or redisclosure.—An authorized recipient of personal information (except a recipient under subsection (b)(11) or (12)) may resell or redisclose the information only for a use permitted under subsection (b) (but not for uses under subsection (b) (11) or (12)). An authorized recipient under subsection (b)(11) may resell or redisclose personal information for any purpose. An authorized recipient under subsection (b)(12) may resell or redisclose personal information pursuant to subsection (b)(12). Any authorized recipient (except a recipient under subsection (b) (11)) that resells or rediscloses personal information covered by this chapter must keep for a period of 5 years records identifying each person or entity that receives information and the permitted purpose for which the information will be used and must make such records available to the motor vehicle department upon request.

18 U.S.C. § 2721(c). The Act does not define "authorized recipient."

The DPPA establishes criminal and civil penalties to be imposed on those who fail to comply with its provisions. Violators are subject to a criminal fine. 18 U.S.C. §§ 2723(a), 2725(2). Also, private persons who knowingly obtain, disclose, or use personal information from a DMV for a purpose not permitted under the DPPA may be subject to liability in civil action brought by the driver to whom the information pertains. 18 U.S.C. § 2724(a). DPPA violators may be liable for the following: (1) actual damages (not less than liquidated damages in the amount of $2,500); (2) punitive damages; (3) attorneys' fees and other litigation costs; and (4) preliminary and equitable relief. 18 U.S.C. § 2724(b). * * *

The Court agrees with defendant Reed Elsevier that plaintiffs may not maintain a DPPA claim for improper obtainment under 18 U.S.C. § 2724(a) without alleging an accompanying impermissible use. The plain language of the DPPA permits entities like Reed Elsevier to obtain drivers' personal information from DMVs and subsequently resell that information to third parties with a permissible use.

When interpreting a statute, courts must begin with an analysis of the statute's actual words because when "the language of the federal statute is plain and unambiguous, it begins and ends [the court's] inquiry." * * *

Congress could have limited resale and redisclosure to "permissible users," keeping in line with 18 U.S.C. § 2721(b)'s theme of permissible use, but instead Congress employed the term "authorized recipient" in § 2721(c). This deliberate word choice reveals congressional intent to allow states and their DMVs to authorize persons and entities to receive drivers' information for resale. In enacting the DPPA, Congress intended to strike "a critical balance between legitimate governmental and business needs for this information, and the fundamental right of our people to privacy and safety." 139 Cong. Rec. S15, 763 (1993). Congress was well aware of the economic value of DMV records and of the common state practice of selling drivers' personal information to private resellers. The inclusion of the term "authorized recipient" and the exclusion of any reference to "users" in DPPA § 2721(c) indicates an intent on behalf of Congress to delegate authorization to the states and thereby permit personal information resellers like Reed Elsevier who are authorized by the state or its DMV to obtain drivers' personal information for the purpose redistribution to persons with "permissible uses."

The plain language of the DPPA is written in terms of permissible "uses" rather than permissible "users." Defendant contends that this congressional linguistic choice, among others, reveals an intent to allow companies like Reed Elsevier to obtain and resell drivers' personal information to parties with a permissible use under the DPPA. The Court agrees. Congress' intent to regulate the use of drivers' personal information rather than the user is evident from its DPPA word choice as well as the language it employed in several other privacy-related statutes. If Congress had intended to require that the "authorized recipient" of personal information also be a user of that information, it could have written the DPPA exceptions explicitly to that effect. Congress could have referred to "permissible users" rather than "permissible uses" in 18 U.S.C. § 2721(b). Instead, Congress opted to describe DPPA disclosure exceptions in terms of use.

Indeed, in other privacy acts Congress has restricted disclosure exceptions to specific users. For example, in the 1998 Video Privacy Protection Act, 18 U.S.C. § 2710, et seq., Congress wrote:

A video tape service provider may disclose personally identifiable information concerning any consumer—

(A) to the consumer;

(B) to any person with the informed, written consent * * *

(C) to a law enforcement agency * * *

(D) to any person if the disclosure is solely of the names and addresses * * *

(E) to any person if the disclosure is incident to the ordinary course of business * * *

18 U.S.C. § 2710(b)(2). Similarly, in the Family Education Rights Privacy Act, U.S.C. § 1232g, et seq., Congress explicitly limited personal informa-

tion release to school officials, teachers, authorized federal representatives, state and local officials, parents, and others, rather than merely regulating the types of use those persons might undertake. * * *

Plaintiffs' reliance on the Iowa Supreme Court opinion in Locate.Plus.com, Inc. v. Iowa D.O.T, 650 N.W. 2d 609, 617–8 (Iowa 2002), is misplaced. Locate.Plus.com does not bind this Court. That decision is both factually and procedurally distinguishable from the case at hand. Furthermore, Locate.Plus.com neglects to provide a meaningful analysis of the DPPA's statutory language and corresponding congressional intent, especially as they relate the common definitions of key DPPA terms and to other federal privacy acts. As a result, the Locate.Plus.com holding cannot apply to the instant plaintiffs' improper obtainment claims, which must be dismissed. * * *

Plaintiffs also cite to language in Reno v. Condon, 528 U.S. 141 (2000), to support her claim. Reno upheld the constitutionality of the DPPA, but the issue of improper obtainment was not before the court. In Reno, the Supreme Court focused on the principles of federalism and the Tenth Amendment, not on the precise meaning and scope of the statute, and certainly not as applied to the facts in this case. This Court finds plaintiffs' reliance on Reno to be unavailing.

For reasons stated above, plaintiffs' DPPA improper obtainment claims must be dismissed * * *. Defendant's obtainment of plaintiffs' personal DMV records for the sole purpose of resale and redisclosure does not entitle plaintiff to relief under the DPPA.

FIDELITY FEDERAL BANK & TRUST v. KEHOE

547 U.S. 1051 (2006), cert. denied.

JUSTICE SCALIA, with whom JUSTICE ALITO joins, concurring.

This case presents an important question of statutory construction—whether "actual damages" must be shown before a plaintiff may recover under the Driver's Privacy Protection Act of 1994, 18 U.S.C. § 2724(b)(1). The Florida Department of Highway Safety and Motor Vehicles sold to petitioner, for a penny apiece, the names and addresses of 565,600 individuals in three counties who registered cars with the DMV—the total cost was thus $5,656. Petitioner intended to mail these individuals a solicitation to refinance their automobile loans. However, because Florida—alone among the States—had not immediately amended its law to comply with the Act, none of these people had given their "express consent" to the release of this information, as the Act requires. § 2721(b)(12). Petitioner [Fidelity Federal Bank and trust] now faces a possible $1.4 billion judgment—$2,500 per violation. Because of other class actions currently pending in Florida, involving the same question, the total amount at stake may reach $40 billion. This enormous potential liability, which turns on a question of federal statutory interpretation, is a strong factor in deciding whether to grant certiorari. * * *

Nonetheless, I concur in the denial of certiorari. A second and equally important legal question is bound up in this case—namely, whether petitioner can be held liable under the Act if it did not know that the State had failed to comply with the Act's "express consent" requirement. The District Court did not reach this issue since it awarded summary judgment to petitioner on the actual damages question. The scienter question remains open in light of the Eleventh Circuit's judgment reversing and remanding the case. See 421 F.3d 1209 (2005). Depending on the course of proceedings below, it may later be appropriate for us to consider granting certiorari as to either or both issues. But because I agree that our consideration of the case would be premature now, I concur in the denial of certiorari.

2. THE REAL ID ACT OF 2005

NOTE: A NATIONAL IDENTIFICATION CARD?

The REAL ID Act of 2005 was signed into law as part of the "Emergency Supplemental Appropriations Act for Defense, the Global War on Terror, and Tsunami Relief Act," Public Law 109–13 (May 11, 2005). Congress gave the Department of Homeland Security authority to promulgate rules under the Act. The Act was originally scheduled to go fully into effect in May 2008, but the period of compliance was twice extended. States making progress towards implementation have been given the option of seeking an extension until May 10, 2011. Individuals from states that have not complied with the Act or its extension provisions could be denied access to commercial aircraft and some federal facilities and nuclear power plants. According to the National Conference of State Legislatures, Congress has appropriated only $200 million to assist states with implementation of the REAL ID; yet, implementation will cost the states an estimated $3.9 billion.

One objective of the REAL ID Act is to implement the recommendation of the 9/11 Commission to enhance the security and integrity of driver's licenses. The 9/11 terrorists used authentic drivers' licenses that they obtained on the basis of unverified identification. In March 2007, DHS announced a proposal to establish minimum standards for state-issued drivers' licenses and identification cards.

Does the REAL ID Act essentially mandate a national identification card? Is a national identification standard, if a not a national identification card, a good idea?

Former Homeland Security Secretary Michael Chertoff explained that: "Raising the security standards on driver's licenses establishes another layer of protection to prevent terrorists from obtaining and using fake documents to plan or carry out an attack. These standards correct glaring vulnerabilities exploited by some of the 9/11 hijackers who used fraudulently obtained drivers licenses to board the airplanes in their attack against America." The new rules would prescribe verification standards and security features for state-issued ID cards. As previously noted, the rules would also make presentation of an identification card that complies with federal standards a condition of boarding most commercial aircraft, and entering federal buildings or nuclear power plants.

Although federal funds would pay for a part of the states' obligations to implement REAL ID, many states have expressed opposition to a policy of national identification standards. Marc Rotenberg, Executive Director of the Electronic Privacy Information Center (EPIC), has argued that the REAL ID Act's proposed system of national identification will be costly and may be vulnerable to unforeseen security risks. Rotenberg and EPIC caution against the proposed DHS regulations for REAL ID on several grounds: The rules would (1) impose more difficult standards for acceptable identification documents that could limit the ability of individuals to get a state driver's license; (2) compel data verification procedures that the federal government itself is not capable of following; (3) mandate minimum data elements required on the face of and in the machine-readable zone of the card; (4) require changes to the design of licenses and identification cards; (5) expand schedules and procedures for retention and distribution of identification documents and other personal data; and (6) dictate security standards for the card, state motor vehicle facilities, and the personal data and documents collected in state motor vehicle databases.

In the article excerpted below Michael Froomkin suggested that the REAL ID era may be a good time for government to bargain with the private sector over privacy standards. The general public has an interest in private businesses adhering to fair information practices, and private businesses have an interest in the general public with whom it transacts business holding reliable, verified identification. Standardization of official state and federal identification could be joined with offering the private sector a voluntary opportunity to use the new government identification system on the condition that it agrees to adhere to strict fair information practices. Do you think U.S. companies are prepared to adopt a version of the Organization for Economic Cooperation and Development privacy principles that Froomkin says he favors? (A statement of the principles follows Froomkin's article.) Would a "more standardization for more privacy" *quid pro quo* make U.S. residents more comfortable with REAL ID's full implementation?

MICHAEL FROOMKIN, CREATING A VIRAL FEDERAL PRIVACY STANDARD

48 B.C. L. Rev. 55, 60–61, 85 (2007).

Although national ID cards are common in many parts of the world, it is an article of faith in many quarters that the United States does not have one. In fact, rather than one ID card we have many: notably, voter ID cards, SSNs, driver's licenses, and credit cards, to name only the most common. Each type of ID was created for a limited purpose, and each is significantly flawed or insecure. As businesses and government have felt a greater need to find a way to authenticate individuals and associate them with existing records, the private sector has come to rely on existing forms of government-issued identification. * * *

Although perhaps not formally mandatory, SSNs are necessary if one wishes to take paid employment or participate in the banking system.

Cars are a practical necessity for most Americans who live outside the largest urban areas, making a driver's license a practical necessity for most as well. A government-produced ID is currently demanded for travel not only behind the wheel of a car, but also as a passenger on airlines, trains, intercity buses, and even local buses. Although such demands are increasingly common, their legal status remains debated. * * *

Many private-sector transactions, particularly those that involve the creation of an ongoing relationship or obligation, also involve the exchange of identification data, including name, address, telephone number, and SSN or driver's license number. Together, these data ordinarily permit the merchant to link a customer to transaction and credit histories maintained by commercial data brokers such as Experian and Choice-Point. Merchants' reasons for requesting ID often depend on the nature of the transaction. For example, by associating a consumer with a set of records such as a credit history, a business can estimate the likelihood of current or future payment. Verifying address and employment information provides some guarantee of recovery by suit or garnishment if payments stop. And, in other types of transactions, the firm may be required to do a records check to comply with regulatory requirements such as "know your customer" rules in financial transactions. In the absence of a regulatory duty, the firm's primary motive may be to enable demographic analysis of the customer database, or to permit future targeted marketing.

The databases maintained by private firms on U.S. persons are remarkably large. Experian, for example, brags that its "North America databases contain more than 65 terabytes (65 trillion bytes) of data" including "credit information on approximately 215 million U.S. consumers and more than 15 million U.S. businesses" and "demographic information on approximately 215 million consumers in 110 million living units across the United States."

These large databases contain many inaccuracies. And from a firm's perspective, the process of matching a given person with the right set of records can be quite difficult, especially if the person has a common name. There are many John Smiths in the United States. Between data entry errors, and inconsistent methods of data acquisition, firms' records can get mixed up. Pulling together an accurate set of data regarding a given person becomes even more difficult when dealing with distributed databases. In theory, as data storage gets cheaper and electronic communication becomes almost costless, it should be easy to tie together disparate sets of records to produce a single, giant, virtual dossier about each of us. But in fact it is not easy, which is why firms like Experian and Choice-Point have something valuable to sell. * * *

The introduction of a new standard REAL ID has created an opportunity for the federal government to use its power creatively. The carrot of lower transaction costs dangled by easy, secure, reliable, and cheap identification might suffice to create market-based incentives for businesses to accept the stick of adherence to substantive privacy conditions. [A sensible national data privacy plan would seek to buy into a full-blown set of Fair Information Practices. My personal preference is to require, at a minimum, that the United States commit itself to an updated and improved version of the 1980 Organization for Economic Co-operation and Development privacy guidelines.] By defining a standard for data access and numbering, and by retaining ownership of the standard and especially the data, the government could give itself the leverage to offer a deal to firms desiring to take advantage of the new credential. A ubiquitous and reliable numbering system should be very attractive to businesses, and they might be willing to accept the obligations of Fair Information Practices as the price of admission. Making the privacy program formally voluntary, in the sense that only those who used the new cards or the new numbers would be required to follow the privacy standard, would also make it more likely to be politically acceptable.

One important consequence of this proposal is that it would centralize and nationalize the data privacy debate. Although there have been successes, the explosion of privacy-destroying technologies within the last two decades suggests pretty strongly that standards and practices unfriendly to data privacy are being set more quickly and in more places than the privacy community can handle. A perverse advantage of a centralized national ID regime would be that it would create a very visible, single target for debate about privacy regulation. This is only a mixed blessing, for centralization also allows the interests that tend to oppose restrictions on the use of personal data to unite their lobbying efforts in one massive push for the goldfish bowl society.

ORGANIZATION FOR ECONOMIC COOPERATION AND DEVELOPMENT PRIVACY GUIDELINES

http://www.cdt.org/privacy/guide/basic/oecdguidelines.html.

In late 1980, the Organization for Economic Cooperation and Development issued a set of Guidelines concerning the privacy of personal records. Although broad, the OECD guidelines set up important standards for future governmental privacy rules. These guidelines underpin most current international agreements, national laws, and self-regulatory policies. Although the guidelines were voluntary, roughly half of OECD member-nations had already passed or proposed privacy-protecting legislation by 1980. * * * The OECD Guidelines are as follows:

    1.   Collection Limitation Principle

There should be limits to the collection of personal data and any such data should be obtained by lawful and fair means and, where appropriate, with the knowledge or consent of the data subject.

    2.   Data Quality Principle

Personal data should be relevant to the purposes for which they are to be used, and, to the extent necessary for those purposes, should be accurate, complete and kept up-to-date.

3. Purpose Specification Principle

The purposes for which personal data are collected should be specified not later than at the time of data collection and the subsequent use limited to the fulfillment of those purposes or such others as are not incompatible with those purposes and as are specified on each occasion of change of purpose.

4. Use Limitation Principle

Personal data should not be disclosed, made available or otherwise used for purposes other than those specified in accordance with Paragraph 9 except:

    a) with the consent of the data subject; or

    b) by the authority of law.

5. Security Safeguards Principle

Personal data should be protected by reasonable security safeguards against such risks as loss or unauthorized access, destruction, use, modification or disclosure of data.

6. Openness Principle

There should be a general policy of openness about developments, practices and policies with respect to personal data. Means should be readily available of establishing the existence and nature of personal data, and the main purposes of their use, as well as the identity and usual residence of the data controller.

7. Individual Participation Principle

An individual should have the right:

    a) to obtain from a data controller, or otherwise, confirmation of whether or not the data controller has data relating to him;

    b) to have communicated to him, data relating to him within a reasonable time; at a charge, if any, that is not excessive; in a reasonable manner; and in a form that is readily intelligible to him;

    c) to be given reasons if a request made under subparagraphs (a) and (b) is denied, and to be able to challenge such denial; and

    d) to challenge data relating to him and, if the challenge is successful to have the data erased, rectified, completed or amended.

8. Accountability Principle

A data controller should be accountable for complying with measures which give effect to the principles stated above.

C. SCHOOL RECORDS—FAMILY EDU-CATIONAL RIGHTS AND PRIVACY ACT OF 1974 (FERPA)

The Family Educational Rights and Privacy Act of 1974 (FERPA), 88 Stat. 571, 20 U.S.C. § 1232g, 34 CFR Part 99, is one of the oldest federal privacy statutes. It regulates the disclosure of students' academic transcripts and other personal information maintained by public or private schools, colleges and universities receiving federal funding. While a student's name, address and years of attendance receive a low level of protection, a student's grades receive a high level of protection.

In the case of minors, parents have the right to exercise FERPA rights and may block the disclosure of academic information to many third parties. In the case of students over eighteen, the students' prior permission must generally be obtained if transcripts are to be released to parents. Exceptions embodied in the statute permit disclosures without consent as needed for safety, law enforcement, research and other purposes.

FAMILY EDUCATIONAL RIGHTS AND PRIVACY ACT (FERPA)

http://www.ed.gov/policy/gen/guid/fpco/ferpa/index.html.

FERPA gives parents certain rights with respect to their children's education records. These rights transfer to the student when he or she reaches the age of 18 or attends a school beyond the high school level. Students to whom the rights have transferred are "eligible students."

- Parents or eligible students have the right to inspect and review the student's education records maintained by the school. Schools are not required to provide copies of records unless, for reasons such as great distance, it is impossible for parents or eligible students to review the records. Schools may charge a fee for copies.

- Parents or eligible students have the right to request that a school correct records which they believe to be inaccurate or misleading. If the school decides not to amend the record, the parent or eligible student then has the right to a formal hearing. After the hearing, if the school still decides not to amend the record, the parent or eligible student has the right to place a statement with the record setting forth his or her view about the contested information.

- Generally, schools must have written permission from the parent or eligible student in order to release any information from a student's education record. However, FERPA allows schools to disclose those records, without consent, to the following parties or under the following conditions (34 CFR § 99.31): School officials with legitimate educational interest; Other schools to which a student is transferring; Specified officials for audit or evaluation purposes;

> Appropriate parties in connection with financial aid to a student; Organizations conducting certain studies for or on behalf of the school; Accrediting organizations; To comply with a judicial order or lawfully issued subpoena; Appropriate officials in cases of health and safety emergencies; and State and local authorities, within a juvenile justice system, pursuant to specific State law.

Schools may disclose, without consent, "directory" information such as a student's name, address, telephone number, date and place of birth, honors and awards, and dates of attendance. However, schools must tell parents and eligible students about directory information and allow parents and eligible students a reasonable amount of time to request that the school not disclose directory information about them. Schools must notify parents and eligible students annually of their rights under FERPA. The actual means of notification (special letter, inclusion in a PTA bulletin, student handbook, or newspaper article) is left to the discretion of each school.

NOTE: HOW FAR FERPA?

How far does FERPA go to safeguard pupil privacy? Does it go far enough, or are the exceptions to the consent rule too liberal? Does FERPA accord with fair information practice principles? Which ones?

Does FERPA prohibit outsiders from visiting the campus of a public school for emotionally disturbed children? See *Connecticut v. Hartford Board of Education*, 464 F.3d 229 (2d Cir. 2006), in which a school district raised but dropped such a claim. The Court of Appeals held that state investigators were entitled under federal monitoring standards, including the Protection and Advocacy for Individuals with Mental Illness statute, 42 U.S.C. § 10801(b)(2), to visit campus to discern whether children protected by the Individuals with Disabilities Education Act were being mistreated. Would FERPA prevent university officials from disclosing a student's potentially dangerous mental illness to fellow students and professors?

Only a couple of FERPA cases have made their way to the U.S. Supreme Court. They both appear in this section. Why did the Court bother to decide the issue of peer grading raised by the *Owasso* case on the merits, since, as the court held the same term in *Gonzaga*, FERPA does not provide for a private right of action?

1. PEER GRADING

OWASSO INDEP. SCH. DIST. NO. I–011 v. FALVO

534 U.S. 426 (2002).

JUSTICE KENNEDY delivered the opinion of the Court.

Teachers sometimes ask students to score each other's tests, papers, and assignments as the teacher explains the correct answers to the entire class. Respondent contends this practice, which the parties refer to as peer grading, violates the Family Educational Rights and Privacy Act of 1974 (FERPA or Act), 88 Stat. 571, 20 U.S.C. § 1232g. We took this case to resolve the issue. * * *

Under FERPA, schools and educational agencies receiving federal financial assistance must comply with certain conditions. § 1232g(a)(3). One condition specified in the Act is that sensitive information about students may not be released without parental consent. The Act states that federal funds are to be withheld from school districts that have "a policy or practice of permitting the release of education records (or personally identifiable information contained therein * * *) of students without the written consent of their parents." § 1232g(b)(1). The phrase "education records" is defined, under the Act, as "records, files, documents, and other materials" containing information directly related to a student, which "are maintained by an educational agency or institution or by a person acting for such agency or institution." § 1232g(a)(4)(A). The definition of education records contains an exception for "records of instructional, supervisory, and administrative personnel * * * which are in the sole possession of the maker thereof and which are not accessible or revealed to any other person except a substitute." § 1232g(a)(4)(B)(i). The precise question for us is whether peer-graded classroom work and assignments are education records.

Three of respondent Kristja J. Falvo's children are enrolled in Owasso Independent School District No. I–011, in a suburb of Tulsa, Oklahoma. The children's teachers, like many teachers in this country, use peer grading. In a typical case, the students exchange papers with each other and score them according to the teacher's instructions, then return the work to the student who prepared it. The teacher may ask the students to report their own scores. In this case it appears the student could either call out the score or walk to the teacher's desk and reveal it in confidence, though by that stage, of course, the score was known at least to the one other student who did the grading. Both the grading and the system of calling out the scores are in contention here.

Respondent claimed the peer grading embarrassed her children. She asked the school district to adopt a uniform policy banning peer grading and requiring teachers either to grade assignments themselves or at least to forbid students from grading papers other than their own. The school district declined to do so, and respondent brought a class action pursuant to Rev. Stat. § 1979, 42 U.S.C. § 1983 (1994 ed., Supp. V), against the school district, Superintendent Dale Johnson, Assistant Superintendent Lynn Johnson, and Principal Rick Thomas (petitioners). Respondent alleged the school district's grading policy violated FERPA and other laws not relevant here. * * *

 We granted certiorari to decide whether peer grading violates FERPA. 533 U.S. 927 (2001). Finding no violation of the Act, we reverse.

At the outset, we note it is an open question whether FERPA provides private parties, like respondent, with a cause of action enforceable under

§ 1983. We have granted certiorari on this issue in another case. *See Gonzaga Univ. v. Doe*, 534 U.S. 1103 (2002). * * *

The parties appear to agree that if an assignment becomes an education record the moment a peer grades it, then the grading, or at least the practice of asking students to call out their grades in class, would be an impermissible release of the records under § 1232g(b)(1) * * * Without deciding the point, we assume for the purposes of our analysis that they are correct. The parties disagree, however, whether peer-graded assignments constitute education records at all. The papers do contain information directly related to a student, but they are records under the Act only when and if they "are maintained by an educational agency or institution or by a person acting for such agency or institution." § 1232g(a)(4)(A).

Petitioners, supported by the United States as amicus curiae, contend the definition covers only institutional records—namely, those materials retained in a permanent file as a matter of course. They argue that records "maintained by an educational agency or institution" generally would include final course grades, student grade point averages, standardized test scores, attendance records, counseling records, and records of disciplinary actions—but not student homework or classroom work.

Respondent, adopting the reasoning of the Court of Appeals, contends student-graded assignments fall within the definition of education records. That definition contains an exception for "records of instructional, supervisory, and administrative personnel * * * which are in the sole possession of the maker thereof and which are not accessible or revealed to any other person except a substitute." § 1232g(a)(4)(B)(i). The Court of Appeals reasoned that if grade books are not education records, then it would have been unnecessary for Congress to enact the exception. Grade books and the grades within, the court concluded, are "maintained" by a teacher and so are covered by FERPA. 233 F.3d at 1215. The court recognized that teachers do not maintain the grades on individual student assignments until they have recorded the result in the grade books. It reasoned, however, that if Congress forbids teachers to disclose students' grades once written in a grade book, it makes no sense to permit the disclosure immediately beforehand. Id., at 1216. The court thus held that student graders maintain the grades until they are reported to the teacher. Ibid.

The Court of Appeals' logic does not withstand scrutiny. Its interpretation, furthermore, would effect a drastic alteration of the existing allocation of responsibilities between States and the National Government in the operation of the Nation's schools. We would hesitate before interpreting the statute to effect such a substantial change in the balance of federalism unless that is the manifest purpose of the legislation. This principle guides our decision.

Two statutory indicators tell us that the Court of Appeals erred in concluding that an assignment satisfies the definition of education records as soon as it is graded by another student. First, the student papers are not, at that stage, "maintained" within the meaning of § 1232g(a)(4)(A).

The ordinary meaning of the word "maintain" is "to keep in existence or continuance; preserve; retain." Random House Dictionary of the English Language 1160 (2d ed. 1987). Even assuming the teacher's grade book is an education record—a point the parties contest and one we do not decide here—the score on a student-graded assignment is not "contained therein," § 1232g(b)(1), until the teacher records it. The teacher does not maintain the grade while students correct their peers' assignments or call out their own marks. Nor do the student graders maintain the grades within the meaning of § 1232g(a)(4)(A). The word "maintain" suggests FERPA records will be kept in a filing cabinet in a records room at the school or on a permanent secure database, perhaps even after the student is no longer enrolled. The student graders only handle assignments for a few moments as the teacher calls out the answers. It is fanciful to say they maintain the papers in the same way the registrar maintains a student's folder in a permanent file.

The Court of Appeals was further mistaken in concluding that each student grader is "a person acting for" an educational institution for purposes of § 1232g(a)(4)(A). 233 F.3d at 1216. The phrase "acting for" connotes agents of the school, such as teachers, administrators, and other school employees. * * *

Under the Court of Appeals' broad interpretation of education records, every teacher would have an obligation to keep a separate record of access for each student's assignments. Indeed, by that court's logic, even students who grade their own papers would bear the burden of maintaining records of access until they turned in the assignments. We doubt Congress would have imposed such a weighty administrative burden on every teacher, and certainly it would not have extended the mandate to students.

Also FERPA requires "a record" of access for each pupil. This single record must be kept "with the education records." This suggests Congress contemplated that education records would be kept in one place with a single record of access. By describing a "school official" and "his assistants" as the personnel responsible for the custody of the records, FERPA implies that education records are institutional records kept by a single central custodian, such as a registrar, not individual assignments handled by many student graders in their separate classrooms.

FERPA also requires recipients of federal funds to provide parents with a hearing at which they may contest the accuracy of their child's education records. § 1232g(a)(2). The hearings must be conducted "in accordance with regulations of the Secretary," ibid., which in turn require adjudication by a disinterested official and the opportunity for parents to be represented by an attorney. 34 CFR § 99.22 (2001). It is doubtful Congress would have provided parents with this elaborate procedural machinery to challenge the accuracy of the grade on every spelling test and art project the child completes.

Respondent's construction of the term "education records" to cover student homework or classroom work would impose substantial burdens on teachers across the country. It would force all instructors to take time, which otherwise could be spent teaching and in preparation, to correct an assortment of daily student assignments. Respondent's view would make it much more difficult for teachers to give students immediate guidance. The interpretation respondent urges would force teachers to abandon other customary practices, such as group grading of team assignments. Indeed, the logical consequences of respondent's view are all but unbounded. At argument, counsel for respondent seemed to agree that if a teacher in any of the thousands of covered classrooms in the Nation puts a happy face, a gold star, or a disapproving remark on a classroom assignment, federal law does not allow other students to see it.

We doubt Congress meant to intervene in this drastic fashion with traditional state functions. Under the Court of Appeals' interpretation of FERPA, the federal power would exercise minute control over specific teaching methods and instructional dynamics in classrooms throughout the country. The Congress is not likely to have mandated this result, and we do not interpret the statute to require it.

For these reasons, even assuming a teacher's grade book is an education record, the Court of Appeals erred, for in all events the grades on students' papers would not be covered under FERPA at least until the teacher has collected them and recorded them in his or her grade book. We limit our holding to this narrow point, and do not decide the broader question whether the grades on individual student assignments, once they are turned in to teachers, are protected by the Act.

2.　NO PRIVATE RIGHT OF ACTION

GONZAGA UNIV. v. DOE

536 U.S. 273 (2002).

CHIEF JUSTICE REHNQUIST delivered the opinion of the Court. * * *

Respondent John Doe is a former undergraduate in the School of Education at Gonzaga University, a private university in Spokane, Washington. He planned to graduate and teach at a Washington public elementary school. Washington at the time required all of its new teachers to obtain an affidavit of good moral character from a dean of their graduating college or university. In October 1993, Roberta League, Gonzaga's "teacher certification specialist," overheard one student tell another that respondent engaged in acts of sexual misconduct against Jane Doe, a female undergraduate. League launched an investigation and contacted the state agency responsible for teacher certification, identifying respondent by name and discussing the allegations against him. Respondent did not learn of the investigation, or that information about him had been disclosed, until March 1994, when he was told by League and others that he would not receive the affidavit required for certification as a Washington schoolteacher.

Respondent then sued Gonzaga and League (petitioners) in state court. He alleged violations of Washington tort and contract law, as well as a pendent violation of § 1983 for the release of personal information to an "unauthorized person" in violation of FERPA. * * *

Congress enacted FERPA under its spending power to condition the receipt of federal funds on certain requirements relating to the access and disclosure of student educational records. The Act directs the Secretary of Education to withhold federal funds from any public or private "educational agency or institution" that fails to comply with these conditions. * * *

Respondent contends that [FERPA] confers upon any student enrolled at a covered school or institution a federal right, enforceable in suits for damages under § 1983, not to have "education records" disclosed to unauthorized persons without the student's express written consent. But we have never before held, and decline to do so here, that spending legislation drafted in terms resembling those of FERPA can confer enforceable rights. * * *

We made clear that unless Congress "speaks with a clear voice," and manifests an "unambiguous" intent to confer individual rights, federal funding provisions provide no basis for private enforcement by § 1983. [Our recent decisions have rejected attempts to infer enforceable rights from Spending Clause statutes.] * * *

We now reject the notion that our cases permit anything short of an unambiguously conferred right to support a cause of action brought under § 1983. Section 1983 provides a remedy only for the deprivation of "rights, privileges, or immunities secured by the Constitution and laws" of the United States. Accordingly, it is rights, not the broader or vaguer "benefits" or "interests," that may be enforced under the authority of that section. This being so, we further reject the notion that our implied right of action cases are separate and distinct from our § 1983 cases. To the contrary, our implied right of action cases should guide the determination of whether a statute confers rights enforceable under § 1983. * * *

With this * * * in mind, there is no question that FERPA's nondisclosure provisions fail to confer enforceable rights. To begin with, the provisions entirely lack the sort of "rights-creating" language critical to showing the requisite congressional intent to create new rights. Alexander v. Sandoval, 532 U.S. at 288–289; Cannon, supra, at 690, n. 13. Unlike the individually focused terminology of Titles VI and IX ("no person shall be subjected to discrimination"), FERPA's provisions speak only to the Secretary of Education, directing that "no funds shall be made available" to any "educational agency or institution" which has a prohibited "policy or practice." 20 U.S.C. § 1232g(b)(1). This focus is two steps removed from the interests of individual students and parents and clearly does not confer the sort of "individual entitlement" that is enforceable under § 1983. Blessing, 520 U.S. at 343. * * *

Our conclusion that FERPA's nondisclosure provisions fail to confer enforceable rights is buttressed by the mechanism that Congress chose to provide for enforcing those provisions. Congress expressly authorized the Secretary of Education to "deal with violations" of the Act, § 1232g(f), and required the Secretary to "establish or designate [a] review board" for investigating and adjudicating such violations, § 1232g(g). Pursuant to these provisions, the Secretary created the Family Policy Compliance Office (FPCO) "to act as the Review Board required under the Act and to enforce the Act with respect to all applicable programs." 34 CFR 99.60(a) and (b) (2001). The FPCO permits students and parents who suspect a violation of the Act to file individual written complaints. § 99.63. If a complaint is timely and contains required information, the FPCO will initiate an investigation, §§ 99.64(a)–(b), notify the educational institution of the charge, § 99.65(a), and request a written response, § 99.65. If a violation is found, the FPCO distributes a notice of factual findings and a "statement of the specific steps that the agency or institution must take to comply" with FERPA. §§ 99.66(b) and (c)(1). These administrative procedures squarely distinguish this case from Wright and Wilder, where an aggrieved individual lacked any federal review mechanism, and further counsel against our finding a congressional intent to create individually enforceable private rights.

Congress finally provided that "except for the conduct of hearings, none of the functions of the Secretary under this section shall be carried out in any of the regional offices" of the Department of Education. 20 U.S.C. § 1232g(g). This centralized review provision was added just four months after FERPA's enactment due to "concern that regionalizing the enforcement of [FERPA] may lead to multiple interpretations of it, and possibly work a hardship on parents, students, and institutions." Cf. Wright, 479 U.S. at 426 ("Congress' aim was to provide a decentralized * * * administrative process" (internal quotation marks omitted)). It is implausible to presume that the same Congress nonetheless intended private suits to be brought before thousands of federal-and state-court judges, which could only result in the sort of "multiple interpretations" the Act explicitly sought to avoid.

In sum, if Congress wishes to create new rights enforceable under § 1983, it must do so in clear and unambiguous terms—no less and no more than what is required for Congress to create new rights enforceable under an implied private right of action. FERPA's nondisclosure provisions contain no rights-creating language, they have an aggregate, not individual, focus, and they serve primarily to direct the Secretary of Education's distribution of public funds to educational institutions. They therefore create no rights enforceable under § 1983. Accordingly, the judgment of the Supreme Court of Washington is reversed, and the case is remanded for further proceedings not inconsistent with this opinion.

D. HEALTH RECORDS AND HEALTH INFORMATION

1. HEALTH INSURANCE PORTABILITY AND ACCOUNTABILITY ACT OF 1996 ("HIPAA") AND AMERICAN RECOVERY AND REINVESTMENT ACT OF 2009 (ARRA)

NOTE: MEDICAL PRIVACY AND CONFIDENTIALITY

Medical information is among the most sensitive types of personal information. The disclosure of medical information can lead to discomfort, embarrassment and discrimination. The confidentiality of the provider-patient relationship may encourage people to seek vital medical attention and to be honest with their physicians. As we saw in Chapter 1 of this textbook, medical patients and consumers have often taken advantage of state tort and statutory remedies for invasions of privacy and breaches of confidentiality by physicians and other healthcare providers.

Federal medical privacy and confidentiality laws are of relatively recent vintage. The Health Insurance Portability and Accountability Act (HIPAA), Public Law 104–191, was enacted in 1996. Through HIPAA, Congress delegated authority to enact national medical data privacy and security standards to the Department of Health and Human Services (DHHS or HHS). The DHHS Office for Civil Rights is responsible for implementing and enforcing the privacy rule.

Congress enacted the Patient Protection and Affordable Care Act (2010) to broaden access to affordable health care. A year earlier, Congress amended HIPAA through provisions of the American Recovery and Reinvestment Act of 2009 (ARRA). ARRA "includ[es] more than $49 billion in discretionary appropriations in mandatory spending to support and promote the adoption of [electronic health records] and the diffusion of [health information technology]." See Melissa Goldstein, "Law and the Public's Health: The Health Privacy Provisions in the American Recovery and Reinvestment Act of 2009: Implications for Public Health Policy and Practice," *125 Public Health Reports 234* (2010).

The HIPAA privacy rule applies to "covered entities," defined as health care providers who engage in certain electronic transactions, health plans, and so-called health care clearinghouses. DHHS defines a "health care clearinghouse" as a public or private entity, such as a hospital's billing service, that either "(1) processes or facilitates the processing of health information received from another entity in a nonstandard format or containing nonstandard data content into standard data elements or a standard transaction; or (2) receives a standard transaction from another entity and processes or facilitates the processing of health information into nonstandard format or nonstandard data content for the receiving entity." See Part II, 45 CFR 160.103.

These "covered entities" are prohibited from using or disclosing individually identifiable "protected health information" without consent, except as provided in the rule. HIPAA limits the right of covered entities to share medical data for purpose of marketing products and services to patients. Mental health information is subject to heightened protection under the HIPAA rule. Major health care providers and insurers were asked to comply with the privacy rule by April 2001. Smaller entities were given until 2004.

"Individually identifiable" information is defined under the HIPAA rule as information that: "relates to the past, present, or future physical or mental health or condition of an individual; the provision of health care to an individual; or the past, present, or future payment for the provision of health care to an individual; and that identifies the individual; or with respect to which there is a reasonable basis to believe the information can be used to identify the individual." See Part II, 45 CFR 164.501. Such information might include a person's names, exact postal addresses, telephone and fax numbers, e-mail addresses, social security number, medical record numbers, health plan beneficiary numbers, driver's license numbers, auto tag numbers, biometric identifiers, and photographs. See the DHHS OCR privacy rule page at http://www.hhs.gov/ocr/hipaa/privruletxt.txt.

HIPAA permits disclosure of health information without consent for many routine purposes. It also permits disclosures for purpose of scientific research and judicial process. HIPAA does not address concerns of modesty or dignity that patients may have in health-care settings. There is little a privacy law can do to get around the fact that health-care delivery requires bodily exposure, nudity and intimate touching.

As summarized by Melissa Goldstein: "Taken together, ARRA's provisions strengthen the level of individual control over and access to information contained in an [electronic health record]; broaden the definition of who is a business associate of covered entities and increase business associate duties; create new notification duties in the event of security breaches; placed new restrictions on marketing, fundraising, and the sale of protected health information (PHI); require the development of guidelines regarding the use of limited data sets and de-identified data; and increase penalties for violations of HIPPA and add new enforcement provisions." *Goldstein, supra.*

ORIGINS OF HIPAA

http://www.hhs.gov/ocr/hipaa/privruletxt.txt.

Congress recognized the importance of protecting the privacy of health information given the rapid evolution of health information systems in the Health Insurance Portability and Accountability Act of 1996 (HIPAA), Public Law 104–191, which became law on August 21, 1996. HIPAA's Administrative Simplification provisions, sections 261 through 264 of the statute, were designed to improve the efficiency and effectiveness of the health care system by facilitating the electronic exchange of information with respect to certain financial and administrative transactions carried out by health plans, health care clearinghouses, and health care providers who transmit information electronically in connection with such transactions. To implement these provisions, the statute directed HHS to adopt a suite of uniform, national standards for transactions, unique health identifiers, code sets for the data elements of the transactions, security of health information, and electronic signature.

At the same time, Congress recognized the challenges to the confidentiality of health information presented by the increasing complexity of the health care industry, and by advances in the health information systems technology and communications. Thus, the Administrative Simplification provisions of HIPAA authorized the Secretary to promulgate standards for the privacy of individually identifiable health information if Congress did not enact health care privacy legislation by August 21, 1999. HIPAA also required the Secretary of HHS to provide Congress with recommendations for legislating to protect the confidentiality of health care information. The Secretary submitted such recommendations to Congress on September 11, 1997, but Congress did not pass such legislation within its self-imposed deadline.

With respect to these regulations, HIPAA provided that the standards, implementation specifications, and requirements established by the Secretary not supersede any contrary State law that imposes more stringent privacy protections. * * *

HHS published a proposed Rule setting forth privacy standards for individually identifiable health information on November 3, 1999 (64 FR 59918). The Department received more than 52,000 public comments in response to the proposal. After reviewing and considering the public comments, HHS issued a final Rule (65 FR 82462) on December 28, 2000, establishing "Standards for Privacy of Individually Identifiable Health Information" ("Privacy Rule").

In an era where consumers are increasingly concerned about the privacy of their personal information, the Privacy Rule creates, for the first time, a floor of national protections for the privacy of their most sensitive information—health information. Congress has passed other laws to protect consumers' personal information contained in bank, credit card, other financial records, and even video rentals. These health privacy protections are intended to provide consumers with similar assurances that their health information, including genetic information, will be properly protected. Under the Privacy Rule, health plans, health care clearinghouses, and certain health care providers must guard against misuse of individuals' identifiable health information and limit the sharing of such information, and consumers are afforded significant new rights to enable them to understand and control how their health information is used and disclosed.

HIPAA PRIVACY AND SECURITY RULES
ENFORCEMENT HIGHLIGHTS

http://www.hhs.gov/ocr/privacy/hipaa/enforcement/highlights/index.html.

Privacy Rule Enforcement Results as of the Date of This Summary [July 31, 2010]

- HHS / OCR has investigated and resolved over 11,421 cases by requiring changes in privacy practices and other corrective actions by the covered entities. Corrective actions obtained by HHS from these entities have resulted in change that is systemic and that affects all the individuals they serve. HHS has successfully enforced the Privacy Rule by applying corrective measures in all cases where an investigation indicates noncompliance by the covered entity. OCR has investigated complaints against many different types of entities including: national pharmacy chains, major medical centers, group health plans, hospital chains, and small provider offices.

- In another 5,960 cases, our investigations found no violation had occurred.

- In the rest of our completed cases (31,194), HHS determined that the complaint did not present an eligible case for enforcement of the Privacy Rule. These include cases in which:

  - OCR lacks jurisdiction under HIPAA—such as a complaint alleging a violation prior to the compliance date or alleging a violation by an entity not covered by the Privacy Rule;

  - the complaint is untimely, or withdrawn or not pursued by the filer;

  - the activity described does not violate the Rule—such as when the covered entity has disclosed protected health information in circumstances in which the Rule permits such a disclosure.

- In summary, since the compliance date in April 2003, HHS has received over 53,789 HIPAA Privacy complaints. We have resolved over ninety percent of complaints received (over 48,575): through investigation and enforcement (over 11,421); through investigation and finding no violation (5,960); and through closure of cases that were not eligible for enforcement (31,194).

From the compliance date to the present, the compliance issues investigated most are, compiled cumulatively, in order of frequency:

1. Impermissible uses and disclosures of protected health information;

2. Lack of safeguards of protected health information;

3. Lack of patient access to their protected health information;

4. Uses or disclosures of more than the Minimum Necessary protected health information; and

5. Complaints to the covered entity.

The most common types of covered entities that have been required to take corrective action to achieve voluntary compliance are, in order of frequency:

1. Private Practices;

2. General Hospitals;

3. Outpatient Facilities;

4. Health Plans (group health plans and health insurance issuers); and,

5. Pharmacies.

Security Rule Enforcement Results as of the Date of This Summary [July 31, 2010]

● Since OCR began reporting its Security Rule enforcement results in October 2009, HHS has received approximately 145 complaints alleging a violation of the Security Rule. During this period, we closed 50 complaints after investigation and appropriate corrective action. As of July 31, 2010, OCR had 180 open complaints and compliance reviews.

HHS DEPARTMENT OF CIVIL RIGHTS: EXAMPLES OF HIPAA ENFORCEMENT ACTIONS

http://www.hhs.gov/ocr/office/index.html.

Hospital Implements New Polices for Telephone Messages

Covered Entity: General Hospital

Issue: Minimum Necessary; Confidential Communications

A hospital employee did not observe minimum necessary requirements when she left a telephone message with the daughter of a patient that detailed both her medical condition and treatment plan. An OCR investigation also indicated that the confidential communications requirements were not followed, as the employee left the message at the patient's home telephone number, despite the patient's instructions to contact her through her work number. To resolve the issues in this case, the hospital developed and implemented several new procedures. One addressed the issue of minimum necessary information in telephone message content. Employees were trained to provide only the minimum necessary information in messages, and were given specific direction as to what information could be left in a message. Employees also were trained to review registration information for patient contact directives regarding leaving messages. The new procedures were incorporated into the standard staff privacy training, both as part of a refresher series and mandatory yearly compliance training.

Hospital Issues Guidelines Regarding Disclosures to Avert Threats to Health or Safety

Covered Entity: General Hospital

Issue: Safeguards; Impermissible Uses and Disclosures; Disclosures to Avert a Serious Threat to Health or Safety

After treating a patient injured in a rather unusual sporting accident, the hospital released to the local media, without the patient's authorization, copies of the patient's skull x-ray as well as a description of the complainant's medical condition. The local newspaper then featured on its front page the individual's x-ray and an article that included the date of the accident, the location of the accident, the patient's gender, a description of patient's medical condition, and numerous quotes from the hospital about such unusual sporting accidents. The hospital asserted that the disclosures were made to avert a serious threat to health or safety; however, OCR's investigation indicated that the disclosures did not meet the Privacy Rule's standard for such actions. The investigation also indicated that the disclosures did not meet the Rule's de-identification standard and therefore were not permissible without the individual's authorization. Among other corrective actions to resolve the specific issues in the case, OCR required the hospital to develop and implement a policy regarding disclosures related to serious threats to health and safety, and to train all members of the hospital staff on the new policy.

Large Medicaid Plan Corrects Vulnerability that Had Resulted in Wrongful Disclosure
Covered Entity: Health Plans
Issue: Impermissible Uses and Disclosures; Safeguards

A municipal social service agency disclosed protected health information while processing Medicaid applications by sending consolidated data to computer vendors that were not business associates. Among other corrective actions to resolve the specific issues in the case, OCR required that the social service agency develop procedures for properly disclosing protected health information only to its valid business associates and to train its staff on the new processes. The new procedures were instituted in Medicaid offices and independent health care programs under the jurisdiction of the municipal social service agency.

Public Hospital Corrects Impermissible Disclosure of Protected Health Information in Response to a Subpoena
Covered Entity: General Hospital
Issue: Impermissible Uses and Disclosures

A public hospital, in response to a subpoena (not accompanied by a court order), impermissibly disclosed the protected health information (PHI) of one of its patients. Contrary to the Privacy Rule protections for information sought for administrative or judicial proceedings, the hospital failed to determine that reasonable efforts had been made to insure that the individual whose PHI was being sought received notice of the request and/or failed to receive satisfactory assurance that the party seeking the information made reasonable efforts to secure a qualified protective order. Among other corrective actions to remedy this situation, OCR required that the hospital revise its subpoena processing procedures. Under the revised process, if a subpoena is received that does not meet the requirements of the Privacy Rule, the information is not disclosed; instead, the hospital contacts the party seeking the subpoena and the requirements of the Privacy Rule are explained. The hospital also trained relevant staff members on the new procedures.

Dentist Changes Process to Safeguard PHI
Covered Entity: Health Care Provider
Issue: Safeguards, Minimum Necessary

An OCR investigation confirmed allegations that a dental practice flagged some of its medical records with a red sticker with the word "AIDS" on the outside cover, and that records were handled so that other patients and staff without need to know could read the sticker. When notified of the complaint filed with OCR, the dental practice immediately removed the red AIDS sticker from the complainant's file. To resolve this matter, OCR also required the practice to revise its policies and operating procedures and to move medical alert stickers to the inside cover of the records. Further, the covered entity's Privacy Officer and other representatives met with the patient and apologized, and followed the meeting with a written apology.

Mental Health Center Provides Access after Denial
Covered Entity: Mental Health Center
Issue: Access, Authorization

The complainant alleged that a mental health center (the "Center") improperly provided her records to her auto insurance company and refused to provide her with a copy of her medical records. The Center provided OCR with a valid authorization, signed by the complainant, permitting the release of information to the auto insurance company. OCR also determined that the Center denied the complainant's request for access because her therapists believed providing the records to her would likely cause her substantial harm. The Center did not, however, provide the complainant with the opportunity to have the denial reviewed, as required by the Privacy Rule. Among other corrective action taken to resolve this issue, the Center provided the complainant with a copy of her records.

Private Practice Revises Policies and Procedures Addressing Activities Preparatory to Research
Covered Entity: Private Practice
Issue: Impermissible Disclosure–Research

A private practice physician who was the principal investigator of a clinical research study disclosed a list of patients and diagnostic codes to a contract research organization to telephone patients for recruitment purposes. The disclosure was not consistent with documents approved by the Institutional Review Board (IRB). The private practice maintained that the disclosure to the contract research organization was permissible as a review preparatory to research. Activities considered "preparatory to research" include: preparing a research protocol; developing a research hypothesis; and identifying prospective research participants. Contacting individuals to participate in a research study is a use or disclosure of protected health information (PHI) for recruitment, as it is part of the research and is not an activity preparatory to research. To remedy this situation, the private practice revised its policies and procedures regarding the disclosure of PHI and trained all physicians and staff members on the new policies and procedures. Under the revised policies and procedures, the practice may use and disclose PHI for research purposes, including recruitment, only if a valid authorization is obtained from each individual or if the covered entity obtains documentation that an alteration to or a waiver of the authorization requirement has been approved by an IRB or a Privacy Board.

Pharmacy Chain Institutes New Safeguards for Protected Health Information

Covered Entity: Pharmacies
Issue: Safeguards

A grocery store based pharmacy chain maintained pseudoephedrine log books containing protected health information in a manner so that individual protected health information was visible to the public at the pharmacy counter. Initially, the pharmacy chain refused to acknowledge that the log books contained protected health information. OCR issued a written analysis and a demand for compliance. Among other corrective actions to resolve the specific issues in the case, OCR required that the pharmacy chain implement national policies and procedures to safeguard the log books. Moreover, the entity was required to train of all staff on the revised policy. The chain acknowledged that log books contained protected health information and implemented the required changes.

a. No Private Right of Action

ACARA v. BANKS

470 F.3d 569 (5th Cir. 2006).

Before DeMoss, Stewart, and Prado, Circuit Judges.

Per Curiam:

Appellant Margaret Acara ("Acara") filed suit against Appellee Dr. Bradley Banks ("Dr. Banks") in Louisiana district court for disclosing her medical information during a deposition without her consent. Acara's complaint claimed subject matter jurisdiction based entirely upon an alleged violation of the Health Insurance Portability and Accountability Act of 1996 ("HIPAA"), Pub. L. No. 104–191, 110 Stat. 1936 (1996) (codified primarily in Titles 18, 26 and 42 of the United States Code). * * * The district court held that HIPAA does not give rise to a private cause of action, and therefore no subject matter jurisdiction existed. * * * This timely appeal followed. For the reasons stated below, we affirm. * * *

Whether or not HIPAA provides for a private cause of action is a question of statutory interpretation subject to de novo review. HIPAA generally provides for confidentiality of medical records. 42 U.S.C. §§ 1320d–1 to d–7. Private rights of action to enforce federal law must be created by Congress. Alexander v. Sandoval, 532 U.S. 275, 286 (2001). HIPAA has no express provision creating a private cause of action, and therefore we must determine if such is implied within the statute. Banks v. Dallas Hous. Auth., 271 F.3d 605, 608 (5th Cir. 2001). "The judicial task is to interpret the statute Congress has passed to determine whether it displays an intent to create not just a private right but also a private remedy. Statutory intent on this latter point is determinative." Id. In addition, the plaintiff has the relatively heavy burden to show Congress intended private enforcement, and must overcome the presumption that Congress did not intend to create a private cause of action. Casas v. Am. Airlines, Inc., 304 F.3d 517, 521–22 (5th Cir. 2002).

HIPAA does not contain any express language conferring privacy rights upon a specific class of individuals. Instead, it focuses on regulating persons that have access to individually identifiable medical information and who conduct certain electronic health care transactions. HIPAA provides both civil and criminal penalties for improper disclosures of medical information. However, HIPAA limits enforcement of the statute to the Secretary of Health and Human Services. Id. Because HIPAA specifically delegates enforcement, there is a strong indication that Congress intended to preclude private enforcement. Alexander, 532 U.S. at 286–87 ("The express provision of one method of enforcing [a statute] suggests Congress intended to preclude others.").

While no other circuit court has specifically addressed this issue, we are not alone in our conclusion that Congress did not intend for private enforcement of HIPAA. Every district court that has considered this issue is in agreement that the statute does not support a private right of action.

Furthermore, Acara provides no authority to support her assertion that a private right of action exists under HIPAA, and her policy arguments are unpersuasive. We hold there is no private cause of action under HIPAA and therefore no federal subject matter jurisdiction over Acara's asserted claims.

NOTE: DE NOVO REVIEW

The court in the preceding case, as in other cases in this chapter, faced a question of statutory interpretation. Courts commonly face the need to resolve disputes about the meaning of a statute. When a court resolves a dispute in favor of one party or another, the losing party often appeals to a higher body. An adverse administrative agency ruling may be appealed to a trial court. An adverse trial court ruling may be appealed to a court of appeals.

The 5th Circuit Court of Appeals in *Acara v. Banks* concluded that: "Whether or not HIPAA provides for a private cause of action is a question of statutory interpretation subject to *de novo* review." What is *de novo* review?

The general rule is that questions of statutory interpretation are decided *de novo*, anew, without deference to conclusions reached by the court from which the appeal was taken. *De novo* review asks a court to "review the matter anew, the same as if it had not been heard before, and as if no decision previously had been rendered." See *Ness v. Commissioner*, 954 F.2d 1495, 1497 (9th Cir. 1992).

Suppose, for example, that a party asks to a federal circuit court of appeal to review an adverse decision rendered by a federal district court, and that the issue on appeal is the meaning of the provision of a federal statute. The appeals court will take up the question of statutory interpretation afresh. It will not give weight to the district court's conclusions. Instead, the appeals court will undertake its own independent examination of the controverted provision. The appeals court will probably begin with the "plain meaning" of the text and recognized canons of statutory construction. It may then turn to consider legislative history, intent and purposes to resolve inconsistencies and ambiguities.

An appeals court may ultimately come to the same conclusion reached by the trial court; but it is free to reach a different conclusion. *De novo* review is independent, but not blind to precedent. How sister and higher courts in other cases have interpreted the same regulation has relevance as persuasive and binding authority, respectively.

De novo review is not limited to questions of statutory interpretation. Punitive damage awards, for example, are subject to *de novo* appellate court review. See *Cooper Industries, Inc. v. Leatherman Tool Group*, 532 U.S. 424 (2001).

b. The "Routine Uses" Rule Is Valid

CITIZENS FOR HEALTH v. LEAVITT

428 F.3d 167 (3rd Cir. 2005).

RENDELL, CIRCUIT JUDGE.

Appellant Citizens for Health, along with nine other national and state associations and nine individuals (collectively "Citizens"), brought this action against the Secretary of the United States Department of Health and Human Services ("HHS" or "Agency") challenging a rule promulgated * * * pursuant to [HIPAA] * * *. Citizens allege that the "Privacy Rule"—officially titled "Standards for Privacy of Individually Identifiable Health Information"—is invalid because it unlawfully authorizes health plans, health care clearinghouses, and certain health care providers to use and disclose personal health information for so-called "routine uses" without patient consent. The relevant part of the specific offending provision of the Privacy Rule reads:

(a) Standard: Permitted uses and disclosures. Except with respect to uses or disclosures that require an authorization under § 164.508(a)(2) [relating to psychotherapy notes] and (3) [relating to marketing], a covered entity may use or disclose protected health information for treatment, payment, or health care operations * * * provided that such use or disclosure is consistent with other applicable requirements of this subpart.

(b) Standard: Consent for uses and disclosures permitted. (1) A covered entity may obtain consent of the individual to use or disclose protected health information to carry out treatment, payment, or health care operations.

(2) Consent, under paragraph (b) of this section, shall not be effective to permit a use or disclosure of protected health information when an authorization, under § 164.508, is required or when another condition must be met for such use or disclosure to be permissible under this subpart. * * *

Citizens challenge subsection (a) as authorizing disclosures that, they contend, violate individual privacy rights.

HIPAA was passed by Congress in August 1996 to address a number of issues regarding the national health care and health insurance system. The statutory provisions relevant to the issues in this case are found in Subtitle F of Title II. Aimed at "administrative simplification," HIPAA Sections 261 through 264 provide for "the establishment of standards and requirements for the electronic transmission of certain health information." More specifically, these provisions direct the Secretary to adopt uniform national standards for the secure electronic exchange of health information.

Section 264 prescribes the process by which standards regarding the privacy of individually identifiable health information were to be adopted. § 264(a), 110 Stat. at 2033. This process contemplated that, within a year of HIPAA's enactment, the Secretary would submit detailed recommendations on such privacy standards, including individual rights concerning individually identifiable health information, procedures for exercising such rights, and the "uses and disclosures of such information that should be authorized or required," to Congress. If Congress did not enact further legislation within three years of HIPAA's enactment, the Secretary was directed to promulgate final regulations implementing the standards within 42 months of HIPAA's enactment. The Act specified that any regulation promulgated pursuant to the authority of Section 264 would provide a federal baseline for privacy protection, but that such regulations would "not supercede a contrary provision of State law, if the provision of State law imposes requirements, standards, or implementation specifications that are more stringent than the requirements, standards, or implementation specifications imposed under the regulation."

Because Congress did not enact privacy legislation by its self-imposed three-year deadline, the Secretary promulgated the privacy standards contemplated in Section 264 through an administrative rulemaking process. During this process, the Rule went through four iterations: the Proposed Original Rule, the Original Rule, the Proposed Amended Rule, and the Amended Rule. The Original Rule required covered entities to seek individual consent before using or disclosing protected health information for routine uses. Before the Original Rule could take effect, however, the Secretary was inundated with unsolicited criticism, principally from health care insurers and providers, warning that the Original Rule's mandatory consent provisions would significantly impact the ability of the health care industry to operate efficiently. He responded by reopening the rulemaking process. The final result was the Amended Rule—the currently effective, codified version of the Privacy Rule, see generally 45 C.F.R. pts. 160 & 164, which is the subject of Citizens' challenge here.

The Amended Rule retains most of the Original Rule's privacy protections. It prohibits "covered entities"—defined as health plans, health care clearinghouses, and health care providers who transmit any health information in electronic form in connection with a transaction covered by the regulations—from using or disclosing an individual's "protected health information"—defined as individually identifiable health information maintained in or transmitted in any form or media including electronic media—except as otherwise provided by the Rule. Covered entities must seek authorization from individuals before using or disclosing information unless a specific exception applies. Uses and disclosures that the Amended Rule allows must be limited to the "minimum necessary" to accomplish the intended purpose.

The Amended Rule departs from the Original Rule in one crucial respect. Where the Original Rule required covered entities to seek individual consent to use or disclose health information in all but the narrowest of circumstances, the Amended Rule allows such uses and disclosures without patient consent for "treatment, payment, and health care operations"—so-called "routine uses." "Health care operations," the broadest category under the routine use exception, refers to a range of management functions of covered entities, including quality assessment, practitioner evaluation, student training programs, insurance rating, auditing services, and business planning and development. The Rule allows individuals the right to request restrictions on uses and disclosures of protected health information and to enter into agreements with covered entities regarding such restrictions, but does not require covered entities to abide by such requests or to agree to any restriction. The Rule also permits, but does not require, covered entities to design and implement a consent process for routine uses and disclosures.

Importantly, the Rule contains detailed preemption provisions, which are consistent with HIPAA Sections 1178(a)(2)(B) and 264(c)(2). These provisions establish that the Rule is intended as a "federal floor" for privacy protection, allowing state law to control where a "provision of State law relates to the privacy of individually identifiable health information and is more stringent than a standard, requirement, or implementation specification adopted under [the Privacy Rule]." * * *

On appeal, Citizens reassert the claims they made before the District Court, that the Secretary, by promulgating the Privacy Rule, (1) unlawfully infringed Citizens' fundamental rights to privacy in personal health information under due process principles of the Fifth Amendment of the United States Constitution; (2) unlawfully infringed Citizens' rights to communicate privately with their medical practitioners under the First Amendment of the Constitution; (3) contravened Congress's intent in enacting HIPAA by eliminating Citizens' reasonable expectations of medical privacy; and (4) violated the APA by arbitrarily and capriciously reversing a settled course of behavior and adopting a policy that he had previously rejected. * * *

We begin our analysis with the premise that the right to medical privacy asserted by Citizens is legally cognizable under the Due Process Clause of the Fifth Amendment, although, as Citizens themselves concede, its "boundaries * * * have not been exhaustively delineated." Whatever those boundaries may be, it is undisputed that a violation of a citizen's right to medical privacy rises to the level of a constitutional claim only when that violation can properly be ascribed to the government. The Constitution protects against state interference with fundamental rights. It only applies to restrict private behavior in limited circumstances. Because such circumstances are not present in this case, and because the "violations" of the right to medical privacy that Citizens have asserted, if they amount to violations of that right at all, occurred at the hands of private entities, the protections of the Due Process Clause of the Fifth Amendment are not implicated in this case. We will accordingly affirm the District Court's finding that the Secretary did not violate Citizens' constitutional rights when he promulgated the Amended Rule. * * *

Citizens' First Amendment claim is that the Amended Rule infringes individuals' right to confidential communications with health care practitioners, i.e., a right to refrain from public speech regarding private personal health information. Citizens argue that the effect of the Amended Rule is to chill speech between individuals and their health care practitioners because the possibility of nonconsensual disclosures makes individuals less likely to participate fully in diagnosis and treatment and more likely to be evasive and withhold important information. Further, because the Rule applies to "health information * * * whether oral or recorded in any form or medium * * *," 45 C.F.R. § 160.103, Citizens argue that the Rule is a content-based regulation reviewable under strict scrutiny.

We believe that a First Amendment claim is an ill-suited challenge to the Amended Rule. The cases on which Citizens rely are not authoritative on the precise issue before us. See Bartnicki v. Vopper, 532 U.S. 514, 533 (2001) (suggesting that "the fear of public disclosure of private conversations might well have a chilling effect on private speech," but ultimately holding that any such interest was outweighed in that case by the media's countervailing First Amendment interest in publishing truthful information of public concern); Jaffee v. Redmond, 518 U.S. 1, 11–12 (1996) (citing the "public interest" in confidential communications between a psychotherapist and her patient as justification for recognizing a psychotherapist-patient privilege in federal courts). And, more to the point, Citizens'

First Amendment claim fails on the same grounds as their Fifth Amendment claim: the potential "chilling" of patients' rights to free speech derives not from any action of the government, but from the independent decisions of private parties with respect to the use and disclosure of individual health information. For all of the reasons enumerated above, the decisions of the private parties to use or disclose private health information in reliance on the Amended Rule, which may or may not "chill" expression between health care providers and their patients, does not implicate the government in a way that gives rise to a constitutional claim. We will therefore affirm the District Court's grant of summary judgment to the Secretary on Citizens' First Amendment claim. * * *

In claims based on HIPAA's statutory language, Citizens argue (1) that the Secretary exceeded the regulatory authority delegated by HIPAA because the Act only authorizes the Secretary to promulgate regulations that enhance privacy and (2) that the Amended Rule impermissibly retroactively rescinded individual rights created by the Original Rule and disturbed Citizens' "settled expectations" in the privacy of their health information. We find the District Court's analysis of these statutory claims to be cogent. Citizens argue that the Secretary has eliminated their reasonable expectations of medical privacy retroactively and prospectively and that such action is inconsistent with Congress's intent in enacting HIPAA. However, Citizens' argument that the controlling policy underlying HIPAA is medical privacy and that the Amended Rule wholly sacrifices this interest to covered entities' interests in efficiency and flexibility ignores the Act's stated goals of "simplifying the administration of health insurance," * * *. As the District Court aptly explained, HIPAA requires the Secretary to "balance privacy protection and the efficiency of the health care system—not simply to enhance privacy." * * * We thus conclude that Citizens' first HIPAA claim lacks merit.

We also agree with the District Court's finding that the Amended Rule does not retroactively eliminate rights that Citizens enjoyed under the Original Rule or under various laws or standards of practice that existed before the Amended Rule went into effect. Because the Original Rule was amended before its compliance date, "covered entities were never under a legal obligation to comply with the Original Rule's consent requirement." * * * Citizens, therefore, never enjoyed any rights under the Original Rule at all. * * *

Lastly, Citizens challenge the rulemaking process under the APA, contending that (1) the Secretary's rulemaking was arbitrary and capricious, in violation of 5 U.S.C. § 706(2)(A), and (2) the Secretary failed to provide adequate notice of the rescission of the consent requirement of the Original Rule, a violation of 5 U.S.C. § 553(b)(3). Citizens argue that the Secretary acted arbitrarily and capriciously by failing to adequately explain the rescission of the consent requirement, ignoring earlier findings, and failing to respond to public comments. * * *

[T]he Secretary's decision to respond to the unintended negative effects and administrative burdens of the Original Rule by rescinding the consent requirement for routine uses and implementing more stringent notice requirements was explained in a detailed analysis that rationally connected the decision to the facts. "Normally, an agency rule would be arbitrary and capricious if the agency has relied on factors which Congress has not intended it to consider, entirely failed to consider an important aspect of the problem, offered an explanation for its decision that runs counter to the evidence before the agency, or is so implausible that it could not be ascribed to a difference in view or the product of agency expertise." * * * The Secretary has not failed in any of these respects, and, hence, we agree with the District Court's analysis and conclusion that the Secretary's decision was reasonable given the findings and that the Secretary did not act arbitrarily and capriciously in violation of the APA. Accordingly, we will affirm the grant of summary judgment to the Secretary on these claims. * * *

c. Limits on Ex Parte Communication With a Physician Witness

LAW v. ZUCKERMAN

307 F. Supp. 2d 705 (D. Md. 2004).

JUDGE CHARLES B. DAY

The Court is faced with an apparent issue of first impression in the Fourth Circuit in this medical malpractice action. The question presented is whether adverse counsel's ex parte discussions with a treating physician regarding the scope of the physician's care violates the Health Insurance and Portability Accountability Act of 1996, 42 U.S.C. 1320d et seq. ("HIPAA"). The Court finds that in the absence of strict compliance with HIPAA such discussions are prohibited. * * *

A jury trial commenced in this case on January 6, 2004. Plaintiff [Rosalynn Law] alleged that the surgical treatment she received from Defendant [David J. Zuckerman, M.D.] rendered her cervix incompetent. * * * Among Plaintiff's alleged damages were the costs and injuries associated with the placement of a permanent cerclage by Dr. Pinckert.

At the end of the second day of trial, Plaintiff raised an objection to ex parte communications that may have occurred between Dr. Thomas Pinckert and Defendant's counsel. * * * Defendant's counsel met with Dr. Pinckert after Plaintiff provided her medical records to Defendant as part of discovery. Plaintiff was never notified in advance that Defendant's counsel would pursue ex parte communications with her treating physician. Plaintiff asserts that any attempt by the defense to have such communications is a violation of HIPAA.

Plaintiff's sole request is for the issuance of an order precluding Dr. Pinckert from discussing Plaintiff's treatment and care with defense counsel or, in the alternative, to order Defendant to disclose all communications held with Dr. Pinckert and the details of Dr. Pinckert's expected testimony at trial. * * *

Defendant's counsel has argued that the Maryland Confidentiality of Medical Records Act, ("MCMRA"), governs this case and not HIPAA because MCMRA's rule governing disclosure is mandatory and therefore more restrictive than HIPAA's permissive rule governing disclosure. * * * MCMRA is applicable to cases where the patient has sued her health care provider alleging medical malpractice. MCMRA states that in such an instance, a health care provider shall disclose patient records without authorization from the patient. Conversely, HIPAA states that a health care provider may disclose patient records after using certain procedures. For the reasons set forth below, the Court does not agree that MCMRA is "more stringent" than HIPAA's requirements. Accordingly, HIPAA preempts MCMRA and is controlling on the issue of ex parte communications. * * *

HIPAA's permissive disclosure requirements give each patient more control over the dissemination of their medical records than MCMRA, while MCMRA sacrifices the patient's control of their private health information in order to expedite malpractice litigation. If state law can force disclosure without a court order, or the patient's consent, it is not "more stringent" than the HIPAA regulations. MCMRA is designed to give adverse counsel access to a patient's medical records without consent. Since Maryland law fails to satisfy the "more stringent" standard, federal law is controlling and all ex parte communications must be conducted in accordance with the procedures set forth in HIPAA. * * *

The recently enacted HIPAA statute has radically changed the landscape of how litigators can conduct informal discovery in cases involving medical treatment. In times past, given Maryland's reluctance to embrace the physician-patient privilege, ex parte contacts with an adversary's treating physician may have been a valuable tool in the arsenal of savvy counsel. The element of surprise could lead to case altering, if not case dispositive results. Ngo v. Standard Tools & Equipment, Co., Inc., 197 F.R.D. 263 (D. Md. 2000) (defendant was free to converse with and use Plaintiff's treating physician as a witness contrary to Plaintiff's wishes). Counsel should now be far more cautious in their contacts with medical fact witnesses when compared to other fact witnesses to ensure that they do not run afoul of HIPAA's regulatory scheme. Wise counsel must now treat medical witnesses similar to the high ranking corporate employee of an adverse party. See Camden v. Maryland, 910 F. Supp. 1115 (D. Md. 1996) (holding that counsel may not have ex parte contact with the former employee of an adverse party when the lawyer knows or should know that the former employee has been extensively exposed to confidential client information); Accord Zachair, Ltd. v. Driggs, 965 F. Supp. 741 (D. Md. 1997); But see Davidson Supply Co., Inc. v. P.P.E., Inc., 986 F. Supp. 956 (D. Md. 1997).

HIPAA outlines the steps to follow in order to obtain protected health information during a judicial proceeding in 45 C.F.R. § 164.512(e). There are three ways. First, counsel may obtain a court order which allows the health care provider to disclose "only the protected health information expressly authorized by such order." 45 C.F.R. § 164.512(e)(1)(i). In the absence of a court order, §§ 164.512(e)(1)(ii)(A) and (B) provide two additional methods available when used in conjunction with more traditional means of discovery. * * *

To the extent there was a disclosure of individually identifiable health information, Defendant's pretrial contacts with Dr. Pinckert were in violation of HIPAA. However, the remedy sought by Plaintiff precluding Defendant's counsel from speaking further with Dr. Pinckert about Plaintiff's treatment is not appropriate here.

The civil remedies for failure to comply with the requirements and standards of HIPAA are found under 42 U.S.C. § 1320d–5. The Secretary shall fine any person who violates a provision of HIPAA "not more than $100 for each such violation." 42 U.S.C. § 1320d–5(a)(1). * * * Since HIPAA does not include any reference to how a court should treat such a violation during discovery or at trial, the type of remedy to be applied is within the discretion of the Court * * *.

Notwithstanding the Court's disagreement with Defendant's counsel's analysis, it is clear that he exercised more than reasonable diligence when determining that his contacts with Dr. Pinckert did not violate HIPAA. On January 8, 2004, the Court did not find at the time that HIPAA applied in the instant case. Transcript, January 8, 2004 at 5–6. However, in the event that Defendant's contact with Dr. Pinckert triggered a HIPAA violation, the Court ordered that either party could speak with Dr. Pinckert before he testified about the issues set forth in Plaintiff's medical records. The Court also stated that if Dr. Pinckert strayed in his testimony from the medical records and offered any opinions beyond his experience as Plaintiff's treating physician such testimony would be prohibited. While the Court finds upon further review that HIPAA was applicable to any pre-trial disclosure of Plaintiff's medical information, it is also apparent that the Court's Order effectively remedied any potential violation. * * *

Therefore, for the reasons stated above, Plaintiff's Motion to preclude Dr. Pinckert from discussing the Plaintiff's treatment with defense counsel is denied.

NOTE: GENETIC WRONGS

The discovery of genetic bases for many illnesses has opened the possibility of treating individuals before symptoms develop and may lead to new genetic information-based medicines. These developments have the potential to improve health and decrease costs. Simultaneously, the proliferation of genetic information enlarges the potential for privacy violations. Since individuals fear that insurers or employers will discriminate against them based on their genes, many avoid genetics-based care. In the 1970s, African Americans were discriminated against in employment and insurance coverage based on their risk of acquiring sickle cell anemia. More recently, it was discovered that some companies had been performing genetic tests on their employees without informing the employees or getting their consent. Since 1991, thirty-four states have responded with laws protecting genetic information. For a nationwide solution, Representative Louise Slaughter (D–NY) introduced the Genetic Information Non-discrimination Act (GINA) in 1995. We take a closer look at GINA and its final passage in 2008 a little later.

U.S. EQUAL OPPORTUNITY EMPLOYMENT COMMISSION, EMPLOYER DNA TESTING PRESS RELEASE

Feb. 9, 2001.

WASHINGTON—The U. S. Equal Employment Opportunity Commission (EEOC) today filed its first court action challenging genetic testing [in] a Petition for a Preliminary Injunction against Burlington Northern Santa Fe Railroad to end genetic testing of employees who have filed claims for work-related injuries based on carpal tunnel syndrome. EEOC alleges that the employees are not told of the genetic test, or asked to consent to it, and that at least one individual who has refused to provide a blood sample because he suspected it would be used for genetic testing has been threatened with imminent discharge if he fails to submit the sample.

"This is EEOC's first lawsuit challenging genetic testing. As science and technology advance, we must be vigilant and ensure that these new developments are not used in a manner that violate workers' rights," said EEOC Chairwoman Ida L. Castro. "Today, the Commission has shown that we will act quickly when confronted with such an egregious violation of the Americans with Disabilities Act as is presented here."

In its Petition, filed in U. S. District Court for the Northern District of Iowa, located in Sioux City, Iowa, the EEOC asks the Court to order the railroad to end its nationwide policy of requiring employees who have submitted claims of work-related carpal tunnel syndrome to provide blood samples which are then used for a genetic DNA test for Chromosome 17 deletion, which is claimed to predict some forms of carpal tunnel syndrome. EEOC also seeks to halt any disciplinary action or termination of the employee who has refused to submit a blood sample.

EEOC Commissioner Paul Steven Miller explained, "The Commission takes the position that basing employment decisions on genetic testing violates the ADA. In particular, employers may only require employees to submit to any medical examination if those examinations are job related and consistent with business necessity. Any test which purports to predict future disabilities, whether or not it is accurate, is unlikely to be relevant to the employee's present ability to perform his or her job."

Chester V. Bailey, Director of EEOC's Milwaukee District Office, noted that the action is based on six charges of discrimination filed with the office. Four of the charges were filed by affected individuals; two were filed by officials of the Brotherhood of Maintenance of the Way Employees on behalf of all affected union members. Bailey certified that EEOC had determined after a preliminary investigation that "the employees would suffer irreparable injury through the invasion of their most intimate privacy rights if the practice of testing is not ended."

EEOC is the federal agency responsible for enforcing the ADA, which prohibits discrimination against qualified individuals with disabilities, including prohibiting an employer from seeking disability related information not related to an employee's ability to perform his or her job. In addition, EEOC enforces Title VII of the Civil Rights Act of 1964, which prohibits discrimination on the bases of race, color, religion, sex or national origin; the Age Discrimination in Employment Act, which protects workers age 40 and older; and the Equal Pay Act which prohibits sex-based differences in compensation.

NOTE: DNA OWNERSHIP AND PRIVACY

In May 2002, while admitting no guilt, the Burlington Northern Santa Fe Railroad agreed to paid $2.2 million to settle claims brought by 36 of its workers whose DNA was tested without their consent.

Is DNA property? Who owns DNA? Does it make sense to ascribe property rights in DNA to the individuals from whom it is taken? See Margaret Everett, The Social Life of Genes, Privacy, Property and the New Genetics, in *Information Ethics: Privacy, Property and Power* (ed. Adam Moore, 2005) 226: "With the development of the biotechnology industry, genes have taken on a (social) life of their own. The commodification of DNA has also met with resistance on the part of research subjects as well as the general public, all potential DNA donors. The construction of DNA as property with commercial value, the identification of the self with DNA, and the objectification of body parts are all necessary to this process of commodification." *Id.* at 245.

The potential of the concept of proprietary privacy in DNA was tested in *Moore v. Regents of UCLA,* 793 P.2d 479 (Cal. 1990). An unwitting biomedical research subject, whose DNA was collected and a potentially profitable cell line developed, sued the University of California. Mr. John Moore claimed that the research physicians, who had originally treated him for leukemia, violated his rights of privacy and property in his DNA.

The court rejected Moore's attempt to draw analogies between his case and privacy tort cases: "Not only are the wrongful-publicity cases irrelevant * * * but the analogy to them seriously misconceives the nature of the genetic materials and research involved in this case. Moore * * * argues that '[i]f the courts have found a sufficient proprietary interest in one's persona, how could one not have a right in one's own genetic material, something far more profoundly the essence of one's human uniqueness than a name or a face?' However, as the defendants' patent makes clear * * * the goal and result of defendants' efforts has been to manufacture lymphokines. Lymphokines, unlike a name or a face, have the same molecular structure in every human being and the same, important functions in every human being's immune system. Moreover, the particular genetic material which is responsible for the natural production of lymphokines, and which defendants use to manufacture lymphokines in the laboratory, is also the same in every person; it is no more unique to Moore than the number of vertebrae in the spine or the chemical formula of hemoglobin." The court endorsed an action for lack of informed consent, but rejected privacy and property based theories of liability.

Note: Genetic Information Nondiscrimination Act of 2008 (GINA)

The Genetic Information Nondiscrimination Act (GINA), Public Law 110–233, became law on May 21, 2008. GINA prohibits genetic discrimination in health insurance coverage (Title I) and employment (Title II). Title I of GINA amended several federal statutes—the Employee Retirement Income Security Act of 1974 (ERISA), the Public Health Service Act (PHS Act), the Internal Revenue Code of 1986 (Code), and the Social Security Act (SSA)—to prohibit discrimination in health coverage based on genetic information. GINA built on existing protections of HIPAA which already prohibited a group health plan or group health insurance issuer from (1) imposing a preexisting condition exclusion based solely on genetic information or (2) discriminating against an individual in eligibility, benefits, or premiums based on genetic information and other health factors of the individual or a dependent of the individual. *See Federal Register,* Vol. 74, No. 193, Wednesday, October 7, 2009. GINA addresses access and equality concerns raised in the past by health law experts. *Cf.* Radhika Rao, A Veil of Genetic Ignorance? Protecting Genetic Privacy to Ensure Equality, 51 *Vill. L. Rev.* 827 (2006). A proposed rule issued on October 1, 2009 would "clarify that genetic information is health information" and "prohibit the use and disclosure of genetic information by covered health plans for underwriting purposes, which include eligibility determinations, premium computations, applications of any pre-existing condition exclusions, and any other activities related to the creation, renewal, or replacement of a contract of health insurance or health benefits". http://www.hhs.gov/ocr/privacy/hipaa/understanding/special/genetic/

GINA does not create "ownership" in DNA as such. It does, however, address the problem of nonconsensual testing and discrimination attacked by the EEOC in the Burlington Railroad case. Would the GINA address all of the consequences of genomics raised by Yael Bregman–Eschet in the excerpt that follows? In particular, would it address concerns about the implications of biobanking? What sort of industry specific fair information practices (something Bregman–Eschet calls for) might beneficially govern biobanking?

YAEL BREGMAN–ESCHET, GENETIC DATABASES AND BIOBANKS: WHO CONTROLS OUR GENETIC PRIVACY?

23 Santa Clara Computer & High Tech. L.J. 1, 7–11 (2006).

In 2000, two teams—one privately owned and the other publicly funded—announced the mapping of the human genome. In the wake of this scientific breakthrough, and the better understanding of various genetic disorders and physical and psychological traits that it promised, expectations for the development of new treatments and cures for various medical conditions has grown tremendously. The Human Genome Project was therefore accompanied by multiple superlatives: the genome itself was described as the "book of life" and the mapping of the human genome was compared to the search for the Holy Grail. However, this new genetic research also posed a growing threat to personal privacy, as vast amounts of medical and genetic information could now be better understood, compiled, and linked together. * * *

Medical data is considered to be highly sensitive, personal information. According to the Ninth Circuit, "[o]ne can think of few subject areas more personal and more likely to implicate privacy interests than that of one's health or genetic make-up." Despite the sensitive and personal nature of medical information, certain proponents of the free market, namely Richard Posner and Richard Epstein, call for open access to medical and genetic information in the name of economic efficiency. However, open access to both medical and genetic information may have far reaching social implications in the form of social stigma and genetic determinism that may lead to problems such as employment and insurance discrimination, which are socially as well as economically undesirable. For this reason, the free market may fail to adequately protect medical privacy. Medical information thus requires considerable privacy protections and confidentiality, necessities long recognized by the Hippocratic Oath.

Genetic information is a sub-class of medical information. It includes information that may be retrieved from an individual's DNA that, with the growing understanding of the human genome and its mapping, may reveal three levels of sensitive information: personal information about the individual such as genes, traits, and predisposition to certain diseases; medical information about an individual's kinship that can be attributed to one's genes; and information about the heritage of the individual, e.g. the routes and origin of her ancestors.

Despite the sensitivity of the information that may be retrieved from one's DNA and tissue samples, the degree of privacy protection that should be granted to genetic information is disputed. Bioethicist George Annas considers genetic information to be especially sensitive medical information because of the different levels of personal information it may reveal: not only about the individual, but also regarding her relatives. According to Annas, our DNA is a reflection of our "future diaries," with the ability to reveal predisposition to illnesses, traits, and even life span.

However, this "future diary" metaphor has been widely contested by others. It has been argued that "genetic information is neither unique nor distinctive in its ability to offer probabilistic peeks into our future health," and that any potential difference between genetic information and other classes of medical information is at most that of degree, not of kind.

Others see genetic data as distinct from other types of medical information, but not unique. Similarly, the Ninth Circuit concluded, in a majority opinion, that a blood sample is not substantially different than fingerprinting. However, in a dissenting opinion Judge Nelson found that: "DNA genetic pattern analysis catalogs uniquely private genetic facts about the individual that should be subject to rigorous confidentiality requirements even broader than the protection of an individual's medical records," thus differentiating genetic information from other classes of medical data or fingerprint records.

When referring to genetic databanks, one must distinguish between two types of repositories: genetic databases, which consist of information derived from individual genetic material and DNA; and DNA banks or biobanks that hold collections of tissue samples, such as blood, saliva, or hair, from which DNA can be derived. Both types of banks pose potential threats to privacy: genetic databases do so via the accumulation of genetic information in a single electronic form; while DNA banks allow for the possibility of making endless amounts of DNA copies from one single tissue sample for different uses, some of which might not have been originally consented to.

Computerization and the creation of electronic dossiers is one of the greatest challenges to medical and genetic privacy in the information technology age. The computerization of medical records makes the medical process more efficient, optimizes health care, and enhances research. But, the compilation of vast amounts of sensitive data, consisting of both medical and genetic information, in a single electronic database to which numerous people in different locations have access, also undermines personal privacy.

Biobanks, on the other hand, create a somewhat different challenge focused on the autonomy of the individual. The ability to store tissue and DNA samples for long periods of time and the possibility to create endless numbers of DNA copies from a single sample, give rise to the concern that these samples could potentially be used for purposes other than those for which they were originally intended. For instance, stored tissue samples collected before genetic testing was even available, can now be used to create DNA databanks to facilitate research that could not have been anticipate at the time the sample was collected. According to the recommendations of the European society of Human Genetics, anonymous samples may be used for purposes other than those originally intended for, provided that these samples are irreversible and cannot be linked back to the name of the donor. Along these lines, the U.K. Human Genetics Commission found it acceptable to conduct research on old collections of samples, for which informed consent was not sought, as long as the samples were anonymized.

Alternatively, many biobanks ask their research subjects for open-ended permission to use their genetic information for future research. This type of broad permission is a weak form of consent because the research subject provides consent without being aware of the specific uses for which the samples might be used, or of possible future uses, which are yet unknown. Genuine informed consent can only be given if the research subjects understand and agree to the general nature of the research, are asked for additional consent if different purposes are sought in the future, have the power to oppose specific uses of their information, and the ability to withdraw from the research at any time.

Hence, the privacy and autonomy threats that accompany the information technology age and its mega databases that hold immense amounts of personal information are not necessarily new. Nonetheless, the challenges of protecting medical and genetic privacy have been growing. One reason is the increasing linkages between medical information and the two types of genetic banks: genetic databases and biobanks. These linkages, which are increasingly being implemented to facilitate scientific progress, create, absent sufficient safeguards, new dimensions to the existing privacy concerns relating to medical and genetic information.

Furthermore, the private sector is becoming increasingly involved in the collection, assembly, and linkage of medical and genetic information, both independently and through partnerships with government or research institutions that willingly transfer individuals' genetic material and/or information to the hands of the private sector. This partnership between the public and private sectors is evident in the Icelandic model, as well as in private agreements between hospitals and commercial biotech companies in the United States.

Although, the involvement of the private sector is crucial for efficient technological development, the growing control that the private industry has over personal medical information and genetic material is problematic. First, unlike the public and non-profit sectors, whose primary goals are (or at least should be) increasing public welfare, the private sector is primarily concerned with its own financial gain and the maximization of shareholder profits. Because of this, the danger exists that, absent adequate safeguards, the private sector may misuse this sensitive information in times of economic crises, such as selling it in the event of bankruptcy. The existing legal framework is not always sufficient to prevent this type of conduct, which undermines the research subjects' genetic privacy, autonomy, and interests.

Finally, absent sufficient restrictions and guidelines for the storage of genetic information, each commercial company is free to choose the level of security placed on the genetic information it collects and stores. As a result, we are witnessing incoherency in the manner in which sensitive information is stored and handled, a phenomenon that not only undermines the privacy interests of the research subjects, but is also claimed to create difficulties in the conduct of genetic research.

The growing control that private commercial companies have over medical and genetic information and material; the lack of sufficient safeguards in place to protect personal privacy; and potential partnerships between the public and the private sectors that bestow additional power to the hands of the private sector, all intensify the threat to personal autonomy and genetic privacy. Hence, this article calls for greater caution in the collection, usage, and assembly of genetic information and material and its linkage to other types of medical information. For this reason, the industry is encouraged to embrace industry-specific fair information practices that will place limitations and restrictions on the compilation and usage of genetic data.

NOTE: ROK LAMPE, PRINCIPLES TO LIVE BY

The Convention on Human Rights and Biomedicine which entered into force on December 1, 1999, is the first legally-binding international document designed to preserve human dignity, rights and freedoms, through a series of principles and prohibitions against the misuse of biological and medical advances. Are the confidentiality and non-discrimination values undergirding HIPAA and GINA reflected in the Convention?

COUNCIL OF EUROPE, CONVENTION FOR THE PROTECTION OF HUMAN RIGHTS AND DIGNITY OF THE HUMAN BEING WITH REGARD TO THE APPLICATION OF BIOLOGY AND MEDICINE: CONVENTION ON HUMAN RIGHTS AND BIOMEDICINE

CETS No.: 164, Oviedo, 4.IV.1997.

Preamble

The member States of the Council of Europe, the other States and the European Community, signatories hereto, * * *

Have agreed as follows:

Chapter I—General provisions

Article 1—Purpose and object

Parties to this Convention shall protect the dignity and identity of all human beings and guarantee everyone, without discrimination, respect for their integrity and other rights and fundamental freedoms with regard to the application of biology and medicine.

Each Party shall take in its internal law the necessary measures to give effect to the provisions of this Convention.

Article 2—Primacy of the human being

The interests and welfare of the human being shall prevail over the sole interest of society or science.

Article 3—Equitable access to health care

Parties, taking into account health needs and available resources, shall take appropriate measures with a view to providing, within their jurisdiction, equitable access to health care of appropriate quality.

Article 4—Professional standards

Any intervention in the health field, including research, must be carried out in accordance with relevant professional obligations and standards.

Chapter II—Consent

Article 5—General rule

An intervention in the health field may only be carried out after the person concerned has given free and informed consent to it.

This person shall beforehand be given appropriate information as to the purpose and nature of the intervention as well as on its consequences and risks.

The person concerned may freely withdraw consent at any time.

Article 6—Protection of persons not able to consent

1. Subject to Articles 17 and 20 below, an intervention may only be carried out on a person who does not have the capacity to consent, for his or her direct benefit.

2. Where, according to law, a minor does not have the capacity to consent to an intervention, the intervention may only be carried out with the authorisation of his or her representative or an authority or a person or body provided for by law. The opinion of the minor shall be taken into consideration as an increasingly determining factor in proportion to his or her age and degree of maturity.

3. Where, according to law, an adult does not have the capacity to consent to an intervention because of a mental disability, a disease or for similar reasons, the intervention may only be carried out with the authorisation of his or her representative or an authority or a person or body provided for by law. The individual concerned shall as far as possible take part in the authorisation procedure.

4. The representative, the authority, the person or the body mentioned in paragraphs 2 and 3 above shall be given, under the same conditions, the information referred to in Article 5.

5. The authorisation referred to in paragraphs 2 and 3 above may be withdrawn at any time in the best interests of the person concerned.

Article 7—Protection of persons who have a mental disorder

Subject to protective conditions prescribed by law, including supervisory, control and appeal procedures, a person who has a mental disorder of a serious nature may be subjected, without his or her consent, to an intervention aimed at treating his or her mental disorder only where, without such treatment, serious harm is likely to result to his or her health.

Article 8—Emergency situation

When because of an emergency situation the appropriate consent cannot be obtained, any medically necessary intervention may be carried out immediately for the benefit of the health of the individual concerned.

Article 9—Previously expressed wishes

The previously expressed wishes relating to a medical intervention by a patient who is not, at the time of the intervention, in a state to express his or her wishes shall be taken into account.

Chapter III—Private life and right to information

Article 10—Private life and right to information

1. Everyone has the right to respect for private life in relation to information about his or her health.

2. Everyone is entitled to know any information collected about his or her health. However, the wishes of individuals not to be so informed shall be observed.

3. In exceptional cases, restrictions may be placed by law on the exercise of the rights contained in paragraph 2 in the interests of the patient.

Chapter IV—Human genome

Article 11—Non-discrimination

Any form of discrimination against a person on grounds of his or her genetic heritage is prohibited.

Article 12—Predictive genetic tests

Tests which are predictive of genetic diseases or which serve either to identify the subject as a carrier of a gene responsible for a disease or to detect a genetic predisposition or susceptibility to a disease may be performed only for health purposes or for scientific research linked to health purposes, and subject to appropriate genetic counselling.

Article 13—Interventions on the human genome

An intervention seeking to modify the human genome may only be undertaken for preventive, diagnostic or therapeutic purposes and only if its aim is not to introduce any modification in the genome of any descendants.

Article 14—Non-selection of sex

The use of techniques of medically assisted procreation shall not be allowed for the purpose of choosing a future child's sex, except where serious hereditary sex-related disease is to be avoided.

Chapter V—Scientific research

Article 15—General rule

Scientific research in the field of biology and medicine shall be carried out freely, subject to the provisions of this Convention and the other legal provisions ensuring the protection of the human being.

Article 16—Protection of persons undergoing research

Research on a person may only be undertaken if all the following conditions are met:

   i. there is no alternative of comparable effectiveness to research on humans;
   ii. the risks which may be incurred by that person are not disproportionate to the potential benefits of the research;
   iii. the research project has been approved by the competent body after independent examination of its scientific merit, including assessment of the importance of the aim of the research, and multidisciplinary review of its ethical acceptability;
   iv. the persons undergoing research have been informed of their rights and the safeguards prescribed by law for their protection;
   v. the necessary consent as provided for under Article 5 has been given expressly, specifically and is documented. Such consent may be freely withdrawn at any time.

Article 17—Protection of persons not able to consent to research

   1. Research on a person without the capacity to consent as stipulated in Article 5 may be undertaken only if all the following conditions are met:

      i. the conditions laid down in Article 16, sub-paragraphs i to iv, are fulfilled;
      ii. the results of the research have the potential to produce real and direct benefit to his or her health;
      iii. research of comparable effectiveness cannot be carried out on individuals capable of giving consent;
      iv. the necessary authorisation provided for under Article 6 has been given specifically and in writing; and
      v. the person concerned does not object.

   2. Exceptionally and under the protective conditions prescribed by law, where the research has not the potential to produce results of direct benefit to the health of the person concerned, such research may be authorised subject to the conditions laid down in paragraph 1, sub-paragraphs i, iii, iv and v above, and to the following additional conditions:

      i. the research has the aim of contributing, through significant improvement in the scientific understanding of the individual's condition, disease or disorder, to the ultimate attainment of results capable of conferring benefit to the person concerned or to other persons in the same age category or afflicted with the same disease or disorder or having the same condition;

    ii. the research entails only minimal risk and minimal burden for the individual concerned.

Article 18—Research on embryos *in vitro*

1. Where the law allows research on embryos *in vitro*, it shall ensure adequate protection of the embryo.

2. The creation of human embryos for research purposes is prohibited.

Chapter VI—Organ and tissue removal from living donors for transplantation purposes

Article 19—General rule

1. Removal of organs or tissue from a living person for transplantation purposes may be carried out solely for the therapeutic benefit of the recipient and where there is no suitable organ or tissue available from a deceased person and no other alternative therapeutic method of comparable effectiveness.

2. The necessary consent as provided for under Article 5 must have been given expressly and specifically either in written form or before an official body.

Article 20—Protection of persons not able to consent to organ removal

1. No organ or tissue removal may be carried out on a person who does not have the capacity to consent under Article 5.

2. Exceptionally and under the protective conditions prescribed by law, the removal of regenerative tissue from a person who does not have the capacity to consent may be authorised provided the following conditions are met:

    i. there is no compatible donor available who has the capacity to consent;
    ii. the recipient is a brother or sister of the donor;
    iii. the donation must have the potential to be life-saving for the recipient;
    iv. the authorisation provided for under paragraphs 2 and 3 of Article 6 has been given specifically and in writing, in accordance with the law and with the approval of the competent body;
    v. the potential donor concerned does not object.

Chapter VII—Prohibition of financial gain and disposal of a part of the human body

Article 21—Prohibition of financial gain

The human body and its parts shall not, as such, give rise to financial gain.

Article 22—Disposal of a removed part of the human body

When in the course of an intervention any part of a human body is removed, it may be stored and used for a purpose other than that for which it was removed, only if this is done in conformity with appropriate information and consent procedures.

Chapter VIII—Infringements of the provisions of the Convention

Article 23—Infringement of the rights or principles

The Parties shall provide appropriate judicial protection to prevent or to put a stop to an unlawful infringement of the rights and principles set forth in this Convention at short notice.

Article 24—Compensation for undue damage

The person who has suffered undue damage resulting from an intervention is entitled to fair compensation according to the conditions and procedures prescribed by law.

Article 25—Sanctions

Parties shall provide for appropriate sanctions to be applied in the event of infringement of the provisions contained in this Convention.

Chapter IX—Relation between this Convention and other provisions

Article 26—Restrictions on the exercise of the rights

1. No restrictions shall be placed on the exercise of the rights and protective provisions contained in this Convention other than such as are prescribed by law and are necessary in a democratic society in the interest of public safety, for the prevention of crime, for the protection of public health or for the protection of the rights and freedoms of others.

2. The restrictions contemplated in the preceding paragraph may not be placed on Articles 11, 13, 14, 16, 17, 19, 20 and 21.

Article 27—Wider protection

None of the provisions of this Convention shall be interpreted as limiting or otherwise affecting the possibility for a Party to grant a wider measure of protection with regard to the application of biology and medicine than is stipulated in this Convention.

Chapter X—Public debate

Article 28—Public debate

Parties to this Convention shall see to it that the fundamental questions raised by the developments of biology and medicine are the subject of appropriate public discussion in the light, in particular, of relevant medical, social, economic, ethical and legal implications, and that their possible application is made the subject of appropriate consultation.

Chapter XI—Interpretation and follow-up of the Convention

Article 29—Interpretation of the Convention

The European Court of Human Rights may give, without direct reference to any specific proceedings pending in a court, advisory opinions on legal questions concerning the interpretation of the present Convention at the request of:

- the Government of a Party, after having informed the other Parties;

- the Committee set up by Article 32, with membership restricted to the Representatives of the Parties to this Convention, by a decision adopted by a two-thirds majority of votes cast.

Article 30—Reports on the application of the Convention

On receipt of a request from the Secretary General of the Council of Europe any Party shall furnish an explanation of the manner in which its internal law ensures the effective implementation of any of the provisions of the Convention.

Chapter XII—Protocols

Article 31—Protocols

Protocols may be concluded in pursuance of Article 32, with a view to developing, in specific fields, the principles contained in this Convention.

The Protocols shall be open for signature by Signatories of the Convention. They shall be subject to ratification, acceptance or approval. A Signatory may not ratify, accept or approve Protocols without previously or simultaneously ratifying accepting or approving the Convention.

Chapter XIII—Amendments to the Convention

Article 32—Amendments to the Convention

1. The tasks assigned to "the Committee" in the present article and in Article 29 shall be carried out by the Steering Committee on Bioethics (CDBI), or by any other committee designated to do so by the Committee of Ministers.

2. Without prejudice to the specific provisions of Article 29, each member State of the Council of Europe, as well as each Party to the present Convention which is not a member of the Council of Europe, may be represented and have one vote in the Committee when the Committee carries out the tasks assigned to it by the present Convention.

3. Any State referred to in Article 33 or invited to accede to the Convention in accordance with the provisions of Article 34 which is not Party to this Convention may be represented on the Committee by an observer. If the European Community is not a Party it may be represented on the Committee by an observer.

4. In order to monitor scientific developments, the present Convention shall be examined within the Committee no later than five years from its entry into force and thereafter at such intervals as the Committee may determine.

5. Any proposal for an amendment to this Convention, and any proposal for a Protocol or for an amendment to a Protocol, presented by a Party, the Committee or the Committee of Ministers shall be communicated to the Secretary General of the Council of Europe and forwarded by him to the member States of the Council of Europe, to the European Community, to any Signatory, to any Party, to any State invited to sign this Convention in accordance with the provisions of Article 33 and to any State invited to accede to it in accordance with the provisions of Article 34.

6. The Committee shall examine the proposal not earlier than two months after it has been forwarded by the Secretary General in accordance with paragraph 5. The Committee shall submit the text adopted by a two-thirds majority of the votes cast to the Committee of Ministers for approval. After its approval, this text shall be forwarded to the Parties for ratification, acceptance or approval.

7. Any amendment shall enter into force, in respect of those Parties which have accepted it, on the first day of the month following the expiration of a period of one month after the date on which five Parties, including at least four member States of the Council of Europe, have informed the Secretary General that they have accepted it.

In respect of any Party which subsequently accepts it, the amendment shall enter into force on the first day of the month following the expiration of a period of one month after the date on which that Party has informed the Secretary General of its acceptance.

Chapter XIV—Final clauses

Article 33—Signature, ratification and entry into force

1. This Convention shall be open for signature by the member States of the Council of Europe, the non-member States which have participated in its elaboration and by the European Community.

2. This Convention is subject to ratification, acceptance or approval. Instruments of ratification, acceptance or approval shall be deposited with the Secretary General of the Council of Europe.

3. This Convention shall enter into force on the first day of the month following the expiration of a period of three months after the date on which five States, including at least four member States of the Council of Europe, have expressed their

consent to be bound by the Convention in accordance with the provisions of paragraph 2 of the present article.

4. In respect of any Signatory which subsequently expresses its consent to be bound by it, the Convention shall enter into force on the first day of the month following the expiration of a period of three months after the date of the deposit of its instrument of ratification, acceptance or approval.

Article 34—Non-member States

1. After the entry into force of this Convention, the Committee of Ministers of the Council of Europe may, after consultation of the Parties, invite any non-member State of the Council of Europe to accede to this Convention by a decision taken by the majority provided for in Article 20, paragraph d, of the Statute of the Council of Europe, and by the unanimous vote of the representatives of the Contracting States entitled to sit on the Committee of Ministers.

2. In respect of any acceding State, the Convention shall enter into force on the first day of the month following the expiration of a period of three months after the date of deposit of the instrument of accession with the Secretary General of the Council of Europe.

Article 35—Territories

1. Any Signatory may, at the time of signature or when depositing its instrument of ratification, acceptance or approval, specify the territory or territories to which this Convention shall apply. Any other State may formulate the same declaration when depositing its instrument of accession.

2. Any Party may, at any later date, by a declaration addressed to the Secretary General of the Council of Europe, extend the application of this Convention to any other territory specified in the declaration and for whose international relations it is responsible or on whose behalf it is authorised to give undertakings. In respect of such territory the Convention shall enter into force on the first day of the month following the expiration of a period of three months after the date of receipt of such declaration by the Secretary General.

3. Any declaration made under the two preceding paragraphs may, in respect of any territory specified in such declaration, be withdrawn by a notification addressed to the Secretary General. The withdrawal shall become effective on the first day of the month following the expiration of a period of three months after the date of receipt of such notification by the Secretary General.

Article 36—Reservations

1. Any State and the European Community may, when signing this Convention or when depositing the instrument of ratification, acceptance, approval or accession, make a reservation in respect of any particular provision of the Convention to the extent that any law then in force in its territory is not in conformity with the provision. Reservations of a general character shall not be permitted under this article.

2. Any reservation made under this article shall contain a brief statement of the relevant law.

3. Any Party which extends the application of this Convention to a territory mentioned in the declaration referred to in Article 35, paragraph 2, may, in respect of the territory concerned, make a reservation in accordance with the provisions of the preceding paragraphs.

4. Any Party which has made the reservation mentioned in this article may withdraw it by means of a declaration addressed to the Secretary General of the Council of Europe. The withdrawal shall become effective on the first day of the month following the expiration of a period of one month after the date of its receipt by the Secretary General.

Article 37—Denunciation

1. Any Party may at any time denounce this Convention by means of a notification addressed to the Secretary General of the Council of Europe.

2. Such denunciation shall become effective on the first day of the month following the expiration of a period of three months after the date of receipt of the notification by the Secretary General.

Article 38—Notifications

The Secretary General of the Council of Europe shall notify the member States of the Council, the European Community, any Signatory, any Party and any other State which has been invited to accede to this Convention of:

a. any signature;

b. the deposit of any instrument of ratification, acceptance, approval or accession;

c. any date of entry into force of this Convention in accordance with Articles 33 or 34;

d. any amendment or Protocol adopted in accordance with Article 32, and the date on which such an amendment or Protocol enters into force;

e. any declaration made under the provisions of Article 35;

f.   any reservation and withdrawal of reservation made in pursuance of the provisions of Article 36;

g.   any other act, notification or communication relating to this Convention.

In witness whereof the undersigned, being duly authorised thereto, have signed this Convention.

Done at Oviedo (Asturias), this 4th day of April 1997, in English and French, both texts being equally authentic, in a single copy which shall be deposited in the archives of the Council of Europe. The Secretary General of the Council of Europe shall transmit certified copies to each member State of the Council of Europe, to the European Community, to the non-member States which have participated in the elaboration of this Convention, and to any State invited to accede to this Convention.

E.   CONSUMER FINANCIAL PRIVACY

Note: The Implications of 2010 Financial Reform Legislation

The Dodd–Frank Wall Street Reform and Consumer Protection Act of 2010, Public Law No: 111–203, was passed by Congress and signed into law by President Barack Obama in an effort to stabilize the US financial system through increased regulation of securities, banking and consumer financial products. The Act authorized the creation of a new Consumer Financial Protection Bureau (CFPB) to regulate the offering and provision of consumer financial products or services.

An array of federal agencies and statutes regulated consumers' financial privacy prior to the Dodd–Frank Act. How, if at all, is the Act expected to affect regulation in this vital area?

Privacy experts Mark MacCarthy and Robert Gellman have argued that the new Consumer Financial Protection Bureau should include a Privacy Office, "an institutional mechanism to help ensure that existing financial products and services, developments in the use of technologies and the innovations in the design of new products and services sustain privacy protections relating to the collection, use, dissemination, and maintenance of personal information." See Mark MacCarthy and Robert Gellman, "The Consumer Financial Protection Bureau Needs a Privacy Office," *Privacy & Security Law Report*, 9 PVLR 32, 08/09/2010.

A Privacy Office is badly needed, these experts maintain, since: "It is inevitable that the Bureau will be the leading government regulator of consumer financial privacy because the legislation gives the Bureau authority to write rules for and to oversee the two major statutes that govern the use of personal information by financial institutions. The first is the Fair Credit Reporting Act (FCRA), which generally regulates credit bureaus. The FCRA governs how information can be furnished to the bureaus, defines permissible purposes for use of credit reports (such as credit, insurance, and employment screening). * * * The second financial privacy statute that the Bureau is responsible for is the Gramm–Leach–Bliley Act (GLB). The authority under GLB to write and enforce information security rules and rules on identity theft remains under the control of the traditional banking agencies and the FTC." *Id.*

There are other reasons for the new Bureau to include a Privacy Office, MacCarthy and Gellman persuasively argue: "In addition to its express jurisdiction over specific legislation, the Bureau has broad rulemaking powers relative to unfairness, deception, and abuse. This authority could and should be used to address privacy issues that are not specifically addressed in these substantive statutes. The Bureau also has jurisdiction over numerous other 'enumerated consumer laws' that may affect privacy in some way, although not as directly as the FCRA and GLB. Any additional laws affecting financial privacy are likely to be administered by the Bureau as well." *Id.*

Finally, conclude MacCarthy and Gellman, "It will be impossible for the Bureau to carry out its mission to regulate financial offerings to consumers without addressing privacy. The collection, use, maintenance, and disclosure of consumer information is an essential part of any consumer financial transaction. * * * [P]rivacy, like consumer information itself, is an integral part of financial activity. Consumer information is also at the heart of illegal activities, such as identity theft, that threaten both consumers and financial institutions." *Id.*

As highlighted by MacCarthy and Gellman, consumer financial privacy is regulated by the Fair Credit Reporting Act and by the Gramm–Leach–Bliley Act. Consumer financial privacy is also regulated by a Right to Financial Privacy Act, an Identity Theft and Deterrence Act, and indirectly through the FTC's unfair and deceptive trade practices authority. All of these mechanism of financial privacy protection these are treated below, with the understanding that the Dodd–Frank Act may in time visibly alter the landscape.

1. RIGHT TO FINANCIAL PRIVACY ACT OF 1978

CHAO v. COMMUNITY TRUST COMPANY

474 F.3d 75 (3d Cir. 2007).

ROTH, CIRCUIT JUDGE:

[The Right to Financial Privacy Act (RFPA), 12 U.S.C. § 3401, was enacted by Congress in 1978] "to protect the customers of financial institutions from unwarranted intrusion into their records while at the same time permitting legitimate law enforcement activity." The RFPA seeks to strike a balance between the right of privacy of customers and the need for law enforcement agencies to obtain financial records as a part of legitimate investigations. * * *

The RFPA provides that, unless a statutory exception applies: "no Government authority may have access to or obtain copies of, or the information contained in the financial records of any customer from a financial institution unless the financial records are reasonably described and—* * * such financial records are disclosed in response to an administrative subpoena or summons * * *." 12 U.S.C. § 3402 * * *

The RFPA defines "customer" as: "any person or authorized representative of that person who utilized or is utilizing any service of a financial institution, or for whom a financial institution is acting or has acted as a fiduciary, in relation to an account maintained in the person's name." 12 U.S.C. § 3401(5). The RFPA defines "person," in turn, as "an individual or a partnership of five or fewer individuals." * * *

Congress enacted the RFPA in response to United States v. Miller, 425 U.S. 435 (1976), in which the Supreme Court held that there is no constitutional right to privacy of financial records. * * *

UNITED STATES v. MILLER

425 U.S. 435 (1976).

MR. JUSTICE POWELL delivered the opinion of the Court.

Respondent was convicted of possessing an unregistered still, carrying on the business of a distiller without giving bond and with intent to defraud the Government of whiskey tax, possessing 175 gallons of whiskey upon which no taxes had been paid, and conspiring to defraud the United States of tax revenues. * * * Prior to trial respondent moved to suppress copies of checks and other bank records obtained by means of allegedly defective subpoenas duces tecum served upon two banks at which he had accounts. The records had been maintained by the banks in compliance with the requirements of the Bank Secrecy Act of 1970 * * *.

[The] District Court overruled respondent's motion to suppress, and the evidence was admitted. The Court of Appeals for the Fifth Circuit reversed on the ground that a depositor's Fourth Amendment rights are violated when bank records maintained pursuant to the Bank Secrecy Act are obtained by means of a defective subpoena. It held that any evidence so obtained must be suppressed. Since we find that respondent had no protectable Fourth Amendment interest in the subpoenaed documents, we reverse the decision below. * * *

The banks did not advise respondent that the subpoenas had been served but ordered their employees to make the records available and to provide copies of any documents the agents desired. At the Bank of Byron, an agent was shown microfilm records of the relevant account and provided with copies of one deposit slip and one or two checks. At the Citizens & Southern National Bank microfilm records also were shown to the agent, and he was given copies of the records of respondent's account during the applicable period. These included all checks, deposit slips, two financial statements, and three monthly statements. The bank presidents were then told that it would not be necessary to appear in person before the grand jury. * * *

We find that there was no intrusion into any area in which respondent had a protected Fourth Amendment interest and that the District Court therefore correctly denied respondent's motion to suppress. Because we reverse the decision of the Court of Appeals on that ground alone, we do not reach the Government's latter two contentions. * * *

In Hoffa v. United States, 385 U.S. 293, 301–302 (1966), the Court said that "no interest legitimately protected by the Fourth Amendment" is implicated by governmental investigative activities unless there is an intrusion into a zone of privacy, into "the security a man relies upon when he places himself or his property within a constitutionally protected area." The Court of Appeals * * * assumed that respondent had the necessary Fourth Amendment interest, pointing to the language in Boyd v. United States * * * which describes that Amendment's protection against the "compulsory production of a man's private papers." We think that the Court of Appeals erred in finding the subpoenaed documents to fall within a protected zone of privacy.

On their face, the documents subpoenaed here are not respondent's "private papers." Unlike the claimant in Boyd, respondent can assert neither ownership nor possession. Instead, these are the business records of the banks. As we said in California Bankers Assn. v. Shultz * * * "[b]anks are * * * not * * * neutrals in transactions involving negotiable instruments, but parties to the instruments with a substantial stake in their continued availability and acceptance." The records of respondent's accounts, like "all of the records [which are required to be kept pursuant to the Bank Secrecy Act,] pertain to transactions to which the bank was itself a party." * * *

Respondent urges that he has a Fourth Amendment interest in the records kept by the banks because they are merely copies of personal records that were made available to the banks for a limited purpose and in which he has a reasonable expectation of privacy. He relies on this Court's statement in Katz v. United States, 389 U.S. 347, 353 (1967), quoting Warden v. Hayden, 387 U.S. 294, 304 (1967), that "we have * * * departed from the narrow view" that " 'property interests control the right of the Government to search and seize,' " and that a "search and seizure" become unreasonable when the Government's activities violate "the privacy upon which [a person] justifiably relie[s]." But in Katz the Court also stressed that "[w]hat a person knowingly exposes to the public * * * is not a subject of Fourth Amendment protection." 389 U.S., at 351. We must examine the nature of the particular documents sought to be protected in order to determine whether there is a legitimate "expectation of privacy" concerning their contents. Cf. Couch v. United States, 409 U.S. 322, 335 (1973).

Even if we direct our attention to the original checks and deposit slips, rather than to the microfilm copies actually viewed and obtained by means of the subpoena, we perceive no legitimate "expectation of privacy" in their contents. The checks are not confidential communications but negotiable instruments to be used in commercial transactions. All of the documents obtained, including financial statements and deposit slips, contain only information voluntarily conveyed to the banks and exposed to their employees in the ordinary course of business. The lack of any legitimate expectation of privacy concerning the information kept in bank records was assumed by Congress in enacting the Bank Secrecy Act, the expressed purpose of which is to require records to be maintained because they "have a high degree of usefulness in criminal, tax, and regulatory investigations and proceedings." * * *

The depositor takes the risk, in revealing his affairs to another, that the information will be conveyed by that person to the Government. United States v. White, 401 U.S. 745, 751–752 (1971). This Court has held repeatedly that the Fourth Amendment does not prohibit the obtaining of information revealed to a third party and conveyed by him to Government authorities, even if the information is revealed on the assumption that it will be used only for a limited purpose and the confidence placed in the third party will not be betrayed. * * *

Since no Fourth Amendment interests of the depositor are implicated here, this case is governed by the general rule that the issuance of a subpoena to a third party to obtain the records of that party does not violate the rights of a defendant, even if a criminal prosecution is contemplated at the time the subpoena is issued.

2. FAIR CREDIT REPORTING ACT OF 1970 (FCRA)

FEDERAL TRADE COMMISSION, WHAT IS A CREDIT REPORT?

http://www.ftc.gov/bcp/menus/consumer/credit/rights.shtm.

A credit report includes information on where you live, how you pay your bills, and whether you've been sued, arrested, or filed for bankruptcy. Nationwide consumer reporting companies [Equifax, Experian, and TransUnion] sell the information in your report to creditors, insurers, employers, and other businesses that use it to evaluate your applications for credit, insurance, employment, or renting a home. [The Fair Credit Reporting Act (FCRA) requires each of the nationwide consumer reporting companies to provide consumers with a free copy of their upon request, once every 12 months.]

NOTE: *FCRA* AND THE *FTC*

The Fair Crediting Reporting Act of 1970 (FCRA), 16 U.S.C. § 1681 et seq., was first enacted in 1970 and has been amended numerous times. It predates the Privacy Act by four years, but has the hallmarks of a fair information practices law. The FCRA is enforced by the Federal Trade Commission, which, "as a public service," posts a version of the complex, amended law on its website. See http://www.ftc.gov/os/statutes/fcradoc.pdf.

The FCRA governs the assembly, maintenance and disclosure of consumer files by "consumer reporting agencies," to insure that these businesses operate fairly, impartially and with respect for privacy. A "consumer reporting agency" is a company, such as a credit bureau, that compiles and sells information from a credit report. Consumer reporting agencies "may sell information about you to creditors, employers, insurers, and other businesses in the form of a consumer report." See http://www.ftc.gov/privacy/privacy initiatives/credit.html.

The FCRA seeks to insure the accuracy of consumer files and the privacy of the information in them. As explained by the FTC, a consumer file is likely to come into existence whenever an individual applies for credit, a loan, insurance, or employment. A "credit report" is a record that "contains information on where you work and live, how you pay your bills and whether you've been sued, arrested, or have filed for bankruptcy." *Id.*

a. Who Is a "Consumer Reporting Agency" or "User of Consumer Credit Information"?

i. *Prospective Employer Excluded*

PELLER v. RETAIL CREDIT COMPANY ET AL.

359 F. Supp. 1235 (N.D. Ga. 1973).

O'KELLEY, DISTRICT JUDGE * * *

The complaint alleges that on or about January 26, 1973, the plaintiff applied for employment with defendant Robley and was requested by that defendant to submit to a polygraph examination administered by defendant Zonn. After being told that this was the normal and customary employment practice of defendant Robley, the plaintiff voluntarily submitted to the polygraph examination. The following day, an agent of defendant Robley informed the plaintiff that he had not passed the polygraph examination and would not be hired. Subsequently, the plaintiff obtained a position with the Arthur Andersen Company. He continued working with Arthur Andersen until February 7, 1973, when he was involuntarily discharged by the personnel manager of said company. The Arthur Andersen Company gave as the reason for the termination, the fact that in checking the Consumer Credit Report of the plaintiff on file with defendant Retail Credit Company, the Arthur Andersen Company learned that the results of the polygraph examination administered to the plaintiff indicated certain adverse information including the fact that the plaintiff had used Marijuana in the past. On February 8, 1973, the plaintiff went to the national headquarters of Retail Credit in Atlanta, Georgia, and confirmed the fact that the plaintiff's Consumer Credit Report contained information allegedly obtained from the polygraph examination.

Having reviewed the provisions of the Fair Credit Reporting Act, the Court hereby determines that the provisions of that Act are not applicable to defendants Zonn and Robley. The Act places certain requirements on consumer reporting agencies and on users of consumer credit information. Civil liability is provided for * * * in cases of willful and negligent noncompliance with these requirements. * * * Under the facts as alleged, it does not appear that Zonn or Robley [a retained polygrapher and an employer] engages in whole or in part in the process of assembling or evaluating consumer credit information or other information on consumers for the purpose of furnishing consumer reports. Likewise, information given by Zonn to its clients does not constitute a consumer report as the Act specifically excludes from its definition of "consumer report," "any report containing information solely as to transactions or experiences between the consumer and the person making the report." * * *

Since the plaintiff has not alleged malice or willful intent by these two defendants, there can be no action for libel, slander, or invasion of right of privacy under this Act.

ii. Credit Card Issuer Excluded

LEMA v. CITIBANK, N.A.

935 F. Supp. 695, 697 (D. Md. 1996).

KAUFMAN, SENIOR DISTRICT JUDGE

[P]laintiff, a consumer, alleges that defendants violated the Fair Credit Reporting Act ("FCRA"), 15 U.S.C. § 1681, et seq., when they provided inaccurate and derogatory information regarding plaintiff's account to one or more credit reporting agencies. * * *

In May, 1989, defendants issued plaintiff a Visa credit card. In September, 1990, plaintiff's account became delinquent. Plaintiff contacted defendants immediately and, by May 1991, made arrangements to settle his account by paying 70% of the balance due, then $3,090. Plaintiff paid the agreed amount, completing the required payments in November 1991. In March 1992, plaintiff began receiving collection notices regarding his account which reported a balance of $3,272.43. In July 1992, the defendants placed an R9 rating, apparently the most unfavorable rating, on the plaintiff's account. Credit companies other than defendants subsequently denied plaintiff consumer credit.

Plaintiff informed defendants in October 1992 of the alleged inaccuracies regarding his account, apparently without any satisfactory response on their part. Thereafter, in December 1994, defendants stated that plaintiff owed an additional sum, which plaintiff paid in March 1995. When plaintiff filed this suit in October 1995, the R9 rating remained on his account. * * *

Plaintiff alleges that defendants are liable to him for violations of the FCRA. The FCRA imposes civil liability only on consumer reporting agencies and users of consumer information. Thus, plaintiff must show that defendants are either of those entities in order to withstand defendants' summary judgment motion.

The FCRA defines a consumer reporting agency as "any person which, for monetary fees * * * regularly engages in whole or in part in the practice of assembling or evaluating consumer credit information

* * * for the purpose of furnishing consumer reports to third parties." 15 U.S.C. § 1681a(f). By definition, a consumer report does not include "any report containing information solely as to transactions or experiences between the consumer and the person making the report." Plaintiffs allege only that defendants reported to third parties information regarding transactions between defendants and plaintiff. Defendants did not therefore furnish a consumer report regarding plaintiff, nor did they act as a consumer reporting agency with respect to him. * * *

The FCRA does not expressly define the term "users of information" which is employed in §§ 1681n and 1681o of the FCRA. However, § 1681m, entitled "Requirements on users of consumer reports," requires users of consumer information who deny credit or increase rates for the same due to information contained in a consumer report to supply the consumer with the name and address of the consumer reporting agency that furnished the report. Here, plaintiff does not allege in his complaint that defendants denied him credit or insurance or increased the rates charged to him based on information obtained from a consumer report. Plaintiff merely alleges that defendants reported information obtained through their transactions with plaintiff to a consumer reporting agency. For that reason, defendants are apparently not users of information for purposes of the FCRA.

Even if defendants are users as defined by the FCRA, plaintiff has not alleged any conduct on their part which violates the FCRA. The FCRA requires consumer reporting agencies, not those who merely report information to them, to report accurate information. * * *

§ 1681h does not create a federal cause of action against persons who allegedly furnish false information regarding a consumer. Instead, it grants both users of information and consumer reporting agencies "a qualified immunity from common law actions based on information which a consumer reporting agency was required by the [FCRA] to disclose. This immunity * * * is the quid pro quo for compulsory disclosure." Thus, all this section does is to allow a plaintiff to bring a state law claim of defamation, invasion of privacy or negligence, provided such plaintiff alleges that defendants acted with malice or willful intent to injure plaintiff.

b. Liability for Obtaining Credit Report Under False Pretenses or for Improper Purposes

HANSEN v. MORGAN

582 F.2d 1214 (9th Cir. 1978).

JUDGE CARTER * * *

This case grew out of a strenuous campaign for the 1974 Republican candidacy for the United States Congress in the Second District of Idaho. Orval Hansen, the incumbent congressman, was defeated in the Republican primary election by appellant George Hansen. Thereafter two Idaho citizens filed complaints with the clerk of the United States House of Representatives alleging improper campaign financing procedures by George Hansen. This caused an investigation of George Hansen by the House Administration Committee, of which incumbent Orval Hansen was a member until his term as Congressman expired. * * *

Appellee Melvin Morgan is the principal stockholder and chief executive of appellee Nate Morgan Jewelers of Pocatello, a corporation. The corporation is a member of the Pocatello Credit Bureau, entitled to receive credit reports from the Bureau. On about August 10, 1974, Melvin Morgan received a telephone call from Rose Bowman which he construed to be a request for a credit report on George Hansen. Morgan contends he agreed to obtain the report upon the belief that it was desired by Orval Hansen to assist the House Administration Committee's investigation of George Hansen. Upon Melvin Morgan's request the credit report was provided without question by the Pocatello Credit Bureau. The report was issued in the names of both George V. Hansen and his wife, Connie. It contained no information adverse to either of them.

When he received the report, Morgan delivered it personally to Orval Hansen's office in Washington D. C. Eventually the report reached the House Administration Committee.

Upon learning of the existence of the credit report, George and Connie Hansen filed suit against [Morgan's family]. * * * Their amended complaint alleged that the Morgans, by willfully or negligently failing to comply with the requirements of * * * the FCRA, unlawfully violated the Hansens' right to privacy. Damages were sought under §§ 1681n and 1681O which authorize civil causes of action for noncompliance with the requirements of the act. * * *

Before the trial judge the Morgans contended the credit report obtained on the Hansens was not a "consumer report" within the meaning of the FCRA. * * *

Section 1681a(d) of Title 15 defines "consumer report" to be:

" * * * Any written, oral, or other communication of any information by a consumer reporting agency bearing on a consumer's credit worthiness, credit standing, credit capacity, character, general reputation, personal characteristics, or mode of living which is used or expected to be used or collected in whole or in part for the purpose of serving as a factor in establishing the consumer's eligibility for (1) credit or insurance to be used primarily for personal, family, or household purposes, or (2) employment purposes, or (3) other purposes authorized under section 1681b of this title. * * * "

The credit report issued on the Hansens in this case falls directly within this definition. Since the Pocatello Credit Bureau knew nothing of the Morgans' real reason for requesting the report, it must have supplied this information with the expectation that the Morgans would use it for purposes consistent both with the FCRA and with the Bureau's form membership contract which closely correlated with the restrictions in the act. And unless the Bureau was generally collecting such information for purposes not permitted by the FCRA, it must have collected the information in the report for use consistent with the purposes stated in the act. There has been no suggestion otherwise. Accordingly, the credit report is (1) a written communication of information (2) by a consumer reporting agency (3) bearing on the Hansens' credit worthiness, credit standing or credit capacity (4) which was both expected to be used, and collected in whole or in part, for the purpose of establishing the Hansens' consumer eligibility for credit transactions. As such it is a consumer report under the FCRA. * * *

The standard for determining when a consumer report has been obtained under false pretenses will usually be defined in relation to the permissible purposes of consumer reports which are enumerated in 15 U.S.C. § 1681b. This is because a consumer reporting agency can legally issue a report only for the purposes listed in § 1681b. If the agency is complying with the statute, then a user cannot utilize an account with a consumer reporting agency to obtain consumer information for a purpose not permitted by § 1681b without using a false pretense.

We hold that obtaining a consumer report in violation of the terms of the statute without disclosing the impermissible purpose for which the report is desired can constitute obtaining consumer information under false pretenses, and that the facts in this case demonstrate that the consumer report was so obtained. * * *

Noncompliance * * * thereby forms a basis of civil liability under [the FCRA]. The Hansens' claim states a valid cause of action under these sections and there were sufficient issues of fact to withstand summary judgment. * * *

The judgment of the district court is reversed and remanded for a trial.

YOHAY v. CITY OF ALEXANDRIA EMPLOYEES CREDIT UNION, INC.

827 F.2d 967 (4th Cir. 1987).

KAUFMAN, SENIOR DISTRICT JUDGE

At the time of the incident in question [attorney Patricia Ryan and her ex husband Stephen Yohay] were engaged in a state court custody trial concerning their son. * * *

[Ryan's clients happened to include the City of Alexandria Employees Credit Union, which routinely requested credit reports from CBI—the Credit Bureau of Georgia, Inc.]

Ryan testified that she had sought information from CBI regarding Yohay's credit in order to compare the numbers of Yohay's credit card accounts with their earlier established joint credit card accounts to ensure that Yohay was no longer using those previously established joint credit arrangements. Also during the trial, Andrea Martin, the Credit Union's assistant manager, testified that Donna Hatton, an employee of the Credit Union, had told her (Martin) that she (Hatton) had obtained the credit report on Yohay from CBI at the request of George Filopovich, the Credit Union's manager * * *.

The Credit Union had a contract with CBI permitting the Credit Union to obtain credit information from CBI for appropriate purposes. The trial testimony revealed that the Credit Union had posted no rules or guidelines concerning the running of credit checks and that seemingly anyone, who could obtain physical access to the computer on the Credit Union's premises, could access CBI's files for any reason.

Yohay first became aware that CBI had furnished credit information to the Credit Union when Yohay obtained from CBI a copy of his credit records in March, 1984. Those records revealed that a credit check of Yohay had been run by the Credit Union on July 26, 1983. Since Yohay had had no relationship with the Credit Union, Yohay wrote a letter to the Credit Union inquiring as to the reason for the credit check. The president of the Credit Union, in responding to such inquiry, informed Yohay that the Credit Union had run the check at the request of Ryan.

Yohay filed the within action against the Credit Union pursuant to the Fair Credit Reporting Act (FCRA), 15 U.S.C. § 1681 et seq., seeking punitive damages, costs, and attorneys' fees, but not seeking compensatory damages. The Credit Union filed a third-party complaint against Ryan for indemnification. * * *

The Credit Union and Ryan were "user[s] of information" obtained from CBI, "a consumer reporting agency." See discussion infra slip op. at 16–18. As such, if either the Credit Union or Ryan "willfully fail[ed] to comply with any requirement imposed" by the FCRA, each is liable to the "consumer"—in these cases Yohay—for actual and punitive damages as well as costs and attorney's fees. See 15 U.S.C. § 1681n.

Accordingly, each of the two users—the Credit Union and Ryan—is subject to civil liability under section 1681n if each user's individual noncompliance with section 1681b was willful. * * * The trial record discloses more than sufficient evidence to support the jury's implicit conclusion that the Credit Union acted willfully. For example, the evidence of the friendly relationship between the manager of the Credit Union, Filopovich, and Ryan and her second husband, Justice, indicated that Filopovich was cognizant of Ryan's improper purpose. * * *

The FCRA specifically provides that punitive damages may be awarded "as the court may allow," 15 U.S.C. § 1681n(2), if the defendant's noncompliance with the provisions of the Act is willful. Actual damages are not a statutory prerequisite to an award of punitive damages under the Act. The award of punitive damages in the absence of any actual damages, in an appropriate case, comports with the underlying deterrent purpose of the FCRA. * * *

Seemingly, anyone who used the Credit Union's computer to access CBI's files appeared—from CBI's perspective—to have authority to gain such access. In that regard it is to be noted that the Credit Union had not posted any guidelines to users of the computer informing them of the circumstances under which such credit information could be obtained. Indeed, the Credit Union had posted the code which provided access to the computer system, enabling anyone with the physical opportunity to use the system to access CBI's files. The record also indicates that the credit check was run by Donna Hatton, an employee of the Credit Union, at the direction of George Filopovich, the manager of the Credit Union. There is little or no question about the apparent, if not the actual, authority of Filopovich to have ordered a credit check from CBI. Accordingly, the Credit Union would be liable to Yohay for Ryan's actions, regardless of whether Ryan had actual or apparent authority to obtain the information about Yohay from CBI.

c. Liability for Maintaining Inaccurate Records

THOMPSON v. SAN ANTONIO RETAIL MERCHANTS ASSO.

682 F.2d 509 (5th Cir.1982).

RUBIN, JOHNSON and GARWOOD, CIRCUIT JUDGES, PER CURIAM

This case involves the liability of [a computerized credit reporting service, the San Antonio Retail Merchants Association (SARMA)] for an inaccurate credit report. * * *

In early 1978, the plaintiff, William Douglas Thompson, III, applied for credit with Gulf and with Ward's in San Antonio. He listed his social security as 407–86–4065, his address as 6929 Timbercreek, his occupation as grounds keeper, and his wife as Deborah C. On February 9, 1978, Gulf's terminal operator mistakenly accepted file number 5867114 as that of the plaintiff. SARMA's computer thereupon automatically captured various information about William Douglas Thompson, III, including his social security number, into file number 5867114. At that point, the original file, which was on William Daniel Thompson, Jr., became a potpourri of information on both the plaintiff and the original William Daniel Thompson, Jr. The name on the file remained that of William Daniel Thompson, Jr. The social security number became that of the plaintiff, the current address and employer became that of the plaintiff, a former address and employer became that of William Daniel Thompson, Jr., and the wife's name became that of the plaintiff's wife. Shortly thereafter, Ward's terminal operator ran a credit check on the plaintiff, was given the garbled data, and accepted file number 5867114 as that of the plaintiff. As a result of the adverse information regarding the Gordon's [Jewelers] account, Ward's denied the plaintiff credit. The plaintiff applied for credit at Ward's in May 1979 and was again rejected. * * *

The adverse information remained in the plaintiff's file during 1978 and the first five and a half months of 1979. During all of this time the plaintiff thought he had been denied credit from Ward's and Gulf because of a 1976 Texas felony conviction for burglary. He had received a five-year probationary sentence, but subsequently gained fulltime employment and straightened out his life. In June of 1979, plaintiff's wife learned from her credit union in processing an application for a loan that her husband's adverse credit rating resulted from a bad debt at Gordon's. The plaintiff knew he had never had an account at Gordon's so he and his wife went directly to their place of business. After waiting some two hours he was informed that there had indeed been a mistake, their credit record was for William Daniel Thompson, Jr.

The plaintiff and his wife went to SARMA with this information in an attempt to purge the erroneous credit information. They spoke with an individual and showed birth registration and drivers license information revealing his name to be William Douglas Thompson III. The entire process required some three hours. Nevertheless SARMA thereafter mailed appellee a letter addressed to William Daniel Thompson III. Appellee's wife again returned to SARMA. Following this SARMA once again addressed appellee in another letter as William Daniel Thompson III. Appellee again returned to SARMA—yet again SARMA wrote still another letter with the same incorrect name. * * *

SARMA had no way of knowing if the information supplied by the subscriber was correct. Although SARMA did conduct spot audits to verify social security numbers, it did not audit all subscribers. With respect to the second act of negligence, SARMA's verification process failed to uncover the erroneous social security number even though Gulf made a specific request for a "revision" to check the adverse credit history ascribed to the plaintiff. SARMA's manager, Mr. Zepeda, testified that what should have been done upon the request for a revision, was to pick up the phone and check with Gordon's and learn, among other things, the social security number for William Daniel Thompson, Jr. It was the manager's further testimony that the social security number is the single most important information in a consumer's credit file. In light of this evidence, this Court cannot conclude that the district court was clearly erroneous in finding negligent violation of section 1681e(b). * * *

The district court's award of $10,000 in actual damages was based on humiliation and mental distress to the plaintiff. Even when there are no out-of-pocket expenses, humiliation and mental distress do constitute recoverable elements of damage under the Act. * * * In the instant case, the amount of damages is a question of fact which may be reversed by this Court only if the district court's findings are clearly erroneous. Fed. R.Civ.P. 52(a).

SARMA asserts that Thompson failed to prove any actual damages, or at best proved only minimal damages for humiliation and mental distress. There was evidence, however, that Thompson suffered humiliation and embarrassment from being denied credit on three occasions. Thompson testified that the denial of credit hurt him deeply because of his mistaken belief that it resulted from his felony conviction:

"I was trying to build myself back up, trying to set myself up, get back on my feet again. I was working sixty hours a week and sometimes seventy. I went back to school. I was going to school at night three nights a week, four nights a week, three hours a night, and [denial of credit] really hurt. It made me disgusted with myself * * *. [I needed credit to] be able to obtain things that everybody else is able to obtain, to be able to buy clothes or set myself up where I can show my ability to be trusted. We didn't even have a bed. It was pretty bad. We were hurting. Everything we had to do, we had to save up and pay cash for strictly. It was just impossible to do it any other way."

Further, the inaccurate information remained in SARMA's files for almost one and one-half years after the inaccurate information was inserted. Even after the error was discovered, Thompson spent months pressing SARMA to correct its mistakes and fully succeeded only after bringing a lawsuit against SARMA. This Court is of the opinion that the [district court] trial judge was entitled to conclude that the humiliation and mental distress were not minimal but substantial.

d. Duty of Reasonable Investigation

JOHNSON v. MBNA

357 F.3d 426, 429 (4th Cir. 2004).

WILKINS, CHIEF JUDGE: * * *

The account at issue, an MBNA [America Bank, N.A.] MasterCard account, was opened in November 1987. The parties disagree regarding who applied for this account and therefore who was legally obligated to pay amounts owed on it. It is undisputed that one of the applicants was Edward N. Slater, whom Johnson married in March 1991. MBNA contends that Johnson was a co-applicant with Slater, and thus a co-obligor on the account. Johnson claims, however, that she was merely an authorized user and not a co-applicant.

In December 2000, Slater filed for bankruptcy, and MBNA promptly removed his name from the account. That same month, MBNA contacted Johnson and informed her that she was responsible for the approximately $17,000 balance on the account. After obtaining copies of her credit report from the three major credit reporting agencies—Experian, Equifax, and Trans Union—Johnson disputed the MBNA account with each of the credit reporting agencies. In response, each credit reporting agency sent to MBNA an automated consumer dispute verification (ACDV). The ACDVs that Experian and Trans Union sent to MBNA specifically indicated that Johnson was disputing that she was a co-obligor on the account. * * * The ACDV that Equifax sent to MBNA stated that Johnson disputed the account balance.

In response to each of these ACDVs, MBNA agents reviewed the account information contained in MBNA's computerized Customer Information System (CIS) and, based on the results of that review, notified the credit reporting agencies that MBNA had verified that the disputed information was correct. Based on MBNA's responses to the ACDVs, the credit reporting agencies continued reporting the MBNA account on Johnson's credit report.

Johnson subsequently sued MBNA, claiming, inter alia, that it had violated the FCRA by failing to conduct a proper investigation of her dispute. * * *

MBNA argues that the language of § 1681s–2(b)(1)(A), requiring furnishers of credit information to "conduct an investigation" regarding disputed information, imposes only a minimal duty on creditors to briefly review their records to determine whether the disputed information is correct. Stated differently, MBNA contends that this provision does not contain any qualitative component that would allow courts or juries to assess whether the creditor's investigation was reasonable. By contrast, Johnson asserts that § 1681s–2(b)(1)(A) requires creditors to conduct a reasonable investigation. We review this question of statutory interpretation de novo. *See Holland v. Pardee Coal Co.*, 269 F.3d 424, 430 (4th Cir. 2001).

The key term at issue here, "investigation," is defined as "[a] detailed inquiry or systematic examination." Am. Heritage Dictionary 920 (4th ed. 2000); see Webster's Third New Int'l Dictionary 1189 (1981) (defining "investigation" as "a searching inquiry"). Thus, the plain meaning of "investigation" clearly requires some degree of careful inquiry by creditors. Further, § 1681s–2(b)(1)(A) uses the term "investigation" in the context of articulating a creditor's duties in the consumer dispute process outlined by the FCRA. It would make little sense to conclude that, in creating a system intended to give consumers a means to dispute—and, ultimately, correct—inaccurate information on their credit reports, Congress used the term "investigation" to include superficial, unreasonable inquiries by creditors. We therefore hold that § 1681s–2(b)(1) requires creditors, after receiving notice of a consumer dispute from a credit reporting agency, to conduct a reasonable investigation of their records to determine whether the disputed information can be verified. * * *

MBNA next contends that even if § 1681s–2(b)(1) requires creditors to conduct reasonable investigations of consumer disputes, no evidence here supports a determination by the jury that MBNA's investigation of Johnson's dispute was unreasonable. * * *

As explained above, MBNA was notified of the specific nature of Johnson's dispute—namely, her assertion that she was not a co-obligor on the account. Yet MBNA's agents testified that their investigation was primarily limited to (1) confirming that the name and address listed on the ACDVs were the same as the name and address contained in the CIS, and (2) noting that the CIS contained a code indicating that Johnson was the sole responsible party on the account. The MBNA agents also testified that, in investigating consumer disputes generally, they do not look beyond the information contained in the CIS and never consult underlying documents such as account applications. Based on this evidence, a jury could reasonably conclude that MBNA acted unreasonably in failing to verify the accuracy of the information contained in the CIS. * * *

MBNA first argues that the district court erred in instructing the jury that, in determining whether MBNA's investigation was reasonable, it should consider "the cost of verifying the accuracy of the information versus the possible harm of reporting inaccurate information." * * * [W]e believe that the general balancing test articulated by the district court—weighing the cost of verifying disputed information against the possible harm to the consumer—logically applies in determining whether the steps taken (and not taken) by a creditor in investigating a dispute constitute a reasonable investigation. The district court therefore did not abuse its discretion in giving this instruction.

For the reasons set forth above, we affirm the [jury verdict and] judgment of the district court.

3. THE FINANCIAL MODERNIZATION ACT OF 1999, GRAMM–LEACH–BLILEY ("GLB")

FEDERAL TRADE COMMISSION

http://www.ftc.gov.

The Financial Modernization Act of 1999, also known as the "Gramm–Leach–Bliley Act" or GLB Act, includes provisions to protect consumers' personal financial information held by financial institutions. [See Title V, Subtitle A of the Gramm–Leach–Bliley Act, Pub. L. No. 106–102, 113 Stat. 1338 (1999) (codified as amended at *15 U.S.C.A. § 6801* et seq. (2000)).] There are three principal parts to the privacy requirements: the Financial Privacy Rule, Safeguards Rule and pretexting provisions. The GLB Act gives authority to eight federal agencies and the states to administer and enforce the Financial Privacy Rule and the Safeguards Rule.

The Financial Privacy Rule governs the collection and disclosure of customers' personal financial information by financial institutions. It also applies to companies, whether or not they are financial institutions, who receive such information.

The Safeguards Rule requires all financial institutions to design, implement and maintain safeguards to protect customer information. The Safeguards Rule applies not only to financial institutions that collect information from their own customers, but also to financial institutions "such as credit reporting agencies" that receive customer information from other financial institutions. * * *

The Gramm–Leach–Bliley Act prohibits "pretexting," the use of false pretenses, including fraudulent statements and impersonation, to obtain consumers' personal financial information, such as bank balances. This law also prohibits the knowing solicitation of others to engage in pretexting. The Commission has been active in bringing cases to halt the operations of companies and individuals that allegedly practice pretexting and sell consumers' financial information.

FEDERAL TRADE COMMISSION

http://www.ftc.gov/bcp/edu/pubs/business/idtheft/bus53.shtm.

In Brief: The Financial Privacy Requirements of the Gramm–Leach–Bliley Act

Protecting the privacy of consumer information held by "financial institutions" is at the heart of the financial privacy provisions of the Gramm–Leach–Bliley Financial Modernization Act of 1999. The GLB Act requires companies to give consumers privacy notices that explain the institutions' information-sharing practices. In turn, consumers have the right to limit some—but not all—sharing of their information. * * *

Financial Institutions

The GLB Act applies to "financial institutions"—companies that offer financial products or services to individuals, like loans, financial or investment advice, or insurance. The Federal Trade Commission has authority to enforce the law with respect to "financial institutions" that are not covered by the federal banking agencies, the Securities and Exchange Commission, the Commodity Futures Trading Commission, and state insurance authorities. Among the institutions that fall under FTC jurisdiction for purposes of the GLB Act are non-bank mortgage lenders, loan brokers, some financial or investment advisers, tax preparers, providers of real estate settlement services, and debt collectors. At the same time, the FTC's regulation applies only to companies that are "significantly engaged" in such financial activities.

The law requires that financial institutions protect information collected about individuals; it does not apply to information collected in business or commercial activities.

Consumers and Customers

A company's obligations under the GLB Act depend on whether the company has consumers or customers who obtain its services. A consumer is an individual who obtains or has obtained a financial product or service from a financial institution for personal, family or household reasons. A customer is a consumer with a continuing relationship with a financial institution. Generally, if the relationship between the financial institution and the individual is significant and/or long-term, the individual is a customer of the institution. For example, a person who gets a mortgage from a lender or hires a broker to get a personal loan is considered a customer of the lender or the broker, while a person who uses a check-cashing service is a consumer of that service.

Why is the difference between consumers and customers so important? Because only customers are entitled to receive a financial institution's privacy notice automatically. Consumers are entitled to receive a privacy notice from a financial institution only if the company shares the consumers' information with companies not affiliated with it, with some exceptions. Customers must receive a notice every year for as long as the customer relationship lasts.

The privacy notice must be given to individual customers or consumers by mail or in-person delivery; it may not, say, be posted on a wall. Reasonable ways to deliver a notice may depend on the type of business the institution is in: for example, an online lender may post its notice on its website and require online consumers to acknowledge receipt as a necessary part of a loan application.

The Privacy Notice

The privacy notice must be a clear, conspicuous, and accurate statement of the company's privacy practices; it should include what information the company collects about its consumers and customers, with whom it shares the information, and how it protects or safeguards the information. The notice applies to the "nonpublic personal information" the company gathers and discloses about its consumers and customers; in practice, that may be most—or all—of the information a company has about them. For example, nonpublic personal information could be information that a consumer or customer puts on an application; information about the individual from another source, such as a credit bureau; or information about transactions between the individual and the company, such as an account balance. Indeed, even the fact that an individual is a consumer or customer of a particular financial institution is nonpublic person information. But information that the company has reason to believe is lawfully public—such as mortgage loan information in a jurisdiction where that information is publicly recorded—is not restricted by the GLB Act.

Opt–Out Rights

Consumers and customers have the right to opt out of—or say no to—having their information shared with certain third parties. The privacy notice must explain how—and offer a reasonable way—they can do that. For example, providing a toll-free telephone number or a detachable form with a pre-printed address is a reasonable way for consumers or customers to opt out; requiring someone to write a letter as the only way to opt out is not.

The privacy notice also must explain that consumers have a right to say no to the sharing of certain information—credit report or application information—with the financial institution's affiliates. An affiliate is an entity that controls another company, is controlled by the company, or is under common control with the company. Consumers have this right under a different law, the Fair Credit Reporting Act. The GLB Act does not give consumers the right to opt out when the financial institution shares other information with its affiliates.

The GLB Act provides no opt-out right in several other situations: For example, an individual cannot opt out if:

- a financial institution shares information with outside companies that provide essential services like data processing or servicing accounts;
- the disclosure is legally required;
- a financial institution shares customer data with outside service providers that market the financial company's products or services.

Receiving Nonpublic Personal Information

The GLB Act puts some limits on how anyone that receives nonpublic personal information from a financial institution can use or re-disclose the information. Take the case of a lender that discloses customer information to a service provider responsible for mailing account statements, where the consumer has no right to opt out: The service provider may use the information for limited purposes—that is, for mailing account statements. It may not sell the information to other organizations or use it for marketing.

However, it's a different scenario when a company receives nonpublic personal information from a financial institution that provided an opt-out notice—and the consumer didn't opt out. In this case, the recipient steps into the shoes of the disclosing financial institution, and may use the information for its own purposes or re-disclose it to a third party, consistent with the financial institution's privacy notice. That is, if the privacy notice of the financial institution allows for disclosure to other unaffiliated financial institutions—like insurance providers—the recipient may re-disclose the information to an unaffiliated insurance provider.

Other Provisions

Other important provisions of the GLB Act also impact how a company conducts business. For example, financial institutions are prohibited from disclosing their customers' account numbers to non-affiliated companies when it comes to telemarketing, direct mail marketing or other marketing through e-mail, even if the individuals have not opted out of sharing the information for marketing purposes.

Another provision prohibits "pretexting"—the practice of obtaining customer information from financial institutions under false pretenses.

The FTC has brought several cases against information brokers who engage in pretexting.

* * * The FTC is one of eight federal regulatory agencies that has the authority to enforce the financial privacy law, along with the state insurance authorities. The federal banking agencies, the Securities and Exchange Commission and the Commodity Futures Trading Commission have jurisdiction over banks, thrifts, credit unions, brokerage firms and commodity traders.

a. Validity and Constitutionality of GLB Privacy Regs

INDIVIDUAL REFERENCE SERVS. GROUP, INC. v. FTC

145 F. Supp. 2d 6 (D.D.C. 2001).

JUDGE ELLEN SEGAL HUVELLE

Plaintiffs bring this action * * * seeking judicial review of regulations (the "Regulations") that were promulgated by the defendant agencies to implement Title V, Subtitle A of the Gramm–Leach–Bliley Act, Pub. L. No. 106–102, 113 Stat. 1338 (1999) (codified as amended at 15 U.S.C.A. § 6801 et seq. (2000)) (the "GLB Act"), which addresses the responsibility of financial institutions to protect the privacy of the personal financial information of their customers. * * *

Plaintiffs contend that the Regulations are both unlawful and unconstitutional. They argue that the Regulations are invalid for five reasons: a) the definition of "nonpublic personal information" in the Regulations contravenes the statutory requirement that only financial information is subject to the GLB Act; b) the Regulations constitute an impermissible regulation of non-financial institutions by the agencies; c) the Regulations contradict a provision of the GLB Act that exempts consumer reporting agencies from the statute's prohibition of the use of account numbers for marketing purposes; d) the Regulations impose a restriction on the use of nonpublic personal information that is inconsistent with the statute; and e) the Regulations modify the operation of the Fair Credit Reporting Act, 15 U.S.C. § 1681 et seq. (the "FCRA"), in contravention of the savings clause of the GLB Act. In addition, plaintiffs allege that the Regulations * * * are overbroad and improperly restrict plaintiffs' speech in violation of the First Amendment * * *. Upon consideration of the pleadings and the record herein, this Court concludes the Regulations are lawful and constitutional. Summary judgment is therefore granted for defendants as to all counts. * * *

Plaintiff Trans Union * * * is a "consumer reporting agency" ("CRA"), as defined in the FCRA, and it provides "consumer reports," as defined at 15 U.S.C. § 1681a(d). The foundation of Trans Union's business is its database, CRONUS, which contains information about consumers that is used to generate credit reports. * * * Although Trans Union gathers this data from over 85,000 entities, its main source of information is financial institutions, which generally provide this information in the form of accounts receivable tapes. * * * These tapes contain information—the name, address, zip code, and social security number, as well as information regarding the account itself—about each consumer that is reported by the financial institution. * * *

Trans Union maintains this information in CRONUS, from which it generates credit reports. These reports contain two types of information: identifying information for each individual, and tradeline information describing the consumer's account and payment history. * * * The identifying information includes the name, address, social security number, and telephone number of the consumers, and since this data is printed at the top of the report, it is typically referred to as "credit header" information. * * * Although financial institutions are the primary source of the identifying information, plaintiffs allege that the resulting credit header is the product of various sources, and that it therefore does not reveal the existence of a customer relationship with any specific financial institution.

Trans Union alleges that three of its product lines will be affected by the Regulations and are therefore at issue in this litigation. First are Trans Union's credit header products. In addition to including the header information in its credit reports, Trans Union sells this data separately to a number of business and governmental entities, which then use the information for both commercial and noncommercial purposes, including target marketing and fraud prevention. * * * These products include "Trace," which allows a customer of Trans Union to input an individual's social security number and receive, in return, the name and address of that person * * *; "Retrace," which enables a customer who has an individual's name and address to obtain that person's social security and phone numbers * * *; and "ID Search," which permits a customer with a person's name and phone number to obtain that individual's social security number and current and former addresses from Trans Union. * * * Trans Union and other CRAs also sell credit header information to individual reference services, which typically work with government agencies to identify and locate individuals for a variety of purposes, including the prosecution of financial crimes and enforcement of child support orders. * * * Similarly, private companies hire individual reference services to help detect and prevent fraud, and health organizations use their products to identify blood and organ donors. Media and political campaign organizations may use individual references services to verify the identities of campaign donors. * * *

Second, Trans Union offers a line of target marketing products that provide both credit header and tradeline information. These target marketing lists are designed to identify consumers who may be interested in purchasing the particular goods or services that are offered by customers of Trans Union. * * * Typically, a targeting marketing list provides a customer with the names and addresses of individuals who live in a household that meets particular criteria, such as having a bank card or a home mortgage. * * * One of these products is "TransLink," a program that allows a retailer to identify the names and addresses of customers who have made purchases from that retailer with a credit card. A retailer who has obtained the name and credit account number of a customer sends this information to Trans Union, which in response provides a corresponding name and address using the information stored in CRO-NUS. * * *

Third, Trans Union uses information that it receives from financial institutions to prepare aggregate or average data on consumers. Trans Union's SUM-it product, for example, creates aggregate financial information, such as the average mortgage and bank card balance, for consumers who live within a particular zip code, zip code-plus-two digits, or zip code-plus-four digits. * * * The information in the SUM-it database is then used to create models that predict consumers' financial characteristics or their propensity to purchase certain goods or services. This aggregate information is then made available to marketing firms. * * * Individual information reported by financial institutions about particular customers is not disclosed in this material. * * *

Plaintiff Individual Reference Services Group, Inc. is a non-stock corporation organized exclusively as a nonprofit trade association under the laws of the state of Maryland. (IRSG Statement P1.) IRSG represents leading information industry companies, including major CRAs, that provide information to help identify, verify, or locate individuals. IRSG represents CRAs, which obtain credit header information directly from financial institutions, and other entities to whom the CRAs provide credit header data. Trans Union is a member of IRSG.

Plaintiff IRSG contests only the regulation of credit header information under the GLB Act; unlike Trans Union, it does not challenge the effects of the agencies' Final Rules on target marketing lists or aggregate data. * * *

The defendants in this action are the Federal Trade Commission ("FTC"), Board of Governors of the Federal Reserve System ("Board"), Federal Deposit Insurance Corporation ("FDIC"), Office of the Comptroller of the Currency ("OCC"), Office of Thrift Supervision ("OTS"), the National Credit Union Administration ("NCUA"), and their respective heads. These agencies are responsible for the administration and enforcement of Title V of the GLB Act, as well as other related statutes. * * *

The Federal Financial Modernization Act, commonly known as the Gramm–Leach–Bliley Act, was passed by Congress and signed by President Clinton in November 1999. The purpose of the GLB Act was "to enhance competition in the financial services industry by providing a prudential framework for the affiliation of banks, securities firms, insurance companies, and other financial service providers * * *." Congress intended that increased competition would benefit consumers by enhancing the availability of financial products and services and by allowing domestic financial services firms to better compete globally.

At the same time, Congress realized that such a structure could exacerbate the concerns of consumers regarding the dissemination of personal financial information. For example, banks, insurance companies, and securities firms have the capacity to know more about an individual's spending habits than ever before, and could use this information for many purposes, including unwanted marketing and solicitation. * * * To balance these interests, the Act provides consumers with the power to choose how their personal information will be shared by financial institutions. As the Act states, "It is the policy of the Congress that each financial institution has an affirmative and continuing obligation to respect the privacy of its customers and to protect the security and confidentiality of those customers' nonpublic personal information." * * * During debates in Congress, legislators noted that the proposed Act would "provide some of the strongest privacy protections to ever be enacted into any federal law," * * * and would "represent the most comprehensive federal privacy protections ever enacted by Congress." * * *

Whether the phrase "personally identifiable financial information" is an unambiguous term—and, as a corollary, whether defendants' interpretation violates any plain meaning of that term—presents a challenging question. However, based on the language, structure, and legislative history of the GLB Act, this Court concludes that "personally identifiable financial information" is an ambiguous term in the Act and that the agencies' interpretation is therefore entitled to deference. * * *

Next, Trans Union contends it is a non-financial institution, and as such, defendants have no authority to regulate it. Specifically, plaintiff argues that CRAs are not financial institutions under the GLB Act, and that Congress intended to give the FTC enforcement, but not rulemaking, authority over these entities. In support of these arguments, plaintiffs spin complex arguments about both the legislative history of the GLB Act and the interplay between that statute and the FCRA in terms of agency authority.

In actuality, however, the grant of rulemaking authority to the agencies over CRAs is unambiguously provided for under the GLB Act, when read in conjunction with other existing statutes and regulations that are cross-referenced in the GLB Act. * * *

The GLB Act created a means to ensure that consumers retain control over their nonpublic personal information. When consumers provide this information to a financial institution, that institution may not disclose the information to third parties, unless the consumer has permitted this through the notice and opt-out procedure specified in the Act. *15 U.S.C. § 6802.* The Act does, however, specify limited circumstances under which nonpublic personal information may be disclosed to a third party without notice and opt-out—including to a CRA in accordance with the FCRA. See § 6802(e)(6). The statute limits the redisclosure of this information by the CRAs, but is silent on the reuse of information disclosed under this exception. Nonetheless, the agencies found that "although section 502(c) does not expressly address use, reuse limitations are, as indicated, implicit in the provisions authorizing or permitting disclosures." * * *

The Court agrees. The statute's legislative history and structure indicate that Congress intended the § 502(e) exceptions to be limited in scope and purpose. * * *

Plaintiffs argue that the Regulations violate their First Amendment right of free speech * * *.

Plaintiffs' primary constitutional argument is that the Regulations violate their First Amendment right to free speech. Plaintiffs' argument is premised on the notion that the use and dissemination of credit header information is speech that is protected by the Constitution, and therefore, the agencies' overbroad definition of "personally identifiable financial information" and flat ban on the use and disclosure of FCRA data impinge on this speech in violation of the First Amendment. The Court disagrees, particularly in light of this Circuit's recent decision in Trans Union v. FTC, which addressed very similar issues. * * *

Defendants argue that the dissemination of credit header information should be protected to the same extent as commercial speech, whereas plaintiffs contend that such expression should be accorded full First Amendment protection. However, plaintiffs offer little to distinguish this case from the precedents of the Supreme Court and this Circuit, which recognized the limited nature of First Amendment protection for the commercial activities of information-based businesses. * * *

In the instant action, plaintiffs' speech is the dissemination of credit header information by financial institutions. This speech does not involve any matter of public concern, but consists of information of interest solely to the speaker and the client audience. Thus, restrictions on the dissemination of this nonpublic personal information does not impinge upon any public debate. Moreover, even if the credit header information that is disseminated by plaintiffs is not commercial speech per se, it is entitled to the same level of protection. * * *

The asserted governmental interest that the Regulations seek to protect is the privacy of consumers—particularly the security and confidentiality of their nonpublic personal information. 15 U.S.C. § 6801(a). According to defendants, customer privacy is violated when an individual is required to relinquish the ability to control the dissemination of personal information in order to obtain financial services. Courts have repeatedly recognized that the protection of consumer privacy—in various forms—is a substantial governmental interest. * * *

Finally, plaintiffs contend that the Final Rules are more extensive than necessary to achieve the government's interest. * * *

The Final Rules do not directly prohibit the use and disclosure of nonpublic personal information, but instead, they require financial institutions to provide customers with notice and the opportunity to opt out. Plaintiffs argue, however, that defendants' use and disclosure restrictions on a CRA's ability to use and disclose credit header information are tantamount to an outright prohibition on such activities, because financial institutions have indicated that they will not provide the required notice and opt-out for CRAs' use of credit headers. As a result, plaintiffs claim that the Regulations are far broader than necessary and that the fit between the use restriction and the interest to be served is disparate.

Plaintiffs have again mischaracterized the nature of the governmental interest at stake, and have compounded that error by overstating the effect of the Regulations on CRAs. The Regulations do not impose any restrictions on CRAs that are not also applicable to all other institutions that receive nonpublic personal information. Like every other third party, Trans Union and other CRAs can still use and disclose this information— except as provided in one of the limited exceptions—as long as the individual consumer is given notice and the opportunity to opt out. This scheme reflects the purpose of the Act—to allow consumers to retain control over their personal financial information. The Rules do not ban speech and are no more extensive than necessary to serve the substantial governmental interest of protecting consumer privacy over personal financial information. For these reasons, the Regulations * * * comport with the requirements of the First Amendment. * * *

For the above reasons, the Court finds that defendants' regulations are neither unlawful nor unconstitutional.

b. Judicial Process Exception

EX PARTE NATIONAL WESTERN
LIFE INSURANCE COMPANY

899 So. 2d 218 (Ala. 2004).

HOUSTON, JUSTICE. * * *

Terrill W. Sanders, as administrator of the estate of John W. Guthrie, deceased ("the respondent"), filed an action based upon an alleged negligent issuance of a life-insurance policy, naming as defendants the petitioners, among others. In pursuing this claim, the respondent sought discovery from the petitioners of insurance policies and any other insurance documents of several individuals who are not parties to, and who have no interest in, this action. The petitioners objected to the respondent's request, asserting that the documents, which contain medical histories, Social Security numbers, marital status, occupation, height, weight, date and location of birth, address, day and evening telephone numbers, and insurance choices, premiums, and benefits, are confidential and private. * * *

[T]he court ordered the petitioners to produce the documents. * * *

The general prohibition in the GLBA on disclosure of nonpublic personal information is subject to certain exceptions, which, in light of the express purposes behind the GLBA, have been properly held to be "limited in scope and purpose." One of those exceptions is § 6802(e)(8), which provides: " * * * this section shall not prohibit the disclosure of nonpublic personal information * * * to comply with Federal, State, or local laws, rules, and other applicable legal requirements; to comply with a properly authorized civil, criminal, or regulatory investigation or subpoena or summons by Federal, State, or local authorities; or to respond to judicial process or government regulatory authorities having jurisdiction over the financial institution for examination, compliance, or other purposes as authorized by law."

In this case, there is no dispute that the petitioners are bound by the GLBA, that the information sought by the respondent is "nonpublic personal information," and that the respondent is a "nonaffiliated third party." The sole issue, therefore, is whether 15 U.S.C. § 6802 (e)(8) allows the petitioners to disclose the requested information to the respondent. * * *

The handful of courts in other jurisdictions that have interpreted the provision have arrived at conflicting opinions as to whether 15 U.S.C. § 6802(e)(8) allows disclosure of nonpublic personal information by a financial institution to a private plaintiff in a civil action, and, if it does, under which part of the provision disclosure is allowed. * * *

We begin our analysis with the petitioners' only concrete suggested interpretation. However, guided not only by the statutory language but also by other evidence to the contrary, we cannot accept the petitioners' argument that "judicial process" is limited to that process "having jurisdiction over the financial institution for examination, compliance, or other purposes as authorized by law." * * *

[T]he use of the unmodified phrase "to respond to judicial process" as an exception to a prohibition on disclosure of personal information was not unfamiliar to Congress when it enacted the GLBA. In 1998, one year before the enactment of the GLBA, Congress enacted the Children's Online Privacy Protection Act of 1998, 15 U.S.C. § 6501 et seq. ("COPPA"). The privacy provision in COPPA, which has a somewhat similar structure to the one in the GLBA, prohibits the disclosure by operators of Internet Web sites of personal information obtained from children unless the operators provide notice of the operator's disclosure policy and receive "verifiable parental consent" for the disclosure. Like the GLBA, COPPA provides certain exceptions to its general prohibition on disclosure, allowing disclosure without parental consent under certain circumstances: "The regulations shall provide that verifiable parental consent * * * is not required * * * ['to respond to judicial process']". * * *

Simply put, we find no sufficient basis to justify a "narrowing" of the "judicial process" exception. The petitioners and amici curiae have presented persuasive arguments that the "judicial process" exception, if it is interpreted in its broad, but plainest sense—as we today interpret it—is seemingly out of proportion with the more narrow exceptions listed in § 6802(e), and possibly with the generalized policies stated in § 6801.

However, the petitioners have not presented to this Court any justifiable way of reading the "judicial process" language, or any specific evidence of a Congressional intent to read that language, more narrowly than what the phrase "judicial process" most plainly means. A perceived lack of proportionality in a statute, like a perceived lack of wisdom in a statute, does not empower this Court to rewrite the statute, even if we wanted to do so.

We hold that the phrase "judicial process" in § 6802(e)(8) encompasses a court order.

c.   No GLB Coverage for an Attorney Practicing Law

AMERICAN BAR ASSOCIATION v. FEDERAL TRADE COMMISSION

368 U.S. App. D.C. 368, 430 F.3d 457 (D.C. Cir. 2005).

SENTELLE, CIRCUIT JUDGE: * * *

Effective November 12, 1999, Congress enacted the Gramm–Leach–Bliley Financial Modernization Act, Pub. L. No. 106–102, 113 Stat. 1338. The Act declared it to be "the policy of the Congress that each financial institution has an affirmative and continuing obligation to respect the privacy of its customers and to protect the security and confidentiality of those customers' nonpublic personal information." 15 U.S.C. § 6801(a). To further that goal, Congress enacted broad privacy protective provisions * * *.

Upon the passage of the Act, the FTC * * * undertook a rulemaking. In May 2000, the FTC concluded the rulemaking and issued regulations. * * * Although the FTC relied in the first instance on Congress's definition of "financial institution" as "an institution the business of which is engaging in financial activities," the Commission restated the definition: "An institution that is significantly engaged in financial activities is a financial institution." 16 C.F.R. § 313.3(k)(1).

Like the statute, the regulations at no point describe the statutory or regulatory scheme as governing the practice of law as such. Indeed, the phrase "practice of law" never appears in part 313, and the word "attorneys," while present in two places, appears in the context of describing persons to whom financial institutions can make release of customer information, if authorized, not in the context of defining "financial institutions" as including attorneys. Nonetheless, the breadth of the FTC's regulation, apparently taken in conjunction with statements to or by news media, caused concern among representatives of the bar. Therefore, various bar associations, including the American Bar Association, made inquiry of the Commission as to whether the Commission was taking a position that privacy provisions of the GLBA and the regulations made pursuant thereto governed attorneys engaged in the practice of law.

On April 8, 2002, the Director of the Bureau of Consumer Protection at the Commission sent a letter to the President and the Director of Governmental Affairs of the ABA "in response to your correspondence regarding the application of Title V, Subtitle A, of the Gramm–Leach–Bliley Act, 15 U.S.C. 6801 et seq. * * * and the Federal Trade Commission's Rule, Privacy of Consumer Financial Information * * * to attorneys at law." * * * [T]he Director only directly addressed the ABA's request for exemption. However, in rejecting that request, the Director made it plain that the Commission was purporting to regulate attorneys engaged in the practice of their profession and asserted that "the GLB Act itself states that entities engaged in 'financial activities' are subject to the Act." * * *

As we analyze [on this appeal] the FTC's arguments for the proposition that Congress in the privacy provisions of the GLBA enabled the Commission to regulate the practice of law, we are reminded repeatedly of a recent admonition from the Supreme Court: "[Congress] does not * * * hide elephants in mouseholes." Whitman v. Am. Trucking Ass'ns, 531 U.S. 457 (2001). The FTC begins its defense of its attempted turf expansion in the correct place, that is, by recognizing that "the starting point in any case involving the meaning of a statute[] is the language of the statute itself." Group Life & Health Ins. Co. v. Royal Drug Co., 440 U.S. 205, 210 (1979). The Commission argues, as it did before the District Court, that the language of the statute evidences a congressional intent to empower the Commission to regulate attorneys engaged in certain types of law practice as "financial institutions" under the privacy regulations promulgated pursuant to the GLBA privacy provisions. More specifically, the Commission notes that the legislation defines "financial institution" quite broadly as "any institution the business of which is engaging in financial activities as described in section 1843(k) of Title 12." The statute in turn deems as "financial in nature" various listed activities, together with those not expressly listed but theretofore listed by the Federal Reserve Board in Regulation Y. Regulation Y * * * includes the activities "providing real estate settlement services," and "providing tax-planning and tax-preparation services to any person." 12 C.F.R. § 225.28(b)(2)(viii), (b)(6)(vi) (2001). The Commission then asserts, "thus, under the terms of the statute, any institution that is in the business of engaging in a financial activity listed in section 4(k) of the BHCA, including those set forth in Regulation Y, qualifies as a 'financial institution.'" That statement by the Commission is unassailable: Indeed, it does no more than restate the provisions of that statute. That is precisely the problem. The Commission's reasoning, doing no more than restating the statute, leaves as open as ever the question of whether an attorney practicing law is an "institution engaging in the business of financial activities."

The statute certainly does not so plainly grant the Commission the authority to regulate attorneys engaged in the practice of law as to entitle the Commission to what is called a "Chevron One" disposition. That is, rather simply we cannot hold that Congress has directly and plainly granted the Commission the authority to regulate practicing attorneys as the Commission attempts. See Chevron U.S.A. Inc. v. NRDC, 467 U.S. 837, 842–43 * * *.

The first question, whether there is such an ambiguity, is for the court, and we owe the agency no deference on the existence of ambiguity. Deference to the agency's interpretation under Chevron is warranted only where "Congress has left a gap for the agency to fill pursuant to an express or implied 'delegation of authority to the agency.'" * * *

The Commission apparently assumed—without reasoning—that it could extend its regulatory authority over attorneys engaged in the practice of law with no other basis than the observation that the Act did not provide for an exemption. * * *

An attorney, or even a law firm, does not fit very neatly into the niche of a "financial institution." Even if one concedes—and it is quite a concession—that Congress would have intended the word "institution" to include an attorney, or even a law firm, it still requires quite a stretch to conclude that such an institution is a "financial institution." It trims the stretch little, if at all, to read the entire statutory definition of "financial institution" as "any institution the business of which is engaging in financial activities as described in section 1843(k) of Title 12" (set forth above). Without reiterating the language of the incorporated statute, attorneys and law firms, even if viewed as "institutions," are not institutions "the business of which is engaging in financial activities," as defined in the statute. The Commission itself seems to recognize the improbability of Congress's having intended to include law firms within the designation "institutions" in the letter under review, in which it conspicuously substituted the word "entities" for "institutions." Such a dramatic rewriting of the statute is not mere interpretation. Even if we accept the inclusion of "entities" such as law firms within the meaning of "institutions," the "business" of a law firm (if the practice of a profession is properly viewed as business) is the practice of the profession of law. * * *

The reasoning in the brief relies on the language of Regulation Y, the second tier incorporation. As noted above, Regulation Y, in its original application, described the "closely related nonbanking activities" in which a bank holding company or its subsidiaries might engage. Within that voluminous listing, the regulation included two activities, "providing real estate settlement services," and "providing tax-planning and tax-preparation services," in which attorneys sometimes, and apparently in the view of the Commission, significantly engage. See 16 C.F.R. § 313.3(k)(1). Again, if Congress intended to empower a federal financial regulator to undertake regulation of the practice of law, this seems a strangely unclear method of doing so. The statute after all defined a "financial institution" as "an institution the business of which is engaging in financial activities." Congress did not adopt the approach of the Commission by covering "an institution that is significantly engaged in financial activities." Certainly it did not extend that definition to cover all "entities." In sum,

Congress did not leave an ambiguity on the question before us—that is, the power of the Commission to regulate the practice of law—sufficient to compel deference to the Commission's determination to do so.

We further determine that even if we err in our conclusion that the regulation fails at Chevron Step One, we are satisfied that the interpretation afforded by the Commission is not sufficiently reasonable to survive that deference at Step Two. * * *

[W]e hold that the Commission's interpretation is not entitled to Chevron deference. We further hold that, even if we afford the interpretation deference, the Commission's interpretation is not a reasonable one. We therefore conclude and hold that the judgment appealed from is affirmed.

d. Financial Data Security Requirements

GUIN v. BRAZOS HIGHER EDUCATION SERVICE
2006 WL 288483 at 5 (D. Minn. 2006).

JUDGE RICHARD H. KYLE

Plaintiff Stacy Guin alleges that Defendant Brazos Higher Education Service Corporation, Inc. ("Brazos") negligently allowed an employee to keep unencrypted nonpublic customer data on a laptop computer that was stolen from the employee's home during a burglary on September 24, 2004. * * *

Brazos, a non-profit corporation with headquarters located in Waco, Texas, originates and services student loans. * * * Brazos has approximately 365 employees, including John Wright, who has worked as a financial analyst for the company since November 2003.

Wright works from an office in his home in Silver Spring, Maryland. * * * As a financial analyst for Brazos, Wright analyses loan portfolios for a number of transactions, including purchasing portfolios from other lending organizations and selling bonds financed by student loan interest payments. Prior to performing each new financial analysis, Wright receives an electronic database from Brazos's Finance Department in Texas. The type of information needed by Wright to perform his analysis depends on the type of transaction anticipated by Brazos. When Wright is performing asset-liability management for Brazos, he requires loan-level details, including customer personal information, to complete his work.

On September 24, 2004, Wright's home was burglarized and a number of items were stolen, including the laptop computer issued to Wright by Brazos. [Neither the police nor private detectives hired by Brazos were able to recover the lap top.]

With the laptop missing, Brazos sought to determine what customer data might have been stored on the hard drive and whether the data was accessible to a third party. Based on internal records, Brazos determined that Wright had received databases containing borrowers' personal information on seven occasions prior to September 24, 2004. * * *

Without the ability to ascertain which specific borrowers might be at risk, Brazos considered whether it should give notice of the theft to all of its customers. In addition to contemplating guidelines recommended by the Federal Trade Commission ("FTC"), Brazos learned that it was required by California law to give notice to its customers residing in that State. Brazos ultimately decided to send a notification letter (the "Letter") to all of its approximately 550,000 customers. The Letter advised borrowers that "some personal information associated with your student loan, including your name, address, social security number and loan balance, may have been inappropriately accessed by the third party." The Letter also urged borrowers to place "a free 90–day security alert" on their credit bureau files and review consumer assistance materials published by the FTC. In addition, Brazos established a call center to answer further questions from customers and track any reports of identity theft. * * *

Plaintiff Stacy Guin, who acquired a student loan through Brazos in August 2002, received the Letter. * * * Guin did not find any indication that a third party had accessed his personal information and, to this date, has not experienced any instance of identity theft or any other type of fraud involving his personal information. * * * To Brazos's knowledge, none of its borrowers has experienced any type of fraud as a result of the theft of Wright's laptop.

[Guin commenced this action and now brings a] "negligence claim * * * on behalf of" all other Brazos customers whose confidential information was inappropriately accessed by a third party * * *.

In his negligence claim, Guin alleges that "[Brazos] owe[d] him a duty to secure [his] private personal information and not put it in peril of loss, theft, or tampering," and "[Brazos's] delegation or release of [Guin's] personal information to others over whom it lacked adequate control, supervision or authority was a result of [Brazos's] negligence * * *." As a result of such conduct, Guin allegedly "suffered out-of-pocket loss, emotional distress, fear and anxiety, consequential and incidental damages." * * *

In order to prevail on a claim for negligence, a plaintiff must prove four elements: (1) the existence of a duty of care, (2) a breach of that duty, (3) an injury, and (4) the breach of the duty was the proximate cause of the injury. Elder v. Allstate Ins. Co., 341 F. Supp. 2d 1095, 1099 (D. Minn. 2004), citing Lubbers v. Anderson, 539 N.W.2d 398, 401 (Minn. 1995). In support of its instant Motion, Brazos advances three arguments: (1) Brazos did not breach any duty owed to Guin, (2) Guin did not sustain an injury, and (3) Guin cannot establish proximate cause. * * *

In order to prove a claim for negligence, Guin must show that Brazos breached a legal duty owed to him under the circumstances alleged in this case. * * * Guin argues that the Gramm–Leach–Bliley Act (the "GLB Act"), 15 U.S.C. § 6801, establishes a statutory-based duty for Brazos "to protect the security and confidentiality of customers' nonpublic personal information." (Mem. in Opp'n at 8.) For the purposes of this Motion only, Brazos concedes that the GLB Act applies to these circumstances and establishes a duty of care. * * * The GLB Act was created "to protect against unauthorized access to or use of such records which could result in substantial harm or inconvenience to any customer [of a financial institution]." 15 U.S.C. § 6801(b)(3). Under the GLB Act, a financial institution must comply with several objectives, including:

> Develop, implement, and maintain a comprehensive written information security program that is written in one or more readily accessible parts and contains administrative, technical, and physical safeguards that are appropriate to your size and complexity, the nature and scope of your activities, and the sensitivity of any customer information at issue;

> Identify reasonably foreseeable internal and external risks to the security, confidentiality, and integrity of customer information that could result in the unauthorized disclosure, misuse, alteration, destruction or other compromise of such information, and assess the sufficiency of any safeguards in place to control these risks; and

> Design and implement information safeguards to control the risks you identify through risk assessment, and regularly test or otherwise monitor the effectiveness of the safeguards' key controls, systems, and procedures.

16 C.F.R. § 314.4(a)–(c). * * *

The Court concludes that Guin has not presented sufficient evidence from which a fact finder could determine that Brazos failed to comply with the GLB Act. In September 2004, when Wright's home was burglarized and the laptop was stolen, Brazos had written security policies, current risk assessment reports, and proper safeguards for its customers' personal information as required by the GLB Act. * * * Brazos authorized Wright to have access to customers' personal information because Wright needed the information to analyze loan portfolios as part of Brazos's asset-liability management function for other lenders. * * * Thus, his access to the personal information was within "the nature and scope of [Brazos's] activities." See 16 C.F.R. § 314.4(a). Furthermore, the GLB Act does not prohibit someone from working with sensitive data on a laptop computer in a home office. Despite Guin's persistent argument that any nonpublic personal information stored on a laptop computer should be encrypted, the GLB Act does not contain any such requirement. Accordingly, Guin has not presented any evidence showing that Brazos violated the GLB Act requirements. * * *

In addition, Guin argues that Brazos failed to comply with the self-imposed reasonable duty of care listed in Brazos's privacy policy—that Brazos will "restrict access to nonpublic personal information to authorized persons who need to know such information." * * * Brazos concedes that under this policy, it owed Guin a duty of reasonable care, but argues that it acted with reasonable care in handling Guin's personal information. * * * The Court agrees. Brazos had policies in place to protect the personal information, trained Wright concerning those policies, and transmitted and used data in accordance with those policies. * * * Wright lived in a relatively "safe" neighborhood and took necessary precautions to secure his house from intruders. * * * [Since there was not breach of a legal duty, Brazos cannot be liable for negligence.]

The facts of this case are closely analogous to Stollenwerk v. Tri–West Healthcare Alliance, No. Civ. 03–0185, 2005 WL 2465906 (D. Ariz. Sept. 6, 2005). In Stollenwerk, the defendant's corporate office was burglarized and a number of items stolen, including computer hard drives containing the personal information of defendant's customers. * * * After the burglary, several customers brought suit against the company asserting claims for consumer fraud, invasion of privacy and negligence. * * * In support of their negligence claim, two plaintiffs relied on the opinion of an expert who described their injury as "an increased risk of experiencing identity fraud for the next seven years." * * * The district court expressly rejected the expert testimony because "the affidavit of plaintiffs' expert conclusorily posits that plaintiffs risk of identity fraud is significantly increased without quantifying the risk." * * * In granting summary judgment for the defendant on the negligence claim, the district court determined that the two plaintiffs had failed to establish an injury for the purpose of proving negligence: "absent evidence that the data was targeted or actually accessed [by the burglars], there is no basis for a reasonable jury to determine that sensitive personal information was significantly exposed."

Like Stollenwerk, in this case Guin has failed to present evidence that his personal data was targeted or accessed by the individuals who burglarized Wright's home in September 2004. The record shows that Brazos is uncertain whether Guin's personal information was even on the hard drive of Wright's laptop computer at the time it was stolen in September 2004. * * * To this date, Guin has experienced no instance of identity theft or any other type of fraud involving his personal information. In fact, to Brazos's knowledge, none of its borrowers has been the subject of any type of fraud as a result of the theft of Wright's laptop computer. * * * Furthermore, Guin has provided no evidence that his identity has been "transferred, possessed, or used" by a third party with "with the intent to commit, aid, or abet any unlawful activity." * * * No genuine issue of material fact exists concerning whether Guin has suffered an injury. Accordingly, he cannot sustain a claim for negligence.

FTC, GUIDELINES FOR DEALING
WITH A DATA BREACH

http://www.ftc.gov/bcp/edu/microsites/idtheft/business/data-breach.html.

Information Compromise and the Risk of Identity Theft: Guidance for Your Business

These days, it is almost impossible to be in business and not collect or hold personally identifying information—names and addresses, Social Security numbers, credit card numbers, or other account numbers—about your customers, employees, business partners, students, or patients. If this information falls into the wrong hands, it could put these individuals at risk for identity theft.

Still, not all personal information compromises result in identity theft, and the type of personal information compromised can significantly affect the degree of potential damage. What steps should you take and whom should you contact if personal information is compromised? Although the answers vary from case to case, the following guidance from the Federal Trade Commission (FTC), the nation's consumer protection agency, can help you make smart, sound decisions. Check federal and state laws or regulations for any specific requirements for your business.

Notifying Law Enforcement

When the compromise could result in harm to a person or business, call your local police department immediately. Report your situation and the potential risk for identity theft. The sooner law enforcement learns about the theft, the more effective they can be. If your local police are not familiar with investigating information compromises, contact the local office of the FBI or the U.S. Secret Service. For incidents involving mail theft, contact the U.S. Postal Inspection Service. Check the blue pages of your telephone directory or an online search engine for the number of the nearest field office.

Notifying Affected Businesses

Information compromises can have an impact on businesses other than yours, such as banks or credit issuers. If account access information—say, credit card or bank account numbers—has been stolen from you, but you do not maintain the accounts, notify the institution that does so that it can monitor the accounts for fraudulent activity. If you collect or store personal information on behalf of other businesses, notify them of any information compromise, as well.

If names and Social Security numbers have been stolen, you can contact the major credit bureaus for additional information or advice. If the compromise may involve a large group of people, advise the credit bureaus if you are recommending that people request fraud alerts for their files. Your notice to the credit bureaus can facilitate customer assistance.

Equifax

U.S. Consumer Services
Equifax Information Services, LLC.
Phone: 678–795–7971
Email: businessrecordsecurity@equifax.com

Experian

Experian Security Assistance
P.O. Box 72
Allen, TX 75013
Email: BusinessRecordsVictimAssistance@experian.com

TransUnion

Phone: 1–800–372–8391

If the information compromise resulted from the improper posting of personal information on your Web site, immediately remove the information from your site. Be aware that Internet search engines store, or "cache," information for a period of time. You can contact the search engines to ensure that they do not archive personal information that was posted in error.

Notifying Individuals

Generally, early notification to individuals whose personal information has been compromised allows them to take steps to mitigate the misuse of their information. In deciding if notification is warranted, consider the nature of the compromise, the type of information taken, the likelihood of misuse, and the potential damage arising from misuse. For example, thieves who have stolen names and Social Security numbers can use this information to cause significant damage to a victim's credit record. Individuals who are notified early can take some steps to prevent or limit any harm.

When notifying individuals, the FTC recommends that you:

● consult with your law enforcement contact about the timing of the notification so it does not impede the investigation.

● designate a contact person within your organization for releasing information. Give the contact person the latest information about the breach, your response, and how individuals should respond. Consider using letters (see sample below), Web sites, and toll-free numbers as methods of communication with those whose information may have been compromised.

It is important that your notice:

● describes clearly what you know about the compromise. Include how it happened; what information was taken, and, if you know, how the thieves have used the information; and what actions you have taken already to remedy the situation. Explain how to reach the contact person in your organization. Consult with your law enforcement contact on exactly what information to include so your notice does not hamper the investigation.

● explains what responses may be appropriate for the type of information taken. For example, people whose Social Security numbers have been stolen should contact the credit bureaus to ask that fraud alerts be placed on their credit reports. See www.ftc.gov/idtheft for more complete information on appropriate follow-up after a compromise.

● includes current information about identity theft. The FTC's Web site at www.ftc.gov/idtheft has information to help individuals guard against and deal with identity theft.

● provides contact information for the law enforcement officer working on the case (as well as your case report number, if applicable) for victims to use. Be sure to alert the law enforcement officer working your case that you are sharing this contact information. Identity theft victims often can provide important information to law enforcement. Victims should request a copy of the police report and make copies for creditors who have accepted unauthorized charges. The police report is important evidence that can help absolve a victim of fraudulent debts.

● encourages those who discover that their information has been misused to file a complaint with the FTC at www.ftc.gov/idtheft or at 1–877–ID–THEFT (877–438–4338). Information entered into the Identity Theft Data Clearinghouse, the FTC's database, is made available to law enforcement.

* * *

4. FINANCIAL IDENTITY THEFT AND PRETEXTING

FTC, PRETEXTING: YOUR PERSONAL INFORMATION REVEALED

http://www.ftc.gov/bcp/conline/pubs/credit/pretext.htm.

When you think of your own personal assets, chances are your home, car, and savings and investments come to mind. But what about your Social Security number (SSN), telephone records and your bank and credit card account numbers? To people known as "pretexters," that information is a personal asset, too.

Pretexting is the practice of getting your personal information under false pretenses. Pretexters sell your information to people who may use it to get credit in your name, steal your assets, or to investigate or sue you. Pretexting is against the law. * * *

Pretexters use a variety of tactics to get your personal information. For example, a pretexter may call, claim he's from a survey firm, and ask you a few questions. When the pretexter has the information he wants, he uses it to call your financial institution. He pretends to be you or someone with authorized access to your account. He might claim that he's forgotten his checkbook and needs information about his account. In this way, the pretexter may be able to obtain personal information about you such as your SSN, bank and credit card account numbers, information in your credit report, and the existence and size of your savings and investment portfolios.

Keep in mind that some information about you may be a matter of public record, such as whether you own a home, pay your real estate taxes, or have ever filed for bankruptcy. It is not pretexting for another person to collect this kind of information. * * *

Under federal law—the Gramm–Leach–Bliley Act—it's illegal for anyone to:

- use false, fictitious or fraudulent statements or documents to get customer information from a financial institution or directly from a customer of a financial institution.

- use forged, counterfeit, lost, or stolen documents to get customer information from a financial institution or directly from a customer of a financial institution.

- ask another person to get someone else's customer information using false, fictitious or fraudulent statements or using false, fictitious or fraudulent documents or forged, counterfeit, lost, or stolen documents.

The Federal Trade Commission Act also generally prohibits pretexting for sensitive consumer information. * * *

Pretexting can lead to identity theft. Identity theft occurs when someone hijacks your personal identifying information to open new charge accounts, order merchandise, or borrow money. Consumers targeted by identity thieves often don't know they've been victimized until the hijackers fail to pay the bills or repay the loans, and collection agencies begin dunning the consumers for payment of accounts they didn't even know they had.

According to the Federal Trade Commission (FTC), the most common forms of identity theft are: *Credit Card Fraud*—a credit card account is opened in a consumer's name or an existing credit card account is "taken over"; *Communications Services Fraud*—the identity thief opens telephone, cellular, or other utility service in the consumer's name; *Bank Fraud*—a checking or savings account is opened in the consumer's name, and/or fraudulent checks are written; and *Fraudulent Loans*—the identity thief gets a loan, such as a car loan, in the consumer's name.

The Identity Theft and Assumption Deterrence Act makes it a federal crime when someone: "knowingly transfers or uses, without lawful authority, a means of identification of another person with the intent to commit, or to aid or abet, any unlawful activity that constitutes a violation of federal law, or that constitutes a felony under any applicable state or local law."

Under the Identity Theft Act, a name or SSN is considered a "means of identification." So is a credit card number, cellular telephone electronic serial number or any other piece of information that may be used alone or in conjunction with other information to identify a specific individual.

HUGGINS v. CITIBANK

355 S.C. 329, 585 S.E.2d 275 (S.C. 2003).

Plaintiff P. Kenneth Huggins, Jr., (Huggins) brought this action in federal court against Defendants Citibank, N.A., Capital One Services, Inc., and Premier Bankcard, Inc., (the Banks) claiming the Banks negligently issued credit cards to an unknown imposter, "John Doe." The complaint alleged Doe applied for a credit card, asserting he was Huggins. Doe then used the credit cards, but failed to pay the Banks.

Huggins alleged the Banks were negligent in various ways: 1) issuing the credit cards without any investigation, verification, or corroboration of Doe's identity; 2) failing to adopt policies reasonably designed to verify the identity of credit card applicants; 3) adopting policies designed to result in the issuance of credit cards without verifying the identity of applicants; and 4) attempting to collect Doe's debt from Huggins. Huggins asserted, as a result of the Banks' issuance of credit cards to Doe, his credit was damaged, he was "hounded by collection agencies," he was distressed and embarrassed, and he expended much time and effort attempting to rectify the damage, with only partial success. * * *

In Polzer v. TRW, Inc., 256 A.D.2d 248, 682 N.Y.S.2d 194 (N.Y. App. Div. 1998), individuals in whose names an imposter had obtained credit cards sued the credit card issuers for negligent enablement of imposter fraud. A New York appellate division court held summary judgment was properly granted because New York did not recognize a cause of action for negligent enablement of imposter fraud. The court stated the defendant credit card issuers "had no relationship either with the imposter who stole the plaintiffs' credit information and fraudulently obtained credit cards, or with plaintiffs, with whom they stood simply in a creditor/debtor relationship." * * *

We are greatly concerned about the rampant growth of identity theft and financial fraud in this country. Moreover, we are certain that some identity theft could be prevented if credit card issuers carefully scrutinized credit card applications. Nevertheless, we agree with the New York appellate court decision in Polzer v. TRW, Inc., supra, and decline to recognize a legal duty of care between credit card issuers and those individuals whose identities may be stolen. The relationship, if any, between credit card issuers and potential victims of identity theft is far too attenuated to rise to the level of a duty between them. * * *.

Finally, we note that various state and national legislation provides at least some remedy for victims of credit card fraud. See Pub. L. No. 107–56, 115 Stat. 272 (Uniting and Strengthening America by Providing Appropriate Tools Required to Intercept and Obstruct Terrorism Act of 2001); 15 U.S.C.A. § 1681 (Fair Credit Reporting Act) (1998); 15 U.S.C.A. § 1692(d)

(1998) (Fair Debt Collection Practices Act); S.C. Code Ann. § 16–13–500 to–530 (2003) (South Carolina Personal Financial Security Act); S.C. Code Ann. § 37–5–108(2) (2002) (South Carolina Consumer Protection Code). While these regulations may not fully compensate victims of identity theft for all of their injury, we conclude the legislative arena is better equipped to assess and address the impact of credit card fraud on victims and financial institutions alike.

IDENTITY THEFT AND ASSUMPTION DETERRENCE ACT

http://www.consumer.gov/idtheft/law_laws_criminal.htm.

In October 1998, Congress passed the Identity Theft and Assumption Deterrence Act of 1998 (Identity Theft Act) to address the problem of identity theft. Specifically, the Act amended 18 U.S.C. § 1028 to make it a federal crime when anyone: "knowingly transfers or uses, without lawful authority, a means of identification of another person with the intent to commit, or to aid or abet, any unlawful activity that constitutes a violation of Federal law, or that constitutes a felony under any applicable State or local law."

Violations of the Act are investigated by federal investigative agencies such as the U.S. Secret Service, the FBI, and the U.S. Postal Inspection Service and prosecuted by the Department of Justice.

PREPARED STATEMENT OF THE FEDERAL TRADE COMMISSION ON

IDENTITY THEFT

Before the

COMMITTEE ON BANKING AND FINANCIAL SERVICES UNITED STATES HOUSE OF REPRESENTATIVES

Washington, D.C.

September 13, 2000

I. The Federal Trade Commission's Role in Combating Identity Theft

A. The Identity Theft and Assumption Deterrence Act of 1998

The Identity Theft and Assumption Deterrence Act of 1998 addresses identity theft in two significant ways. First, the Act strengthens the criminal laws governing identity theft. Specifically, the Act amends 18 U.S.C. § 1028 ("Fraud and related activity in connection with identification documents") to make it a federal crime to:

> knowingly transfer [ ] or use [ ], without lawful authority, a means of identification of another person with the intent to commit, or to aid or abet, any unlawful activity that constitutes a violation of Federal law, or that constitutes a felony under any applicable State or local law.

The second way in which the Act addresses the problem of identity theft is by focusing on consumers as victims. In particular, the Act provides for a centralized complaint and consumer education service for victims of identity theft and gives the responsibility of developing this function to the Commission. The Act directs that the Commission establish procedures to: (1) log the receipt of complaints by victims of identity theft; (2) provide identity theft victims with informational materials; and (3) refer complaints to appropriate entities, including the major national consumer reporting agencies and law enforcement agencies.

B. *The FTC's Response to Identity Theft*

In enacting the Identity Theft Act, Congress recognized that coordinated efforts are essential to best serve the needs of identity theft victims because these fraud victims often need assistance both from government agencies at the national and state or local level and from private businesses. Accordingly, the FTC's role under the Act is primarily one of facilitating information sharing among public and private entities.

In order to fulfill the purposes of the Act, the Commission has developed and begun implementing a plan that centers on three principal components:

(1) *Toll-free telephone hotline.* The Commission has established a toll-free telephone number, 1–877–ID THEFT (438–4338), that consumers can call to report identity theft. Consumers who call the hotline receive telephone counseling from specially trained personnel to help them resolve credit-related problems that may have resulted from the misuse of their identities. In addition, the hotline counselors enter information from consumers' complaints into the Identity Theft Data Clearinghouse (the "Clearinghouse")—a centralized database used to aid law enforcement and prevent identity theft.

The identity theft hotline has been in operation since November 1, 1999. The hotline answered an average of over 1000 calls per week in the months of July and August, 2000.

About forty percent of consumers who call the FTC identity theft hotline inquire about how to guard against identity theft. The counselors suggest steps consumers should take to minimize their risk. This information has been developed from the Commission's extensive experience in advising consumers on how to avoid credit and charge card fraud and maintain financial privacy.

Around sixty percent of consumers who call the FTC identity theft hotline have already become victims of identity theft. The counselors give them specific information about preventing additional harm to their finances and credit histories. Consumers are instructed to contact each of the three national consumer reporting agencies to obtain copies of their credit reports and request that a fraud alert be placed on their credit reports. The counselors also advise consumers to review carefully the information on the reports to detect any additional evidence of identity theft. Consumers are informed of their rights under the Fair Credit Reporting Act and are given the procedures for correcting misinformation on their credit reports. Consumers are also advised to contact each of the creditors or service providers where the identity thief has established or accessed an account to request that the account be closed. The counselors also inform consumers of their rights under the Fair Credit Billing Act and the Truth in Lending Act, which, among other things, limit their responsibility for unauthorized charges to fifty dollars in most instances. Consumers who have been contacted by a debt collector concerning debts incurred by the identity thief are advised of their rights under the Fair Debt Collection Practices Act, which prescribes debt collectors' practices.

The FTC counselors advise consumers to notify their local police departments, both because local law enforcement may be in the best position to catch and prosecute identity thieves, and because a police report often helps consumers demonstrate to would-be creditors and debt collectors that they are genuine victims of identity theft. Nearly 75% of the states have enacted their own identity theft laws and counselors, in appropriate circumstances, will refer consumers to other state and local authorities.

Lastly, where investigation and resolution of the identity theft falls under the jurisdiction of another regulatory agency that has a program in place to assist consumers, callers are referred to those agencies. For example, consumers who complain that someone has been using their Social Security number for employment are advised to report this to the Social Security Administration's fraud hotline and to request a copy of their Social Security Statement to verify the accuracy of the earnings reported to their Social Security number.

(2) *Identity theft complaint database.* Detailed information from the complaints received on the FTC's identity theft hotline is entered into the FTC's Identity Theft Data Clearinghouse. The information in the Clearinghouse is available to law enforcement agencies nationwide via the FTC's secure law enforcement website, *Consumer Sentinel.* Access to the Clearinghouse information supports law enforcement agencies' efforts to combat identity theft by providing a range of complaints from which to spot patterns of illegal activity. For example, federal law enforcement agencies may be able to more readily identify organized or large-scale identity theft rings. The Commission expects that the Clearinghouse will allow the many agencies involved in combating identity theft to share data, enabling these offices to work more effectively to track down identity thieves and assist consumers.

In addition, the Clearinghouse facilitates the referral process mandated by the Identity Theft Act. Clearinghouse members can access directly the database from their desktops in order to support their investigations and identify emerging trends and patterns in identity theft in their geographic areas. The Commission also plans to disseminate complaint information through customized reports, extracting for our law enforcement partners the Clearinghouse complaints that meet the criteria they have designated.

For agencies that have their own sophisticated data-mining tools, Commission staff will provide large batches of raw data for further analysis. Staff will notify our law enforcement partners when we identify trends or patterns in the data that appear to have ramifications for them. Finally, the Clearinghouse information provides policy makers with a sense of the extent of identity theft activity and the forms it is taking (*e.g.,* credit card vs. phone fraud, latest scams, etc).

(3) *Consumer education.* The FTC has taken the lead in coordinating with other government agencies and organizations the development and dissemination of comprehensive consumer education materials for victims of identity theft and those concerned with preventing this crime. The results of the FTC's extensive, multi-media campaign include print materials, media mailings and interviews and a website, located at www.consumer.gov/idtheft. This collaborative consumer education effort is ongoing; the Commission hopes to continue this effort with many of the private sector financial institutions that have an interest in preventing and remedying identity theft. * * *

II. What the Clearinghouse Tells Us About Identity Theft

A. *A Serious Problem*

By now, many people have encountered, directly or indirectly through another person, some form of identity theft: Someone has used their name to open up a credit card account; their identifying information—name, social security number, mother's maiden name, or other personal information—has been used by another to commit fraud or engage in other unlawful activities. Other common forms of identity theft include taking over an existing credit card account and making unauthorized charges on it (typically, the identity thief forestalls discovery by the victims by contacting the credit card issuer and changing the billing address on the account); taking out loans in another person's name; writing fraudulent checks using another person's name and/or account number; and opening a telephone or wireless service account in another person's name. In extreme cases, the identity thief may completely take over the victim's identity—opening a bank account, obtaining multiple credit cards, buying a car, getting a home mortgage and even working under the victim's name.

Unavoidable. Although there are many steps consumers can take to minimize their risk of identity theft, there is no way to completely avoid it. One out of eight victims that call the Commission's identity theft hotline report that they have been victimized by someone they know— either a family member, a neighbor or workplace acquaintance, someone employed by a financial institution they do business with, or in some other way known to them. Incidences of workplace identity theft appear to be increasing. Since November 1999, the Commission has received reports of hospitals, schools, and other employers whose personnel records had been compromised by an identity thief. Each such instance has the potential to translate into hundreds of identity theft victims. In these cases, where someone has access to personal information because of their relationship to the victim, identity theft is practically unavoidable.

The majority of victims do not know how their identifying information was compromised. The question these victims most commonly ask when they call the FTC's identity theft hotline is, "how could this have happened to me?" Our answer is that it could have arisen in a multitude of ways. For example, identity theft can arise from simple, low-tech practices such as stealing someone's mail or "dumpster diving" through their trash to collect credit card offers or obtain identifying information such as account numbers or social security numbers. There are also far more sophisticated practices being employed. In a practice known as "skimming," identity thieves use computers to read and store the information encoded on the magnetic strip of an ATM or credit card when that card is inserted through either a specialized card reader or a legitimate payment mechanism (*e.g.,* the card reader used to pay for gas at the pump in a gas station). Once stored, that information can be re-encoded onto any other card with a magnetic strip, instantly transforming a blank card into a machine-readable ATM or credit card identical to that of the victim.

The Internet has dramatically altered the potential occurrence and impact of identity theft. First, the Internet provides access to identifying information, through both illicit and legal means. The global publication of identifying details that previously were available only to a select few increases the potential for misuse of that information. Second, the ability of the identity thief to purchase goods and services from innumerable e-merchants expands the potential harm to the victim through numerous purchases. The explosion of financial services offered on-line, such as mortgages, credit cards, bank accounts and loans, provides a sense of anonymity to those potential identity thieves who would not risk committing identity theft in a face-to-face transaction.

Undetectable. In many instances, identity theft goes undetected by creditors, law enforcement and the victims for months or even years. One caller to the FTC's identity theft hotline reported that his wallet was stolen in 1992. This consumer was unaware that he was the victim of identity theft until seven years later, when, in the summer of 1999, he was arrested on an outstanding warrant for an offense committed by the identity thief in 1993. The consumer spent several nights in jail and was forced to post $15,000 bond. He was also shocked and dismayed to discover multiple outstanding criminal charges against him in several states as a result of the identity thief's activities. This example, while unusual, is not unique. The FTC has received numerous reports from consumers who were not aware that they had been victimized by an identity thief until four or more years after the first fraudulent transaction.

Unstoppable. For victims of identity theft, the costs can be significant and long-lasting. Where the identity thief has committed a crime in the victim's name, the harm is especially pernicious. In the worst cases, the negative consequences are never completely eradicated. For example, one consumer who called the FTC identity theft hotline reported that her income tax refund was withheld due to past child support she was believed to have owed. She found out that a child was born to a person using her name and social security number in a state she had never even visited. Another consumer reported that he is unable to renew his driver's license or register to vote because, due to crimes committed in his name by another person, he is considered to be on probation for federal law violations including possession of drugs with intent to distribute and fraud. More than one consumer has been denied employment when a background check or security clearance showed criminal records relating to an offense committed by someone using their names and social security numbers. Another consumer lost his job when, as part of his promotion review, a background check indicated that he had a criminal record. Although the consumer went to court and obtained a declaration that he did not have a criminal record, he lost his job because the company that performed the background check said that it could not clear his record.

Identity thieves can run up debts in the tens of thousands of dollars under their victims' names. Even where the individual consumer is not legally liable for these debts, the consequences to the consumer are often considerable. A consumer's credit history is frequently scarred and he or she typically must spend numerous hours over the course of months or even years contesting bills and correcting credit reporting errors. Creditors for the fraudulent accounts often continue to harass the consumer. In the interim, the consumer victim may be denied loans, mortgages and employment; a bad credit report may even prevent him or her from something as simple as opening up a new bank account at a time when other accounts are tainted and a new account is essential. Moreover, even after the initial fraudulent bills are resolved, new fraudulent charges may continue to appear, requiring ongoing vigilance and effort by the victimized consumer.

B. *Patterns and Practices: Specific Complaint Data*

The Identity Theft Data Clearinghouse provides law enforcement with the first opportunity to collect and consolidate identity theft complaints on a nationwide basis. The fruits of this effort are already evident. The basic complaint data show that the most common forms of identity theft reported during the first ten months of operation were:

- *Credit Card Fraud*—Approximately 55% of consumers reported credit card fraud—*i.e.,* a credit card account opened in their name or a "takeover" of their existing credit card account;

- *Communications Services*—Approximately 28% reported that the identity thief opened up telephone, cellular, or other utility service in their name;

- *Bank Fraud*—Approximately 18% reported that a checking or savings account had been opened in their name, and/or that fraudulent checks had been written; and

- *Fraudulent Loans*—Approximately 11% reported that the identity thief obtained a loan, such as a car loan, in their name.

Of consumer identity theft complaints related to credit cards, 72% involved the establishment of a new credit card account in the victim's name and 24% involved the takeover of an existing account. Among reports of identity theft related to a checking or savings account, 44% involved the use of unauthorized checks, 28% involved the establishment of a new checking account in the victim's name and 19% involved unauthorized electronic funds transfer.

Not surprisingly, the states with the largest populations account for the largest numbers of complainants and suspects. California, New York, Florida, Texas and Illinois, in descending order, represent the states with the highest number of complainants. About 55% of victims calling the identity theft hotline report their age. Of these, 40% fall between 30 and 44 years of age. Approximately 27% are between age 45 and 64 and another 22% are between age 19 and 29. About 8% of those reporting their ages are 65 and over; and over 3% are age 18 and under.

Consumers also report the harm to their reputation or daily life. The most common non-monetary harm reported by consumers is damage to their credit report through derogatory, inaccurate information. The negative credit information leads to the other problems most commonly reported by victims, including loan denials, bounced checks and rejection of credit cards. Identity theft victims also report repeated contacts by debt collectors for the bad debt incurred by the identity thief. Many consumers report that they have to spend significant amounts of time resolving these problems.

Consumers also report problems with the banks and other institutions that provided the credit, goods or services to the identity thief in the consumer's name. These institutions often attempt to collect the bad debt from the victim, or report the bad debt to a consumer reporting agency, even after the victim believes that he or she has demonstrated the fraud. Of consumers lodging identity theft-related complaints with the Clearinghouse, 29% reported complaints about a bank credit card issuer, 25% reported complaints about a bank creditor and 22% reported complaints about a depository institution.

The majority of consumer complaints related to bank credit card issuers, bank creditors and depository institutions fall into three categories: (1) the institution refused to correct information or close the disputed account; (2) customer service personnel were not helpful; and (3) the institution's security procedures were inadequate.

The Clearinghouse data also reveal that consumers are often dissatisfied with the consumer reporting agencies. The leading complaints by identity theft victims against the consumer reporting agencies are that they provide inadequate assistance over the phone, or that they will not reinvestigate or correct an inaccurate entry in the consumer's credit report. * * *

B. *Gramm–Leach–Bliley Act Implementation*

Section 521(a) of the Gramm–Leach–Bliley Act (the "GLB Act") prohibits obtaining or attempting to obtain customer information of a financial institution relating to another person by fraud or misrepresentation—a practice often referred to as "pretexting" or "pretext calling." Pretexting by an identity thief who seeks consumers' account information for the purpose of defrauding the consumer would likely constitute a violation of both the Identity Theft Act and the GLB Act. The Identity Theft Data Clearinghouse collects information, if known by a complainant, as to how an identity thief obtained the complainant's personal information. This information is useful to law enforcement prosecuting identity theft under both statutes. Indeed, the Commission is beginning to receive complaints that identity thieves have accessed private information by pretexting financial institutions or by otherwise forging documents provided to a financial institution. The GLB Act provides for enforcement by the Commission for entities under its jurisdiction and provides criminal penalties for use by criminal law enforcement. * * *

V. Conclusion

The Identity Theft Data Clearinghouse demonstrates that identity theft is a serious and growing problem, but it also reveals ways to halt this growth. * * *

5. SIDELIGHTS—CONSUMER BANKRUPTCY DATA, WILLS AND TRUSTS

LUIS SALAZAR, PRIVACY AND BANKRUPTCY LAW

26 *Am. Bankr. Inst. J.* 44 (Feb. 2007).

Privacy provisions governing consumer bankruptcy filings * * * originated in 2001 with the Subcommittee on Privacy and Electronic Access to Case Files of the Court Administration and Case Management Committee of the Judicial Committee of the United States. * * * [I]t was the subcommittee's task to reconcile the court's growing online, electronic access, the public's right to access information, and the risk that the information contained in court files would be put to criminal purposes. This task was particularly critical in the bankruptcy courts, where a typical case filed would include a debtor's name, address, social security number, bank accounts, minor children's names and more. All this information could make an identity thief's job easy.

The subcommittee ultimately proposed a privacy plan that, insofar as bankruptcy files are concerned, primarily work to suppress social security numbers. Fed. R. Bank. R. 1007(f) therefore requires each debtor to submit a verified statement containing their full social security number. That statement, however, does not become part of the court record. A debtor is only required to submit the last four digits of his social security number on the petition and schedules. To allow creditors to identify creditors, the § 341 notice and proofs of claim sent to creditors must contain the full social security number, but the copies of these pleadings in the court file may not.

Additionally, amended § 107(c)(1) empowers the bankruptcy court for cause to protect an individual to the extent the court finds that disclosure of either information that constitutes a means of identification * * * that is contained in a paper to be filed with the court to the extent that the court finds that disclosure of that information would create undue risk of identity theft or other unlawful injury to the individual or the individual's property. The U.S. Trustee and panel trustee nonetheless will have full access to all such papers.

FRANCES H. FOSTER, PRIVACY AND THE ELUSIVE QUEST FOR UNIFORMITY IN THE LAW OF TRUSTS

38 Ariz. St. L.J. 713, 714 (2006).

On July 9, 2004, Marlon Brando's will was filed for probate in Los Angeles Superior Court. A media feeding frenzy ensued. Reporters from across the globe scoured Brando's probate file for intimate details about the reclusive actor's personal life. Within hours, "enquiring minds" learned that Brando left a $21.6 million estate and a truly complex and fractured family. What even the most intrepid reporter could not discover, however, is how Brando's property will be divided. Except for "certain monthly payments" to two female friends, Brando's will devises his entire estate to his "[l]iving [t]rust," a document that is not part of the public probate file. Thus, Brando's trust gave him after death what he most craved during life—privacy.

The Brando case illustrates a curious distinction between two "functional equivalents," the will and the revocable inter vivos or "living" trust ("revocable trust"). If the decedent devises her estate by will, the will becomes public record after her death, available to beneficiaries, heirs, thieves, reporters, and the "just plain curious" alike. If the decedent makes the identical disposition of her estate by a revocable trust, however, the document remains private. Indeed, in most states, even current beneficiaries of a revocable trust cannot view in full the trust document that defines their rights and interests.

At first glance, trust privacy has considerable appeal. It responds to an almost visceral human need to keep one's private life private and to protect one's survivors from the glare of publicity. * * *

[Yet, trust privacy has impeded two of the most significant modern reform efforts in the trusts and estates field. It has undermined efforts] to unify the law of wills and will substitutes. In addition the effort to make trust law uniform across states through the promulgation and enactment of a Uniform Trust Code has been frustrated.

NOTE: A PLEA FOR RATIONALITY

Does the United States need a general financial privacy statute? Could a single statute unify the treatment of financial data in banking, lending, credit, employment, bankruptcy, tax litigation and trusts and estates?

F. EMPLOYEE POLYGRAPH PROTECTION ACT OF 1988

NOTE: LIE DETECTORS

The plaintiff in *Campbell v. Woodard Photographic* (2006), excerpted below, lost his job after stealing from his employer. His fate was sealed when his boss discovered an incriminating eBay transaction receipt on an office computer printer tray. Plaintiff Campbell had tried to sell stolen office property over the internet.

Despite being caught red-handed, Campbell brought invasion of privacy tort claim against his former employer for reading the eBay transaction receipt and, in addition, for examining pain medicine found among Campbell's possessions during a theft investigation of the office. The district court frowned on the privacy torts claims, arguing that the plaintiff had spoken freely about his health problems to co-workers and had left the eBay receipt in plain view. Did the plaintiff suffer a "highly offensive" intrusion?

Plaintiff Campbell also claimed a violation of the Employee Polygraph Protection Act of 1988 (EPPA). This act of Congress makes it a federal offense for an employer to force or threaten lie-detection testing: "An employer need not actually administer a polygraph test to be liable." What is the primary purpose of the EPPA? The Department of Labor's description of the EPPA and its purposes precedes the *Campbell* case.

US DEPARTMENT OF LABOR, EMPLOYEE POLYGRAPH PROTECTION ACT OF 1988

http://www.dol.gov/whd/regs/compliance/whdfs36.htm.

The Department of Labor administers and enforces the Employee Polygraph Protection Act of 1988 (the Act) through the Wage and Hour Division of the Employment Standards Administration. The Act generally prevents employers engaged in interstate commerce from using lie detector tests either for pre-employment screening or during the course of employment, with certain exemptions. The Act, signed by the President on June 27, 1988, became effective on December 27, 1988.

Under the Act, the Secretary of Labor is directed to distribute a notice of the Act's protections, to issue rules and regulations, and to enforce the provisions of the Act. The Act empowers the Secretary of Labor to bring injunctive actions in U.S. district courts to restrain violations, and to assess civil money penalties up to $10,000 against employers who violate any provision of the Act. Employers are required to post notices summarizing the protections of the Act in their places of work.

Definitions

- A <u>lie detector</u> includes a polygraph, deceptograph, voice stress analyzer, psychological stress evaluator or similar device (whether mechanical or electrical) used to render a diagnostic opinion as to the honesty or dishonesty of an individual.

- A <u>polygraph</u> means an instrument that records continuously, visually, permanently, and simultaneously changes in cardiovascular, respiratory and electrodermal patterns as minimum instrumentation standards and is used to render a diagnostic opinion as to the honesty or dishonesty of as individual.

Prohibitions

An employer shall not:

- Require, request, suggest or cause an employee or prospective employee to take or submit to any lie detector test.

- Use, accept, refer to, or inquire about the results of any lie detector test of an employee or prospective employee.

- Discharge, discipline, discriminate against, deny employment or promotion, or threaten to take any such action against an employee or prospective employee for refusal to take a test, on the basis of the results of a test, for filing a complaint, for testifying in any proceeding or for exercising any rights afforded by the Act.

Exemptions

Federal, state and local governments are excluded. In addition, lie detector tests administered by the Federal Government to employees of Federal contractors engaged in national security intelligence or counterintelligence functions are exempt. The Act also includes limited exemptions where **polygraph** tests (but no other lie detector tests) may be administered in the private sector, subject to certain restrictions:

- To employees who are reasonably suspected of involvement in a workplace incident that results in economic loss to the employer and who had access to the property that is the subject of an investigation; and

- To prospective employees of armored car, security alarm, and security guard firms who protect facilities, materials or operations affecting health or safety, national security, or currency and other like instruments; and

- To prospective employees of pharmaceutical and other firms authorized to manufacture, distribute, or dispense controlled substances who will have direct access to such controlled substances, as well as current employee who had access to persons or property that are the subject of an ongoing investigation.

Qualifications of examiners

An examiner is required to have a valid and current license if required by a State in which the test is to be conducted, and must maintain a minimum of $50,000 bond or professional liability coverage.

Employee/prospective employee rights

An employee or prospective employee must be given a written notice explaining the employee's or prospective employee's rights and the limitations imposed, such as prohibited areas of questioning and restriction on the use of test results. Among other rights, an employee or prospective employee may refuse to take a test, terminate a test at any time, or decline to take a test if he/she suffers from a medical condition. The results of a test alone cannot be disclosed to anyone other than the employer or employee/prospective employee without their consent or, pursuant to court order, to a court, government agency, arbitrator or mediator.

Under the exemption for ongoing investigations of work place incidents involving economic loss, a written or verbal statement must be provided to the employee prior to the polygraph test which explains the specific incident or activity being investigated and the basis for the employer's reasonable suspicion that the employee was involved in such incident or activity.

Where polygraph examinations are permitted under the Act, they are subject to strict standards concerning the conduct of the test, including the pre-test, testing and post-test phases of the examination.

Civil actions may be brought by an employee or prospective employee in Federal or State court against employers who violate the Act for legal or equitable relief, such as employment reinstatement, promotion, and payment of lost wages and benefits. The action must be brought within 3 years of the date of the alleged violation.

CAMPBELL v. WOODARD PHOTOGRAPHIC, INC.

433 F.Supp.2d 857 (N.D. Ohio 2006).

JAMES G. CARR, CHIEF JUDGE.

Woodard and Wilburn own WPI, a photography business in Northwest Ohio. The company employed Campbell as a production manager at its Bellevue facility from April 3, 2001, to December 2, 2004. Throughout that term of employment, Campbell was an at-will employee.

In the late Summer of 2004, several thefts of cash, equipment, and other valuables occurred at WPI locations. On November 10, 2004, a "memory-mate envelope" containing $2,700 in cash, checks, and receivables disappeared from the Bellevue store.

Two days later, Woodard and Wilburn held a meeting with their employees to discuss that most recent theft. They informed the staff that

WPI would conduct an investigation and mentioned the possibility of using polygraph examinations. The parties dispute what the defendants said precisely regarding those tests. * * *

Woodard and Wilburn requested Campbell and two others, who, as did the plaintiff, had access to the missing envelope, to detail in writing their movements on November 10, 2004. Campbell complied, stating that he did not leave the premises during work hours that day.

Following the meeting, WPI retained CIC, and its employee Johnson, to conduct an inquiry. CIC does not use polygraph tests during its investigations.

Johnson requested all WPI employees to complete questionnaires regarding the incident. In addition, Woodard examined key card entry logs which the company keeps to track employees' comings and goings. From these records, he determined Campbell had left the premises for forty-three minutes on the day of the theft, in direct contradiction to Campbell's written statement. Campbell contends he left the office to purchase a pack of cigarettes and that his failure to include such in his written statement was an oversight.

Woodard claims he also discovered a printout detailing Campbell's recent eBay transactions, in the printer tray in Campbell's office. That document listed several items identical to equipment missing from WPI. Further, maintenance employees reported seeing Campbell outside an inventory room where WPI kept such items.

Because of that information, inconsistencies between Campbell's oral and written statements, and his conduct in the interviews, WPI decided to terminate Campbell, Woodard, subsequently, contacted the Bellevue Police Department to inform it of the company's findings. * * *

Under the EPPA [Employee Polygraph Protection Act of 1988], an employer may not "directly or indirectly, require, request, suggest, or cause any employee or prospective employee to take or submit to any lie detector test." 29 U.S.C. § 2002(1). An employer need not actually administer a polygraph test to be liable. Polkey v. Transtecs Corp., 404 F.3d 1264, 1267–68 (11th Cir.2005).

Here, Campbell submitted the deposition testimony of Kathleen Ordway, an employee present at the November 12, 2006, meeting. She stated Woodard told his employees at the meeting, "[t]hat everyone would have to take a polygraph." That testimony tracks the statute's language and Campbell, therefore, has made out a prima facie case on this claim.

Defendants respond that any potential use of polygraph tests occurred during an investigation, which the statute permits. 29 U.S.C. § 2006(d). That exception, however, requires the employer have a "reasonable suspicion," 29 U.S.C. § 2006(d)(3), which the applicable regulations define as, "an observable, articulable basis in fact which indicates that a particular employee was involved, or responsible for, an economic loss." 20 C.F.R. § 801.129(f)(1). Here, however, at the time of the meeting, defendants had no particularized suspicions whatsoever. They only focused on Campbell later in the inquiry. Consequently, defendants may not avail themselves of the statutory exception and summary judgment is inappropriate for WPI and Woodard.

G.   VIDEO PRIVACY PROTECTION ACT OF 1988

NOTE: BORK'S LAW

The Video Privacy Protection Act of 1988 (VPPA), 18 U.S.C. § 2710 (2002) is remarkable for its genesis and for its narrow, specific scope.

Judge Robert Bork was nominated to the Supreme Court. A former Yale law professor, Bork was a scholarly critic of the reasoning of *Griswold v. Connecticut* and *Roe v. Wade*. In Congressional hearings on his nomination, he stood by his view that the constitution was not a valid source of a "right to privacy." Bork's nomination fell through. But before Judge Bork left the public stage, someone got hold of his video rental records, which were published in a local Washington D.C. newspaper, the *City Paper*. Bork's taste in movies turned out to be perfectly innocuous, but many people were outraged that no law expressly prohibited a video store from handing over rental records to third-parties.

Enacted in the era of the VCR (video cassette recorder), the VPPA prohibits a "video tape service provider" from disclosing without consent "personally identifiable information concerning any consumer," including rental records of "prerecorded video cassette tapes or similar audio visual material." Suits in federal court may be brought against "video tape service provider" violators. Courts may award: "(A) actual damages but not less than liquidated damages in an amount of $2,500; (B) punitive damages; (C) reasonable attorneys' fees and other litigation costs reasonably incurred; and (D) such other preliminary and equitable relief as the court determines to be appropriate." The statute also expressly provides for an exclusionary rule as follows: "Personally identifiable information obtained in any manner other than as provided in this section shall not be received in evidence in any trial, hearing, arbitration, or other proceeding in or before any court, grand jury, department, officer, agency, regulatory body, legislative committee, or other authority of the United States, a State, or a political subdivision of a State." Finally, the statute instructs video providers to "destroy personally identifiable information as soon as practicable, but no later than one year from the date the information is no longer necessary for the purpose for which it was collected and there are no pending requests or orders for access to such information * * *." Why prohibit data retention? Are there data government might prefer that entities preserve, such as data held by internet service providers, telephone companies and libraries?

The VPPA has proven to be a potential weapon against data sharing by the distinctly 21st century video providers Blockbuster and Netflix.

1. COMMERCIAL ADULT VIDEO ARCADES

BAMON CORP. v. CITY OF DAYTON

730 F. Supp. 80 (S.D. Ohio 1990).

WALTER HERBERT RICE, UNITED STATES DISTRICT JUDGE * * *

On October 18, 1989, the City Commission of Dayton, Ohio, passed an ordinance (hereinafter "the Ordinance") regulating the design and occupancy of video booths located in "Amusement Arcades" and in which a "film or video viewing devices used to exhibit material depicting certain enumerated sexual acts and bodily functions." Section 136.08 of the Ordinance defines an "Amusement Arcade" as "any place of business [other than hotels or motels] in which a film or video viewing service or devices are located for the use of entertainment of a person or persons patronizing the place of business." If the material depicted by "film or video viewing devices" within an amusement arcade depicts any of the enumerated subjects listed in Section 136.09(A), every video booth in which such material is shown must comply with the following requirements:

(1) Be visible from a well-illuminated continuous main aisle;

(2) Not be obscured by any curtain, door or other enclosure;

(3) All side or rear walls must be without holes or openings;

(4) Shall not be occupied by more than one patron at a time;

(5) Be illuminated by a light bulb of a wattage of no less than 25 watts.

Section 136.09(B). The Ordinance further provides that any "owner, operator, employee, or agent of an amusement arcade" who violates these requirements, and/or who allows or permits a violation thereof, and any patron who violates the one-patron-per booth requirement, is guilty of a first degree misdemeanor.

Plaintiff Bamon Corporation ("Plaintiff") is an Ohio corporation which has been doing business as McCook Theatre at the same location in the City of Dayton for the past ten years. * * * Plaintiff's business, which consists of a theatre, boutique and "entertainment facility," * * * primarily involves the sale of "Adult" books and magazines, the sale and/or rental and exhibition of "Adult" films and videotapes, and the exhibition of "Adult" live entertainment. * * * It is undisputed that the sexually explicit materials comprising Plaintiff's stock in trade are not classified as legally obscene; they are, therefore, protected under the first amendment. * * *

There are thirty-five viewing booths on Plaintiff's premises in which a pre-set movie may be seen for a fee of twenty-five cents, four booths in which a videotape rented for five dollars may be viewed, and thirteen booths in which may be viewed live nude and/or semi-nude entertainment by a performer separated from the viewer by a glass plate. * * * All of the booths in Plaintiff's establishment are totally enclosed, having neither windows nor other "viewing portholes," and have a full-length door which patrons may lock. * * *

Plaintiff filed the instant action on November 13, 1989, seeking an order of this Court declaring the Ordinance unconstitutional and permanently enjoining its enforcement. * * *

At several places in the Complaint, Plaintiff asserts that the Ordinance violates the rights of its patrons to view constitutionally protected material in private. * * * Plaintiff argues that its viewing booths, as currently constructed, are "private places" in which Plaintiff's patrons' "privacy right" is to be protected. * * * The origin of this right to privacy within the booths is, according to the Complaint, grounded both in the United States Constitution and in federal law. * * *

It is unclear whether Plaintiff has standing to assert his patrons' privacy rights. The Court is willing to assume such standing, arguendo, in order to reach the merits of Plaintiff's privacy claim; however, the Court has found, and Plaintiff has cited, no caselaw supporting Plaintiff's proposition that its patrons have an inherent right to view sexually explicit, non-obscene material in the privacy of an enclosed video booth located in a public business establishment. Plaintiff's assertion to the contrary notwithstanding, * * * neither the Supreme Court's decision in Stanley v. Georgia, 394 U.S. 557 (1969) (holding that the viewing of obscene materials in one's home is constitutionally protected), nor its decision in Paris Adult Theatre I v. Slaton, 413 U.S. 49 (1973) (holding that there is no privacy right to view obscene movies in places of public accommodation), supports Plaintiff's proposition. It is insufficient simply to distinguish these decisions on the ground that they involve the right to view obscene materials. Indeed, the broader language of Paris Adult Theatre, distinguishing Stanley, is most persuasive and relevant herein:

> It is unavailing to compare a theater, open to the public for a fee, with the private home of [Stanley] * * *. This Court has, on numerous occasions, refused to hold that commercial ventures such as a motion-picture house are "private" for the purpose of civil rights litigation and civil rights statutes.

413 U.S. at 65 (citations omitted). Given this language, and the fact that the right of privacy has not been extended to public businesses, the Court declines to broaden that right to include a right to view non-obscene movies or live entertainment in an enclosed booth in Plaintiff's place of business. * * *

Plaintiff also alleges that the Video Privacy Protection Act of 1988, 18 U.S.C. § 2710, preempts the Ordinance at issue in this case. Plaintiff asserts that enforcement of the Ordinance will force the public disclosure of its patrons' "purchase, rental or viewing" of videotaped materials and that such disclosure violates privacy rights inherent in this Act. Id. at PP 25–26. Plaintiff misconstrues the nature of the disclosure which the Act regulates. As its legislative history makes clear, the Act was intended to prohibit, except in limited circumstances, the disclosure to public or private entities of records (or information derived from those records) kept by video tape service providers and linking the names of customers with the subject matter of the videotaped materials they have rented or purchased.

Although Plaintiff is correct in noting the privacy concerns "inherent" in the Act, nothing in its legislative history or its language suggests that it protects against the possibility that a patron's choice of viewing material might be "disclosed" to others by virtue of the removal of the door of a video booth. Moreover, as Defendants rightly point out, the Ordinance does not require that amusement arcades disclose to anyone their patrons' choices of videotaped subject matter. The federal Act, in terms, preempts only those provisions of local law that require the disclosure prohibited by the Act.

2. WARRANT REQUIREMENT FOR LAW ENFORCEMENT ACCESS TO VIDEO RENTAL DATA

CAMFIELD v. CITY OF OKLAHOMA CITY

248 F.3d 1214 (10th Cir. 2001).

BRISCOE, CIRCUIT JUDGE

This appeal arises from a well-publicized decision by the Oklahoma City Police Department (OCPD) to remove the Academy Award-winning film The Tin Drum from public access after a state judge opined in an ex parte hearing that the movie contained child pornography in violation of Oklahoma law. Michael Camfield, whose rented copy of the movie was obtained from him at his apartment by three OCPD officers, sued the City of Oklahoma City (City), several members of the OCPD and two state prosecutors under 42 U.S.C. § 1983, alleging violations of his First, Fourth and Fourteenth Amendment rights. He also sought declaratory relief under the * * * Video Privacy Protection Act (VPPA), 18 U.S.C. § 2710. * * *

Tin Drum, a German language film with English subtitles, received the 1979 Academy Award for best foreign language film and shared the Palme D'Or Award at the Cannes International Film Festival that same year. Based on the 1959 novel of the same name by Gunter Grass, the film has been described as a complex allegorical fantasy intended to symbolize the rise of Nazism and the corresponding decline of morality in Nazi Germany. The movie opens in Danzig in the 1930s when the main character, Oskar Matzerath, decides to stop growing at the age of three in order to "protest against the absurdities and obscenities of the adult world" during the rise of Nazism. * * * Throughout the approximately eighteen years depicted in the film, Oskar remains diminutive in size and appears to be a very young boy, while those around him continue to age normally. Not until the end of the film and near the end of World War II, when Oskar is twenty-one years old, does he express a desire to resume growing again. The movie, which has been in public circulation around the world for over twenty years, has received critical acclaim and been discussed in several academic articles and books related to film studies.

In June 1997, a citizen complained to OCPD Maj. William Citty that The Tin Drum contains child pornography. Maj. Citty contacted vice division Lt. Gregory Taylor, advised him of the complaint and asked him to obtain a copy of the movie. Lt. Taylor did so and assigned the case to Sgt. Se Kim. Sgt. Kim watched the movie, observed certain scenes he believed contained child pornography and, in accordance with a common vice division practice, took the movie to the county courthouse to request judicial confirmation of his opinion. A state judge agreed to watch the movie and give his own opinion.

On the morning of June 24, 1997, Sgt. Kim and Sgt. Britt High met with the judge, who advised the officers he believed The Tin Drum contained child pornography in violation of Okla. Stat. tit. 21, § 1021.2. The judge communicated his decision orally and did not issue a written ruling or specify which scenes violated the law. However, the judge later explained that he based his opinion on three scenes in the movie, which have been referred to in this litigation as (1) the bathhouse scene, (2) the bedroom scene, and (3) the sitting room scene. All three scenes portray Oskar and a female character named Maria Matzerath as being sixteen years old, although at the time of filming the actor playing Oskar was eleven years old and the actress playing Maria was twenty-four. According to the judge, the bathhouse scene shows Oskar "engaged in or portrayed, depicted or represented to be engaging in an act of cunnilingus with" Maria. * * * In the bedroom scene, Oskar "begins to engage in or is portrayed, depicted, or represented as engaging in an act of sexual intercourse * * * with" Maria. Id. Finally, in the sitting room scene, Oskar observes Maria and an adult male "engaged in or portrayed, depicted, * * * or represented as engaging in sexual intercourse" on a couch. * * *

The next day, on June 25, 1997, Sgt. High proposed a plan in which the officers would go to video stores in Oklahoma City that rented The Tin Drum and ask the employees to voluntarily relinquish their store's copies of the movie; if any copies were checked out, the officers would ask the employees to provide each renter's name and address. * * *

That evening, Sgt. High, Sgt. Kim, and a third officer, Sgt. Matt French, went to several video stores in Oklahoma City and obtained all available copies of The Tin Drum. They also asked for and received the names and addresses of several customers who were renting the movie. One of those customers was Michael Camfield, and the officers went to his apartment to ask for his copy of the movie. Camfield is the Development Director of the American Civil Liberties Union of Oklahoma. He had recently learned of the controversy surrounding The Tin Drum and was watching the film to formulate rebuttals and policy responses on behalf of the ACLU when the officers knocked on his door. Sgt. High told Camfield that the film contained child pornography under Oklahoma law; Camfield responded that he disagreed with the judge's determination. A "great debate" concerning the artistic merits of the movie ensued, * * * but Camfield eventually turned over his copy of the videotape to the officers. As a result of the voluntary surrender plan, the OCPD removed a total of nine copies of the movie from public circulation. No warrants were issued for any of the videotapes. Although Camfield and other parties later revoked their consent and demanded the return of their videotapes, the OCPD refused.

Camfield subsequently sued the City, DA Macy, Sgt. High and Sgt. Kim in federal court. He alleged that the defendants violated the VPPA, 18 U.S.C. § 2710, and infringed his rights under the First, Fourth and Fourteenth Amendments to the United States Constitution, in violation of 42 U.S.C. § 1983. * * *

With regard to Camfield's claim under the VPPA, the district court held that Sgts. High, Kim and French violated the Act as a matter of law when they obtained Camfield's name and address from the video store without a warrant or court order. The district court subsequently held that the City was liable for any damages that Camfield incurred as a result of this violation because the officers were acting within the scope of their employment. However, because the actual amount of Camfield's damages involved questions of fact, the district court left that issue for the jury.

After a three-day trial, the jury found in favor of Sgts. High, Kim and French on Camfield's Fourth Amendment claims and awarded Camfield the statutory minimum of $2500 in liquidated damages on his VPPA claim.

3. WHO IS A "VIDEO TAPE SERVICE PROVIDER"?

DANIEL v. CANTRELL

375 F.3d 377 (6th Cir. 2004).

CUDAHY, CIRCUIT JUDGE

The plaintiff, Alden Joe Daniel, Jr. (Daniel) was charged with and eventually pleaded guilty to the sexual molestation of three underage girls. Allegedly, part of his modus operandi was showing pornographic movies to the underage girls. * * * Therefore, as part of the criminal investigation into his conduct, law enforcement officials sought and were able to obtain his video rental records. On March 27, 2000, Daniel's state-appointed attorney, James F. Logan, filed a motion to suppress the disclosures. The motion argued that these video rental records were obtained in violation of the [Video Privacy Protection Act (the Act), 18 U.S.C. § 2710]. It is unclear whether or not this motion was granted; however, between May and August of 2000, Daniel pleaded guilty to one count of rape, five counts of statutory rape, two counts of sexual battery by an authority figure and failure to appear.

On June 10, 2002, Daniel filed a pro se complaint in the United States District Court for the Eastern District of Tennessee alleging that numerous defendants obtained and disclosed private information regarding his rental of pornographic videos in violation of the Act. * * *

In his complaint, Daniel asserts that video rental store owners and their employees disclosed personally identifiable information about his video rentals to [law enforcement] defendants Estes, the Cantrells, Stabler, Jenne, Kimbrell and Alvarez. These defendants then disclosed this information to a Bradley County Grand Jury. Daniel alleges that these disclosures violated his right to privately rent video tapes under the Act. According to Daniel's complaint, the disclosures began as early as January 11, 1998, and were ongoing and continuous up to the last two civil suits against him that were filed in September, 2001. To support this latter contention, Daniel submitted the sworn affidavits of his mother and father. * * *

Reading Daniel's complaint broadly, it appears that he may be asserting claims under two sections of the Act: §§ 2710(b) and (d). We discuss section (b) first. Section (b) provides that "[a] video tape service provider who knowingly discloses, to any person, personally identifiable information concerning any consumer of such provider shall be liable to the aggrieved person for the relief provided in subsection (d)." * * * Therefore, under the plain language of the statute, only a "video tape service provider" (VTSP) can be liable. The term VTSP is defined by the statute to mean "any person, engaged in the business, in or affecting interstate or foreign commerce, of rental, sale, or delivery of prerecorded video cassette tapes or similar audio video materials["]. * * *

Daniel argues, however, that any person, not just a VTSP, can be liable under the Act based on Dirkes v. Borough of Runnemede, 936 F. Supp. 235 (D.N.J. 1996). Dirkes did reach this conclusion but only by misreading the Act. The court in Dirkes was focused on language in the Act stating that "any person aggrieved by any act of a person in violation of this section may bring a civil action in the United States district court." * * * Because the statute states that a suit can be based upon an act of "a person" rather than an act of "a VTSP," Dirkes found that any person can be liable under the Act. Dirkes, 936 F. Supp. at 240. Dirkes, however, ignored the rest of the sentence. A lawsuit under the Act must be based on an "act of a person in violation of this section["]. * * * The statute makes it clear that only a VTSP can be in violation of section 2710(b). See § 2710(b)(1) [A "video tape service provider" who knowingly discloses personally identifiable information shall be liable.]. Moreover, if any person could be liable under the Act, there would be no need for the Act to define a VTSP in the first place. * * * We avoid interpretations of a statute which would render portions of it superfluous. * * *

Because the following defendants do not fit into the definition of a VTSP necessary for liability under section (b) and because section (d) is not the basis for a private cause of action, we affirm the district court in its dismissal of all claims against Ellie M. Cantrell, Michael Cantrell, Lee Ann Stabler, Roger E. Jenne, Jerry N. Estes, Joseph V. Hoffer, Stephen D. Crump, Chuck Kimbrell and Tony Alvarez. * * *

NOTE: BORROWING MOVIES, BUYING BOOKS

Would it violate the Video Privacy protection Act for a public library or bookstore to give the police a list of the video tapes a person borrowed or purchased, respectively? Would it run afoul of any law for a bookstore to give police a list of the books a person purchased? See Jared N. Klein, The Right to Privacy in What You Read: the Fourth Amendment Implications of a Book Store Search, 13 *Temp. Pol. & Civ. Rts. L. Rev.* 361 (2003).

HARRIS v. BLOCKBUSTER

No. 3:09–cv–217–M (N. D. Texas).

Memorandum Denying Motion to Compel Arbitration

This case arises out of alleged violations of the Video Privacy Protection Act by Defendant Blockbuster Inc. ("Blockbuster"). Blockbuster operates a service called Blockbuster Online, which allows customers to rent movies through the internet. Blockbuster entered into an agreement with Facebook ("the Blockbuster contract") which caused Blockbuster's customers' movie rental choices to be disseminated on the customers' Facebook accounts through Facebook's "Beacon" program. In short, when a customer rented a video from Blockbuster Online, the Beacon program would transmit the customer's choice to Facebook, which would then broadcast the choice to the customer's Facebook friends.

Plaintiff claims that this arrangement violated the Video Privacy Protection Act, 18 U.S.C. § 2710, which prohibits a videotape service provider from disclosing personally identifiable information about a customer unless given informed, written consent at the time the disclosure is sought. The Act provides for liquidated damages of $2,500 for each violation. Blockbuster attempted to invoke an arbitration provision in its "Terms and Conditions," which includes a paragraph governing "Dispute Resolution" that states, in pertinent part: "[a]ll claims, disputes or controversies ... will be referred to and determined by binding arbitration." It further purportedly waives the right of its users to commence any class action. As a precondition to joining Blockbuster Online, customers were required to click on a box certifying that they had read and agreed to the Terms and Conditions.

On August 30, 2008, before the case was transferred to this Court, the Defendant moved to enforce the arbitration provision. The Plaintiffs argued that the arbitration provision is unenforceable, principally for two reasons: (1) it is illusory; and (2) it is unconscionable. Because the Court concludes that the arbitration provision is illusory, the Court does not reach the unconscionability issue.

Analysis

The basis for the Plaintiffs' claim that the arbitration provision is illusory is that Blockbuster reserves the right to modify the Terms and Conditions, including the section that contains the arbitration provision, "at its sole discretion" and "at any time," and such modifications will be effective immediately upon being posted on the site. Under the heading "Changes to Terms and Conditions," the contract states: "Blockbuster may at any time, and at its sole discretion, modify these Terms and Conditions of Use, including without limitation the Privacy Policy, with or without notice. Such modifications will be effective immediately upon posting. You agree to review these Terms and Conditions of Use periodically and your continued use of this Site following such modifications will indicate your acceptance of these modified Terms and Conditions of Use. If you do not agree to any modification of these Terms and Conditions of Use, you must immediately stop using this Site."

The Court concludes that the Blockbuster arbitration provision is illusory for the same reasons as that in *Morrison*. Here, as in *Morrison*, there is nothing in the Terms and Conditions that prevents Blockbuster from unilaterally changing any part of the contract other than providing that such changes will not take effect until posted on the website. There are likewise no "*Halliburton* type savings clauses," as there is "nothing to suggest that once published the amendment would be inapplicable to disputes arising, or arising out of events occurring, before such publication." The Fifth Circuit in *Morrison* noted the lack of an "express exemption" of the ability to unilaterally modify all rules, which the Blockbuster agreement also does not contain. The Blockbuster contract only states that modifications "will be effective immediately upon posting," and the natural reading of that clause does not limit application of the modifications to earlier disputes. * * *

NOTE: BLOCKBUSTER

In 2009 Facebook agreed to shut down its Beacon program and to create a foundation to promote online privacy, safety and security as part of a $9.5 million settlement in *Harris v. Blockbuster*, a class action suit brought in 2008, see above. Explain how Blockbuster Beacon may have violated the Video Privacy Protection Act.

Why did the district court deny defendant's motion to compel arbitration? The Electronic Information Privacy Center opposed enforcing the mandatory arbitration agreement and filed an amicus brief explaining why: "Mandatory arbitration clauses implicate privacy interests, as they prevent consumers from availing themselves of strong statutory protections already in place. In *Blockbuster*, Harris sued under the Video Privacy Protection Act, which provides for civil penalties of at least $2,500 per violation. However, Blockbuster's arbitration clause would have prevented users from litigating claims in court, and as a result, benefiting from the Act's privacy protections. Consumers simply do not have the same privacy rights in arbitration proceedings than in court proceedings, where they are protected by state and federal statutes." http://epic.org/amicus/blockbuster/default.html#int

NOTE: NETFLIX

Explain whether Netflix was liable to its customers for violations of the Video Privacy Protection Act, as suggested by the FTC in the Closing Letter that follows.

FEDERAL TRADE COMMISSION LETTER TO NETFLIX, MARCH 12, 2010

http://www.ftc.gov/os/closings/100312netflixletter.pdf.

Reed Freeman
Morrison & Foerster LLP
2000 Pennsylvania Ave., NW
Washington, DC 20006

Dear Mr. Freeman:

On October 13, 2009, staff from the FTC's Division of Privacy and Identity Protection contacted your client, Netflix, Inc. ("Netflix"), regarding the privacy implications of Netflix's planned release of customer movie viewing data in connection with the company's efforts to improve its movie recommendation algorithm. Specifically, staff expressed concern that, despite Netflix's efforts to "anonymize" the customer data prior to its release, it would be possible to re-identify specific customers and thereby associate them with their movie viewing histories and preferences.

Staff's concerns about Netflix's planned release stemmed from research published after the company released a similar data set on October 2, 2006. According to news reports and Netflix's website, Netflix released the first data set as part of its Netflix Prize 1 contest ("Prize 1"), through which researchers competed to improve the algorithm Netflix uses to recommend movies to its subscribers. Netflix's algorithm takes into account past viewing habits and movie preferences of each of its subscribers. The Prize 1 data set represented the movies rated by over 480,000 Netflix customers and the date each rating was given. In an apparent effort by Netflix to anonymize the data, the company replaced customers' names with unique numbers and did not include addresses, phone numbers, or other direct identifiers.

Following the conclusion of Prize 1, two researchers at the University of Texas, Arvind Narayanan and Vitaly Shmatikov, published a research paper demonstrating that it is possible to re-identify particular individuals within the Prize 1 data set using a minimal amount of outside information. With this minimal information, one could determine all of the Netflix movies that a subscriber had rated for a given period of time.

Notwithstanding the research and its attendant publicity, Netflix announced on August 6, 2009, its intention to create a second contest, Netflix Prize 2 ("Prize 2"). Prize 2 would involve the release of a data set based on Netflix customers' movie viewing habits and preferences. In addition, the Prize 2 data set would contain certain demographic data about Netflix customers.

In light of the Narayanan and Shmatikov research, Netflix's intention to release a second data set one containing a richer portfolio of consumer information raised serious concerns about the risk that Netflix's customers would be re-identified and associated with their potentially sensitive movie viewing histories and preferences. Due to advances in technology that allow for vast amounts of data to be collected, stored, accessed, and combined, staff encourages companies to be cautious when releasing data presumed to be "anonymous" or "not personally identifiable," especially when those representations are made to consumers.

Consequently, in a letter to Netflix dated November 3, 2009, staff identified a number of concerns related to Prize 2. These include the risk of re-identification and the extent to which Netflix's previous representations to its customers about disclosure of their information would raise concerns under Section 5 of the FTC Act. Following a number of productive discussions between staff and Netflix, the company sent a letter to staff stating that it intended to suspend plans for Prize 2. Further, Netflix stated that if it releases a second data set in the future, it would not do so publicly; rather, it would release such data only to researchers who contractually agree to specific limitations on its use. In addition, Netflix stated that it would implement a number of operational safeguards to prevent the data from being used to re-identify consumers. Finally, Netflix agreed to further discussion with FTC staff prior to releasing the data.

Based upon these assurances, staff has determined to close the investigation. The company's swift response and willingness to take steps to protect consumer data represents a meaningful commitment to protecting the privacy of consumers. We encourage Netflix to maintain this commitment as it develops future policies and practices involving consumer data. The closing of this investigation is not to be construed as a determination that a violation may not have occurred, just as the pendency of an investigation should not be construed as a determination that a violation has occurred. The Commission reserves the right to take such further action as the public interest may require.

Sincerely,

Maneesha Mithal
Associate Director
Division of Privacy and Identity Protection
Federal Trade Commission

NETFLIX CANCELS CONTEST OVER PRIVACY CONCERNS

Epic.org
March 15, 2010.

Netflix canceled its second $1 million Netflix Prize after privacy concerns from the FTC and a federal lawsuit alleging invasion of privacy and violations of the Video Privacy Protection Act. [The lawsuit filed in December 2009 had alleged that: "A Netflix member's movie data may reveal that member's private information such as sexuality, religious beliefs, or political affiliations. Such data may also reveal a member's personal struggles with issues such as domestic violence, adultery, alcoholism or substance abuse."] * * * After productive discussions with the FTC over reidentification concerns * * * Netflix and the federal agency reached an understanding on how Netflix would use user data in the future. Netflix also settled the VPPA lawsuit.

H.   REGULATING COMPUTERS, INTERNET USE AND DATA FLOW

1.   LEGISLATION REGULATING THE INTERNET

NOTE: RULES COMBATING PERILS

The internet is a phenomenal resource. It is a resource for communication, commerce, education, entertainment, art, friendship, charity and politics. Why, if at all, should society regulate the internet through legislation? The internet comes with major problems and costs, some of which are, arguably, most effectively addressed through legal rules. In May 2010, U.S. Representatives Rick Boucher (VA–09), Chairman of the Subcommittee on Communications, Technology, and the Internet, and Cliff Stearns, Ranking Member of the Subcommittee, released a discussion draft of legislation to protect the privacy of information about individuals on the Internet and offline as well.

More than a decade ago, Professor Yochai Benkler characterized many of the problems spawned by the internet as "destabilization" of traditional information flows in everyday life. Yochai Benkler, Net Regulation, Taking Stock and Looking Forward, 71 *U. Colo. L. Rev.* 1203 (2000). Perhaps society should regulate the internet to restore information flows to preferred, pre-internet channels. Or, perhaps, without regard to previous patterns and expectations of privacy, government should regulate the internet to address what strike the public today as serious dangers attendant to internet use.

The perils of internet use include the dignitarian and reputational harm that befalls individuals when internet use enables the government or other third-parties to gain access to personal data and communications. Privacy protection measures applicable to the internet, such as commercial anonymizers and privacy laws, decrease the danger that persons will be "judged, fairly or unfairly, on the basis of isolated bits of personal information that are taken out of context." See Jeffrey Rosen, *The Unwanted Gaze* (2000) at 200.

The internet exposes users to financial peril. Failure to use secure websites, websites with meaningful privacy policies, and privacy enhancing technologies (such as encryption, digital signatures and pseudonyms) can lead to inadvertent disclosures of sensitive financial data or personal identifiers. Disclosures of personal data can mean financial losses, consumer inconvenience and identity theft.

Internet users have been tricked into giving bank account numbers, passwords and social security numbers to sham website operators pretending to be legitimate banks or other businesses. Users have responded to their detriment to spam and phishing email ensnaring them with false promises of riches into bogus investments and pyramid schemes. Internet users have been victimized by "spyware".

The internet can be an exhilarating domain for social experimentation and personal growth. Cf. Jerry Kang, Cyber–Race, 113 *Harv. L. Rev.* 1130 (2000). But racism, anti-Semitism and sexism pervade cyberspace. Sexism and objectification of women on the web replicates demeaning conditions off-line. In a noteworthy instance, a woman was emotionally jolted by the virtual rape of a virtual person she role-played in an online game. See Julian Dibble, *My Tiny Life* (1999). See generally Ann Bartow, Our Data, Ourselves: Privacy, Propertization, and Gender, 34 *U.S.F. L. Rev.* 633 (2000); see also, Anita L. Allen, Gender and Privacy in Cyberspace, 52 *Stan. L. Rev.* 1175 (2000). Women and children have been victimized off-line by sexual predators first met online.

Social networking spaces, for example, Facebook.com, Twitter.com, Linked-in.com and MySpace.com, provide engaging opportunities for forging relationships with peers and obtaining information. Entertainment spaces, such as YouTube and celebrity gossip blogs also form social networking functions. The seeming anonymity and freedom of the internet may encourage people to let down their guard in ways they come to regret. Incivility, crime and terrorism that can be perpetrated or facilitated on-line may be especially tempting. Cf. Neal Katyal, Criminal Law in Cyberspace, 149 *U. Pa. L. Rev.* 1003 (2001). Non-criminal opportunities to "misbehave" on-line can have off-line consequences. People who post lewd photographs or vulgar content on a social networking website may find that their reputations are damaged in ways that affect school admissions or employment.

Using the internet exposes children to sexual predators, adult content and e-businesses out to sell them something or collect commercially valuable information. As a result of the Children's Online Privacy Protection Act of 1998 ("COPPA"), discussed below, websites aimed at minors under 13 generally offer opportunities to play and network on an anonymous basis or with parental consent. A February 2007 FTC report, "Implementing the Children's Online Privacy Protection Act," concluded that COPPA has been an effective data protection measure without significantly diminishing the amount of meaningful internet content available to children. Some, but not all, of the problems attendant to internet use will be susceptible to straightforward regulatory responses.

Not all the problems that arise in connection with the internet relate to dignitarian, reputational or financial harm that can stem from disclosures of sensitive information. Another type of problem that has arisen is disagreement over authority to regulate the Internet. Do customers have a right to monopolize provider (e.g., Comcast) bandwith with peer-to-peer networking applications, and does the Federal Communications Commission (FCC) have the authority to decide such questions through either rule-making or adjudication. See *Comcast Corp. v. FCC*, 600 F. 3d 642 (2010), holding that the FCC lacks authority to regulate an Internet service provider's network management practices. Notwithstanding the Comcast decision, on June 17, 2010 the Federal Communications Commission opened a new proceeding to reclassify the Internet—classified as an information service since 2002—as a telephone service, under Title II of the 1934 Telecommunications Act. If reclassification were accomplished, the FCC could presumably set net neutrality rules and regulate the Internet. Another regulatory issue, again involving the FCC, is whether the FCC should subject Internet telephony (voice over Internet protocol) to state telecommunications fees for the Universal Service Fund, a program that subsidizes telecommunications costs in low-income and rural areas.

YOCHAI BENKLER, NET REGULATION: TAKING STOCK AND LOOKING FORWARD

71 U. Colo. L. Rev. 1203 (2000).

[Legislative efforts to regulate the internet] can be organized usefully into three clusters. In the first cluster, legislation attempts to harness technology to serve what are perceived to be governmental goals unrelated to the Net. These include: enhancing education by providing school access and teacher training; funding internet access in libraries; publishing government information and information required by law to be published by non-government actors; and communicating with government by opening up the process of public comment on regulations. * * *

As more public functions are performed on the Net, and are enhanced and altered by the Net, its role in people's lives is affected. The machine through which you debate political issues with your community plays a different role in your life than the machine through which you shop for Christmas presents. The social construction of the Net is affected by the extent to which it is understood and treated as a means for public participation, as a means for study and education, or as the great shopping mall in the sky. That social construction will be affected by the extent to which, and the way in which, the public uses the Net to provide traditional public goods like education, civic participation, or information about the world we share as citizens and autonomous persons.

The second cluster of legislative actions encompasses efforts aimed directly at fostering the advancement of Net infrastructure. These include primarily physical infrastructure regulation, as well as investment in research and development of the intellectual infrastructure. This is not to say that all such investments are apolitical, aimed solely at some commonly-held sense of optimal development * * *. There are questions of just how freely the market can provide for infrastructure, both physical and intellectual. Investments in research and development indicate at least some concern that markets will not invest optimally; regulation of incumbent carriers suggests the same for the physical infrastructure market. There are disagreements over which set of regulations will best achieve infrastructural development—whether, for example, cable carriers who offer broadband data carriage must interconnect with competing ISPs or not * * *.

The third cluster of issues * * * directly concerns control over information. These efforts at regulation respond to radical changes that the Net has wrought on traditional structures of control over information flows. Where doors and locked bureaus could once protect privacy, data-mining and encryption now do battle over whether there will be more privacy than in the pre-Net environment, or less. Where clearly-demarcated copies of information goods—like books or records—once defined the boundaries of control that intellectual property owners had over their products, technological protection measures and licenses do battle with digital duplication and transmission to determine whether owners or users will gain more control over the information products they own, or use, respectively. Where brown paper wraps, the watchful eye of the store keeper or the parent, and government and social regulation once controlled access to "dangerous materials," kids more technologically attuned than their parents and users who seek out or provide "dangerous materials" can now produce and access these materials at lower cost, and much freer of the traditional means of social surveillance, than ever before. This third cluster is a series of laws attempting to establish the terms of control over information flows, given the shake-up of the technological parameters that defined the boundaries of control before the Net * * *.

The introduction of the Net caused a much more significant disturbance than any previous technological change since the abandonment of the general acceptability of morality regulation per se. This is so for a number of reasons. The most important reason is organizational. The Net eliminated the intermediaries that, in previous technologies, were used as gatekeepers to control the dissemination of, and access to, pornographic materials. Gone were the editor, the magazine or video store owner, the broadcasters, the cable operator, or even the telephone company. Anything that anyone was willing to put online was available directly to anyone else, using facilities that saw nothing but streams of zeros and ones. This not only eliminated organizational control points, but also social approbation control points—the need to look someone in the eye in order to rent or buy the thing. [T]he Net dramatically reduced producers' production and distribution costs. Anyone could put his or her fantasies online at a cost of no more than spare time, or exhibit their photographs at the cost of scanning them.

NOTE: PRIVATE VS. PUBLIC SOLUTIONS

In the late 1990's, Lawrence Lessig made a striking contribution to the debates about Internet regulation. See Lawrence Lessig, *Code and Other Laws of Cyberspace* (1999). The question of the day was whether the government should enact laws regulating the internet or leave regulation to the market and technologists. Lessig discussed both how government might intentionally regulate the internet and how other entities, social forces and structures could regulate the internet by design and default. Lessig argued that in the absence of government regulation or other collective, democratic interventions, the architecture of the internet, its code, becomes law.

Lessig's efforts to assess alternative schemes for regulating privacy on the Internet were met with serious objections. See, e.g., Paul M. Schwartz, Beyond Lessig's Code for Internet Privacy: Cyberspace Filters, Privacy–Control, and Fair Information Practices, 2000 *Wis. L. Rev.* 743 (2000); Internet Privacy and the State, 32 *Conn. L. Rev.* 815 (2000). Marc Rotenberg, Executive Director of the Electronic Privacy Information Center, was one of Lessig's most knowledgeable critics. Rotenberg argued that Lessig underestimated the capacity of government and public values to beneficially regulate the Internet to protect privacy. According to Rotenberg, a fundamental misunderstanding of the origins, scope and polices behind pre-existing U.S. and European privacy law undercut the cogency of Lessig's intriguing case for P3P and other "code".

MARC ROTENBERG, FAIR INFORMATION PRACTICES AND THE ARCHITECTURE OF PRIVACY: (WHAT LARRY DOESN'T GET)

2001 Stan. Tech. L. Rev. 1 (2001).

Larry Lessig's *Code and Other Laws of Cyberspace* has popularized the view that "code is law." The observation, roughly stated, is that decisions regarding the architecture of the evolving communications infrastructure exercise control over individuals much like legal code, and therefore should be subject to democratic considerations such as accountability and public participation. The argument has attracted critics from the libertarian wing of the cyberintelligentsia who see it as an invitation to government intervention and supporters on the liberal/communitarian/progressive (choose one) side who at last have a richly argued intellectual framework with which to explore the role of the public in the decisions made by large private entities. * * *

Lessig's characterization of the development of actual privacy law and specifically the EU Data Directive is simply not accurate. * * *

While it is true that the [1996 European Union] Data Directive takes a more comprehensive approach to privacy protection in the private sector than does current U.S. law, it can easily be shown that the EU Data Directive came about in response to the economic requirements of the integration of the European national markets in the early 1990's. The harmonization of national law was necessary to promote the free flow of goods, services, labor and capital across the EU's internal borders. United States privacy law, in contrast, is derived from an effort to regulate intrusive monitoring practices made possible by new technologies * * *.

He next says that the basis of the EU Data Directive is "notice and choice," which is an odd reformulation of a comprehensive legal framework that addresses a wide range of privacy interests, from access and control to security and remedies. The * * * "notice and choice" formulation of privacy protection is a relatively recent creation of the U.S. marketing industry that, embraced by the Federal Trade Commission, almost purposefully attempts to negate the range of rights that are to be found in the EU Data Directive. Prior to the recent efforts of industry to develop a self-regulatory alternative to the EU Directive, European privacy law would have been characterized as "omnibus," by way of contrast to U.S. privacy law, which was termed "sectional." There was no general disagreement about the underlying interests that the law would protect, just differences in the scope of application. * * * [T]he structure, purpose and provisions of privacy law between the U.S. and the European countries revealed a high degree of similarity.

The traditional complement to "notice" had long been "consent," and the problem that attracted privacy scholars and policymakers was to determine what would constitute adequate or meaningful consent. Under the EU privacy regime, meaningful consent typically required "opt-in," i.e., in the absence of affirmative action by the individual, the company simply could not make use of personal information for purposes unrelated to the transaction at hand. U.S. privacy law also followed an opt-in regime, particularly in the medical records field. However, industry groups and the Direct Marketing Association in particular urged the less burdensome "opt-out" regime, which allows businesses to go forward with various uses of personal data as long as there are some means (however burdensome or inefficient) for consumer objections. In the United States, the opt-out regime was typically viewed as what industry was prepared to do and not what the public wanted done.

The "notice and choice" formulation put forward by the Direct Marketing Association in 1996 provided an opportunity for the marketing industry to avoid resolving the difficult problem of what would constitute meaningful consent. But it had this odd (and for business, highly advantageous) consequence: while both opt-in and opt-out presumed a limited, purpose-specific disclosure of personal information, albeit with differing allocations of burden, the "choice" formulation opened the policy world to the notion that there could be many diverse uses for personal information; instead of asking about a narrow and unrelated use of personal data, companies now were free to propose a wide range of uses for information that might otherwise be kept confidential * * *.

This approach was clearly at odds with the general aim of privacy law in both the United States and Europe to limit the collection and use of personal data; it went against the specific European principle of "finality" that makes clear the need to limit data collection to a specific purpose. Indeed, much of privacy law is premised on the idea of discrete transactions involving the transfer of personal information from individual to institution where it is the individual's expectation—and the institution's responsibility—to ensure that the information will only be used for a well-defined, stated purpose. When you provide information to a state Department of Motor Vehicles, for example, what "choices" over the use of that data, other than to enable your receipt of a license, would you exercise? Likewise, when you answer your doctor's question about the whether you have been sleeping well at night, what choice would you exercise other than to obtain appropriate care from the doctor?

The problems with the choice formulation also become apparent if one is willing to analogize privacy protection to other forms of health and safety protection. How much choice, for example, should consumers have in the quality of car brakes or airbags? The choice concept also imagines the creation of perfect market conditions where consumers are suddenly negotiating over a range of uses for personal information. Subtly, but powerfully and profoundly, the substitution of "notice and choice" for "notice and consent" transferred the protection of privacy from the legal realm, and from an emphasis on the articulation of rights and responsibilities, to the marketplace, where consumers would now be forced to pay for what the law could otherwise provide. * * *

Lessig [goes on to support a technique of privacy protection called] Platform for Privacy Preferences. This system facilitates the collection of personal information from individuals visiting commercial websites by enabling a "negotiation" over privacy "preferences." (The P3P standard was developed by a group of private companies, known as the World Wide Web Consortium, that attempt to control many of the technical standards for the Internet.) Lessig notes that P3P is not without faults; he says that the larger point is to "imagine an architecture, tied to the market, that protects privacy rights * * *." To make P3P viable, Lessig says that it would be necessary to establish property rights in personal information. "P3P is the architecture to facilitate that negotiation; the law is the rule that says negotiation must occur."

Lessig treats those who might be skeptical of the P3P/property regime dismissively, as extremists or leftists. This is convenient shorthand that avoids the need to actually engage in a substantive discussion. But the more telling problem with the proposal is that Lessig does not attempt to place his solution in the context of any other regime for privacy protection. P3P simply exists as an opportunity to code a solution. * * *

Still, the argument over P3P is not simply a debate over the pros and cons of a particular approach to the privacy problem. It is rather a battle over public code versus private code, an argument about whether the designers of the communications infrastructure should be accountable to the views of lawyers, policymakers and especially citizens, or whether they should be free to pursue whatever architecture provides private advantage. P3P is a form of private code, much like the Windows operating system, that reflects a particular institution's views of how choices and behavior should be constrained in cyberspace. It elevates notice and choice as a preferred method for privacy protection and downplays the role and history of Fair Information Practices. It maps nicely to the anti-regulatory views espoused by industry but not at all to the well-established tradition of privacy protection in law. P3P is in the end an invitation to reject privacy as a political value that can be protected in law and to ask individuals to now bargain with those in possession of their secrets over how much privacy they can afford. * * *

P3P arose at a particular point in time. There was growing support in the United States for comprehensive privacy legislation and the U.S. trading partners favored this outcome as well. But business was reluctant to support this approach and did not want its new practices, its code, to be subject to public regulation. And so an extended architecture of notice and choice was put forward as a privacy solution. This was, at the end of the day, little more than the old "opt-out" box offered by the Direct Marketing Association whenever the DMA was pressed to provide a privacy solution. All of the problems of compliance, burden, enforcement, and effectiveness that were known about the DMA's opt-out program were present in the design of P3P. * * *

Lessig [too quickly] tosses aside his own calls for the development of code that reflects public values and public interests. Even Lessig's call for a property-based notion of privacy in the context of his other arguments in favor of government regulation seems odd and out of place. Lessig expresses a preference for property regimes over privacy legislation, what he calls liability regimes. The preference for a property regime over a liability regime is that it allows individuals to exercise choice, to negotiate, and to obtain value.

This analysis presupposes that individuals have a general interest in alienating the value of private information in the marketplace. Admittedly this is a popular argument in some corners, but where is the proof? Whereas Lessig analogizes the exercise of property rights in personal information to the sale of a used car, a common commercial transaction, the better analogy may be to vacation photographs or a high school diploma. Both the photographs and the diploma are items personal to the individual. A property regime allows the individual to exercise control over these items, to exclude others from use, but it is hardly intended to facilitate sale. It could well be argued that those items that are most personal to us are those where the disparity between what a willing buyer and a willing seller will pay is the largest. Do we really want to create markets in these circumstances so that individuals are encouraged to disclose—to alienate in the market—their HIV status, their email correspondence with colleagues, or their love letters from high school? Certainly it is a property-based regime that allows an individual to exercise control over these items and incidents of private life, but this is not a regime that, generally understood, encourages one to sell these things to others.

Brandeis and Warren understood the problem with market-based approaches to privacy when they wrote the article on the right to privacy more than a century ago. They purposefully distinguished a privacy right from an intellectual property claim, noting that copyright typically protects an interest once publication occurs, privacy protects a right to simply not publish. * * *

A regulatory regime brings other benefits. In the privacy field, it will likely mean a government office with the expertise and authority to advocate on privacy matters. When, for example, a proposal is put forward by law enforcement to develop techniques for wiretapping, governments with privacy agencies, that is to say governments that have a regulatory structure to protect privacy which includes a privacy agency, will have also to contend with the competing claims of citizens' privacy interests. Indeed, this has happened repeatedly in the last few years as countries with privacy regulations and privacy offices have rebuffed calls for expanded police surveillance while those that lack such agencies have remained in control of law enforcement agencies.

Privacy agencies also provide an effective resource for consumers with privacy concerns and are often times able to respond to privacy complaints without extensive and costly litigation. Such agencies also provide a source of expertise and advice for emerging privacy issues. This has been the experience not only of privacy agencies in Europe but also of those in Canada.

A property-based regime of the type Lessig describes lacks any commitment to an institutional structure (or more broadly democratic institutions) that could be established to protect an underlying public interest. Privacy interests that cannot be expressed in the marketplace through the exercise of P3P preferences simply do not exist. Again interests of common concern are pushed aside in the name of promoting market-based negotiation. Such an approach implicates not only public values but also public debate and public institutions.

A regulatory regime also allows the design of an architecture that reflects public values as opposed to simply private market power. Consider, once again, the resolution of the Caller ID debate. What would the result have been in the absence of a regulatory framework? The telephone companies would simply have announced that the new network architecture enables the disclosure of calling numbers to call recipients and the blocking of such numbers by call recipients. The telephone company would have offered services that allowed customers, for a price, to obtain the number of the calling party or, for a price, to withhold disclosure of one's number when calling another person. If ideal market conditions prevailed, it is even conceivable that the telephone company could price such services on a call by call basis. The telephone company would, under this scenario, become a very rich auctioneer, while telephone customers collectively would see the control of disclosure over personal information significantly diminished.

Why does Lessig settle for P3P? It is possible he genuinely believes it will work. It may also be, consistent with the somewhat pessimistic conclusion of the book, that he simply assumes that government will not succeed in its efforts to regulate the Internet to protect privacy.

DISCUSSION DRAFT OF PRIVACY LEGISLATION

(May 4, 2010).

U.S. Representatives Rick Boucher (VA), Chairman of the Subcommittee on Communications, Technology, and the Internet and Cliff Stearns (FLA) Ranking Member of the Subcommittee

PRIVACY DISCUSSION DRAFT EXECUTIVE SUMMARY

Broadband networks are a primary driver of the national economy, and it is fundamentally in the nation's interest to encourage their expanded use. One clear way Congress can promote greater use of the Internet is to assure individuals a high degree of privacy protection, including transparency about the collection, use and sharing of information about them, and to give them control over that collection, use and sharing, both online and offline.

A set of meaningful privacy protections for Internet users will be particularly important as a means of encouraging the trend toward cloud computing.

Online advertising supports much of the commercial content, applications and services that are available on the Internet today without charge, and this legislation will not disrupt this well established and successful business model. It simply extends to consumers these baseline privacy protections:

Disclosure of privacy practices: Any company that collects personally identifiable information about individuals must conspicuously display a clearly-written, understandable privacy policy that explains how information about individuals is collected, used and disclosed.

Collection and use of information: As a general rule, companies may collect information about individuals unless an individual affirmatively opts out of that collection. Opt-out consent also applies when a website relies upon services delivered by another party to effectuate a first party transaction, such as the serving of ads on that website.

No consent is required to collect and use operational or transactional data—the routine web logs or session cookies that are necessary for the functioning of the website—or to use aggregate data or data that has been rendered anonymous.

Companies need an individual's express opt-in consent to knowingly collect sensitive information about an individual, including information that relates to an individual's medical records, financial accounts, Social Security number, sexual orientation, government-issued identifiers and precise geographic location information.

Disclosure of information to unaffiliated parties: An individual has a reasonable expectation that a company will not share that person's information with unrelated third parties. If a company wants to share an individual's personally-identifiable information with unaffiliated third parties other than for an operational or transactional purpose, the individual must grant affirmative permission for that sharing.

Many websites work with third-party advertising networks, which collect information about a person or an IP address from numerous websites, create a profile and target ads based on that profile. The bill creates an exception to the opt-in consent requirement for third-party information sharing by applying opt-out consent to the sharing of an individual's information with a third-party ad network if there is a clear, easy-to-find link to a webpage for the ad network that allows a person to edit his or her profile, and if he chooses, to opt out of having a profile, provided that the ad network does not share the individual's information with anyone else.

Implementation and enforcement: The Federal Trade Commission would adopt rules to implement and enforce the measure. States may also enforce the FTC's rules through State attorneys general or State consumer protection agencies.

2. CHILDREN'S ONLINE PRIVACY PROTECTION ACT OF 1998 (COPPA)

a. Design and Purposes of COPPA—Data Protection

FEDERAL TRADE COMMISSION—PRIVACY INITIATIVES, CHILDREN'S ONLINE PRIVACY PROTECTION ACT (COPPA), 15 U.S.C. § 6501–06

http://www.ftc.gov/privacy/privacyinitiatives/childrens.html.

Children's Privacy: The Children's Online Privacy Protection Act

The primary goal of the Children's Online Privacy Protection Act (COPPA) Rule is to give parents control over what information is collected from their children online and how such information may be used.

The Rule applies to:

● Operators of commercial Web sites and online services directed to children under 13 that collect personal information from them;

● Operators of general audience sites that knowingly collect personal information from children under 13; and

● Operators of general audience sites that have a separate children's area and that collect personal information from children under 13.

The Rule requires operators to:

● Post a privacy policy on the homepage of the Web site and link to the privacy policy on every page where personal information is collected.

- Provide notice about the site's information collection practices to parents and obtain verifiable parental consent before collecting personal information from children.

- Give parents a choice as to whether their child's personal information will be disclosed to third parties.

- Provide parents access to their child's personal information and the opportunity to delete the child's personal information and opt-out of future collection or use of the information.

- Not condition a child's participation in a game, contest or other activity on the child's disclosing more personal information than is reasonably necessary to participate in that activity.

- Maintain the confidentiality, security and integrity of personal information collected from children.

In order to encourage active industry self-regulation, COPPA also includes a *safe harbor* provision allowing industry groups and others to request Commission approval of self-regulatory guidelines to govern participating Web sites' compliance with the Rule.

ANITA L. ALLEN, MINOR DISTRACTIONS

38 Houston L. Rev. 751 (2001).

Policymakers, business concerns, educators, and parents who supported passage of COPPA believed the legislation could reduce the risk of one class of harms posed by the new economy to children who use computers: imprudent disclosures of personal information by children to e-businesses. A 1996 report of the Center for Media Education noted that the "interactive nature of the Internet gives marketers unprecedented power to gather detailed personal information from children." In May 2000, researchers at the University of Pennsylvania's Annenberg Public Policy Center released a study showing that children are more likely to reveal personal family information than their parents online.

COPPA, like the Family Educational Rights and Privacy Act of 1976 ("FERPA"), purports to protect children's informational privacy by investing parents with the right to bar certain disclosures of information to third parties. Some privacy advocates argue that COPPA's paternalism is more problematic than FERPA's because COPPA limits children's access to the World Wide Web, the most powerful single source of knowledge and vehicle of communication of all time.

COPPA requires "verifiable parental consent for the collection, use or disclosure of personal information" obtained from children. Under COPPA Section 1302 (1): "The term 'child' means any individual under the age of 13." The statute applies to children under 13, although older children disclose financial information about themselves and their household's as well. In fact a study by Professor Joseph Turow of the University of Pennsylvania suggested that teenagers may be a bigger problem for online disclosures private information about their households than children under 13.

Fair information practice standards first promulgated in the 1970s are embodied in COPPA's requirements of notice, access, and security. COPPA requires certain fair information practices of covered Web sites. For example, operators must provide clear "notice" on the web site of what information the operator collects and how the operator will use and/or disclose information collected from children. COPPA requires that operators provide parents with: (1) "a description of the specific types of personal information collected from the child by [the] operator"; (2) "the opportunity at any time to refuse to permit the operator's further use or maintenance * * * of personal information from that child"; and (3) "a means that is reasonable * * * for the parent to obtain any personal information collected from that child."

The second requirement, that parents be permitted to prohibit further use of information at any time, is a particularly strong consumer right vis-à-vis the commercial sector. This requirement merits special emphasis. The right of parents is not simply an ordinary right to "opt out" of unwanted third-party disclosures, or even a right to limit secondary uses of information. These ordinary rights appear in many formulations of fair information practices. Under COPPA, parents are ascribed a powerful right to veto primary collection, primary use, secondary use, and even maintenance of data. This strong right goes beyond typical formulations of fair information practices.

The strong veto right is needed to further the objectives of the statute. COPPA's parental veto rule is clearly needed to effect meaningful parental control. COPPA confers to parents the power to function as gatekeepers of children and families' personal information; and because small children sometimes slip personal information under the gate, parental power to recapture information previously disclosed is critical. An adult lacks the power to recapture personal data concerning household income and habits that he, she, a spouse or older teen have rashly disclosed. But under COPPA that same adult is able to recapture data imprudently disclosed by a young child. COPPA has no exceptions for "mature minors," analogous to the required exceptions to laws requiring parental notification or consent for abortion services. In the realm of data privacy, unlike the realm of reproductive privacy, for children under thirteen, parents rule absolutely.

Parents cannot waive the protection entailed by certain COPPA requirements and prohibitions. For example, COPPA requires operators to establish procedures to protect the "confidentiality, security, and integrity of personal information collected from children." This obligation cannot be avoided through parental waivers. Nor can COPPA's prohibition against operators conditioning a child's participation in online activities (for example, games and prizes) on the provision of more personal information than is reasonably necessary to participate in the activity. This last prohibition disables the use of incentives that would turn simple children's games into data bonanzas for online businesses. Policymakers did not want e-commerce to have this ability even if particular parents are indifferent.

COPPA section 6503 provides a safe harbor for operators who follow Commission-approved self-regulatory guidelines issued by representatives of the marketing or online industries or other designated persons. Several groups and companies applied for safe harbor status right away. To encourage compliance and limit the need for formal enforcement actions, the FTC seeks to educate the public. The FTC operates multiple Web sites designed to educate the public about privacy online. For example, colorful, consumer-friendly FTC Web site called "Kidzprivacy" seeks to educate parents and children about online informational privacy, and about their rights and powers under COPPA.

COPPA authorizes the FTC to enforce its provisions. The FTC can bring enforcement actions under COPPA and impose civil penalties. Even before COPPA went into effect, the FTC displayed an interest in the privacy of young families. The FTC's first internet privacy complaint was a deceptive practices suit brought and settled in 1998 against GeoCities. The Commission alleged that "GeoCities misled its customers, both children and adults, by not telling the truth about how it was using their personal information." The settlement required GeoCities to ensure parental control by obtaining parental consent prior to collecting personal information from children twelve and under. According to the FTC, industry self-regulatory guidelines already in effect in 1998 but ignored by GeoCities, urged sites to obtain parental consent for at least some transactions with children.

In another pre-COPPA case, on May 6, 1999, the FTC announced that The Young Investor Web site operated by Liberty Financial Services, a large Massachusetts asset management company, had settled an action alleging false promises of anonymity. As reported by the FTC, the Web site operators used contests, prizes and promises of anonymity to induce children to provide detailed financial data about their allowances, stocks, bonds, mutual funds, spending habits, college plans, and family finances.

The FTC initiated its first enforcement action under COPPA in a case alleging a violation of the provision against the conditioning of participation in a contest on disclosures of personal information. On July 21, 2000, the Commission filed an enforcement action under COPPA against Toysmart.com, concurrent with its settlement of charges that Toysmart had violated its own privacy policy when it sought to sell its customer database to discharge obligations in bankruptcy. The firm's policy had been reviewed and approved by TRUSTe, an industry self-regulation group. The COPPA violation alleged against Toysmart was that a trivia contest, which first appeared on the Toysmart Web site in May 2000, collected personal information from children under thirteen without obtaining the consent of the children's parents. The contest conditioned participation on the disclosure of personal information.

On April 19, 2001, the FTC announced the settlements of its first line of civil penalty cases brought under COPPA. Monarch Services, Inc. and Girls Life, Inc., operators of www.girlslife.com; Bigmailbox.com, Inc., and Nolan Quan, operators of www.bigmailbox.com; and Looksmart Ltd., operator of www.insidetheweb.com, were charged with violating COPPA by illegally collecting personal information from children under thirteen years of age without parental consent and requiring children to disclose more personal information than was needed for participation in the activities involved. To settle the charges, the operators agreed to pay $100,000 in civil penalties. Furthermore, the settlements bar any future COPPA violations and require the companies to delete all personally identifying information collected from children online at any time since COPPA became effective. In addition, the operators will post a privacy policy on their Web site that complies with the law, as well as a link to www.ftc.gov/kidzprivacy, the FTC's site that provides information about COPPA.

b.   FTC COPPA Compliance Actions/ http://www.ftc.gov/

"ICONIX BRAND GROUP SETTLES CHARGES ITS APPAREL WEB SITES VIOLATED CHILDREN'S ONLINE PRIVACY PROTECTION ACT"

October 20, 2009.

Company Will Pay $250,000 Civil Penalty

Iconix Brand Group, Inc. will pay a $250,000 civil penalty to settle Federal Trade Commission charges that it violated the Children's Online Privacy Protection Act (COPPA) and the FTC's COPPA Rule by knowingly collecting, using, or disclosing personal information from children online without first obtaining their parents' permission.

Iconix owns, licenses, and markets—both offline and online—several popular apparel brands that appeal to children and teens, including Mudd, Candie's, Bongo, and OP. Iconix required consumers on many of its brand-specific Web sites to provide personal information, such as full name, e-mail address, zip code, and in some cases mailing address, gender, and phone number—as well as date of birth—in order to receive brand updates, enter sweepstakes contests, and participate in interactive brand-awareness campaigns and other Web site features. Since 2006, Iconix knowingly collected and stored personal information from approximately 1,000 children without first notifying their parents or obtaining parental consent, according to the FTC's complaint. On one Web site, MyMudd-World.com, Iconix also enabled girls to publicly share personal stories and photos online, according to the complaint.

"Companies must provide parents with the opportunity to say 'no thanks' to the collection and disclosure of their children's personal information," said FTC Chairman Jon Leibowitz. "Children's privacy is paramount, and Iconix really missed the boat by denying parents control over their kids' information online."

COPPA requires operators of Web sites directed to children under 13 years old that collect personal information from them—and operators of general audience Web sites that knowingly collect personal information from children under 13—to notify parents and obtain their consent before collecting, using, or disclosing any such information. One requirement of the COPPA Rule is that Web site operators post a privacy policy that is clear, understandable, and complete.

The Commission's complaint also charges Iconix with violating both COPPA and the Federal Trade Commission Act by falsely stating in its privacy policy that it would not seek to collect personal information from children without obtaining prior parental consent, and that it would delete any children's personal information about which it became aware. According to the FTC complaint, Iconix knowingly collected personal information from children without obtaining prior parental consent and did not delete it.

The settlement order requires Iconix to pay a $250,000 civil penalty. The order also specifically prohibits Iconix from violating any provision of the FTC's COPPA Rule, and requires the company to delete all personal information collected and maintained in violation of COPPA. The company is required to distribute the order and the FTC's "How to Comply with the Children's Online Privacy Protection Rule" to company personnel. The order also contains standard compliance, reporting, and record-keeping provisions to help ensure the company abides by its terms.

To provide resources to parents and their children about COPPA and about children's privacy in general, the order requires the company to link to the Commission's www.OnGuardOnline.gov Web site on any Iconix Web site that collects or discloses children's personal information, and on any Iconix site that offers the opportunity to upload writings or images, to create publicly viewable user profiles, or to interact online with other Iconix site visitors.

The Commission vote approving the complaint and consent order was 4–0. On behalf of FTC, the Department of Justice is filing the complaint today in the U.S. District Court for the Southern District of New York, and submitting the consent order for the court's approval.

"XANGA.COM TO PAY $1 MILLION FOR VIOLATING COPPA PRIVACY PROTECTION RULE"

September 7, 2006.

Civil Penalty Against Social Networking Site Is Largest Ever for a COPPA Violation

Social networking Web site operators Xanga.com, Inc. and its principals, Marc Ginsburg and John Hiler, will pay a $1 million civil penalty for allegedly violating the Children's Online Privacy Protection Act (COPPA) and its implementing Rule, under the terms of a settlement with the Federal Trade Commission announced today.

According to the FTC, Xanga.com collected, used, and disclosed personal information from children under the age of 13 without first notifying parents and obtaining their consent. The penalty is the largest ever assessed by the FTC for a COPPA violation, and is more than twice the next largest penalty.

The complaint charges that the defendants had actual knowledge they were collecting and disclosing personal information from children. The Xanga site stated that children under 13 could not join, but then allowed visitors to create Xanga accounts even if they provided a birth date indicating they were under 13. Further, they failed to notify the children's parents of their information practices or provide the parents with access to and control over their children's information. The defendants created 1.7 million Xanga accounts over the past five years for users who submitted age information indicating they were under 13.

"Protecting kids' privacy online is a top priority for America's parents, and for the FTC," said FTC Chairman Deborah Platt Majoras. "COPPA requires all commercial Web sites, including operators of social networking sites like Xanga, to give parents notice and obtain their consent before collecting personal information from kids they know are under 13. A million-dollar penalty should make that obligation crystal clear."

Xanga.com—Xanga.com is one of the most popular social networking sites on the Internet. After setting up a personal profile, users can post information about themselves for other users to read and respond to. On Xanga.com, users can create their own pages or Web logs (blogs) that contain profile information, online journals, text, hypertext images, as well as links to audio, video, and other files or sites. Information on the Xanga site is available to the general public through the use of global search engines such as Google and Yahoo.

Incorporated in 1999 and based in New York City, privately held Xanga.com, Inc. was founded by Ginsburg and Hiler. In 2005, Xanga had about 25 million registered accounts.

The Commission's Complaint—According to the Commission's complaint, the defendants violated COPPA, the COPPA Rule, and the FTC Act by collecting personal information from children with actual knowledge that they were under the age of 13, failing to post on their site sufficient notice of their information practices regarding children, failing to notify parents directly about their information practices regarding children, and failing to obtain verifiable parental consent before collecting, using, or disclosing children's personal information. The complaint also alleges the defendants failed to provide parents with reasonable access to and control over their children's information on the Xanga.com site.

The Consent Order—The consent order is designed to prohibit Xanga, Ginsburg, and Hiler from violating COPPA and the COPPA Rule in the future. Accordingly, it contains strong conduct provisions that will be monitored by the FTC. The order specifically prohibits the defendants from violating any provision of the Rule and requires them to delete all personal information collected and maintained by the site in violation of the Rule. The defendants further must distribute the order and the FTC's How to Comply with the Children's Online Privacy Protection Rule to certain company personnel. The order also contains standard compliance, reporting, and record keeping provisions to help ensure the defendants abide by its terms.

To provide resources to parents and their children about the risks associated with social networking sites, the order additionally requires the defendants to provide links on certain of their sites to FTC consumer education materials for the next five years. First, the defendants must include a link to the Children's Privacy section of the Commission's ftc.gov site on any site they operate that is subject to COPPA. Second, the defendants must include links to the Commission's recently published safety tips for social networking on any of their social networking sites.

The order requires the defendants to pay a civil penalty of $1 million for violating the COPPA Rule, as detailed above.

The Commission vote approving the complaint and consent decree and order was 5–0. They were filed by the Department of Justice on the FTC's behalf on September 7, 2006, in the U.S. District Court for the Southern District of New York.

"FTC RECEIVES LARGEST COPPA CIVIL PENALTIES TO DATE IN SETTLEMENTS WITH MRS. FIELDS COOKIES AND HERSHEY FOODS"

February 27, 2003.

FTC Alleges Companies' Web Sites Violated Children's Online Privacy Protection Act

Mrs. Fields Cookies and Hershey Foods Corporation have each agreed to settle Federal Trade Commission charges that their Web sites violated the Children's Online Privacy Protection Act (COPPA) Rule by collecting personal information from children without first obtaining the proper parental consent. Mrs. Fields will pay civil penalties of $100,000 and Hershey will pay civil penalties of $85,000. The separate settlements bar the companies from violating the Rule in the future and represent the biggest COPPA penalties awarded to date.

"These settlements offer food for thought for anyone who operates a Web site that caters to kids," said Howard Beales, Director of the FTC's Bureau of Consumer Protection. "If your Web site collects personal information from children, comply with the law or face the consequences."

The COPPA Rule applies to operators of commercial Web sites and online services directed to children under the age of 13 and to general audience Web sites and online services that knowingly collect personal information from children under 13. Among other things, the Rule requires that Web site operators obtain verifiable consent from a parent or guardian *before* they collect personal information from children.

According to the FTC complaints, the Mrs. Fields and Hershey sites each violated the COPPA Rule when they failed to obtain verifiable parental consent before collecting personal information from children under 13. In addition, the sites allegedly failed to post adequate privacy policies, to provide direct notice to parents about the information they were collecting and how it would be used, and to provide a reasonable means for parents to review the personal information collected from their children and to refuse to permit its further use.

Mrs. Fields Cookies

According to the FTC, portions of Mrs. Fields' Web sites—mrsfields.com, pretzeltime.com, and pretzelmaker.com—were directed to children. These Web pages offered birthday clubs for children 12 or under and provided birthday greetings and coupons for free cookies or pretzels. While Mrs. Fields did not disseminate the information it collected to third parties, the company allegedly collected personal information—including full name, home address, e-mail address and birth date—from more than 84,000 children, without first obtaining parental consent.

Hershey Foods Corporation

Hershey operates more than 30 Web sites—many of which are candy-related sites directed to children. On a number of these sites, the company allegedly employed a method of obtaining parental consent that does not meet the standard delineated under the COPPA Rule. Specifically, Hershey instructed children under 13 to have their parents fill in an online parental consent form. The FTC alleges the company took no steps to ensure that a parent or guardian saw or filled out the consent forms. The FTC further alleges that even if a parent or guardian did not submit information on the consent form, the company proceeded to collect personal information—including full name, home address, e-mail address and age—from children. According to the complaint, this method of obtaining parental consent was not reasonably calculated to ensure that the person providing consent was the child's parent. This is the first COPPA case to challenge a company's method of obtaining parental consent.

The settlements bar future COPPA violations, require that the companies delete any information collected in violation of COPPA, require civil penalty payments, and contain certain record-keeping requirements to allow the FTC to monitor the companies' compliance with the order.

The Commission vote to approve the complaints and consent decrees was 5–0. The U.S. Department of Justice filed the Hershey Foods complaint and consent decree in the U.S. District Court for the Middle District of Pennsylvania in Harrisburg, and the Mrs. Fields complaint and consent decree were filed in the U.S. District Court for the District of Utah, Central Division on February 26, 2003 at the request of the FTC.

"FTC ANNOUNCES SETTLEMENT WITH BANKRUPT WEBSITE, TOYSMART.COM, REGARDING ALLEGED PRIVACY POLICY VIOLATIONS"

July 21, 2000.

In a settlement announced today by the Federal Trade Commission, Toysmart.com ("Toysmart") has agreed to settle charges the company violated Section 5 of the FTC Act by misrepresenting to consumers that personal information would never be shared with third parties and then disclosing, selling, or offering that information for sale in violation of the company's own privacy statement. The agreement forbids the sale of this customer information except under very limited circumstances.

The Commission also announced today that it will file an amended complaint with the U.S. District Court in Massachusetts alleging that Toysmart collected personal information from children in violation of the Children's Online Privacy Protection Act of 1998 ("COPPA") and its implementing regulations. The FTC's regulations went into effect on April 21, 2000, and this is the first complaint the Commission has filed alleging a violation of COPPA. COPPA requires that operators of commercial Web sites and online services directed to children under 13, and general audience sites that know that they are collecting personal information from children, obtain parents' consent before personal information is collected from their children. The amended complaint against Toysmart alleges that the site collected names, e-mail addresses, and ages of children under 13 without notifying parents or obtaining parental consent.

"Customer data collected under a privacy agreement should not be auctioned off to the highest bidder," according to Jodie Bernstein, Director of the FTC's Bureau of Consumer Protection. "This settlement protects consumers from a winner-take-all bid in bankruptcy court, ensuring only a family-oriented Web site willing to buy the entire Toysmart Web site has the ability to do so."

Bernstein added: "The settlement also protects customers of Toysmart from unilateral privacy policy changes in the future by a bankruptcy purchaser. Any change in the original Toysmart policy will have to be approved by consumers on an 'opt-in' basis before the successor company can make such a change."

Bernstein also stated that "this settlement shows that the FTC is serious about enforcing the Children's Online Privacy Protection Act. This is the first charge brought under COPPA, and is only the start of our efforts to ensure that Web sites that gather information from children under 13 comply with the parental notification requirements of the law."

Until recently, Toysmart was a popular Web site that marketed and sold educational and non-violent children's toys over the Internet. Through its Web site, Toysmart collected detailed personal information about its visitors, including name, address, billing information, shopping preferences, and family profiles—which included the names and birthdates of children. Since September 1999, Toysmart has posted a privacy policy which states that information collected from customers will never be shared with third parties. When it ran into financial difficulties, however, it attempted to sell all of its assets, including its detailed customer databases, and on July 10, 2000, the FTC filed a lawsuit in the U.S. District Court for the District of Massachusetts against Toysmart to prevent the sale of the customer information.

The settlement announced today resolves the issues in that lawsuit. The company is currently in Chapter 11 bankruptcy, in a case pending in the U.S. Bankruptcy Court for the District of Massachusetts, in Boston. Toysmart's motion to sell its assets, including the customer information, is set for hearing July 26, 2000.

Under the settlement agreement, Toysmart will file an order today in Bankruptcy Court ("Bankruptcy Order"), prohibiting Toysmart from selling the customer list as a stand-alone asset. The settlement only allows a sale of such lists as a package which includes the entire Web site, and only to a "Qualified Buyer"—an entity that is in a related market and that expressly agrees to be Toysmart's successor-in-interest as to the customer information.

The Qualified Buyer must abide by the terms of the Toysmart privacy statement. If the buyer wishes to make changes to that policy, it must follow certain procedures to protect consumers. It may not change how the information previously collected by Toysmart is used, unless it provides notice to consumers and obtains their affirmative consent ("opt-in") to the new uses.

In the event that the Bankruptcy Court does not approve the sale of the customer information to a Qualified Buyer or a plan of reorganization within the next year, Toysmart must delete or destroy all customer information. In the interim, Toysmart is obligated to abide by its privacy statement.

After the Bankruptcy Order is approved, the FTC will also file a stipulated consent agreement and final order before the U.S. District Court, Massachusetts ("District Court Order"), enjoining the unlawful practices alleged in the Complaint, prohibiting Toysmart from making any false or misleading statements about the disclosure of personal information to third parties, and prohibiting Toysmart from disclosing, selling, or offering for sale to any third party any customer information, except as provided for in the Bankruptcy Order.

The District Court Order requires that Toysmart immediately delete or destroy all information collected in violation of COPPA. The District Court Order also requires that Toysmart confirm through a sworn statement under penalty of perjury that it has never previously violated its privacy statement.

The Commission vote to approve the settlement was 3–2, with Commissioners Sheila F. Anthony and Orson Swindle voting against the settlement, and with Commissioner Mozelle W. Thompson issuing a separate statement.

In her statement, Commissioner Anthony declared that the terms of the negotiated settlement were insufficient to protect consumer privacy. Anthony stated: "To accept the bankruptcy settlement would place business concerns ahead of consumer privacy. Although the proposed settlement's definition of a qualified buyer attempts to ensure that only an entity 'similar' to Toysmart is eligible to purchase the list, I do not believe that this limitation is an adequate proxy for consumer privacy interests. In my view, consumer privacy would be better protected by requiring that consumers themselves be given notice and choice before their detailed personal information is shared with or used by another corporate entity— especially where, as here, consumers provided that information pursuant to a promise not to transfer it."

Commissioner Swindle argued against any sale of the consumer information collected by Toysmart. Swindle said: "I agree that a sale to a third party under the terms of the Bankruptcy Order would be a substantial improvement over the sale that likely would have occurred without Commission action. Nevertheless, I do not think that the Commission should allow the sale.

If we really believe that consumers attach great value to the privacy of their personal information and that consumers should be able to limit access to such information through private agreements with businesses, we should compel businesses to honor the promises they make to consumers to gain access to this information. Toysmart promised its customers that their personal information would *never* be sold to a third party, but the Bankruptcy Order in fact would allow a sale to a third party. In my view, such a sale should not be permitted because 'never' really means never."

In his statement approving the settlement, Commissioner Thompson underlined the fact that Toysmart's customer database—its most valuable asset in bankruptcy—is intrinsically linked to its privacy policy. "In building this asset, however, Toysmart made a covenant with its customers; the company's lack of success does not extinguish this important obligation which forms the very basis for the existence of the asset." Thompson added that his "decision to approve the settlement is not without reservation. Like my colleagues Commissioner Anthony and Commissioner Swindle, I think that consumers would benefit from notice and choice before a company transfers their information to a corporate successor." He concluded by urging "any successor to provide Toysmart customers with notice and an opportunity to 'opt out' as a matter of good will and business practice."

3. CHILD ONLINE PROTECTION ACT OF 1998 (COPA)

a. Design and Purposes of COPA—Child Safety

Note: *COPA* Versus *COPPA*

The Children's Online Privacy Protection Act (COPPA) and the Child Online Protection Act (COPA) are two statutes from roughly the same era with similar names. But the laws had different purposes. The purpose of COPA was to protect children who use the internet from encountering adult content online. The purpose of COPPA was to make it more difficult for children to disclose personal information to website operators. COPA was beset by constitutional challenges that were never a problem for COPPA. The Supreme Court upheld COPA's reliance on community standards. But in March 2007, the Eastern District Court of Pennsylvania ruled in *ACLU v. Gonzales*, that COPA violates the First and Fifth Amendments. The court permanently enjoined federal prosecutors from enforcing the troubled statute. In January 2009, to the relief of civil libertarians, the Supreme Court denied cert.—placing a nail in COPA's coffin. See the complex string of litigation, American Civil Liberties Union v. Reno, 31 F. Supp.2d 473 (E.D. Pa. 1999), aff'd, 217 F.3d 162 (3d Cir. 2000), vacated and remanded sub nom. Ashcroft v. American Civil Liberties Union, 535 U.S. 564 (2002), aff'd on remand, 322 F.3d 240 (3d Cir. 2003), aff'd and remanded, 542 U.S. 656 (2004), judgment entered by American Civil Liberties Union v. Gonzales, 478 F.Supp.2d 775 (E.D. Pa. 2007), aff'd sub nom. American Civil Liberties Union v. Mukasey, 534 F.3d 181 (3rd Cir. 2008), cert. denied, ___ U.S. ___, 129 S.Ct. 1032 (2009).

Is there something fundamentally misguided about trying to protect children from adult internet content? What type of statute could get around the perceived First Amendment problems? Are there technological solutions to the problem that could circumvent the need for prohibitive laws? Could placing filters on computers used by children do the trick?

b. Constitutional Problems, Privacy Problems

ASHCROFT v. ACLU

535 U.S. 564 (2002).

Justice Thomas announced the judgment of the Court * * *

Congress first attempted to protect children from exposure to pornographic material on the Internet by enacting the Communications Decency Act of 1996 (CDA), 110 Stat. 133. The CDA prohibited the knowing transmission over the Internet of obscene or indecent messages to any recipient under 18 years of age. * * * It also forbade any individual from knowingly sending over or displaying on the Internet certain "patently offensive" material in a manner available to persons under 18 years of age. * * * [I]n Reno v. American Civil Liberties Union, we held that the CDA's regulation of indecent transmissions, and the display of patently offensive material, ran afoul of the First Amendment. We concluded that "the CDA lacked the precision that the First Amendment requires when a statute regulates the content of speech" because, "in order to deny minors access to potentially harmful speech, the CDA effectively suppressed a large amount of speech that adults had a constitutional right to receive and to address to one another." * * *

After our decision in Reno v. American Civil Liberties Union, Congress explored other avenues for restricting minors' access to pornographic material on the Internet. In particular, Congress passed and the President signed into law the Child Online Protection Act. * * * COPA prohibits any person from "knowingly and with knowledge of the character of the material, in interstate or foreign commerce by means of the World Wide Web, making any communication for commercial purposes that is available to any minor and that includes any material that is harmful to minors." 47 U.S.C. § 231 (a)(1).

Apparently responding to our objections to the breadth of the CDA's coverage, Congress limited the scope of COPA's coverage in at least three ways. First, while the CDA applied to communications over the Internet as a whole, including, for example, e-mail messages, COPA applies only to material displayed on the World Wide Web. Second, unlike the CDA, COPA covers only communications made "for commercial purposes." Ibid. And third, while the CDA prohibited "indecent" and "patently offensive" communications, COPA restricts only the narrower category of "material that is harmful to minors." Ibid.

Drawing on the three-part test for obscenity set forth in Miller v. California, 413 U.S. 15 (1973), COPA defines "material that is harmful to minors" as

> "any communication, picture, image, graphic image file, article, recording, writing, or other matter of any kind that is obscene or that—
>
> "(A) the average person, applying contemporary community standards, would find, taking the material as a whole and with respect to minors, is designed to appeal to, or is designed to pander to, the prurient interest;
>
> "(B) depicts, describes, or represents, in a manner patently offensive with respect to minors, an actual or simulated sexual act or sexual contact, an actual or simulated normal or perverted sexual act, or a lewd exhibition of the genitals or post-pubescent female breast; and
>
> "(C) taken as a whole, lacks serious literary, artistic, political, or scientific value for minors." 47 U.S.C. § 231 (e)(6).

Like the CDA, COPA also provides affirmative defenses to those subject to prosecution under the statute. An individual may qualify for a defense if he, "in good faith, has restricted access by minors to material that is harmful to minors—(A) by requiring the use of a credit card, debit account, adult access code, or adult personal identification number; (B) by accepting a digital certificate that verifies age; or (C) by any other reasonable measures that are feasible under available technology.'' § 231(c)(1). Persons violating COPA are subject to both civil and criminal sanctions. A civil penalty of up to $50,000 may be imposed for each violation of the statute. Criminal penalties consist of up to six months in prison and/or a maximum fine of $50,000. An additional fine of $50,000 may be imposed for any intentional violation of the statute. § 231(a).

One month before COPA was scheduled to go into effect, respondents filed a lawsuit challenging the constitutionality of the statute in the United States District Court for the Eastern District of Pennsylvania. Respondents are a diverse group of organizations, most of which maintain their own Web sites. * * * Respondents' Web sites contain ''resources on obstetrics, gynecology, and sexual health; visual art and poetry; resources designed for gays and lesbians; information about books and stock photographic images offered for sale; and online magazines.'' Id., at 484.

In their complaint, respondents alleged that, although they believed that the material on their Web sites was valuable for adults, they feared that they would be prosecuted under COPA because some of that material ''could be construed as 'harmful to minors' in some communities. App. 63. Respondents' facial challenge claimed, inter alia, that COPA violated adults' rights under the First and Fifth Amendments because it (1) ''created an effective ban on constitutionally protected speech by and to adults''; (2) ''[was] not the least restrictive means of accomplishing any compelling governmental purpose''; and (3) ''[was] substantially overbroad.'' Id., at 100–101. * * *

The CDA's use of community standards to identify patently offensive material, however, was particularly problematic in light of that statute's unprecedented breadth and vagueness. The statute covered communications depicting or describing ''sexual or excretory activities or organs'' that were ''patently offensive as measured by contemporary community standards''—a standard somewhat similar to the second prong of Miller's three-prong test. But the CDA did not include any limiting terms resembling Miller's additional two prongs. It neither contained any requirement that restricted material appeal to the prurient interest nor excluded from the scope of its coverage works with serious literary, artistic, political, or scientific value. Ibid. The tremendous breadth of the CDA magnified the impact caused by differences in community standards across the country, restricting Web publishers from openly displaying a significant amount of material that would have constituted protected speech in some communities across the country but run afoul of community standards in others.

COPA, by contrast, does not appear to suffer from the same flaw because it applies to significantly less material than did the CDA and defines the harmful-to-minors material restricted by the statute in a manner parallel to the Miller definition of obscenity. See supra, at 5–6, 10. To fall within the scope of COPA, works must not only ''depict, describe, or represent, in a manner patently offensive with respect to minors,'' particular sexual acts or parts of the anatomy, they must also be designed to appeal to the prurient interest of minors and "taken as a whole, lack serious literary, artistic, political, or scientific value for minors." 47 U.S.C. § 231 (e)(6).

These additional two restrictions substantially limit the amount of material covered by the statute. Material appeals to the prurient interest, for instance, only if it is in some sense erotic * * *. Of even more significance, however, is COPA's exclusion of material with serious value for minors. In Reno, we emphasized that the serious value "requirement is particularly important because, unlike the 'patently offensive' and 'prurient interest' criteria, it is not judged by contemporary community standards." 521 U.S. at 873 * * *. This is because "the value of [a] work [does not] vary from community to community based on the degree of local acceptance it has won." Id., at 500. Rather, the relevant question is "whether a reasonable person would find * * * value in the material, taken as a whole." Thus, the serious value requirement "allows appellate courts to impose some limitations and regularity on the definition by setting, as a matter of law, a national floor for socially redeeming value." Reno, supra, at 873, a safeguard nowhere present in the CDA. * * *

When the scope of an obscenity statute's coverage is sufficiently narrowed by a "serious value" prong and a "prurient interest" prong, we have held that requiring a speaker disseminating material to a national audience to observe varying community standards does not violate the First Amendment. * * *

While Justice Kennedy and Justice Stevens question the applicability of this Court's community standards jurisprudence to the Internet, we do not believe that the medium's "unique characteristics" justify adopting a different approach than that set forth in [precedent]. * * *

Respondents argue that COPA is "unconstitutionally overbroad" because it will require Web publishers to shield some material behind age verification screens that could be displayed openly in many communities across the Nation if Web speakers were able to limit access to their sites on a geographic basis. Brief for Respondents 33–34. "To prevail in a facial challenge," however, "it is not enough for a plaintiff to show 'some' overbreadth." Reno, supra, at 896 (O'CONNOR, J., concurring in judgment in part and dissenting in part). Rather, "the overbreadth of a statute must not only be real, but substantial as well." Broadrick v. Oklahoma, 413 U.S. 601, 615 (1973). At this stage of the litigation, respondents have failed to satisfy this burden, at least solely as a result of COPA's reliance on community standards. Because Congress has narrowed the range of content restricted by COPA in a manner analogous to Miller's definition of obscenity, we conclude, consistent with our holdings in Hamling and Sable, that any variance caused by the statute's reliance on community standards is not substantial enough to violate the First Amendment. * * *

We hold only that COPA's reliance on community standards to identify "material that is harmful to minors" does not by itself render the statute substantially overbroad for purposes of the First Amendment. We do not express any view as to whether COPA suffers from substantial overbreadth for other reasons, whether the statute is unconstitutionally vague, or whether the District Court correctly concluded that the statute likely will not survive strict scrutiny analysis once adjudication of the case is completed below. While respondents urge us to resolve these questions at this time, prudence dictates allowing the Court of Appeals to first examine these difficult issues.

4.   THE CAN–SPAM ACT OF 2003

a.   CAN–SPAM's Purpose

NOTE: ANTI-SPAM LEGISLATION

The Controlling the Assault of Non–Solicited Pornographic and Marketing ("CAN–SPAM") Act of 2003, 15 U.S.C. §§ 7701 et seq., forbids sending certain types of electronic communications—"spam". "Spam" is a term used to refer to unsolicited commercial email sent in bulk, often repeatedly. The term "spam" apparently comes from a 1970 Monty Python Flying Circus skit. In a characteristically wacky scene, a server in a restaurant presents a customer with a menu consisting of nothing but "egg and spam; egg bacon and spam; egg bacon sausage and spam; spam bacon sausage and spam; spam egg spam spam bacon and spam; spam sausage spam spam bacon spam tomato and spam * * *." See David Crystal, *Language and the Internet* (2001), 53.

Like unwanted postal mail and telemarketing telephone calls, a flurry of spam can violate a recipient's sense of privacy. A primary purpose of the CAN–SPAM Act, however, was to address the problem of unsolicited commercial emails with explicit adult, pornographic content. Why did Congress not go after all forms of spam?

The CAN–SPAM Act prohibits false and misleading transmissions of information, and prohibits deceptive subject headings. It regulates the use of return addresses, opt-out options, and automatic creation of multiple email accounts. Special provisions of the Act require that persons sending unsolicited email with adult content label the email appropriately. See *United States v. Cyberheat, Inc.*, 2007 WL 686678 (D. Ariz. 2007). The Act authorizes enforcement actions by the Federal Trade Commission. Substantial penalties are provided for by the statute and at least one court has held that plaintiffs need not mitigate their damages. See *Phillips v. Netblue, Inc.*, 2006 WL 3647116 (N.D. Cal. 2006).

b.   May a State University Block Legal Spam?

WHITE BUFFALO VENTURES v. UNIVERSITY OF TEXAS

420 F.3d 366 (5th Cir. 2005).

JERRY E. SMITH, CIRCUIT JUDGE:

This case involves the regulation of unsolicited, commercial mass electronic messages ("emails") (a species belonging to the larger communication genus often referred to as "spam"). Plaintiff White Buffalo Ventures, LLC ("White Buffalo"), operates several online dating services, including longhornsingles.com, which targets students at the University of Texas at Austin ("UT"). Pursuant to its internal anti-solicitation policy, UT blocked White Buffalo's attempts to send unsolicited bulk commercial email. * * *

The parties do not dispute the facts. UT provides, free of charge, Internet access and email addresses to faculty, staff, and students at the domain "utexas.edu." Owners of electronic mail accounts can access those accounts either on-grounds (by means of wireless connections or of wired, authenticated clusters) or remotely (by means of some other Internet access provider). An owner of a UT user account may, for example, log on from any third-party dial-up or broadband service provider and check for email residing on one of UT's 178 email servers.

UT has a policy of blocking many types of incoming spam, irrespective of commercial content or source authenticity. Under the Regents' Rules, the technology department (the "ITC") implements procedures (1) to block incoming unsolicited, commercial emails and (2) to stop the transmission of such emails.

White Buffalo operates several online dating services, including one, called "longhornsingles.com," that targets UT students. In February 2003, White Buffalo submitted a Public Information Act request seeking all "non-confidential, non-exempt email addresses" held by UT, which responded by disclosing all qualifying email addresses. In April 2003, White Buffalo began sending legal commercial spam to targeted members of the UT community.

UT received several complaints regarding unsolicited email blasts from White Buffalo. UT investigated and determined that White Buffalo had indeed sent unsolicited emails to tens of thousands of UT email account-holders, at which point UT issued a cease and desist letter. White Buffalo refused to comply with that letter, so UT blocked all email ingress from the IP address that was the source address for the unsolicited White Buffalo spam. The filter blocked all email sent from that IP address to addresses containing the "@utexas.edu" string. * * *

In part, CAN–SPAM prohibits fraudulent, abusive and deceptive commercial email, 15 U.S.C. §§ 7703, 7704; provides for enforcement of the Act by federal agencies, states, and Internet service providers ("ISPs"), id. § 7706; and provides for the issuance of regulations to implement the purposes of the Act, id. § 7711. The parties have agreed, in the district court and on appeal, that White Buffalo complied with the requirements of the CAN–SPAM Act. Its email blasts were not unlawful.

Most relevant to White Buffalo's claim is CAN–SPAM'S preemption clause: "This chapter supersedes any statute, regulation, or rule of a State or political subdivision of a State that expressly regulates the use of electronic mail to send commercial messages, except to the extent that any such statute, regulation, or rule prohibits falsity or deception in any portion of a commercial electronic mail message or information attached thereto." § 7707(b)(1). * * *

There are two competing interpretations, both rooted firmly in the text of the Act, of the degree of authority state actors may wield in response to commercial spam. Under the first, state entities may not regulate commercial speech except where that regulation relates to the authenticity of the speech's source and content. Under the second, state entities may implement a variety of non-authenticity related commercial speech restrictions, provided the state entity implementing them is an "Internet access provider."

As a result of Congress's apparent failure to contemplate this question, we must not infer preemption. The textual ambiguity triggers the strong presumption against such a finding, and we cannot be sure whether UT's regulations fall within the ambit of the express preemption clause. UT may therefore implement the Regents' Rules without violating the Supremacy Clause. * * *

CAN–SPAM does not preempt the Regents' Rules, because § 7701(b)(1) is in tension with plain text found elsewhere in the Act, and that tension triggers the presumption against preemption. * * *

White Buffalo contends that the district court erred in granting summary judgment on its First Amendment claim. Whether UT has violated White Buffalo's First Amendment rights turns on the resolution of the four-part commercial speech test in Central Hudson Gas & Electric Corp. v. Public Service Commission, 447 U.S. 557 (1980). * * *

Commercial speech is "expression related solely to the economic interests of the speaker and its audience." Central Hudson, 447 U.S. at 561. No one seriously disputes the commercial character of the speech at issue here. * * *

Under the first Central Hudson prong, we must determine whether the speech is unlawful or misleading. See id. Both parties agree that White Buffalo's commercial solicitations are legal and that they contain factually accurate information. * * *

Under the second Central Hudson prong we must assess the "substantiality" of the government's proffered interests. See id. UT advances two primary interests: (1) safeguarding the time and interests of those with UT email accounts ("user efficiency") and (2) protecting the efficiency of its networks and servers ("server efficiency"). * * *

For purposes of evaluating the summary judgment, we acknowledge as substantial the government's gatekeeping interest in protecting users of its email network from the hassle associated with unwanted spam. Also substantial is the "server efficiency" interest, but it must independently satisfy a "goodness of fit" inquiry under the fourth prong of Central

Hudson. "Suffer the servers" is among the most chronically over-used and under-substantiated interests asserted by parties (both government and private ones) involved in Internet litigation, and rules imposed pursuant to such interests require more than a judicial rubber-stamp * * *.

Pursuant to the third Central Hudson prong, we must next determine whether the UT policy directly advances both proffered substantial interests: (1) UT's interest in sanitizing the network for its email account-holders (user efficiency) and (2) its interest in preserving the operating efficiency of its servers (server efficiency). See id. at 569. Again, there can be no serious dispute that UT's anti-spam policy, which blocks specific incoming commercial spam after account-holders have complained about it, directly advances both interests. One can hardly imagine a more direct means of preventing commercial spam from appearing in account-holders' inboxes and occupying server space than promulgating a policy that excludes such material from the email network. * * *

Having resolved the first three Central Hudson questions in UT's favor, we must finally conduct the most difficult inquiry—whether the ITC policy is no more extensive than necessary to achieve at least one of the two substantial state interests. * * *

With respect to the first proffered substantial state interest, which is promoting user efficiency, the ITC policy is no more extensive than necessary. We have little problem affirming the proposition that, to keep community members from wasting time identifying, deleting, and blocking unwanted spam, UT may block otherwise lawful commercial spam (as long as the blocks are content-and viewpoint-neutral). * * *

We reject, however, the proposition that the ITC policy is no more extensive than necessary to secure the state's second substantial interest, which is the efficiency of its servers.

We must * * * consider the evidence in the light most favorable to the nonmovant. Moreover, the challenged regulation should indicate that its proponent "carefully calculated the costs and benefits associated with the burden on speech imposed by its prohibition." There is record testimony that White Buffalo can send a restricted volume of email at off-peak times, so as not to impede server efficiency. * * *

A governmental entity may assert that a statute serves multiple interests, and only one of those need be substantial. See Bolger v. Youngs Drug Prods. Corp., 463 U.S. 60, 71–73 (1983). The ITC policy survives First Amendment scrutiny despite its failure to justify that policy in relationship to the server efficiency interest. We therefore decide that UT's anti-spam policy is constitutionally permissible under Central Hudson. Because we so decide, we need not address what type of First Amendment forum a public university email network constitutes.

c. FTC Enforcement

FTC, ADULT WEBSITE OPERATION SETTLES FTC CHARGES UNWITTING CONSUMERS EXPOSED TO X–RATED SPAM

Press Release, March 4, 2008.

An X-rated Web operation that paid affiliates who used illegal e-mail to drive customers to its Web sites will pay a $413,000 civil penalty under a settlement reached with the FTC and the Department of Justice. The settlement also bars the illegal marketing practices in the future and requires the operator to monitor its affiliates to ensure that they are complying with the law.

In 2005, the FTC cracked down on seven companies that illegally exposed unwitting consumers, including children, to graphic sexual content, in violation of federal laws. Five of those cases were previously settled. The settlement announced today with Cyberheat, Inc., ends the litigation in that case, and brings the total combined civil penalty amount in these cases to over $1.6 million.

The FTC's Adult Labeling Rule and the CAN–SPAM Act require commercial e-mailers of sexually-explicit material to use the phrase "SEXUALLY EXPLICIT:" in the subject line of the e-mail message and to ensure that the initially viewable area of the message does not contain graphic sexual images. The Rule and the Act also require that unsolicited commercial e-mail contain an opportunity for consumers to opt out of receiving future e-mail and provide a postal address, among other things. The FTC charged that the affiliate marketers sent sexually-explicit e-mail messages that:

- Violated the Adult Labeling Rule requirements;
- Violated the requirement to provide a clear and conspicuous opt-out mechanism; and
- Violated the requirement to provide a postal address.

While Cyberheat did not send e-mail directly to consumers, they operated an "affiliate marketing" program in which they paid others who used spam to drive traffic to Cyberheat's Web sites. The government's complaint alleged that under the CAN–SPAM Act, the defendant is liable for the illegal spam sent by its affiliates because the defendant induced them to send it by offering to pay those who successfully attracted subscriber to its Web sites.

The settlement bars future violations of the CAN–SPAM Act and the Adult Labeling Rule and requires the defendant to closely monitor its affiliates to ensure that they are complying with the law. In addition the defendant will pay $413,000 in civil penalties. The settlement contains standard bookkeeping and record keeping provisions to allow the FTC to monitor the company for compliance.

The Commission vote to accept the settlement was 5–0.

d. From Spam to Phishing and Spyware

NOTE: ANNOYANCES

"Spyware" is a program installed on an internet user's computer, generally without fully informed consent, to track web transactions or other online behavior. "Phishing" is a kind of internet-based pretexting. It involves using the internet to fraudulently obtain personal information, money or other things of value. A phisher might pretend to be a bank and send an email to an individual requesting her account number or social security number, supposedly to "verify" transactions. The phisher might direct the email recipient to a phony website that resembles that of a legitimate business.

Congress has considered a number of proposals to enhance privacy and security on the internet to address "phishing" and "spyware" abuses. See Ira Rubinstein, Privacy and Security Legislation and Policy: The Last Twelve Months, *Seventh Annual Institute on Privacy Law: Evolving Laws and Practices in a Security Driven World* (ed. Practicing Law Institute 2006), 65–89. An Anti–Phishing Act of 2005 was introduced into the House and Senate. Anti-spyware bills have also been introduced into the House, the "SPY Act," and an "I–SPY Prevention Act of 2005." The SPYLOCK Act was introduced into the Senate in 2004. A "SAFEWEB Act" was introduced into the Senate in 2006. This law would grant the FTC additional authority to work with foreign agencies to address problems of cross-border spam, spyware and phishing. How serious are these problems? The Internet Spyware Prevention Act of 2007 was approved by the U.S. House of Representatives in May 2007.

INTERNET SPYWARE PREVENTION ACT OF 2007—BILL SUMMARY & STATUS

110th Congress (2007–2008) H.R.1525.

All Information

Internet Spyware (I–SPY) Prevention Act of 2007—(Sec. 2) Amends the federal criminal code to impose a fine and/or prison term of up to five years for intentionally accessing a protected computer (a computer exclusively for the use of a financial institution or the U.S. government or which is used in or affects interstate or foreign commerce or communication) without authorization, or exceeding authorized access, by causing a computer program or code to be copied onto the protected computer and intentionally using that program or code in furtherance of another federal criminal offense.

Imposes a fine and/or prison term of up to two years if such unauthorized access of a protected computer is for the purpose of: (1) intentionally obtaining or transmitting personal information (including a Social Security number or other government-issued identification number, a bank or credit card number, or an associated password or access code) with intent to defraud or injure a person or cause damage to a protected computer; or

(2) intentionally impairing the security protection of a protected computer with the intent to defraud or injure a person or damage such computer.

Prohibits any person from bringing a civil action under state law premised upon the defendant's violating this Act.

Exempts any lawfully authorized investigative, protective, or intelligence activity of the United States, a state, or a local law enforcement agency or of an U.S. intelligence agency from the prohibitions of this Act.

(Sec. 3) Authorizes appropriations for FY2008–FY2011 to the Attorney General for prosecutions needed to discourage the use of spyware and practices commonly called phishing and pharming.

(Sec. 4) Expresses the sense of Congress that the Department of Justice should vigorously prosecute those who use spyware to commit crimes and those that conduct phishing and pharming scams.

5. RESPONSIBILITY FOR DATA SECURITY BREACHES

NOTE: SECURITY BREACHES

The Massachusetts-based TJX company revealed in January 2007 that it had lost customer data to hackers in a data security breach of systems used to process customer transactions data. At the time of the breach, popular TJX retailers in the U.S. included close to 2,000 stores in the T.J. Maxx, Marshalls, HomeGoods, A.J. Wright, and Bob's Stores chains. Additional TJX stores are located in Canada and Europe.

A breach of a security system has been defined as "an unauthorized acquisition of computerized data that compromises the security, confidentiality, or integrity of personal information maintained by a person or business." See Catherine M. Bump et al., "Summary of State Data Security Laws as of March 2006," *Seventh Annual Institute on Privacy Law: Evolving Laws and Practices in a Security Driven World* (ed. Practicing Law Institute 2006) 39–63. See generally, John Kennedy, "Slouching Towards Security Standards: The Legacy of California's SB 1386," in Id., 91–168 (assessing laws governing breaches of public and private data systems).

A data security breach can be the intentional act of a malicious hacker or industrial spy, as appears to have been the case in the TJX incident. But it can also be an accident, as where (1) an employee misplaces a lap-top computer that has not been password-protected and contains unencrypted personal data, (2) a firm's back-up storage devices are misplaced, or (3) someone carelessly uploads sensitive data to a publicly accessible website. A single security breach in the data system of a hospital or financial institution can compromise the informational privacy of millions of individuals.

Security breaches in the financial services industry have been especially worrisome. They risk disclosure of social security numbers, account numbers and other highly sensitive banking and credit information. The Federal Reserve System, the Federal Deposit Insurance Corporation, The Office of the Comptroller of the Currency, and the Office of Thrift Supervision joined forces to issue guidelines on data security. Their report, "Inter-agency Guidance on Response Programs for Unauthorized Access to Customer Information and Customer Notice," was issued in 2005.

Security breaches are not inevitable, although even a very careful firm can be victimized. Prompt notice of breaches affords affected individuals an opportunity to protect themselves against identity theft and embarrassment. Providing notice to consumers is thus a major focus of the recently enacted state data security breach laws. California led the nation with the first state data breach statute mandating consumer notification. See California Civil Code section 1798.82 (requiring disclosure of security breaches of "unencrypted personal information * * * in the most expedient time possible and without unreasonable delay"). About half the states now have laws that require companies to guard against data breaches and to publicize breaches through the media, mail, and/or email.

In response to a bevy of high-profile data breaches in recent years, a plethora of data security breach bills have been introduced into Congress. In the meantime, the Federal Trade Commission (FTC) has taken an active interest in sanctioning firms with inadequate security practices, which the Commission generally frames as "unfair trade practices." In the words of FTC Chair, Deborah Platt Majoras, "Consumers must have the confidence that companies that possess their confidential information will handle it with due care and appropriately provide for its security."

Paul M. Schwartz and Edward J. Janger have proposed creating an official coordinated response architecture and a "Coordinated Response Agent" to automatically notify consumers of data security breaches, coordinate information sharing among affected entities, and improve data security in the future. Paul M. Schwartz and Edward J. Janger, Notification of Data Security Breaches, 105 *Mich. L. Rev.* 913 (2007).

FTC, "BJ'S WHOLESALE CLUB SETTLES FTC CHARGES"

Press Release, June 16, 2005.

BJ's Wholesale Club, Inc. has agreed to settle Federal Trade Commission charges that its failure to take appropriate security measures to protect the sensitive information of thousands of its customers was an unfair practice that violated federal law. According to the FTC, this information was used by an unauthorized person or persons to make millions of dollars of fraudulent purchases. The settlement will require BJ's to implement a comprehensive information security program and obtain audits by an independent third party security professional every other year for 20 years.

Natick, Massachusetts-based BJ's operates 150 warehouse stores and 78 gas stations in 16 states in the Eastern United States. Approximately 8 million consumers are currently members, with net sales totaling about $6.6 billion in 2003.

"Consumers must have the confidence that companies that possess their confidential information will handle it with due care and appropriately provide for its security," said Deborah Platt Majoras, Chairman of the FTC. "This case demonstrates our intention to challenge companies that fail to protect adequately consumers' sensitive information."

According to the FTC's complaint, BJ's uses a computer network to obtain bank authorization for credit and debit card purchases and to track inventory. For credit and debit card purchases at its stores, BJ's collects information, such as name, card number, and expiration date, from the magnetic stripe on the back of the cards. The information is sent from the computer network in the store to BJ's central datacenter computer network and from there through outside computer networks to the bank that issued the card.

The FTC charged that BJ's engaged in a number of practices which, taken together, did not provide reasonable security for sensitive customer information. Specifically, the agency alleges that BJ's:

- Failed to encrypt consumer information when it was transmitted or stored on computers in BJ's stores;

- Created unnecessary risks to the information by storing it for up to 30 days, in violation of bank security rules, even when it no longer needed the information;

- Stored the information in files that could be accessed using commonly known default user IDs and passwords;

- Failed to use readily available security measures to prevent unauthorized wireless connections to its networks; and

- Failed to use measures sufficient to detect unauthorized access to the networks or to conduct security investigations.

The FTC's complaint charges that the fraudulent purchases were made using counterfeit copies of credit and debit cards used at BJ's stores, and that the counterfeit cards contained the same personal information BJ's had collected from the magnetic stripes of the cards. After the fraud was discovered, banks cancelled and re-issued thousands of credit and debit cards, and consumers experienced inconvenience, worry, and time loss dealing with the affected cards. Since then, banks and credit unions have filed lawsuits against BJ's and pursued bank procedures seeking the return millions of dollars in fraudulent purchases and operating expenses. According to BJ's SEC filings, as of May 2005, the amount of outstanding claims was approximately $13 million.

The FTC alleges that BJ's failure to secure customers' sensitive information was an unfair practice because it caused substantial injury that was not reasonably avoidable by consumers and not outweighed by offsetting benefits to consumers or competition. The settlement requires BJ's to establish and maintain a comprehensive information security program that includes administrative, technical, and physical safeguards. The settlement also requires BJ's to obtain an audit from a qualified, independent, third-party professional that its security program meets the standards of the order, and to comply with standard book keeping and record keeping provisions.

The Commission vote to accept the proposed consent agreement was 5–0. The FTC will publish an announcement regarding the agreement in the Federal Register shortly. The agreement will be subject to public comment for 30 days, beginning today and continuing through July 16, 2005, after which the Commission will decide whether to make it final. Comments should be addressed to the FTC, Office of the Secretary, Room H–159, 600 Pennsylvania Avenue, N.W., Washington, D.C. 20580. The FTC is requesting that any comment filed in paper form near the end of the public comment period be sent by courier or overnight service, if possible, because U.S. postal mail in the Washington area and at the Commission is subject to delay due to heightened security precautions.

6. BROKEN PROMISES AND MISLEADING STATEMENTS

NOTE: PROMISES, PROMISES

It is generally agreed that companies with websites should post appropriate privacy policies, limit information sharing with third parties, and moderate undisclosed use of cookies, Internet tags/web beacons, or other tracking capabilities. They should also avoid sending unsolicited email or spam; avoid making misleading statements; and child-proof their websites to be COPPA complaint. Finally, companies with web sites should never make promises that they cannot keep. See Ruth Hill Bro, "Top Ten Web Site Mistakes of U.S. Companies," *Seventh Annual Institute on Privacy Law: Evolving Laws and Practices in a Security Driven World* (ed. Practicing Law Institute 2006), 405–419.

Companies that transact business online often represent to consumers that their personal information will not be shared. What happens when privacy and security promises are broken, whether through an intentional data transfer or a security breach?

The Attorney General of New York has been especially active in the area of suing firms that break such promises; other states, like California and Vermont, have gotten tough as well. See generally Kenneth M. Dreifach, "Data Privacy, Web Security and Attorney General Enforcement," *Seventh Annual Institute on Privacy Law: Evolving Laws and Practices in a Security Driven World* (ed. Practicing Law Institute 2006), pp. 355–385. On the federal side, broken promises and misleading statements are viewed in a negative light by the FTC, as the ChoicePoint case, below, demonstrates.

FTC, "CHOICEPOINT SETTLES DATA SECURITY BREACH CHARGES; TO PAY $10 MILLION IN CIVIL PENALTIES, $5 MILLION FOR CONSUMER RE-DRESS"

Press Release, January 26, 2006.

Consumer data broker ChoicePoint, Inc., which last year acknowledged that the personal financial records of more than 163,000 consumers in its database had been compromised, will pay $10 million in civil penalties and $5 million in consumer redress to settle Federal Trade Commission charges that its security and record-handling procedures violated consumers' privacy rights and federal laws. The settlement requires ChoicePoint to implement new procedures to ensure that it provides consumer reports only to legitimate businesses for lawful purposes, to establish and maintain a comprehensive information security program, and to obtain audits by an independent third-party security professional every other year until 2026.

"The message to ChoicePoint and others should be clear: Consumers' private data must be protected from thieves," said Deborah Platt Majoras, Chairman of the FTC. "Data security is critical to consumers, and protecting it is a priority for the FTC, as it should be to every business in America."

ChoicePoint is a publicly traded company based in suburban Atlanta. It obtains and sells to more than 50,000 businesses the personal information of consumers, including their names, Social Security numbers, birth dates, employment information, and credit histories.

The FTC alleges that ChoicePoint did not have reasonable procedures to screen prospective subscribers, and turned over consumers' sensitive personal information to subscribers whose applications raised obvious "red flags." Indeed, the FTC alleges that ChoicePoint approved as customers individuals who lied about their credentials and used commercial mail drops as business addresses. In addition, ChoicePoint applicants reportedly used fax machines at public commercial locations to send multiple applications for purportedly separate companies.

According to the FTC, ChoicePoint failed to tighten its application approval procedures or monitor subscribers even after receiving subpoenas from law enforcement authorities alerting it to fraudulent activity going back to 2001.

The FTC charged that ChoicePoint violated the Fair Credit Reporting Act (FCRA) by furnishing consumer reports—credit histories—to subscribers who did not have a permissible purpose to obtain them, and by failing to maintain reasonable procedures to verify both their identities and how they intended to use the information.

The agency also charged that ChoicePoint violated the FTC Act by making false and misleading statements about its privacy policies. Choicepoint had publicized privacy principles that address the confidentiality and security of personal information it collects and maintains with statements such as, "ChoicePoint allows access to your consumer reports only by those authorized under the FCRA * * *" and "Every ChoicePoint customer must successfully complete a rigorous credentialing process. ChoicePoint does not distribute information to the general public and monitors the use of its public record information to ensure appropriate use."

The stipulated final judgment and order requires ChoicePoint to pay $10 million in civil penalties—the largest civil penalty in FTC history—and to provide $5 million for consumer redress. It bars the company from furnishing consumer reports to people who do not have a permissible purpose to receive them and requires the company to establish and maintain reasonable procedures to ensure that consumer reports are provided only to those with a permissible purpose. ChoicePoint is required to verify the identity of businesses that apply to receive consumer reports, including making site visits to certain business premises and auditing subscribers' use of consumer reports.

The order requires ChoicePoint to establish, implement, and maintain a comprehensive information security program designed to protect the security, confidentiality, and integrity of the personal information it collects from or about consumers. It also requires ChoicePoint to obtain, every two years for the next 20 years, an audit from a qualified, independent, third-party professional to ensure that its security program meets the standards of the order. ChoicePoint will be subject to standard record-keeping and reporting provisions to allow the FTC to monitor compliance. Finally, the settlement bars future violations of the FCRA and the FTC Act.

This case is being brought with the invaluable assistance of the U.S. Department of Justice and the Securities and Exchange Commission.

The Commission vote to accept the settlement was 5–0.

FTC, WIDESPREAD DATA BREACHES UNCOVERED BY FTC PROBE; FTC WARNS OF IMPROPER RELEASE OF SENSITIVE CONSUMER DATA ON P2P FILE–SHARING NETWORKS

Press Release, February 22, 2010.

The Federal Trade Commission has notified almost 100 organizations that personal information, including sensitive data about customers and/or employees, has been shared from the organizations' computer networks and is available on peer-to-peer (P2P) file-sharing networks to any users of those networks, who could use it to commit identity theft or fraud. The agency also has opened non-public investigations of other companies whose customer or employee information has been exposed on P2P networks. To help businesses manage the security risks presented by file-sharing software, the FTC is releasing new education materials that present the risks and recommend ways to manage them.

Peer-to-peer technology can be used in many ways, such as to play games, make online telephone calls, and, through P2P file-sharing software, share music, video, and documents. But when P2P file-sharing software is not configured properly, files not intended for sharing may be accessible to anyone on the P2P network.

"Unfortunately, companies and institutions of all sizes are vulnerable to serious P2P-related breaches, placing consumers' sensitive information at risk. For example, we found health-related information, financial records, and drivers' license and social security numbers—the kind of information that could lead to identity theft," said FTC Chairman Jon Leibowitz. "Companies should take a hard look at their systems to ensure that there are no unauthorized P2P file-sharing programs and that authorized programs are properly configured and secure. Just as important, companies that distribute P2P programs, for their part, should ensure that their software design does not contribute to inadvertent file sharing."

As the nation's consumer protection agency, the FTC enforces laws that require companies in various industries to take reasonable and appropriate security measures to protect sensitive personal information, including the Gramm–Leach–Bliley Act and Section 5 of the FTC Act. Failure to prevent such information from being shared to a P2P network may violate such laws. Information about the FTC's privacy and data security enforcement actions can be found at www.ftc.gov/privacy/privacy initiatives/ promises_enf.html.

The notices went to both private and public entities, including schools and local governments, and the entities contacted ranged in size from businesses with as few as eight employees to publicly held corporations employing tens of thousands. In the notification letters, the FTC urged the entities to review their security practices and, if appropriate, the practices of contractors and vendors, to ensure that they are reasonable, appropriate, and in compliance with the law. The letters state, "It is your responsibility to protect such information from unauthorized access, including taking steps to control the use of P2P software on your own networks and those of your service providers."

The FTC also recommended that the entities identify affected customers and employees and consider whether to notify them that their information is available on P2P networks. Many states and federal regulatory agencies have laws or guidelines about businesses' notification responsibilities in these circumstances.

7. NO HARM, NO FOUL?

HAMMOND v. THE BANK OF NEW YORK MELLON CORP.

2010 WL 2643307 (S.D.N.Y.).

I. Introduction

This case is one of many similar litigations (most brought as purported class actions) in which plaintiffs seek damages for the loss of personal identification information through accident or theft. * * * While there is a split in authority as to how to analyze these cases, every court to do so has ultimately dismissed under Rule 12(b)(6) of the Federal Rules of Civil Procedure ("Fed. R. Civ.P.") or under Rule 56 following the submission of a motion for summary judgment. Several courts, including federal district courts in Arkansas, Missouri, New Jersey, Ohio, and the District of Columbia, have determined that the potential risk of identity theft resulting from the loss of personal information is not an "injury-in-fact" within the meaning of Article III of the United States Constitution and have dismissed these cases after concluding that plaintiffs lacked "standing." *See, e.g., Randolph,* 486 F.Supp.2d at 1, 8–9 ("Plaintiffs' claims that they are subject to an increased risk of identity theft and inconvenience" as a result of the theft of a laptop containing their names, addresses, and Social Security numbers fail to allege an injury in fact and "Plaintiffs' allegation that they have incurred or will incur costs in an attempt to protect themselves against their alleged increased risk of identity theft fails to demonstrate an injury that is sufficiently 'concrete and particularized' and 'actual or imminent.' ") * * *.

Other courts have determined that similarly situated plaintiffs had standing but concluded, for one reason or another, that loss of identity information is not a legally cognizable claim. *See, e.g., Pisciotta,* 499 F.3d at 634 ("Without more than allegations of increased risk of future identity theft, the plaintiffs have not suffered a harm that the law is prepared to remedy. Plaintiffs have not come forward with a single case or statute, from any jurisdiction, authorizing the kind of action they now ask this federal court * * * to recognize as a valid theory of recovery [.]"); *McLoughlin,* 2009 WL 2843269, at *4; *Caudle,* 580 F.Supp.2d at 280; *Ruiz III,* 2010 WL 2170993, at *1; *see also Forbes,* 420 F.Supp.2d at 1020–21 (where the Court rejected plaintiffs' breach of contract and negligence claims and plaintiffs' contention that they had suffered damage as a result of the time and money they had spent to monitor their credit).

For the reasons set forth below, this Court concludes that Plaintiffs here do not have Article III standing (*i.e.,* there is no "case or controversy") because they claim to have suffered little more than an increased risk of future harm from the loss (whether by accident or theft) of their personal information. The opinion goes on to say that even if, *arguendo,* Plaintiffs had demonstrated standing, their claims properly would be dismissed. * * *

II. Background

On April 22, 2009, Tom Hammond ("Hammond"), William H. Wicks ("Wicks"), Linda Young ("Young"), Lois Giordano ("Giordano"), Debbie Bernstein ("Bernstein"), Alyson Kanney ("Kanney"), and Ken Witek ("Witek"), on behalf of themselves and all others similarly situated (collectively, "Plaintiffs"), filed a second amended putative class action complaint ("Complaint") against the Bank of New York Mellon Corporation ("BNY" or "Defendant"). Plaintiffs assert common law claims of negligence, negligence *per se,* breach of implied contract, and breach of fiduciary duty, as well as statutory claims under [various states' consumer protection laws].

Plaintiffs' claims arise out of two incidents (referred to herein as the "tape losses") in which it is alleged that the "names, addresses, Social Security numbers, bank account information, financial data, debit or credit card, checking account numbers and information and/or shareholder account information (the 'Sensitive Personal Information') was stolen, accessed and/or compromised by third parties while entrusted to Defendant[.]" Specifically, Plaintiffs allege that, in February 2008, "a BNY metal box with six to ten unencrypted computer back-up tapes containing the Sensitive Personal Information of consumers was 'lost' from a truck operated by a transport company hired by BNY," and that, in April 2008, "a backup data storage tape containing images of scanned checks and other payment documents was 'lost' while being transported from Philadelphia to Pittsburgh" by an outside carrier. Plaintiffs seek actual damages, equitable relief, fees, costs, and expenses.

On December 2, 2009, Defendant moved for dismissal as follows: (1) pursuant to Fed.R.Civ.P. 12(b)(1), arguing that Plaintiffs lack standing to sue because the "mere increased risk of harm" resulting from the tape losses is "not an actual or imminent injury"; and (2) pursuant to Fed. R.Civ.P. 56(c), arguing that summary judgment should be granted because "neither an increased risk of future identity theft nor the emotional distress and worry relating to the increased risk constitute 'harm' that the law is prepared to remedy." * * *

Defendant BNY "is a financial institution comprised of a number of business units" including, among others, Shareowner Services and Working Capital Solutions ("WCS").

"Shareowner Services and WCS produced back-up Tapes of computer information and used third party vendors to transport and, in some instances, store those Tapes in secure storage facilities." "In late February 2008, Archive Systems, Inc. ('Archive'), a vendor transporting Shareowner Services' back-up tapes by truck, discovered that one of ten boxes was missing" "A separate incident, involving WCS, occurred in April 2008 when a national courier service lost a back-up tape with payment information" ("April 2008 tape loss"). According to Plaintiffs, the missing tapes "contained the unencrypted Sensitive Data of approximately 12.5 million individuals[.]" In the months following the February 2008 and April 2008 tape losses, BNY notified the affected individuals by letter. ("Dear Sir or Madam, We are writing to let you know that computer tapes containing some of your personal information were lost while being transported to an off-site storage facility by our archive services vendor. While we have no reason to believe that this information has been accessed or used inappropriately, we deeply regret that this incident occurred and we wanted to explain the precautionary steps we have taken to help protect you.").) And, "[a]t no cost, BNY Mellon offered the individuals affected by the February and April tape losses the following services: a minimum of 24 months of credit monitoring, $25,000 of identity theft insurance (where permitted by applicable law), reimbursement for certain credit freeze costs, and a toll-free number to handle inquiries." * * *

Plaintiffs now seek remedies beyond those already (voluntarily) provided by Defendant, including compensatory damages for: the "value of their Sensitive Personal Information that was improperly stolen, misplaced and/or compromised"; the "unauthorized disclosure and/or compromise of their Sensitive Personal Information"; "monetary losses for money stolen from their accounts and/or fraudulent charges made on their accounts"; the "value of all time expended and/or out-of-pocket expenses incurred to proactively safeguard and/or repair their credit"; and "the burden and expense of comprehensive credit monitoring." Plaintiffs also seek equitable relief, "to wit, [the] creation of a fund for comprehensive credit monitoring for more than two (2) years into the future, as well as * * * the appointment of an administrator and advisory panel * * * so as to prevent any additional harm and remedy actual harm, that has or will occur."

Of the seven named Plaintiffs, only Hammond, Kanney, and Bernstein claim to have suffered "unauthorized credit transactions" after the tapes were lost. Both Hammond and Kanney acknowledge that they were reimbursed for any unauthorized charges they encountered. Bernstein acknowledges that the unauthorized charge which she encountered and which was not reimbursed "was unrelated to the tape loss." The Court concludes that Plaintiffs lack standing because their claims are future-oriented, hypothetical, and conjectural. There is no "case or controversy." And, as noted, several other courts have reached the same conclusion in factually similar cases, both where data have been lost and where data have been stolen. For example, in *Randolph,* where a laptop computer belonging to defendant's employee and containing the personal data of some 13,000 individuals was stolen from the employee's home, plaintiffs alleged that they had been "placed at a substantial risk of harm in the form of identity theft" and that they had "incurred and will incur actual damages in an attempt to prevent identity theft by purchasing services to monitor their credit information." * * *

Negligence

Under New York law, "the elements of a negligence claim are the existence of a duty, a breach of that duty, and damages proximately caused by that breach of duty." *Rangon v. Skillman Ave. Corp.,* No. 37311/07, 2010 WL 2197787, at *2 (N.Y. Sup.Ct. June 3, 2010); *Shmushkina v. Price is Right of Brooklyn, Inc.,* 839 N.Y.S.2d 683, 684 (Sup.Ct.2007). * * * Summary judgment for Defendant would be granted because, among other reasons, Plaintiffs cannot establish that Defendant owed them any duty. *See Silverman Partners L.P. v. First Bank,* 687 F.Supp.2d 269, 281 (E.D.N.Y.2010). None of the named Plaintiffs had any direct dealings with Defendant. * * * Because there is no duty owed by the Defendant to the Plaintiffs, Plaintiffs also cannot establish breach of duty, and summary judgment would be appropriate for that reason as well. * * *

Breach of Fiduciary Duty

The elements of this claim are: "breach by a fiduciary of a duty owed to plaintiff; defendant's knowing participation in the breach; and damages." *SCS Commc'ns, Inc. v. Herrick Co.,* 360 F.3d 329, 342 (2d Cir. 2004). "Absent extraordinary circumstances * * * parties dealing at arms length in a commercial transaction lack the requisite level of trust or confidence between them necessary to give rise to a fiduciary obligation." *U.S. Bank Nat'l Ass'n v. Ables & Hall Builders,* ___ F.Supp.2d ___, No. 08 Civ. 2540, 2010 WL 996761, at *10 (S.D.N.Y. Mar. 19, 2010) (quoting *Henneberry v. Sumitomo Corp. of Am.,* 415 F.Supp.2d 423, 460 (S.D.N.Y. 2006)). * * * Summary judgment would be granted for Defendant because there is no proof of the existence of a fiduciary relationship between Defendant and Plaintiffs. * * *

Breach of Implied Contract

"To form a valid contract under New York law, there must be an offer, acceptance, consideration, mutual assent and intent to be bound." *Leibowitz v. Cornell Univ.,* 584 F.3d 487, 507 (2d Cir.2009). "A contract implied in fact may result as an inference from the facts and circumstances of the case," *Jemzura v. Jemzura,* 330 N.E.2d 414, 420 (N.Y.1975), and requires proof of the elements of an express contract. *Leibowitz,* 584 F.3d at 507 (citing *Maas,* 94 N.Y.2d at 93). * * * Plaintiffs have adduced no evidence of Defendant's "assent" to be contractually bound to any named Plaintiff. * * *

State Consumer Protection Claims

Plaintiffs cannot establish that Defendant engaged in consumer-oriented fraud or other misconduct which caused actual damages within the meaning of the laws of their respective states. * * *

V.   Conclusion and Order

For the reasons stated herein, Defendant's motion for summary judgment is granted. Plaintiffs' cross-motion for class certification is denied as moot. The Clerk of Court is respectfully requested to close this case.

NOTE: CLOUD COMPUTING AND PRIVACY

The term "cloud computing" refers to the practice of storing information created on a physical device under a user's control—such as desktop computer, laptop, cell phone—elsewhere, with future internet/web-based accessibility. There are three basic types of cloud computing, see http://epic.org/privacy/cloudcomputing/#Types:

1. Software as a Service (SaaS) is the most common and widely known type of cloud computing. SaaS applications provide the function of software that would normally have been installed and run on the user's desktop. With SaaS, however, the application is stored on the cloud computing service provider's servers and run through the user's web browser over the Internet. Examples of SaaS include: Gmail, Google Apps, and Salesforce.

2. Platform as a Service (PaaS) cloud computing provides a place for developers to develop and publish new web applications stored on the servers of the PaaS provider. Customers use the Internet to access the platform and create applications using the PaaS provider's API, web portal, or gateway software. Examples of PaaS include: Saleforce's Force.com, Google App Engine, Mozilla Bespin, Zoho Creator.

3. Infrastructure as a Service (IaaS) seeks to obviate the need for customers to have their own data centers. IaaS providers sell customers access to web storage space, servers, and Internet connections. The IaaS provider owns and maintains the hardware and customers rent space according to their current needs. An example of Iaas is Amazon Web Services. IaaS is also known as utility computing.

According to a 2010 survey of more than 800 experts, conducted by the Pew Research Center Internet & American Life Project and Elon University's Imagining the Internet Center, cloud computing is expected to grow in popularity and overtake local storage: "A solid majority of technology experts and stakeholders * * * expect that by 2020 most people will access software applications online and share and access information through the use of remote server networks, rather than depending primarily on tools and information housed on their individual, personal computers. They say that cloud computing will become more dominant than the desktop in the next decade. In other words, most users will perform most computing and communicating activities through connections to servers operated by outside firms."

Cloud computing already enjoys enormous popularity. Again, according to Pew: "Among the most popular cloud services now are social networking sites (the 500 million people using Facebook are being social in the cloud), webmail services like Hotmail and Yahoo mail, microblogging and blogging services such as Twitter and WordPress, video-sharing sites like YouTube, picture-sharing sites such as Flickr, document and applications sites like Google Docs, social-bookmarking sites like Delicious, business sites like eBay, and ranking, rating and commenting sites such as Yelp and TripAdvisor." Cloud computing potentially increases the amount of data a person or business can accumulate. It also potentially provides a more reliable back-up than the ordinary home or office computer. Yet cloud computing raises obvious data privacy and security concerns. The more sensitive and essential the data, the more trust consumers and industry will have to have that data stored in the cloud will be protected from unintentional and unauthorized disclosures or inadvertent destruction. At present, "Legal rights and regulatory authority for the protection of the privacy of cloud computing users are not well defined. Data stored in the cloud may be subject to less stringent legal protection than data stored on a personal computer. Under the Electronic Communications Privacy Act, data stored in the cloud may be subject to a lesser standard for law enforcement to gain access to it than if the data were stored on a personal computer." See http://epic.org/privacy/cloudcomputing/#Types.

8.   COMPUTER FRAUD AND ABUSE ACT OF 1986

COMPUTER FRAUD AND ABUSE ACT

http://www.justice.gov/criminal/cybercrime/ccmanual/01ccma.pdf.

In the early 1980s law enforcement agencies faced the dawn of the computer age with growing concern about the lack of criminal laws available to fight the emerging computer crimes. Although the wire and mail fraud provisions of the federal criminal code were capable of addressing some types of computer-related criminal activity, neither of those statutes provided the full range of tools needed to combat these new crimes. *See* H.R. Rep. No. 98–894, at 6 (1984), *reprinted in* 1984 U.S.C.C.A.N. 3689, 3692.

In response, Congress included in the Comprehensive Crime Control Act of 1984 provisions to address the unauthorized access and use of computers and computer networks. The legislative history indicates that Congress intended these provisions to provide "a clearer statement of proscribed activity" to "the law enforcement community, those who own and operate computers, as well as those who may be tempted to commit crimes by unauthorized access." *Id.* Congress did this by making it a felony to access classified information in a computer without authorization, and a misdemeanor to access financial records or credit histories stored in a financial institution or to trespass into a government computer. In so doing, Congress opted not to add new provisions regarding computers to existing criminal laws, but rather to address federal computer-related offenses in a single, new statute, 18 U.S.C. § 1030.

Even after enacting section 1030, Congress continued to investigate problems associated with computer crime to determine whether federal criminal laws required further revision. Throughout 1985, both the House and the Senate held hearings on potential computer crime bills, continuing the efforts begun in the year before. These hearings culminated in the Computer Fraud and Abuse Act (CFAA), enacted by Congress in 1986, which amended 18 U.S.C. § 1030.

In the CFAA, Congress attempted to strike an "appropriate balance between the Federal Government's interest in computer crime and the interests and abilities of the States to proscribe and punish such offenses."

See S. Rep. No. 99–432, at 4 (1986), *reprinted in* 1986 U.S.C.C.A.N. 2479, 2482.

Congress addressed federalism concerns in the CFAA by limiting federal jurisdiction to cases with a compelling federal interest—i.e., where computers of the federal government or certain financial institutions are involved, or where the crime itself is interstate in nature. *See id.*

In addition to clarifying a number of the provisions in the original section 1030, the CFAA also criminalized additional computer-related acts. For example, Congress added a provision to penalize the theft of property via computer that occurs as a part of a scheme to defraud. Congress also added a provision to penalize those who intentionally alter, damage, or destroy data belonging to others. This latter provision was designed to cover such activities as the distribution of malicious code and denial of service attacks. Finally, Congress also included in the CFAA a provision criminalizing trafficking in passwords and similar items.

As computer crimes continued to grow in sophistication and as prosecutors gained experience with the CFAA, the CFAA required further amendment, which Congress did in 1988, 1989, 1990, 1994, 1996, 2001, and 2002. * * *

In some circumstances, the CFAA allows victims who suffer specific types of loss or damage as a result of a violations of the Act to bring civil actions against the violators for compensatory damages and injunctive or other equitable relief. 18 U.S.C. § 1030(g). * * *

In 2001, the USA PATRIOT Act amended the definition of "protected computer" to make clear that this term includes computers outside of the United States so long as they affect "interstate or foreign commerce or communication of the United States." 18 U.S.C. § 1030(e)(2)(B) (2001). As a result of this amendment, a protected computer is now defined as a computer "exclusively for the use of a financial institution or the United States Government, or, in the case of a computer not exclusively for such use, used by or for a financial institution or the United States Government and the conduct constituting the offense affects that use by or for the financial institution or the Government" or a computer "used in interstate or foreign commerce or communication, including a computer located outside the United States that is used in a manner that affects interstate or foreign commerce or communication of the United States." 18 U.S.C. § 1030(e)(2).

UNITED STATES v. MILLOT
433 F.3d 1057 (8th Cir. 2006).

HEANEY, CIRCUIT JUDGE.

On June 15, 2004, a jury found Thomas S. Millot guilty of unauthorized computer intrusion, in violation of the Computer Fraud and Abuse Act (CFAA), 18 U.S.C. § 1030(a) et seq. The district court sentenced Millot to three months of imprisonment, three months of home detention, three years of supervised release, a $5,000 fine, and restitution in the amount of $20,350. Millot appeals his conviction * * *. We affirm.

In 2000, Millot worked as a systems analyst in the Information Access Management Group for Aventis Pharmaceuticals. The Information Access Management Group managed the day-to-day computer security duties at Aventis's Kansas City, Missouri facility. Millot was responsible for administration of the SecureID cards and accounts. A SecureID card is an active device that generates a number that, in combination with a user name and personal identification number, allows Aventis employees to remotely access the Aventis computer system in order to check email and perform other job-related functions. An employee's remote access level depends on the individual's responsibilities for the company. As a systems analyst, Millot's access level was the highest available.

Millot had the lead responsibility for disabling remote access accounts when individuals left employment and collecting and tracking returned SecureID cards. On or around August 2000, Millot reassigned the access account of former employee Gernot Fromm to one of the inventoried SecureID cards, and increased the account access level to the highest level available.

In October of 2000, Aventis Pharmaceuticals outsourced its security functions to International Business Machines (IBM). Although several members of the Information Access Group were subsequently hired by IBM, Millot was not offered a job with IBM, and left employment with Aventis in September 2000. When he left employment, he kept the SecureID card he assigned to the Fromm account. To keep the card active he periodically accessed the network. Millot used the Fromm account to access the Aventis computer network nine times between August 26 and December 16, 2000. On December 16, 2000, he used the SecureID card and the Fromm account to log onto the Aventis system and delete Jeff Jernigan's account. Jernigan was the manager of Technical Services for Aventis, and his ability to remotely access and monitor the network was essential to his job. December 16, 2000, was a Saturday, and Jernigan unsuccessfully attempted to access the Aventis system from his home. Although Geoffery Bridges was able to rebuild Jernigan's account within a matter of hours, Jernigan continued to experience problems with his account for the following three weeks.

Bridges and Lori Meyer, former Aventis employees then working for IBM, performed the bulk of the activities in response to Millot's intrusion into the Aventis computer system. Bridges rebuilt the Jernigan account and investigated the intrusion while Meyer performed a security audit to verify that all existing access accounts belonged to current employees, and that each account's access level was appropriate. Bridges spent 31 hours restoring Jernigan's account and investigating the computer intrusion, and Meyers spent 376 hours on the audit for a total of 407 hours. IBM billed its staff's services at fifty dollars per hour, for a total cost of $20,350.

Investigators traced the unauthorized remote access back to Millot's personal internet access account. On March 3, 2003, Millot confessed that he had taken over the Fromm account, repeatedly contacted the Aventis computer system, and deleted the Jernigan account. The grand jury issued an indictment alleging that "it cost more than Five Thousand Dollars ($5,000) [to at least one or more persons] to conduct a damage assessment of, verify the security of, and restore the integrity of the Aventis network computer system." * * *

Millot admitted the underlying conduct, but challenged the government's allegation that the loss caused by his conduct amounted to the $5,000 minimum required for a conviction under the CFAA. * * * Millot alleges the government failed to prove damage of at least $5,000 because the district court erred in finding IBM a "victim" under the CFAA. * * *

To determine whether we should overturn Millot's conviction, we must determine whether the district court properly classified IBM as a potential victim under the CFAA, and if so, whether the government's evidence was sufficient for a jury to find that the loss exceeded $5,000. * * *

Millot argues that any costs incurred by IBM should not have been considered in determining whether the loss amounted to the statutory minimum because the system was owned by Aventis and IBM was a "volunteer" fixing the system. This argument lacks merit. The CFAA provides for a fine and imprisonment up to five years for an individual who "intentionally accesses a protected computer without authorization, and as a result of such conduct, recklessly causes damage" and that conduct causes "loss to 1 or more persons during any 1–year period * * * aggregating at least $5,000 in value." Although the damage was done to the Aventis computer system, the statute does not restrict consideration of losses to only the person who owns the computer system, and the district court properly instructed the jury to consider losses sustained by IBM in determining whether the statutory minimum was met.

Next we address the sufficiency of the evidence. Millot contends that the government's evidence was insufficient to establish that the actual loss exceeded the $5,000 minimum, because there was no evidence that IBM specifically billed Aventis the amount alleged. * * *

At Millot's trial, the government presented undisputed evidence regarding the hours spent by Bridges and Meyers in response to the unauthorized intrusion, and that the time spent was valued at fifty dollars per hour. IBM undoubtedly paid Meyers and Bridges for their time, and the work was done on behalf of Aventis to remedy damage to Aventis's computer system that Millot admits he caused. Millot's own expert agreed that the work done by Meyers and Bridges was a reasonable response to the discovery of a breach in the security of the computer system. Millot argues that the cost of the work performed was absorbed by IBM under its existing contract with Aventis. This argument neglects the fact that the hours spent by Bridges and Meyers addressing the issues caused by

Millot's unauthorized intrusion could have been spent on other duties under the contract.

Accordingly, we find that the evidence presented was sufficient to support the conviction.

9.   PRIVACY PROTECTION ACT OF 1980

NOTE: TREAT TENDERLY THE PRESS

"The Privacy Protection Act (PPA) [42 U.S.C. § 2000aa–7(b)] makes it unlawful for a government officer or employee, in connection with the investigation or prosecution of a criminal offense, to search for or seize documentary materials * * * possessed by a person in connection with a purpose to disseminate to the public a newspaper, book, broadcast, or other similar form of public communication * * *." *See S.H.A.R.K. v. Metro Parks Serving Summit County*, 2006 WL 1705009 (N.D. Ohio 2006). The remedies for violations of the PPA include civil damages against the government entity whose agents engaged in the search or the agents themselves.

Congress enacted the PPA to provide journalists with greater protection against searches and seizures, in response to the Supreme Court ruling in *Zurcher v. Stanford Daily* (1978), below. A story and photograph appeared in the *Stanford Daily* student newspaper reporting on a campus riot. Police did not suspect the newspaper itself or its employees of participating in the violence, but obtained a warrant to search the newspaper's offices, looking for any evidence it might contain of the identities of wrongdoers. The Court upheld the warrant in question, outraging the national press.

The Sixth Circuit has held that incidental seizure of First Amendment materials in connection with evidence gathering for a crime does not give rise to claims under the PPA. *Guest v. Leis*, 255 F.3d 325 (6th Cir. 2001). The materials in question in *Guest* were servers that hosted bulletin boards that may have been used for illegal purposes.

In 1980, Congress could not have anticipated the role computers and the internet would come to play in everyday life. On the face of it, the PPA applies to material produced and stored on computers, since they might include journalists' "work products," "mental impressions, conclusions or theories" referenced by the PPA. But should the PPA be construed to apply with equal force to the computer-stored work product of an amateur blogger and a professional? Is it significant, in this regard, that the newspaper in the *Stanford Daily* case was a student paper and not the *New York Times?*

Consider this: Jason Chen was the editor of the technology blog *Gizmodo* on April 23, 2010 when California's Rapid Enforcement Allied Computer Team (REACT) entered his residence without his permission and seized four computers and two servers. They had obtained a search warrant and were investigating the disappearance of an Apple iPhone prototype. Gizmodo had published stories reporting on the phone, allegedly purchased from a college student who claimed to have found the device in a bar. (Gizmodo returned the phone to Apple.) California has a shield law, Cal. Penal. Code § 1524(g) and

Cal. Evid. Code § 1070, which prohibits the issuance of warrants for journalists' work products, apparently including professional bloggers.

ZURCHER v. STANFORD DAILY

436 U.S. 547 (1978).

MR. JUSTICE WHITE delivered the opinion of the Court. * * *

Late in the day on Friday, April 9, 1971, officers of the Palo Alto Police Department and of the Santa Clara County Sheriff's Department responded to a call from the director of the Stanford University Hospital requesting the removal of a large group of demonstrators who had seized the hospital's administrative offices and occupied them since the previous afternoon. After several futile efforts to persuade the demonstrators to leave peacefully, more drastic measures were employed. The demonstrators had barricaded the doors at both ends of a hall adjacent to the administrative offices. The police chose to force their way in at the west end of the corridor. As they did so, a group of demonstrators emerged through the doors at the east end and, armed with sticks and clubs, attacked the group of nine police officers stationed there. * * *

On Sunday, April 11, a special edition of the Stanford Daily (Daily), a student newspaper published at Stanford University, carried articles and photographs devoted to the hospital protest and the violent clash between demonstrators and police. The photographs carried the byline of a Daily staff member and indicated that he had been at the east end of the hospital hallway where he could have photographed the assault on the nine officers. The next day, the Santa Clara County District Attorney's Office secured a warrant from the Municipal Court for an immediate search of the Daily's offices for negatives, film, and pictures showing the events and occurrences at the hospital on the evening of April 9. * * * The warrant affidavit contained no allegation or indication that members of the Daily staff were in any way involved in unlawful acts at the hospital.

The search pursuant to the warrant was conducted later that day by four police officers and took place in the presence of some members of the Daily staff. The Daily's photographic laboratories, filing cabinets, desks, and wastepaper baskets were searched. Locked drawers and rooms were not opened. * * *. The search revealed only the photographs that had already been published on April 11, and no materials were removed from the Daily's office.

A month later the Daily and various members of its staff, respondents here, brought a civil action in the United States District Court for the Northern District of California seeking declaratory and injunctive relief under 42 U.S.C. 1983 against the police officers who conducted the search, the chief of police, the district attorney and one of his deputies, and the judge who had issued the warrant. The complaint alleged that the search of the Daily's office had deprived respondents under color of state law of rights secured to them by the First, Fourth, and Fourteenth Amendments of the United States Constitution. * * *

The issue here is how the Fourth Amendment is to be construed and applied to the "third party" search, the recurring situation where state authorities have probable cause to believe that fruits, instrumentalities, or other evidence of crime is located on identified property but do not then have probable cause to believe that the owner or possessor of the property is himself implicated in the crime that has occurred or is occurring. * * *

First, * * * it is apparent that whether the third-party occupant is suspect or not, the State's interest in enforcing the criminal law and recovering the evidence remains the same; and it is the seeming innocence of the property owner that the District Court relied on to foreclose the warrant to search. But, as respondents themselves now concede, if the third party knows that contraband or other illegal materials are on his property, he is sufficiently culpable to justify the issuance of a search warrant. Similarly, if his ethical stance is the determining factor, it seems to us that whether or not he knows that the sought-after articles are secreted on his property and whether or not he knows that the articles are in fact the fruits, instrumentalities, or evidence of crime, he will be so informed when the search warrant is served, and it is doubtful that he should then be permitted to object to the search, to withhold, if it is there, the evidence of crime reasonably believed to be possessed by him or secreted on his property, and to forbid the search and insist that the officers serve him with a subpoena duces tecum.

Second, we are unpersuaded that the District Court's new rule denying search warrants against third parties and insisting on subpoenas would substantially further privacy interests without seriously undermining law enforcement efforts. Because of the fundamental public interest in implementing the criminal law, the search warrant, a heretofore effective and constitutionally acceptable enforcement tool, should not be suppressed on the basis of surmise and without solid evidence supporting the change. As the District Court understands it, denying third-party search warrants would not have substantial adverse effects on criminal investigations because the nonsuspect third party, once served with a subpoena, will preserve the evidence and ultimately lawfully respond. The difficulty with this assumption is that search warrants are often employed early in an investigation, perhaps before the identity of any likely criminal and certainly before all the perpetrators are or could be known. The seemingly blameless third party in possession of the fruits or evidence may not be innocent at all; and if he is, he may nevertheless be so related to or so sympathetic with the culpable that he cannot be relied upon to retain and preserve the articles that may implicate his friends, or at least not to notify those who would be damaged by the evidence that the authorities are aware of its location. In any event, it is likely that the real culprits will have access to the property, and the delay involved in employing the subpoena duces tecum, offering as it does the opportunity to litigate its validity, could easily result in the disappearance of the evidence, whatever the good faith of the third party.

Forbidding the warrant and insisting on the subpoena instead when the custodian of the object of the search is not then suspected of crime, involves hazards to criminal investigation much more serious than the District Court believed; and the record is barren of anything but the District Court's assumptions to support its conclusions. At the very least, the burden of justifying a major revision of the Fourth Amendment has not been carried.

We are also not convinced that the net gain to privacy interests by the District Court's new rule would be worth the candle. In the normal course of events, search warrants are more difficult to obtain than subpoenas, since the latter do not involve the judiciary and do not require proof of probable cause. Where, in the real world, subpoenas would suffice, it can be expected that they will be employed by the rational prosecutor. On the other hand, when choice is available under local law and the prosecutor chooses to use the search warrant, it is unlikely that he has needlessly selected the more difficult course. His choice is more likely to be based on the solid belief, arrived at through experience but difficult, if not impossible, to sustain in a specific case, that the warranted search is necessary to secure and to avoid the destruction of evidence. * * *

There is no reason to believe * * * that magistrates cannot guard against searches of the type, scope, and intrusiveness that would actually interfere with the timely publication of a newspaper. Nor, if the requirements of specificity and reasonableness are properly applied, policed, and observed, will there be any occasion or opportunity for officers to rummage at large in newspaper files or to intrude into or to deter normal editorial and publication decisions. The warrant issued in this case authorized nothing of this sort. * * *

The fact is that respondents and amici have pointed to only a very few instances in the entire United States since 1971 involving the issuance of warrants for searching newspaper premises. This reality hardly suggests abuse; and if abuse occurs, there will be time enough to deal with it. Furthermore, the press is not only an important, critical, and valuable asset to society, but it is not easily intimidated—nor should it be. * * *

We accordingly reject the reasons given by the District Court and adopted by the Court of Appeals for holding the search for photographs at the Stanford Daily to have been unreasonable within the meaning of the Fourth Amendment and in violation of the First Amendment. Nor has anything else presented here persuaded us that the Amendments forbade this search. It follows that the judgment of the Court of Appeals is reversed.

I. TELEPHONE AND CABLE PRIVACY STATUTES

1. TELEPHONE CONSUMER PROTECTION ACT OF 1991 AND THE NATIONAL DO–NOT–CALL REGISTRY

Note: Subscriber Protections

This section examines federal statutes whose aim is to curb telemarketing abuses and secure the confidentiality of information telephone and cable customers routinely entrust to their service providers. Laws that regulate wiretapping and other interceptions of communications are examined in detail in Chapter 4.

a. Constitutionality of the Federal Registry

MAINSTREAM MKTG. SERVS. v. FTC

358 F.3d 1228 (10th Cir. 2004).

Ebel, Circuit Judge.

The four cases consolidated in this appeal involve challenges to the national do-not-call registry, which allows individuals to register their phone numbers on a national "do-not-call list" and prohibits most commercial telemarketers from calling the numbers on that list. The primary issue in this case is whether the First Amendment prevents the government from establishing an opt-in telemarketing regulation that provides a mechanism for consumers to restrict commercial sales calls but does not provide a similar mechanism to limit charitable or political calls. We hold that the do-not-call registry is a valid commercial speech regulation because it directly advances the government's important interests in safeguarding personal privacy and reducing the danger of telemarketing abuse without burdening an excessive amount of speech. In other words, there is a reasonable fit between the do-not-call regulations and the government's reasons for enacting them.

As we discuss below in greater detail, four key aspects of the do-not-call registry convince us that it is consistent with First Amendment requirements. First, the list restricts only core commercial speech—i.e., commercial sales calls. Second, the do-not-call registry targets speech that invades the privacy of the home, a personal sanctuary that enjoys a unique status in our constitutional jurisprudence. See Frisby v. Schultz, 487 U.S. 474, 484 (1988). Third, the do-not-call registry is an opt-in program that puts the choice of whether or not to restrict commercial calls entirely in the hands of consumers. Fourth, the do-not-call registry materially furthers the government's interests in combating the danger of abusive telemarketing and preventing the invasion of consumer privacy, blocking a significant number of the calls that cause these problems. Under these circumstances, we conclude that the requirements of the First Amendment are satisfied.

A number of additional features of the national do-not-call registry, although not dispositive, further demonstrate that the list is consistent with the First Amendment rights of commercial speakers. The challenged regulations do not hinder any business' ability to contact consumers by other means, such as through direct mailings or other forms of advertising. Moreover, they give consumers a number of different options to avoid calls they do not want to receive. Namely, consumers who wish to restrict some but not all commercial sales calls can do so by using company-specific do-not-call lists or by granting some businesses express permission to call. In addition, the government chose to offer consumers broader options to restrict commercial sales calls than charitable and political calls after finding that commercial calls were more intrusive and posed a greater danger of consumer abuse. The government also had evidence that the less restrictive company-specific do-not-call list did not solve the problems caused by commercial telemarketing, but it had no comparable evidence with respect to charitable and political fundraising.

The national do-not-call registry offers consumers a tool with which they can protect their homes against intrusions that Congress has determined to be particularly invasive. Just as a consumer can avoid door-to-door peddlers by placing a "No Solicitation" sign in his or her front yard, the do-not-call registry lets consumers avoid unwanted sales pitches that invade the home via telephone, if they choose to do so. We are convinced that the First Amendment does not prevent the government from giving consumers this option. * * *

In 2003, two federal agencies—the Federal Trade Commission (FTC) and the Federal Communications Commission (FCC)—promulgated rules that together created the national do-not-call registry. The national do-not-call registry is a list containing the personal telephone numbers of telephone subscribers who have voluntarily indicated that they do not wish to receive unsolicited calls from commercial telemarketers. Commercial telemarketers are generally prohibited from calling phone numbers that have been placed on the do-not-call registry, and they must pay an annual fee to access the numbers on the registry so that they can delete those numbers from their telephone solicitation lists. So far, consumers have registered more than 50 million phone numbers on the national do-not-call registry.

The national do-not-call registry's restrictions apply only to telemarketing calls made by or on behalf of sellers of goods or services, and not to charitable or political fundraising calls. Additionally, a seller may call consumers who have signed up for the national registry if it has an established business relationship with the consumer or if the consumer has given that seller express written permission to call. Telemarketers generally have three months from the date on which a consumer signs up for the registry to remove the consumer's phone number from their call lists. Consumer registrations remain valid for five years, and phone numbers that are disconnected or reassigned will be periodically removed from the registry.

The national do-not-call registry is the product of a regulatory effort dating back to 1991 aimed at protecting the privacy rights of consumers and curbing the risk of telemarketing abuse. In the Telephone Consumer Protection Act of 1991 ("TCPA")—under which the FCC enacted its do-not-call rules—Congress found that for many consumers telemarketing sales calls constitute an intrusive invasion of privacy. See Pub. L. No. 102–243, 105 Stat. 2394 at § 2 (1991). Moreover, the TCPA's legislative history cited statistical data indicating that "most unwanted telephone solicitations are commercial in nature" and that "unwanted commercial calls are a far bigger problem than unsolicited calls from political or charitable organizations." H.R. Rep. No. 102–317 at 16 (1991). The TCPA therefore authorized the FCC to establish a national database of consumers who object to receiving "telephone solicitations," which the act defined as commercial sales calls.

Furthermore, in the Telemarketing and Consumer Fraud and Abuse Prevention Act of 1994 ("Telemarketing Act")—under which the FTC enacted its do-not-call rules—Congress found that consumers lose an estimated $40 billion each year due to telemarketing fraud. Therefore, Congress authorized the FTC to prohibit sales calls that a reasonable consumer would consider coercive or abusive of his or her right to privacy. Id. at § 3.

The FCC and FTC initially sought to accomplish the goals of the TCPA and the Telemarketing Act by adopting company-specific do-not-call lists, requiring sellers to maintain lists of consumers who have requested not to be called by that particular solicitor, and requiring telemarketers to honor those requests. See Rules and Regulations Implementing the Telephone Consumer Protection Act of 1991. * * * Yet in enacting the national do-not-call registry, the agencies concluded that the company-specific lists had failed to achieve Congress' objectives. * * * Among other shortfalls, the agencies explained that the large number of possible telephone solicitors made it burdensome for consumers to assert their rights under the company-specific rules, and that commercial telemarketers often ignored consumers' requests not to be called. Accordingly, the agencies decided to keep the company-specific rules as an option available to consumers, but to supplement them with the national do-not-call registry.

In this appeal we have consolidated four cases challenging various aspects of the national do-not-call registry. Cases Nos. 03–1429, 03–6258 and 03–9571 involve First Amendment attacks on the do-not-call list and its registry fees. We address these issues in parts III and IV(A) respectively. Case No. 03–9594 involves a challenge to the FCC rule's established business relationship exception on administrative law grounds. We address this issue in part IV(B). Finally, in part IV(C), we address the alternative argument that the FTC lacked statutory authority to enact its do-not-call regulations, an argument that the district court relied upon in case No. 03–6258. We conclude that all of the telemarketers' challenges lack merit and we uphold the do-not-call list in its entirety. * * *

The national do-not-call registry's telemarketing restrictions apply only to commercial speech. Like most commercial speech regulations, the do-not-call rules draw a line between commercial and non-commercial speech on the basis of content. * * *

Central Hudson Gas & Elec. Corp. v. Public Serv. Comm'n., 447 U.S. 557, 566 (1980) established a three-part test governing First Amendment challenges to regulations restricting non-misleading commercial speech that relates to lawful activity. First, the government must assert a substantial interest to be achieved by the regulation. Central Hudson, 447 U.S. at 564. Second, the regulation must directly advance that governmental interest, meaning that it must do more than provide "only ineffective or remote support for the government's purpose." Id. Third, although the regulation need not be the least restrictive measure available, it must be narrowly tailored not to restrict more speech than necessary. Together, these final two factors require that there be a reasonable fit between the government's objectives and the means it chooses to accomplish those ends. United States v. Edge Broad. Co., 509 U.S. 418, 427–28 (1993).

The government bears the burden of asserting one or more substantial governmental interests and demonstrating a reasonable fit between those interests and the challenged regulation. Utah Licensed Beverage Ass'n v. Leavitt, 256 F.3d 1061, 1069 (10th Cir. 2001). The government is not limited in the evidence it may use to meet its burden. For example, a commercial speech regulation may be justified by anecdotes, history, consensus, or simple common sense. Went For It, 515 U.S. at 628. Yet we may not take it upon ourselves to supplant the interests put forward by the state with our own ideas of what goals the challenged laws might serve. Edenfield v. Fane, 507 U.S. 761, 768 (1993).

A. Governmental Interests

The government asserts that the do-not-call regulations are justified by its interests in 1) protecting the privacy of individuals in their homes, and 2) protecting consumers against the risk of fraudulent and abusive solicitation. Both of these justifications are undisputedly substantial governmental interests.

In Rowan v. United States Post Office Dep't, the Supreme Court upheld the right of a homeowner to restrict material that could be mailed to his or her house. 397 U.S. 728 (1970). The Court emphasized the importance of individual privacy, particularly in the context of the home, stating that "the ancient concept that 'a man's home is his castle' into which 'not even the king may enter' has lost none of its vitality." Id. at 737. In Frisby v. Schultz, the Court again stressed the unique nature of the home and recognized that "the State's interest in protecting the well-being, tranquility, and privacy of the home is certainly of the highest order in a free and civilized society." As the Court held in Frisby: "One important aspect of residential privacy is protection of the unwilling listener. * * * [A] special benefit of the privacy all citizens enjoy within their own walls, which the State may legislate to protect, is an ability to avoid intrusions. Thus, we have repeatedly held that individuals are not required to welcome unwanted speech into their own homes and that the government may protect this freedom." * * *

Likewise, in Hill v. Colorado, the Court called the unwilling listener's interest in avoiding unwanted communication part of the broader right to be let alone that Justice Brandeis described as "the right most valued by civilized men.". The Court added that the right to avoid unwanted speech has special force in the context of the home. FCC v. Pacifica Found., 438 U.S. 726 (1978) ("In the privacy of the home * * * the individual's right to be left alone plainly outweighs the First Amendment rights of an intruder.").

Additionally, the Supreme Court has recognized that the government has a substantial interest in preventing abusive and coercive sales practices. Edenfield v. Fane, 507 U.S. 761 (1993) ("The First Amendment * * * does not prohibit the State from insuring that the stream of commercial information flows cleanly as well as freely.") * * *

B.   Reasonable Fit

A reasonable fit exists between the do-not-call rules and the government's privacy and consumer protection interests if the regulation directly advances those interests and is narrowly tailored. See Central Hudson, 447 U.S. at 564–65. In this context, the "narrowly tailored" standard does not require that the government's response to protect substantial interests be the least restrictive measure available. All that is required is a proportional response.

In other words, the national do-not-call registry is valid if it is designed to provide effective support for the government's purposes and if the government did not suppress an excessive amount of speech when substantially narrower restrictions would have worked just as well. See Central Hudson, 447 U.S. at 564–65. These criteria are plainly established in this case. The do-not-call registry directly advances the government's interests by effectively blocking a significant number of the calls that cause the problems the government sought to redress. It is narrowly tailored because its opt-in character ensures that it does not inhibit any speech directed at the home of a willing listener.

1.   Effectiveness

The telemarketers assert that the do-not-call registry is unconstitutionally underinclusive because it does not apply to charitable and political callers. First Amendment challenges based on underinclusiveness face an uphill battle in the commercial speech context. As a general rule, the First Amendment does not require that the government regulate all aspects of a problem before it can make progress on any front. United States v. Edge Broad. Co., 509 U.S. 418 (1993). "Within the bounds of the general protection provided by the Constitution to commercial speech, we allow room for legislative judgments." Id. The underinclusiveness of a commercial speech regulation is relevant only if it renders the regulatory framework so irrational that it fails materially to advance the aims that it was purportedly designed to further. * * *

Yet so long as a commercial speech regulation materially furthers its objectives, underinclusiveness is not fatal under Central Hudson. * * *

As discussed above, the national do-not-call registry is designed to reduce intrusions into personal privacy and the risk of telemarketing fraud and abuse that accompany unwanted telephone solicitation. The registry directly advances those goals. So far, more than 50 million telephone numbers have been registered on the do-not-call list, and the do-not-call regulations protect these households from receiving most unwanted telemarketing calls. * * *

To be sure, the do-not-call list will not block all of these calls. Nevertheless, it will prohibit a substantial number of them, making it difficult to fathom how the registry could be called an "ineffective" means of stopping invasive or abusive calls, or a regulation that "furnishes only speculative or marginal support" for the government's interests. * * *

Finally, the type of unsolicited calls that the do-not-call list does prohibit—commercial sales calls—is the type that Congress, the FTC and the FCC have all determined to be most to blame for the problems the government is seeking to redress. According to the legislative history accompanying the TCPA, "complaint statistics show that unwanted commercial calls are a far bigger problem than unsolicited calls from political or charitable organizations." * * * Similarly, the FCC determined that calls from solicitors with an established business relationship with the recipient are less problematic than other commercial calls. * * *

Additionally, the FTC has found that commercial callers are more likely than non-commercial callers to engage in deceptive and abusive practices. * * * Specifically, the FTC concluded that in charitable and political calls, a significant purpose of the call is to sell a cause, not merely to receive a donation, and that non-commercial callers thus have stronger incentives not to alienate the people they call or to engage in abusive and deceptive practices. * * * The speech regulated by the do-not-call list is therefore the speech most likely to cause the problems the government sought to alleviate in enacting that list, further demonstrating that the regulation directly advances the government's interests. * * *

2. Narrow Tailoring * * *

We hold that the national do-not-call registry is narrowly tailored because it does not over-regulate protected speech; rather, it restricts only calls that are targeted at unwilling recipients. The do-not-call registry prohibits only telemarketing calls aimed at consumers who have affirmatively indicated that they do not want to receive such calls and for whom such calls would constitute an invasion of privacy. See Hill v. Colorado, 530 U.S. 703 (2000) (the right of privacy includes an unwilling listener's interest in avoiding unwanted communication).

The Supreme Court has repeatedly held that speech restrictions based on private choice (i.e.—an opt-in feature) are less restrictive than laws that prohibit speech directly. In Rowan, for example, the Court approved a law under which an individual could require a mailer to stop all future mailings if he or she received advertisements that he or she believed to be erotically arousing or sexually provocative. 397 U.S. at 729–30, 738. Although it was the government that empowered individuals to avoid materials they considered provocative, the Court emphasized that the mailer's right to communicate was circumscribed only by an affirmative act of a householder. Id. at 738. "Congress has erected a wall—or more accurately permits a citizen to erect a wall—that no advertiser may penetrate without his acquiescence. * * * The asserted right of a mailer, we repeat, stops at the outer boundary of every person's domain." Id.

Likewise, in rejecting direct prohibitions of speech (even fully protected speech), the Supreme Court has often reasoned that an opt-in regulation would have been a less restrictive alternative. * * *

The idea that an opt-in regulation is less restrictive than a direct prohibition of speech applies not only to traditional door-to-door solicitation, but also to regulations seeking to protect the privacy of the home from unwanted intrusions via telephone, television, or the Internet. * * *

Like the do-not-mail regulation approved in Rowan, the national do-not-call registry does not itself prohibit any speech. Instead, it merely "permits a citizen to erect a wall * * * that no advertiser may penetrate without his acquiescence." See Rowan, 397 U.S. at 738. Almost by definition, the do-not-call regulations only block calls that would constitute unwanted intrusions into the privacy of consumers who have signed up for the list. Moreover, it allows consumers who feel susceptible to telephone fraud or abuse to ensure that most commercial callers will not have an opportunity to victimize them. Under the circumstances we address in this case, we conclude that the do-not-call registry's opt-in feature renders it a narrowly tailored commercial speech regulation.

The do-not-call registry's narrow tailoring is further demonstrated by the fact that it presents both sellers and consumers with a number of options to make and receive sales offers. From the seller's perspective, the do-not-call registry restricts only one avenue by which solicitors can communicate with consumers who have registered for the list. In particular, the do-not-call regulations do not prevent businesses from corresponding with potential customers by mail or by means of advertising through other media. * * *

From the consumer's perspective, the do-not-call rules provide a number of different options allowing consumers to dictate what telemarketing calls they wish to receive and what calls they wish to avoid.

Consumers who would like to receive some commercial sales calls but not others can sign up for the national do-not-call registry but give written permission to call to those businesses from whom they wish to receive offers. * * * Alternatively, they may decline to sign up on the national registry but make company-specific do-not-call requests with those particular businesses from whom they do not wish to receive calls. * * * Therefore, under the current regulations, consumers choose between two default rules—either that telemarketers may call or that they may not. Then, consumers may make company-specific modifications to either of these default rules as they see fit, either granting particular sellers permission to call or blocking calls from certain sellers. * * *

In sum, the do-not-call registry is narrowly tailored to restrict only speech that contributes to the problems the government seeks to redress, namely the intrusion into personal privacy and the risk of fraud and abuse caused by telephone calls that consumers do not welcome into their homes. No calls are restricted unless the recipient has affirmatively declared that he or she does not wish to receive them. Moreover, telemarketers still have the ability to contact consumers in other ways, and consumers have a number of different options in determining what telemarketing calls they will receive. Finally, there are not numerous and obvious less-burdensome alternatives that would restrict less speech while accomplishing the government's objectives equally as well. * * *

We hold that 1) the do-not-call list is a valid commercial speech regulation under Central Hudson because it directly advances substantial governmental interests and is narrowly tailored; 2) the registry fees telemarketers must pay to access the list are a permissible measure designed to defray the cost of legitimate government regulation; 3) it was not arbitrary and capricious for the FCC to adopt the established business relationship exception; and 4) the FTC has statutory authority to establish and implement the national do-not-call registry.

b. FTC Do–Not–Call Registry Enforcement

FTC SUES TO STOP ROBOCALLS WITH DECEPTIVE CREDIT CARD INTEREST–RATE REDUCTION CLAIMS

Press Release, December 8, 2009.

The Federal Trade Commission today announced its second major law enforcement effort this year targeting telemarketers who violated the Do Not Call Rule and other laws by making hundreds of thousands or even millions of pre-recorded robocalls to consumers. The cases announced today target three groups that allegedly made robocalls to sell worthless credit-card interest-rate reduction programs for hefty up-front fees of as much as $1,495. At the FTC's request, in each case, the court has issued an order temporarily halting the robocalls pending trial.

"The FTC has heard the public outcry against robocalls and has taken swift action to stop them. During these difficult economic times, the last thing anyone needs is to be bombarded by robocalls pitching worthless interest-rate reduction programs," FTC Chairman Jon Leibowitz said. "The lawsuits announced today are not the first, nor will they be the last, that the agency brings to protect consumers from intrusive, illegal, and deceptive telemarketing robocalls."

The three complaints announced today follow two filed in May that led to court orders stopping other telemarketers from using robocalls with deceptive claims about extended auto warranties. Since September 1, 2009, virtually all robocalls have been illegal, unless the recipients have provided written authorization to receive the pre-recorded calls (see press release at: http://www.ftc.gov/opa/2009/08/robocalls.shtm).

The Commission today also issued a new publication, the National Do Not Call Registry Data Book for Fiscal Year 2009, which contains information about the Registry, along with a breakdown of consumer complaints about companies violating the Do Not Call rules. According to the Data Book, there are more than 191 million numbers on the Do Not Call Registry.

According to the three FTC complaints, Economic Relief Technologies, LLC, Dynamic Financial Group (U.S.A.) Inc., and JPM Accelerated Services (JPM) and related defendants made illegal pre-recorded robocalls to consumers, using names like "card services," "credit card services" or "account services." The robocalls allegedly claimed the defendants' services could lower the interest rate on consumers' credit cards. In each case, consumers who pressed 1 after hearing the automated call were transferred to live telemarketers who allegedly misrepresented that consumers could dramatically lower the rates on their credit card. The telemarketers also said consumers would save thousands of dollars in a short period of time by lowering their interest rates and would be able to pay off their debts faster—for an up-front fee ranging from $495 to $1,495. The defendants then falsely stated that if consumers did not save a "guaranteed" amount—typically $2,500 or more—they could get a full refund of the up-front fee. However, after securing the fee, the defendants allegedly did not negotiate lower rates on behalf of consumers and provided few refunds to those who were dissatisfied with the service.

The Economic Relief Technologies defendants also allegedly operated a related scam: using names like "Auto Protection Center" and "Warranty Services," they tricked consumers into believing they were affiliated with their vehicle manufacturer or dealership, and falsely stated that the consumers' vehicles' warranties were about to expire. The scheme is similar to several stopped by a court order at the FTC's request earlier this year (see press release at http://www.ftc.gov/opa/2009/05/robocalls.shtm).

The lawsuits allege the defendants broke the law by making illegal robocalls to consumers, and that their deceptive sales pitches violated the FTC Act and the FTC's Telemarketing Sales Rule. Additional charges include: 1) calling consumers whose phone numbers are on the National

Do Not Call Registry; 2) calling consumers who had previously asked not to be called; 3) failing to transmit their caller ID information, as required; 4) "spoofing" or masking their caller ID information; 5) failing to promptly identify themselves, the purpose of their call, and/or the nature of the goods or services they were selling; 6) improperly abandoning calls; and 7) failing to make required disclosures in their robocalls. * * *

FTC, "FTC ENFORCEMENT AGAINST COLUMBIA HOUSE"

Press Release, July 15, 2005.

Columbia House Settles FTC Charges of Do Not Call Violations

The Columbia House Company, a well-known direct marketer of home entertainment products, has settled Federal Trade Commission charges that it violated federal law by calling existing or past subscribers of its home entertainment clubs after the subscribers had placed their telephone numbers on the National Do Not Call Registry, and after the subscribers had made specific requests to the company that they not be called. Columbia House will pay a $300,000 civil penalty and is barred from making illegal telemarketing calls in the future.

Columbia House markets its home entertainment products to consumers through a variety of membership clubs, including a DVD club, a video club, and music clubs. Consumers who join the clubs receive a number of DVDs, CDs, or videos at a reduced price if they sign on to purchase a designated number of additional products over the next two years. According to a complaint filed by the Department of Justice on the FTC's behalf, Columbia House conducts telemarketing campaigns to existing and former members of its home entertainment clubs, soliciting former members to rejoin one of its clubs and existing members to purchase additional products.

Under the Do Not Call Rule, a company may call consumers whose telephone numbers are on the National Registry if the company has an established business relationship with the consumer, unless the consumer has asked not to be called. Companies with whom a consumer has an existing business relationship may call the consumer for up to 18 months after the consumer's last business transaction with the company. In addition, since 1995, the FTC's Telemarketing Sales Rule (TSR) has required companies to keep a company-specific do not call list and to honor consumers' specific requests that they not be called. Such a request must be honored even if the company has an established business relationship with the consumer. Companies are not permitted to call former customers whose numbers appear on the National Registry after the 18–month period has elapsed.

According to the FTC, from October 2003 through March 2004, Columbia House placed tens of thousands of calls to former members whose phone numbers were registered on the National Registry, after the company no longer had an established business relationship with those members as defined by the law. The FTC's complaint further alleged that, since December 1995, Columbia House violated the company-specific do not call provision of the TSR by calling consumers who had previously asked that they not be called. The FTC's complaint stated that although the company had implemented procedures to attempt to prevent future calls to such consumers, those procedures had proven ineffective in preventing the alleged calls.

The stipulated judgment and order bars Columbia House from calling any consumer who has previously asked not to be called. It also prohibits Columbia House from calling any consumer whose number is registered on the National Do Not Call Registry, unless the company has received a request, in writing, from the consumer permitting future calls; or the company has an established business relationship with the consumer and the consumer has not previously requested to be removed from the company's call list. The order further requires Columbia House to pay a $300,000 civil penalty. The order contains recordkeeping provisions to assist the FTC in monitoring the company's compliance.

The FTC reminds businesses that, before calling a former customer based on an established business relationship, they must ensure that the relationship has not expired and that the customer has not made a specific request not to be called. Entities that hire third parties to telemarket on their behalf are responsible for ensuring that the telemarketers comply with federal law by downloading the appropriate area codes of data from the Registry; scrubbing their call lists every 31 days; making sure established business relationships are current before calling consumers whose numbers are registered; and honoring company-specific do not call requests.

The Commission vote to refer the complaint and stipulated judgment and order to the Department of Justice for filing was 5–0. The complaint and stipulated judgment and order were filed on July 14, 2005, in the U.S. District Court for the Northern District of Illinois, Eastern Division, by the Department of Justice at the request of the FTC.

c. A Stricter, State Do–Not–Call Law

NATIONAL COALITION OF PRAYER v. CARTER
455 F.3d 783 (7th Cir. 2006).

FLAUM, CHIEF JUDGE.

Plaintiffs are charities that Indiana's Telephone Privacy Act ("the Act") precludes from fundraising through professional telemarketers. They claim that the Act violates their First Amendment right to freedom of speech because it is content-based, underbroad, and a prior restraint on speech. The district court granted summary judgment to the State, and Plaintiffs now appeal. For the following reasons, we affirm the decision of the district court. * * *

In May 2001, Indiana's governor signed into law the Indiana Telephone Privacy Act, codified at Indiana Code § 24–4.7. The Act creates a statewide do-not-call list and allows Indiana residential telephone customers to add themselves to this list. Once citizens affirmatively place their telephone numbers on the list, "telephone solicitors" cannot legally call the numbers for a "telephone sales call." The Act defines a "telephone solicitor" as "an individual, a firm, an organization, a partnership, an association, or a corporation * * * doing business in Indiana." A "telephone sales call" is any call made to "solicit[]" a "sale of consumer goods or services" or a "charitable contribution," or to "obtain[] information that will or may be used for the direct solicitation of a sale of consumer goods or services or an extension of credit for such purposes."

The Act exempts certain calls from its purview. Most relevant to this case, the Act permits "telephone call[s] made on behalf of a charitable organization that is exempt from federal income taxation under Section 501 of the Internal Revenue Code, but only if * * * [t]he telephone call is made by a volunteer or an employee of the charitable organization[, and] the telephone solicitor who makes the telephone call immediately discloses * * * [his or her] true first and last name [and t]he name, address, and telephone number of the charitable organization." * * *

The Plaintiffs in this case are all tax-exempt charities. They wish to use telemarketers to solicit donations for their charitable causes. They claim that the Act violates their First Amendment rights, because it prohibits them from using telemarketers to call the numbers registered on the do-not-call list. On cross motions for summary judgment, the district court found in favor of the State, and Plaintiffs now appeal. * * *

The State's argument is primarily based on Rowan [v. United States Postal Service, 397 U.S. 728 (1970)]. In that case, the Supreme Court reviewed a law that allowed customers of the U.S. Postal Service to prohibit delivery of sales literature for items "which the addressee in his sole discretion believes to be erotically arousing or sexually provocative." The Court upheld the statute, citing the need for a person to be safe from any unwanted message—even a "valid message"—in his or her own home. * * *

We find the State's Rowan analogy persuasive, and choose to adopt it here. * * *

We conclude that the Act places the Attorney General of Indiana in a "ministerial" role * * * analogous to that of the Postmaster General in the final legislation in Rowan[.] * * * The telephone calls that the Attorney General must allow to be placed to numbers on the do-not-call list are very well defined. For example, it involves little discretion to decide if the call was placed on behalf of a tax-exempt charity, or if the person who placed the call was a volunteer or employee of that charity. * * *

Because the Act sharply curtails telemarketing—the speech that was most injurious to residential privacy—while excluding speech that historically enjoys greater First Amendment protection, we are satisfied that the Act is not underbroad. Therefore, applying Rowan, we believe that the state's interest in protecting residents' right not to endure unwanted speech in their own homes outweighs any First Amendment interests the Plaintiffs possess. * * *

For the foregoing reasons, we affirm the district court's grant of summary judgment for the State of Indiana and its denial of the Plaintiffs' motion for summary judgment.

2. CABLE COMMUNICATIONS POLICY ACT OF 1984

Note: Privacy Rights for Cable Subscribers

The Cable Communications Policy Act ("CCPA"), 47 U.S.C. § 551 et seq., regulates the informational privacy of persons who subscribe to cable services. Contemporary cable companies (e.g., Comcast Cable and Time–Warner Cable) provide television, internet and telephone services. The Cable Communications Policy Act was amended by the USA PATRIOT Act to make it clear that federal wiretap rules that apply to telephones also apply to internet and telephone services provided by cable companies. To what extent does this statute specifically reflect fair information practice principles? Look closely at the major requirements of sections (c)–(h) of the Act. Would you describe the privacy protections outlined in the CCPA as weak or strong?

CABLE COMMUNICATIONS POLICY ACT 47 U.S.C. § 551 ET SEQ.

§ 551. Protection of subscriber privacy * * *

(c) Disclosure of personally identifiable information.

(1) Except as provided in paragraph (2), a cable operator shall not disclose personally identifiable information concerning any subscriber without the prior written or electronic consent of the subscriber concerned and shall take such actions as are necessary to prevent unauthorized access to such information by a person other than the subscriber or cable operator.

(2) A cable operator may disclose such information if the disclosure is—

(A) necessary to render, or conduct a legitimate business activity related to, a cable service or other service provided by the cable operator to the subscriber;

(B) subject to subsection (h), made pursuant to a court order authorizing such disclosure, if the subscriber is notified of such order by the person to whom the order is directed;

(C) a disclosure of the names and addresses of subscribers to any cable service or other service, if—

    (i) the cable operator has provided the subscriber the opportunity to prohibit or limit such disclosure, and

    (ii) the disclosure does not reveal, directly or indirectly, the—

        (I) extent of any viewing or other use by the subscriber of a cable service or other service provided by the cable operator, or

        (II) the nature of any transaction made by the subscriber over the cable system of the cable operator; or

(D) to a government entity as authorized under chapters 119, 121, or 206 of title 18, United States Code [18 USCS §§ 2510 et seq., 2701 et seq., or 3121 et seq.], except that such disclosure shall not include records revealing cable subscriber selection of video programming from a cable operator.

(d) Subscriber access to information. A cable subscriber shall be provided access to all personally identifiable information regarding that subscriber which is collected and maintained by a cable operator. Such information shall be made available to the subscriber at reasonable times and at a convenient place designated by such cable operator. A cable subscriber shall be provided reasonable opportunity to correct any error in such information.

(e) Destruction of information. A cable operator shall destroy personally identifiable information if the information is no longer necessary for the purpose for which it was collected and there are no pending requests or orders for access to such information under subsection (d) or pursuant to a court order.

(f) Civil action in United States district court; damages; attorney's fees and costs; nonexclusive nature of remedy.

    (1) Any person aggrieved by any act of a cable operator in violation of this section may bring a civil action in a United States district court. * * *

(h) Disclosure of information to governmental entity pursuant to court order. Except as provided in subsection (c)(2)(D), a governmental entity may obtain personally identifiable information concerning a cable subscriber pursuant to a court order only if, in the court proceeding relevant to such court order—

    (1) such entity offers clear and convincing evidence that the subject of the information is reasonably suspected of engaging in criminal activity and that the information sought would be material evidence in the case; and

    (2) the subject of the information is afforded the opportunity to appear and contest such entity's claim.

MARCY E. PEEK, "THE CABLE COMMUNICATIONS POLICY ACT OF 1984"

The Encyclopedia of Privacy (ed. William G. Staples 2007).

The Cable Communications Policy Act of 1984 dictates the privacy practices of cable companies. Under the act, default privacy protections are minimal. For example, although customers must sometimes give consent for their cable companies to collect personally identifiable information, consent is easily obtained and is often not required. First, nothing in the act prevents a cable company from obtaining the required consent via the standard cable agreement or via another standardized process such as a "click through" agreement on the company's website. Second, even without such consent, cable operators may collect such information in order to "obtain information necessary to render a cable service or other service provided by the cable operator to the subscriber" or to "detect unauthorized reception of cable communications."

3. TELECOMMUNICATIONS ACT OF 1996— CUSTOMER PROPRIETARY NETWORK INFORMATION (CPNI) PRIVACY

NOTE: OPT-IN VERSUS OPT-OUT

U.S. West v. FCC attracted wide interest. It considered, head-on, the relative constitutionality of "opt-in" versus "opt-out" data protection laws. The court sided with opt-out approaches, on First Amendment grounds, disappointing some consumer privacy advocates. But see, Fred Cate, "Protecting Privacy in the New Millenium: The Fallacy of 'Opt-in'," arguing that "opt-in provides no greater privacy protection then opt-out but imposes significantly higher costs with dramatically different legal and economic implications," see www.bbbonline.org/UnderstandingPrivacy/library/whitepapers/fallacyofoptin.pdf. Professor Cate stresses that both opt-in and opt-out give customers the final say. Does Professor Cate have a point? Is the case correctly decided? The dissenting opinion offers grounds for arguing that it was not. Who gets it right?

U.S. WEST v. FEDERAL COMMUNICATIONS COMMISSION

182 F.3d 1224 (10th Cir. 1999).

TACHA, CIRCUIT JUDGE. * * *

This case involves classic issues of separation of powers and the courts' necessary role as guardians of constitutional interests. It is seductive for us to view this as just another case of reviewing agency action. However, this case is a harbinger of difficulties encountered in this age of exploding information, when rights bestowed by the United States Constitution must be guarded as vigilantly as in the days of handbills on public sidewalks. In the name of deference to agency action, important civil liberties, such as the First Amendment's protection of speech, could easily be overlooked. Policing the boundaries among constitutional guarantees, legislative mandates, and administrative interpretation is at the heart of our responsibility. This case highlights the importance of that role. * * *

The dispute in this case involves regulations the FCC promulgated to implement provisions of 47 U.S.C. § 222, which was enacted as part of the Telecommunications Act of 1996. Section 222, entitled "Privacy of customer information," states generally that "every telecommunications carrier has a duty to protect the confidentiality of proprietary information of, and relating to * * * customers." 47 U.S.C. § 222(a). To effectuate that duty, § 222 places restrictions on the use, disclosure of, and access to certain customer information. At issue here are the FCC's regulations clarifying the privacy requirements for CPNI [customer proprietary network information] * * *. Therefore, the essence of the statutory scheme requires a telecommunications carrier to obtain customer approval when it wishes to use, disclose, or permit access to CPNI in a manner not specifically allowed under § 222. * * *

The [FCC] regulations also describe the means by which a carrier must obtain customer approval. Section 222(c)(1) did not elaborate as to what form that approval should take. The FCC decided to require an "opt-in" approach, in which a carrier must obtain prior express approval from a customer through written, oral, or electronic means before using the customer's CPNI. See 47 C.F.R. § 64.2007(b). The government acknowledged that the means of approval could have taken numerous other forms, including an "opt-out" approach, in which approval would be inferred from the customer-carrier relationship unless the customer specifically requested that his or her CPNI be restricted. * * *

Petitioner argues that the [FCC's] CPNI regulations interpreting 47 U.S.C. § 222 violate the First Amendment. The First Amendment states, "Congress shall make no law * * * abridging the freedom of speech." U.S. Const. amend. I. Although the text of the First Amendment refers to legislative enactments by Congress, it is actually much broader in scope and encompasses, among other things, regulations promulgated by administrative agencies. * * *

As a threshold requirement for the application of the First Amendment, the government action must abridge or restrict protected speech. The government argues that the FCC's CPNI regulations do not violate or even infringe upon petitioner's First Amendment rights because they only prohibit it from using CPNI to target customers and do not prevent petitioner from communicating with its customers or limit anything that it might say to them. This view is fundamentally flawed. Effective speech has two components: a speaker and an audience. A restriction on either of these components is a restriction on speech. * * *

Privacy considerations of some sort clearly drove the enactment of § 222. The concept of privacy, though, is multi-faceted. Indeed, one can apply the moniker of a privacy interest to several understandings of privacy, such as the right to have sufficient moral freedom to exercise full individual autonomy, the right of an individual to define who he or she is by controlling access to information about him or herself, and the right of an individual to solitude, secrecy, and anonymity. * * * The breadth of the concept of privacy requires us to pay particular attention to attempts by the government to assert privacy as a substantial state interest. * * *

In the context of a speech restriction imposed to protect privacy by keeping certain information confidential, the government must show that the dissemination of the information desired to be kept private would inflict specific and significant harm on individuals, such as undue embarrassment or ridicule, intimidation or harassment, or misappropriation of sensitive personal information for the purposes of assuming another's identity. Although we may feel uncomfortable knowing that our personal information is circulating in the world, we live in an open society where information may usually pass freely. A general level of discomfort from knowing that people can readily access information about us does not necessarily rise to the level of a substantial state interest under Central Hudson for it is not based on an identified harm.

Neither Congress nor the FCC explicitly stated what "privacy" harm § 222 seeks to protect against. The CPNI Order notes that "CPNI includes information that is extremely personal to customers * * * such as to whom, where, and when a customer places a call, as well as the types of service offerings to which the customer subscribes," and it summarily finds "call destinations and other details about a call * * * may be equally or more sensitive [than the content of the calls]". The government never states it directly, but we infer from this thin justification that disclosure of CPNI information could prove embarrassing to some and that the government seeks to combat this potential harm.

We have some doubts about whether this interest, as presented, rises to the level of "substantial." We would prefer to see a more empirical explanation and justification for the government's asserted interest. * * * [N]otwithstanding our reservations, we assume for the sake of this appeal that the government has asserted a substantial state interest in protecting people from the disclosure of sensitive and potentially embarrassing personal information. * * *

Under * * * Central Hudson, the government must "demonstrate that the harms it recites are real and that its restriction will in fact alleviate them to a material degree." Edenfield v. Fane, 507 U.S. 761, 771 (1993); accord Rubin v. Coors Brewing Co., 514 U.S. 476, 487 (1995). "This burden is not satisfied by mere speculation or conjecture." Edenfield, 507 U.S. at 770. On the record before us, the government fails to meet its burden. * * *

[T]he FCC can theorize that allowing existing carriers to market new services with CPNI will impede competition for those services, but it provides no analysis of how or if this might actually occur. Beyond its own speculation, the best the government can offer is that "the vigor of US

West's protests against the rules * * * indicates that US West also believes that this restriction will be effective in promoting Congress's competitive interest." Appellees Br. at 30. This is simply additional conjecture, and it is inadequate to justify restrictions under the First Amendment. See Edenfield, 507 U.S. 761 at 770–71. * * *

Even assuming, arguendo, that the state interests in privacy and competition are substantial and that the regulations directly and materially advance those interests, we do not find, on this record, the FCC rules regarding customer approval properly tailored. * * *

Even assuming that telecommunications customers value the privacy of CPNI, the FCC record does not adequately show that an opt-out strategy would not sufficiently protect customer privacy. The respondents merely speculate that there are a substantial number of individuals who feel strongly about their privacy, yet would not bother to opt-out if given notice and the opportunity to do so. Such speculation hardly reflects the careful calculation of costs and benefits that our commercial speech jurisprudence requires. * * *

In sum, even assuming that respondents met the prior two prongs of Central Hudson, we conclude that based on the record before us, the agency has failed to satisfy its burden of showing that the customer approval regulations restrict no more speech than necessary to serve the asserted state interests. Consequently, we find that the CPNI regulations interpreting the customer approval requirement of 47 U.S.C. § 222(c) violate the First Amendment.

BRISCOE, CIRCUIT JUDGE, dissenting: * * *

Dissatisfied with the FCC's selection of the "opt-in" approach, rather than its suggested opt-out approach (which is allegedly cheaper and results in a higher "approval" rate than the opt-in approach), US West filed this action challenging the validity of the FCC's CPNI Order. * * *

In my view, § 222, in particular subsection (c)(1), is unambiguous in the sense that Congress made it abundantly clear it intended for telecommunications carriers to obtain customer "approval" prior to using, disclosing, or permitting access to individually identifiable CPNI. Although Congress did not specifically define the term "approval" in the statute, its ordinary and natural meaning clearly "implies knowledge and exercise of discretion after knowledge." * * *

Because the approval requirement imposed by Congress in § 222 is fairly rigorous in that it requires customer knowledge and exercise of discretion after knowledge, the methods available for obtaining such approval were obviously limited. * * * [I]nterested parties proposed only three possible methods for obtaining approval: (1) requiring express written approval, (2) requiring express written, oral, or electronic approval (the opt-in method), or (3) requiring only implied approval by allowing carriers to notify customers of their intent to use CPNI and affording customers a mechanism to "opt-out" if they did not want their CPNI to be used (the opt-out method). After quickly disposing of the most restrictive of these three options (i.e., the method requiring express written approval), the FCC carefully weighed the advantages and disadvantages of the two remaining options, i.e., the opt-in and the opt-out approaches. CPNI Order at 67–85. Ultimately, the FCC concluded the opt-in approach was best suited to forwarding the purpose of the statute * * *.

After reviewing the CPNI Order and the administrative record, I am convinced the FCC's interpretation of § 222, more specifically its selection of the opt-in method for obtaining customer approval, is entirely reasonable. * * *

US West contends the CPNI Order "violates the First Amendment by requiring that carriers secure prior affirmative consents from customers before using individually-identifiable customer information to speak with their customers on an individualized basis about services beyond the 'categories' of telecommunications services to which they currently subscribe." In other words, US West suggests the CPNI Order unduly limits its ability to engage in commercial speech with its existing customers regarding new products and services it may offer. US West also claims the CPNI Order "restricts the ability of carriers to share and use CPNI internally—to have different divisions, affiliates, and personnel within the same carrier communicate information to each other (i.e., to speak to each other), absent a prior affirmative consent from the customer." Id.

The problem with US West's arguments is they are more appropriately aimed at the restrictions and requirements outlined in § 222 rather than the approval method adopted in the CPNI Order. As outlined above, it is the statute, not the CPNI Order, that prohibits a carrier from using, disclosing, or permitting access to individually identifiable CPNI without first obtaining informed consent from its customers. Yet US West has not challenged the constitutionality of § 222, and this is not the proper forum for addressing such a challenge even if it was raised. Thus, we must assume the restrictions and requirements outlined in the statute are constitutional. More specifically, we must assume the statute's restrictions on the use of CPNI, and its requirement that a carrier obtain customer approval prior to using, disclosing, or permitting access to individually identifiable CPNI, do not violate the First Amendment. * * *

US West also contends the FCC's restrictions on the disclosure of CPNI are so severe they constitute a regulatory taking of property without just compensation, in violation of the Takings Clause of the Fifth Amendment.

In addressing US West's takings argument, the threshold question is whether CPNI constitutes "property" for purposes of the Takings Clause. US West gives short shrift to this issue, arguing the decision in Ruckelshaus v. Monsanto Co., 467 U.S. 986 (1984), establishes that CPNI is protectable property for purposes of the Takings Clause. In Monsanto, plaintiff Monsanto, a pesticide manufacturer doing business in Missouri, filed suit challenging certain amendments to the Federal Insecticide,

Fungicide, and Rodenticide Act (FIFRA), 7 U.S.C. § 136 et seq., requiring it to disclose to the EPA various health, environmental, and safety data related to its products. In addressing Monsanto's assertion that the challenged regulations constituted a takings under the Fifth Amendment, the Court held "that to the extent that Monsanto had an interest in its health, safety, and environmental data cognizable as a trade secret property right under Missouri law, that property right was protected by the Taking Clause of the Fifth Amendment." 467 U.S. at 1003–04.

Although Monsanto certainly sets the stage for treatment of CPNI as property for Fifth Amendment purposes, US West has failed to take the requisite step of demonstrating that CPNI qualifies as trade secret property, or any other kind of protectable property interest, under state law. Therefore, there is no basis for concluding US West has presented a "grave" or "serious" Fifth Amendment challenge to the CPNI Order.

4. TELEPHONE PRETEXTING

FCC, FCC STRENGTHENS TELEPHONE PRETEXTING RULES

Press Release, April 2, 2007.

Washington, D.C.—The Federal Communications Commission has strengthened its privacy rules by requiring telephone and wireless carriers to adopt additional safeguards to protect the personal telephone records of consumers from unauthorized disclosure. These new safeguards will help prevent unauthorized access to customer proprietary network information, or CPNI.

The new safeguards include:

- Carrier Authentication Requirements. Carriers are prohibited from releasing a customer's phone call records when a customer calls the carrier except when the customer provides a password. If a customer does not provide a password, carriers may not release the customer's phone call records except by sending it to an address of record or by the carrier calling the customer at the telephone of record. Carriers are required to provide mandatory password protection for online account access. Carriers are permitted to provide all CPNI, including customer phone call records, to customers based on in-store contact with a valid photo ID.

- Notice to Customer of Account Changes. Carriers are required to notify the customer immediately when the following are created or changed: (1) a password; (2) a back-up for forgotten passwords; (3) an online account; or (4) the address of record.

- Notice of Unauthorized Disclosure of CPNI. A notification process is established for both law enforcement and customers in the event of a CPNI breach.

- Joint Venture and Independent Contractor Use of CPNI. Consent rules are modified to require carriers to obtain explicit consent from a customer before disclosing a customer's CPNI to a carrier's joint venture partners or independent contractors for the purposes of marketing communications-related services to that customer.

- Annual CPNI Certification. Certification rules are amended to require carriers to file with the Commission an annual certification, including an explanation of any actions taken against data brokers and a summary of all consumer complaints received in the previous year regarding the unauthorized release of CPNI.

- CPNI Regulations Applicable to Providers of Interconnected VoIP Service. All CPNI rules are extended to cover providers of interconnected voice over Internet Protocol (VoIP) service.

- Business Customers. In limited circumstances, carriers may bind themselves contractually to authentication regimes other than those adopted in this Order for services they provide to their business customers that have a dedicated account representative and contracts that specifically address the carrier's protection of CPNI.

The Commission also adopted a Further Notice of Proposed Rulemaking seeking comment on what additional steps, if any, the Commission should take to further protect the privacy of consumers.

Action by the Commission, March 13, 2007, by Report and Order and Further Notice of Proposed Rulemaking (FCC 07–22). Chairman Martin and Commissioner McDowell, with Commissioners Copps and Adelstein dissenting in part, and Commissioner Tate concurring in part. Separate statements issued by Chairman Martin, Commissioners Copps, Adelstein, Tate and McDowell.

J. EUROPEAN DATA PROTECTION: STANDARDS AND STATUTES

1. COUNCIL OF EUROPE AND ECHR

Note: Rok Lampe, Data Protection and the Council of Europe

Data protection is an essential component of every individual's private life. The European Court of Human Rights—applying Article 8 of the European Convention for the Protection of Human Rights and Fundamental Freedoms (ECHR)—has traditionally protected the gathering, storing, processing and disposal of personal information. Recognizing the seriousness of data protection for enjoyment of the right to privacy, the members of the Council of Europe adopted a special treaty on data protection in 1981. This *Convention for the Protection of Individuals with Regard to Automatic Processing of Personal Data (ETS 108)* entered into force in 1985. Designed to protect the individual against abuses which may accompany the collection and processing of personal data, the Convention outlawed the processing of "sensitive" data concerning a person's race, politics, health, religion, sexual life, criminal record, etc., in the absence of proper legal safeguards. The Convention also enshrined the individual's right to know that information about him or her is stored and, if necessary, to have it corrected. Restrictions on the rights laid down in the Convention are only possible when overriding interests, e.g. State security, defence, etc., are at stake.

One of the most interesting and controversial European cases related to data protection is *Z v. Finland* (judgment of 25 Feb. 1997). The applicant—a wife of an African suspected of a sex crime—complained that details of her medical records, including her HIV status, were revealed for the purposes of her husband's criminal trial, violating her right to privacy under Article 8. The Court's response was to find that "In view of the highly intimate and sensitive nature of information concerning a person's HIV status, any State measures compelling communication or disclosure of such information without the consent of the patient call for the most careful scrutiny on the part of the Court, as do the safeguards designed to secure an effective protection." The Court also accepted, however, that the interests of a patient and the community as a whole in protecting the confidentiality of medical data may be outweighed by the interest in investigation and prosecution of crime and in the publicity of court proceedings. Each case must thus be considered on its own merits and must take into account the margin of appreciation that the State enjoys in such an area. The Court's conclusion in *Z v. Finland* was that the disclosure of the witness's medical records was "necessary", within the meaning of Article 8 paragraph 2, for the purposes of a trial. However, the Court went on to find that the publication of the witness's name and HIV status in the appeal court judgment was not justified as necessary for any legitimate aim. Supporting the finding was the fact that the criminal files containing details of Z's medical records (HIV status) would be made public within 10 years, while she might still be alive.

COUNCIL OF EUROPE, CONVENTION FOR THE PROTECTION OF INDIVIDUALS WITH REGARD TO AUTOMATIC PROCESSING OF PERSONAL DATA (1981)

http://www.coe.int/t/e/legal_affairs/legal_co-operation/data_protection/.

Chapter I—General provisions

Article 1—Object and purpose

The purpose of this convention is to secure in the territory of each Party for every individual, whatever his nationality or residence, respect for his rights and fundamental freedoms, and in particular his right to privacy, with regard to automatic processing of personal data relating to him ("data protection").

Article 2—Definitions

For the purposes of this convention:

a "personal data" means any information relating to an identified or identifiable individual ("data subject");

b "automated data file" means any set of data undergoing automatic processing;

c "automatic processing" includes the following operations if carried out in whole or in part by automated means: storage of data, carrying out of logical and/or arithmetical operations on those data, their alteration, erasure, retrieval or dissemination;

d "controller of the file" means the natural or legal person, public authority, agency or any other body who is competent according to the national law to decide what should be the purpose of the automated data file, which categories of personal data should be stored and which operations should be applied to them.

Article 3—Scope

1 The Parties undertake to apply this convention to automated personal data files and automatic processing of personal data in the public and private sectors.

* * *

Chapter II—Basic principles for data protection

Article 4—Duties of the Parties

1 Each Party shall take the necessary measures in its domestic law to give effect to the basic principles for data protection set out in this chapter.

2 These measures shall be taken at the latest at the time of entry into force of this convention in respect of that Party.

Article 5—Quality of data

Personal data undergoing automatic processing shall be:

a obtained and processed fairly and lawfully;

b stored for specified and legitimate purposes and not used in a way incompatible with those purposes;

c adequate, relevant and not excessive in relation to the purposes for which they are stored;

d accurate and, where necessary, kept up to date;

e preserved in a form which permits identification of the data subjects for no longer than is required for the purpose for which those data are stored.

Article 6—Special categories of data

Personal data revealing racial origin, political opinions or religious or other beliefs, as well as personal data concerning health or sexual life, may not be processed automatically unless domestic law provides appropriate safeguards. The same shall apply to personal data relating to criminal convictions.

Article 7—Data security

Appropriate security measures shall be taken for the protection of personal data stored in automated data files against accidental or unauthorised destruction or accidental loss as well as against unauthorised access, alteration or dissemination.

Article 8—Additional safeguards for the data subject

Any person shall be enabled:

a   to establish the existence of an automated personal data file, its main purposes, as well as the identity and habitual residence or principal place of business of the controller of the file;

b   to obtain at reasonable intervals and without excessive delay or expense confirmation of whether personal data relating to him are stored in the automated data file as well as communication to him of such data in an intelligible form;

c   to obtain, as the case may be, rectification or erasure of such data if these have been processed contrary to the provisions of domestic law giving effect to the basic principles set out in Articles 5 and 6 of this convention;

d   to have a remedy if a request for confirmation or, as the case may be, communication, rectification or erasure as referred to in paragraphs b and c of this article is not complied with.

Article 9—Exceptions and restrictions

1   No exception to the provisions of Articles 5, 6 and 8 of this convention shall be allowed except within the limits defined in this article.

2   Derogation from the provisions of Articles 5, 6 and 8 of this convention shall be allowed when such derogation is provided for by the law of the Party and constitutes a necessary measure in a democratic society in the interests of:

a   protecting State security, public safety, the monetary interests of the State or the suppression of criminal offences;

b   protecting the data subject or the rights and freedoms of others.

3   Restrictions on the exercise of the rights specified in Article 8, paragraphs b, c and d, may be provided by law with respect to automated personal data files used for statistics or for scientific research purposes when there is obviously no risk of an infringement of the privacy of the data subjects.

Article 10—Sanctions and remedies

Each Party undertakes to establish appropriate sanctions and remedies for violations of provisions of domestic law giving effect to the basic principles for data protection set out in this chapter.

Article 11—Extended protection

None of the provisions of this chapter shall be interpreted as limiting or otherwise affecting the possibility for a Party to grant data subjects a wider measure of protection than that stipulated in this convention.

Chapter III—Transborder data flows

Article 12—Transborder flows of personal data and domestic law

1   The following provisions shall apply to the transfer across national borders, by whatever medium, of personal data undergoing automatic processing or collected with a view to their being automatically processed.

2   A Party shall not, for the sole purpose of the protection of privacy, prohibit or subject to special authorisation transborder flows of personal data going to the territory of another Party.

3   Nevertheless, each Party shall be entitled to derogate from the provisions of paragraph 2:

a   insofar as its legislation includes specific regulations for certain categories of personal data or of automated personal data files, because of the nature of those data or those files, except where the regulations of the other Party provide an equivalent protection;

b   when the transfer is made from its territory to the territory of a non Contracting State through the intermediary of the territory of another Party, in order to avoid such transfers resulting in circumvention of the legislation of the Party referred to at the beginning of this paragraph.

* * *

2. UNITED NATIONS

NOTE: *ROK LAMPE, GENERAL ASSEMBLY GUIDELINES FOR THE REGULATION OF COMPUTERIZED PERSONAL DATA FILES (RESOLUTION 45/95 OF 14 DECEMBER 1990).*

In 1990 the General Assembly of the United Nations issued Guidelines for the Regulation of Computerized Personal Data Files ((E/CN.4/1990/72), Resolution 45/95 of 14 December 1990). These Guidelines included ten general rules applicable to States on data flow protection which should be regarded as minimum standards for national legislation, in Europe and in other parts of the world governed by the United Nations:

1.   Principle of lawfulness and fairness

Information about persons should not be collected or processed in unfair or unlawful ways, nor should it be used for ends contrary to the purposes and principles of the Charter of the United Nations.

2.   Principle of accuracy

Persons responsible for the compilation of files or those responsible for keeping them have an obligation to conduct regular checks on the accuracy and relevance of the data recorded and to ensure that they are kept as complete as possible in order to avoid errors of omission and that they are kept up to date regularly or when the information contained in a file is used, as long as they are being processed.

3. Principle of the purpose-specification

The purpose which a file is to serve and its utilization in terms of that purpose should be specified, legitimate and, when it is established, receive a certain amount of publicity or be brought to the attention of the person concerned, in order to make it possible subsequently to ensure that:

> (a) All the personal data collected and recorded remain relevant and adequate to the purposes so specified;

> (b) None of the said personal data is used or disclosed, except with the consent of the person concerned, for purposes incompatible with those specified;

> (c) The period for which the personal data are kept does not exceed that which would enable the achievement of the purposes so specified.

4. Principle of interested-person access

Everyone who offers proof of identity has the right to know whether information concerning him is being processed and to obtain it in an intelligible form, without undue delay or expense, and to have appropriate rectifications or erasures made in the case of unlawful, unnecessary or inaccurate entries and, when it is being communicated, to be informed of the addressees. Provision should be made for a remedy, if need be with the supervisory authority specified in principle 8 below. The cost of any rectification shall be borne by the person responsible for the file. It is desirable that the provisions of this principle should apply to everyone, irrespective of nationality or place of residence.

5. Principle of non-discrimination

Subject to cases of exceptions restrictively envisaged under principle 6, data likely to give rise to unlawful or arbitrary discrimination, including information on racial or ethnic origin, colour, sex life, political opinions, religious, philosophical and other beliefs as well as membership of an association or trade union, should not be compiled.

6. Power to make exceptions

Departures from principles 1 to 4 may be authorized only if they are necessary to protect national security, public order, public health or morality, as well as, inter alia, the rights and freedoms of others, especially persons being persecuted (humanitarian clause) provided that such departures are expressly specified in a law or equivalent regulation promulgated in accordance with the internal legal system which expressly states their limits and sets forth appropriate safeguards. Exceptions to principle 5 relating to the prohibition of discrimination, in addition to being subject to the same safeguards as those prescribed for exceptions to principles I and 4, may be authorized only within the limits prescribed by the International Bill of Human Rights and the other relevant instruments in the field of protection of human rights and the prevention of discrimination.

7. Principle of security

Appropriate measures should be taken to protect the files against both natural dangers, such as accidental loss or destruction and human dangers, such as unauthorized access, fraudulent misuse of data or contamination by computer viruses.

8.   Supervision and sanctions

The law of every country shall designate the authority which, in accordance with its domestic legal system, is to be responsible for supervising observance of the principles set forth above. This authority shall offer guarantees of impartiality, independence vis-a-vis persons or agencies responsible for processing and establishing data, and technical competence. In the event of violation of the provisions of the national law implementing the aforementioned principles, criminal or other penalties should be envisaged together with the appropriate individual remedies.

9.   Transborder data flows

When the legislation of two or more countries concerned by a transborder data flow offers comparable safeguards for the protection of privacy, information should be able to circulate as freely as inside each of the territories concerned. If there are no reciprocal safeguards, limitations on such circulation may not be imposed unduly and only in so far as the protection of privacy demands.

10.   Field of application

The present principles should be made applicable, in the first instance, to all public and private computerized files as well as, by means of optional extension and subject to appropriate adjustments, to manual files. Special provision, also optional, might be made to extend all or part of the principles to files on legal persons particularly when they contain some information on individuals.

3.   EUROPEAN UNION

ROK LAMPE, THE RIGHT TO PRIVACY AND DATA PROTECTION IN THE EUROPEAN UNION

Economic integration demanded that the European Union become, not only an association based on economic grounds, but also a compact transnational system which offers protection of fundamental rights defined in the European Charter on Fundamental Rights. Drafted in 2000 and coming into legal effect in 2009 with the Lisbon Treaty, the Charter includes key provisions for privacy protection in its Articles 7 and 8.

Article 7 of the Charter of Fundamental Rights of the European Union protects the right to privacy on the EU level with a general provision: *"Everyone has the right to respect for his or her private and family life, home and communications."* The rights guaranteed in Article 7 of the Charter correspond to the those guaranteed by Article 8 of the European Convention on Human Rights (ECHR), except that, to take account of developments in technology, the drafters of Article 7 replaced the old fashioned word "correspondence" with the more contemporary "communications". Article 7 of the

Charter must be read in tandem with its Article 52, a general provision setting out the scope and limitations of civil and political rights as follows:

1. Any limitation on the exercise of the rights and freedoms recognized by this Charter must be provided for by law and respect the essence of those rights and freedoms. Subject to the principle of proportionality, limitations may be made only if they are necessary and genuinely meet objectives of general interest recognized by the Union or the need to protect the rights and freedoms of others.

2. Rights recognized by this Charter which are based on the Community Treaties or the Treaty on European Union shall be exercised under the conditions and within the limits defined by those Treaties.

3. Insofar as this Charter contains rights which correspond to rights guaranteed by the Convention for the Protection of Human Rights and Fundamental Freedoms, the meaning and scope of those rights shall be the same as those laid down by the said Convention. This provision shall not prevent Union law providing more extensive protection.

This rather complex approach was explained officially by the presidium—the founder of the Draft Charter of Fundamental Rights of the European Union (http://www.europarl.europa.eu/charter/pdf/04473_en.pdf). A main objective was to ensure the necessary consistency between the Charter and the ECHR.

Data Protection in the European Union has its roots in international as well European fundamental documents. EU data protection regulations were influenced both by ECHR Article 8 and by the 1990 UN Guidelines Concerning Computerized Personal Data Files. Significantly, EU data protection regulations also reflect the influence of the Organisation for Economic Co-operation and Development (OECD) Guidelines Governing the Protection of Privacy and Transborder Flows of Personal Data, adopted by the OECD Council September 23, 1980. The recommendations of the OECD were based on several premises, namely that: (1) member countries have a common interest in protecting privacy and individual liberties, and in reconciling fundamental but competing values such as privacy and the free flow of information; (2) that automatic processing and transborder flows of personal data create new forms of relationships among countries and require the development of compatible rules and practices; (3) that transborder flows of personal data contribute to economic and social development; (4) that domestic legislation concerning privacy protection and transborder flows of personal data may hinder such transborder flows; and that (5) it is important to advance the free flow of information between Member countries and to avoid the creation of unjustified obstacles to the development of economic and social relations among Member countries. The OECD recommended that Member countries take into account in their domestic legislation the principles concerning the protection of privacy and individual liberties set forth in the Guidelines to remove or avoid creating, in the name of privacy protection, unjustified obstacles to transborder flows of personal data.

OECD GUIDELINES GOVERNING THE PROTECTION OF PRIVACY AND TRANSBORDER FLOWS OF PERSONAL DATA (1980)

Part one

General definitions

1.   For the purposes of these Guidelines:

"data controller" means a party who, according to domestic law, is competent to decide about the contents and use of personal data regardless of whether or not such data are collected, stored, processed or disseminated by that party or by an agent on its behalf;

"personal data" means any information relating to an identified or identifiable individual (data subject);

"transborder flows of personal data" means movements of personal data across national borders.

Scope of Guidelines

2.   These Guidelines apply to personal data, whether in the public or private sectors, which, because of the manner in which they are processed, or because of their nature or the context in which they are used, pose a danger to privacy and individual liberties.

3.   These Guidelines should not be interpreted as preventing:

the application, to different categories of personal data, of different protective measures depending upon their nature and the context in which they are collected, stored, processed or disseminated; the exclusion from the application of the Guidelines of personal data which obviously do not contain any risk to privacy and individual liberties; or the application of the Guidelines only to automatic processing of personal data.

4.   Exceptions to the Principles contained in Parts Two and Three of these Guidelines, including those relating to national sovereignty, national security and public policy ("order public"), should be:

as few as possible, and made known to the public.

5.   In the particular case of Federal countries the observance of these Guidelines may be affected by the division of powers in the Federation.

6.   These Guidelines should be regarded as minimum standards which are capable of being supplemented by additional measures for the protection of privacy and individual liberties.

Part two:

Basic principles of national application

Collection Limitation Principle

7. There should be limits to the collection of personal data and any such data should be obtained by lawful and fair means and, where appropriate, with the knowledge or consent of the data subject:

Data Quality Principle

8. Personal data should be relevant to the purposes for which they are to be used, and, to the extent necessary for those purposes, should be accurate, complete and kept up-to-date.

Purpose Specification Principle

9. The purposes for which personal data are collected should be specified not later than at the time of data collection and the subsequent use limited to the fulfilment of those purposes or such others as are not incompatible with those purposes and as are specified on each occasion of change of purpose.

Use Limitation Principle

10. Personal data should not be disclosed, made available or otherwise used for purposes other than those specified in accordance with Paragraph 9 except: with the consent of the data subject; or by the authority of law.

Security Safeguards Principle

11. Personal data should be protected by reasonable security safeguards against such risks as loss or unauthorised access, destruction, use, modification or disclosure of data.

Openness Principle

12. There should be a general policy of openness about developments, practices and policies with respect to personal data. Means should be readily available of establishing the existence and nature of personal data, and the main purposes of their use, as well as the identity and usual residence of the data controller.

Individual Participation Principle

13. An individual should have the right:

to obtain from a data controller, or otherwise, confirmation of whether or not the data controller has data relating to him; to have communicated to him, data relating to him within a reasonable time; at a charge, if any, that is not excessive; in a reasonable manner; and in a form that is readily intelligible to him; to be given reasons if a request made under subparagraphs (a) and (b) is denied, and to be able to challenge such denial; and to challenge data relating to him and, if the challenge is successful, to have the data erased, rectified, completed or amended.

Accountability Principle

14. A data controller should be accountable for complying with measures which give effect to the principles stated above.

Part three:

Principles of international application free flow and legitimate restrictions

15. Member countries should take into consideration the implications for other Member countries of domestic processing and re-export of personal data.

16. Member countries should take all reasonable and appropriate steps to ensure that transborder flows of personal data, including transit through a Member country, are uninterrupted and secure.

17. A Member country should refrain from restricting transborder flows of personal data between itself and another Member country except where the latter does not yet substantially observe these Guidelines or where the re-export of such data would circumvent its domestic privacy legislation. A Member country may also impose restrictions in respect of certain categories of personal data for which its domestic privacy legislation includes specific regulations in view of the nature of those data and for which the other Member country provides no equivalent protection.

18. Member countries should avoid developing laws, policies and practices in the name of the protection of privacy and individual liberties, which would create obstacles to transborder flows of personal data that would exceed requirements for such protection.

Part four:

National implementation

19. In implementing domestically the principles set forth in Parts Two and Three, Member countries should establish legal, administrative or other procedures or institutions for the protection of privacy and individual liberties in respect of personal data. Member countries should in particular endeavour to:

adopt appropriate domestic legislation; encourage and support self-regulation, whether in the form of codes of conduct or otherwise; provide for reasonable means for individuals to exercise their rights; provide for adequate sanctions and remedies in case of failures to comply with measures which implement the principles set forth in Parts Two and Three; and ensure that there is no unfair discrimination against data subjects.

Part five:

International co-operation

20. Member countries should, where requested, make known to other Member countries details of the observance of the principles set forth in these Guidelines. Member countries should also ensure that procedures for transborder flows of personal data and for the protection of privacy and individual liberties are simple and compatible with those of other Member countries which comply with these

Guidelines.

21.   Member countries should establish procedures to facilitate: information exchange related to these Guidelines, and mutual assistance in the procedural and investigative matters involved.

22.   Member countries should work towards the development of principles, domestic and international, to govern the applicable law in the case of transborder flows of personal data.

NOTE: ROK LAMPE, ARTICLE 8 OF THE *EU* CHARTER AND ITS INFLUENCES

Although Article 7 of the Charter on Fundamental Rights of the European Union offers solid ground for protection on the right to private and family life in general, the European legislature decided to include a special provision on data protection in the Charter, Article 8. Article 8 ("Protection of personal data") reads as follows:

1.   Everyone has the right to the protection of personal data concerning him or her.

2.   Such data must be processed fairly for specified purposes and on the basis of the consent of the person concerned or some other legitimate basis laid down by law. Everyone has the right of access to data which has been collected concerning him or her, and the right to have it rectified.

3.   Compliance with these rules shall be subject to control by an independent authority.

The language of this Article is based on Article 286 of the Treaty establishing the European Community; Directive 95/46/EC of the European Parliament and of the Council on the protection of individuals with regard to the processing of personal data and on the free movement of such data (OJ L 281, 23.11.1995); Article 8 of the ECHR; and on the Council of Europe Convention of 28 January 1981 for the Protection of Individuals with regard to Automatic Processing of Personal Data, which had been previously ratified by all the Member States.

The right to the protection of personal data may be limited under the conditions set out by Article 52 of the Charter. However Article 52 does not prevent and has not prevented EU law from providing more extensive protection than the legal and aspirational human rights documents by which it was influenced. Data protection is today regarded as one of the fundamental rights in the European Union—anchored in the Article 8 of the Charter on Fundamental Rights. Beside protecting personal data as one of the key human rights, it also struggles to include data protection into its main regulative field—regulation of a common market which is based on the free movement of persons, goods, services and capital. In last two decades the European Union has passed the following Directives on data protection, which demand their implementation in national legislation of Member States, so called harmonization on the EU level, and which form the solid frame of the EU regulative approach to data protection:

— Directive 95/46/EC of the European Parliament and of the Council of 24 October 1995 on the protection of individuals with regard to the processing of personal data and on the free movement of such data;

— Directive 97/66/EC of the European Parliament and of the Council of 15 December 1997 concerning the processing of personal data and the protection of privacy in the telecommunications sector;

— Directive 2002/58/EC of the European Parliament and of the Council of 12 July 2002 concerning the processing of personal data and the protection of privacy in the electronic communications sector; and

— Directive 2006/24/EC of the European Parliament and of the Council of 15 March 2006 on the retention of data generated or processed in connection with the provision of publicly available electronic communications services or of public communications networks and amending Directive 2002/58/EC.

NOTE: ROK LAMPE, THE EUROPEAN DATA PROTECTION DIRECTIVE 95/46/EC

When US commentators speak of the "EU Directive" and of its creation of an comprehensive, "omnibus", approach to data protection by contrast to the sectoral approach found in the US, they generally mean to refer to Directive 95/46/EC and its telecommunication, electronic communications, and data retention companions and amendments just listed. This European Data Protection Directive 95/46/EC—formally known in English as Directive 95/46/EC of the European Parliament and of the Council on the protection of individuals with regard to the processing of personal data and on the free movement of such data of 24 October 1995 (Official Journal L 281, 23/11/1995 P. 0031—0050)—is a main legal source of data protection in the European Union.

The European Data Protection Directive was passed on October 24, 1995 and came into effect on October 25, 1998. The objective of the Directive is to harmonize data protection regulation among member states. Members' obligations are defined in the Directive, understood as a key element of the smooth functioning of the internal EU market. The Directive is based on the idea, recited in its preamble, that "the difference in levels of protection of the rights and freedoms of individuals, notably the right to privacy, with regard to the processing of personal data afforded in the Member States may prevent the transmission of such data from the territory of one Member State to that of another Member State [and that] this difference may therefore constitute an obstacle to the pursuit of a number of economic activities at Community level, distort competition and impede authorities in the discharge of their responsibilities under Community law". With solid regulation of data protection, free movement of goods, persons, services and capital is enabled. The Directive not only requires that personal data should be able to flow freely from one Member State to another, but also that the fundamental rights of individuals should be safeguarded in the process.

Personal data is defined broadly by the 1995 EU Directive to include "sensitive information" such as "racial or ethnic origin, political opinions, religious or philosophical beliefs, trade union membership" and data concerning "health or sex life." The Directive does not apply to public sector data transfers having to do with criminal law enforcement and national security; or to the communications of natural persons concerning "purely personal" or "household" matters.

The Directive 95/46/EC defines the following terms, which form the common terminology in all member states:

(a) 'personal data' shall mean any information relating to an identified or identifiable natural person ('data subject'); an identifiable person is one who can be identified, directly or indirectly, in particular by reference to an identification number or to one or more factors specific to his physical, physiological, mental, economic, cultural or social identity;

(b) 'processing of personal data' ('processing') shall mean any operation or set of operations which is performed upon personal data, whether or not by automatic means, such as collection, recording, organization, storage, adaptation or alteration, retrieval, consultation, use, disclosure by transmission, dissemination or otherwise making available, alignment or combination, blocking, erasure or destruction;

(c) 'personal data filing system' ('filing system') shall mean any structured set of personal data which are accessible according to specific criteria, whether centralized, decentralized or dispersed on a functional or geographical basis;

(d) 'controller' shall mean the natural or legal person, public authority, agency or any other body which alone or jointly with others determines the purposes and means of the processing of personal data; where the purposes and means of processing are determined by national or Community laws or regulations, the controller or the specific criteria for his nomination may be designated by national or Community law;

(e) 'processor' shall mean a natural or legal person, public authority, agency or any other body which processes personal data on behalf of the controller;

(f) 'third party' shall mean any natural or legal person, public authority, agency or any other body other than the data subject, the controller, the processor and the persons who, under the direct authority of the controller or the processor, are authorized to process the data;

(g) 'recipient' shall mean a natural or legal person, public authority, agency or any other body to whom data are disclosed, whether a third party or not; however, authorities which may receive data in the framework of a particular inquiry shall not be regarded as recipients;

(h) 'the data subject's consent' shall mean any freely given specific and informed indication of his wishes by which the data subject signifies his agreement to personal data relating to him being processed.

The Directive consists of 34 Articles divided into seven Chapters. Chapter II regulates general rules on the lawfulness of the processing of personal data. According to Article 6 of the Directive, Member States shall ensure that personal data is:

(a) processed fairly and lawfully;

(b) collected for specified, explicit and legitimate purposes and not further processed in a way incompatible with those purposes. Further processing of data for historical, statistical or scientific purposes shall not be considered as incompatible provided that Member States provide appropriate safeguards;

(c) adequate, relevant and not excessive in relation to the purposes for which they are collected and/or further processed;

(d) accurate and, where necessary, kept up to date; every reasonable step must be taken to ensure that data which are inaccurate or incomplete, having regard to the purposes for which they were collected or for which they are further processed, are erased or rectified;

(e) kept in a form which permits identification of data subjects for no longer than is necessary for the purposes for which the data were collected or for which they are further processed. Member States shall lay down appropriate safeguards for personal data stored for longer periods for historical, statistical or scientific use.

Article 7 of the Directive regulates criteria for making data processing legitimate. Under this provision Member States must ensure that personal data is processed only if:

(a) the data subject has unambiguously given his consent; or

(b) processing is necessary for the performance of a contract to which the data subject is party or in order to take steps at the request of the data subject prior to entering into a contract; or

(c) processing is necessary for compliance with a legal obligation to which the controller is subject; or

(d) processing is necessary in order to protect the vital interests of the data subject; or

(e) processing is necessary for the performance of a task carried out in the public interest or in the exercise of official authority vested in the controller or in a third party to whom the data are disclosed; or

(f) processing is necessary for the purposes of the legitimate interests pursued by the controller or by the third party or parties to whom the data are disclosed, except where such interests are overridden by the interests for fundamental rights and freedoms of the data subject which require protection under Article 1 (1).

NOTE: ROK LAMPE, THE SWEDISH CASE

CASE C–101/01 BODIL LINDQVIST v. ÅKLAGARKAM-MAREN I JÖNKÖPING (REFERENCE FOR A PRELIM-INARY RULING FROM THE GÖTA HOVRÄTTEN) (DI-RECTIVE 95/46/EC—SCOPE)

JUDGMENT OF THE COURT OF THE EUROPEAN UNION
6 November 2003.

[In this decision the Court interpreted various parts of the Directive 95/46, especially with regards to publication of personal data on the internet, place of publication, definition of transfer of personal data to third countries and compatibility with Directive 95/46 of greater protection for personal data under the national legislation of a Member State. ECJ Case C–101/01 has important implications for the posting of personal data on the Internet. Through this case, the court has clarified that posting personal data on the Internet amounts to processing personal data for the purposes of the Data Protection Directive. The court's finding highlights the fact that Europe's data protection regime is extremely far reaching.

The case was brought to the Court by Swedish Court of Appeal in 2001, for a preliminary ruling under Article 234 EC. Seven questions were raised concerning *inter alia* the interpretation of Directive 95/46/EC. (The Directive 95/46 was already at that time implemented in Swedish law by the Personuppgiftslag (SFS 1998:204)—the Swedish law on personal data, 'the PUL'). Those questions were raised in criminal proceedings before that court against Mrs Lindqvist, who was charged with breach of the Swedish legislation on the protection of personal data for publishing on her internet site personal data on a number of people working with her on a voluntary basis in a parish of the Swedish Protestant Church.]

* * *

12. In addition to her job as a maintenance worker, Mrs Lindqvist worked as a catechist in the parish of Alseda (Sweden). She followed a data processing course on which she had inter alia to set up a home page on the internet. At the end of 1998, Mrs Lindqvist set up internet pages at home on her personal computer in order to allow parishioners preparing for their confirmation to obtain information they might need. At her request, the administrator of the Swedish Church's website set up a link between those pages and that site.

13. The pages in question contained information about Mrs Lindqvist and 18 colleagues in the parish, sometimes including their full names and in other cases only their first names. Mrs Lindqvist also described, in a mildly humorous manner, the jobs held by her colleagues and their hobbies. In many cases family circumstances and telephone numbers and other matters were mentioned. She also stated that one colleague had injured her foot and was on half-time on medical grounds.

14. Mrs Lindqvist had not informed her colleagues of the existence of those pages or obtained their consent, nor did she notify the Datainspektionen (the supervisory authority for the protection of electronically transmitted data) of her activity. She removed the pages in question as soon as she became aware that they were not appreciated by some of her colleagues.

15. The public prosecutor brought a prosecution against Mrs Lindqvist charging her with breach of the PUL on the grounds that she had:

— processed personal data by automatic means without giving prior written notification to the Datainspektionen (Paragraph 36 of the PUL);

— processed sensitive personal data (injured foot and half-time on medical grounds) without authorisation (Paragraph 13 of the PUL);

— transferred processed personal data to a third country without authorisation (Paragraph 33 of the PUL).

[Mrs Lindqvist was fined SEK 4 000 (approximately EUR 450) for processing personal data by automatic means without notifying the Datainspektion (Swedish supervisory authority for the protection of electronically transmitted data) in writing, for transferring data to third countries without authorisation and for processing sensitive personal data (a foot injury and part time work on medical grounds).

She appealed against that decision to the Göta hovrätt, which asked the Court of Justice of the EC whether the activities with which Mrs Lindqvist was charged are contrary to the provisions of the data protection directive, which is intended to ensure the same level of protection in all the Member States for the rights and freedoms of individuals.

Mrs Lindqvist accepted the facts but disputed that she was guilty of an offence. Mrs Lindqvist was fined by the Eksjö tingsrätt (District Court) (Sweden) and appealed against that sentence to the referring court. As it had doubts as to the interpretation of the Community law applicable in this area, *inter alia* Directive 95/46, the Göta hovrätt decided to stay proceedings and refer the following questions to the Court for a preliminary ruling:] * * *

'(1) Is the mention of a person—by name or with name and telephone number—on an internet home page an action which falls within the scope of [Directive 95/46]? Does it constitute "the processing of personal data wholly or partly by automatic means" to list on a self-made internet home page a number of persons with comments and statements about their jobs and hobbies etc.?

(2) If the answer to the first question is no, can the act of setting up on an internet home page separate pages for about 15 people with links between the pages which make it possible to search by first name be considered to constitute "the processing otherwise than by automatic means of personal data which form part of a filing system or are intended to form part of a filing system" within the meaning of Article 3(1)?

If the answer to either of those questions is yes, the hovrätt also asks the following questions:

(3) Can the act of loading information of the type described about work colleagues onto a private home page which is none the less accessible to anyone who knows its address be regarded as outside the scope of [Directive 95/46] on the ground that it is covered by one of the exceptions in Article 3(2)?

(4) Is information on a home page stating that a named colleague has injured her foot and is on half-time on medical grounds personal data concerning health which, according to Article 8(1), may not be processed?

(5) [Directive 95/46] prohibits the transfer of personal data to third countries in certain cases. If a person in Sweden uses a computer to load personal data onto a home page stored on a server in Sweden—with the result that personal data become accessible to people in third countries—does that constitute a transfer of data to a third country within the meaning of the directive? Would the answer be the same even if, as far as known, no one from the third country had in fact accessed the data or if the server in question was actually physically in a third country?

(6) Can the provisions of [Directive 95/46], in a case such as the above, be regarded as bringing about a restriction which conflicts with the general principles of freedom of expression or other freedoms and rights, which are applicable within the EU and are enshrined in inter alia Article 10 of the European Convention on the Protection of Human Rights and Fundamental Freedoms? * * *

(7) Can a Member State, as regards the issues raised in the above questions, provide more extensive protection for personal data or give it a wider scope than the directive, even if none of the circumstances described in Article 13 exists?' * * *

[The Court submitted the answers and rulings as follows:]

1. The act of referring, on an internet page, to various persons and identifying them by name or by other means, for instance by giving their telephone number or information regarding their working conditions and hobbies, constitutes 'the processing of personal data wholly or partly by automatic means' within the meaning of Article 3(1) of Directive 95/46/EC of the European Parliament and of the Council of 24 October 1995 on the protection of individuals with regard to the processing of personal data and on the free movement of such data.

2. Such processing of personal data is not covered by any of the exceptions in Article 3(2) of Directive 95/46.

3. Reference to the fact that an individual has injured her foot and is on half-time on medical grounds constitutes personal data concerning health within the meaning of Article 8(1) of Directive 95/46.

4. There is no 'transfer [of data] to a third country' within the meaning of Article 25 of Directive 95/46 where an individual in a Member State loads personal data onto an internet page which is stored on an internet site on which the page can be consulted and which is hosted by a natural or legal person who is established in that State or in another Member State, thereby making those data accessible to anyone who connects to the internet, including people in a third country.

5. The provisions of Directive 95/46 do not, in themselves, bring about a restriction which conflicts with the general principles of freedom of expression or other freedoms and rights, which are applicable within the European Union and are enshrined inter alia in Article 10 of the European Convention for the Protection of Human Rights and Fundamental Freedoms signed at Rome on 4 November 1950. It is for the national authorities and courts responsible for applying the national legislation implementing Directive 95/46 to ensure a fair balance between the rights and interests in question, including the fundamental rights protected by the Community legal order.

6. Measures taken by the Member States to ensure the protection of personal data must be consistent both with the provisions of Directive 95/46 and with its objective of maintaining a balance between freedom of movement of personal data and the protection of private life. However, nothing prevents a Member State from extending the scope of the national legislation implementing the provisions of Directive 95/46 to areas not included in the scope thereof provided that no other provision of Community law precludes it.

NOTE: NOTEWORTHY PROVISIONS OF THE DIRECTIVE 95/46/EC

Noteworthy provisions of the Directive include these:

1. Right of individual to access personal information about themselves. Articles 10 and 11.

2. Right of Member states to withhold information in the name of national security, defense, public security, criminal law enforcement, financial interests of Members of the EU, personal privacy or rights of a data subject or other individuals. Article 13.

3. Right of data subjects to object to the processing of information about them. Article14.

4. Rights to remedies, including monetary compensation. Articles 22–24.

NOTE: ROK LAMPE, THE DUTCH CASE

CASE C–553/07 COLLEGE VAN BURGEMEESTER EN WETHOUDERS VAN ROTTERDAM v. M.E.E. RIJKEBOER

JUDGMENT OF THE COURT OF EUROPEAN UNION
7 May 2009.

This decision is an important interpreter of person's rights regarding data protection under the Directive 95/46, especially of the right of access to data and to information on the recipients of data. The case was brought to the courts as a reference for a preliminary ruling from the Dutch court (Raad van State). The reference for a preliminary ruling relates to the interpretation of Article 12(a) of Directive 95/46/EC. This reference has been made in the context of proceedings between Mr Rijkeboer and the College van burgemeester en wethouders van Rotterdam (Board of Aldermen of Rotterdam; "the College") regarding the partial refusal of the College to grant Mr Rijkeboer access to information on the disclosure of his personal data to third parties during the two years preceding his request for that information.

The factual situation can be submitted as follows. By letter of 26 October 2005, Mr Rijkeboer requested the College to notify him of all instances in which data relating to him from the local authority personal records had, in the two years preceding the request, been disclosed to third parties. He wished to know the identity of those persons and the content of the data disclosed to them. Mr Rijkeboer, who had moved to another municipality, wished to know in particular to whom his former address had been disclosed.

Communication of the data is registered and stored in electronic form in accordance with the "Logisch Ontwerp GBA" (GBA Logistical Project). This is an automated system established by the Ministerie van Binnenlandse Zaken en Koninkrijkrelaties (Netherlands Ministry of the Interior and Home Affairs). It is apparent from the reference for a preliminary ruling that the data requested by Mr Rijkeboer dating from more than one year prior to his request were automatically erased, which accords with the provisions of Article 110 of the Wet GBA.

By decisions of 27 October and 29 November 2005, the College complied with that request only in part by notifying him only of the data relating to the period of one year preceding his request, by application of Article 103(1) of the Wet GBA. Mr Rijkeboer lodged a complaint with the College against the refusal to give him the information relating to the recipients to whom data regarding him had been disclosed during the period before the year preceding his request. That complaint having been rejected by decision of 13 February 2006, Mr Rijkeboer brought an action before the court (Rechtbank) in Rotterdam. That court upheld the action, taking the view that the restriction on the right to information on provision of data to the year before the request, as provided for in Article 103(1) of the Wet GBA, is at variance with Article 12 of the Directive. It also held that the exceptions referred to in Article 13 of that directive are not applicable.

The College appealed against that decision to the Raad van State. That court finds that Article 12 of the Directive on rights of access to data does not indicate any time period within which it must be possible for those rights to be exercised. In its view, that article does not necessarily, however, preclude Member States from imposing a time restriction in their national legislation on the data subject's right to information concerning the recipients to whom personal data have been provided, but the court has doubts in that regard. In those circumstances the Raad van State decided to stay the proceedings and to refer the following question to the Court for a preliminary ruling:

" 'Is the restriction, provided for in the [Netherlands] Law [on local authority personal records], on the communication of data to one year prior to the relevant request compatible with Article 12(a) of [the] Directive ..., whether or not read in conjunction with Article 6(1)(e) of that directive and the principle of proportionality?' "

Accordingly, the question referred by the national court should be understood, essentially, as seeking to determine whether, pursuant to the Directive and, in particular, to Article 12(a) thereof, an individual's right of access to information on the recipients or categories of recipient of personal data regarding him and on the content of the data communicated may be limited to a period of one year preceding his request for access.

The court highlighted two provisions of the Directive, namely Article 6(1)(e) on the storage of personal data and Article 12(a) on the right of access to those data. However, neither that court nor any of the parties which submitted observations to the Court raised the question of the exceptions set out in Article 13 of the Directive. (Article 6 of the Directive deals with the quality of the data. Article 6(1)(e) requires Member States to ensure that personal data are kept for no longer than is necessary for the purposes for which the data were collected or for which they are further processed. The data must therefore be erased when those purposes have been served.)

Article 12(a) of the Directive provides that Member States are to guarantee data subjects a right of access to their personal data and to information on the recipients or categories of recipient of those data, without setting a time-limit. Article 12 of the Directive, entitled 'Right of access', states as follows:

'Member States shall guarantee every data subject the right to obtain from the controller:

(a) without constraint, at reasonable intervals and without excessive delay or expense:

— confirmation as to whether or not data relating to him are being processed and information at least as to the purposes of the processing, the categories of data concerned, and the recipients or categories of recipients to whom the data are disclosed,

— communication to him in an intelligible form of the data undergoing processing and of any available information as to their source,

— knowledge of the logic involved in any automatic processing of data concerning him at least in the case of the automated decisions referred to in Article 15(1);

(b) as appropriate the rectification, erasure or blocking of data the processing of which does not comply with the provisions of this Directive, in particular because of the incomplete or inaccurate nature of the data;

(c) notification to third parties to whom the data have been disclosed of any rectification, erasure or blocking carried out in compliance with (b), unless this proves impossible or involves a disproportionate effort.'

Those two articles seek, therefore, to protect the data subject. The national court sought to know whether there is a link between those two articles. Does the right of access to information on the recipients or categories of recipient of personal data and information on the content of the data disclosed, depend on the length of time for which those data have been stored?

In the decision the Court of European Union highlighted that the right to privacy, set out in Article 1(1) of Directive 95/46 on the protection of individuals with regard to the processing of personal data and on the free movement of such data, means that the data subject may be certain that his personal data are processed in a correct and lawful manner, that is to say, in particular, that the basic data regarding him are accurate and that they are disclosed to authorised recipients. As is stated in recital 41 in the preamble to the directive, in order to carry out the necessary checks, the data subject must have a right of access to the data relating to him which are being processed.

Subsequently it answered to the question referred:

— "Article 12(a) of the Directive requires Member States to ensure a right of access to information on the recipients or categories of recipient of personal data and on the content of the data disclosed not only in respect of the present but also in respect of the past. It is for Member States to fix a time-limit for storage of that information and to provide for access to that information which constitutes a fair balance between, on the one hand, the interest of the data subject in protecting his privacy, in particular by way of his rights to object and to bring legal proceedings and, on the other, the burden which the obligation to store that information represents for the controller."

— "Rules limiting the storage of information on the recipients or categories of recipient of personal data and on the content of the data disclosed to a period of one year and correspondingly limiting access to that information, while basic data is stored for a much longer period, do not constitute a fair balance of the interest and obligation at issue, unless it can be shown that longer storage of that information would constitute an excessive burden on the controller. It is, however, for national courts to make the determinations necessary."

NOTE: ROK LAMPE, NONDISCRIMINATION PRINCIPLE

Article 3(2) of Directive 95/46 excludes from its scope of application, *inter alia*, the processing of personal data concerning public security, defense, state security and the activities of the State in areas of criminal law. It follows that, while the processing of personal data for the purposes of the application of the legislation relating to the right of residence and for statistical purposes falls within the scope of application of Directive 95/46, the position is otherwise where the objective of processing those data is connected with the fight against crime.

CASE C–524/06 HEINZ HUBER v. BUNDESREPUBLIK DEUTSCHLAND (REFERENCE FOR A PRELIMINARY RULING FROM THE OBERVERWALTUNGSGERICHT FÜR DAS LAND NORDRHEIN–WESTFALEN)

JUDGMENT OF THE COURT OF EUROPEAN UNION
16 December 2008.

[In this case Mr Huber, an Austrian national, moved to Germany in 1996 in order to carry on business there as a self-employed insurance agent. In accordance with Paragraph 1(1) of the Law on the central register of foreign nationals (Gesetz über das Ausländerzentralregister) of 2 September 1994 (BGBl. 1994 I, p. 2265), as amended by the Law of 21 June 2005 (BGBl. 1994 I, p. 1818) ("the AZRG"), the Bundesamt, which is attached to the Federal Ministry of the Interior, is responsible for the management of the AZR, a centralised register which contains certain personal data relating to foreign nationals who, inter alia, are resident in Germany on a basis which is not purely temporary. The foreign nationals concerned are those who reside in that territory for a period of more than three months, as is shown by the general administrative circular of the Federal Ministry of the Interior relating to the AZRG and to the regulation implementing that Law (Allgemeine Verwaltungsvorschrift des Bundesministeriums des Innern zum Gesetz über das AZR und zur AZRG–Durchführungsverordnung) of 4 June 1996. That information is collected in two databases which are managed separately. One contains personal data relating to foreign nationals who live or have lived in Germany and the other to those who have applied for a visa.]

* * *

20 In accordance with Paragraph 3 of the AZRG, the first database contains, in particular, the following information:

— the name of the authority which provided the data;

— the reference number allocated by the Bundesamt;

— the grounds of registration;

— surname, surname at birth, given names, date and place of birth, sex and nationality;

— previous and other patronymics, marital status, particulars of identity documents, the last place of residence in the country of origin, and information supplied on a voluntary basis as to religion and the nationality of the spouse or partner;

— particulars of entries into and exits from the territory, residence status, decisions of the Federal Employment Agency relating to a work permit, refugee status granted by another State, date of death;

— decisions relating, inter alia, to any application for asylum, any previous application for a residence permit, and particulars of, inter alia, any expulsion proceedings, arrest warrants, suspected contraventions of the laws on drugs or immigration, and suspected participation in terrorist activities, or convictions in respect of such activities; and

— search warrants.

21 As the authority entrusted with the management of the AZR, the Bundesamt is responsible for the accuracy of the data registered in it.

22 According to Paragraph 1(2) of the AZRG, by registering and supplying personal data relating to foreign nationals, the Bundesamt assists the public authorities responsible for the application of the law on foreign nationals and the law on asylum, together with other public bodies.

Responsible authority stored in the AZR the following data of Mr Huber, due to the fact that he was a foreign national:

— his name, given name, date and place of birth, nationality, marital status, sex;

— a record of his entries into and exits from Germany, and his residence status;

— particulars of passports issued to him;

— a record of his previous statements as to domicile; and

— reference numbers issued by the Bundesamt, particulars of the authorities which supplied the data and the reference numbers used by those authorities.

32 Since he took the view that he was discriminated against by reason of the processing of the data concerning him contained in the AZR, in particular because such a database does not exist in respect of German nationals, Mr Huber requested the deletion of those data on 22 July 2000. That request was rejected on 29 September 2000 by the administrative authority which was responsible for maintaining the AZR at the time.

33 The challenge to that decision also having been unsuccessful, Mr Huber brought an action before the Verwaltungsgericht Köln (Administrative Court, Cologne) which upheld the action by judgment of 19 December 2002. The Verwaltungsgericht Köln held that the general processing, through the AZR, of data regarding a Union citizen who is not a German national constitutes a restriction of Articles 49 EC and 50 EC which cannot be justified by the objective of the swift treatment of cases relating to the right of residence of foreign nationals. In addition, that court took the view that the storage and processing of the data at issue were contrary to Articles 12 EC and 18 EC, as well as Articles 6(1)(b) and 7(e) of Directive 95/46.

34 The Bundesrepublik Deutschland, acting through the Bundesamt, brought an appeal against that judgment before the Oberverwaltungsgericht für das Land Nordrhein–Westfalen (Higher Administrative Court for the *Land* North–Rhine Westphalia), which considers that certain of the

questions of law raised before it require an interpretation of Community law by the Court.

35   First, the national court notes that, according to the Court's case-law, a citizen of the European Union lawfully resident in the territory of a Member State of which he is not a national can rely on Article 12 EC in all situations which fall within the scope of Community law. It refers in that regard to Case C–85/96 *Martínez Sala* [1998] ECR I–2691, paragraph 63; Case C–184/99 *Grzelczyk* [2001] ECR I–6193, paragraph 32; and Case C–209/03 *Bidar* [2005] ECR I–2119, paragraph 32. Accordingly, having exercised the right to the freedom of movement conferred on him by Article 18(1) EC, Mr Huber was entitled to rely on the prohibition of discrimination laid down by Article 12 EC.

36   The national court states that the general processing of personal data relating to Mr Huber in the AZR differs from the processing of data relating to a German national in two respects: first, some of the data relating to Mr Huber are stored not only in the register of the district in which he resides but also in the AZR, and, secondly, the AZR contains additional data.

37   The national court doubts whether such a difference in treatment can be justified by the need to monitor the residence of foreign nationals in Germany. It also raises the question whether the general processing of personal data relating to Union citizens who are not German nationals and who reside or have resided in Germany is proportionate to the objective of protecting public security, inasmuch as the AZR covers all of those citizens and not only those who are subject to an expulsion order or a prohibition on residing in Germany.

38   Secondly, the national court is of the opinion that, in the circumstances of the main proceedings, Mr Huber falls within the scope of application of Article 43 EC. Since the freedom of establishment extends not only to the taking up of activities as a self-employed person but also the framework conditions for that activity, the national court raises the question whether the general processing of data relating to Mr Huber in the AZR is liable to affect those conditions to such an extent that it comprises a restriction on the exercise of that freedom.

39   Thirdly, the national court raises the question whether the criterion of necessity imposed by Article 7(e) of Directive 95/46 can be a criterion for assessing a system of general data processing such as the system put in place under the AZR. The national court does not, in fact, rule out the possibility that the directive may leave it open to the national legislature itself to define that requirement of necessity. However, should that not be the case, the question arises how that requirement is to be understood, and more particularly whether the objective of administrative simplification might justify data processing of the kind put in place by the AZRG.

40   In those circumstances, the Oberverwaltungsgericht für das Land Nordrhein–Westfalen decided to stay the proceedings and refer the following questions to the Court of Justice for a preliminary ruling:

'(1) Is the general processing of personal data of foreign citizens of the Union in a central register of foreign nationals compatible with ... the prohibition of discrimination on grounds of nationality against citizens of the Union who exercise their right to move and reside freely within the territory of the Member States (Article 12(1) EC, in conjunction with Articles 17 EC and 18(1) EC)[?]

(2) [Is such processing compatible with] the prohibition of restrictions on the freedom of establishment of nationals of a Member State in the territory of another Member State (first paragraph of Article 43 EC)[?]

(3) [Is such treatment compatible with] the requirement of necessity under Article 7(e) of Directive 95/46?'

* * *

The Grand Chamber of the Court of the European Union ruled:

1. A system for processing personal data relating to Union citizens who are not nationals of the Member State concerned, such as that put in place by the Law on the central register of foreign nationals (Gesetz über das Ausländerzentralregister) of 2 September 1994, as amended by the Law of 21 June 2005, and having as its object the provision of support to the national authorities responsible for the application of the law relating to the right of residence does not satisfy the requirement of necessity laid down by Article 7(e) of Directive 95/46/EC of the European Parliament and of the Council of 24 October 1995 on the protection of individuals with regard to the processing of personal data and on the free movement of such data, interpreted in the light of the prohibition on any discrimination on grounds of nationality, unless:

— it contains only the data which are necessary for the application by those authorities of that legislation, and

— its centralised nature enables the legislation relating to the right of residence to be more effectively applied as regards Union citizens who are not nationals of that Member State.

It is for the national court to ascertain whether those conditions are satisfied in the main proceedings.

The storage and processing of personal data containing individualised personal information in a register such as the Central Register of Foreign Nationals for statistical purposes cannot, on any basis, be considered to be necessary within the meaning of Article 7(e) of Directive 95/46.

2. Article 12(1) EC must be interpreted as meaning that it precludes the putting in place by a Member State, for the purpose of fighting crime, of a system for processing personal data specific to Union citizens who are not nationals of that Member State.

To conclude the judgment of the Court—system for processing personal data relating to Union citizens who are not nationals of the Member State concerned, putting in place a central register of foreign nationals and having as its object the provision of support to the national authorities responsible for the application of the law relating to the right of residence does not satisfy the requirement of necessity laid down by Article 7(e) of Directive 95/46 on the protection of individuals with regard to the processing of personal data and on the free movement of such data, interpreted in the light of the prohibition on any discrimination on grounds of nationality, unless:

— it contains only the data which are necessary for the application by those authorities of that legislation, and

— its centralised nature enables that legislation to be more effectively applied as regards the right of residence of Union citizens who are not nationals of that Member State.

It is for the national court to ascertain whether those conditions are satisfied. Having regard to the objective of Directive 95/46 of ensuring an equivalent level of protection in all Member States, the concept of necessity laid down by Article 7(e) of the directive cannot have a meaning which varies between the Member States. It follows that what is at issue is a concept which has its own independent meaning in Community law.

As regards the use of a central register of foreign nationals for the purpose of the application of the legislation relating to the right of residence, it is necessary for a Member State, within the meaning of Article 7(e), to have the relevant particulars and documents available to it in order to ascertain, within the framework laid down under the applicable Community legislation, whether a right of residence in its territory exists in relation to a national of another Member State and to establish that there are no grounds which would justify a restriction on that right. It follows that the use of a register for the purpose of providing support to the authorities responsible for the application of the legislation relating to the right of residence is, in principle, legitimate and, having regard to its nature, compatible with the prohibition of discrimination on grounds of nationality laid down by Article 12(1) EC. However, such a register must not contain any information other than what is necessary for that purpose. In that regard, as Community law presently stands, the processing of personal data contained in the documents referred to in Articles 8(3) and 27(1) of Directive 2004/38 on the right of citizens of the Union and their family members to move and reside freely within the territory of the Member States amending Regulation No 1612/68 and repealing Directives 64/221, 68/360, 72/194, 73/148, 75/34, 75/35, 90/364, 90/365 and 93/96 must be considered to be necessary, within the meaning of Article 7(e) of Directive 95/46, for the application of the legislation relating to the right of residence.

With respect to the necessity that a centralised register be available in order to meet the requirements of the authorities responsible for the application of the legislation relating to the right of residence, even if it were to be assumed that decentralised registers such as district population registers contain all the data which are relevant for the purposes of allowing the authorities to undertake their duties, the centralisation of those data could be necessary, within the meaning of Article 7(e) of Directive 95/46, if it contributes to the more effective application of that legislation as regards the right of residence of Union citizens who wish to reside in a Member State of which they are not nationals.

The storage and processing of personal data containing individualised personal information in such a register for statistical purposes cannot, on any basis, be considered to be necessary within the meaning of Article 7(e) of Directive 95/46. While Community law has not excluded the power of Member States to adopt measures enabling the national authorities to have an exact knowledge of population movements affecting their territory, the exercise of that power does not, of itself, mean that the collection and storage of individualised personal information is necessary. It is only anonymous information that requires to be processed in order for such an objective to be attained.

Article 12(1) EC must be interpreted as meaning that it precludes the putting in place by a Member State, for the purpose of fighting crime, of a system for processing personal data specific to Union citizens who are not nationals of that Member State.

The principle of non-discrimination, which has its basis in Articles 12 EC and 43 EC, requires that comparable situations must not be treated differently and that different situations must not be treated in the same way. Such treatment may be justified only if it is based on objective considerations independent of the nationality of the persons concerned and is proportionate to the objective being legitimately pursued.

While it is true that the objective of fighting crime is a legitimate one, it cannot be relied on in order to justify the systematic processing of personal data when that processing is restricted to the data of Union citizens who are not nationals of the Member State concerned. The fight against crime necessarily involves the prosecution of crimes and offences committed, irrespective of the nationality of their perpetrators. It follows that, as regards a Member State, the situation of its nationals cannot, as regards the objective of fighting crime, be different from that of Union citizens who are not nationals of that Member State and who are resident in its territory. Therefore, a difference in treatment between those nationals and those Union citizens which arises by virtue of the systematic processing of personal data relating only to Union citizens who are not nationals of the Member State concerned for the purposes of fighting crime constitutes discrimination which is prohibited by Article 12(1) EC.

NOTE: TRANSFER OF PERSONAL DATA TO THIRD COUNTRIES

Chapter IV (article 25) of the Directive 95/46 regulates transfer of personal data to third countries with the following principles:

1. The Member States shall provide that the transfer to a third country of personal data which are undergoing processing or are intended for

processing after transfer may take place only if, without prejudice to compliance with the national provisions adopted pursuant to the other provisions of this Directive, the third country in question ensures an adequate level of protection.

2.   The adequacy of the level of protection afforded by a third country shall be assessed in the light of all the circumstances surrounding a data transfer operation or set of data transfer operations; particular consideration shall be given to the nature of the data, the purpose and duration of the proposed processing operation or operations, the country of origin and country of final destination, the rules of law, both general and sectoral, in force in the third country in question and the professional rules and security measures which are complied with in that country.

3.   The Member States and the Commission shall inform each other of cases where they consider that a third country does not ensure an adequate level of protection within the meaning of paragraph 2.

4.   Where the Commission finds, under the procedure provided for in Article 31 (2), that a third country does not ensure an adequate level of protection within the meaning of paragraph 2 of this Article, Member States shall take the measures necessary to prevent any transfer of data of the same type to the third country in question.

5.   At the appropriate time, the Commission shall enter into negotiations with a view to remedying the situation resulting from the finding made pursuant to paragraph 4.

6.   The Commission may find, in accordance with the procedure referred to in Article 31 (2), that a third country ensures an adequate level of protection within the meaning of paragraph 2 of this Article, by reason of its domestic law or of the international commitments it has entered into, particularly upon conclusion of the negotiations referred to in paragraph 5, for the protection of the private lives and basic freedoms and rights of individuals.

Many U.S. companies are multi-national enterprises conducting business in Europe. U.S. corporations have affiliates and divisions in Europe, and they employ European workers. For American multi-national corporations, global data transfers are imperative. For example, business and human resource information may need to flow electronically from New York and Paris to Miami and Tokyo for operational and audit purposes.

The EU Directive prohibits the transfer of personal data to countries that do not meet the Directive's "adequacy" standards for privacy protection. Lacking an omnibus privacy protection law or equivalent combination of laws, the United States does not meet the EU standard. Indeed, the United States and the European Union have significantly different approaches to consumer privacy protection. The EU law requires registration of data bases with data protection agencies. Moreover, the EU often requires consent of the data subject and "opt in" as opposed to "opt out" consent for data collection and transfer.

To enable U.S. multi-national organizations to transfer data outside the EU, and to thereby preserve a several hundred billion dollar international trade relationship, the U.S. and the EU successfully negotiated a "Safe Harbor" agreement in 2000. The European Parliament adopted the safe harbor plan and it has been implemented. The accord was designed to protect the privacy of European citizens, while avoiding the need for U.S. firms to enter individual data-protection contracts with Europeans; or for the U.S. government to mandate EU-style privacy rules for all U.S. firms.

As explained by the Commerce Department: "The safe harbor is a mechanism which, through an exchange of documents, enables the EU to certify that participating U.S. companies meet the EU requirements for adequate privacy protection. Participation in the safe harbor is voluntarily. Organizations will need to adhere to the privacy requirements laid out in the safe harbor documents for all data received from the EU." See http://www.export.gov/safeharbor/sh_overview.html.

Under the agreement, U.S. firms may transfer data from Europe if they participate in a voluntary program of certification. The required certification is a self-certification process. U.S. companies wishing to participate must join a self-regulatory privacy program (such as TRUSTe) and develop a policy that conforms to the Safe Harbor. TRUSTe, one of several industry self-regulators, maintains an online privacy seal program that went into effect in 1997. To receive the TRUSTe seal of approval and the right to carry the seal on its websites' home pages, a company must agree to submit to TRUSTe oversight and to cooperate with TRUSTe's dispute resolution process. The Department of Commerce maintains a list of all organizations that have filed self-certification letters, and makes the self-certification letters publicly available.

Certifying firms are expected to adopt a published privacy policy and adhere to the seven Safe Harbor principles: (1) notice of purposes of data collection; (2) choice—including opt-in choice if sensitive data is to be transferred to third-parties; (3) access to personal information for purposes of verification and correction; (4) "onward transfer"—which forbids transfer of information to third-parties who do not subscribe to the Safe Harbor or EU Directive; (5) security; (6) data integrity—which requires that data be collected for relevant purposes; and (7) enforcement—a readily available means of recourse for violations of other six Safe Harbor principles.

The implementation of the Safe Harbor has not been without difficulties. From the perspective of the European Commission, some companies enrolled in the safe harbor program need an improved understanding of the Safe Harbor principles. The Commission has drafted model privacy policies and maintains a website for the benefit of participating firms.

Primarily the enforcement of the Safe Harbor rests in the hands of private sector self-regulators and dispute resolution mechanisms charged to hold companies to their voluntary commitments. However, alleging "unfair trade practices" the FTC is authorized to take action against a company whose practices diverged from its published privacy policies. Penalties of up to $12,000 per day may be assessed. The False Statements Act (18 U.S.C. Sec. 1001) could provide a further remedy.

In addition, a Data Protection Panel created under the Safe Harbor agreement is charged with investigating and resolving complaints about the infringement of the Safe Harbor principles. The Panel consists of representatives of EU data protection authorities. As explained by the Data Protection Panel, a potential infringement of a Safe Harbor Principle would include this: "If your EU based employer transferred your personal data to the U.S. based headquarters operating under the Safe Harbor agreement and the latter disclosed such information without your consent, this action may be tantamount to a violation of the onward transfer principle. In this case, the data protection panel would be competent to investigate whether such action constitutes an infringement of the Safe Harbor principles."

Privacy advocates and consumer groups have criticized the Safe Harbor agreement. Critics say the agreement lets the U.S. off the hook for its failure to adopt stronger privacy protection laws for its own residents. Critics point out that privacy is recognized in the international context as a human right. Article 12 of the United Nations Universal Declaration of Human Rights explicitly affirms the right to privacy, as does Article 8 of the European Convention for the Protection of Human Rights and Fundamental Freedoms. The Organization for Economic Cooperation and Development (OECD) adopted privacy guidelines in 1980. The U.S. has not passed comprehensive privacy laws enacted by virtually all other OECD members.

Many Asian and South American countries now have data-protection laws. Is the U.S. likely to raise its domestic privacy standards through comprehensive legislation in response to EU or other international standards? See Gregory Shaffer, Globalization and Social Protection: The Impact of EU and International Rules in the Ratcheting Up of U.S. Privacy Standards, 25 *Yale J. Int'l L.* 1 (2000). Writing in the year 2000, Shaffer argued that despite "transnational institutional interdependence" and "foreign market power" stricter domestic data-protection laws in the U.S. were not inevitable. After September 11, 2001 terrorist attacks on U.S. soil, the EU and the U.S. negotiated an agreement on the "Processing and transfer of passenger name record (PNR) data by air carriers to the United States Department of Homeland Security". (The agreement was renegotiated in June 2007, reducing to 19 the types of data collected by U.S. officials, but extending approved data retention from 3 to 15 years. The EU also agreed to U.S. use of data on European financial transactions derived from the Belgian consortium, SWIFT.)

Under the original PNR Agreement it signed with the US, EU member states must transfer records of air passengers who fly to the United States to the United States Bureau of Customs and Border Protection. European institutions jointly brought the original PNR Agreement to the European Court of Justice, questioning its legality under EU legislation. See European Parliament v. Council of the European Union and Commission of the European Communities, C–317/04 and C–318/04. To be precise, the Court tested the legality of the Council Decision 2004/496/EC and the Commission Decision 2004/535/EC which EU institutions passed in the process of ratification of the Agreement.

The Court based its decision on Article 25 of the Directive 95/46 (transfer of data to third countries). It decided that Decision 2004/496 on the conclusion of an Agreement between the European Community and the United States of America on the processing and transfer of PNR (Passenger Name Record) data by Air Carriers to the United States Department of Homeland Security, Bureau of Customs and Border Protection, cannot have been validly adopted on the basis of Article 95 EC, read in conjunction with Article 25 of Directive 95/46 on the protection of individuals with regard to the processing of personal data and on the free movement of such data.

The Court concluded, however, that the agreement related to data processing operations which concern public security and the activities of the State in areas of criminal law. As such they are excluded from the scope of Directive 95/46 by virtue of Article 3(2) of that directive:

"Decision 2004/535 on the adequate protection of personal data contained in the Passenger Name Record of air passengers transferred to the United States Bureau of Customs and Border Protection relates to personal-data processing operations concerning public security and the activities of the State in areas of criminal law, operations which are excluded from the scope of Directive 95/46 on the protection of individuals with regard to the processing of personal data and on the free movement of such data, by virtue of the first indent of Article 3(2) of that directive. The fact that the personal data are collected by private operators for commercial purposes and it is they who arrange for their transfer to a third country does not alter such a conclusion, inasmuch as their transfer falls within a framework established by the public authorities that relates to public security, and is not necessary for the supply of services by those operators."

NOTE: DIRECTIVE 97/66—TELECOMMUNICATIONS DIRECTIVE

Whereas Directive 95/46/EC requires Member States to ensure the rights and freedoms of natural persons with regard to the processing of personal data, and in particular their right to privacy, the aim of the Directive 97/66 (formally titled Directive 97/66/EC of the European Parliament and of the Council of 15 December 1997 concerning the processing of personal data and the protection of privacy in the telecommunications sector) was to ensure the free flow of personal data in the European Union. How do the two aims differ? Directive 97/66 is no longer in force, having been repealed and replaced by Directive 2002/59/EC.

NOTE: DIRECTIVE 2002/58/EC AND DIRECTIVE 2006/24/EC—DIRECTIVES ON PRIVACY AND ELECTRONIC COMMUNICATIONS

The EU Directive on Privacy and Electronic Communications, formally known as, the "Directive 2002/58/EC of the European Parliament and of the Council of 12 July 2002 concerning the processing of personal data and the protection of privacy in the electronic communications sector," is a main legal source on protection of privacy in the area of electronic communication.

It was amended in 2006 by the EU Directive on Data Retention, formally "Directive 2006/24/EC of the European Parliament and of the Council of 15 March 2006 on the retention of data generated or processed in connection with the provision of publicly available electronic communications services or of public communications networks and amending Directive 2002/58/EC."

The text of these directives are found below and conclude this chapter. What are the analogues in the US law to the substantive provisions of these

Directives? Consider this question carefully as you examine each section. Try to name the "sectoral" U.S. privacy statute each substantive provision of this "omnibus" law corresponds to, if any. Some provisions correspond to the Electronic Communications Privacy Act of 1986 ("ECPA"), the federal electronic communications statute whose Wiretap Act, Stored Communications Act, and Pen Register Acts are detailed in Chapter 4 of this textbook? You can return to this question after studying Chapter 4.

DIRECTIVE ON PRIVACY AND ELECTRONIC COMMUNICATIONS

Directive 2002/58/EC of the European Parliament and of the Council Of 12 July 2002 Concerning the Processing of Personal Data and the Protection of Privacy in the Electronic Communications Sector.

Article 1

Scope and aim

1. This Directive harmonises the provisions of the Member States required to ensure an equivalent level of protection of fundamental rights and freedoms, and in particular the right to privacy, with respect to the processing of personal data in the electronic communication sector and to ensure the free movement of such data and of electronic communication equipment and services in the Community.

2. The provisions of this Directive particularise and complement Directive 95/46/EC for the purposes mentioned in paragraph 1. Moreover, they provide for protection of the legitimate interests of subscribers who are legal persons.

3. This Directive shall not apply to activities which fall outside the scope of the Treaty establishing the European Community, such as those covered by Titles V and VI of the Treaty on European Union, and in any case to activities concerning public security, defence, State security (including the economic well-being of the State when the activities relate to State security matters) and the activities of the State in areas of criminal law.

Article 2

Definitions

Save as otherwise provided, the definitions in Directive 95/46/EC and in Directive 2002/21/EC of the European Parliament and of the Council of 7 March 2002 on a common regulatory framework for electronic communications networks and services (Framework Directive)(8) shall apply.

The following definitions shall also apply:

(a) "user" means any natural person using a publicly available electronic communications service, for private or business purposes, without necessarily having subscribed to this service;

(b) "traffic data" means any data processed for the purpose of the conveyance of a communication on an electronic communications network or for the billing thereof;

(c) "location data" means any data processed in an electronic communications network, indicating the geographic position of the terminal equipment of a user of a publicly available electronic communications service;

(d) "communication" means any information exchanged or conveyed between a finite number of parties by means of a publicly available electronic communications service. This does not include any information conveyed as part of a broadcasting service to the public over an electronic communications network except to the extent that the information can be related to the identifiable subscriber or user receiving the information;

(e) "call" means a connection established by means of a publicly available telephone service allowing two-way communication in real time;

(f) "consent" by a user or subscriber corresponds to the data subject's consent in Directive 95/46/EC;

(g) "value added service" means any service which requires the processing of traffic data or location data other than traffic data beyond what is necessary for the transmission of a communication or the billing thereof;

(h) "electronic mail" means any text, voice, sound or image message sent over a public communications network which can be stored in the network or in the recipient's terminal equipment until it is collected by the recipient.

Article 3

Services concerned

1. This Directive shall apply to the processing of personal data in connection with the provision of publicly available electronic communications services in public communications networks in the Community.

2. Articles 8, 10 and 11 shall apply to subscriber lines connected to digital exchanges and, where technically possible and if it does not require a disproportionate economic effort, to subscriber lines connected to analogue exchanges.

3. Cases where it would be technically impossible or require a disproportionate economic effort to fulfil the requirements of Articles 8, 10 and 11 shall be notified to the Commission by the Member States.

Article 4

Security

1. The provider of a publicly available electronic communications service must take appropriate technical and organisational measures to safeguard security of its services, if necessary in conjunction with the provider of the public communications network with respect to network security. Having regard to the state of the art and the cost of their implementation, these measures shall ensure a level of security appropriate to the risk presented.

2. In case of a particular risk of a breach of the security of the network, the provider of a publicly available electronic communications service

must inform the subscribers concerning such risk and, where the risk lies outside the scope of the measures to be taken by the service provider, of any possible remedies, including an indication of the likely costs involved.

Article 5

Confidentiality of the communications

1.   Member States shall ensure the confidentiality of communications and the related traffic data by means of a public communications network and publicly available electronic communications services, through national legislation. In particular, they shall prohibit listening, tapping, storage or other kinds of interception or surveillance of communications and the related traffic data by persons other than users, without the consent of the users concerned, except when legally authorised to do so in accordance with Article 15(1). This paragraph shall not prevent technical storage which is necessary for the conveyance of a communication without prejudice to the principle of confidentiality.

2.   Paragraph 1 shall not affect any legally authorised recording of communications and the related traffic data when carried out in the course of lawful business practice for the purpose of providing evidence of a commercial transaction or of any other business communication.

3.   Member States shall ensure that the use of electronic communications networks to store information or to gain access to information stored in the terminal equipment of a subscriber or user is only allowed on condition that the subscriber or user concerned is provided with clear and comprehensive information in accordance with Directive 95/46/EC, inter alia about the purposes of the processing, and is offered the right to refuse such processing by the data controller. This shall not prevent any technical storage or access for the sole purpose of carrying out or facilitating the transmission of a communication over an electronic communications network, or as strictly necessary in order to provide an information society service explicitly requested by the subscriber or user.

Article 6

Traffic data

1.   Traffic data relating to subscribers and users processed and stored by the provider of a public communications network or publicly available electronic communications service must be erased or made anonymous when it is no longer needed for the purpose of the transmission of a communication without prejudice to paragraphs 2, 3 and 5 of this Article and Article 15(1).

2.   Traffic data necessary for the purposes of subscriber billing and interconnection payments may be processed. Such processing is permissible only up to the end of the period during which the bill may lawfully be challenged or payment pursued.

3.   For the purpose of marketing electronic communications services or for the provision of value added services, the provider of a publicly

available electronic communications service may process the data referred to in paragraph 1 to the extent and for the duration necessary for such services or marketing, if the subscriber or user to whom the data relate has given his/her consent. Users or subscribers shall be given the possibility to withdraw their consent for the processing of traffic data at any time.

4.   The service provider must inform the subscriber or user of the types of traffic data which are processed and of the duration of such processing for the purposes mentioned in paragraph 2 and, prior to obtaining consent, for the purposes mentioned in paragraph 3.

5.   Processing of traffic data, in accordance with paragraphs 1, 2, 3 and 4, must be restricted to persons acting under the authority of providers of the public communications networks and publicly available electronic communications services handling billing or traffic management, customer enquiries, fraud detection, marketing electronic communications services or providing a value added service, and must be restricted to what is necessary for the purposes of such activities.

6.   Paragraphs 1, 2, 3 and 5 shall apply without prejudice to the possibility for competent bodies to be informed of traffic data in conformity with applicable legislation with a view to settling disputes, in particular interconnection or billing disputes.

Article 7

Itemised billing

1.   Subscribers shall have the right to receive non-itemised bills.

2.   Member States shall apply national provisions in order to reconcile the rights of subscribers receiving itemised bills with the right to privacy of calling users and called subscribers, for example by ensuring that sufficient alternative privacy enhancing methods of communications or payments are available to such users and subscribers.

Article 8

Presentation and restriction of calling and connected line identification

1.   Where presentation of calling line identification is offered, the service provider must offer the calling user the possibility, using a simple means and free of charge, of preventing the presentation of the calling line identification on a per-call basis. The calling subscriber must have this possibility on a per-line basis.

2.   Where presentation of calling line identification is offered, the service provider must offer the called subscriber the possibility, using a simple means and free of charge for reasonable use of this function, of preventing the presentation of the calling line identification of incoming calls.

3.   Where presentation of calling line identification is offered and where the calling line identification is presented prior to the call being established, the service provider must offer the called subscriber the possibility, using a simple means, of rejecting incoming calls where the presentation

of the calling line identification has been prevented by the calling user or subscriber.

4. Where presentation of connected line identification is offered, the service provider must offer the called subscriber the possibility, using a simple means and free of charge, of preventing the presentation of the connected line identification to the calling user.

5. Paragraph 1 shall also apply with regard to calls to third countries originating in the Community. Paragraphs 2, 3 and 4 shall also apply to incoming calls originating in third countries.

6. Member States shall ensure that where presentation of calling and/or connected line identification is offered, the providers of publicly available electronic communications services inform the public thereof and of the possibilities set out in paragraphs 1, 2, 3 and 4.

Article 9

Location data other than traffic data

1. Where location data other than traffic data, relating to users or subscribers of public communications networks or publicly available electronic communications services, can be processed, such data may only be processed when they are made anonymous, or with the consent of the users or subscribers to the extent and for the duration necessary for the provision of a value added service. The service provider must inform the users or subscribers, prior to obtaining their consent, of the type of location data other than traffic data which will be processed, of the purposes and duration of the processing and whether the data will be transmitted to a third party for the purpose of providing the value added service. Users or subscribers shall be given the possibility to withdraw their consent for the processing of location data other than traffic data at any time.

2. Where consent of the users or subscribers has been obtained for the processing of location data other than traffic data, the user or subscriber must continue to have the possibility, using a simple means and free of charge, of temporarily refusing the processing of such data for each connection to the network or for each transmission of a communication.

3. Processing of location data other than traffic data in accordance with paragraphs 1 and 2 must be restricted to persons acting under the authority of the provider of the public communications network or publicly available communications service or of the third party providing the value added service, and must be restricted to what is necessary for the purposes of providing the value added service.

Article 10

Exceptions

Member States shall ensure that there are transparent procedures governing the way in which a provider of a public communications network and/or a publicly available electronic communications service may override:

(a) the elimination of the presentation of calling line identification, on a temporary basis, upon application of a subscriber requesting the tracing of malicious or nuisance calls. In this case, in accordance with national law, the data containing the identification of the calling subscriber will be stored and be made available by the provider of a public communications network and/or publicly available electronic communications service;

(b) the elimination of the presentation of calling line identification and the temporary denial or absence of consent of a subscriber or user for the processing of location data, on a per-line basis for organisations dealing with emergency calls and recognized as such by a Member State, including law enforcement agencies, ambulance services and fire brigades, for the purpose of responding to such calls.

Article 11

Automatic call forwarding

Member States shall ensure that any subscriber has the possibility, using a simple means and free of charge, of stopping automatic call forwarding by a third party to the subscriber's terminal.

Article 12

Directories of subscribers

1. Member States shall ensure that subscribers are informed, free of charge and before they are included in the directory, about the purpose(s) of a printed or electronic directory of subscribers available to the public or obtainable through directory enquiry services, in which their personal data can be included and of any further usage possibilities based on search functions embedded in electronic versions of the directory.

2. Member States shall ensure that subscribers are given the opportunity to determine whether their personal data are included in a public directory, and if so, which, to the extent that such data are relevant for the purpose of the directory as determined by the provider of the directory, and to verify, correct or withdraw such data. Not being included in a public subscriber directory, verifying, correcting or withdrawing personal data from it shall be free of charge.

3. Member States may require that for any purpose of a public directory other than the search of contact details of persons on the basis of their name and, where necessary, a minimum of other identifiers, additional consent be asked of the subscribers.

4. Paragraphs 1 and 2 shall apply to subscribers who are natural persons. Member States shall also ensure, in the framework of Community law and applicable national legislation, that the legitimate interests of subscribers other than natural persons with regard to their entry in public directories are sufficiently protected.

Article 13

Unsolicited communications

1. The use of automated calling systems without human intervention (automatic calling machines), facsimile machines (fax) or electronic mail for the purposes of direct marketing may only be allowed in respect of subscribers who have given their prior consent.

2. Notwithstanding paragraph 1, where a natural or legal person obtains from its customers their electronic contact details for electronic mail, in the context of the sale of a product or a service, in accordance with Directive 95/46/EC, the same natural or legal person may use these electronic contact details for direct marketing of its own similar products or services provided that customers clearly and distinctly are given the opportunity to object, free of charge and in an easy manner, to such use of electronic contact details when they are collected and on the occasion of each message in case the customer has not initially refused such use.

3. Member States shall take appropriate measures to ensure that, free of charge, unsolicited communications for purposes of direct marketing, in cases other than those referred to in paragraphs 1 and 2, are not allowed either without the consent of the subscribers concerned or in respect of subscribers who do not wish to receive these communications, the choice between these options to be determined by national legislation.

4. In any event, the practice of sending electronic mail for purposes of direct marketing disguising or concealing the identity of the sender on whose behalf the communication is made, or without a valid address to which the recipient may send a request that such communications cease, shall be prohibited.

5. Paragraphs 1 and 3 shall apply to subscribers who are natural persons. Member States shall also ensure, in the framework of Community law and applicable national legislation, that the legitimate interests of subscribers other than natural persons with regard to unsolicited communications are sufficiently protected.

Article 14

Technical features and standardisation

1. In implementing the provisions of this Directive, Member States shall ensure, subject to paragraphs 2 and 3, that no mandatory requirements for specific technical features are imposed on terminal or other electronic communication equipment which could impede the placing of equipment on the market and the free circulation of such equipment in and between Member States.

2. Where provisions of this Directive can be implemented only by requiring specific technical features in electronic communications networks, Member States shall inform the Commission in accordance with the procedure provided for by Directive 98/34/EC of the European Parliament and of the Council of 22 June 1998 laying down a procedure for the

provision of information in the field of technical standards and regulations and of rules on information society services(9).

3. Where required, measures may be adopted to ensure that terminal equipment is constructed in a way that is compatible with the right of users to protect and control the use of their personal data, in accordance with Directive 1999/5/EC and Council Decision 87/95/EEC of 22 December 1986 on standardisation in the field of information technology and communications(10).

Article 15

Application of certain provisions of Directive 95/46/EC

1. Member States may adopt legislative measures to restrict the scope of the rights and obligations provided for in Article 5, Article 6, Article 8(1), (2), (3) and (4), and Article 9 of this Directive when such restriction constitutes a necessary, appropriate and proportionate measure within a democratic society to safeguard national security (i.e. State security), defence, public security, and the prevention, investigation, detection and prosecution of criminal offences or of unauthorised use of the electronic communication system, as referred to in Article 13(1) of Directive 95/46/EC. To this end, Member States may, inter alia, adopt legislative measures providing for the retention of data for a limited period justified on the grounds laid down in this paragraph. All the measures referred to in this paragraph shall be in accordance with the general principles of Community law, including those referred to in Article 6(1) and (2) of the Treaty on European Union.

2. The provisions of Chapter III on judicial remedies, liability and sanctions of Directive 95/46/EC shall apply with regard to national provisions adopted pursuant to this Directive and with regard to the individual rights derived from this Directive.

3. The Working Party on the Protection of Individuals with regard to the Processing of Personal Data instituted by Article 29 of Directive 95/46/EC shall also carry out the tasks laid down in Article 30 of that Directive with regard to matters covered by this Directive, namely the protection of fundamental rights and freedoms and of legitimate interests in the electronic communications sector.

Article 16

Transitional arrangements

1. Article 12 shall not apply to editions of directories already produced or placed on the market in printed or off-line electronic form before the national provisions adopted pursuant to this Directive enter into force.

2. Where the personal data of subscribers to fixed or mobile public voice telephony services have been included in a public subscriber directory in conformity with the provisions of Directive 95/46/EC and of Article 11 of Directive 97/66/EC before the national provisions adopted in pursuance of this Directive enter into force, the personal data of such subscribers may

remain included in this public directory in its printed or electronic versions, including versions with reverse search functions, unless subscribers indicate otherwise, after having received complete information about purposes and options in accordance with Article 12 of this Directive.

* * *

NOTE: THE LESS POPULAR DIRECTIVE

One of the EU's Data Directives has not been uniformly well received by member states and privacy advocates. The EU Data Retention Directive [Council Directive 2006/24/EC] has been highly controversial. A few member states, communication providers and human rights organizations have objected to it. Soon after the directive was promulgated, Ireland, supported by the Slovak Republic, filed a motion with the European Court of Justice (ECJ) to nullify the directive on procedural grounds [Case C–301/06, *Ireland v. European Parliament and Council of the European Union*, 2009 E.C.R. I–82]. With Ireland's petition, forty three civil liberties organizations submitted amicus briefs, arguing that the directive violated the following rights: Respect for private life guaranteed by Article 8 of the European Convention for the Protection of Human Rights and Fundamental Rights [ECHR]; freedom of expression guaranteed by article 10 of ECHR; and the protection of property guaranteed by Article 1 of ECHR. Critics of the directive suggest that it does not call for adequate measures to ensure that collected data remains confidential. For example, the directive does not require that the government secure a judicial warrant in order to access information. Further, the directive arguably violates the right to protection of property because it places significant financial burden on communication providers who are obliged by the directive to store large amounts of information. Opponents to the directive argue that the directive is too lax in its lack of standardization of the period of time that a communication company should retain data (the directive stipulates anywhere between six and twenty four months) and in its lack of specification with regard to the exact cases in which member states can request data. The directive provides only very general guidance: information can be used "for purpose[s] of the investigation, detection, and prosecution of serious crime...." Thus, there is a risk that information would be abused by the authorities. Many opponents to the directive also fear the "big brother" effect; if people know that their actions are being documented, citizens will be suspicious of the government for purposes other than persecution of serious crimes. The ECJ dismissed Ireland's claim holding that the directive was enacted through appropriate legal process; the ECJ did not address the privacy concerns raised by human rights organizations and others because they were not included in Ireland's petition.

In 2009, the Romanian Constitutional Court found the implementation of the directive to be unconstitutional, *inter alia*, because it violates the right to privacy of Article 8 of the ECHR. For analysis see, Cristian Gânj, The Lives of Other Judges: Effects of the Romanian Data Retention Judgment (December 4, 2009). Available at SSRN: http://ssrn.com/abstract=1558043. In March 2010, the German Constitutional Court declared the implementation of the directive to be unconstitutional, because it enormously burdened fundamental rights guaranteed by the German Basic Law. See, Christian DeSimone, Pitting Karlsruhe against Luxembourg? German Data Protection and the Contested Implementation of the EU Data Retention Directive, 11 German L.J. 291 (2010). It is assumed that a petition to the ECJ concerning the human rights aspects of the directive will soon be submitted. Meanwhile, the European Commission called Sweden to the European Court of Justice because it did not implement the directive. In response, Sweden implemented the directive's requirement by passing an appropriate state law.

The text of the controversial data retention directive follows. Would a federal statute with similar provisions be as controversial in the U.S. context?

RETENTION OF DATA DIRECTIVE 2006/24

Directive 2006/24/EC of the European Parliament and of the Council of 15 March 2006 on the Retention of Data Generated or Processed in Connection With the Provision of Publicly Available Electronic Communications Services or of Public Communications Networks and Amending Directive 2002/58/EC.

Whereas:

(1) Directive 95/46/EC of the European Parliament and of the Council of 24 October 1995 on the protection of individuals with regard to the processing of personal data and on the free movement of such data [3] requires Member States to protect the rights and freedoms of natural persons with regard to the processing of personal data, and in particular their right to privacy, in order to ensure the free flow of personal data in the Community.

(2) Directive 2002/58/EC of the European Parliament and of the Council of 12 July 2002 concerning the processing of personal data and the protection of privacy in the electronic communications sector (Directive on privacy and electronic communications) [4] translates the principles set out in Directive 95/46/EC into specific rules for the electronic communications sector.

(3) Articles 5, 6 and 9 of Directive 2002/58/EC lay down the rules applicable to the processing by network and service providers of traffic and location data generated by using electronic communications services. Such data must be erased or made anonymous when no longer needed for the purpose of the transmission of a communication, except for the data necessary for billing or interconnection payments. Subject to consent, certain data may also be processed for marketing purposes and the provision of value-added services.

(4) Article 15(1) of Directive 2002/58/EC sets out the conditions under which Member States may restrict the scope of the rights and obligations provided for in Article 5, Article 6, Article 8(1), (2), (3) and (4), and Article 9 of that Directive. Any such restrictions must be necessary, appropriate and proportionate within a democratic society for specific public order purposes, i.e. to safeguard national security (i.e. State security), defence, public security or the prevention, investigation, detection and prosecution

of criminal offences or of unauthorised use of the electronic communications systems.

(5) Several Member States have adopted legislation providing for the retention of data by service providers for the prevention, investigation, detection, and prosecution of criminal offences. Those national provisions vary considerably.

(6) The legal and technical differences between national provisions concerning the retention of data for the purpose of prevention, investigation, detection and prosecution of criminal offences present obstacles to the internal market for electronic communications, since service providers are faced with different requirements regarding the types of traffic and location data to be retained and the conditions and periods of retention.

(7) The Conclusions of the Justice and Home Affairs Council of 19 December 2002 underline that, because of the significant growth in the possibilities afforded by electronic communications, data relating to the use of electronic communications are particularly important and therefore a valuable tool in the prevention, investigation, detection and prosecution of criminal offences, in particular organised crime.

(8) The Declaration on Combating Terrorism adopted by the European Council on 25 March 2004 instructed the Council to examine measures for establishing rules on the retention of communications traffic data by service providers.

(9) Under Article 8 of the European Convention for the Protection of Human Rights and Fundamental Freedoms (ECHR), everyone has the right to respect for his private life and his correspondence. Public authorities may interfere with the exercise of that right only in accordance with the law and where necessary in a democratic society, inter alia, in the interests of national security or public safety, for the prevention of disorder or crime, or for the protection of the rights and freedoms of others. Because retention of data has proved to be such a necessary and effective investigative tool for law enforcement in several Member States, and in particular concerning serious matters such as organised crime and terrorism, it is necessary to ensure that retained data are made available to law enforcement authorities for a certain period, subject to the conditions provided for in this Directive. The adoption of an instrument on data retention that complies with the requirements of Article 8 of the ECHR is therefore a necessary measure.

(10) On 13 July 2005, the Council reaffirmed in its declaration condemning the terrorist attacks on London the need to adopt common measures on the retention of telecommunications data as soon as possible.

(11) Given the importance of traffic and location data for the investigation, detection, and prosecution of criminal offences, as demonstrated by research and the practical experience of several Member States, there is a need to ensure at European level that data that are generated or processed, in the course of the supply of communications services, by provid-

ers of publicly available electronic communications services or of a public communications network are retained for a certain period, subject to the conditions provided for in this Directive.

(12) Article 15(1) of Directive 2002/58/EC continues to apply to data, including data relating to unsuccessful call attempts, the retention of which is not specifically required under this Directive and which therefore fall outside the scope thereof, and to retention for purposes, including judicial purposes, other than those covered by this Directive.

(13) This Directive relates only to data generated or processed as a consequence of a communication or a communication service and does not relate to data that are the content of the information communicated. Data should be retained in such a way as to avoid their being retained more than once. Data generated or processed when supplying the communications services concerned refers to data which are accessible. In particular, as regards the retention of data relating to Internet e-mail and Internet telephony, the obligation to retain data may apply only in respect of data from the providers' or the network providers' own services.

(14) Technologies relating to electronic communications are changing rapidly and the legitimate requirements of the competent authorities may evolve. In order to obtain advice and encourage the sharing of experience of best practice in these matters, the Commission intends to establish a group composed of Member States' law enforcement authorities, associations of the electronic communications industry, representatives of the European Parliament and data protection authorities, including the European Data Protection Supervisor.

(15) Directive 95/46/EC and Directive 2002/58/EC are fully applicable to the data retained in accordance with this Directive. Article 30(1)(c) of Directive 95/46/EC requires the consultation of the Working Party on the Protection of Individuals with regard to the Processing of Personal Data established under Article 29 of that Directive.

(16) The obligations incumbent on service providers concerning measures to ensure data quality, which derive from Article 6 of Directive 95/46/EC, and their obligations concerning measures to ensure confidentiality and security of processing of data, which derive from Articles 16 and 17 of that Directive, apply in full to data being retained within the meaning of this Directive.

(17) It is essential that Member States adopt legislative measures to ensure that data retained under this Directive are provided to the competent national authorities only in accordance with national legislation in full respect of the fundamental rights of the persons concerned.

(18) In this context, Article 24 of Directive 95/46/EC imposes an obligation on Member States to lay down sanctions for infringements of the provisions adopted pursuant to that Directive. Article 15(2) of Directive 2002/58/EC imposes the same requirement in relation to national provisions adopted pursuant to Directive 2002/58/EC. Council Framework

Decision 2005/222/JHA of 24 February 2005 on attacks against information systems [5] provides that the intentional illegal access to information systems, including to data retained therein, is to be made punishable as a criminal offence.

(19) The right of any person who has suffered damage as a result of an unlawful processing operation or of any act incompatible with national provisions adopted pursuant to Directive 95/46/EC to receive compensation, which derives from Article 23 of that Directive, applies also in relation to the unlawful processing of any personal data pursuant to this Directive.

(20) The 2001 Council of Europe Convention on Cybercrime and the 1981 Council of Europe Convention for the Protection of Individuals with Regard to Automatic Processing of Personal Data also cover data being retained within the meaning of this Directive.

(21) Since the objectives of this Directive, namely to harmonise the obligations on providers to retain certain data and to ensure that those data are available for the purpose of the investigation, detection and prosecution of serious crime, as defined by each Member State in its national law, cannot be sufficiently achieved by the Member States and can therefore, by reason of the scale and effects of this Directive, be better achieved at Community level, the Community may adopt measures, in accordance with the principle of subsidiarity as set out in Article 5 of the Treaty. In accordance with the principle of proportionality, as set out in that Article, this Directive does not go beyond what is necessary in order to achieve those objectives.

(22) This Directive respects the fundamental rights and observes the principles recognized, in particular, by the Charter of Fundamental Rights of the European Union. In particular, this Directive, together with Directive 2002/58/EC, seeks to ensure full compliance with citizens' fundamental rights to respect for private life and communications and to the protection of their personal data, as enshrined in Articles 7 and 8 of the Charter.

(23) Given that the obligations on providers of electronic communications services should be proportionate, this Directive requires that they retain only such data as are generated or processed in the process of supplying their communications services. To the extent that such data are not generated or processed by those providers, there is no obligation to retain them. This Directive is not intended to harmonise the technology for retaining data, the choice of which is a matter to be resolved at national level.

(24) In accordance with paragraph 34 of the Interinstitutional agreement on better law-making [6], Member States are encouraged to draw up, for themselves and in the interests of the Community, their own tables illustrating, as far as possible, the correlation between this Directive and the transposition measures, and to make them public.

(25) This Directive is without prejudice to the power of Member States to adopt legislative measures concerning the right of access to, and use of, data by national authorities, as designated by them. Issues of access to data retained pursuant to this Directive by national authorities for such activities as are referred to in the first indent of Article 3(2) of Directive 95/46/EC fall outside the scope of Community law. However, they may be subject to national law or action pursuant to Title VI of the Treaty on European Union. Such laws or action must fully respect fundamental rights as they result from the common constitutional traditions of the Member States and as guaranteed by the ECHR. Under Article 8 of the ECHR, as interpreted by the European Court of Human Rights, interference by public authorities with privacy rights must meet the requirements of necessity and proportionality and must therefore serve specified, explicit and legitimate purposes and be exercised in a manner that is adequate, relevant and not excessive in relation to the purpose of the interference,

HAVE ADOPTED THIS DIRECTIVE:

Article 1

Subject matter and scope

1. This Directive aims to harmonise Member States' provisions concerning the obligations of the providers of publicly available electronic communications services or of public communications networks with respect to the retention of certain data which are generated or processed by them, in order to ensure that the data are available for the purpose of the investigation, detection and prosecution of serious crime, as defined by each Member State in its national law.

2. This Directive shall apply to traffic and location data on both legal entities and natural persons and to the related data necessary to identify the subscriber or registered user. It shall not apply to the content of electronic communications, including information consulted using an electronic communications network.

Article 2

Definitions

1. For the purpose of this Directive, the definitions in Directive 95/46/ EC, in Directive 2002/21/EC of the European Parliament and of the Council of 7 March 2002 on a common regulatory framework for electronic communications networks and services (Framework Directive) [7], and in Directive 2002/58/EC shall apply.

2. For the purpose of this Directive:

(a) "data" means traffic data and location data and the related data necessary to identify the subscriber or user;

(b) "user" means any legal entity or natural person using a publicly available electronic communications service, for private or business purposes, without necessarily having subscribed to that service;

(c) "telephone service" means calls (including voice, voicemail and conference and data calls), supplementary services (including call forwarding and call transfer) and messaging and multi-media services (including short message services, enhanced media services and multi-media services);

(d) "user ID" means a unique identifier allocated to persons when they subscribe to or register with an Internet access service or Internet communications service;

(e) "cell ID" means the identity of the cell from which a mobile telephony call originated or in which it terminated;

(f) "unsuccessful call attempt" means a communication where a telephone call has been successfully connected but not answered or there has been a network management intervention.

Article 3

Obligation to retain data

1. By way of derogation from Articles 5, 6 and 9 of Directive 2002/58/EC, Member States shall adopt measures to ensure that the data specified in Article 5 of this Directive are retained in accordance with the provisions thereof, to the extent that those data are generated or processed by providers of publicly available electronic communications services or of a public communications network within their jurisdiction in the process of supplying the communications services concerned.

2. The obligation to retain data provided for in paragraph 1 shall include the retention of the data specified in Article 5 relating to unsuccessful call attempts where those data are generated or processed, and stored (as regards telephony data) or logged (as regards Internet data), by providers of publicly available electronic communications services or of a public communications network within the jurisdiction of the Member State concerned in the process of supplying the communication services concerned. This Directive shall not require data relating to unconnected calls to be retained.

Article 4

Access to data

Member States shall adopt measures to ensure that data retained in accordance with this Directive are provided only to the competent national authorities in specific cases and in accordance with national law. The procedures to be followed and the conditions to be fulfilled in order to gain access to retained data in accordance with necessity and proportionality requirements shall be defined by each Member State in its national law, subject to the relevant provisions of European Union law or public international law, and in particular the ECHR as interpreted by the European Court of Human Rights.

Article 5

Categories of data to be retained

1. Member States shall ensure that the following categories of data are retained under this Directive:

(a) data necessary to trace and identify the source of a communication:

(1) concerning fixed network telephony and mobile telephony:

(i) the calling telephone number;

(ii) the name and address of the subscriber or registered user;

(2) concerning Internet access, Internet e-mail and Internet telephony:

(i) the user ID(s) allocated;

(ii) the user ID and telephone number allocated to any communication entering the public telephone network;

(iii) the name and address of the subscriber or registered user to whom an Internet Protocol (IP) address, user ID or telephone number was allocated at the time of the communication;

(b) data necessary to identify the destination of a communication:

(1) concerning fixed network telephony and mobile telephony:

(i) the number(s) dialled (sic) (the telephone number(s) called), and, in cases involving supplementary services such as call forwarding or call transfer, the number or numbers to which the call is routed;

(ii) the name(s) and address(es) of the subscriber(s) or registered user(s);

(2) concerning Internet e-mail and Internet telephony:

(i) the user ID or telephone number of the intended recipient(s) of an Internet telephony call;

(ii) the name(s) and address(es) of the subscriber(s) or registered user(s) and user ID of the intended recipient of the communication;

(c) data necessary to identify the date, time and duration of a communication:

(1) concerning fixed network telephony and mobile telephony, the date and time of the start and end of the communication;

(2) concerning Internet access, Internet e-mail and Internet telephony:

(i) the date and time of the log-in and log-off of the Internet access service, based on a certain time zone, together with the IP address, whether dynamic or static, allocated by the Internet access service provider to a communication, and the user ID of the subscriber or registered user;

(ii) the date and time of the log-in and log-off of the Internet e-mail service or Internet telephony service, based on a certain time zone;

(d) data necessary to identify the type of communication:

(1) concerning fixed network telephony and mobile telephony: the telephone service used;

(2) concerning Internet e-mail and Internet telephony: the Internet service used;

(e) data necessary to identify users' communication equipment or what purports to be their equipment:

(1) concerning fixed network telephony, the calling and called telephone numbers;

(2) concerning mobile telephony:

(i) the calling and called telephone numbers;

(ii) the International Mobile Subscriber Identity (IMSI) of the calling party;

(iii) the International Mobile Equipment Identity (IMEI) of the calling party;

(iv) the IMSI of the called party;

(v) the IMEI of the called party;

(vi) in the case of pre-paid anonymous services, the date and time of the initial activation of the service and the location label (Cell ID) from which the service was activated;

(3) concerning Internet access, Internet e-mail and Internet telephony:

(i) the calling telephone number for dial-up access;

(ii) the digital subscriber line (DSL) or other end point of the originator of the communication;

(f) data necessary to identify the location of mobile communication equipment:

(1) the location label (Cell ID) at the start of the communication;

(2) data identifying the geographic location of cells by reference to their location labels (Cell ID) during the period for which communications data are retained.

2. No data revealing the content of the communication may be retained pursuant to this Directive.

Article 6

Periods of retention

Member States shall ensure that the categories of data specified in Article 5 are retained for periods of not less than six months and not more than two years from the date of the communication.

Article 7

Data protection and data security

Without prejudice to the provisions adopted pursuant to Directive 95/46/EC and Directive 2002/58/EC, each Member State shall ensure that providers of publicly available electronic communications services or of a public communications network respect, as a minimum, the following data security principles with respect to data retained in accordance with this Directive:

(a) the retained data shall be of the same quality and subject to the same security and protection as those data on the network;

(b) the data shall be subject to appropriate technical and organisational measures to protect the data against accidental or unlawful destruction, accidental loss or alteration, or unauthorised or unlawful storage, processing, access or disclosure;

(c) the data shall be subject to appropriate technical and organisational measures to ensure that they can be accessed by specially authorised personnel only;

and

(d) the data, except those that have been accessed and preserved, shall be destroyed at the end of the period of retention.

Article 8

Storage requirements for retained data

Member States shall ensure that the data specified in Article 5 are retained in accordance with this Directive in such a way that the data retained and any other necessary information relating to such data can be transmitted upon request to the competent authorities without undue delay.

Article 9

Supervisory authority

1. Each Member State shall designate one or more public authorities to be responsible for monitoring the application within its territory of the provisions adopted by the Member States pursuant to Article 7 regarding the security of the stored data. Those authorities may be the same authorities as those referred to in Article 28 of Directive 95/46/EC.

2. The authorities referred to in paragraph 1 shall act with complete independence in carrying out the monitoring referred to in that paragraph.

Article 10

Statistics

1. Member States shall ensure that the Commission is provided on a yearly basis with statistics on the retention of data generated or processed in connection with the provision of publicly available electronic communications services or a public communications network. Such statistics shall include:

— the cases in which information was provided to the competent authorities in accordance with applicable national law,

— the time elapsed between the date on which the data were retained and the date on which the competent authority requested the transmission of the data,

— the cases where requests for data could not be met.

2. Such statistics shall not contain personal data.

Article 11

Amendment of Directive 2002/58/EC

The following paragraph shall be inserted in Article 15 of Directive 2002/58/EC:

"1a. Paragraph 1 shall not apply to data specifically required by Directive 2006/24/EC of the European Parliament and of the Council of 15 March 2006 on the retention of data generated or processed in connection with the provision of publicly available electronic communications services or of public communications networks [] to be retained for the purposes referred to in Article 1(1) of that Directive.

Article 12

Future measures

1. A Member State facing particular circumstances that warrant an extension for a limited period of the maximum retention period referred to in Article 6 may take the necessary measures. That Member State shall immediately notify the Commission and inform the other Member States of the measures taken under this Article and shall state the grounds for introducing them.

2. The Commission shall, within a period of six months after the notification referred to in paragraph 1, approve or reject the national measures concerned, after having examined whether they are a means of arbitrary discrimination or a disguised restriction of trade between Member States and whether they constitute an obstacle to the functioning of the internal market. In the absence of a decision by the Commission within that period the national measures shall be deemed to have been approved.

3. Where, pursuant to paragraph 2, the national measures of a Member State derogating from the provisions of this Directive are approved, the Commission may consider whether to propose an amendment to this Directive.

Article 13

Remedies, liability and penalties

1. Each Member State shall take the necessary measures to ensure that the national measures implementing Chapter III of Directive 95/46/EC providing for judicial remedies, liability and sanctions are fully implemented with respect to the processing of data under this Directive.

2. Each Member State shall, in particular, take the necessary measures to ensure that any intentional access to, or transfer of, data retained in accordance with this Directive that is not permitted under national law

adopted pursuant to this Directive is punishable by penalties, including administrative or criminal penalties, that are effective, proportionate and dissuasive.

Article 14

Evaluation

1. No later than 15 September 2010, the Commission shall submit to the European Parliament and the Council an evaluation of the application of this Directive and its impact on economic operators and consumers, taking into account further developments in electronic communications technology and the statistics provided to the Commission pursuant to Article 10 with a view to determining whether it is necessary to amend the provisions of this Directive, in particular with regard to the list of data in Article 5 and the periods of retention provided for in Article 6. The results of the evaluation shall be made public.

2. To that end, the Commission shall examine all observations communicated to it by the Member States or by the Working Party established under Article 29 of Directive 95/46/EC.

Article 15

Transposition

1. Member States shall bring into force the laws, regulations and administrative provisions necessary to comply with this Directive by no later than 15 September 2007. They shall forthwith inform the Commission thereof. When Member States adopt those measures, they shall contain a reference to this Directive or shall be accompanied by such reference on the occasion of their official publication. The methods of making such reference shall be laid down by Member States.

2. Member States shall communicate to the Commission the text of the main provisions of national law which they adopt in the field covered by this Directive.

3. Until 15 March 2009, each Member State may postpone application of this Directive to the retention of communications data relating to Internet Access, Internet telephony and Internet e-mail. Any Member State that intends to make use of this paragraph shall, upon adoption of this Directive, notify the Council and the Commission to that effect by way of a declaration. The declaration shall be published in the Official Journal of the European Union.

NOTE: WHICH IS BETTER, SECTORAL OR OMNIBUS?

So which approach to privacy regulation is better, sectoral as in the US or omnibus as in the EU? Prof. Schwartz asks an important additional question: whether the national approach is sectoral or omnibus, when should national rules be designed to preempt state ones? As to the first question, surely the goals of regulation are pertinent, as well as the background conditions of law and tradition. Should then the next step for the US be to enact more sectoral privacy laws, to enact better sectoral privacy laws, or to pursue a new regime of fewer and more comprehensive federal data protection rules that work in tandem with state rules?

PAUL M. SCHWARTZ, PREEMPTION AND PRIVACY

118 Yale L.J. 902 (2009) (footnotes omitted).

* * *

B.   Omnibus and Sectoral Privacy Laws: U.S. and European Regulatory
     Paths

The world's first comprehensive information privacy statute was a
state law; the Hessian Parliament enacted this statute in Wiesbaden,
Germany, on September 30, 1970. * * * This law was followed by those of
other German states, which then influenced the form and content of a
federal omnibus law, the Federal German Data Protection Act (Bundesda-
tenschutzgesetz, or BDSG). The term, "data protection," is the standard
nomenclature in Europe for information privacy. The 1977 BDSG establishes standards for information processing by public and private entities
alike.

The German preference for anchoring data protection law in omnibus
privacy statutes is typical of European data protection law. The European
Union's adoption in 1995 of the Data Protection Directive has played a
key role in this process. The Data Protection Directive envisions that all
EU member states follow its requirements by "transposing" them into
national law. It leaves the choice of specific legal instruments to each
member state, and, at least theoretically, an EU member state could
choose to enact a combination of sectoral laws to comply with the
Directive. Yet all member states have enacted omnibus laws to transpose
the Directive into national law. * * *

In the United States, by contrast, FIPs have generally developed
through laws that regulate information use exclusively on a sector-by-
sector basis. The one partial exception in the United States is the Privacy
Act of 1974, * * * which is an omnibus law for the public sector, albeit a
narrow one. The Privacy Act only regulates certain kinds of federal
agencies, and only certain kinds of information use. * * *

In contrast to * * * omnibus privacy laws, a sectoral approach is
necessarily more narrowly tailored and its terms, by their nature, are
more specific. The U.S. Video Privacy Protection Act of 1988 (VPPA)
provides a good example. Its jurisdictional sweep is limited to a "video
tape service provider," which is defined in technology-neutral terms. As a
result, the law has been easily extended to DVDs. The VPPA contains
FIPs, but these are necessarily tailored to the specific context of the
"rental, sale, or delivery of prerecorded video cassette tapes or similar
audio visual materials." A description of its customization will provide a
useful illustration of the basics of a sectoral information privacy statute.
* * *

I now return to the question of why the United States and Europe have taken divergent paths. The United States continues to lack an omnibus bill that covers the private sector and has, at best, only a relatively limited omnibus bill for part of the public sector. In contrast, as new countries have joined the EU, they have commenced their regulation of information privacy with omnibus laws and have supplemented these statutes with sectoral ones. In my view, the continuing differences can best be explained by a modest account that looks at (1) initial choices followed by path dependency, and (2) the usefulness of omnibus laws in multination systems that wish to harmonize their regulations.

1. The U.S. Path

* * * [T]here was considerable caution in the United States in the 1970s against a broad regulation of information use that would include the private and public sectors in one fell swoop. This orientation demonstrates an ideology that I term "regulatory parsimony." As the medical profession expresses the idea, "above all, do no harm." The same perspective is demonstrated in aspects of the Privacy Act of 1974, which, though a kind of omnibus bill for the public sector, is more limited than the typical omnibus EU law for the public sector. * * *

2. The EU Path

* * * Regarding the decision to enact omnibus laws from the first era of data protection law in Europe, Spiros Simitis observes that the European lawmaker began with the idea that it was necessary to analyze problems that cut across individual contexts of processing and for which, therefore, a uniform solution expressed in a single statute should be developed. At the same time, the European legislator was also confronted with a considerable challenge because data processing was in its infancy and, therefore, the subject of regulation lacked clear contours.

Despite uncertainty, European lawmakers decided to enact omnibus data protection statutes. Abraham Newman has identified different historically contingent factors that smoothed the path to enactment of data protection statutes in the 1970s in France and Germany, two leaders in information privacy law. For example, Newman shows how French industry's potential opposition to the proposed French data protection legislation was muted by the past nationalization of many affected companies and the centralization of these industries, which minimized the impact of the statute. As a further example, in Germany, a pro-privacy alliance benefited at the critical point in the late 1970s from a "particular alignment of political actors at that time [who] neutralized key barriers to the passage of the policy."

After the initial choice in key European nations to enact omnibus laws, the EU's "harmonizing" project in the field of data protection exercised a strong influence on other nations. This term of European Community law refers to formal attempts to increase the similarity of legal measures in member states. As Joachim Jacob, the Federal Data Protection Commissioner of Germany, observed, "the European Community is also becoming an information and data community." European integration increased the sharing of data among EU Member Nations and created new demands for personal information. Due to this data sharing throughout the EU, nations with privacy statutes had incentives to advocate equivalent safeguards in all member states. Without such shared levels of protection, previous efforts within individual nations to ensure privacy for their citizens' data would be for naught. The information could easily be transferred to other member states with weaker levels of data protection.

The resulting policy response was the movement to harmonize privacy law throughout the EU. Through the Data Protection Directive, the EU obliged lagging nations within its ranks to protect personal information and to follow the omnibus approach. Moreover, as Newman has observed, the national data protection commissioners, already in place by the 1980s, played an important transgovernmental role in shaping the Directive and expanding privacy protection in Europe. National privacy regulators worked so that their national legislation would be "exported upward regionally." The benefit of an omnibus law for this project is that it provides a relatively limited series of benchmarks and sets them within a single statute. In contrast, an exclusively sectoral approach would lead to far greater complexity in assessing the "equivalency" of data protection for each of the now twenty-seven EU member states. * * *

C. Recent Federal and State Trends and the Role of Preemption

This Essay's brief history of information privacy in U.S. law has traced its roots from tort law to the start of the modern era. It also has drawn on comparative examples to illustrate U.S. regulatory exceptionalism centered on its lack of an omnibus statute for the private sector. To bring this account up to the present, this Essay returns to the formative decade for information privacy law in the United States—the 1970s. During this period, the U.S. Congress enacted Title III of the Omnibus Crime Control and Safe Streets Act of 1968 (the Wiretap Act), the Fair Credit Reporting Act in 1970, the Family Educational Rights and Privacy Act of 1974, and the Right to Financial Privacy Act of 1978. All of these laws are sector-specific except for the Privacy Act of 1974.

Against this background, the states in the United States have been especially important laboratories for innovations in information privacy law. As noted, the state tradition begins with the recognition of privacy torts throughout the twentieth century. Other innovations followed. Already in 1977, the blue ribbon Privacy Protection Study Commission commented on "the significant increase in State regulatory efforts to protect the interests of the individual in records kept about him ... [which had] already led a number of States to try out innovative protections, particularly in their regulation of private-sector organizations." * * *

State privacy law has started the twenty-first century with renewed activity. * * * As examples from a different area of privacy law, New York and Connecticut are now considering bills that would set limits on companies that track consumers across websites to deliver targeted advertisements based on their behavior. * * *

Second, states have provided innovative approaches. * * * [S]tates have taken legislative action to restrict the use of social security numbers. They also have granted consumers who are victims of identity theft the ability to place freezes on their credit reports, and have obliged businesses to supply these victims with the relevant records of transactions associated with their stolen identity. Moreover, state law preceded federal law in granting identity theft victims a right to free copies of their credit reports.

Third, states have created an opportunity for simultaneous experiments with different policies. As Malcolm Feeley and Edward Rubin dryly observe of the general idea of states-as-laboratories, these experiments are "desirable, presumably * * * not because of an abiding national commitment to pure research but because the variations may ultimately provide information about a range of alternative government policies and enable the nation to choose the most desirable one." Justice Louis Brandeis famously pointed to this benefit of state regulation and also identified the ability of these "novel social and economic experiments" to take place, at least some of the time, "without risk to the rest of the country." As an illustration of these simultaneous policy solutions, data breach notification statutes vary in their notification "triggers"—that is, the standard under which a company must share information about a data security incident. * * *

[Some federal privacy statutes establish standards ("floors") below which state privacy laws cannot fall, and preempt weaker state standards.]

The Wiretap Act [which will be examined in this textbook in Chapter 4] provides [a]. . . classic example of a federal privacy "floor." This federal statute permits the recording of telephone conversations by private parties if one party to the conversation has consented. It also allows states to enact more restrictive laws. As the Wiretap Act's legislative history notes, "The proposed provision envisions that States would be free to adopt more restrictive legislation, or no legislation at all, but not less restrictive legislation." Twelve states have enacted "all party" consent statutes. Under these laws, all parties to a phone call must agree to have their telephone call recorded.

Another federal law with a similar approach to state regulation is the Gramm–Leach–Bliley Act (GLB Act), Title V of which regulates the personal information processing of financial institutions. This statute also sets a federal "floor" for privacy. For example, the GLB Act allows states to set higher privacy standards regarding how financial institutions share personal information with outside organizations (termed "non-affiliated entities" in the statute).

Federal privacy legislation has also preempted state legislation with the effect of weakening existing state standards. A statute from 2003, FACTA, which amends the Fair Credit Reporting Act, contains examples of such a downward revision. * * *

Here, then, is the landscape against which Bill Gates and others have called for a federal omnibus statute for privacy—and one with strong preemption requirements. Industry in the United States also has made clear that strong ceiling preemption is an essential condition of its support for any comprehensive legislation. As a Microsoft white paper from 2005 states, "federal privacy legislation should pre-empt state laws that impose requirements for the collection, use, disclosure and storage of personal information." Any single drop of preemption language in a federal statute is, moreover, likely to go a long way. In recent litigation concerning other areas of law, the Supreme Court has demonstrated a willingness in the face of statutory ambiguity to identify a congressional intent to occupy a regulatory field and impose a "ceiling."

II. A FEDERAL OMNIBUS PRIVACY LAW: STRENGTHS AND WEAKNESSES

* * *

There are three potential problems with a federal omnibus law. These are (1) the costs of an extra layer of regulation, (2) the harms from disregard of the parsimony principle, and (3) the danger of ossification in the federal omnibus law itself. Under federal omnibus legislation, regulated entities would bear the cost of compliance with not only any sector regulation, federal or state, but also the federal omnibus law as it applies to their activities. To some extent FTC enforcement actions are already partial gap-fillers in regulatory coverage, and thereby increase the costs of compliance for private organizations that process personal information. Yet the existing FTC privacy principles are far from comprehensive, and a federal omnibus law will, therefore, add in some fashion to the regulatory weight. At the same time, by leveling the privacy regulatory field, an omnibus law would also ameliorate inconsistencies that flow from convergence.

As for the parsimony principle, it warns against taking action—and especially broad action—under conditions of uncertainty. This principle was at work in 1974 during the debate about S. 3418 and then the Privacy Act. An analogy can also be drawn from environmental law. In this area, Congress has not enacted a federal gap-filling statute modeled on nuisance law. Instead, federal environmental law emerged in targeted areas— through sectoral regulations, as it were—as represented by the Clean Air Act, the Clean Water Act, the Endangered Species Act, and so on. Nuisance law is left as a gap-filler on the state level, where it is left to develop and be applied in a fashion that is attuned to local conditions, including aggregate local policy preferences.

Finally, a federal omnibus law might be difficult to amend. This flaw in a potential omnibus privacy law can be usefully compared to this flaw in the labor law context. Cynthia Estlund has demonstrated how an "ossification" of American labor law has taken place and contributed significantly to its ineffectuality. * * * The risk of ossification following enactment of a federal omnibus privacy law is also great. Such an omnibus law, like the NLRA, would be difficult to amend—industry, privacy advocates, and other parties may be able to muster enough congressional support to block any significant changes to it. Yet technological change will wreak havoc over time with such a statute's regulatory assumptions, both explicit and implicit. This example illustrates the negative side of the promise of an omnibus law in responding to telecommunications convergence.

* * *

Overall, federal sectoral law can have the potential to build on the results of state law. The devil is in the details, however, and one cannot state at an abstract level that a federal sectoral law is necessarily preferable to the messier universe of different and unconsolidated state sectoral statutes. Whether one is a privacy advocate or skeptic, history teaches that the federal government and the states may switch back and forth in their concern for and level of attention to this issue. * * *

There has been a noticeable lack of gridlock at the state sectoral level. The website of the California Office of Information Security and Privacy Protection displays an impressive list of privacy legislation enacted in 2008 alone or currently pending. Among the recent legislation are statutes that make it a misdemeanor to eavesdrop intentionally on Radio Frequent Identification devices, that increase penalties for hospital employees that snoop through medical records, and that simplify the procedures for consumers to place a security freeze on their credit files. An interesting regulatory lever has been the public's strong interest in privacy. This interest has been reflected in countywide privacy regulations—such as northern California's financial privacy ordinances—and a successful use of a privacy referendum in North Dakota and the threat of such a referendum in California.

Like environmental law, privacy is also an attractive area for politicians and private advocates seeking a field for policy entrepreneurship. * * *

Thus, gridlock has not kept states from enacting privacy statutes. States are also not competing for business with each other by failing to regulate privacy with sufficient rigor. There certainly has been no race to the bottom, which also has been termed the "race of laxity." In the context of environmental law, there is a rich scholarly debate regarding whether or not states have competed to offer weaker regulatory regimes to curry favor with business. In the area of information privacy, there is scant room for such a debate. Even if there is no indication of a race to the top, states are far from enacting successive waves of information privacy statutes with weaker protections for consumers and more favorable conditions for businesses. In other words, California privacy initiatives have not encouraged Nevada or other states, neighboring or otherwise, to enact weaker regulations in the same area. At any rate, state legislative activities will continue and will drive a flight by businesses to Washington for federal solutions. Over the next decade and beyond, continuing waves of state privacy lawmaking will provoke industry activity to seek federal legislation.

CHAPTER 4

FEDERAL SURVEILLANCE LAW

■ ■ ■

Introduction

Has the United States become a problematic "surveillance" society? Through the materials in this Chapter, which continue the survey of federal privacy statutes, begun in Chapter 3, you can judge for yourself whether the government has appropriate or inappropriate access to knowledge of personal conduct and conversations. That the government has lawful means of access to virtually all mechanisms of communication stands beyond dispute. Whether government is sufficiently respectful of privacy and publicly accountable for its surveillance activities remains open for debate.

Commentators began expressing concerns about surveillance and surveillance technologies decades ago. See, generally, Alan F. Westin, Science, Privacy, and Freedom: Issues and Proposals for the 1970's, 66 *Columbia L. Rev.* 1003, 1006–09 (1966). Before email and its interception were dreamt of, people worried about the invasive potential of wiretapping, tape recording, tiny microphones and cameras. A "Cold War" with the Soviet Union followed World War II. It placed espionage into the forefront of the American consciousness. Techniques used to detect foreign spies and traitors might as easily be used to keep track of loyal Americans. "McCarthyism" and the "Red Scare" doubtlessly contributed to a sense of vulnerability. Westin warned in 1966 that autonomy plus all four "states of privacy"—solitude, intimacy, anonymity and reserve—were in jeopardy. Crucial to autonomy, Westin explained, is the "individual's sense that it is he [or she] who decides when to 'go public.'"

Close surveillance of travelers, shoppers, suspects, and pedestrians on the street has become more prevalent in the years since the terrorist attacks of September 11, 2001. We have already encountered examples of post 9/11 government surveillance in Chapter 2 of this textbook, in connection with the unit on airport security and the Fourth Amendment. This Chapter focuses on the statutes that govern common forms of surveillance and spying, some of which have been in place a long time. After 9/11, the USA PATRIOT Act was enacted and it substantially amended existing laws to make government surveillance outside bounds of the Fourth Amendment easier and more effective.

Crafted by Congress to control the reach of 20th century technology, a complex set of federal statutes regulate investigative surveillance and other acquisition of communications. The federal statutes examined in this Chapter extensively regulate wiretapping, voice-recording, and access to others' telephone records, voice mail and email. These statutes describe in detail the judicial procedures and standards that should be followed by law enforcement, executive agencies, private firms and individuals to avoid evidence exclusion, or civil and criminal penalties. The complex provisions of these statutes are presented here through engaging judicial opinions that seek to interpret them in real-world contexts.

Privacy is important, yet it goes without saying that effective law enforcement and national security measures benefit from covert investigations. The federal surveillance statutes establish the extent to which government officials—who must also avoid running afoul of the Constitution and state laws—may secretly investigate groups, organizations and individuals.

Like government, the private sector also relies on covert investigations. Accordingly, the federal surveillance statutes fix the extent to which private individuals may lawfully snoop, as they frequently do, in business, employment and personal life.

Soon after the invention of the telephone, law enforcement officials realized that tapping into telephone lines to overhear private conversations could help put criminals behind bars. The practice became common. In *Olmstead v. United States*, 277 U.S. 438 (1928) (Brandeis, dissenting), the Supreme Court ruled that a phone tap that could be accomplished without trespassing onto private property did not violate the Fourth Amendment. "There was no searching. There was no seizure." 277 U.S. at 464. It took an act of Congress six years later to give conversational privacy its due by restricting unauthorized wiretapping.

Section 605 of the Federal Communications Act of 1934 was the nation's first major anti-wiretapping statute. It provided that: "No person not being authorized by the sender shall intercept any communication and divulge or publish the existence, contents, substance, purport, effect or meaning of such intercepted communication to any person * * *." The historic Act prohibited wiretapping, but little else. Moreover, it did not have much muscle. It failed to preempt weaker, state wiretapping laws, and was thought by some jurists only to apply if an offender divulged the contents of an unauthorized interception.

Title III of the Omnibus Crime Control and Safe Streets Act of 1968 ("Title III"), 47 U.S.C. § 3711 was the country's second major federal statute limiting surveillance, and it went much further. Title III attempted to balance concerns about personal privacy with concerns about efficient law enforcement and security. Preempting weaker state laws, Title III regulated both face-to-face oral communications, which could be secretly transmitted and recorded, and analog telephone calls placed through common carriers over wire, which could be intercepted. Title III was complemented by the Foreign Intelligence Surveillance Act of 1978, 50 U.S.C. §§ 1801 et seq. ("FISA"), to specifically address the special demands of national security and foreign espionage. The FISA established a procedure through which government agencies could obtain expedited, top-secret approval for national security-related surveillance from a federal judge.

Although the term "Title III" survives as a nickname for the federal wiretapping laws, the statute itself was supplanted over twenty years ago by a revised set of rules. The Electronic Communications Privacy Act of 1986 ("ECPA") expanded and reorganized Title III, to take into account major changes in technology—the rise of electronic and digital communications.

Title I of ECPA, the Wire and Electronic Communications Interception Act, 18 U.S.C. §§ 2510 et seq. ("Wiretap Act"), prohibits intercepting oral, wire or electronic communications during their transmission. Title I covers all telephone calls placed on any landline, cell phone or cordless phone (except a telephone that is part of a purely private system that does not affect interstate commerce, such as a phone that is connected only to an internal company communication system or intercom). It also covers satellite communications, and email transmissions "in flight" and in transient storage during transmission. Title I governs the recording, sharing and piracy of intercepted communications.

Title II of ECPA, the Stored Wire and Electronic Communications Act, 18 U.S.C. §§ 2701 et seq. ("Stored Communications Act") makes it a crime to obtain, alter or block access to a wire or electronic communication in electronic storage. Title II governs access to stored email and voice mail. It governs the ability of internet service providers to provide third-party access to user and subscriber data.

Title III of ECPA, the Pen Register Act, 18 U.S.C. §§ 3121 et seq. ("Pen Register Act"), regulates the use of pen registers and the capture of the non-content portions of wire and electronic communications. It also regulates caller identification equipment, and other "trap and trace" devices that capture outgoing or in-coming phone numbers.

ECPA has been amended several times, and will undoubtedly be amended again. The Digital Telephony Act, also known as the Communications Assistance for Law Enforcement Act of 1994 ("CALEA"), amended ECPA to enhance law enforcement. CALEA reflected concern that emerging technologies would frustrate law enforcement surveillance. CALEA thus requires, in the words of the Federal Communications Commission, that "telecommunications carriers and manufacturers of telecommunications equipment modify and design their equipment, facilities, and services to ensure that they have the necessary surveillance capabilities". See http://www.fcc.gov/calea/. The Digital Telephony Act also extended the protection of ECPA Title I to cordless telephones. Despite their functional equivalence to land lines and cellular telephones, cordless telephones been excluded from protection because they made use of radio-b technology, rather than wires, electronic technology or switching stations.

The Uniting and Strengthening America by Providing Appropriate Tools Required to Intercept and Obstruct Terrorism Act of 2001 ("USA PATRIOT Act" or "PATRIOT Act") made numerous changes to ECPA. Its changes were aimed at facilitating the government's global "war on terrorism." The Cyber Security Enhancement Act of the Homeland Security Act of 2002 amended ECPA Title II to battle computer crime and release internet service providers from liability for good faith disclosure to government of customer information held in electronic storage.

Not all popular surveillance techniques and technologies are regulated by ECPA and its amendments. The courts have generally, but not universally, agreed that ECPA does not specifically regulate the use of video-only camera surveillance, for example. Still, covert video surveillance inside someone else's home or office would presumably violate state privacy laws and would require a warrant under the Fourth Amendment. EPCA does not provide crystal clear guidance on the use of GPS (global positioning satellite) and cell phone tower-based data gathering.

We begin this Chapter with some background reflections on the lure of technology for secret observation, and the ethics of spying and other surveillance. See generally, Jan Goldman (ed.), *Ethics of Spying: a Reader for the Intelligence Professional* (2006).

NOTE: THE LURE OF SURVEILLANCE AND TECHNOLOGY

As characterized by scholar Bilge Yesil, *Video Surveillance: Power and Privacy in Everyday Life* 6 (2009):

> Surveillance is the systematic investigation or monitoring of the actions or communications of one or more persons. Its primary objective is to collect information about the individuals concerned, their activities or actions. Its secondary purpose is to deter a whole population from engaging in certain kinds of activities. Surveillance can be undertaken by public or private entities, in different domains that range from administration, commerce, and employment to policing and security.

Who engages in surveillance? Why do they do it? What techniques and technologies do they employ? In Book II of Plato's *Republic*, Glaucon narrates the story of a poor shepherd who finds a magic ring. The ring—think of it as a kind of "new technology"—gives him the unprecedented power of invisibility. He uses this power innocuously at first, to spy casually on his friends. But he eventually uses the power of invisibility to seduce the king's wife, kill the king, and seize the king's riches.

Powered by science rather than magic, contemporary surveillance technology confers extraordinary powers of invisibility on the people who possess it. At first, the shepherd is playful and curious in using his power to see and hear without being detected; but eventually, he becomes murderous. The story of the magic ring is a cautionary tale worth remembering. The power of perfect invisibility corrupts even the just.

THE MYTH OF GYGES PLATO, THE REPUBLIC BOOK II (360 BC)

Translated by Benjamin Jowett, 1873.

[H]aving given both to the just and the unjust power to do what they will, let us watch and see whither desire will lead them; then we shall discover in the very act the just and unjust man to be proceeding along the same road, following their interest, which all natures deem to be their good, and are only diverted into the path of justice by the force of law. The liberty which we are supposing may be most completely given to them in the form of such a power as is said to have been possessed by Gyges the ancestor of Croesus the Lydian.

According to the tradition, Gyges was a shepherd in the service of the king of Lydia; there was a great storm, and an earthquake made an opening in the earth at the place where he was feeding his flock. Amazed at the sight, he descended into the opening, where, among other marvels, he beheld a hollow brazen horse, having doors, at which he stooping and looking in saw a dead body of stature, as appeared to him, more than human, and having nothing on but a gold ring; this he took from the finger of the dead and reascended.

Now the shepherds met together, according to custom, that they might send their monthly report about the flocks to the king; into their assembly he came having the ring on his finger, and as he was sitting among them he chanced to turn the collet of the ring inside his hand, when instantly he became invisible to the rest of the company and they began to speak of him as if he were no longer present. He was astonished at this, and again touching the ring he turned the collet outwards and reappeared; he made several trials of the ring, and always with the same result—when he turned the collet inwards he became invisible, when outwards he reappeared. Whereupon he contrived to be chosen one of the messengers who were sent to the court; where as soon as he arrived he seduced the queen, and with her help conspired against the king and slew him, and took the kingdom.

Suppose now that there were two such magic rings, and the just put on one of them and the unjust the other; no man can be imagined to be of such an iron nature that he would stand fast in justice. No man would keep his hands off what was not his own when he could safely take what he liked out of the market, or go into houses and lie with any one at his pleasure, or kill or release from prison whom he would, and in all respects be like a God among men. Then the actions of the just would be as the actions of the unjust; they would both come at last to the same point.

And this we may truly affirm to be a great proof that a man is just, not willingly or because he thinks that justice is any good to him individually, but of necessity, for wherever any one thinks that he can safely be unjust, there he is unjust. For all men believe in their hearts that injustice is far more profitable to the individual than justice, and he who argues as I have been supposing, will say that they are right. If you could imagine any one obtaining this power of becoming invisible, and never doing any wrong or touching what was another's, he would be thought by the lookers-on to be a most wretched idiot, although they would praise him to one another's faces, and keep up appearances with one another from a fear that they too might suffer injustice.

ANITA L. ALLEN, THE VIRTUOUS SPY: PRIVACY AS AN ETHICAL LIMIT

91 The Monist: An International Quarterly Journal
of General Philosophical Inquiry 1 (Jan. 2008).

Is there any reason not to spy on other people as necessary to get the facts straight, especially if you can put the facts you uncover to good use?

To "spy" is secretly to monitor or investigate another's beliefs, intentions, actions, omissions, or capacities, particularly as revealed in otherwise concealed or confidential conduct, communications and documents. By definition, spying involves secret covert activity, though not necessarily lies, fraud or dishonesty. Nor does spying necessarily involve the use of special equipment, such as a tape recorder or high-powered binoculars. Use of a third party agent, such as a "private eye" or Central Intelligence Agency operative is not necessary for surveillance to count as spying.

By "spying" I mean something different from unwanted open surveillance of people who know they are being observed or investigated; and I mean something different from openly prying into others' affairs by plying them with meddlesome questions. Like spying, open surveillance and prying raise moral concerns. Notably, all three—spying, open surveillance and prying, potentially interfere with expectations of privacy. People want to be let alone. But spying is morally troublesome both because it violates privacy norms and because it relies on secrecy and, perhaps, nefarious deception.

Contemporary technologies of data collection make secret, privacy-invading surveillance easy and nearly irresistible. For every technology of confidential personal communication—telephone, mobile phone, computer email—there are one or more counter-technologies of eavesdropping. But covert surveillance conducted by amateur and professional spies still includes old-fashioned techniques of stealth, trickery and deception known a half century ago: shadowing by car, peeking at letters and diaries, donning disguises, breaking and entering, taking photographs, and tape recording conversations. The ethical examination of spying cannot be reduced to a conversation about reigning in the mischief potential of twenty-first century technology. We do need to concern ourselves with what tomorrow's spies will do with nanotechnology, but plenty of spying is

)le with the time-tested techniques of the Baby Boomers, or even, for
natter, the Victorians.

Consider three interrelated ideas. The first idea is one I will call the
anti-spying principle: spying on other adults is prima facie unethical.
Spying ought always to be approached with caution and circumspection.
Regardless of its motive, spying carries an ethical cloud. Spying is like
cheating. It exploits confidence in the rules of the game. Spying inherently
involves taking advantage of those who place their confidence in the social
norms that shape a cooperative communal life. Spying should be presumed
wrong because it often uses secrecy to unfair advantage and interferes
with the enjoyment of beneficial modes of personal privacy that individuals expect others to respect. The second idea is an exception to the anti-
spying principle: spying on others is ethically permissible, even mandatory, in certain situations, where the ends are good. In the situations I have
in mind, spying is prompted by genuine obligations of caretaking, defense
of others or self-defense. Having to spy can make a person uneasy. Yet
spying can be a good way to take care of your children, yourself and the
people for whom you are professionally responsible. Privacy is extremely
important, but it is not everything. The third and final idea is a constraint
on exceptions to the anti-spying principle: where spying is ethically
permitted or required, there are ethical limits on the methods of spying.
The virtuous spy will violate privacy and transparency norms, of course;
but he or she will, to the extent possible, continue to act with respect for
the moral autonomy and for the moral and legal interests of the investigative target. Adhering to fair information principles and minimization rules
are helpful in this regard.

Surveillance professionals confront the complex ethics of spying all
the time. Yet the ethics of spying is not a subject matter solely for
surveillance professionals, who surely ought to think hard through questions of right and wrong tied to their work. All of us are potential spies—
every parent, lover, neighbor or employer. And as citizens of a democracy,
we are accountable for the spying our representatives authorize our
government to perform. The questions "when is it ethical to spy on other
people?" and "what is the ethical way to spy, when spying needs to be
done?" are of general interest and importance.

DANIEL J. SOLOVE, A TAXONOMY
OF PRIVACY: SURVEILLANCE

154 University of Pennsylvania Law Review 477, 498 (2006).

For a long time, surveillance has been viewed as problematic. The
term "Peeping Tom" originates from a legend dating back to 1050. When
Lady Godiva rode naked on a horse in the city of Coventry to protest
taxes, a young man named Tom gawked at her, and he was punished by
being blinded. Today, many states have Peeping Tom laws. South Carolina, for example, criminalizes "peep[ing] through windows, doors, or
other like places, on or about the premises of another, for the purpose of

spying upon or invading the privacy of the persons spied upon and any other conduct of a similar nature, that tends to invade the privacy of others." Some states prohibit two-way mirrors in certain areas.

As with visual surveillance, audio surveillance has long been viewed as troubling. William Blackstone noted that eavesdropping was a common law crime, and defined it as "listen[ing] under walls or windows, or the eaves of a house, to hearken after discourse, and thereupon to frame slanderous and mischievous tales." These attitudes persisted after the emergence of electronic eavesdropping. As early as 1862, California prohibited the interception of telegraph communications. Soon after telephone wiretapping began in the 1890s, several states prohibited it, such as California in 1905. By 1928, over half the states had made wiretapping a crime. Justice Holmes referred to wiretapping as a "dirty business," and Justice Frankfurter called it "odious." When the Supreme Court held in the 1928 case Olmstead v. United States that the Fourth Amendment did not protect against wiretapping, Congress responded six years later by making wiretapping a federal crime. In 1967, the Supreme Court changed its position on wiretapping, overruling Olmstead in Katz v. United States. One year later, Congress passed the Omnibus Crime Control and Safe Streets Act of 1968, Title III of which provided comprehensive protection against wiretapping. Title III required law enforcement officials to obtain a warrant before wiretapping and criminalized wiretaps by private parties. Congress amended Title III in 1986 with the Electronic Communications Privacy Act (ECPA), expanding Title III's protections from wiretapping to additional forms of electronic surveillance.

What is the harm if people or the government watch or listen to us? Certainly, we all watch or listen, even when others may not want us to, and we often do not view this as problematic. However, when done in a certain manner—such as continuous monitoring—surveillance has problematic effects. For example, people expect to be looked at when they ride the bus or subway, but persistent gawking can create feelings of anxiety and discomfort.

Not only can direct awareness of surveillance make a person feel extremely uncomfortable, but it can also cause that person to alter her behavior. Surveillance can lead to self-censorship and inhibition. Because of its inhibitory effects, surveillance is a tool of social control, enhancing the power of social norms, which work more effectively when people are being observed by others in the community. John Gilliom observes: "Surveillance of human behavior is in place to control human behavior, whether by limiting access to programs or institutions, monitoring and affecting behavior within those arenas, or otherwise enforcing rules and norms by observing and recording acts of compliance and deviance." This aspect of surveillance does not automatically make it harmful, though, since social control can be beneficial and every society must exercise a sizeable degree of social control. For example, surveillance can serve as a deterrent to crime. Many people desire the discipline and control surveillance can bring. Jeff Rosen observes that Britain's closed circuit television (CCTV)—a network of over four million public surveillance cameras—is widely perceived as "a friendly eye in the sky, not Big Brother but a kindly and watchful uncle or aunt."

Too much social control, however, can adversely impact freedom, creativity, and self-development. According to Julie Cohen, "pervasive monitoring of every first move or false start will, at the margin, incline choices toward the bland and the mainstream." Monitoring constrains the "acceptable spectrum of belief and behavior," and it results in "a subtle yet fundamental shift in the content of our character, a blunting and blurring of rough edges and sharp lines." Surveillance thus "threatens not only to chill the expression of eccentric individuality, but also, gradually, to dampen the force of our aspirations to it." Similarly, Paul Schwartz argues that surveillance inhibits freedom of choice, impinging upon self-determination.

In many instances, people are not directly aware that they are being observed. Does covert surveillance cause a problem? Under one view, surveillance is a prima facie wrong, whether overt or covert, for it demonstrates a lack of respect for its subject as an autonomous person. Philosopher Stanley Benn explains that overt surveillance does so by threatening its target's "consciousness of pure freedom as subject, as originator and chooser." As Benn contends, "[f]inding oneself an object of scrutiny, as the focus of another's attention, brings one to a new consciousness of oneself, as something seen through another's eyes." Turning to covert observation, Benn explains that it "is objectionable because it deliberately deceives a person about his world, thwarting, for reasons that cannot be his reasons, his attempts to make a rational choice."

Although concealed spying is certainly deceptive, Benn's argument is unconvincing. It is the awareness that one is being watched that affects one's freedom, and Benn fails to explain why covert surveillance has any palpable effect on a person's welfare or activities. A more compelling reason why covert surveillance is problematic is that it can have a chilling effect on behavior. In fact, there can be an even greater chilling effect when people are generally aware of the possibility of surveillance, but are never sure if they are being watched at any particular moment. This phenomenon is known as the Panoptic effect, based on Jeremy Bentham's 1791 architectural design for a prison called the Panopticon. The prison was set up with the inmates' cells arrayed around a central observation tower. Most importantly, the guards could see each prisoner from the tower, but the prisoners could not see the guards from their cells. In Michel Foucault's words, the cells were akin to "small theatres, in which each actor is alone, perfectly individualized and constantly visible." The prisoner's "only rational option" was to conform with the prison's rules because, at any moment, it was possible that they were being watched.

Thus, awareness of the possibility of surveillance can be just as inhibitory as actual surveillance.

One might attempt to imagine surveillance so covert that its subjects are completely unaware of even the possibility of being observed. While such well-concealed surveillance might eliminate the potential for any discomfort or chilling effect, it would still enable the watchers to gather a substantial degree of information about people, creating an architectural problem. Surveillance is a sweeping form of investigatory power. It extends beyond a search, for it records behavior, social interaction, and potentially everything that a person says and does. Rather than targeting specific information, surveillance can ensnare a significant amount of data beyond any originally sought. If watched long enough, a person might be caught in some form of illegal or immoral activity, and this information could then be used to discredit or blackmail her. A prime example is the FBI's extensive wiretapping of Martin Luther King, Jr., widely believed to have been initiated in order to expose King's alleged communist ties. Though the surveillance failed to turn up any evidence of such ties, it did reveal King's extramarital affairs. The FBI then attempted to blackmail King with the information, and FBI officials leaked it in order to discredit King. * * *

[A]lthough the law often focuses on whether surveillance occurs in a public or private place, surveillance is harmful in all settings, not just private ones. Surveillance in public can certainly cause uneasiness, as illustrated by the example of being stared at continuously in public. As Alan Westin observes: "Knowledge or fear that one is under systematic observation in public places destroys the sense of relaxation and freedom that men seek in open spaces and public arenas." Moreover, public surveillance can have chilling effects that make people less likely to associate with certain groups, attend rallies, or speak at meetings. Espousing radical beliefs and doing unconventional things takes tremendous courage; the attentive gaze, especially the government's, can make these acts seem all the more daring and their potential risks all the more inhibitory.

NOTE: NEW TECHNOLOGIES AND FEDERAL CRIMINAL INVESTIGATIONS—THE LEGAL FRAMEWORK

Federal law enforcement officials investigating criminal conduct are required to conform to the standards of the Fourth Amendment, as amplified by the Federal Rules of Criminal Procedure, the Electronic Communications Privacy Act, and case law. Judges and magistrates responsible for issuing warrants must understand how complex law enforcement surveillance techniques work and then fairly and pragmatically apply existing legal frameworks to regulate their use.

IN THE MATTER OF THE APPLICATION OF THE UNITED STATES OF AMERICA FOR AN ORDER: (1) AUTHORIZING THE USE OF A PEN REGISTER AND TRAP AND TRACE DEVICE; (2) AUTHORIZING RELEASE OF SUBSCRIBER AND OTHER INFORMATION; AND (3) AUTHORIZING THE DISCLOSURE OF LOCATION–BASED SERVICES

2010 WL 3021950 (W.D.Tex. 2010).

ANDREW W. AUSTIN, UNITED STATES MAGISTRATE JUDGE.

In general terms, federal law authorizes the use of four types of electronic surveillance as criminal investigative tools. The tools can be viewed on a graduating scale—as the intrusiveness of each increases, the legal standard that the law enforcement agency must satisfy to use that tool increases accordingly.

Pen registers and trap and trace devices, in most contexts the least invasive tools, require a law enforcement officer to certify that the information likely to be obtained by the pen register or trap and trace device "is relevant to an ongoing criminal investigation." 18 U.S.C. § 3122(b)(2) [Pen Register Act, ECPA, Title III]. [A "pen register" is a "device or process which records or decodes dialing, routing, addressing, or signaling information transmitted by an instrument or facility from which a wire or electronic communication is transmitted, provided, however, that such information shall not include the contents of any communication . . ." 18 U.S.C. § 3127(3). A "trap and trace device" is "a device or process that captures the incoming electronic or other impulses which identify the originating number" or other identifiers "reasonably likely to identify the source of a wire or electronic communication, provided, however, that such information not include the contents of any communication." 18 U.S.C. § 3127(4).]

Stored communications and subscriber or customer account records require (generally speaking) "specific and articulable facts showing that there are reasonable grounds to believe that the records or other information sought are relevant and material to an ongoing criminal investigation." 18 U.S.C. § 2703(d) * * * ["Stored Communications Act," ECPA Title II].

Search and seizure warrants are covered by FED.R.CRIM.P. 41 and its "probable cause" standard. [generally, the Fourth Amendment Standard]

Finally, wiretap orders have the highest legal standard, as they are governed by a detailed set of procedures laid out in 18 U.S.C. § 2501, *et. seq.* [The Wiretap Act, ECPA, Title I/previously denoted "Title III"] Wiretaps are often referred to as "super-warrants" because of the additional requirements beyond probable cause necessary for their issuance.
* * *

The Court's focus in the present application is on cellular site location information ("CSLI"), which is information that resides on computer servers of telecommunications providers which allows law enforcement agencies to locate a cell phone, and its user, in both real time and, by accessing historical data, in the past. A request for CSLI presents a number of legal issues, and a growing number of decisions addressing these many have been handed down by magistrate and district judges in the past few years. The primary issue presented in those cases is the standard the Government's evidence must meet for it to obtain an order requiring the disclosure of CSLI, and whether that standard is different depending upon the type of information sought (historical v. prospective data), or the means by which the information is to be acquired (single tower, multiple towers, or GPS data). * * *

Beginning in 2005, magistrate and district judges began issuing published decisions addressing many of the questions raised by applications for CSLI. The first comprehensive opinion was issued by Magistrate Judge Stephen Wm. Smith of Houston. *In re Application for Pen Register and Trap/Trace Device with Cell Site Location Authority,* 396 F.Supp.2d 747 (S.D.Tex.2005) (hereinafter *Houston 2005 Order*). In that decision, Judge Smith rejected what was termed the government's "hybrid theory," by which it contended that CSLI was obtainable with less than probable cause through a hybridization of the authorities granted by the pen/trap statute and the Stored Communications Act ("SCA"). He concluded that CSLI required a showing of probable cause, as it was properly considered akin to a tracking device. Several courts followed with decisions reaching the same overall conclusion regarding probable cause. The first opinion to reach the opposite conclusion—that probable cause was not required for cell site information—came in December 2005 from Judge Gorenstein of the Southern District of New York. *New York 2005 Order,* 405 F.Supp.2d 435 (S.D.N.Y.2005). Although Judge Gorenstein accepted the government's "hybrid theory," he made it clear that his decision was restricted to the facts before him, in which the government was only requesting "cell-site information concerning the physical location of the antenna towers associated with the beginning and termination of calls to and from" the subject phone. *Id.* at 437.

Magistrate and district judges across the country then began to weigh in on the issue. To date, a strong majority have reached the same conclusion as Judge Smith. Since Judge Gorenstein's opinion, several courts have followed his lead and distinguished between CSLI obtained from a single cell tower and CSLI obtained from multiple towers or with GPS technology. In these courts' view, making this distinction was warranted because triangulation (via information from multiple towers) and GPS provide more precise location capabilities, and thus CSLI from these sources is more invasive. The majority approach, however, has been to require the same "probable cause" showing for CSLI regardless of the means by which the information is to be acquired. Significantly, although a minority of decisions have allowed limited CSLI with only a showing of "specific and articulable facts," there are no published decisions permitting multiple tower or GPS-based CSLI without a showing of "probable cause." * * *

The question thus becomes, what is the authority for granting the Government access to CSLI * * * ? In short, the answer would seem to be the Fourth Amendment, in conjunction with FED.R.CRIM.P. 41. * * *

> "Americans do not generally know that a record of their whereabouts is being created whenever they travel about with their cell phones, or that such record is likely maintained by their cell phone providers and is potentially subject to review by interested Government officials. And second . . . most Americans would be appalled by the notion that the Government could obtain such a record without at least a neutral, judicial determination of probable cause."

Moreover, when presented with whether use of investigatory techniques that do not fit easily within the statutorily or constitutionally-authorized tools constitute "searches" under the Fourth Amendment, the Supreme Court has fallen back to these same basic principles. For example, in a recent case involving the use of a thermal imaging device, the Supreme Court concluded that when the government uses a device not in general public use to "explore details of the home that would previously not have been knowable without physical intrusion, the surveillance is a 'search' and is presumptively unreasonable without a warrant." *Kyllo v. United States,* 533 U.S. 27, 40 (2001). * * *

* * * [T]he Government [in this case] suggests that an application that requests only single tower information may be granted under the pen/trap statute and/or the SCA on a showing of less than probable cause, on the theory that such data does not amount to tracking information, because it cannot precisely locate the phone user, but rather only provides information regarding the location of the phone provider's cell tower. * * *

* * *[C]ell phone technology is moving quickly to the point where debates about single tower v. multiple tower triangulation are academic. Estimates from three years ago were that over 90% of cell phones then in use had GPS capabilities, through which the target phone could be located to within as little as 50 feet. The Federal Communications Commission and its Enhanced 911 initiative requires cell phone carriers to be able to pinpoint the location of their customers in case of an emergency call. And although the main motivation behind the 911 initiative has been public safety, it is not surprising that companies are now trying to turn those required investments into commercial opportunities by offering non-emergency tracking for a monthly fee. For example, by paying a monthly fee and subscribing to MobileMe, an iPhone user can determine exactly where his or her phone is (a very handy "app" when a user misplaces their phone). The bottom line is that cell phones undoubtedly have become "electronic . . . device[s] which permit [ ] the tracking of the movement of a person or object." 18 U.S.C. § 3117. They *are* tracking devices. * * *

What is the significance of the conclusion that a cell phone acts as a tracking device when it transmits information about its location? The significance is that if cell phones squarely meet the definition of "tracking devices" it is time to stop treating them as something else, at least when the Government seeks to use them to track a person's movements. Rule 41 contains express procedures governing tracking device warrants, and those procedures need to be followed with regard to future requests for CSLI. This means several things. First, in past applications, the Government has taken the position that it has no obligation to provide notice of the tracking to the cell phone user, as its notice obligation was met by service of the order on the telecommunications provider from whom it received the CSLI. This does not meet the requirements of Rule 41, which provides that when a tracking device warrant is authorized, "the officer must serve a copy of the warrant on the person who was tracked or whose property was tracked." FED.R.CRIM.P. 41(f)(2)(C). Thus, warrants seeking CSLI must meet this obligation of Rule 41. Similarly, a return must be filed, as with all other warrants. FED.R.CRIM.P. 41(f)(2)(B).

In sum, there are difficult questions presented by the probable cause determination on CSLI applications, and it is not obvious what the answers to those questions are (at least it is not obvious to me what the answers are). Accordingly, until there is more guidance from Congress and the courts on these issues, I will take a cautious approach toward CSLI requests.

First, I will insist on strict adherence to the requirements of Rule 41 on all requests for CSLI, including requests for historical data. The warrants will be granted only on a showing of probable cause, may only last 45 days (in the case of prospective warrants), and notice on the person tracked is required (although it may be delayed). The warrants must be returned to the magistrate judge identified on the warrant. I will further require that warrants for CSLI be "stand alone" documents, and not be included as part of an application for a pen register, trap and trace, or subscriber records. With regard to probable cause, I will not take as narrow an approach * * * and insist that the CSLI must itself qualify as "evidence of a crime." But the warrant affidavit must demonstrate that there is probable cause to believe that tracking the phone will *lead* to evidence of a crime. One example of evidence that would meet this standard is evidence that the phone to be tracked is intimately involved in the crime being investigated; for example, where the sole or dominant purpose of the target phone is its use in a drug trafficking organization to make and receive calls related to the drug business. Evidence that a person has a cell phone and is engaged in criminal conduct is not enough to meet this standard. In investigations, being granted a warrant for CSLI should be the exception, not the rule, and if all the Government must prove to receive CSLI is that the target has a cell phone and probably engages in crime, then a CSLI warrant would be issued in *every* criminal investigation. As a result, I will require that there be more than this contained within the Government's application. What this will be is necessarily a fact-intensive question, and all that can be provided at this point are the general guidelines just discussed. In other words, we will have to make law on this issue the old-fashioned way, case by case.

NOTE: FEDERAL RULES OF CRIMINAL PROCEDURE

We will examine the text and interpretations of the ECPA titles referred to in Magistrate Austin's thoughtful opinion in the sections ahead, starting with the Wiretap Act, Title I, the source of the most stringent protections and requirements, followed by the Stored Communications Act, Title II, and the Pen Register Act, Title III.

In his opinion Magistrate Austin refers to Rule 41 of the *Federal Rules of Criminal Procedure*. The text of the important rule follows. By comparison, the language of the Fourth Amendment is broad and abstract, offering little specific guidance to law enforcement or the courts: "The right of the people to be secure in their persons, houses, papers, and effects, against unreasonable searches and seizures, shall not be violated, and no Warrants shall issue, but upon probable cause, supported by Oath or affirmation, and particularly describing the place to be searched, and the persons or things to be seized."

FEDERAL RULES OF CRIMINAL PROCEDURE

Rule 41. Search and Seizure.

(a) Scope and Definitions.

(1) *Scope.*

This rule does not modify any statute regulating search or seizure, or the issuance and execution of a search warrant in special circumstances.

(2) *Definitions.*

The following definitions apply under this rule:

(A) "Property" includes documents, books, papers, any other tangible objects, and information.

(B) "Daytime" means the hours between 6:00 a.m. and 10:00 p.m. according to local time.

(C) "Federal law enforcement officer" means a government agent (other than an attorney for the government) who is engaged in enforcing the criminal laws and is within any category of officers authorized by the Attorney General to request a search warrant.

(D) "Domestic terrorism" and "international terrorism" have the meanings set out in 18 U.S.C. § 2331.

(E) "Tracking device" has the meaning set out in 18 U.S.C. § 3117(b).

(b) Authority to Issue a Warrant.

At the request of a federal law enforcement officer or an attorney for the government:

(1) a magistrate judge with authority in the district—or if none is reasonably available, a judge of a state court of record in the district—has authority to issue a warrant to search for and seize a person or property located within the district;

(2) a magistrate judge with authority in the district has authority to issue a warrant for a person or property outside the district if the person or property is located within the district when the warrant is issued but might move or be moved outside the district before the warrant is executed;

(3) a magistrate judge—in an investigation of domestic terrorism or international terrorism—with authority in any district in which activities related to the terrorism may have occurred has authority to issue a warrant for a person or property within or outside that district;

(4) a magistrate judge with authority in the district has authority to issue a warrant to install within the district a tracking device; the warrant may authorize use of the device to track the movement of a person or property located within the district, outside the district, or both; and

(5) a magistrate judge having authority in any district where activities related to the crime may have occurred, or in the District of Columbia, may issue a warrant for property that is located outside the jurisdiction of any state or district, but within any of the following:

(A) a United States territory, possession, or commonwealth;

(B) the premises—no matter who owns them—of a United States diplomatic or consular mission in a foreign state, including any appurtenant building, part of a building, or land used for the mission's purposes; or

(C) a residence and any appurtenant land owned or leased by the United States and used by United States personnel assigned to a United States diplomatic or consular mission in a foreign state.

(c) Persons or Property Subject to Search or Seizure.

A warrant may be issued for any of the following:

(1) evidence of a crime;

(2) contraband, fruits of crime, or other items illegally possessed;

(3) property designed for use, intended for use, or used in committing a crime; or

(4) a person to be arrested or a person who is unlawfully restrained.

(d) Obtaining a Warrant.

(1) *In General.* After receiving an affidavit or other information, a magistrate judge—or if authorized by Rule 41(b), a judge of a state court of record—must issue the warrant if there is probable cause to

search for and seize a person or property or to install and use a tracking device.

(2) *Requesting a Warrant in the Presence of a Judge.*

  (A) *Warrant on an Affidavit.*

  When a federal law enforcement officer or an attorney for the government presents an affidavit in support of a warrant, the judge may require the affiant to appear personally and may examine under oath the affiant and any witness the affiant produces.

  (B) *Warrant on Sworn Testimony.*

  The judge may wholly or partially dispense with a written affidavit and base a warrant on sworn testimony if doing so is reasonable under the circumstances.

  (C) *Recording Testimony.*

  Testimony taken in support of a warrant must be recorded by a court reporter or by a suitable recording device, and the judge must file the transcript or recording with the clerk, along with any affidavit.

(3) *Requesting a Warrant by Telephonic or Other Means.*

  (A) *In General.*

  A magistrate judge may issue a warrant based on information communicated by telephone or other appropriate means, including reliable electronic means.

  (B) *Recording Testimony.*

  Upon learning that an applicant is requesting a warrant under Rule 41(d)(3)(A), a magistrate judge must:

      (i) place under oath the applicant and any person on whose testimony the application is based; and

      (ii) make a verbatim record of the conversation with a suitable recording device, if available, or by a court reporter, or in writing.

  (C) *Certifying Testimony.*

  The magistrate judge must have any recording or court reporter's notes transcribed, certify the transcription's accuracy, and file a copy of the record and the transcription with the clerk. Any written verbatim record must be signed by the magistrate judge and filed with the clerk.

  (D) *Suppression Limited.*

  Absent a finding of bad faith, evidence obtained from a warrant issued under Rule 41(d)(3)(A) is not subject to suppression on the ground that issuing the warrant in that manner was unreasonable under the circumstances.

(e) Issuing the Warrant.

(1) *In General.* The magistrate judge or a judge of a state court of record must issue the warrant to an officer authorized to execute it.

(2) *Contents of the Warrant.*

(A) *Warrant to Search for and Seize a Person or Property.* Except for a tracking-device warrant, the warrant must identify the person or property to be searched, identify any person or property to be seized, and designate the magistrate judge to whom it must be returned. The warrant must command the officer to:

(i) execute the warrant within a specified time no longer than 14 days;

(ii) execute the warrant during the daytime, unless the judge for good cause expressly authorizes execution at another time; and

(iii) return the warrant to the magistrate judge designated in the warrant.

(B) *Warrant Seeking Electronically Stored Information.* A warrant under Rule 41(e)(2)(A) may authorize the seizure of electronic storage media or the seizure or copying of electronically stored information. Unless otherwise specified, the warrant authorizes a later review of the media or information consistent with the warrant. The time for executing the warrant in Rule 41(e)(2)(A) and (f)(1)(A) refers to the seizure or on-site copying of the media or information, and not to any later off-site copying or review.

(C) *Warrant for a Tracking Device.* A tracking-device warrant must identify the person or property to be tracked, designate the magistrate judge to whom it must be returned, and specify a reasonable length of time that the device may be used. The time must not exceed 45 days from the date the warrant was issued. The court may, for good cause, grant one or more extensions for a reasonable period not to exceed 45 days each. The warrant must command the officer to:

(i) complete any installation authorized by the warrant within a specified time no longer than 10 calendar days;

(ii) perform any installation authorized by the warrant during the daytime, unless the judge for good cause expressly authorizes installation at another time; and

(iii) return the warrant to the judge designated in the warrant.

(3) *Warrant by Telephonic or Other Means.* If a magistrate judge decides to proceed under Rule 41(d)(3)(A), the following additional procedures apply:

(A) *Preparing a Proposed Duplicate Original Warrant*. The applicant must prepare a "proposed duplicate original warrant" and must read or otherwise transmit the contents of that document verbatim to the magistrate judge.

(B) *Preparing an Original Warrant*. If the applicant reads the contents of the proposed duplicate original warrant, the magistrate judge must enter those contents into an original warrant. If the applicant transmits the contents by reliable electronic means, that transmission may serve as the original warrant.

(C) *Modification*. The magistrate judge may modify the original warrant. The judge must transmit any modified warrant to the applicant by reliable electronic means under Rule 41(e)(3)(D) or direct the applicant to modify the proposed duplicate original warrant accordingly.

(D) *Signing the Warrant*. Upon determining to issue the warrant, the magistrate judge must immediately sign the original warrant, enter on its face the exact date and time it is issued, and transmit it by reliable electronic means to the applicant or direct the applicant to sign the judge's name on the duplicate original warrant.

(f) Executing and Returning the Warrant.

   (1) *Warrant to Search for and Seize a Person or Property*.

(A) *Noting the Time*. The officer executing the warrant must enter on it the exact date and time it was executed.

(B) *Inventory*. An officer present during the execution of the warrant must prepare and verify an inventory of any property seized. The officer must do so in the presence of another officer and the person from whom, or from whose premises, the property was taken. If either one is not present, the officer must prepare and verify the inventory in the presence of at least one other credible person. In a case involving the seizure of electronic storage media or the seizure or copying of electronically stored information. the inventory may be limited to describing the physical storage media that were seized or copied. The officer may retain a copy of the electronically stored information that was seized or copied.

(C) *Receipt*. The officer executing the warrant must give a copy of the warrant and a receipt for the property taken to the person from whom, or from whose premises, the property was taken or leave a copy of the warrant and receipt at the place where the officer took the property.

(D) *Return*. The officer executing the warrant must promptly return it, together with a copy of the inventory, to the magistrate judge designated on the warrant. The judge must, on request, give a copy of the inventory to the person from whom, or from whose premises, the property was taken and to the applicant for the warrant.

(2) *Warrant for a Tracking Device.*

(A) *Noting the Time.* The officer executing a tracking-device warrant must enter on it the exact date and time the device was installed and the period during which it was used.

(B) *Return.* Within 10 calendar days after the use of the tracking device has ended, the officer executing the warrant must return it to the judge designated in the warrant.

(C) *Service.* Within 10 calendar days after the use of the tracking device has ended, the officer executing a tracking-device warrant must serve a copy of the warrant on the person who was tracked or whose property was tracked. Service may be accomplished by delivering a copy to the person who, or whose property, was tracked; or by leaving a copy at the person's residence or usual place of abode with an individual of suitable age and discretion who resides at that location and by mailing a copy to the person's last known address. Upon request of the government, the judge may delay notice as provided in Rule 41(f)(3).

(3) *Delayed Notice.* Upon the government's request, a magistrate judge—or if authorized by Rule 41(b), a judge of a state court of record—may delay any notice required by this rule if the delay is authorized by statute.

(g) Motion to Return Property.

A person aggrieved by an unlawful search and seizure of property or by the deprivation of property may move for the property's return. The motion must be filed in the district where the property was seized. The court must receive evidence on any factual issue necessary to decide the motion. If it grants the motion, the court must return the property to the movant, but may impose reasonable conditions to protect access to the property and its use in later proceedings.

(h) Motion to Suppress.

A defendant may move to suppress evidence in the court where the trial will occur, as Rule 12 provides.

(i) Forwarding Papers to the Clerk.

The magistrate judge to whom the warrant is returned must attach to the warrant a copy of the return, of the inventory, and of all other related papers and must deliver them to the clerk in the district where the property was seized.

(*As amended Dec. 27, 1948, eff. Oct. 20, 1949; Apr. 9, 1956, eff. July 8, 1956; Apr. 24, 1972, eff. Oct. 1, 1972; Mar. 18, 1974, eff. July 1, 1974; Apr.*

26 and July 8, 1976, eff. Aug. 1, 1976; July 30, 1977, eff. Oct. 1, 1977; Apr. 30, 1979, eff. Aug. 1, 1979; Mar. 9, 1987, eff. Aug. 1, 1987; Apr. 25, 1989, eff. Dec. 1, 1989; May 1, 1990, eff. Dec. 1, 1990; Apr. 22, 1993, eff. Dec. 1, 1993; Oct. 26, 2001; Apr. 29, 2002, eff. Dec. 1, 2002; Apr. 12, 2006, eff. Dec. 1, 2006.)

A. "TITLE III" AND ITS SUCCESSOR, THE ELECTRONIC COMMUNICATIONS PRIVACY ACT OF 1986 (ECPA), TITLE I, THE WIRETAP ACT

LAM LEK CHONG v. U.S. DRUG ENFORCEMENT ADMINISTRATION

929 F.2d 729 (C.A.D.C. 1991).

In enacting Title III, Congress sought to regulate comprehensively both the use of electronic surveillance as an investigative tool and the disclosure of materials obtained through such surveillance. The purpose of the statute is to control the conditions under which interception will be permitted in order to safeguard the privacy of wire and oral communications. Animating the whole of Title III is "an overriding congressional concern" with the protection of individual privacy.

Title III safeguards privacy in the first instance by significantly restricting the initiation of electronic surveillance. Surveillance techniques are authorized only in the investigation of specified serious offenses. All surveillance is subject to prior judicial approval, issued in accordance with detailed application procedures and on a showing and finding of probable cause. Moreover, the government may not resort to electronic surveillance unless normal investigative methods are demonstrably infeasible.

Congressional sensitivity to privacy rights is perhaps most evidently reflected in Title III's strictly limited disclosure provisions. Apart from two instances in which judges authorizing interception may, at their discretion, release intercepted material to parties overheard, use and disclosure is governed by section 2517 of the statute. Section 2517 permits disclosure of intercepted communications in three circumstances only:

(1) Any investigative or law enforcement officer who, by any means authorized by this chapter, has obtained knowledge of the contents of any wire, oral, or electronic communication * * * may disclose such contents to another investigative or law enforcement officer to the extent that such disclosure is appropriate to the proper performance of the official duties of the officer making or receiving the disclosure.

(2) Any investigative or law enforcement officer * * * may use such contents to the extent such use is appropriate to the proper performance of his official duties.

(3) Any person who has received, by any means authorized by this chapter, any information concerning a wire, oral, or electronic communica-

tion * * * may disclose the contents * * * while giving testimony under oath * * *.

Moreover, Title III explicitly authorizes the recovery of civil damages by persons whose communications are disclosed in violation of the statute. Taken together, these provisions represent a comprehensive statutory scheme dedicated to preserving personal privacy by sharply limiting the circumstances under which surveillance may be undertaken and its fruits disclosed.

RICHARD C. TURKINGTON, GENERAL ANALYSIS OF ECPA TITLE I ("TITLE III") CASES

Privacy Law (2002), 297.

A general four step analysis should be utilized in evaluating Title I cases. First there must be a determination as to whether there was an "interception" of a "wire, oral or electronic communication" within the meaning of Section 2510. Title I does not apply to the case unless this has occurred. * * * [T]he second step * * * is to determine whether one of the Section 2511 exceptions applies to the case. If there is a Section 2510 interception and no exception applies to the case, the interception is a in violation of Title I, unless it is authorized by a court order that satisfies the requirements of Section 2518. Section 2518 establishes the necessary procedure for obtaining a court ordered electronic surveillance. Section 2518 also imposes restrictions on the scope and duration of the surveillance. * * * If there has been a violation of Title I, the fourth step is to consider the applicability of a criminal sanction, civil remedy or right to exclude the contents of the illegal interception in court proceedings.

1. INTERCEPTING AND RECORDING CALLS

a. Domestic Use Exceptions—Spouses' and Children's Conversational Privacy

UNITED STATES v. JONES

542 F.2d 661 (6th Cir. 1976).

CELEBREZZE, CIRCUIT JUDGE.

This is an appeal by the Government from the dismissal of an indictment against William Allan Jones which charged him with intercepting telephone conversations of his estranged wife and using the contents of the intercepted communications in violation of [Title III] 18 U.S.C. §§ 2511(1)(a) and (d) (1970). Relying principally on the decision of the Fifth Circuit in Simpson v. Simpson, 490 F.2d 803 (5th Cir. 1974), the District Court held that Title III of the Omnibus Crime Control and Safe Streets Act of 1968 was not intended to reach interspousal wiretaps placed on telephones in the marital home. On appeal the Government argues * * * that there is no statutory exception for interspousal wiretaps. * * *

Appellee submitted an affidavit with exhibits attached wherein he stated that he paid the rent on the premises and the telephone bills during the period in question; that he and his wife continued a sexual relationship even though he had moved out of the house in late July of 1974; that he returned to the house on occasion to babysit; that on October 18, 1974 while babysitting he became suspicious that his wife was involved in an extramarital affair and placed a recording device on the telephone; that the recordings of the intercepted phone calls confirmed his suspicions; and that he used the recordings to obtain a divorce. On December 3, 1975, District Judge Bailey Brown, sitting by designation, ruled on the basis of the proffered materials that Appellee's conduct fell within an implied exception to 18 U.S.C. § 2511(1)(a) for purely interspousal wiretaps placed on telephones within the marital home and he dismissed all counts of the indictment. * * *

As the Supreme Court stated in United States v. Giordano, 416 U.S. 505 (1974), "[the] purpose of the legislation * * * was effectively to prohibit * * * all interceptions of oral and wire communications, except those specifically provided for in the Act * * *." Despite the unambiguous language of the statute, the District Court chose to follow the Fifth Circuit's holding in Simpson v. Simpson, 490 F.2d 803 (5th Cir. 1974), that this section was not intended to prohibit purely interspousal wiretaps placed on telephones in the marital home. Because we interpret the statute's legislative history differently than did the Court in Simpson and because we believe that this case is distinguishable from Simpson both legally and factually, we reverse.

Simpson v. Simpson was a civil suit under 18 U.S.C. § 2520 (1970), brought by a woman against her former husband. The husband, harboring uncertainties as to his wife's faithfulness, attached a recording device to the telephone lines at their home and recorded conversations between his wife and another man which the Court described as "mildly compromising." 490 F.2d at 804. He used the recordings to obtain an uncontested divorce. Id. Although the Simpson Court admitted that the "naked language" of Title III was all-inclusive, they concluded that Congress did not intend to intrude into domestic conflicts normally left to state law. The Simpson Court reviewed the Act's legislative history and based their conclusion on the lack of a positive expression of Congressional intent to include purely interspousal wiretaps within the Act's prohibitions. The Court distinguished electronic surveillance by a third-party, which they stated would violate the Act even if instigated by a spouse, because they viewed it as "an offense against a spouse's privacy of a much greater magnitude than is personal surveillance by the other spouse." * * *

Ordinarily a court will not refer to legislative history in construing a statute which is clear on its face. See e.g., United States v. Oregon, 366 U.S. 643, 648 (1961). The language of § 2511(1)(a) quite clearly expresses a blanket prohibition on all electronic surveillance except under circumstances specifically enumerated in the statute. * * * The natural presumption when construing a statute is that Congress meant what it said.

However, the Simpson Court concluded that, despite the literal language of the section, the absence of positive proof of congressional intent to include interspousal wiretaps in the Act's prohibitions indicated that Congress did not intend to reach that activity. * * * The District Court in this case adopted Simpson's analysis of the statute's legislative history and concluded that, as a matter of law, Appellee was immune from prosecution for intercepting and recording his wife's telephone conversations. This conclusion is untenable because it contradicts both the explicit language of the statute and the clear intent of Congress expressed in the Act's legislative history.

This section was enacted as part of Title III of the Omnibus Crime Control and Safe Streets Act of 1968. * * * Title III was drafted to fill loopholes in the existing law. * * * The Senate Report on the bill described the problem addressed by Title III:

> The tremendous scientific and technological developments that have taken place in the last century have made possible today the widespread use and abuse of electronic surveillance techniques. As a result of these developments, privacy of communication is seriously jeopardized by these techniques of surveillance. Commercial and employer-labor espionage is becoming widespread. It is becoming increasingly difficult to conduct business meetings in private. Trade secrets are betrayed. Labor and management plans are revealed. No longer is it possible, in short, for each man to retreat into his home and be left alone. Every spoken word relative to each man's personal, marital, religious, political, or commercial concerns can be intercepted by an unseen auditor and turned against the speaker to the auditor's advantage.

S. REP. No. 1097, Reprinted In U.S. Code Cong. & Admin. News 1968, 90th Cong., 2d Sess., at 2154. Although the primary target of the bill was organized crime, the Senate Report makes it clear that the purpose of the bill was to establish an across-the-board prohibition on all unauthorized electronic surveillance:

> Title III has as its dual purpose (1) protecting the privacy of wire and oral communications, and (2) delineating on a uniform basis the circumstances and conditions under which the interception of wire and oral communications may be authorized. To assure the privacy of oral and wire communications, title III prohibits all wiretapping and electronic surveillance by persons other than duly authorized law enforcement officers engaged in the investigation or prevention of specified types of serious crimes, and only after authorization of a court order obtained after a showing and finding of probable cause.

Id. at 2153.

[T]he legislative history leaves no doubt that the Act was intended to reach private electronic surveillance and that Congress was aware that a major area of use for surveillance techniques was the preparation of domestic relations cases. Professor Robert Blakey, publicly credited with being the author of Title III, testified before the Subcommittee on Administrative Practice and Procedure of the Senate Judiciary Committee that:

> [Private] bugging in this country can be divided into two broad categories, commercial espionage and marital litigation.

Congressional awareness that the Act's prohibition of private surveillance would be applicable to domestic relations investigations is reflected in the comments of Senator Hruska, one of the co-sponsors of the bill, which were joined by Senators Dirksen, Scott and Thurmond:

> A broad prohibition is imposed on private use of electronic surveillance, particularly in domestic relations and industrial espionage situations.

Our review of the legislative history of this section, testimony at congressional hearings, and debates on the floor of Congress, inescapably lead to the conclusion that 18 U.S.C. § 2511(1)(a) establishes a broad prohibition on all private electronic surveillance and that a principal area of congressional concern was electronic surveillance for the purposes of marital litigation. * * *

For purposes of federal wiretap law, it makes no difference whether a wiretap is placed on a telephone by a spouse or by a private detective in the spouse's employ. The end result is the same—the privacy of the unconsenting parties to the intercepted conversation has been invaded. It is important to recognize that it is not just the privacy of the targeted spouse which is being violated, but that of the other party to the conversation as well. * * * Justice Brandeis aptly described the "evil" of wiretapping in his dissenting opinion to Olmstead v. United States, 277 U.S. 438 (1928) (Brandeis, J., dissenting):

> The evil incident to invasion of the privacy of the telephone is far greater than that involved in tampering with the mails. Whenever a telephone line is tapped, the privacy of the persons at both ends of the line is invaded and all conversations between them upon any subject, and although proper, confidential and privileged, may be overheard. Moreover, the tapping of one man's telephone line involves the tapping of the telephone of every other person whom he may call or who may call him. As a means of espionage, writs of assistance and general warrants are but puny instruments of tyranny and oppression when compared with wire-tapping.

The view expressed by Justice Brandeis in Olmstead that there is a constitutional right to privacy in wire communications was later accepted by a majority of the Supreme Court in Berger v. New York (1967), and in Katz v. United States (1967). Title III was drafted to meet the standards enunciated in Berger for constitutional electronic surveillance and to conform with Katz. The implication is clear then that the Congress enacted Title III to protect the privacy of all persons conversing over the telephone and that their privacy is shielded from invasion by third parties and spouses alike.

As a matter of statutory construction, the conclusion reached in Simpson is also questionable. The explicit language of 18 U.S.C. § 2511(1)(a) is that "any person" who violates the section is liable to punishment "except as otherwise specifically provided." If Congress had intended to create another exception to Title III's blanket prohibition of unauthorized wiretaps they would have included a specific exception for interspousal wiretaps in the statute. * * *

This interpretation is consistent with the pervasive theme of Title III that electronic surveillance should be sharply curtailed and in no instance be undertaken without strict judicial authorization and supervision. * * *

Even if Simpson was correctly decided on its facts, this case is clearly distinguishable. In Simpson the Court was concerned about the scope of the civil remedies under § 2520. The Court stated that Congress had not sought to create "a federal remedy for marital grievances" when it provided civil remedies for aggrieved persons. * * *

This case is also distinguishable on its facts. In Simpson the wiretapping incident took place while the couple were living together as man and wife. Here, it is undisputed that Appellee and his wife were separated at the time of the electronic surveillance. Appellee had moved out of the house in July of 1974 and by October 18th when the surveillance device was installed he was under a restraining order from the Chancery Court to prevent him from "coming about" his wife. * * *

The allegations in the indictment clearly state violations of 18 U.S.C. § 2511(1)(a) and (d), for wrongful interception and use of wire communications. We reach this conclusion reluctantly because we share the concern of other courts which have grappled with this problem that application of federal wiretap law to essentially domestic conflicts may lead to harsh results in individual cases. However, the plain language of the section and the Act's legislative history compels interpretation of the statute to include interspousal wiretaps. It is not for this Court to question the wisdom of Congress and to establish an implied exception to a federal statute by judicial fiat. Only Congress has the authority to amend 18 U.S.C. § 2511. Accordingly, the judgment of the District Court is reversed and the case is remanded for trial.

H.J. McCLOSKEY, THE POLITICAL IDEAL OF PRIVACY

21 The Philosophical Quarterly 303–314 (1971).

[L]ove, and like it respect for persons, may dictate invasions of privacy. The lover, because of his love, wants to know all about his loved one, because he loves her, and wants to know her more fully as the person she is. * * * Love, and equally respect for persons, may dictate the seeking of knowledge against the wishes of the person concerned. The lover * * * may suspect that she has a serious disease and is afraid to have it diagnosed and treated * * *.

NOTE: SUPPRESSION OF EVIDENCE GAINED IN VIOLATION OF TITLE I

A suspicious husband extensively spied on his wife in the year preceding the couple's separation, *Potter v. Havlicek*, 2007 WL 539534 (S.D. Ohio 2007). The husband used various means of surveillance including: video recording; collecting files and cookies from the family's shared computer; monitoring his wife's computer activity using software that tracks usage including keyboard strokes, display screens, and website logs; and accessing electronic mail sent to third parties and received from third parties through stored "remember me" password-saved accounts.

The man later attempted to introduce intercepted electronic communications into a child custody proceeding. His wife and one of her friends whose communications were unlawfully intercepted sought suppression of the evidence under ECPA Title I. The court held that ECPA provides the suppression remedy only in cases of *wire or oral* communications interceptions in violation of the statute—not *electronic* communications. Courts have held on the basis of statutory interpretation that the suppression of evidence remedy is limited to unlawful interceptions of wire and oral communications, and does not apply to unlawfully intercepted electronic communications, such as email. "[W]e cannot under the ECPA grant appellant's requested remedy—suppression. The ECPA does not provide an independent statutory remedy of suppression for interceptions of electronic communications." *United States v. Meriwether*, 917 F.2d 955, 960 (6th Cir.1990) (citing 18 U.S.C. § 2518(10)(c) (1988); and S.Rep. No. 99–541, 99th Cong., 2d Sess. 23, reprinted in 1986 U.S.Code Cong. & Admin. News 3555, 3577). Suppression provisions of ECPA apply neither to electronic communications, covered by ECPA Title I or stored communications covered by Title II. See *United States v. Smith*, 155 F.3d 1051, 1056 (9th Cir. 1998) (Section 2708 precludes suppression as a remedy for violation of the Store Communications Act). Other statutory remedies would apply, however, including civil damages.

NEWCOMB v. INGLE

944 F.2d 1534 (10th Cir. 1991).

ANDERSON, CIRCUIT JUDGE * * *

Defendant Jean A. Mackey, with the help of her father, defendant Howard Q. Day, intercepted and recorded telephone conversations of her minor son Brent, within her own home without Brent's knowledge or consent. Brent's parents were divorced at the time, and Mackey had custody of Brent and his younger brother.

In one instance, Mackey recorded a conversation in which Brent's father, Harold Newcomb (Newcomb), instructed Brent and his brother as they set fire to their home. Thereafter, Mackey told a fire investigator of the existence of the tapes. After the tapes were recovered, Mackey sent them to defendant Nancy Ingle, an assistant county attorney. Based on the recorded conversation, Ingle brought criminal charges against Newcomb resulting in a conviction. In juvenile court, Newcomb stipulated to the severance of his parental rights. All charges against Brent were dismissed after Newcomb and Mackey stipulated to the designation of Brent and his brother as children in need of care.

Upon reaching majority, Brent brought this suit alleging violations of 18 U.S.C. §§ 2510–2520, 42 U.S.C. § 1983, and the first, fourth, fifth, sixth, and fourteenth amendments. Brent alleged that Ingle intercepted conversations between him and Newcomb, unlawfully arrested him, denied him counsel, forced him to sign away his rights, and incarcerated him. Brent also alleged that Mackey and Day unlawfully installed the wiretap device; disclosed the contents of Brent's conversations with Newcomb to friends and relatives; and, on the day of the fire, intercepted the conversation "for the purpose of commiting (sic) criminal or tortuious (sic) act."

Defendants filed motions for summary judgment which the district court granted. The court held that Brent had failed to prove any causal connection between the recordings and his alleged injury: "What happened to you was brought about because of the actions that you and your brother took, that was the source of your problem or any damage that occurred to you, not the fact that your mother recorded those conversations." Rec. Supp. Vol. I at 38. The court found "that reasonable men and women could not differ, that there is totally lacking the willfulness of intentional wrongdoing or reckless disregard of known legal duty that is a requisite to the willfully component of Section 2511 of Title 18." Id. at 40. The court held that Ingle had acted at all times within the confines of her official duties and did not in any way act in a malicious manner. Therefore, Ingle was entitled to qualified immunity.

The issue here is whether Title III of the Omnibus Crime Control and Safe Streets Act of 1968, 18 U.S.C. §§ 2510–2520, applies in a situation such as this where a minor child sues his custodial parent for telephone interceptions made within the family home. Title III makes it unlawful for any person to "willfully intercept[], endeavor[] to intercept, or procure[] any other person to intercept or endeavor to intercept, any wire or oral communication." 18 U.S.C. § 2511(1)(a). A civil cause of action is provided by 18 U.S.C. § 2520.

No cases address the situation we have here. The closest analogy is where spouses have tapped one another, but that is still qualitatively different from a custodial parent tapping a minor child's conversations within the family home.

We hold that the interception at issue here is not reached by Title III. The interception of a family member's telephone conversations by use of an extension phone in the family home is arguably permitted by a broad reading of the exemption contained in 18 U.S.C. § 2510(5)(a)(i). There is no persuasive reason why Congress would exempt a business extension and not one in the home. The difference between listening on the extension and tapping the line within the home in the context here is not material. "We think the (5)(a)(i) exemption is indicative of Congress's intention to abjure from deciding a very intimate question of familial relations, that of the extent of privacy family members may expect within the home vis-a-vis each other." Simpson, 490 F.2d at 809. Further, because no violation of Title III by Mackey is present, no violation by Day or Ingle can be established.

b. The Minimization Requirement

SCOTT v. UNITED STATES
436 U.S. 128 (1978).

MR. JUSTICE REHNQUIST delivered the opinion of the Court.

In 1968, Congress enacted Title III of the Omnibus Crime Control and Safe Streets Act of 1968, which deals with wiretapping and other forms of electronic surveillance. 18 U.S.C. §§ 2510–2520 (1976 ed.). In this Act Congress, after this Court's decisions in Berger v. New York, 388 U.S. 41 (1967), and Katz v. United States, 389 U.S. 347 (1967), set out to provide law enforcement officials with some of the tools thought necessary to combat crime without unnecessarily infringing upon the right of individual privacy. See generally S. Rep. No. 1097, 90th Cong., 2d Sess. (1968). We have had occasion in the past, the most recent being just last Term, to consider exactly how the statute effectuates this balance. This case requires us to construe the statutory requirement that wiretapping or electronic surveillance "be conducted in such a way as to minimize the interception of communications not otherwise subject to interception under this chapter * * *."

In January 1970, Government officials applied, pursuant to Title III, for authorization to wiretap a telephone registered to Geneva Jenkins. The supporting affidavits alleged that there was probable cause to believe nine individuals, all named, were participating in a conspiracy to import and distribute narcotics in the Washington, D. C., area and that Geneva Jenkins' telephone had been used in furtherance of the conspiracy, particularly by petitioner Thurmon, who was then living with Jenkins. The District Court granted the application on January 24, 1970, authorizing agents to "[intercept] the wire communications of Alphonso H. Lee, Bernis Lee Thurmon, and other persons as may make use of the facilities hereinbefore described." App. 80. The order also required the agents to conduct the wiretap in "such a way as to minimize the interception of communications that are [not] otherwise subject to interception" under the Act and to report to the court every five days "the progress of the interception and the nature of the communication intercepted." Ibid. Interception began that same day and continued, pursuant to a judicially authorized extension, until February 24, 1970, with the agents making the periodic reports to the judge as required. Upon cessation of the interceptions, search and arrest warrants were executed which led to the arrest of 22 persons and the indictment of 14. * * *

Petitioners' principal contention is that the failure to make good-faith efforts to comply with the minimization requirement is itself a violation of

§ 2518 (5). They urge that it is only after an assessment is made of the agents' good-faith efforts, and presumably a determination that the agents did make such efforts, that one turns to the question of whether those efforts were reasonable under the circumstances. ... Thus, argue petitioners, Agent Cooper's testimony, which is basically a concession that the Government made no efforts which resulted in the noninterception of any call, is dispositive of the matter. * * *

The Government responds that petitioners' argument fails to properly distinguish between what is necessary to establish a statutory or constitutional violation and what is necessary to support a suppression remedy once a violation has been established. In view of the deterrent purposes of the exclusionary rule, consideration of official motives may play some part in determining whether application of the exclusionary rule is appropriate after a statutory or constitutional violation has been established. But the existence vel non of such a violation turns on an objective assessment of the officer's actions in light of the facts and circumstances confronting him at the time. Subjective intent alone, the Government contends, does not make otherwise lawful conduct illegal or unconstitutional.

We think the Government's position, which also served as the basis for decision in the Court of Appeals, embodies the proper approach for evaluating compliance with the minimization requirement. Although we have not examined this exact question at great length in any of our prior opinions, almost without exception in evaluating alleged violations of the Fourth Amendment the Court has first undertaken an objective assessment of an officer's actions in light of the facts and circumstances then known to him. The language of the Amendment itself proscribes only "unreasonable" searches and seizures. In Terry v. Ohio, 392 U.S. 1, 21–22 (1968), the Court emphasized the objective aspect of the term "reasonable."

"And in justifying the particular intrusion the police officer must be able to point to specific and articulable facts which, taken together with rational inferences from those facts, reasonably warrant that intrusion. The scheme of the Fourth Amendment becomes meaningful only when it is assured that at some point the conduct of those charged with enforcing the laws can be subjected to the more detached, neutral scrutiny of a judge who must evaluate the reasonableness of a particular search or seizure in light of the particular circumstances. And in making that assessment it is imperative that the facts be judged against an objective standard; would the facts available to the officer at the moment of the seizure or the search 'warrant a man of reasonable caution in the belief' that the action taken was appropriate?" (Footnotes omitted.)

Petitioners do not appear, however, to rest their argument entirely on Fourth Amendment principles. Rather, they argue in effect that regardless of the search-and-seizure analysis conducted under the Fourth Amendment, the statute regulating wiretaps requires the agents to make good-faith efforts at minimization, and the failure to make such efforts is itself a violation of the statute which requires suppression.

This argument fails for more than one reason. In the first place, in the very section in which it directs minimization Congress, by its use of the word "conducted," made it clear that the focus was to be on the agents' actions not their motives. Any lingering doubt is dispelled by the legislative history which, as we have recognized before in another context, declares that § 2515 was not intended "generally to press the scope of the suppression role beyond present search and seizure law."

We turn now to the Court of Appeals' analysis of the reasonableness of the agents' conduct in intercepting all of the calls in this particular wiretap. Because of the necessarily ad hoc nature of any determination of reasonableness, there can be no inflexible rule of law which will decide every case. The statute does not forbid the interception of all nonrelevant conversations, but rather instructs the agents to conduct the surveillance in such a manner as to "minimize" the interception of such conversations. Whether the agents have in fact conducted the wiretap in such a manner will depend on the facts and circumstances of each case.

We agree with the Court of Appeals that blind reliance on the percentage of nonpertinent calls intercepted is not a sure guide to the correct answer. Such percentages may provide assistance, but there are surely cases, such as the one at bar, where the percentage of nonpertinent calls is relatively high and yet their interception was still reasonable. The reasons for this may be many. Many of the nonpertinent calls may have been very short. Others may have been one-time only calls. Still other calls may have been ambiguous in nature or apparently involved guarded or coded language. In all these circumstances agents can hardly be expected to know that the calls are not pertinent prior to their termination.

In determining whether the agents properly minimized, it is also important to consider the circumstances of the wiretap. For example, when the investigation is focusing on what is thought to be a widespread conspiracy more extensive surveillance may be justified in an attempt to determine the precise scope of the enterprise. And it is possible that many more of the conversations will be permissibly interceptible because they will involve one or more of the co-conspirators. The type of use to which the telephone is normally put may also have some bearing on the extent of minimization required. For example, if the agents are permitted to tap a public telephone because one individual is thought to be placing bets over the phone, substantial doubts as to minimization may arise if the agents listen to every call which goes out over that phone regardless of who places the call. On the other hand, if the phone is located in the residence of a person who is thought to be the head of a major drug ring, a contrary conclusion may be indicated.

Other factors may also play a significant part in a particular case. For example, it may be important to determine at exactly what point during the authorized period the interception was made. During the early stages of surveillance the agents may be forced to intercept all calls to establish categories of nonpertinent calls which will not be intercepted thereafter. Interception of those same types of calls might be unreasonable later on, however, once the nonpertinent categories have been established and it is clear that this particular conversation is of that type. Other situations may arise where patterns of nonpertinent calls do not appear. In these circumstances it may not be unreasonable to intercept almost every short conversation because the determination of relevancy cannot be made before the call is completed.

After consideration of the minimization claim in this case in the light of these observations, we find nothing to persuade us that the Court of Appeals was wrong in its rejection of that claim. Forty percent of the calls were clearly narcotics related and the propriety of their interception is, of course, not in dispute. Many of the remaining calls were very short, such as wrong-number calls, calls to persons who were not available to come to the phone, and calls to the telephone company to hear the recorded weather message which lasts less than 90 seconds. In a case such as this, involving a wide-ranging conspiracy with a large number of participants, even a seasoned listener would have been hard pressed to determine with any precision the relevancy of many of the calls before they were completed. A large number were ambiguous in nature, making characterization virtually impossible until the completion of these calls. And some of the nonpertinent conversations were one-time conversations. Since these calls did not give the agents an opportunity to develop a category of innocent calls which should not have been intercepted, their interception cannot be viewed as a violation of the minimization requirement.

We are thus left with the seven calls between Jenkins and her mother. The first four calls were intercepted over a three-day period at the very beginning of the surveillance. They were of relatively short length and at least two of them indicated that the mother may have known of the conspiracy. The next two calls, which occurred about a week later, both contained statements from the mother to the effect that she had something to tell Jenkins regarding the "business" but did not want to do so over the phone. The final call was substantially longer and likewise contained a statement which could have been interpreted as having some bearing on the conspiracy, i. e., that one "Reds," a suspect in the conspiracy, had called to ask for a telephone number. Although none of these conversations turned out to be material to the investigation at hand, we cannot say that the Court of Appeals was incorrect in concluding that the agents did not act unreasonably at the time they made these interceptions. Its judgment is accordingly Affirmed.

MR. JUSTICE BRENNAN with whom MR. JUSTICE MARSHALL joins, dissenting.

In 1968, Congress departed from the longstanding national policy forbidding surreptitious interception of wire communications, by enactment of Title III of the Omnibus Crime Control and Safe Streets Act of 1968, 18 U.S.C. §§ 2510–2520 (1976 ed.). That Act, for the first time authorizing law enforcement personnel to monitor private telephone conversations, provided strict guidelines and limitations on the use of wiretaps as a barrier to Government infringement of individual privacy. One of the protections thought essential by Congress as a bulwark against unconstitutional governmental intrusion on private conversations is the "minimization requirement" of § 2518 (5). The Court today eviscerates this congressionally mandated protection of individual privacy, marking the third decision in which the Court has disregarded or diluted congressionally established safeguards designed to prevent Government electronic surveillance from becoming the abhorred general warrant which historically had destroyed the cherished expectation of privacy in the home. * * *

The District Court's findings of fact, not challenged here or in the Court of Appeals, plainly establish that this requirement was shamelessly violated. The District Court found: "[The] monitoring agents made no attempt to comply with the minimization order of the Court but listened to and recorded all calls over the [subject] telephone. They showed no regard for the right of privacy and did nothing to avoid unnecessary intrusion."

The District Court further found that the special agent who conducted the wiretap testified under oath that "he and the agents working under him knew of the minimization requirement but made no attempt to comply therewith." * * * The District Court found a "knowing and purposeful failure" to comply with the minimization requirements. * * *

[T]he Court manifests a disconcerting willingness to unravel individual threads of statutory protection without regard to their interdependence and to whether the cumulative effect is to rend the fabric of Title III's "congressionally designed bulwark against conduct of authorized electronic surveillance in a manner that violates the constitutional guidelines announced in Berger v. New York, 388 U.S. 41 (1967), and Katz v. United States, 389 U.S. 347 (1967)." This process of myopic, incremental denigration of Title III's safeguards raises the specter that, as judicially "enforced," Title III may be vulnerable to constitutional attack for violation of Fourth Amendment standards, thus defeating the careful effort Congress made to avert that result.

NOTE: *A BULWARK*

Minimization is a key limitation on covert surveillance, with an important role in Wiretap Act and FISA cases. How is the minimization requirement, in the words of the *Scott* dissent, "a bulwark against unconstitutional governmental intrusion on private conversations"? Does the majority's analysis undermine the requirement, in the way the dissent describes? Did the police flout the requirement, or simply act pragmatically?

c. "Consent" and "Business Extension" Exceptions

DEAL v. SPEARS

980 F.2d 1153 (8th Cir. 1992).

BOWMAN, CIRCUIT JUDGE.

This civil action is based on Title III of the Omnibus Crime Control and Safe Streets Act of 1968, 18 U.S.C. §§ 2510–2520. Plaintiffs Sibbie Deal and Calvin Lucas seek damages against Deal's former employers, defendants Newell and Juanita Spears, doing business as the White Oak Package Store, for the intentional interception and disclosure of plaintiffs' telephone conversations. After a bench trial, the District Court awarded statutory damages to Deal and Lucas in the amount of $40,000 and granted their request for attorney fees in accordance with Title III's fee-shifting provision. Newell and Juanita Spears appeal. * * * We affirm. * * *

Newell and Juanita Spears have owned and operated the White Oak Package Store near Camden, Arkansas, for about twenty years. The Spearses live in a mobile home adjacent to the store. The telephone in the store has an extension in the home, and is the only phone line into either location. The same phone line thus is used for both the residential and the business phones.

Sibbie Deal was an employee at the store from December 1988 until she was fired in August 1990. The store was burglarized in April 1990 and approximately $16,000 was stolen. The Spearses believed that it was an inside job and suspected that Deal was involved. Hoping to catch the suspect in an unguarded admission, Newell Spears purchased and installed a recording device on the extension phone in the mobile home. When turned on, the machine would automatically record all conversations made or received on either phone, with no indication to the parties using the phone that their conversation was being recorded. Before purchasing the recorder, Newell Spears told a sheriff's department investigator that he was considering this surreptitious monitoring and the investigator told Spears that he did not "see anything wrong with that." Id. at 619.

Calls were taped from June 27, 1990, through August 13, 1990. During that period, Sibbie Deal, who was married to Mike Deal at the time, was having an extramarital affair with Calvin Lucas, then married to Pam Lucas. Deal and Lucas spoke on the telephone at the store frequently and for long periods of time while Deal was at work. (Lucas was on 100% disability so he was at home all day.) Based on the trial testimony, the District Court concluded that much of the conversation between the two was "sexually provocative." Deal also made or received numerous other personal telephone calls during her workday. Even before Newell Spears purchased the recorder, Deal was asked by her employers to cut down on her use of the phone for personal calls, and the Spearses told her they might resort to monitoring calls or installing a pay phone in order to curtail the abuse.

Newell Spears listened to virtually all twenty-two hours of the tapes he recorded, regardless of the nature of the calls or the content of the conversations, and Juanita Spears listened to some of them. Although there was nothing in the record to indicate that they learned anything about the burglary, they did learn, among other things, that Deal sold Lucas a keg of beer at cost, in violation of store policy. On August 13, 1990, when Deal came in to work the evening shift, Newell Spears played a few seconds of the incriminating tape for Deal and then fired her. Deal and Lucas filed this action on August 29, 1990, and the tapes and recorder were seized by a United States deputy marshal pursuant to court order on September 3, 1990.

Mike Deal testified that Juanita Spears told him about the tapes, and that she divulged the general nature of the tapes to him. Pam Lucas testified that Juanita Spears intimated the contents of the tapes to her but only after Pam asked about them, and she also testified that Juanita told her to tell Sibbie to drop a workers compensation claim she had made against the store or "things could get ugly." Transcript at 67. Pam Lucas also testified that Juanita Spears "never told me what was on the tapes." Transcript at 68. Juanita testified that she discussed the tapes and the nature of them, but only in general terms.

The Spearses challenge the court's finding of liability. They admit the taping but contend that the facts here bring their actions under two statutory exceptions to civil liability. Further, Juanita Spears alleges that she did not disclose information learned from the tapes, thus the statutory damages assessed against her on that ground were improper. For their part Deal and Lucas challenge the court's failure to award them punitive damages as permitted by statute.

The elements of a violation of the wire and electronic communications interception provisions (Title III) of the Omnibus Crime Control and Safe Streets Act of 1968 are set forth in the section that makes such interceptions a criminal offense. Under the relevant provisions of the statute, criminal liability attaches and a federal civil cause of action arises when a person intentionally intercepts a wire or electronic communication or intentionally discloses the contents of the interception. The successful civil plaintiff may recover actual damages plus any profits made by the violator. If statutory damages will result in a larger recovery than actual damages, the violator must pay the plaintiff "the greater of $100 a day for each day of violation or $10,000." Further, punitive damages, attorney fees, and "other litigation costs reasonably incurred" are allowed.

The Spearses first claim they are exempt from civil liability because Sibbie Deal consented to the interception of calls that she made from and received at the store. Under the statute, it is not unlawful "to intercept a wire, oral, or electronic communication * * * where one of the parties to the communication has given prior consent to such interception," and thus no civil liability is incurred. The Spearses contend that Deal's consent may be implied because Newell Spears had mentioned that he might be forced to monitor calls or restrict telephone privileges if abuse of the store's telephone for personal calls continued. They further argue that the extension in their home gave actual notice to Deal that her calls could be overheard, and that this notice resulted in her implied consent to interception. We find these arguments unpersuasive.

There is no evidence of express consent here. Although constructive consent is inadequate, actual consent may be implied from the circumstances. See Griggs–Ryan v. Smith, 904 F.2d 112, 116 (1st Cir. 1990). Nevertheless, "consent under title III is not to be cavalierly implied * * *. Knowledge of the capability of monitoring alone cannot be considered implied consent."

We do not believe that Deal's consent may be implied from the circumstances relied upon in the Spearses' arguments. The Spearses did not inform Deal that they were monitoring the phone, but only told her they might do so in order to cut down on personal calls. Moreover, it seems clear that the couple anticipated Deal would not suspect that they were intercepting her calls, since they hoped to catch her making an admission about the burglary, an outcome they would not expect if she knew her calls were being recorded. As for listening in via the extension, Deal testified that she knew when someone picked up the extension in the residence while she was on the store phone, as there was an audible "click" on the line.

Given these circumstances, we hold as a matter of law that the Spearses have failed to show Deal's consent to the interception and recording of her conversations.

The Spearses also argue that they are immune from liability under what has become known as an exemption for business use of a telephone extension. The exception is actually a restrictive definition. Under Title III, a party becomes criminally and civilly liable when he or she "intercepts" wire communications. " 'Intercept' means the aural or other acquisition of the contents of any wire, electronic, or oral communication through the use of any electronic, mechanical, or other device[.]" 18 U.S.C. § 2510(4). Such a device is "any device or apparatus which can be used to intercept a wire, oral, or electronic communication" except when that device is a[:]

> telephone * * * instrument, equipment or facility, or any component thereof, (i) furnished to the subscriber or user by a provider of wire or electronic communication service in the ordinary course of its business and being used by the subscriber or user in the ordinary course of its business or furnished by such subscriber or user for connection to the facilities of such service and used in the ordinary course of its business[.]

Id. § 2510(5)(a)(i) (1988).

Thus there are two essential elements that must be proved before this becomes a viable defense: the intercepting equipment must be furnished to the user by the phone company or connected to the phone line, and it must be used in the ordinary course of business. The Spearses argue that the extension in their residence, to which the recorder was connected, meets the equipment requirement, and the listening-in was done in the ordinary course of business. We disagree.

* * * The calls would not have been heard or otherwise acquired—that is, intercepted—at all but for the recording device, as the Spearses did not spend twenty-two hours listening in on the residential extension. When turned on, the recorder was activated automatically by the lifting of the handset of either phone, even though it was connected only to the extension phone. Further, Deal ordinarily would know (by the "click" on the line) when the residential extension was picked up while she was using the store phone; thus her calls likely would not have been intercepted if the recorder had not been in place.

It seems far more plausible to us that the recording device, and not the extension phone, is the instrument used to intercept the call. We do not believe the recording device falls within the statutory exemption. The recorder was purchased by Newell Spears at Radio Shack, not provided by the telephone company. Further, it was connected to the extension phone, which was itself the instrument connected to the phone line. There was no evidence that the recorder could have operated independently of the telephone.

We hold that the recording device, and not the extension phone, intercepted the calls. But even if the extension phone intercepted the calls, we do not agree that the interception was in the ordinary course of business.

We do not quarrel with the contention that the Spearses had a legitimate business reason for listening in: they suspected Deal's involvement in a burglary of the store and hoped she would incriminate herself in a conversation on the phone. Moreover, Deal was abusing her privileges by using the phone for numerous personal calls even, by her own admission, when there were customers in the store. The Spearses might legitimately have monitored Deal's calls to the extent necessary to determine that the calls were personal and made or received in violation of store policy.

But the Spearses recorded twenty-two hours of calls, and Newell Spears listened to all of them without regard to their relation to his business interests. Granted, Deal might have mentioned the burglary at any time during the conversations, but we do not believe that the Spearses' suspicions justified the extent of the intrusion. See Watkins, 704 F.2d at 583 ("We hold that a personal call may not be intercepted in the ordinary course of business under the exemption in section 2510(5)(a)(i), except to the extent necessary to guard against unauthorized use of the telephone or to determine whether a call is personal or not."); Briggs v. American Air Filter Co., 630 F.2d 414, 420 n.9 ("A general practice of surreptitious monitoring would be more intrusive on employees' privacy than monitoring limited to specific occasions."). We conclude that the scope of the interception in this case takes us well beyond the boundaries of the ordinary course of business.

For the reasons we have indicated, the Spearses cannot avail themselves of the telephone extension/business use exemption of Title III.

Juanita Spears also contends that she did not communicate the information on the tapes, and thus she is not liable for disclosure under the statute. Liability attaches when a party "intentionally discloses * * * to any other person the contents of any wire, oral, or electronic communication, knowing or having reason to know that the information was obtained" through an interception illegal under Title III. 18 U.S.C. § 2511(1)(c). The statutory definition of "contents," a term of art under Title III, brings Juanita's alleged disclosures within the purview of the statute; she need not play the tapes or repeat conversations to be liable. " 'Contents', when used with respect to any wire, oral, or electronic communication, includes any information concerning the substance, purport, or meaning of that communication[.]" Id. § 2510(8) (1988). Based on the testimony of plaintiffs and their witnesses, which the trial court credited, Juanita Spears disclosed enough of the "contents" of the taped conversations between Deal and Lucas to incur liability. We have reviewed the record in this case, including the trial transcript and the depositions offered as evidence, and we cannot say that the District Court's finding that Juanita Spears disclosed the "contents" of the tapes is clearly erroneous.

NOTE: ROK LAMPE, WORK PHONES AND EMAIL— EXPECTATIONS OF PRIVACY

The European Court of Human Rights has incorporated a "reasonable expectation of privacy principle" into European privacy law. The leading case is *Halford v. U.K.* (1997). The Court debated whether surveillance of the applicant Halford's telephone in her office at Merseyside police headquarters fell within the scope of "private life" and "correspondence" under Article 8 of the Covenant for the Protection of Human Rights and Fundamental Freedoms.

EUROPEAN COURT OF HUMAN RIGHTS CASE OF HALFORD v. UNITED KINGDOM

(73/1996/692/884)
19 March and 27 May 1997.

As Assistant Chief Constable, Ms Halford was provided with her own office and two telephones, one of which was for private use. These telephones were part of the Merseyside police internal telephone network, a telecommunications system outside the public network. No restrictions were placed on the use of these telephones and no guidance was given to her * * *.

* * *

17.   She alleges that calls made from her home and her office telephones were intercepted for the purposes of obtaining information to use against her in the discrimination proceedings. In support of these allegations she adduced various items of evidence before the Commission. In addition, she informed the Court that she was told by an anonymous source on 16 April 1991 that, shortly before, the source had discovered the Merseyside police checking transcripts of conversations made on her home telephone.

For the purposes of the case before the Court, the Government accepted that the applicant had adduced sufficient material to establish a reasonable likelihood that calls made from her office telephones were intercepted. They did not, however, accept that she had adduced sufficient material to establish such a reasonable likelihood in relation to her home telephone.

18.   Ms Halford raised her concerns about the interception of her calls before the Industrial Tribunal on 17 June 1992. On 2 July 1992, in the course of the hearing, counsel for the Home Secretary expressed the opinion that it was not possible for her to adduce evidence about the alleged interceptions before the Industrial Tribunal because section 9 of the Interception of Communications Act 1985 ("the 1985 Act") expressly excluded the calling of evidence before any court or tribunal which tended to suggest that an offence under section 1 of the Act had been committed.

* * *

A.   The office telephones

1.   Applicability of Article 8 (art. 8) to the complaint relating to the office telephones

42.   The applicant argued, and the Commission agreed, that the calls made on the telephones in Ms Halford's office at Merseyside police headquarters fell within the scope of "private life" and "correspondence" in Article 8 para. 1 (art. 8–1), since the Court in its case-law had adopted a broad construction of these expressions (see, for example, the Klass and Others v. Germany judgment of 6 September 1978, Series A no. 28, p. 21, para. 41; the Huvig v. France judgment of 24 April 1990, Series A no. 176–B, p. 41, para. 8, and p. 52, para. 25; the Niemietz v. Germany judgment of 16 December 1992, Series A no. 251–B; and the A. v. France judgment of 23 November 1993, Series A no. 277–B).

43.   The Government submitted that telephone calls made by Ms Halford from her workplace fell outside the protection of Article 8, because she could have had no reasonable expectation of privacy in relation to them. At the hearing before the Court, counsel for the Government expressed the view that an employer should in principle, without the prior knowl-

edge of the employee, be able to monitor calls made by the latter on telephones provided by the employer.

44.   In the Court's view, it is clear from its case-law that telephone calls made from business premises as well as from the home may be covered by the notions of "private life" and "correspondence" within the meaning of Article 8 para. 1 (art. 8–1) (see the above-mentioned Klass and Others judgment, loc. cit.; the Malone v. the United Kingdom judgment of 2 August 1984, Series A no. 82, p. 30, para. 64; the above-mentioned Huvig judgment, loc. cit.; and, mutatis mutandis, the above-mentioned Niemietz judgment, pp. 33–35, paras. 29–33).

45.   There is no evidence of any warning having been given to Ms Halford, as a user of the internal telecommunications system operated at the Merseyside police headquarters, that calls made on that system would be liable to interception. She would, the Court considers, have had a reasonable expectation of privacy for such calls, which expectation was moreover reinforced by a number of factors. As Assistant Chief Constable she had sole use of her office where there were two telephones, one of which was specifically designated for her private use. Furthermore, she had been given the assurance, in response to a memorandum, that she could use her office telephones for the purposes of her sex-discrimination case.

46.   For all of the above reasons, the Court concludes that the conversations held by Ms Halford on her office telephones fell within the scope of the notions of "private life" and "correspondence" and that Article 8 (art. 8) is therefore applicable to this part of the complaint.

2.   Existence of an interference

47.   The Government conceded that the applicant had adduced sufficient material to establish a reasonable likelihood that calls made from her office telephones had been intercepted. The Commission also considered that an examination of the application revealed such a reasonable likelihood.

48.   The Court agrees. The evidence justifies the conclusion that there was a reasonable likelihood that calls made by Ms Halford from her office were intercepted by the Merseyside police with the primary aim of gathering material to assist in the defence of the sex-discrimination proceedings brought against them. This interception constituted "interference by a public authority", within the meaning of Article 8 para. 2, with the exercise of Ms Halford's right to respect for her private life and correspondence.

3.   Whether the interference was "in accordance with the law"

49.   Article 8 para. 2 further provides that any interference by a public authority with an individual's right to respect for private life and correspondence must be "in accordance with the law".

According to the Court's well-established case-law, this expression does not only necessitate compliance with domestic law, but also relates to the quality of that law, requiring it to be compatible with the rule of law. In the context of secret measures of surveillance or interception of communications by public authorities, because of the lack of public scrutiny and the risk of misuse of power, the domestic law must provide some protection to the individual against arbitrary interference with Article 8 rights. Thus, the domestic law must be sufficiently clear in its terms to give citizens an adequate indication as to the circumstances in and conditions on which public authorities are empowered to resort to any such secret measures (see the above-mentioned Malone judgment, p. 32, para. 67; and, mutatis mutandis, the Leander v. Sweden judgment of 26 March 1987, Series A no. 116, p. 23, paras. 50–51).

50. In the present case, the Government accepted that if, contrary to their submission, the Court were to conclude that there had been an interference with the applicant's rights under Article 8 in relation to her office telephones, such interference was not "in accordance with the law" since domestic law did not provide any regulation of interceptions of calls made on telecommunications systems outside the public network.

51. The Court notes that the 1985 Act does not apply to internal communications systems operated by public authorities, such as that at Merseyside police headquarters, and that there is no other provision in domestic law to regulate interceptions of telephone calls made on such systems (see paragraphs 36–37 above). It cannot therefore be said that the interference was "in accordance with the law" for the purposes of Article 8 para. 2 of the Convention since the domestic law did not provide adequate protection to Ms Halford against interferences by the police with her right to respect for her private life and correspondence.

It follows that there has been a violation of Article 8 in relation to the interception of calls made on Ms Halford's office telephones.

EUROPEAN COURT OF HUMAN RIGHTS CASE OF COPLAND v. THE UNITED KINGDOM

ECHR 62617/00
3 April 2007.

* * *

31. The Government accepted that the College was a public body for whose actions the State was directly responsible under the Convention.

32. Although there had been some monitoring of the applicant's telephone calls, e-mails and internet usage prior to November 1999, this did not extend to the interception of telephone calls or the analysis of the content of websites visited by her. The monitoring thus amounted to nothing more than the analysis of automatically generated information to determine whether College facilities had been used for personal purposes

which, of itself, did not constitute a failure to respect private life or correspondence. The case of P.G. and J.H. v. the United Kingdom, no. 44787/98, ECHR 2001–IX, could be distinguished since there actual interception of telephone calls occurred. There were significant differences from the case of Halford v. the United Kingdom, judgment of 25 June 1997, Reports of Judgments and Decisions 1997–III, where the applicant's telephone calls were intercepted on a telephone which had been designated for private use and, in particular her litigation against her employer.

33. In the event that the analysis of records of telephone, e-mail and internet use was considered to amount to an interference with respect for private life or correspondence, the Government contended that the interference was justified.

34. First, it pursued the legitimate aim of protecting the rights and freedoms of others by ensuring that the facilities provided by a publicly funded employer were not abused. Secondly, the interference had a basis in domestic law in that the College, as a statutory body, whose powers enable it to provide further and higher education and to do anything necessary and expedient for those purposes, had the power to take reasonable control of its facilities to ensure that it was able to carry out its statutory functions. It was reasonably foreseeable that the facilities provided by a statutory body out of public funds could not be used excessively for personal purposes and that the College would undertake an analysis of its records to determine if there was any likelihood of personal use which needed to be investigated. In this respect, the situation was analogous to that in Peck v. the United Kingdom, no. 44647/98, ECHR 2003–I.

35. Finally, the acts had been necessary in a democratic society and were proportionate as any interference went no further than necessary to establish whether there had been such excessive personal use of facilities as to merit investigation.

* * *

36. The applicant did not accept that her e-mails were not read and that her telephone calls were not intercepted but contended that, even if the facts were as set out by the Government, it was evident that some monitoring activity took place amounting to an interference with her right to respect for private life and correspondence.

37. She referred to legislation subsequent to the alleged violation, namely the Regulation of Investigatory Powers Act 2000 and the Telecommunications Regulations 2000 (see paragraph 20 above), which she claimed were an explicit recognition by the Government that such monitoring amounted to interference under Article 8 and required authorisation in order to be lawful. Since these laws came into force in 2000, the legal basis for such interference post-dated the events in the present case. Thus, the interference had no basis in domestic law and was entirely different from the position in Peck (see paragraph 34 above) where the local authority was specifically empowered by statute to record visual images of events

occurring in its area. In the present case there was no such express power for the College to carry out surveillance on its employees and the statutory powers did not make such surveillance reasonably foreseeable.

38. The applicant asserted that the conduct of the College was neither necessary nor proportionate. There were reasonable and less intrusive methods that the College could have used such as drafting and publishing a policy dealing with the monitoring of employees' usage of the telephone, internet and e-mail.

    B.   The Court's assessment

39. The Court notes the Government's acceptance that the College is a public body for whose acts it is responsible for the purposes of the Convention. Thus, it considers that in the present case the question to be analysed under Article 8 relates to the negative obligation on the State not to interfere with the private life and correspondence of the applicant and that no separate issue arises in relation to home or family life.

40. The Court further observes that the parties disagree as to the nature of this monitoring and the period of time over which it took place. However, the Court does not consider it necessary to enter into this dispute as an issue arises under Article 8 even on the facts as admitted by the Government.

    1.   Scope of private life

41. According to the Court's case-law, telephone calls from business premises are prima facie covered by the notions of "private life" and "correspondence" for the purposes of Article 8 § 1 (see Halford, cited above, § 44 and Amann v. Switzerland [GC], no. 27798/95, § 43, ECHR 2000–II). It follows logically that e-mails sent from work should be similarly protected under Article 8, as should information derived from the monitoring of personal internet usage.

42. The applicant in the present case had been given no warning that her calls would be liable to monitoring, therefore she had a reasonable expectation as to the privacy of calls made from her work telephone (see Halford, § 45). The same expectation should apply in relation to the applicant's e-mail and internet usage.

    2.   Whether there was any interference with the rights guaranteed under Article 8.

43. The Court recalls that the use of information relating to the date and length of telephone conversations and in particular the numbers dialled can give rise to an issue under Article 8 as such information constitutes an "integral element of the communications made by telephone" (see Malone v. the United Kingdom, judgment of 2 August 1984, Series A no. 82, § 84). The mere fact that these data may have been legitimately obtained by the College, in the form of telephone bills, is no bar to finding an interference with rights guaranteed under Article 8 (ibid). Moreover, storing of personal data relating to the private life of an individual also falls within the application of Article 8 § 1 (see Amann, cited above, § 65). Thus, it is

irrelevant that the data held by the college were not disclosed or used against the applicant in disciplinary or other proceedings.

44. Accordingly, the Court considers that the collection and storage of personal information relating to the applicant's telephone, as well as to her e-mail and internet usage, without her knowledge, amounted to an interference with her right to respect for her private life and correspondence within the meaning of Article 8.

3. Whether the interference was "in accordance with the law"

45. The Court recalls that it is well established in the case-law that the term "in accordance with the law" implies—and this follows from the object and purpose of Article 8—that there must be a measure of legal protection in domestic law against arbitrary interferences by public authorities with the rights safeguarded by Article 8 § 1. This is all the more so in areas such as the monitoring in question, in view of the lack of public scrutiny and the risk of misuse of power (see Halford, cited above, * * *).

46. This expression not only requires compliance with domestic law, but also relates to the quality of that law, requiring it to be compatible with the rule of law (see, inter alia, Khan v. the United Kingdom, judgment of 12 May 2000, Reports of Judgments and Decisions 2000–V, § 26; P.G. and J.H. v. the United Kingdom, cited above, § 44). In order to fulfil the requirement of foreseeability, the law must be sufficiently clear in its terms to give individuals an adequate indication as to the circumstances in which and the conditions on which the authorities are empowered to resort to any such measures (see Halford, cited above, * * *).

47. The Court is not convinced by the Government's submission that the College was authorised under its statutory powers to do "anything necessary or expedient" for the purposes of providing higher and further education, and finds the argument unpersuasive. Moreover, the Government do not seek to argue that any provisions existed at the relevant time, either in general domestic law or in the governing instruments of the College, regulating the circumstances in which employers could monitor the use of telephone, e-mail and the internet by employees. Furthermore, it is clear that the Telecommunications (Lawful Business Practice) Regulations 2000 (adopted under the Regulation of Investigatory Powers Act 2000) which make such provision were not in force at the relevant time.

48. Accordingly, as there was no domestic law regulating monitoring at the relevant time, the interference in this case was not "in accordance with the law" as required by Article 8 § 2 of the Convention. The Court would not exclude that the monitoring of an employee's use of a telephone, e-mail or internet at the place of work may be considered "necessary in a democratic society" in certain situations in pursuit of a legitimate aim. However, having regard to its above conclusion, it is not necessary to pronounce on that matter in the instant case.

49. There has therefore been a violation of Article 8 in this regard.

d. Prison Equipment, "Ordinary Course of Duty" Exception

UNITED STATES v. PAUL

614 F.2d 115 (6th Cir. 1980).

JUDGE KEITH

On March 30, 1978, Corrections Officers at the Ashland Kentucky Federal Correctional Institution monitored a telephone conversation between inmate Arnold Pierce and an unidentified female. The Officers overheard Pierce tell the woman to "bring the material," and that he would "have the money." The next morning, Corrections Officers stopped and searched Pierce and removed a $5.00 bill from his person. In addition, one Susan Paul presented herself at the institution to visit Pierce. Paul was taken to the Warden's office and strip searched, but no contraband was found.

Later that day, Corrections Officers monitored a conversation between inmate Bill Grimes and a woman identified as Susan. The woman stated that she was scared in that she had been taken to the Warden's office, but that she "had ditched the stuff under the chair and they didn't find anything on her." The Warden's office was searched and a quantity of hashish found. Based largely on the above testimony, Pierce and Paul were tried and convicted of violating 18 U.S.C. § 1791, which makes it unlawful for anyone to introduce, on the grounds of a federal prison, anything contrary to a rule of the Attorney General.

The sole question raised on appeal is whether the district court erred in refusing to suppress testimony regarding the monitored telephone conversations. Defendants contend that the government monitoring violated Title III of the Omnibus Crime Control and Safe Streets Act, 18 U.S.C. §§ 2510 Et seq. The issue before us is whether Title III applies to the monitoring of telephone calls to or from inmates at a prison and, if so, whether Title III was violated.

We note that defendants' claim is purely statutory. It still appears to be good law that so far as the Fourth Amendment is concerned, jail officials are free to intercept conversations between a prisoner and a visitor. * * *

Title III's broad prohibition on most forms of warrantless wiretapping presents a more troublesome issue, however. We do not question the government's need to monitor prisoners' telephone calls as a security measure. Nor do we doubt that the result of a ruling invalidating such monitoring would result in the elimination of telephone privileges for many prisoners. The problem is that Congress apparently never specifically considered the issue which is before us when it passed Title III.

The government takes the broad view that Title III does not apply at all because it was merely intended to codify the Supreme Court's constitutional decisions in Berger v. New York, 388 U.S. 41 (1967), and Katz v. United States. According to the government, surveillance which does not require a warrant under the Fourth Amendment should be automatically permissible under Title III.

We have problems with this view. It is true that Congress passed Title III in response to Berger and Katz. However, the statutory language speaks for itself and covers areas not addressed in Berger or Katz. * * *

The district court took the view that Title III did apply, but that the prison monitoring was excepted under 18 U.S.C. § 2510(5)(a) which excludes from the ambit of Title III the interception of communications over equipment used by "an investigative or law enforcement officer in the ordinary course of his duties * * *."

We agree with the district court. The monitored calls in this case came in over the prison switchboard and were then routed to telephones provided for inmate use within the institution. The district court found that the telephone monitoring took place pursuant to a policy statement issued by the Federal Bureau of Prisons as well as local prison rules. Although the issue was disputed, the court found that the telephone rules were posted and that the inmates had reasonable notice that monitoring of telephone conversations might occur.

Under these circumstances, we conclude, as did the district court, that the monitoring took place within the ordinary course of the Correctional Officers' duties and was thus permissible under 18 U.S.C. § 2510(5)(a). This factual situation distinguishes the only other case we have found on the prison wiretapping question, Campiti v. Walonis, 453 F. Supp. 819 (D.Mass.1978), Aff'd, 611 F.2d 387 (1st Cir. 1979). There, the monitoring was not shown to be related to prison security and was not done pursuant to a posted prison regulation. District Judge Hermansdorfer properly denied the motion to suppress. The judgments of conviction are affirmed.

e.   Preserving Evidence of "Injurious Act" Exception

MOORE v. TELFON COMMUNICATIONS

589 F.2d 959 (9th Cir. 1978).

Judge Sneed

Telfon operated a radio broadcasting correspondence school known as "Columbia School of Broadcasting." Although its principal place of business was San Francisco, courses were marketed nationwide through franchised distributors. Moore, a resident of New York, contacted Anderson, the creator and founder of the school, for the purpose of obtaining a franchise in 1966.

Although Moore desired the New York franchise, he ultimately purchased the Hartford, Connecticut franchise. The New York franchise was beyond Moore's means and Anderson intended to reserve that market for Columbia itself. Nevertheless, Moore extended his operations into the New York area, violating a Telfon agreement with Columbia Broadcasting Systems. Anderson and Moore entered into negotiations over this and other problems arising from Moore's activities in the course of which Moore threatened to institute a multi-million dollar antitrust suit if Anderson did not buy him out at an equal figure. * * *

On July 6, 1970, Telfon instituted an action to terminate the franchise agreement. Moore filed a counterclaim against Telfon, Anderson, and Bear Stearns, alleging antitrust violations, as well as breach of contract. Discovery disclosed that Anderson had recorded several conversations with Moore during the course of their business relationship. It had been a common practice for Anderson to record conversations with franchisees pertaining to statistical information and advertising leads. Anderson did not regard these conversations as confidential because the information was to be related to other officers and employees. During the period when Moore was threatening to institute lawsuits, Anderson recorded seven conversations without Moore's consent for the purpose of documenting threats of extortion. On the basis of these conversations Moore sued Anderson and Telfon * * *.

The privacy action involved three theories of law. The first alleged violation of the California common law right to privacy. Implicit in the verdict is the finding that Anderson's recordation of conversations with Moore was not an unauthorized or unwarranted intrusion into Moore's personal affairs either (1) because there was no serious and unreasonable invasion of privacy or (2) because the defendants were permitted to record and disclose the conversations.

The second theory was California Penal Code sections 630–637.2. Section 632 prohibits recording, intentionally and without the consent of all parties, a confidential communication. The definition of "confidential communication" excludes communications made in "circumstances in which the parties to the communication may reasonably expect that the communication may be overheard or recorded." Cal.Pen.C. § 632(c). Section 633.5 provides that nothing in § 632 shall be construed as prohibiting one party to a confidential communication from recording such communication for the purpose of obtaining evidence reasonably believed to relate to the commission of the crime of extortion. The verdict for Telfon and Anderson means that the jury alternatively found either that Moore impliedly consented, the communication was not confidential, or Anderson recorded the conversation for the purpose of obtaining evidence reasonably believed to relate to the crime of extortion.

The final theory of the privacy action is an alleged violation of 18 U.S.C. § 2511 which prohibits the willful interception of any wire or oral communication. However, for a person who is a party to the communication and not acting under color of law an interception is unlawful only if done for the purpose of committing a criminal, tortious or injurious act. 18 U.S.C. § 2511(2)(a)(d). The jury must have found that Anderson did not record the conversation for any such purpose. * * *

Congress did not define the meaning of "injurious act." While we acknowledge that the term embraces acts not easily classified as either "criminal" or "tortious," we cannot believe that Congress intended it to be read to embrace every act which disadvantages the other party to this communication. Such a reading would nullify the exemption created by § 2511(2) (a)(d). Presumably there is some disadvantage in having any conversation intercepted in the absence of consent of all parties. Congress, we believe, intended to permit one party to record conversation with another when the recorder is acting "out of a legitimate desire to protect himself."

The Eighth Circuit, in Meredith v. Gavin, 446 F.2d 794 (8th Cir. 1971), after reasoning that "a perfectly legitimate act may often be injurious," held that the conduct Congress intended to prohibit was the "interception by a party to the conversation with an intent to use that interception against the non-consenting party in some harmful way and in a manner in which the offending party had no right to proceed." Id. at 799. It further decided the scope of harmful conduct within the meaning of "injurious act" was to be determined on an ad hoc basis. We align ourselves with these views. It follows that Congress did not intend to prohibit recording a conversation when its purpose was to preserve evidence of extortion directed against the recorder to be used later for the purpose of terminating a franchise agreement. The district court's instructions to that effect were not erroneous.

f. First Amendment "Clean Hands" Defense

BARTNICKI v. VOPPER

532 U.S. 514 (2001).

JUSTICE STEVENS delivered the opinion of the Court.

These cases raise an important question concerning what degree of protection, if any, the First Amendment provides to speech that discloses the contents of an illegally intercepted communication. That question is both novel and narrow. Despite the fact that federal law has prohibited such disclosures since 1934, this is the first time that we have confronted such an issue.

The suit at hand involves the repeated intentional disclosure of an illegally intercepted cellular telephone conversation about a public issue. The persons who made the disclosures did not participate in the interception, but they did know—or at least had reason to know—that the interception was unlawful. Accordingly, these cases present a conflict between interests of the highest order—on the one hand, the interest in the full and free dissemination of information concerning public issues, and, on the other hand, the interest in individual privacy and, more specifically, in fostering private speech. The Framers of the First Amendment surely did not foresee the advances in science that produced the conversation, the interception, or the conflict that gave rise to this action. It is therefore not surprising that Circuit judges, as well as the Members of this Court, have come to differing conclusions about the First Amendment's application to this issue. Nevertheless, having considered the interests at stake, we are firmly convinced that the disclosures made by respondents in this suit are protected by the First Amendment. * * *

During 1992 and most of 1993, the Pennsylvania State Education Association, a union representing the teachers at the Wyoming Valley West High School, engaged in collective-bargaining negotiations with the school board. Petitioner Kane, then the president of the local union, testified that the negotiations were " 'contentious' " and received "a lot of media attention." * * * In May 1993, petitioner Bartnicki, who was acting as the union's "chief negotiator," used the cellular phone in her car to call Kane and engage in a lengthy conversation about the status of the negotiations. An unidentified person intercepted and recorded that call.

In their conversation, Kane and Bartnicki discussed the timing of a proposed strike, * * * difficulties created by public comment on the negotiations, * * * and the need for a dramatic response to the board's intransigence. At one point, Kane said: " 'If they're not gonna move for three percent, we're gonna have to go to their, their homes * * * To blow off their front porches, we'll have to do some work on some of those guys. (PAUSES). Really, uh, really and truthfully because this is, you know, this is bad news. (UNDECIPHERABLE).' " Ibid.

In the early fall of 1993, the parties accepted a non-binding arbitration proposal that was generally favorable to the teachers. In connection with news reports about the settlement, respondent Vopper, a radio commentator who had been critical of the union in the past, played a tape of the intercepted conversation on his public affairs talk show. Another station also broadcast the tape, and local newspapers published its contents. After filing suit against Vopper and other representatives of the media, Bartnicki and Kane (hereinafter petitioners) learned through discovery that Vopper had obtained the tape from Jack Yocum, the head of a local taxpayers' organization that had opposed the union's demands throughout the negotiations. Yocum, who was added as a defendant, testified that he had found the tape in his mailbox shortly after the interception and recognized the voices of Bartnicki and Kane. Yocum played the tape for some members of the school board, and later delivered the tape itself to Vopper. * * *

In their amended complaint, petitioners alleged that their telephone conversation had been surreptitiously intercepted by an unknown person using an electronic device, that Yocum had obtained a tape of that conversation, and that he intentionally disclosed it to Vopper, as well as other individuals and media representatives. Thereafter, Vopper and other members of the media repeatedly published the contents of that conversation. The amended complaint alleged that each of the defendants "knew or had reason to know" that the recording of the private telephone conversation had been obtained by means of an illegal interception. Relying on both federal and Pennsylvania statutory provisions, petitioners sought actual damages, statutory damages, punitive damages, and attorney's fees and costs. [Title 18 U.S.C. § 2511(1)(c) provides that any person who "intentionally discloses, or endeavors to disclose, to any other person the contents of any wire, oral, or electronic communication, knowing or having reason to know that the information was obtained through the interception of a wire, oral, or electronic communication in violation of this subsection; * * * shall be punished * * *." The Pennsylvania Act contains a similar provision. Title 18 U.S.C. § 2511(1)(a) provides: "(1) Except as otherwise specifically provided in this chapter [§§ 2510–2520 (1994 ed. and Supp. V)] any person who—(a) intentionally intercepts, endeavors to intercept, or procures any other person to intercept or endeavor to intercept, any wire, oral, or electronic communication; * * * shall be punished * * *."]

The constitutional question before us concerns the validity of the statutes as applied to the specific facts of this case. Because of the procedural posture of the case, it is appropriate to make certain important assumptions about those facts. We accept petitioners' submission that the interception was intentional, and therefore unlawful, and that, at a minimum, respondents "had reason to know" that it was unlawful. Accordingly, the disclosure of the contents of the intercepted conversation by Yocum to school board members and to representatives of the media, as well as the subsequent disclosures by the media defendants to the public, violated the federal and state statutes. Under the provisions of the federal statute, as well as its Pennsylvania analog, petitioners are thus entitled to recover damages from each of the respondents. The only question is whether the application of these statutes in such circumstances violates the First Amendment.

In answering that question, we accept respondents' submission on three factual matters that serve to distinguish most of the cases that have arisen under § 2511. First, respondents played no part in the illegal interception. Rather, they found out about the interception only after it occurred, and in fact never learned the identity of the person or persons who made the interception. Second, their access to the information on the tapes was obtained lawfully, even though the information itself was intercepted unlawfully by someone else. Cf. Florida Star v. B. J. F., 491 U.S. 524 (1989) ("Even assuming the Constitution permitted a State to proscribe receipt of information, Florida has not taken this step"). Third, the subject matter of the conversation was a matter of public concern. If the statements about the labor negotiations had been made in a public arena—during a bargaining session, for example—they would have been newsworthy. This would also be true if a third party had inadvertently overheard Bartnicki making the same statements to Kane when the two thought they were alone. * * *

We agree with petitioners that § 2511(1)(c), as well as its Pennsylvania analog, is in fact a content-neutral law of general applicability. "Deciding whether a particular regulation is content based or content neutral is not always a simple task * * *. As a general rule, laws that by their terms distinguish favored speech from disfavored speech on the basis of the ideas or views expressed are content based." Turner Broadcasting System, Inc. v. FCC, 512 U.S. 622, 642–643 (1994). In determining whether a regulation is content based or content neutral, we look to the purpose behind the regulation; typically, "government regulation of expressive activity is content neutral so long as it is 'justified without reference to the content of the regulated speech.'" Ward v. Rock Against Racism, 491 U.S. 781, 791 (1989).

In this case, the basic purpose of the statute at issue is to "protect the privacy of wire and oral communications." S. Rep. No. 1097, 90th Cong., 2d Sess., 66 (1968). The statute does not distinguish based on the content of the intercepted conversations, nor is it justified by reference to the content of those conversations. Rather, the communications at issue are singled out by virtue of the fact that they were illegally intercepted—by virtue of the source, rather than the subject matter. * * *

As a general matter, "state action to punish the publication of truthful information seldom can satisfy constitutional standards." Smith v. Daily Mail Publishing Co., 443 U.S. 97, 102 (1979). More specifically, this Court has repeatedly held that "if a newspaper lawfully obtains truthful information about a matter of public significance then state officials may not constitutionally punish publication of the information, absent a need * * * of the highest order." Id., at 103; see also Florida Star v. B. J. F., 491 U.S. 524 (1989) * * *.

Accordingly, in New York Times Co. v. United States, 403 U.S. 713 (per curiam), the Court upheld the right of the press to publish information of great public concern obtained from documents stolen by a third party. In so doing, that decision resolved a conflict between the basic rule against prior restraints on publication and the interest in preserving the secrecy of information that, if disclosed, might seriously impair the security of the Nation. In resolving that conflict, the attention of every Member of this Court was focused on the character of the stolen documents' contents and the consequences of public disclosure. Although the undisputed fact that the newspaper intended to publish information obtained from stolen documents was noted in Justice Harlan's dissent, id., at 754, neither the majority nor the dissenters placed any weight on that fact.

However, New York Times v. United States raised, but did not resolve the question "whether, in cases where information has been acquired unlawfully by a newspaper or by a source, government may ever punish not only the unlawful acquisition, but the ensuing publication as well." Florida Star, 491 U.S. at 535, n. 8. The question here, however, is a narrower version of that still-open question. Simply put, the issue here is this: "Where the punished publisher of information has obtained the information in question in a manner lawful in itself but from a source who has obtained it unlawfully, may the government punish the ensuing publication of that information based on the defect in a chain?" Boehner, 191 F.3d at 484–485 (Sentelle, J., dissenting). * * *

The Government identifies two interests served by the statute—first, the interest in removing an incentive for parties to intercept private conversations, and second, the interest in minimizing the harm to persons whose conversations have been illegally intercepted. We assume that those interests adequately justify the prohibition in § 2511(1)(d) against the interceptor's own use of information that he or she acquired by violating § 2511(1)(a), but it by no means follows that punishing disclosures of lawfully obtained information of public interest by one not involved in the initial illegality is an acceptable means of serving those ends.

The normal method of deterring unlawful conduct is to impose an appropriate punishment on the person who engages in it. If the sanctions that presently attach to a violation of § 2511(1)(a) do not provide sufficient deterrence, perhaps those sanctions should be made more severe. But it would be quite remarkable to hold that speech by a law-abiding possessor of information can be suppressed in order to deter conduct by a non-law-abiding third party. Although there are some rare occasions in which a law suppressing one party's speech may be justified by an interest in deterring criminal conduct by another, see, e.g., New York v. Ferber, 458 U.S. 747 (1982), this is not such a case.

With only a handful of exceptions, the violations of § 2511(1)(a) that have been described in litigated cases have been motivated by either financial gain or domestic disputes. In virtually all of those cases, the identity of the person or persons intercepting the communication has been known. Moreover, petitioners cite no evidence that Congress viewed the prohibition against disclosures as a response to the difficulty of identifying persons making improper use of scanners and other surveillance devices and accordingly of deterring such conduct, and there is no empirical evidence to support the assumption that the prohibition against disclosures reduces the number of illegal interceptions.

Although this case demonstrates that there may be an occasional situation in which an anonymous scanner will risk criminal prosecution by passing on information without any expectation of financial reward or public praise, surely this is the exceptional case. Moreover, there is no basis for assuming that imposing sanctions upon respondents will deter the unidentified scanner from continuing to engage in surreptitious interceptions. Unusual cases fall far short of a showing that there is a "need of the highest order" for a rule supplementing the traditional means of deterring antisocial conduct. The justification for any such novel burden on expression must be "far stronger than mere speculation about serious harms." United States v. National Treasury Employees Union, 513 U.S. 454 (1995). Accordingly, the Government's first suggested justification for applying § 2511(1)(c) to an otherwise innocent disclosure of public information is plainly insufficient.

The Government's second argument, however, is considerably stronger. Privacy of communication is an important interest, Harper & Row, Publishers, Inc. v. Nation Enterprises, 471 U.S. 539, 559 (1985), and Title

III's restrictions are intended to protect that interest, thereby "encouraging the uninhibited exchange of ideas and information among private parties * * *." Brief for United States 27. Moreover, the fear of public disclosure of private conversations might well have a chilling effect on private speech. * * *

Accordingly, it seems to us that there are important interests to be considered on both sides of the constitutional calculus. In considering that balance, we acknowledge that some intrusions on privacy are more offensive than others, and that the disclosure of the contents of a private conversation can be an even greater intrusion on privacy than the interception itself. As a result, there is a valid independent justification for prohibiting such disclosures by persons who lawfully obtained access to the contents of an illegally intercepted message, even if that prohibition does not play a significant role in preventing such interceptions from occurring in the first place.

We need not decide whether that interest is strong enough to justify the application of § 2511(c) to disclosures of trade secrets or domestic gossip or other information of purely private concern. In other words, the outcome of the case does not turn on whether § 2511(1)(c) may be enforced with respect to most violations of the statute without offending the First Amendment. The enforcement of that provision in this case, however, implicates the core purposes of the First Amendment because it imposes sanctions on the publication of truthful information of public concern.

In this case, privacy concerns give way when balanced against the interest in publishing matters of public importance. As Warren and Brandeis stated in their classic law review article: "The right of privacy does not prohibit any publication of matter which is of public or general interest." The Right to Privacy, 4 Harv. L. Rev. 193, 214 (1890). One of the costs associated with participation in public affairs is an attendant loss of privacy. * * *

Our opinion in New York Times Co. v. Sullivan, 376 U.S. 254 (1964), reviewed many of the decisions that settled the "general proposition that freedom of expression upon public questions is secured by the First Amendment." * * * [A] stranger's illegal conduct does not suffice to remove the First Amendment shield from speech about a matter of public concern. The months of negotiations over the proper level of compensation for teachers at the Wyoming Valley West High School were unquestionably a matter of public concern, and respondents were clearly engaged in debate about that concern. That debate may be more mundane than the Communist rhetoric that inspired Justice Brandeis' classic opinion in Whitney v. California, 274 U.S. at 372, but it is no less worthy of constitutional protection.

CHIEF JUSTICE REHNQUIST, with whom JUSTICE SCALIA and JUSTICE THOMAS join, dissenting.

Technology now permits millions of important and confidential conversations to occur through a vast system of electronic networks. These advances, however, raise significant privacy concerns. We are placed in the uncomfortable position of not knowing who might have access to our personal and business e-mails, our medical and financial records, or our cordless and cellular telephone conversations. In an attempt to prevent some of the most egregious violations of privacy, the United States, the District of Columbia, and 40 States have enacted laws prohibiting the intentional interception and knowing disclosure of electronic communications. The Court holds that all of these statutes violate the First Amendment insofar as the illegally intercepted conversation touches upon a matter of "public concern," an amorphous concept that the Court does not even attempt to define. But the Court's decision diminishes, rather than enhances, the purposes of the First Amendment: chilling the speech of the millions of Americans who rely upon electronic technology to communicate each day.

Over 30 years ago, with Title III of the Omnibus Crime Control and Safe Streets Act of 1968, Congress recognized that the "tremendous scientific and technological developments that have taken place in the last century have made possible today the widespread use and abuse of electronic surveillance techniques. As a result of these developments, privacy of communication is seriously jeopardized by these techniques of surveillance * * *. No longer is it possible, in short, for each man to retreat into his home and be left alone. Every spoken word relating to each man's personal, marital, religious, political, or commercial concerns can be intercepted by an unseen auditor and turned against the speaker to the auditor's advantage." * * *

This concern for privacy was inseparably bound up with the desire that personal conversations be frank and uninhibited, not cramped by fears of clandestine surveillance and purposeful disclosure: "In a democratic society privacy of communication is essential if citizens are to think and act creatively and constructively. Fear or suspicion that one's speech is being monitored by a stranger, even without the reality of such activity, can have a seriously inhibiting effect upon the willingness to voice critical and constructive ideas." * * *

To effectuate these important privacy and speech interests, Congress and the vast majority of States have proscribed the intentional interception and knowing disclosure of the contents of electronic communications. See, e.g., 18 U.S.C. § 2511(1)(c) (placing restrictions upon "any person who * * * intentionally discloses, or endeavors to disclose, to any other person the contents of any wire, oral, or electronic communication, knowing or having reason to know that the information was obtained through the interception of a wire, oral, or electronic communication"). * * *

Surely "the interest in individual privacy," * * * must embrace the right to be free from surreptitious eavesdropping on, and involuntary broadcast of, our cellular telephone conversations. The Court subordinates that right, not to the claims of those who themselves wish to speak, but to the claims of those who wish to publish the intercepted conversations of others. Congress' effort to balance the above claim to privacy against a marginal claim to speak freely is thereby set at naught.

NOTE: INCENTIVES?

Does the holding in *Bartnicki* encourage unlawful interception, recording and disclosure of communications protected by ECPA? Does the dissent in this case offer a persuasive, alternative analysis?

g. Cordless Telephone Recording—Are There "Public Interest" and "Re-publication" Defenses?

SPETALIERI v. KAVANAUGH

36 F. Supp. 2d 92 (N.D.N.Y. 1998).

McAvoy, Chief Judge * * *

At all times relevant hereto, Plaintiff Steven A. Spetalieri ("plaintiff") was the head of the Narcotics Bureau for the City of Kingston Police Department ("KPD"). Defendant Joan Williams Washington ("Washington") is a resident of the City of Kingston and lives in close proximity to plaintiff's friend, Rachel Bloom ("Bloom"). Washington is a member of the neighborhood watch program and has frequent contact with the KPD. Washington owns a scanner that she uses to monitor police and fire department activity, and radio communications of the City of Kingston (the "City") Department of Public Works, where her husband is employed.

In the spring or summer of Washington's scanner picked up telephone conversations between plaintiff and Bloom. Bloom was using a cordless telephone. Plaintiff, on the other hand, was using a traditional, hard-wired telephone. In the telephone conversations, plaintiff frequently used profanity and spoke in a denigrating manner about African–Americans.

Washington apparently recognized plaintiff as a party to the conversations. Because she believed that plaintiff's speech was inappropriate, especially in light of his position as head of the KPD Narcotics Bureau, Washington locked her scanner on the particular frequency that received plaintiff's telephone conversation and tape recorded three telephone conversations (two of which were between plaintiff and Bloom).

Washington did not do anything with the tape until on or about July 12, 1996, when she gave the tape to Defendant McShell Moye–Clarke ("Clarke"), president of the Kingston Branch of the NAACP. Washington apparently urged Clarke to listen to the tape and take appropriate action. Washington, however, did not want to be identified as the source of the tape for fear of reprisal. As a condition of obtaining the tape, Clarke apparently promised Washington that the NAACP would protect her.

Clarke listened to the tape and played it for other members of the NAACP.

On July 15, 1996, Clarke and other members of the NAACP delivered the tape to District Attorney Investigator Junious Harris ("Harris") of the Ulster County District Attorney's Office. Clarke did not advise Harris of the source of the tape and claimed that the recording came from conversations that had been inadvertently heard over someone's television. Clarke also apparently stated that she did not know the source of the tape, but that she found it in her mailbox.

Defendant Michael Kavanagh, the Ulster County District Attorney ("Kavanagh" or the "District Attorney"), also listened to a portion of the tape. Kavanagh directed Harris to copy the tape and have Clarke deliver the tape to Defendant Deputy Police Chief Paul Watzka ("Watzka"), which she did, again claiming that the tape had been anonymously left in her mailbox. Kavanagh also contacted Watzka and recommended that plaintiff be suspended or put on limited duty pending an internal investigation. Kavanagh immediately drafted a memorandum to all Assistant District Attorneys requesting a list of all County Court cases in which plaintiff played a key role in the investigation and prosecution. Concerned over plaintiff's credibility as a witness, Kavanagh believed that the tape and any investigation thereof would have to be disclosed pursuant to Brady v. Maryland, 373 U.S. 83 (1963), in the prosecutions of African–Americans in which plaintiff was going to testify. Accordingly, Kavanagh decided not to use plaintiff as a witness in any criminal cases prosecuted by his office. As a result, the District Attorney's office reviewed those cases in which plaintiff would be an essential witness and offered plea bargains.

Watzka informed the Chief of Police for the KPD (the "Chief") that he received a tape recording from the NAACP involving a police officer making racial slurs. The Chief advised Watzka to contact Defendant City of Kingston Mayor T. R. Gallo ("Gallo"). Gallo stated that a meeting of the Board of Police Commissioners should be convened and that Watzka should review the matter and conduct an investigation.

A meeting of the Board of Police Commissioners (the "Board") was convened on July 16, 1996. Present at the meeting were, inter alios, Defendants Kay Quick ("Quick"), a member of the Board; Gallo; and Reverend Willie Hardin ("Hardin"), Director of Human Rights for the City of Kingston. The Board recommended that plaintiff be suspended for thirty days without pay and instructed Watzka to investigate the origin of the tape. Upon the expiration of the thirty-day suspension, the Board met again and continued the suspension with pay.

Beginning on July 16, 1996, articles began to appear in local newspapers regarding the taped conversations. Various reporters contacted Kavanagh who publicly commented that an avowed racist should not be in law enforcement and urged either that plaintiff retire from the KPD or be terminated. Gallo and Clarke also commented to the press.

After the Board meeting, plaintiff was served with Disciplinary Charges and a hearing officer was appointed to review the matter. Plaintiff ultimately negotiated a settlement with the City in satisfaction of the Disciplinary Charges whereby plaintiff agreed to retire from the KPD in exchange for certain financial compensation.

Thereafter, plaintiff commenced the instant litigation against the defendants asserting various claims pursuant to § 1983, a claim pursuant to New York Executive Law § 296, and a common-law claim for defamation. In response, Washington filed a Third–Party Complaint against the NAACP, Hazel Dukes, President of the New York State Conference of NAACP Branches, and Clarke, as president of the Ulster County Branch of the NAACP (the "third-party defendants") claiming that the third-party defendants had agreed to defend and indemnify her for any damages, attorneys' fees and other expenses she might incur by reason of having given the tape to Clarke.

The defendants and third-party defendants have now moved for summary judgment dismissing the Complaint and Third–Party Complaint, respectively, in their entirety. Plaintiff has cross-moved for leave to amend the Complaint to add causes of action for violations of 18 U.S.C. § 2510, et seq. (the "Wiretap Statute") * * *.

It is now axiomatic that leave to amend shall be freely granted unless it would be futile, cause undue delay or prejudice, or when it is sought in bad faith. Foman v. Davis, 371 U.S. 178, 182 (1962). For the following reasons plaintiff is granted leave to amend the Complaint to assert a cause of action for violations of 18 U.S.C. § 2510 * * *.

Although the defendants predictably claim that they will be prejudiced and that the amendment would be futile, the Court disagrees. The alleged violation of 18 U.S.C. § 2511 arises out of the very same conduct as that alleged in the original Complaint. Further, much of the discovery conducted in the case would readily lend itself to a prosecution or defense of a claim pursuant to 18 U.S.C. § 2520. Thus, there is no prejudice. Furthermore, as will be discussed, § 2520 applies to all cordless telephone conversations and, therefore, the amendment would not be futile. * * *.

Whether the 1994 amendments to Title III of the Omnibus Crime Control and Safe Streets Act of 1968 (the "Amendments") apply to all cordless telephones [—even those without scrambling technology to thwart interception—] appears to be an issue of first impression. The Court has not found, and the parties have not presented, any case applying the Amendments to cordless telephone conversations. * * *

In 1994, Congress amended the ECPA to remove the exception for cordless telephones from the definition of wire or electronic communications, P.L. 103–414, § 202(a), and amended the penalty provisions to include the interception of cordless telephones conversations. P.L. 103–414, § 202(b). Nothing in the statute or the legislative history indicates Congress' intent to protect modern, expensive, high-tech cordless phones with scrambling technology and not lower-cost, non-scrambling cordless telephones. To the contrary, Congress found that cordless telephones play an integral part of our society, that people expect that such telephone calls will be private and, accordingly, amended § 2511 to protect cordless telephone calls. Congress succinctly stated that "the [ECPA] * * * exempted from the protection of the Act 'the radio portion of a cordless telephone' * * *. The bill deletes the exceptions for cordless phones and imposes a penalty * * * for intentionally intercepting such communications."

The House Report specifically stated that "while the portion of cordless telephone communications occurring between the handset and the base unit was excluded from ECPA's privacy protections, the 1991 Privacy and Technology Task Force found that 'the cordless phone, far from being a novelty item used only at "poolside", has become ubiquitous * * * More and more communications are being carried out by people [using cordless phones] in private, in their homes and offices, with an expectation that such calls are just like any other phone call.' "

Further, the language of § 2511(4)(b) demonstrates that Congress intended to cover all cordless telephone conversations. Section 2511(4)(b) provides that "if the offense is a first offense * * * and is not for a tortious or illegal purpose or for purposes of * * * commercial advantage or private commercial gain, and the wire or electronic communication with respect to which the offense under paragraph (a) is a radio communication that is not scrambled, encrypted, or transmitted using modulation techniques * * * then * * * if the communication is the radio portion of * * * a cordless telephone communication that is transmitted between cordless telephone handset and the base unit * * * the offender shall be fined under this title." This language makes it particularly clear that Congress did not intend to exempt non-scrambling, less sophisticated cordless telephones from the privacy protections. * * *

Defendant Clarke further claims that this cause of action is futile because the record does not establish that she possessed the conscious objective to violate the statute, her distribution of the tape is protected by the First Amendment, and the statute cannot punish telephone conversations that do not affect interstate commerce.

The Wiretap Statute is not violative of the First Amendment on its face. Clarke cites In re: King World Productions, 898 F.2d 56, 59 (6th Cir. 1990), for the proposition that her First Amendment rights trump the ECPA. * * *

Clarke also maintains that her actions are protected by the First Amendment because she was petitioning the government "to take action to repudiate plaintiff's racist comments." Clarke Reply Memo. of Law, p. 8. For the reasons that follow, the Court need not resolve this Constitutional issue. * * *

Clarke admits to having: (1) listened to the tape, and (2) disclosed the tape to the executive committee of the NAACP, the Ulster County District Attorney's Office, and the KPD. * * * Section 2520 provides a civil cause of action for the intentional disclosure of a wire, oral, or electronic communication "knowing or having reason to know that the information was obtained through the interception of a wire, oral, or electronic communication in violation of this subsection." * * *

A genuine issue of material fact remains regarding whether Clarke violated § 2511; that is, whether she intentionally used, endeavored to use, disclosed, or endeavored to disclose any protected communication that she knew or had reason to know was obtained in violation of the Wiretap Statute. Clarke expressed her reservations regarding the legality of the tape, but nevertheless listened to it and disclosed it to the NAACP and others. Thus, this issue and the amount of any damages is for a jury. * * *

The City and County Defendants further argue that amending the Complaint would be futile because their conduct is exempt from the Wiretap Statute. Specifically, these defendants maintain that 18 U.S.C. §§ 2517(1) and (2) authorize them to disclose the tape to and within the KPD for investigation purposes. Defendants further assert that they are immune from liability because they disclosed the tape to the media after it had become common knowledge.

Defendants rely on Forsyth v. Barr, 19 F.3d 1527 (5th Cir. 1994), cert. denied, 115 S. Ct. 195 (1994), for the argument that they were permitted to use and disclose the tape to the KPD pursuant to 18 U.S.C. § 2517(1) and (2). The Forsyth court concluded that "disclosure and use under §§ 2517(1) and (2) of unlawfully intercepted information that is otherwise conveyed lawfully to law enforcement officers is permitted; in sum, that information disclosed or used under those subsections need not be only that which is intercepted 'in accordance with' the Act." * * * The Fifth Circuit apparently believed that law enforcement may use illegally intercepted communications provided they took no part in the illegal interception. In United States v. Murdock, 63 F.3d 1391, 1404 (6th Cir.1995), cert. denied, 517 U.S. 1187 (1996), the Sixth Circuit reached a similar result recognizing a clean hands exception allowing for the introduction of evidence obtained by an illegal wiretap where the government took no part in the interception. * * *

* * * A plain and fair reading of the statute evinces that Congress intended to limit law enforcement officers' use or disclosure of information that was lawfully obtained. See 18 U.S.C. § 2517. Because of the serious privacy concerns involved even in a legal wiretap, Congress sought to impose limits upon the use of information derived therefrom. These limitations are contained in § 2517. * * *

Thus, § 2517 does not insulate the City or County Defendants from liability unless they can demonstrate that they obtained the tape recordings "by any means authorized by this chapter" or, of course, unless they demonstrate that they did not have the requisite degree of knowledge to invoke § 2511.

The Court also rejects the County Defendants' assertion that they are insulated from liability for disclosing the tape because the contents of the tape had become common knowledge. The County Defendants both used and disclosed the tape recordings to the KPD before the media reports. As previously noted, for purposes of statutory damages, there is only one violation of the statute for disclosing an impermissibly intercepted communication regardless of the actual number of disclosures. Similarly, there is but one violation of the statute for using impermissible intercepted tapes, regardless of the actual number of uses. Thus, it is irrelevant for purposes of this motion whether the contents of the tape recordings had become common knowledge after it had been used and disclosed by the County Defendants. Triable issues of fact remain regarding whether the City and/or County Defendants knew that the tape had been obtained in violation of the Wiretap Statute, which City Defendants used or disclosed the tape recording, and whether the contents of the tape had, indeed, become public knowledge at the time of disclosure.

2. INTERCEPTING EMAIL IN FLIGHT AND IN TEMPORARY STORAGE

UNITED STATES v. COUNCILMAN

418 F.3d 67 (1st Cir. 2005).

Lipez, Circuit Judge.

This case presents an important question of statutory construction. We must decide whether interception of an e-mail message in temporary, transient electronic storage states an offense under the Wiretap Act, as amended by the Electronic Communications Privacy Act of 1986, 18 U.S.C. §§ 2510–2522. The government believes it does, and indicted Councilman under that theory. The district court disagreed and dismissed the indictment. * * *

The Internet is a network of interconnected computers. Data transmitted across the Internet are broken down into small "packets" that are forwarded from one computer to another until they reach their destination, where they are reconstituted. See Orin S. Kerr, Internet Surveillance Law After the USA Patriot Act: The Big Brother that Isn't, 97 Nw. U. L. Rev. 607, 613–14 (2003). Each service on the Internet—e.g., e-mail, the World Wide Web, or instant messaging—has its own protocol for using packets of data to transmit information from one place to another. The e-mail protocol is known as Simple Mail Transfer Protocol ("SMTP").

After a user composes a message in an e-mail client program, a program called a mail transfer agent ("MTA") formats that message and sends it to another program that "packetizes" it and sends the packets out to the Internet. Computers on the network then pass the packets from one to another; each computer along the route stores the packets in memory, retrieves the addresses of their final destinations, and then determines where to send them next. At various points the packets are reassembled to form the original e-mail message, copied, and then re-packetized for the next leg of the journey. Sometimes messages cannot be transferred immediately and must be saved for later delivery. Even when delivery is immediate, intermediate computers often retain backup copies, which they delete later. This method of transmission is commonly called "store and forward" delivery.

Once all the packets reach the recipient's mail server, they are reassembled to form the e-mail message. A mail delivery agent ("MDA") accepts the message from the MTA, determines which user should receive the message, and performs the actual delivery by placing the message in that user's mailbox. One popular MDA is "procmail," which is controlled by short programs or scripts called "recipe files." These recipe files can be used in various ways. For example, a procmail recipe can instruct the MDA to deposit mail addressed to one address into another user's mailbox (e.g., to send mail addressed to "help" to the tech support department), to reject mail from certain addresses, or to make copies of certain messages.

Once the MDA has deposited a message into the recipient's mailbox, the recipient simply needs to use an e-mail client program to retrieve and read the message. While the journey from sender to recipient may seem rather involved, it usually takes just a few seconds, with each intermediate step taking well under a second. * * *

Defendant-appellee Bradford C. Councilman was Vice President of Interloc, Inc., which ran an online rare and out-of-print book listing service. As part of its service, Interloc gave book dealer customers an e-mail address at the domain "interloc.com" and acted as the e-mail provider. Councilman managed the e-mail service and the dealer subscription list.

According to the indictment, in January 1998, Councilman directed Interloc employees to intercept and copy all incoming communications to subscriber dealers from Amazon.com, an Internet retailer that sells books and other products. Interloc's systems administrator modified the server's procmail recipe so that, before delivering any message from Amazon.com to the recipient's mailbox, procmail would copy the message and place the copy in a separate mailbox that Councilman could access. Thus, procmail would intercept and copy all incoming messages from Amazon.com before they were delivered to the recipient's mailbox, and therefore, before the intended recipient could read the message. This diversion intercepted thousands of messages, and Councilman and other Interloc employees routinely read the e-mail messages sent to Interloc subscribers in the hope of gaining a commercial advantage. * * *

On July 11, 2001, a grand jury returned a two-count indictment against Councilman. Count One charged him under 18 U.S.C. § 371, the general federal criminal conspiracy statute, for conspiracy to violate the Wiretap Act, 18 U.S.C. § 2511, by intercepting electronic communications, disclosing their contents, using their contents, and causing a person providing an electronic communications service to divulge the communications' contents to persons other than the addressees. The object of the conspiracy was to exploit the content of e-mail from Amazon.com to dealers in order to develop a list of books, learn about competitors, and attain a commercial advantage for Interloc and its parent company. [Councilman moved to dismiss the indictment. The district court granted the motion, which a divided panel of this court affirmed. The United States appeals.] * * *

Because this is an appeal of an order dismissing an indictment on "purely legal" grounds, our review is de novo, United States v. Lopez–Lopez, 282 F.3d 1, 9 (1st Cir. 2002), and we assume the truth of the facts alleged in the indictment, see Bank of Nova Scotia v. United States, 487 U.S. 250, 261 (1988). * * *

The Wiretap Act of 1968 specified, inter alia, the conditions under which law enforcement officers could intercept wire communications, and the penalties for unauthorized private interceptions of wire communications. As amended by the Electronic Communications Privacy Act of 1986, Pub. L. No. 99–508, 100 Stat. 1848 ("ECPA"), the Act makes it an offense to "intentionally intercept[], endeavor[] to intercept, or procure[] any other person to intercept or endeavor to intercept, any wire, oral, or electronic communication." 18 U.S.C. § 2511(1). Two terms are at issue here: "electronic communication" and "intercept."

Councilman contends that the e-mail messages he obtained were not, when procmail copied them, "electronic communications," and moreover the method by which they were copied was not "interception" under the Act. Because these contentions raise important questions of statutory construction with broad ramifications, we discuss in some detail the Act's text, structure, and legislative history. We conclude that Councilman's interpretation of the Wiretap Act is inconsistent with Congress's intent. * * *

We begin, as we must, with the statute's text. United States v. Rosa–Ortiz, 348 F.3d 33, 36 (1st Cir. 2003). As noted above, the statutory definition of "electronic communication" is broad and, taken alone, would appear to cover incoming e-mail messages while the messages are being processed by the MTA. * * *

As often happens under close scrutiny, the plain text is not so plain. The statute contains no explicit indication that Congress intended to exclude communications in transient storage from the definition of "electronic communication," and, hence, from the scope of the Wiretap Act. Councilman, without acknowledging it, looks beyond the face of the statute and makes an inferential leap. He infers that Congress intended to exclude communications in transient storage from the definition of "electronic communication," regardless of whether they are in the process of being delivered, simply because it did not include the term "electronic storage" in that definition. This inferential leap is not a plain text reading of the statute. * * *

The question, then, is whether Councilman's inferential leap, based on a canon of construction, is justified. The Russello maxim—which is simply a particular application of the classic principle expressio unius est exclusio alterius—assumes that Congress acts carefully and deliberately in including terms in one part of a statute and omitting them in another. [See Russello v. United States, 464 U.S. 16 (1983).]

The maxim upon which Councilman relies is most apt when Congress enacts a new, self-contained statute, and two provisions of that act, drafted with parallel language, differ in that one provision uses a term, but the other provision, where it would be equally sensible to use that term if Congress desired it to apply, conspicuously omits it. Under such conditions, the maxim's interpretive value is at its apex because the underlying inference of legislative intent is most plausible. See Field v. Mans, 516 U.S. 59 (1995) ("The more apparently deliberate the contrast, the stronger the inference, as applied, for example, to contrasting statutory sections originally enacted simultaneously in relevant respects.")

If the statute's language, structure, or circumstances of enactment differ from that idealized picture, the canon's force is diminished. For example, if the language of the two provisions at issue is not parallel, then Congress may not have envisioned that the two provisions would be closely compared in search of terms present in one and absent from the other. "The Russello presumption—that the presence of a phrase in one provision and its absence in another reveals Congress'[s] design—grows weaker with each difference in the formulation of the provisions under inspection." Similarly, where the history of the two provisions is complex, the canon may be a less reliable guide to Congressional intent. For example, if the first provision was already part of the law, whereas the second is entirely new, Congress may have paid less attention to subtle differences between the two.

In attempting to determine whether Congress intended the term "electronic communication" to exclude communications in momentary storage, the expressio unius maxim is not particularly helpful. Put differently, though it may be "presumed that Congress acts intentionally and purposely in the disparate inclusion or exclusion," Russello, 464 U.S. at 23, that presumption may be rebutted. That is the case here.

First, the definitions of "wire communication" and "electronic communication" in the Wiretap Act are not parallel. The former is defined in a single lengthy clause that specifies multiple independent criteria, with the electronic storage clause tacked onto the end. The revised definition hews closely to its original definition in the 1968 Wiretap Act; the ECPA simply amended that definition by replacing the phrase "communication" with "aural transfer," making certain modifications not relevant here, and, of course, adding the clause "and such term includes any electronic storage of such communication." See ECPA § 101(a)(1)(D), 100 Stat. at 1848. By contrast, "electronic communication" is first defined in broad terms which are narrowed by four specific exclusions enumerated in separate subparagraphs. See 18 U.S.C. § 2510(12). The definition was drafted from scratch as part of the ECPA. ECPA § 101(a)(6), 100 Stat. at 1848–49.

Second, any expressio unius inference that can be drawn from the presence of the electronic storage clause in one definition and its absence from another is in tension with a much more compelling—and directly contrary—expressio unius inference drawn from the same statutory provisions: Congress knew how to, and in fact did, explicitly exclude four specific categories of communications from the broad definition of "electronic communication." See ECPA § 101(a)(6)(C). Yet Congress never added the exclusion urged by Councilman: "any electronic communication in electronic storage." This interpretative principle then applies: "Where Congress explicitly enumerates certain exceptions to a general prohibition, additional exceptions are not to be implied, in the absence of evidence of a contrary legislative intent." TRW v. Andrews, 534 U.S. 19, 28 (2001) (quotation marks and citation omitted). * * *

In short, the ECPA's plain text does not clearly state whether a communication is still an "electronic communication" within the scope of the Wiretap Act when it is in electronic storage during transmission. Applying canons of construction does not resolve the question. Given this continuing ambiguity, we turn to the legislative history. * * *

By the early 1980s, the advent of electronic communications, principally e-mail, suggested to many that the Wiretap Act needed revision. To update the Act, Senator Patrick Leahy introduced the Electronic Communications Privacy Act of 1985. See S. 1667, 99th Cong. (1985), reprinted in 131 Cong. Rec. S11,795 (Sept. 19, 1985). That bill would have amended the Act by striking out the existing definition of "wire communication," substituting the phrase "electronic communication" for "wire communication" throughout the Act, and subsuming wire communications within the newly-defined term "electronic communication." See id. § 101.

Shortly after the bill was introduced, the Congressional Office of Technology Assessment released a long-awaited study of the privacy implications of electronic surveillance. See Office of Technology Assessment, Federal Government Information Technology: Electronic Surveillance and Civil Liberties, available at http://www.wws.princeton.edu/ota/disk2/1985/8509_n.html (Oct. 1985) ("OTA Report"). The report identified the different points at which an e-mail message could be intercepted:

> There are at least five discrete stages at which an electronic mail message could be intercepted and its contents divulged to an unintended receiver: at the terminal or in the electronic files of the sender, while being communicated, in the electronic mailbox of the receiver, when printed into hardcopy, and when retained in the files of the electronic mail company for administrative purposes. Existing law offers little protection.

Id. at 48. It emphasized that "interception of electronic mail at any stage involves a high level of intrusiveness and a significant threat to civil liberties." Id. at 50.

The Department of Justice ("DOJ") was the principal opponent of the original bill. * * * DOJ asked Congress to treat prospective surveillance of electronic communications differently from surveillance of wire communications in three specific respects that are related solely to law enforcement and are not relevant here. DOJ's willingness to extend some of the Wiretap Act's protections to e-mail did not, however, extend to "the time after a specific communication has been sent and while it is in the electronic mail firm's computers but has not been delivered, or has been delivered to the electronic mailbox but has not been received by the recipient." In such cases, DOJ suggested, the message should be treated like first-class mail, and law enforcement should be able to seize it with an ordinary search warrant. Id.

A new version of the bill was introduced to meet some, but not all, of DOJ's concerns. See Electronic Communications Privacy Act of 1986, S. 2575, 99th Cong. (1986). The new bill rejected DOJ's preferred solution and instead added electronic communications to the Wiretap Act's existing prohibitions on interception of wire communications. As the House report made clear, Congress intended to give the term "electronic communication" a broad definition:

> The term 'electronic communication' is intended to cover a broad range of communication activities * * *. As a rule, a communication is an electronic communication if it is neither carried by sound waves nor can fairly be characterized as one containing the human voice (carried in part by wire). Communications consisting solely of data, for example * * * would be electronic communications.

H.R. Rep. No. 99–647 (1986), at 35. By incorporating electronic communications into the wiretap act, the bill largely rejected DOJ's view that e-mail should receive no (or little) more protection than first class mail. See H.R. Rep. No. 99–647, at 22 (explaining why e-mail differs from regular mail). Nevertheless, because some of DOJ's specific concerns were addressed, DOJ acknowledged that "the bill has been substantially modified to accommodate our concerns" and supported it. Id. at 30–31. * * *

Responding to concerns raised in the OTA Report, Congress sought to ensure that the messages and by-product files that are left behind after transmission, as well as messages stored in a user's mailbox, are protected from unauthorized access. E-mail messages in the sender's and recipient's computers could be accessed by electronically "breaking into" those computers and retrieving the files. Before the ECPA, the victim of such an attack had few legal remedies for such an invasion. Furthermore, the e-mail messages retained on the service provider's computers after transmission—which, the report noted, are primarily retained for "billing purposes and as a convenience in case the customer loses the message"— could be accessed and possibly disclosed by the provider. Before the ECPA, it was not clear whether the user had the right to challenge such a disclosure. Id. Similar concerns applied to temporary financial records and personal data retained after transmission.

Given this background and the evidence in the legislative history that Congress responded to the OTA Report in refining the legislation, see, e.g., House Hearings at 42–73, it appears that Congress had in mind these types of pre- and post-transmission "temporary, intermediate storage of a wire or electronic communication incidental to the electronic transmission thereof," see 18 U.S.C. § 2510(17), when it established the definition of "electronic storage." Its aim was simply to protect such data. See infra Part II.C.1 (describing the Stored Communications Act). There is no indication that it meant to exclude the type of storage used during transmission from the scope of the Wiretap Act. * * *

The original version of the ECPA of 1986 included the definition of "electronic storage" as it reads today, but did not include electronic storage in the definition of "wire communication." 132 Cong. Rec. S7,991 (June 19, 1986). Neither Senator Leahy's floor statement upon introducing the bill nor the staff bill summary mentioned voice mail in the context of the Wiretap Act amendments. See id.; cf. H.R. Rep. No. 99–647, at 63 (mentioning voice mail in the context of Stored Communications Act). Voice mail had not, apparently, been a major subject of discussion in the context of the ECPA. * * *

If the addition of the electronic storage clause to the definition of "wire communication" was intended to remove electronic communications from the scope of the Wiretap Act for the brief instants during which they are in temporary storage en route to their destinations—which, as it turns out, are often the points where it is technologically easiest to intercept those communications—neither of the Senate co-sponsors saw fit to mention this to their colleagues, and no one, evidently, remarked upon it. No document or legislator ever suggested that the addition of the electronic storage clause to the definition of "wire communication" would take messages in electronic storage out of the definition of "electronic communication." * * *

In sum, the legislative history indicates that Congress included the electronic storage clause in the definition of "wire communication" provision for the sole reason that, without it, access to voicemail would have been regulated solely by the Stored Communications Act. Indeed, that is exactly what happened when Congress later removed the explicit reference to "electronic storage" from the definition of "wire communication" in the Uniting and Strengthening America by Providing Appropriate Tools Required to Intercept and Obstruct Terrorism (USA PATRIOT) Act, Pub. L. No. 107–56, tit. II, § 209(1)(A), 115 Stat. 272, 283 (2001). See Robert A. Pikowsky, An Overview of the Law of Electronic Surveillance Post September 11, 2001, 94 Law Libr. J. 601, 608 (2002) ("The USA PATRIOT Act amended the statutory scheme and unambiguously brought voicemail under the Stored Communications Act."). * * *

We conclude that the term "electronic communication" includes transient electronic storage that is intrinsic to the communication process for such communications. That conclusion is consistent with our precedent. See Blumofe v. Pharmatrak, Inc. (In re Pharmatrak Privacy Litig.), 329 F.3d 9, 21 (1st Cir. 2003) (a rigid "storage-transit dichotomy * * * may be less than apt to address current problems"); see also Hall v. EarthLink Network, Inc., 396 F.3d 500, 503 n.1 (2d Cir. 2005) (rejecting arguments that "communication over the Internet can only be electronic communication while it is in transit, not while it is in electronic storage"). Consequently, in this context we reject Councilman's proposed distinction between "in transit" and "in storage." * * *

Even though we conclude that the temporarily stored e-mail messages at issue here constitute electronic communications within the scope of the Wiretap Act, the statute also requires the conduct alleged in the indictment to be an "interception." 18 U.S.C. § 2511(1) (making it an offense to "intentionally intercept[], endeavor[] to intercept, or procure[] any other person to intercept or endeavor to intercept, any * * * electronic communication"). The term "intercept" is defined broadly as "the aural or other acquisition of the contents of any wire, electronic, or oral communication through the use of any electronic, mechanical, or other device." Id. § 2510(4).

Councilman's core argument on appeal is that because the messages at issue, when acquired, were in transient electronic storage, they were not "electronic communications" and, therefore, section 2511(1)'s prohibition on "interception" of any "electronic communication" did not apply. That is the argument that we have now rejected in holding that an e-mail message does not cease to be an "electronic communication" during the momentary intervals, intrinsic to the communication process, at which the message resides in transient electronic storage. See supra Part II. * * *

Councilman's appeal does not provide any other basis for finding that the acquisitions were not "interceptions" of "electronic communications." To be sure, Councilman does argue that "Congress intended 'intercept' to cover acquisitions 'contemporaneous with transmission.'" However, his entire argument on this point is based on the theory, as he writes in his brief, that "courts uniformly have understood 'electronic storage' to negate the 'contemporaneous with transmission' element of a Wiretap Act 'intercept,'" and therefore "an e-mail in 'electronic storage' * * * cannot by definition be acquired 'contemporaneous with transmission.'" That argument is simply a variation on, and entirely subsumed within, his primary argument concerning "storage"—the very argument that we have now rejected.

Consequently, this appeal does not implicate the question of whether the term "intercept" applies only to acquisitions that occur contemporaneously with the transmission of a message from sender to recipient or, instead, extends to an event that occurs after a message has crossed the finish line of transmission (whatever that point may be). * * *

That ends this aspect of the matter. Because the facts of this case and the arguments before us do not invite consideration of either the existence or the applicability of a contemporaneity or real-time requirement, we need not and do not plunge into that morass. * * *

Thus far we have considered only the Wiretap Act, not the Stored Communications Act, 18 U.S.C. §§ 2701–2712, because the indictment only alleged a violation of the former. Councilman argues that acquisition of electronic communications in temporary electronic storage is regulated by the Stored Communications Act. From this he infers that such acquisition is not regulated by the Wiretap Act, or that, at minimum, the potential overlap implicates the rule of lenity or other doctrines of "fair warning." Consequently, we must delve into the "complex, often convoluted" intersection of the Wiretap Act and Stored Communications Act. United States v. Smith, 155 F.3d 1051, 1055 (9th Cir. 1998). * * *

While drafting the ECPA's amendments to the Wiretap Act, Congress also recognized that, with the rise of remote computing operations and large databanks of stored electronic communications, threats to individual privacy extended well beyond the bounds of the Wiretap Act's prohibition against the "interception" of communications. These types of stored communications—including stored e-mail messages—were not protected by the Wiretap Act. Therefore, Congress concluded that "the information [in these communications] may be open to possible wrongful use and public disclosure by law enforcement authorities as well as unauthorized private parties." S. Rep. No. 99–541, at 3 (1986), reprinted in 1986 U.S.C.C.A.N. 3555, 3557.

Congress added Title II to the ECPA to halt these potential intrusions on individual privacy. This title, commonly referred to as the Stored Communications Act, established new punishments for accessing, without (or in excess of) authorization, an electronic communications service facility and thereby obtaining access to a wire or electronic communication in electronic storage. 18 U.S.C. § 2701 (a). Another provision bars electronic communications service providers from "divulging to any person or entity the contents of a communication while in electronic storage by that service." Id. § 2702(a)(1).

The privacy protections established by the Stored Communications Act were intended to apply to two categories of communications defined by the statutory term "electronic storage":

(A) any temporary, intermediate storage of a wire or electronic communication incidental to the electronic transmission thereof; and

(B) any storage of such communication by an electronic communication service for purposes of backup protection of such communication.

18 U.S.C. § 2510(17); id. § 2701(a) (incorporating Wiretap Act definitions into Stored Communications Act). The first category, which is relevant here, refers to temporary storage, such as when a message sits in an e-

mail user's mailbox after transmission but before the user has retrieved the message from the mail server.

Councilman's conduct may appear to fall under the Stored Communications Act's main criminal provision:

(a) Offense. Except as provided in subsection (c) of this section whoever—

(1) intentionally accesses without authorization a facility through which an electronic communication service is provided; or

(2) intentionally exceeds an authorization to access that facility;

and thereby obtains, alters, or prevents authorized access to a wire or electronic communication while it is in electronic storage in such system shall be punished * * *.

18 U.S.C. § 2701(a). At the same time, Councilman would arguably be exempted by the Stored Communications Act's provider exception: "Subsection (a) of this section does not apply with respect to conduct authorized (1) by the person or entity providing a wire or electronic communications service." Id. § 2701(c). Under this theory, § 2701(c)(1) establishes virtually complete immunity for a service provider that "obtains, alters, or prevents authorized access to" e-mail that is "in electronic storage" in its system. See Fraser, 352 F.3d at 115 ("We read § 2701(c) literally to except from Title II's protection all searches by communications service providers."). The district court surmised that § 2701(a) would have covered Councilman's conduct but that § 2701(c)(1) exempted him. Councilman, 245 F. Supp. 2d at 320.

A second provision of the Stored Communications Act prohibits "a person or entity providing an electronic communication service to the public [from] knowingly divulging to any person or entity the contents of a communication while in electronic storage by that service." 18 U.S.C. § 2702(a)(1). Yet this provision, too, has service provider exceptions, permitting a provider to divulge an electronic communication "to a person employed or authorized or whose facilities are used to forward such communication to its destination," id. § 2702(b)(4), or "as may be necessarily incident to the rendition of the service or to the protection of the rights or property of the provider of that service," id. § 2702(b)(5). We assume, dubitante, that one or both of these provisions would exempt Councilman under § 2702.

On this premise, he argues that if he is not liable under the Stored Communications Act, then he cannot be liable under the Wiretap Act either. Since Congress enacted the ECPA as a package, he says, it did not intend to lay traps in the overlap between the two titles. If conduct that potentially falls under both titles is exempt from one of them, then that exemption provides a "safe harbor" and the conduct does not violate the other title either.

We find this argument unpersuasive. In general, if two statutes cover the same conduct, the government may charge a violation of either. * * *

We therefore conclude that the term "electronic communication" includes transient electronic storage that is intrinsic to the communication process, and hence that interception of an e-mail message in such storage is an offense under the Wiretap Act. * * *

NOTE: *CARNIVORE—DCS1000*

DCS1000, once known as "Carnivore," was a special government software email monitoring capability, no longer in use at the Federal Bureau of Investigation. A "packet sniffer," DCS1000/Carnivore analyzed "data flowing through computer networks, allowing law enforcement officials to monitor e-mail messages of criminal suspects." *Judicial Watch, Inc. v. Federal Bureau of Investigation*, 190 F. Supp. 2d 29 (D.D.C. 2002). "Carnivore" was controversial because "of the potential Fourth Amendment search and seizure concerns," id. at 29, raised by tapping into the internet with the aid of internet service providers to read emails and other online communications transmitted by suspected criminals, terrorists and spies. The FBI now uses commercially available internet surveillance technology, instead of DCS1000/Carnivore. For a history of DCS1000/Carnivore and attempts by public interest lawyers and civil libertarians to find out more about it, see the website of the Electronic Privacy Information Center (EPIC), http://www.epic.org/privacy/carnivore/foia_documents.html.

3. INTERCEPTING SATELLITE TELEVISION BROADCASTS

DIRECTV, INC. v. PEPE

431 F.3d 162 (3d Cir. 2005).

Van Antwerpen, Circuit Judge * * *

These cases arise as part of a program of litigation undertaken by DIRECTV to deter the illegal interception of the company's encrypted satellite broadcasts. * * *

DIRECTV * * * asserted first that the "defendants have received and/or assisted others in receiving DIRECTV's satellite transmissions of television programming without authorization, in violation of 47 U.S.C. § 605(a) [§ 705 of the Communications Act]." App. 70 & 83. Section 605 provides a civil remedy for the unauthorized use or publication of various wire or radio communications, including encrypted satellite broadcasts. See 47 U.S.C. § 605. Second, DIRECTV claimed that "by using Pirate Access Devices to decrypt and view DIRECTV's satellite transmissions of television programming, defendants intentionally intercepted, endeavored to intercept, or procured other persons to intercept or endeavor to intercept, DIRECTV's satellite transmission of television programming, in violation of 18 U.S.C. § 2511(1)(a)." § 2511(1)(a) prohibits the intentional and unauthorized interception of "electronic communication[s]." Third, DIRECTV alleged that "defendants possessed and used Pirate Access Devices, knowing or having reason to know that the design of such devices render then primarily useful for the purpose of surreptitious interception of DIRECTV's satellite transmissions of television programming, and that such devices, or any component thereof, have been or will be sent through the mail or transported via interstate or foreign commerce, in violation of 18 U.S.C. § 2512(1)(b)." App. 72 & 85. Section 2512(1)(b) criminalizes the manufacture, assembly, possession, or sale of so-called "Pirate Access Devices" in interstate or foreign commerce. With each claim, DIRECTV alleged that it suffered lost revenue, breach of its security and accounting systems, infringement of its proprietary information and trade secrets, and interference with business relations. On these bases, it sought damages, attorneys fees, costs, and injunctive relief. * * *

The District Court concluded that the legislative history of the ECPA, case law, and a comparison of the damages provisions of 47 U.S.C. § 605 and 18 U.S.C. § 2520, which admittedly overlap, all indicate that private claims cannot arise under § 2511(1)(a). In the view of the District Court, 47 U.S.C. § 605, provided DIRECTV's sole remedy. We find that the plain language of § 2511 compels the opposite result, a conclusion that is supported—not contradicted, as the District Court found—by the legislative history. Accordingly, we are constrained to reverse. * * *

As a threshold matter, we must decide whether DIRECTV's satellite television transmissions are "electronic communications" within the meaning of the ECPA. We hold that they are. The ECPA defines "electronic communication" as "any transfer of signs, signals, writing, images, sounds, data, or intelligence of any nature transmitted in whole or in part by a wire, radio, electromagnetic, photoelectronic or photooptical system that affects interstate or foreign commerce." 18 U.S.C. § 2510(12). A television broadcast is self-evidently a "transfer of * * * signals," including, at the very least, images and sounds. The means of transmission is by radio wave from the satellite to a ground-based antenna. We conclude, therefore, that DIRECTV's satellite broadcasts are "electronic communications" as defined by the ECPA. Where our sister courts of appeals have considered the issue, they have reached the same conclusion. * * *

The plain language of § 2511(1)(a) and § 2520(a) compels us to conclude that private parties can bring a cause of action for damages and injunctive relief where aggrieved by a defendant's violation of § 2511(1)(a). Where we are called upon to interpret a statute, we must always begin with its plain language. Robinson v. Shell Oil Co., 519 U.S. 337, 340 (1997). Where "the statutory language is unambiguous and 'the statutory scheme is coherent and consistent,'" we cannot look further. Id. (quoting United States v. Ron Pair Enters., Inc., 489 U.S. 235, 240 (1989)).

Section 2511 provides in relevant part that "except as otherwise specifically provided in this chapter any person who * * * intentionally intercepts * * * any * * * electronic communication" is subject to criminal penalties or civil suit by the federal government. 18 U.S.C. § 2511(1)(a). Appearing later in the same chapter, § 2520 expressly authorizes private suits by "any person whose * * * electronic communication is intercepted * * * in violation of this chapter." 18 U.S.C. § 2520(a). Both sections reference the interception of electronic communications. The linguistic interlock between the two provisions could not be tighter, nor more obviously deliberate: § 2511(1)(a) renders unlawful the unauthorized interception of electronic communications, including encrypted satellite television broadcasts, while § 2520(a) authorizes private suit against those who have engaged in such activities.

To illustrate the point, we observe that the ECPA excepts a number of activities from its reach; however, it nowhere provides an exception for the interception of electronic communications in the form of encrypted satellite television broadcasts. For example, another subsection of § 2511 excludes interception of certain unencrypted satellite transmissions from its scope, but is silent on encrypted satellite television broadcasts:

> Conduct otherwise an offense under this subsection that consists of or relates to the interception of a satellite transmission that is not encrypted or scrambled and that is transmitted—
>
> > (i) to a broadcasting station for purposes of retransmission to the general public; or
> >
> > (ii) as an audio subcarrier intended for redistribution to facilities open to the public, but not including data transmissions or telephone calls,
>
> is not an offense under this subsection unless the conduct is for the purposes of direct or indirect commercial advantage or private financial gain.

18 U.S.C. § 2511(4)(b). The clear implication, for present purposes, is that encrypted satellite transmissions are not excepted from § 2511. In § 2511(4)(b), Congress made express provision for "conduct otherwise an offense" under § 2511 relating to unencrypted, non-scrambled satellite transmissions to except it out of the general rule that such interceptions would indeed violate § 2511. See Lande, 968 F.2d at 909–10 (holding that § 2511(1) bars unauthorized interception of encrypted satellite television broadcasts because "no exception is 'specifically provided' for the unauthorized viewing of [such] signals").

Furthermore, as DIRECTV correctly observes, § 2511(1)(a) cannot be read to exclude the interception of encrypted satellite television broadcasts from its reach without rendering § 2511(4)(b) meaningless. * * * Here, Congress included § 2511(4)(b) to provide a specific exception for the interception of certain unencrypted satellite transmissions where the purpose is neither commercial nor for private financial gain. To read § 2511(1)(a) as excluding from its reach the interception of satellite transmissions in general, encrypted or not, would be to obviate the need for a particularized exception for unencrypted satellite transmissions.

Our conclusion that § 2511(1)(a) supports a civil claim comports with that of every other court of appeals to have considered the question. See, e.g., DIRECTV Inc. v. Robson, 420 F.3d 532, 537 (5th Cir. 2005); Nicholas, 403 F.3d at 226. Having concluded that § 2511(1)(a) renders the interception of encrypted satellite television broadcasts unlawful, it is plain that § 2520(a), as discussed above, authorizes private suit for such activity: "any person whose * * * electronic communication is intercepted * * * in violation of this chapter may in a civil action recover from the person or entity * * * which engaged in that violation such relief as may be appropriate." * * *

Relying on the statute's legislative history, case law, and a comparison of the damages provisions in the ECPA and the Communications Act, the District Court concluded that 47 U.S.C. § 605 supplants a private cause of action under the ECPA's provision in 18 U.S.C. § 2511(1)(a) for the interception of encrypted satellite television broadcasts. * * * [T]hese considerations do not overcome the plain language of the statute, which controls our analysis. * * *

In refusing to find a cause of action under § 2511(1)(a), the District Court also relied on the pro-privacy policy considerations underlying the ECPA as expressed in our opinion in Bartnicki v. Vopper, 200 F.3d 109, 122 (3d Cir. 1999). In adjudicating the First Amendment questions at issue in Bartnicki, we noted that § 2511(1) protected victims from "the surreptitious interception of private communications" and "the dissemination of private information so obtained." 200 F.3d at 122. In this case the District Court took our language in Bartnicki to mean that § 2511(1) would apply only to wrongs against private persons, and not piracy against a commercial service such as DIRECTV.

Again, the plain language of the ECPA trumps other considerations, and compels an opposite conclusion. Section 2520(a) provides that "any person whose * * * electronic communication is intercepted * * * "can recover for violations of the ECPA. In turn, § 2510(6) defines "person" to include "any individual, partnership, association, joint stock company, trust, or corporation." As a corporation, DIRECTV is a "person" within the meaning of the ECPA, and can therefore bring suit under it. * * *

For the foregoing reasons, we conclude that Congress has made a private right of action available under §§ 2511(1)(a) and 2520 of the ECPA for the unauthorized interception of encrypted satellite television broadcasts. Accordingly, we reverse the District Court's Orders in both cases to the extent that they deny DIRECTV's claims under 18 U.S.C. §§ 2511(1)(a) and 2520(a), and remand both cases for further proceedings consistent with this opinion.

NOTE: VOICE OVER *IP*, WIRETAPPING AND *CALEA*

Are VoIP services subject to "wiretap" interception and ECPA? "VoIP" (voice over Internet protocol) refers to facilities used to deliver voice information over the Internet. VoIP involves transmitting voice information in digital form in discrete packets. Traditional telephony employs the circuitry of a public switched telephone network. A major advantage of VoIP and Internet telephony is that it avoids the tolls charged by ordinary telephone service. See Search VoIP.com, http://searchvoip.techtarget.com/sDefinition/. Law enforcement officials prefer that the principles of CALEA are applied to VoIP new technologies, requiring VoIP service providers to make their networks interceptible. See http://www.fcc.gov/voip/.

In 2004 the American Civil Liberties Union wrote a letter to the Senate Commerce, Science and Transportation Committee, expressing concerns about S. 2281, the VOIP Regulatory Freedom Act of 2004, and opposing interpretations of the law which might extend the Communications Assistance to Law Enforcement Act (CALEA) to voice over Internet protocol (VoIP) applications.

The ACLU argued that: (1) "ECPA allows law enforcement to obtain surveillance warrants for the entire range of IP applications, making the extension of CALEA to VoIP unnecessary. ECPA requires that all communications providers, including those offering VoIP, comply with a lawful wiretap order and the communications industry has fully complied with that legal requirement. Furthermore, law enforcement has provided no evidence to suggest that wiretapping existing, non-CALEA-compliant IP networks has been more difficult than wiretapping CALEA-compliant public switched telephone networks ("PSTN"). Thus, there is no compelling reason to extend CALEA to VoIP."; that (2) "[E]xtending CALEA to the Internet would endanger the privacy of every American. Building in a "back-door" to provide easy access for law enforcement also creates a loophole that can be exploited by hackers, criminals and terrorists. Furthermore, over the last decade, law enforcement has used its ability to set standards to push for increasing amounts of information under more limited trap and trace orders that are not supposed to contain the content of calls. As the line between content and location information blurs with greater Internet communications, this problem will only grow worse."; and that (3) "[A]pplying CALEA to the Internet presents a possibly insurmountable technical nightmare. Telephone networks run on the same PSTN standard regardless of carrier; whereas, different Internet service providers employ different network designs. This non-standard architecture would make application of CALEA to VoIP an expensive proposition and perhaps technically impossible. Finally, retrofitting VoIP networks with interception capability would be cost prohibitive for VoIP service providers."

In 2005 the FCC announced that facilities-based providers and "interconnected" VoIP service providers who enabled calls to public switched telephone networks would be subject to CALEA. Providers were expected to be in compliance with CALEA by May 2007.

FCC, LAW ENFORCEMENT ACCESS TO BROADBAND AND VoIP SERVICE PROVIDERS

May 3, 2006.

The Federal Communications Commission today adopted a Second Report and Order and Memorandum Opinion and Order (Order) that addresses several issues regarding implementation of the Communications

Assistance for Law Enforcement Act (CALEA), enacted in 1994. The primary goal of the Order is to ensure that Law Enforcement Agencies (LEAs) have all of the resources that CALEA authorizes to combat crime and support homeland security, particularly with regard to facilities-based broadband Internet access providers and interconnected voice over Internet protocol (VOIP) providers. The Order balances the needs of Law Enforcement with the competing aims of encouraging the development of new communications services and technologies and protecting customer privacy.

The current CALEA proceeding was initiated in response to a Joint Petition filed by the Department of Justice, Federal Bureau of Investigation, and Drug Enforcement Administration in March 2004. These parties asked the Commission to address several issues so that industry and Law Enforcement would have clear guidance as CALEA implementation moves forward. The First Report and Order in this proceeding concluded that facilities-based broadband Internet access and interconnected VOIP providers were covered by CALEA. This Order addresses remaining issues raised in this proceeding and provides certainty that will help achieve CALEA compliance, particularly for packet-mode technologies.

First, the Order affirms that the CALEA compliance deadline for facilities-based broadband Internet access and interconnected VoIP services will be May 14, 2007, as established by the First Report and Order in this proceeding. The Order concludes that this deadline gives providers of these services sufficient time to develop compliance solutions, and notes that standards developments for these services are already well underway. * * *

Seventh, the Order concludes that carriers are responsible for CALEA development and implementation costs for post-January 1, 1995 equipment and facilities, and declines to adopt a national surcharge to recover CALEA costs. The Order finds that it would not serve the public interest to implement a national surcharge because such a mechanism would increase the administrative burden placed upon the carriers and provide little incentive for them to minimize their costs. * * *

NOTE: *AOL SEARCH QUERY DISCLOSURE CASE*

Plaintiffs alleged an ECPA violation in a 2010 case against AOL. What is the arguable ECPA violation where the facts are as follows? AOL is an Internet Service Provider that allows its members to conduct Internet searches by entering keyword search queries. According to Plaintiffs, AOL collected, over the course of a three-month period, the search queries of over 650,000 of its members without their knowledge, and assembled the data into a database. In late July 2006, AOL published this database on the Internet, allegedly rendering members' private and personal information available to the general public for ten days. AOL acknowledges that such a disclosure occurred, but claims that the data was anonymous. In addition, AOL asserts that it took immediate corrective action and that Plaintiffs did not suffer any injury as a result of the disclosure. See Doe v. AOL LLC., 2010 WL 431890 (N.D.Cal.).

Note: Rok Lampe, Does Wiretapping Violate a Human Right? The Van Hulst Case

A Human Rights Committee was formed pursuant to the International Covenant on Civil and Political Rights. The Committee hears complaints brought by nations or individuals claiming human rights violations. One of the most notable privacy-related cases brought to the Human Rights Committee under a Protocol of the Covenant concerned the scope of data surveillance. The author (plaintiff) of the communication (complaint) was Antonius Cornelis Van Hulst, a Dutch citizen. Mr. Van Hulst claimed to be a victim of violations by the Netherlands of articles 17 (right to privacy) and 14 (right to a fair trial) of the Covenant. Specifically, he maintained that, during a preliminary inquiry against Mr. A.T.M.M., the author's lawyer, telephone conversations between A.T.M.M. and the author were intercepted and recorded. On the basis of the information obtained by this phone surveillance, a preliminary inquiry was opened against Van Hulst himself, and the tapping of his own telephone line was wrongly authorized.

HUMAN RIGHTS COMMITTEE, COMMUNICATION NO 903/1999: NETHERLANDS. 15/11/2004

CCPR/C/82/D/903/1999.

The facts as submitted by the author * * *

2.2   By judgment of 4 September 1990, the District Court of 's-Hertogenbosch (Netherlands) convicted the author of the complaint of participation in a criminal organization, persistent acquisition of property without intent to pay, fraud and attempted fraud, extortion, forgery and handling stolen goods, and sentenced him to six years' imprisonment.

2.3   During the criminal proceedings, counsel for the author contended that the public prosecutor's case should not be admitted, because the prosecution's case contained a number of reports on telephone calls between the author and his lawyer, A.T.M.M, which it was unlawful to receive in evidence. Counsel argued that, in accordance with article 125h, paragraph 2, read in conjunction with Section 218, of the Code of Criminal Procedure, the evidence obtained unlawfully should have been discarded.

2.4   Although the District Court agreed with the author that the telephone calls between him and A.T.M.M., could not be used as evidence, insofar as the latter acted as the author's lawyer and not as a suspect, it rejected the author's challenge to the prosecution's case, noting that the prosecutor had not relied on the contested telephone conversations in establishing the author's guilt. While the Court ordered their removal from the evidence, it admitted and used as evidence other telephone conversations, which had been intercepted and recorded in the context of the preliminary inquiry against A.T.M.M., in accordance with Section

125g of the Code of Criminal Procedure, and which did not concern the lawyer-client relationship with the author.

2.5 On appeal, the author's defence counsel argued that not all records of the tapped telephone calls, which should have been destroyed pursuant to Section 125h, paragraph 2, had in fact been destroyed. However, by judgment of 10 April 1992, the's-Hertogenbosch [sic] Court of Appeal rejected this defence, stating that the author's request to examine whether the reports in question had been destroyed would be irrelevant, "as their absence from the case file would provide no certainty about [their destruction]." The Court convicted the author of persistent acquisition of property without intent to pay, forgery, and resort to physical threats, without making use of the telephone records, and sentenced him to five years' imprisonment.

2.6 Before the Supreme Court, the author's defence counsel stated that the Court of Appeal had not responded to his defence that the records of the telephone conversations with his lawyer had been illegally obtained without having subsequently been destroyed. The Supreme Court rejected this argument and, by decision of 30 November 1993, for different reasons, it partially quashed the judgment of the Court of Appeal on two counts, as well as the sentence, and referred the matter back to the Arnhem Court of Appeal.

2.7 On 24 March 1995, the Arnhem Court of Appeal acquitted the author on one count and sentenced him to three years' imprisonment on the other counts. In his cassation appeal against this judgment, the author contended that his defence relating to the tapped telephone calls had still not been responded to. On 16 April 1996, the Supreme Court dismissed the appeal, without reasons, referring to Section 101a of the Judiciary Act.

*   *   *

The complaint

3.1 The author claims that the Supreme Court's dismissal, by mere reference to Section 101a of the Judiciary Act, of his defence relating to the tapped telephone calls, as well as the admission as evidence and use of reports on tapped telephone calls between him and his lawyer, violated his rights under article 14 (procedural guarantees) of the Covenant, and that the interference with his right to confidential communication with his lawyer was unlawful and arbitrary, in violation of article 17 of the Covenant.

*   *   *

3.6 With regard to his claim under article 17, the author submits that, as a client of Mr. A.T.M.M., he should have been accorded judicial protection from the wire tapping and recording of his telephone conversations with his lawyer, since he could not know that the latter was a suspect in criminal investigations. The right to consult a lawyer of one's own choice is undermined if the protection of confidentiality depends on whether a lawyer is himself a criminal suspect or not.

3.7 The author submits that his right, under article 17, not to be subjected to arbitrary or unlawful interference with his privacy includes a right to confidential communication with his lawyer, which can only be restricted

(a) in accordance with the law;

(b) for a legitimate purpose; and

(c) if the interference is proportionate to the aim pursued.

3.8 Although the author concedes that combating crime is a legitimate purpose, he challenges the Supreme Court's jurisprudence that Section 125h, paragraph 2, of the Code of Criminal Procedure, while requiring the destruction of reports on tapped telephone calls involving a person entitled to decline to give evidence, does not preclude that cognizance may be taken of information which falls within the scope of Section 218 of the Code of Criminal Procedure, as it is not clear in advance whether the conversation involves a person bound by law to observe confidentiality. Rather, Section 125h, paragraph 2, should be read to forbid strictly the tapping of telephone connections of a lawyer/suspect, "as all confidential conversations must immediately be destroyed." Otherwise information could be gathered by means of interception and recording, which could normally not be obtained through the statements of witnesses or suspects. The author adds that the tapping of telephone calls between him and his lawyer was a disproportionate measure.

The State party's observations on admissibility and merits

4.1 In its observations dated 23 April 2003, the State party, while not contesting the admissibility of the communication, argues that neither the Supreme Court's reference to Section 101a of the Judiciary Act, nor the admission as evidence of tapped telephone conversations between the author and Mr. A.T.M.M., violated the author's right to a fair trial under article 14, and that the interference with his privacy and correspondence was neither unlawful nor arbitrary.

* * *

4.5 As to the admission as evidence of certain recorded telephone conversations between the author and Mr. A.T.M.M., the State party submits that it is generally for the national courts, and not for the Committee, to assess the evidence before them, unless there are clear indications of a violation of article 14. For the State party, the proceedings as a whole must be considered fair because: (a) the District Court only admitted recordings of conversations between the author and his lawyer, insofar as they related to the latter's involvement in the commission of a criminal offence, and made it clear that neither the public prosecutor nor the Court itself based their findings on protected lawyer-client conversations; (b) no transcripts of the recordings were made or introduced in the case file, the recordings merely having been mentioned at trial, [. . .]; (c) the reliability of the evidence was never disputed by the author, who merely complained that the information should have been erased; and (d) because the case file indicates that the author's conviction was not based on tapped conversations in which Mr. A.T.M.M. acted as a lawyer rather than a suspect.

4.6 Regarding the author's claim under article 17, the State party concedes that telephone calls made from or to a law firm may be covered by the notions of "privacy" or "correspondence" and that the interception of the author's telephone calls constituted "interference" within the meaning of this provision. By reference to the Committee's General Comment 16, it denies that this interference was unlawful or arbitrary within the meaning of article 17, which only prohibits interference not envisaged by law ("unlawful"), and which itself must comply with the provisions, aims and objectives of the Covenant, or which is not reasonable in the in the particular circumstances ("arbitrary").

4.7 The State party argues that the applicable law at the time, i.e. Sections 125 litera f to h of the Code of Criminal Procedure, did not forbid the tapping of telephone conversations with persons bound by law to secrecy. The legislator, when enacting these provisions in 1971, did not indicate that they should not apply to persons bound by law to secrecy, within the meaning of Section 218 of the Code of Criminal Procedure. Moreover, the applicable law, which then included detailed Guidelines for the Examination of Telephone Conversations, was sufficiently precise to authorize interference with the right to privacy, setting out procedural safeguards against abuse of power, such as the requirement of a judicial authorization of telephone taps and provision for the preparation and, in certain cases, destruction of official records on any interception.

4.8 The State party argues that the interference with the author's right to privacy pursued a legitimate purpose (combating crime) and was proportionate, as the District Court ensured that the tapped conversations, in which Mr. A.T.M.M. acted as the author's lawyer, rather than a suspect of criminal offences, were not taken into account in the criminal proceedings against the author. As for the conversations which were intercepted because A.T.M.M. was a suspect, thus not involving professional communication between a lawyer and his client, the State party argues that it is unreasonable to expect total impunity for the author and A.T.M.M. on the mere basis that the latter is also a lawyer.

* * *

Issues and proceedings before the Committee

Consideration of admissibility

* * *

6.7 The Committee considers that the author has substantiated, for purposes of admissibility, that the interception of telephone conversations between him and his lawyer, as well as the State party's failure to destroy the recordings of certain tapped calls, may raise issues under article 17 of the Covenant. It therefore concludes that the communication is admissible insofar as it raises issues under article 17.

Consideration of the merits

7.1 The Human Rights Committee has considered the present communication in the light of all the information made available to it by the parties, as provided in article 5, paragraph 1, of the Optional Protocol.

7.2 The issue before the Committee is whether the interception and recording of the author's telephone calls with Mr. A.T.M.M. constituted an unlawful or arbitrary interference with his privacy, in violation of article 17 of the Covenant.

7.3 The Committee recalls that, in order to be permissible under article 17, any interference with the right to privacy must cumulatively meet several conditions set out in paragraph 1, i.e.

— it must be provided for by law,

— be in accordance with the provisions, aims and objectives of the Covenant and

— be reasonable in the particular circumstances of the case.

7.4 The Committee notes that Section 125g of the Dutch Code of Criminal Procedure authorizes the investigating judge to order, during the preliminary judicial investigation, the interception or recording of data traffic, in which the suspect is believed to be taking part, provided that this is strictly required in the interests of the investigation and relates to an offence for which pre-trial detention may be imposed. The author has not contested that the competent authorities acted in accordance with the requirements of this provision. The Committee is therefore satisfied that the interference with his telephonic conversations with Mr. A.T.M.M. was lawful within the meaning of article 17, paragraph 1, of the Covenant.

7.5 One other question which arises is whether the State party was required by Section 125h, paragraph 2, read in conjunction with Section 218 of the Code of Criminal Procedure, to discard and destroy any information obtained as a result of the interception and recording of the author's conversations with Mr. A.T.M.M., insofar as the latter acted as his lawyer and as such was subject to professional secrecy. The Committee notes, in this regard, that the author challenges the Supreme Court's jurisprudence that cognizance may be taken of tapped telephonic conversations involving a person entitled to decline evidence, even though Section 125h, paragraph 2, provides that the reports on such conversations must be destroyed. The Committee considers that an interference is not "unlawful", within the meaning of article 17, paragraph 1, if it complies with the relevant domestic law, as interpreted by the national courts.

7.6 Finally, the Committee must consider whether the interference with the author's telephonic conversations with Mr. A.T.M.M. was arbitrary or reasonable in the circumstances of the case. The Committee recalls its jurisprudence that the requirement of reasonableness implies that any interference with privacy must be proportionate to the end sought, and must be necessary in the circumstances of any given case (Communication

No. 488/1992, Toonen v. Australia, at para. 8.3.). The Committee has noted the author's argument that clients can no longer rely on the confidentiality of communication with their lawyer, if there is a risk that the content of such communication may be intercepted and used against them, depending on whether or not their lawyer is suspected of having committed a criminal offence, and irrespective of whether this is known to the client. While acknowledging the importance of protecting the confidentiality of communication, in particular that relating to communication between lawyer and client, the Committee must also weigh the need for States parties to take effective measures for the prevention and investigation of criminal offences.

7.7   The Committee recalls that the relevant legislation authorizing interference with one's communications must specify in detail the precise circumstances in which such interference may be permitted and that the decision to allow such interference can only be taken by the authority designated by law, on a case-by-case basis (General Comment 16 [32], at para. 8.). It notes that the procedural and substantive requirements for the interception of telephone calls are clearly defined in Section 125g of the Dutch Code of Criminal Procedure and in the Guidelines for the Examination of Telephone Conversations of 2 July 1984. Both require interceptions to be based on a written authorization by the investigating judge.

7.8   The Committee considers that the interception and recording of the author's telephone calls with A.T.M.M. did not disproportionately affect his right to communicate with his lawyer in conditions ensuring full respect for the confidentiality of the communications between them, as the District Court distinguished between tapped conversations in which A.T.M.M. participated as the author's lawyer, and ordering their removal from the evidence, and other conversations, which were admitted as evidence because they were intercepted in the context of the preliminary inquiry against A.T.M.M. Although the author contested that the State party accurately made this distinction, he has failed to substantiate this challenge.

7.9   Insofar as the author claims that the reports of the tapped conversations between him and his lawyer should have been destroyed immediately, the Committee notes the State party's uncontested argument that the records of the tapped conversations were kept intact in their entirety, separately from the case file, for possible inspection by the defence. As the right to privacy implies that every individual should have the right to request rectification or elimination of incorrect personal data in files controlled by public authorities (Ibid., at para. 10.), the Committee considers that the separate storage of the recordings of the author's tapped conversations with Mr. A.T.M.M. cannot be regarded as unreasonable for purposes of article 17 of the Covenant.

7.10   In the light of the foregoing, the Committee concludes that the interference with the author's privacy in regard to his telephone conversations with A.T.M.M. was proportionate and necessary to achieve the legitimate purpose of combating crime, and therefore reasonable in the particular circumstances of the case, and that there was accordingly no violation of article 17 of the Covenant.

7.11   The Human Rights Committee, acting under article 5, paragraph 4, of the Optional Protocol, is of the view that the facts before it do not disclose any violation of article 17 of the Covenant.

B.   THE ELECTRONIC COMMUNICATIONS PRIVACY ACT OF 1986 (ECPA), TITLE II, THE STORED ELECTRONIC INFORMATION ("STORED COMMUNICATIONS") ACT

1.   ACCESS TO STORED EMAIL, CIVIL LIABILITY

JENNINGS v. JENNINGS

___ S.E.2d ___, 2010 WL 2813307 (S.C.App. 2010).

On June 21, 2006, Husband's wife, Gail Jennings (Wife), discovered a card for flowers in her car. Suspecting the flowers were not for her, Wife questioned Husband, who had recently borrowed her car, about the card. To Wife's dismay, Husband informed Wife that he had bought the flowers for another woman, with whom he had fallen in love. Although Husband refused to tell Wife the woman's full name, he mentioned that he had been corresponding with her via email at his office. That same day, the couple separated.

A few days later, Wife's daughter-in-law, Holly Broome (Broome), visited Wife at her home. Wife, who was extremely upset, told Broome about the separation and the conversation she had had with Husband. The next day, Broome, who had previously worked for Husband, logged onto Husband's Yahoo account from her personal computer by changing Husband's password. Broome proceeded to read emails that had been sent between Husband and his girlfriend. After reading a few of the emails, Broome called Wife, who came over to Broome's home. Broome printed the emails, and she and Wife made copies of them. They then gave one set of the emails to Neal, Wife's divorce attorney, and another set to Brenda Cooke (Cooke), a private investigator from the BJR International Detective Agency, Inc. (BJR) whom Wife had hired.

Broome subsequently logged onto Husband's Yahoo account on five or six additional occasions. Information she obtained about Husband's girlfriend as a result was communicated to Neal and Cooke. According to Broome, she never accessed any of Husband's unopened emails.

On June 29, 2006, Wife initiated an action in family court for divorce and separate support and maintenance. During the course of that litigation, which is still pending, Husband learned that Broome had accessed emails from his Yahoo account and that copies of those emails had been disseminated to Cooke and BJR.

In February 2007, Husband commenced this action against Wife, Broome, Cooke, and BJR, alleging causes of action for invasion of privacy (publicizing of private affairs and wrongful intrusion), conspiracy to intercept and disseminate private electronic communications, and violation of the South Carolina Homeland Security Act, S.C.Code Ann. §§ 17–30–10 to –145 (Supp.2009) (HSA). The parties filed cross-motions for summary judgment in May 2007.

In June 2007, Husband filed a motion to amend his complaint, which was granted pursuant to a Consent Order to Amend issued July 13, 2007. Later that July, Husband filed his amended complaint, adding allegations of violations of the following statutes: (i) the South Carolina Computer Crime Act (CCA), S.C.Code Ann. §§ 16–16–10 to–40 (2003 & Supp.2009); (ii) Title I of the Federal Electronic Communications Privacy Act (ECPA), 18 U.S.C. §§ 2510–2522 (2006); and (iii) Title II of the ECPA, 18 U.S.C. §§ 2701–2712 (2006), which is separately known as the Stored Communications Act (SCA). * * *

I.   Did the circuit court err in determining that Husband failed to allege all of the elements of a cause of action under section 2701 of the SCA?

Section 2701(a) of the SCA provides:

> Except as provided in subsection (c) of this section whoever—
>
> > (1) intentionally accesses without authorization a facility through which an electronic communication service is provided; or
> >
> > (2) intentionally exceeds an authorization to access that facility;
>
> *and thereby obtains, alters, or prevents authorized access to a wire or electronic communication while it is in electronic storage in such system* shall be punished as provided in subsection (b) of this section.

18 U.S.C. § 2701(a) (2006) (emphasis added).

Husband contends that the circuit court erred by determining that he failed to allege all of the elements of a cause of action under Section 2701. We agree. * * *

In the present case, Husband introduced evidence showing that Broome logged onto Husband's Yahoo email account without authorization by changing Husband's password. He also presented evidence that Broome, without Husband's consent, read and printed emails that were stored in Husband's Yahoo email account. Importantly, at least one court has held that comparable proof was sufficient to withstand a summary judgment motion in a section 2701 action. *See Fischer v. Mt. Olive Lutheran Church, Inc.,* 207 F.Supp.2d 914, 924–26 (W.D.Wis.2002) (denying summary judgment to defendants in a cause of action for a violation of section 2701 where evidence was presented to show that defendants logged onto plaintiff's Hotmail account without authorization and printed plaintiff's emails). Because the circuit court was ruling on motions for summary judgment, it was required to consider the evidence presented by Husband. Accordingly, we conclude that the circuit court erred by granting summary judgment to Respondents based merely upon the fact that Husband failed to expressly allege in his complaint that Respondents "obtain[ed], alter[ed], or prevent[ed] authorized access to a wire or electronic communication while it [was] in electronic storage." *See* 18 U.S.C. § 2701(a) (2006). * * *

II.   Did the circuit court err in holding that the emails were not in "electronic storage" as contemplated by 18 U.S.C. § 2510(17)?

By its terms, section 2701(a) applies only to communications that are in "electronic storage." *See* 18 U.S.C. § 2701(a) (2006). Section 2510(17) defines "electronic storage" as:

(A) any temporary, intermediate storage of a wire or electronic communication incidental to the electronic transmission thereof; and

(B) any storage of such communication by an *electronic communication service* for purposes of *backup protection* of such communication.

18 U.S.C. § 2510(17) (2006) (emphasis added). In the present case, Husband contends that the emails in question fell within subsection (B) of section 2510(17) and that the circuit court therefore erred by holding that the emails were not in "electronic storage." We agree. * * *

An ECS is defined as "any service which provides to users thereof the ability to send or receive wire or electronic communications." 18 U.S.C. § 2510(15) (2006). In the present case, the circuit court denied recovery to Husband based in part on its finding that "Plaintiff has not asserted or provided evidence from which to conclude he is an 'electronic communication service.'" Although we agree with the circuit court that Husband is not an ECS, the circuit court framed the issue incorrectly. Specifically, the circuit court should have addressed whether Yahoo was an ECS, rather than whether Husband was an ECS. Here, the emails in question were stored on servers operated by Yahoo. Therefore, the emails were stored "by" Yahoo. *See Quon v. Arch Wireless Operating Co., Inc.,* 529 F.3d 892, 901 (9th Cir.2008) ("By archiving the text messages on its server, Arch Wireless certainly was 'storing' the messages."), *rev'd on other grounds sub nom. City of Ontario v. Quon,* No. 08–1332, 2010 WL 2400087 (U.S. June 17, 2010). Although any emails stored by Husband on the hard drive of his computer would not be covered by the SCA, in this case, Broome did not access the emails in question from Husband's hard drive. Instead, she logged directly onto Yahoo's system and retrieved the emails from there. Accordingly, the relevant issue here is whether Yahoo constitutes an ECS. * * *

Turning to that question, we hold that Yahoo is an ECS. Yahoo unquestionably provides its users with the ability to send or receive electronic communications. Any doubt regarding whether Yahoo constitutes an ECS is removed by the SCA's legislative history, which provides that "electronic mail companies are providers of electronic communication services." S. REP. NO. 99–541, at 14 (1986); *see also* H.R. REP. NO. 99–647, at 63 (1986) ("An 'electronic mail' service ... would be subject to Section 2701."). * * *

B.   Were the emails being stored "for purposes of backup protection"?

As noted above, to fall within section 2510(17)(B), a communication must not only be stored by an ECS, it must also be stored "for purposes of backup protection." In *Theofel v. Farey–Jones,* 359 F.3d 1066 (9th Cir. 2004), the Ninth Circuit addressed whether previously delivered emails held by an internet service provider (ISP) were stored "for purposes of backup protection" as contemplated by section 2510(17)(B). The court concluded that they were, explaining:

> An obvious purpose for storing a message on an ISP's server after delivery is to provide a second copy of the message in the event that the user needs to download it again—if, for example, the message is accidentally erased from the user's own computer. The ISP copy of the message functions as a "backup" for the user. Notably, nothing in the Act requires that the backup protection be for the benefit of the ISP rather than the user. Storage under these circumstances thus literally falls within the statutory definition.

Id. at 1075.

Like the Ninth Circuit, we believe that one of the purposes of storing a backup copy of an email message on an ISP's server after it has been opened is so that the message is available in the event that the user needs to retrieve it again. In the present case, the previously opened emails were stored on Yahoo's servers so that, if necessary, Husband could access them again. Accordingly, we hold that the emails in question were stored "for purposes of backup protection" as contemplated by section 2510(17)(B).

C.   Does the SCA apply to emails in a "post-transmission" state?

Respondents also argue for affirmance of the circuit court's decision on the ground that the emails in question were not in "electronic storage" as contemplated by section 2510(17) because they were in a "post-transmission" state. In making this argument, Respondents rely upon *Fraser v. Nationwide Mut. Ins. Co.,* 135 F.Supp.2d 623 (E.D.Pa.2001), *aff'd on other grounds,* 352 F.3d 107 (3rd Cir.2003). In *Fraser,* the court addressed whether an employer violated the SCA when it accessed emails of its employee that were stored on the employer's server. *Id.* at 632. The court held that there was no violation because the emails were in "post-transmission" storage, meaning that they had already been retrieved by the intended recipient. *Id.* at 636. The court concluded that the SCA "provides protection only for messages while they are in the course of transmission." *Id.*

However, the district court's decision in *Fraser* was subsequently appealed to the Third Circuit, which affirmed on different grounds. *See Fraser v.*

Nationwide Mut. Ins. Co., 352 F.3d 107 (3rd Cir.2003). Specifically, the Third Circuit held that the employer's actions fell within the exception set forth in section 2701(c)(1) because the employer administered the email system and thus was acting as the ECS. *Id.* at 114–15. Importantly, in reaching that result, the Third Circuit expressed skepticism regarding the district court's ruling that the emails were not in electronic storage, stating:

> [A]ccording to the District Court, the e-mail was in a state it de-scribed as "post-transmission storage." We agree that Fraser's e-mail was not in temporary, intermediate storage. But to us it seems questionable that the transmissions were not in backup storage—a term that neither the statute nor the legislative history defines. Therefore, while we affirm the District Court, we do so through a different analytical path, *assuming without deciding that the e-mail in question was in backup storage.*

Id. at 114 (emphasis added).

Moreover, in *Theofel,* the Ninth Circuit declined to follow the district court's holding in *Fraser,* reasoning:

> In contrast to subsection (A), subsection (B) [of section 2510(17)] does not distinguish between intermediate and post-transmission storage. Indeed, *Fraser's* interpretation renders subsection (B) essentially su-perfluous, since temporary backup storage pending transmission would already seem to qualify as "temporary, intermediate storage" within the meaning of subsection (A). *By its plain terms, subsection (B) applies to backup storage regardless of whether it is intermediate or post-transmission.*

Theofel, 359 F.3d at 1075–76 (emphasis added). Similarly, in *Quon v. Arch Wireless Operating Co., Inc.,* 309 F.Supp.2d 1204 (C.D.Cal.2004), the court rejected the contention that the SCA did not apply to emails in a "post-transmission" state, explaining: "Part (B) [of section 2510(17)] states that the storage must be 'for the purpose of backup protection.' Backup protection clearly may be needed after transmission." *Id.* at 1208. For the foregoing reasons, we decline to follow the district court's decision in *Fraser.* * * *

Alternatively, Wife, Cooke and BJR contend that, even if the emails were in "electronic storage," the circuit court's grant of summary judg-ment as to them should be affirmed because they [unlike Broome] did not engage in a violation of section 2701. We agree. * * *

Importantly, section 2707 extends civil liability only to "the person or entity ... which engaged in [the] violation." 18 U.S.C. § 2707(a) (2006). * * * Here there is no evidence that Wife, Cooke, or BJR accessed Husband's email account. Although Wife disclosed some of Husband's emails to Cooke and BJR, who allegedly used the emails to obtain additional information about Husband's affair, the SCA does not punish such conduct. *See Cardinal Health,* 582 F.Supp.2d at 976 ("While [the]

SCA punishes the act of accessing a 'facility through which an electronic communication service is provided' in an unauthorized manner, the SCA does not punish disclosing and using the information obtained therefrom."). Accordingly, the circuit court did not err by granting summary judgment to Wife, Cooke, and BJR. *See Fischer,* 207 F.Supp.2d at 926 (granting summary judgment to defendants who did not access plaintiff's email accounts); *Cardinal Health,* 582 F.Supp.2d at 977–79 (same); *see also Freeman v. DirecTV, Inc.,* 457 F.3d 1001 (9th Cir.2006) (holding that civil liability under section 2707 does not extend to those who aid, abet, or conspire with a person or entity engaging in a violation of section 2702); *Doe v. GTE Corp.,* 347 F.3d 655 (7th Cir.2003) (holding that an ISP was not liable under sections 2511 and 2520 of the ECPA for aiding and abetting defendants who intercepted and disclosed oral communications).

2. INTERNET SERVICE PROVIDER LIABILITY FOR DISCLOSING STORED EMAIL TO POLICE

FREEDMAN v. AMERICA ONLINE, INC.

303 F.Supp.2d 121 (D.Conn. 2004).

On or about April 1, 2003, Defendants William Young and David Bensey executed a State of Connecticut Superior Court Search and Seizure Warrant Application. Defendants allege that Young completed the Warrant Application and that Bensey witnessed his signature on the document. * * * The Warrant Application did not bear a judicial signature and was never submitted to a Judge for his/her signature verifying its being subscribed and sworn before him/her. The actual form was not filled out nor was it signed by a Judge. It thus constituted a legal nullity. Young and Bensey sent the warrant application to America Online, Inc. ("AOL") via facsimile without further communication.

On April 7, 2003, AOL responded to Young and Bensey's submission by faxing Plaintiff's subscriber information to Young. This information included Plaintiff's name, address, phone numbers, account status, membership information, software information, billing and account information, and his other AOL screen names.

During the course of these actions, Young and Bensey were police officers acting in the official capacities in the performance of their duties, within the scope of their employment as police officers of the Town of Fairfield, Connecticut.

Plaintiff filed an eleven count complaint, alleging * * * violation of the Electronic Communication Privacy Act against all Defendants * * * violation of the Fourth and First Amendments against Young and Bensey (Counts Four and Five); * * * [and] invasion of privacy against Young and Bensey (Count Eight) * * *.

Plaintiff moves for partial summary judgment * * * arguing that Defendants are liable for violating § 2703(c) of the Electronic Communications Privacy Act of 1986 ("ECPA"), 18 U.S.C. § 2701 et seq. Plaintiff alleges that Young and Bensey violated the ECPA by soliciting an information disclosure by AOL with an invalid search warrant. * * *

The ECPA distinguishes between the rights of government entities and the rights of private entities regarding the disclosure of subscriber information by an internet service provider ("ISP"). Section 2703(c)(1) of the ECPA provides that a governmental entity seeking such information from an ISP must comply with specific legal process, e.g. a proper search warrant, court order, or subpoena, or must obtain the subscriber's consent. * * * In enacting the ECPA, Congress created a private right of action for parties aggrieved by violation of the statute. * * * "Governmental 'entities' are subject to liability * * *."

Plaintiff argues that Defendants violated § 2703(c) by using an invalid warrant to solicit his subscriber information from AOL. He contends that McVeigh v. Cohen, 983 F. Supp. 215 (D.D.C. 1998) supports his position that the government is liable for soliciting subscriber information without complying with the ECPA's legal process requirements.

In McVeigh, a Navy officer contacted AOL and requested information about the identity of an AOL customer (the plaintiff, also a Navy officer). McVeigh, 983 F. Supp. at 217. AOL disclosed the information, and consequently the Navy advised the plaintiff that it was commencing an administrative discharge proceeding against him on the basis that he was involved in homosexual conduct violating the "Don't Ask, Don't Tell" policy. Id. The plaintiff sought a preliminary injunction, arguing that the defendants violated his rights under the ECPA. Id. at 216.

In considering the substantial likelihood of success on the merits, the court noted that the Navy's actions were "likely illegal under the * * * ECPA." Id. at 219. The court stated that "in soliciting and obtaining * * * personal information about the Plaintiff from AOL" the government failed to comply with the ECPA's requirements that it either (1) had a valid warrant or (2) gave the plaintiff prior notice and sought a subpoena or court order. Id. at 219. The court found it "unlikely" that the government would prevail in its argument that 18 U.S.C. § 2703(c)(1)(B) "puts the obligation on the online service provider to withhold information from the government, and not vice versa." Id. at 220. In soliciting the information from AOL, "the government knew, or should have known, that by turning over the information without a warrant, AOL was breaking the law." Id.

The McVeigh court rejected the defendants' argument that pursuant to Tucker v. Waddell, 83 F.3d 688 (4th Cir. 1996), there is no cause of action against the government under § 2703(c). McVeigh, 983 F. Supp. at 220. In Tucker, the court analyzed the statutory language and found that although the government may be liable for violations of §§ 2703(a) or (b), "the language of § 2703(c) does not prohibit any governmental conduct, and thus a governmental entity may not violate that subsection by simply accessing information improperly." Tucker, 83 F.3d at 693. However, Tucker acknowledged the possibility that a governmental entity might violate § 2703(c) by aiding, abetting, or conspiring in the provider's violation. Id. at 693 n.6. McVeigh rejected Tucker because the sections of § 2703 "were intended to work in tandem to protect consumer privacy." McVeigh, 983 F. Supp. at 220.

Tucker is now rejected for other reasons as well. As Plaintiff argues, since Tucker was decided Congress amended the ECPA and removed the textual distinctions within § 2703 relied on by Tucker. * * * Therefore, Tucker does not foreclose government liability under § 2703(c), and in fact supports the conclusion that the government can be liable under the present text of § 2703(c). To conclude that the government may circumvent the legal processes set forth in the ECPA by merely requesting subscriber information from an ISP contradicts Congress's intent to protect personal privacy.

In light of legal precedent, the framework of the statute, and the legislative intent, governmental entities can be liable under § 2703(c) for soliciting information from an ISP without complying with the legal processes specified in the statute. * * *

Plaintiff alleges that Young and Bensey violated the ECPA by soliciting disclosure by AOL with a defective search warrant. Compl. P 32; Pl. Mem. at 1. Defendants respond that (1) they merely requested and did not "require" AOL to disclose Plaintiff's subscriber information, (2) there is a genuine issue of material fact as to whether AOL disclosed Plaintiff's information pursuant to the emergency exception, (3) there is a genuine issue of material fact as to whether Plaintiff consented to have this information disclosed and (4) Bensey did not violate the ECPA because he merely witnessed Young's signature on the Warrant Application. * * *

Young and Bensey argue that they are not liable because, in accordance with the plain language of the statute, they did not "require" AOL to disclose Plaintiff's information. As noted above, the ECPA provides that a governmental entity may require a provider of electronic communication service * * * to disclose a record or other information pertaining to a subscriber * * * only when the governmental entity—(A) obtains a warrant issued using the procedures described in the Federal Rules of Criminal Procedure by a court with jurisdiction over the offense under investigation or equivalent State warrant. * * *

Defendants' argument that they merely requested but did not require AOL to disclose the information is disingenuous and does not absolve them from liability under the ECPA. The ECPA imposes an obligation on governmental entities to follow specific legal processes when seeking such information. 18 U.S.C. § 2703(c). Congress designed such procedures to both (1) protect personal privacy against unwarranted government searches and (2) preserve the legitimate needs of law enforcement. S. REP. NO. 99–541 (1986). To conclude that Defendants did not act improperly upon merely requesting such information without following the ECPA procedural safeguards ignores the fact that a request accompanied by a court form has substantial resemblance to a compulsory court order. The deficiency would have excused AOL from complying. In what was submitted Young and Bensey clearly intended that AOL supply the information sought. That AOL responded was nothing less than what was intended and cannot be found to be otherwise. To hold that AOL was less than expected, i.e. required to respond, would erode Congress's intended protection in the ECPA and would undermine personal privacy rights. In soliciting the information from AOL, Defendants knew, or should have known, that AOL was requested to violate the ECPA. See McVeigh, 983 F. Supp. 215 at 220. Even if AOL acted without lawful authority in disclosing the information, this does not absolve Defendants from unlawfully requesting or soliciting AOL's disclosure. Putting the burden and obligation on both the government and ISPs is consistent with Congress' intent to protect personal privacy. Violation by one does not excuse the other. Accordingly, Defendants' argument that they merely requested, but did not require, AOL to disclose Plaintiff's subscriber information does not absolve them from liability for their violation of the ECPA. * * *

Defendants contend that there is a genuine issue of material fact whether AOL disclosed Plaintiff's subscriber information pursuant to the ECPA emergency disclosure exception. Def. Opp. at 10. They argue that § 2703(c) does not expressly prohibit a governmental entity from requesting information from an ISP, and that to read § 2703(c) as prohibiting a request from a governmental entity would nullify other ECPA provisions. Def. Opp. at 8. For example, they note that the ECPA provides that "A provider * * * may divulge a record or other information pertaining to a subscriber * * * (4) to a governmental entity, if the provider reasonably believes that an emergency involving immediate danger of death or serious physical injury to any person justifies disclosure of the information." 18 U.S.C. § 2702(c). They argue that the statute does not prohibit governmental entities from providing information about such an emergency situation, and that AOL "may have reasonably believed" that the recipients of Plaintiff's e-mails "faced an emergency situation involving immediate danger of death or serious physical injury." Def. Opp. at 9, 11 (citing 18 U.S.C. § 2702(c)(4)).

Defendants' argument is flawed. First, their conclusory speculation about what AOL "may have believed" is not only lacking in any evidentiary substantiation, but it is also insufficient to raise a genuine issue of material fact to survive summary judgment. They offer no evidence from which a reasonable juror could conclude that AOL believed the e-mail recipients were in immediate danger. See Delaware & H. R. Co. v. Conrail, 902 F.2d 174, 178 (2d Cir. 1990) ("conclusory allegations will not suffice to create a genuine issue"). Second, as Plaintiff notes, it took AOL over six days to respond to the officers' request for information, a delayed response which severely undermines Defendants' conclusory allegation that AOL "may have believed" the e-mail recipients were in immediate danger.

Under the circumstances of this case, Defendants fail to raise a genuine issue of material fact whether AOL disclosed Plaintiff's subscriber information pursuant to the ECPA emergency disclosure exception. The government may not circumvent the legal process specified in the ECPA pursuant to the "emergency" exception on such a speculative basis. This is not a situation where, on its own initiative, AOL voluntarily disclosed Plaintiff's subscriber information to the government. Instead, the government's request, submitted with an invalid warrant, triggered AOL's response, six days later. The Court declines to speculate whether it would ever be appropriate, under exigent circumstances when it would not be feasible to get a signed warrant or comply with other legal process, for the government to notify the ISP of an emergency and receive subscriber information without conforming with the ECPA. * * *

For the reasons stated herein, Plaintiff's motion for partial summary judgment * * * is granted to the extent he seeks a finding that Defendants Young and Bensey violated the ECPA by soliciting subscriber information without complying with 18 U.S.C. § 2703(c).

3. PRIVATE LITIGANT LIABILITY FOR EMAIL ACQUISITION VIA OVERBROAD SUBPOENA

THEOFEL v. FAREY–JONES

359 F.3d 1066 (9th Cir. 2004).

KOZINSKI, CIRCUIT JUDGE:

We consider whether defendants violated federal electronic privacy and computer fraud statutes when they used a "patently unlawful" subpoena to gain access to e-mail stored by plaintiffs' Internet service provider.

Plaintiffs Wolf and Buckingham, officers of Integrated Capital Associates, Inc. (ICA), are embroiled in commercial litigation in New York against defendant Farey–Jones. In the course of discovery, Farey–Jones sought access to ICA's e-mail. He told his lawyer Iryna Kwasny to subpoena ICA's ISP, NetGate.

Under the Federal Rules, Kwasny was supposed to "take reasonable steps to avoid imposing undue burden or expense" on NetGate. Fed. R. Civ. P. 45(c)(1). One might have thought, then, that the subpoena would request only e-mail related to the subject matter of the litigation, or maybe messages sent during some relevant time period, or at the very least those sent to or from employees in some way connected to the litigation. But Kwasny ordered production of "all copies of emails sent or received by anyone" at ICA, with no limitation as to time or scope.

NetGate, which apparently was not represented by counsel, explained that the amount of e-mail covered by the subpoena was substantial. But defendants did not relent. NetGate then took what might be described as the "Baskin–Robbins" approach to subpoena compliance and offered defendants a "free sample" consisting of 339 messages. It posted copies of the messages to a NetGate website where, without notifying opposing counsel, Kwasny and Farey–Jones read them. Most were unrelated to the litigation, and many were privileged or personal.

When Wolf and Buckingham found out what had happened, they asked the court to quash the subpoena and award sanctions. Magistrate Judge Wayne Brazil soundly roasted Farey–Jones and Kwasny for their conduct, finding that "the subpoena, on its face, was massively overbroad" and "patently unlawful," that it "transparently and egregiously" violated the Federal Rules, and that defendants "acted in bad faith" and showed "at least gross negligence in the crafting of the subpoena." He granted the motion to quash and socked defendants with over $9000 in sanctions to cover Wolf and Buckingham's legal fees. Defendants did not appeal that award.

Wolf, Buckingham and other ICA employees whose e-mail was included in the sample also filed this civil suit against Farey–Jones and Kwasny. They claim defendants violated the Stored Communications Act, 18 U.S.C. § 2701 et seq., the Wiretap Act, 18 U.S.C. § 2511 et seq., and the Computer Fraud and Abuse Act, 18 U.S.C. § 1030, as well as various state laws. The district court held that none of the federal statutes applied, and dismissed the claims without leave to amend. It declined jurisdiction over the state law claims under 28 U.S.C. § 1367(c)(3). Plaintiffs now appeal.
* * *

1. The Stored Communications Act provides a cause of action against anyone who "intentionally accesses without authorization a facility through which an electronic communication service is provided * * * and thereby obtains, alters, or prevents authorized access to a wire or electronic communication while it is in electronic storage." 18 U.S.C. §§ 2701(a)(1), 2707(a). "Electronic storage" means either "temporary, intermediate storage * * * incidental to * * * electronic transmission," or "storage * * * for purposes of backup protection." Id. § 2510(17). The Act exempts, inter alia, conduct "authorized * * * by the person or entity providing a wire or electronic communications service," id. § 2701(c)(1), or "by a user of that service with respect to a communication of or intended for that user," Id. § 2701(C)(2).

The district court dismissed on the ground that NetGate had authorized defendants' access. It held that this consent was not coerced, because the subpoena itself informed NetGate of its right to object. Plaintiffs contend that NetGate's authorization was nonetheless invalid because the subpoena was patently unlawful. Their claim turns on the meaning of the word "authorized" in section 2701. We have previously reserved judgment on this question, see Konop v. Hawaiian Airlines, Inc., 302 F.3d 868, 879 n.8 (9th Cir. 2002), while other circuits have considered related issues, see, e.g., EF Cultural Travel BV v. Explorica, Inc., 274 F.3d 577, 582 n.10 (1st Cir. 2001) (holding access might be "unauthorized" under the Computer

Fraud and Abuse Act if it is "not in line with the reasonable expectations" of the party granting permission (internal quotation marks omitted)); United States v. Morris, 928 F.2d 504, 510 (2d Cir. 1991) (holding access unauthorized where it is not "in any way related to [the system's] intended function").

We interpret federal statutes in light of the common law. See Beck v. Prupis, 529 U.S. 494, 500–01 (2000). Especially relevant here is the common law of trespass. Like the tort of trespass, the Stored Communications Act protects individuals' privacy and proprietary interests. The Act reflects Congress's judgment that users have a legitimate interest in the confidentiality of communications in electronic storage at a communications facility. Just as trespass protects those who rent space from a commercial storage facility to hold sensitive documents, cf. Prosser and Keeton on the Law of Torts § 13, at 78 (W. Page Keeton ed., 5th ed. 1984), the Act protects users whose electronic communications are in electronic storage with an ISP or other electronic communications facility.

A defendant is not liable for trespass if the plaintiff authorized his entry. See Prosser & Keeton § 13, at 70. But "an overt manifestation of assent or willingness would not be effective * * * if the defendant knew, or probably if he ought to have known in the exercise of reasonable care, that the plaintiff was mistaken as to the nature and quality of the invasion intended." Id. § 18, at 119; cf. Restatement (Second) of Torts §§ 173, 892B(2). Thus, the busybody who gets permission to come inside by posing as a meter reader is a trespasser. J.H. Desnick, M.D., Eye Servs., Ltd. v. ABC, 44 F.3d 1345, 1352 (7th Cir. 1995). So too is the police officer who, invited into a home, conceals a recording device for the media. Cf. Berger v. Hanlon, 129 F.3d 505, 516–17 (9th Cir. 1997), vacated, 526 U.S. 808 (1999), reinstated in relevant part, 188 F.3d 1155, 1157 (9th Cir. 1999).

Not all deceit vitiates consent. "The mistake must extend to the essential character of the act itself, which is to say that which makes it harmful or offensive, rather than to some collateral matter which merely operates as an inducement." Prosser & Keeton § 18, at 120 (footnote omitted). In other words, it must be a "substantial mistake[] * * * concerning the nature of the invasion or the extent of the harm." Restatement (Second) of Torts § 892B(2) cmt. g. Unlike the phony meter reader, the restaurant critic who poses as an ordinary customer is not liable for trespass, Desnick, 44 F.3d at 1351; nor, unlike the wired cop, is the invitee who conceals only an intent to repeat what he hears, cf. Dietemann v. Time, Inc., 449 F.2d 245, 249 (9th Cir. 1971) (invasion of privacy claim). These results hold even if admission would have been refused had all the facts been known.

These are fine and sometimes incoherent distinctions. See Med. Lab. Mgmt. Consultants v. ABC, 30 F. Supp. 2d 1182, 1201–04 (D. Ariz. 1998), aff'd, 306 F.3d 806 (9th Cir. 2002). But the theory is that some invited mistakes go to the essential nature of the invasion while others are merely collateral. Classification depends on the extent to which the intrusion trenches on "the specific interests that the tort of trespass seeks to protect." Desnick, 44 F.3d at 1352; see also Lewis v. United States, 385 U.S. 206, 211 (1966); Food Lion, Inc. v. Capital Cities/ABC, Inc., 194 F.3d 505, 517–18 (4th Cir. 1999).

We construe section 2701 in light of these doctrines. Permission to access a stored communication does not constitute valid authorization if it would not defeat a trespass claim in analogous circumstances. Section 2701(c)(1) therefore provides no refuge for a defendant who procures consent by exploiting a known mistake that relates to the essential nature of his access.

Under this standard, plaintiffs have alleged facts that vitiate Net-Gate's consent. NetGate disclosed the sample in response to defendants' purported subpoena. Unbeknownst to NetGate, that subpoena was invalid. This mistake went to the essential nature of the invasion of privacy. The subpoena's falsity transformed the access from a bona fide state-sanctioned inspection into private snooping. See Restatement (Second) of Torts § 174 (addressing "consent induced by fraud or mistake as to the validity of purported legal authority"); cf. Bumper v. North Carolina, 391 U.S. 543, 549 (1968) ("A search conducted in reliance upon a warrant cannot later be justified on the basis of consent if it turns out that the warrant was invalid."). The false subpoena caused disclosure of documents that otherwise would have remained private; it effected an "invasion * * * of the specific interests that the [statute] seeks to protect." Desnick, 44 F.3d at 1352.

Defendants had at least constructive knowledge of the subpoena's invalidity. It was not merely technically deficient, nor a borderline case over which reasonable legal minds might disagree. It "transparently and egregiously" violated the Federal Rules, and defendants acted in bad faith and with gross negligence in drafting and deploying it. They are charged with knowledge of its invalidity. See Prosser & Keeton § 18, at 119 (consent likely vitiated where defendants "ought to have known in the exercise of reasonable care" of the mistake).

That NetGate could have objected is immaterial. The subpoena may not have been coercive, but it was deceptive, and that is an independent ground for invalidating consent. See Restatement (Second) of Torts § 892B(2)–(3). It was a piece of paper masquerading as legal process. NetGate produced the sample in response and doubtless would not have done so had it known the subpoena was void—particularly in light of its own legal obligation not to disclose such messages to third parties, see 18 U.S.C. § 2702(a)(1). That NetGate could have objected proves disclosure was not an inevitable consequence, but it was still a foreseeable one (and the intended one).

Allowing consent procured by known mistake to serve as a defense would seriously impair the statute's operation. A hacker could use some-one else's password to break into a mail server and then claim the server "authorized" his access. Congress surely did not intend to exempt such intrusions—indeed, they seem the paradigm of what it sought to prohibit. Cf. Morris, 928 F.2d at 510 (access gained by guessing someone else's password is not "authorization" under the Computer Fraud and Abuse Act).

The subpoena power is a substantial delegation of authority to private parties, and those who invoke it have a grave responsibility to ensure it is not abused. Informing the person served of his right to object is a good start, see Fed. R. Civ. P. 45(a)(1)(D), but it is no substitute for the exercise of independent judgment about the subpoena's reasonableness. Fighting a subpoena in court is not cheap, and many may be cowed into compliance with even overbroad subpoenas, especially if they are not represented by counsel or have no personal interest at stake. Because defendants procured consent by exploiting a mistake of which they had constructive knowledge, the district court erred by dismissing based on that consent.

Defendants ask us to affirm on the alternative ground that the messages they accessed were not in "electronic storage" and therefore fell outside the Stored Communications Act's coverage. See 18 U.S.C. § 2701(a)(1). The Act defines "electronic storage" as "(A) any temporary, intermediate storage of a wire or electronic communication incidental to the electronic transmission thereof; and (B) any storage of such communication by an electronic communication service for purposes of backup protection of such communication." Id. § 2510(17), incorporated by id. § 2711(1). Several courts have held that subsection (A) covers e-mail messages stored on an ISP's server pending delivery to the recipient. See In re Doubleclick, Inc. Privacy Litig., 154 F. Supp. 2d 497, 511–12 (S.D.N.Y. 2001); Fraser v. Nationwide Mut. Ins. Co., 135 F. Supp. 2d 623, 635–36 (E.D. Pa. 2001); cf. Steve Jackson Games, Inc. v. U.S. Secret Serv., 36 F.3d 457, 461–62 (5th Cir. 1994) (messages stored on a BBS pending delivery). Because subsection (A) applies only to messages in "temporary, intermediate storage," however, these courts have limited that subsection's coverage to messages not yet delivered to their intended recipient. See Doubleclick, 154 F. Supp. 2d at 512; Fraser, 135 F. Supp. 2d at 636.

Defendants point to these cases and argue that messages remaining on an ISP's server after delivery no longer fall within the Act's coverage. But, even if such messages are not within the purview of subsection (A), they do fit comfortably within subsection (B). There is no dispute that messages remaining on NetGate's server after delivery are stored "by an electronic communication service" within the meaning of 18 U.S.C. § 2510 (17)(B). Cf. Doubleclick, 154 F. Supp. 2d at 511 (holding that subsection (B) did not apply because the communications at issue were not being stored by an electronic communication service). The only issue, then, is whether the messages are stored "for purposes of backup protection." 18 U.S.C. § 2510(17)(B). We think that, within the ordinary meaning of those terms, they are.

An obvious purpose for storing a message on an ISP's server after delivery is to provide a second copy of the message in the event that the user needs to download it again—if, for example, the message is accidentally erased from the user's own computer. The ISP copy of the message functions as a "backup" for the user. Notably, nothing in the Act requires that the backup protection be for the benefit of the ISP rather than the user. Storage under these circumstances thus literally falls within the statutory definition.

One district court reached a contrary conclusion, holding that "backup protection" includes only temporary backup storage pending delivery, and not any form of "post-transmission storage." See Fraser, 135 F. Supp. 2d at 633–34, 636. We reject this view as contrary to the plain language of the Act. In contrast to subsection (A), subsection (B) does not distinguish between intermediate and post-transmission storage. Indeed, Fraser's interpretation renders subsection (B) essentially superfluous, [*1076] since temporary backup storage pending transmission would already seem to qualify as "temporary, intermediate storage" within the meaning of subsection (A). By its plain terms, subsection (B) applies to backup storage regardless of whether it is intermediate or post-transmission.

The United States, as amicus curiae, disputes our interpretation. It first argues that, because subsection (B) refers to "any storage of such communication," it applies only to backup copies of messages that are themselves in temporary, intermediate storage under subsection (A). The text of the statute, however, does not support this reading. Subsection (A) identifies a type of communication ("a wire or electronic communication") and a type of storage ("temporary, intermediate storage * * * incidental to the electronic transmission thereof"). The phrase "such communication" in subsection (B) does not, as a matter of grammar, reference attributes of the type of storage defined in subsection (A). The government's argument would be correct if subsection (B) referred to "a communication in such storage," or if subsection (A) referred to a communication in temporary, intermediate storage rather than temporary, intermediate storage of a communication. However, as the statute is written, "such communication" is nothing more than shorthand for "a wire or electronic communication."

The government's contrary interpretation suffers from the same flaw as Fraser's: It drains subsection (B) of independent content because virtually any backup of a subsection (A) message will itself qualify as a message in temporary, intermediate storage. The government counters that the statute requires only that the underlying message be temporary, not the backup. But the lifespan of a backup is necessarily tied to that of the underlying message. Where the underlying message has expired in the normal course, any copy is no longer performing any backup function. An ISP that kept permanent copies of temporary messages could not fairly be described as "backing up" those messages.

The United States also argues that we upset the structure of the Act by defining "electronic storage" so broadly as to be superfluous and by rendering irrelevant certain other provisions dealing with remote computing services. The first claim relies on the argument that any copy of a message necessarily serves as a backup to the user, the service or both. But the mere fact that a copy could serve as a backup does not mean it is stored for that purpose. We see many instances where an ISP could hold messages not in electronic storage—for example, e-mail sent to or from the ISP's staff, or messages a user has flagged for deletion from the server. In both cases, the messages are not in temporary, intermediate storage, nor are they kept for any backup purpose.

Our interpretation also does not render irrelevant the more liberal access standards governing messages stored by remote computing services. See 18 U.S.C. §§ 2702(a)(2), 2703(b). The government's premise is that a message stored by a remote computing service "solely for the purpose of providing storage or computer processing services to [the] subscriber," id. §§ 2702(a)(2)(B), 2703(b)(2)(B), would also necessarily be stored for purposes of backup protection under section 2510(17)(B), and thus would be subject to the more stringent rules governing electronic storage. But not all remote computing services are also electronic communications services and, as to those that are not, section 2510(17)(B) is by its own terms inapplicable. The government notes that remote computing services and electronic communications services are "often the same entities," but "often" is not good enough to make the government's point. Even as to remote computing services that are also electronic communications services, not all storage covered by sections 2702(a)(2)(B) and 2703(b)(2)(B) is also covered by section 2510(17)(B). A remote computing service might be the only place a user stores his messages; in that case, the messages are not stored for backup purposes.

Finally, the government invokes legislative history. It cites a passage from a 1986 report indicating that a committee intended that messages stored by a remote computing service would "continue to be covered by section 2702(a)(2)" if left on the server after user access. H.R. Rep. No. 647, 99th Cong., at 65 (1986). The cited discussion addresses provisions relating to remote computing services. We do not read it to address whether the electronic storage provisions also apply. See id. at 64–65. The committee's statement that section 2702(a)(2) would "continue" to cover e-mail upon access supports our reading. If section 2702(a)(2) applies to e-mail even before access, the committee could not have been identifying an exclusive source of protection, since even the government concedes that unopened e-mail is protected by the electronic storage provisions.

The government also points to a subsequent, rejected amendment that would have made explicit the electronic storage definition's coverage of opened e-mail. See H.R. Rep. No. 932, 106th Cong., at 7 (2000). This sort of legislative history has very little probative value; Congress might have rejected the amendment precisely because it thought the definition already applied.

Finally, the government points to a passing reference in another recent report. The discussion addresses an unrelated issue and merely assumes that the definition only applies to unopened e-mail. This assumption was natural given that Fraser had recently been decided.

We acknowledge that our interpretation of the Act differs from the government's and do not lightly conclude that the government's reading is erroneous. Nonetheless, for the reasons above, we think that prior access is irrelevant to whether the messages at issue were in electronic storage. Because plaintiff's e-mail messages were in electronic storage regardless of whether they had been previously delivered, the district court's decision cannot be affirmed on this alternative ground.

2.   Plaintiffs also claim a violation of the Wiretap Act, which authorizes suit against those who "intentionally intercept[] * * * any wire, oral, or electronic communication." 18 U.S.C. §§ 2511(1)(a), 2520(a). We recently held in Konop v. Hawaiian Airlines, Inc., 302 F.3d 868 (9th Cir. 2002), that the act applies only to "acquisition contemporaneous with transmission." Id. at 878. Specifically, "Congress Did Not Intend For 'intercept' To Apply To 'electronic Communications' When Those Communications Are In 'electronic Storage.'" id. at 877 (quoting Steve Jackson Games, 36 F.3d at 462). Konop is dispositive, and the district court correctly dismissed the claim.

3.   Plaintiffs finally claim a violation of the Computer Fraud and Abuse Act, which provides a cause of action against one who, inter alia, "intentionally accesses a computer without authorization or exceeds authorized access, and thereby obtains * * * Information from any protected computer if the conduct involved an interstate or foreign communication." 18 U.S.C. § 1030(a)(2)(C), (g). The conduct must involve one of five factors listed in 18 U.S.C. § 1030(a)(5)(B), which include a loss in excess of $5000. Id. § 1030(a)(5)(B)(i), (g).

The district court dismissed without leave to amend on the theory that the Act does not apply to unauthorized access of a third party's computer. It also dismissed for failure to allege damages or loss, though it noted that this omission might be cured by amendment. Plaintiffs do not dispute the latter defect, but urge us to reverse as to the former ground so they can amend.

The district court erred by reading an ownership or control requirement into the Act. The civil remedy extends to "any person who suffers damage or loss by reason of a violation of this section." 18 U.S.C. § 1030(g). "The word 'any' has an expansive meaning, that is, 'one or some indiscriminately of whatever kind.'" HUD v. Rucker, 535 U.S. 125 (2002) (quoting United States v. Gonzales, 520 U.S. 1, 5 (1997)). Nothing in the provision's language supports the district court's restriction. Individuals other than the computer's owner may be proximately harmed by unauthorized access, particularly if they have rights to data stored on it.

Defendants argue in the alternative that NetGate authorized their access. Our earlier discussion disposes of this defense. They further contend that any damages or loss plaintiffs suffered do not fall within the Act's ambit. Because plaintiffs have not yet alleged the damages or loss they suffered, it would be premature to consider the argument.

4. Defendants contend they are immune from liability under the Noerr–Pennington doctrine, which exempts petitioning of public authorities from civil liability on First Amendment grounds. See Manistee Town Ctr. v. City of Glendale, 227 F.3d 1090, 1092 (9th Cir. 2000); Kottle v. Northwest Kidney Ctrs., 146 F.3d 1056, 1059 (9th Cir. 1998). Lawsuits are protected by the doctrine because they are essentially petitions to the courts for redress of grievances. See Cal. Motor Transp. Co. v. Trucking Unlimited, 404 U.S. 508, 510 (1972). The doctrine is typically invoked to immunize the act of petitioning itself—i.e., the filing of the lawsuit. But it has been extended to certain conduct "incidental to the prosecution of the suit," for example, deciding whether to settle a claim. See Columbia Pictures Indus., Inc. v. Prof'l Real Estate Investors, Inc., 944 F.2d 1525, 1528–29 (9th Cir. 1991), aff'd, 508 U.S. 49 (1993). Defendants seize on this language from Columbia Pictures and argue that, because the subpoena was incidental to their litigation, they are entitled to immunity.

We are skeptical that Noerr–Pennington applies at all to the type of conduct at issue. Subpoenaing private parties in connection with private commercial litigation bears little resemblance to the sort of governmental petitioning the doctrine is designed to protect. Nevertheless, assuming arguendo the defense is available, it fails. Noerr–Pennington does not protect "objectively baseless" sham litigation. See Prof'l Real Estate Investors, Inc. v. Columbia Pictures Indus., Inc., 508 U.S. 49 (1993). The magistrate judge found that the subpoena was "transparently and egregiously" overbroad and that defendants acted with gross negligence and in bad faith. This is tantamount to a finding that the subpoena was objectively baseless.

Defendants urge us to look only at the merits of the underlying litigation, not at the subpoena. They apparently think a litigant should have immunity for any and all discovery abuses so long as his lawsuit has some merit. Not surprisingly, they offer no authority for that implausible proposition. Assuming Noerr–Pennington applies at all, we hold that it is no bar where the challenged discovery conduct itself is objectively baseless.

5. * * * We reverse dismissal of the Stored Communications Act Claim, affirm dismissal of the Wiretap Act claim, and reverse dismissal with prejudice of the Computer Fraud and Abuse Act claim with instructions to dismiss with leave to amend. We also reverse dismissal of the state claims.

NOTE: NSA ACQUISITION OF TELEPHONE CALL AND SUBSCRIBER INFORMATION

After September 11, 2001, AT&T began regularly providing the National Security Agency (NSA) with residential customer telephone calling records and access to other information about their customers and subscribers. On May 26, 2006, plaintiffs went to state court to enjoin AT&T Corporation's and, in a separate suit, Verizon Communications, Inc.'s, disclosure of their California customers' telephone records to the NSA. The suits alleged that the privacy provisions of the California Constitution and the California Public Utilities Code barred the disclosures.

The phone companies removed the lawsuits against them to federal district court, where they were consolidated. See *In re National Security Agency Telecommunications Records Litigation*, 2007 WL 163106 (N.D. Cal.). The phone companies argued in federal court, on plaintiffs' motion to remand back to state court, that the plaintiffs' claims were completely preempted by the Foreign Intelligence Surveillance Act and ECPA's Stored Communications Act. Federal law governing national security, "leaves no room for plaintiffs' state law privacy claims," urged the phone companies. However, the court held that neither FISA, ECPA Title II, nor federal common law completely preempts state law claims for greater privacy protection. The court did, however, refuse the plaintiffs' request that it remand the litigation to state court. The United States had filed a formal "statement of interest" in the case and opposed remand; therefore "remand would be futile because intervention by the government in state court would render this action removable pursuant to [the California code of civil procedure] § 1442(a)."

4. WHO IS AN "ELECTRONIC COMMUNICATION SERVICE" UNDER TITLE II?—THE AIRLINE PASSENGER DATA SYSTEM EXCLUSION

DYER v. NORTHWEST AIRLINES CORPS.

334 F.Supp.2d 1196 (D.N.D. 2004).

JUDGE DANIEL L. HOVLAND * * *

Following September 11, 2001, the National Aeronautical and Space Administration ("NASA") requested system-wide passenger data from Northwest Airlines for a three-month period in order to conduct research for use in airline security studies. Northwest Airlines complied and, unbeknownst to its customers, provided NASA with the names, addresses, credit card numbers, and travel itineraries of persons who had flown on Northwest Airlines between July and December 2001.

The discovery of Northwest Airlines' disclosure of its customers' personal information triggered a wave of litigation. Eight class actions— seven in Minnesota and one in Tennessee—were filed in federal court prior to March 19, 2004. The seven Minnesota actions were later consolidated into a master file.

The Plaintiffs initiated the above-entitled action in state court in North Dakota on March 19, 2004. The complaint alleges that Northwest Airlines' unauthorized disclosure of customers' personal information constituted a violation of the Electronic Communications Privacy Act

("ECPA"), 18 U.S.C. §§ 2702(a)(1) and (a)(3), and a breach of contract.
* * *

The ECPA defines "electronic communication service" as "any service which provides the users thereof the ability to send or receive wire or electronic communications." 18 U.S.C. § 2510(15). In construing this definition, courts have distinguished those entities that sell access to the internet from those that sell goods or services on the internet. 18 U.S.C. § 2702(a)(3) prescribes the conduct only of a "provider of a remote computing service or electronic communication service to the public." A provider under the ECPA is commonly referred to as an internet service provider or ISP. There is no factual allegation that Northwest Airlines, an airline that sells airline tickets on its website, provides internet services.

Courts have concluded that "electronic communication service" encompasses internet service providers as well as telecommunications companies whose lines carry internet traffic, but does not encompass businesses selling traditional products or services online. See In re Doubleclick Inc. Privacy Litig., 154 F.Supp.2d 497, 511, n. 20. (S.D.N.Y. 2001); In re Northwest Airlines Privacy Litig. (D. Minn. June 6, 2004) ("Defining electronic communications service to include online merchants or service providers like Northwest stretches the ECPA too far"); Crowley v. Cybersource Corp., 166 F.Supp.2d 1263 (N.D. Cal. 2001) (finding that an online retailer did not constitute an electronic communication service provider); Andersen Consulting LLP v. UOP, 991 F.Supp. 1041 (N.D.Ill.1998) (finding that users and providers of electronic communication services are not necessarily synonymous); but see United States v. Mullins, 992 F.2d 1472, 1478 (9th Cir. 1993) (stating that an airline, though a computerized travel reservation system accessed through terminals by travel agencies, constituted a provider of electronic communication services).

The distinction is critical in this case. Northwest Airlines is not an electronic communications service provider as contemplated by the ECPA. Instead, Northwest Airlines sells its products and services over the internet as opposed to access to the internet itself. The ECPA definition of "electronic communications service" clearly includes internet service providers such as America Online, as well as telecommunications companies whose cables and phone lines carry internet traffic. However, businesses offering their traditional products and services online through a website are not providing an "electronic communication service". As a result, Northwest Airlines falls outside the scope of 18 U.S.C. § 2702 and the ECPA claim fails as a matter of law. The facts as pled to not give rise to liability under the ECPA. 18 U.S.C. § 2702(a) does not prohibit or even address the dissemination of business records of passenger flights and information as described in the complaint. Instead, the focus of 18 U.S.C. § 2702(a) is on "communications" being stored by the communications service provider for the purpose of subsequent transmission or for backup purposes. * * *

The Plaintiffs base their breach of contract claim on Northwest Airlines' alleged violation of the privacy policy posted on its website. Northwest Airlines contends that a policy posted on its website does not constitute a contract. In addition, Northwest Airlines argues that even if the policy did constitute a contract, the Plaintiffs claim fails because they have not alleged any contract damages. * * *

Having carefully reviewed the complaint, the Court finds the Plaintiffs' breach of contract claim fails as a matter of law. First, broad statements of company policy do not generally give rise to contract claims. * * * Second, nowhere in the complaint are the Plaintiffs alleged to have ever logged onto Northwest Airlines' website and accessed, read, understood, actually relied upon, or otherwise considered Northwest Airlines' privacy policy. Finally, even if the privacy policy was sufficiently definite and the Plaintiffs had alleged they did read the policy prior to providing personal information to Northwest Airlines, the Plaintiffs have failed to allege any contractual damages arising out of the alleged breach. * * * The breach of contract claim is subject to dismissal as a matter of law.

IN RE JETBLUE AIRWAYS CORP. PRIVACY LITIGATION

379 F.Supp.2d 299 (E.D.N.Y. 2005).

JUDGE CAROL BAGLEY AMON * * *

JetBlue has a practice of compiling and maintaining personal information, known in the airline industry as Passenger Name Records ("PNRs"), on each of its adult and minor passengers. Information contained in PNRs includes, for example, passenger names, addresses, phone numbers, and travel itineraries. (Am. Compl. ¶ 38; Pl.'s Mem. at 4–5.) The PNRs are maintained, or temporarily stored, on JetBlue's computer servers, and passengers are able to modify their stored information. (Am. Compl. ¶ 39.) Acxiom, a world leader in customer and information management solutions, maintains personally-identifiable information on almost eighty percent of the U.S. population, including many JetBlue passengers, which it uses to assist companies such as JetBlue in customer and information management solutions. * * *

The personal information that forms the basis of JetBlue's PNRs is obtained from its passengers over the telephone and through its Internet website during the selection and purchase of travel arrangements. In order to encourage the provision of personal information in this manner, JetBlue created a privacy policy which provided that the company would use computer IP addresses only to help diagnose server problems, cookies to save consumers' names, e-mail addresses to alleviate consumers from having to re-enter such data on future occasions, and optional passenger contact information to send the user updates and offers from JetBlue. * * * The JetBlue privacy policy specifically represented that any financial and personal information collected by JetBlue would not be shared with third parties and would be protected by secure servers. JetBlue also purported to have security measures in place to guard against the loss, misuse, or alteration of consumer information under its control. * * *

In the wake of September 11, 2001, Torch, a data mining company similar to Acxiom, presented the Department of Defense ("DOD") with a data pattern analysis proposal geared toward improving the security of military installations in the United States and possibly abroad. Torch suggested that a rigorous analysis of personal characteristics of persons who sought access to military installations might be used to predict which individuals pose a risk to the security of those installations. DOD showed interest in Torch's proposal and added Torch as a subcontractor to an existing contract with SRS so that Torch could carry out a limited initial test of its proposed study. The SRS contract was amended to include airline PNRs as a possible data source in connection with Torch's study. Because Torch needed access to a large national-level database of personal information and because no federal agencies approached by Torch would grant access to their own governmental databases, Torch independently contacted a number of airlines in search of private databases that might contain adequate information to serve its requirements. These airlines declined to share their passengers' personal information unless the Department of Transportation ("DOT") and/or the Transportation Security Administration ("TSA") were involved and approved of such data sharing.

Unable to obtain the data through its own devices, Torch asked members of Congress to intervene on its behalf with the airlines or federal agencies. (Id. ¶ 47.) Torch also contacted the DOT directly. Following a series of meetings, the DOT and the TSA agreed to assist Torch in obtaining consent from a national airline to share its passenger information. (Id. ¶ 51.) On July 30, 2002, the TSA sent JetBlue a written request to supply its data to the DOD, and JetBlue agreed to cooperate. (Id. ¶¶ 53–54.) In September 2002, JetBlue and Acxiom collectively transferred approximately five million electronically-stored PNRs to Torch in connection with the SRS/DOD contract. (Id. ¶¶ 53, 55.) Then, in October 2002, Torch separately purchased additional data from Acxiom for use in connection with the SRS contract. This data was merged with the September 2002 data to create a single database of JetBlue passenger information including each passenger's name, address, gender, home ownership or rental status, economic status, social security number, occupation, and the number of adults and children in the passenger's family as well as the number of vehicles owned or leased. Using this data, Torch began its data analysis and created a customer profiling scheme designed to identify high-risk passengers among those traveling on JetBlue.

In or about September 2003, government disclosures and ensuing public investigations concerning the data transfer to Torch prompted JetBlue Chief Executive Officer David Neelman to acknowledge that the transfer had been a violation of JetBlue's privacy policy. (Id. ¶¶ 63, 65–66.) A class of plaintiffs whose personal information was among that transferred now brings this action against JetBlue, Torch, Acxiom, and

SRS, seeking monetary damages, including punitive damages, and injunctive relief. (Id. ¶ 5.) Plaintiffs assert five causes of action against all defendants: (1) violation of the Electronic Communications Privacy Act of 1986 ("ECPA"), 18 U.S.C. § 2701, et seq., (2) violation of the New York General Business Law and other similar state consumer protection statutes, (3) trespass to property, (4) unjust enrichment, and (5) declaratory judgment. In addition, plaintiffs bring a sixth claim for breach of contract against JetBlue. All defendants have moved for dismissal pursuant to Rule 12(b)(6) of the Federal Rules of Civil Procedure. Defendants argue that plaintiffs have failed to state a claim under federal or state law and that the state law claims asserted are expressly preempted by the Airline Deregulation Act, 49 U.S.C. § 41713(b) (1997), or impliedly preempted by the federal government's pervasive occupation of the field of aviation security. The federal government filed a statement of interest arguing that no defendant violated the ECPA and urging dismissal of the federal claim. * * *

Plaintiffs allege that all defendants violated § 2702 of the Electronic Communications Privacy Act of 1986 ("ECPA"), 18 U.S.C. § 2701, et seq. (1986), by divulging stored passenger communications without the passengers' authorization or consent. * * * The statute defines "electronic communication service" as "any service which provides to users the ability to send or receive wire or electronic communications." 18 U.S.C. § 2510(15). The term "electronic communication" includes "any transfer of signs, signals, writing, images, sounds, data, or intelligence of any nature transmitted in whole or in part by wire, radio, electronic, photoelectronic or photoptical system that affects interstate or foreign commerce." 18 U.S.C. § 2510(12). "Remote computing service" refers to "the provision to the public of computer storage or processing services by means of an electronic communication system." 18 U.S.C. § 2711(2).

Plaintiffs allege that the JetBlue Passenger Reservation Systems constitute an "electronic communication service" within the meaning of the statute. * * *

Plaintiffs argue that the decisions in the Northwest Airlines cases are not persuasive because they rely on questionable and inapposite authorities. Specifically, plaintiffs observe that the cases rest heavily on Crowley, which in turn rests principally on Andersen. Because Andersen concerned a company that only provided e-mail services to a hired contractor for use in connection with a specific project, and because that company did not provide the general public with the ability to send or receive wire or electronic communications, plaintiffs argue that the import of the case is limited to private communications loops and does not reach the JetBlue or Amazon.com models, which, through their websites, offer their products and services to the public at large. However, apart from considering the limited scope of the e-mail system at issue, the Andersen case also addressed the significance under the ECPA of the fact that Andersen, the hired contractor, could communicate with third-parties over the Internet using the e-mail capabilities provided by the defendant company. The court held that "the fact that Andersen could communicate to third-parties over the Internet and that third-parties could communicate with it did not mean that [the hiring company] provided an electronic communication service to the public." Andersen, 991 F.Supp. at 1043. Indeed, as discussed, the hiring company was not considered an independent provider of Internet services for the simple reason that, like any other consumer, it had to purchase Internet access from an electronic communication service provider. Id. This particular distinction did not turn on the existence of there being a private communication loop. * * *

Plaintiffs' attempt to distinguish the case law is unavailing. They contend that Doubleclick and Crowley bear little if any relation to this case because the plaintiffs in those cases failed to allege that any party was a provider of an electronic communication service. * * * Although it is true that the plaintiffs in Crowley initially failed to make such an allegation, it is clear from the court's opinion that they ultimately did argue that Amazon.com is an electronic communication service provider. That argument was considered by the court and rejected on the merits. Crowley, 166 F.Supp.2d at 1270. And though the plaintiffs in Doubleclick did not allege that any party was an electronic communication service provider, see Doubleclick, 154 F.Supp.2d at 511 n.20, the court had cause to undertake a detailed analysis of the meaning of the term as set forth in § 2510(15) of the ECPA. See id. at 508–12. As § 2510(15) contains the sole definition of "electronic communication service" that applies throughout the statute, the Doubleclick court's analysis of that term is relevant to the instant case.

Based upon the foregoing, this Court finds as a matter of law that JetBlue is not an electronic communication service provider within the meaning of the ECPA. * * *

Plaintiffs have also failed to establish that JetBlue is a remote computing service. Plaintiffs simply make the allegation without providing any legal or factual support for such a claim. * * * Although plaintiffs allege that JetBlue operates a website and computer servers, no facts alleged indicate that JetBlue provides either computer processing services or computer storage to the public. As such, under the plain meaning of the statute, JetBlue is not a remote computing service.

For the foregoing reasons, JetBlue as a matter of law is not liable under § 2702 of the ECPA. Because the sole basis for plaintiffs' ECPA claim against Torch, Acxiom, and SRS is an aiding and abetting or conspiracy theory, the claim against those defendants cannot stand absent liability on the part of JetBlue. Accordingly, all defendants' motions to dismiss are granted with respect to the ECPA claim.

5. NATIONAL SECURITY LETTERS, AND THE PATRIOT ACT'S "GAG" REQUIREMENT FOR "ELECTRONIC COMMUNICATION SERVICE PROVIDERS"

DOE v. GONZALES

449 F.3d 415 (2d Cir. 2006).

PER CURIAM:

This consolidated appeal calls on us to consider 18 U.S.C. § 2709, a statute that governs the Federal Bureau of Investigation's (FBI) issuance of National Security Letters (NSLs) to wire or electronic communication service providers. An NSL is an administrative subpoena that allows the FBI to gain access to, inter alia, "subscriber information * * * or electronic communication transactional records" held by internet service providers, when this information is "relevant to an authorized investigation to protect against international terrorism or clandestine intelligence activities * * *." 18 U.S.C. §§ 2709(a) & (b)(2). [Plaintiffs] are internet service providers who received NSLs and commenced proceedings in the Southern District of New York and the District of Connecticut (respectively) challenging the constitutionality of § 2709.

Section 2709 was originally enacted as part of Title II of the Electronic Communication Privacy Act of 1986 ("ECPA"), Pub. L. No. 99–508, § 201, 100 Stat. 1848, 1867–68 (1986), and was amended in 1993 and 1996. See generally FBI Access to Telephone Records, Pub. L. No. 103–142, § 1, 107 Stat. 1491, 1491–92 (1993); Intelligence Authorization Act for Fiscal Year 1997, Pub. L. No. 104–293, § 601(a), 110 Stat. 3461, 3469 (1996). Shortly after the terrorist attacks of September 11, 2001, however, Congress again amended § 2709 by means of Title V, Section 505 of the Uniting and Strengthening America by Providing Appropriate Tools Required to Intercept and Obstruct Terrorism Act of 2001 ("USA PATRIOT Act"), Pub. L. 107–56, 115 Stat. 272, 365 (Oct. 26, 2001).

Both the Southern District of New York in Doe v. Ashcroft ("Doe I"), 334 F.Supp.2d 471 (S.D.N.Y. 2004), and the District of Connecticut in Doe v. Gonzales ("Doe II"), 386 F.Supp.2d 66 (D. Conn. 2005), ruled on the constitutionality of § 2709 (as amended by the USA PATRIOT Act). However, while this appeal was pending, Congress passed the USA PATRIOT Improvement and Reauthorization Act of 2005, Pub. L. No. 109–177, 120 Stat. 192 (Mar. 9, 2006) (the "Reauthorization Act" or the "Act"). This Act dramatically altered § 2709, and added several new procedures codified at 18 U.S.C. § 3511, which now govern judicial review of the FBI's requests for information through NSLs. In light of the significant changes to § 2709 in the Reauthorization Act, this Court issued an order on March 15, 2006 requesting supplemental letter briefs from the parties on the impact of the Reauthorization Act on this case.

Having reviewed the Government's Letter Brief dated March 29, 2006 ("Gov't Ltr. Br."), the Plaintiffs' Letter Brief dated April 7, 2006 ("Pls. Ltr. Br."), and the Government's Reply Letter Brief dated April 18, 2006 ("Gov't Reply Ltr. Br."), we dispose of Doe I and Doe II as follows.

I. Doe I, No. 05–0570 * * *

[T]he Southern District of New York held that the then-applicable version of § 2709 was unconstitutional as applied to John Doe I under the Fourth Amendment because it was denied pre-enforcement judicial review. Doe I, 334 F.Supp.2d at 494–511. The Southern District of New York also held that the permanent nondisclosure requirement (also known as the "gag order" provision) of the then-applicable version of § 2709(c) was unconstitutional on its face under the First Amendment because it operated as a content-based prior restraint on speech that was not sufficiently narrowly tailored to achieve a compelling governmental interest. Doe I, 334 F.Supp.2d at 511–26.

The Reauthorization Act has substantially shifted the legal footing on which Doe I stands. * * *

The new § 2709(c) now explicitly allows an NSL recipient to talk with an attorney "to obtain legal advice or legal assistance with respect to the request." 18 U.S.C. § 2709(c)(1); see Gov't Ltr. Br. at 2. The Reauthorization Act also added procedures for the judicial review of the terms and conditions of nondisclosure imposed on a recipient of an NSL. See 18 U.S.C. § 3511(b). However, Plaintiffs argue that the revised version of § 2709(c), as amended and supplemented by the Reauthorization Act, still violates John Doe I's First Amendment rights. See Pls. Ltr. Br. at 2–4. The Government responds that the Reauthorization Act and the new procedures found in 18 U.S.C. § 3511 solve the purported First Amendment problems that the nondisclosure provisions of the prior version of § 2709(c) had raised. * * *

We do not believe that it would be prudent to resolve these novel First Amendment issues as a part of this appeal. Therefore, we also vacate the First Amendment portion of Doe I, and we remand this case so that the Southern District of New York, in the first instance, can address the First Amendment issues presented by the revised version of § 2709(c), and the Reauthorization Act's new procedures and standards for judicial review found at 18 U.S.C. § 3511. On remand, the district court will, as appropriate, have the opportunity to receive amended pleadings, request new briefs, conduct oral argument, and, in due course, furnish its views on the constitutionality of the revised version of § 2709(c) and the Reauthorization Act.

II. Gonzales v. Doe II, No. 05–4896

In Doe II, on a motion for preliminary injunction, the District of Connecticut enjoined the Government from enforcing the gag order imposed on John Doe II under § 2709(c) insofar as it prevented John Doe II from revealing its identity as a recipient of an NSL. In granting its motion for a preliminary injunction, the District of Connecticut held that John Doe II had demonstrated irreparable harm from the suppression of its speech, and a likelihood of success on the merits that § 2709(c) violated John Doe II's First Amendment rights as a content-based, prior restraint on speech. See Doe II, 386 F.Supp.2d at 72–82. * * *

In light of the Reauthorization Act, the Government now asserts that John Doe II should move in the District of Connecticut, under the new procedures in 18 U.S.C. § 3511(b), for a modification of the terms of its § 2709(c) non-disclosure requirements so that it can reveal its identity.

CARDAMONE, CIRCUIT JUDGE, Concurring:

I concur in the judgment of the court. I write separately to address an argument the government continues to press notwithstanding the recent amendments to 18 U.S.C. § 2709(c). The question previously before us was whether subsection (c), which imposed a permanent ban on speech, ran afoul of the First Amendment. The Reauthorization Act has altered the functioning and perhaps the scope of § 2709(c)'s gag provision, and that is why we are remanding the New York case (Doe I) for further proceedings and dismissing the Connecticut case (Doe II). Yet, in its recent letter briefings to the panel, the government perseveres, insisting that a permanent ban on speech is permissible under the First Amendment. This issue warrants comment, especially because I suspect that a perpetual gag on citizen speech of the type advocated so strenuously by the government may likely be unconstitutional.

Prior to the passage of the Reauthorization Act the government sought enforcement of 18 U.S.C. § 2709 (as amended by the USA PATRI-OT Act), and specifically § 2709(c), the non-disclosure provision at the heart of the two appeals. Section 2709(c) provided that no recipient of a National Security Letter (NSL) "shall disclose to any person" that they received such a letter. 18 U.S.C. § 2709(c) (2000). By its terms the statute permanently prohibited a recipient from ever disclosing the fact of having received an NSL. See Butterworth v. Smith, 494 U.S. 624 (1990) (finding similarly worded statute as permanently prohibiting disclosure of grand jury testimony). The government, while conceding the permanent bar, nonetheless declared that § 2709's non-disclosure provision was fully consistent with the First Amendment. Such a proposition should be greeted with a healthy dose of judicial skepticism. A permanent ban on speech seems highly unlikely to survive the test of strict scrutiny, one where the government must show that the statute is narrowly tailored to meet a compelling government interest. See Ashcroft v. ACLU, 542 U.S. 656, 665–66 (2004); Kamasinski v. Judicial Review Council, 44 F.3d 106, 109 (2d Cir. 1994) (applying strict scrutiny to Connecticut judicial investigation gag statute).

It seems to me that courts resolve the tension between the government's interest in maintaining the integrity of its investigative process and the First Amendment in favor of the government so long as the ban on disclosure is limited. The cases also hold that a ban on speech is not constitutionally permissible once the investigation ends. For instance, the Supreme Court in Butterworth teaches that a "permanent ban on disclosure of [a witness's] own testimony once a grand jury has been discharged" violates the First Amendment. Similarly in Kamasinski, we "conclude[d] that [a] limited ban on disclosure of the fact of filing or the fact that testimony was given does not run afoul of the First Amendment." But, we further held that "the ban on disclosure is constitutional only so long as the [government] acts in its investigatory capacity."

The government advanced the "mosaic theory" as one of the reasons to support a permanent ban on speech. That theory envisions thousands of bits and pieces of apparently innocuous information, which when properly assembled create a picture. At bottom the government's assertion is simply that antiterrorism investigations are different from other investigations in that they are derivative of prior or concurrent investigations. Thus, permanent non-disclosure is necessary because, implicitly in the government's view, all terrorism investigations are permanent and unending.

The government's urging that an endless investigation leads logically to an endless ban on speech flies in the face of human knowledge and common sense: witnesses disappear, plans change or are completed, cases are closed, investigations terminate. Further, a ban on speech and a shroud of secrecy in perpetuity are antithetical to democratic concepts and do not fit comfortably with the fundamental rights guaranteed American citizens. Unending secrecy of actions taken by government officials may also serve as a cover for possible official misconduct and/or incompetence.

Moreover, with regard to having something be secret forever, most Americans would agree with Benjamin Franklin's observation on our human inability to maintain secrecy for very long. He wrote "three may keep a secret, if two of them are dead." Benjamin Franklin, Poor Richard's Almanack 8 (Dean Walley ed., Hallmark 1967) (1732). In fact, what happened in the Connecticut case bears out Franklin's astute observation. While striving to keep the identities of the Connecticut plaintiffs secret, the government inadvertently revealed their identities through public court filings. This revelation was widely reported in the media. Thus, the case assumed the awkward posture where the identities of the Connecticut plaintiffs were published, yet the government continued to insist that the Connecticut plaintiffs may not identify themselves and that their identities must still be kept secret. This is like closing the barn door after the horse has already bolted.

Since the passage of the Reauthorization Act, the government asserts that we should vacate the District of Connecticut's preliminary injunction rather than leaving it unreviewed on appeal. See per curiam, supra at 7–8. To me, the government's request for vacatur in the Connecticut case is not surprising, but right in line with the pervasive climate of secrecy. It sought to prevent, through § 2709(c), the Doe plaintiffs from ever revealing that they were subjects of an NSL, effectively keeping that fact secret forever. Then, by requesting vacatur of the decision below, the government attempts to purge from the public record the fact that it had tried and failed to silence the Connecticut plaintiffs.

While everyone recognizes national security concerns are implicated when the government investigates terrorism within our Nation's borders, such concerns should be leavened with common sense so as not forever to trump the rights of the citizenry under the Constitution. As Justice Black wrote in New York Times Co. v. United States, 403 U.S. 713 (1971): "The word 'security' is a broad, vague generality whose contours should not be invoked to abrogate the fundamental law embodied in the First Amendment. The guarding of military and diplomatic secrets at the expense of informed representative government provides no real security for our Republic." Id. at 719 (Black, J., concurring).

Although I concur in the per curiam that declines to resolve the novel First Amendment issue before us on this appeal, that does not mean I think that issue unworthy of comment. Hence, this concurrence.

NOTE: NATIONAL SECURITY LETTER LIBRARY EXCEPTION

The National Security Letter authorization was amended in response to outcry from professional librarians about the loss of confidentiality and anonymity enjoyed by library patrons as a result of the "war on terror". The change means that most libraries would not qualify as a "wire or electronic communication service provider" for purposes of ECPA despite making internet-linked computers available to patrons: "(f) Libraries.—A library, as that term is defined in section 213(1) of the Library Services and Technology Act (20 U.S.C. 9122(1)), the services of which include access to the Internet, books, journals, magazines, newspapers, or other similar forms of communication in print or digitally by patrons for their use, review, examination, or circulation, is not a wire or electronic communication service provider for purposes of this section, unless the library is providing the services defined in section 2510(15) ("electronic communication service") of this title." See 18 U.S.C. § 2709. Critics of the "Privacy Protection for Library Patrons" exclusion fear that a library that provides users with the ability to send and receive emails or other communications may still qualify as a "wire or electronic communications service provider." Yet the library's ISP, not the library, is arguably the "provider" in such an instance. See www.fas.org/sgp/crs/intel/RS 22384.pdf.

SUSAN N. HERMAN, THE USA PATRIOT ACT AND THE SUBMAJORITARIAN FOURTH AMENDMENT

41 Harv. C.R.–C.L. L. Rev. 67, 78 (2006).

This * * * discussion of four of the most controversial surveillance provisions of the Patriot Act [Uniting and Strengthening America by Providing Appropriate Tools Required to Intercept and Obstruct Terrorism Act of 2001] will show the roles that Congress, the executive branch, and the courts have played in deciding what level of surveillance is reasonable. Secrecy and executive branch control over the flow of information have undermined both political and judicial accountability.

A. Section 215: Librarians and Beyond * * *

Section 215, titled "Access to Records and Other Items Under the Foreign Intelligence Surveillance Act," authorizes the government to acquire records and tangible things from custodians—including educational or financial institutions, Internet service providers, or even indignant librarians—under a court order. * * * The Patriot Act vastly expanded the kinds of records and objects the government could acquire under this provision, which now covers any type of record and tangible thing, and eliminated the requirement that the government demonstrate any form of individualized suspicion. * * * [S]ection 215 only requires that the affiant, a highly placed designee of the Director of the FBI, certify that he or she believes that information relevant to an investigation against "international terrorism or clandestine intelligence activities" may be obtained. Once the affiant has done this, the court "shall" enter an ex parte order, "as requested, or as modified, approving the release of records."

Section 215 contains a broad gag order that prohibits any person from disclosing to anyone "other than those persons necessary to produce the tangible things" that the FBI has sought or obtained tangible things under this section. Other than this narrow pragmatic exception, there is no boundary or time limit to the nondisclosure provision. Not only is the custodian never to tell the target that his or her records have been requested or turned over, but the statute contains no exception allowing custodians to consult counsel, to ask a court to lift the prohibition, or to report to the Inspector General or the press that the government has made such a request, even if they do not reveal the name of the target or the nature of the information requested.

The chief criticisms leveled against this provision target each feature described above. First, the provision allegedly violates Fourth Amendment principles of antecedent review by not requiring a court to find individualized suspicion before issuing the order. The government may gather sensitive information, including medical, religious, or library records, about anyone even if there is no reason to suspect the person whose records are sought of any sort of misconduct or connection with terrorists. Because there is no requirement of any form of individualized suspicion, the court issuing the order has less to decide and less of a role than a court issuing a traditional search warrant (where the court would evaluate the existence of probable cause to believe the individual is involved in criminal activity). Second, the gag order allegedly violates the Fourth Amendment because—unlike searches pursuant to a warrant or electronic surveillance in criminal investigations—it does not provide for notice to the target, even after the fact. Because the target never learns of the issuance of the order (unless and until a criminal prosecution is brought), the potential safeguard of giving the target an opportunity to invoke judicial review of any sort is eliminated.

First Amendment concerns are also raised about this section, as it allows the gathering of information about an individual's reading habits, Internet activities, or religious practices. Even if the discretion to investigate is not actually used in such a manner, the specter of such use might chill people from engaging in lawful and valued forms of speech and association, like taking books out of a library or attending a mosque. In a nod to First Amendment values, Congress had provided in FISA that "United States persons" may not be subjected to FISA surveillance "solely upon the basis of activities protected by the first amendment * * *." Section 215 did not rescind this prohibition, but the protection is of limited value. United States persons may still be investigated based in part on First Amendment protected activities (including protected speech or association), non-United States persons may be investigated "solely" on the basis of their speech or association, and the gag order makes it impossible for targets to challenge politically or religiously motivated investigations because they will not know that such investigations are taking place.

The government, on the other hand, can plausibly argue that section 215 actually provides more process than is constitutionally necessary. The Supreme Court has held that targets have no Fourth Amendment rights with respect to governmental demands for business records held by a third party because such a demand does not count as a "search" within the meaning of the Fourth Amendment. If the Fourth Amendment does not apply, no prior judicial approval or showing of individualized suspicion is required. Thus, even if Congress leaves the section unamended, it will have exceeded the constitutional mark. * * *

Despite the paucity of public information about implementation, a number of Arab and Muslim groups in Detroit, Michigan, brought a constitutional challenge to section 215 in Muslim Community Association of Ann Arbor v. Ashcroft ("MCA"). The plaintiffs asserted that they had a "well-founded belief that they and their members, clients and constituents * * * have been or are currently the targets of investigations conducted under Section 215." One of the plaintiffs, an Islamic Center, contended that it was likely to be asked to provide records of its members and, due to the gag order, would be unable to challenge the constitutionality of such an order. Some of the plaintiffs also alleged that concern about the potential use of this Patriot Act power was causing community members to be "afraid to attend a mosque, practice their religion, or express their opinions about religious and political issues." This type of harm may be suffered even by those who do not know whether the government is screening their records. The First Amendment chilling effect claim, unlike the Fourth Amendment claims, is not contingent on whether the power in question has actually been used. * * *

Because of the secrecy surrounding the implementation of section 215, targets could not join the litigation, custodians had difficulty establishing both standing and ripeness, critical aspects of the litigation took place ex parte and in camera, and the plaintiffs' attorney was at a disadvantage without equal access to the facts on which arguments could be based. Because the Attorney General could decide whether and when to divulge information about the implementation of section 215, one party— the government—gained a considerable measure of control over multiple aspects of the litigation. * * *

B.   Section 505: National Security Letters * * *

Section 505 goes even further than section 215 in circumventing judicial oversight of the government's collection of information from third party custodians. It allows the government to obtain records from a communications provider by issuing its own administrative subpoena, called a National Security Letter ("NSL"), to seek various types of information about the customers of communications providers, including telephone companies, Internet service providers, and libraries with computer terminals. Section 505 both dispenses with any showing of individualized suspicion and any form of antecedent judicial review. The Patriot Act eliminated the previous requirement of a showing that "specific and articulable facts existed" that the target was a "foreign power" or "agent of a foreign power." Now, the government only needs to certify that information relevant to a terrorism investigation may be obtained. Section 505 also carries a nondisclosure provision even more broadly worded than the gag order of section 215, prohibiting any provider or agent served with an NSL from disclosing to "any person" that the FBI has sought or obtained records pursuant to this authority.

The critique of this provision is the same as the critique of section 215—the judicial role is inadequate and the gag order overly restrictive— but is even more fervent because section 505 contemplates no judicial role at all and institutes a more comprehensive gag order. The government has ardently defended its administrative subpoena power and sought to expand its use, arguing that the NSL is comparable to a grand jury subpoena.

The public learned from a 2005 Washington Post article, rather than a government report or court order, that the FBI has issued more than 30,000 National Security Letters a year, an astronomical increase over "historic norms."

The Justice Department had argued that, as with section 215, all information about use of this authority, even statistical information, should be exempt from disclosure to the public. * * *

Two attempts to litigate the constitutionality of this section bear marks of the same distortions in the litigation process that plagued the section 215 litigation: the impact of secrecy, the difference between the rights of targets and custodians, and the privileged position of First Amendment compared to Fourth Amendment claims. The first lawsuit challenging this section was brought by an Internet service provider who was served with an NSL. Instead of complying with the NSL, as virtually all other recipients had, this provider consulted counsel, even though the gag order on its face contained no exception for consulting counsel or anyone else. The provider's counsel, the ACLU, filed a John Doe complaint claiming that section 505 violated the First, Fourth, and Fifth Amendments. * * *

The government argued that the court could find section 505 constitutional by construing it to allow the NSL recipient to consult with counsel and to bring a judicial proceeding contesting the constitutionality of the particular demand for information. The court rejected this argument, finding that the statute, in the manner in which it was being applied, exerted an "undue coercive effect" on NSL recipients because the recipient was not told that counsel could be consulted or that any form of judicial review might be available. All but the most "mettlesome and undaunted" providers, the judge observed, would feel coerced into complying with the demand for information and the demand of absolute and permanent silence. Focusing on the statute as applied, the court did not address the issue of whether the statute was indeed violative of the Fourth Amendment on its face. It instead found that section 505 could be used in a manner that infringed the First Amendment rights of subscribers and that the broad nondisclosure provision of section 505 violated the First Amendment. * * *

The Senate Patriot Act renewal bill amended section 505 along the lines suggested by the government in litigating the Doe case. House bill also allowed recipients of NSLs to bring a court challenge and to move to set aside the secrecy order under a comparable standard. It also provided new, explicit penalties for violating the gag order. Nonetheless, neither bill provided for any standard of individualized suspicion or even a statement of facts for a reviewing court to consult in determining whether the NSL is oppressive or unreasonable.

C. Section 218: Foreign Intelligence Surveillance * * *

Section 218 expands the power of the government to use [Foreign Intelligence Surveillance Act ("FISA")] warrants to conduct electronic surveillance instead of proceeding under the more demanding standards of Title III, which covers criminal investigations. The actual provision in the Patriot Act enigmatically provides, in its entirety, that two specified sections of FISA "are each amended by striking 'the purpose' and inserting 'a significant purpose.'" This seemingly trivial semantic amendment effected a major expansion of the government's authority to conduct electronic surveillance. The government now only needs to persuade the FISA court that there is probable cause to believe that the target is an "agent of a foreign power," rather than persuading a regular court that there is probable cause to believe that the target is involved in criminal activity. Critics described section 218 as razing the wall that previous law had erected between criminal law enforcement and intelligence gathering, while others maintained that no such wall had actually existed under the earlier law. Although the import of this amendment has been debated, the principal constitutional challenge to this expanded authority remains the same: that electronic surveillance should not be permitted in the absence of a more traditional judicial finding of probable cause.

As was the case with other Patriot Act provisions, section 218 was not the first or only expansion of the power conferred under FISA or the first contraction of FISA's initial safeguards. Questions were raised about the constitutionality of FISA's compromise long before critics leveled similar charges at the Patriot Act, claiming that the statute dispenses with a finding of traditional probable cause, requires less particularity, has no provision for even post hoc notice to the target (unless the government decides to use evidence derived from a FISA search in court), and allows a secret ex parte court to issue surveillance orders. On the other hand, the original statute did include a number of safeguards similar to those required when electronic surveillance is conducted in connection with a criminal investigation—like some judicial review of the government's reasons for selecting a target, and some minimization requirement. The Supreme Court has never ruled on the constitutionality of FISA, although there may be claims of unconstitutionality in both directions—that FISA grants too much or too little power to the executive.

Here, as with the sections previously described, targets and people who might be "aggrieved" by the use of such surveillance powers cannot avail themselves of any judicial remedy because they are not given notice of the fact that they have been the subject of a search. Such notice presumably would be given in a criminal prosecution where the government is planning to introduce evidence obtained under FISA, so the government can again control the existence and timing of litigation by not bringing to trial criminal prosecutions supported by evidence derived from FISA-based surveillance. Nevertheless, the constitutionality of section 218 has been the subject of a judicial opinion, handed down in a highly unusual ex parte proceeding. * * *

According to Attorney General Gonzales, the government has submitted seventy-four percent more applications to the FISA court since the Patriot Act was enacted, all of which have been granted. Although these numbers are available, there is no way for the public to evaluate how many applications would not have met the standards of Title III, how much useful information has been obtained as a result of such surveillance, or whether any of this information has prevented terrorist actions. The only case thus far concerning the constitutionality of section 218 took place in a unique context where the government was the only party to the litigation. Perhaps due to the distortions of the procedural context, the special court hearing the case essentially replicated legislative reasoning in concluding that the provision is reasonable. * * *

Because the statutory scheme and constitutional law involved are so complex, it would be unrealistic to expect meaningful public assessment of the changes effected by section 218. Academic commentators have, for the most part, been critical of the substantial expansion of the FISA surveillance authority. * * *

During the sunset debates, both houses of Congress voted to renew section 218 without amendment and without sunset. Courts other than the [FISA Court of Review], including the Supreme Court, are not likely to have occasion to review the constitutionality of this section unless the government is willing to provoke a challenge by relying on evidence obtained under section 218 in a criminal prosecution. Here too, the legislative debate followed the public's lack of concern or perhaps lack of knowledge about the content of this provision, and the courts did not impose any limitation on the executive branch beyond what Congress had provided.

D. Section 213: "Sneak And Peek" * * *

Section 213, the so-called "sneak and peek" provision, applies in cases where the government has honored the Fourth Amendment norm by obtaining a search warrant based on probable cause. This provision allows the government to ask a court for permission to defer notifying the target that a search (or sometimes even a seizure) has taken place on a finding, inter alia, that immediate notification might have "an adverse result." The delay in notification may be extended, apparently indefinitely, "for good cause shown." This authority is not limited to terrorism investigations and was not scheduled to sunset. Courts are left a great deal of discretion: The statute provides no time limit, the standard to be applied is fairly open ended, and notification of seizures as well as searches may be deferred.

Critics of this section claim that the Fourth Amendment requires notice prior to a search. The searches affected by this provision are conducted pursuant to a search warrant, and frequently take place in homes—a venue the Supreme Court has found to enjoy special protection. Moreover, the Supreme Court has held, although only relatively recently, that searches are presumptively unreasonable unless law enforcement officials "knock and announce" themselves before executing a warrant. Having an opportunity to view the search warrant gives the target a chance to point out any mistakes—perhaps the address is wrong—and to ensure that the search does not exceed the scope authorized.

Lack of notice of a seizure allegedly constitutes a denial of due process. Earlier Supreme Court case law also suggested that when law enforcement agents seize property pursuant to a search warrant, due process requires that they take "reasonable steps to give notice that the property has been taken so the owner can pursue available remedies for its return." Without notification, the target of a seizure might conclude that she or he was the victim of a burglary or might be entirely unaware of the government's seizure, as might happen if the government copies the hard drive of the target's computer. Thus, the individual may not have any opportunity to challenge the validity of the warrant or the propriety of the scope of its execution. In this section, unlike the other Patriot Act provisions described, a judge makes the decision in each individual case whether the statutory standard, however elastic, has been met. * * *

There appears to have been no litigation over the constitutionality of this provision. The very secrecy targets might wish to contest prevents targets from learning whether they have been affected by this provision. The odds that this section will be the subject of litigation may be greater because it applies not only to terrorism investigations, where the government's priority may be prevention rather than prosecution, but to all crimes. * * *

Respondents in the Gallup Poll had the most negative reaction to this provision. Seventy-one percent of those surveyed disapproved of allowing agents to search a home secretly and, for an unspecified period of time, not to inform the person of that search. A number of commentators have likewise been critical of this provision. * * *

The 2001 Congress evidently did not anticipate this level of controversy. The Patriot Act did not provide for section 213 to sunset. During the sunset debates, however, the provision was discussed and the resulting Senate bill proposed amending this section by providing time limits circumscribing the period of delay and requiring more specific reporting to Congress about the provision's use. The time limits, however, included very elastic provisions allowing exceptions, making the amendments vulnerable to the criticism that they do not implement any real reform. The House bill imposed outer limits on delayed notification and also enhanced oversight provisions.

The draft conference report proposed some time limits, but the limits were similarly elastic and subject to renewal. * * *

Overall, the history of these four Patriot Act provisions shows that secrecy and other forces have impeded both political and judicial accountability. Three of these four provisions were among the chief subjects of debate during the sunset hearings and virtually the only provisions either the House or Senate even considered amending. But although many people were troubled by the breadth of these particular powers, the public did not have enough information to evaluate how the powers had been used or whether they had been abused. * * *

[T]he bulk of the Patriot Act provisions hastily passed in October 2001 seem destined to become permanent law. Attention will now turn to the courts.

C. THE ELECTRONIC COMMUNICATIONS PRIVACY ACT OF 1986 (ECPA), TITLE III, THE PEN REGISTER ACT

NOTE: CONTENTS, NON-CONTENT AND SOMETHING IN BETWEEN

The case that follows, *In the Matter of the Application of the U.S.A.*, examines the federal Pen Register Act (ECPA, Title III) in a contemporary setting. It describes the history and purposes of the Act, however. It also examines how the Act was amended to facilitate law enforcement by passage of the Communications Assistance for Law Enforcement Act of 1994 (CALEA) and the Uniting and Strengthening America by Providing Appropriate Tools Required to Intercept and Obstruct Terrorism Act of 2001 (USA PATRIOT Act). Why does ECPA provide different levels of protection for communications "contents" and non-content information?

IN THE MATTER OF THE APPLICATION OF THE U.S.A.

441 F.Supp.2d 816 (S.D. Tex. 2006).

JUDGE STEPHEN WM. SMITH

This opinion addresses * * * whether the Government may obtain "post-cut-through dialed digits" containing communication contents under the authority of the Pen/Trap Statute. * * *

"Post-cut-through dialed digits" are any numbers dialed from a telephone after the call is initially setup or "cut-through." Sometimes these digits are other telephone numbers, as when a party places a credit card call by first dialing the long distance carrier access number and then the phone number of the intended party. Sometimes these digits transmit real information, such as bank account numbers, Social Security numbers, prescription numbers, and the like. In the latter case, the digits represent communications content; in the former, they are non-content call processing numbers. U.S. Telecom, 227 F.3d at 462.

Because of this dual capacity, post-cut-through dialed digits occupy a doubtful position under federal electronic surveillance laws, which are founded upon the fundamental (indeed, constitutional) distinction between communications content and non-content. It is well-established that the content of telephone communications is protected by the Fourth Amendment. Katz v. United States, 389 U.S. 347, 353–54 (1967). In order to gain authorization to intercept content, the Government must obtain a special wiretap warrant that satisfies not only the usual probable cause standard but also additional threshold requirements set out in Title III of the Omnibus Crime Control and Safe Streets Act of 1968 (commonly referred to as the "Wiretap Act").

By contrast, there is no Fourth Amendment protection for telephone numbers dialed to connect a call. Smith v. Maryland, 442 U.S. 735, 745–46 (1979). In 1986, Congress enacted the ECPA to regulate the process under which law enforcement could install pen registers, which capture phone numbers of outgoing calls, and trap and trace devices, which capture phone numbers of incoming calls. Although a court order was required, the threshold for obtaining the order was very low: a Government attorney need only certify that "the information likely to be obtained is relevant to an ongoing criminal investigation." 18 U.S.C. § 3122(b)(2). Because pen register technology at that time was unable to obtain contents, the question of law enforcement access to dialed numbers straddlng the line between content and non-content was simply not contemplated when the ECPA was enacted. * * *

Telecommunications technology did not stand still, of course, and within a few years law enforcement became very concerned that criminal investigations were being hindered by the technical inability of telecommunications carriers to provide authorized electronic surveillance. In response to these concerns, Congress enacted the Communications Assistance for Law Enforcement Act of 1994 (CALEA). Under this law, telecommunication companies were directed to build into their networks the technical capability to assist law enforcement with authorized interception of communications and "call-identifying information." See 47 U.S.C. § 1002. Congress intended CALEA to preserve the status quo, and therefore the new statute did not modify the legal standards for electronic surveillance via wiretap or pen/trap devices.

One of the new technological wrinkles discussed during congressional deliberations on CALEA was the capacity of pen registers to capture content information in the form of post-cut-through dialed digits. This is reflected in the following exchange between Senator Leahy and FBI Director Freeh:

> Sen. Leahy: You say this would not expand law enforcement's authority to collect data on people, and yet if you're going to the new technologies, where you can dial up everything from a video movie to do your banking on it, you are going to have access to a lot more data, just because that's what's being used for doing it.

> Mr. Freeh: I don't want that access, and I'm willing to concede that. What I want with respect to pen registers is the dialing information, telephone numbers which are being called, which I have now under pen register authority. As to the banking accounts and what movie somebody is ordering in Blockbuster, I don't want it, don't need it, and I'm willing to have technological blocks with respect to that information, which I can get with subpoenas or other process. I don't want that in terms of my access, and that's not the transactional data that I need.

Accordingly, CALEA was amended to address the post-cut-through dialed digits issue, by inserting the following limitation into the Pen/Trap Statute's provision authorizing pen registers:

> (c) Limitation.—A government agency authorized to install and use a pen register under this chapter or under State law shall use technology reasonably available to it that restricts the recording or decoding of electronic or other impulses to the dialing and signaling information utilized in call processing.

Pub. L. No. 103–414, § 207, 108 Stat. 4279, 4292 (1994) (codified at 18 U.S.C. § 3121(c)).

Subsequent to CALEA's passage, attention turned to the development of specific technological standards through which telecommunications carriers would comply with their obligation to assist law enforcement by providing "call-identifying information." Development of such standards was left to the telecommunications industry, in consultation with law enforcement agencies and consumers, under the auspices of the Federal Communications Commission. 47 U.S.C. § 1006. In 1999, the FCC issued a ruling on the proposed technical standards (referred to as the "J–Standard"), finding among other things that the J–Standard must include the capability for "post-cut-through dialed digit extraction." This capability required carriers to use tone-detection equipment to generate a list of all digits dialed after a call has been connected, including numbers dialed after connecting to a long distance carrier (such as 1–800–CALL–ATT), or to an automated telephone service, such as bank account or credit card numbers. * * *

Several entities challenged the FCC decision and the petitions for review were consolidated in United States Telecom Assoc. v. Federal Communications Comm'n, 343 U.S.App.D.C. 278, 227 F.3d 450 (D.C. Cir. 2000). Petitioners contended that the CALEA obligation to produce "call-identifying information" should be limited to telephone numbers only, and that the FCC exceeded its authority by including the broader dialed digit extraction capability in the J–Standard. Applying the usual Chevron deference standard of review, the D.C. Circuit first determined that CALEA was ambiguous with respect to its definition of call-identifying information. The court rejected the contention that the definition should be read in parity with ECPA definitions of "pen register" and "trap and trace device," which are limited to phone numbers: "CALEA neither cross-references nor incorporates ECPA's definitions of pen registers and trap and trace devices. Moreover, the fact that CALEA's definition of 'call-identifying information' differs from the ECPA's description of the information obtainable by pen registers and trap and trace devices reinforces the statute's inherent ambiguity." Id. at 459.

Next, the court determined that the FCC's ruling as to dialed digit extraction reflected a lack of reasoned decision-making. In particular, the FCC failed to explain how the dialed digit extraction capability would meet the statutory requirements of a "cost-effective" method that would "protect the privacy and security of communications not authorized to be intercepted." Id. at 461–62 (citing 47 U.S.C. § 1006(b)(1) & (2)). The Government had argued that the FCC's ruling adequately protected privacy because a law enforcement agency is entitled to receive all post-cut-through digits with a pen register order, subject to CALEA's "reasonably available technology" caveat (18 U.S.C. § 3121(c)). The court effectively side-stepped this argument, observing that "[n]o court has yet considered that contention, however, and it may be that a Title III warrant is required to receive all post-cut-through digits." Id. at 462. Because the FCC had not given "any meaningful consideration" to protecting the privacy of dialed digit contents, its order regarding dialed digit extraction was vacated and remanded for further proceedings. * * *

Congress returned to the dialed digits issue in the fall of 2001 during its consideration of the USA PATRIOT Act. Among the law enforcement enhancements within the initial DOJ-proposed bill was a provision amending the Pen/Trap Statute to include all "dialing, routing, addressing, or signaling information," thereby extending its coverage to Internet communications. See Orin S. Kerr, Internet Surveillance Law After the USA PATRIOT Act: The Big Brother That Isn't, 97 Nw.U.L.Rev. 607, 637 (Winter 2003). Privacy advocates objected to this broadened definition, concerned that it might allow the Government to obtain the contents of communications without a wiretap order. Id. at 640–41. Senator Leahy, who had been instrumental in passing the CALEA "reasonably available technology" limitation, declared on the Senate floor that § 3121(c) had so far not achieved its purpose of protecting dialed digit contents from collection by pen registers:

> When I added the direction on use of reasonably available technology (codified as 18 U.S.C. 3121(c)) to the pen register statute as part of the Communications Assistance for Law Enforcement Act (CALEA) in 1994, I recognized that these devices collected content and that such collection was unconstitutional on the mere relevance standard. Nevertheless, the FBI advised me in June 2000, that pen register devices for telephone services "continue to operate as they have for decades" and that "there has been no change * * * that would better restrict the recording or decoding of electronic or other impulses to the dialing and signaling information utilized in call processing." Perhaps, if there were meaningful judicial review and accountability, the FBI would take the statutory direction more seriously and actually implement it.

147 Cong. Rec. S11000 (Oct. 25, 2001) (remarks of Sen. Leahy).

To alleviate this concern that had not been fully alleviated by CALEA, Congress amended the Pen/Trap Statute in three ways: (1) the phrase "shall not include the contents of any communication" was added to the pen register definition at § 3127(3); (2) the same phrase was added to the trap and trace device definition at § 3127(4); and (3) the phrase "so as not to include the contents of any wire or electronic communications" was added to the reasonably available technology limitation at § 3121(c). Senator Leahy explained the significance of the latter amendment on the Senate floor:

> The USA PATRIOT Act also requires the government to use reasonably available technology that limits the interceptions under the pen/trap device laws "so as not to include the contents of any wire or electronic communications." This limitation on the technology used by the government to execute pen/trap orders is important since as the FBI advised me in June 2000, pen register devices "do capture all electronic impulses transmitted by the facility on which they are attached, including such impulses transmitted after a phone call is connected to the called party." The impulses made after the call is

connected could reflect the electronic banking transactions a caller makes, or the electronic ordering from a catalogue that a customer makes over the telephone, or the electronic ordering of a prescription drug.

This transactional data intercepted after the call is connected is "content."

Id.; see also Beryl A. Howell, Seven Weeks: The Making of the USA PATRIOT Act, 72 GEO. WASH. L. REV. 1145, 1198 (2004).

On May 24, 2002, Deputy Attorney General Larry D. Thompson issued a memorandum setting out DOJ policy on post-cut-through dialed digits in light of the PATRIOT Act amendments. This policy consists of two "basic principles": (1) law enforcement would use reasonably available technology to minimize over-collection of contents, while still allowing collection of all non-content digits; and (2) no affirmative investigative use would be made of any content digits incidentally collected. * * *

In response to the briefing order in this case, the Government has filed a submission that "technology currently is not reasonably available which would permit law enforcement to reliably discern and then separately collect only those post-cut-through digits that are call processing information from those that may constitute content." For this reason, the Government apparently employs no filtering technology at this time, and seeks this court's authorization to gather all dialed digits, content and non-content, in reliance on its pledge to make no affirmative investigative use of content digits. * * *

The starting point of statutory interpretation is always the wording of the statute. If its meaning is plain and unambiguous, the job is done and further inquiry moot. See, e.g., Barnhart v. Sigmon Coal Co., 534 U.S. 438, 450 (2002). Here we begin with the relevant definitions. In pertinent part, "pen register" is defined as:

A device or process which records or decodes dialing, routing, addressing, or signaling information transmitted by an instrument or facility from which a wire or electronic communication is transmitted, provided, however, that such information shall not include the contents of any communication * * *

18 U.S.C. § 3127(3). Similarly, "trap and trace device" is defined in pertinent part as:

A device or process which captures the incoming electronic or other impulses which identify the originating number or other dialing, routing, addressing, or signaling information reasonably likely to identify the source of a wire or electronic communication, provided, however, that such information shall not include the contents of any communication * * *

18 U.S.C. § 3127(4). The emphasized passages plainly declare that, by definition, pen/trap devices must not obtain information that includes contents. This proscription against content is unqualified.

The term "contents" of communication is defined as "any information concerning the substance, purport, or meaning of that communication." 18 U.S.C. §§ 2510(8), 3127(1). It is undisputed that post-cut-through dialed digits can and often do include call content. See United States Telecom., 227 F.3d at 462. As the D.C. Circuit explained:

> For example, subjects calling automated banking services enter account numbers. When calling voicemail systems, they enter passwords. When calling pagers, they dial digits that convey actual messages. And when calling pharmacies to renew prescriptions, they enter prescription numbers.

Id. Some post-cut-through digits are non-content telephone numbers, as when a party places a credit card call by first dialing a long distance carrier access number, and then, after the initial call is "cut through," dialing the number of the intended party. Id. The Government's application covers all post-cut-through dialed digits, both content and non-content.

> Even in this latter example, however, the calling party may be required to enter content information such as an account number before the carrier will proceed with the call. The Government argues that account number digits dialed in this manner actually become non-content call set-up information, thereby losing their "protected" content status. Resolution of this particular question is immaterial here, because the Government's application seeks access to all digits dialed, before and after call set-up.

The Government contends that the seemingly unconditional command of § 3127 is relieved by § 3121(c), which reads in its entirety:

> (c) Limitation.—A government agency authorized to install and use a pen register or trap and trace device under this chapter or under State law shall use technology reasonably available to it that restricts the recording or decoding of electronic or other impulses to the dialing, routing, addressing, and signaling information utilized in the processing and transmitting of wire or electronic communications so as not to include the contents of any wire or electronic communications.

18 U.S.C. § 3121(c). On its face, however, this section does not expressly authorize anything. Instead, it imposes an affirmative obligation ("shall use technology") upon a law enforcement agency which has already been "authorized to install and use" a pen/trap device. * * *

There are numerous difficulties with the Government's construction. First, it rests almost entirely upon legislative silence. Section 3121(c) does not say what the outcome would be if technology could not separate all content from non-content dialed digits. The most natural reading of the provision is that Congress assumed that such technology would be available, and for that reason did not address or even contemplate the contrary scenario. If Congress did contemplate the possibility that technology would not be available, then it is certainly curious why it did not explicitly declare content digits as fair game, especially since the statute elsewhere excludes content in unqualified terms. Of course, this anomaly disappears if the passage is construed not to allow acquisition of contents in this situation * * *.

The Government incorrectly argues that its interpretation is the only way to avoid rendering § 3121(c) superfluous. According to the DOJ Memo: "This provision imposes an affirmative obligation to operate a pen register or trap and trace device in a manner that, to the extent feasible with reasonably available technology, will minimize any possible overcollection while still allowing the device to collect all of the limited information authorized." * * * [T]he DOJ's gloss on the passage, * * * can be reduced to the following maxim: "minimize content, but allow all non-content." This is admittedly one possible way to read § 3121(c), but there is another—that the Government must use technology reasonably at hand to gather as many non-content digits as possible, without also including contents. In other words, "maximize non-content, but disallow all content." This "maximization" reading is not only inherently plausible, but also in harmony with the unqualified content proscription found in the concluding passage of § 3121(c) ("so as not to include the contents of any wire or electronic communications"). By contrast, the Government's minimization reading contradicts, or at least creates serious tension with, the explicit content prohibitions inserted into the statute by the PATRIOT Act. The operative canon of statutory construction here is not the rule against superfluity, but rather the rule that statutory provisions be construed in harmony with one another. See Food and Drug Admin. v. Brown & Williamson Tobacco Corp., 529 U.S. 120, 133 (2000) ("A court must therefore interpret the statute as a symmetrical and coherent regulatory scheme, and fit, if possible, all parts into an harmonious whole * * *." (internal quotations and citations omitted)). Thus, the Government is the party at odds with traditional canons of construction, not amici.

In practice, it appears the Government has not even adhered to its own view that the statute imposes an affirmative obligation to minimize content collection. According to its submissions, the Government has concluded that no technology currently available would permit law enforcement to isolate call processing digits from content digits with 100% accuracy. Apparently for that reason, the Government is not currently using any minimization technology at all. Instead, it asks this court to authorize the collection of all digits dialed, before and after call set-up, and to rely upon the Government's promise not to make affirmative investigative use of contents. But the Government's affirmative obligation under § 3121(c) is not a mere contingency, lying dormant until some future day when a foolproof filter is found. It is, as the DOJ memo appears to recognize, a continuing obligation to use whatever technology is available at any given time to avoid collection of contents. That technology need not be perfect, only reasonably available, and if so it must be used. * * *

Courts should not be in the business of crafting exceptions to unqualified proscriptions handed down by Congress. "Shall not include contents" is not a precatory suggestion, it is a plain commandment. While not etched upon a tablet of stone, this edict from Capitol Hill is no less binding upon those who must interpret and execute it. * * *

Because the text of the statute is so plain, there is no need to resort to legislative history for clearer signs of congressional intent. Even so, the legislative history already recited in this opinion abundantly confirms the plain meaning of the statute.

Briefly summarized, that history reflects persistent Congressional efforts to assure that communications contents retain their protected legal status in the face of changing technology and law enforcement capabilities. The initial Pen/Trap Statute, part of the ECPA, was "primarily a privacy law." Kerr, 97 Nw. L. Rev. at 638. It regulated the phone number collection that would otherwise have been unregulated after Smith v. Maryland. Because existing pen register technology in the 1980s did not allow over-collection of content, there was no need for Congress to address the contents problem in that portion of the ECPA. When Congress became aware of the issue in 1994, it passed the CALEA amendment to the Pen/Trap Statute imposing an affirmative obligation to use technology to restrict the information collected to call-processing numbers. See 18 U.S.C. § 3121(c). Advised in 2001 that pen registers continued to collect content despite CALEA's technology limitation, Congress acted again by inserting into the Patriot Act not one but three separate directives placing contents out of bounds for pen/trap devices. 18 U.S.C. §§ 3121(c), 3127(3) & (4). * * *

Also questionable is the Government's apparent presumption that the pre-PATRIOT Act version of § 3121(c) was intended to authorize the collection of content so long as filtering technology was unavailable. One respected authority, in an article addressing what he considered unfounded criticism of the PATRIOT Act by privacy advocates, noted that despite "ambiguous language in the pen register statute dating from 1986 * * * no one had ever thought that the contents of communications that happen to include numbers were somehow exempted from the Wiretap Act." See Kerr, 97 Nw. U.L. Rev. at 642; see also id. at 641 (characterizing such an interpretation as "fanciful" and "difficult to imagine."). While there is no need for the court to definitively construe previous versions of the Pen/Trap Statute, it is appropriate to note that the fundamental premise of the Government's argument from legislative history is highly dubious.

Post-cut-through dialed digit contents may be intercepted by law enforcement under the Wiretap Act, and collected from electronic storage under the SCA. They are not available to law enforcement under the Pen/Trap Statute. Section 3121(c) is a limitation, not a license. Because the Pen/Trap Statute triply forbids what the Government requests, the application to acquire post-cut-through dialed digits must be denied.

D. VIDEO SURVEILLANCE: BEYOND THE BOUNDS OF ECPA

1. ORWELL'S DYSTOPIA

GEORGE ORWELL,

1984 (1949).

The hallway smelt of boiled cabbage and old rag mats. At one end of it a coloured poster, too large for indoor display, had been tacked to the wall. It depicted simply an enormous face, more than a metre wide: the face of a man of about forty-five, with a heavy black moustache and ruggedly handsome features. Winston made for the stairs. It was no use trying the lift. Even at the best of times it was seldom working, and at present the electric current was cut off during daylight hours. It was part of the economy drive in preparation for Hate Week. The flat was seven flights up, and Winston, who was thirty-nine and had a varicose ulcer above his right ankle, went slowly, resting several times on the way. On each landing, opposite the lift-shaft, the poster with the enormous face gazed from the wall. It was one of those pictures which are so contrived that the eyes follow you about when you move. BIG BROTHER IS WATCHING YOU, the caption beneath it ran.

Inside the flat a fruity voice was reading out a list of figures which had something to do with the production of pig-iron. The voice came from an oblong metal plaque like a dulled mirror which formed part of the surface of the right-hand wall. Winston turned a switch and the voice sank somewhat, though the words were still distinguishable. The instrument (the telescreen, it was called) could be dimmed, but there was no way of shutting it off completely. He moved over to the window: a smallish, frail figure, the meagreness of his body merely emphasized by the blue overalls which were the uniform of the party. His hair was very fair, his face naturally sanguine, his skin roughened by coarse soap and blunt razor blades and the cold of the winter that had just ended. * * *

Behind Winston's back the voice from the telescreen was still babbling away about pig-iron and the overfulfilment of the Ninth Three–Year Plan. The telescreen received and transmitted simultaneously. Any sound that Winston made, above the level of a very low whisper, would be picked up by it, moreover, so long as he remained within the field of vision which the metal plaque commanded, he could be seen as well as heard. There was of course no way of knowing whether you were being watched at any given moment. How often, or on what system, the Thought Police plugged in on any individual wire was guesswork. It was even conceivable that they watched everybody all the time. But at any rate they could plug in your wire whenever they wanted to. You had to live—did live, from habit that became instinct—in the assumption that every sound you made was overheard, and, except in darkness, every movement scrutinized.

Winston kept his back turned to the telescreen. It was safer, though, as he well knew, even a back can be revealing. * * *

Winston turned round abruptly. He had set his features into the expression of quiet optimism which it was advisable to wear when facing the telescreen.

2. SETTING LEGAL LIMITS ON VIDEO SURVEILLANCE—PARTICULARITY

NOTE: BIG BROTHER

The government installs a video camera in your residence. You are detected committing a crime. Can the video be placed into evidence at your criminal trial?

What bodies of law regulate video surveillance? What relevance do the Fourth Amendment, ECPA, FISA and state surveillance laws have when video-only technologies are at issue? Why doesn't ECPA expressly protect against video-only surveillance? How does the "particularity" requirement differ from the "minimization" requirement? *See U.S. v. Torres* for answers.

UNITED STATES v. TORRES

751 F.2d 875 (7th Cir. 1984).

POSNER, CIRCUIT JUDGE.

This appeal by the United States raises two novel and important questions: whether the federal government may ever secretly televise the interior of a private building as part of a criminal investigation and use the videotapes in a criminal trial, and if so whether the warrants under which television surveillance was conducted in this case complied with constitutional requirements. A federal grand jury indicted the four defendants, who are members of the FALN (Fuerzas Armadas de Liberacion Nacional Puertorriquena), on charges of seditious conspiracy (18 U.S.C. § 2384) and related weapons and explosives violations. On the eve of trial, the district judge ordered the suppression of videotapes that the FBI had made as part of its surveillance of two FALN safe houses. 583 F. Supp. 86, 99–105 (N.D. Ill. 1984). The government appeals this order under 18 U.S.C. § 3731. The videotapes had no sound track; but at the same time that the FBI was televising the interiors of the safe houses it was recording the sounds on different equipment. The judge refused to order suppression of the sound tapes, and they are not issue in this appeal.

The FALN is a secret organization of Puerto Rican separatists that has been trying to win independence for Puerto Rico by tactics that include bombing buildings in New York, Chicago, and Washington. The bombs are assembled and stored, and members of the organization meet, in safe houses rented under false names. The bombings have killed several people, injured many others, and caused millions of dollars of property damage. * * *

The background to the present case is the arrest in 1980 in a Chicago suburb of several members of the FALN, one of whom agreed to help the FBI's investigation of the organization. He identified as members two of the people later charged in this case. FBI agents followed one, who unwittingly led the agents to an apartment in Chicago that was being used as an FALN safe house. The U.S. Attorney obtained from Chief Judge McGarr of the Northern District of Illinois an order authorizing the FBI to make surreptitious entries into the apartment to install electronic "bugs" and television cameras in every room. The FBI wanted to see as well as hear because it had reason to believe that the people using the safe houses, concerned they might be bugged, would play the radio loudly when they were speaking to each other and also would speak in code, and that the actual assembly of bombs would be carried on in silence. The television surveillance of the first apartment paid off: the FBI televised two of the defendants assembling bombs. On the basis of these observations the FBI obtained a search warrant for the apartment and found dynamite, blasting caps, guns, and maps showing the location of prisons. Tailing the same two defendants led to the second safe house involved in this appeal. Again a warrant was obtained to conduct electronic, including television, surveillance; and it was by televising meetings in this safe house that the other two defendants in this case were identified.

The trial judge held that there was no statutory or other basis for Chief Judge McGarr's order authorizing television surveillance of the safe houses and that therefore the fruits of the surveillance, including the videotapes, would be inadmissible in the defendants' forthcoming trial. 583 F. Supp. at 105. The defendants and amici curiae advance the following additional grounds for this result: television surveillance in criminal investigations (other than of foreign agents) is forbidden by federal statute; it is in any event so intrusive—so reminiscent of the "telescreens" by which "Big Brother" in George Orwell's 1984 maintained visual surveillance of the entire population of "Oceania," the miserable country depicted in that anti-utopian novel—that it can in no circumstances be authorized (least of all, one imagines, in the year 1984) without violating both the Fourth Amendment and the Fifth Amendment's due process clause; and even if all this is wrong, still the particular orders ("warrants," as we shall call them) in this case did not satisfy the requirements of the Fourth Amendment's warrant clause.

The trial judge appears, however, to have overlooked United States v. New York Tel. Co., 434 U.S. 159 (1977), where the Supreme Court held that Rule 41 of the Federal Rules of Criminal Procedure, which authorizes the issuance of search warrants, embraces orders to install "pen registers" (devices that record the phone numbers that a telephone subscriber is dialing). * * * We cannot think of any basis on which the rule might be thought sufficiently flexible to authorize a pen register, bug, or wiretap, but not a camera. It is true that secretly televising people (or taking still or moving pictures of them) while they are in what they think is a private place is an even greater intrusion on privacy than secretly recording their conversations. But the fact that electronic eavesdropping is more intrusive than conventional searching did not prevent the Supreme Court in the New York Telephone case from reading Rule 41—very broadly in view of its language—to embrace electronic eavesdropping. The next step, to television surveillance, is smaller than the one the Court took.

There is another basis, besides Rule 41, for the issuance of warrants for television surveillance. * * * [T]he power to issue a search warrant was historically, and is still today, an inherent (by which we mean simply a nonstatutory, or common law) power of a court of general jurisdiction. * * *

The power to issue a search warrant is a common law power in America as well as England, and in the federal system as well as in the states. While "the whole criminal jurisdiction of the courts of the United States [is] derived from Acts of Congress," Jones v. United States, 137 U.S. 202 (1890), this does not mean that every procedural incident of their jurisdiction is statutory. * * *

The defendants argue, however, that Title III of the Omnibus Crime Control and Safe Streets Act of 1968, 18 U.S.C. §§ 2510–2520, as amended by the Foreign Intelligence Surveillance Act of 1978, 50 U.S.C. §§ 1801 et seq., deprives the federal courts of the power they would otherwise have to issue a warrant for television surveillance. Title III authorizes federal judges to issue warrants (called "orders") for wiretapping and bugging, and establishes elaborate requirements for such warrants. But it does not authorize warrants for television surveillance. The statute regulates only the "interception of wire or oral communications." A man televised while silently making a bomb is not engaged in any form of communication, let alone "wire or oral communication." Any possible doubt on this score is dispelled by the statutory definition of "intercept" as "the aural acquisition of the contents of any wire or oral communication through the use of any electronic, mechanical, or other device." A visual observation is in no possible sense an "aural acquisition," or an acquisition, of any kind, of a "wire or oral communication." Nor would a camera meet the statutory definition of "electronic, mechanical, or other device." The Senate committee report, after repeating the statutory definition of "aural acquisition," remarks: "Other forms of surveillance are not within the proposed legislation."

It does not follow, however, that because Title III does not authorize warrants for television surveillance, it forbids them. The motto of the Prussian state—that everything which is not permitted is forbidden—is not a helpful guide to statutory interpretation. Television surveillance (with no soundtrack) just is not within the statute's domain. The legislative history does not refer to it, probably because television cameras in 1968 were too bulky and noisy to be installed and operated surreptitiously. It would be illogical to infer from Congress's quite natural omission to deal with a nonproblem that it means to tie the federal courts' hands when and if the problem arose.

The defendants appeal to the spirit of Title III, which was, they say, the protection of privacy, and from which they infer that Congress meant to forbid any electronic investigative techniques that it did not authorize. But this description of the spirit of Title III is incomplete. Enacted in the wake of Katz v. United States, supra, which has held that electronic eavesdropping was subject to the Fourth Amendment, Title III established procedures to facilitate the use of wiretapping and bugging (subject to appropriate safeguards) in federal criminal investigations. Protecting privacy was a goal of the statute but not the only or even the paramount goal. The Senate report states that "Title III has as its dual purpose (1) protecting the privacy on a uniform basis the circumstances and conditions under which the interception of wire and oral communications may be authorized." The second formulation seems an allusion to the law-enforcement objectives of Title III, elsewhere in the report described as paramount. "The major purpose of title III is to combat organized crime"; and "intercepting the communications of organized criminals is the only effective method of learning about their activities." Id. at 70, 72.

The Foreign Intelligence Surveillance Act established procedures for electronic surveillance of foreign agents. Reflecting changes in technology in the decade that had passed since the enactment of Title III, the Act defines electronic surveillance broadly enough to cover television, by including in the definition the use of "an electronic, mechanical, or other surveillance device * * * for monitoring to acquire information, other than from a wire or radio communication * * *." Although the procedures in the Act have no direct application to this case—these defendants are not agents of a foreign power, and the government does not argue that the Act authorized television surveillance of them—the Act also amended Title III as follows: "procedures in [Title III] and the Foreign Intelligence Surveillance Act of 1978 shall be the exclusive means by which electronic surveillance, as defined [in the Foreign Intelligence Surveillance Act], and the interception of domestic wire and oral communications may be conducted." 18 U.S.C. § 2511(2)(f). The defendants read this to mean that television surveillance, a form of electronic surveillance that does not involve the interception of wire or oral communications, may be conducted only in accordance with the Foreign Intelligence Surveillance Act; since that Act did not authorize the surveillance in this case, section 2511(2)(f) forbids it.

All this section means to us, however, is that the Foreign Intelligence Surveillance Act is intended to be exclusive in its domain and Title III in its. The powers that the Act gives the government to keep tabs on agents of foreign countries are not to be used for purely domestic investigations, and conversely the limitations that Title III places on wiretapping and bugging are not to be used to hobble the government's activities against foreign agents. To read the Foreign Intelligence Surveillance Act as the defendants would have us do would give a statute designed to regularize the government's broad powers to deal with the special menace posed by agents of foreign powers the side effect of curtailing the government's powers in domestic law enforcement. This is not what Congress intended in making what the Senate report on the bill that became the Foreign Intelligence Surveillance Act described as a "technical and conforming" amendment to Title III. S. Rep. No. 604, supra, at 3. * * *

The fact is that Congress has never addressed the issue of judicial authorization of television surveillance in federal criminal investigations. But of course that observation cannot be the end of our analysis. It is too late in the day to argue that the Fourth Amendment regulates only the types of search that were technically feasible in the eighteenth century. The government therefore quite properly does not argue that television surveillance is outside the scope of the Fourth Amendment. We think it also unarguable that television surveillance is exceedingly intrusive, especially in combination (as here) with audio surveillance, and inherently indiscriminate, and that it could be grossly abused—to eliminate personal privacy as understood in modern Western nations.

The precise application of the Fourth Amendment to television surveillance has, therefore, now to be considered. The Fourth Amendment provides: "[1] The right of the people to be secure in their persons, houses, papers, and effects, against unreasonable searches and seizures, shall not be violated, and [2] no Warrants shall issue, but upon probable cause, supported by Oath or affirmation, and particularly describing the place to be searched, and the persons or things to be seized." The usual way in which judges interpreting the Fourth Amendment take account of the fact that searches vary in the degree to which they invade personal privacy is by requiring a higher degree of probable cause (to believe that the search will yield incriminating evidence), and by being more insistent that a warrant be obtained if at all feasible, the more intrusive the search is. But maybe in dealing with so intrusive a technique as television surveillance, other methods of control as well, such as banning the technique outright from use in the home in connection with minor crimes, will be required, in order to strike a proper balance between public safety and personal privacy. That question is not before us, but we mention it to make clear that in declining to hold television surveillance unconstitutional per se we do not suggest that the Constitution must be interpreted to allow it to be used as generally as less intrusive techniques can be used. * * *

The FALN has the plans, the materials, and the know-how to kill in gross. A sophisticated as well as lethal practitioner of urban terrorism, it meets to plan its operations and assemble bombs in safe houses leased under false names. Alert to the possibility that its safe houses might be bugged by the FBI, it takes effective steps to defeat this form of electronic surveillance, making it highly resistant to conventional methods of law enforcement even as enhanced by modern techniques for overhearing conversations. We do not think the Fourth Amendment prevents the government from coping with the menace of this organization by installing and operating secret television cameras in the organization's safe houses. The benefits to the public safety are great, and the costs to personal privacy are modest. A safe house is not a home. No one lives in these apartments, amidst the bombs and other paraphernalia of terrorism. They are places dedicated exclusively to illicit business; and though the Fourth Amendment protects business premises as well as homes, the invasion of privacy caused by secretly televising the interior of business premises is less than that caused by secretly televising the interior of a home, while the social benefit of the invasion is greater when the organization under investigation runs a bomb factory than it would be if it ran a chop shop or a numbers parlor. There is no right to be let alone while assembling bombs in safe houses.

Having concluded that the district court could validly authorize television surveillance in this case, we come to the question whether the two warrants complied with the requirements of the Fourth Amendment's warrant clause. * * *

The government asked for the warrants in its applications for Title III warrants—applications the government had to make because it wanted to record the sounds in the apartments at the same time that it was televising the interiors—and the warrants it got covered both methods of surveillance. Title III imposes many restrictions on intercept warrants. Those related to the constitutional requirement of particularity are that the judge must certify that "normal investigative procedures have been tried and have failed or reasonably appear to be unlikely to succeed if tried or to be too dangerous," 18 U.S.C. § 2518(3)(c), and that the warrant must contain "a particular description of the type of communication sought to be intercepted, and a statement of the particular offense to which it relates," § 2518(4)(c), must not allow the period of interception to be "longer than is necessary to achieve the objective of the authorization, nor in any event longer than thirty days" (though renewals are possible), § 2518(5), and must require that the interception "be conducted in such a way as to minimize the interception of communications not otherwise subject to interception under [Title III]," id. Each of these four requirements is a safeguard against electronic surveillance that picks up more information than is strictly necessary and so violates the Fourth Amendment's requirement of particular description.

After stating that there was probable cause to believe both that the individuals named in the warrant were using the specified premises (the safe house) in connection with specified federal crimes and that intercepts of oral and wire communications at this address would yield evidence concerning these crimes, after stating that normal investigative methods had been tried and had failed, and after authorizing intercepts at the address, each of the original warrants in this case went on to authorize the FBI "to install [at the address] devices that will visually monitor and record the activity taking place in furtherance of the above-described [illegal] purposes." Each warrant then specified the number of surreptitious entries that the FBI was authorized to make to install, adjust, and remove both the audio and video equipment (a total of 34 separate entries were authorized), required progress reports to be made to the court every five days, required that the electronic surveillance cease "upon the attainment of the authorized objective," and put a deadline of 30 days on both the audio and video surveillance. One of the warrants was renewed a total of four times, so that it authorized a total of 150 days of surveillance, and the other was renewed twice; and in all, 130 hours of videotape were made. The renewal warrants were essentially identical to the original ones, but were supported by even more compelling showings of probable cause, based on information yielded by the execution of the original warrants.

In short, the warrants complied with all four of the requirements of Title III that implement the constitutional requirements of particularity. In fact, the only requirement of Title III that the government may not have complied with in its television surveillance was the requirement that the application be authorized by the Attorney General or an Assistant Attorney General specially designated by him. Actually, the authorization was obtained; it just was not communicated to the district judge. * * *

If Title III and the Foreign Intelligence Surveillance Act were inconsistent, then we would have to make a choice, and in doing so we might unavoidably be exercising something resembling a legislature's discretion. But there is no inconsistency. The two statutes govern nonoverlapping domains. And television surveillance for domestic criminal investigations is in neither statute's domain. No doubt this is, as we have said, anomalous; it may seem fairly to cry out for congressional attention; but it does not create ambiguity as to the legal duties under which the government labors in conducting television surveillance of domestic criminal suspects. The only legal duties are those imposed by the Fourth Amendment. And we therefore go as far as is proper for us to go when we use a part of Title III to give meaning to the Fourth Amendment's requirement of particularity as applied to television surveillance. Since the Fourth Amendment has long been held fully applicable to the states through the Fourteenth Amendment, state and local officers who might want to use television surveillance in criminal investigations will be under the same restraints as we impose on federal officers today.

The defendants complain, finally, that the warrants in this case did not explain the basis of the judge's finding of probable cause and did not identify as safe houses the addresses at which the surveillance was to be conducted. This complaint misapprehends the purpose of a search warrant, which is twofold: to show that a judicial officer authorized the search, and to indicate to the government agents who will execute the warrant what the limits of the authorization are. A warrant is not a judicial opinion, and the basis for the warrant is not in the warrant itself; * * * it is in the application for the warrant. The application in this case set forth in full and convincing detail the reasons for thinking that the addresses where the surveillance was to be conducted were FALN safe houses, that normal investigative methods would be unavailing, and that television surveillance was an appropriate supplement to electronic eaves-dropping. The truth of the recitals in the application is not controverted, and they provided an adequate factual basis for the warrants.

The order of suppression is reversed and the case remanded for trial.

UNITED STATES v. MESA–RINCON

911 F.2d 1433 (10th Cir. 1990).

McKay, Circuit Judge. * * *

On March 15, 1988, the United States Secret Service applied for an order to authorize the interception of nonverbal conduct via closed circuit television to be installed by surreptitious entry. The application was approved by the district court the same day it was filed. The district court's order authorized the interception and recordation of nonverbal conduct in a specified building in Lenexa, Kansas. The order also authorized the surreptitious entry by Secret Service agents to install and maintain the video surveillance equipment.

On March 16, 1988, the Secret Service installed a television camera at the authorized location. Government agents later used the television camera to observe and record both defendants counterfeiting United States currency. The agents also observed other activities, including an apparent act of masturbation by an unknown male who had entered the premises in a manner not known to those conducting the surveillance.

Defendants moved to suppress all video evidence in the district court. The district court denied the suppression motion * * *. Defendants now challenge the video evidence on three grounds. First, they claim that the district court did not have statutory or inherent power to authorize this type of search. Second, defendants argue that the application for surveillance did not satisfy traditional fourth amendment requirements. Finally, defendants claim that the government failed to follow the limitations for television surveillance required by United States v. Torres, 751 F.2d 875 (7th Cir. 1984). * * *

Defendants argue that the district court is without statutory or inherent power to order covert television surveillance. We hold that Fed.R.Crim.P. 41(b) grants authority to the district court to authorize the surveillance that took place in this case. * * * The Supreme Court has interpreted Rule 41 to authorize the issuance of a search warrant to install a "pen register," a device that records the phone numbers dialed from a telephone. United States v. New York Telephone Co., 434 U.S. 159 (1977). The New York Telephone Court stated that Rule 41 "is sufficiently flexible to include within its scope electronic intrusions authorized upon a finding of probable cause." Thus, although the language of Rule 41 concerns conventional searches, the Supreme Court has interpreted the rule to cover "electronic intrusions," including wiretaps. New York Telephone, 434 U.S. at 169.

Relying primarily on New York Telephone, two circuit courts have held that Rule 41 authorizes district courts to issue warrants for video surveillance. See United States v. Torres, 751 F.2d 875, 877–78 (7th Cir. 1984), cert. denied, 470 U.S. 1087 (1985); United States v. Biasucci, 786 F.2d 504, 509 (2d Cir. 1986). We are in agreement with the Seventh Circuit's statement that "we cannot think of any basis on which the rule might be thought sufficiently flexible to authorize a pen register, bug, or wiretap, but not a camera." Torres, 751 F.2d at 877–78. Thus, we conclude that Rule 41(b) provides the district court with authority to issue the order involved in this case. * * *

Although Congress has not yet delineated the requirements for video surveillance, we find guidance in case law and congressional enactments concerning similar search and seizure techniques. We have considered carefully the underlying purposes of the fourth amendment and the intrusiveness of video surveillance. Having done so, we now adopt the following five requirements for video surveillance that define more specifically the probable cause and particularity requirements of the fourth amendment. These requirements have been formulated for other search techniques, and we hold that they must be satisfied before video surveillance will be permitted. An order permitting video surveillance shall not be issued unless: (1) there has been a showing that probable cause exists that a particular person is committing, has committed, or is about to commit a crime; (2) the order particularly describes the place to be searched and the things to be seized in accordance with the fourth amendment; (3) the order is sufficiently precise so as to minimize the recording of activities not related to the crimes under investigation; (4) the judge issuing the order finds that normal investigative procedures have been tried and have failed or reasonably appear to be unlikely to succeed if tried or appear to be too dangerous; and (5) the order does not allow the period of interception to be longer than necessary to achieve the objective of the authorization, or in any event no longer than thirty days.

We adopt these five requirements from three separate sources that discuss search techniques similar to video surveillance: Title III of the Omnibus Crime Control and Safe Streets Act of 1968, 18 U.S.C. §§ 2510–20 (1988), the court here means; the Foreign Intelligence Surveillance Act, 50 U.S.C. §§ 1801–11 (1982); and the common law concerning audio surveillance prior to the passage of Title III. [Editor's Note: ECPA was enacted in 1986, so Title III is really Title I, the Wiretap Act.] Each of these sources contains at least four of the five requirements.

Title III establishes elaborate warrant requirements for wiretapping and bugging. See 18 U.S.C. §§ 2516, 2518 (1988). Unfortunately, Title III does not discuss television surveillance in any way. Thus, its requirements are not binding on this court in the context of video surveillance. However, the fact that Title III does not discuss television surveillance is no authority for the proposition that Congress meant to outlaw the practice. Despite Congress' silence concerning video surveillance, we believe that Title III's provisions provide strong guidance for establishing video surveillance requirements. For example, Title III provides requirements for the surreptitious interception of oral communications within a private or business dwelling. We believe that the interception of oral communications provides a strong analogy to video surveillance even though video surveillance can be vastly more intrusive, as demonstrated by the surveillance in this case that recorded a person masturbating before the hidden camera.

All five of the requirements we adopt for video surveillance are found in Title III. These five requirements are the only requirements of Title III that deal with the probable cause and particularity requirements of the fourth amendment. We do not apply the remaining statutory provisions of Title III to video surveillance because we believe such a course to require congressional action. The provisions we do not adopt are not required by the fourth amendment. We simply look to Title III for guidance in implementing the fourth amendment in an area that Title III does not specifically cover.

Three United States circuit courts have adopted at least four of these requirements from Title III in television surveillance cases. Our holding puts us into substantial agreement with these three courts. We simply articulate the additional requirement of probable cause, almost certainly assumed by all three courts. * * *

We next look for guidance to the only congressional enactment that specifically addresses video surveillance, namely, the Foreign Intelligence Surveillance Act (FISA). See 50 U.S.C. §§ 1801–11 (1982). FISA establishes procedures for the electronic surveillance, including television surveillance, of foreign agents. The act applies only to the surveillance of foreign agents. Thus, the act does not apply to the kind of domestic surveillance that took place in this case. However, we believe that FISA provides strong guidance as to the minimum requirements for domestic surveillance. FISA was enacted in the face of the President's strong constitutional authority over foreign affairs. See U.S. Const. art. II, §§ 2–3. Thus, FISA covers an area in which there is more deference to governmental searches than in the area of domestic surveillance. In light of this fact, we believe that FISA provides strong guidance for the minimum standards of domestic surveillance.

FISA contains language closely approximating four of the five requirements we have adopted. The statute requires the government submission requesting video surveillance to include: (1) "a statement of the proposed minimization procedures"; (2) "a detailed description of the nature of the information sought and the type of communications or activities to be subjected to the surveillance"; (3) "a certification * * * that such information cannot reasonably be obtained by normal investigative techniques"; and (4) "a statement of the period of time for which the electronic surveillance is required to be maintained." * * * "An order issued under this section may approve an electronic surveillance for the period necessary to achieve its purpose, or for ninety days, whichever is less."

FISA contains requirements that are nearly identical to the ones we adopt in this case concerning domestic video surveillance. The only differences are that FISA allows ninety days while we provide for only thirty days, with the possibility of extensions, and that FISA does not require a probable cause finding. Thus, we find FISA's provisions supportive of the requirements we adopt in domestic video surveillance cases.

Finally, we look to Supreme Court case law for guidance in identifying the requirements for video surveillance. The Supreme Court has not specifically dealt with the constitutionality of video surveillance. However, the Court's discussions, prior to the enactment of Title III, of surreptitiously installed listening devices provides substantial guidance as to the requirements we should impose on video surveillance in the absence of congressional action.

The Supreme Court found the interception of oral communications through surreptitiously installed listening devices unconstitutional in two cases predating Title III. See Berger v. New York, 388 U.S. 41 (1967); Katz v. United States, 389 U.S. 347 (1967). In Berger, the Court specifically outlined several deficiencies in a New York statute covering listening devices. In so doing, the Court condemned the absence of the five minimum requirements that we apply to video surveillance in this case. The weaknesses of the statute were: (1) "eavesdropping is authorized without requiring belief that any particular offense has been or is being committed," Berger, 388 U.S. at 58–59; (2) "likewise the statute's failure to describe with particularity the conversations sought gives the officer a roving commission to 'seize' any and all conversations," id. at 59; (3) The statute does not require minimization by allowing "eavesdropping for a two-month period * * *. During such a long and continuous (24 hours a day) period the conversations of any and all persons coming into the area covered by the device will be seized indiscriminately and without regard to their connection with the crime under investigation," id.; (4) "the statute places no termination date on the eavesdrop once the conversation sought is seized," id. at 59–60; and (5) the statute "permits uncontested entry without any showing of exigent circumstances," id. at 60. Thus, analogous Supreme Court precedent supports our adoption of the five requirements for domestic video surveillance.

Our adoption of the five requirements for valid domestic video surveillance leaves us with the task of applying the requirements to the facts of this case.

A. Probable Cause

Defendants suggest that the order authorizing video surveillance in this case was not supported by probable cause because the government only alleged lawful conduct in its affidavit supporting the request for the order. Probable cause is a common-sense standard that requires facts sufficient "to warrant a man of reasonable caution in the belief that an offense has been or is being committed." * * *

The supporting affidavit alleges that the following conduct was observed. The defendants legally purchased all of the printing equipment and accessories necessary for the printing process most commonly used by counterfeiters. When making these purchases, defendants used aliases and on one occasion gave a fictitious address. There were large purchases of white bond paper similar to the weight used to print genuine United States currency. Although the defendants were purportedly setting up a printing business, they did not obtain a business permit. No telephone was located in the warehouse, and there was no sign indicating the location of the business. The window to the warehouse was covered with duct tape, and a printing press serviceman was required to wait outside when he returned to the warehouse to retrieve a tool he had left. The defendants were also observed carrying bags of trash out of the warehouse and disposing of them at defendant Stoppe's rural residence. * * *

We hold that the above information allows a reasonable person to conclude that an offense had been or was being committed and that a search would uncover evidence of wrongdoing. Thus, we hold that probable cause existed to issue the order contested in this case.

B. Particularization

The second requirement we have imposed upon video surveillance orders is particularization. The fourth amendment states that warrants shall "particularly describ[e] the place to be searched, and the persons or things to be seized." U.S. Const. amend. IV. The purpose of this requirement is to provide guidance to police and to avoid general searches without specific limits.

Title III requires

> a particular description of the nature and location of the facilities from which or the place where the communication is to be intercepted, * * * a particular description of the type of communications sought to be intercepted, * * * the identity of the person, if known, committing the offense and whose communications are to be intercepted.

18 U.S.C. § 2518(1)(b) (1988). Thus, particularization under Title III requires three things: (1) a description of the place to be put under surveillance; (2) a description of the type of activity sought to be intercepted; and (3) the identity of the person committing the offense. Three other cases have adopted a fourth requirement that the warrant must also particularly describe the crime under investigation. See United States v. Cox, 449 F.2d 679, 687 (10th Cir. 1971) (outlining all four requirements); United States v. Tortorello, 480 F.2d 764, 779–80 (2d Cir.), cert. denied, 414 U.S. 866 (1973); Teicher, 439 N.Y.S.2d at 854, 422 N.E.2d at 514. We apply all four particularity requirements to video surveillance.

The order in this case identified the place to be searched by its address and further described it as a unit in a one-story rectangular warehouse-style building. * * * We hold that this description satisfies the first particularity requirement of describing the place to be put under surveillance. * * *

The order in this case also authorized the interception of nonverbal conduct "concerning offenses involving the counterfeiting of obligations or securities of the United States, or the uttering of counterfeit United States obligations or securities, in violation of Sections 471 and 472 of Title 18, United States Code." * * * We hold that this language contains an adequate description of the type of activity sought to be captured by the camera, the second requirement, and an adequate description of the crimes under investigation, the fourth requirement.

The third requirement of particularity requires the specific identification of individuals committing the offense under investigation. The order in this case authorized televised surveillance of "Peter Scott Stoppe, Joaquin Emilio Mesa, and others as yet unknown * * *." We hold that this language sufficiently identifies defendants Stoppe and Mesa–Rincon. In addition, the Supreme Court has held that "the failure to identify additional persons who are likely to be overheard engaging in incriminating conversations could hardly invalidate an otherwise lawful judicial authorization." * * * Thus, the order in this case fulfilled the requirement of identifying the individuals to be observed.

We conclude that the order of the district court in this case satisfied the requirements of particularity.

C. Minimization

The purpose of the minimization requirement is to avoid the recording of activity by persons with no connection to the crime under investigation who happen to enter an area covered by a camera. "The minimization question is one of reasonableness." United States v. Apodaca, 820 F.2d 348, 350 (10th Cir. 1987). Title III

> does not forbid the interception of all nonrelevant conversations, but rather instructs the agents to conduct the surveillance in such a manner as to 'minimize' the interception of such conversations. Whether the agents have in fact conducted the wiretap in such a manner will depend on the facts and circumstances of each case.

Scott v. United States, 436 U.S. 128, 139–40 (1978). We hold that the order involved in this case required adequate minimization procedures.

The order required that:

> Interception shall be conducted in such a manner as to minimize the interception of visual, non-verbal conduct when it is determined that a named interceptee's conduct is not criminal in nature * * *.

> IT IS FURTHER ORDERED that when it is determined that none of the named interceptees nor any person subsequently identified as an

accomplice who uses the premises to commit or converse about the designated offenses is inside the premises, interception of visual, non-verbal conduct shall be discontinued, except that if such a determination is made, visual monitoring ceases, and agents are thereafter unable to ascertain whether any of the aforementioned persons is inside the premises, agents may engage in spot monitoring to determine whether any of the persons is once again inside the premises. Whenever it is determined that any of the aforementioned persons is within the premises, interception of visual, non-verbal conduct may be initiated to determine whether such conduct involves the designated offenses. If the conduct relates to such offenses, it may be intercepted.

Order, March 15, 1988, at 4. This order specifically requires minimization and outlines the procedures to be followed. Although the sentence structure of the order concerning when visual monitoring is to stop is somewhat difficult to follow, we believe that it provides adequate guidance. * * *

The order in this case required surveillance to minimize the interception of conduct when it was determined that the conduct was not criminal in nature. The order also allowed spot checks to see if the targets of the investigation were in the building. We hold that on its face the order fulfilled the minimization requirement.

D. Alternative Investigation Techniques

The fourth amendment protects us against "unreasonable searches and seizures." To determine whether a search is "reasonable" we must balance the intrusiveness of the method used and the expectation of privacy in the premises searched with the government's showing of necessity for the search. "Unfortunately, there can be no ready test for determining reasonableness other than by balancing the need to search against the invasion which the search entails." Camara v. Municipal Court, 387 U.S. 523 (1967). Thus, as the intrusiveness of the method used increases and the expectation of privacy in the premises searched increases, the government's showing of necessity increases and must be more clearly established.

Title III requires a search warrant application to contain "a full and complete statement as to whether or not other investigative procedures have been tried and failed or why they reasonably appear to be unlikely to succeed if tried or to be too dangerous." 18 U.S.C. § 2518(1)(c) (1988). In Berger v. New York, the Court refused to uphold a warrant statute that "permit[ted] unconsented entry without any showing of exigent circumstances." "Such a showing of exigency, in order to avoid notice, would appear more important in eavesdropping [and we add in video surveillance], with [their] inherent dangers, than that required when conventional procedures of search and seizure are utilized." We adopt these requirements in the video surveillance context by holding that the government must use the least intrusive means available to obtain the needed information.

The showing of necessity needed to justify the use of video surveillance is higher than the showing needed to justify other search and seizure methods, including bugging. The use of a video camera is an extraordinarily intrusive method of searching. Here, the incident in which an unidentified individual was observed masturbating provides an excellent example of this intrusiveness. No other technique would have recorded—at least in graphic visual detail—an apparently innocent individual engaging in this very personal and private behavior. "Television surveillance is identical in its indiscriminate character to wiretapping and bugging. [However,] it is even more invasive of privacy, just as a strip search is more invasive than a pat-down search * * *." Because of the invasive nature of video surveillance, the government's showing of necessity must be very high to justify its use.

Another element of the intrusiveness equation that affects the government's required showing of necessity is the nature of the premises to be put under surveillance. Our expectation of privacy lessens as we move from a private home to a public business. For example, an ordinary individual has a right to expect greater privacy in his own home than does an individual owning a business into which he invites the public. The Seventh Circuit emphasized the high expectation of privacy in the home when it stated: "Maybe in dealing with so intrusive a technique as television surveillance, other methods of control as well, such as banning the technique outright from use in the home in connection with minor crimes, will be required, in order to strike a proper balance between public safety and personal privacy."

The business involved in this case falls somewhere between a private home, in which there is a high expectation of privacy, and a public business, in which there is a lower expectation of privacy. This business was not a home. There were no bedroom or living areas. We think that it is fair to say that the government reasonably did not expect someone to masturbate in the building. However, the business was not open to the general public. The windows had been taped over and no signs invited public traffic. We conclude that the expectation of privacy was less than in a private home, but higher than in a public business. We also conclude that the use of a highly intrusive video camera in a building in which there was at least a "medium" expectation of privacy created a high degree of intrusiveness. Consequently, the government had a high burden to meet in showing the necessity of video surveillance.

In the affidavit supporting the application for a video surveillance order, the government outlined the general surveillance techniques that had been used without success. "The U. S. Secret Service has exhausted all investigative leads, and * * * there is a possibility when Stoppe and Mesa counterfeit money it could be done without detection with the current surveillance techniques." The affidavit also explained that two other techniques would not work in this case. "An audio intercept has also not been requested and this is based on my experience that Stoppe and Mesa could counterfeit U.S. currency without discussing the process to each other, and it is not practical since the noise of the printing press could drown out any type of audio intercept." "The U. S. Secret Service has been unable to develop an inside confidential informant in this case." Id.

The application for the order also described three types of information necessary for the conviction of defendants that only video surveillance could provide:

    a. Information indicating the precise nature, scope, extent, and methods of operation of the participants in the illegal activities referred to above;

    b. Information reflecting the identities and roles of all accomplices, aiders and abettors, co-conspirators and participants in the illegal activities referred to above; and

    c. Admissible evidence of commission of the offenses described above.

Application, March 15, 1988, at 2–3. This information formed the government's showing of necessity.

This court has previously held that the provisions of Title III "are not designed to force the government to exhaust all other conceivable investigative procedures before resorting to wiretapping." Apodaca, 820 F.2d at 350. In addition, this court has previously used the identification of all of the members of a conspiracy, learning the precise nature and scope of the illegal activity, the apprehension of accomplices, and the determination of the dimensions of an extensive conspiracy as sufficient justification for the use of electronic surveillance. * * *

In another television surveillance case, the Second Circuit held that an affidavit, describing the techniques that had been attempted and those that the government did not consider worth pursuing, sufficiently demonstrated that video surveillance was necessary. See Biasucci, 786 F.2d at 511. This holding was contrasted with a prior case in which the Second Circuit held that the government had failed to establish that other investigative procedures were unlikely to succeed when it merely asserted that no other investigative method existed to determine the identity of individuals who might be involved in drug transactions. * * *

We do not require the government to explain why all conceivable investigatory methods would not work. See Apodaca, 820 F.2d at 350. Instead, we require the government to prove exhaustion—either by attempt or explanation of why the method would not work—of all "reasonable" investigatory methods. We will find authorization of video surveillance improper only when the government fails to attempt or explain its failure to attempt all reasonable alternative investigatory techniques. The determination of reasonableness will be based on the individual facts of each case.

Although existing case law seems to support the order in this case, we believe that the highly intrusive nature of a video camera requires further analysis to determine whether any less intrusive means could reasonably have been used. See Teicher, 439 N.Y.S.2d at 855, 422 N.E.2d at 515. The legislative history of Title III suggests a few other techniques that should be considered. "Normal investigative procedure would include, for example, standard visual or aural surveillance * * * general questioning or interrogation under an immunity grant, use of regular search warrants, and the infiltration of conspiratorial groups by undercover agents or informants." S. Rep. No. 1097, 90th Cong., 2d Sess. 101 (1968).

With respect to standard visual or aural surveillance, the government's affidavit specifically explains that defendants could counterfeit money without detection using current visual surveillance techniques. See Affidavit, March 15, 1988, at 27. The government also explained that an audio intercept was not requested because money could be counterfeited without verbal discussion and the printing presses could drown out any type of audio intercept. See id. at 20. It seems likely, however, that use of standard visual surveillance of the business would disclose the identities of most accomplices. Nevertheless, as the government points out, at least two of its goals from video surveillance could not be achieved through standard visual or audio surveillance.

It is possible that interrogation of one of the suspects under a grant of immunity would have been a fruitful course. However, only two suspects were involved in the case; and the government was unsure of the role of either party. The process of arrest or grand jury subpoena could have raised suspicion in others likely to prevent successful completion of the investigation. Although the government did not discuss this option in its affidavit, we do not believe that interrogation under a grant of immunity would have been a reasonable alternative in this case. Government explanation of the unreasonableness of this alternative would have been helpful in this case. Yet, we do not strictly require the government to discuss its reasons for rejecting alternatives that appear unreasonable under a recitation of the facts of the case.

The government also did not specifically discuss why a standard search of the premises was not practical. Again, we only require the government to discuss reasonable alternatives. While a normal search could have produced some circumstantial evidence, it is also quite likely that the key evidence of actual counterfeit bills might not be found. If the Secret Service had searched the business before any money was counterfeited, they would have obtained no direct evidence of the counterfeiting operation.

Regarding infiltration, it would be very difficult for an agent to penetrate an operation involving only two people without arousing great suspicion. The government's affidavit specifically explained that the Secret Service had been unable to develop an inside confidential informant in this case. * * *

We conclude that the government made the necessary showing that other investigative techniques had or would have failed.

In summary, this case involves a situation in which the government has demonstrated a pressing need for video surveillance, and we have determined that the resulting search would involve a high degree of intrusiveness. To determine the reasonableness of this search we are required to balance the government's showing of need with the intrusiveness of the search. Thus, although we find video surveillance extremely intrusive, we hold that the expectation of privacy in this business premises was low enough as to be outweighed by the government's specific showing of a need for video surveillance.

Our holding is narrowly limited to business premises. We leave to another day the details of the higher showing that would a fortiori be required to justify video surveillance of the central bastion of privacy—the home. * * *

E. Time Limitations on Video Surveillance

Title III does not allow electronic surveillance "for any period longer than is necessary to achieve the objective of the authorization, nor in any event longer than thirty days." 18 U.S.C. § 2518(5) (1988). The order authorizing video surveillance in this case stated that surveillance was to continue until three types of conduct were intercepted or for a period of thirty days from the date of the order, whichever was earlier. Thus, the order fully complied with the time requirements that would apply to audio surveillance under Title III. Although video surveillance is more intrusive than the methods allowed under Title III, we see no reason to add additional time restraints on video surveillance. Therefore, we hold that the order in this case satisfied proper time limitations.

In conclusion, we hold that the order issued by the district court in this case complied with all the requirements necessary to make the search a reasonable one under the fourth amendment. * * *

We hold that the district court has power to authorize covert television surveillance. We also hold that the district court's order authorizing video surveillance in this case complied with all the requirements we now impose on video surveillance. * * *

The district court's disposition of this case is affirmed.

NOTE: *FISA*

The previous two cases referred extensively to the FISA and the principles of monitored surveillance for which it stands. The next section considers in detail the FISA; its post 9/11 Patriot Act and 2008 Amendments; and the jurisdiction and influence of the top secret FISA court. The USA PATRIOT Act amended the FISA expressly to permit the flow of information between foreign intelligence operations and law enforcement. But the FISA court seemed unwilling to let go of what came to be know as the "wall requirement," setting the stage for an unusual appeal of a FISA court decision to the FISA court of appeals. In 2008, the FISA statute was further amended to make some types of foreign intelligence gathering easier.

E. FOREIGN INTELLIGENCE SURVEILLANCE ACT OF 1978 (FISA)

THE FISA AND THE FISC

http://www.fas.org/irp/agency/doj/fisa/court2010.html.

The Foreign Intelligence Surveillance Act of 1978 prescribes procedures for requesting judicial authorization for electronic surveillance and physical search of persons engaged in espionage or international terrorism against the United States on behalf of a foreign power. * * *

The Foreign Intelligence Surveillance Court was created by section 103(a) of the Foreign Intelligence Surveillance Act of 1978 (50 U.S.C. 1803(a)). It was originally comprised of seven district judges from seven circuits named by the Chief Justice of the United States to serve a maximum of 7 years. In 2001, the U.S.A. Patriot Act (section 208) amended the Foreign Intelligence Surveillance Act to increase the number of FIS Court judges from seven to eleven, "of whom no fewer than 3 shall reside within 20 miles of the District of Columbia." * * *

The Foreign Intelligence Surveillance Court of Review was created by the Foreign Intelligence Surveillance Act of 1978 to review applications that were denied by the FIS Court. The Court of Review is comprised of three judges, one of whom is designated as the presiding judge, named by the Chief Justice of the United States from the U.S. district or appellate courts. Judges serve a maximum of seven years and are not eligible for redesignation.

ANNUAL FISA REPORT OFFICE OF THE ASSISTANT ATTORNEY GENERAL U.S. DEPARTMENT OF JUSTICE

http://www.fas.org/irp/agency/doj/fisa/2009rept.pdf
April 30, 2010.

The Honorable Joseph R. Biden, Jr.
President
United States Senate
Washington, D.C. 20510

Dear Mr. President:

This report is submitted pursuant to sections 107 and 502 of the Foreign Intelligence Surveillance Act of 1978 (the "Act"), as amended, 50 U.S.C. § 1801 *et seq.*, and section 118 of USA PATRIOT Improvement and Reauthorization Act of 2005, Pub. L. No. 109–177 (2006). In accordance with those provisions, this report covers all applications made by the Government during calendar year 2009 for authority to conduct electronic surveillance for foreign intelligence purposes under the Act, all applications made by the Government during calendar year 2009 for access to certain business records (including the production of tangible things) for foreign intelligence purposes, and certain requests made by the Federal

Bureau of Investigation pursuant to national security letter authorities. In addition, while not required to do so by statute, the Government is providing information concerning the number of applications made during calendar year 2009 for authority to conduct physical searches for foreign intelligence purposes.

Applications for Electronic Surveillance Made During Calendar Year 2009 * * *

During calendar year 2009, the Government made 1,376 applications to the Foreign Intelligence Surveillance Court (hereinafter "FISC") for authority to conduct electronic surveillance and physical searches for foreign intelligence purposes. The 1,376 applications include applications made solely for electronic surveillance, applications made solely for physical search, and combined applications requesting authority for electronic surveillance and physical search. Of these, 1,329 applications included requests for authority to conduct electronic surveillance.

Of these 1,329 applications, eight were withdrawn by the Government. The FISC denied one application in whole, and one in part, and made modifications to the proposed orders in fourteen applications. Thus, the FISC approved collection activity in a total of 1,320 of the applications that included requests for authority to conduct electronic surveillance.

Applications for Access to Certain Business Records (Including the Production of Tangible Things) Made During Calendar Year 2009 * * *

During calendar year 2009, the Government made twenty-one applications to the FISC for access to certain business records (including the production of tangible things) for foreign intelligence purposes. The FISC did not deny, in whole or in part, any such application filed by the Government during calendar year 2009. The FISC made modifications to nine proposed orders in applications for access to business records.

Requests Made for Certain Information Concerning Different United States Persons Pursuant to National Security Letter Authorities During Calendar Year 2009 * * *

Pursuant to Section 118 of the USA PATRIOT Improvement and Reauthorization Act, Pub. L. 109–177 (2006), the Department of Justice provides Congress with annual reports regarding requests made by the Federal Bureau of Investigation (FBI) pursuant to the National Security Letter (NSL) authorities provided in 12 U.S.C. § 3414, 15 U.S.C. § 1681u, 15 U.S.C. § 1681v, 18 U.S.C. § 2709, and 50 U.S.C. § 436.

In 2009, the FBI made 14,788 NSL requests (excluding requests for subscriber information only) for information concerning United States persons. These sought information pertaining to 6,114 different United States persons.

Sincerely,
Ronald Welch
Assistant Attorney General

AMNESTY INTERNATIONAL USA v. JOHN McCONNELL

646 F.Supp.2d 633 (2009).

JOHN G. KOELTL, DISTRICT JUDGE.

This is a facial challenge to the constitutionality of Section 702 of the Foreign Intelligence Surveillance Act of 1978 ("FISA"), 50 U.S.C. § 1881a, which was added to FISA by Section 101(a)(2) of the FISA Amendments Act of 2008 (the "FAA"). In relevant part, the FAA amended FISA by creating a new framework within which federal officials may seek approval from the Foreign Intelligence Surveillance Court (the "FISC") to authorize surveillance targeting non-United States persons located outside the United States to acquire foreign intelligence information.

The plaintiffs are attorneys and organizations in the United States whose work necessitates international communications with people and organizations they believe to be likely targets of surveillance under the FAA. The defendants are the Director of National Intelligence, the Director of the National Security Agency and Chief of the Central Security Service, and the Attorney General of the United States.

The plaintiffs fear that their international communications will be monitored under the FAA. They make no claim that their communications have yet been monitored, and they make no allegation or showing that the surveillance of their communications has been authorized or that the Government has sought approval for such surveillance. However, the plaintiffs assert that they have an "actual and well-founded fear" of surveillance under the FAA and claim already to have incurred significant costs in taking steps to protect their international communications from surveillance. The plaintiffs challenge the FAA as unconstitutional under the Fourth Amendment, the First Amendment, and Article III of the Constitution.

The Government contends as a threshold matter that the plaintiffs lack standing to challenge the FAA. The Government also contends that the lawsuit lacks merit in any event because the FAA is constitutional on its face.

* * * The parties have filed cross-motions for summary judgment. For the reasons explained below, the plaintiffs have failed to show that they have standing to bring their facial challenge to the statute. * * *

Prior to the passage of the FAA, FISA created a framework for federal officials to apply for and obtain orders authorizing electronic surveillance where a significant purpose of the surveillance was to obtain foreign intelligence information. * * * FISA established the FISC, comprised of judges appointed by the Chief Justice of the United States, with jurisdiction to hear applications for and to grant orders approving electronic surveillance "in aid of protecting the United States against attack by foreign governments or international terrorist groups." * * *

FISA required that each application for an order approving electronic surveillance be made by a federal officer upon oath or affirmation after approval by the Attorney General. * * * An application was required to set forth the identity of the federal officer making the application; the identity, if known, of the target of the electronic surveillance; the facts upon which the applicant relied in concluding that the target of the electronic surveillance was a foreign power or an agent of a foreign power and that each of the facilities or places at which the surveillance was directed was being used, or was about to be used, by a foreign power or agent thereof; a statement of proposed minimization procedures; the type of information sought and the means by which surveillance would be effected; a statement concerning the previous applications sought; and a statement of the period of time for which the surveillance was required to be maintained. * * *

The application had to be approved by the Attorney General upon the Attorney General's finding that it satisfied the criteria and requirements of such an application. * * * The application had to include a certification from a high ranking executive officer employed in the area of national security or defense that the information sought was foreign intelligence information as defined by 50 U.S.C. § 1801(e). 50 U.S.C. § 1804(a)(6). Foreign intelligence information included information relating to the ability of the United States to protect against international terrorism, and "information with respect to a foreign power or foreign territory that relates to ... the conduct of the foreign affairs of the United States," among other things. * * *. FISA required that the certification include a statement that the information sought could not reasonably be obtained by normal investigative techniques and designating the type of foreign intelligence information sought in accordance with § 1801(e). 50 U.S.C. § 1804(a)(6). Finally, after the passage of the Patriot Act, the executive officer was required to certify that "a significant purpose of the surveillance is to obtain foreign intelligence information." 50 U.S.C. § 1804(a)(6).

Prior to approving the requested electronic surveillance, a FISC judge had to find that: (1) the application was made by a federal officer and approved by the Attorney General; (2) there was probable cause on the basis of the application to believe that the target of the electronic surveillance was a foreign power or agent of a foreign power, and that each of the facilities or places at which the electronic surveillance was directed was being used, or was about to be used, by a foreign power or an agent of a foreign power; (3) the proposed minimization procedures met the definition of minimization procedures set forth in § 1801(h); and (4) the application contained all statements and certifications required under § 1804. 50 U.S.C. § 1805(a).

Pursuant to FISA, a FISC judge who was satisfied that an application met the statutory requirements was required to enter an ex parte order approving the requested electronic surveillance. 50 U.S.C. § 1805(a). Such an order was required to specify the identity of the target of the surveillance; the location of each of the facilities or places at which the surveillance would be directed; the type of information sought and communications or activities to be subjected to the surveillance; the means by which the surveillance would be effected; and the period of time for which the surveillance was approved; and to direct that the minimization procedures be followed. 50 U.S.C. § 1805(c).

The FISA framework governed applications for orders authorizing electronic surveillance to obtain foreign intelligence information, including surveillance of communications between persons located within the United States ("domestic communications") and surveillance of communications between persons located within the United States and persons located outside the United States ("international communications"). FISA defined "electronic surveillance" to include:

> (1) the acquisition by an electronic, mechanical, or other surveillance device of the contents of any wire or radio communication sent by or intended to be received by a particular, known United States person who is in the United States, if the contents are acquired by intentionally targeting that United States person, under circumstances in which a person has a reasonable expectation of privacy and a warrant would be required for law enforcement purposes;

> (2) the acquisition by an electronic, mechanical, or other surveillance device of the contents of any wire communication to or from a person in the United States, without the consent of any party thereto, if such acquisition occurs in the United States, but does not include the acquisition of those communications of computer trespassers that would be permissible under section 2511(2)(i) of Title 18;

> (3) the intentional acquisition by an electronic, mechanical, or other surveillance device of the contents of any radio communication, under circumstances in which a person has a reasonable expectation of privacy and a warrant would be required for law enforcement purposes, and if both the sender and all intended recipients are located within the United States; or

> (4) the installation or use of an electronic, mechanical, or other surveillance device in the United States for monitoring to acquire information, other than from a wire or radio communication, under circumstances in which a person has a reasonable expectation of privacy and a warrant would be required for law enforcement purposes.

50 U.S.C. § 1801(f). The FISA requirements thus applied to the surveillance of international wire communications (including telephone and email communications) provided that the surveillance occurred in the United States. 50 U.S.C. § 1801(f)(2). The FISA requirements did not apply to the surveillance of international radio communications, or to surveillance of international wire communications that did not take place in the United States, unless such surveillance targeted a known United States person located in the United States. *See* 50 U.S.C. §§ 1801(f)(1–2).

B

The FAA was signed into law on July 10, 2008. The FAA leaves much of the preexisting FISA framework intact. However, new Section 702 of FISA, added by Section 101(a)(2) of the FAA and codified at 50 U.S.C. § 1881a, sets forth a new framework displacing the preexisting FISA framework where the Government seeks approval from the FISC to authorize surveillance targeting non-United States persons located outside the United States to acquire foreign intelligence information. Under the FAA, "[n]otwithstanding any other provision of law, upon the issuance of an order in accordance with [50 U.S.C. § 1881a(i)(3)] or a determination under [50 U.S.C. § 1881a(c)(2)], the Attorney General and the Director of National Intelligence may authorize jointly, for a period of up to 1 year from the effective date of the authorization, the targeting of persons reasonably believed to be located outside the United States to acquire foreign intelligence information." 50 U.S.C. § 1881a(a).

In order to authorize surveillance under the FAA, the Attorney General and the Director of National Intelligence must apply for and obtain an order authorizing such surveillance from the FISC. 50 U.S.C. §§ 1881a(a) & (i)(3). The application consists of providing a written certification and any supporting affidavit, under oath and under seal, to the FISC. The certification must attest, among other things, that a significant purpose of the requested surveillance is to obtain foreign intelligence information; that the surveillance involves obtaining such information from or with the assistance of an electronic communications service provider; and that the surveillance complies with certain limitations set forth in § 1881a(b). 50 U.S.C. § 1881a(g)(2)(A)(v–vii).

Pursuant to the limitations set forth in § 1881a(b), the requested surveillance may not intentionally target any person known at the time of the surveillance to be located in the United States; any person reasonably believed to be located outside the United States if the purpose of such surveillance is to target a particular, known person reasonably believed to be in the United States; or any United States person reasonably believed to be located outside the United States. 50 U.S.C. § 1881a(b)(1–3). Moreover, the requested surveillance may not intentionally acquire communications known at the time of the surveillance to be domestic communications, 50 U.S.C. § 1881a(b)(4), although it may intentionally acquire international communications. Section 1881a(b) also provides that the requested surveillance must be conducted in a manner consistent with the Fourth Amendment. 50 U.S.C. § 1881a(b)(5).

The certification must attest that guidelines have been adopted in accordance with 50 U.S.C. § 1881a(f) to ensure compliance with the limitations in § 1881a(b) and to ensure that an application for a court order is filed as required by § 1881a. 50 U.S.C. § 1881a(g)(2)(A)(iii). In addition, such guidelines must be provided to the congressional intelligence committee and the Committees on the Judiciary of the Senate and the House of Representatives, as well as the FISC. 50 U.S.C. § 1881a(f)(2).

The certification must attest that such guidelines are consistent with the Fourth Amendment. 50 U.S.C. § 1881a(g)(2)(A)(iv).

The certification must attest that the Government has targeting and minimization procedures in place that have been approved by the FISC or have been submitted to the FISC for approval or will be submitted with the certification. 50 U.S.C. § 1881a(g)(2)(A)(i–ii). The certification must also include the actual procedures and attest that they comply with the Fourth Amendment. 50 U.S.C. § 1881a(g)(2)(B) & (g)(2)(A)(iv). "Targeting procedures" are procedures reasonably designed to ensure that the requested surveillance is limited to targeting persons reasonably believed to be located outside the United States, and to prevent the intentional surveillance of communications known to be domestic communications at the time of the surveillance. 50 U.S.C. § 1881a(d)(1) & (g)(2) (A)(i). "Minimization procedures" for purposes of electronic surveillance under the FAA must meet the definition of minimization procedures for purposes of electronic surveillance under FISA. Minimization procedures are:

> (1) specific procedures, which shall be adopted by the Attorney General, that are reasonably designed in light of the purpose and technique of the particular surveillance, to minimize the acquisition and retention, and prohibit the dissemination, of nonpublicly available information concerning unconsenting United States persons consistent with the need of the United States to obtain, produce, and disseminate foreign intelligence information;

> (2) procedures that require that nonpublicly available information, which is not foreign intelligence information, as defined in [50 U.S.C. § 1801(e)(1)], shall not be disseminated in a manner that identifies any United States person, without such person's consent, unless such person's identity is necessary to understand foreign intelligence information or assess its importance; [and]

> (3) notwithstanding paragraphs (1) and (2), procedures that allow for the retention and dissemination of information that is evidence of a crime which has been, is being, or is about to be committed and that is to be retained or disseminated for law enforcement purposes[.]

50 U.S.C. § 1801(h).

The certification required by the FAA must be supported, as appropriate, by the affidavit of any appropriate official in the area of national security who is appointed by the President, by and with the advice and consent of the Senate, or who is the head of an element of the intelligence community. 50 U.S.C. § 1881a(g)(2)(C). The certification must include an effective date for the authorization that is at least 30 days after the submission of the certification to the FISC; or, if the acquisition has begun or the effective date is less than 30 days after the submission of the certification to the FISC, the date the acquisition began or the effective date of the acquisition. 50 U.S.C. § 1881a(g)(2)(D).

The FISC has jurisdiction to review a certification for electronic surveillance under the FAA, including the targeting and minimization procedures that were adopted by the Attorney General in consultation with the Director of National Intelligence. 50 U.S.C. § 1881a(i)(1)(A). The FAA provides that the FISC shall review the certification, the targeting procedures and the minimization procedures to ensure that they comply with all of the requirements discussed above. 50 U.S.C. § 1881a(i)(2). If the FISC finds that the certification contains all the required elements and the targeting and minimization procedures are in compliance with the statute and with the Fourth Amendment, it must issue an order granting the Government approval to authorize the requested surveillance. 50 U.S.C. § 1881a(i)(3)(A). The FISC must complete its review and issue an order with respect to an application for an order authorizing surveillance no more than 30 days after the date on which the certification and the targeting and minimization procedures are submitted for approval. 50 U.S.C. § 1881a(i)(1)(B).

The FAA allows for the Government to appeal an order rejecting an application for a surveillance order to the FISA Court of Review. The Court of Review must decide an appeal no more than 60 days from the date the appeal is filed. The Government is permitted to continue any surveillance affected by a FISC order while an appeal to the Court of Review is pending, or while any rehearing of the FISC order by the FISC en banc is pending. The Government may file a petition for a writ of certiorari with the Supreme Court for review of a decision of the Court of Review. 50 U.S.C. § 1881a(i)(4).

The FAA provides for a semiannual assessment of compliance with the targeting and minimization procedures adopted in accordance with 50 U.S.C. §§ 1881a(d) and (e) and the guidelines adopted in accordance with § 1881a(f). The FAA provides that each assessment shall be made by the Attorney General and the Director of National Intelligence, and submitted to the FISC, the congressional intelligence committees, and the Committees on the Judiciary of the House of Representatives and the Senate. 50 U.S.C. § 1881a(*l*).

The FAA also provides that the Inspector General of the Department of Justice and the Inspector General of each element of the intelligence community authorized to acquire foreign intelligence information under § 1881a are authorized to review compliance with the targeting and minimization procedures adopted under §§ 1881a(d) and (e) and the guidelines adopted under § 1881a(f). With respect to surveillance authorized under § 1881a, those officials are required to review the number of disseminated intelligence reports containing a reference to a United States person identity and the number of United States person identities subsequently disseminated by the element concerned in response to requests for identities that were not referred to by name or title in the original reporting. They are also required to review the number of targets that were later determined to be located in the United States and, to the extent possible, whether communications of such targets were reviewed. They must provide each such review to the Attorney General, the Director of National Intelligence, the congressional intelligence committees, and the Committees on the Judiciary of the House of Representatives and the Senate. 50 U.S.C. § 1881a(*l*)(2).

Finally, the FAA provides for the head of each element of the intelligence community conducting surveillance authorized under § 1881a to conduct an annual review to determine whether there is reason to believe that foreign intelligence information has been or will be obtained from the surveillance. The annual review is required to provide an accounting of the number of disseminated intelligence reports containing a reference to a United States person identity; an accounting of the number of United States person identities subsequently disseminated by that element in response to requests for identities that were not referred to by name or title in the original reporting; the number of targets that were later determined to be located in the United States and, to the extent possible, whether communications of such targets were reviewed; and a description of any procedures developed by the head of such element of the intelligence community and approved by the Director of National Intelligence to assess, in a manner consistent with national security, operational requirements and the privacy interests of United States persons, the extent to which the surveillance authorized under § 1881a acquires the communications of United States persons, and the results of any such assessment. 50 U.S.C. § 1881a(*l*)(3)(A). The purpose of the annual review is to evaluate the adequacy of the minimization procedures used and, as appropriate, the application of the minimization procedures to a particular surveillance. 50 U.S.C. § 1881a(*l*)(3)(B). The annual reviews are to be provided to the FISC, the Attorney General, the Director of National Intelligence, the congressional intelligence committees, and the Committees on the Judiciary of the House of Representatives and the Senate. 50 U.S.C. § 1881a(*l*)(3)(C).

In applying for an order from the FISC approving the authorization of surveillance under the FAA, the Government is not required to identify the specific facilities, places, premises, or property at which the surveillance will be directed or conducted. 50 U.S.C. § 1881g(4). The Government is also not required to identify the specific targets of the requested surveillance or to show probable cause that the prospective targets of the surveillance are foreign powers or agents thereof.

II

The plaintiffs move for summary judgment declaring the FAA unconstitutional, and the Government moves for summary judgment dismissing the plaintiffs' constitutional challenge. Summary judgment may not be granted unless "the pleadings, the discovery and disclosure materials on file, and any affidavits show that there is no genuine issue as to any material fact and that the movant is entitled to judgment as a matter of law." * * *

* * * The plaintiffs are attorneys and human rights, labor, legal, and media organizations whose work requires them to engage in sensitive and sometimes privileged telephone and email communications with colleagues, clients, journalistic sources, witnesses, experts, foreign governmental officials, and victims of human rights abuses located outside the United States. (Pl.'s 56.1 Stmt. ¶ 9(A).) Some of the plaintiffs communicate by telephone and email with people the United States Government believes or believed to be associated with terrorist organizations. (Pl.'s 56.1 Stmt. ¶ 9(B).) Some of the plaintiffs communicate by telephone and email with political and human rights activists who oppose governments that are supported economically or militarily by the United States Government. (Pl.'s 56.1 Stmt. ¶ 9(C).) Some of the plaintiffs communicate by telephone and email with people located in geographic areas that are a special focus of the United States Government's counterterrorism or diplomatic efforts. (Pl.'s 56.1 Stmt. ¶ 9(D).)

All of the plaintiffs exchange information that constitutes foreign intelligence information within the meaning of the FAA. (Pl.'s 56.1 Stmt. ¶ 9(E).) The plaintiffs believe that their communications will be monitored under the FAA, and that those communications will be retained, analyzed, and disseminated by the Government. (Pl.'s 56.1 Stmt. ¶ 9(F).) This belief has affected the way the plaintiffs do their jobs. (Pl.'s 56.1 Stmt. ¶ 9(G).) Namely, the plaintiffs feel constrained in locating witnesses, cultivating sources, gathering information, and communicating confidential information to their clients, among other things. (Pl.'s 56.1 Stmt. ¶ 9(H).) The plaintiffs have ceased engaging in certain conversations on the telephone and by email. (Pl.'s 56.1 Stmt. ¶ 9(I).) The attorney plaintiffs have an ethical obligation to avoid communicating confidential information about client matters over telephone, fax, or email if they have reason to believe that it is likely to be intercepted by others. (Pl.'s Supplemental 56.1 Stmt. ¶ 2(J).)

The plaintiffs have incurred costs in seeking to protect the confidentiality of sensitive and privileged communications. (Pl.'s 56.1 Stmt. ¶ 9(J).) Some of the plaintiffs now travel long distances to meet personally with individuals instead of communicating with those individuals over telephone or email. (Pl.'s 56.1 Stmt. ¶ 9(K).) On the whole, the plaintiffs' reaction to the FAA has affected their work more than their reaction to previous regulatory enactments providing frameworks for Government surveillance. (Pl.'s 56.1 Stmt. ¶ 9(L).)

III

The plaintiffs argue that on its face, the FAA violates the Fourth Amendment, the First Amendment, and Article III of the Constitution. The plaintiffs argue under the Fourth Amendment that the FAA fails to protect the privacy interest of Americans in the content of their telephone calls and emails. They argue under the First Amendment that the FAA chills the constitutionally protected speech of Americans who fear that their telephone calls and emails will be subject to surveillance. They argue under Article III that the process of judicial review set forth in the FAA violates the principle of the separation of powers by allowing the FISC to issue orders approving the authorization of surveillance in the absence of any case or controversy and by allowing for the Government to continue surveillance while an appeal to the FISC Court of Review is pending.

In order to reach the merits of the plaintiffs' constitutional arguments, the Court must first determine whether the plaintiffs have standing to bring this action. * * *

Article III of the Constitution limits the jurisdiction of federal courts to "Cases" and "Controversies." *Lujan v. Defenders of Wildlife,* 504 U.S. 555, 559, 112 S.Ct. 2130, 119 L.Ed.2d 351 (1992). To satisfy the irreducible constitutional minimum of Article III standing, a plaintiff must show that (1) it has suffered an actual or imminent injury in fact, that is concrete and particularized, and not conjectural or hypothetical; (2) there is a causal connection between the injury and the defendant's actions; and (3) it is likely that a favorable decision in the case will redress the injury. *Id.* at 560–61, 112 S.Ct. 2130. "The party invoking federal jurisdiction bears the burden of establishing these elements." *Id.* at 561, 112 S.Ct. 2130. * * *

Apart from the irreducible constitutional minimum, the Supreme Court has also recognized other prudential limitations on the class of persons who may invoke the federal judicial power. "[T]he Court has held that when the asserted grievance is a 'generalized grievance' shared in substantially equal measure by all or a large class of citizens, that harm alone normally does not warrant exercise of jurisdiction." *Warth,* 422 U.S. at 499, 95 S.Ct. 2197. The Court has also held that the plaintiff must generally assert the plaintiff's own rights, and cannot rest on the legal rights or interests of third parties. *Id.* This case turns on whether the plaintiffs have met the irreducible constitutional minimum of personal, particularized, concrete injury in fact without turning to the additional prudential aspects of standing.

The plaintiffs advance what they characterize as two independent bases for Article III standing to challenge the constitutionality of the FAA. First, the plaintiffs argue that they have standing on the basis of their fear that their communications will be monitored under the FAA because that fear is "actual and well-founded." Second, the plaintiffs argue that they have standing on the basis of the costs they have incurred in taking measures to protect the confidentiality of their international communications, in light of their fear of surveillance. The Court addresses each proffered basis for standing in turn.

A

* * *

The Government argues that the plaintiffs' fear that their communications will be monitored under the FAA does not confer standing on the plaintiffs to challenge the constitutionality of that statute. The Government contends that standing to make a pre-enforcement challenge to a statute may only be found "where there is a threat of imminent enforcement of a specific proscription that demonstrably applies to a plaintiff's actions" (Gov't Reply Br. 2–3), and that no such basis for a pre-enforcement challenge to the FAA exists here.

The plaintiffs have failed to establish standing to challenge the constitutionality of the FAA on the basis of their fear of surveillance. The plaintiffs can only demonstrate an abstract fear that their communications will be monitored under the FAA. The FAA creates a framework within which intervening federal officials may apply for approval from the FISC to authorize surveillance targeting non-United States persons located outside the United States to acquire foreign intelligence information. The FAA sets forth the requirements that an application to obtain a surveillance order from the FISC must satisfy. Contrary to the characterization of the statute in the plaintiffs' motion papers, the FAA itself does not authorize the surveillance of the plaintiffs' communications. Indeed, the FAA neither authorizes surveillance nor identifies on its face a class of persons that includes the plaintiffs. Rather the FAA authorizes specified federal officials to seek a surveillance order from the FISC. That order cannot target the plaintiffs and whether an order will be sought that affects the plaintiffs' rights, and whether such an order would be granted by the FISC, is completely speculative.

1.

Courts have explicitly rejected standing based on a fear of surveillance in circumstances similar to those in this case. * * * The * * * plaintiffs in this case have not shown that any specific action is threatened or even contemplated against them. They have not shown or alleged that the Government has sought or obtained approval from the FISC to authorize surveillance of their communications. They have not shown or alleged that surveillance of their communications has ever taken place under the challenged statute. They only allege a fear, based on a perceived likelihood, that their communications will be surveilled. But absent any showing that such surveillance has been conducted, authorized or even contemplated, the plaintiffs' fear is speculative. * * *

1. PULLING DOWN THE "WALL" AFTER THE USA PATRIOT ACT

IN RE SEALED CASE NO. 02–001
310 F.3d 717 (Foreign Int.Surv.Ct.Rev. 2002).

GUY, SENIOR CIRCUIT JUDGE, Presiding; SILBERMAN and LEAVY, SENIOR CIRCUIT JUDGES.

United States Foreign Intelligence Surveillance Court of Review

Per Curiam: This is the first appeal from the Foreign Intelligence Surveillance Court to the Court of Review since the passage of the Foreign

Intelligence Surveillance Act (FISA), 50 U.S.C. §§ 1801–1862 (West 1991 and Supp. 2002), in 1978. This appeal is brought by the United States from a FISA court surveillance order which imposed certain restrictions on the government. Since the government is the only party to FISA proceedings, we have accepted briefs filed by the American Civil Liberties Union (ACLU) and the National Association of Criminal Defense Lawyers (NACDL) as amici curiae.

Not surprisingly this case raises important questions of statutory interpretation, and constitutionality. After a careful review of the briefs filed by the government and amici, we conclude that FISA, as amended by the Patriot Act, supports the government's position, and that the restrictions imposed by the FISA court are not required by FISA or the Constitution.

I.

The court's decision from which the government appeals imposed certain requirements and limitations accompanying an order authorizing electronic surveillance of an "agent of a foreign power" as defined in FISA. There is no disagreement between the government and the FISA court as to the propriety of the electronic surveillance; the court found that the government had shown probable cause to believe that the target is an agent of a foreign power and otherwise met the basic requirements of FISA. The government's application for a surveillance order contains detailed information to support its contention that the target, who is a United States person, is aiding, abetting, or conspiring with others in international terrorism. The FISA court authorized the surveillance, but imposed certain restrictions, which the government contends are neither mandated nor authorized by FISA. Particularly, the court ordered that law enforcement officials shall not make recommendations to intelligence officials concerning the initiation, operation, continuation or expansion of FISA searches or surveillances. Additionally, the FBI and the Criminal Division [of the Department of Justice] shall ensure that law enforcement officials do not direct or control the use of the FISA procedures to enhance criminal prosecution, and that advice intended to preserve the option of a criminal prosecution does not inadvertently result in the Criminal Division's directing or controlling the investigation using FISA searches and surveillances toward law enforcement objectives. * * *

These restrictions * * * [appear] to proceed from the assumption that FISA constructed a barrier between counterintelligence/intelligence officials and law enforcement officers in the Executive Branch—indeed, it uses the word "wall" popularized by certain commentators (and journalists) to describe that supposed barrier. Yet the opinion does not support that assumption with any relevant language from the statute.

The "wall" emerges from the court's implicit interpretation of FISA. The court apparently believes it can approve applications for electronic surveillance only if the government's objective is not primarily directed toward criminal prosecution of the foreign agents for their foreign intelligence activity. But the court neither refers to any FISA language supporting that view, nor does it reference the Patriot Act amendments, which the government contends specifically altered FISA to make clear that an application could be obtained even if criminal prosecution is the primary counter mechanism.

Instead the court relied for its imposition of the disputed restrictions on its statutory authority to approve "minimization procedures" designed to prevent the acquisition, retention, and dissemination within the government of material gathered in an electronic surveillance that is unnecessary to the government's need for foreign intelligence information. 50 U.S. In the Matter of the Application of the United States of America C. § 1801(h). * * *

II.

We turn first to the statute as enacted in 1978. It authorizes a judge on the FISA court to grant an application for an order approving electronic surveillance to "obtain foreign intelligence information" if "there is probable cause to believe that * * * the target of the electronic surveillance is a foreign power or an agent of a foreign power," and that "each of the facilities or places at which the surveillance is directed is being used, or is about to be used, by a foreign power or an agent of a foreign power." 50 U.S.C. § 1805(a)(3). As is apparent, the definitions of agent of a foreign power and foreign intelligence information are crucial to an understanding of the statutory scheme. The latter means

> (1) information that relates to, and if concerning a United States person is necessary to, the ability of the United States to protect against—
>
> > A) actual or potential attack or other grave hostile acts of a foreign power or an agent of a foreign power;
> >
> > B) sabotage or international terrorism by a foreign power or an agent of a foreign power; or
> >
> > C) clandestine intelligence activities by an intelligence service or network of a foreign power or by an agent of a foreign power. Id. § 1801(e)(1).

The definition of an agent of a foreign power, if it pertains to a U.S. person (which is the only category relevant to this case), is closely tied to criminal activity. The term includes any person who "knowingly engages in clandestine intelligence gathering activities * * * which activities involve or may involve a violation of the criminal statutes of the United States," or "knowingly engages in sabotage or international terrorism, or activities that are in preparation therefor." Id. §§ 1801(b)(2)(A), (C). International terrorism refers to activities that "involve violent acts or acts dangerous to human life that are a violation of the criminal laws of the United States or of any State, or that would be a criminal violation if committed within the jurisdiction of the United States or any State." Id. § 1801(c)(1). Sabotage means activities that "involve a violation of chapter 105 of [the criminal code], or that would involve such a violation if committed against the United States." Id. § 1801(d). For purposes of clarity in this opinion we will refer to the crimes referred to in section 1801(a)–(e) as foreign intelligence crimes.

In light of these definitions, it is quite puzzling that the Justice Department, at some point during the 1980s, began to read the statute as limiting the Department's ability to obtain FISA orders if it intended to prosecute the targeted agents—even for foreign intelligence crimes. * * *

The government argues persuasively that arresting and prosecuting terrorist agents of, or spies for, a foreign power may well be the best technique to prevent them from successfully continuing their terrorist or espionage activity. The government might wish to surveil the agent for some period of time to discover other participants in a conspiracy or to uncover a foreign power's plans, but typically at some point the government would wish to apprehend the agent and it might be that only a prosecution would provide sufficient incentives for the agent to cooperate with the government. Indeed, the threat of prosecution might be sufficient to "turn the agent." * * *

The origin of what the government refers to as the false dichotomy between foreign intelligence information that is evidence of foreign intelligence crimes and that which is not appears to have been a Fourth Circuit case decided in 1980. United States v. Truong Dinh Hung, 629 F.2d 908 (4th Cir. 1980). That case, however, involved an electronic surveillance carried out prior to the passage of FISA and predicated on the President's executive power. In approving the district court's exclusion of evidence obtained through a warrantless surveillance subsequent to the point in time when the government's investigation became "primarily" driven by law enforcement objectives, the court held that the Executive Branch should be excused from securing a warrant only when "the object of the search or the surveillance is a foreign power, its agents or collaborators," and "the surveillance is conducted 'primarily' for foreign intelligence reasons." Targets must "receive the protection of the warrant requirement if the government is primarily attempting to put together a criminal prosecution." Id. at 916. Although the Truong court acknowledged that "almost all foreign intelligence investigations are in part criminal" ones, it rejected the government's assertion that "if surveillance is to any degree directed at gathering foreign intelligence, the executive may ignore the warrant requirement of the Fourth Amendment." Id. at 915.

Several circuits have followed Truong in applying similar versions of the "primary purpose" test, despite the fact that Truong was not a FISA decision. * * *

[T]he First Circuit, seeing Duggan as following Truong, explicitly interpreted FISA's purpose wording in section 1804(a)(7)(B) to mean that "although evidence obtained under FISA subsequently may be used in criminal prosecutions, the investigation of criminal activity cannot be the primary purpose of the surveillance." United States v. Johnson, 952 F.2d

565, 572 (1st Cir. 1991) (citations omitted), cert. denied, 506 U.S. 816 (1992). * * *

In sum, we think that the FISA as passed by Congress in 1978 clearly did not preclude or limit the government's use or proposed use of foreign intelligence information, which included evidence of certain kinds of criminal activity, in a criminal prosecution.

Apparently to avoid running afoul of the primary purpose test used by some courts, the 1995 Procedures [adopted by the Attorney General] limited contacts between the FBI and the Criminal Division in cases where FISA surveillance or searches were being conducted by the FBI for foreign intelligence (FI) or foreign counterintelligence (FCI) purposes. The procedures state that "the FBI and Criminal Division should ensure that advice intended to preserve the option of a criminal prosecution does not inadvertently result in either the fact or the appearance of the Criminal Division's directing or controlling the FI or FCI investigation toward law enforcement objectives." 1995 Procedures at 2, P6. Although these procedures provided for significant information sharing and coordination between criminal and FI or FCI investigations, based at least in part on the "directing or controlling" language, they eventually came to be narrowly interpreted within the Department of Justice, and most particularly by OIPR, as requiring OIPR to act as a "wall" to prevent the FBI intelligence officials from communicating with the Criminal Division regarding ongoing FI or FCI investigations. * * * Thus, the focus became the nature of the underlying investigation, rather than the general purpose of the surveillance. Once prosecution of the target was being considered, the procedures, as interpreted by OIPR in light of the case law, prevented the Criminal Division from providing any meaningful advice to the FBI. Id.

The Department's attitude changed somewhat after the May 2000 report by the Attorney General and a July 2001 Report by the General Accounting Office both concluded that the Department's concern over how the FISA court or other federal courts might interpret the primary purpose test has inhibited necessary coordination between intelligence and law enforcement officials. * * * In August 2001, the Deputy Attorney General issued a memorandum clarifying Department of Justice policy governing intelligence sharing and establishing additional requirements. (These actions, however, did not replace the 1995 Procedures.) But it does not appear that the Department thought of these internal procedures as "minimization procedures" required under FISA. Nevertheless, the FISA court was aware that the procedures were being followed by the Department and apparently adopted elements of them in certain cases.

The Patriot Act and the FISA Court's Decision

The passage of the Patriot Act altered and to some degree muddied the landscape. In October 2001, Congress amended FISA to change "the purpose" language in 1804(a)(7)(B) to "a significant purpose." It also added a provision allowing "Federal officers who conduct electronic surveillance to acquire foreign intelligence information" to "consult with

Federal law enforcement officers to coordinate efforts to investigate or protect against" attack or other grave hostile acts, sabotage or international terrorism, or clandestine intelligence activities, by foreign powers or their agents. 50 U.S.C. § 1806(k)(1). And such coordination "shall not preclude" the government's certification that a significant purpose of the surveillance is to obtain foreign intelligence information, or the issuance of an order authorizing the surveillance. Id. § 1806(k)(2). [T]he Patriot Act amendments to FISA expressly sanctioned consultation and coordination between intelligence and law enforcement officials * * *.

On March 6, 2002, the Attorney General approved new "Intelligence Sharing Procedures" to implement the Act's amendments to FISA. The 2002 Procedures supersede prior procedures and were designed to permit the complete exchange of information and advice between intelligence and law enforcement officials. * * *

Unpersuaded by the Attorney General's interpretation of the Patriot Act, the court ordered that the 2002 Procedures be adopted, with modifications, as minimization procedures to apply in all cases. * * *

Essentially, the FISA court took portions of the Attorney General's augmented 1995 Procedures—adopted to deal with the primary purpose standard—and imposed them generically as minimization procedures. In doing so, the FISA court erred. It did not provide any constitutional basis for its action—we think there is none—and misconstrued the main statutory provision on which it relied. The court mistakenly categorized the augmented 1995 Procedures as FISA minimization procedures and then compelled the government to utilize a modified version of those procedures in a way that is clearly inconsistent with the statutory purpose. * * *

The FISA court's decision and order not only misinterpreted and misapplied minimization procedures it was entitled to impose, but as the government argues persuasively, the FISA court may well have exceeded the constitutional bounds that restrict an Article III court. The FISA court asserted authority to govern the internal organization and investigative procedures of the Department of Justice which are the province of the Executive Branch (Article II) and the Congress (Article I). Subject to statutes dealing with the organization of the Justice Department, however, the Attorney General has the responsibility to determine how to deploy personnel resources. As the Supreme Court said in Morrison v. Olson in cautioning the Special Division of the D.C. Circuit to avoid unauthorized administrative guidance of Independent Counsel, "the gradual expansion of the authority of the Special Division might in another context be a bureaucratic success story, but it would be one that would have serious constitutional ramifications." * * *

We also think the refusal by the FISA court to consider the legal significance of the Patriot Act's crucial amendments was error. The government, in order to avoid the requirement of meeting the "primary purpose" test, specifically sought an amendment to section 1804(a)(7)(B) which had required a certification "that the purpose of the surveillance is to obtain foreign intelligence information" so as to delete the article "the" before "purpose" and replace it with "a." The government made perfectly clear to Congress why it sought the legislative change. Congress, although accepting the government's explanation for the need for the amendment, adopted language which it perceived as not giving the government quite the degree of modification it wanted. Accordingly, section 1804(a)(7)(B)'s wording became "that a significant purpose of the surveillance is to obtain foreign intelligence information." There is simply no question, however, that Congress was keenly aware that this amendment relaxed a requirement that the government show that its primary purpose was other than criminal prosecution. * * *

In sum, there can be no doubt as to Congress' intent in amending section 1804(a)(7)(B). Indeed, it went further to emphasize its purpose in breaking down barriers between criminal law enforcement and intelligence (or counterintelligence) gathering by adding section 1806(k):

(k) Consultation with Federal law enforcement officer

(1) Federal officers who conduct electronic surveillance to acquire foreign intelligence information under this title may consult with Federal law enforcement officers to coordinate efforts to investigate or protect against

(A) actual or potential attack or other grave hostile acts of a foreign power or an agent of a foreign power; or

(B) sabotage or international terrorism by a foreign power or an agent of a foreign power; or

(C) clandestine intelligence activities by an intelligence service or network of a foreign power or by an agent of a foreign power. * * *

The FISA court noted this amendment but thought that Congress' approval of consultations was not equivalent to authorizing law enforcement officers to give advice to officers who were conducting electronic surveillance nor did it sanction law enforcement officers "directing or controlling" surveillances. However, dictionary definitions of "consult" include giving advice. See, e.g., OXFORD ENGLISH DICTIONARY ONLINE (2d ed. 1989). Beyond that, when Congress explicitly authorizes consultation and coordination between different offices in the government, without even suggesting a limitation on who is to direct and control, it necessarily implies that either could be taking the lead. * * *

Accordingly, the Patriot Act amendments clearly disapprove the primary purpose test. And as a matter of straightforward logic, if a FISA application can be granted even if "foreign intelligence" is only a significant—not a primary—purpose, another purpose can be primary. One other legitimate purpose that could exist is to prosecute a target for a foreign intelligence crime. We therefore believe the Patriot Act amply supports the government's alternative argument but, paradoxically, the

Patriot Act would seem to conflict with the government's first argument because by using the term "significant purpose," the Act now implies that another purpose is to be distinguished from a foreign intelligence purpose. * * *

That leaves us with something of an analytic conundrum. On the one hand, Congress did not amend the definition of foreign intelligence information which, we have explained, includes evidence of foreign intelligence crimes. On the other hand, Congress accepted the dichotomy between foreign intelligence and law enforcement by adopting the significant purpose test. Nevertheless, it is our task to do our best to read the statute to honor congressional intent. The better reading, it seems to us, excludes from the purpose of gaining foreign intelligence information a sole objective of criminal prosecution. * * *

The government claims that even prosecutions of non-foreign intelligence crimes are consistent with a purpose of gaining foreign intelligence information so long as the government's objective is to stop espionage or terrorism by putting an agent of a foreign power in prison. That interpretation transgresses the original FISA. It will be recalled that Congress intended section 1804(a)(7)(B) to prevent the government from targeting a foreign agent when its "true purpose" was to gain non-foreign intelligence information—such as evidence of ordinary crimes or scandals. (If the government inadvertently came upon evidence of ordinary crimes, FISA provided for the transmission of that evidence to the proper authority. 50 U.S.C. § 1801(h)(3).) It can be argued, however, that by providing that an application is to be granted if the government has only a "significant purpose" of gaining foreign intelligence information, the Patriot Act allows the government to have a primary objective of prosecuting an agent for a non-foreign intelligence crime. Yet we think that would be an anomalous reading of the amendment. For we see not the slightest indication that Congress meant to give that power to the Executive Branch. Accordingly, the manifestation of such a purpose, it seems to us, would continue to disqualify an application. That is not to deny that ordinary crimes might be inextricably intertwined with foreign intelligence crimes. For example, if a group of international terrorists were to engage in bank robberies in order to finance the manufacture of a bomb, evidence of the bank robbery should be treated just as evidence of the terrorist act itself. But the FISA process cannot be used as a device to investigate wholly unrelated ordinary crimes. * * *

III.

Having determined that FISA, as amended, does not oblige the government to demonstrate to the FISA court that its primary purpose in conducting electronic surveillance is not criminal prosecution, we are obliged to consider whether the statute as amended is consistent with the Fourth Amendment. * * *

Comparison of FISA Procedures with Title III

It is important to note that while many of FISA's requirements for a surveillance order differ from those in Title III, few of those differences have any constitutional relevance. In the context of ordinary crime, beyond requiring searches and seizures to be reasonable, the Supreme Court has interpreted the warrant clause of the Fourth Amendment to require three elements: First, warrants must be issued by neutral, disinterested magistrates. Second, those seeking the warrant must demonstrate to the magistrate their probable cause to believe that "the evidence sought will aid in a particular apprehension or conviction" for a particular offense. Finally, "warrants must particularly describe the 'things to be seized,'" as well as the place to be searched. Dalia v. United States, 441 U.S. 238, 255 (1979) (citations omitted).

With limited exceptions not at issue here, both Title III and FISA require prior judicial scrutiny of an application for an order authorizing electronic surveillance. 50 U.S.C. § 1805; 18 U.S.C. § 2518. And there is no dispute that a FISA judge satisfies the Fourth Amendment's requirement of a "neutral and detached magistrate." * * *

The statutes differ to some extent in their probable cause showings. Title III allows a court to enter an ex parte order authorizing electronic surveillance if it determines on the basis of the facts submitted in the government's application that "there is probable cause for belief that an individual is committing, has committed, or is about to commit" a specified predicate offense. 18 U.S.C. § 2518(3)(a). FISA by contrast requires a showing of probable cause that the target is a foreign power or an agent of a foreign power. 50 U.S.C. § 1805(a)(3). We have noted, however, that where a U.S. person is involved, an "agent of a foreign power" is defined in terms of criminal activity. Admittedly, the definition of one category of U.S. person—agents of foreign powers—that is, persons engaged in espionage and clandestine intelligence activities for a foreign power—does not necessarily require a showing of an imminent violation of criminal law. * * * Congress clearly intended a lesser showing of probable cause for these activities than that applicable to ordinary criminal cases. * * *

Turning then to the first of the particularity requirements, while Title III requires probable cause to believe that particular communications concerning the specified crime will be obtained through the interception, 18 U.S.C. § 2518(3)(b), FISA instead requires an official to designate the type of foreign intelligence information being sought, and to certify that the information sought is foreign intelligence information. When the target is a U.S. person, the FISA judge reviews the certification for clear error, but this "standard of review is not, of course, comparable to a probable cause finding by the judge." Nevertheless, FISA provides additional protections to ensure that only pertinent information is sought. The certification must be made by a national security officer—typically the FBI Director—and must be approved by the Attorney General or the Attorney General's Deputy. * * *

With respect to the second element of particularity, although Title III generally requires probable cause to believe that the facilities subject to surveillance are being used or are about to be used in connection with commission of a crime or are leased to, listed in the name of, or used by the individual committing the crime, FISA requires probable cause to believe that each of the facilities or places at which the surveillance is directed is being used, or is about to be used, by a foreign power or agent. In cases where the targeted facilities are not leased to, listed in the name of, or used by the individual committing the crime, Title III requires the government to show a nexus between the facilities and communications regarding the criminal offense. The government does not have to show, however, anything about the target of the surveillance; it is enough that "an individual"—not necessarily the target—is committing a crime. * * * On the other hand, FISA requires probable cause to believe the target is an agent of a foreign power (that is, the individual committing a foreign intelligence crime) who uses or is about to use the targeted facility. Simply put, FISA requires less of a nexus between the facility and the pertinent communications than Title III, but more of a nexus between the target and the pertinent communications. * * *

Amici particularly focus on the differences between the two statutes concerning notice. Title III requires notice to the target (and, within the discretion of the judge, to other persons whose communications were intercepted) once the surveillance order expires. 18 U.S.C. § 2518(8)(d). FISA does not require notice to a person whose communications were intercepted unless the government "intends to enter into evidence or otherwise use or disclose" such communications in a trial or other enumerated official proceedings. 50 U.S.C. § 1806(c). As the government points out, however, to the extent evidence obtained through a FISA surveillance order is used in a criminal proceeding, notice to the defendant is required. Of course, where such evidence is not ultimately going to be used for law enforcement, Congress observed that "the need to preserve secrecy for sensitive counterintelligence sources and methods justifies elimination of the notice requirement." S. REP. at 12.

Based on the foregoing, it should be evident that while Title III contains some protections that are not in FISA, in many significant respects the two statutes are equivalent, and in some, FISA contains additional protections. Still, to the extent the two statutes diverge in constitutionally relevant areas—in particular, in their probable cause and particularity showings—a FISA order may not be a "warrant" contemplated by the Fourth Amendment. * * *

The main purpose of ordinary criminal law is twofold: to punish the wrongdoer and to deter other persons in society from embarking on the same course. The government's concern with respect to foreign intelligence crimes, on the other hand, is overwhelmingly to stop or frustrate the immediate criminal activity. As we discussed in the first section of this opinion, the criminal process is often used as part of an integrated effort to counter the malign efforts of a foreign power. Punishment of the terrorist or espionage agent is really a secondary objective; indeed, punishment of a terrorist is often a moot point.

Supreme Court's Special Needs Cases

The distinction between ordinary criminal prosecutions and extraordinary situations underlies the Supreme Court's approval of entirely warrantless and even suspicionless searches that are designed to serve the government's "special needs, beyond the normal need for law enforcement." * * *

A recent case, City of Indianapolis v. Edmond, 531 U.S. 32 (2000), is relied on by both the government and amici. In that case, the Court held that a highway check point designed to catch drug dealers did not fit within its special needs exception because the government's "primary purpose" was merely "to uncover evidence of ordinary criminal wrongdoing." The Court rejected the government's argument that the "severe and intractable nature of the drug problem" was sufficient justification for such a dragnet seizure lacking any individualized suspicion. Id. at 42. Amici particularly rely on the Court's statement that "the gravity of the threat alone cannot be dispositive of questions concerning what means law enforcement officers may employ to pursue a given purpose." * * *.

The Court emphasized that it was decidedly not drawing a distinction between suspicionless seizures with a "non-law-enforcement primary purpose" and those designed for law enforcement. Id. at 44 n. 1. Rather, the Court distinguished general crime control programs and those that have another particular purpose, such as protection of citizens against special hazards or protection of our borders. The Court specifically acknowledged that an appropriately tailored road block could be used "to thwart an imminent terrorist attack." Id. at 44. The nature of the "emergency," which is simply another word for threat, takes the matter out of the realm of ordinary crime control.

Conclusion

FISA's general programmatic purpose, to protect the nation against terrorists and espionage threats directed by foreign powers, has from its outset been distinguishable from "ordinary crime control." After the events of September 11, 2001, though, it is hard to imagine greater emergencies facing Americans than those experienced on that date. * * *

Although the Court in City of Indianapolis cautioned that the threat to society is not dispositive in determining whether a search or seizure is reasonable, it certainly remains a crucial factor. Our case may well involve the most serious threat our country faces. Even without taking into account the President's inherent constitutional authority to conduct warrantless foreign intelligence surveillance, we think the procedures and government showings required under FISA, if they do not meet the minimum Fourth Amendment warrant standards, certainly come close.

We, therefore, believe firmly, * * * that FISA as amended is constitutional because the surveillances it authorizes are reasonable.

Accordingly, we reverse the FISA court's orders in this case to the extent they imposed conditions on the grant of the government's applications, vacate the FISA court's Rule 11, and remand with instructions to grant the applications as submitted and proceed henceforth in accordance with this opinion.

NOTE: MIXING NATIONAL SECURITY WITH LAW ENFORCEMENT INTERNATIONALLY—ECHELON

The top secret Echelon System of global communications interception has its own version of the "wall" problem analyzed in the *FISA* case. Critics believe the blurring of international-national security efforts and international-criminal law enforcement efforts results in unbridled spying and eavesdropping outside any rule of law and against the spirit of international standards.

PRIVACY INTERNATIONAL: NATIONAL SECURITY, INTELLIGENCE AGENCIES AND THE "ECHELON SYSTEM"

http://www.privacyinternational.org.

In the past several years, there has been considerable attention given to mass surveillance by intelligence agencies of international and national communications. Investigations have been opened and hearings held in parliaments around the world about the "Echelon" system coordinated by the United States.

Immediately following the Second World War, in 1947, the governments of the United States, the United Kingdom, Canada, Australia and New Zealand signed a National Security pact known as the "Quadripartite," or "United Kingdom–United States" (UKUSA) agreement. Its intention was to seal an intelligence bond in which a common national security objective was created. Under the terms of the agreement, the five nations carved up the earth into five spheres of influence, and each country was assigned particular signals intelligence (SIGINT) targets.

The UKUSA Agreement standardized terminology, code words, intercept handling procedures, arrangements for cooperation, sharing of information, Sensitive Compartmented Information (SCI) clearances, and access to facilities. One important component of the agreement was the exchange of data and personnel.

The strongest alliance within the UKUSA relationship is the one between the United States National Security Agency (NSA), and Britain's Government Communications Headquarters (GCHQ). The NSA operates under a 1952 presidential mandate, National Security Council Intelligence Directive (NSCID) Number 6, to eavesdrop on the world's communications networks for intelligence and military purposes. In doing so, it has built a vast spying operation that can reach into the telecommunications systems of every country on earth. Its operations are so secret that this activity, outside the United States, occurs with little or no legislative or judicial oversight. The most important facility in the alliance is Menwith Hill, a Royal Air Force base in the north of England. With over two dozen domes and a vast computer operations facility, the base has the capacity to eavesdrop on vast chunks of the communications spectrum. With the creation of Intelsat and digital telecommunications, Menwith Hill and other stations developed the capability to eavesdrop on an extensive scale on satellite-borne fax, telex and voice messages.

The current debate over NSA activities has focused on the existence of a signals intelligence system known as "Echelon." United States officials have refused to confirm the existence of this or any other surveillance systems. In May 2001, the European Parliament's Temporary Committee on the Echelon Interception System (established in July 2000) issued a report concluding that "the existence of a global system for intercepting communications * * * is no longer in doubt." According to the committee, the Echelon system (reportedly run by the United States in cooperation with Britain, Canada, Australia and New Zealand) was set up at the beginning of the Cold War for intelligence gathering and has developed into a network of intercept stations around the world. Its primary purpose, according to the report, is to intercept private and commercial communications, not military intelligence. * * *

[A]s long as the UK–USA SIGINT partners police and govern their own operations outside of actual effective parliamentary and judicial oversight, there is good reason to believe that SIGINT can be turned against individuals and groups exercising civil and political rights. There is ample evidence that the activities of Greenpeace, Christian Aid, Amnesty International, the International Committee to Ban Landmines, the Tibetan government-in-exile, various anti-globalization movements like the Independent Media Center, and the International Committee of the Red Cross have been targeted by UKUSA agencies.

Second, there is an increasing blurring between the activities of intelligence agencies and law enforcement. The creation of a seamless international intelligence and law enforcement surveillance system has resulted in the potential for a huge international network that may, in practice, negate current rules and regulations prohibiting domestic communications surveillance by national intelligence agencies.

The use of Echelon to target diplomatic communications was highlighted as a result of disclosures made in 2003 by a British intelligence employee, former United Nations officials, and a former British Cabinet Minister concerning eavesdropping by the US NSA and the British GCHQ over UN Secretary General Kofi Annan's telephone communications and private conversations. The issue of eavesdropping on the diplomatic communications of the UN and its member nations' missions is covered by four international conventions: the Universal Declaration of Human

Rights (Article 12), the 1961 Vienna Convention on Diplomatic Relations (Article 27), the 1947 Headquarters Agreement between the UN and the United States, and the 1946 Convention on the Privileges and Immunities of the UN (Article 2).

F. FEDERAL ENCRYPTION POLICY

The Wassenaar Arrangement on Export Controls for Conventional Arms and Dual–Use Goods and Technologies is a multinational agreement in which the United States participates. As explained by the U.S. Bureau of Industry and Security, the arrangement "establishes a list of items for which member countries are to apply export controls. Member governments implement these controls to ensure that transfers of the controlled items do not contribute to the development or enhancement of military capabilities that undermine the goals of the Arrangement, and are not diverted to support such capabilities." See http://www.bxa.doc.gov/ Wassenaar/Default.htm.

Encryption tools are one of the items listed in the arrangement and therefore subject to export controls. Take a look at the brief description of the federal encryption export control policies, below. Then read the interesting cases of a graduate student and a professor who got into trouble for possible violations of the policies. How did the First Amendment come into play?

1. ENCRYPTION LICENSING PROCEDURES

U.S. ENCRYPTION EXPORT CONTROL POLICY

http://www.bxa.doc.gov/Encryption/EncFactSheet12_09_04 December 9, 2004.

U.S. encryption export policy continues to rest on three principles: review of encryption products prior to sale, streamlined post-export reporting, and license review of certain exports and reexports of strong encryption to foreign governments. Effective December 9, 2004, the Export Administration Regulations (EAR) have been amended in order to streamline and strengthen export and reexport controls on encryption items, in keeping with these principles. * * *

(1) All encryption items are eligible for 30 day review based on a more clearly articulated set of eligibility criteria. * * *

(2) The European Union "license-free zone" has been updated

This rule expands the list (Supplement No. 3 to part 740 of the EAR) of countries to which certain encryption items may be sent immediately (i.e., without a 30 day waiting period), once a review request is submitted to the U.S. Government. * * * To further ensure that companies in the U.S. can effectively trade with their "license-free zone" partners, this rule allows encryption items and related technical assistance to private sector end-users headquartered in Canada or any country listed * * * [in the

Supplement] for internal company use in the development of new products, without prior technical review. However, review is still required for new products produced or developed with an item that had been exported or reexported without review for such internal company use, before the products are transferred to others. * * *

2. DOES THE FIRST AMENDMENT CONSTRAIN ENCRYPTION POLICY?—TWO VIEWS

BERNSTEIN v. U.S. DEP'T OF STATE

974 F. Supp. 1288 (N.D. Cal. 1997).

JUDGE MARILYN HALL PATEL

At the time this action was filed, plaintiff was a PhD candidate in mathematics at University of California at Berkeley working in the field of cryptography, an area of applied mathematics that seeks to develop confidentiality in electronic communication. Plaintiff is currently a Research Assistant Professor in the Department of Mathematics, Statistics and Computer Science at the University of Illinois at Chicago. * * *

Encryption basically involves running a readable message known as "plaintext" through a computer program that translates the message according to an equation or algorithm into unreadable "ciphertext." Decryption is the translation back to plaintext when the message is received by someone with an appropriate "key." The message is both encrypted and decrypted by compatible keys. The uses of cryptography are far-ranging in an electronic age, from protecting personal messages over the Internet and transactions on bank ATMs to ensuring the secrecy of military intelligence. In a prepublication copy of a report done by the National Research Council ("NRC") at the request of the Defense Department on national cryptography policy, the NRC identified four major uses of cryptography: ensuring data integrity, authenticating users, facilitating nonrepudiation (the linking of a specific message with a specific sender) and maintaining confidentiality. * * *

Once a field dominated almost exclusively by governments concerned with protecting their own secrets as well as accessing information held by others, the last twenty years has seen the popularization of cryptography as industries and individuals alike have increased their use of electronic media and have sought to protect their electronic products and communications. * * *

As a graduate student, Bernstein developed an encryption algorithm he calls "Snuffle." He describes Snuffle as a zero-delay private-key encryption system. * * * Bernstein has articulated his mathematical ideas in two ways: in an academic paper in English entitled "The Snuffle Encryption System," and in "source code" written in "C", a high-level computer programming language, detailing both the encryption and decryption, which he calls "Snuffle.c" and "Unsnuffle.c", respectively. Once source code is converted into "object code," a binary system consisting of a series of 0s and 1s read by a computer, the computer is capable of encrypting and decrypting data.

In 1992 plaintiff submitted a commodity jurisdiction ("CJ") request to the State Department to determine whether Snuffle.c and Unsnuffle.c (together referred to as Snuffle 5.0), each submitted in C language source files, and his academic paper describing the Snuffle system, were controlled by [International Traffic in Arms Regulations ("ITAR"), 22 C.F.R. §§ 120–30 (1994)]. The [government] determined that the commodity Snuffle 5.0 was a defense article * * * subject to licensing by the Department of State prior to export. The ODTC identified the item as a "stand-alone cryptographic algorithm which is not incorporated into a finished software product." * * *

Alleging that he was not free to teach, publish or discuss with other scientists his theories on cryptography embodied in his Snuffle program, plaintiff brought this action challenging the AECA and the ITAR on the grounds that they violated the First Amendment. * * *

Plaintiff contends that * * * the [encryption regulations and recent] amendments regulating encryption items, both facially and as applied, constitutes a prior restraint on plaintiff's right to free speech, is unconstitutionally vague and overbroad, is content-based, and violates his freedom of association. * * *

The encryption regulations * * * [are] specifically directed at speech protected by the First Amendment. The Department of Commerce requires a license to export * * *. And as made explicit by the new regulations, export includes publication where publication is or could be made electronic and even where the information to be published is already publicly available. * * *

[T]he exception for printed materials, while at first glance a concession to the speech interests involved, is so irrational and administratively unreliable that it may well serve to only exacerbate the potential for self-censorship * * *.

[T]he Supreme Court's recent decision in Reno v. American Civil Liberties Union * * * suggests that not only is the distinction between print and electronic media increasingly untenable, but that the Internet is subject to the same exacting level of First Amendment scrutiny as print media. * * *

[T]he court declares that the Export Administration Regulations, 15 C.F.R. Pt. 730 et seq.(1997) and all rules, policies and practices promulgated or pursued thereunder insofar as they apply to or require licensing for encryption and decryption software and related devices and technology are in violation of the First Amendment on the grounds of prior restraint and are, therefore, unconstitutional as discussed above, and shall not be applied to plaintiff's publishing of such items, including scientific papers, algorithms or computer programs * * *.

[D]efendants are permanently enjoined from doing or causing to be done the following acts:

a) further and future enforcement, operation or execution of the statutes, regulations, rules, policies and practices declared unconstitutional under this order, including criminal or civil prosecutions with respect to plaintiff or anyone who uses, discusses or publishes or seeks to use, discuss or publish plaintiff's encryption program and related materials described in paragraph 5) of this order; and

b) threatening, detaining, prosecuting, discouraging or otherwise interfering with plaintiff or any other person described in paragraph 6) above in the exercise of their federal constitutional rights as declared in this order.

JUNGER v. DALEY

8 F.Supp.2d 708 (N.D. Ohio 1998).

JUDGE JAMES S. GWIN, UNITED STATES DISTRICT JUDGE. * * *

Plaintiff Junger seeks injunctive and declaratory relief from the government's enforcement of export controls on encryption software. In support of his motion for injunctive relief, Junger claims the Export Administration Regulations ("Export Regulations") * * * violate rights protected by the First Amendment.

The government denies that the Export Regulations implicate First Amendment rights. The government says its licensing requirement seeks only to restrict the distribution of encryption software itself, not ideas on encryption. Stated otherwise, the government says it seeks to control only the engine for encrypting data. The government says it controls the distribution of sophisticated encryption software for valid national security purposes. * * *

The Court finds that the Export Regulations are constitutional because encryption source code is inherently functional, because the Export Regulations are not directed at source code's expressive elements, and because the Export Regulations do not reach academic discussions of software, or software in print form. For these reasons, the Court grants the government's motion for summary judgment and denies Junger's motion for summary judgment. * * *

Once almost the exclusive province of military and governmental bodies, cryptography is now increasingly available to businesses and private individuals wishing to keep their communications confidential. See Bernstein v. United States Dep't of State, 974 F. Supp. 1288, 1292 (N.D. Cal. 1997) ("Bernstein III"). To keep their communications confidential, users encrypt and decrypt communications, records and other data. Through encryption, users seek to prevent the unauthorized interception, viewing, tampering, and forging of such data. Without encryption, information sent by a computer is unsecured. Without encryption those other than the intended recipient may view sensitive information. * * *

Encryption has been used for decades although the methods of encryption have changed. Until the end of World War II, mechanical devices commonly did encryption, such as Nazi Germany's Enigma machines. Today, computers and electronic devices have largely replaced mechanical encryption. In using electronic devices, encryption can be done with dedicated hardware (such as a telephone scrambler's electronic circuitry) or with computer software. Encryption software carries out a cryptographic "algorithm," which is a set of instructions that directs computer hardware to encrypt plaintext into an encoded ciphertext. Mathematical functions or equations usually make up the instructions.

Like all software, encryption programs can take two general forms: object code and source code. Source code is a series of instructions to a computer in programming languages such as BASIC, PERL, or FORTRAN. Object code is the same set of instructions translated into binary digits (1's and 0's). Thus, source code and object code are essentially interchangeable. While source code is not directly executable by a computer, the computer can easily convert it into executable object code with "compiler" or "interpreter" software. * * *

Plaintiff Junger is a law professor. He teaches a course titled "Computers and the Law" at Case Western Reserve University Law School in Cleveland, Ohio. Junger maintains sites on the World Wide Web that include information about courses that he teaches, including a computers and law course. His web sites also set out documents involved with this litigation. Plaintiff Junger uses his web site to describe the process of this litigation through press releases and filed materials. Besides descriptions of this lawsuit, the web site has information from Junger's courses and other topics of interest to him.

Plaintiff Junger wishes to post to his web site various encryption programs that he has written to show how computers work. Such a posting is an export under the Export Regulations. See 15 C.F.R. § 734.2(b)(9).

On June 12, 1997, Plaintiff Junger submitted three applications to the Commerce Department requesting determination of commodity classifications for encryption software programs and other items. With these applications, Plaintiff Junger sought a Commerce Department determination whether they restricted the materials from export. On July 4, 1997, the Bureau of Export Administration told Junger that Export Classification Number 5D002 covered four of the five software programs he had submitted, and therefore were subject to the Export Regulations. Although it found that four programs were subject to the Export Regulations, the Commerce Department found that the first chapter of Junger's textbook, Computers and the Law, was an allowed unlicensed export. While deciding that the printed book chapter containing encryption code could be exported, the Commerce Department said that export of a software program itself would need a license. After receiving the classification determination, Junger has not applied for a license to export his classified encryption software. * * *

The scrutiny the Court will apply to the Export Regulations depends upon whether the export of encryption source code is expressive, and whether the Export Regulations are directed at the content of ideas. Prior restraints on expressive materials bear a heavy presumption against their constitutional validity, and are subject to the strictest judicial scrutiny. See New York Times Co. v. United States, 403 U.S. 713 (1971) (per curiam).

If a law distinguishes among types of speech based on their content of ideas, the Court reviews it under strict scrutiny. See Turner Broadcasting System, Inc. v. FCC, 512 U.S. 622 (1994). To survive strict scrutiny, the government must employ narrowly tailored means that are necessary to advance a compelling government interest. See id.

If a law does not distinguish among types of speech based upon the content of the speech, the law will not be subject to strict scrutiny. Turner, 512 U.S. at 658 (laws favoring broadcast programs over cable programs are not subject to strict scrutiny unless the laws reflect government preference for the content of one speaker). As described in Turner: "It would be error to conclude, however, that the First Amendment mandates strict scrutiny for any speech regulation that applies to one medium (or a subset thereof) but not others." Id. at 660.

If the Export Regulations are not expressive and if the Export Regulations are not aimed at the content of the ideas, then the Court reviews the regulations under an intermediate scrutiny standard. See id. at 662. Under intermediate scrutiny, a law is constitutional if it furthers a substantial governmental interest, if the interest is unrelated to the suppression of free expression, and if the restriction is no greater than is essential to the furtherance of that interest. See id. (citing United States v. O'Brien, 391 U.S. 367, 377 (1968)). * * *

The most important issue in the instant case is whether the export of encryption software source code is sufficiently expressive to merit First Amendment protection. This is a matter of first impression in the Sixth Circuit. Indeed, the Court is aware of only two other courts in the United States that have addressed this question, and they reached opposite results. This Court finds that although encryption source code may occasionally be expressive, its export is not protected conduct under the First Amendment. * * *

Plaintiff Junger urges that the Export Regulations are invalid on their face as an unconstitutional prior restraint on the export of encryption source code. * * *

Prior restraints on publication of expressive materials are anathema to American constitutionalism. As the Supreme Court has recognized, "it has been generally, if not universally, considered that it is the chief purpose of the [First Amendment's free press] guaranty to prevent previous restraints upon publication." * * *

In order for a licensing law to be invalidated by a prior restraint facial challenge, it "must have a close enough nexus to expression, or to conduct commonly associated with expression, to pose a real and substantial threat" of censorship. * * * A facial attack upon legislation on First Amendment grounds is appropriate only where the challenged statute "is directed narrowly and specifically at expression or conduct commonly associated with expression." See Lakewood, 486 U.S. at 760.

Exporting encryption source code is not an activity that is "commonly associated with expression." Source code is a set of instructions to a computer that is commonly distributed for the wholly non-expressive purpose of controlling a computer's operation. It may, as the Court has noted, occasionally be exported for expressive reasons. Nevertheless, the prior restraint doctrine is not implicated simply because an activity may on occasion be expressive. * * *

Plaintiff Junger urges this Court to review the Export Regulations under a strict scrutiny standard. He argues that strict scrutiny is appropriate because where the government seeks to "suppress, disadvantage, or impose differential burdens on speech because of its content," such regulations must be subject to the most searching judicial review. * * *

Junger first alleges that the Export Regulations discriminate because of content because they treat other types of software more favorably than encryption software. Plaintiff Junger is correct that the government subjects encryption software to heightened licensing regulations that do not apply to other types of software. Under the Export Administration Act, all types of software are regulated as "technology." 50 U.S.C. App. § 2415(4). However, encryption software is categorized under the stricter "commodity" standard. * * *

The Export Regulations are not content based, however, because the regulations burden encryption software without reference to any views it may express. As the President has made clear, encryption software is regulated because it has the technical capacity to encrypt data and by that jeopardize American security interests, not because of its expressive content. * * *

Because the Export Regulations are content neutral, the Court must evaluate the licensing scheme under intermediate scrutiny. A content neutral government regulation passes constitutional muster if " 'it furthers an important or substantial governmental interest; if the governmental interest is unrelated to the suppression of free expression; and if the incidental restriction of alleged First Amendment freedoms is no greater than is essential to the furtherance of that interest.' "

The "important interest" prong is satisfied because the government is properly concerned with controlling the export of encryption software to potentially hostile countries or individuals to protect national security.

The use of encryption products by foreign intelligence targets can have "a debilitating effect" on the National Security Agency's "ability to collect and report * * * critical foreign intelligence." * * *

The government's important interest in controlling the spread of encryption software is not diminished even if certain forms of encryption software are already available abroad. Whatever the present foreign availability of encryption software, the government has a substantial interest to limit future distribution. The government also has an interest in ensuring that the most complex and effective encryption programs, such as 128–bit key length software, are not widely released abroad. * * *

The Export Regulations are "unrelated to the suppression of free expression," O'Brien, 391 U.S. at 377, for the same reasons that they are content neutral. The Export Regulations are not designed to limit the free exchange of ideas about cryptography. Instead, the government regulates encryption software because it does the function of actually encrypting data.

Besides meeting the "important interest" and "unrelated" prongs, the Export Regulations also satisfy the "narrow tailoring" requirement. The narrow tailoring prong does not require that the government employ the least speech-restrictive means to achieve its purposes. Instead, narrow tailoring requires that the law not "burden substantially more speech than is necessary to further the government's legitimate interests." Ward, 491 U.S. at 799. * * *

The government's interest in controlling the spread of encryption software and gathering foreign intelligence surely would be "achieved less effectively" absent the export controls. Encryption software posted on the Internet or on computer diskette can be converted from source code into workable object code with a single keystroke. Elimination of export controls would permit the unrestricted export of encryption software to any person, organization, or country, without regard to the strength of the software, the identity of the recipients, or the uses to which it might be put.

The export controls at issue do not "burden substantially more speech than is necessary to further the government's legitimate interests," Ward, 491 U.S. at 799, for the same reason they are not overbroad. Export controls are targeted at precisely the activity that threatens the government's legitimate interests. * * * The licensing requirements are tailored to the risks presented, with less restrictive requirements for exports that pose lesser risks, such as 40–bit mass market and key-recovery software. See 15 C.F.R. § 742.15(b)(1)–(2). Finally, the Export Regulations do not reach print publications. Thus, they "leave open ample alternative channels of communication," Ward, 491 U.S. at 802, for the exchange of information and ideas regarding cryptography.

Because the content neutral export regulations at issue enable the government to collect vital foreign intelligence, are not directed at a source code's ideas, and do not burden more speech than necessary, they satisfy intermediate scrutiny. * * *

Plaintiff Junger alleges that the Export Regulations violate his First Amendment rights of academic freedom and freedom of association by restricting his ability to teach, publish, and distribute encryption software. Neither Junger nor the defendants address this issue in the briefs submitted to the Court. The Court therefore considers that Junger has waived the academic freedom and freedom of association claims. * * *

Plaintiff Junger claims that executive regulation of encryption exports under the International Emergency Economic Powers Act is an impermissibly broad delegation of authority and, therefore, a violation of the separation of powers. Specifically, he alleges that the President does not have the statutory authority under the International Emergency Economic Powers Act to extend regulatory control to encryption software. Instead, encryption software is exempt from regulation under the International Emergency Economic Powers Act because it is "informational material." * * *

The Court lacks jurisdiction to review Junger's claim that the President exceeded his authority under the International Emergency Economic Powers Act when he directed that encryption products be controlled for export. "Longstanding authority holds that such review is not available when the statute in question commits the decision to the discretion of the President." Dalton v. Specter, 511 U.S. 462, 474 (1994).

The President clearly has statutory authority under the International Emergency Economic Powers Act to extend export controls in general. See United States v. Spawr Optical Research, Inc., 685 F.2d 1076, 1079–1082 (9th Cir. 1982), cert. denied, 461 U.S. 905 (1983). Congress has recognized and approved of this practice, see id. 685 F.2d at 1081, and courts have consistently held that the President's decision to invoke the International Emergency Economic Powers Act to regulate international trade is unreviewable. * * *

For these reasons, plaintiff's motion for summary judgment is denied, and defendants' motion for summary judgment is granted.

Note: The Clipper Chip Story

An April 15, 1993 White House memorandum, reprinted below, describes the "Clipper Chip" encryption initiative. The White House publicly announced authorization of the initiative a day later, on April 16. President Bill Clinton directed federal authorities to "request manufacturers of communications hardware which incorporates encryption to install the U.S. government-developed key-escrow microcircuits in their products." The move was designed to thwart criminals and terrorists who might seek to use new technologies to send secret messages that could not be intercepted and deciphered by law enforcement or national security officials.

Private industry rejected the idea: "Silicon Valley staunchly opposed the Clipper Chip, which would have given the government a back-door key to all

U.S. encrypted data." Thomas L. Friedman, Webbed, Wired and Worried, *New York Times*, May 26, 2002. Largely because industry balked, the "Clipper Chip eventually went the way of clipper ships * * * and researchers showed its cryptographic approach was flawed anyway." Brian Bergstein, Fight Over Surveillance Law Continues, *TechwebNews*, November 6, 2005.

The Clipper Clip initiative has been denigrated as government "micromanaging" and "blamed for discouraging" innovative technology. Id. Especially in light of federal encryption export controls, there was reason in the early 1990s to question the wisdom of the Clipper Chip, both from privacy and from innovation perspectives. See Michael Froomkin, The Metaphor is the Key: Cryptography, the Clipper Chip and the Constitution, 143 *U. Penn. L. Rev.* 709 (1995); It Came from Planet Clipper, 1996 *U. Chi. L. Forum* 15 (1996).

Ironically, the federal government's policies may have indirectly discouraged encryption innovation in the past, but today the government is prepared to punish firms that fail to use encryption to secure consumer data and thereby enable data breaches. Stanford University Professor Dan Boneh, co-inventor of identity-based encryption, has noted that government has gone from stalling deployment of cryptography to mandating it with regulations such as Sarbanes–Oxley and HIPAA: "There's been a complete flip, recognizing that encryption is there to help us, not just to help our enemies." See Paul Krill, Public Key Cryptography Celebrates Anniversary, InfoWorld Daily, October 27, 2006.

PRESIDENT WILLIAM J. CLINTON, CLASSIFIED MEMO AUTHORIZING CLIPPER CHIP ENCRYPTION PROGRAM

April 15, 1993.

Advanced telecommunications and commercially available encryption are part of a wave of new computer and communications technology. Encryption products scramble information to protect the privacy of communications and data by preventing unauthorized access. Advanced telecommunications systems use digital technology to rapidly and precisely handle a high volume of communications. These advanced telecommunications systems are integral to the infrastructure needed to ensure economic competitiveness in the information age.

Despite its benefits, new communications technology can also frustrate lawful government electronic surveillance. Sophisticated encryption can have this effect in the United States. When exported abroad, it can be used to thwart foreign intelligence activities critical to our national interests. In the past, it has been possible to reserve a government capability to conduct electronic surveillance in furtherance of legitimate law enforcement and national security interests, while at the same time protecting the privacy and civil liberties of all citizens. As encryption technology improves, doing so will require new, innovative approaches.

In the area of communications encryption, the U.S. government has developed a microcircuit that not only provides privacy through encryption that is substantially more robust than the current government standard, but also permits escrowing of the keys needed to unlock the encryption. The system for the escrowing of keys will allow the government to gain access to encrypted information only with appropriate legal authorization.

To assist law enforcement and other government agencies to collect and decrypt, under legal authority, electronically transmitted information, I hereby direct the following, action to be taken:

Installation of Government–Developed Microcircuits

The Attorney General of the United States or her representative, shall request manufacturers of communications hardware which incorporates encryption to install the U.S. government-developed key-escrow microcircuits in their products. The fact of law enforcement access to the escrowed keys will not be concealed from the American public. All appropriate steps shall be taken to ensure that any existing or future versions of the key-escrow microcircuit are made widely available to U.S. communications hardware manufacturers, consistent with the need to ensure the security of the key-escrow system. In making this decision, I do not intend to prevent the private sector from developing, or the government from approving, other microcircuits or algorithms that are equally effective in assuring both privacy and a secure key-escrow system.

Key–Escrow

The Attorney General shall make all arrangements with appropriate entities to hold the keys for the key-escrow microcircuits installed in communications equipment. In each case, the key holder must agree to strict security procedures to prevent unauthorized release of the keys. The keys shall be released only to government agencies that have established their authority to acquire the content of those Communications that have been encrypted by devices containing the microcircuits. The Attorney General shall review for legal sufficiency the procedures by which an agency establishes its authority to acquire the content of such communications.

Procurement and Use of Encryption Devices

The Secretary of Commerce, in consultation with other appropriate U.S. agencies, shall initiate a process to write standards to facilitate the procurement and use of encryption devices fitted with key-escrow microcircuits in federal communications systems that process sensitive but unclassified information. Expect this process to proceed on a schedule that will permit promulgation of final standard within six months of this directive.

The Attorney General will procure and utilize encryption devices to the extent needed to preserve the government's ability to conduct lawful electronic surveillance and to fulfill the need for secure law enforcement communications. Further, The Attorney General shall utilize funds from the Department of Justice Asset Forfeiture Super Surplus Fund to effect this purchase.

/s/ William J. Clinton

G. UNLEASHING SURVEILLANCE

WHAT IS TIA?

What is.com (August 1, 2006).

Total Information Awareness (TIA) is the name of a massive U.S. data mining project focused on scanning travel, financial and other data from public and private sources with the goal of detecting and preventing transnational threats to national security. TIA has also been called Terrorism Information Awareness. The program was part of the Homeland Security Act and, after its creation in January 2003, was managed by the Defense Advanced Research Projects Agency (DARPA). In September 2003, U.S. Congressional negotiators agreed to terminate the program and ceased funding. In 2006, however, news agencies reported that software developed for it had been shifted to other agencies, specifically the National Security Agency (NSA).

TIA initiatives included a massive counter-terrorism database and advanced methods for data collection, processing and analysis. At the time, technology capable of accomplishing some of the program's data mining goals had not yet been invented. For example, one component of the system was a technology that enabled unilingual English speakers to monitor information in other languages. To that end, DARPA began awarding contracts for the design and development of TIA system components in August, 2002.

A number of privacy rights organizations, such as the American Civil Liberties Union (ACLU), expressed concerns that the program would gather the personal information of private citizens indiscriminately and would not be held publicly accountable. While legislative negotiators in Congress (who terminated the project under DARPA) agreed, many of the programs developed under TIA are currently used to gather and analyze data at the NSA.

NOTE: ROK LAMPE, SURVEILLANCE AND THE RIGHT TO PRIVACY IN EUROPE

Article 8 of the Covenant for the Protection of Human Rights and Fundamental Freedoms was designed to protect individuals' right to privacy primarily against the public authority. Surveillance—including wiretapping, photographs and video recording—by public law enforcement and government intelligence gathering authorities implicates Article 8's privacy protections.

The terrorist attacks of September 11, 2001 in the United States and subsequent terrorist attacks in London and Madrid arguably pointed to the need for more aggressive law enforcement and intelligence gathering in Europe. Even the social riots in Paris suggested to some that public authorities should engage in more vigilant monitoring and surveillance than in the past.

The European Court for Human Rights has held that secret surveillance of citizens is tolerable under the Convention, but only in so far as strictly necessary for safeguarding democratic institutions. In this regard, the Court has been influenced by the modern reality that democratic societies find themselves threatened by highly sophisticated forms of espionage and by terrorism within their jurisdictions.

In one of the leading pre 9/11 cases the Court upheld the legitimacy of secret surveillance of the mail and telecommunications in the interests of national security or for the prevention of disorder or crime. *See Klass v. Germany*, judgment of 6 Sept 1978, paragraph 48. In *Klass* the Court addressed whether German legislation which authorized opening of letters and wire-tapping in order to safeguard national security and to prevent disorder and crime, violated the plaintiffs' right to privacy under Article 8. Five "applicants" (plaintiffs), among them a lawyer, claimed that Article 10 paragraph 2 of the German Constitution (*Grundgesetz* or Basic Law) and a statute enacted in pursuance of that provision, namely the Act of 13 August 1968 on Restrictions on the Secrecy of the Mail, Post and Telecommunications (referred to as "the G 10"), were contrary to the Convention. The applicants did not dispute that the State has the right to have recourse to the surveillance measures contemplated by the legislation; they challenged the legislation on the ground that it permits those measures without obliging the authorities in every case to notify the persons concerned after the event, and excludes a remedy before the courts against the ordering and execution of such measures. The Court ultimately approved the German system. But in doing so it stressed that adequate and effective guarantees against abuse must be a part of any surveillance regime.

EUROPEAN COURT OF HUMAN RIGHTS CASE OF KLASS AND OTHERS v. GERMANY

(Application no. 5029/71)
6 September 1978.

* * *

51. According to the G 10, a series of limitative conditions have to be satisfied before a surveillance measure can be imposed. Thus, the permissible restrictive measures are confined to cases in which there are factual indications for suspecting a person of planning, committing or having committed certain serious criminal acts; measures may only be ordered if the establishment of the facts by another method is without prospects of success or considerably more difficult; even then, the surveillance may cover only the specific suspect or his presumed "contact-persons". Consequently, so-called exploratory or general surveillance is not permitted by the contested legislation.

Surveillance may be ordered only on written application giving reasons, and such an application may be made only by the head, or his substitute, of certain services; the decision thereon must be taken by a Federal Minister empowered for the purpose by the Chancellor or, where appropriate, by the supreme Land authority. Accordingly, under the law there exists an administrative procedure designed to ensure that measures are not ordered haphazardly, irregularly or without due and proper consideration. In addition, although not required by the Act, the competent Minister in practice and except in urgent cases seeks the prior consent of the G 10 Commission.

52. The G 10 also lays down strict conditions with regard to the implementation of the surveillance measures and to the processing of the information thereby obtained. The measures in question remain in force for a maximum of three months and may be renewed only on fresh application; the measures must immediately be discontinued once the required conditions have ceased to exist or the measures themselves are no longer necessary; knowledge and documents thereby obtained may not be used for other ends, and documents must be destroyed as soon as they are no longer needed to achieve the required purpose.

As regards the implementation of the measures, an initial control is carried out by an official qualified for judicial office. This official examines the information obtained before transmitting to the competent services such information as may be used in accordance with the Act and is relevant to the purpose of the measure; he destroys any other intelligence that may have been gathered.

60. In the light of these considerations and of the detailed examination of the contested legislation, the Court concludes that the German legislature was justified to consider the interference resulting from that legislation with the exercise of the right guaranteed by Article 8 para. 1 (art. 8–1) as being necessary in a democratic society in the interests of national security and for the prevention of disorder or crime (Article 8 para. 2) (art. 8–2). Accordingly, the Court finds no breach of Article 8 (art. 8) of the Convention.

EUROPEAN COURT OF HUMAN RIGHTS CASE OF MURRAY v. THE UNITED KINGDOM

(Application no. 14310/88)
28 October 1994.

* * *

V. ALLEGED VIOLATION OF ARTICLE 8 (art. 8) OF THE CONVENTION

83. All six applicants claimed to be the victims of a violation of Article 8 (art. 8) of the Convention, which provides:

"1. Everyone has the right to respect for his private and family life, his home and his correspondence.

2. There shall be no interference by a public authority with the exercise of this right except such as is in accordance with the law and is necessary

in a democratic society in the interests of national security, public safety or the economic well-being of the country, for the prevention of disorder or crime, for the protection of health or morals, or for the protection of the rights and freedoms of others."

A. Arguments before the Court

84. The first applicant complained of the manner in which she was treated both in her home and at the Army centre; in the latter connection she objected to the recording of personal details concerning herself and her family, as well as the photograph which was taken of her without her knowledge or consent. All six applicants contended that the entry into and search of their family home by the Army, including the confinement of the second, third, fourth, fifth and sixth applicants for a short while in one room, violated Article 8.

85. Both the Government and the Commission considered that the matters complained of were justified under paragraph 2 of Article 8 as being lawful measures necessary in a democratic society for the prevention of crime in the context of the fight against terrorism in Northern Ireland.

B. Interference

86. It was not contested that the impugned measures interfered with the applicants' exercise of their right to respect for their private and family life and their home.

C. "In accordance with the law"

87. On the other hand, the applicants did not concede that the resultant interferences had been "in accordance with the law". They disputed that the impugned measures all formed an integral part of Mrs Murray's arrest and detention or that the domestic courts had affirmed their lawfulness, in particular as concerns the retention of the records including the photograph of Mrs Murray.

88. Entry into and search of a home by Army personnel such as occurred in the present case were explicitly permitted by section 14 (3) of the 1978 Act for the purpose of effecting arrests under that section. The Court of Appeal upheld the legality of the search in the present case. The short period of restraint endured by the other members of Mrs Murray's family when they were asked to assemble in one room was held by the House of Lords to be a necessary and proper part of the procedure of arrest of Mrs Murray. The Court of Appeal and the House of Lords also confirmed that the Army's implied lawful authority under section 14 extended to interrogating a detained person and to recording personal details of the kind contained in the standard record form. It is implicit in the judgments of the national courts that the retention of such details was covered by the same lawful authority derived from section 14. The taking and, by implication, also the retention of a photograph of the first applicant without her consent had no statutory basis but, as explained by the trial court judge and the Court of Appeal, were lawful under the common law.

The impugned measures thus had a basis in domestic law. The Court discerns no reason, on the material before it, for not concluding that each of the various measures was "in accordance with the law", within the meaning of Article 8 para. 2.

D. Legitimate aim

89. These measures undoubtedly pursued the legitimate aim of the prevention of crime.

E. Necessity in a democratic society

90. It remains to be determined whether they were necessary in a democratic society and, in particular, whether the means employed were proportionate to the legitimate aim pursued. In this connection it is not for the Court to substitute for the assessment of the national authorities its own assessment of what might be the best policy in the field of investigation of terrorist crime (see the above-mentioned Klass and Others judgment, p. 23, para. 49). A certain margin of appreciation in deciding what measures to take both in general and in particular cases should be left to the national authorities.

91. The present judgment has already adverted to the responsibility of an elected government in a democratic society to protect its citizens and its institutions against the threats posed by organised terrorism and to the special problems involved in the arrest and detention of persons suspected of terrorist-linked offences. These two factors affect the fair balance that is to be struck between the exercise by the individual of the right guaranteed to him or her under paragraph 1 of Article 8 and the necessity under paragraph 2 for the State to take effective measures for the prevention of terrorist crimes (see, mutatis mutandis, the above-mentioned Klass and Others judgment, p. 28, para. 59).

92. The domestic courts held that Mrs Murray was genuinely and honestly suspected of the commission of a terrorist-linked crime. The European Court, for its part, has found on the evidence before it that this suspicion could be regarded as reasonable for the purposes of sub-paragraph (c) Article 5 para. 1 of the European Convention on Human Rights. The Court accepts that there was in principle a need both for powers of the kind granted by section 14 of the 1978 Act and, in the particular case, to enter and search the home of the Murray family in order to arrest Mrs Murray.

Furthermore, the "conditions of extreme tension", as Lord Griffiths put it in his speech in the House of Lords, under which such arrests in Northern Ireland have to be carried out must be recognised. The Court notes the analysis of Lord Griffiths, when he:

"The search cannot be limited solely to looking for the person to be arrested and must also embrace a search whose object is to secure that the arrest should be peaceable. I ... regard it as an entirely reasonable precaution that all the occupants of the house should be asked to assemble in one room. ... It is in everyone's best interest that the arrest is peaceably effected and I am satisfied that the procedures adopted by the Army are sensible, reasonable and designed to bring about the arrest with the minimum of danger and distress to all concerned."

These are legitimate considerations which go to explain and justify the manner in which the entry into and search of the applicants' home were carried out. The Court does not find that, in relation to any of the applicants, the means employed by the authorities in this regard were disproportionate to the aim pursued.

93.   Neither can it be regarded as falling outside the legitimate bounds of the process of investigation of terrorist crime for the competent authorities to record and retain basic personal details concerning the arrested person or even other persons present at the time and place of arrest. None of the personal details taken during the search of the family home or during Mrs Murray's stay at the Army centre would appear to have been irrelevant to the procedures of arrest and interrogation.

Similar conclusions apply to the taking and retention of a photograph of Mrs Murray at the Army centre. In this connection too, the Court does not find that the means employed were disproportionate to the aim pursued.

94.   In the light of the particular facts of the case, the Court finds that the various measures complained of can be regarded as having been necessary in a democratic society for the prevention of crime, within the meaning of Article 8 para. 2.

    F.   Conclusion

95.   In conclusion there has been no violation of Article 8 in respect of any of the applicants.

NOAH SHACHTMAN, PENTAGON KILLS LIFELOG PROJECT

Wired News, February 2004.

The Pentagon canceled its so-called LifeLog project, an ambitious effort to build a database tracking a person's entire existence. Run by DARPA, the Defense Department's research arm, LifeLog aimed to gather in a single place just about everything an individual says, sees or does: the phone calls made, the TV shows watched, the magazines read, the plane tickets bought, the e-mail sent and received. Out of this seemingly endless ocean of information, computer scientists would plot distinctive routes in the data, mapping relationships, memories, events and experiences. Life-Log's backers said the all-encompassing diary could have turned into a near-perfect digital memory, giving its users computerized assistants with an almost flawless recall of what they had done in the past. But civil libertarians immediately pounced on the project when it debuted last spring, arguing that LifeLog could become the ultimate tool for profiling potential enemies of the state. Researchers close to the project say they're not sure why it was dropped late last month. DARPA hasn't provided an explanation for LifeLog's quiet cancellation. "A change in priorities" is the only rationale agency spokeswoman Jan Walker gave to Wired News.

LIFELOG PROJECT

http://www.darpa.mil/ipto/solicitations/closed/03–30_PIP.htm.

The Information Processing Technology Office (IPTO) of the Defense Advanced Research Projects Agency (DARPA) is soliciting proposals to develop an ontology-based (sub)system that captures, stores, and makes accessible the flow of one person's experience in and interactions with the world in order to support a broad spectrum of associates/assistants and other system capabilities. The objective of this "LifeLog" concept is to be able to trace the "threads" of an individual's life in terms of events, states, and relationships.

Functionally, the LifeLog (sub)system consists of three components: data capture and storage, representation and abstraction, and data access and user interface. LifeLog accepts as input a number of raw physical and transactional data streams. Through inference and reasoning, LifeLog generates multiple layers of representation at increasing levels of abstraction. The input data streams are abstracted into sequences of events and states, which are aggregated into threads and episodes to produce a timeline that constitutes an "episodic memory" for the individual. Patterns of events in the timeline support the identification of routines, relationships, and habits. Preferences, plans, goals, and other markers of intentionality are at the highest level.

LifeLog is interested in three major data categories: physical data, transactional data, and context or media data. "Anywhere/anytime" capture of physical data might be provided by hardware worn by the LifeLog user. Visual, aural, and possibly even haptic sensors capture what the user sees, hears, and feels. GPS, digital compass, and inertial sensors capture the user's orientation and movements. Biomedical sensors capture the user's physical state. LifeLog also captures the user's computer-based interactions and transactions throughout the day from email, calendar, instant messaging, web-based transactions, as well as other common computer applications, and stores the data (or, in some cases, pointers to the data) in appropriate formats. Voice transactions can be captured through recording of telephone calls and voice mail, with the called and calling numbers as metadata. FAX and hardcopy written material (such as postal mail) can be scanned. Finally, LifeLog also captures (or at least captures pointers to) the tremendous amounts of context data the user is exposed to every day from diverse media sources, including broadcast television and radio, hardcopy newspapers, magazines, books and other documents, and softcopy electronic books, web sites, and database access.

LifeLog can be used as a stand-alone system to serve as a powerful automated multimedia diary and scrapbook. By using a search engine interface, the user can easily retrieve a specific thread of past transactions, or recall an experience from a few seconds ago or from many years earlier in as much detail as is desired, including imagery, audio, or video replay of the event. In addition to operating in this stand-alone mode, LifeLog can also serve as a subsystem to support a wide variety of other applications, including personal, medical, financial, and other types of assistants, and various teaching and training tools. As increasing numbers of people acquire LifeLogs, collaborative tasks could be facilitated by the interaction of LifeLogs, and properly anonymized access to LifeLog data might support medical research and the early detection of an emerging epidemic. Application of the LifeLog abstraction structure in a synthesizing mode will eventually allow synthetic game characters and humanoid robots to lead more "realistic" lives. However, the initial LifeLog development is tightly focused on the stand-alone system capabilities, and does not include the broader class of assistive, training, and other applications that may ultimately be supported.

LifeLog technology will support the long-term IPTO vision of a new class of truly "cognitive" systems that can reason in a variety of ways, using substantial amounts of appropriately represented knowledge; can learn from experiences so that their performance improves as they accumulate knowledge and experience; can explain their actions and can accept direction; can be aware of their own behavior and reflect on their own capabilities; and can respond in a robust manner to surprises.

WILLIAM NEW, CONGRESS FUNDS DEFENSE, KILLS INFORMATION AWARENESS

National Journal's Technology Daily, September 25, 2003.

Congress on Thursday completed the fiscal 2004 Defense Department appropriations bill that permanently kills a far-reaching technology research program that set off a furor over rights to citizens' personal information.

"Total Information Awareness [TIA] is no more," said Sen. Ron Wyden, D–Ore., a key player in blocking the program. * * *

The Defense Advanced Research Projects Agency (DARPA) will continue its mission of developing visionary defense technologies. The appropriations bill eliminates the Information Awareness Office under which TIA was being developed, but transfers certain technologies deemed non-controversial to other places within DARPA. These include technologies related to biowarfare, wargaming and speech recognition.

The provision also "does not restrict the national foreign intelligence program from using processing, analysis and collaboration tools for counterterrorism foreign intelligence purposes." * * *

PRESIDENT GEORGE W. BUSH, THE INTELLIGENCE REFORM AND TERRORISM PREVENTION ACT OF 2004

December 17, 2004.

Under this new law, our vast intelligence enterprise will become more unified, coordinated and effective. It will enable us to better do our duty, which is to protect the American people. * * *

Nearly six decades ago, our nation and our allies faced a new—the new world of the Cold War and the dangers of a new enemy. To defend the free world from an armed empire bent on conquest, visionary leaders created new institutions such as the NATO alliance. The NATO alliance was begun by treaty in this very room. President Truman also implemented a sweeping reorganization of the federal government. He established the Department of Defense, the Central Intelligence Agency, and the National Security Council.

America, in this new century, again faces new threats. Instead of massed armies, we face stateless networks; we face killers who hide in our own cities. We must confront deadly technologies. To inflict great harm on our country, America's enemies need to be only right once. Our intelligence and law enforcement professionals in our government must be right every single time. Our government is adapting to confront and defeat these threats. We're staying on the offensive against the enemy. We'll take the fight to the terrorists abroad so we do not have to face them here at home.

And here at home, we're strengthening our homeland defenses. We created the Department of Homeland Security. We have made the prevention of terror attacks the highest priority of the Department of Justice and the FBI. We'll continue to work with Congress to make sure they've got the resources necessary to do their jobs. We established the National Counterterrorism Center where all the available intelligence on terrorist threats is brought together in one place and where joint action against the terrorists is planned.

We have strengthened the security of our nation's borders and ports of entry and transportation systems. The bill I sign today continues the essential reorganization of our government. Those charged with protecting America must have the best possible intelligence information, and that information must be closely integrated to form the clearest possible picture of the threats to our country.

A key lesson of September the 11th, 2001 is that America's intelligence agencies must work together as a single, unified enterprise. The Intelligence Reform and Terrorism Prevention Act of 2004 creates the position of Director of National Intelligence, or DNI, to be appointed by the President with the consent of the Senate.

The Director will lead a unified intelligence community and will serve as the principal advisor to the President on intelligence matters. The DNI will have the authority to order the collection of new intelligence, to ensure the sharing of information among agencies and to establish common standards for the intelligence community's personnel. It will be the DNI's responsibility to determine the annual budgets for all national intelligence agencies and offices and to direct how these funds are spent. These authorities vested in a single official who reports directly to me will make all our intelligence efforts better coordinated, more efficient, and more effective.

The Director of the CIA will report to the DNI. The CIA will retain its core of responsibilities for collecting human intelligence, analyzing intelligence from all sources, and supporting American interests abroad at the direction of the President.

The new law will preserve the existing chain of command and leave all our intelligence agencies, organizations, and offices in their current departments. Our military commanders will continue to have quick access to the intelligence they need to achieve victory on the battlefield. And the law supports our efforts to ensure greater information sharing among federal departments and agencies, and also with appropriate state and local authorities.

The many reforms in this act have a single goal: to ensure that the people in government responsible for defending America have the best possible information to make the best possible decisions. The men and women of our intelligence community give America their very best every day, and in return we owe them our full support. As we continue to reform and strengthen the intelligence community, we will do all that is necessary to defend its people and the nation we serve.

H. KEEPING TRACK: GPS, RFID AND NANOTECHNOLOGY

NOTE: GLOBAL POSITIONING SATELLITE TECHNOLOGY

Global position technologies enable users to locate targets of interest in geographic space. GPS was developed by the U.S. Department of Defense for military purposes, and is now available as a public service. Anyone with a GPS receiver can make use of the system. Popular applications enable drivers to navigate their way through unfamiliar neighborhoods and cities. What privacy concerns are raised by GPS technologies?

UNDERSTANDING GPS

http://www.faa.gov.

The Global Positioning System (GPS) is a space-based radio-navigation system consisting of a constellation of satellites and a network of ground stations used for monitoring and control. A minimum of 24 GPS satellites orbit the Earth at an altitude of approximately 11,000 miles providing users with accurate information on position, velocity, and time anywhere in the world and in all weather conditions.

GPS is operated and maintained by the Department of Defense (DoD). The National Space–Based Positioning, Navigation, and Timing (PNT) Executive Committee manages GPS, while the U.S. Coast Guard acts as the civil interface to the public for GPS matters. * * *

History and Development

The Global Positioning System, formally known as the Navstar Global Positioning System, was initiated in 1973 to reduce the proliferation of navigation aids. By creating a system that overcame the limitations of many existing navigation systems, GPS became attractive to a broad spectrum of users worldwide. The Global Positioning System has been successful in virtually all navigation applications, and because its capabilities are accessible using small, inexpensive equipment, GPS is being utilized in a wide variety of applications across the globe. * * *

Satellite Navigation is based on a global network of satellites that transmit radio signals in medium earth orbit. Users of Satellite Navigation are most familiar with the 24 Global Positioning System (GPS) satellites. The United States, who developed and operates GPS, and Russia, who developed a similar system known as GLONASS, have offered free use of their respective systems to the international community. The International Civil Aviation Organization (ICAO), as well as other international user groups, have accepted GPS and GLONASS as the core for an international civil satellite navigation capability known as the Global Navigation Satellite System (GNSS).

The basic GPS service provides users with approximately 100–meter accuracy, 95% of the time, anywhere on or near the surface of the earth. To accomplish this, each of the 24 satellites emits signals to receivers that determine their location by computing the difference between the time that a signal is sent and the time it is received. GPS satellites carry atomic clocks that provide extremely accurate time. The time information is placed in the codes broadcast by the satellite so that a receiver can continuously determine the time the signal was broadcast. The signal contains data that a receiver uses to compute the locations of the satellites and to make other adjustments needed for accurate positioning. The receiver uses the time difference between the time of signal reception and the broadcast time to compute the distance, or range, from the receiver to the satellite. The receiver must account for propagation delays, or decreases in the signal's speed caused by the ionosphere and the troposphere. With information about the ranges to three satellites and the location of the satellite when the signal was sent, the receiver can compute its own three-dimensional position. An atomic clock synchronized to GPS is required in order to compute ranges from these three signals. However, by taking a measurement from a fourth satellite, the receiver avoids the need for an atomic clock. Thus, the receiver uses four satellites to compute latitude, longitude, altitude, and time.

GPS is comprised of three segments: [a control segment, a space segment and a user segment].

* * *

The user segment includes the equipment of the military personnel and civilians who receive GPS signals. Military GPS user equipment has been integrated into fighters, bombers, tankers, helicopters, ships, submarines, tanks, jeeps, and soldiers' equipment. In addition to basic navigation activities, military applications of GPS include target designation, close air support, "smart" weapons, and rendezvous.

With more than 500,000 GPS receivers, the civilian community has its own large and diverse user segment. Surveyors use GPS to save time over standard survey methods. GPS is used by aircraft and ships for enroute navigation and for airport or harbor approaches. GPS tracking systems are used to route and monitor delivery vans and emergency vehicles. In a method called precision farming, GPS is used to monitor and control the application of agricultural fertilizer and pesticides. GPS is available as an in-car navigation aid and is used by hikers and hunters. GPS is also used on the Space Shuttle. Because the GPS user does not need to communicate with the satellite, GPS can serve an unlimited number of users.

The aviation community is using GPS extensively. Aviation navigators, equipped with GPS receivers, use satellites as precise reference points to trilaterate the aircraft's position anywhere on or near the earth. GPS is already providing benefits to aviation users, but relative to its potential, these benefits are just the beginning. The foreseen contributions of GPS to aviation promise to be revolutionary. With air travel nearly doubled in the 21st Century, GPS can provide a cornerstone of the future air traffic management (ATM) system that will maintain high levels of safety, while reducing delays and increasing airway capacity. To promote this future ATM system, the FAA's objective is to establish and maintain a satellite-based navigation capability for all phases of flight.

NOTE: ARE SOME USES OF *GPS* TOO SNEAKY?

GPS products help people avoid getting lost. They can also enhance safety by discouraging detectable misconduct and facilitating emergency interventions. But GPS products raise privacy and autonomy concerns. See Waseem Karim, The Privacy Implications of Personal Locators: Why You Should Think Twice Before Voluntarily Availing Yourself to GPS Monitoring, 14 *Wash. U. J.L. & Pol'y* 485 (2004).

A worried parent may place GPS in a teenager's car or phone. A car rental business might install GPS technology to keep track of where customers go in their rental cars. See *Turner v. American Car Rental, Inc.*, 92 Conn.App. 123, 884 A.2d 7 (2005), holding that whether installing GPS in a rental car was an invasion of privacy was a question of fact for a jury. May private employers require employees to carry GPS technology for monitoring and tracking purposes? See Donna M. D. Thomas, Gotcha—GPS Invasion of Worker Privacy, 37 *Maryland Bar Journal* 55 (January/February, 2004).

How do the state and federal governments use GPS for surveillance purposes? Is its use subject to the Fourth Amendment? Two recent courts have held that the use of GPS by law enforcement requires a warrant, United States v. Maynard, 615 F.3d 544 (D.C.Cir.2010); Commonwealth v. Connolly, 454 Mass. 808, 913 N.E.2d 356 (Mass., September 17, 2009). But see United States v. Garcia, 474 F.3d 994 (7th Cir. 2007).

UNITED STATES v. GARCIA

474 F.3d 994 (7th Cir. 2007).

JUDGE POSNER * * *

The defendant had served time for methamphetamine offenses. Shortly after his release from prison, a person who was a known user of meth reported to police that the defendant had brought meth to her and her husband, consumed it with them, and told them he wanted to start manufacturing meth again. Another person told the police that the defendant had bragged that he could manufacture meth in front of a police station without being caught. A store's security video system recorded the defendant buying ingredients used in making the drug.

From someone else the police learned that the defendant was driving a borrowed Ford Tempo. They went looking for it and found it parked on a public street near where the defendant was staying. The police placed a GPS (global positioning system) "memory tracking unit" underneath the rear bumper of the Ford. Such a device, pocket-sized, battery-operated, commercially available for a couple of hundred dollars (see, e.g., Vehicle–Tracking, Incorporated, "GPS Vehicle Tracking with the Tracking Key," www.vehicle-tracking.com/products/Tracking–Key.html, visited Jan. 21, 2007), receives and stores satellite signals that indicate the device's location. So when the police later retrieved the device (presumably when the car was parked on a public street, as the defendant does not argue that the retrieval involved a trespass), they were able to learn the car's travel history since the installation of the device. One thing they learned was that the car had been traveling to a large tract of land. The officers obtained the consent of the tract's owner to search it and they did so and discovered equipment and materials used in the manufacture of meth. While the police were on the property, the defendant arrived in a car that the police searched, finding additional evidence.

The police had not obtained a warrant authorizing them to place the GPS tracker on the defendant's car. * * * The government argues that they needed nothing because there was no search or seizure within the meaning of the Fourth Amendment. * * *

The Fourth Amendment forbids unreasonable searches and seizures. There is nothing in the amendment's text to suggest that a warrant is required in order to make a search or seizure reasonable. All that the amendment says about warrants is that they must describe with particularity the object of the search or seizure and must be supported both by an oath or affirmation and by probable cause, which is understood, in the case of searches incident to criminal investigations, to mean probable cause that the search will turn up contraband or evidence of crime. * * *

The Supreme Court, however, has created a presumption that a warrant is required, unless infeasible, for a search to be reasonable. * * *

The defendant's contention that by attaching the memory tracking device the police seized his car is untenable. The device did not affect the car's driving qualities, did not draw power from the car's engine or battery, did not take up room that might otherwise have been occupied by passengers or packages, did not even alter the car's appearance, and in short did not "seize" the car in any intelligible sense of the word. But was there a search? The Supreme Court has held that the mere tracking of a vehicle on public streets by means of a similar though less sophisticated device (a beeper) is not a search. * * *

If a listening device is attached to a person's phone, or to the phone line outside the premises on which the phone is located, and phone conversations are recorded, there is a search (and it is irrelevant that there is a trespass in the first case but not the second), and a warrant is required. But if police follow a car around, or observe its route by means of cameras mounted on lampposts or of satellite imaging as in Google Earth, there is no search. Well, but the tracking in this case was by satellite. Instead of transmitting images, the satellite transmitted geophysical coordinates. The only difference is that in the imaging case nothing touches the vehicle, while in the case at hand the tracking device does. But it is a distinction without any practical difference.

There is a practical difference lurking here, however. It is the difference between, on the one hand, police trying to follow a car in their own car, and, on the other hand, using cameras (whether mounted on lampposts or in satellites) or GPS devices. In other words, it is the difference between the old technology–the technology of the internal combustion engine–and newer technologies (cameras are not new, of course, but coordinating the images recorded by thousands of such cameras is). But GPS tracking is on the same side of the divide with the surveillance cameras and the satellite imaging, and if what they do is not searching in Fourth Amendment terms, neither is GPS tracking.

This cannot be the end of the analysis, however, because the Supreme Court has insisted, ever since Katz v. United States, 389 U.S. 347 (1967), that the meaning of a Fourth Amendment search must change to keep pace with the march of science. So the use of a thermal imager to reveal details of the interior of a home that could not otherwise be discovered without a physical entry was held in Kyllo v. United States, 533 U.S. 27, 34 (2001), to be a search within the meaning of the Fourth Amendment. But Kyllo does not help our defendant, because his case unlike Kyllo is not one in which technology provides a substitute for a form of search unequivocally governed by the Fourth Amendment. The substitute here is for an activity, namely following a car on a public street, that is unequivocally not a search within the meaning of the amendment.

But while the defendant's efforts to distinguish the GPS case from the satellite-imaging and lamppost-camera cases are futile, we repeat our earlier point that there is a difference (though it is not the difference involved in Kyllo) between all three of those situations on the one hand and following suspects around in a car on the other. The new technologies enable, as the old (because of expense) do not, wholesale surveillance. One can imagine the police affixing GPS tracking devices to thousands of cars at random, recovering the devices, and using digital search techniques to identify suspicious driving patterns. One can even imagine a law requiring all new cars to come equipped with the device so that the government can keep track of all vehicular movement in the United States. It would be premature to rule that such a program of mass surveillance could not possibly raise a question under the Fourth Amendment—that it could not be a search because it would merely be an efficient alternative to hiring another 10 million police officers to tail every vehicle on the nation's roads.

Of course the amendment cannot sensibly be read to mean that police shall be no more efficient in the twenty-first century than they were in the eighteenth. There is a tradeoff between security and privacy, and often it favors security. Even at the height of the "Warren Court," the Court held over a strong dissent by Justice Brennan that the planting of an undercover agent in a criminal gang does not become a search just because the agent has a transmitter concealed on his person, even though the invasion of privacy is greater when the suspect's words are recorded and not merely recollected. Lopez v. United States, 373 U.S. 427 (1963).

Yet Chief Justice Warren, while concurring in the judgment in Lopez, remarked "that the fantastic advances in the field of electronic communication constitute a great danger to the privacy of the individual; that indiscriminate use of such devices in law enforcement raises grave constitutional questions under the Fourth and Fifth Amendments; and that these considerations impose a heavier responsibility on this Court in its supervision of the fairness of procedures in the federal court system." Id. at 441, 83 S.Ct. 1381. These "fantastic advances" continue, and are giving the police access to surveillance techniques that are ever cheaper and ever more effective. Remember the beeper in Knotts? "Officers installed a beeper inside a five-gallon container of chloroform * * * [and] followed the car in which the chloroform had been placed, maintaining contact by using both visual surveillance and a monitor which received the signals sent from the beeper." United States v. Knotts, supra, 460 U.S. at 278, 103 S.Ct. 1081. That was only a modest improvement over following a car by means of unaided human vision.

Technological progress poses a threat to privacy by enabling an extent of surveillance that in earlier times would have been prohibitively expensive. Whether and what kind of restrictions should, in the name of the Constitution, be placed on such surveillance when used in routine criminal enforcement are momentous issues that fortunately we need not try to resolve in this case. So far as appears, the police of Polk County (a rural county in northwestern Wisconsin), where the events of this case unfolded, are not engaged in mass surveillance. They do GPS tracking only when they have a suspect in their sights. They had, of course, abundant grounds for suspecting the defendant. Should government someday decide to institute programs of mass surveillance of vehicular movements, it will be time enough to decide whether the Fourth Amendment should be interpreted to treat such surveillance as a search.

NOTE: *RADIO FREQUENCY IDENTIFICATION*

Radio Frequency Identification (RFID) technology is big business, raising eyebrows and raising hopes. Cf. *Albrecht v. Metropolitan Pier and Exposition Authority*, 338 F.Supp.2d 914 (N.D. Ill. 2004), contesting denial of the right to protest at a symposium advocating RFID to tag and track individual consumer products. But see Jerry Brito, Relax Don't Do It: Why RFID Privacy Concerns Are Exaggerated and Legislation Is Premature, 2004 *UCLA J. L. & Tech.* 5 (2004). Commercial applications of RFID technology have improved the efficiency of commerce, voting and emergency response capabilities. See RFID Applications Case Studies, http://www.aimglobal.org/casestudies/RFID.asp. Agricultural uses have public health benefits, but have proven controversial. See e.g., *Farm–To–Consumer Legal Defense Fund v. Vilsack,* 636 F.Supp.2d 116 (D.D.C. 2009) (plaintiffs object to government system requiring that cattle bear RFID identification tags). Why is RFID controversial from a privacy perspective?

REEPAL S. DALAL, CHIPPING AWAY AT THE CONSTITUTION: THE INCREASING USE OF RFID CHIPS COULD LEAD TO AN EROSION OF PRIVACY RIGHTS

86 B.U. L. Rev. 485, 486–94 (2006).

Radio Frequency Identification, or RFID, is one of the latest technologies that will revolutionize the way we live. An RFID system involves the communication of digital data from an RFID chip or tag to a reader through radio waves. * * * As with many earlier tracking and surveillance technologies, the rise of such a vast information-gathering system implicates privacy concerns. An important question is where to strike the balance between the use of the technology to gather information for a more efficient society and the protection of individuals' Fourth Amendment rights against unreasonable search and seizure. As new technology is developed, the definition and scope of the Fourth Amendment must be revisited and interpreted in light of such advances.

RFID is a method of identifying items using radio waves. There are two main components to an RFID system: a transponder, sometimes called a tag or a microchip, and a reader. Generally, tags are attached to items and hold digital information about the item; the reader is used to extract the information held on the tag.

The standardized coding system used to hold the information is called the Electronic Product Code, or EPC. The EPC is conceptually similar to the UPC used in barcodes, but EPCs are more versatile than UPCs and can hold much more information. While UPC barcodes can only store seven bits of information, EPC RFID tags can store up to 256 bits. In fact, the EPC system has enough capacity "to provide unique identifiers for all items produced worldwide." Information can be 'written onto' an EPC while it is affixed to an item, allowing the tag to continually update the item's information. This means that as an item moves from one place to the next, the EPC is updated with information regarding its exact location. Furthermore, the EPC system does not require line of sight in order to read information. Therefore, a reader can pick up a signal emitted from an RFID tag without making a direct scan of the tag. A variety of information can be transmitted by the tag. * * *

Government Use Privacy Concerns

The most significant concern surrounding government use of RFID is the limitless surveillance potential. Government use of various technologies for surveillance purposes has always been a highly litigated issue, and the Supreme Court has been frequently called upon to strike a balance between proper and improper uses of technology. Surveillance technology is ever-advancing and the courts must continually interpret and draw lines between permissible uses and those which violate individuals' Fourth Amendment rights. The potential government applications of RFID technology examined in the following sections justify the growing concern about widespread government surveillance.

1.   Passport / Driver's License Concerns

Although equipping passports and driver's licenses with RFID tags presents many advantages for security, there is also a downside. Passports and driver's licenses contain highly sensitive personal information about citizens' whereabouts and identity. The recent attention given to identity theft has shed light on the immense harm that could result if personal information falls in the wrong hands. However, privacy advocates are more concerned that government officials will be able to lawfully access personal information from citizens' passports and driver's licenses without citizens' knowledge or consent. Because the information from the chips can be read remotely, "[p]utting the chips in passports would enable the government to read personal information from more than 50 feet away." Eventually "[i]nformation from card readers could also be coupled with global positioning system data and relayed to satellites, helping the government form a comprehensive picture of the comings and goings of its citizens."

2.   Toll Collection Concerns

While the use of RFID in toll collection booths has produced immediate and noticeable improvements in traffic to many commuters, this too has a downside. This use allows information to be gathered regarding the travel of citizens' cars on highways. The surveillance potential is immense. "Investigators in criminal investigations already regularly subpoena E–Z Pass automatic toll records, which come from RFID readers, to figure out where an individual's car was at a particular time." The possibility of the government profiling individuals is also a concern raised by government use of RFID. Much like the concern that the government will purchase information from private companies to create profiles, the government could also use the information it obtains through its own uses to create such profiles. The government's own implementation of RFID systems simply eliminates the need to contract with a private company; instead government officials have direct access to information regarding individuals' whereabouts and lifestyles. Profiling can be seen and is analyzed as an enhanced form of surveillance.

The potential for abuse created by these surveillance capabilities by the government has fueled a "big brother" scare which seems to have been reignited by the recently passed USA PATRIOT Act ("Act"). The Act broadens federal law enforcement's authority by expanding terrorism laws to include "domestic terrorism." The Act also increases, among other things, law enforcement's power to conduct searches, as well as its ability to use phone and internet surveillance techniques This legislation has prompted significant opposition in light of its threats to citizens' civil liberties. Given this expanded government authority, concerns are brewing regarding the potential for government use of RFID technology to infringe on citizens' Fourth Amendment rights.

THE SMART GRID

epic.org/privacy/smartgrid.

[In September 2010, the National Institute of Standards and Technology (NIST) created a 15–member Smart Grid Advisory Committee composed of representatives from industry, academia, and trade and professional organizations. See generally http://www.nist.gov/public_affairs/releases/smartgrid_092710.cfm. Earlier in 2010, the Electronic Information Privacy Center's Associate Director Lillie Coney testified before the House Committee on Science and Technology concerning what she called "thorny privacy issues" raised by the Smart Grid. The following is EPIC's overview of the technology and the extraordinary surveillance threat it may pose for consumers of electricity.]

* * *

On December 19, 2007, the Energy Independence and Security Act of 2007 was enacted as Public Law 110–140. The bill, among other things, directed that Smart Grid technology be studied for its potential "to maintain a reliable and secure electricity infrastructure that can meet future demand growth." * * *

The term "Smart Grid" encompasses a host of inter-related technologies rapidly moving into public use to reduce or better manage electricity consumption. Smart grid systems may be designed to allow electricity service providers, users, or third party electricity usage management service providers to monitor and control electricity use. The electricity service providers may view a smart grid system as a way to precisely locate power outages or other problems so that technicians can be dispatched to mitigate problems. Pro-environment policymakers may view a smart grid as key to protecting the nation's investment in the future as the world moves toward renewable energy. Another view of smart grid systems is that it would support law enforcement by making it easier to identify, track, and manage information or technology that is associated with people, places, or things involved in an investigations. National security and defense supporters may see the efficient and exacting ability of smart grid systems to manage and redirect the flow of electricity across large areas as critical to assuring resources for their use. Marketers may view smart grid systems as another opportunity to learn more about consumers and how they use the items they purchase. Finally, consumers, if given control over some smart grid features, may see smart grid systems as tools to assist them in making better informed decisions regarding their energy consumption.

Smart meter technology is the first remote communication device designed for smart grid application. These meters have moved into the marketplace and are poised to change how data on home or office consumption of electricity is collected by service providers. Additional changes that smart grid systems may bring are not limited to meters but extend to monitoring other devices, e.g. washing machines, hot water heaters, pool pumps, entertainment centers, lighting fixtures, and heating and cooling systems. Consuming electricity will take on new meaning in the context of privacy rights. A Fayetteville, NC smart grid pilot project in claims that it can manage over 250 devices within a customer's home. The system would be able to selectively reduce demand among its 80,000 customers by turning off devices in homes that are part of the smart grid program. * * *

Privacy implications for smart grid technology deployment centers on the collection, retention, sharing, or reuse of electricity consumption information on individuals, homes, or offices. Fundamentally, smart grid systems will be multi-directional communications and energy transfer networks that enable electricity service providers, consumers, or third party energy management assistance programs to access consumption data. Further, if plans for national or transnational electric utility smart grid systems proceed as currently proposed these far reaching networks will enable data collection and sharing across platforms and great distances. * * *

Plans are underway to support smart grid system applications that will monitor any device transmitting a signal, which may include non-energy-consuming end use items that are only fitted with small radio frequency identification devices (RFID) tags may be possible. RFID tags are included in most retail purchases for clothing, household items, packaging for food, and retail items.

NANOTECHNOLOGY: A POLICY PRIMER,
JOHN F. SARGENT JR.

March 12, 2010.
http://www.nanolawreport.com/uploads/file/Nanotechnology
%20A%20Policy%20Primer%20RL34511.pdf.

Nanoscale science, engineering and technology—commonly referred to collectively as nanotechnology—is believed by many to offer extraordinary economic and societal benefits. Congress has demonstrated continuing support for nanotechnology and has directed its attention primarily to three topics that may affect the realization of this hoped for potential: federal research and development (R & D) in nanotechnology; U.S. competitiveness; and environmental, health, and safety (EHS) concerns. This report provides an overview of these topics—which are discussed in more detail in other CRS reports—and two others: nanomanufacturing and public understanding of and attitudes toward nanotechnology.

The development of this emerging field has been fostered by significant and sustained public investments in nanotechnology R & D. Nanotechnology R & D is directed toward the understanding and control of matter at dimensions of roughly 1 to 100 nanometers. At this size, the properties of matter can differ in fundamental and potentially useful ways from the properties of individual atoms and molecules and of bulk matter. Since the launch of the National Nanotechnology Initiative (NNI) in 2000 through FY2010, Congress has appropriated approximately $12.4 billion for nanotechnology R & D. In addition, the President requested an additional $1.8 billion in funding for nanotechnology R & D for FY2011. More than 60 nations have established similar programs. In 2006 alone, total global public R & D investments reached an estimated $6.4 billion, complemented by an estimated private sector investment of $6.0 billion. Data on economic outputs that are used to assess competitiveness in mature technologies and industries, such as revenues and market share, are not available for assessing nanotechnology. Alternatively, data on inputs (e.g., R & D expenditures) and non-financial outputs (e.g. scientific papers, patents) may provide insight into the current U.S. position and serve as bellwethers of future competitiveness. By these criteria, the United States appears to be the overall global leader in nanotechnology, though some believe the U.S. lead may not be as large as it has been for previous emerging technologies.

Some research has raised concerns about the safety of nanoscale materials. There is general agreement that more information on EHS implications is needed to protect the public and the environment; to assess and manage risks; and to create a regulatory environment that fosters prudent investment in nanotechnology-related innovation. Nanomanufacturing—the bridge between nanoscience and nanotechnology products—may require the development of new technologies, tools, instruments, measurement science, and standards to enable safe, effective, and affordable commercial-scale production of nanotechnology products. Public understanding and attitudes may also affect the environment for R&D,

regulation, and market acceptance of products incorporating nanotechnology.

In 2003, Congress enacted the 21st Century Nanotechnology Research and Development Act providing a legislative foundation for some of the activities of the NNI, addressing concerns, establishing programs, assigning agency responsibilities, and setting authorization levels. Both the House of Representatives and the Senate remain actively engaged in the NNI. Legislation has been introduced in the House (H.R. 554) and Senate (S. 1482) that would amend the act. The House passed H.R. 554 on February 11, 2009. The Senate has not acted on this legislation. The 111th Congress may address policy issues related to the NNI through this or other legislation.

Note: Nanotechnology—Even Sneakier?

Could teeny-tiny technologies constitute a major privacy headache in the near future? According to the National Nanotechnology Initiative, nanotechnology involves: "(1) Research and technology development at the atomic, molecular or macromolecular levels, in the length scale of approximately 1 to 100 nanometer range; (2) creating and using structures, devices and systems that have novel properties and functions because of their small and/or intermediate size; and (3) the ability to control or manipulate on the atomic scale." See generally Ronald Sandler and W. D. Kay, The National Nanotechnology Initiative and the Social Good, 34 *J.L. Med. & Ethics* 675 (2006). At present, the applications of nanotechnology have been mainly limited to industrial manufacturing. Tennis balls, beer bottles, and drill bits have been made with the help of nanotechnology. Someday, nanotechnology could serve as the basis for monitoring and surveillance devices, since "A variety of nanotechnology applications may hold the potential for improving the density of memory storage. For example, IBM has demonstrated the potential to create high-density memory devices (with an estimated storage capacity of 1 terabyte per square inch) by storing information mechanically using thermal-mechanical nanoscale probes to punch nanoscale indentations into a thin plastic film. The probes can be used to read and write data in parallel." John F. Sargent Jr., Nanotechnology: A Policy Primer 2 (March 12, 2010). High-density memory devices? This is where the privacy concerns kick in.

EVA GUTIERREZ, "PRIVACY IMPLICATIONS OF NANOTECHNOLOGY"

http://www.epic.org/privacy/nano/.

This technology has the potential to revolutionize our concept of individual privacy. We should be mindful of the fact that as nanotechnology makes computing capabilities increasingly smaller and more efficient, collecting, storing, sharing and processing large amounts of information will become easier and cheaper. Nanotechnology has the capability of dramatically improving surveillance devices and producing new weapons, thus leading to an increase in incentives to private companies producing security nanotechnology.

When examining the potential privacy risks that nanotechnology may bring it is important to first determine what type of technical and legal barriers will define the norms for the use of this technology. Historically, Congress has acted in anticipation of potential risk by passing legislation in advance of product introduction into the market. For example, Congress passed the Cable Communications Policy Act in 1984 envisioning the advent of two-way cable. The possibility of the cable operator viewing the habits of subscribers motivated Congress to pass strong opt-in protections for the use of individuals' data. Similarly, Congress acted to prohibit telemarketing to cellular telephones in 1991 with the Telephone Consumer Protection Act, long before the devices became into popular use.

It would be wise for Congress to enact legislation in advance of the adoption of nanotechnology innovations to guard against threats posed to the environment, health, safety, public welfare, and privacy. Taking action prior to the adoption of nanotechnology innovations may allow for circumvention of problems because this technology may allow for very few or limited opportunities to make post-implementation corrections to processes associated with the technology. For example, if Congress waits to pass privacy-protective legislation until after the technology is prevalent in society, then it may be too difficult to deviate or restrict nano surveillance technology's use. It is important to note that historically privacy-protective legislation has not been designed to limit the use of the new technology, but instead to ensure that "the data collection is fair, transparent, and subject to law," in order to "build consumer confidence, establish a stable business environment, and allow for the benefits of new technology while safeguarding key interests."This rule of law should also apply to new nanotech devices intended for surveillance purposes.

With nanotechnology bringing new types of devices appropriate for surveillance and with the potential to invade individual privacy, legislation should be passed not necessarily to prohibit the ability to engage in surveillance, but to ensure that such surveillance is consistent with the Fourth Amendment. * * *

Specifically, one of the primary privacy risks related to nanotechnology is the potential to implant microchips into humans. Researchers acknowledge that nanotech microchips could provide a great deal of added benefits, such as dispensing customized amounts of drugs, or alternatively aiding Alzheimer's patients through an implanted "assisted cognition" device to ensure these patients do not get lost. These goals are laudable, but must be accompanied by the consideration that many technologies tend to "creep" into other areas. Should such technology come available it would not only be sold as a way of monitoring or controlling the behavior of Alzheimer's patients, but may be suggested as a means of controlling or monitoring the behavior of those incarcerated or on parole, those receiving public assistance, school aged children, employees, and even wayward spouses.

MICHAEL FROOMKIN, THE DEATH OF PRIVACY?

52 Stanford Law Review 1461 (2000).

[T]echnological change has not yet moved so far or so quickly as to make legal approaches to privacy protection irrelevant. There is much the law can do, only a little of which has been tried. * * * Whenever the law can address the issue of data collection itself, however, it reduces the pressure on data protection law and contributes greatly to data privacy protection * * *.

There is no magic bullet, no panacea. If the privacy pessimists are to be proved wrong, the great diversity of new privacy-destroying technologies will have to be met with a legal and social response that is at least as subtle and multifaceted as the technological challenge. Given the rapid pace at which privacy-destroying technologies are being invented and deployed, a legal response must come soon, or it will be too late.

US HOUSE OF REPRESENTATIVES HOMELAND SECURITY COMMITTEE HEARING "VIEWPOINTS ON HOMELAND SECURITY: A DISCUSSION WITH THE 9/11 COMMISSIONERS."

May 19, 2010.
2010 WLNR 10399465.

I. INTRODUCTION

* * * We are very happy to be before this committee this morning * * * to discuss the challenges the serious and evolving terrorist threat poses to our nation.

Today, we are appearing in our capacity as co-chairmen of the Bipartisan Policy Center's National Security Preparedness Group (NSPG), a successor to the 9/11 Commission. Drawing on a strong roster of national security professionals, the NSPG works as an independent, bipartisan group to monitor the implementation of the 9/11 Commission's recommendations and address other emerging national security issues. * * *

We believe the strength of our group will allow us to be a voice on national security issues and a resource to you and the executive branch. First and foremost, we are here to help play a constructive role in support of your work.

Recent events have reminded us, especially the failed attempts on 12/25 and in Times Square, that the country needs to continue to improve its defenses and strengthen governmental institutions designed to fight international terrorism and other threats to the United States. At the Bipartisan Policy Center, our National Security Preparedness Group has been studying the implementation of the 9/11 Commission's recommendations, especially those regarding intelligence reform, and new threats to our national security.

We look forward to working with you, and benefiting from the work of this committee, as our study continues.

Today we would like to discuss with you two ongoing projects that have a direct bearing on the important work of this committee.

First, as we testified in January, the threat from al Qaeda, remains serious. What we and other experts are studying is how the threat of terrorism is evolving. The conventional wisdom for years has been that al Qaeda's preferred method was a spectacular attack like 9/11. But the defining characteristic of today's threat seems to be its diversity.

Second, the 5 year anniversary of the Intelligence Reform and Terrorism Prevention Act recently passed. Our group marked this anniversary by hosting a conference on the State of Intelligence Reform. The Director of National Intelligence and host of other former intelligence officials participated in the conference and I will share with you today some of the conclusions from the discussion.

The Terrorist Threat

The defining trait of today's terrorist threat is its diversity. As you well know, the Attorney General has stated that the Times Square attempted attack was directed by the Pakistani Taliban. The attempted attack in December was the work of al Qaeda in the Arabian Peninsula. In both of these cases, al Qaeda affiliates thought previously as regional or local threats demonstrated their ability to reach the United States. We're well aware of the threat emanating from the tribal regions of Pakistan. We've also come to appreciate the increasing threat of homegrown terrorism as some Americans have become radicalized.

As we have come to recognize the evolving nature of the threat, we as a country need to consider what policy recommendations should follow this new assessment. Our National Security Preparedness Group is studying this issue. Professor Bruce Hoffman from Georgetown and Peter Bergen of the New America Foundation are leading a series of interviews and meetings with terrorism experts to take a fresh look at the nature of the threat in light of the increased activity. We will work over the summer to complete this work and draw conclusions and recommendations that Congress and the Administration can utilize. We have already arranged for Bergen and Hoffman to testify on this assessment in September, along with homeland security experts Fran Townsend and Steven Flynn. We look forward to working with you on this study and the opportunity to return in the fall to your committee.

State of Intelligence Reform

The determination of terrorists to attack the homeland remains unabated, reminding us of the need for viable and agile governmental institutions to counter the threat. To us, these episodes further suggest the importance of creating a Director of National Intelligence and a National Counter Terrorism Center in the first place. At their core, the problems evident on September 11, 2001, reflected failures of information sharing among the federal partners charged with protecting the country. No one in the federal government was charged with fusing intelligence derived from multiple foreign and domestic sources. The DNI has been charged with breaking down bureaucratic, cultural, technological, and policy barriers to the sharing of information among federal agencies and the NCTC has been successful in thwarting a number of potential terrorist attacks.

There has been good work done since September 11, 2001, but we need to continue down the path toward further integration and insist on a greater level of effectiveness within the intelligence community. To further these goals, we hosted a conference on the State of Intelligence Reform in April with Director Blair, General Hayden, Admiral McConnell, Fran Townsend, Jane Harman, John McLaughlin and Steve Cambone. The conference was a success in highlighting the importance of the issues this committee is dedicated to, including information-sharing and improved counter-terrorism policy within our borders.

Today, we are releasing a brief summary of the proceedings, and we would like to offer you several key observations.

First, the President needs to be very active in defining roles and responsibilities within the intelligence community. We think the conference showed that the DNI has achieved a meaningful measure of success in its first years—that has made it worth the inevitable turmoil—but that the successes relied too heavily on key personalities within the executive branch. We want to continue to look closely at the authorities of the DNI to make sure he has the authority to do his work, but it is our sense that the success of the DNI in the short term is not dependent on additional statutory adjustments to IRTPA.

Nonetheless, there are still ambiguities that can contribute to mission confusion and lack of clarity about lanes in the road. This is perhaps the greatest challenge facing the DNI. Is the DNI a strong leader of the intelligence community empowered to lead the IC as an enterprise? Or is the DNI a mere coordinator, a convening authority charged with helping facilitate common inter-intelligence agency agreement? The lack of clarity in its mission invites a host of other criticisms, including that the ODNI is too large, too intrusive, and too operational.

The burden is on the President to clarify who is in charge of the Intelligence Community and where final authority lies on budget, personnel, and other matters. In our estimation, we need a strong DNI who is a leader of the intelligence community. The DNI must be the person who drives inter-agency coordination and integration. At the same time, the DNI's authorities must be exercised with discretion and consideration of the priorities and sensitivities of other intelligence agencies. But the President's leadership is crucial and must be enduring or we run the risk of mission confusion and decrease the prospect of achieving long and lasting reform that was recommended after September 11, 2001. The

DNI's ability to lead the Intelligence Community depends on the President defining his role and giving him the power and authority to act.

Second, the nature of the domestic intelligence mission demands greater clarity. The Intelligence Community must become more competent in obtaining and using appropriate information on people who cross borders and may have nefarious intent, including Americans. The failed attack of 12/25, cross-border drug violence, and other events last year highlighted the challenges we face due to our porous borders and the rapid mobility of modern society. In addition, we have seen that some of our practices, such as no-fly lists, must be more dynamic and responsive, capable of triggering quick action, including warnings based on incomplete information. Our procedures for collecting and using US person data must adapt to these new challenges. Lastly, the Attorney General's guidelines for intelligence agencies operating domestically needs to be updated and harmonized so that the IC can perform its mission successfully.

It was clear in the conference that in many ways, "domestic intelligence" has not received enough attention especially in light of the evolving nature of the terrorist threat. The 9/11 Commission placed great emphasis on the need for the FBI to reform itself and build an organization that placed more emphasis on preventing attacks. To refocus attention on these issues, we will host a conference in the fall with top government officials and other experts to ensure we are taking the right steps along the path of reform.

Third, as evidenced by the reviews following the failed attempt on 12/25, the DNI needs to be a leader in managing and improving analysis in an Intelligence Community awash with data. In an age when we are collecting more information than ever before, a major challenge is understanding, managing, and integrating a huge amount of information. The DNI needs to develop ways of dealing with intelligence information overload. The good news is that the technology to do the job exists. We need to continue to push forward on policy innovations to ensure that we manage the data properly and that the right people get the information they need, while protecting civil liberties. We're cosponsoring a series of events with the Markle Foundation to continue to push for innovative policies, including making information discoverable and building interfaces that allow for its efficient exchange while at the same time protecting civil liberties. Making progress on these issues is critical to mounting an effective fight against increasingly sophisticated terrorists.

PRIVACY AND CIVIL LIBERTIES

The balance between security and liberty will always be a part of the struggle against terrorism. America must not sacrifice one for the other. Following the 9/11 Commission recommendations, the Bush Administration created a Privacy and Civil Liberties Oversight Board to advise the executive branch and oversee government efforts to defend civil liberties. The board was staffed and became operational in 2006. In 2007, Congress restructured the Board as an independent agency outside the White

House. Despite early criticisms of undue delay and inadequate funding, the Board held numerous sessions with national security and homeland security advisers, the attorney general, and the FBI Director, among others, on terrorist surveillance and other issues arising from intelligence collection.

However, the Board has been dormant since that time. With massive capacity to develop data on individuals, the Board should fight to ensure that collection capabilities do not violate privacy and civil liberties. Mr. Chairman we support the sentiment expressed in your letter to President Obama, supported by many members of this committee, that he should quickly appoint members to the Board. We continue to believe that the Board provides critical functions and we urge President Obama its swift reconstitution.

CONGRESSIONAL OVERSIGHT

Third, the DNI and IC must provide greater transparency, foster greater trust with the American people, and avoid over-reaction during troubled times. While much intelligence must remain classified and out of public view, the Intelligence Community still needs support from the media, Congress, users of intelligence, and foreign partners, among others, to successfully pursue our national goals. The DNI should work to promote a robust relationship/partnership with Congress, which serves as the proxy for the public in overseeing the IC and affirming its direction.

The 9/11 Commission also placed great emphasis on rigorous congressional oversight. This recommendation helped precipitate the creation of a House Homeland Security Committee and a Senate Homeland Security and Governmental Affairs Committee. However, enduring fractured and overlapping committee jurisdictions on both sides of the hill have left Congressional oversight in an unsatisfactory state. DHS entities still report to dozens of separate committees hundreds of times per year, which constitutes a serious drain of time and resources for senior DHS officials. Furthermore, the jurisdictional melee among the scores of Congressional committees has led to conflicting and contradictory tasks and mandates for DHS. Without taking serious action, we fear this unworkable system could make the country less safe.

The 9/11 Commission also called congressional oversight over intelligence dysfunctional. We made recommendations to strengthen the oversight committees which were not accepted by the Congress, though some progress has been made. Today we want to emphasize the enormous importance we attach to rigorous oversight of the intelligence community.

Congress is the only source of independent advice to the president on intelligence matters. Such oversight requires changes in the structure of Congressional committees, specifically the creation of powerful oversight committees in both the House and Senate. Today, the appropriations committees' monopoly on the provision of funding weakens the ability of the intelligence authorization committees to perform oversight and wastes much of their expertise.

Congressional oversight can help ensure the intelligence community is operating effectively and help resolve disputes about conflicting roles and missions. We urge the Congress to take action to strengthen the oversight capabilities of the intelligence committees.

INDEX

References are to Pages

†